Exceptional Children

Exceptional Children

AN INTRODUCTION TO SPECIAL EDUCATION

FIFTH EDITION

WILLIAM L. HEWARD
The Ohio State University

Merrill, an imprint of Prentice Hall
Upper Saddle River, New Jersey   Columbus, Ohio

Library of Congress Cataloging-in-Publication Data

Heward, William L.
    Exceptional children : an introduction to special education/
William L. Heward.—5th ed.
        p.   cm.
    Includes bibliographical references and indexes.
    ISBN 0-13-366956-4
    1. Special education—United States. 2. Exceptional children—United States.I. Title.
LC3981.H49   1996
    371.9—dc20   95-6916
                                                                              CIP

Cover photo: Scott Cunningham
Editor: Ann Castel Davis
Developmental Editor: Carol S. Sykes
Production Editor: Mary Irvin
Photo Editor: Anne Vega
Design Coordinator: Jill E. Bonar
Text Designer: Frankenberry Design
Cover Designer: Proof Positive/Farrowlyne Associates, Inc.
Production Manager: Patricia A. Tonneman
Electronic Text Management: Marilyn Wilson Phelps, Matthew Williams,
    Karen L. Bretz, Tracey Ward
Illustrations: Romark Illustrations

This book was set in Garamond by Prentice Hall and was printed and bound by R.R.
Donnelley/Ohio. The cover was printed by Phoenix Color Corp.

 © 1996 by Prentice-Hall, Inc.
Simon & Schuster/A Viacom Company
Upper Saddle River, New Jersey 07458

Earlier editions © 1992 by Macmillan Publishing and © 1988, 1984, 1980 by Merrill Publishing
Company.

Photo credits: See p. xx

Printed in the United States of America

10 9 8 7 6 5 4 3 2

ISBN: 0-13-366956-4

Prentice-Hall International (UK) Limited, *London*
Prentice-Hall of Australia Pty. Limited, *Sydney*
Prentice-Hall of Canada, Inc., *Toronto*
Prentice-Hall Hispanoamericana, S. A., *Mexico*
Prentice-Hall of India Private Limited, *New Delhi*
Prentice-Hall of Japan, Inc., *Tokyo*
Simon & Schuster Asia Pte. Ltd., *Singapore*
Editora Prentice-Hall do Brasil, Ltda., *Rio de Janeiro*

About the Author

William Lee Heward grew up in Three Oaks, Michigan. He majored in psychology and sociology as an undergraduate at Western Michigan University, earned his doctorate in special education at the University of Massachusetts, and has been a member of the special education faculty at The Ohio State University since 1975. Bill has had several opportunities to teach and lecture abroad, most recently in 1993 when he served as a Visiting Professor at Keio University in Tokyo, Japan. He is a recipient of Ohio State University's highest honor for teaching excellence, the Alumni Association's Distinguished Teaching Award.

Bill's current research interests focus on "low technology" methods that classroom teachers can use to increase the frequency with which each student actively responds and participates during instruction. His research has appeared in many of the field's leading professional journals, including *Behavioral Disorders*, *Exceptional Children*, *Journal of Applied Behavior Analysis*, *Learning Disability Quarterly*, *Research in Developmental Disabilities*, *Teacher Education and Special Education*, *Teaching Exceptional Children*, and *The Elementary School Journal*.

Bill has coauthored five other textbooks, including *Applied Behavior Analysis* (Merrill, 1987) and the forthcoming *A Dozen Teaching Mistakes and What To Do Instead* (Merrill/Prentice Hall). He has also written for the popular market. His book *Some Are Called Clowns* chronicled his five summers as a pitcher for the Indianapolis Clowns, the last of the barnstorming baseball teams.

For my children:
to Lee, for typing the references; and
to Lynn, for checking on me in the night.

Preface

Special education is the story of people. It is the story of the parents and teachers who work together to meet the needs of a preschool child with multiple disabilities. It is the story of the fourth-grader with learning disabilities who encounters both regular and special teachers in her public school. It is the story of the gifted and talented child who brings new insights to old problems, the high school student with cerebral palsy who is learning English as his second language, and the woman who has recently moved into a group home after spending most of her life in a large institution. Special education is all of their stories.

When Mike Orlansky and I began writing the first edition of *Exceptional Children* nearly 20 years ago, we sought to convey the diversity and excitement of special education and to tell the story of the many people who participate in it. Those objectives remain unchanged. I have tried, in this edition, to present a comprehensive, current, and up-to-date survey of professional research, practice, and trends in the education of people with special needs.

I hope you will find the Fifth Edition of *Exceptional Children* an informative, readable, and challenging introduction to special education, a rapidly changing discipline that is still in its formative years. Whether you are a beginner or a person with years of experience, I hope you continue your study and involvement with children and adults who have special needs. For you, too, can make a worthwhile contribution to the still-unfinished story of special education.

✸ Organization, Structure, and Special Features

The book begins with "A Personal View of Special Education"—eight perspectives on the purpose and responsibilities of special education—which sets the stage for the chapters that follow. The book's 15 chapters are organized into three parts. Part One—Foundations for Understanding Special Education—presents an overview of terminology, laws, policies, and practices that are consistent with the exceptional child's right to receive an appropriate education in the least restrictive environment, and examines the importance of understanding and appreciating the cultural and linguistic differences children bring to the classroom. Part Two—Students with Exceptional Educational Needs—surveys nine specific categories of exceptionality, introducing definitions, prevalence, causes, historical background, assessment techniques, strategies for education and treatment, and current and future trends. Part Three—Family and Life-Span Issues—considers three topics of importance to all special educators: parent and family involvement, early intervention, and transitions to adulthood.

Teaching & Learning Boxes

New to this edition are Teaching & Learning boxes that describe a wide range of effective interventions—from classroom performance and classroom management to organizational checklists and communication tips. These features highlight innovative strategies for improving the achievement and independence of students with disabilities—from using guided notes to help students with learning disabilities to teaching students who are blind to cook with tape-recorded recipes to using the "Idea Bunny" to help preschoolers learn to work independently.

Profiles & Perspectives Boxes

Profiles & Perspectives boxes include two types of essays. One type highlights the personal struggles, triumphs, and stories of persons with disabilities, such as an interview with the student leaders of the Gallaudet University uprising to hire a president who is deaf; two pieces contributed by Stephen W. Hawking, the world-renowned theoretical physicist whose severe disabilities are paled by his scholarly accomplishments; and a story about Sebine Johnson, who was featured on the cover of the Second Edition and is now a 22-year-old facing the excitement and challenges of life in the adult world. The second type of Profiles & Perspectives box consists of essays by special educators, parents, and journalists who share their personal perspectives about where special education is, or should be, going. Examples include "What Special Educators Should Know," by Tom Lovitt; "My Return Voyage," by Patty Barbetta; and "Perspectives On Educating Young Children Prenatally Exposed to Illegal Drugs" by Judy Carta.

Focus Questions

Each chapter begins with five questions that provide a framework for studying the chapter and its implications. These Focus Questions can serve as discussion starters for introducing, overviewing, concluding, or reviewing. Points to consider in discussing these questions can be found in both the Instructor's Manual and Student Study Guide, thus helping integrate this feature with the core content of each chapter, as well as with the broad scope of special education.

Margin Notes

Numerous margin notes throughout each chapter provide additional commentary and perspectives on the accompanying content and frequently direct students to related material in other chapters or professional resources or to articles from the January, 1995, issue of *Educational Leadership*.

Chapter Summaries

Chapter summaries, organized by the main headings from the chapter, use a bulleted list to overview the major principles and key points for each chapter. When used with the Chapter Overviews in the Instructor's Manual and Student Study Guide, these Summaries provide succinct review packages for students and offer checkpoints (for students and professors) for coverage of chapter contents.

For More Information

These end-of-chapter sections provide additional resources for students and professors: journals, books, organizations, and special services. These are particularly helpful for outside assignments, extended research, graduate-level projects, and professional contacts once students become practicing professionals. The items in this section complement the references that appear at the end of the text.

Key Terms/Glossary

More than 250 key terms appears in **boldface** the first time they appear in the text. These terms are included in the Glossary, which serves as a convenient guide to the professional terminology of special education. The key terms also appear in the "Chapter-at-a-Glance" charts included in both the Instructor's Manual and Student Study Guide, allowing for a quick overview of the sections in which they appear.

References/New Research and Conceptual Developments

Special education does not stand still for long. Since the previous edition was published, the field has been changed by many new research studies, theoretical contributions, and innovative approaches to education and training. Citations to more than 1,000 new references have been added to this edition. The complete list of nearly 2,200 references that appears at the end of the text provides students with a compendium of recent research and other scholarly work in the field of special education.

✸ *Supplements to Accompany the Text*
Material for the Instructor

Instructor's Manual

An expanded and improved Instructor's Manual is fully integrated with the text and includes numerous recommendations for presenting and extending the content of the chapters. The manual consists of recommendations for using overhead projectors, a section on audiovisual supplements, lists of introductory or enrichment activities, and chapter-by-chapter sections. Individual chapter guides include Chapter Outlines, Chapter-at-a-Glance charts, Chapter Overviews, answers to Focus Questions, and "To Focus Your Teaching" sections. Each of these features assists the instructor in enhancing the text and its presentation to students.

Overhead Transparencies

A package of nearly 150 two- and four-color acetate transparencies is available for use with the text. The transparencies highlight key concepts, summarize content, and illustrate figures and charts from the text.

Test Bank

A printed test bank of approximately 1,000 test questions also accompanies the text. A variety of objective and essay questions are provided for each chapter. A computerized version, available in Macintosh and IBM, has also been prepared and allows for customizing assessment for individual classrooms.

For the Student

Educational Leadership

A copy of the January, 1995, issue of *Educational Leadership* entitled "The Inclusive School" is provided free with each copy of the text. Included in the issue are 18 articles that discuss the pros and cons of including students with disabilities into the regular classroom. Contributors to the issue include, among others, John O'Neil, Douglas and Lynn Fuchs, Joseph Renzulli, and Jean Schumaker and Don Deshler. Reference to these articles throughout the text and supplements support interactive class discussions about inclusion.

Student Study Guide

The Student Study Guide uses an interactive approach to reinforce the content of the text. Individual chapter sections include answers to Focus Questions; Chapter Overviews; Chapter-at-a-Glance charts; an Interactive Chapter Review that walks students through the contents, invites reflection, presents study tips and explanations of content—all in a conversational and personal tone; and a chapter Self-Check Quiz with answers.

Acknowledgments

Many people contributed ideas, suggestions, insights, and constructive criticism during the preparation of *Exceptional Children*. The fifth edition has been enhanced by the combined efforts of a talented team of professionals at Merrill and Prentice Hall. My editor, Ann Castel Davis, has provided unwavering support and enthusiasm for the fifth edition. I really appreciate Ann for this; in addition, she's a Cubs fan. Developmental Editor Carol Sykes deserves a medal for putting up with me throughout more than a year of researching, writing, and revising the fifth edition. Carol's gentle but effective "author handling" skills are appreciated. Linda Poderski and Laura Larson copyedited the manuscript with a fine balance of technical skill and respect for the author's writing style. If it were not for the hard work and professionalism of Production Editor Mary Irvin, the fifth edition would never have seen the light of day. Mary didn't even blink when I handed her the "mother of all reference lists." The effective and meaningful portrayal of special education requires excellent photographs, and the contributions of Photo Editor Anne Vega and photographer Scott Cunningham are evident throughout this edition. I'm confident you'll share my appreciation of their considerable talents. I am grateful for the assistance of each of the following people who arranged photo shoots: Don Cantrell, Debra Edwards and Anne Gibson, Columbus Public Schools; Ron Heath, Ohio School for the Blind. Susan Frankenberry's talents as a text designer are apparent in the book's attractive appearance and functional layout.

No single author can capture the many perspectives and areas of expertise that make up special education. The currency and quality of this edition have been enhanced tremendously by Profiles & Perspectives and Teaching & Learning essays authored exclusively for this text by the following people: Patricia M. Barbetta, Florida International University; Sue Brewster and Lyn Doll, Toledo Public Schools; Judith J. Carta, Juniper Gardens Children's Center, Kansas City, KS; Vivian I. Correa, University of Florida; Jill C. Dardig, Ohio Dominican College; Marsha Forest and Jack Pearpoint, Centre for Integrated Education and Community, Toronto; Douglas Fuchs and Lynn S. Fuchs, Vanderbilt University; Stephen W. Hawking, Cambridge University; Michael F. Giangreco, University of Vermont; Richard D. Howell, The Ohio State University; Thomas C. Lovitt, University of Washington; Margo A. Mastropieri and Thomas E. Scruggs, Purdue University; Jane Piirto, Ashland University; Diane M. Sainato, The Ohio State University; and Barbara L. Schirmer, Lewis and Clark College.

Other individuals who provided me with material and information that greatly enriched the fifth edition are Teresa A. Grossi, University of Toledo; Cecelia Johnson, Marietta, Georgia; Maria do Carmo Braga de Cruz, Oporto, Portugal; Ronni Hochman, Upper Arlington Schools; Bruce and Cynthie Johnson, Columbus, Ohio; Sandy Letham and Dennis Higgins, Zuni Elementary School, Albuquerque, NM; Sandie Trask-Tyler, Westerville City Schools; and David W. Test, University of North Carolina at Charlotte. I am honored by their participation and owe a great debt of gratitude to each of these scholars, teachers, and parents for their contributions to this text.

The following professors—all of whom have served as instructors of introductory special education courses at other colleges and universities—provided timely and helpful reviews of the previous edition: Bruce Baum, State University at Buffalo; Jim Burns, The College of St. Rose; Peter Carullias, II, University of Cincinnati; Carol Chase Thomas, University of North Carolina at Wilmington; Alice E. Christie, University of Akron; Sheila Drake, Kansas Wesleyan University; Pamela J. Gent, Clarion University of Pennsylvania; Joan M. Goodship, University of Richmond; Sheldon Maron, Portland State University; James M. Patton, College of William and Mary; Leonila P. Rivera, Southwest Missouri State University; James A. Siders, University of Southern Mississippi; and Scott Sparks, Ohio University. Their perspectives, experience, and recommendations helped guide the revision process.

I am indebted to Vivian I. Correa, University of Florida, for coauthoring Chapter 3—Special Education in a Culturally and Linguistically Diverse Society—and to my Ohio State colleagues, Richard D. Howell and Raymond H. Swassing, for coauthoring Chapter 12—Gifted and Talented Students. Rodney A. Cavanaugh, State University of New York at Plattsburgh, and Patricia M. Barbetta, Florida International University, coauthored the Student Study Guide and the Instructor's Manual. Rodney and Patty's work has greatly strengthened the scope and quality of the ancillary package and I am confident that instructors and students will appreciate their hard work and creativity. The reference list would never have been completed without many hours of gracious, late-night help of doctoral students—Sheila Alber, Concepcion Ortiz Blake, Paul Malanga, Kristyn Sheldon, Stacy Martz, Randy Seevers, and Brian Kai Yung Tam—and my colleagues Tim Heron and Jose Navarro. Sheila and Brian also deserve thanks for compiling the name index.

I will always be grateful to Mike Orlansky, a friend, former colleague, and coauthor of four previous editions of *Exceptional Children*. Mike, I hope you'll be pleased with the latest rendition of "H&O." Finally, I would be remiss if I failed to mention Tom Hutchinson and Francie Margolin. Tom was the moving force behind the first edition; he first suggested that I write an introduction to special education text, outlined the book on a restaurant napkin, and brought Mike and me together. Francie worked closely with us on the first three editions.

Most of all, I appreciate and wish to acknowledge the support of my family—Jill, Lee, and Lynn—who had to endure the unsightly aftermath of too many all-nighters.

Contents

C H A P T E R *7*

Students with Communication Disorders   *291*

C H A P T E R *8*

Students Who Are Deaf or Hard-of-Hearing   *335*

C H A P T E R *9*

Students Who Are Blind or Have Low Vision   *387*

C H A P T E R *10*

Students with Physical and Health Impairments   *433*

Special Features

✳ *Profiles & Perspectives*

Photo Credits

Exceptional Children

A Personal View of Special Education

My primary goal in revising this book is to explain the history, practices, advances, problems, and challenges that make up the complex and dynamic field called special education in as complete, clear, up-to-date, and objective a manner as possible. This, of course, is much easier said than done: an author's personal views are surely implicit in those explanations—between the lines, as they say. Because my personal beliefs and assumptions about special education—which are by no means unique, but neither are they universally held by everyone in the field—affect both the substance and the tone of the entire book, I believe I owe you an explicit summary of those views.

People with disabilities have a fundamental right to live and participate fully in settings and programs—in school, at home, in the workplace, and in the community—that are as normalized as possible. That is, the settings and programs in which children and adults with disabilities learn, live, work, and play should, to the greatest extent possible, be the same settings and programs in which people without disabilities participate. A defining feature of normalized settings and programs is the integration of persons with and without disabilities.

Individuals with disabilities have the right to as much independence as we can help them achieve. Special educators have no more important teaching task than that of helping children and adults with disabilities learn how to increase the level of decision making and control over their own lives. Thus, self-management and self-advocacy skills should be significant curriculum components for students with disabilities.

Special education must continue to expand its efforts to recognize and respond appropriately to all learners with exceptional educational needs—the gifted and talented child, the preschooler with disabilities, the infant who is at risk for a future learning problem, the exceptional child from a different cultural background, and the adult with disabilities. In support of this belief, this text includes a chapter on each of these critical areas of special education.

Professionals have too long ignored the needs of parents and families of exceptional children, often treating them as patients, clients, or even adversaries, instead of realizing that they are partners with the same goals. Some special educators have too often given the impression (and, worse, believed it to be true) that parents are there to serve professionals, when in fact the opposite is more correct. We have long neglected to recognize parents as a child's first—and in many ways best—teachers. Learning to work effectively with parents is one of the most important skills the special educator can acquire. Thus, a chapter is devoted to the importance of the parent-professional partnership.

The efforts of special educators are most effective when they incorporate the input and services of all of the disciplines in the helping professions. It is foolish to argue over territorial rights when we can accomplish more by working together within an interdisciplinary team that includes our colleagues in psychology, medicine, social services, and vocational rehabilitation.

All students have the right to an effective education. As educators, our primary responsibility is to design and implement effective instruction for personal, social, vocational, and academic skills. These skills are the same ones that determine the quality of our lives: working effectively and efficiently on our jobs; being productive members of our communities; maintaining a comfortable lifestyle in our homes; communicating with our friends and family; using our leisure time meaningfully and enjoyably. Instruction is ultimately effective when it helps the individuals we serve to acquire and maintain positive lifestyle changes. To put it another way: the proof of the process is in the product. Therefore . . .

Teachers must demand effectiveness from their instructional approaches. For many years conventional wisdom has fostered the belief that it takes unending patience to teach children with disabilities. I believe this view is a disservice to students with special needs and to the educators—both special and general education teachers—whose job it is to teach them. Teachers should not wait patiently for exceptional students to learn, attributing lack of progress to some inherent attribute or faulty process within the child, such as mental retardation, learning disability, attention-deficit disorder, or emotional disturbance. Instead, the teacher should use direct and frequent measures of the student's performance as the primary guide for modifying the instructional program in order to improve its effectiveness. This, I believe, is the real work of the educator. Numerous examples of instructional strategies and tactics that have been empirically demonstrated to be effective are described and illustrated throughout the text. Although you will not know how to teach exceptional children after reading this or any other introductory text, you will gain an appreciation for the importance of direct, systematic instruction and an understanding of the kinds of teaching skills the special educator must have.

Finally, the future for individuals with disabilities holds great promise. We have only begun to discover the myriad ways to improve teaching, increase learning, prevent or minimize the conditions that cause disabilities, encourage acceptance, and use technology to compensate for disabilities. Although I make no specific predictions for the future, I am certain that we have not come as far as we can in learning how to help exceptional individuals build and enjoy fuller, more independent lives in the school, community, and workplace.

Foundations for Understanding Special Education

Keys to Special Education

* When is special education needed? How do we know?

* If categorical labels do not help a teacher decide what and how to teach, why are they used so frequently?

* Why have court cases and federal legislation been required to ensure that children with disabilities receive an appropriate education?

* Can a special educator provide all three kinds of intervention—*preventive*, *remedial*, and *compensatory*—on behalf of an individual child?

* What do you think are the three most important challenges facing special education today? Why? Read your answer again after completing this textbook.

*E*ducating children with special needs or abilities presents a difficult challenge. Teachers and related professionals who have accepted that challenge—special educators—work in an exciting and rapidly changing field. This introductory text captures for you some of the action and excitement that characterize this important and dynamic field. Throughout the book, specific information about exceptional children is presented, both proven and promising instructional techniques are described, some of the accomplishments that can be attained when professionals and parents work together are shared, and areas that present continuing difficulty and concern for the future are examined. Presented first are the background information, concepts, and perspectives that are basic to an understanding of exceptional children and special education.

✳ *Who Are Exceptional Children?*

Let's begin by defining four terms: *exceptional children, disability, handicap,* and *at risk.* All children exhibit differences from one another in terms of their physical attributes (e.g., some are shorter, some are stronger) and learning abilities (e.g., some learn quickly and generalize what they learn to new situations; others need repeated practice and have difficulty remembering and using what they have been taught). The differences among most children are relatively small, enabling these children to benefit from the general education program. The physical attributes and/or learning abilities of some children, however—those called **exceptional children**—differ from the norm (either below or above) to such an extent that an individualized program of special education is required to meet these children's needs. The term *exceptional children* includes children who experience difficulties in learning and children whose performance is so superior that special education is necessary to help them fulfill their potential. Thus, *exceptional children* is an inclusive term that refers to children with learning and/or behavior problems, children with physical disabilities or sensory impairments, and children who are intellectually gifted or have a special talent.

Disability refers to reduced function or loss of a particular body part or organ; it is often used interchangeably with the term *impairment.* A disability limits the ability to perform certain tasks (e.g., to see, hear, walk) in the same way that most persons do. A person with a disability is not handicapped, however, unless the physical disability leads to educational, personal, social, vocational, or other problems. If a child who has lost a leg, for example, can learn to use an artificial limb and thus function in and out of school without problems, he or she is not handicapped. The term *students with disabilities* is more restrictive than *exceptional children* in that it does not include gifted and talented children.

Handicap refers to a problem a person with a disability or impairment encounters in interacting with the environment. A disability may pose a handicap in one environment but not in another. The child with an artificial limb may be handicapped when competing against nondisabled peers on the basketball court but may experience no handicap in the classroom. Individuals with disabilities also experience handicaps that have nothing to do with their disabilities, but rather are the result of negative attitudes and behavior of others that needlessly restrict their access and ability to participate fully in the community. Although there are technical differences between *disability* and *handicap,* traditionally the two terms have been used interchangeably. The descriptor *with disabilities* is preferred today.

At risk refers to children who, although not currently identified as having a disability, are considered to have a greater-than-usual chance of developing a disability. The term is often applied to infants and preschoolers who, because of conditions surrounding their births or home environments, may be expected to experience developmental problems at a later time. The term also refers to students who are experiencing learning problems in the regular classroom and are therefore "at risk" of school failure or of being identified for special education services.

> The word *handicapped* is derived from "cap in hand" and conjures up the image of a person with disabilities begging in the street. *Handicapism* refers to the negative stereotyping and unequal and unjust treatment of people with disabilities.

In separate chapters, we examine the defining characteristics and educational implications of each of the following so-called categories of exceptional children:

- Mental retardation
- Learning disabilities
- Emotional and behavioral disorders
- Communication (speech and language) disorders
- Hearing impairments
- Visual impairments
- Physical and other health impairments
- Severe disabilities
- Gifted and talented

> Physicians also use the term *at risk* (or *high risk)* to identify pregnancies with a greater-than-normal probability of producing babies with disabilities. For example, a pregnancy may be considered "high risk" if the pregnant woman is above or below typical childbearing age, uses alcohol heavily, or is drug-dependent.

It is a mistake, however, to think that there are two distinct kinds of children—that is, those who are special and those who are regular. Exceptional children are more like other children than they are different. All children are unique individuals who require individual attention, nurturing, and caring. As stated earlier, all children differ from one another in individual characteristics along a continuum; exceptional children are those whose differences from the norm are large enough to require an individually designed program of instruction—in other words, special education—if they are to benefit fully from education.

✳ *How Many Exceptional Children Are There?*

Each year, the U.S. Department of Education reports to Congress on the education of the country's children with disabilities. As this book went to press, the most recent data available pertained to the 1992-93 school year (U.S. Department of Education, 1994).

Let's take a quick look at some of the numerical facts about special education in the United States.

- More than 5.1 million children with disabilities, or 7.4% of the resident population from birth to age 21, received special education services during the 1992-93 school year.

> Table 1.1 shows the number of students aged 6 through 21 who received special education during the 1992-93 school year under each of the 12 disability categories used by the federal government.

- The number of children and youth who receive special education has grown every year since a national count was begun in 1976, with an overall increase of 39% since the 1976-77 school year.
- New early intervention programs have been major contributors to the increases since 1986. During the 1992-93 school year, 459,728 preschoolers (4% of the population aged 3 to 5) and 143,392 infants and toddlers (1.2% of all children from birth through age 2) were among those receiving special education.
- Children with disabilities in special education represent approximately 8% of the entire school-age population.
- The number of children who receive special education increases from age 3 through age 9. The number served decreases gradually with each successive age year after age 9 until age 17. Thereafter, the number of students receiving special education decreases sharply.
- Ninety-four percent of all school-age children receiving special education are reported under four disability categories: (a) learning disabilities (52.4%), (b) speech and language impairment (22.2%), (c) mental retardation (10.9%), and (d) emotional disturbance (8.3%).
- The percentage of school-age students receiving special education under the learning disabilities category has grown dramatically (from 23.8% to 52.4%), whereas the percentage of students with mental retardation has decreased (from 24.9% to 10.9%) since the federal government began collecting and reporting child count data in 1976-77.
- About twice as many males as females receive special education.
- The vast majority—approximately 90%—of school-age children receiving special education have "mild disabilities."
- The "typical" child receiving special education in the United States is a 9-year-old boy with learning disabilities who spends part of each school day in the regular classroom and part in a resource room (U.S. Department of Education, 1990).

What factors might be responsible for the huge increase in the number of children identified as learning disabled? Why has the number of children identified as mentally retarded decreased in recent years? Compare your ideas with what you learn later in Chapters 4 and 5.

Although special education for children who are gifted and talented is not mandated by federal law as it is for children with disabilities, approximately 2 million children are being served in public school programs for gifted and talented students (U.S. Department of Education, 1993). This number ranks gifted and talented stu-

Although children with disabilities have special instructional needs, they are, above all, children.

TABLE 1.1
Number of students aged 6 through 21 who received special education services under each of the 12 disability categories used by the federal government, school year 1992-93

Disability	Number	Percentage
Specific learning disabilities	2,333,571	52.4
Speech or language impairments	990,718	22.2
Mental retardation	484,871	10.9
Serious emotional disturbance	368,545	8.3
Multiple disabilities	86,179	1.9
Hearing impairments	43,707	1.0
Orthopedic impairments	46,498	1.0
Other health impairments	63,982	1.4
Visual impairments	18,129	0.4
Autism	12,238	0.3
Deaf-blindness	773	0.0
Traumatic brain injury	2,906	0.1
All disabilities	4,452,117	100.0

Source: From *Sixteenth Annual Report to Congress on the Implementation of the Individuals with Disabilities Education Act,* p. 12, 1994, U.S. Department of Education.

dents as the second largest group of exceptional children receiving special education services. On the basis of an estimate that gifted and talented children may comprise as much as 5% of the school-age population, approximately 2.5 million additional gifted and talented children may need special education (Clark, 1992). This discrepancy between need and the level of service may make gifted and talented children the most underserved group of exceptional children.

> In 1988 Congress passed the *Jacob K. Javits Gifted and Talented Students Education Act,* which provides federal funds in support of research, teacher training, and program development.

To state precisely how many exceptional children live in the United States is virtually impossible for many reasons: (a) the different criteria that states and local school systems use to identify exceptional children; (b) the relative ability of a school system to provide effective instructional support to the regular classroom teacher so that an at-risk student does not become a special education student; (c) the imprecise nature of assessment; (d) the large part that subjective judgment plays in interpretation of assessment data; and (e) the fact that a child may be diagnosed as disabled at one time in his or her school career and not disabled (or included in a different disability category) at another time.

✳ *Problems of Labeling and Classifying Exceptional Children*

Centuries ago, the labeling and classifying of people was of little importance: Survival was the main concern. Those whose disabilities prevented their full participation in the activities necessary for survival were left on their own to perish or, in some instances, were even killed. In later years, derogatory labels like "dunce," "imbecile," and "fool" were applied to people with mental retardation or behavior problems, and other demeaning words were used for persons with other disabilities or physical deformities. In each instance, however, the purpose of classification was the same: to exclude the person with disabilities from the activities, privileges, and facilities of "normal" society.

The Pros and Cons

Many educators believe that the labeling and classifying of exceptional children functions to exclude them from normal society. Others argue that a workable system of classifying exceptional children (or their exceptional learning needs) is a prerequisite to providing the special educational programs those children require if they are to be integrated into normal society. Although the pros and cons of using disability category labels have been widely debated for more than two decades, research has shed little light on the problem. Most of the studies conducted to assess the effects of labeling have produced inconclusive, often contradictory, evidence and have generally been marked by methodological weakness (MacMillan, 1982).

Classification is a complex issue involving emotional, political, and ethical considerations, in addition to scientific, fiscal, and educational interests. As with most complex questions, there are valid arguments on both sides. Here are the reasons most often cited for and against the classification and labeling of exceptional children.

Possible Benefits of Labeling

- Categories can relate diagnosis to specific types of education or treatment.
- Labeling may lead to a "protective" response in which children are more accepting of the atypical behavior by a peer with disabilities than they would be if that same behavior were emitted by a child without disabilities (MacMillan, 1982).
- Labeling helps professionals communicate with one another and classify and assess research findings.
- Funding of special education programs is often based on specific categories of exceptionality.
- Labels enable disability-specific advocacy groups (e.g., parents of children with autism) to promote specific programs and to spur legislative action.
- Labeling helps make exceptional children's special needs more visible to the public.

Possible Disadvantages of Labeling

- Because labels usually focus on disability, impairment, and performance deficits, some people may think only in terms of what the individual *cannot do* instead of what he or she *can or might be able to learn to do.*
- Labels may cause others to hold low expectations for and to differentially treat a child on the basis of the label, which may result in a *self-fulfilling prophecy.* For example, in one study, student teachers gave a child labeled "autistic" more praise and rewards and less verbal correction for *incorrect* responses than they gave a child labeled "normal" (Eikeseth & Lovaas, 1992). Such differential treatment could hamper a child's acquisition of new skills and contribute to the development and maintenance of a level of performance consistent with the label's prediction.
- Labels that describe a child's performance deficit often mistakenly acquire the role of explanatory constructs (e.g., "Sherry acts that way *because* she is emotionally disturbed").

A protective response—whether by peers, parents, or teachers—toward a child with a disability can be a disadvantage if it creates a "learned helplessness" and diminishes the labeled child's chances to develop independence (Weisz, 1981; Weisz, Bromfield, Vines, & Weiss, 1985).

- Labels suggest that learning problems are primarily the result of something wrong within the child, thereby reducing the systematic examination of and accountability for instructional variables as the cause of performance deficits. This is an especially damaging outcome when the label provides educators with a built-in excuse for ineffective instruction (e.g., "Jalen hasn't learned to read because he's _____ ").
- A labeled child may develop a poor self-concept.
- Labels may lead peers to reject or ridicule the labeled child.
- Special education labels have a certain permanence; once labeled, it is difficult for a child to ever again achieve the status of simply being "just another kid."
- Labels often provide a basis for keeping children out of the regular classroom.
- A disproportionate number of children from diverse cultural, ethnic, and linguistic groups have been inaccurately labeled as disabled, especially under the category mild mental retardation.
- Classification of exceptional children requires the expenditure of a great amount of money and professional and student time that could better be spent in planning and delivering instruction.

Clearly, there are strong arguments both for and against the classification and labeling of exceptional children. Let's look more closely at how the use of categorical labels affects a child's access to special education services and the quality of instruction that he or she receives.

Labeling and Services

On one level, the various labels given to children with special learning needs can be viewed as a means of organizing the funding and administration of special education services in the schools. To receive special education services, a child must be identified as having a disability and, with few exceptions, must be further classified into one of that state's categories, such as mental retardation or learning disabilities. In practice, therefore, a student becomes eligible for various kinds of special education and related services because of membership in a given category. If losing one's label also means loss of needed services, the trade-off is not likely to be beneficial for the child. In the 1970s, for example, the definition of mental retardation was changed, and children who had previously been classified under the subcategory of "borderline mental retardation" no longer met the definition; as a result, they were no longer eligible for special education services designed for children with mental retardation. Although many of this large group of youngsters receive services under other disability categories, most notably learning disabilities, some do not receive needed services (MacMillan, 1989; Zetlin & Murtaugh, 1990).

Arguing that labels are necessary for students with emotional and behavioral disorders, Braaten, Kauffman, Braaten, Polsgrove, and Nelson (1988) write:

> We share the concern regarding the stigma of the label "behaviorally disordered," even more the stigma of "seriously emotionally disturbed." The label itself has little value other than channeling services. But to argue that BD students' stigma derives from their label misses the point that these students become social outcasts before they are referred for special education. . . . Serious problems must be talked about with serious language at an "official" level, else the students' difficulties are trivialized. Descriptions such as "naughty in class" (e.g., Shepard, 1987) and other euphemisms used to characterize LD and other mildly handicapped students—and

Not all labels used to classify children with disabilities are considered equally negative or stigmatizing. One factor possibly contributing to the large number of children identified as *learning disabled* is that many parents view "learning disabilities" as a socially acceptable classification (Algozzine & Korinek, 1985; Lieberman, 1985).

In the early 1970s, the U.S. government commissioned a comprehensive study of the classification of exceptional children. The results of this project can be found in *Classification of Children* (Vols. 1 and 2), edited by the project's director, Nicholas Hobbs (Hobbs, 1976a, 1976b). A third book, *The Futures of Children* (Hobbs, 1975), contains summaries of findings and recommendations. Other reviews of the labeling and classification of exceptional children can be found in MacMillan (1982) and Smith, Neisworth, and Hunt (1983). None of these discussions has produced conclusive arguments that could lead to total acceptance or absolute rejection of labeling practices.

by implication BD students—suggest that their problems are minor. The likely consequence of such language will be reduction in services for an already underserved group. (p. 23)*

Although identification and classification of exceptional children appear necessary, no one is happy with the current system of categorical labels. Labels signify eligibility for services, but they have proven unreliable in many cases. For example, one study that examined the classification of 523 students with mild disabilities found that 24% had been given two or more labels during their school years and that 17% of those who were moved from their initial category to another category were later reassigned to their initial classification (Wolman, Thurlow, & Bruininks, 1989). Similar results were reported by Halgren and Clarizio (1993), who reported that 16.3% of the 654 students with various disabilities in 10 school districts were reclassified during a 3-year period.

Reynolds, Wang, and Walberg (1987), who are strong opponents of the present system of identifying and labeling children for special education services, believe that "the boundaries of the categories have shifted so markedly in response to legal, economic, and political forces as to make diagnosis largely meaningless" (p. 396). Some special educators believe that the classification of exceptional children by disability category may actually interfere with the assessment and instructional planning that is directed toward each student's real learning needs. Stainback and Stainback (1984) argue:

> These categories often do not reflect the specific educational needs and interests of students in relation to such services. For example, some students categorized as visually handicapped may not need large-print books, while others who are not labeled visually impaired and thus are ineligible for large-print books could benefit from their use. Similarly, not all students labeled behaviorally disordered may need self-control training, while some students not so labeled may need self-control training as a part of their educational experience. (p. 105)

Impact on Instruction

What we can say about the possible benefits of classifying exceptional children is that, on the one hand, most are experienced not by individual children, but rather by groups of children, parents, and professionals who are associated with a certain category. On the other hand, all of the negative aspects of labeling affect the individual child who has been labeled. Of the possible advantages of labeling listed earlier, only the first two could be said to benefit an individual child. However, the argument that labels associate diagnosis with proper treatment is tenuous at best, particularly when the kinds of labels used in special education are considered. Written 25 years ago, this quote states clearly what many special educators have long believed about the irrelevance of categorical labels to instruction:

> The children are given various labels including deaf, blind, orthopedically handicapped, trainable mentally retarded, educable mentally retarded, autistic, socially

Unlike school-age children, the provision of special services for preschoolers does not require the use of specific disability labels. Children from birth through age 5 can receive early intervention services under a generic at-risk category if they are experiencing established biological (e.g., low birth weight) or environmental conditions (e.g., extremely impoverished home environment) that often result in a developmental delay or disability. We examine early intervention in Chapter 14.

---

*Excerpt from The Regular Education Initiative (REI): Patent Medicine for Behavioral Disorders. By Braaten, S., et al. (1988). *Exceptional Children, 55,* 21-27. Copyright (1988) by The Council for Exceptional Children. Reprinted by permission.

maladjusted, perceptually handicapped, brain-injured, emotionally disturbed, disadvantaged, and those with learning disabilities. For the most part the labels are not important. They rarely tell the teacher who can be taught in what way. One could put five or six labels on the same child and still not know what to teach him or how. (Becker, Engelmann, & Thomas, 1971, pp. 435-436)

A number of special educators have proposed alternative approaches to classifying exceptional children that focus on educationally relevant variables (e.g., Iscoe & Payne, 1972; Quay, 1968; Reynolds, Zetlin, & Wang, 1993; Sontag, Sailor, & Smith, 1977). Lovitt (1982) suggests classifying exceptional children according to the curriculum and skill areas they need to learn.

> "What should we call the special children who are sent to our classes?" This question might be asked by regular education teachers who are about to have special education children mainstreamed in their classes. Should they carefully study the dossiers of the children to figure out what others have called them? Should a regular teacher, for instance, try to remember that Roy, who will soon be sent to his regular class, was called emotionally disturbed by two school psychologists, a social worker, and a reading teacher (even though he was referred to as learning disabled by another school psychologist)? Should he hang on to the fact that Amy was called mentally retarded by most of the people who wrote reports for her folder? Likewise, should he make every effort to recall that Tim was most often referred to as learning disabled?
>
> No. Those labels do not help teachers design effective programs for the special children they will teach. They won't help teachers decide where to seat the children; they certainly won't help them to design educational and management strategies.
>
> But if we shouldn't refer to these special children by using those old labels, then how should we refer to them? For openers, call them Roy, Amy, and Tim. Beyond that, refer to them on the basis of what you're trying to teach them. For example, if a teacher wants to teach Roy to compute, read, and comprehend, he might call him a student of computation, reading, and comprehension. We do this all the time with older students. Sam, who attends Juilliard, is referred to as "the trumpet student"; Jane, who attends Harvard, is called "the law student." (Lovitt, 1979, p. 5)

In a system such as this, called **curriculum-based assessment,** students would be assessed and classified relative to the degree to which they are learning specific curriculum content (Howell, Fox, & Morehead, 1993; Potter & Wamre, 1990; Salvia & Hughes, 1990). The fundamental question in curriculum-based assessment is: How is the student progressing in the curriculum of the local school? (Tucker, 1985). Educators who employ curriculum-based assessment believe that it is more important to assess (and thereby classify) students in terms of acquisition of the skills and knowledge included in the school's curriculum than to determine the degree to which they differ from the normative score of all children in some general physical attribute or learning characteristic.

Even though curriculum-based assessment is being used more frequently, use of the traditional labels and categories of exceptional children is likely to continue. The continued development and use of educationally relevant classification systems, however, make it more likely that diagnosis and assessment will lead to meaningful instructional programs for children, promote more educationally meaningful communication and research by professionals, and perhaps decrease some of the negative aspects of the current practice of labeling children.

As an alternative to the traditional, categorical-driven model of special education, Reynolds, Zetlin, and Wang (1993) have proposed a system called "20/20 Analysis." All students showing the least progress (below the 20th percentile) and the most progress (above the 80th percentile) toward a school's important objectives would be identified and eligible for "broad (noncategorical) approaches to improvement of learning opportunities" (p. 294). For a critique and discussion of the possible merits and disadvantages of 20/20 Analysis, see Soodak and Podell (1994) and Reynolds, Zetlin, and Wang (1994).

What's in a Name?

The Labels and Language of Special Education

Some years ago at the annual convention of the Council for Exceptional Children, hundreds of attendees were wearing big yellow and black buttons that were very popular that year. The buttons proclaimed "Label jars, not children!" Wearers of the buttons were presumably making a statement about one or more of the criticisms leveled at categorizing and labeling exceptional children, such as labeling is negative; it focuses only on the child's deficits in learning or behavior; labeling makes it more likely that others (teachers, parents, peers) will expect poor performance and bad behavior from the labeled child; and labels may hurt the child's self-esteem.

Labels, in and of themselves, are not the problem. The dictionary defines *label* as "a descriptive word or phrase applied to a person, group, theory, etc., as a convenient generalized classification" (*Webster's New World Dictionary,* 1986, p. 785). Most professionals in special education agree that a common language for referring to children who share common instructional and related service needs is necessary. The kinds of words that we use as labels, and even the order in which they are spoken or written, do, however, influence the degree to which a particular label serves as an appropriate generalized classification for communicating variables relevant to the design and provision of educational and other human services. For exam-

ple, although they may refer to a common set of educational needs, terms such as "the handicapped," "the retarded," and "blind children" also imply negative connotations that are unwarranted and inappropriate. Such blanket labels imply that all persons in the group being labeled are alike; individuality has been lost. At the personal level, when we describe a child as a "physically handicapped boy," we place too much emphasis on the disability, suggesting the deficits caused by the disability are the most important thing to know about him.

How, then, should we refer to exceptional children? At the personal level, we can and should follow Tom Lovitt's advice and call them by their names: Linda, Shawon, and Jackie. Referring to a child as "Molly, a fifth-grade student with learning disabilities" helps us focus on the individual child and her primary role as a student. Such a description does not ignore or gloss over the learning problems that challenge Molly, but it does acknowledge that there are other things we should know about her.

It is important for everyone, not just special educators, to speak, write, and think about exceptional children and adults in ways that respect each person's individuality and recognize strengths and abilities instead of focusing only on disabilities. Simply changing the way we talk about an individual with a disability, however, will not make the needs and challenges posed by his or her disability go away. Many individuals with disabilities have begun to speak up against the efforts by those without disabilities to assuage their feelings with language that may be politically correct but that ignores the reality of a disability. Judy Heumann (1993), Director of the U.S. Department of Education's Office of Special Education and Rehabilitation Services and a person who has used a wheel-

chair since she was 18 months old, explains her position:

> As our movement has evolved, we have been plagued by people, almost always not themselves disabled, attempting to change what we call ourselves. If we are "victims" of anything, it is of such terms as physically challenged, able-disabled, differently abled, handi-capables, and people with differing abilities, to name just a few. Nondisabled people's discomfort with reality-based terms such as disabled led them to these euphemisms. I believe these euphemisms have the effect of depoliticizing our own terminology and devaluing our own view of ourselves as disabled people. . . .
>
> I have a physical disability that results in my inability to walk and perform a number of other significant tasks without the assistance of another person. This cannot be labeled away and I am not ashamed of it. I feel no need to change the word "disabled." For me, there is no stigma. I am not driven to call myself a "person with a disability." I know I am a person; I do not need to tell myself that I am. I also do not believe that being called a "person with a disability" results in my being treated any more like a human being. Maybe putting the word "disabled" first makes people stop and look at what, as a result of society's historical indifference to and/or hatred of people like me, is a critical part of my existence. . . .
>
> Let the disabled people who are politically involved and personally affected determine our own language. . . . A suggestion to those of you who do not know what to call me: ask!

Donald Cook, an educational researcher, contributed these comments to a discussion of how to speak to and about people with disabilities that took place on an internet bulletin board:

> I am handicapped by post polio syndrome and must use a wheelchair

and/or a walker. The other day I was referred to, for the first time, as "differently-abled." The context was benign: the speaker had noticed a beach with special wheelchairs that went across sand and into the water, and thought I would like to know about it. Still the term "differently-abled" stunned me. I asked whose feelings were being spared here, mine or hers? This question angered

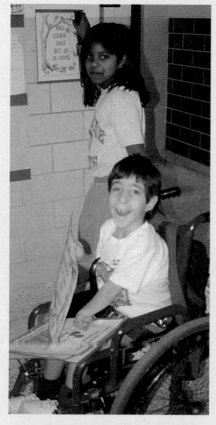

Changing the label used to identify or classify Jeffrey's disability won't lessen the severity of his handicap. But referring to him as "Jeffrey, a third grader," instead of a "multi-handicapped boy," helps us recognize his strengths and abilities—what he can do—instead of focusing on the disability as if it were his defining characteristic.

her—a possible sign of a question with a point. It seems clear to me that my condition is not merely different in some abstract dimension but one of a loss of function. So I prefer "handicapped" or some term which acknowledges that. It is NOT the case that there is some "compensation" such as the ability to extract square roots lightening fast with my left toe, or any other. (*CompuServe Education Forum,* July 11, 1994)

Bernard Rimland (1993a), director of the Autism Research Institute in San Diego and the father of a son with autism, is a severe critic of those who are trying to change the language of special education under the

> . . . arrogant assumption of the moral high ground . . . certain that their way is the only way. . . . They insist that words such as "autistic," "retarded," and "handicapped" not be used. They insist that the silly euphemism "challenging" be used to describe severely self-injurious or assaultive behavior. . . . It deprives the handicapped of their most valuable asset—the recognition of their disability by the rest of us. Yes, there are people on the borderline between normal and handicapped. Does that mean that no one is handicapped? Yes, there are shades of gray. Does that mean there is no black and white? Does twilight disprove the difference between day and night? (p. 1)

The following commentary, written by Michael Goldfarb, Executive Director of the Association for the Help of Retarded Children, offers some provocative and insightful thoughts on the "language of special education."

> Even after it had become fashionable to use the phrase "Down syndrome," Louis Striar insisted on calling his son a mongoloid. He enjoyed the shocked look on people's faces when he stubbornly clung to the old label. He consistently refused to trade in a phrase he was used to for one that was used by others. I always

thought that Louie did this simply to shock people, because he enjoyed that.

I now realize that his real goal, as a Board member of AHRC and as a parent of a disabled son, was to demonstrate that no new label, however popular, would solve his son's problem with society or society's problem with his son. No matter what label you used, Martin was retarded. Louie was attempting to teach us a very painful lesson, one which we still have not learned, namely, that linguistic reform alone can't really change the world. It has taken me a dozen years to figure out what he meant.

Consider the following lists of words:

crippled
handicapped
disabled
challenged

inmate
patient
resident
client
program participant

feeble minded
retarded
person with mental retardation
person

institution
state school
developmental center

Consider the words on the top of each list, the old and unfashionable ones. The names at the bottom are new and more acceptable. Many professionals in this field have made it a matter of deep personal commitment to get you to use the most up-to-date expressions.

Every one of these changes has been presented as an essential act of consciousness raising. Every one of these changes has been proposed by numbers of enlightened, progressive, and intelligent professionals with the genuine intent of changing the image and role of disabled people in this society. Every one of these linguistic reforms has been followed several years later by newer and "better" names. Every one of these changes has failed to make the world different.

Linguistic reform without systemic change conceals unhappy truths. Social problems may be reflected in the way we speak, but they are rarely, if ever, cured by changes in language. It is certainly true that liberals feel better when they use the most acceptable phrase, but this should not obscure the fact that the oppressed continue to be oppressed under any label. (Perhaps we should not call people "the oppressed"; perhaps it would be better to call them "people with oppression.")

Our real problem in this and many other societies is that we respect only intelligence, stylish good looks, and earning potential. This society denigrates people who are not intelligent, who are deemed unattractive, or who are poor. Referring to retarded people as "people with mental retardation" will not make them brighter, prettier, richer. These names leave the old prejudices intact. Society's attitudes and the values that underlie them must be changed. This will take far more than trivial linguistic changes. Can you imagine a Planning Board meeting at which a local resident says, "We don't want any retarded people living in our neighborhood! But people with mental retardation? That's

different. They can move in anytime." I can't.

Changing attitudes and values is more difficult than changing language. Perhaps that is why we spend so much time changing language. ✳

From M. Goldfarb, Executive Director's Report, *AHRC Chronicle,* Spring 1990. Adapted by permission.
Excerpt from Heumann, J. (1993). Building Our Own Boats: A Personal Perspective on Disability Policy. In Gostin & Beyer (Eds.), *Implementing the Americans with Disabilities Act: Rights and Responsibilities of all Americans,* Paul H. Brookes Publishing, P.O. Box 10624, Baltimore MD 21285-0624. Reprinted by permission of the publisher and author.

✳ *Special Education as Civil Rights: Litigation and Legislation Affecting Exceptional Children*

It is said that a society can be judged by the way it treats those who are different. By this criterion, our educational system has less than a distinguished history. Children who are different because of race, culture, language, gender, or exceptionality have often been denied full and fair access to educational opportunities (Banks & Banks, 1993).

Although exceptional children have always been with us, attention has not always been paid to their special needs. In the past, many children with disabilities were entirely excluded from any publicly supported program of education. Prior to the 1970s, many states had laws permitting public schools to deny enrollment to children with disabilities (Heward & Cavanaugh, 1993). Local school officials had no legal obligation to grant students with disabilities the same educational access that nondisabled students enjoyed. One state law, for example, allowed schools to refuse to serve "children physically or mentally incapacitated for school work"; another state had a law stipulating that children with "bodily or mental conditions rendering attendance inadvisable" could be turned away. When these laws were contested, the nation's courts generally supported exclusion. In a 1919 case, for example, a 13-year-old student with physical disabilities (but normal intellectual ability) was excluded from his local school because he "produces a depressing and nauseating effect upon the teachers and school children. . . . [H]e takes up an undue portion of the teacher's time and attention, distracts attention of other pupils, and interferes generally with the discipline and progress of the school" (T. P. Johnson, 1986, p. 2). Many communities had no facilities or services whatsoever to help exceptional children and their families.

Past practices were not entirely negative. Long before there was any legal requirement to do so, many children with special needs were educated by devoted parents and teachers.

The fundamental question of curriculum-based assessment is "How is the student progressing in the curriculum of the local school?"

When local public schools began to accept a measure of responsibility for educating certain exceptional students, a philosophy of segregation prevailed—a philosophy that continued unchanged until recently. Integration of exceptional children into regular schools and classes is a relatively recent phenomenon. Children received labels—such as mentally retarded, crippled, or emotionally disturbed—and were confined to isolated and segregated classrooms, kept apart from the other children and teachers in the regular education program. One special education teacher describes the sense of isolation she felt and the crude facilities in which her special class operated in the 1960s.

> I accepted my first teaching position, a special education class in a basement room next door to the furnace. Of the 15 "educable mentally retarded" children assigned to work with me, most were simply nonreaders from poor families. One child had been banished to my room because she posed a behavior problem to her fourth-grade teacher.
>
> My class and I were assigned a recess spot on the opposite side of the play yard, far away from the "normal" children. I was the only teacher who did not have a lunch break. I was required to eat with my "retarded" children while other teachers were permitted to leave their students. . . . Isolated from my colleagues, I closed my door and did my thing, oblivious to the larger educational circles in which I was immersed. Although it was the basement room, with all the negative perceptions that arrangement implies, I was secure in the knowledge that despite the ignominy of it all I did good things for children who were previously unloved and untaught. (Aiello, 1976)

Children with mild learning and behavioral disorders usually remained in the regular classroom but received no special treatment. If their deportment in class exceeded the teacher's tolerance for misbehavior, they were labeled "disciplinary problems" and suspended from school. If they did not make satisfactory academic progress, they were termed "slow learners," "failures," or "ineducable." Children with more severe disabilities—including many with visual, hearing, and physical or health impairments—were usually placed into segregated schools or institutions or kept at home. Children who were gifted and talented seldom received special attention in schools. They could make it on their own, it was thought, without help.

Society's response to exceptional children has come a long way. As our concepts of equality, freedom, and justice have expanded, children with disabilities and the families have moved from isolation to participation. Although the speed of these changes has been described as a "painfully slow process of integration and participation" (Cremins, 1983, p. 3), the "history of special education can be summarized quite well in two words: 'progressive integration' " (Reynolds, 1989, p. 7).

Society no longer regards children with disabilities as beyond the responsibility of the local public schools. No longer may a child who is different from the norm be turned away from school because someone believes that he or she is "unable to appropriately benefit from typical instruction." Recent legislation and court decisions confirm that all children with disabilities, no less than any other citizen, have the right to a *free, appropriate program of public education in the least restrictive environment.*

The provision of equitable educational opportunities to exceptional children has not come about by chance. Many laws and court cases have had important effects on public education in general and on the education of children with special needs in particular. And the process of change is never finished. As Prasse (1986) notes, legal influences on special education are not fixed or static, but rather fluid and dynamic.

Brown v. Board of Education

The recent history of special education, especially in regard to the education of children with disabilities in regular schools, is related to the civil rights movement. Special education was strongly influenced by social developments and court decisions in the 1950s and 1960s, especially the landmark case of *Brown v. Board of Education* [of Topeka], 347 U.S. 483 (1954). This case challenged the practice of segregating students according to race. In its ruling in the *Brown* case, the U.S. Supreme Court declared that education must be made available to all children on equal terms:

> Today, education is perhaps the most important function of state and local governments. Compulsory school attendance laws and the great expenditure for education both demonstrate our recognition of the importance of education to our democratic society. It is required in the performance of our most basic responsibilities. . . . In these days, it is doubtful that any child may reasonably be expected to succeed in life if he is denied the opportunity of an education. (*Brown v. Board of Education,* 1954)

The *Brown* decision and the ensuing extension of public school education to African American and White children on equal terms began a period of intense concern and questioning among parents of children with disabilities, who asked why the same principles of equal access to education did not apply to their children. Numerous court cases were initiated in the 1960s and early 1970s by parents and other advocates dissatisfied with an educational system that denied equal access to children with disabilities. Generally, the parents based their arguments on the Fourteenth Amendment to the Constitution, which provides that no state shall deny any person within its jurisdiction the equal protection of the law and that no state shall deprive any person of life, liberty, or property without due process of law. The concepts of equal protection and due process are so fundamentally important in special education that we discuss them in some detail.

Equal Protection

In the past, children with disabilities usually received differential treatment; that is, they were excluded from certain educational programs or were given special education only in segregated settings. Basically, when the courts have been asked to rule on the practice of denial and segregation, judges have examined whether such treatment is *rational* and whether it is *necessary* (Williams, 1977). One of the most historically significant cases to examine these questions was the class action suit *Pennsylvania Association for Retarded Children v. Commonwealth of Pennsylvania* (1972). The association (PARC) challenged a state law that denied public school education to certain children considered "unable to profit from public school attendance."

> A *class action* lawsuit is one made on behalf of a group of people. In the PARC case, the class of people was school-age children with mental retardation living in Pennsylvania.

The lawyers and parents supporting PARC argued that even though the children had intellectual disabilities, it was neither rational nor necessary to assume they were ineducable and untrainable. Because the state was unable to prove that the children were, in fact, ineducable or to demonstrate a rational basis for excluding them from public school programs, the court decided that the children were entitled to receive a free, public education. In addition, the court maintained that parents had the right to be notified before any change was made in their children's educational program.

These and other rights are guaranteed under the equal protection clause of the Fourteenth Amendment, which holds that people may not be deprived of their equality or liberty because of any classification (e.g., race, nationality, religion). The courts have often regarded people with disabilities as belonging to a minority group that has a history of discrimination, political powerlessness, and unequal treatment (Thomas, 1985). Thus, equal protection and certain procedures known as due process of law must be provided to ensure that children with disabilities and their families are fully informed of their rights and are treated fairly and reasonably as citizens.

The wording of the PARC decision proved particularly important because of its influence on subsequent federal legislation. Not only did the court rule that all children with mental retardation were entitled to a free, appropriate public education, but the ruling also stipulated that placements in regular classrooms and regular public schools were preferable to segregated settings.

> It is the Commonwealth's obligation to place each mentally retarded child in a free, public program of education and training appropriate to the child's capacity. . . . [P]lacement in a regular public school class is preferable to placement in a special public school class and placement in a special public school is preferable to placement in any other type of program of education and training. An assignment to homebound instruction shall be re-evaluated not less than every 3 months, and notice of the evaluation and an opportunity for a hearing thereon shall be accorded to the parent or guardian. (*Pennsylvania Association for Retarded Children v. Commonwealth of Pennsylvania,* 1972)

Due Process

In the past, students with disabilities (and some nondisabled students as well) were not always considered "people" in the eyes of the law. Several recent laws and court decisions, however, have clearly established that students are, indeed, people, entitled to exercise such rights as privacy, freedom of travel, the practice of religion, and personal rights, such as choosing their own clothing and hairstyles. Although school officials may enforce reasonable regulations, they may not operate unfairly or arbitrarily, and they do not have absolute authority over students.

An important element of due process in special education is the acknowledgment of a student as a person, with important rights and responsibilities. Some people have questioned why highly specific legal safeguards are necessary to protect the rights of children with disabilities: Aren't they protected by the same laws and due process procedures that apply to all citizens? Reviewing how children with disabilities have been treated in the past by schools (and by society in general), we find that existing laws and legal procedures were often not equally applied. Meyen (1978) cites five reasons for the necessity of specific legal safeguards for children with disabilities.

1. Once placed in a special education program, many children with disabilities remained there for the rest of their educational careers. This type of system permanently excluded many children from regular classrooms once they were placed elsewhere.
2. Decisions to place students in special education programs were often made primarily on the basis of teacher recommendation or the results of a single test.
3. Children with severe disabilities were routinely excluded from public school programs. If they received any education at all, their parents usually had to pay for it.
4. A disproportionate number of children from minority cultural groups were placed in special education programs.
5. The level of educational services provided to residents of institutions was often extremely low or nonexistent.

These circumstances led to higher levels of activism by parents of exceptional children and by lawyers, educators, and other advocates who were concerned that these children were not being treated fairly. Many legislators and judges agreed. The concept of due process for students with disabilities and their parents within the public educational system is now embodied in law. Key elements of due process as it relates to special education are the parents' right to

- Be notified in writing before the school takes any action that may alter their child's program (testing, reevaluation, change in placement)
- Give or withhold permission to have their child tested for eligibility for special education services, reevaluated, or placed into a different classroom or program
- See all school records about their child
- Have a hearing before an impartial party (not an employee of the school district) to resolve disagreements with the school system
- Receive a written decision following any hearing
- Appeal the results of a due process hearing to the state department of education (school districts may also appeal)

Ann and Rud Turnbull (1990), who are special educators and parents of a young man with disabilities, describe due process as the legal technique that seeks to achieve fair treatment, accountability, and a new and more equal "balance of power" between professionals, who have traditionally wielded power, and families, who have thought they could not affect their children's education.

Other Important Court Cases

In addition to the *PARC* case, several other judicial decisions have had far-reaching effects on special education. The rulings of some of these cases have been incorporated into subsequent federal legislation, most notably PL 94–142, the Individuals with Disabilities Education Act.

Table 1.2 is a summary of key judicial decisions that have had significant impact on special education and the lives of individuals with disabilities.

Hobson v. Hansen (1967)

In this case, the court ruled against the so-called tracking system, in which children were placed into either regular or special classes according to their scores on intelligence tests. Most of the tests had been standardized on a population of White middle-class children. *Hobson v. Hansen* involved African American working-class children, who made up most of the student population of the Washington, DC, public schools. The court decided that these children were not being classified according to their ability to learn, but rather according to environmental and social factors irrelevant to their learning ability and potential.

Diana v. State Board of Education (1970)

On the basis of the results of intelligence tests given in English, a Spanish-speaking student in California had been placed into a special class for children with mental retardation. The court ruled that this placement was inappropriate and that the child must be given another evaluation in her native language.

Standardized intelligence tests are discussed in Chapter 4.

Mills v. Board of Education (1972)

Seven children had been excluded from the public schools in Washington, DC, because of learning and behavior problems. The school district contended that it did not have enough money to provide special education programs for them. The court held that lack of funds is no excuse for failing to educate the children and ordered the schools to readmit and serve them appropriately. Even if funds are limited (as is often the case), children with disabilities may not be denied access to public schools. Financial problems cannot be allowed to have a greater impact on children with disabilities than on students without disabilities.

Larry P. v. Riles (1979)

This California case found the placement of African American children in special classes inappropriate because of unfair testing. The IQ tests that were used failed to recognize the children's cultural background and the learning that took place in their homes and communities. When different tests were used, it was found that the children were not mentally retarded. The court ordered that IQ tests could not be used as the sole basis for placing children into special classes.

These cases and many others helped establish the schools' responsibility to provide education for children with disabilities and to treat them fairly. Exceptional children, who suffered from exclusion and segregation in the past, are today moving toward greater inclusion and integration in the schools. Gilhool (1976), an attorney

TABLE 1.2
Major court cases that have affected special education and the lives of individuals with disabilities

YEAR	COURT CASE
1954	*Brown v. Board of Education of Topeka* (Kansas) Established the right of all children to an equal opportunity for an education.
1967	*Hobson v. Hansen* (Washington, D.C.) Declared the track system, which used standardized tests as a basis for special education placement, unconstitutional because it discriminated against African American and poor children.
1970	*Diana v. State Board of Education* (California) Declared that children cannot be placed in special education on the basis of culturally biased tests or tests given in other than the child's native language.
1972	*Mills v. Board of Education of the District of Columbia* Established the right of every child to an equal opportunity for education; declared that lack of funds was not an acceptable excuse for lack of educational opportunity.
1972	*Pennsylvania Association for Retarded Citizens v. the Commonwealth of Pennsylvania* Class action suit that established the right to free public education for all children with mental retardation.
1972	*Wyatt v. Stickney* (Alabama) Declared that individuals in state institutions have the right to appropriate treatment within those institutions.
1979	*Larry P. v. Riles* (California) First brought to court in 1972; ruled that IQ tests cannot be used as the sole basis for placing children in special classes.
1979	*Armstrong v. Kline* (Pennsylvania) Established the right of some children with severe disabilities to an extension of the 180-day public school year.
1982	*Board of Education of the Hendrik Hudson Central School District v. Rowley* (New York) First case based on PL 94–142 to reach the U.S. Supreme Court; while denying plaintiff's specific request, upheld for each child with disabilities the right to a personalized program of instruction and necessary supportive services.
1983	*Abrahamson v. Hershman* (Massachusetts) Ruled that residential placement in a private school was necessary for a child with multiple disabilities who needed around-the-clock training; required the school district to pay for the private placement.

instrumental in the *PARC* case, aptly summarized the focus of judicial and social developments: "Integration is a central constitutional value. Not integration that denies differences, but rather integration that accommodates difference."

Turnbull (1993)—an attorney, nationally recognized expert on special education law, and the father of a son with severe disabilities—provides an in-depth but very readable explanation of special education law and related court cases.

✳ *The Individuals with Disabilities Education Act*

In 1975 the United States Congress passed Public Law 94–142, the *Individuals with Disabilities Education Act (IDEA)*. Shortly after its passage, PL 94–142 was called "blockbuster legislation" (Goodman, 1976) and hailed as the law that "will probably become known as having the greatest impact on education in history" (Stowell & Terry, 1977, p. 475). These predictions have proven accurate; the IDEA is a landmark piece of legislation that has changed the face of education in this country. This law has affected every school in the country and has changed the roles of regular and

YEAR	COURT CASE
1984	*Department of Education v. Katherine D.* (Hawaii) Ruled that a homebound instructional program for a child with multiple health impairments did not meet the least-restrictive-environment standard; called for the child to be placed in a class with children without disabilities and provided with related medical services.
1984	*Irving Independent School District v. Tatro* (Texas) Ruled that catheterization was necessary for a child with physical disabilities to remain in school and that it could be performed by a nonphysician, thus obligating the school district to provide that service.
1984	*Smith v. Robinson* (Rhode Island) Ordered the state to pay for the placement of a child with severe disabilities into a residential program and ordered the school district to reimburse the parents' attorney fees. U.S. Supreme Court later ruled that PL 94–142 did not entitle parents to recover such fees, but Congress subsequently passed an "Attorney's Fees" bill, leading to enactment of PL 99–372.
1985	*Cleburne v. Cleburne Living Center* (Texas) U.S. Supreme Court ruled unanimously that communities cannot use a discriminatory zoning ordinance to prevent establishment of group homes for persons with mental retardation.
1988	*Honig v. Doe* (California) Ruled that children with disabilities could not be excluded from school for any misbehavior that is "disability-related" (in this case, "aggressive behavior against other students" on the part of two "emotionally handicapped" students) but that educational services could cease if the misbehavior is not related to the disability.
1989	*Timothy W. v. Rochester School District* (New Hampshire) A U.S. Appeals Court upheld the literal interpretation that PL 94–142 requires that *all* children with disabilities be provided with a free, appropriate public education. The three-judge Appeals Court overturned the decision of a District Court judge, who had ruled that the local school district was not obligated to educate a 13-year-old boy with multiple and severe disabilities because he could not "benefit" from special education.

special educators, school administrators, parents, and many others involved in the educational process. Its passage marked the culmination of the efforts of a great many educators, parents, and legislators to bring together in one comprehensive bill this country's laws regarding the education of children with disabilities. The law reflects society's concern for treating people with disabilities as full citizens, with the same rights and privileges that all other citizens enjoy.

The IDEA mandates that all children with disabilities between the ages of 3 and 21, regardless of the type or severity of their disability, shall receive a *free, appropriate public education.* This education must be provided at public expense—that is, without cost to the child's parents. The IDEA is directed primarily at the states, which are responsible for providing education to their citizens. Each state education agency must comply with the law by locating and identifying all children with disabilities. The majority of the many rules and regulations defining how the IDEA operates are related to six major principles that have remained unchanged since 1975 (Strickland & Turnbull, 1993; Turnbull, 1993):

1. *Zero reject.* Schools must enroll every child, regardless of the nature or severity of his or her disabilities; no child with disabilities may be excluded from a public education.
2. *Nondiscriminatory testing.* Schools must use nonbiased, multifactored methods of evaluation to determine whether a child has a disability and, if so, whether spe-

Federal legislation is identified by a numerical system. PL 94–142, for example, was the 142nd bill passed by the 94th Congress. PL 94–142 was originally called the *Education for All Handicapped Children Act.* Since it became law in 1975, Congress has amended PL 94–142 three times: in 1983, in 1986, and again in 1990. The 1990 amendments renamed the law the *Individuals with Disabilities Education Act*—often referred to by its acronym, the IDEA.

cial education is needed. Testing and evaluation procedures must not discriminate on the basis of race, culture, or native language. All tests must be administered in the child's native language, and identification and placement decisions must not be made on the basis of a single test score.

3. *Appropriate education.* Schools must develop and implement an **individualized education program (IEP)** for each student with a disability. The IEP must be individually designed to meet the child's unique needs.

4. ***Least restrictive environment (LRE).*** Schools must educate students with disabilities with children who do not have disabilities to the maximum extent possible.

5. *Due process.* Schools must provide safeguards to protect the rights of children with disabilities and their parents by ensuring due process, confidentiality of records, and parental involvement in educational planning and placement decisions.

6. *Parent participation.* Schools must collaborate with the parents of students with disabilities in the design and implementation of special education services.

The *individualized education program (IEP)* and the *least restrictive environment (LRE)* are examined in detail in Chapter 2.

Education of students with disabilities is expensive. Laws and regulations calling for special education would be of limited value if the schools lacked the necessary financial resources. Congress backed up its mandate for free, appropriate public education by providing federal funds to help school districts meet the additional costs of educating children with disabilities (many of whom had not previously been served by public schools). Congress allocates funds to each state yearly to help implement the IDEA's goals and policies. Each state then directs most of the money it receives from the federal government to local school districts to provide services to students with disabilities.

The original intent of Congress was that approximately 40% of the total cost of educating each child with a disability would be covered by federal funds. Many state and local educational administrators, however, contend that federal financial assistance for the education of students with disabilities has not been sufficient and that their schools are hard-pressed to meet the costs of educating children with disabilities. School districts spend about twice as much money on each student in special education as they do on each student in regular education. Chaikind, Danielson, and Brauen (1993) reported a per pupil annual cost of approximately $7,800 in 1989-90 dollars, or about 2.3 times the cost of educating each pupil in regular education. They found that costs of special education services varied considerably by disability category, ranging from under $1,000 per student with speech and language impairments to over $30,000 per student with deaf-blindness.

When Congress passed the IDEA in 1975, it authorized the federal government to provide up to 40% of the average per child expenditure in public elementary and secondary schools to assist states in meeting the needs of children with disabilities. According to spending levels during the 1992-93 school year, however, Congress provided only 8.3% of average per child expenditures (U.S. Department of Education, 1994).

Other Provisions of the Law

Two priorities were set forth in the IDEA for the expenditure of funds to educate children with disabilities. The first priority was to children who were currently unserved by any kind of educational program. The second priority was to children who were currently inadequately served. Many previously unserved and inadequately served children were those with severe and multiple disabilities; many had been kept at home or in institutions.

The IDEA also stipulates that, in cases in which an appropriate education cannot be provided in the public schools, children with disabilities may be placed in private school programs at no cost to their parents. This has proven to be a particularly controversial aspect of the law. Parents and school officials have frequently disagreed over whether private school placement at public expense is the most appropriate way to meet the needs of an exceptional child. Children with disabilities have sometimes been prevented from attending regular schools by circumstances other than educational performance. A child who uses a wheelchair, for example, may require a specially equipped school bus. A child with special health problems may require medication several times a day. The law calls for schools to provide any **related services**—such as special transportation, counseling, physical therapy, and other supportive assistance—that a child with disabilities may need in order to benefit from special education. Figure 1.1 provides definitions of the 15 types of related services included in the IDEA regulations. This provision has also been highly controversial, with much disagreement over what kinds of related services are necessary and reasonable for the schools to provide and what services should be the responsibility of the child's parents.

In addition, each state is required to develop a comprehensive system for personnel development, including inservice training programs for regular education teachers, special education teachers, school administrators, and other support personnel. Finally, each state must submit to the federal government an annual plan describing how it ensures the education of all children with disabilities in the state.

Amendments to PL 94–142

Like other comprehensive federal laws, PL 94–142 periodically undergoes reauthorization and amendment in response to changing circumstances. Since its passage, PL 94–142 has been amended three times. In 1982 the administrative branch of the federal government initiated action to revise some of the rules and regulations of PL 94–142. The proposed changes, which would have softened the law in several respects, were met with overwhelming opposition by parent advocacy and professional groups. As a result, when the law was amended for the first time in 1983 (PL 98–199), Congress passed a strong reaffirmation of all major provisions of PL 94–142, including an expansion of research and services for the transition of secondary students from school to work, and modest increases in funding levels for various programs.

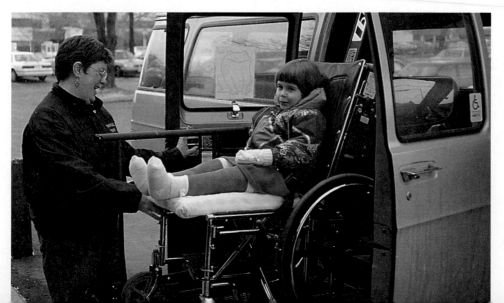

School districts must provide related services to students with disabilities—such as this adapted wheelchair lift that enables Tammy to travel to and from school—so they may have access to and benefit from a public education.

FIGURE 1.1

Types and definitions of related services that students with disabilities may need in order to benefit from education

1. <u>Audiology</u> includes identification of children with hearing loss; determination of the range, nature, and degree of hearing loss; and creation and administration of programs for [treatment and] prevention of hearing loss.

2. <u>Counseling services</u> means services provided by qualified social workers, psychologists, guidance counselors, or other qualified personnel.

3. <u>Early identification and assessment of disabilities in children</u> means the implementation of a formal plan for identifying a disability as early as possible in a child's life.

4. <u>Medical services</u> means services provided by a licensed physician to determine a child's medically related disability that results in the child's need for special education and related services.

5. <u>Occupational therapy</u> includes improving, developing, or restoring functions impaired or lost through illness, injury, or deprivation.

6. <u>Parent counseling and training</u> means assisting parents in understanding the special needs of their child and providing parents with information about child development.

7. <u>Physical therapy</u> means services provided by a qualified physical therapist.

8. <u>Psychological services</u> includes administering psychological and educational tests, and other assessment procedures; interpreting assessment results; obtaining, integrating, and interpreting information about child behavior and conditions relating to learning; consulting with other staff members in planning school programs to meet the special needs of children as indicated by psychological tests, interviews, and behavioral evaluations; and planning and managing a program of psychological services, including psychological counseling for children and parents.

9. <u>Recreation</u> includes assessment of leisure function, therapeutic recreation services, recreation programs in schools and community agencies, and leisure education.

10. <u>Rehabilitative counseling services</u> means services that focus specifically on career development, employment preparation, achieving independence, and integration in the workplace and community of a student with a disability.

11. <u>School health services</u> means services provided by a qualified school nurse or other qualified person.

12. <u>Social work services in schools</u> includes preparing a social or developmental history on a child with a disability, group and individual counseling with the child and family, working with those problems in a child's living situation (home, school, and community) that affect the child's adjustment in school, and mobilizing school and community resources to enable the child to learn as effectively as possible in his or her educational program.

13. <u>Speech pathology</u> includes identification, diagnosis, and appraisal of specific speech or language impairments, provision of speech and language services, and counseling and guidance of parents, children, and teachers regarding speech and language impairments.

14. <u>Transportation</u> includes travel to and from school and between schools, travel in and around school buildings, and specialized equipment (e.g., special or adapted buses, lifts, and ramps), if required to provide special transportation for a child with a disability.

15. <u>Assistive technology and services</u> are devices and related services that restore lost capacities or improve impaired capacities.

Source: Adapted from 20 U.S. Code, Sec. 1401(a)(17).

PL 99–457: Extending Special Education to Infants, Toddlers, and Preschoolers

A significant series of changes to PL 94–142 occurred with the passage of Public Law 99–457, the *Education of the Handicapped Act Amendments* of 1986. Noting that more than 30 states and territories still did not require preschool services for all 3- to 5-year-old children with disabilities, Congress included provisions in PL 99–457 to expand services for this segment of the population. Beginning with the 1990–91 school year, each state was required to serve all preschool children with disabilities fully—that is, with the same services and protections available to school-age children—or lose all future federal funds for preschoolers with disabilities. PL 99–457 includes a formula for awarding money to each state on the basis of number of preschool children with disabilities identified and served.

PL 99–457 encourages the provision of special education services to infants and toddlers with disabilities—that is, children from birth through age 2 who need early intervention services because they are experiencing developmental delays or because they have a diagnosed physical or mental impairment with a high probability of resulting in developmental delays. The law states that Congress has found "an urgent and substantial need" to

1. enhance the development of infants and toddlers with disabilities and to minimize their potential for developmental delay,
2. reduce the educational costs to our society, including our Nation's schools, by minimizing the need for special education and related services after infants and toddlers with disabilities reach school age,
3. minimize the likelihood of institutionalization of individuals with disabilities and maximize their potential for independent living in society, and
4. enhance the capacity of families to meet the special needs of their infants and toddlers with disabilities. (PL 99–457, Sec. 1471)

Rather than mandate special services for this age-group, PL 99–457 encourages each state to "develop and implement a statewide, comprehensive, coordinated, multidisciplinary, interagency program of early intervention services for infants and toddlers with disabilities and their families." The encouragement is in the form of a gradually increasing amount of federal money to be awarded to states that agree to identify and serve all infants and toddlers with disabilities. Various education and human services agencies within each state work together to provide such services as medical and educational assessment, physical therapy, speech and language intervention, and parent counseling and training. These early intervention services are prescribed and implemented according to an **individualized family services plan (IFSP)** written by a multidisciplinary team that includes the child's parents.

> Early intervention for infants, toddlers, and preschoolers with disabilities is the subject of Chapter 14.

> IFSPs are described in Chapter 14.

PL 101–476: Education of the Handicapped Act Amendments of 1990

In 1990, PL 94–142 was amended by Congress for the third time. This law changed the title "Education of the Handicapped Act" to "Individuals with Disabilities Education Act," commonly referred to as the IDEA, and made the same title change in all other laws making reference to the original EHA. The new law retained all of the basic provisions of PL 94–142 but made several important additions.

- **Autism** and **traumatic brain injury** were added as two new categories of disability.
- Schools are now required to provide transition services to students with disabilities, as dictated by individual needs. **Transition services** are defined as "a coordinated set of activities for a student, designed within an outcome-oriented process, which promotes movement from school to post-school activities, including post-secondary education, vocational training, integrated employment, contin-

uing and adult education, adult services, independent living, or community partic
ipation." (Sec. 602(a) (19))

- IEPs must now contain a statement of the needed transition services for students beginning no later than age 16 (at a younger age when determined appropriate for the individual) and annually thereafter.
- Rehabilitation counseling and social work services were added to the definition of related services.

Legal Challenges Based on PL 94–142

Although PL 94–142 has resulted in dramatic increases in the numbers of students receiving special education services and in greater recognition of the legal rights of children with disabilities and their families, it has also brought about an ever-increasing number of disputes concerning the education of students with disabilities. Thousands of due process hearings and numerous court cases have been brought about by parents and other advocates. Due process hearings and court cases often place parents and schools in confrontation with each other and are expensive and time-consuming. For these reasons, or perhaps because there are now fewer disagreements between parents and schools, the number of due process hearings has dropped significantly since the years immediately following passage of PL 94–142 (Singer & Butler, 1987).

It is difficult to generalize how judges and courts have resolved the various legal challenges based on PL 94–142. There have been many different interpretations of such concepts as *free, appropriate education* and *least restrictive environment.* The law uses these terms repeatedly, but in the view of many parents, educators, judges, and attorneys, the law does not define them with sufficient clarity. Thus, the questions of what is appropriate and least restrictive for a particular child and whether a public school district should be compelled to provide a certain service must often be decided by judges and courts on consideration of the evidence presented to them.

Most public school programs operate for approximately 180 school days per year. Parents and educators have argued that, for some children with disabilities, particularly those with severe and multiple disabilities, a 180-day school year is not sufficient to meet their needs. In *Armstrong v. Kline* (1979), the parents of five students with severe disabilities claimed that their children tended to regress during the usual breaks in the school year and called on the schools to provide a period of instruction longer than 180 days. The court agreed and ordered the schools to extend the school year for these students. Several states and local districts now provide year-round educational programs for some students with disabilities, but there are no clear and universally accepted guidelines as to which students are entitled to free public education for a longer-than-usual school year.

Browder, Lentz, Knos-
ter, and Wilansky
(1988) discuss the
extended school year.

The first case based on the IDEA to reach the U.S. Supreme Court was *Board of Education of the Hendrick Hudson Central School District v. Rowley* (1982). Amy Rowley was a fourth grader who, because of her hearing impairment, needed special education and related services. The school district had originally provided Amy with a hearing aid, speech therapy, a tutor, and a sign language interpreter to accompany her in the regular classroom. The school withdrew the sign language services after the interpreter reported that Amy did not make use of her services: Amy reportedly looked at the teacher to read her lips and asked the teacher to repeat instructions, rather than get the information from the interpreter. Amy's parents contended that she was missing up to 50% of the ongoing instruction (her hearing impairment was estimated to have left her with 50% residual hearing) and was therefore being denied an appropriate public school education. The school district's position was that Amy, with the help of the other special services she was still receiving, was passing from grade to grade without an interpreter. School personnel thought, in fact, that an interpreter might hinder Amy's interactions with her teacher and peers. It was also noted that this service would cost the school district as much as $25,000 per year. The Supreme Court ruled that Amy, who was making satisfactory progress in school without an interpreter, was receiving an adequate education and that the school district could not be compelled to hire a full-time interpreter.

The second PL 94–142 case to reach the Supreme Court was *Irving Independent School District v. Tatro* (1984). In this case, the Court decided that a school district was obligated to provide catheterization and other related medical services to enable a young child with physical impairments to attend school. (See Chapter 10 for further discussion of this case.)

Some cases have resulted from parents' protesting the suspension or expulsion of children with disabilities. The case of *Stuart v. Nappi* (1978), for example, concerned a high school student who spent much of her time wandering in the halls even though she was assigned to special classes. The school sought to have the student expelled on disciplinary grounds because her conduct was considered detrimental to order in the school. The court agreed with the student's mother that expulsion would deny the student a free, appropriate public education as called for in the IDEA. In other cases, expulsion or suspension of students with disabilities has been upheld if the school could show that the grounds for expulsion did not relate to the student's disability. In 1988, however, the Supreme Court ruled in *Honig v. Doe* that a student with disabilities could not be expelled from school for disciplinary reasons, which meant that, for all practical purposes, schools cannot recommend expulsion or suspend a student with disabilities for more than 10 days.

The case of *Timothy W. v. Rochester School District* threatened the "zero reject" philosophy of the IDEA. In July 1988, Judge Loughlin of the district court in New Hampshire ruled that a 13-year-old boy with severe disabilities and quadriplegia was ineligible for education services because he could not "benefit" from special education. The judge ruled in favor of the Rochester School Board, which claimed that the IDEA was not intended to provide educational services to "*all* handicapped students." In his decision, the judge determined that the federal law was not explicit regarding a "rare child" with severe disabilities and declared that special evaluations and examinations should be used to determine "qualifications for education under PL 94–142."

In May 1989, a court of appeals overturned the lower court's decision, ruling that public schools must educate all children with disabilities regardless of how little they might benefit or the nature or severity of their disabilities. The three-judge panel concluded that "schools cannot avoid the provisions of EHA by returning to the practices that were widespread prior to the Act's passage . . . unilaterally excluding certain handicapped children from a public education on the ground that they are uneducable." In summarizing the case, Buchanan and Kochar (1989) express the concerns of many parents and special educators:

> If the Loughlin decision stood, how would the language of PL 94–142 have changed? Would *all* have become *some*? Would the law only apply to "mildly and moderately

The Rowley case marked the first time a deaf attorney had ever argued a case before the U.S. Supreme Court.

The National School Boards Association (NSBA) defended the Rochester School Board when the district court's decision was appealed. The NSBA stated that local schools have no obligation to serve children on the "low end of the spectrum . . . because they have no capacity to benefit from special education."

impaired" children, and would "free appropriate public education" only be for students who were allowed to attend school? . . . If the Loughlin decision was upheld, years of research in education for new and innovative methods of teaching the handicapped may have been lost. . . . This case underscores the need for vigilance in our watch for shifts in interpretations of EHA that subtly modify the essential foundations of zero reject and protection from functional exclusion. (p. 3)

Challenges to existing services and differing views on whether a particular program is appropriate or least restrictive are certain to continue. The high costs of providing special education and related services, although clearly not a valid basis for excluding students with disabilities, will likely be more often taken into consideration by judges and courts as they determine what schools may reasonably be expected to do. In Kauffman's (1985) words, "One of the problems we are going to have to resolve in the next decade or so is what the limits of special education are, where it stops" (p. 14). Some observers predict a lack of further expansion of related services for children with disabilities; others are more optimistic. H. R. Turnbull (1986), for example, notes that although the Supreme Court decided against the provision of related services in the *Rowley* case and in favor of them in the *Tatro* case, the decisions are consistent: The Court recognized the need for integration of children with disabilities with nondisabled children in both cases and kept the student's individualized education program as "the focal point of appropriateness" (p. 351). Although the courts will probably grant some requests in the future and deny others, it is now a well-established principle that each student with disabilities is entitled to a personalized program of instruction and supportive services that will enable him or her to benefit from an education in as integrated a setting as possible.

Related Legislation

Gifted and Talented Children

Although PL 94–142 does not apply to gifted and talented children, other federal legislation has addressed the specialized needs of this population. Public Law 95–561, the *Gifted and Talented Children's Education Act* of 1978, provides financial incentives for state and local education agencies to develop programs for students who are gifted and talented. PL 95–561 provides for the identification of gifted and talented children and includes special procedures for identifying and educating those from disadvantaged backgrounds. The law makes funding available for inservice training programs, research, and other projects aimed at meeting the needs of gifted and talented students.

In 1982 the Education Consolidation Act phased out the federal Office of Gifted and Talented and merged gifted education with 29 other programs. Federal dollars to support these 30 wide-ranging education programs (K–12) are sent to the states in the form of "block grants." Each state has the responsibility to determine what portion, if any, of the block grant funds will be used to support programs and services for students who are gifted and talented.

Congress passed the *Jacob K. Javits Gifted and Talented Student Education Act* in 1988 as part of the Elementary and Secondary Education Bill. This act provided $8 million for the identification and service of gifted students, the professional development and training of teachers, and the creation of a National Center for the Education of the Gifted. Although no federal legislation requires states to provide special education programs for students who are gifted, Sisk (1984) found that 47 states had appointed a state consultant or director of gifted programs, compared with Marland's (1971) earlier report that only 10 state departments of education had a consultant for the gifted on their staff.

Section 504 of the Rehabilitation Act of 1973

Another important law that extends civil rights to people with disabilities is *Section 504 of the Rehabilitation Act* of 1973. This regulation states, in part, that "no otherwise qualified handicapped individual shall, solely by reason of his handicap, be excluded from the participation in, be denied the benefits of, or be subjected to discrimination in any program or activity receiving federal financial assistance." This law, worded almost identically to the Civil Rights Act of 1964 (which prohibited discrimination based on race, color, or national origin), has expanded opportunities to children and adults with disabilities in education, employment, and various other settings. It requires provision of "auxiliary aids for students with impaired sensory, manual, or speaking skills"—for example, readers for students who are blind, and people to assist students with physical disabilities in moving from place to place. This requirement does not mean that schools, colleges, and employers must have *all* such aids available at *all* times; it simply demands that no person with disabilities may be excluded from a program because of the lack of an appropriate aid.

Section 504 is not a federal grant program; unlike the IDEA, it does not provide any federal money to assist people with disabilities. Rather, it "imposes a duty on every recipient of federal funds not to discriminate against handicapped persons" (T. P. Johnson, 1986, p. 8). "Recipient," of course, includes public school districts, virtually all of which receive federal support. Most colleges and universities have also been affected; even many students in private institutions receive federal financial aid. The Office of Civil Rights conducts periodic compliance reviews and acts on complaints when parents, disabled individuals, or others contend that a school district is violating Section 504.

Architectural accessibility for students, teachers, and others with physical and sensory impairments is an important feature of Section 504; however, the law does not call for a completely barrier-free environment. Emphasis is on accessibility to programs, not on physical modification of all existing structures. If a chemistry class is required for a premedical program of study, for example, a college might make this program accessible to a student with physical disabilities by reassigning the class to an accessible location or by providing assistance to the student in traveling to an otherwise inaccessible location. All sections of all courses need not be made accessible, but a college should not segregate students with disabilities by assigning them all to a particular section regardless of disability. Like PL 94–142, Section 504 calls for nondiscriminatory placement in the "most integrated setting appropriate" and has served as the basis for many court cases over alleged discrimination against individuals with disabilities, particularly in their right to employment.

Americans with Disabilities Act

The *Americans with Disabilities Act* (PL 101–336) was signed into law on July 26, 1990. Patterned after Section 504 of the Rehabilitation Act of 1973, the Americans with Disabilities Act (ADA) extends civil rights protection to persons with disabilities in private sector employment, all public services, public accommodation, transporta-

Table 1.3 is a summary of federal legislation regarding the education and rights of individuals with disabilities.

TABLE 1.3
Federal legislation concerning the education and rights of individuals with disabilities

YEAR	LEGISLATION
1958	National Defense Education Act (PL 85–926) Provided funds for training professionals to train teachers of children with mental retardation.
1961	Special Education Act (PL 87–276) Provided funds for training professionals to train teachers of deaf children.
1963	Mental Retardation Facility and Community Center Construction Act (PL 88–164) Extended support given in PL 85–926 to training teachers of children with other disabilities.
1965	Elementary and Secondary Education Act (PL 89–10) Provided money to states and local districts for developing programs for economically disadvantaged and disabled children.
1966	Amendment to Title I of the Elementary and Secondary Education Act (PL 89–313) Provided funding for state-supported programs in institutions and other settings for children with disabilities.
1966	Amendments to the Elementary and Secondary Education Act (PL 89–750) Created the Bureau of Education for the Handicapped.
1968	Handicapped Children's Early Assistance Act (PL 90–538) Established the "first chance network" of experimental programs for preschool children with disabilities (see Chapter 14).
1969	Elementary, Secondary, and Other Educational Amendments (PL 91–230) Defined learning disabilities; provided funds for state-level programs for children with learning disabilities.
1973	Section 504 of the Rehabilitation Act (PL 93–112) Declared that a person cannot be excluded on the basis of disability alone from any program or activity receiving federal funds (adopted 1977).
1974	Education Amendments (PL 93–380) Extended previous legislation; provided money to state and local districts for programs for gifted and talented students for the first time. Also protected rights of children with disabilities and their parents in placement decisions.
1975	Developmental Disabilities Assistance and Bill of Rights Act (PL 94–103) Affirmed rights of citizens with mental retardation and cited areas where services must be provided for people with mental retardation and other developmental disabilities.
1975	Individuals with Disabilities Education Act (PL 94–142) Originally named the Education for All Handicapped Children Act (EHA), PL 94–142 mandates free, appropriate public education for all children with disabilities regardless of degree of severity of handicap; protects rights of children with disabilities and their parents in educational decision making; requires development of an individualized education program (IEP) for each child with a disability; states that students with disabilities must receive educational services in the least restrictive environment.

tion, and telecommunications. A person with a disability is defined in the ADA as a person (a) with a mental or physical impairment that substantially limits that person in a major life activity (e.g., walking, talking, working, self-care); (b) with a record of such an impairment (e.g., a person who no longer has heart disease but who is discriminated against because of that history); or (c) who is regarded as having such an impairment (e.g., a person with significant facial disfiguration due to a burn who is not limited in any major life activity but is discriminated against). The major provisions of the ADA are as follows:

YEAR	LEGISLATION
1983	Amendments to the Education of the Handicapped Act (PL 98–199) Required states to collect data on the number of youth with disabilities exiting their systems and to address the needs of secondary students making the transition to adulthood (see Chapter 15). Also gave incentives to states to provide services to infants and preschool children with disabilities.
1984	Developmental Disabilities Assistance and Bill of Rights Acts (PL 98–527) Mandated development of employment related training activities for adults with disabilities.
1986	Handicapped Children's Protection Act (PL 99–372) Provided authority for reimbursement of attorney's fees to parents who must go to court to secure an appropriate education for their child. Parents who prevail in a hearing or court case may recover the costs incurred for lawyers to represent them, retroactive to July 4, 1984.
1986	Education of the Handicapped Act Amendments of 1986 (PL 99–457) Encouraged states to develop comprehensive interdisciplinary services for infants and toddlers (birth through age 2) with disabilities and to expand services for preschool children (aged 3 through 5). After the 1990–91 school year, states must provide free, appropriate education to all 3- to 5-year-olds with disabilities to be eligible to apply for federal preschool funding (see Chapter 14).
1986	Rehabilitation Act Amendments (PL 99–506) Set forth regulations for development of supported employment programs for adults with disabilities (see Chapter 15).
1990	Americans with Disabilities Act (PL 101–336) Provides civil rights protection against discrimination to citizens with disabilities in private sector employment, access to all public services, public accommodations, transportation, and telecommunications.
1990	Education of the Handicapped Act Amendments of 1990 (PL 101–476) In addition to renaming the EHA as the Individuals with Disabilities Education Act, this law added autism and traumatic brain injury as two new categories of disability, required all IEPs to include a statement of needed transition services no later than age 16, and expanded the definition of related services to include rehabilitation counseling and social work services.
1994	Goals 2000: Educate America Act (PL 103–227) Provides federal funds to state and local education agencies for the development and implementation of educational reforms to help achieve eight national education goals by the year 2000.

- Employers with 15 or more employees may not refuse to hire or promote a person because of a disability if that person is qualified to perform the job. Also, the employer must make reasonable accommodations that will allow a person with a disability to perform essential functions of the job. Such modifications in job requirements or situation must be made if they will not impose undue hardship on the employer.
- All new vehicles purchased by public transit authorities must be accessible to people with disabilities. All rail stations must be made accessible, and at least one car per train in existing rail systems must be made accessible.
- It is illegal for public accommodations to exclude or refuse persons with disabilities. Public accommodations are everyday businesses and services, such as hotels, restaurants, grocery stores, and parks. All new buildings must be made accessible, and existing facilities must remove barriers if the removal can be accomplished without much difficulty or expense.

The Americans with Disabilities Act requires employers to make reasonable accommodations to allow a person with disabilities to perform essential job functions.

- Companies offering telephone service to the general public must offer relay services to individuals who use telecommunications devices for the deaf (e.g., TDDs) 24 hours per day, 7 days per week.

Goals 2000: Educate America Act

The 1989 Governors' Education Summit was chaired by then-governor of Arkansas, Bill Clinton.

The most recent federal legislation on education is the *Goals 2000: Educate America Act* (PL 103–227), passed by Congress in March 1994. The bill codifies a set of proposals for reforming American education advocated by President Bush and all 50 state governors who participated in a national education summit in 1989. The law identifies specific objectives designed to help the country achieve eight national education goals by the year 2000 (see Table 1.4).

Goals 2000 provides monetary resources to states and communities to assist in the development and implementation of educational reforms related to virtually every aspect of education, including curriculum and textbooks, teaching practices, use of educational technology, evaluation and measurement of student progress, teacher training and inservice development, parent and community involvement, and school administration and management. All reform efforts are to be focused on student outcomes, in particular helping all students reach high academic and occupational skill standards.

Exactly how Goals 2000 will affect special education is unknown at this time. That the authors of the new legislation intended the goals and objectives to include exceptional children, however, is clear in the bill's definition of "all students" and "all children."

> The terms "all students" and "all children" mean students or children from a broad range of backgrounds and circumstances, including disadvantaged students and children, students or children with diverse racial, ethnic, and cultural background, Amer-

TABLE 1.4
The Goals 2000: Educate America Act

Public Law 103-227 identifies the following eight goals to be achieved by the Year 2000:

Goal 1   All children in America will start school ready to learn.

Goal 2   The high school graduation rate will increase to at least 90 percent.

Goal 3   All students will leave grades 4, 8, and 12 having demonstrated competency over challenging subject matter, including English, mathematics, science, foreign languages, civics and government, economics, arts, history, and geography.

Goal 4   United States students will be first in the world in mathematics and science achievement.

Goal 5   Every adult American will be literate and will possess the knowledge and skills necessary to compete in a global economy and exercise the right and responsibilities of citizenship.

Goal 6   Every school in the United States will be free of drugs, violence, and the unauthorized presence of firearms and alcohol and will offer a disciplined environment conducive to learning.

Goal 7   The nation's teaching force will have access to programs for the continued improvement of their professional skills and the opportunity to acquire the knowledge and skills needed to instruct and prepare all American students for the next century.

Goal 8   Every school will promote partnerships that will increase parental involvement and participation in promoting the social, emotional, and academic growth of children.

ican Indians, Alaska Natives, Native Hawaiians, students or children with disabilities, students or children with limited English proficiency, school-aged students or children who have dropped out of school, migratory students or children, and academically talented students and children. (Public Law 103–227)

✳ *A Definition of Special Education*

Special education can be defined from many perspectives. One may, for example, view special education as a legislatively governed enterprise. From this viewpoint, one would be concerned about the legal implications of informing parents of students with disabilities about their right to help plan their children's individualized education programs. From a purely administrative point of view, special education might be seen as the part of a school system's operation that requires certain teacher-pupil ratios in the classroom and that has special formulas for determining levels of funding according to the category of exceptional children served. From a sociological or political perspective, special education can be seen as an outgrowth of the civil rights movement, a demonstration of society's changing attitudes about people with disabilities in general. Each perspective has some validity, and each continues to play a role in defining what special education is and how it is practiced. None of these views, however, would yield the essence of special education.

Special Education as Teaching

Ultimately, *teaching* is what special education is most about. But the same can be said of all of education. What, then, is *special* about special education? One way to answer that question is to look at special education in terms of the *who, what, where,* and *how* of its teaching.

Who?

Are there jobs in special education? Yes. During the 1992–93 school year, 308,904 special education teachers were employed in the United States, with a reported 27,282 more needed (U.S. Department of Education, 1994). During the same year, 311,488 special education personnel other than teachers were employed, with a reported shortage of 13,665.

We have already identified the most important *who* in special education: the children whose exceptional educational needs necessitate an individually planned program of education. Teachers, both general education classroom teachers and special educators—teachers who have completed specialized training programs in preparation for their work with students with special needs—provide the instruction that is the heart of each child's individualized program of education. Working with special educators and regular classroom teachers are many other professionals—including school psychologists, speech-language pathologists, physical therapists, counselors, and medical specialists, to name only a few—who help provide the educational and related services that exceptional children need. This interdisciplinary team of professionals, working together with parents and families, bears the primary responsibility for helping exceptional children learn despite their differences and special needs.

What?

Special education can sometimes be differentiated from regular education by its curriculum—that is, by *what* is taught. Some children with disabilities need intensive, systematic instruction to learn skills that typically developing children acquire naturally. For example, self-help skills, such as dressing, eating, and toileting, are not part of the regular education curriculum, yet these skills are an important part of the curriculum for many students with severe disabilities. Also, some children are taught certain skills to compensate for or reduce the handicapping effects of a disability. A child who is blind may receive special training in reading and writing braille, whereas

Most of all, special education is about teaching.

a seeing child does not need these skills. It can be said that in regular education the school system dictates the curriculum but that in special education the child's individual needs dictate the curriculum (Lieberman, 1985). We should not forget, however, that approximately 70% of children with disabilities are educated in regular classrooms for at least part of the day—meaning that most students in special education experience the regular school curriculum.

Where?

Special education can sometimes be identified by *where* it takes place. Although most children with disabilities receive much of their education in regular classrooms, the others are someplace else—mostly in separate classrooms and separate residential and day schools. And many of those in regular classrooms spend a portion of each day in a resource room, where they receive individualized instruction. Special educators also teach in many environments not usually thought of as "school." An early childhood special educator may spend much of his or her time teaching parents how to work with their infant or toddler at home. Special education teachers, particularly those who work with students with severe disabilities, are increasingly conducting **community-based instruction,** helping their students learn and practice functional daily living and job skills in the actual settings where they must be used (Beck, Brocrs, Hogue, Shipstead, & Knowlton, 1994).

Approximately 70% of all children with disabilities received at least part of their education in regular classrooms during the 1992–93 school year (Figure 1.2). This includes 34.9% who were served in the regular classroom and 36.3% who were served for part of each school day in a resource room, a special setting in which a

Functional curriculum is the term often used to describe the knowledge and skills needed by students with disabilities to achieve as much success and independence as they can in daily living, personal-social, community, and work settings (Clark, 1994).

Table 1.5 provides the definitions of six educational placements used by the U.S. Department of Education.

FIGURE 1.2
Percentage of all students with disabilities aged 6 through 21 served in six educational placements

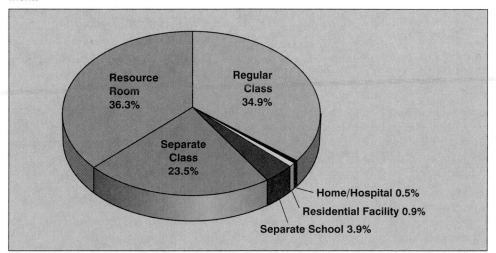

Notes: Separate school includes both public and private separate school facilities. Residential facility includes both public and private residential facilities

Source: From *Sixteenth Annual Report to Congress on the Implementation of the Individuals with Disabilities Education Act,* p. 12, 1994, U.S. Department of Education.

TABLE 1.5
Definitions of six educational placements for students with disabilities

PLACEMENT	DEFINITION
Regular class	Students receive a majority of their education in a regular class and receive special education and related services for less than 21% of the school day. Includes children placed in a regular class and receiving special education within the regular class, as well as children placed in a regular class and receiving special education outside the regular class.
Resource room	Students receive special education and related services for 60% or less of the school day and at least 21% of the school day. May include resource rooms with part-time instruction in the regular class.
Separate class	Students receive special education and related services for more than 60% of the school day and are placed in self-contained special classrooms with part-time instruction in regular class or placed in self-contained classes full-time on a regular school campus.
Separate school facility	Students receive special education and related services in separate day schools for students with disabilities for greater than 50% of the school day.
Residential facility	Students receive education in a public or private residential facility at public expense for greater than 50% of the school day.
Homebound/hospital environment	Students placed in and receiving education in hospital or homebound programs.

Source: Adapted from *Twelfth Annual Report to Congress on the Implementation of the Education of the Handicapped Act,* pp. 18-19, 1990, Washington, DC: U.S. Department of Education.

Where students with disabilities are educated—in particular, the extent to which they are included as meaningful participants in the instructional and social life of the regular classroom—is the most hotly debated issue in special education today. In Chapter 2, we examine the issues of *inclusion* and the integration of special and regular education into one service delivery system.

special educator provides individualized instruction. About one fourth of all children with disabilities are educated in separate classrooms within a regular school. About 1 in 20 school-age students with disabilities—usually the student with more severe disabilities—is educated in special schools. Residential schools serve less than 1% of all children with disabilities, as do nonschool environments such as homebound or hospital programs.

The vast majority of children in the two largest groups of students with disabilities spend at least part of the school day in regular classrooms: 79% of children with learning disabilities and 95% of children with speech or language impairments (Table 1.6). In contrast, only 30% of children with mental retardation, 24% of children with multiple disabilities, and 12% of children with deaf-blindness were educated in regular classrooms during the 1992–93 school year, although these figures represent increases over those of previous years.

TABLE 1.6

Percentage of students aged 6 through 21 served in six educational environments during the 1991–92 school year

DISABILITY	EDUCATIONAL ENVIRONMENT[a]					
	REGULAR CLASS	RESOURCE ROOM	SEPARATE CLASS	SEPARATE SCHOOL	RESIDENTIAL FACILITY	HOMEBOUND/ HOSPITAL
Specific learning disabilities	24.7	54.2	20.0	0.9	0.1	0.1
Speech or language impairments	85.5	9.1	3.9	1.4	0.1	0.1
Mental retardation	5.1	25.4	59.2	8.8	1.2	0.3
Serious emotional disturbance	15.8	27.8	36.9	13.9	4.0	1.5
Multiple disabilities	7.2	18.1	47.1	22.6	3.8	2.2
Hearing impairments	27.0	20.5	31.2	9.6	11.5	0.1
Orthopedic impairments	32.4	21.0	34.3	7.3	0.9	4.1
Other health impairments	36.3	27.6	21.4	3.3	0.5	11.8
Visual impairments	39.6	21.2	19.6	8.5	10.6	0.4
Autism	4.7	6.9	48.5	35.9	3.1	0.9
Deaf-blindness	5.8	6.2	36.3	21.2	28.6	1.8
Traumatic brain injury	7.8	9.0	23.7	53.4	3.7	2.4
All disabilities	34.9	36.3	23.5	3.9	0.9	0.5

[a]Data for students placed in public and private separate schools and in public and private residential facilities have been combined for presentation in this table.

Source: From *Sixteenth Annual Report to Congress on the Implementation of the Individuals with Disabilities Act*, p. 14, 1994, Washington, DC: U. S. Department of Education.

41

Signaling for Help

·························

Resource rooms are busy places. Students come and go throughout the day, each according to an individualized schedule. Each student who comes to the resource room does so because of a need for intensive individualized instruction. The IEP objectives for any given group of students in a resource room at any one time typically cover a wide range of academic and social skills. Because of the varied skill levels and the ever-changing student groupings in the resource room, the resource room teacher is usually managing several types and levels of instruction at once. To accomplish this, students are often assigned individualized learning activities. Resource room teachers face a difficult challenge: the need to be in several places at once. While students work at their desks, the teacher moves about the room, providing individual students with prompts, encouragement, praise, and/or corrective feedback as needed.

Students in a resource room are usually working on those skills in which they need the most help. Therefore, an effective and efficient system with which students can signal the resource room teacher for assistance is a must. Hand raising, the typical

attention-getting signal, poses several problems. It is difficult to continue to work while holding one's hand in the air, a situation that results in a great deal of "down" time as students wait for the teacher to get to them. In addition, if several students are waving their hands in competition for the teacher's attention, it is distracting to other students and to the teacher. If unsuccessful in getting the teacher's help, students may give up trying whenever they run into difficulty. Even worse, students who are unsuccessful in obtaining the teacher's assistance may stop discriminating their need for help and simply continue to practice errors.

One solution is both simple and effective. Students need an easy, quiet means of signaling for help that allows them to keep working, with the assurance that their teacher will recognize their need for help. In Ronni Hochman's resource room for middle school students with learning disabilities, each student has a small flag made of colored felt, a dowel rod, and a 1¼-inch cube of wood. When one of Ronni's students needs assistance or wants her to check completed work, the student simply stands the flag up on his or her desk. While waiting for the teacher, the student can either go on to another item or work on materials in a special folder. With this simple and inexpensive system, down time is greatly reduced, and neither Ronni nor her students are distracted by hand waving or calling out. (Kerr & Nelson [1989], describe a signaling device made from an empty can wrapped with red and green construction paper. Students turn the can on one end or the other to signal "I'm working" or "I need help.")

Ronni asked her students to write what they thought of the signal flag system after using it for about 3 months.

> This is one of the best way to work in sted of raising your hand you raise your flag and keep on working but if you raise you hand you can't keep working. That is special because I get more work done. If she is working with some one els you raise it and she will get to you as fast as she can.—Brent

> The flags in Miss Hochmans room are used for assistance from the teacher. When Miss Hochman is working you rais you flag and she will help you as soon as she has time. But you keep on working, like going on to the next problem.—Pam

Signal flags are a simple and effective way for students to obtain teacher assistance and feedback.

How?

How special educators teach can, at times, be differentiated from the methods used by regular education teachers. One special educator may use sign language to communicate with the students. Another special educator may use a carefully structured procedure for gradually withdrawing visual prompts in helping a student learn to discriminate his or her own name from others. But for the most part, effective special education teachers employ the same set of fundamental teaching skills that all good teachers use. There are not two distinct sets of instructional methods—one to use with special students, the other to use with regular students. Nor is there a certain set of teaching methods appropriate for students within a given disability category that differs significantly from effective teaching methods for students in another category. Morsink, Thomas, and Smith-Davis (1987) reviewed the literature and found no evidence that specific teaching methods are differentially effective with students labeled as learning disabled, mildly mentally retarded, and emotionally disturbed. Instead, all special educators should be skilled in the procedures for systematically designing, implementing, and evaluating instruction (e.g., Mercer & Mercer, 1993; Polloway & Patton, 1993; Snell, 1993).

Special Education as Intervention

Intervention is a general name for all efforts on behalf of individuals with disabilities. The overall goal of intervention is to eliminate or at least reduce the obstacles that might keep a child or adult with disabilities from full and active participation in school and society. The three basic kinds of intervention efforts are

- *Preventive.* Keeping possible problems from becoming a serious disability
- *Remedial.* Overcoming disability through training or education
- *Compensatory.* Giving the individual new ways to deal with the disability

Preventive Techniques

Preventive efforts are most promising when they begin early—even before birth, in many cases. In later chapters, we explore some of the exciting new methods available for preventing disabilities. We also explore the efforts in social and educational programs to stimulate infants and very young children to acquire skills that most children learn without special help. Unfortunately, prevention programs have only just begun to affect the number and severity of disabilities in this country. And it is likely that we will be well into the 21st century before we achieve a significant reduction of disabilities. In the meantime, we must count on remedial and compensatory efforts to help people with disabilities achieve fuller and more independent lives.

Early intervention with infants, toddlers, and preschoolers with disabilities is the subject of Chapter 14.

Remedial Programs

Remedial programs are supported largely by educational institutions and social agencies. In fact, the word *remediation* is primarily an educational term; the word *rehabilitation* is used more often by social service agencies. Both have a common purpose: to teach the person with disabilities basic skills for independence. In school, those skills may be academic (reading, writing, speaking, computing), social (getting along with others; following instructions, schedules, and other daily routines), or personal (feeding, dressing, using the toilet without assistance). Increasingly, schools

Programs for helping secondary students with disabilities make the transition from school to adulthood are discussed in Chapter 15.

are also teaching career and job skills to prepare youngsters with special needs for life as adults in the community. In doing so, schools are sharing more of the responsibilities that social services agencies have historically accepted. Vocational training, or **vocational rehabilitation,** includes preparation to develop work habits and work attitudes, as well as specific training in a particular skill such as auto mechanics, carpentry, or assembly-line work. The underlying assumption of both remedial and rehabilitative programs is that a person with disabilities needs special help to succeed in the normal settings.

Compensatory Efforts

Still another intervention approach is to compensate for a person's disability by helping him or her learn to use a substitute skill or device. For example, a child with cerebral palsy can be trained to make maximum use of her hands, but the use of a headstick and a template placed over a regular typewriter may effectively compensate for lack of muscle control by letting her type instead of write lessons by hand. Compensatory efforts aim to give the individual with a disability some kind of asset that nondisabled individuals do not need—whether it be a device such as a headstick, or special training such as mobility instruction for a child without vision.

What, then, is special education? At one level, it is a profession, with tools, techniques, and research efforts focused on evaluating and meeting the learning needs of exceptional children and adults. At a more practical level, **special education** is individually planned, systematically implemented, and carefully evaluated instruction to help exceptional learners achieve the greatest possible personal self-sufficiency and success in present and future environments.

✳ Current Challenges

Special education has accomplished a great deal during the past 25 years, and there is legitimate reason for those in the field to feel good about the progress. Much has been accomplished in terms of making a free, appropriate education available to many children with disabilities who were previously denied access to an education. Much has been learned about how to effectively teach children with severe disabilities—children who many had thought were not capable of learning. Special educators and parents have learned to work together on behalf of exceptional children. Technological advances have helped many students overcome physical or communication disabilities. Throughout the remaining chapters, we describe many of these advances, but attempting to reveal the state of the art in an ever-changing discipline like special education is difficult.

Although the beginnings of special education can be traced back several centuries, in many respects the field is still in its formative years. There is much to learn about teaching exceptional children and much to be done to make special education most useful to those who need it most. Here are four areas that most in the field consider critical.

See the January, 1995, issue of *Educational Leadership*, pp. 42–45, and pp. 46–49.

1. *Least restrictive environment.* We must maximize the movement of students with disabilities, particularly those with severe disabilities, into educational settings that are as normalized as possible. Even though 7 of 10 students with disabilities do spend part of each day in a regular classroom, for many children with disabili-

ties a *special education means a separate education.* (Chapter 2 examines the concept of educating exceptional children in the least restrictive environment; various strategies and techniques for integrating students with disabilities into the regular classroom are presented throughout the book.)

2. *Early intervention.* We must make special education and related services more widely available for infants and toddlers who have disabilities or are at risk for developmental delay. The number of preschool children who receive special education is likely to grow significantly during the coming years. (Chapter 14 is devoted to early intervention.)

3. *Transition to adulthood.* We must improve the ability of young people to leave secondary special education programs and live and work independently in their communities. (Chapter 15 is devoted to the special needs of adults with disabilities and to educational programs to promote a successful transition from school to adulthood.)

4. *Special education–regular education relationship.* It has been estimated that, in addition to the children with disabilities who receive special education, another 10% to 20% of the student population have mild to moderate learning problems that interfere with their ability to progress and succeed in a regular education program (Will, 1986). Both special and regular educators must develop strategies for working together and sharing their skills and resources to prevent these millions of at-risk students from becoming failures of our educational system.

These four areas are by no means the only important issues in special education today. We could easily identify other challenges that many in the field would argue are equally or even more important. For example,

• Increasing the availability and quality of special education programs for gifted and talented students
• Developing teaching strategies that enable students with severe disabilities to generalize newly learned skills to other settings
• Applying advances in high technology to greatly reduce or eliminate the disabling effects of physical and sensory impairments

The ultimate effectiveness of special education must be measured by its ability to help secondary students with disabilities make a successful transition to adult life.

- Combating the pervasive effects of childhood poverty on development and success in school (1 in 5 American children under the age of 5 is living in poverty)
- Developing effective methods for providing education and related services to the growing numbers of children entering school whose development and learning are affected by prenatal exposure to drugs or alcohol
- Improving the behavior and attitudes of people without disabilities toward those with disabilities
- Opening up more opportunities for individuals with disabilities to participate in the full range of residential, employment, and recreational options available to nondisabled persons

We do not know how successful special education will be in meeting these challenges. Only time will tell. And, of course, special educators do not face these challenges alone. General education; adult service agencies, such as vocational rehabilitation, social work, and medicine; and society as a whole must all help find the solutions to these problems. But we do know that a large and growing group of people are working hard to make these predictions become reality—people with and without disabilities, people within and outside special education. Whatever professional and career goals you follow, your introductory study of special education will help you make a personal commitment to be part of that group.

Summary

Who Are Exceptional Children?

- *Exceptional children* are those whose physical attributes and/or learning abilities differ from the norm, either above or below, to such an extent that an individualized program of special education is indicated.
- *Disability* refers to the reduced function or loss of a particular body part or organ.
- *Handicap* refers to the problems a person with a disability or impairment encounters when interacting with the environment.
- A child who is *at risk* is not currently identified as having a disability, but rather is considered to have a greater-than-usual chance of developing a disability if intervention is not provided.

How Many Exceptional Children Are There?

- Children in special education represent approximately 8% of the school-age population.
- The four largest categories of children with disabilities receiving special education are learning disabilities, speech and language impairments, mental retardation, and emotional disturbance.

- Ninety percent of children receiving special education have "mild disabilities."
- Approximately 70% of students with disabilities receive at least part of their education in regular classrooms.

Problems of Labeling and Classifying Exceptional Children

- Some believe that labels lead to exclusion of exceptional children from normal society; others believe that labeling is necessary to provide appropriate programs.
- Labels can be convenient for communicating about disabilities.
- Labels can also have a negative effect on the child and on others' perceptions of him or her.

Special Education as Civil Rights

- The move to extend educational opportunities to children with disabilities is an outgrowth of the civil rights movement.
- All children are now recognized to have the right to equal protection under the law, which has been interpreted to mean the right to a free public education in the least restrictive environment.

- All children and their parents have the right to due process under the law, which includes the rights to be notified of any decision affecting the child's educational placement, to have a hearing and present a defense, to see a written decision, and to appeal any decision.

- Court decisions have also established the rights of children with disabilities to fair assessment in their native language and to education at public expense, regardless of the school district's financial constraints.

The Individuals with Disabilities Education Act (IDEA)

- The IDEA (PL 94–142) made many trends in special education part of federal law. It extends public education to all children with disabilities between the ages of 3 and 21.

- The IDEA requires that students with disabilities be educated in the *least restrictive environment* (LRE). LRE is a relative concept (the regular classroom is not necessarily the best placement for every student) stipulating that, to the maximum extent possible, students with disabilities are to be educated with students without disabilities in regular educational environments. The law also sets out requirements for diagnosis, nondiscriminatory assessment, individualization of programming, and personnel development.

- Court cases have challenged the way particular school districts implement specific provisions of the IDEA. No trend has emerged, but rulings from the various cases have established the principle that each student with disabilities is entitled to a personalized program of instruction and supportive services that will enable him or her to benefit from an education in as integrated a setting as possible.

- The Education for the Handicapped Act Amendments of 1986 (PL 99–457) required states to provide special education services to all preschoolers with disabilities aged 3 to 5 by 1991 or lose all future federal funds for preschoolers with disabilities. This law also makes available federal money to encourage states to develop early intervention programs for disabled and at-risk infants and toddlers from birth to age 2. Early intervention services must be coordinated by an individualized family services plan.

- The Gifted and Talented Children's Education Act (PL 95–561) provides financial incentives to states for developing programs for gifted and talented students.

- Section 504 of the Rehabilitation Act forbids discrimination in all federally funded programs, including educational and vocational programs, on the basis of disability alone.

- The Americans with Disabilities Act (PL 101–336) extends the civil rights protections for persons with disabilities to private sector employment, all public services, public accommodations, transportation, and telecommunications.

A Definition of Special Education?

- *Special education* is individually planned, systematically implemented, and carefully evaluated instruction to help exceptional children achieve the greatest possible personal self-sufficiency and success in present and future environments.

- Intervention efforts are of three kinds: preventive, remedial, and compensatory.

Current Challenges

- Four major challenges that special education faces are:

  educating children with disabilities in the least restrictive environment

  making early intervention programs more widely available to infants and toddlers who have disabilities or are at risk for developing a disability

  improving the ability of young adults with disabilities to make a successful transition from school to community life

  improving the relationship with regular education to better serve the many students who have not been identified as disabled but who are not progressing in the general education program

· ·

For More Information

Journals

Education & Treatment of Children. A quarterly journal devoted to the dissemination of information concerning the development and improvement of services for children and youths. Includes original research, reviews of the literature, and descriptions of innovative intervention and treatment programs. Published by PRO-ED, 8700 Shoal Creek Boulevard, Austin, TX 78758-6897.

Exceptionality. Quarterly journal of original research on the education of exceptional learners. Published by the

Council for Exceptional Children, 1920 Association Drive, Reston, VA 22091-1589.

Exceptional Children. The official journal of the Council for Exceptional Children. Publishes original research, position papers, debates, and reviews of the literature related to contemporary issues concerning the education of exceptional children. Designed to assist all professionals who work with exceptional children, including school psychologists, counselors, and administrators. Published six times per year by the Council for Exceptional Children, 1920 Association Drive, Reston, VA 22091-1589.

Intervention in School and Clinic. An interdisciplinary journal directed toward an international audience of teachers, parents, educational therapists, and specialists in all fields who deal with the day-to-day aspects of special and remedial education. Published five times per year by PRO-ED, 8700 Shoal Creek Boulevard, Austin, TX 78758-6897.

Elementary School Journal. A widely disseminated journal of research, reviews, and position papers concerning all aspects of elementary education. Published five times per year by the University of Chicago Press, Journals Division, 5720 South Woodlawn Avenue, Chicago, IL 60637.

Journal of Special Education. A quarterly journal that publishes articles from all disciplines; deals with research, theory, opinion, and reviews of the literature in special education. Published by PRO-ED, 8700 Shoal Creek Boulevard, Austin, TX 78758-6897.

Phi Delta Kappan. A highly regarded journal that publishes articles of general interest on all aspects of education, a good source for information on current trends and issues. Eighth and Union, P.O. Box 789, Bloomington, IN 47402.

Preventing School Failure. Published six times per year by PRO-ED, 8700 Shoal Creek Boulevard, Austin, TX 78758-6897.

Remedial and Special Education. Devoted to discussion of issues involving the education of persons for whom typical instruction is not effective. Emphasizes interpretation of research literature and recommendations for the practice of remedial and special education. Published six times per year by PRO-ED, 8700 Shoal Creek Boulevard, Austin, TX 78758-6897.

Teacher Education and Special Education. Quarterly journal of research, program descriptions, and discussion articles on issues and methods pertaining to the education of teachers and other educational personnel for exceptional children. Published by the Teacher Education Division of CEC, 1920 Association Drive, Reston, VA 22091-1589.

Teaching Exceptional Children. A practitioner's journal designed to assist both regular and special education classroom teachers of children with disabilities, as well as those who are gifted and talented. Most articles feature practical methods and materials for classroom use. Also includes a teacher idea exchange, reviews of books and instructional materials, descriptions of selected materials from the ERIC Clearinghouse on Disabilities and Gifted Education, and information on national meetings and inservice training opportunities. Published quarterly by the Council for Exceptional Children, 1920 Association Drive, Reston, VA 22091-1589.

Books

Lovitt, T. C. (1995). *Tactics for teaching* (2nd ed.). Englewood Cliffs, NJ: Prentice Hall.

Pullen, P. L., & Kauffman, J. M. (1987). *What should I know about special education? Answers for classroom teachers.* Austin, TX: PRO-ED.

Rothstein, L. F. (1995). *Special education law* (2nd ed.). Reston, VA: Council for Exceptional Children.

Smarte, L., & McLane, K. (1994). *How to find answers to your special education questions* (rev. ed.). Reston, VA: Council for Exceptional Children.

Turnbull, H. R., III. (1993). *Free appropriate public education: The law and children with disabilities* (4th ed.). Denver: Love.

Wang, M., Reynolds, M. C., & Walberg, H. J. (Eds.). (1987). *Handbook of special education: Research and practice* (Vol. 1). New York: Pergamon Press.

Ysseldyke, J. E., Algozzine, B., & Thurlow, M. L. (1992). *Critical issues in special education* (2nd ed.). Boston: Houghton Mifflin.

Organization

Council for Exceptional Children (CEC), 1920 Association Drive, Reston, VA, 22091-1589. Includes more than 50,000 teachers, teacher educators, administrators, researchers, and other professionals involved in the education of exceptional children and adults.

Planning and Providing Special Education Services

- Can the quality of an individualized education program be judged by examining the document itself?

- Is the least restrictive environment always the regular classroom?

- Why is collaboration and teaming so critical to the planning and provision of effective special education services?

- What are the similarities and differences among *least restrictive environment, mainstreaming,* and *full inclusion?*

- If special and regular education merge into one educational system in which all students with disabilities are fully included in the regular classroom, how might the education of children with disabilities and the progress they make change as a result?

Special education can be viewed as a system for the delivery of services to children with special needs, rather than as a separate, specialized content area apart from regular education. The regular classroom teacher who works with Sharon, the speech-language pathologist who consults with Sharon's teacher twice each week, and the resource room teacher who works directly with Sharon and communicates with her regular class teacher are all members of a team that plans and delivers a program of education and related services designed to meet Sharon's individual needs. In this chapter, we examine three critical aspects of that system: (a) the individualized education plan (IEP), (b) least restrictive environment (LRE), and (c) the importance of teaming and collaboration among professionals. We also look at some of the challenges and concerns facing special education today.

✳ *Individualized Education Program (IEP)*

Individualized family service plans (IFSP) are developed for infants and toddlers (from birth until age 3) with disabilities. IFSPs are described in Chapter 15.

For ideas on how students with disabilities can participate in the IEP process, see "Someone's Missing" later in this chapter. Van Reusen and Bos (1990, 1994) offer additional information on how to involve students in the IEP conference.

The IDEA requires that an **individualized education program (IEP)** be developed and implemented for every student with disabilities between the ages of 3 and 21. The law is specific as to what an IEP must include and who is to take part in its formulation. Each IEP must be the product of the joint efforts of the members of a *child study team,* which must include at least (a) the child's teacher(s), (b) a representative of the local school district other than the child's teacher, (c) the child's parents or guardian, and (d) whenever appropriate, the child him- or herself. Other professionals, such as physical educators, speech-language pathologists, and physical therapists, may also be involved in the IEP conference.

The IDEA requires that all IEPs include the following:

1. A statement of the child's present levels of educational performance, including academic achievement, social adaptation, prevocational and vocational skills, psychomotor skills, and self-help skills
2. A statement of annual goals describing the educational performance to be achieved by the end of each school year
3. A statement of short-term instructional objectives presented in measurable, intermediate steps between the present level of educational performance and the annual goals
4. A statement of specific educational services needed by the child, including a description of
   a. all special education and related services needed to meet the unique needs of the child (determined without regard to the availability of those services), including the physical education program
   b. any special instructional media and materials that are needed
5. A statement of the needed transition services for students, beginning no later than age 16 and annually thereafter (when determined appropriate for the individual, beginning at age 14 or younger), including, when appropriate, a state-

ment of the interagency responsibilities or linkages (or both) before the student leaves the school setting

6. The date when those services will begin and the length of time the services will be given
7. A description of the extent to which the child will participate in regular education programs
8. A justification for the type of educational placement the child will have
9. A list of the individuals who are responsible for implementing the IEP
10. Objective criteria, evaluation procedures, and schedules of determining, at least annually, whether the short-term instructional objectives are being achieved

Figure 2.1 shows one example of an IEP. IEP formats vary widely across school districts, and schools may go beyond the requirements of the law and include additional information. Each child's IEP must be reviewed and, if necessary, revised at least once each year. The child's parent or guardian must consent to the IEP and must receive a copy of the document.

One of the most difficult tasks for the child study team is determining how inclusive the IEP document should be. Strickland and Turnbull (1993) state that the definition of special education as "specially designed instruction" should be a key element in determining what should go into a student's IEP.

> The determination of whether instruction is "specially designed" must be made by comparing the nature of the instruction for the student with a disability to instructional practices used with typical students at the same age and grade level. If the instructional adaptations that a student with a disability requires are (1) significantly different from adaptations normally expected or made for typical students in that setting, and if (2) the adaptations are necessary to offset or reduce the adverse effect of the disability on learning and educational performance, then these adaptations should be considered "specially designed instruction" and should be included as part of the student's IEP, regardless of the instructional setting. (p. 13)

The IEP is a system for spelling out where the child is, where he should be going, how he will get there, how long it will take, and how to tell when he has arrived. The IEP is a measure of accountability for teachers and schools. Whether a particular school or educational program is effective will be judged, to some extent, by how well it is able to help children meet the goals and objectives set forth in their IEPs. Like other professionals, teachers are being called on to demonstrate effectiveness, and the IEP provides one way for them to do so. The IEP is not, however, a legally binding contract. A child's teacher and school cannot be prosecuted in the courts if the child does not achieve the goals set forth in the IEP. Nevertheless, the school must be able to document that a conscientious and systematic effort was made to achieve those goals. The IEP is, however, much more than an accountability device. Its potential benefits are improved planning (including planning for the student's needs after leaving school), consistency, regular evaluation, and clearer communication among parents, teachers, and others involved in providing services to the student.

Although many educators note that "the plan for the IEP is grand and has great potential" (Morse, 1985, p. 182), inspection and evaluation of IEPs often do not reveal consistency between what is written on the document and the instruction that students experience in the classroom (Nevin, McCann, & Semmel, 1983; Smith, 1990b). Of all the requirements of the IDEA, the IEP is "probably the single most

Transition services are detailed in an **individualized transition plan (ITP)**, which becomes part of each student's IEP. ITPs are described in Chapter 14.

Strickland and Turnbull (1993) provide detailed procedures for systematic development and implementation of IEPs.

FIGURE 2.1

Portion of a completed IEP for a 5th-grade student

INDIVIDUAL EDUCATION PROGRAM

Date _____ 3-1-96 _____

(1) Student

Name: Joe S.

School: Adams

Grade: 5

Current Placement: Regular Class/Resource Room

Date of Birth: 10-1-84   **Age:** 11-5

(2) Committee

		Initial
Mrs. Wrens	Principal	*Ga.W.*
Mrs. Snow	Regular Teacher	*g.s.*
Mr. LaJoie	Counselor	
Mr. Thomas	Resource Teacher	*M.T.*
Mr. Ryan	School Psychologist	*H.RR.*
Mrs. S.	Parent	*J.S.*
Joe S.	Student	*Joe S.*

EP from ___3-15-96___ to ___3-15-97___

(3) Present Level of Educational Functioning	(4) Annual Goal Statements	(5) Instructional Objectives	(6) Objective Criteria and Evaluation
MATH Strengths 1. Can successfully compute addition and subtraction problems to two places with regrouping and zeros. 2. Knows 100 basic multiplication facts. Weaknesses 1. Frequently makes computational errors on problems with which he has had experience. 2. Does not complete seatwork. Key Math total score of 2.1 Grade Equivalent.	Joe will apply knowledge of regrouping in addition and renaming in subtraction to four-digit numbers.	1. When presented with 20 addition problems of 3-digit numbers requiring two renamings, the student will compute answers at a rate of one problem per minute and an accuracy of 90%. 2. When presented with 20 subtraction problems of 3-digit numbers requiring two renamings, the student will compute answers at a rate of one problem per minute with 90% accuracy. 3. When presented with 20 addition problems of 4-digit numbers requiring three renamings, the student will compute answers at a rate of one problem per minute and an accuracy of 90%. 4. When presented with 20 subtraction problems of 4-digit numbers requiring three renamings, the student will compute answers at a rate of one problem per minute with 90% accuracy.	Teacher-made tests (weekly) Teacher-made tests (weekly) Teacher-made tests (weekly)
READING Woodcock Reading Mastery Tests Grade Equivalent Letter identification 3.0 Word identification 1.0 Word attack 2.0 Word comprehension 4.3	The student's oral reading rate for reading material at his comfortable reading level will increase from 30 words per minute to 36 words per minute. Student will improve reading fluency.	1. When presented with a list of 250 basic sight vocabulary words listed in order of difficulty and\or commonly taught, the student will correctly pronounce 200 of them by the end of the year. 2. When presented with a list of 37 direction words listed in order of difficulty and/or commonly taught, the student will correctly pronounce 24 of them. 3. When presented with a list of 40 words and phrases frequently seen on signs listed in order of difficulty, the student will correctly pronounce 30 of them.	Brigance Diagnostic Inventory of Basic Skills, (after 4 and 9 mos.) Teacher observation (daily) Brigance Diagnostic Inventory of Basic Skills, (after 4 and 9 mos.) Teacher observation (daily) Brigance Diagnostic Inventory of Basic Skills, (after 4 and 9 mos.) Teacher observation (daily)

(3) Present Level of Educational Functioning	(4) Annual Goal Statements	(5) Instructional Objectives	(6) Objective Criteria and Evaluation
SOCIAL EMOTIONAL <u>Strengths</u> 1. Joe cooperates in group activities. 2. Attentive and cooperative in class. <u>Weaknesses</u> 1. Reluctant participant on playground. 2. Makes derogatory comments about himself frequently during the school day. 3. Has few friends, is ignored by peers.	Joe will speak about himself in a positive manner. Joe will participate with peers in small groups on the playground and in class.	1. In a one-to-one situation with the teacher Joe will talk about his personal strengths for five min. a day. 2. In a one-to-one situation with the teacher Joe will state 5 strengths he possesses for 3 days in a row. 3. After a small-group activity (3-4 students), Joe will tell the teacher 3 things he did well in the group. 4. After a small-group activity Joe will tell the teacher 6 things he did well in the group. 5. In a small-group activity Joe will ask a peer for help instead of asking an adult: a) With verbal reminders from an adult in 80% of opportunities. b) With nonverbal reminders in 80% of opportunities. c) With no signals in 80% of opportunities. 6. In a small-group activity Joe will offer assistance to a peer: a) With verbal reminders from an adult in 80% of opportunities. b) With nonverbal reminders in 80% of opportunities. c) With no signals in 80% of opportunities.	Teacher observation (daily) for 15 days. Anecdotal records (daily) Anecdotal records (daily) 3 consecutive days Anecdotal records (daily) 5 consecutive days Anecdotal records (daily) 5 consecutive days Teacher observation. Data collected 30 min. a day, 3 days a week Teacher observation. Data collected 30 min. a day, 3 days a week

(7) Educational Services to be Provided

Services Required	Date initiated	Duration of Service	Individual Responsible for the Service
Regular Reading-Adapted	3-15-96	3-15-97	Reading Improvement Specialist and Special Education Teacher
Resource Room	3-15-96	3-15-97	Special Education Teacher
Counselor Consultant	3-15-96	3-15-97	Counselor
Monitoring diet and general health	3-15-96	3-15-97	School Health Nurse

Extent of time in the regular education program: 60% increasing to 80%
Justification of the educational placement:

It is felt that the structure of the resource room can best meet the goals stated for Joe; especially when coordinated with the regular classroom.

It is also felt that Joe could profit enormously from talking with a counselor. He needs someone with whom to talk and with whom he can share his feelings.

(8) I have had the opportunity to participate in the development of the Individual Education Program.
I agree with Individual Education Program   (✓)
I disagree with the individual Education Program   ( )

Parent's Signature ___*Mrs J.*___

Source: From *Developing and Implementing Individualized Education Programs* (3rd ed.) (pp. 308, 311, 313, 316) by B. B. Strickland and A. P. Turnbull, 1993, New York: Macmillan. Reprinted by permission.

A child study team meets to develop an IEP and then reviews and revises the IEP at least once a year.

unpopular aspect of the law, not only because it requires a great deal of work, but because the essence of the plan itself seems to have been lost in the mountains of paperwork" (Gallagher, 1984, p. 228). Several studies of actual IEPs seem to support Gallagher's contention (Fiedler & Knight, 1986; Schenck, 1980; Smith 1990a). Smith and Simpson (1989), for example, evaluated the IEPs of 214 students with behavioral disorders and found that one third of the IEPs lacked necessary mandated components.

But proper inclusion of all mandated components in an IEP is no guarantee that the document will guide the student's learning and teacher's teaching in the classroom, as intended by the IDEA. A harsh critic of many current practices in special education, Algozzine (1993) writes:

> An individualized education plan (IEP) was at the heart of educational reform policy set forth in Public Law 94–142. The intent was to identify and provide services on an individualized basis for all students requiring special education. The concept was good, but the outcomes after 15 years of professional practice have been less than stellar. For the most part, documents developed to provide control and assurance for IEPs have become merely records illustrating compliance. Federal, state, and local evaluations of IEPs have concentrated on the extent to which required components are present, rather than on the extent to which what is actually written in required components assures appropriate education. Independent research has failed to elevate IEPs above the compliance document stage. (p. 463)

Many special and regular educators are working to create procedures for developing IEPs that go beyond compliance with the law and actually serve as a meaningful guide for the "specially designed instruction" a student with disabilities needs. For example, Giangreco, Cloninger, and Iverson (1993) have developed and field-tested an IEP process called COACH, which guides child study teams through the assessment and planning stages of IEP development in a way that results in learning goals and objectives directly related to functional skills in integrated settings.

No matter how appropriate the goals and objectives specified on a student's IEP are, the document's usefulness is limited without direct and ongoing monitoring of student progress (Fuchs & Fuchs, 1986; Wesson, King, & Deno, 1984). Unfortunately, many teachers do not collect and use student performance data to evaluate the effectiveness of their instruction. Although three fourths of the 510 special education teachers in one survey indicated that frequently collected student performance data are "important," many indicated they most often relied on anecdotal observations and subjective measures (e.g., checklists, letter grades) for determining whether or not IEP objectives were met, and 85% said they "never" or "seldom" collected and charted student performance data to make instructional decisions (Cooke, Heward, Test, Spooner, & Courson, 1991).

Some observers have asked, "If children with disabilities must have IEPs, then why not extend this requirement to all children in the public schools?" Indeed, some states and local school districts now use individualized educational planning for all students. Utah, for example, has adopted the requirement that an "individual education plan for the projected education program [being] pursued by each student during membership in the school" (Robinson, 1982, p. 205) be developed cooperatively by teachers, parents, and the student. This requirement has reportedly led to more conferences, better career planning, and greater parental involvement. Although some teachers view IEPs as an added burden of paperwork and some parents do not wish to become involved in the planning process, all students can benefit from accurate specification of individual goals, periodic evaluation, parent involvement, and contributions from various disciplines that the IEP offers.

> Giek (1992) and Farlow and Snell (1994) describe a variety of practical procedures for obtaining and using student performance data to monitor student progress toward IEP objectives.

> Parental involvement in the IEP process is examined in Chapter 13.

✳ *The Least Restrictive Environment*

The IDEA requires that every student with disabilities be educated in the **least restrictive environment (LRE).** Specifically, the law stipulates that

> to the maximum extent appropriate, children with disabilities, including children in public or private institutions or other care facilities, [be] educated with children who are not disabled, and that special classes, separate schooling, or other removal of children with disabilities from the regular educational environment [occur] only when the nature or severity of the disability is such that education in regular classes with the use of supplementary aids and services cannot be achieved satisfactorily. (20 U.S.C. § 1412(5) (B))

Thus, the LRE is the setting that is closest to a regular school program and that also meets the child's special educational needs. Least restrictive environment is a relative concept; the LRE for one child might be inappropriate for another. Since the passage of the IDEA, there have been many differences of opinion over which type of setting is least restrictive and most appropriate for students with disabilities. Some educators and parents consider any decision to place a student with disabilities outside the regular classroom to be overly restrictive; most, however, recognize that a regular class placement can be restrictive and inappropriate if the child's instructional and social needs are not adequately met. It is also generally accepted that there are wide individual differences among children and that there can be more than one "best" way to provide appropriate educational services to a child with disabilities. As Taylor, Biklen, and Searl (1986) observe, decisions concerning a child's

Someone's Missing
························

The Student as an Overlooked Participant in the IEP Process

by Mary T. Peters

Classroom teachers, specialists, administrators, and parents meet with each other once a year at the IEP conference. The group meets to share progress by the student, discuss future goals and objectives, and determine needed services and placement for the student. But where is the student?

Although the regulations for the Individuals with Disabilities Education Act (IDEA) state that "the child, wherever appropriate" be included, rarely does the student play an active role in the IEP process. Gillespie (1981) found that more than 90% of students with disabilities and 75% of their parents had no knowledge of the student participation provision in the IDEA.

Students with disabilities are often not perceived by administrators, teachers, or parents as an integral part of the IEP team, with the right (if not the responsibility) to assist in developing and implementing their own special education programs. Students are more likely to be viewed as the recipients of special services. When they are empowered as active team members in all aspects of the IEP process, however, students have an opportunity to heighten their independence, self-advocacy skills, and self-esteem. Also, students may be able to offer insightful perceptions and valuable contributions. All students with disabilities can and should be involved in the IEP process.

How Can Students Participate?

The IEP conference is just one part of the entire IEP process. Students may be involved at any stage. Figure A illustrates strategies that facilitate student participation in the three major stages of assessment, the IEP conference itself, and instruction.

Assessment

All students should actively participate in the assessment and evaluation of their skills and preferences.

Student Determination of Preferences. For all students, participation in the IEP process can begin with determining preferences. By sharing their likes and dislikes, students provide input from which teachers can identify objectives, goals, and potential reinforcers. Students sometimes make inappropriate or unrealistic choices. In these cases, teachers should counsel students and present them with a variety of more likely alternatives.

Student Self-Evaluation. Students can be further involved in the assessment phase by engaging in self-evaluation. They can use a teacher-made self-rating scale or checklist to determine perceived strengths, weaknesses, competencies, and successes in goal attainment. This information can help teachers devise goals that focus on the student's strong points and address deficit areas that are important to the student.

Goal Setting. Students who are trained to assess their own skills and goal achievement may be better able to set realistic expectations for themselves. Other valuable information that can contribute to the assessment phase is student identification of future goals and ambitions. A wish list can help students identify future plans, expectations, and skills they wish to acquire. Pictures, photos, checklists, and classroom activities can help students identify goals that are then incorporated into their IEPs. Computer software such as Be A Winner: Set Your Goals (M.C.E., Inc., 1988) offers adolescents and adults an interactive program for choosing long- and short-term goals.

The IEP Conference

The degree to which a student may participate in the IEP conference will vary. The highest degree of involvement for students is their acceptance as full team members and opportunities to act as self-advocates. There are also many opportunities for partial participation by students unable to be fully involved.

Preconference Preparation. Students need to be informed about the intent and significance of the meeting, the roles of each team member, and procedures that will be followed. Videotaped presentations of real or staged IEP meetings can be an excellent way to prepare students for their own conference. Role playing can also help emphasize and define the responsibilities of all team members, including those

FIGURE A
Strategies to promote student involvement in three phases of the IEP process

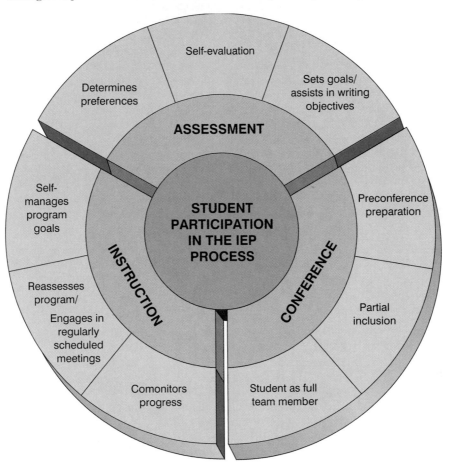

of the student. Students should rehearse appropriate and expected behaviors. The following are suggested rules for student behavior during the IEP conference:

- Remain seated throughout the meeting.
- Maintain eye contact with those who are addressing you.
- Respect others as they speak by listening without interruption.
- If you don't understand, excuse yourself politely and ask them to explain again.
- Wait your turn before offering your opinion and recommendations.
- When you disagree, state your case without being loud or impatient; offer your own suggestions instead.

- Respond to direct questions.

Creative intervention by teachers is sometimes necessary to convince parents of the advantages of student involvement in the IEP conference. Parents may be persuaded by talking to others who have involved their child in the IEP conference. Parents can be invited to participate in or view videotapes of classroom preconference activities. In some cases, administrators may also need to be reminded of students' right to participate and be encouraged to advocate for them in this regard.

Conference Participation. Students who have been involved in other phases of the IEP process will be better prepared for the conference experience. The more active the student has been, the more likely he will be successful in the IEP meeting itself. When something should not be discussed in front of the child (e.g., controversial issues, policy decisions, disagreements), the student can enter the meeting near its conclusion to meet with team members, listen to suggested goals and objectives, and hear comments relating to his or her progress.

With parental cooperation, team commitment, prior preparation, and involvement in other phases of the IEP process, students can be successfully integrated as team members. The student might report his or her own progress, contribute to discussions, and help formulate goals and objectives at the conference. Once these are agreed on, the student should cosign the completed document, just as other team members do.

Instruction

In comonitoring their progress, students participate in classroom activities that remind them of the goals they have helped set. Daily, weekly, and monthly activities can be designed to include students in the ongoing collection of data, assessment of progress, and reevaluation of goals. Teachers can help students tally stickers, tokens, points, or grades they have earned. These can be recorded on a chart or other visual representation related to identified student goals. Younger students can color bar graphs or collect small items or cards to signify their progress.

Students can also comonitor their progress in meetings with other students. These meetings should be positive, encouraging group cooperation, support, and problem-solving opportunities. Self-management, self-monitoring, and self-instruction techniques may also help students meet the goals they have helped set (Heward, 1987b; Kerr & Nelson, 1989; Lovitt, 1995).

Including students in a process designed expressly for them is often overlooked, but there are numerous possibilities for student participation in the IEP process for educators who wish to implement instruction with students—not just for them.

Adapted from "Someone's Missing: The Student as an Overlooked Participant in the IEP Process" by Mary T. Peters, 1990, *Preventing School Failure, 34*(4), pp. 32-36. Reprinted with permission of the Helen Dwight Reid Educational Foundation. Published by Holdref Publications, 1319 Eighteenth St., N.W., Washington, DC 20036-1802. © 1990.

educational program should be based on consideration of that child's needs. Not all children with the same disability should be placed in the same setting; the goal, instead, is to find the appropriate LRE for each child.

Recognizing the importance of the academic and social interactions that the child experiences over the physical characteristics of where special education takes place, Heron and Skinner (1981) define the least restrictive environment as

> that educational setting which maximizes the . . . student's opportunity to respond and achieve, permits the regular education teacher to interact proportionally with all the students in the classroom, and fosters acceptable social relations between nonhandicapped and [handicapped] students. (p. 116)

A Continuum of Services

Children with disabilities and their families need a wide range of special education and related services from time to time. Today, most schools provide a *continuum of services*—that is, a range of placement and service options to meet the individual needs of students with disabilities. The continuum is often symbolically depicted as a pyramid, with placements ranging from least restrictive (regular classroom placement) at the bottom to most restrictive (special schools and residential programs) at the top (see Figure 2.2). The fact that the pyramid is widest at the bottom indicates that the greatest number of children are served in regular classrooms and that the number of children who require more restrictive, intensive, and specialized placements gets smaller as we move up. As already noted, the majority of children receiving special education services have mild disabilities. The number of children with mild mental retardation, for example, is far greater than those who experience severe retardation. Likewise, children with mild or moderate behavior problems greatly outnumber those with severe emotional and behavioral disorders. As the severity of the disability increases, the need for more specialized services also increases, but the number of students involved decreases.

Five of the seven levels of service depicted in Figure 2.2 are available in regular public school buildings. Children at Levels 1 through 4 attend regular classes with peers without disabilities; supportive help is given by special teachers who provide consultation to the children's regular teachers or in special resource rooms. In a **resource room,** a special educator provides instruction to students with disabilities for part of the school day, either individually or in small groups. Children at Level 5, who require full-time placement in a **self-contained class,** are with other children with disabilities for most of the school day and only interact with children without disabilities at certain times, such as during lunch, recess, or perhaps art and music. Although the self-contained classroom provides significantly fewer opportunities for interaction with nondisabled children than the regular classroom, it provides more integration than placement in a special school or residential facility attended only by children with disabilities.

> The definitions of six educational placements used by the U.S. Department of Education are shown in Chapter 1. Wiederholt and Chamberlain (1989) describe types of resource room programs and review the research conducted on their effects.

FIGURE 2.2
Continuum of educational services for students with disabilities

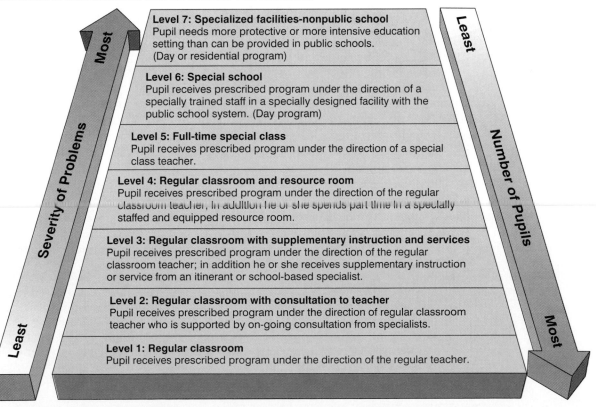

Source: From Montgomery County Public Schools, Rockville, MD. Reprinted by permission.

Maynard Reynolds, who was among the first to propose the continuum of services concept, believes that it is time to make some changes in the model—specifically, to do away with the two most restrictive placements.

> In this writer's view, we are prepared now to lop off the top two levels of the continuum. . . . [I]t is now well demonstrated that we can deliver special education and related services within general school buildings and at a continuum level no higher than the special class. Thus, we can foresee the undoing or demise of special schools (day and residential) as delivery mechanisms for special education—at least in the United States. (1989, p. 8)

Not all special educators would agree with Reynolds. As we will see throughout this text, the relative value of providing services to students with disabilities outside the regular classroom, and especially in separate classrooms and schools, is a hotly contested issue in special education.

Placement of a student with disabilities at any level on the continuum of services is not to be regarded as permanent. The continuum concept is intended to be flexible, with students moving from one placement to another as dictated by their current educational needs. Teachers, parents, and administrators should periodically review the specific goals and objectives for each child—they are required to do so at least annually—and make new placement decisions if warranted. A child may be placed in a less integrated setting for a limited time; then, when a performance review shows that certain goals have been achieved, the child should be returned to a more normalized setting.

Current interpretation of the LRE, based on recent court cases, is that a child should be removed from the regular school program only to the extent there is clear evidence that removal is necessary for the child to receive appropriate educational services. The child's parents must be informed whenever any change in placement is being considered so that they can either consent or object to the change and can present additional information if they wish. No removal from the regular school program should be regarded as permanent; a plan should be made for returning the child to as normal a setting as possible as soon as certain needs or conditions are met. Thus, each student with disabilities must have access to educational experiences appropriate to that student's special needs and as similar as possible to those a student without disabilities would have.

Because neither the IDEA nor the regulations that accompany it specify exactly how a school district is to determine LRE, numerous conflicts have arisen; some have led to court cases. After reviewing the rulings of four LRE disputes that reached U.S. courts of appeals, Yell (1995) concluded that the IDEA does not require the placement of students with disabilities into the regular classroom but does fully support the continuum of services.

> At times, the mainstream will be the appropriate placement; however, IDEA and case law interpreting the LRE mandate are clear that for some students with disabilities, the appropriate and least restrictive setting will not be the regular education classroom. As the *Daniel* court stated, "Mainstreaming a child who will suffer from the experience would violate [IDEA's] mandate for a free appropriate public education." . . . The IEP team, as the courts have indicated, needs to employ a balancing test, weighing the desirability of integration against the obligation to furnish an appropriate education. (p. 402)

Other placement and service delivery alternatives not shown in the Figure 2.2 continuum have been developed. One example is the integrated classroom model, in which a teacher and a teacher aide provide all instruction in a classroom of students with and without disabilities (Affleck, Madge, Adams, & Lowenbraun, 1988).

Yell (1995) provides a checklist that schools can follow to determine whether the LRE requirements of the IDEA have been met.

Mainstreaming

The word **mainstreaming** describes the process of integrating children with disabilities into regular classrooms. Much discussion and controversy and many misconceptions have arisen regarding the education of students with disabilities in regular classes—the so-called mainstream of our public school system. Some people view mainstreaming as placing all students with disabilities into regular classrooms with no additional supportive services; others have the idea that mainstreaming can mean completely segregated placement of children with disabilities as long as they interact with nondisabled peers in a few activities (perhaps at lunch or on the playground). Many parents strongly support the placement of their children into regular classes; others have resisted it just as strongly, thinking that the regular classroom does not offer the intense, individualized education their children need. For example, a recent study found that most parents of elementary students with learning disabilities who received reading instruction in resource rooms had strong positive attitudes toward the resource room program and were reluctant to have their children reintegrated into general education classes for reading instruction (Green & Shinn, 1995).

> Although often confused, the terms *mainstreaming* and *least restrictive environment* are not synonymous. Mainstreaming is the placement of students with disabilities into regular classrooms; the LRE principle requires that students with disabilities must be educated in settings as close to the regular class as possible.

Interestingly, the word *mainstreaming* does not appear in the IDEA, the federal legislation that generated most of the discussion and debate. As we have seen, what the law does call for is the education of each child with disabilities in the least restrictive environment, removed no farther than necessary from the regular public school program.

The IDEA does not require placement of all children with disabilities in regular classes, call for children with disabilities to remain in regular classes without necessary supportive services, or suggest that regular teachers should educate students with disabilities without help from special educators and other specialists. It does, however, specifically call for regular and special educators to cooperate in providing an equal educational opportunity to every student with disabilities.

We know that simply placing a child with disabilities into a regular classroom does not mean that the child will learn and behave appropriately or be socially accepted by children without disabilities (Gresham, 1982). It is important for special educators to teach appropriate social skills and behavior to the child with disabilities and to educate nondisabled children about their classmates. Examples of effective mainstreaming programs can be found at age levels ranging from preschool (Esposito & Reed, 1986; Jenkins, Speltz, & Odom, 1985) to high school (Warger, Aldinger, & Okun, 1983), and they include children whose disabilities range from mild (Algozzine & Korinek, 1985; Thomas & Jackson, 1986) to severe (Brinker, 1985; Condon, York, Heal, & Fortschneider, 1986). Numerous strategies for mainstreaming students with special needs can be found in Lewis and Doorlag (1995); Salend (1994); and Wood (1992, 1993).

> Classwide peer tutoring is one proven method for successfully including students with disabilities into the academic and social life of the regular classroom. See "Classwide Peer Tutoring" later in this chapter.

Successful mainstreaming requires that teachers, parents, administrators, and students all work together. Heron and Harris (1993) describe consultation and collaboration procedures that special educators can use in working with regular educators to plan and deliver needed services to students with disabilities in the mainstream. Figure 2.3 shows a checklist that planning teams can use to evaluate the likelihood of a successful mainstreaming experience.

Peer tutoring enables students with and without disabilities to learn from one another.

✳ The Importance of Teaming and Collaboration

Collaboration, once a "buzzword" for futurists' conceptualizations of the effective schools in the 21st century (Benjamin, 1989), has become common and necessary practice in the 1990s. Teachers who work with students with disabilities and other students who are difficult to teach have discovered they are better able to diagnose and solve learning and behavior problems in the classroom when they work together. Pfeiffer (1982) concluded that team decision making was generally consistent, effective, and superior to individual decision making in the placement of exceptional children. "A cooperative work group brings to bear on a complex task differing values as well as unique professional perspectives. This enhances the problem-solving effectiveness that is required" (p. 69) when determining the most appropriate educational program for an exceptional child.

Various types of teams have been developed. Some schools use *intervention assistance teams* to help classroom teachers devise and implement adaptations for a student who is experiencing either academic or behavioral difficulties so that he or she can remain in the regular classroom. This approach is commonly called "prereferral intervention" because successful intervention avoids the costly and time-consuming process of assessment for special education placement (Graden, Casey, & Christenson, 1985). Fuchs, Fuchs, Bahr, Fernstrom, and Stecker (1990) note that prereferral intervention

> is often "brokered" by one or more support staff, such as a special educator or school psychologist, who works indirectly with a targeted difficult-to-teach (DTT) student through consultation with the teacher. Implicit in this definition is a preven-

Carter and Sugai (1989) found that, although not required by federal law, 23 states required prereferral interventions for students suspected of having a disability, and 11 additional states recommended that local school districts use prereferral systems. Descriptions of prereferral intervention models and related research can be found in Fuchs, Fuchs, and Bahr (1990); Graden (1989); and Pugach and Johnson (1989b).

FIGURE 2.3

A mainstreaming preparation checklist

Teachers, parents, and administrators must be committed to carrying out the least restrictive environment concept. If individuals with disabilities are ever to become full participants in society, meaningful inclusion in integrated settings must occur as early and as widely as possible. Educators should be willing to put forth their best efforts to make a regular class experience rewarding and enriching for students with disabilities. Special educators can do much to make this happen.

Preparation is the key to a successful mainstreaming experience. This checklist can serve as a guide for the special educator, not only for preparing the student with disabilities, but also for working with the other people who must support the mainstreaming effort. The teacher should examine and work on each element of the checklist and not place a student with disabilities into a mainstream setting until most, if not all, of the "yes" boxes can be checked. For more information on each item in the checklist, see Dardig (1981).

1. Student with disabilities:

Yes   No
☐   ☐   Is familiar with rules and routine of the regular classroom?
☐   ☐   Follows verbal and written directions used in the regular classroom?
☐   ☐   Remains on-task for adequate time periods?
☐   ☐   Has expressed a desire to participate in the regular class setting?
☐   ☐   Reacts appropriately to teasing, questions, criticism, etc.?
☐   ☐   Student's IEP objectives match instructional objectives in regular class?

2. Regular class teacher:

Yes   No
☐   ☐   Has been given rationale for mainstreaming activities and asked to cooperate?
☐   ☐   Has information about student's needs, present skills, and current learning objectives?
☐   ☐   Has been provided with special materials and/or support services as needed?
☐   ☐   Has prepared class for mainstreaming?
☐   ☐   Has acquired special helping skills if necessary?
☐   ☐   Will be monitored regularly to identify any problems that arise?

3. Nondisabled peers:

Yes   No
☐   ☐   Have been informed about student's participation and about disability (if appropriate) with the opportunity to ask questions?
☐   ☐   Have been asked for their cooperation and friendship toward the student?
☐   ☐   Have learned helping skills and praising behaviors?

4. Parents of student with disabilities:

Yes   No
☐   ☐   Have received verbal or written information about mainstreaming situation?
☐   ☐   Have been asked to praise and encourage child's progress in regular and special classes?

5. Nondisabled student's parents:

Yes   No
☐   ☐   Have been informed about mainstreaming activities at PTA meeting, conferences, or through other vehicle, and asked for their cooperation?

6. School administrator:

Yes   No
☐   ☐   Has been informed about specifics of mainstreaming activities?
☐   ☐   Has indicated specific steps she or he will take to encourage and support these activities?

Source: Adapted from "Helping Teachers Integrate Handicapped Students into the Regular Classroom" by J. C. Dardig, 1981, *Educational Horizons, 59,* pp. 124–130. Reprinted with permission of Educational Horizons, quarterly journal, published by Pi Lambda Theta, an international honor and professional association in education, Bloomington, IN 47407-6626.

Classwide Peer Tutoring

Integrating Students with Disabilities into the Regular Classroom

Meaningful inclusion of a student with disabilities into the academic and social life of the regular classroom presents a difficult challenge. The regular classroom teacher is expected to deliver individualized instruction to the mainstreamed student, maintain effective programming for the rest of the class, and help the mainstreamed child become socially integrated into the classroom. In-class tutoring is one method that has been used successfully to individualize instruction for students with disabilities without requiring them to leave the regular classroom. Certified tutors, classroom aides, parent and grandparent volunteers, and older students have all served as effective in-class tutors for students with disabilities. But obtaining extra adult help or out-of-class students as tutors on a regular basis is frequently a problem.

An often-untapped but always-available source of tutoring help in every classroom is the students themselves. Although the idea of peer tutoring (same-age classmates teaching one another) is not new (Lancaster, 1806), it has recently become the focus of renewed interest and research. As it is often implemented, peer tutoring involves singling out students with disabilities or low achievers who have not mastered a particular skill for special help from a few high-achieving students who are assigned as tutors. In contrast, a *classwide peer-tutoring system* includes mainstreamed students as full participants in an ongoing whole-class activity. Direct, individualized instruction is provided to every student in the class, and positive social interactions between students with disabilities and their classmates are encouraged. One classwide peer-tutoring program that has been developed for teaching basic reading and math skills in the primary grades is described here (Cooke, Heron, & Heward, 1983).

Tutoring Folder

Every student in the class has a tutoring folder containing 10 flashcards in a GO pocket (see Figure A).

Each card has one word (sound or math fact) to be taught to the child's partner. Each child serves as both tutor and student each day. When in the role of student, each child practices words from an individualized list of unknown words determined by a teacher-given pretest.

Tutor Huddle

The daily peer tutoring session begins with children getting their folders and participating in a 5-minute "tutor huddle" with two or three other tutors (Heward, Heron, & Cooke, 1982). The children take turns presenting and orally reading the words they will shortly be responsible for teaching to their partners. (Meanwhile, their partners are in other tutor huddles working on the words they, too, will soon be teaching.) Fellow tutors confirm correct responses by saying "Yes" and help identify words a tutor doesn't know. The teacher circulates around the room, helping tutor huddles that cannot identify or agree on a given word.

Practice

After tutor huddle, partners join one another on the floor to practice their words. One child begins in the role of tutor, presenting the set of word cards as many times as possible during the 5-minute practice period. Tutors are trained to praise their students from time to time for correct responses. When a student makes an error, the tutor says, "Try again." If the student still does not respond correctly, the tutor says, "The word is *tree;* say *tree.*" A timer signals the end of the first practice period, and the partners switch roles.

Testing

After the second practice period, the children reverse roles again, and the first tutor tests her partner by presenting each sight word once, providing no prompts or cues. Words the student reads correctly are placed in one pile, and missed words in another. Roles are then switched again, and the first tutor is

FIGURE A
Peer tutoring folder

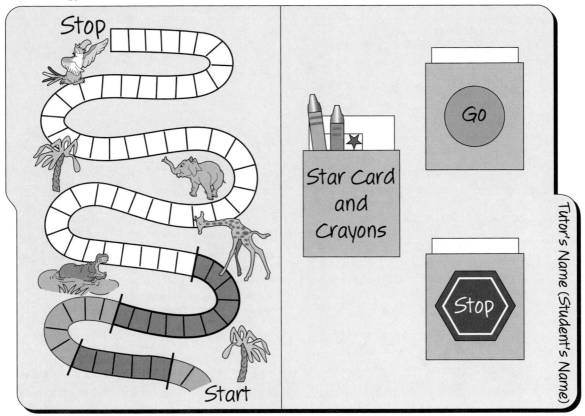

Adapted from "Peer Tutoring: Implementing Classwide Programs in the Primary Grades" by N. L. Cooke, T. E. Heron, & W. L. Heward, 1983, p. 14. Columbus, OH: Special Press. Used by permission.

now tested on the words she practiced. The peer-tutoring session ends with the tutors marking on a chart the number of words their partners said correctly during the test and praising one another for their good work. When a child correctly reads a word on the test for three consecutive sessions, that word is considered learned and is moved to the folder's STOP pocket. When all 10 words have been learned, a new set of words is placed in the GO pocket.

Results

This peer tutoring system was originally developed and evaluated during a 5-month period in a first-grade classroom of 28 children. The class included a boy with learning disabilities and a girl with mental retardation, both of whom attended a special education resource room for part of the school day. All children in the classroom learned sight words at a rapid, consistent pace (Heron, Heward, Cooke, & Hill, 1983). The children also retained the words they had taught one another. The class average on 10-word review tests given 1 week after each set of words was learned was 8.9 words correct. Of particular interest was the performance of the two mainstreamed children. The boy with learning disabilities functioned successfully both as a student and as a tutor. Although the child with mental retardation did not serve as a tutor, she participated as a student, learning at the rate of almost 1 new word per day. Her sight word vocabulary increased from a pretest score of 4 to a total of 51 words by the end of the study

FIGURE B

Examples of peer-tutoring flashcards in different subject areas showing variations in presentation and response modes. Tutor marks plus and minus signs to record partner's performance during testing.

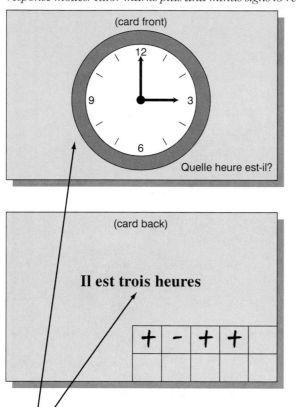

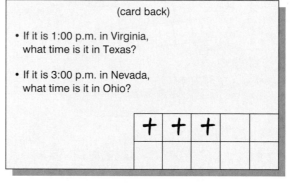

Vary cards to show other clock faces and times

Vary to include generalization questions: If you left California at 10:00 a.m. traveling 600 miles per hour, and you flew for 5 hours to New York, what time would it be when you arrived. (Give reverse problem).

(Cooke, Heron, Heward, & Test, 1982). She, too, remembered the words she had learned, averaging 8.7 words correct out of a possible 10 on the 1-week review tests. And both she and her tutor enjoyed the daily sessions. When the long program ended, her tutor wrote, "I like peer tutoring. I liked my student vary [sic] much." The positive social interactions of a classwide peer-tutoring program may, in the long run, prove to be of equal or even greater benefit to the children involved than the actual learning gains themselves.

Variations

The program described here is one of a number of similar classwide peer-tutoring models that reliably produce significant academic gains by students with disabilities in regular classrooms (e.g., Delquadri, Greenwood, Whorton, Carta, & Hall, 1986; Greenwood, Maheady, & Carta, 1991; Maheady, Harper, & Mallette, 1991; Mathes, Fuchs, Fuchs, Henley, & Sanders, 1994; Miller, Barbetta, & Heron, 1994). This system has been replicated in hundreds of classrooms with sight words, math facts, and other subject areas. Figure B shows examples of peer-tutoring flashcard variations across different subject areas and levels of difficulty. To see how high school students with learning disabilities used the system to teach Spanish to one another, see pages "Somos Todos Ayudantes Y Estudiantes!" in Chapter 5.

FIGURE B (continued)

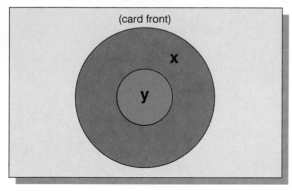

(card front)

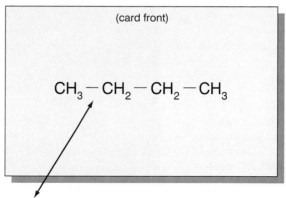

(card front)

Vary to show other chemical formulas.

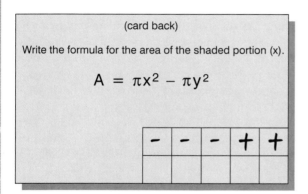

(card back)

Write the formula for the area of the shaded portion (x).

$$A = \pi x^2 - \pi y^2$$

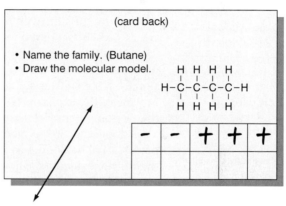

(card back)

• Name the family. (Butane)
• Draw the molecular model.

Vary to show other geometric formulas.

Vary by having the student draw other molecular models.

Adapted from "START tutoring: Designing, training, implementing, adapting, and evaluating tutoring programs for school and home settings" by A. D. Miller, P. M. Barbetta, & T. E. Heron, 1994. In R. Gardner III, D. M. Sainato, J. O. Cooper, T. E. Heron, W. L. Heward, J. Eshleman, & T. A. Grossi (Eds.), *Behavior analysis in education: Focus on measurably superior instruction* (pp. 274–275). Pacific Grove, CA: Brooks/Cole. Used by permission.

tative intent; that is, (a) eliminating inappropriate referrals while increasing the legiti-macy of those that are initiated and (b) reducing future student problems by strengthening the teacher's capacity to intervene effectively with a greater diversity of children. (p. 495)

Educators are also teaming with one another to serve students with disabilities in regular classrooms. Often called *teacher assistance teams* or *cooperative educa-tion teams,* these collaborative teaching efforts have become the subject of much research and interest (Chalfant & Pysh, 1989; Villa & Thousand, 1993). Henderson (1986) describes the functioning of a "building planning and placement team," a group of full-time and part-time professionals assigned to a given school building to diagnose special needs, deliver services, and review children's placements.

"Here's another idea we could try." Intervention assistance teams plan strategies to help children with learning or behavioral problems remain in the regular classroom.

Although *paraprofessionals*—paid (and occasionally volunteer) workers who provide direct instructional and support services to students with disabilities under such titles as classroom aides and teacher assistants—are critically important members of the special education team, relatively little attention has been paid to their training and supervision. For suggestions on how to effectively use paraprofessionals in special education, see Blalock (1991); Courson and Heward (1988); and Jones and Bender (1993).

Figure 2.4 shows the relationships among professionals and the student that are likely to develop with each of the three types of teams.

Many students with disabilities need services from several disciplines. One survey of preschool children with disabilities in a noncategorical public school program found that, of the 81 children receiving services, 56 were served by four or more professionals, 16 were served by three professionals, and 9 were served by two professionals. No child was served by only one professional (Northcott & Erickson, 1977). In view of the expansion of services to infants, toddlers, and preschool children and the ongoing concern for planning transitional services for young adults after they leave programs of special education, the practice of involving professional and paraprofessional personnel as a team to assess students and plan cooperatively to meet their diverse needs is gaining even wider acceptance.

Although there are many variations of the team approach in terms of size and structure, each member of a team generally assumes certain clearly assigned responsibilities and recognizes the importance of learning from, contributing to, and interacting with the other members of the team. Many believe that the consensus and group decisions arising from a team's involvement provide a form of insurance against erroneous or arbitrary conclusions in the complex issues that face educators of students with disabilities.

In practice, three team models have emerged (Giangreco, York, & Rainforth, 1989; Woodruff & McGonigel, 1988). *Multidisciplinary teams* are composed of professionals from different disciplines who work independently of one another. Each team member conducts assessments, plans interventions, and delivers services. Teams that operate according to a multidisciplinary structure risk the danger of not providing services that recognize the child as an integrated whole; they tend to "splinter" the child into segments along disciplinary lines. (An old saying described the child with disabilities as giving "his hands to the occupational therapist, his legs to the physical therapist, and his brain to the teacher" [Williamson, 1978].) Another concern is the lack of communication among team members.

Interdisciplinary teams are characterized by formal channels of communication between members. Although each professional usually conducts discipline-specific assessments, the interdisciplinary team meets to share information and to develop intervention plans. Each team member is generally responsible for implementing a portion of the service plan related to his or her discipline.

FIGURE 2.4

Relationships among professionals from various disciplines and the learner in three team models

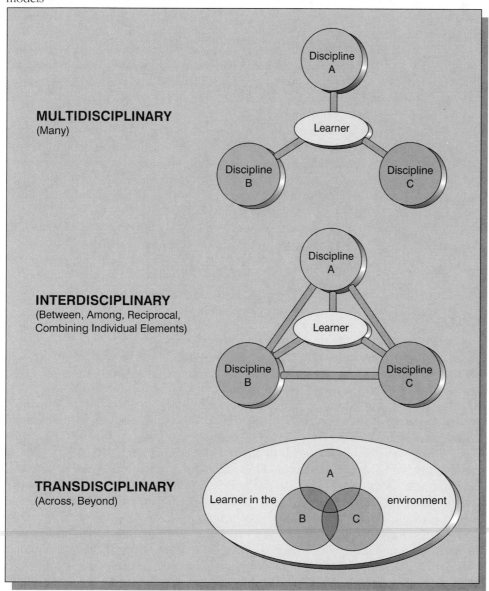

Source: From "Providing Related Services to Learners with Severe Handicaps in Educational Settings: Pursuing the Least Restrictive Option" by M. F. Giangreco, J. York, and B. Rainforth, 1989, *Pediatric Physical Therapy, 1*(2), p. 57. Reprinted by permission.

The highest level of team involvement, but also the most difficult to accomplish, is the *transdisciplinary team.* Members of transdisciplinary teams seek to provide services in a uniform and integrated fashion by conducting joint assessments, sharing information and expertise across discipline boundaries, and selecting goals and interventions that are discipline-free (Gallivan-Fenlon, 1994; Giangreco, Edel-

Regardless of the team model, team members must learn to put aside professional rivalries and work for the benefit of the student. See "Interactive Teaming" later in this chapter.

man, & Dennis, 1991; Giangreco, York, & Rainforth, 1989). Members of transdisciplinary teams also share roles (often referred to as *role release*); in contrast, members of multidisciplinary and interdisciplinary teams generally operate in isolation and may not coordinate their services in order to achieve the integrated delivery of related services.

The team approach is thought to be more cost-effective because professionals can share their expertise and serve a greater number of children through consultation. An effective team, with all members sharing their expertise and skills, can do much to provide an appropriate and consistent educational program for students with disabilities and to enhance the individual effectiveness of each of its members. Of course, not all of these advantages are realized in all cases. It is sometimes difficult for members of an interdisciplinary team to agree on which learning objectives are most important for the child. In response to this problem, various strategies have been developed to help IEP planning teams set priorities for a child's learning goals while giving equal consideration to each member's input (Dardig & Heward, 1981; Giangreco, Cloninger, & Iverson, 1993). Recently, educators have recognized the importance of including the student with disabilities as an integral member of the team (Peters, 1990; Van Reusen & Bos, 1994; Villa & Thousand, 1992).

✳ *Regular and Special Education: A New Relationship?*

How can special education and regular education work together most effectively for the benefit of all students? Every child with a disability, regardless of the service setting, must have an IEP developed specially to suit his or her individual abilities and needs. Thus, special educators, regular educators, and parents should not be in an us-versus-them relationship. Instead, they should all work together to individualize instruction, manage behavior, and plan cooperatively to meet students' immediate and long-range needs.

Although not all children with disabilities attend regular classes, it is true that regular classroom teachers are expected to deal with a much wider variety of learning, behavioral, sensory, and physical differences among their students than was the case just a few years ago. Thus, provision of inservice training for regular educators is an important (and sometimes overlooked) requirement of the IDEA. Regular classroom teachers are understandably wary of having children with disabilities placed into their classes if little or no training or support is provided. The role of regular classroom teachers is already a demanding one; they do not want their classes to become any larger, especially if they perceive exceptional children as unmanageable. Regular classroom teachers are entitled to be involved in decisions about children who are placed into their classes and to be offered continuous consultation and other supportive services from special educators (Heron & Harris, 1993; Idol, 1989; West & Idol, 1990).

The Regular Education Initiative

The relationship between special education and regular education has been the subject of a great deal of debate and discussion in recent years. Stainback and Stainback (1984) were among the first to call for a merger of special and regular education, contending that the current dual system is inefficient and outdated: "It is time to stop developing criteria for who does or does not belong in the mainstream and instead turn the spotlight to increasing the capabilities of the regular school environment, the mainstream, to meet the needs of all students" (p. 110).

Proponents of a merger between regular and special education cite the following as major problems as evidence that such a merger is warranted:

- Overlapping of programs for low-achieving students and students with mild disabilities
- High costs of assessing and placing students with disabilities in "pull-out" programs of questionable effectiveness
- Large numbers of children in regular classrooms who are failing or academically at risk but whose needs are not being met because they do not meet the eligibility criteria for special education (e.g., Gartner & Lipsky, 1987; Wang, Reynolds, & Walberg, 1985; Will, 1986)

Most often referred to as the **regular education initiative (REI)**, the proposed merger would consist of the "joining of demonstrably effective practices from special, compensatory, and general education to establish a general education system that is more inclusive and better serves all students, particularly those who require greater-than-usual educational support" (Reynolds, Wang, & Walberg, 1987, p. 394).

Lilly (1986) contends that the barriers between general and special education are gradually being broken down and that, although supportive services are needed by many students who have difficulty in learning and behaving, "we need not and should not offer these services through special education. . . . A single coordinated system of service delivery is preferable to the array of special programs currently offered in the schools" (p. 10).

The idea of merging general and special education is by no means universally popular. Mesinger (1985) describes Stainback and Stainback as holding "a distinctly minority viewpoint" and explains, "I am reluctant to abandon special education as a system until I see evidence of a drastic improvement in regular educational teacher training and professional practice in the public schools" (p. 512). Similarly, Lieberman (1985) calls for special education to maintain its separate identity because, among other reasons, "in regular education, the system dictates the curriculum; in special education, the child dictates the curriculum" (p. 514).

Partly in response to the REI, a number of research and demonstration projects have been developed and tested to restructure the delivery of educational services to children with disabilities in the regular classroom. Two of the most well known are the Adaptive Learning Environments Model (ALEM), developed by Wang (1980) and her colleagues, and Mainstreaming Experiences for Learning Disabled Students (Project MELD), developed by Zigmond and Baker (1987). Zigmond and Baker (1990) acknowledge the difficulty of ensuring quality instructional services for students with disabilities in their report of a 2-year study of the academic progress and social behavior of 13 students with learning disabilities who participated in a Project MELD school.

> A successful alternative to pull-out (resource or self-contained) special education programs requires more than the administrative fiat to "put children back." Returning students with learning disabilities to the mainstream should be the catalyst for a schoolwide improvement effort. The current data make it clear that such students will not make progress if teachers continue with "business as usual." (p. 185)

For additional arguments and supportive data in favor of REI, see Bilken and Zollers (1986); Stainback and Stainback (1987); and Wang and Walberg (1988).

For additional arguments and supportive data questioning the wisdom of merging regular and special education, see Hallahan, Keller, McKinney, Lloyd, and Bryan (1988); Kauffman, Gerber, and Semmel (1988); Kauffman and Pullen (1989); Keogh (1988); and Schumaker and Deschler (1988).

Interactive Teaming

························

by Vivian I. Correa

Vignette #1

Gail Miller, the school liaison at a local elementary school, has asked that a team meeting be held to discuss the referral of Jacque, a 3-year-old Haitian child, to special education. Jacque was brought to the United States to live with his grandmother a year ago, and his diagnosis of cerebral palsy qualified him to receive early intervention services at a local day-care center. Gail Miller is worried. Jacque is now eligible for preschool special education services at the elementary school, but no one at the school speaks French Creole and Jacque's custodial grandmother speaks little English. According to the IDEA, children must be assessed in their native language. Gail Miller is at a loss for what to do.

Vignette #2

Claire, a 16-year-old with learning disabilities, is asking her parents to assist her in getting an after-school job at the mall like her friends. Claire's parents ask Tom Greco, the high school transition specialist, to arrange a meeting with the principal and teachers regarding this request. Tom Greco is concerned about this situation. What should he do?

Vignette #3

Audrey is 8 years old and has been diagnosed with autism. Her teacher, Ms. Jones, is a beginning teacher at the local elementary school. Audrey's family is concerned that Audrey's self-injurious behaviors have increased within the last few weeks. Ms. Jones has noticed this increase as well and has tried some strategies to redirect the behavior, with no positive results. Ms. Jones is worried about the situation and would like some assistance. What is she to do?

Interactive Teaming

Collaboration and teaming have become critical parts of the way educators do their work in schools today.

Solving the problems described in the three vignettes will require teaming and collaboration. Whether working with families, community agencies, or other educators, collaboration is a complex task that requires special knowledge and skills. We often assume that all education personnel and families know how to collaborate and team. It seems like common sense. Administrators, for example, often ask teachers to work together to solve a problem, assuming that they understand the intricacies of the collaboration process. Yet, what often results from the interactions among the teachers are problems associated with poor interpersonal communication, role ambiguity, turf wars, lack of leadership support, and time constraints. Many educators have not learned the skills necessary for collaboration and lack the basic knowledge for understanding the dynamic process of interactive teaming.

Interactive teaming occurs when there is mutual or reciprocal effort among and between members of the team to meet the goal of providing the best possible education program for a student (Thomas, Correa, & Morsink, 1995). The purpose of interactive teaming is to share information and expertise in order to ensure that the best possible decisions are made and that effective programs are implemented.

Collaborating with professionals and families within an interactive team model has its benefits and its barriers. The benefits of teaming, however, far outweigh the difficulties that may occur. For example, when individuals team, there is a sense of camaraderie, friendship, and mutuality. Effective teaming produces effective ideas and comprehensive solutions that one person alone may not have been able to achieve.

What, then, are the important skills that education personnel need in order to become effective team members? It is not surprising that one of the most important skills necessary for interactive teaming is the ability to communicate well. Effective *interpersonal communication* involves the ability to be empathic, genuine, positive, open, clear, and assertive. Both verbal and nonverbal communication skills can be developed in individuals through training and practice.

A second skill necessary for interactive teaming is *role clarification*. Each member of a team must understand his or her own role and responsibilities and those of other members. If confusion or overlapping interests occur among team members, effective teaming may be jeopardized. Members who are unsure of their roles and responsibilities may blame others by making statements such as, "I thought that was what you were supposed to do," or, "No one told me I was responsible for this." Avoiding ambiguity of roles and responsibilities from the onset of interactive teaming is critical.

A third skill involved in interactive teaming relates to adult learning. Effective team members can *role release* to other members by teaching them about basic procedures and practices associated with their profession. For example, an occupational therapist can teach a classroom teacher and a parent how to implement oral motor exercises on a child prior to meals. Thus, educating and learning from other adults become core skills necessary for implementing the best integrated educational strategies for students.

Interactive team members must also become culturally competent. The first step for developing *cultural competence* is to become self-aware of one's own attitudes, values, biases, and stereotypes of ethnic minorities (e.g., African Americans, Native Americans, Asians, Hispanics) and non-ethnic minorities (e.g., individuals who are homeless, gays and lesbians, those living in poverty). Team members must understand the impact that ethnic or non-ethnic diversity plays in the interactions among professional team members, as well as among the students and families with whom they work. Teams must develop culturally responsive services for students and families from many diverse groups. (The characteristics of culturally responsive services are discussed in Chapter 3.)

Suggested Steps

The procedures involved in interactive teaming are listed below. The procedures may vary, however, depending on such factors as the age of the child, the severity of the problem, and the types of professionals available.

1. Designate a team leader and make sure all persons involved are notified of the meeting time and place.

2. Introduce all team members and state the purpose of the meeting.
3. Describe, in detail, the problem situation and allow team members to ask questions for purposes of clarification.
4. Reach consensus on a specific, measurable, and observational definition of the problem.
5. Prioritize the problems, if there are more than one, on the basis of the needs of the student and the family.
6. Determine the history and frequency of the problem.
7. Discuss any previous interventions that have been attempted.
8. Brainstorm possible interventions, encouraging full team participation.
9. Establish procedures for collecting data.
10. Determine how long the intervention will be applied.
11. Clarify the responsibilities of each team member.
12. Develop timelines for activities and schedule a follow-up meeting.
13. Evaluate the intervention regularly with team members and make modifications if necessary.
14. Provide consultative and collaborative assistance to each member as needed.
15. Evaluate the team's effectiveness and determine whether any changes need to be made in operating procedures, team composition, or other areas.

Interactive teaming can be extremely successful in solving problems for special education teachers working within today's inclusive school environments. The benefits of teaming are the development of effective strategies and solutions for students with disabilities and their families. The skills required for effective collaboration and teaming, however, are complex and must be demonstrated by all team members. It is imperative that college and university programs in teacher education teach the skills of teaming and collaboration and allow preservice students to practice them. As educators prepare for the increasing challenges of tomorrow's schools, a collaborative model like interactive teaming may well be the major pattern for future service delivery for students with disabilities and their families.

Collaboration Activities

1. Think about the last time you worked on a project with a group of peers (e.g., planning a party or

campus activity). Did everything go smoothly? Which individuals worked well together? Which ones did not? Why? What problems did you encounter? Why do you think those problems occurred? How were they resolved?

2. Form small teams and choose one of the three vignettes to tackle. Have each person take a role (e.g., special educator, regular classroom teacher, parent) and role-play a problem-solving conference. Use the steps described above to come to some solutions. Share the results of your interactive teaming experience with the larger group. How did each team member feel about the con-

ference? What problems or barriers emerged? How were those resolved? What were the solutions that resulted from the collaboration?

Vivian I. Correa is Professor of Special Education at the University of Florida and coauthor of *Interactive Teaming: Consultation and Collaboration in Special Programs* (Thomas, Correa, & Morsink, 1995). She is well known for her work in helping teachers plan and deliver effective instruction for students from culturally and linguistically diverse backgrounds. Dr. Correa is also coauthor of Chapter 3 of this text, "Special Education in a Culturally and Linguistically Diverse Society."

Although Wang and Walberg (1988) claim success for most students with mild disabilities served by the ALEM model, Fuchs and Fuchs (1988a, 1988b) reviewed research on ALEM and concluded that the "jury is still out" (Fuchs & Fuchs, 1988a, p. 125).

> Before establishing a merger between special and general education, we hope parents, teachers, researchers, and policymakers insist on additional empirical studies of full-time, large-scale mainstreaming and persuasive evidence that such programs indeed work as their creators claim they do. If these programs are implemented widely without sufficient validation, we fear many handicapped children and teachers may suffer. (p. 126)

Inclusive Education

Most recently, the term **inclusive education** has replaced the REI as the focal point for special education reform. Some special educators believe that the continuum of services should give way to regular classroom placement for all students with disabilities. For example, Taylor (1988) suggests that the LRE and continuum of services model

> 1. *Legitimates restrictive environments.* To conceptualize services in terms of restrictiveness is to legitimize more restrictive settings. As long as services are conceptualized in this manner, some people will end up in restrictive environments. Some people will continue to support institutions and other segregated settings merely by defining them as the LRE for certain people.
> 2. *Confuses segregation and integration with intensity of services.* As represented by the continuum, LRE equates segregation with the most intensive services and integration with the least intensive services. The principle assumes that the least restrictive, most integrated settings are incapable of providing the intensive services needed by people with severe disabilities. However, segregation and integration on the one hand and intensity of services on the other are separate dimensions.
> 3. *[Is] based on a "readiness model."* Implicit in LRE is the assumption that people with developmental disabilities must earn the right to move to the least restrictive environment. In other words, the person must "get ready" or "be prepared" to live, work, or go to school in integrated settings.

4. *Supports the primacy of professional decision making.* As Biklen (1988) notes, integration is ultimately a moral and philosophical issue, not a professional one. Yet LRE invariably is framed in terms of professional judgments regarding "individual needs." The phrase "least restrictive environment" is almost always qualified with words such as "appropriate," "necessary," "feasible," and "possible" (and never with "desired" or "wanted").

5. *Sanctions infringements on people's rights.* When applied to people with disabilities, the LRE principle sanctions infringements on basic rights to freedom and community participation beyond those imposed on nondisabled people. The question imposed by LRE is not whether people with disabilities should be restricted, but to what extent.

6. *Implies that people must move as they develop and change.* As LRE is commonly conceptualized, people with disabilities are expected to move toward increasingly less restrictive environments. Even if people moved smoothly through a continuum, their lives would be a series of stops between transitional placements.

7. *Directs attention to physical settings rather than to the services and supports people need.* By its name, the principle of the LRE emphasizes facilities and environments designed specifically for people with disabilities. The field has defined the mission in terms of creating "facilities," first large ones and now smaller ones, and "programs," rather than providing the services and supports to enable people with disabilities to participate in the same settings used by other people. (pp. 45-48)

There is yet no clear consensus in the field about the meaning of inclusion. To some, inclusion means full-time placement of all students with disabilities into regular classrooms; to others, the term refers to any degree of integration in the mainstream. Stainback and Stainback (1992), strong advocates and leaders of the "inclusion movement," define an *inclusive school* as "a place where everyone belongs, is accepted, supports, and is supported by his or her peers and other members of the school community in the course of having his or her educational needs met" (p. 3).

Giangreco, Cloninger, Dennis, and Edelman (1994) contend that inclusive education is in place only when all five components shown in Figure 2.5 "occur on an ongoing, daily basis" (p. 321).

Virtually all special educators support the inclusion of students with disabilities in regular classrooms and the development and evaluation of new models for work-

See the January, 1995, issue of *Educational Leadership*, pp. 7–11 and 52–55.

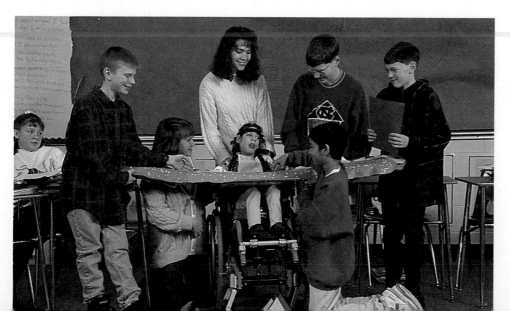

Shared activities with individualized outcomes and a sense of belonging and group membership for all students are two defining features of inclusive education.

FIGURE 2.5

Components of inclusive education

Inclusive education is in place when each of these five features occurs on an ongoing, daily basis.

1. *Heterogeneous Grouping* All students are educated *together* in groups where the number of those with and without disabilities approximates the *natural proportion*. The premise is that "students develop most when in the physical, social, emotional, and intellectual presence of nonhandicapped persons in reasonable approximations to the natural proportions" (Brown, Ford, Nisbet, Sweet, Donnellan, & Gruenewald, 1983, p. 17). Thus, in a class of 25 students, perhaps there is one student with significant disabilities, a couple of others with less significant disabilities, and many students without identified disabilities working at various levels.

2. *A Sense of Belonging to a Group* All students are considered members of the class rather than visitors, guests, or outsiders. Within these groups, students who have disabilities are welcomed, as are students without disabilities.

3. *Shared Activities with Individualized Outcomes* Students share educational experiences (e.g., lessons, labs, field studies, group learning) at the same time (Schnorr, 1990). Even though students are involved in the same activities, their learning objectives are individualized and, therefore, may be different. Students may have different objectives in the same curriculum area (e.g., language arts) during a shared activity. This is referred to as *multi-level instruction* (Campbell, Campbell, Collicott, Perner, & Stone, 1988; Collicott, 1991; Giangreco & Meyer, 1988; Giangreco & Putnam, 1991). Within a shared activity, a student also may have individualized objectives from a curriculum area (e.g., social skills) other than that on which other students are focused (e.g., science). This practice is referred to as *curriculum overlapping* (Giangreco & Meyer, 1988; Giangreco & Putnam, 1991).

4. *Use of Environments Frequented by Persons without Disabilities* Shared educational experiences take place in environments predominantly frequented by people without disabilities (e.g., general education classrooms, community worksites).

5. *A Balanced Educational Experience* Inclusive education seeks an individualized balance between the academic/functional and social/personal aspects of schooling (Giangreco, 1992). For example, teachers in inclusion-oriented schools would be as concerned about students' self-image and social network as they would be about developing literacy competencies or learning vocational skills.

Source: From "Problem-Solving Methods to Facilitate Inclusive Education" by M.F. Giangreco, C.J. Cloninger, R.E. Dennis, & S.W. Edelman, 1994. *In Creativity and Collaborative Learning: A Practical Guide to Empowering Students and Teachers* by J.S. Thousand, R.A. Villa, & A.I. Nevin (Eds.), p. 322. Baltimore, MD: Brookes. Reprinted by permission.

Position statements on inclusion by the Council for Learning Disabilities, the Learning Disabilities Association of America, and The Association for Persons with Severe Handicaps (TASH) can be found in Chapters 5 and 11. The discussion of inclusion and where students with disabilities are best served continues throughout the text.

ing more cooperatively with general educators to serve all students. Most, however, are not in favor of eliminating the LRE concept and dismantling the continuum of alternative placements. The Council for Exceptional Children, the major professional organization in special education, supports inclusion as a "meaningful goal" to be pursued by schools but believes that the continuum of services and program options must be maintained and that IEP planning teams must make placement and decisions based on the student's individual educational needs (see Figure 2.6).

Fuchs and Fuchs (1994), who are concerned that reform in special education is being "radicalized" by a minority who want to do away with all special education placements in favor of full inclusion, write:

Special education has big problems. Not the least of which is that it must redefine its relationship with general education. Now is the time to hear from inventive pragmatists, not extremists on the right or the left. Now is the time for leadership that recognizes the need for change; appreciates the importance of consensus building; looks at general education with a sense of what is possible; respects special education's traditions and values and the law that undergirds them; and seeks to strengthen the mainstream, as well as other educational potions that can provide more intensive services, to enhance the learning and lives of all children. (p. 305)

See "A Case for Special Education Placements" beginning on the next page.

✳ *Where Does Special Education Go from Here?*

The promise of a free, appropriate public education for all children with disabilities is indeed an ambitious one. The process of bringing this goal about has been described in such lofty terms as a "new Bill of Rights" and a "Magna Carta" for children with disabilities (Goodman, 1976). Weintraub and Abeson (1974) wrote more than 20 years ago in support of the IDEA: "At the minimum, it will make educational opportunities a reality for all handicapped children. At the maximum, it will make our schools healthier learning environments for all our children" (p. 529). Today, most observers acknowledge that substantial progress has been made toward fulfillment of that promise.

Turnbull et al. (1986) observe that the IDEA has had far-reaching effects: "The student is no longer required to fit the school, but the school is required to fit the student" (p. 183). Schools today provide far more than academic training. In effect, they have become diversified agencies offering such services as medical support, physical therapy, vocational training, parent counseling, recreation, special transportation, and inservice education for staff members. In place of the once-prevalent practice of

FIGURE 2.6
CEC policy on inclusive schools

CEC Policy on Inclusive Schools

The Council for Exceptional Children (CEC) believes all children, youth, and young adults with disabilities are entitled to a free and appropriate education and/or services that lead to an adult life characterized by satisfying relations with others, independent living, productive engagement in the community, and participation in society at large. To achieve such outcomes, there must exist for all children, youth, and young adults with disabilities a rich variety of early intervention, educational, and vocational program options and experiences. Access to these programs and experiences should be based on individual educational need and desired outcomes. Furthermore, students and their families or guardians, as members of the planning team, may recommend the placement, curriculum option, and the exit document to be pursued.

CEC believes that a continuum of services must be available for all children, youth, and young adults. CEC also believes that the concept of inclusion is a meaningful goal to be pursued in our schools and communities. In addition, CEC believes children, youth, and young adults with disabilities should be served whenever possible in general education classrooms in inclusive neighborhood schools and community settings. Such settings should be strengthened and supported by an infusion of specially trained personnel and other appropriate supportive practices according to the individual needs of the child.

Adopted by the CEC Delegate Assembly, 1993, San Antonio, Texas.

Source: From Supplement to *Teaching Exceptional Children,* Vol. 25, No. 4, May 1993. Copyright (1993) by The Council for Exceptional Children. Reprinted by permission.

A Case for Special Education Placements

by Douglas Fuchs and Lynn S. Fuchs

In the 1980s, there was the regular education initiative (REI)—a misnamed movement supported by many special educators that called for a merger of special education and general education, modifications in special education funding formulas, and changes in the responsibilities of special educators. The REI went nowhere, in large part, because of the profound disinterest in the proposal by general education. Recently, a different and smaller group of special educators and advocates with primary concern for children with severe disabilities have seized the leadership of the special education reform movement and are marching under the banner of "full inclusion."

There are two types of full inclusionists. The first type argues for a complete dismantling of special education: no more special education placements, no more special education teachers, and no more special education students (e.g., Stainback & Stainback, 1992). The second type of full inclusionist says special educators should provide services to students with disabilities, but only in regular classrooms (e.g., Giangreco, Dennis, Engelman, & Schattman, 1993). What both groups have in common—what makes them, in our opinion, full inclusionists—is the belief that *all* children with disabilities should be in the education mainstream full time.

We believe that full inclusion is a mistake, that an appropriate education for some students with disabilities requires some special education services be delivered outside the regular classroom. Before describing a rationale for full inclusion and why we think it is a mistake, we will review a basic principle underlying the provision of a free, appropriate education for students with disabilities: the least restrictive environment (LRE).

LRE and the Continuum of Alternate Placements

Advocates of full inclusion reject the LRE principle, which is central to the Individuals with Disabilities Education Act (IDEA). The LRE concept has two parts. First, it encourages the *social interaction* between students with disabilities and their nondisabled peers by mandating that to "the maximum extent appropriate, children with disabilities are to be educated with children who are not disabled." As a practical matter, this part of the LRE principle promotes the mainstreaming of students with disabilities into regular classrooms as much as possible.

The second part of the LRE concept requires that special needs students be provided an *appropriate education,* or one that permits the child to benefit from instruction. It says: "special classes, separate schooling, or other removal of children with disabilities from the regular educational environment occurs only when the nature or severity of the disability is such that education in regular classes with the use of supplementary aids and services cannot be achieved satisfactorily." Implicit in this statement is the recognition that the mainstream may not be capable of providing an appropriate education for every student with disabilities. Senator Robert Stafford of Vermont, one of the original sponsors of the IDEA, said that when developing the LRE notion, Congress was well aware that the regular classroom may be harmful to some special needs students (Stafford, 1978). Accordingly, Congress developed a "continuum of alternate placements"—from part-time resource room programs to self-contained classrooms in regular schools to separate day schools and residential facilities.

A majority of the special education community in this country supports the two-part definition of the LRE—an individually determined placement that is as close as possible to that of normally developing, same-age peers while providing an education appropriate to the student's individualized learning needs. Nevertheless, there is a small but influential group of advocates and special educators who reject this . . . and more.

A Case for Inclusion

Advocates of full inclusion believe that schools should have two essential and related goals for children with disabilities: (a) to improve their social competence and acceptance and (b) to change the attitudes of teachers and students without disabilities, who someday will become parents, taxpayers, and service providers. They believe that this can happen only when special needs students are placed in mainstream or integrated settings: "The rationale for educating students with severe disabilities in integrated settings is to ensure their normalized community participation by providing them . . . instruction in the skills . . . essential to their success in the social . . . [settings] in which they will ultimately use these skills" (Gartner & Lipsky, 1987, p. 386).

Full inclusionists refuse to accept the idea that social integration and appropriate education are not one in the same, that they can be different objectives that sometimes compete with one another. Rather, they believe that the two are the same, that social interaction with and acceptance by nondisabled peers is *the* appropriate education for students with disabilities. It follows that any placement outside the regular classroom is inappropriate and that the principle of LRE and the entire continuum of special education placements must be rejected. Therefore, full inclusionists advance a policy whereby literally all children with disabilities would be in regular classrooms full time.

Why must all children be placed into regular classrooms? Because adherents believe that as long as special education placements exist, the children they care about most will surely be placed in them. They offer two reasons for this view. First, special education historically has served as general education's "dumping ground"; special education has made it too easy for classroom teachers to rid themselves of their "undesirables" and "unteachables." Second, children with severe disabilities are frequently viewed by classroom teachers as the most undesirable and unteachable pupils. Only by abolishing resource rooms, separate classes, and special schools will regular educators be forced to deal with those students they heretofore have avoided. In the process, all of education will be transformed into a more responsible, resourceful, and humane system.

And how will this transformation be bankrolled? After the special education system and its separate placements are dismantled, say the full inclusionists, more than enough money will be available to hire specialists of all kinds to support regular classroom teachers. Full inclusionists implore the rest of us to resist being bound by what is and to develop instead a vision of what might be. Or, as Ken Kesey used to say to the Merry Pranksters, Get on the bus!

What full inclusionists fail to realize, however, is that supporters of special education placements have visions of their own.

A Case for Special Education Placements

Although it has become fashionable to complain that special education flatout doesn't work (e.g., National Association of State Boards of Education, 1992; Shapiro, Loeb, Bowermaster, & Toch, 1993), reviews of research on the effectiveness of resource rooms and self-contained classrooms indicate that many special education programs are superior to regular classrooms for some types of students (e.g., Carlberg & Kavale, 1980; Madden & Slavin, 1983; Sindelar & Deno, 1979). Furthermore, descriptive studies suggest that the organization, intensity, and systematicity of instruction provided by effective special education teachers may help their students outperform students in the mainstream (e.g., Howard-Rose & Rose, 1994). Good special education is characterized by the use of a variety of instructional techniques, curricula, materials, motivational strategies, grouping patterns, and an evaluation system that monitors each student's progress. The selection, combination, and recombination of these instructional elements by the well-trained special educator are ongoing, dynamic processes guided by individual student performance data. This level of individualization is in marked contrast to the "one-size-fits-all" approach observed in many regular classrooms (e.g., Fuchs, Fuchs, & Bishop, 1992).

Gerry Rosenberg, father of 5-year-old Danny, who has cognitive and physical disabilities, recently told Congress why his family chose Longview School, a publicly supported day treatment program in Gaithersburg, Maryland. Commenting on special education's approach to individualizing

For some children with disabilities, separate placements such as resource rooms and self-contained classrooms may provide more of the intensive, systematic instruction they need than the regular classroom.

instruction, Rosenberg (1994) said, "For students like our son, there are no bright road markers to assist in indicating what teaching techniques will work. Longview serves as a laboratory in diagnostic and teaching techniques. [The staff's] wealth of experience allows for constant experimentation in what is appropriate educationally for Danny."

Well-regarded special education day schools and residential programs also offer a comprehensive setting in which instruction can be interwoven throughout the day. This "wrap-around" environment is evident in Cohen's (1994) description of the Lexington School for the Deaf in Queens, New York: "Few public schools can offer what most prelingually deaf children need: a visually oriented setting, communication access to all activities, interaction with deaf peers and deaf adults, and at least minimal sign language fluency on the part of teachers and peers. And no public school can offer the richness and nurturance of a deaf cultural environment" (pp. 55–56).

Those who work with children with severe emotional and behavior problems refer to this comprehensive environment as *milieu therapy,* an "environment in which everyday events are turned to therapeutic use. Any activity in a child's day—from refusing to get dressed in the morning to answering a question correctly at school to picking a fight—offers the child-care worker an opportunity to teach, change, or reinforce behavior through therapeutic intervention" (Weisman, 1994, p. 46). Exemplary residential schools for children with severe emotional and behavior problems, programs like The Villages, Woodland Hills, The Walker School, Green Chimneys, and Boys Town, "offer . . . children a chance at a second childhood" (Weisman, 1994, p. 52), one that is highly structured, predictable, and safe.

We are not suggesting that all students with disabilities require settings like Longview School, Lexington School for the Deaf, or Boys Town. In fact, relatively few special education students require such organized, intensive, systematic, and comprehensive approaches. Nor do we think that all special education placements are successful; alas, they are not. Moreover, we would be among the first to assert that too many children with disabilities have and continue to be placed into separate special education settings. But none of this diminishes the fact that for some children, separate is better, and that to abolish special education placements in the name of full inclusion would be to deny an appropriate education for many children with disabilities.

What the Majority Wants

Despite the fact that most full inclusionists are primarily concerned with students with severe disabilities (a group that constitutes about 10% of all special-needs students), they presume to speak for everyone when they state without qualification that the regular classroom is the only acceptable placement for children with disabilities. They presume to know what is best for all as they push for an end to special education placements. However, official position statements by professional and advocacy groups, such as the American Council on the Blind, the Commission on the Education of the Deaf, the Council for Exceptional Children, the Council for Children with Behavior Disorders, and The Learning Disabilities Association, strongly endorse the LRE concept and the continuum of special education placement options and either implicitly or explicitly reject full inclusion.

Are these supporters of special education placements less concerned about social competence, acceptance, and opportunities for meaningful participation in integrated environments than full inclusionists? Not at all. Supporters and critics of special education placements are equally invested in integration. Supporters, however, recognize that the successful inclusion of some children may be a long-term goal; that an immediate placement of these youngsters in the regular classroom could mean closing the door on their opportunities to learn to read and write; to control their behavior and to learn to like themselves; to go to college or vocational school; and to become responsible and productive citizens. In short, supporters of the LRE principle see the continuum of special education placements as a means toward helping students with disabilities achieve meaningful participation and membership in integrated schools, communities, and employment settings.

At the same time, the professional and grassroots groups that support special education placements do not presume to dictate the best placement for other students. As Bernard Rimland, the father of a son with autism and a well-known advocate, puts it, "I have no quarrel with inclusionists if they are content to insist upon inclusion for *their* children. But when they try to force me and other unwilling parents to dance to their tune, I find it highly objectionable and quite intolerable. Parents need options" (Rimland, 1993, p. 3).

Yes, in certain school districts many students with disabilities spend too much time in separate special education placements. But we think a policy that would eliminate the continuum of alternative placements and place all children with disabilities into regular classrooms is wrongheaded. Full inclusion should be rejected on many counts, but the basic one is this: Its one-size-fits-all approach fails to recognize that "special needs students" refers to a diverse group with many different needs. No one teacher, curriculum, instructional strategy, or placement—however cleverly conceived or shrewdly packaged—will ensure an *appropriate* education for all children with disabilities. ✺

Douglas Fuchs and Lynn Fuchs are Professors of Special Education at Vanderbilt University. Their research interests focus on developing classroom-based techniques like curricular-based measurement and peer-assisted learning strategies that strengthen the academic performance and social integration of students with and without disabilities. They are the coeditors of the *Journal of Special Education.*

excluding children with disabilities from programs, schools now seek the most appropriate ways of including them. Schools are committed to providing wide-ranging services to children from differing backgrounds and with differing characteristics.

Many citizens—both within and outside the field of education—have welcomed the recognition of the rights of children with disabilities in their schools and communities. Additionally, the greater involvement of parents and families in the educational process and the emphasis on team planning to meet individual needs throughout the life span are widely regarded as positive developments. Reports from teachers and students, as well as a growing number of data-based studies, indicate that many children with disabilities are being successfully educated in regular schools and that, for the most part, they are well accepted by their nondisabled schoolmates.

Despite this ample evidence of progress toward providing equal educational opportunity, it is equally true that many people—again, inside and outside the field of education—have detected significant problems in the implementation of the IDEA. Many school administrators maintain that the federal government has never granted sufficient financial resources to the states and local school districts to assist them in providing special services, which are often very costly. Special education teachers express dissatisfaction over excessive paperwork, unclear guidelines, and inappropriate grouping of students with disabilities. General education teachers contend that they receive little or no training or support when students with disabilities are placed into their classes. Some parents of children with disabilities have voiced opposition to full inclusion. Some observers find that the schedules and procedures used in mainstreaming programs actually allow for relatively little integration (Sansone & Zigmond, 1986). There are many other problems, real and perceived, and no "quick fix" or easy solution can be offered.

Special education is at a crossroads. Once, access to educational opportunity was the primary issue for individuals with disabilities. Would they receive an education at all? Could they be served in their local community? Some access problems persist (e.g., particularly for children who live in poverty or in extremely isolated areas), but now "the primary issue of contention in special education is whether students will receive a quality education in regular public schools" (Biklen, 1985, p. 174).

Can we fulfill the promise of a free, appropriate public education for all students with disabilities? The answer depends on the readiness of professionals to work together, assume new roles, communicate with each other, and involve parents, families, and individuals with disabilities themselves.

Ultimately, educators must realize that regardless of where services are delivered, the most crucial variable is the quality of instruction that children receive. Keogh's (1990) conclusion regarding the greatest challenge for special education reform is right on target:

> It is clear that major changes are needed in the delivery of services to problem learners, and that these services need to be the responsibility of regular as well as special educators. It is also clear that teachers are the central players in bringing about change in practice. It follows, then, that our greatest and most pressing challenge in the reform effort is to determine how to improve the quality of instruction at the classroom level. (p. 190)

Special education is serious business. The learning and adjustment problems faced by students with disabilities are real, and their prevention and remediation require effective intervention. Regardless of who does it or where it takes place, good teaching must occur. Exceptional children deserve no less.

See the January, 1995, issue of *Educational Leadership*, p. 33–35, 36–40, 42–45, and 50–51.

Over 55% of the 15,000 members surveyed by CEC's Division for Learning Disabilities reported that much of the paperwork required by the IDEA is unnecessary, duplicative, and costly (*The DLD Times*, Fall, 1994). These teachers believed that excessive paperwork interfered with time available for providing services to students and contributed to some special education teachers leaving the field.

For an in-depth look at different perspectives on the evolving theory and practice of special education during the past 25 years, with recommendations and predictions for the future, see the winter 1994 issue of the *Journal of Special Education*.

See "What Special Educators Need to Know" beginning on the next page.

What Special Educators Need to Know

by Thomas C. Lovitt

I have been troubled for some time that special education teachers seem so uninterested in instruction. I don't mean they are not interested in doing what is best for children and youths with disabilities; most care deeply about the youngsters they serve. But it has been my experience when teaching classes, conducting inservices, and simply chatting with special education teachers that many simply do not know enough about the business of teaching. When asked, for example, how they would go about teaching an academic skill or how they would deal with a behavior problem, these virtuous and noble instructors can usually come up with only a few potential solutions.

My first shocking and disappointing experience with this inability to name teaching tactics was about 12 years ago when I asked a large group of teachers how they would manage a certain obstreperous behavior. I provided a hypothetical situation in which a 10-year-old boy of normal intelligence had been hitting and terrorizing children on the playground. His fights were unsettling to the principal, the teachers (including his fourth-grade teacher), and especially his victims. As I described this situation, the teachers at that workshop nodded, indicating they were familiar with this kind of problem. But when asked to come up with interventions to deal with it, they initially named only four: (a) expel the scoundrel from school, (b) lecture the

pugnacious pupil, (c) call the belligerent boy's parents, and (d) send the rascal to the principal's office. Sensing that the group might be screening their suggestions or were otherwise inhibiting their recommendations, I told them to let loose, that for this exercise there were no restraints. I pleaded with them to name as many possible solutions as they could, even if they seemed bizarre, unreasonable, or unacceptable. But all the coaxing and cuing stimulated only a few more suggestions.

Since that time, I have repeated this exercise with classes and inservice groups, using the same example and others pertaining to academic instruction. Sadly, the results are generally the same. When asked to name techniques to either accelerate a particular skill or decelerate a problem behavior, a group of 25 or more special education teachers will predictably come up with just a few responses, and this despite the fact that they are told to use a no-holds-barred approach.

Not only are special education teachers slow in coming up with instructional solutions in these simulated exercises, but most of the ones they do identify are not actual instructional techniques. They are often related to who should carry out the teaching, how many pupils should be taught at a time, and the sort of attitude the teacher should have while instructing.

That special education teachers are limited in their ability to name instructional techniques and often confuse instructional practices with other aspects of education was vividly pointed out in a study we recently carried out (Lovitt, in press). The main purpose of that research was to identify and describe the various curricular offerings and accompanying delivery systems available for secondary students with disabilities. We interviewed 30 special education teachers from six

high schools; 13 worked with students with mild disabilities, 7 with youths with moderate to severe disabilities, and 10 with students with emotional and behavioral disorders.

We asked several questions about curriculum, delivery systems, IEPs, working with parents, collaborating with others, and evaluating performance. Then we asked: "What instructional techniques or approaches seem to work well with your students?" Disappointingly, their responses replicated the replies from previous groups of teachers: few possible solutions were named, and most of those were only indirectly related to instruction. Allow me to take a critical, if somewhat caustic, look at the categories into which their "teaching tactics" fell.

No One Method Works

At first, the most common response by teachers that "no one method will work for all students" seems unarguable. Certainly, there are differences among pupils and they must be recognized and dealt with. No quarrel there. But simply saying that students are different just won't cut it in the classroom. Regardless of how many types of learners there are, teachers must have a ready supply of instructional techniques from which to draw and should be able to name them. One could easily argue that the more differences there are among and across individuals, the larger the teacher's warehouse of techniques should be.

One-to-One Instruction

The next most common solution by teachers was to provide "one-on-one instruction." That, too, on first blush, appears to be an honorable reply. But think about it. A totally inept teacher, one who knew absolutely nothing about teaching beginning reading, could be paired one-to-one with a child who needed early reading instruction. It is doubtful that child would learn about reading, early or otherwise. There is more to effective instruction than working one-to-one. For openers, the one doing the instructing must have considerable knowledge and skills related to what is to be taught and *how to teach it*.

Individualized Instruction

"Individualized instruction" implies that a child is instructed differently from all others. That could be good, but it might also be bad or irrelevant. What if a girl were given individualized instruction on something beyond her ability level, on something she already knew or could do, or on something she would be better off not knowing? Simply saying that individualized instruction is a terrific way to teach is as weak as saying that instruction should be one-on-one.

Collaborative/Peer-Mediated Learning

Another technique our teachers mentioned was "peer-mediated instruction." Although peer tutoring and cooperative learning are often effective ways to *deliver* instruction, they are not instructional techniques in my way of thinking. As I lampooned the preceding techniques, one can imagine "cooperative learning" situations that, of themselves, failed to teach students an intended skill, concept, or attribute. A history teacher could set up a cooperative learning group in which each member was assigned a different role and informed to work with others to learn about the Lincoln and Douglas debates. But suppose that instead of refining their understandings of those famous arguments, the children cooperatively plan to kidnap the principal, hold her hostage, and demand a plane to take them to Disneyland. Although that teacher had been duly "Johnsoned" and "Slavinized," he failed mis-

erably to emphasize curriculum or instruction.

Good Relationships

The next set of approaches from the teachers dealt with "building good relationships." Again, a commendable thought. It is no doubt better for a teacher to develop trust and understanding with students and to be happy and enthusiastic while teaching than to be untrustworthy and grumpy. But that's only the beginning. A trustworthy clown could waltz into a classroom and engage children in some type of activity, but unless the erstwhile member of Barnum and Bailey's outfit knew about the content of the intended lesson and how to teach it, it is doubtful the children would learn much. At best, the youngsters would be entertained and possibly consider the circus as a career.

Multimodality Instruction

The last set of suggestions from teachers, "multimodality instruction," has been around for ages. Those who endorse the "multi" approach imply that it is a good idea to propel the material to be learned through as many channels as possible: visual, auditory, tactile, and kinesthetic. Although that might seem like a good thing to do, the research on multimodality instruction, of which there is a great deal, would not encourage teachers to buy into the plan.

A few teachers we interviewed passed the "naming instructional techniques test." Teachers of students with behavioral disorders were more explicit about naming instructional practices than were other types of special education teachers. Not infrequently, those instructors of tough youths mentioned the use of behavioral techniques in general, the arrangement of "level systems" based on students' adaptations to a school's

culture, and the involvement of contracts and tokens specifically.

In this day and age of more diversity, not to mention the emphasis on including more children and youths with disabilities in general education classes, it is crucial for teachers to be skilled in the selection and application of a wide range of empirically proven instructional techniques. If asked how to curtail the fighting of a boy on the playground, a teacher should be able to quickly name a dozen potential solutions. Various ways to implement each of the following strategies might be among those in the teacher's repository: self-monitoring, time out, response cost, contingency contracting, reinforcement of other behaviors, reinforcement of low rate of responding, and overcorrection. Similarly, if asked how to teach reading or listening comprehension to students who were capable "decoders," a teacher might cite the following techniques among her arsenal: guided reading, cloze procedure, story grammars, semantic webs, reciprocal teaching, structured dialogue, free description, provided and generated questions, paragraph restatements, mental imagery, summarization, and text structures. To teach vocabulary, for example, teachers should know about the following practices: direct instruction (through modeling, synonyms, and definitions), learning through context, predicting word meanings, and constructing possible sentences.

I believe that teachers must get back to the business of teaching. To do so, they must increase their knowledge and skills about effective instructional strategies. Although it may be more exciting to learn and debate about the policy issues of education, such as school reform, the merger of special and general education, the merits of full inclusion, graduation requirements, class size, co-teaching, and integrated curriculum, knowledge about any of those topics is no substitute for having knowledge and skills of effective instruction.

As I said earlier, and hasten to reemphasize here, it is one thing to simply name and describe instructional techniques and quite another to properly use them. Fortunately, great numbers of proven techniques are at hand, and they come in all shapes and sizes. There is a vast array of empirically demonstrated practices for teachers of children and youths with mild disabilities. Scores of data-based procedures are available for instructors of persons with behavioral disorders and severe disabilities. Likewise, there are exemplary tactics galore for practitioners who serve individuals with sensory impairments. Many of those tactics are introduced and discussed in this textbook. Others are described in dozens of education journals, such as *The Reading Teacher, Intervention in School and Clinic, Education and Treatment of Children, Elementary School Journal, Journal of Behavioral Education, Remedial and Special Education,* and *Teaching Exceptional Children.* (Journals that publish articles evaluating and describing instructional strategies are listed at the end of each chapter in this text.) ✳

Tom Lovitt is Professor of Special Education at the University of Washington in Seattle and the author of *Tactics for Teaching* (in press). In two of his previous books—*In Spite of My Resistance, I've Learned from Children* (1977) and *In Spite of My Persistence, I've Learned from Children* (1982)— Lovitt used his sometimes humorous and poignant encounters with children with learning and behavior problems to dispel some widely held myths and misconceptions about how such students are "supposed" to be taught. Special education teachers and students have benefited from his research on effective teaching practices for more than 30 years. Lovitt's current work focuses on adapting curriculum materials for use by secondary students with learning disabilities in the general education classrooms.

Regardless of where services are delivered, the most crucial variable is the quality of instruction that each child receives.

Summary

Individualized Education Program (IEP)

- An IEP planning team must include at least (a) the child's teacher(s), (b) a representative of the local school district other than the child's teacher, (c) the child's parents or guardian, and (d) whenever appropriate, the child him- or herself.

- Although the formats vary widely from school district to school district, each IEP must include statements about (a) the child's present levels of educational performance, (b) annual goals, (c) short-term instructional objectives, (d) specific educational services needed by the child, (e) transition services for students beginning no later than age 16, (f) the date when services will begin and the length of time the services will be given, (g) the extent to which the child will participate in regular education programs, (h) justification for the type of educational placement, (i) the individuals who will be responsible for implementing the program, and (j) criteria for determining whether the short-term instructional objectives are being achieved.

- Without direct and ongoing monitoring of student progress toward IEP goals and objectives, the document's usefulness is limited.

- The IEP is a measure of accountability for teachers and schools; however, a teacher and school cannot be prosecuted if the child does not achieve all of the goals set forth in the IEP.

The Least Restrictive Environment (LRE)

- The LRE is the setting closest to a regular school program that also meets the child's special educational needs.

- The LRE is a relative concept; the LRE for one child might be inappropriate for another.

- The continuum of services is a range of placement and service options to meet the individual needs of students with disabilities.

- Mainstreaming describes the process of integrating children with disabilities into regular schools and classes. Successful mainstreaming requires that teachers, parents, administrators, and students all work together.

- Studies have shown that well-planned, carefully conducted mainstreaming can be generally effective with students of all ages, types, and degrees of disability.

The Importance of Teaming and Collaboration

- A team approach, in which teachers, other professionals, and parents share information and skills, can help make each student's education as effective and consistent as possible.

- Many schools use intervention assistance teams to help classroom teachers devise and implement adaptations for a student who is experiencing either academic or behavioral difficulties so that he or she can remain in the regular classroom.

- Three team models are multidisciplinary, interdisciplinary, and transdisciplinary. Transdisciplinary teams conduct joint assessments, share information and expertise across discipline boundaries, and select discipline-free goals and interventions.

Regular and Special Education: A New Relationship?

- Some special educators are calling for a merger between regular and special education; this movement is called the regular education initiative (REI).

- Opponents of the REI are concerned that students with disabilities may not receive the services they need in the general education system.

- Some special educators believe that the LRE principle should give way to full inclusion, in which all students with disabilities are served in regular classrooms.

- Most special educators and professional organizations, such as CEC, support inclusion as a "meaningful goal" but believe that the continuum of services and program options must be maintained and that placement decisions must be based on the student's individual educational needs.

Where Does Special Education Go From Here?

- The promise of a free, appropriate public education for all children with disabilities is an ambitious one, but substantial progress has been made toward fulfillment of that promise.

- Implementation of the IDEA has brought problems of funding, inadequate teacher training, and opposition by some to integration of children with disabilities into regular classes.

- Regardless of where services are delivered, the most crucial variable is the quality of instruction that each child receives.

For More Information

Journals

All of the journals listed at the end of Chapter 1 are relevant to the content of Chapter 2.

Journal of Disability Policy Studies. Publishes research, discussion, and review articles addressing a broad range of topics on disability policy from the perspective of a variety of academic disciplines. Published quarterly by the Department of Rehabilitation Education and Research, University of Arkansas, 346 N. West Avenue, Fayetteville, AK 72701.

Journal of Educational and Psychological Consultation. Published quarterly by the Association for Educational and Psychological Consultation, Lawrence Erlbaum Associates, Inc., 365 Broadway, Hillsdale, NJ 07642.

Books

Giangreco, M. F., Cloninger, C. J., & Iverson, V. S. (1993). *Choosing options and accommodations for children.* Baltimore: Paul H. Brookes.

Goodlad, J. I., & Lovitt, T. C. (Eds.). (1993). *Integrating general and special education.* New York: Macmillan.

Heron, T. E., & Harris, K. C. (1993). *The educational consultant: Helping professionals, parents, and mainstreamed students* (3rd ed.). Austin, TX: PRO-ED.

Howell, K. W., Fox, S. L., & Morehead, M. K. (1993). *Curriculum-based evaluation: Teaching and decision making* (2nd ed.). Pacific Grove, CA: Brooks/Cole.

Kauffman, J. M., & Hallahan, D. P. (Eds.). (1995). *The illusion of full inclusion: A comprehensive critique of a current special education bandwagon.* Austin, TX: PRO-ED.

Lewis, R. B., & Doorlag, D. H. (1995). *Teaching special students in the mainstream* (4th ed.). New York: Prentice Hall/Merrill.

Lipsky, D. K., & Gartner, A. (Eds.). (1989). *Beyond separate education: Quality education for all.* Baltimore: Paul H. Brookes.

Salend, S. J. (1994). *Effective mainstreaming: Creating inclusive classrooms* (2nd ed.). New York: Macmillan.

Skrtic, T. M. (1991). *Beyond special education: A critical analysis of professional culture and school organization.* Denver: Love.

Stainback, S., & Stainback, W. (Eds.). (1992). *Curricular considerations in inclusive classrooms: Facilitating learning for all students.* Baltimore: Paul H. Brookes.

Strickland, B. B., & Turnbull, A. P. (1993). *Developing and implementing individualized education programs* (3rd ed.). New York: Macmillan.

Thomas, C. C., Correa, V. I., & Morsink, C. V. (1995). *Interactive teaming: Consultation and collaboration in special programs* (2nd ed.). New York: Prentice Hall/Merrill.

Thousand, J. S., Villa, R. A., & Nevin, A. I. (Eds.). (1994). *Creativity and collaborative learning: A practical guide to empowering students and teachers.* Baltimore: Paul H. Brookes.

Wood, J. W. (1992). *Adapting instruction for mainstreamed students* (2nd ed.). New York: Macmillan.

Special Education in a Culturally and Linguistically Diverse Society

by Vivian I. Correa and William L. Heward

- What are the major issues and concerns affecting educational services for culturally and linguistically diverse students with disabilities and their families?

- How are contemporary views of *culture, cultural pluralism,* and *multicultural education* influencing special education practices for culturally and linguistically diverse students?

- What initial steps can a teacher take to become culturally responsive?

- How should assessment, curriculum, and instructional methods differ for students from culturally or linguistically different backgrounds?

- If a student cannot speak, read, or write English well enough to progress in the school curriculum, does it make any difference whether the limited English proficiency is caused by cultural differences or by a disability?

*T*he following wide-ranging observations illustrate some of the challenges that special educators face:

- By the year 2000, non-European Americans are expected to comprise one third of the U.S. population (Grossman, 1995, p. 1).
- Nearly half (46%) of school-age youths in the United States will be people of color by 2020 (Pallas, Natriello, & McDill, 1989).
- Most teachers in the United States are White; the next largest group, African Americans, comprise less than 5% of all public school teachers (Ladson-Billings, 1994, p. 26).
- Half of American teachers teach a limited-English-proficient (LEP) student at some time in their careers (McKeon, 1994, p. 48).
- The 1990 census recorded 380 language categories in the United States (U.S. Bureau of the Census, 1990).
- The U.S. English political interest group lobbied for federal and state laws that would eliminate the use of any languages other than English in all public and private sectors. By March 1993, 15 states had either amended their constitutions or enacted statutes making English their official language (Banks, 1994b, p. 266).
- For many socially and culturally diverse parents, their own personal school experiences create obstacles to involvement. Those who have dropped out of school do not feel confident in school settings (Finders & Lewis, 1994, p. 51).
- The psychological impact of homelessness is manifested by a greater prevalence and intensity of anxiety, depression, and behavioral disturbances. Homeless children scored significantly higher than housed children on sleep problems, extreme shyness, speech difficulties, withdrawal, and aggression (Pawlas, 1994, p. 80).
- Standardized testing in particular has long been a source of heated debate because, on the basis of test scores, LEP children are often misassigned to lower curriculum tracks or special education (LaCelle-Peterson & Rivera, 1994, as cited in McKeon, 1994, p. 48).
- There is a bitter irony in the fact that an English-speaking student may earn college credit for learning to speak another language, whereas a language-minority child is encouraged not to use, and therefore lose, the same skill (Ada, 1986, p. 387).

Special educators, in facing these challenges, seek to provide a relevant, individualized education to students with disabilities from culturally diverse backgrounds. Our public school system is based, after all, on a philosophy of equal educational opportunity. The IDEA is only one of many significant steps toward implementing equal educational opportunity. Court decisions and legislation, besides prohibiting discrimination in schools because of intellectual or physical disability, have forbidden discrimination in education and employment on the basis of race, nationality, gender, or inability to speak English. Special programs now provide financial support and assistance to schools that serve refugee and migrant students and that provide self-determination in education for Native Americans.

Despite these important efforts, equal educational opportunity for all is not yet a reality (Banks & Banks, 1993; Grossman, 1995). Interestingly, the following statement by the U.S. Department of Education further emphasizes the problem of the high disproportion of minority children in special education; the problem continues to be an issue of national concern and debate:

> Congress . . . suggested that the use of standardized assessment instruments which are racially biased are, at least in part, responsible. Some observers contend that school professionals are more likely to refer and place minority and poor children in special education because of lower expectations regarding the educability of these children. Other observers have noted, however, that it is logical to expect a disproportionate number of poor, minority children being placed in special education given that these children are more likely to have experienced poor prenatal and early childhood nutrition and health care, resulting in actual disabilities. (U.S. Department of Education, 1992, p. 15)

Some students with disabilities still experience discrimination or receive a less-than-adequate education because of their racial, ethnic, social class, or other differences from the majority. In addressing this issue, we are not implying that belonging to a cultural or linguistic group that differs from the majority culture is a disability. One of our society's strengths is its cultural diversity; society has benefited from the contributions of many ethnic groups.

> Ethnic diversity is a positive element in a society because it enriches a nation and increases the ways in which its citizens can perceive and solve personal and public problems. Ethnic diversity also enriches a society because it provides individuals with more opportunities to experience other cultures, and thus, to become more fulfilled as human beings. When individuals are able to participate in a variety of ethnic cultures, they are more able to benefit from the total human experience. (Banks, 1994b, p. 44)

But even though cultural diversity is a strength of our society, being a member of a minority group too often means discrimination and misunderstanding, closed doors, and lowered expectations.

Each child in this classroom benefits from the diverse cultural and ethnic perspectives, values, and problem-solving approaches they experience by working with one another.

✳ *Reasons for Concern*

Why do students from culturally diverse backgrounds merit special concern and attention? First, the achievement of culturally diverse students typically lags behind that of White, mainstream students. Because the achievement of ethnic groups such as African Americans, Hispanics, and Native Americans is similar to White students' in the early grades but falls further behind the longer the students stay in school (Banks, 1994b), there is reason for concern over the role our educational system may be playing in limiting the achievement of students from different cultural groups.

Second, the fact remains that culturally and linguistically diverse students continue to be both underrepresented and overrepresented in special education (Correa, Blanes, & Rapport, 1995). The following facts help illustrate the problem:

* Asian Pacific students are generally underrepresented in disability categories and overrepresented in gifted and talented programs.
* African American students still tend to be overrepresented in classrooms for students with mild mental retardation.
* Latinos are overrepresented in programs for students with learning disabilities and speech-language impairments (as cited in Artiles & Trent, 1994).
* Native Americans are in classes for students with learning disabilities in disproportionately high numbers, whereas their representation in classes for students who are gifted is consistently low (Chinn & Hughes, 1987).
* Ethnically diverse students constitute about 27% of the general school population but only about 18% of all students who are identified as gifted and talented (Chinn & McCormick, 1986).
* Approximately 500,000 migrant students live in the United States, but only 10.7% of them with mild disabilities appear to be identified (Smith & Luckasson, 1995).
* In the 1988–89 school year, 26% of Black and 18% of Hispanic children who received special education services were labeled mentally retarded, whereas only 11% of White children had this label (U.S. Department of Education, 1990).

The postsecondary school adjustment of young adults with disabilities is examined in Chapter 15.

A third reason for concern is the fact that culturally and linguistically diverse students are dropping out of school at a much higher rate than White students. At the beginning of this decade, the dropout rate for Hispanics was 49%; for African Americans, 47%; and for Whites, 33% (De La Rosa & Maw, 1990). It is also estimated that one third of Native American students eventually will drop out of school (Napier, 1992). Compounding this problem is the fact that "about 1 in 4 special education students drop out of high school; 43 percent of those who graduate remain unemployed three to five years after high school, and nearly one third—primarily those with learning and emotional disabilities—are arrested at least once after leaving high school" (Shapiro, Loeb, & Bowermaster, 1993, p. 56). Both the distinguishing characteristics of ethnic background and disability are placing culturally and linguistically diverse students with disabilities in double jeopardy for dropping out and not attaining success in postschool settings. In fact, Utley (1995) observed culturally and linguistically diverse students "face quadruple jeopardy due to a combination of factors, such as poverty, language, culture, and/or disabling condition and this has devastating effects on their educational opportunities and makes them vulnerable to placement in special education" (p. 303).

The fact that culturally diverse children constitute a high percentage of special education students is not, in itself, a problem. Students with special needs should be served in special programs, whatever their ethnic background. The presence of large numbers of culturally diverse students, however, raises several important concerns for special educators:

- *Adequacy of assessment and placement procedures.* Have students received fair and multifaceted assessments before being placed in special education programs? Is referral based on a child's documented special needs, rather than on value judgments about his or her background? Are opportunities available for periodic reassessment and for parent and student involvement in program planning? Are culturally diverse students and students with disabilities included in screenings for gifted and talented children?

- *Provision of appropriate supportive services.* Special efforts may help improve the education and adjustment of students from culturally diverse backgrounds; such services may be provided either by the school or by other agencies. Examples of special efforts that may be appropriate are (a) bilingual aides to assist non-English-speaking students in the classroom and to translate correspondence sent home, (b) inservice training for teachers to encourage sensitivity toward different cultures and to enhance appropriate educational planning, and (c) multicultural education for students to increase awareness of their own and others' backgrounds and to reduce the potential for prejudice by developing positive attitudes about different groups.

- *Interactions between school and cultural background.* School staff generally require or expect certain behaviors of students; for example, it is assumed that most children will learn to respond to the teacher's instructions and will be positively motivated by verbal praise. Children, however, are strongly influenced by their early contacts with family members, neighbors, and friends. If the expectations and values of home and school environments are vastly different, children may have serious problems. Behaviors considered problems by school personnel might be related to differences between the standards of behavior in the home and standards of the school. For example, a child who is silent and shy may be behaving according to the standards of her home. Yet teachers might characterize this child as overly withdrawn and refer the child to a school counselor. The idea of cultural incongruence between home and school can also be seen in instruction. Often the typical mode of instruction in mainstream U.S. classrooms is analytical and verbal, whereas the language learning style of some culturally diverse learners is more imaginative and non-verbal (Harry, 1992). Such conflicts can interfere with a child's learning and behavior and are thus a legitimate concern of special educators.

A Note on Terminology

Many terms have been applied to members of culturally diverse populations. As we saw in Chapter 1, although labels sometimes can serve a useful purpose in identifying relevant factors, they are just as likely to convey misleading or inaccurate generalizations. This unfortunate effect is especially evident in several terms that have been used to refer to children from different cultural backgrounds.

In the United States, the term *minority* essentially represents an attempt to categorize by race, not by culture (Harry, 1992). Figure 3.1 identifies the U.S. Department of Education, Office of Civil Rights' (OCR) (1987) classification of racial groups. These classifications, however, do not address the common occurrence of mixed race origins. Furthermore, the term *minority* implies that the racial group being referred to constitutes a recognizable minority in society. Yet in many communities and regions of the country, "minorities" constitute the predominant population. An African American child in Detroit, a Hispanic child in Miami, or a Navajo child on a reservation in Arizona could be considered part of a "minority" only in respect to the national population, a comparison that would have little relevance to the child's immediate environment. The *majority* of students now enrolled in the 25 largest public school systems in the United States are from ethnically diverse "minority" groups (Smith & Luckasson, 1995). In addition to suggesting that the population of the group is small, the term *minority group* carries some "negative connotations of being less than other groups with respect to power, status, and treatment" (Chinn & Kamp, 1982, p. 383). For example, Brantliner and Guskin (1985) describe a minority individual as someone who (a) is politically excluded from roles of significance and responsibility in institutions; (b) receives a smaller share of goods, services, and prestige; and (c) is perceived by members of the dominant culture as deviant and inferior (or, if viewed positively, as different or interesting). Although such discriminatory outcomes and perceptions still exist, they are inappropriate. As Gollnick and Chinn (1994) observe, the "inability to view other cultures as equally viable alternatives for organizing reality is known as **ethnocentrism.** It is a common characteristic of cultures, whereby one's own cultural traits are viewed as natural, correct, and superior to those of another culture, whose traits are perceived as odd, amusing, inferior, or immoral" (p. 9).

FIGURE 3. 1

Classification of racial groups according to the U.S. Department of Education, Office of Civil Rights (OCR)

American Indian or Alaskan Native – A person having origins in any of the original peoples of North America and who maintains cultural identification through tribal affiliation or community recognition.

Asian or Pacific Islander – A person having origins in any of the original peoples of the Far East, Southeast Asia, the Pacific Islands, or the Indian subcontinent. The areas include, for example, China, India, Japan, Korea, the Philippine Islands, and Samoa.

Hispanic – A person of Mexican, Puerto Rican, Cuban, Central or South American, or other Spanish culture or origin—regardless of race.

Black (not of Hispanic origin) – A person having origins in any of the Black racial groups of Africa.

White (not of Hispanic origin) – A person having origins in any of the original peoples of Europe, North Africa, or the Middle East.

Source: From *1986 Elementary and Secondary School Civil Rights Survey: National Summaries* by U.S. Department of Education, Office of Civil Rights, 1987, Washington, DC: DBS Corporation.

The term *culturally diverse* is preferred when referring to children whose backgrounds are different enough to require, at times, special methods of assessment, instruction, intervention, or counseling. This term implies no judgment of a culture's value and does not equate cultural diversity with disability. Furthermore, the names used to describe ethnic groups have also changed. *Asian American* has replaced *Oriental; African American* has replaced *Black; Latino* in some parts of the country has replaced *Hispanic;* and emphasis is increasing on the use of a specific tribal name, rather than *Native American.* It is important for special educators to respect and keep up with these changes that represent increasing group identity and empowerment (Lynch & Hanson, 1992).

> The Division for Culturally and Linguistically Diverse Exceptional Learners (DDEL), a division of CEC, serves the interests of professionals working with culturally and linguistically diverse students with disabilities and their families.

A Note of Caution

Elsie J. Smith, a counselor who specializes in working with people of diverse cultural backgrounds, finds it helpful to remember the following saying: "Each individual is like all other people, like some other people, and like no other person" (1981, p. 180). We must keep this observation in mind as we consider certain issues that have been of concern to specific cultural groups. The importance of understanding and respecting interindividual and intraindividual differences cannot be stressed too strongly. For example, Native Americans are a heterogeneous group. Although a certain cultural heritage and worldview are shared by many Native Americans, as Little Soldier (1990) points out, "Tribal differences are very real and tribal affiliations are quite important to Indian people. . . . There is no such thing as a single 'Indian' culture. Navajos are as different culturally from the Sioux as Canadians are from Mexicans" (pp. 66, 68).

This point should have been made clear in our discussion of the widely used categories of disabilities in special education. It is known, for example, that two students affected by Down syndrome may display very different academic abilities, social behaviors, and personality traits. We have seen that one child who is blind may read braille fluently and play the piano well, whereas another child who is blind may do neither. Similarly, two members of the same racial or cultural group may function quite differently in school.

We should always be objective observers of students' behavior and avoid stereotypes based on race or culture; nevertheless, a teacher who is oblivious to the typical values and ideas shared by members of different cultural groups can inadvertently present a lesson that is not only ineffective but perhaps also offensive or embarrassing to a child. We hope to present information that will help teachers and others recognize whether their approaches and interactions with members of diverse cultural groups are as effective as they can be. Understanding and appreciation of different cultures can go a long way toward avoiding misinterpretations of children's behavior.

Although this chapter presents information on culturally and linguistically diverse students from African American, Hispanic, Asian, and Native American backgrounds, it is important to define diversity in a much broader way. Cusher, McClelland, and Safford (1992) state that diversity

> encompasses not only those individuals whose ethnic heritage originates in another country, but also those among us who may have special educational and other needs . . . , those who may share significantly different lifestyles (rural and urban children, children who live in extreme poverty, drug dependents), those whose identity is crit-

This student's behavior and values are influenced not only by his membership in a specific cultural group, but by his social class, gender, and exceptionality.

ically influenced by gender, and those who are significantly influenced by variations in class and religion. (p. 7)

In other words, as we think about diversity, we must remember that Appalachian, gay and lesbian, homeless, or Muslim students are diverse and deserve the same respect, understanding, and acceptance from educators as other ethnically diverse groups.

This point cannot be stressed too strongly: Each of the cultural groups discussed is extremely heterogeneous; for example, Native Americans today comprise 510 federally recognized tribes and 278 reservations (e.g., reservations, pueblos, rancherias, communities) and speak 187 languages (Coburn et al., 1995). Asian Americans are an even more diversified group, coming from more than 24 countries and speaking more than 1,000 languages and dialects (Leung, 1988).

The degree to which a child inherits a distinct cultural background also varies immensely. Remember, a student's cultural group is just one of the social groups that influence his or her values and behavior.

> For example, a child in the classroom is not just Asian-American, but also male and middle-class. . . . Therefore, his view of reality and his actions based on that view will differ from those of a middle-class Asian-American girl or a lower-class Asian-American boy. A teacher's failure to consider the integration of race, social class, and gender could lead at times to an oversimplified or inaccurate understanding of what occurs in schools. (Grant & Sleeter, 1989, p. 49)

✳ *Culture, Cultural Pluralism, and Multicultural Education*

What must a classroom teacher know to help culturally diverse students with disabilities achieve? Are special methods of assessment and instruction necessary to work with students whose cultural heritage differs from the majority? If a classroom contains students from four cultural groups, does that mean the teacher must use four ways of teaching? Before a meaningful discussion of these important questions can be attempted, several more fundamental questions must be answered: What is a culture? What does membership in a particular social group mean? How do and should members of different cultural groups view and treat one another? What roles and responsibilities do schools have in teaching children from different cultural backgrounds to interact with one another?

Culture

To survive, a social group must adapt to and modify the environments in which it lives. **Culture** "refers to the many different factors that shape one's sense of group identity: race, ethnicity, religion, geographical locations, income status, gender, and occupations" (Turnbull, Turnbull, Shank, & Leal, 1995, p. 8). Culture can be defined as

> the way of life of a social group; the human-made environment. Although culture is often defined in a way that includes all the material and nonmaterial aspects of group life, most social scientists today emphasize the intangible, symbolic, and ideational aspect of culture. . . . Cultures are dynamic, complex, and changing. (Banks, 1994a, pp. 50–51)

A culture, then, is determined by the "world view, values, styles, and above all language" shared by members of a social group (Hilliard, 1980, p. 585). Even though an "outsider" can learn to speak the language of another social group or to use some of its tools, such accomplishments do not confer complete access to or understanding of the group's culture. Although the language, artifacts, and other things associated with a particular group are sometimes presented as its culture, this view is only partly accurate. Chopsticks, for example, are an important part of the Chinese culture but are not culture in and of themselves.

> Unless we know the meaning of an action such as using chopsticks, these implements remain just bits of wood, bone, or ivory. We have to acquire the knowledge and ideas about what they mean and what they are used for. . . . If we are members of the social group that uses such implements, we will know the code by virtue of knowing the culture. A stranger in the group would have to watch chopstick-using behavior or ask for instructions. . . . Even then, the stranger might not learn all the subtleties of chopstick use immediately but would have to be acquainted with the social group for a long time before finding out that there are rules of politeness and etiquette surrounding the apparently simple process of eating with chopsticks. (Bullivant, 1993, p. 35)

People who share a particular culture's ideas and values usually interpret events in similar ways. Although membership in a specific cultural group does not determine behavior, members are exposed to (socialized by) the same set of expectations and consequences for acting in certain ways. As a result, certain types of behavior become more probable (Banks, 1994b; Skinner, 1974). It is also important

Pazcual Villaronga, a bilingual teacher in New York City's "El Barrio," reflects on his own culture in the poem "The So Called," on the facing page. He states, "The poem's energy is not so much out of anger, but rather more out of a burning desire to celebrate the many cultures within. And especially the ones that make me who I am!" (Villaronga, 1995, p. 260).

to remember that each student is simultaneously a member of multiple groups according to race, ethnicity, social class, religion, gender, and disability. Each of these groups exerts various degrees of influence on the student's ways of interpreting and responding to the world. For example:

> The Commission on Education of the Deaf (1988) has recognized the existence of an identifiable and important deaf culture, suggesting that this culture be tapped by educators to help students who are deaf understand and then cope with their deafness. According to the commission, the psychological and sociological aspects of deafness need to be incorporated into school curricula. They must not be suppressed in a misguided effort to deny the differences inherent in deafness. (Turnbull, Turnbull, Shank, & Leal, 1995, p. 569)

Gollnick and Chinn (1994) outline four basic characteristics of culture that provide a background for considering the special needs of culturally diverse students with disabilities and their families.

1. *Our cultural heritage is learned.* It is not innately based on the culture in which we are born. Vietnamese infants adopted by Italian American, Catholic, middle-class parents will share a cultural heritage with middle-class Italian American Catholics, rather than Vietnamese in Vietnam.
2. *Culture is shared.* Shared cultural patterns and customs bind people together as an identifiable group and make it possible for them to live together and function with ease. Groups may not realize the common cultural aspects as existent in the cultural group—the way they communicate with each other and the foods they eat.
3. *Culture is an adaptation.* Cultures have developed to accommodate certain environmental conditions and available natural and technological resources. Thus, Eskimo who live with extreme cold, snow, ice, seals, and the sea have developed a culture different from the Pacific Islander. The culture of urban residents differs from rural residents, in part, because of the resources available in the different settings.
4. *Culture is a dynamic system that changes continuously.* For example, the replacement of industrial workers by robots is changing the culture of many working-class communities. (pp. 6-7)

In fact, Glenn (1989) stated that "we need an approach to education that takes seriously the lived culture of children and their families, not the fiestas and folklore that had meaning for their grandparents but are not part of the lives of families coming to terms with the losses and gains of immigration" (p. 777).

Cultural Pluralism

Currie (1981) recalls a native Canadian parent who likened cultural pluralism to a bouquet that is "more beautiful because of the diversity of flowers, all of which add to the total beauty, and yet, each is beautiful in its own right. . . . It is the differences which must be recognized and accepted instead of being ignored or rejected" (p. 165).

The United States is a society composed of people from many cultural groups, and the students in our schools reflect this great diversity. **Cultural pluralism** exists when the cultural differences that make up a society are not only mutually respected by all members of the larger society but also fostered and encouraged as well. Janzen (1994) describes the differences between cultural pluralism and *cultural assimilation:*

> The goal of cultural pluralism is that ethnic groups remain intact and that their idiosyncratic ways of knowing and acting will be respected and continued. Assimilationism, on the other hand, accepts the importance of understanding multiple beliefs, but has as its primary goal the amalgamation of all groups into the American mainstream. (p. 9)

The So Called

Pazcual Villaronga

I am mixture
similar to h2O
I am american pie
the black-eyed peas
with plenty of salsa

I am the rhythm and blues
the classical lines
the pru-cu-ta-ca-ca-mambo

I am a potpourri of values and
    attitudes
the fact that men don't cry
but in reality they do
and don't die

I am a mixture
of beautiful paints
that picture
psychedelic tones
african blood
spanish blood
and Indian blood

transported
by economical
social
or political fact

from an island of joy
under a damn
cynical
implemented
ploy

to a jungle of cement
metal
and glass

to become a confused entity
a confused being
of meatloaf
and oxtails
and arroz con pollo

of beethoven
Isaac Hayes
and eddi palmieri

to struggle with my culture
their culture
and the loss of mine

goodbye three kinds
hello christmas
and its mad capitalistic
season

the dropping of my accent
the implementation of
another language

I am Puerto Rico
the u.s. of a.
and new york

spinning
trying to lose myself
in the sun
on the penthouse
in my place
in my slums
trying to become
what will constantly be denied

I am black
white
brown
uptown
downtown
all around
the damn town

I am here
I am there
I am everywhere
spread thin
so that my existence
my consistency
my reality

can be denied
mesmerized
until I boil down to nothing
at the bottom of the pot
"El Pegao"

which they don't know is the best
part of the meal
especially because I survive
to eat it

I am the music you can't exploit
because you don't
understand
comes from our corazones
speaks of our culture
our history
our minds

in a language you find
easier to destroy
because yours is better

I am caught in a flight
over a sea
of controversy

I am a piece of a puzzle
that doesn't fit
here or there

because both my vehicles of
    expression
are dulled and
downed
by my own
and my own

I am what has always been there
only with a different name
to fit the purpose
to play the game,
for someone's fame
other than mine

I am the P.R.
the rican
the spic
the new click
the so called New-Yor-Rican ✴

Pazcual Villaronga is a bilingual teacher in
the Lola Rodriguez de Tio Bilingual School
in Manhattan's District 4, in New York City's
"El Barrio."

Cultural pluralism is promoted when students teach one another about their ethnic, linguistic, and historical backgrounds.

Baca and Cervantes (1989) point out that the term *melting pot* was first used as the title of a Broadway play that debuted in 1908 (Zangwill, 1909).

Belief in cultural pluralism as a positive value is a recent concept. Throughout most of our country's development, cultural assimilation was valued and practiced. This was the so-called *melting pot theory,* wherein all immigrants were expected to relinquish their native language and cultural heritage in exchange for complete adoption of the language, values, and ways of the new "American way of life." During and after World War I, an intensive program of Americanization was put into effect in schools, churches, and the workplace because of concern that some immigrants might support their native countries against the United States (Banks, 1994b).

Even though Americans share an overarching *macroculture* as members of a nation-state, the significant and growing *microcultures* (smaller cultures within the core culture) in the United States are evidence that the melting pot has not been completely successful. As Banks (1994b) points out,

> Every nation-state has overarching values, symbols, and ideations shared to some degree by all microcultures. Various microcultural groups within the nation, however, may mediate, interpret, reinterpret, perceive, and experience these overarching national values and ideals differently. (p. 84)

The melting pot theory, nevertheless, has had tremendous influence on our society's institutions. Janzen (1994) writes that even today "assimilationists fear the strength and solidarity of cultural pluralism, and sometimes they sharply deplore what they see as its end result" (p. 10). Critics contend that one of the undesirable outcomes of attempting to create a monocultural (melting pot) society is an educational system that lacks tolerance for cultural diversity among students.

> America's intolerance of diversity is reflected in an ethnocentric educational system to "Americanize foreigners or those who are seen as culturally different." . . . The ill-disguised contempt for a child's language is part of a broader distaste for the child himself and the culture he represents. Children who are culturally different are said to be culturally "deprived." Their language and culture are seen as "disadvantages." (Kobrick, 1972, p. 54)

Unfortunately, some children from cultural backgrounds that are different from White, middle-class America still encounter the institutionalized discrimination that

Kobrick described more than two decades ago. But there is reason for optimism. Educators are realizing the benefits and necessity, not to mention the ethical and moral correctness, of cultural pluralism. Evidence of this realization is the increasing emphasis on multicultural education.

Multicultural Education

Multicultural education refers to the actualization of cultural pluralism in the schools. According to Turnbull et al. (1995), multicultural education attempts to teach all children in ways that recognize the contributions of many cultures in the United States.

> The multicultural education approach . . . includes attention to staffing, environment, assessment, curricula, materials, and instruction and calls for reorganization that reflects the perspectives of and knowledge about diverse racial and ethnic groups (traditionally oppressed groups as well as Euro-Americans), both sexes, disability groups, and social classes" (Ball & Harry, 1993, p. 432).

Additionally, a multicultural approach also recognizes that families are diverse, and involving them in education requires an understanding of their cultural beliefs and attitudes about education and disabilities. James Banks (1994a), a leading developer and advocate of multicultural education programs, identifies five major goals of the approach:

1. *To help individuals gain a greater self-understanding by viewing themselves from the perspectives of other cultures.* Students taught to understand and value their own culture and to acquaint themselves with other cultures will gain an understanding and respect for other ethnic cultures.
2. *To provide students with cultural and ethnic alternatives.* Schools should move away from the Anglocentric curriculum and teach students about the richness of the music, literature, values, lifestyles, and perspectives that exist among other ethnic groups.
3. *To provide students with the skills, attitudes, and knowledge they need to function within their ethnic culture and the mainstream culture.* Multicultural education prepares students to function successfully in their home and ethnic communities, as well as in the U.S. mainstream.
4. *To reduce the pain and discrimination that members of some ethnic and racial groups experience in schools and in the wider society.* Multicultural education provides ways to reduce prejudice and alienation of ethnically diverse students in schools by empowering them and respecting their ethnic identity.
5. *To help students master essential literacy, numeracy, thinking, and perspective-taking skills.* Multicultural education assumes that students will master important skills if multiethnic and relevant content is embedded in the curriculum.

Some educators erroneously believe they have incorporated multicultural education into their schools simply by offering various units of study on different cultural groups (e.g., "Scientific Contributions by African Americans") or by periodically scheduling special cultural awareness events (e.g., "Hispanic Week"). Such activities are an important part of multicultural education, but they are not sufficient. Leaders of the multicultural education movement believe that to truly put the concept into practice, a complete transformation of the school is necessary. Some experts believe that teachers often present superficial, inaccurate stereotypes. Figure 3.2 illustrates

The BUENO Center for Multicultural Education at the University of Colorado is an excellent source of materials and information for building cultural awareness in students with disabilities. See "For More Information" at the end of this chapter.

> "Never judge another man until you have walked a mile in his moccasins." This North American Indian proverb suggests the importance of understanding the cultural background and experiences of other persons rather than judging them by our own standards (Gollnick & Chinn, 1994, p. 9).

the absurd and yet comical way a teacher might provide superficial coverage of multiethnic information.

Teachers who use units on the foods, clothing, stories, legends, dances, and arts of the major American ethnic groups only on special occasions and holidays would be more effective if they included this content in the ongoing, daily curriculum (Grossman, 1995). Although the tourist approach to multicultural education is a positive first step, experts believe that the major goal of multicultural education is to "transform the school so that . . . students from diverse cultural, social-class, racial, and ethnic groups will experience an equal opportunity to learn in school" (Banks, 1989, pp. 19-20).

✳ *Initial Steps to Becoming Culturally Responsive Educators*

Before teachers can implement culturally responsive assessment, curriculum, and instructional procedures, they must develop a self-awareness and appreciation of diversity.

FIGURE 3.2

A non-Indian story

> You are a "non-Indian." When you arrive in class, the "Indians" are all at the front of the room chatting with the teacher. She looks up. "Ah, the new student. Welcome! Have a seat. You're a non-Indian, aren't you? We were just talking about your people." The children turn to look at you. They giggle and whisper to each other. None of the people in the room look or sound like your family. You look around the room. No dolls in the beds or pictures on the book covers have eyes or hair or noses like those of your family members. Only one of the pictures of faces on the bulletin board looks similar to yours. The bulletin board says "Thanksgiving: A non-Indian Holiday" and has a grotesque picture of a non-Indian woman in Reeboks and a Pilgrim hat, holding a dead turkey in one hand and a machine gun in the other. Your classmates giggle when they look at the bulletin board. "Look at those funny shoes," they whisper. (You look down at your favorite pair of Reeboks and stuff your feet under your chair.)
>
> "Now class, it's very important to remember that our non-Indian friends are not responsible for what their forefathers did. They stole our land and ruined our forests, but that was a long time ago. We're not going to talk about that today. Who knows what kind of houses non-Indians live in? Yes, that's right. They live in square houses with red tile roofs. Who lives in these houses? Mother and father and sister and brother. Yes, that is right. Grandmother? No; they don't live with their grandmothers like we do. They send their grandmothers to special places called retirement homes. Why? I don't know.
>
> "Next week, during Thanksgiving, we'll have a unit on non-Indians. We'll all make a non-Indian town out of clay. It's called a suburb. Can you say suburb? Non-Indians sleep in separate rooms, and they have little houses to keep their cars in. Now this is a non-Indian hat." The teacher pulls out a Pilgrim's hat. "Non-Indians wore these when they first came to our land."

Source: From "Culturally Assaultive Classrooms" by L. Clark, S. DeWolf, & C. Clark, 1992, *Young Children*, *47*(5), 4–9. Reprinted by permission.

Teacher Awareness and Development

Teachers are human beings who bring their cultural perspective, values, hopes, and dreams to the classroom. They also bring their prejudices, stereotypes, and misconceptions to the classroom. The teacher's values and perspective mediate and interact with the teacher and influence the way that messages are communicated and perceived by their students. (Banks, 1994b, p. 159)

Lynch and Hanson (1992) state that to understand and appreciate fully the diversity that exists among the students and families that special educators serve, we must first understand and appreciate our own cultures. Self-awareness is the first step on the journey toward cross-cultural competence. Educators must also become aware of their own biases and prejudices. All cultures have built-in biases, and there are no right or wrong cultural beliefs. Cultural self-awareness is the bridge to learning about other cultures. "It is not possible to be truly sensitive to someone else's culture until one is sensitive to one's own and the impact that cultural customs, values, beliefs, and behaviors have on practice" (Lynch & Hanson, p. 39).

See "A Cultural Journey" later in this chapter.

Fortunately, multicultural education is becoming a required component in many teacher education programs, and educators are learning how to become more accepting and supportive of cultural differences. As a measure of one's beliefs about culture and its importance to teaching, for example, both practicing and prospective teachers can complete an instrument like the Multicultural Self-Report Inventory (Slade & Conoley, 1989) (Figure 3.3). A low score indicates less multicultural bias; a high score suggests greater discomfort with the concept. Slade and Conoley (1989) describe several activities that are part of a 2-week module used in a preservice teacher-training course designed to develop positive attitudes toward cultural diversity in the classroom.

Once teachers are aware of their own ethnic attitudes, behaviors, and perceptions, they can begin an action program designed to change their behavior if necessary (Banks, 1994b) and gain knowledge about other cultures. Methods for gathering information about cultures include but are not limited to reading books, studying ethnograms, and interviewing cultural informants (persons from the culture who are

Multicultural education is most meaningful when multiethnic and relevant content is embedded within the curriculum in a systematic and ongoing way. Children in this school have spent several weeks preparing for a visit by Ashley Bryan, an author of children's books about African culture.

An Ethnic Feelings Book

·······················

The self-contained classroom for students with developmental disabilities consisted of 4 boys and 8 girls from 9 to 12 years old. All of the children were African Americans. Their teacher, Charles Jones, was concerned about his students' self-perceptions and levels of self-esteem. Their informal verbal discussions about themselves, their aspirations, and their interpersonal interactions with each other were often negative. When frustrated academically or socially, the students frequently engaged in ethnic name-calling. The name-calling was often associated with skin color and their African heritage (e.g., "You're black"; "I'm not black"; "You're like those dirty Africans"; "My ancestors don't come from Africa!"). Self-deprecating statements, such as "I'm crazy," were also heard. When asked, "What do you want to do for a living when you're an adult?" the children's responses typically involved sports, working in a fast-food restaurant, and motherhood, suggesting a limited view of future possibilities.

Collectively, the students did not feel good about themselves, nor did they appear comfortable with their ethnicity. Difficulty in performing academic tasks seemed to reinforce their feelings of inadequacy in general and their negative perceptions of their ethnicity in particular. Working with Bridgie Alexis Ford, a faculty member in special education at the University of Akron, Mr. Jones developed and implemented a cultural awareness project for his students. The project was designed to help the students learn factual information about the historic experiences and contributions of African Americans. Jones and Ford believed that as a result of learning about their ancestors' experiences and examining their own feelings about those experiences, the students would develop positive feelings about their ethnic heritage. Positive feelings about one's cultural group are an important factor in developing self-esteem and self-confidence.

The cultural awareness unit took about 30 to 45 minutes each day for 10 weeks and revolved around the creation of an ethnic feelings book. The feelings book included both factual information about African Americans and the students' interpretations of the feelings of their ancestors during various periods. The unit began with the positive aspects of African life prior to the slave-trade era, discussed slavery and segregation, identified actions by African Americans to create freedom and equal opportunity, and focused on the students' positive characteristics and capabilities. After covering each part of the unit, the students created another section of their feelings book. The emphasis throughout the unit was on highlighting positive aspects and contributions and dispelling negative stereotypes.

Historical information and personal accounts were presented via low-vocabulary, high-interest, well-illustrated books and filmstrips, recordings, and West African artifacts. African American leaders from the local community also visited the classroom and discussed their accomplishments and feelings with the students. These were some of the instructional activities that were part of the unit:

- *Brainstorming.* To acquire background information about what the students already knew about their African ancestors.
- *Adoption of a tribe.* Each student adopted one of the tribes portrayed in the books or filmstrips and prepared a report about the tribe. The class selected one of the reports, edited it, and included it in the feelings book.
- *Discussions about negative terminology and stereotypes assigned to slaves.* Ethnic name-calling was also discussed.
- *Segregation simulation.* At the beginning of one school day, half the class tied blue strings around their waists to designate themselves as segregated students (SS). Throughout the rest of that day, these students were treated in a discriminatory manner: They didn't get to use recreational equipment during recess, they could not use the rest rooms at the times the non-SS students were using them, and they received no verbal attention or tangible reinforcement during normal class routines. The next day, the students switched roles so that everyone experienced the feelings of segregation.
- *Identification of positive attributes.* Positive characteristics of relatives and community leaders whom the students admired were discussed. The students submitted typed paragraphs describing

their talents and interests and indicating the types of jobs they believed they could pursue.

The students exhibited a great deal of enthusiasm and cooperative behavior throughout the project. Name-calling decreased, and when it did occur, the students began to reprimand one another. Multicultural activities are often restricted to a special day or week during the school year; for students with learning disabilities, Ford and Jones believe that an ongoing, systematic approach to cultural awareness is imperative.

From "An Ethnic Feelings Book: Created by Students with Developmental Handicaps" by B. A. Ford and C. Jones, 1990, *Teaching Exceptional Children, 22*(4), pp. 36-39. Copyright (1989) by the Council for Exceptional Children. Adapted by permission.

familiar with the families' beliefs and patterns). Teachers should increase their understanding and appreciation of different ethnic and cultural groups by studying the following concepts:

Origins and immigration

Shared culture, values, and symbols

Ethnic identity and sense of peoplehood

Perspectives, worldview, and frames of reference

Ethnic institutions and self-determination

Demographic, social, political, and economic status

Prejudice, discrimination, and racism

Intraethnic diversity

Assimilation and acculturation

Revolution

Knowledge construction (Banks, 1994a, pp. 53-58)

Furthermore, teachers can study the verbal and nonverbal communication styles of ethnic groups. Although mainstream American teachers will probably not

Mr. Bryan signs copies of The Turtle Knows Your Name.

FIGURE 3.3

Multicultural Self-Report Inventory. Items marked by a zero (0) have no positive or negative relevance and are included to lessen the probability of giving answers just because they are socially acceptable. Items that are marked with a minus (–) are scored negatively. The lower the score, the more accepting and supportive the person's attitude about cultural differences.

MULTICULTURAL SELF-REPORT INVENTORY

SA = Strongly Agree
MA = Moderately Agree
U = Undecided
MD = Moderately Disagree
SD = Strongly Disagree

			SA	*MA*	*U*	*MD*	*SD*
	1.	I am interested in exploring cultures different from my own.	1	2	3	4	5
(–)	2.	I have enough experience with cultures different from my own.	1	2	3	4	5
(0)	3.	I seem to like some cultures and ethnic groups better than others.	1	2	3	4	5
(–)	4.	Part of the role of a good teacher is to encourage children to adopt middle class values.	1	2	3	4	5
(–)	5.	I feel that cultural differences in students do not affect students' behavior in school.	1	2	3	4	5
(–)	6.	As students progress through school, they should adopt the mainstream culture.	1	2	3	4	5
	7.	I am comfortable around people whose cultural background is different from mine.	1	2	3	4	5
	8.	I can identify attitudes of my own that are peculiar to my culture.	1	2	3	4	5
	9.	I believe I can recognize attitudes or behaviors in children that are a reflection of cultural or ethnic differences.	1	2	3	4	5

find it feasible to adopt the nonverbal behaviors of another culture, teacher-student and teacher-parent communication may be enhanced by some knowledge of the different significance attached to touch, interpersonal distance, silence, dress, and gestures. It is important to note, however, that "simply recognizing ethnic and cultural diversity is not enough. Understanding and respect for diverse values, traditions, and behaviors are essential if we are to actualize fully our nation's democratic ideals" (Banks, 1994b, p. 287).

In preparing to work with culturally and linguistically diverse students and their families, teachers must also understand that collaboration and teaming are critical. Today's teachers must collaborate with other professionals from various programs (e.g., bilingual and ESL education), culturally diverse community agencies, and social services agencies (Thomas, Correa, & Morsink, 1995). In fact, a recent and promising trend toward full-service schools (Dryfoos, 1994) will require personnel from various agencies to collaborate. Full-service schools provide families and their children with a "one-stop-shopping" approach to receiving all necessary support, such as welfare checks, food stamps, physical examinations and immunizations, employment train-

FIGURE 3.3 *(continued)*

			SA	MA	U	MD	SD
	10.	I feel I can take the point of view of a child from a different culture.	1	2	3	4	5
(–)	11.	It makes me uncomfortable when I hear people talking in a language that I cannot understand.	1	2	3	4	5
(–)	12.	Values and attitudes learned in minority cultures keep children from making progress in school.	1	2	3	4	5
(–)	13.	Only people who are part of a culture can really understand and empathize with children from that culture.	1	2	3	4	5
(–)	14.	I have had few cross-cultural experiences.	1	2	3	4	5
	15.	Multicultural education is an important part of a school curriculum.	1	2	3	4	5
(0)	16.	I am prejudiced in favor of some ethnic or cultural group or groups.	1	2	3	4	5
(–)	17.	Some ethnic groups make less desirable citizens than others.	1	2	3	4	5
	18.	Some ethnic groups are more reluctant to talk about family matters than other cultural groups.	1	2	3	4	5
	19.	Children from differing ethnic groups are likely to differ in their attitudes toward teacher authority.	1	2	3	4	5
(–)	20.	Personally, I have never identified any prejudice in myself.	1	2	3	4	5
(–)	21.	I am prejudiced *against* some ethnic or cultural groups.	1	2	3	4	5
(–)	22.	In the United States, given equal intelligence and physical ability, every individual has equal access to success.	1	2	3	4	5

Source: From "Multicultural Experiences for Special Educators" by J. C. Slade and C. W. Conoley, 1989, *Teaching Exceptional Children, 22*(1), p. 62. Reprinted by permission.

ing and placement, GED instruction, day care, and transportation. Full-service schools are often located on elementary or secondary school campuses and are coordinated by multiple agencies.

Teacher education programs should help pre- and inservice teachers understand the enjoyment and challenges involved with teaching culturally diverse students with disabilities. "Teacher education programs . . . should help teachers explore and clarify their own ethnic and cultural identities and develop more positive attitudes toward other racial, ethnic, and cultural groups" (Banks, 1994b, p. 159). Effective teachers must develop not only cultural sensitivity but also knowledge and skills for implementing a culturally responsive curriculum and pedagogy. Furthermore, a large part of working with students in schools is establishing school-family partnerships. Family involvement becomes an important component to becoming culturally competent.

Involving Culturally and Linguistically Diverse Families

The parent-professional partnership is examined in detail in Chapter 13.

Family involvement in the educational process is considered important for students' success in school. A. J. Reynolds (1992) reports on the positive influence of parental involvement on children's academic achievement and school adjustment. He discusses a strong correlation between parental involvement in school and the at-risk child's development of self-confidence, motivation, and sense of cohesiveness. Furthermore, families of students who did not drop out and who succeeded in school participated in their children's school decisions, demonstrated a motivating and nonpunitive action concerning grades, and were involved to different degrees within the school environment (Rumberger, Ghatak, Polous, Ritter, & Dornbush, 1990).

Involving families who come from diverse backgrounds in school activities is most challenging. Often the demands and challenges faced by families who are less educated, poor, or isolated from the mainstream American culture prevent them from becoming actively involved in school partnerships. The literature on culturally diverse families supports the following six notions about these families (Correa, 1992; Harry, 1992; Lynch & Hanson, 1992; Thomas, Correa, & Morsink, 1995).

1.   *Many families may be potentially English proficient, less well educated, come from low SES, or be undocumented immigrants.* For practitioners, it means that we provide materials in both the native and English language and preferably communicate with the family directly through home visits or by telephone. Some parents are not able to read their native language and may depend on older offspring who are English dominant to translate materials for them.

2.   *Practitioners must understand that although the parents may not have finished school or are unable to read, they are "life educated" and know their child better than anyone else does.* In Spanish, the term *educado* (educated) does not mean "formal schooling," but means that a child is skilled in human relations, well mannered, respectful of adults, and well behaved.

3.   *If families are suspected to be undocumented immigrants, it is natural for them to be fearful of interaction with anyone representing authority.* Our role as special educators is not to engage in the activities of the Office of Immigration and Naturalization Services. Our focus is on educating children, children who—by law—are *not a suspect class* (Correa, Gollery, & Fradd, 1988). Building trust and cooperation from families, even if undocumented immigrants, is important.

4.   *Families from culturally diverse backgrounds tend to be family oriented.* Extended family members—*compadres* or *padrinos* (godparents) in the Hispanic culture—may play important roles in child rearing and family decisions. A child's disability or even a mild language problem may be extremely personal for them to discuss with "outsiders," and solutions for problems may lie within the family structure. For educators it is important to respect this informal kinship system of support. We

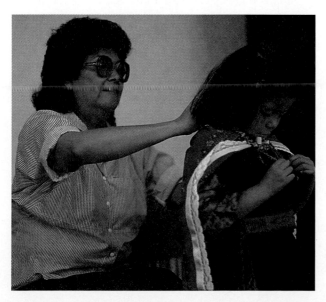

A culturally responsive educator strives to develop awareness of and sensitivity for the beliefs and values held by parents and family members from different cultural groups.

must understand that we may represent a much more formal and impersonal support service for these families. Dunst, Trivette, and Deal (1988) contend that this close, insular aspect in a family is a strength that assists the family in functioning and coping with the stresses sometimes associated with [raising] a child with a disability.

5. *It is important to know that the family may hold idiosyncratic ideologies and practices about illness and disability.* For example, in some Hispanic cultures, parents may believe that a child's disability was caused by *el mal ojo* (the evil eye) or *el susto* (a scare or fright experienced by the pregnant mother). Special educators must understand that families (usually the elders) may believe that, to cure the child, the family must make *mandas* (offerings to God or a Catholic saint) or seek the help of a *curandero* (a local healer). It is important to note, however, that culture is only one influence on a family's reaction to having a child with a disability. Other influences, such as financial status, intactness of the family, external and internal support systems, and coping mechanisms, must also be considered (Correa, 1992; Harry, 1992; Lynch & Hanson, 1992). Interestingly, among many Native American groups, it is not considered negative or tragic to have a child born with a disability; "It is assumed the child has the prenatal choice of how he wishes to be born and, if [disabled], is so by choice" (Stewart, 1977, p. 439).

6. *The educational system—in particular, the special education system—may be extremely intimidating to the family.* Although this may be true for many Anglo American families as well, for the family from a Non-English Language Background (NELB) or a less-educated and poor background, professionals' use of educational language and jargon, their nonverbal communication, and possible insensitivities may be especially intimidating. Interestingly, families may hold the professional up on a pedestal and think the professional is the expert and not question or comment on their own wishes for their child's education.

Florian (1987) states that the modern idea of *consumer involvement* in service delivery has not often been used by ethnically diverse parents of children with disabilities. Parents or caregivers may not participate in a partnership with us because, in the case of parent education groups, the groups do not address their needs; and if groups are relevant, the ways we educate and propose solutions to child-rearing issues may be inappropriate or impractical for the culturally diverse family.

Christensen (1992) advised that teachers should understand a broad range of the families' cultural aspects. The top 12 areas that teachers reported as necessary for understanding families from culturally diverse backgrounds included the following:

General understanding of culture

Child-rearing practices

Family patterns

Views of exceptionality

Availability and use of community resources

Linguistic differences

Acknowledging own culture and biases

Beliefs about professionals

Nonverbal communication styles

Views of medical practices

Sex roles

Religion

Prior to developing services to meet the needs of a child with disabilities from a culturally diverse background, teachers should obtain as much information as possible about the child, the family, and the cultural group. One useful strategy is to interview parents and others who are familiar with the child and his or her particular cultural environment. The following questions might be among those asked in an interview:

- Why have members of the cultural group left their homeland?
- Why have members of the cultural group settled in the local community?
- To what extent do members of the cultural group experience poverty?
- What is the typical family size?
- What roles are assigned to individual family members?
- What customs, values, and beliefs in the culture have relevance in understanding the children's behavior?
- What are the social functions and leisure activities in which members of the cultural group participate?
- How do members of the cultural group view education?
- How do members of the cultural group view [individuals with disabilities]? (Mattes & Omark, 1984, pp. 43-45)

Information gained from such questions can form a basis for determining appropriate and reinforcing activities. It will also enhance the teacher's understanding of a child's behavior in school and facilitate communication with parents.

✳ *Understanding the Educational Needs of Culturally and Linguistically Diverse Students*

Alternative Educational Assessment

Tests are widely used in special education. However, the testing methods used to identify students for special education services represent an inexact science at best and at times little more than guesswork (Correa, Blanes-Reyes, & Rapport, 1995). The likelihood of obtaining valid, accurate, and unbiased assessment results is even less when the student in question is from a culturally different background. Figueroa (1989) calls the current practice of psychological testing of children from culturally and linguistically diverse groups "random chaos" because it is so fraught with problems.

Brown (1982) discusses several ways that tests—traditionally standardized on White, English-speaking, middle-class children—may discriminate against those from different cultural backgrounds.

1. *The tests use formats and items that are more germane to one group than another.* For example, the test may include restrictive time limits, vocabulary tasks that require the child to read the word, and items that require a child to read in a task designed to measure listening comprehension ability.
2. *Children have differing amounts of "test wiseness," which is more likely to be a problem with the preschool-age child than with the school-age child.* For exam-

ple, White, middle-class, preschool-age children tend to be familiar with question-and-answer formats, with puzzles, and with pointing and naming tasks often included on tests. The same degree of familiarity cannot be assumed when evaluating a disadvantaged child.

3. *The skills reflected by the test items may not be relevant to the skills demanded by the disadvantaged and culturally different child's environment.* "The tests, rather than assessing the disadvantaged child's ability, measure the extent to which such children have assimilated aspects of the dominant culture" (p. 164).

The practice of placing children in special education programs for students with disabilities or giftedness solely because of their performance on standardized intelligence tests is rapidly disappearing. It is widely believed that, in the past, over-reliance on IQ tests resulted in the inappropriate labeling and placement of many students from diverse cultural backgrounds; IQ tests do not present a fair or complete measure of the intelligence of culturally diverse students.

> Issues in IQ testing are discussed more fully in Chapters 4 and 12.

Hilliard (1975) calls attention to sources of cultural bias in several widely used tests of cognitive ability. These tests appear to be based on the faulty premise that every child comes to the test with a similar background of life experiences. Hilliard cites the following examples of potentially unfair test items:

> On one test, a child must be familiar with such words as wasp, captain, hive, casserole, shears, cobbler, or hydrant. On another test, a child must know the distance from Boston to London [and] why icebergs melt. . . . The child, in order to get the answers correct, must assume that women are weak and need protection, that policemen are always nice, that labor laws are just. How is the examiner to distinguish ignorance from disagreement? (p. 22)

Some interesting evidence indicates that a child's performance in testing situations may be heavily influenced by the environment and the examiner. Labov (1975) presents a case study of the verbal behavior of an 8-year-old African American child named Leon. When Leon was tested in school by a White interviewer who placed objects on a table and said, "Tell me everything you can about this," his response was minimal, consisting mostly of silence and one-word utterances. It appeared that Leon was functioning well below his age level and perhaps had a serious communication disorder or mental retardation. On another occasion, however, Leon was interviewed by an African American examiner who took him to an apartment in a familiar neighborhood, brought along Leon's best friend and a supply of potato chips, and sat down on the floor with the child. In this situation, Leon spoke much more fluently; he had a great deal to say to the adult and to his friend. Labov has also performed a detailed linguistic analysis of the nonstandard English used by many African American children and has concluded that traditional classroom tests and tasks have little relevance or accuracy. "There is no reason to believe that any non-standard vernacular is in itself an obstacle to learning" (Labov, 1975, p. 127).

Even though Labov's case study illustrates that one child responded differently to different examiners, it should not be assumed that the race, gender, or age of a teacher or examiner will inevitably affect a child's performance. Brown (1982) reviewed several studies of the effects of examiner race on the performance of culturally diverse children and found no general tendency of African American and Hispanic students to score higher or lower when tested by White, African American, or Hispanic examiners. Characteristics such as the examiner's "ability to evidence a warm, responsive, receptive, but firm style" were found to be more important than race or ethnic group in motivating children to do their best. "This does not preclude the possibility that ethnic or racial variables can influence performance, but it does suggest that to study race alone—without considering other interactional variables— is likely to be futile" (Brown, 1982, p. 165).

Alternative, nonstandardized methods of educational assessment with multiple criteria seem to be a more appropriate and effective assessment process for an ethno-linguistically diverse population. Alternative assessment includes an integrated approach using a variety of measures and data collection methods (e.g., observations, self-reports, checklists, portfolios, inventories, curriculum-based assessment). This approach provides teachers with relevant and useful information regarding student performance and is valuable in making appropriate instructional decisions (Fradd & McGee, 1994; Hamayan & Damico, 1991). Furthermore, alternative assessment allows for the exploration of the numerous factors and confounding variables (e.g., environmental deprivation, poverty, health problems, language and cultural differences) that affect the performance of minority students and that could result in a misdiagnosis.

Mercer (1981) suggests that observation of a child's behavior outside school, in the family and neighborhood, may be more valuable than formal tests in determining abilities and needs and in particular may help differentiate students who are learning disabled from those who have mental retardation. If a child is "learning the skills needed to cope intelligently with the nonacademic world, then s/he may be ignorant of the skills needed to succeed in school but is not mentally retarded" (Mercer, 1981, p. 101). Dent (1976) emphasizes the importance of precise descriptions of behaviors—including antecedents and consequences. In certain cultures and settings, loud talking is not always equivalent to boisterous or aggressive behavior. And hitting and name-calling may not be hostile; they may represent a sign of respect or affection (Dent, 1976). Interpretations and value judgments should not be used in reporting children's behavior.

Along with objective recording of behaviors, a child's social and cultural background should be taken into account when assessing performance. What is normal and acceptable in a child's culture may be regarded as abnormal or unacceptable in school and may result in conflict, mislabeling, or punishment. Gallimore, Boggs, and Jordan (1974) offer the example of several native Hawaiian children who sought help from other children on tests and tasks and seemed to pay little attention to the teacher. This behavior was interpreted as cheating and inattentiveness. Closer observation of the children's home and community environments, however, revealed that the Hawaiian children were typically peer oriented. It was normal for them to share in the responsibility of caring for each other, and they often worked cooperatively on tasks, rather than follow the directions of an adult.

Cox and Ramirez (1981) report that even though generalizations cannot be made about the learning styles of any group of students, it appears that many [African American], Hispanic, and other culturally diverse children are more group oriented, more sensitive to the social environment, and more positively responsive to adult modeling than are White students. Students from certain cultural backgrounds may not learn effectively in highly competitive situations or on nonsocial tasks. They may be uncomfortable with trial-and-error approaches and may not be interested in the fine details of certain concepts and materials.

Nondiscriminatory assessment requires that decisions be based on varied and accurate information. Building rapport with children before testing them; observing their behavior in school, home, and play settings; and consulting with their parents can help teachers and examiners become more aware of cultural differences and reduce the number of students inappropriately placed in special education programs. Paraprofessional personnel or volunteers who are familiar with a child's language and/or cultural background have proven to be valuable assistants in many testing situations (Mattes & Omark, 1984).

As J. R. Brown (1982) notes, limited use of language is not synonymous with limited intellectual ability: "Some culturally different children are virtually silent in the testing situation, and the examiner may need to listen to the child in play with other children to hear a representative sample of the child's language" (p. 170). Standardized tests in English are not likely to give an accurate picture of a child's abilities if he or she comes from a non-English-speaking home. "If the student's primary language is Spanish, Navajo, or Thai, the only justification for testing in English is to determine the student's facility in this second language" (Lewis & Doorlag, 1991, p. 361).

The IDEA specifies that assessment for the purpose of identifying and placing children with disabilities must be conducted in the child's native language. Figueroa, Fradd, and Correa (1989), however, point out a serious flaw in the way the law can be implemented:

> A curious and perhaps vicious anomaly exists between the law and its regulations. Whereas the actual legislation defines "native language" as the language of the home, . . . the regulations degenerate the intent of the law by defining "native language" as the language normally used by the child in school. Most bilingual children quickly acquire a conversational English that may not support academic development in English. For them, the regulations in P.L. 94–142 preclude any primary language support. As it has turned out, the act's brand of special education for Hispanic children from native language homes has perpetuated preexisting problems. (p. 175)*

Unfortunately, when an examiner does wish to use the child's native language, not many reliable tests are available in languages other than English, and translation or adaptation of tests into other languages poses certain problems (Cummins, 1989). Alzate (1978), for example, reviewed several studies of the performance of Spanish-

The law also requires that notice of IEP and placement meetings and other important conferences be given to parents in their native language.

---

*Excerpt by Figuero, R. A., Fradd, S.H., & Correa, V. I. (1989). "Bilingual special education and this special issue." *Exceptional Children*, 56, 174–178. Copyright (1989) by the Council for Exceptional Children. Reprinted by permission.

Assessment of children whose native language is not English must be handled with great skill and care.

speaking children on translated versions of English tests and concluded that translated tests are generally unreliable. DeAvila (1976) points out the great variety in language within Hispanic populations and notes that when Mexican American children were given a test in Spanish that was developed with a population of Puerto Rican children, they performed even more poorly than on an admittedly unfair English test. To illustrate the confusion that may result from inappropriate translations, DeAvila observes that a Spanish-speaking child may use any one of several words to describe a kite, depending on the family's country of origin: *cometa, huila, volantin, papalote,* or *chiringa.* Thus, although translation of tests and other materials into a child's native language may be helpful in many instances, care must be taken to avoid an improper translation that may actually do a disservice to the linguistically different child.

It is not always easy to distinguish between children whose learning and communication problems result from disabilities and those who are solely in need of instruction in English. The high number of language-minority students in special education classes, however, implies a need for tests and referral procedures that will "help teachers to distinguish differences from exceptionalities for language minority students" and to accommodate the differences in the least restrictive educational setting (Teacher Education Division, 1986, p. 25).

Bias and discrimination can also occur in the referral process, when children's records are reviewed and decisions are made about what type of services to provide. In the opinion of some educators, a child's race, family background, and economic circumstances—rather than actual performance and needs—unfairly influence the label he or she is likely to receive and the degree to which he or she will be removed from the regular classroom.

The prereferral process shown in Figure 3.4 was initially developed by Ortiz and Garcia (1988) as a means of making sure that curriculum and instruction are responsive to the linguistic and cultural needs of Hispanic students who are experiencing difficulty in the regular classroom *before* they are referred for formal assessment to determine special education placement. Although the model was presented in reference to Spanish-speaking students, it is a sound approach to helping improve the quality of regular education for any student who is experiencing academic difficulty. By systematically addressing the questions as illustrated in the model, both special and regular educators can work together to improve the student's performance in the mainstream classroom prior to movement to a more restrictive environment.

Ortiz (1991a, 1991b) further developed and evaluated the efficacy of the model addressing the issues of prereferral, assessment, and intervention of language-minority students. The *Assessment and Intervention Model for the Bilingual Exceptional Student* (AIM for the BESt) model is a comprehensive service delivery model that was pilot-tested in four elementary schools in central Texas. Two of the schools served as intervention sites; two served as comparison or control sites. The steps and features of the AIM for the BESt model are listed in Figure 3.5.

Culturally Responsive Curriculum and Instructional Methodology

Culturally responsive instructional practices enhance students' opportunities to reach their fullest potential. The need for a culturally responsive pedagogy is even

FIGURE 3.4

A prereferral process for preventing inappropriate placements of culturally diverse students in special education

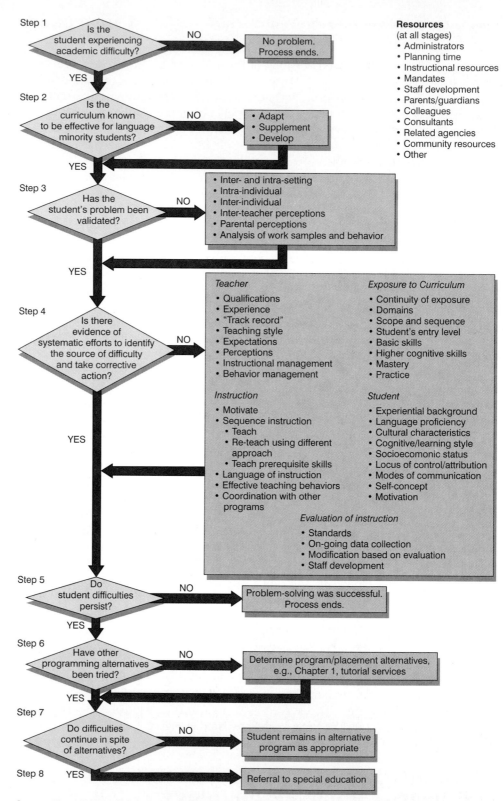

Step 1 — Is the student experiencing academic difficulty? — NO → No problem. Process ends.

YES

Step 2 — Is the curriculum known to be effective for language minority students? — NO → • Adapt • Supplement • Develop

YES

Step 3 — Has the student's problem been validated? — NO → • Inter- and intra-setting • Intra-individual • Inter-individual • Inter-teacher perceptions • Parental perceptions • Analysis of work samples and behavior

YES

Step 4 — Is there evidence of systematic efforts to identify the source of difficulty and take corrective action? — NO →

Teacher
• Qualifications
• Experience
• "Track record"
• Teaching style
• Expectations
• Perceptions
• Instructional management
• Behavior management

Instruction
• Motivate
• Sequence instruction
  • Teach
  • Re-teach using different approach
  • Teach prerequisite skills
• Language of instruction
• Effective teaching behaviors
• Coordination with other programs

Exposure to Curriculum
• Continuity of exposure
• Domains
• Scope and sequence
• Student's entry level
• Basic skills
• Higher cognitive skills
• Mastery
• Practice

Student
• Experiential background
• Language proficiency
• Cultural characteristics
• Cognitive/learning style
• Socioecomonic status
• Locus of control/attribution
• Modes of communication
• Self-concept
• Motivation

Evaluation of instruction
• Standards
• On-going data collection
• Modification based on evaluation
• Staff development

YES

Step 5 — Do student difficulties persist? — NO → Problem-solving was successful. Process ends.

YES

Step 6 — Have other programming alternatives been tried? — NO → Determine program/placement alternatives, e.g., Chapter 1, tutorial services

YES

Step 7 — Do difficulties continue in spite of alternatives? — NO → Student remains in alternative program as appropriate

Step 8 — YES → Referral to special education

Resources
(at all stages)
• Administrators
• Planning time
• Instructional resources
• Mandates
• Staff development
• Parents/guardians
• Colleagues
• Consultants
• Related agencies
• Community resources
• Other

Source: From "A Prereferral Process for Preventing Inappropriate Placements of Culturally Diverse Students in Special Education" by A. A. Ortiz & S. B. Garcia, in *Schools and the Culturally Diverse Exceptional Student: Promising Practices and Future Directions* (p. 9) by A. A. Ortiz and B. A. Ramirez (Eds.), 1988, Reston, VA: Council for Exceptional Children. Reprinted by permission.

more critical when referring to culturally diverse students with disabilities (Moll, 1992). As in virtually all cultures, the family plays a critical role in the early development and socialization of the ethnically different child. The culture of the home and the child's early experiences strongly influence the child's learning and behavioral style at school.

Although it is dangerous to make overgeneralizations of the learning styles of specific ethnic groups of students, some observations may assist special educators in understanding the relationship between culture and school success.

FIGURE 3.5
The AIM for the BESt model for culturally diverse students

The Assessment and Intervention Model for the Bilingual Exceptional Student (AIM for the BESt) describes a service delivery system designed to (a) improve the academic performance of limited English proficient (LEP) students in regular and special education programs, (b) reduce the inappropriate referral of LEP students to special education, and (c) ensure that assessment produces are nonbiased. AIM for the BESt consists of six major steps.

Step 1: The regular classroom teacher uses instructional strategies known to be effective for language-minority students.

The project staff trained general, bilingual, and special education teachers on using a reciprocal interaction approach to oral and written communication that emphasized higher-order thinking and problem solving. In particular, the teachers were introduced to the shared literature (Roser & Firth, 1983) and writing workshop approaches (Graves, 1983).

Step 2: When a student experiences difficulty, the teacher attempts to resolve the difficulty and validates the problem.

The project staff trained the teachers in diagnostic/prescriptive approaches that included sequencing instruction by (a) observing and analyzing student performance to design instructional programs, (b) implementing the program, (c) monitoring the progress, and (d) redesigning instruction as necessary.

Step 3: If the problem is not resolved, the teacher requests assistance from a school-based, problem-solving team.

The project staff, teachers, and support personnel formed cooperative teams to assist teachers with student-related problems by developing interventions and follow-up plans to resolve the difficulties.

Step 4: If the problem is not resolved by the school-based, problem-solving team, a special education referral is initiated.

The team's records describing the intervention plans from Step 3 accompanied the referral for special education services. The records were beneficial in assisting the referral team in designing appropriate evaluations and making recommendations.

Step 5: Assessment personnel incorporate informal assessment procedures into the comprehensive individual assessment.

Project staff trained personnel in using alternative assessment instruments and strategies to support standardized testing. In particular, curriculum-based assessment in both the native language and English were used with the students.

Step 6: If the child had a disability, special educators used instructional strategies known to be effective for language-minority students.

Special education teachers used the reciprocal interactive strategies for instruction. The holistic strategies described in Step 1 also included (a) encouraging expression of students' experiences, language background, and interests to foster success and pride and (b) peer collaboration and peer approval.

Source: From "Assessment and Intervention Model for the Bilingual Exceptional Student (AIM for the BESt)" by A. A. Ortiz and C. Y. Wilkinson (1991), *Teacher Education and Special Education, 14,* 35-42. Adapted by permission.

- Some African Americans believe that actions speak louder than words, that talk is cheap, and that Anglo Americans beguile each other with verbal discourse. Great importance is attached to people's nonverbal behavior; African Americans may spend much time observing others to see "where they are coming from" (Smith, 1981).
- Some African American students engage in conversation without making eye contact at all times. They may even take part in other activities while still paying attention to a conversation.
- The attitudes of some African American parents toward their children with disabilities may seem unfamiliar to non-Black professionals. They may be less inclined than Anglo Americans to blame or punish themselves or to feel guilty for their children's disabilities or behavior problems (Orlion, 1988).
- "Curriculum designed for [African American] students should be a combination of cognitive, affective, and action activities integrated into the subjects they are studying, and they should include a variety of data sources such as scholarly research, oral histories, personal experiences, and ethnic literature" (Gay, 1995, p. 49). African American students should be allowed to tell their own multiple stories in their own diverse voices and according to their own unique cultural styles and esthetics.
- Some Hispanic children are influenced by the patterns of *machismo* associated with males in the culture. Although the mainstream American culture has at times associated this pattern with physical aggressiveness and dominance over women, it actually implies the males' belief in dignity in conduct, respect for others, love for the family, and affection for children.
- Hispanic children typically are treasured and indulged with great amounts of personal and physical affection. They are not without responsibility, however, and this may take precedence over school or personal attainment.
- Hispanic children and families are likely to turn to members of the extended family when they need help, rather than rely on schools or agencies, which they regard as impersonal.
- Some Hispanic children are brought up to believe that contributing to and sacrificing for the benefit of the group is more important than personal aggrandizement. They may prefer to work in groups.
- Mexican American children often respond well to close personalized relationships with teachers.
- Native Americans tend to absorb children with disabilities into the family and community, rather than to segregate them. Non-Native American professionals, in fact, often experience difficulty in setting up programs to identify and serve children with disabilities on Indian reservations or in Native Alaskan communities (particularly if Native people are not involved in planning and carrying out the programs).
- A Native American child may convey attention and respect by avoiding direct eye contact while listening.
- Social and academic competition among Native American children may lead to problems. Activities for some students should emphasize cooperative approaches to problems and de-emphasize competition among peers (Sisk, 1987).
- Asian American students with disabilities are a sizable, growing population but may be hard to identify because cultural attitudes toward disability and achievement. Asian Americans often deal with exceptionality within the family, rather than seek outside services.

Teachers are most effective when curriculum content and instructional methods are responsive to the cultural, ethnic, and linguistic diversity among their students.

- For some Asian American groups, education is highly valued and is viewed as a means of upward mobility. Parents influenced by their traditional cultural heritage believe that no sacrifice is too great to obtain a good education for their children. From the child's viewpoint, scholastic achievement is the highest tribute one could bring to his or her parents and family (Leung, 1988).
- Some educators are concerned, however, that a stereotype of Asian American students as hard-working, successful, and without problems has given them a "success image" that makes it difficult for many to believe that any Asian American student may need special education services (Kim & Harh, 1983; Yee, 1988).
- Some Asian American students may find it difficult to speak of their own accomplishments, to ask or answer questions in class, or to voluntarily express opinions, lest they appear to be showing off. Also, "personal matters that embarrass or cause hurt or stress are not usually discussed with anyone except family and very close friends" (Brower, 1983, p. 114).
- Migrant children, many of whom are from culturally diverse backgrounds, are likely to require special instructional programs.
- Migrant children sometimes speak *pocho,* a mixture of English and Spanish. The teacher should encourage communication by listening first and then modeling standard speech patterns for the child (King-Stoops, 1980).
- Migrant children often have low levels of self-esteem. It is understandable that the mobility, poverty, and other conditions inherent in the migrant lifestyle often adversely affect self-concept development. Teachers should encourage students to share their experiences and travels with other students (Salend, 1990).

Culturally and linguistically diverse students come to school with rich and complex cultural backgrounds that may be influenced by the family, home, and local community. Culturally responsive educators struggle with the balance between accepting and respecting the unique characteristics of students from diverse backgrounds and preparing them for postschool environments in the mainstream American culture. In fact, Brower (1983) suggests that culturally and linguistically diverse students may

See "Refugee Children from Vietnam: Adjusting to American Schools" later in this chapter.

The Migrant Student Record Transfer System (MSRTS) is headquartered in Little Rock, Arkansas. See "For More Information" at the end of this chapter for other organizations that provide educational programming and assistance to migrant students.

need to be taught about American expectations and values so that they can become more forthright and assertive in educational and employment situations.

The first place to begin to prepare students for the "real" world is the classroom. Teachers can begin to balance respect for one's culture and preparedness for postschool settings by accommodating and adapting their instructional programs and curricula and by adopting a culturally responsive pedagogy. Correa, Blanes-Reyes, and Rapport (1995) outline the characteristics of a culturally responsive pedagogy:

1. *Context-embedded instruction.* Context-embedded instruction facilitates the development of responsive classroom environments for all children by providing meaningful content that is culturally responsive and that uses students' experiences as tools for building further knowledge (Baca & Cervantes, 1989; Bennett, 1990; Cummins, 1989; Scarcella, 1990).

2. *Content-rich curriculum.* Researchers have shown that students who receive instruction within a content-rich curriculum develop a positive attitude about learning, a heightened self-concept, and pride in their culture (Duran, 1988; Scarcella, 1990). In addition, a positive vision of culturally and linguistically diverse students by the classroom teacher is essential for an appropriate education (Moll, 1992). Teachers who were convinced that these children from culturally and linguistically diverse backgrounds were competent and capable of learning in an innovative and intellectually challenging curriculum reported higher levels of student achievement.

3. *Equitable pedagogy.* An equitable pedagogy, which varies according to students' needs and teachers' styles, focuses on providing an appropriate educational experience for all children regardless of their disability or ethnolinguistic background. Instructional practices that facilitate and promote academic success among students within a pluralistic and democratic setting allow students to develop positive ethnic and national identifications (Villegas, 1988). In fact, Banks (1994a) advocates for a "*transformative curriculum* that challenges the basic assumptions and implicit values of the Eurocentric, male-dominated curriculum institutionalized in U.S. schools, colleges, and universities. It helps students to view concepts, events, and situations from diverse racial, ethnic, gender, and social-class perspectives. The transformative curriculum also helps students to construct their own interpretations of the past, present, and future" (p. 103).

> Siccone (1995) provides an excellent book that contains more than 75 multicultural activities to enhance self-worth, self-respect, and self-confidence in K-8 students.

Cooperative learning activities provide an excellent way for children to experience and acquire respect for those who are different from themselves.

4. *Interactive and experiential teaching.* Interactive and experiential teaching approaches have been reported by researchers to promote feelings of responsibility, self-pride, and belongingness in diverse learners (Obiakor, Algozzine, & Ford, 1993; Voltz & Damiano-Lantz, 1993). This hands-on approach empowers learners as they share the responsibility for the learning process while teachers provide guidance in the construction of knowledge.

5. *Classroom materials and school environment.* Classroom materials and school environment should reflect students' diverse backgrounds (Freeman & Freeman, 1993). Materials that are selected on the basis of their relevance to the content and their significance to the student generate a more meaningful and student-centered learning experience.

Expanding the teaching strategies that special educators use in serving students with various abilities is critical as more students from diverse backgrounds enter our schools. Although special educators are usually familiar with behavioral teaching approaches, incorporating more constructivist approaches may be necessary for students from culturally and linguistically diverse backgrounds. Matching the learning styles and individualizing teaching for all students are primary goals in special education.

Putnam (1993) supports cooperative learning strategies for educating students from diverse backgrounds: "Our belief is that cooperative learning, to be used most effectively, should be applied at all levels of the educational ecosystem, including cooperative groups of learners, cooperation and teaming among teachers, and cooperation with families and the broader community" (p. 12).

Bilingual Special Education

The National Center for Educational Statistics estimated that in 1980 there were more than 30 million people in the United States whose first language was not English. Today, it is likely that there are more than 8 million school-age children with *limited English proficiency* (LEP) because their first language is not English (Grossman, 1995). Bilingual or language-minority children have "been exposed to two languages in natural speaking contexts [and] come from homes where they have made functional use of a language other than that of the dominant culture during interactions with one or more family members" (Mattes & Omark, 1984, p. 2). Some school districts offer programs of *bilingual education*—the use of two languages as media of instruction for a student or a group of students. Bilingual education programs have as their primary goal "for the LEP student to function effectively in both the native language and English. The student's native language and culture are taught concurrently with English and the dominant culture. The student actually becomes bilingual and bicultural in the process, with neither language surfacing as the dominant one" (Gollnick & Chinn, 1994, p. 242).

For students who are both linguistically different and disabled, their attempts to succeed in school are especially challenging. Not only must they work to overcome the difficulties posed by their disability, but they also must do so in an environment in which instruction takes place in a foreign language and opportunities to use their native language are too infrequent. For these children, a program of bilingual special education may be needed. Baca and Cervantes (1989) define **bilingual special education** as

Refugee Children from Vietnam

Adjusting to American Schools

Tam Thi Dang Wei is a school psychologist who is Vietnamese. Wei points out that many Vietnamese refugee children encounter emotional, social, and educational problems in the United States because of different cultural traditions and expectations. The following incidents illustrate some cross-cultural difficulties that have arisen as Vietnamese students and American schools adjust to each other. Wei interprets each incident.

Incident: A Vietnamese girl in the 10th grade in Missouri reportedly refused to go to her gym class. When asked for a valid reason by the gym teacher, she simply said she did not like gym. Only much later did the real reason appear. The girl revealed to a Vietnamese friend that she objected to being seen bare-legged, wearing gym shorts.

Interpretation: Coming from a region of Vietnam where old customs and traditions were still strong and where women, both young and old, were never to be seen bare-legged, this girl confessed to an intense feeling of discomfort when the gym hour occurred. To provide a sense of measure to this interesting case, however, we must also mention the case of two Vietnamese high school girls, one in Georgia and the other in Maryland, who were drum majorettes for their respective high school bands.

Incident: An 8-year-old Vietnamese boy in an elementary school in Maryland complained of a stomachache every day after lunch. His teacher was mystified because the same food and milk did not make any other child in the class sick. The cause was later identified to be the fresh milk, which was perfectly good, but to which the boy's digestive system was not accustomed.

Interpretation: Food habits are different from one culture to the next. Rice is a staple in the Vietnamese diet, whereas bread is a staple in the American diet. Pork is preferred to beef by most Vietnamese; the reverse is true in the United States. Fresh milk is likely to give some Vietnamese an upset stomach. They are used to boiled rather than homogenized milk, and their bodies are said not to produce the necessary enzyme to digest fresh milk.

Incident: A teacher thought his Vietnamese student had an auditory discrimination problem. He found out later that some sounds in the English language do not exist in the Vietnamese language. The student simply could not hear them and thus could not pronounce them correctly. Another teacher was surprised to see a Vietnamese child color pictures of eggs brown and cows yellow. The surprise turned into laughter when a Vietnamese friend told the teacher that Vietnamese eggs are brown in color and that there are more yellow cows in Vietnam than black or brown cows.

Interpretation: The language problem is still a major handicap for students. It is complicated further by the cultural trait of face-saving, which affects the pride and self-esteem of the Vietnamese and causes them frustration and a loss of motivation. It is important that American teachers understand the consequence of failure for these students.

Refugee children are a unique challenge for educators not only because they can be misdiagnosed, misclassified, or misunderstood but also because they may not receive appropriate services when they indeed have disabling conditions. ✹

From "The Vietnamese Refugee Child: Understanding Cultural Differences" by T. T. D. Wei in *The Bilingual Exceptional Child* (pp. 197-212) by D. R. Omark and J. G. Erickson (Eds.), 1983, San Diego: College-Hill. Adapted by permission.

the use of the home language and the home culture along with English in an individually designed program of special instruction for the student. Bilingual special education considers the child's language and culture as foundations upon which an appropriate education may be built. The primary purpose of bilingual special education is to help each individual student achieve a maximum potential for learning. (p. 18)

In response to the objection to bilingual special education on the basis that it is too much to ask special educators, who already face the difficult task of teaching basic skills to a child with a disability, to do so in a second language, Baca and Cervantes (1989) reply that just the opposite is true:

The imparting of basic skills may be facilitated considerably if one understands that the child's culture and language are the foundations upon which an appropriate edu-

cation may be built. . . . In short, building on children's acquired repertoires is fundamental to sound educational practice. The English language and Anglo cultural skills
are actually the additional materials. (p. 18)

Most bilingual education programs usually emphasize either a *transitional* or a
maintenance approach. In a transitional program, the student's first language and
culture are used only to the extent necessary to function in the school until English
is mastered sufficiently for all instruction. Transitional programs are an assimilationist
approach in which the LEP student is expected to learn to function in English as
soon as possible (Gollnick & Chinn, 1994). The home language is used only to help
the student make the transition to English. The native language is gradually faded
out as the student learns to speak English.

The maintenance approach to bilingual education, however, helps the LEP student function in both the native language and English, encouraging the student to
become bilingual and bicultural in the process. Cummins (1989) stresses the importance of encouraging children to develop their first-language skills (L1). He cites several studies suggesting that a major predictor of academic success for linguistically
different students is the extent to which their native language and culture are incorporated into the school program. Cummins states that even where programs of bilingual education are not offered, school staff can encourage and promote children's
skills and pride in their first language.

Although most bilingual educators support the maintenance approach to bilingual education, the majority of programs in existence are transitional (Gollnick &
Chinn, 1994). In fact, all state and federal laws providing support for bilingual education favor only transitional models. But, as Baca and Cervantes (1989) point out, the
laws do not prevent school districts from offering maintenance programs if their staff
desire to do so.

A *restoration* model of bilingual education seeks to restore the students'
ancestral language and cultural heritage that have been lost or diminished through
cultural assimilation. *Enrichment* programs of bilingual education are designed to
teach a new language and cultural ways to a group of monolingual students; for
example, some school districts now offer language "immersion schools" in which all
or most instruction is provided in a second language (Spanish and French are the
most common).

Educators disagree about the most effective methods for teaching bilingual students. Former U.S. Secretary of Education William J. Bennett (1986) wrote that some
children "come from families who encourage their acquisition of English; some run
in peer groups where the native language is a matter of pride. Some arrive speaking
languages from which the transition to English is relatively easy; others speak languages whose entire structure is perplexingly different from ours" (p. 62). Bennett
maintains that the choice of specific methods to teach bilingual children should be a
local decision, but he argues strongly that "all American children need to learn to
speak, read, and write English as soon as possible" (p. 62). Some professionals and
legislators have called for designating English as the exclusive official language of the
United States. Adopting such a policy, however, probably would discourage schools
from offering instruction in students' native languages.

Conversely, the English Plus group advocates for linguistic pluralism and
encourages educational programs to offer opportunities to learn a second language
and develop cultural sensitivity (National Council for Languages and International
Studies, 1992). Banks (1994b) observes that the nation's language policies and prac-

Figure 3.6 lists several
specific strategies by
which school staff can
create a climate for pro-
moting children's use
of their first language
(L1).

FIGURE 3.6

Strategies for encouraging children to develop proficiency in their first language (L1)

- Reflect the various cultural groups in the school district by providing signs in the main office and elsewhere that welcome people in the different languages of the community.
- Encourage students to use their L1 around the school.
- Provide opportunities for students from the same ethnic group to communicate with one another in their L1.
- Recruit people who can tutor students in their L1.
- Provide books written in the various languages in the classroom and in the school library.
- Incorporate greetings and information in the various languages in newsletters and other school communications.
- Provide bilingual and multilingual signs.
- Display pictures and objects of the various cultures in the school.
- Create study units that incorporate the students' L1.
- Encourage students to write contributions in their L1 for school newspapers and magazines.
- Provide opportunities for students to study their L1 in elective subjects and in extracurricular clubs.
- Encourage parents to help in the classroom, library, playground, and in clubs.
- Invite second-language learners to use their L1 during assemblies and other official school functions.
- Invite people from ethnic minority communities to act as resource people and to speak to students in both formal and informal settings.

Source: From *New Voices: Second Language Learning and Teaching: A Handbook for Primary Teachers* by New Zealand Department of Education, 1988, Wellington; cited in "A Theoretical Framework for Bilingual Special Education" by J. Cummins, 1989, *Exceptional Children, 56,* p. 113-114.

tices are at a crossroads and exemplify the second-language ambivalence held by people in the United States.

Research in bilingual education has not provided clear guidelines to methodology. There is general agreement, however, that children acquire English most effectively through interactions with teachers, parents, and peers. A child who engages in and talks about interesting experiences will be more likely to develop good English skills than a child who is limited to classroom instruction and teacher correction of errors. Efforts should be made to give bilingual exceptional children a wide variety of opportunities to explore the world through language. Briggs (1991) recommends that teachers use the following strategies for getting their "point across" when working with limited-English-proficient students:

- Use gestures.
- Use visuals.
- Write down important information.
- Check frequently for understanding.

- Actively involve students.
- Use cooperative learning and other types of pair and group work.
- Focus on communication.
- Discuss learning strategies.
- Use students' experiences and interests.
- Have varied ways of assessing your students.
- Make sure you and your students are organized.
- Allow more time for reaction.
- Use the students' primary language.
- Use notes and tapes.
- Give the students as much support as you can in class. (pp. 11-14)

✳ *In Closing: How Many Different Teaching Approaches Are Needed?*

How does one integrate the vast amount of information on culturally and linguistically diverse students and their families to serve them effectively? To return to the question posed earlier: Does a teacher with students from four cultural backgrounds need four methods of teaching? The answer is both no and yes. For the first answer, systematic instructional procedures apply to children of all cultural backgrounds. For the most part, good teaching is good teaching. Indeed, when students with disabilities have the additional special need of adjusting to a new or different culture or language, it is even more important for the teacher to plan individualized activities, convey expectations clearly, observe and record behavior precisely, and give the child specific, immediate reinforcement and feedback in response to performance. These procedures, coupled with a helpful and friendly attitude, will increase the culturally different child's motivation and achievement in school. But the systematic teacher, by definition, is responsive to changes (or lack of change) in individual students' performance. So it can also be argued that the effective teacher needs as many different ways of teaching as there are students in the classroom—regardless of cultural backgrounds.

This argument is basically true. But it also begs the real question of how cultural and language differences affect a child's *responsiveness* to instruction and, hence, whether those effects warrant different approaches to teaching. So although the basic methods of systematic instruction remain the same, teachers who will be most effective in helping children with disabilities from culturally diverse backgrounds to achieve will be those who are sensitive to and respectful of their students' heritage and values. A teacher does not have to share her students' culture and native language to serve them effectively, but a teacher will likely be quite ineffective in helping her students achieve in the classroom if she ignores those differences.

The teacher of culturally diverse children with disabilities should adopt a flexible teaching style, establish a positive climate for learning, and use a variety of approaches to meet individual student needs. With a caring attitude, careful assessment and observation of behavior, and the use of appropriate materials and community resources, the teacher can do a great deal to help culturally and linguistically diverse children with disabilities and their families experience success in school.

Summary

Reasons for Concern

- Although cultural diversity is a strength of our society, many students with disabilities still experience discrimination because of cultural, social class, or other differences from the majority. Educators must avoid stereotypes based on race or culture.

- Students who are members of culturally diverse groups are typically underrepresented in gifted programs and overrepresented in special education.

Culture, Cultural Pluralism, and Multicultural Education

- Special educators should be aware of each child's cultural background in evaluating classroom behavior.

- Multicultural education actualizes cultural pluralism.

- As is the case with regular education, the special educator must remember that, within each cultural group, students remain heterogeneous.

Initial Steps in Becoming Culturally Competent

- It is necessary for educators to become culturally self-aware prior to becoming responsive to students and families from diverse backgrounds.

- Teacher education programs should include curriculum and field-based experiences related to teaching culturally diverse students.

- Understanding family values and beliefs about education, disabilities, and school involvement informs teachers about their diverse students.

Understanding the Educational Needs of Culturally Diverse Students with Disabilities

- Assessment of students for placement in special education should be fair; referral should be based on each child's needs, rather than on background.

- Multicultural approaches to curriculum include an equitable pedagogy that matches the student's learning style and the teacher's teaching styles and focus on providing an appropriate educational experience for all children regardless of their disability or ethnolinguistic background.

- Cooperative learning has been an effective strategy for students from diverse backgrounds.

Bilingual Special Education

- Bilingual special education uses the child's home language (L1) and home culture along with English (L2) in an individually designed education program.

- Most bilingual special education programs take either a transitional or a maintenance approach.

How Many Different Teaching Approaches Are Needed?

- Regardless of their cultural background, all children benefit from good, systematic instruction.

- The teacher must be sensitive, however, to the extent to which cultural and language differences affect a child's responsiveness to instruction.

For More Information

Journals

Equity and Choice. Published in cooperation with the Institute for Responsive Education and Center on Families, Communities, and Children's Learning by Corwin Press.

Multicultural Education. Published by the National Association for Multicultural Education by Caddo Gap Press, 3145 Geary Boulevard, Suite 275, San Francisco, CA 94118.

Teaching Tolerance. Published by the Southern Poverty Law Center, 400 Washington Avenue, Montgomery, AL 36104.

Books

Baca, L. M., & Cervantes, H. T. (1989). *The bilingual special education interface* (2nd ed.). New York: Merrill/Macmillan.

Banks, J. A. (1994a). *An introduction to multicultural education.* Needham Heights, MA: Allyn & Bacon.

Banks, J. A. (1994b). *Multiethnic education: Theory and practice* (3rd ed.). Needham Heights, MA: Allyn & Bacon.

Banks, J. A., & Banks, C. A. M. (Eds.). (1996). *Multicultural education: Issues and perspectives* (3rd ed.). Boston, MA: Allyn & Bacon

Cheng, L. L. (1987). *Assessing Asian language performance.* Rockville, MD: Aspen.

Council on Interracial Books for Children. (1984). *Guidelines for selecting bias-free textbooks and story books.* New York: Author.

Cusher, K., McClelland, A., & Safford, P. (1992). *Human diversity in education.* New York: McGraw-Hill.

Derman-Sparks, L., & The A.B.C. Task Force. (1989). *Antibias curriculum: tools for empowering young children.* Washington, DC: National Association for the Education of Young Children.

Fradd, S. H., & Tikunoff, W. J. (Eds.). (1987). *Bilingual education and bilingual special education: A guide for administrators.* Boston: Little, Brown.

Gollnick, D. M., & Chinn, P. C. (1994). *Multicultural education in a pluralistic society* (4th ed.). New York: Macmillan.

Grant, C. A. (1995). *Educating for diversity: An anthology of multicultural voices.* Needham Heights, MA: Allyn & Bacon.

Kitano, M. K., & Chinn, P. C. (Eds.). (1986). *Exceptional Asian children and youth.* Reston, VA: Council for Exceptional Children.

Mattes, L. J., & Omark, D. R. (1984). *Speech and language assessment for the bilingual handicapped.* San Diego: College-Hill.

Ortiz, A. A., & Ramirez, B. A. (Eds.). (1988). *Schools and the culturally diverse exceptional student: Promising practices and future directions.* Reston, VA: Council for Exceptional Children.

Putnam, J. W. (1993). *Cooperative learning and strategies for inclusion: Celebrating diversity in the classroom.* Baltimore: Paul H. Brookes.

Siccone, F. (1995). *Celebrating diversity: Building self-esteem in today's multicultural classrooms.* Needham Heights, MA: Allyn & Bacon.

Tiedt, P. L., & Tiedt, I. M. (1906). *Multicultural teaching: A handbook of activities, information, and resources* (2nd ed.). Needham Heights, MA: Allyn & Bacon.

Willig, A. C., & Greenberg, H. F. (1986). *Bilingualism and learning disabilities: Policy and practice for teachers and administrators.* New York: American Library.

Organizations

BUENO Center for Multicultural Education, College of Education, University of Colorado, Boulder, CO 80309-0249 (Leonard Baca, Director). Conducts research, implements pre- and inservice teacher training programs, and disseminates information about multicultural education through various publications.

Division for Culturally and Linguistically Diverse Exceptional Learners (DDEL), Council for Exceptional Children, 1920 Association Drive, Reston, VA 22091. One of the newest divisions of CEC, publishes the biannual *DDEL Newsletter* and an annual monograph on the needs of culturally diverse exceptional children.

ERIC Clearinghouse on Rural Education and Small Schools, New Mexico State University, Las Cruces, NM 88004. Publishes a directory of organizations and programs involved in the education of migrant students.

Interstate Migrant Education Council, Education Commission of the States, 1860 Lincoln Street, Denver, CO 80203. Acts as a forum for the development of policy issues and information dissemination about migrant education.

Joint National Committee for Languages (JNCL) supports efforts to facilitate laws that will provide funds for second-language education programs.

Migrant Student Record Transfer System (MSRTS), a nationwide computerized transcript and health record service for migrant students; it is located in Little Rock, Arkansas.

National Association of Multicultural Education. Caddo Gap Press, 3145 Geary Boulevard, Suite 275, San Francisco, CA 94118. (415) 750-9978.

National Association of State Directors of Migrant Education, 200 West Baltimore Street, Baltimore, MD 21201. Provides information for teachers and parents about delivery of services to migrant students.

Teachers of English to Speakers of Other Languages (TESOL). 1600 Camron Street, Suite 300, Alexandria, VA 22513-2751 (703) 830-0774.

Students with
Exceptional Educational Needs

Students with Mental Retardation

* Why has the definition of mental retardation changed so much over the years?

* What is most important in determining a person's level of adaptive functioning: intellectual capability or a supportive environment?

* How and why is mental retardation a socially defined phenomenon?

* What should a curriculum for students with mental retardation emphasize?

* How do environmental supports and the principle of normalization interact to influence adaptive behavior in the community?

Most people have some notion of what mental retardation is and what people with mental retardation must be like. Unfortunately, although there is considerable and growing public awareness of mental retardation, much of that awareness still consists of misconceptions and oversimplifications. In this chapter, we examine some key factors in understanding the very complex concept known as mental retardation. We also describe some contemporary teaching methods and service delivery practices that are helping improve the quality of life for individuals with mental retardation.

Mental retardation is the oldest "field" within special education in the United States. The first public school special education programs began in 1896 with classes for children with mental retardation. Of course, things have changed a great deal since then. During the past 25 years, especially, we have witnessed significant improvements in the education and treatment of children and adults with retarded development. After more than a century of virtually complete exclusion and segregation from everyday society, people with mental retardation are beginning to experience some of the benefits and responsibilities of participation in the mainstream.

✳ *Defining Mental Retardation: Emphasizing Measured Intelligence*

Numerous definitions of mental retardation have been proposed, debated, revised, and counterproposed over the years. Because mental retardation is a concept that affects and is affected by people in many different disciplines, it has been defined from many different perspectives. Because physicians were the first professional group to work with people with mental retardation, it is not surprising that most early definitions emphasized biological or medical criteria. A definition used by a professional within a given discipline may be functional only from the perspective of that particular field. Although a definition of mental retardation based on biological or medical criteria may be useful to physicians, a medically oriented definition may be of little value to the teacher or psychologist.

Why is the diagnosis of mental retardation so important? Some children and adults are so clearly deficient in academic, social, and self-care skills that it is obvious to anyone who interacts with them that they require special services and educational programming. For these individuals, how mental retardation is defined is not much of an issue; they experience pervasive and substantial deficits in all or most areas of development and functioning. But this group comprises only a small portion of the total population of persons with mental retardation. The largest segment consists of school-age children with mild retardation. Thus, how mental retardation is defined determines what special educational services many thousands of children are eligible (or ineligible) to receive.

As MacMillan (1982) notes, disagreements among professionals over what constitutes mental retardation are "not merely academic exercises in semantics" (p. 35). A subtle difference between two definitions can determine whether the label mental retardation is associated with a particular child. The critical importance of definitions was recognized as early as 1924 when Kuhlman noted that "definitions of mental deficiency are used to decide the fate of thousands every year" (n.p.).

We will examine how and why the definition of mental retardation has evolved over the years and some of the effects of those changes. First, we will look at the earliest definitions of mental retardation based primarily on the concept of the degree of inherited intelligence. Following a discussion of how intelligence is measured and how the results can be used to classify individuals with mental retardation, we will examine the most recent definition of mental retardation—a definition intended to change the way people think about mental retardation, away from deficits within the individual toward the environment and the kinds and levels of supports needed in order for the individual to function effectively.

The term *mental retardation* is, above all, a label used to identify an observed performance deficit—failure to demonstrate age-appropriate intellectual and social behavior. Mental retardation describes performance; it is not a "thing" a person is born with or possesses.

Early Definitions

In early times, the term *idiocy* (derived from a Greek word meaning "people who did not hold public office" [MacMillan, 1982, p. 38]) was used to identify persons with severe deficits in cognitive functioning or personal competence. In the 19th century, the label *imbecile* (derived from the Latin word for "weak and feeble") indicated a less severe degree of mental retardation. In 1900, Ireland defined the two terms this way:

> Idiocy is mental deficiency, or extreme stupidity, depending upon malnutrition or disease of the nervous centers, occurring either before birth or before the evolution of mental faculties in childhood. The word imbecility is generally used to denote a less decided degree of mental incapacity. (p. 1)

The term *simpleton* eventually was added to refer to persons with mild mental retardation (Clausen, 1967).

The two definitions most widely used during the first half of this century were written by Tredgold and Doll. Tredgold's (1937) reads:

> A state of incomplete mental development of such a kind and degree that the individual is incapable of adapting himself to the normal environment of his fellows in such a way to maintain existence independently of supervision, control, or external support. (p. 4)

In 1941 Doll suggested six criteria essential to the definition and concept of mental retardation: (1) social incompetence, (2) due to mental subnormality, (3) which has been developmentally arrested, (4) which obtains at maturity, (5) is of constitutional origin, and (6) is essentially incurable" (p. 215).

The AAMR's IQ-Based Definition

In 1959 the American Association on Mental Retardation (AAMR) published its first manual on terminology and classification of mental retardation that included a definition; that definition was revised slightly in 1961 to read:

> Mental retardation refers to subaverage general intellectual functioning which originates during the developmental period and is associated with impairment in adaptive behavior. (Heber, 1961, p. 3)

AAMR is an international organization of professionals—in education, medicine, psychology, social work, speech pathology, and so forth—as well as students, parents, and others concerned with the study, treatment, and prevention of mental retardation. Its more than 9,000 members are from 55 countries.

The 1973 definition of mental retardation was incorporated into the IDEA and serves today as the basis by which many states identify children under the disability category of mental retardation.

In 1973 the AAMR made two major changes in the definition of mental retardation. That definition, with minor rewording, was retained in the organization's 1983 manual on terminology:

> Mental retardation refers to significantly subaverage general intellectual functioning resulting in or associated with deficits in adaptive behavior, and manifested during the developmental period. (Grossman, 1983, p. 11)

At first glance, the two definitions may appear the same: They use the same terminology and similar word order. There are, however, important differences. First, according to the 1961 definition, mental retardation is equated with "subaverage general intellectual functioning" *associated with* adaptive behavior impairments. According to the revised definition, however, an individual must be well below average in both intellectual functioning *and* adaptive behavior; that is, intellectual functioning is no longer the sole defining criterion. A second important change is the degree of subaverage intellectual functioning that must be demonstrated before mental retardation is diagnosed. The word *significantly* in the 1973/1983 definition refers to a score of two or more standard deviations below the mean on a standardized intelligence test; the 1961 definition required a score of only one standard deviation below the mean. This change eliminated the category of *borderline* mental retardation. A third change, although not as important as the first two, extended the developmental period from 16 years to 18 years, to coincide with the usual span of public schooling. The definition specifies that the deficits in intellectual functioning and adaptive behavior must occur during the developmental period to help distinguish mental retardation from other disabilities (e.g., impaired performance by an adult due to head injury).

Which girl has mental retardation? The term mental retardation *identifies substantial limitations in present functioning; it is not something inherent within the individual. People with mental retardation also possess strengths and positive attributes.*

Measurement of Intellectual Functioning

Intellectual functioning is most often measured by a standardized intelligence (IQ) test. An IQ test consists of a series of questions and problem-solving tasks assumed to require certain amounts of intelligence to answer or solve correctly. Although an IQ test samples only a small portion of the full range of an individual's skills and abilities, the test taker's performance on those items is used to derive a score representing his or her overall intelligence.

A *standardized* test consists of the same questions and tasks always presented in a certain, specified way, with the same scoring procedures used each time the test is administered. An IQ test has also been *normed;* that is, it has been administered to a large sample of people selected at random from the population for whom the test is intended. Test scores of the people in the random sample are then used as norms, or averages of how people generally perform on the test. On the two most widely used intelligence tests, the *Stanford-Binet Intelligence Scale* (Thorndike, Hagen, & Sattler, 1986) and the revised *Wechsler Intelligence Scale for Children— Revised* (WISC-R) (Wechsler, 1974), the norm or average score is 100. The test taker's age is considered when computing an IQ. For example, to obtain a score of 100, a 5-year-old child must respond correctly to those questions and tasks most 5-year-olds get right. A 16-year-old who responds correctly to only those test items the average 5-year-old gets right would receive a score much lower than 100.

Standard deviation is a mathematical concept. It refers to the amount by which a particular score on a given test varies from the mean, or average score, of all the scores in the norm sample. (See Figure 4.1 for further information about standard deviation.) One standard deviation on the Stanford-Binet is 16 points; on the WISC-R, 15 points. (The difference stems from the difference in the distribution of scores obtained from the samples of children used to derive the norms for the two tests.) Thus, according to the AAMR's first definition, a diagnosis of mental retardation could be determined on the basis of an IQ score as high as 84 or 85, depending on the test used. The subsequent AAMR definition of mental retardation requires an IQ score at least two standard deviations below the mean, which is 68 or 70 on the two tests.

Many professionals supported the shift to a more conservative definition of mental retardation requiring a score of at least two standard deviations (approximately 70 or less) below the mean on an IQ test. Listed here are some of their reasons:

1. *The mental retardation label can be stigmatizing.* Some educators believe that when a child receives the official label *mental retardation,* the damage done by the label itself outweighs any positive effects of special education and treatment that result from the label. Although recent studies have shown that children and adults continue to hold negative misconceptions about mental retardation (e.g., Antonak, Fiedler, & Mulick, 1989; Goodman, 1989), research on whether the label itself is responsible for negative stereotyping has yielded mixed results (MacMillan, Jones, & Aloia, 1974; Rowitz, 1981).

2. *Intelligence tests can be culturally biased.* Both the Binet and Wechsler IQ tests have been heavily criticized for being culturally biased. The tests tend to favor children from the population on which they were normed—primarily White, middle-class children. Some of the questions on an IQ test may tap learning that only a mid-

Traditional methods of standardized assessment do not allow the examiner to give prompts or cues or to interact in any way that might "teach" the child how to respond correctly during the test itself. Some psychologists and educators believe that such strict testing methods do not reveal the child's true learning potential. They recommend an alternative approach to assessment called *dynamic assessment* in which the examiner uses various forms of "guided learning" activities to determine the child's potential for change. To learn more about dynamic assessment, see Jitendra and Kameenui (1993).

Wilson (1992) described the fourth edition of the Stanford-Binet IQ (Thorndike et al., 1986) as a "model of standardized test construction" that should be useful with most school-age children (p. 84). However, when assessing children under the age of 5 who are thought to have mild mental retardation or with anyone thought to have severe mental retardation, he recommends using Form L-M, an earlier edition of the test (Terman & Merrill, 1973).

FIGURE 4.1

IQ scores seem to be distributed throughout the population according to a phenomenon called the *normal curve,* shown here. To describe how one particular score varies from the mean (average score), the population is broken into units called standard deviations. Each standard deviation includes a fixed portion of the population. Theoretically, 34.13% of the population will fall within one standard deviation above the mean, and another 34.13% will be within one standard deviation below "normal." By applying an algebraic formula to the scores achieved by the norm sample on a test, it can be determined what value equals one standard deviation for that test. A person's IQ test score can then be described in terms of how many standard deviations above or below the mean it is. About 2.3% of the population falls two or more standard deviations below the mean, which the AAMR calls "significantly subaverage." Therefore, about 2.3% of the population would be identified if IQ scores were the sole criterion for diagnosing mental retardation.

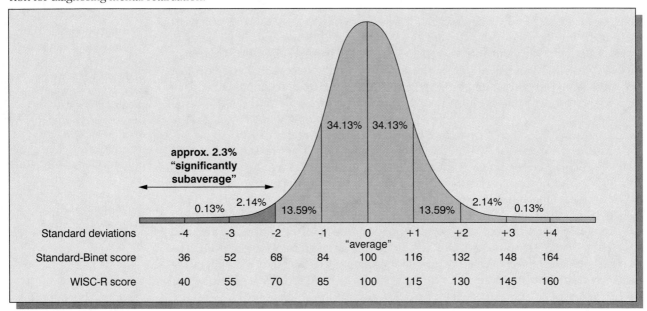

	-4	-3	-2	-1	0 "average"	+1	+2	+3	+4
Standard deviations	-4	-3	-2	-1	0	+1	+2	+3	+4
Standard-Binet score	36	52	68	84	100	116	132	148	164
WISC-R score	40	55	70	85	100	115	130	145	160

A possible negative outcome of being labeled as mentally retarded is that peers may be more likely to avoid or ridicule the child. To find out what two young researchers did to improve children's attitudes about people with mental retardation, read A. Turnbull and Bronicki (1986) and K. Turnbull and Bronicki (1989).

dle-class child is likely to have experienced. Both tests, which are highly verbal, are especially inappropriate for children for whom English is a second language. Mercer (1973a) points out that when an IQ test is used to identify children for special class placement, many more African American, Hispanic, and poor children are identified than are White, middle-class children.

3. *IQ scores can change significantly.* Several studies have shown that IQ scores can change, particularly in the 70–85 range that formerly constituted borderline retardation (MacMillan, 1982). Because of the misconception that mental retardation is a permanent condition even though it is intended to describe only present deficits in performance, there is hesitancy to use the label *mental retardation* on the basis of a test score that might increase by as many as 15 to 20 points after a period of effective instruction.

4. *Intelligence testing is not an exact science.* Even though the major intelligence tests are among the most carefully developed and standardized of all psychological tests, they are still far from perfect. Among the many variables that can affect

an individual's IQ score are motivation, the time and location of the test, and inconsistency or bias on the test giver's part in scoring responses that are not precisely covered by the test manual. Even the choice of which test to use can be critical. For example, Wechsler (1974) reports that the WISC-R and the revised Stanford-Binet correlate with each other at about the 0.70 level. This means that it is possible for a child's performance on one test to fall in the range defined by mental retardation but not if the other test is used.

When the upper IQ limit was reduced from 85 to 70, the largest group of children previously served, those with borderline mental retardation, were no longer identified. Although this may have appeared to be an "overnight cure" of a large portion of mental retardation, some special educators were (and remain today) concerned that many children with mild mental retardation were "being drowned in the mainstream" (Kidd, 1979, p. 75) because they no longer qualified for the special education they needed. The 1983 AAMR manual (Grossman, 1983) emphasizes that the IQ cutoff score of 70 is intended only as a guideline and should not be interpreted as a hard-and-fast requirement. A higher IQ score of 75 or more may be associated with mental retardation if, according to a clinician's judgment, the child exhibits deficits in adaptive behavior thought to be caused by impaired intellectual functioning.

Robinson and Robinson (1976), in their excellent discussion of intelligence testing, summarize some potential values and pitfalls of IQ tests:

> The development and popular utilization of the IQ as a single, simple, objective index of the rate of intellectual growth has been a mixed blessing. When properly understood and carefully used, an IQ test can be valuable in assessing a child's rate of progress, but it refers to only those aspects of mental ability tapped by a particular test. Its measurement is subject to error from a number of sources, some of them capable of drastically affecting scores. There is little doubt that IQs have been seriously misused because of persistent and erroneous notions about their supposed permanence or their magical power to predict future performance. Such a simple index of present behavior as the IQ cannot possibly reflect all the many aspects of the complex developmental phenomenon known as intelligence.
>
> Nowhere has the IQ proved to be a more mixed blessing than in matters concerning the welfare of mentally retarded children. To be sure, the development of intelligence tests provided a means for more objective assessment. Tests have been very useful in helping to identify children who need special training and in establishing more orderly methods for admissions procedures in institutions. Many retarded children have been helped to lead more productive lives because of the early identification of their problems. Other children whose school failures were not due to overall intellectual deficits have also been identified and treated accordingly.
>
> On the other hand, the apparent simplicity of the IQ led to an enthusiastic but largely misguided movement to label or classify children primarily on the basis of their scores on intelligence tests. Accurate classification of intellectual deficit was thought to be all that was required to achieve understanding of retarded children, individual characteristics being grossly underestimated. Furthermore, undue belief in IQ constancy led to a diminution in research and treatment. Professional interest in many complex problems declined over a long period, not to be rejuvenated until the mid-1960s. Fortunately, a more realistic view now prevails. (p. 343)

A recent alternative to traditional tests of intelligence is the *Kaufman Assessment Battery for Children* (K-ABC) (Kaufman & Kaufman, 1983). The K-ABC is based on the theory that intelligence is composed of two information-processing abilities:

MacMillan (1989) provides a thoughtful discussion of concerns regarding marginal learners in the 75–85 IQ range who may "reside in an educational 'DMZ,' or 'no man's land' where students are ineligible for any special educational services" (p. 14).

sequential processing and simultaneous processing. "Sequential processing places a premium on the serial or temporal order of stimuli when solving problems; in contrast, simultaneous processing demands a gestalt-like, frequently spatial, integration of stimuli to solve problems with maximum efficiency" (Kaufman & Kaufman, 1983, p. 2). Some view the K-ABC as a significant advancement in understanding and measuring children's intelligence, and some school psychologists use the test as part of their battery of assessment instruments to determine eligibility for and placement in special education programs. Several authorities on special education assessment suggest, however, that complete acceptance of the new approach be deferred until a significant body of research demonstrates the validity of the K-ABC's constructs and the remedial approach it recommends (McLoughlin & Lewis, 1994; Salvia & Ysseldyke, 1991).

Clearly, intelligence tests have both advantages and disadvantages. Here are several more important considerations to keep in mind:

- *The concept of intelligence is a hypothetical construct.* No one has ever seen a thing called intelligence; it is not a precise entity, but rather something we infer from observed performance. We assume it takes more intelligence to perform some tasks than it does to perform other tasks.
- *There is nothing mysterious or all-powerful about an IQ test.* An IQ test consists of a series of questions and/or problem-solving tasks.
- *An IQ test measures only how a child performs at one point in time on the items included in one test.* We infer from that performance how a child might perform in other situations.
- *IQ tests have proven to be the best single predictor of school achievement.* Because IQ tests are composed largely of verbal and academic tasks—the same things a child must master to succeed in school—they correlate with school achievement more highly than any other kind of test or variable.
- *In the hands of a competent school psychologist, IQ tests can provide useful information, particularly in objectively identifying an overall performance deficit.*
- *Results of an IQ test should never be used as the sole basis for labeling and classifying a child or for making a decision on the provision or denial of special education services.*
- *Results from an IQ test are generally not useful for determining educational objectives or designing instructional strategies for a student.* Results of teacher-administered, criterion-referenced assessments of a student's performance of curriculum-specific skills are generally more useful for planning what to teach. Results of direct and frequent measurement of a student's performance during instruction provide needed information for evaluating and modifying teaching practices. In their analysis of intelligence testing in general, and use of the WISC-R in particular, Macmann and Barnett (1992) conclude that

> it is difficult to imagine a plausible set of circumstances in which inferences about a student's intellectual processing (based on the analysis of WISC-R scores) could markedly improve the quality of instruction that may be afforded through sound instructional principles and the alteration of methods and materials based on careful monitoring of intervention outcomes. (p. 156)

Measurement of Adaptive Behavior

To be classified as mentally retarded, a person must be clearly subnormal in adaptive behavior. It would be pointless to identify and classify as mentally retarded a person

A *criterion-referenced test* for basic math skills, for example, might include 10 single-digit addition problems. Rather than judging the child's ability to compute single-digit math problems by comparing his or her performance with other children's (as in norm-referenced testing) or inferring it from his or her work on other types of math problems, the child's performance on the skill in question is compared with a standard criterion. For example, if the criterion is 9 and the child gets 9 or 10 correct, instruction will not be necessary on that skill; if he or she gets fewer than 9 correct, a teaching program for single-digit addition problems would be implemented.

who faces no unusual problems or whose needs are met without professional attention. Some people with an IQ below 70 do well in school and society. Such people are not mentally retarded, and should not be labeled as such. (MacMillan, 1982, p. 42)

The AAMR manual on terminology defines *adaptive behavior* as "the effectiveness or degree with which the individual meets the standards of personal independence and social responsibility expected of his age and social group" (Grossman, 1983, p. 157).

Adaptive Behavior Scale

A frequently used instrument for assessing adaptive behavior by school-age children is the *AAMR Adaptive Behavior Scale—School* (ABS-S) (Lambert, Nihira, & Leland, 1993). The ABS-S consists of two parts: Part 1 contains nine domains related to independent functioning and daily living skills; Part 2 assesses the individual's level of maladaptive (inappropriate) behavior (see Table 4.1). The ABS-S is long: 104 items with multiple questions per item. A shorter (75 items) adaptation of the scale, called the *Classroom Adaptive Behavior Checklist,* has been developed by Hunsucker, Nelson, and Clark (1986).

Vineland Social Maturity Scale

The *Vineland Social Maturity Scale* (Doll, 1965) is another widely used method for assessing adaptive behavior. The Vineland has recently undergone substantial revision and is now available in three versions under the name *Vineland Adaptive Behavior Scales* (Sparrow, Balla, & Cicchetti, 1984). Two of the versions, the Interview Editions in Survey Form or Expanded Form, are administered by an individual, such as a teacher or direct caregiver, who knows well the person being assessed. The Classroom Edition is designed to be completed by a teacher.

Assessment of Social Competence

One of the most recent adaptive behavior assessment instruments to be developed is the *Assessment of Social Competence* (ASC) (Meyer, Cole, McQuarter, & Reichle, 1990). The ASC, which is intended to measure social competence at all levels of social and intellectual functioning, consists of 252 items organized within 11 social functions (e.g., initiates interactions, follows rules, indicates preferences). Each function is further broken down into eight levels, with the highest level representing performance at an adult level of mastery. Each item is given one of three scores: "no evidence of behavior," "someone else's report of the behavior only," or "direct observation of the behavior."

The Dilemma of Accurate Measurement

Measurement of adaptive behavior has proven difficult, in large part because of the relative nature of social adjustment and competence: What is considered appropriate in one situation or by one group may not be in or by another. Nowhere is there a list that everyone would agree describes exactly those adaptive behaviors all of us should exhibit. As with IQ tests, cultural bias can be a problem in adaptive behavior scales; for instance, one item on some scales requires a child to tie a laced shoe, but

> Measurement of adaptive behavior is important for reasons other than the diagnosis of mental retardation. The severity of maladaptive behavior exhibited by persons with mental retardation is one of the most critical factors in determining their placement and success in most school, work, and residential settings (Campbell, Smith, & Wool, 1982). Because Part 2 of the ABS focuses primarily on the frequency rather than the severity of maladaptive behavior, MacDonald and Barton (1986) have developed a revision that enables an assessment of the severity of a person's maladaptive behavior.

TABLE 4.1
Domains of adaptive functioning covered by the *Adaptive Behavior Scale—School*

PART ONE

I.   Independent Functioning
   A. Eating
   B. Toilet Use
   C. Cleanliness
   D. Appearance
   E. Care of Clothing
   F. Dressing and Undressing
   G. Travel
   H. Other Independent Functioning

II. Physical Development
   A. Development
   B. Motor Development

III. Economic Activity
   A. Money Handling and Budgeting
   B. Shopping Skills

IV. Language Development
   A. Expression
   B. Verbal Comprehension
   C. Social Language Development

V.   Numbers and Time

VI. Prevocational/Vocational Activity

VII. Self-Direction
   A. Initiative
   B. Perseverance
   C. Leisure Time

VIII. Responsibility

IX. Socialization

PART TWO

X.   Social Behavior

XI. Conformity

XII. Trustworthiness

XIII. Stereotyped and Hyperactive Behavior

XIV. Self-Abusive Behavior

XV. Social Engagement

XVI. Disturbing Interpersonal Behavior

Source: From *Adaptive Behavior Scale—School* (2nd ed.) by N. Lambert, K. Nihira, and H. Leland, 1993, Austin, TX: PRO-ED. Reprinted by permission.

some children have never had a shoe with laces. Ongoing research being conducted today on the measurement of adaptive behavior may help resolve these problems.

Some professionals have argued against inclusion of adaptive behavior in the definition of mental retardation (e.g., Clausen, 1972). Zigler, Balla, and Hodapp (1984) contend that mental retardation should be determined only by a score of less than 70 on a standardized IQ test. In a rebuttal that probably reflects the position of most professionals in the field, Barnett (1986) attacks the proposal of Zigler et al. by explaining the necessity of retaining adaptive behavior in the definition of mental retardation if the concept is to remain socially valid.

Despite the fact that most professionals view adaptive behavior as an important component of mental retardation, a child's IQ score remains the primary variable in identifying him or her as mentally retarded. A survey of state departments of education found that although assessment of adaptive behavior is mentioned in the procedures used by 44 states to identify children with mental retardation, 36 of those states used no specific criteria or cutoff scores (Frankenberger & Fronzaglio, 1991). By contrast, only one state allows a child to be identified with mental retardation without falling under a specific cutoff score on an IQ test.

Classification of Mental Retardation Based on Intellectual Ability

As discussed in Chapter 1, classification of exceptional children is a difficult but necessary task. Many systems have been proposed for classifying mental retardation by type or degree of severity. In 1963 Gelof reported that 23 classification systems were

Adaptive behavior includes the ability to work cooperatively with others.

An examination of the guidelines issued by state departments of education found that only 56% of states used the term *mental retardation;* the remaining states classified students with terms such as *developmental disabilities, developmental handicaps,* or *mental disabilities* (Utley, Lowitzer, & Baumeister, 1987).

in use in English-speaking countries. Various systems have been developed that classify mental retardation according to **etiology** (cause) or clinical type (e.g., **Down syndrome**). Although these classification systems are useful to physicians, they generally have limited utility for educators. For example, two children might be classified as having **Down syndrome**, but one functions with little assistance in a regular second grade classroom, while the other is unable to perform the most basic self-help tasks.

Mental retardation has traditionally been classified by the degree or level of intellectual impairment, as measured by an IQ test. The most widely used classification method cited in the professional literature consists of four levels of mental retardation according to the range of IQ scores shown in Table 4.2. The range of scores representing the high and low ends of each level indicates an awareness of the inexactness of intelligence testing and the importance of clinical judgment in determining level of severity.

Educators use different terms for the various levels of mental retardation. For many years, students with mental retardation were classified as either *educable mentally retarded* (EMR) or *trainable mentally retarded* (TMR), which refer to mild and moderate levels of retardation, respectively. (Because children with severe and profound mental retardation were often denied a public education, they were not considered in this two-level classification system.) Although one may still encounter the terms *EMR* or *TMR* today, most educators consider their use inappropriate because of the connotations of predetermined achievement limits.

Mild Retardation

Children with mild retardation have traditionally been educated in self-contained classrooms in the public schools. Today many children with mild mental retardation are being educated in regular classrooms, with a special educator helping the classroom teacher with individualized instruction for the child and providing extra tutoring in a resource room as needed. Many children with mild retardation are not identified until they enter school and sometimes not until the second or third grade, when more difficult academic work is required.

For a review of research on teaching reading to students with mental retardation, see Conners (1992). Chapter 15 offers more information on how adults with mental retardation live and work.

Traditionally, school programs for students with mild mental retardation stressed the basic academic subjects—reading, writing, and arithmetic—during the elementary years, with a shift in emphasis to vocational training and work-study programs in junior high and high school. Schools today are increasingly beginning career education (Brolin, 1995) and instruction on community living skills (Dever, 1989) in the elementary grades. Most students with mild mental retardation master

TABLE 4.2
Classification of mental retardation by measured IQ score

LEVEL	INTELLIGENCE TEST SCORE[*]
Mild retardation	50 – 55 to approximately 70
Moderate retardation	35 – 40 to 50 – 55
Severe retardation	20 – 25 to 35 – 40
Profound retardation	Below 20 – 25

[*]Based on the AAMR's *Classification of Mental Retardation* (Grossman, 1983) and the *Diagnostic and Statistical Manual of Mental Disorders (DSM-IV)* (American Psychiatric Association, 1994).

academic skills up to about the sixth grade level and are able to learn job skills well enough to support themselves independently or semi-independently. Some adults who have been identified with mild mental retardation develop excellent social and communication skills and once they leave school are no longer recognized as having a disability.

Moderate Retardation

Most children with moderate retardation show significant delays in development during their preschool years. As they grow older, discrepancies in overall intellectual, social, and motor development generally grow wider between these children and age-mates without disabilities. Approximately 30% of individuals with moderate mental retardation have Down syndrome, and about 50% have some form of brain damage (Neisworth & Smith, 1978). People with moderate mental retardation are more likely to have physical disabilities and behavior problems than are individuals with mild retardation.

During their school years, children with moderate mental retardation are most often taught in self-contained classrooms with highly structured instructional programs designed to teach daily living skills. Academics may be limited to development of a basic sight-word vocabulary (e.g., "survival" words such as *exit, don't walk, stop*), some functional reading skills (e.g., simple recipes), and basic number concepts. In the past, most persons with moderate mental retardation were removed from society and placed in large institutions, where they had little opportunity to develop and learn how to get along in the world. Today most people with moderate retardation are receiving the individualized levels of support and supervision they require to live and work in the community.

Severe and Profound Retardation

Individuals with severe and profound mental retardation are almost always identified at birth or shortly afterward. Most of these infants have significant central nervous system damage, and many have additional disabilities and/or health conditions. Although IQ scores can serve as the basis for differentiating severe and profound retardation from one another, the difference is primarily one of functional impairment. Until recently, training for individuals with severe retardation focused primarily on self-care skills—toileting, dressing, and eating and drinking—and communication development. A person with profound mental retardation may not be able to care for personal needs, have limited or no independent mobility, and require 24-hour nursing care. Recent developments in instructional technology, however, are showing that many persons with severe and profound mental retardation can learn skills previously thought to be beyond their capability—even to the point of becoming semi-independent adults able to live and work in the community.

Until recently, children with severe and profound mental retardation were virtually shut out by the U.S. educational system. Fortunately, this situation is changing. Litigation and legislation ensuring the rights of individuals with disabilities, regardless of the type or degree of disability, and advances in educational methods (Cipani & Spooner, 1994; Snell, 1993) have contributed to this change. The outlook for these children is improving. An effective advocacy group of researchers, teachers, parents, and other interested individuals—The Association for Persons with Severe Handicaps (TASH)—is working to help that future.

Career education is discussed in Chapter 15. Carroll et al. (1991) describe how students with disabilities can learn needed functional academic and vocational skills by operating a "classroom company."

Mental retardation is seldom a time-limited condition. Although many individuals with mental retardation make tremendous advancements in adaptive skills (some to the point of functioning independently and no longer being considered under any disability category), most are affected throughout their life span (Mulick & Antonak, 1994). In Chapter 15, we examine in detail the transition to adult life by individuals with disabilities.

For information on the prevalence, evaluation, and treatment of individuals with a dual diagnosis of mental retardation and mental illness, see the *Journal of Consulting and Clinical Psychology* (1994, Vol. 62, No. 1).

Instruction in self-contained classrooms for students with mental retardation emphasizes functional skills such as using money.

✳ *Defining Mental Retardation: Emphasizing Individualized Need for Supports*

Numerous alternative definitions of mental retardation have been proposed, spurred in part by questions over the nature and meaning of what is measured by intelligence tests and the steady gains in adaptive functioning by individuals with mental retardation as a result of advancement in effective methods of treatment and education and increased opportunities to participate in schools and the community. Four of the more prominent alternatives define mental retardation from behavioral, sociological, or instructional perspectives.

Alternative Definitions

Bijou's Behavioral Definition

Sidney Bijou (1966) proposed a strictly behavioral definition that states, "A retarded individual is one who has a limited repertoire of behavior shaped by events that constitute his history" (p. 2). Bijou and Dunitz-Johnson (1981) have described an "inter-behavior analysis" view of mental retardation that attributes a limited (retarded) behavioral repertoire to the hampering effects of biomedical impairment, handicapping sociocultural conditions, or both. Biomedical impairment can retard an individual's development through injury to the response equipment or to the internal or external sources of stimulation. Handicapping sociocultural conditions may include an impoverished home environment, limited educational opportunities, and negative parental practices such as indifference or abuse. Bijou's view maintains that if the person's environment provides the proper supports, the deficits in functioning

Response equipment refers to parts of the body that produce movement or responses. It includes the brain, eyes, speech organs, and so forth.

Daniel

"Hey, hey, hey, Fact Track!" The 11-year-old chose one of his favorite programs from the table next to the computer in his parents' dining room. He inserted the floppy disk, booted the system, and waited for the program to load.

"What is your name?" appeared on the monitor.

"Daniel Skandera," he typed. A menu scrolled up, listing the program's possibilities. Daniel chose multiplication facts, Level 1.

"How many problems do you want to do?" the computer asked.

"20."

"Do you want to set a goal for yourself, Daniel?"

"Yes, 80 sec."

"Get ready!"

Daniel Skandera, Jr., was born with Down syndrome, a chromosomal abnormality that usually results in moderate to severe mental retardation. "A psychologist tested Daniel at 12 months and told us he was three standard deviations below normal, untestable. That assessment was the basis for Daniel's being denied enrollment in an infant stimulation program. We knew the tests were invalid and accepted the challenge of teaching Daniel ourselves," explained Daniel's father. "Between Marie [Daniel's mother] and me, we had spent about 10,000 hours working with Daniel by the time he was 5. It's paid off a million times over. He's an inspiration and a joy."

"We believed that we had learned enough about how Daniel learns to work with him confidently," says Marie. "If something doesn't work, if he becomes frustrated, we are challenged to try another approach. Daniel is an only child, and we were older when he was born. When we're gone, we want him to be able to take care of himself, to be a taxpayer instead of a tax burden."

Randomly generated multiplication facts flashed on the screen: "4 × 6," "2 × 9," "3 × 3," "7 × 6." Daniel responded, deftly punching in his answers on the computer's numeric keypad. Twice he recognized errors and corrected them before inputting his answers.

Daniel attends a regular fourth-grade classroom. Academically, he performs at grade level except for two subjects. For math and spelling, his best subjects ("Hooray, I love spellin'!"), he leaves the fourth-grade classroom each day and moves to the fifth grade. Daniel is not a special education student; he has no IEP. His extracurricular activities are those of his classmates and neighborhood friends: riding his bicycle, working out on his regulation-size trampoline, playing along with tape-recorded rock 'n' roll on his six-piece drum set, roughhousing, spending the night at a buddy's.

"Positive expectations are the key words," agreed Daniel's parents. "With Daniel, it might take a little longer, but we get there."

The computer tallied the results. "You completed 20 problems in 66 seconds. You beat your goal. Problems correct = 20. Congratulations, Daniel!" And with that the 11-year-old retreated hastily to the TV room. It was almost tip-off time for an NBA championship game, and Daniel wanted to see the first half before bedtime. ✴

---

associated with mental retardation can be replaced with more adaptive, age-appropriate behavior.

Mercer's Sociological Definition

Jane Mercer, a sociologist, believes that the concept of mental retardation is a sociological phenomenon and that the label mental retardation is "an achieved social status in a social system" (Mercer, 1973a, p. 3). Mercer's research (1973a, 1973b) shows that many children identified as mildly retarded by the school system, especially children from cultural minorities, are labeled because their behavior does not meet the norms of the White, middle-class social system.

Mercer has developed a system for diagnosing mental retardation in children from minority groups. Called SOMPA (System of Multicultural Pluralistic Assessment), it is designed to eliminate cultural bias in intelligence testing. Using SOMPA, the examiner converts the child's WISC-R IQ score into what is called an *estimated learning potential* (ELP) score. The ELP score is affected by such variables as ethnic group membership and family size and structure. Although some school districts use SOMPA, research has not determined how valid and ultimately useful it may be.

Gold's Social Responsibility Definition

The story of Daniel, an 11-year-old with Down syndrome, offers powerful support of Gold's belief in the power of systematic teaching. See the Profiles & Perspectives box, "Daniel", earlier in this chapter.

A definition of mental retardation encompassing both a behavioral and a sociological perspective was proposed by Marc Gold (1980a). According to Gold, mental retardation should be viewed as society's failure to provide sufficient training and education, rather than as a deficit within the individual.

> Mental retardation refers to a level of functioning which requires from society significantly above average training procedures and superior assets in adaptive behavior, manifested throughout life. The mentally retarded person is characterized by the level of power needed in the training process for [the person] to learn, and not by limitations on what [the person] can learn. The height of a retarded person's level of functioning is determined by the availability of training technology and the amount of resources society is willing to allocate and not by significant limitations in biological potential. (p. 148)

Gold's "social responsibility" perspective is a highly optimistic one in its claim that the ultimate level of functioning of a person with mental retardation is determined by the technology available for training and the amount of resources devoted to the task.

Dever's Instructional Definition

Recognizing that definitions both reflect the perceptions of their developers and help shape the perceptions of people entering the field, Dever (1990) believes that mental retardation should be conceptualized from an instructional perspective. He offers the following definition to guide the efforts of personnel who work directly with individuals with mental retardation after they have been identified according to an "administrative" definition such as the AAMR's: "Mental retardation refers to the need for specific training of skills that most people acquire incidentally and that enable individuals to live in the community without supervision" (p. 149).

The alternative definitions of mental retardation proposed by Bijou, Mercer, Gold, and Dever are important ones. Each defines mental retardation as a relative phenomenon that should not be viewed as a permanent condition. Each emphasizes the fundamental notion that mental retardation represents a current level of performance; it is not something a person has in the same way one has the measles or red hair. Furthermore, performance can often be altered significantly by manipulating certain aspects of the environment (teaching adaptive, age-appropriate behavior or, in Mercer's view, altering one's own culturally biased perspective of what constitutes adaptive behavior).

The 1992 System: A Definition Based on Needed Supports

Although none of the alternative definitions was widely adopted, each of the perspectives they represented helped lay the foundation for the AAMR's newest definition of mental retardation. Called the "1992 System" by its developers, the new definition represents a shift away from conceptualizations of mental retardation as an inherent trait or permanent state of being to a description of the individual's present functioning and the environmental supports needed to improve it.

> *Mental retardation* refers to substantial limitations in present functioning. It is characterized by significantly subaverage intellectual functioning, existing concurrently with related limitations in two or more of the following applicable adaptive skill areas: communication, self-care, home living, social skills, community use, self-direction, health and safety, functional academics, leisure, and work. Mental retardation manifests before age 18.
>
> The following four assumptions are essential to the application of the definition:
>
> 1. Valid assessment considers cultural and linguistic diversity as well as differences in communication and behavioral factors;
> 2. The existence of limitations in adaptive skills occurs within the context of community environments typical of the individual's age peers and is indexed to the person's individualized needs for supports;
> 3. Specific adaptive limitations often coexist with strengths in other adaptive skills or other personal capabilities; and
> 4. With appropriate supports over a sustained period, the life functioning of the person with mental retardation will generally improve. (Luckasson et al., 1992, p. 1)

Figure 4.2 shows how the three key elements of the new definition are interrelated. *Capabilities,* on the left side of the triangle, show that functioning is related specifically to limitations in intelligence and adaptive skills. The right side of the triangle represents the *environments* in which limited functioning is meaningful. The bottom of the triangle shows that the presence and absence of supports influence *functioning.* The equilateral triangle emphasizes that all three aspects are necessary

FIGURE 4.2

General structure of the 1992 AAMR definition of mental retardation

Source: From "Mental Retardation: Definition, Classification, and Systems of Supports" (9th ed.) (p. 10), 1992, American Association on Mental Retardation, Washington, DC. Reprinted by permission.

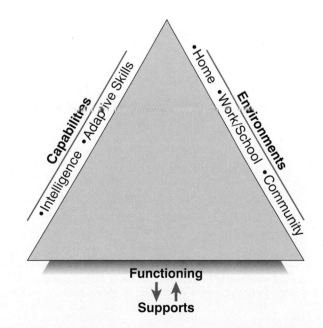

for a full understanding of mental retardation. Mental retardation is defined within the context of the environments in which the individual lives; it exists as a disability (limitations in functioning) as a result of the interaction between limitations in capabilities and demands of the environment.

Classification Based on Intensity of Needed Supports

The 1992 System is more than a definition of mental retardation. It also provides conceptual and procedural recommendations for functionally classifying mental retardation according to a profile of needed supports. This approach represents a change away from classifying mental retardation on the basis of estimates of an individual's deficiencies to estimating the intensities of supports needed to improve functioning in the environments in which the individual lives, goes to school or works, and plays. Needed supports are identified and classified by an interdisciplinary team according to the four levels of intensities shown in Table 4.3.

An interdisciplinary team develops a profile of the types and intensity of needed supports within each of four dimensions:

Dimension I: Intellectual Functioning and Adaptive Skills

Dimension II: Psychological/Emotional Considerations (e.g., behavioral problems)

Dimension III: Physical/Health/Etiology Considerations

Dimension IV: Environmental Considerations (e.g., mobility/access)

TABLE 4.3
Definitions of intensities of supports for individuals with mental retardation

Intermittent	Supports on an "as needed basis." Characterized by episodic nature, person not always needing the support(s), or short-term supports needed during life-span transitions (e.g., job loss or an acute medical crisis). Intermittent supports may be high or low intensity when provided.
Limited	An intensity of supports characterized by consistency over time, time-limited but not of an intermittent nature, may require fewer staff members and less cost than more intense levels of support (e.g., time-limited employment training or transitional supports provided during the school to adult period).
Extensive	Supports characterized by regular involvement (e.g., daily) in at least some environments (such as work or home) and not time-limited (e.g., long-term support and long-term home living support).
Pervasive	Supports characterized by their constancy and high intensity; provided across environments; potential life-sustaining nature. Pervasive supports typically involve more staff members and intrusiveness than do extensive or time-limited supports.

Source: From "Mental Retardation: Definition, Classification, and Systems of Supports: Workbook" (9th ed.) (p. 26), 1992, American Association on Mental Retardation, Washington, DC. Reprinted by permission.

Figure 4.3 is an example of what the profile and intensities of needed supports might look like for Jared, an upper-elementary student who has intellectual limitations and behavioral problems. In developing this profile, the interdisciplinary team incorporated the results of various assessments of Jared's current functioning and knowledge of his experiences and his parents' desires for placement, including the following:

- He frequently displays stereotypic movements of the hands and body.
- He seldom smiles, laughs, or shows affection toward others.
- He has a congenital heart problem.
- He does not initiate routine self-care tasks without prompting and reminding.
- He has been attending a self-contained classroom in a separate school for students with mental retardation since he was 5 years old, despite the fact that he has to ride the bus for 1 hour each way.
- His friends are limited to his immediate family, relatives, and two neighborhood children who sometimes visit.
- His parents are eager for him to attend school with his siblings, neighbors, and peers, and they have noted favorable changes in behavior when he is with peers.
- His teachers have recently reduced his tantrum behavior by equipping him with a radio headset.
- He has acquired some practical skills when taught in community settings (e.g., crossing the street, purchasing a snack).

The authors of the 1992 System believe that classification by levels of needed supports represents a radical and needed improvement over traditional methods of classification based on IQ. Recognizing the administrative ease with which the four traditional IQ-determined levels of intellectual deficiency could be substituted for the four intensity levels of needed support, they cite six reasons why it would be illogical to do so:

1. Intensities of needed supports are based on the individual's strengths and limitations in four dimensions, as opposed to the first dimension only or often just IQ score alone.
2. Assessment of supports involves many disciplines analyzing a variety of assessment findings and is more meaningful than norm-referenced intelligence scores alone.
3. Levels of needed supports are based on the strengths and weaknesses of an individual's capabilities and his or her environments, not simply on an individual's intellectual limitations.
4. Levels of needed support are viewed as potentially changing and thus requiring reassessment, not as static descriptions of an inherent deficit in intellectual ability.
5. An individual's support profile is likely to include a variety of supports at different levels of intensities, making a single, global summary label meaningless.
6. Predictions about needed supports are not predictors of ability. (Adapted from Schalock et al., 1992, p. 186)

The Ever-Changing Definition of Mental Retardation

The conception of mental retardation has undergone numerous changes in terminology, IQ score cutoff, and the relative role of adaptive functioning during the past

FIGURE 4.3

Profile and intensities of supports for Jared, an upper-elementary student with mental retardation

Name	Jared		Date	9/20/96

List the support function, the specific activity, and the level of intensities needed in each of the areas and/or dimensions. (See Activities listed on the back of this page.)

Levels of intensity are: I–Intermittent; L–Limited; E–Extensive; P–Pervasive

Dimension I: Intellectual Functioning and Adaptive Skills

Dimension/Area	Support Function	Activity	Level of Intensity I L E P
Communication	Befriending	Establish an augmentative communication system.	E
Self-care	Health assistance	Assist in developing independent grooming and hygiene.	L
Social skills	Behavior support	Modeling and social skills programming to teach functional communication and other replacement skills, and to decrease escape behaviors.	E
Home living	Behavior support	Teach him to make bed, prepare his sack lunch.	L
Community use	Community access and use	Provide opportunities for recreation and community use activities.	L
Self-direction	Behavior support	Teach problem-solving skills and decision-making.	E
Health and safety	Health assistance	Procure on-going medical/physical exams.	I
Functional academics	Student assistance	Evaluate the efficacy of computer assisted instruction. Provide activity-based instruction in functional academics.	P
Leisure	Community access and use Befriending	Attend and participate in as many games and recreation programs as possible.	I
Work N/A			

four decades. In each case, those changes have reflected an ongoing attempt to better understand mental retardation in order to achieve more effective and reliable systems of identification, classification, research, and habilitation. In a paper describing the implications of the new definition for the field of mental retardation, the members of the AAMR Ad Hoc Committee recognize the need for and inevitability of ongoing change (Schalock et al., 1994):

> The reactions to the 1992 System are not unlike the reactions to a scientific revolution discussed by Kuhn (1970), in which there are doubts or difficulties with a partic-

FIGURE 4.3   *(continued)*

Dimension II: Psychological/Emotional Considerations			
Dimension/Area	Support Function	Activity	Level of Intensity I L E P
	Behavioral support	Teach replacement skills matched to functional assessment. Employ non-aversive strategies.	E

Dimension III: Physical/Health Considerations			
Dimension/Area	Support Function	Activity	Level of Intensity I L E P
	Health assistance	Procure annual physical. Monitor heart defect.	I

Dimension IV: Environment Considerations			
Dimension/Area	Support Function	Activity	Level of Intensity I L E P
	Community access and use	Move into a regular integrated school.	E

Source: From "Mental Retardation: Definition, Classification, and Systems of Supports: Workbook" (pp. 24–25), 1992, American Association on Mental Retardation, Washington, DC. Used by permission.

ular approach, conflict between the "old" and "new" approaches, and the eventual acceptance of a new paradigm whose major characteristics include attracting converts, being sufficiently open-ended so that it is testable, and being attractive and hopeful. . . . [T]he field of mental retardation is in the middle of a paradigm shift and it will continue to undergo significant future changes.

The assessment, diagnostic, and habilitation procedures required by the 1992 System will undoubtedly change and be implemented over time, as was true for the 1983 definitions (Lowitzer, Utley, & Baumeister, 1987). There is already evidence that the 1992 System is taking root. . . . Change never comes easy. However, the challenges and opportunities provided by the changing conception of mental retardation and the 1992 System set an important agenda for the next decade. (pp. 189–190)

Not all professionals in the field of mental retardation share the same level of enthusiasm and optimism for the new definition (e.g., Borthwick-Duffy, 1994; Greenspan, 1994; Jacobsen & Mulick, 1992; MacMillan, Gresham, & Siperstein, 1993). Some of the concerns stated by critics of the new definition are as follows:

- IQ testing will remain a primary (and in practice perhaps the only) means of diagnosis.

- The IQ criterion of 75 will increase the number of persons identified.
- The new definition may fail to differentiate subgroups of mental retardation, particularly by whether the condition is caused by organic impairment or environmental influence.
- The 10 adaptive skill areas do not consider developmental factors and cannot be reliably assessed with current methods.
- The levels of needed supports are too subjective.
- Classification will remain essentially unchanged in practice because the four intensities of supports—intermittent, limited, extensive, and pervasive—will simply replace the four levels of retardation based on IQ scores—mild, moderate, severe, and profound.

In response to these and other criticisms of the new definition, Reiss (1994), a member of the AAMR Ad Hoc Committee on Terminology and Classification that developed the new definition, writes:

> The new AAMR definition does not raise the IQ limit and is not intended to increase the number of people considered to have mental retardation. There is no intent to change who is and who is not considered to have mental retardation. Instead, the intent was to change how people *think* about mental retardation: the old deficiency model is replaced with a new support model. (p. 1)

CEC's Division on Mental Retardation and Developmental Disabilities position on the AAMR 1992 definition is one of cautious support. In an official position statement adopted by its board of directors, CEC-MRDD praises the new definition for focusing greater attention on the needs of individuals instead of on degrees of deficiency residing within the person with mental retardation and for providing the field with a positive stimulus for debate on issues critical to persons with mental retardation. The statement notes, however, that the changes required by and the implications of the new definition are so profound that they "require the most careful consideration before they are implemented in special education practices."

Smith (1994) concludes his presentation and discussion of CEC-MRDD's position on the new definition with this observation:

> The new definition should not be viewed as either tug-of-war or as dogma. . . . [W]hile the revised definition may be a paradigm shift it must be remembered that unlike physics, for example, where a paradigm shift from the worldview of Newton to that of Einstein does nothing to change the reality of the physical universe, a paradigm shift in the field of mental retardation may have profound implications for the education, care and treatment of perhaps millions of human beings. (p. 179)

The debate over the definition of mental retardation will surely continue. We end this discussion of definition with the words of the late Burton Blatt, one of the field's most prolific, influential, and controversial figures, who argues that when all is said and done, mental retardation is best viewed as an administrative category. In his final book *The Conquest of Mental Retardation* (1987), Blatt writes, "Simply stated, someone is mentally retarded when he or she is 'officially' identified as such" (p. 72).

✳ Causes of Mental Retardation

More than 250 causes of mental retardation have been identified. Table 4.4 lists just some of the many hundreds of disorders associated with mental retardation that are

TABLE 4.4
Disorders in which mental retardation may occur

I. PRENATAL CAUSES

   A. Chromosomal Disorders (e.g., Trisomy 21 [Down syndrome], fragile-X syndrome, **Turner syndrome, Klinefelter syndrome**)

   B. Syndrome Disorders (e.g., **Duchenne muscular dystrophy**, **Prader-Willi syndrome**)

   C. Inborn Errors of Metabolism (e.g., phenylketonuria [PKU], Tay-Sachs disease)

   D. Developmental Disorders of Brain Formation (e.g., **anencephaly**, spina bifida, **hydrocephalus**)

   E. Environmental Influences (e.g., maternal malnutrition, **fetal alcohol syndrome**, diabetes mellitus, irradiation during pregnancy)

II. PERINATAL CAUSES

   A. Intrauterine Disorders (e.g., maternal anemia, premature delivery, abnormal presentation, umbilical cord accidents, multiple gestation)

   B. Neonatal Disorders (e.g., intracranial hemorrhage, neonatal seizures, respiratory disorders, meningitis, encephalitis, head trauma at birth)

III. POSTNATAL CAUSES

   A. Head Injuries (e.g., cerebral concussion, contusion, or laceration)

   B. Infections (e.g., **encephalitis**, meningitis, malaria, measles, **rubella**)

   C. Demyelinating Disorders (e.g., postinfectious disorders, postimmunization disorders)

   D. Degenerative Disorders (e.g., **Rett syndrome**, Huntington disease, Parkinson disease)

   E. Seizure Disorders (e.g., **epilepsy**)

   F. Toxic-Metabolic Disorders (e.g., **Reye syndrome**, lead or mercury poisoning)

   G. Malnutrition (e.g., protein-calorie malnutrition)

   H. Environmental Deprivation (e.g., psychosocial disadvantage, child abuse and neglect, chronic social/sensory deprivation)

   I. Hypoconnection Syndrome

Source: From R. Luckasson et al. (Eds.). *Mental Retardation: Definition, Classification, and Systems of Support* (9th ed.), 1992, pp. 81–91. Washington, DC: American Association on Mental Retardation. Used by permission.

categorized by the AAMR (Luckasson et al., 1992) according to **prenatal** (occurring before birth), **perinatal** (occurring during or shortly after birth), and **postnatal** causes. All of these etiologic factors associated with mental retardation can be classified as either organic (biological or medical) or environmental.

For the majority of individuals with mental retardation, however, the exact cause is unknown. Authors of a review of 13 epidemiological studies concluded that for approximately 50% of cases of mild mental retardation and 30% of cases of severe mental retardation, the cause is unknown (McLaven & Bryson, 1987). Nevertheless, knowledge of etiology is critical to efforts designed to prevent the incidence of mental retardation and may have implications for some educational interventions (MacMillan et al., 1993). For example, Hodapp and Dykens (1994) suggest that teach-

The term *syndrome* refers to a number of symptoms that occur together and that provide the defining characteristics of a given disease or condition. **Down syndrome** and **fragile-X syndrome** are the two most common causes of inherited mental retardation. For a discussion of the educator's role in identification, intervention, and prevention of fragile-X syndrome, see Santos (1992).

ers may want to use sign language with students with Down syndrome but avoid using it with males who have **fragile-X syndrome** because of the dramatically different responses to hand movement tasks between children with the two different syndromes.

Organic Causes

All of the known causes of retardation are biological or medical, and these conditions are referred to as *clinical mental retardation* (brain damage). It is important to understand that none of the etiologic factors shown in Table 4.4 *is* mental retardation. These disorders, syndromes, and conditions are commonly associated with mental retardation, but they may or may not result in the deficits of intellectual and social functioning that define mental retardation. Indeed, one or more of these etiologic factors are found in many individuals who do not experience mental retardation.

Environmental Causes

Individuals with mild mental retardation make up 80% to 85% of all individuals with mental retardation. In the vast majority of those cases, etiology is unknown; that is, there is no demonstrable evidence of organic pathology—no brain damage or other physical problem. When no actual organic damage is evident in an individual with mental retardation, the cause is presumed to be **psychosocial disadvantage,** the combination of a poor social and cultural environment early in the child's life. Although there is no direct proof that social and environmental deprivation causes mental retardation, it is generally believed that these influences cause most cases of mild retardation.

The term *developmental retardation* is also used as a synonym for *psychosocial disadvantage* to refer to mental retardation thought to be caused primarily by environmental influences such as minimal opportunities to develop early language, child abuse and neglect, and/or chronic social or sensory deprivation.

Research conducted at the Juniper Gardens Children's Project has led to a hypothesis of developmental retardation as an intergenerational progression in which the cumulative experiential deficits in social and academic stimulation are transmitted to children from low socioeconomic status (SES) environments during their preadult life span (Greenwood et al., 1992; Greenwood, Hart, Walker, & Risley, 1994). Figure 4.4 illustrates the progression of developmental retardation in terms of low academic achievement and early school failure. Key contributors to this cycle of environmentally caused retardation are

1. limited parenting practices that produce low rates of vocabulary growth in early childhood,
2. instructional practices in middle childhood and adolescence that produce low rates of academic engagement during the school years,
3. lower rates of academic achievement and early school failure,
4. early school dropout, and finally
5. parenthood and continuance of the progression into the next generation.

Although this progression represents one of undoubtedly many specific developmental pathways leading to developmental retardation, it does represent an increasingly sophisticated guide for knowing where, when, and why environmental variables affect behavior and outcomes. (Greenwood et al., 1994, p. 216)

This model is much more than intellectual theorizing and conjecture. The Juniper Gardens research team has obtained more than 25 years of research data

FIGURE 4.4

Schematic illustration of the intergenerational progression of developmental retardation

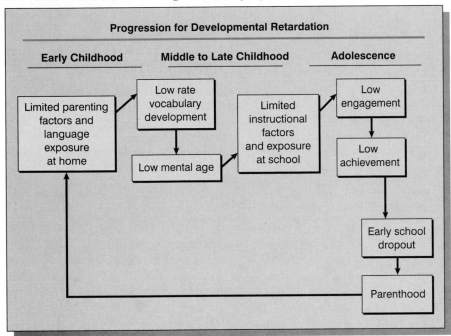

Source: From "The Opportunity to Respond and Academic Performance Revisited: A Behavioral Theory of Developmental Retardation and Its Prevention" by C. R. Greenwood, B. Hart, D. Walker, and T. Risley. In R. Gardner III, D. M. Sainato, J. O. Cooper, T. E. Heron, W. L. Heward, J. W. Eshleman, & T. A. Grossi (Eds.), *Behavior Analysis in Education: Focus on Measurably Superior Instruction*, 1994, p. 216. Pacific Grove, CA: Brooks/Cole. Reprinted by permission.

that show clearly the relationships among parenting, early vocabulary growth, and school failure. For example, a **longitudinal study** of 45 infants and their families from their home environment through their early schooling examined the relations between SES status and parent-child language interactions. The results showed strong correlations between SES status and the amount of exposure to language at home (see Figure 4.5). Young children from poor environments verbally interacted with their parents less often and were exposed to less vocabulary than children from middle- and upper-SES homes. It was also found that observations of natural language use in the home during the first 7 to 36 months of age could be used to predict children's measured IQ and academic achievement at the end of first grade (Hart & Risley, 1992).

Additional support for the hypothesis of developmental retardation is provided by McDermott (1994), who has found that much of the variability in prevalence rates of mental retardation reported by different school districts is explained by SES status. Her findings are "consistent with the notion that a large percentage of mental retardation is based on environmental causes, most notably, deprivation in the early years of life" (p. 182).

A *longitudinal study* follows the development of the same subjects over a period of years.

FIGURE 4.5

Trajectories of parent and child vocabulary use in upper-SES, middle-/lower-SES, and welfare households

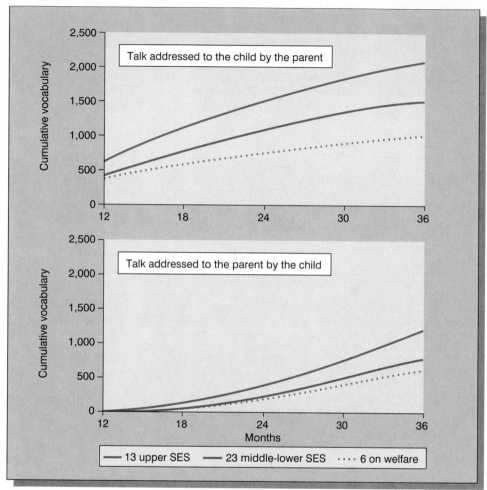

Source: From "The Opportunity to Respond and Academic Performance Revisited: A Behavioral Theory of Developmental Retardation and Its Prevention" by C. R. Greenwood, B. Hart, D. Walker, and T. Risley. In R. Gardner III, D. M. Sainato, J. O. Cooper, T. E. Heron, W. L. Heward, J. W. Eshleman, & T. A. Grossi (Eds.), *Behavior Analysis in Education: Focus on Measurably Superior Instruction,* 1994, p. 217. Pacific Grove, CA: Brooks/Cole. Reprinted by permission.

✹ *Prevalence*

Changing definitions of mental retardation, lack of a nationwide systematic reporting system, and the changing status of schoolchildren with mild mental retardation (most are no longer counted after leaving school) contribute to the difficulty of estimating the number of people with mental retardation. Historically, the federal government estimated the prevalence of mental retardation at 3% of the general population, although recent analyses find little objective support for this figure. When prevalence figures are based on IQ scores alone, approximately 2.3% of the population theoretically scores in the retarded range—two standard deviations below the mean (see Figure 4.1).

Basing prevalence estimates on IQ scores only, however, ignores the other necessary criterion for mental retardation—deficits in adaptive functioning. Because there are as yet no universally accepted measures of adaptive behavior, no major prevalence studies have assessed it. Some professionals believe that if adaptive behavior is included with intellectual ability when estimating prevalence, the figure would drop to about 1% (Baroff, 1982). Baroff has developed a formula for estimating the number of persons with mental retardation. He suggests that 4 people per 1,000 are in the moderate/severe/profound ranges and that 5 people per 1,000 have mild retardation. This 0.9% is about one third of the traditional 3% estimate.

The 1% estimate is consistent with prevalence figures in education. During the 1992–93 school year, 533,715 students age 6 through 21 received special education under the disability category of mental retardation (U.S. Department of Education, 1994). These students represented 11.5% of all school-age children in special education, or about 1.06% of the total school-age population.

Prevalence rates vary greatly from state to state. For example, the prevalence of mental retardation as a percentage of total school enrollment ranged from lows of 0.32% and 0.39% (New Jersey and Colorado) to a high of 3.09% (Alabama). Such large differences in prevalence are no doubt a function of the widely differing criteria for identifying students with mental retardation (Frankenberger & Fronzaglio, 1991). Prevalence figures also vary considerably among districts within a given state (McDermott, 1994).

✳ *Historical Background*

The history of mental retardation is long. No doubt, some people have been slower to learn than others for as long as people have populated the earth. The Greeks in 1552 B.C. and the Romans in 449 B.C. were among the first to recognize people officially as mentally retarded. Even passages in the Bible refer to slow learners (Barr, 1913; Lindman & McIntyre, 1961).

Several special educators and historians have written detailed and interesting accounts of how philosophies about and treatment of people with mental retardation have changed over the years. For example, Hewett and Forness (1977) describe the role and importance of survival, superstition, science, and service in the treatment of people with mental retardation during different historic periods. Gearheart and Litton (1975) characterize the early history of mental retardation (prior to the 1800s) as consisting primarily of superstition and extermination; the 19th century as the era that produced institutions for persons with mental retardation; the 20th century as the era of public school classes; the 1950s and 1960s as the era of legislation and national support; and the 1970s as the era of normalization, child advocacy, and litigation. Here we can only briefly describe some of the changing attitudes and significant events that have affected how persons with mental retardation have been treated over the years.

> Readers wishing to learn more about the history of mental retardation might begin by reading Blatt (1987); Beirne-Smith, Patton, and Ittenbach (1994); MacMillan (1982); Scheerenberger (1984); and Zigler, Hodapp, and Edison (1990).

Attitudes in Early Societies

The primary goal of human beings in primitive societies was survival. The sick, physically disabled, and elderly were often abandoned or even killed to increase the chance of survival by others. The Greeks and the Romans often sent mentally and physically disabled children far away from the community, where they would perish

Even the right to life itself has not always been a given for persons with mental retardation. Euthanasia "mercy killing"—of persons with mental retardation—was viewed by some leaders in the field as a logical means for society to "put an end to the existence of these defective and inefficient members within it" (Tredgold, 1947, p. 491). For information on involuntary sterilization and euthanasia as components of the *eugenics* movement designed to "rid society" of persons with disabilities, see Antonak, Fiedler, and Mulick (1993); Elks (1993); Lusthaus (1985); Smith (1985); and Smith and Polloway (1993).

Many consider Itard to be the father of special education.

on their own. Later, as survival became less a 24-hour concern and society separated into levels, ridicule of people with mental retardation was common. Superstitions and myths developed. Words like *idiot, imbecile,* and *dunce* were used, and some kings and queens and other wealthy people kept "fools" or imbeciles as clowns or court jesters. Bogdan (1986) provides historic documentation of the exhibition of people with mental retardation for amusement and profit during the period 1850 to 1940.

During the Middle Ages, as religion became a dominant force, a more humanitarian view was taken. Asylums and monasteries were opened to care for people with mental retardation. No one thought, however, that the behavior of a person with mental retardation could be altered.

Nineteenth-Century Advancements

At the beginning of the 19th century, the first attempt to educate an individual with mental retardation was recorded. In 1798 three hunters found and captured an 11- or 12-year-old boy in the woods of Aveyron, France. The boy—later called Victor, the Wild Boy of Aveyron (Itard, 1894/1962)—was completely unsocialized and had no language. He was pronounced an "incurable idiot." Jean Marc Gaspard Itard, a physician working at an institution for the deaf, refused to believe that Victor was uneducable. Itard began a program of intensive training with Victor. After almost 5 years, he concluded his work, deeming it a miserable failure because he did not reach his original goals for Victor. The changes that did occur with Victor, however, were significant: He was much more socialized and could read and write a few words. "The French Academy of Science encouraged Itard to publish his memoirs of his work with Victor. Itard did, which not only made Itard very famous, but may have been the single most important event in the creation of what is now viewed as a genuine field" (Blatt, 1987, p. 34).

Another Frenchman, Edouard Seguin, had tremendous influence on the creation of facilities and educational programs for persons with mental retardation in this country. Seguin, who had worked briefly with Itard prior to Itard's death in 1838 and who was inspired by the work with Victor, immigrated to the United States in 1848. He later helped establish the Pennsylvania Training School, an early educational facility.

Advocacy in the United States

The first publicly funded residential school in the United States was the Massachusetts School for Idiotic and Feeble Minded Youth, founded in 1850 by Samuel Gridley Howe. With a powerful letter arguing for the rights of people with mental retardation in a democratic society, Howe, who had already devoted much of his life to educating children who were blind or deaf, persuaded the Massachusetts legislature to override the governor's veto and provide him with $2,500 to begin the school.

During the remainder of the 19th century, large state institutions for individuals with mental retardation or mental illness (they were often viewed as the same) became the primary means of service delivery. As the institutions became overcrowded and understaffed, the optimism sparked by the educational gains produced by Itard, Seguin, and Howe began to wane (Gardner, 1993). State institutions came to be considered custodial, rather than educational, a view that has taken years of effort to change, extending even to the present.

The first public school class for children with mental retardation was formed in 1896 in Providence, Rhode Island. Thus began the special class movement, which saw 87,030 children enrolled in special classes in 1948; 703,800 in 1969; and 1,305,000 in 1974, the year before the signing of the IDEA. The great increases in the number of children being served by the public schools paralleled increases in federal aid to education, particularly to special education, in the 1950s and 1960s.

In recent years, we have witnessed a move away from separate special schools and large state-operated institutions as the most common educational and residential placements for persons with mental retardation. The trend is toward education in the least restrictive environment (which includes the regular classroom for a significant and growing number of children with mental retardation) and more normalized lifestyles for adults with mental retardation.

> In 1950, parents of children with mental retardation formed the National Association for Retarded Children. Known today as The Arc, it remains a powerful and important advocacy organization for persons of all ages with mental retardation.

✹ *Educational Approaches*
Curriculum Goals

What do individuals with mental retardation need to learn? Not too many years ago, children with mild mental retardation were presented with a slowed-down version of the general education curriculum that focused largely on traditional academic subject areas. For example, a group of EMR children might study a geography unit in which they learned the 50 states and their capitals during the course of several weeks. Students with more severe retardation spent many hours of instruction learning isolated skills thought to be prerequisites for other more meaningful activities. Many hundreds of students with mental retardation spent thousands of hours putting pegs into pegboards and sorting plastic sticks by color. Unfortunately, knowing that Boise is the capital of Idaho or being able to sort by color did not help these students become more independent.

> See the Profiles & Perspectives box, "A Case for Teaching Functional Skills" later in this chapter.

Functional Academics

In recent years, identifying functional curriculum goals for students with mental retardation has become a major priority for special educators. All learning activities in a functional curriculum are designed to help students acquire skills that can be used in everyday home, community, and work environments. Clark (1994) points out that what is functional for one student may not necessarily be so for another student. He suggests that teachers determine functional knowledge or skills by seeking answers to these questions:

- Does the content focus on necessary knowledge and skills to function as independently as possible in the home, school, or community?
- Does the content provide a scope and sequence for meeting future needs?
- Do the student's parents think the content is important for both current and future needs?
- Does the student think the content is important for both current and future needs?
- Is the content appropriate for the student's chronological age and current intellectual, academic, or behavioral performance level(s)?
- What are the consequences to the student of not learning the concepts and skills? (p. 37)

"That'll be eighty-five cents, please." Ben's teacher is helping him learn functional vocation skills in the lunchroom bagel shop that he and his classmates operate.

An even simpler approach to determining whether any given skill represents functional curriculum is to contemplate this question from the student's perspective: "Will I need it when I'm 21?"

> All of our curricular decisions hinge on the answer to this question. Young children with mental retardation cannot answer this question for themselves yet, so families and teachers must answer it for them, continuously looking ahead to the future for each child. (Beck, Broers, Hogue, Shipstead, & Knowlton, 1994, p. 45)

FIGURE 4.6

Organization of the Taxonomy of Community Living Skills

Source: From *Community Living Skills: A Taxonomy* by R. B. Dever, 1988, Washington, DC: American Association on Mental Retardation. Copyright 1988 by American Association on Mental Retardation. Reprinted by permission.

A Case for Teaching Functional Skills

"My Brother Darryl"

18 years old, moderately/severely handicapped. Been in school for 12 years. Never been served in any setting other than an elementary school. He has had a number of years of "individualized instruction." He has learned to do a lot of things! Darryl can now do lots of things he couldn't do before.

He can put 100 pegs in a board in less than 10 minutes while in his seat with 95% accuracy, but he can't put quarters in a vending machine.

Upon command he can "touch" his nose, shoulder, leg, hair, ear. He is still working on wrist, ankle, hips, but he can't blow his nose when needed.

He can do a 12-piece Big Bird puzzle with 100% accuracy and color an Easter bunny and stay in the lines. He prefers music, but has never been taught to use a radio or record player.

He can now fold primary paper in halves and even quarters, but he can't sort clothes, white from colors, for washing.

He can roll Play-Doh and make wonderful clay snakes, but he can't roll bread dough and cut out biscuits.

He can string beads in alternating colors and match it to a pattern on a DLM card, but he can't lace his shoes.

He can sing his ABCs and tell me names of all the letters in the alphabet when presented on a card in upper case with 80% accuracy, but he can't tell Men's room from Ladies' when we go to McDonald's.

He can be told it's cloudy/rainy and take a black felt cloud and put it on the day of the week on an enlarged calendar (with assistance), but he still goes out in the rain without a raincoat or hat.

He can identify with 100% accuracy 100 different Peabody Picture Cards by pointing, but he can't order a hamburger by pointing to a picture or gesturing.

He can walk a balance beam forward, sideways, and backward, but he can't walk up the steps of the bleachers unassisted in the gym or go to basketball games.

He can count to 100 by rote memory, but he doesn't know how many dollars to pay the waitress for a $2.59 McDonald coupon special.

He can put a cube in the box, under the box, beside the box, and behind the box, but he can't find the trash bin in McDonald's and empty his trash into it.

He can sit in a circle with appropriate behavior and sing songs and play Duck Duck Goose, but nobody else in his neighborhood his age seems to want to do that.

I guess he's just not ready yet.

From Preston Lewis, Kentucky Department of Education. Reprinted by permission.

Community Living Skills

One organized statement of functional goals that can be used as the framework around which to build a curriculum is *A Taxonomy of Community Living Skills* (Dever, 1989). The taxonomy includes more than 300 instructional goals structured around five domains that represent the person as he or she lives, works, plays, and moves through the community:

- Personal maintenance and development
- Homemaking and community life
- Vocational
- Leisure
- Travel

Figure 4.6 illustrates how the five domains are related to one another; Table 4.5 lists the major goals for each domain.

TABLE 4.5
List of major curriculum goals from the Taxonomy of Community Living Skills

DOMAIN P
PERSONAL MAINTENANCE AND DEVELOPMENT

I. The learner will follow routine body maintenance procedures
  A. Maintain personal cleanliness
  B. Groom self
  C. Dress appropriately
  D. Follow appropriate sleep patterns
  E. Maintain nutrition
  F. Exercise regularly
  G. Maintain substance control

II. The learner will treat illnesses
  A. Use first aid and illness treatment procedures
  B. Obtain medical advice when necessary
  C. Follow required medication schedules

III. The learner will establish and maintain personal relationships
  A. Interact appropriately with family
  B. Make friends
  C. Interact appropriately with friends
  D. Cope with inappropriate conduct of family and friends
  E. Respond to sexual needs
  F. Obtain assistance in maintaining personal relationships

IV. The learner will handle personal "glitches"
  A. Cope with changes in daily schedule
  B. Cope with equipment breakdowns and material depletions

DOMAIN H
HOMEMAKING AND COMMUNITY LIFE

I. The learner will obtain living quarters
  A. Find appropriate living quarters
  B. Rent/buy living quarters
  C. Set up living quarters

II. The learner will follow community routines
  A. Keep living quarters neat and clean
  B. Keep fabrics neat and clean
  C. Maintain interior of living quarters
  D. Maintain exterior of living quarters
  E. Respond to seasonal changes
  F. Follow home safety procedures
  G. Follow accident/emergency procedures
  H. Maintain foodstock
  I. Prepare and serve meals
  J. Budget money appropriately
  K. Pay bills

III. The learner will co-exist in a neighborhood and community
  A. Interact appropriately with community members
  B. Cope with inappropriate conduct of others
  C. Observe requirements of the law
  D. Carry out civic duties

IV. The learner will handle "glitches" in the home
  A. Cope with equipment breakdowns
  B. Cope with depletions of household supplies
  C. Cope with unexpected depletions of funds
  D. Cope with disruptions in routine
  E. Cope with sudden changes in the weather

Source: From *Community Living Skills: A Taxonomy* by R. B. Dever, 1988, Washington, DC: American Association on Mental Retardation. Copyright 1988 by American Association on Mental Retardation. Reprinted by permission.

TABLE 4.5   *(continued)*

DOMAIN V
VOCATIONAL

I.   The learner will obtain work
   A.   Seek employment
   B.   Accept employment
   C.   Use unemployment services
II.   The learner will perform the work routine
   A.   Perform the job routine
   B.   Follow work-related daily schedule
   C.   Maintain work station
   D.   Follow employer rules and regulations
   E.   Use facilities appropriately
   F.   Follow job safety procedures
   G.   Follow accident and emergency procedures

III.   The learner will co-exist with others on the job
   A.   Interact appropriately with others on the job
   B.   Cope with inappropriate conduct of others on the job
IV.   The learner will handle "glitches" on the job
   A.   Cope with changes in work routine
   B.   Cope with work problems
   C.   Cope with supply depletions and equipment breakdowns

DOMAIN L
LEISURE

I.   The learner will develop leisure activities
   A.   Find new leisure activities
   B.   Acquire skills for leisure activities
II.   The learner will follow community routines
   A.   Perform leisure activities
   B.   Maintain leisure equipment
   C.   Follow leisure safety procedures
   D.   Follow accident and emergency procedures

III.   The learner will co-exist with others during leisure
   A.   Interact appropriately with others in a leisure setting
   B.   Respond to the inappropriate conduct of others
IV.   The learner will handle "glitches" during leisure
   A.   Cope with changes in leisure routine
   B.   Cope with equipment breakdowns and material depletions

DOMAIN T
TRAVEL

I.   The learner will travel routes in the community
   A.   Form mental maps of frequented buildings
   B.   Form mental maps of the community
II.   The learner will use conveyances
   A.   Follow usage procedures
   B.   Make decisions preparatory to travel
   C.   Follow travel safety procedures
   D.   Follow accident and emergency procedures

III.   The learner will co-exist with others while traveling
   A.   Interact appropriately with others while traveling
   B.   Respond to the inappropriate conduct of others while traveling
IV.   The learner will handle "glitches"
   A.   Cope with changes in travel schedule
   B.   Cope with equipment breakdowns
   C.   Cope with being lost

Instructional Methodology

Research in specific educational techniques for students with mental retardation began when Itard started his work with Victor, the Wild Boy of Aveyron. But only since the early 1960s has the scientific method been employed systematically in an attempt to discover effective and reliable teaching methods. Although this research is far from finished—indeed, we must continually search for better teaching methods—one approach that has produced consistent educational improvements in students with mental retardation is the behavioral approach, or applied behavior analysis.

Applied behavior analysis can be defined as systematically arranging environmental events to produce desired learning. Behaviorally oriented teachers verify the effects of their instruction by directly measuring student performance. Applied behavior analysis is not a single technique but a systematic approach to teaching based on scientifically demonstrated principles that describe how the environment affects learning (Alberto & Troutman, 1995; Cooper, Heron, & Heward, 1987; Sulzer-Azaroff & Mayer, 1991). Teaching methods derived from applied behavior analysis are used effectively not only with learners who experience mental retardation and other disabilities but also with students in general education.

Although literally hundreds of specific teaching tactics are based on behavior analysis (e.g., Lovitt, 1995), most hold the following six features in common:

1. Precise definition and *task analysis* of the new skill or behavior to be learned
2. *Direct and frequent measurement* of the student's performance of the skill
3. Frequent opportunities for *active student response* during instruction
4. Immediate and *systematic feedback* for student performance
5. Procedures for *transferring stimulus control* of correct student responses from instructional cues or prompts to naturally occurring stimuli
6. Strategies to promote the *generalization and maintenance* of newly learned skills to different, nontraining situations and environments

Task Analysis

An initial step in the behavioral approach to instruction is to specify exactly what skills, or behaviors, the learner is to acquire. **Task analysis** means breaking down complex or multiple-step behaviors or skills into small, easier-to-teach subtasks. The subskills or subtasks are then sequenced, either in the natural order in which they are typically performed or from the easiest to most difficult. Assessing a student's performance on a sequence of task-analyzed subskills helps pinpoint exactly where instruction should begin. Table 4.6 shows a task analysis for eating in a fast-food restaurant.

During the task analysis stage of instructional planning, it is also important to consider the extent to which the natural environment requires performance of the target skill for a given duration or at a minimum rate. For example, Test, Spooner, Keul, and Grossi (1990) included specific time limits for each of the 17 steps in a task analysis used to teach two secondary students with severe mental retardation to use the public telephone to call home. The specific sequence of steps and the time limit for each step were determined by having two adults without disabilities use the telephone.

Direct and Frequent Measurement

Another hallmark of the behavioral approach is direct and frequent measurement. Measurement is direct when it objectively records the learner's performance of the

For a list of textbooks on applied behavior analysis and behavioral teaching methods, see the "For More Information" section at the end of this chapter. The following journals regularly publish applications of behavior analysis with learners with mental retardation and other disabilities: *Behavior Modification, Education & Treatment of Children, Education and Training in Mental Retardation and Developmental Disabilities, Journal of Applied Behavior Analysis, The Journal of The Association for Persons with Severe Handicaps, Journal of Behavioral Education,* and *Research in Developmental Disabilities.*

Excellent descriptions of how to perform and validate task analyses can be found in Bailey and Wolery (1984); Bellamy, Horner, and Inman (1979); Gold (1976); Moyer and Dardig (1978); Snell (1993); and Test and Spooner (in press). A task-analytic procedure based on 17 fundamental motions known as *therbligs* can also be used by special educators (Browder, Lim, Lin, & Belfiore, 1993).

TABLE 4.6   Task analysis of ordering, paying, and eating in a fast-food restaurant

SKILL	APPROPRIATE RESPONSE	INAPPROPRIATE RESPONSE
Locating		
1.1	Does not initiate social interaction. Does not self-stimulate.	Talks/makes manual sign to customer or trainer. Engages in motor/vocal self-stimulation so that customers differentially attend to him.
1.2	Enters double door within 2 min of start.	Uses wrong door. Does not enter within 2 min.
1.3	Goes directly to counter. Does not leave line except to get into shorter line.	Not in line or at counter within 30 sec. Gets out of line.
Ordering		
2.1	Makes ordering response within 10 sec of cue. If written, finishes within 2 min.	Does not respond within 10 sec. Responds before cue. Makes inappropriate (i.e. nonordering-related) verbalization. Not finished writing within 2 min.
2.2	Says "How much for . . . ?" when giving order.	Does not inquire "How much for . . . ?"
2.3	Orders food that he can afford, appropriate item combination (i.e., minimum order—sandwich & drink; maximum—sandwich, drink, side order, & any other item).	Orders more food than he can pay for. Uses inappropriate item combination.
2.4	Says "Eat here" when asked.	Does not say order is to dine in. Says "To go."
Paying		
3.1	Begins to get money within 10 sec of cue. Does not let go of money on counter before cashier cue.	Does not get money within 10 sec. Releases money before cue.
3.2	Hands cashier appropriate combination of bills.	Does not give enough money. Gives too much money so that same bill is returned.
3.3	Displays fingers on at least one hand.	Does not display fingers.
3.4	Inquires "Mistake?" if short billed.	Does not inquire if short billed. Inquires "Mistake?" when change is accurate.
3.5	Puts money in pocket.	Does not take change. Puts money on tray instead of pocket.
3.6	Requests salt, pepper, or catsup.	Does not request any condiments.
3.7	Takes a napkin from dispenser.	Does not take napkin from dispenser.
3.8	Says "Thank you."	Does not say "Thank you."
Eating and Exiting		
4.1	Sits at unoccupied, trashfree table within 1 min of availability.	Sits with other customer. Sits at a table with trash present. Does not sit down within 1 min.
4.2	Eats food placed only on paper.	Eats food off tray, table, etc.
4.3	Puts napkin in lap *and* wipes mouth or hands.	Does not put napkin in lap. Does not wipe hands or mouth on it.
4.4	Does not spill food or drink.	Drops food off tray or spills drink.
4.5	If spills occur, picks up every one, does not eat any spilled item.	Does not pick up or blot. Eats spilled food.
4.6	Puts trash in container, tray on top, within 2 min of finishing eating.	Does not put trash in container within 2 min. Uses inappropriate container. Throws tray in container.
4.7	Exits within 1 min of trash or 3 min of finishing eating.	Does not exit within time limits.

Source: From "Teaching the Handicapped to Eat in Public Places: Acquisition, Generalization, and Maintenance of Restaurant Skills" by R. A. van den Pol, et al., 1981, *Journal of Applied Behavior Analysis, 14,* p. 63. Copyright by the Society for the Experimental Analysis of Behavior, Inc. Reprinted by permission.

Precision teaching, a method of direct and frequent assessment of student performance with specific decision rules indicating when instruction should be modified, is described in Chapter 5.

behavior of interest in the natural environment for that skill. Measurement is frequent when it occurs on a regular basis; ideally, measurement should take place as often as instruction occurs. Academic achievement tests have traditionally been the major source of data for evaluating educational programs. Although achievement data are important, they are not useful for day-to-day planning and evaluation of instruction. Achievement tests are usually given only once or twice a year, and the information they provide is too indirect, requiring that inferences be made about the student's actual classroom performance.

> Two errors of judgment are common for [teachers] who do not collect direct and frequent measurements of their student's performance. First, many ineffective intervention programs are continued. . . . Second, many effective programs are discontinued prematurely because subjective judgment finds no improvement. For example, teachers who do not use direct and frequent measures might discern little difference between a student's reading 40 words per minute with 60% accuracy and 48 words per minute with 73% accuracy. However, direct and frequent data collected on the rate and accuracy of oral reading would show an improved performance. Decision making in education must be based upon performance data; the individual's behavior must dictate the course of action. (Cooper, Heron, & Heward, 1987, p. 60)

For guidelines on how to make instructional decisions based on student performance data, see Farlow and Snell (1994).

Only through diligent direct and frequent measurement of student performance are teachers able to provide the individualized instruction so vital to the growth and progress of children with mental retardation.

Active Student Response

For reviews of research showing the relationship between student participation and achievement in both general and special education, see Brophy and Good (1986); Fisher and Berliner (1985); Greenwood, Delquadri, and Hall (1984); and Greenwood et al. (1994).

Contemporary educational research is unequivocal in its support of the positive relationship between the amount of time children spend actively responding to academic tasks and their subsequent achievement. Students who make many responses during a lesson learn more than students who make few responses or, worse, passively observe the teacher or other students respond. Providing instruction with high levels of active student participation is important for all learners, but it is particularly important for students with disabilities: "For children who are behind to catch up, they simply must be taught more in less time. If the teacher doesn't attempt to teach more in less time . . . the gap in general knowledge between a normal and handicapped student becomes even greater" (Kameenui & Simmons, 1990, p. 11).

Various terms such as *active student response, opportunity to respond,* and *academic learning time* are used to refer to this most important variable.

> Active student response (ASR) can be defined as an observable response made to an instructional antecedent. To say it less technically, ASR occurs when a student emits a detectable response to ongoing instruction. The kinds of responses that qualify as ASR are as varied as the kinds of lessons that are taught. Depending upon the instructional objective, examples of ASR include words read, problems answered, boards cut, test tubes measured, praise and supportive comments spoken, notes or scales played, stitches sewn, sentences written, workbook questions answered, and fastballs pitched. The basic measure of how much ASR a student receives is a frequency count of the number of academic responses emitted within a given period of instruction. (Heward, 1994, p. 286)

When all variables are held constant (e.g., quality of curriculum materials, students' prerequisite skills, motivational variables), an ASR-rich lesson will generally result in more learning than a lesson in which students make few or no responses.

Frequent active student response (ASR) is a fundamental characteristic of numerous instructional methods with empirical support for their effectiveness with students with disabilities, including

- **choral responding** (Heward, Courson, & Narayan, 1989; Kamps, Dugan, Leonard, & Daoust, 1994; Sainato, Strain, & Lyon, 1987)
- **response cards** (see "Everyone Participates in This Science Class" in the Teaching & Learning box in Chapter 6) (Gardner, Heward, & Grossi, 1994; Narayan, Heward, Gardner, Courson, & Omness, 1990)
- **guided notes** (see "Guided Notes" in the Teaching & Learning box in Chapter 5) (Heward, 1994; Lazarus, 1991, 1993)
- repeated reading (O'Shea, Sindelar, & O'Shea, 1985; Weinstein & Cooke, 1992)
- fluency-building activities such as **time-trials** (see "How Many Can You Do in 1 Minute?" in the Teaching & Learning box later in this chapter) (Howell & Lorson-Howell, 1990; Miller & Heward, 1992)
- peer tutoring (see "Somos Todos Ayudantes y Estudiantes!" in the Teaching & Learning box in Chapter 5) (Maheady, Sacca, & Harper, 1988; Miller, Barbetta, & Heron 1994)
- computer-assisted instruction (Lewis, 1995)
- direct instruction (see Chapter 5) (Becker, 1992; Gersten, Carnine, & White, 1984; Weisberg, 1994)

Systematic Feedback

Academic feedback—information provided to students on some aspect of their performance—falls into two broad categories: positive feedback for correct responses and error correction for incorrect responses. Reith and Evertson (1988) note that all major reviews of the literature on effective teaching describe academic feedback as among the most critical instructional variables. *Feedback* refers to all of the information and consequences received by a student after he or she has responded. Correct responses are followed by praise and/or other forms of **positive reinforcement.** Incorrect responses receive systematic error correction.

> See "What to Do When Students Make Mistakes" in the Teaching & Learning box later in this chapter.

Effective instruction for all students is characterized by frequent opportunities for active student response and systematic feedback.

Feedback is generally most effective when it is *specific, immediate, positive, frequent,* and *differential* (comparing the student's present performance with past performance; e.g., "You read 110 words today, Jermon. That's 5 more than yesterday.") (Van Houten, 1980, 1984). But what does *immediate* mean, what aspects of the student's performance should be attended to, and how frequently must feedback be delivered to be effective?

Effective teachers change the focus and timing of the feedback they provide as a student progresses from initial attempts at learning a new skill through practicing a newly acquired skill. The point of contact between the learner and systematic instruction is a three-term relationship, often called a practice trial or learning trial (see Figure 4.7). A **learning trial** consists of three major elements: (a) an instructional antecedent (e.g., a question or item from the curriculum or lesson), (b) the student's response to that item, and (c) instructional feedback following the response. The learning trial serves as a basic unit for analyzing and examining teaching and learning from both the teacher's perspective (as an opportunity to teach) and the student's perspective (as an opportunity to learn). The concept of the three-term learning trial is not limited to structured, teacher-directed instruction. Learning trials occur during incidental teaching, community-based instruction, on the playground, and with social as well as academic skills.

Figure 4.7 illustrates two ways in which a series of learning trials can take place within the ongoing dimension of time. When a student is first learning a new skill or content knowledge, feedback ideally follows each response. Feedback during this initial **acquisition stage of learning** should focus on the accuracy and topography

FIGURE 4.7

Feedback within a series of learning trials during the acquisition and practice stages of learning

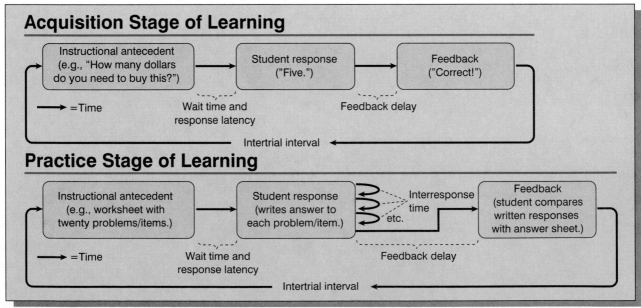

Source: From "Three 'Low-Tech' Strategies for Increasing the Frequency of Active Student Response During Group Instruction," by W. L. Heward. In R. Gardner III, D. M. Sainato, J. O. Cooper, T. E. Heron, W. L. Heward, J. W. Eshleman, & T. A. Grossi (Eds.), 1994, *Behavior Analysis in Education: Focus on Measurably Superior Instruction* (p. 284). Pacific Grove, CA: Brooks/Cole.

of the student's response. By providing feedback after each response, the teacher reduces the likelihood of the student practicing errors (Van Houten, 1984).

During the **practice stage of learning,** when the student can perform the new skill with accuracy, a series of responses can and should be emitted before feedback is obtained (as shown in the bottom half of Figure 4.7). Feedback during the practice stage should emphasize the rate or speed at which the student performs the target skill. Providing feedback after each response during the practice stage of learning may actually have a detrimental effect by blocking the student's chance to develop fluency by "going fast."

Transferring Stimulus Control

Trial-and-error learning is difficult and frustrating, at best, for students without disabilities. For students with mental retardation and other learning problems, it is likely to be a complete waste of time. Instead of waiting to see whether the student will make a correct response, the effective teacher provides a prompt that makes a correct response very probable. The correct response is reinforced, the prompt is repeated, and another correct student response is reinforced. As the response prompts are gradually and systematically withdrawn, the student's behavior comes under the **stimulus control** of the curriculum content or things in the natural environment that typically serve as cues for that skill.

One method for transferring stimulus control is **constant time delay,** a procedure in which the teacher begins by simultaneously presenting the stimulus being taught and a controlling response prompt. For example, as the teacher holds up a flashcard with the word *ball* printed on it, he says, "Ball," which successfully prompts a correct response by the student. After a number of 0-second delay trials, the teacher waits for a fixed amount of time (e.g., 4 seconds) between presentation of the instructional stimulus and the response prompt. Learning trials are repeated with the constant delay until the student begins to respond correctly prior to the teacher's prompt; that is, the student's behavior has come under the control of the instructional stimulus (the printed word), and the response prompt is no longer needed.

Time delay is one of the most well researched strategies for teaching students with mental retardation and severe disabilities (Ault, Gast, Wolery, & Doyle, 1992; Kratzer, Spooner, Test, & Koorland, 1993). See Wolery, Ault, and Doyle (1992) for detailed information on how to use response-prompting strategies with students who have moderate and severe disabilities.

Generalization and Maintenance

Generalization and *maintenance* refers to the extent to which students extend what they have learned across settings and over time. Students with disabilities often have trouble remembering what they have learned and using their new knowledge and skills in settings or situations different from the ones in which they were taught. During the past 20 years, behavior analysts have designed and evaluated a number of effective alternatives to the "train and hope" method of teaching (Stokes & Baer, 1977; Stokes & Osnes, 1989). Although there is still much to be learned about helping students with disabilities get the most out of what they learn, the promising beginnings of a reliable "technology of generalization" have been developed. Four strategies used by special educators to promote the generalization and maintenance of new skills and knowledge are listed starting on p. 175:

Several studies have found a procedure called *instructive feedback,* in which the teacher presents students with information about nontarget content/items, to be effective with students with mental retardation (e.g., Doyle, Gast, Wolery, Ault, & Farmer, 1990; Gast, Doyle, Wolery, Ault, & Baklarz, 1991).

Is constant time delay a difficult procedure to use? No. A recent study found that second- and fourth-grade students could successfully use constant time delay to teach sight words to three peers with mental retardation and other disabilities (Wolery, Werts, Snyder, & Caldwell, 1994).

Two good sources for how-to information for planning and implementing instruction for generalized outcomes are Baer (1981) and Horner, Dunlap, and Koegel (1988).

What to Do When Students Make Mistakes

·························

Providing Effective and Efficient Error Correction

Students make mistakes. Even during the most carefully planned lessons using well-designed instructional materials, student errors occur. Students answer incorrectly, give incomplete answers, or do not respond at all. The importance of providing feedback to students when they make errors is well documented (e.g., Brophy, 1986; Christenson, Ysseldyke, & Thurlow, 1989; Fisher et al., 1980). Despite support for correcting student errors, relatively little experimental research on error correction exists, and that which does is far from conclusive. Teachers are left in the unsettling position of being aware of the importance of correcting student errors but receiving little in the way of empirically supported guidance in how to do so.

Don't Let Students Practice Errors During the Acquisition Stage of Learning

Students "learn by doing," but if errors are repeated, what are they learning? They may be learning how to perform skills incorrectly. Students learn better by "doing with feedback." The biggest problem with delayed feedback is that it allows students to practice errors (Van Houten, 1980, 1984). Practicing errors also wastes valuable instructional time because of the reteaching and relearning that eventually must take place.

Most errors are made during the acquisition stage of learning, when the student is learning how to perform a new skill or to remember and use new knowledge correctly. During the acquisition stage, it is important that feedback be provided *before the student is required to use the skill/knowledge again.* Acquisition stage feedback should be qualitative, focusing on the accuracy of the student's response. For example: "Excellent, Robin. You removed all of the leaves with dark spots. But there's still too much sand on them to serve to our customers. Let me

show you again how to wash it off. Then you can show me."

It is usually not critical that feedback occur within a few seconds or minutes of a student's response. For behaviors that produce a permanent product (e.g., a completed workbook page, a sanded piece of wood), feedback even received a day or two later may still be helpful as long as it occurs before the student must respond again.

Teachers can ensure that students receive feedback after each response by using instructional strategies such as these:

- *Teacher-led group instruction.* Provide frequent opportunities for all students to actively respond with techniques such as choral responding (Heward, Courson, & Narayan, 1989) and response cards (see "Everyone Participates in this Science Class" in Chapter 6).
- *Collaborative learning.* Use a peer tutoring system or small-group activities in which peers provide feedback and error correction to one another after each response (Miller, Barbetta, & Heron, 1994). (See "Classwide Peer Tutoring" in Chapter 2.)
- *Learning centers.* Use instructional materials and computer software that provide feedback on the accuracy of each response.
- *Independent seatwork.* Have students self-score their work and self-correct any errors before proceeding to the next problem or item.
- *Homework.* Avoid assigning homework or independent seatwork activities that do not contain self-scoring and self-correcting components until the student can perform the target skill with some accuracy.

When Errors Occur, Provide Effective and Efficient Error Correction

When handled properly, errors can provide good opportunities for teaching and learning. Too often, however, error correction is carried out ineffectively (the student is still wrong the next time) and inefficiently (it is time-consuming and reduces the total number of learning trials that can be conducted during the lesson). Research suggests that learning is enhanced when error correction has the following qualities:

- *Done right now.* Errors should be corrected before going to the next item or problem. Teachers may be hesitant to "hold up" instruction when a student errs during group instruction, preferring instead to work individually with the student after the conclusion of the lesson. But this approach may allow the student to repeat the error for the remainder of the lesson. Two recent studies compared "right now" and "end-of-the-lesson" error correction during sight word lessons with primary students with mental retardation and science vocabulary lessons with upper elementary-age students with learning disabilities. Error correction immediately after each error was more effective, even when the postlesson error correction consisted of massed practice (repeated trials) (Barbetta, Heward, Bradley, & Miller, 1994; Kleinman et al., 1994).
- *Direct.* Error correction is direct when the feedback relates to the target skill. Several studies have shown that the effectiveness of error correction is improved when students are provided with complete information or a direct model of the missed item (Barbetta, Heward, & Bradley, 1993; Espin & Deno, 1989). That is, instead of offering incomplete or indirect feedback, tell, show, and/or guide the student through the correct response.
- *Quick.* Error correction is quick when the teacher rapidly tells, shows, and/or demonstrates the correct response (e.g., "No. This word is *circus.*"). Correcting an error in 3 or 4 seconds is better than discussing the student's mistake for a minute or longer. In trying to help students "understand" their error, teachers often spend a great deal of time talking. Although detailed explanation is sometimes necessary and helpful, often students just get confused or lose interest during all of the teacher talk. The time lost to hashing over the previous error would be better used for conducting several more complete learning trials (Heron, Heward, Cooke, & Hill, 1983).
- *Ends with the student making the correct response.* When a student errs, teachers often hint, probe, tell, show, and eventually provide the correct response or ask another student to answer. The student who made the original error

passively observes. Results from several studies show that feedback is more effective when the student who erred is given an opportunity to emit the corrected response (Barbetta & Heward, 1993; Dalrymple & Feldman, 1992; Drevno et al., 1994). For example, Barbetta, Heron, and Heward (1993) examined the effects of active student response during the correction of errors made by primary students with mental retardation during sight word lessons. Half of each week's set of 20 unknown words were taught with No Response (NR) error correction (after each error, the teacher modeled the correct response while the student looked at the word); the remaining 10 words were taught with Active Student Response (ASR) error correction (the student repeated the word after the teacher's model). ASR error correction was more effective for all six children on all five measures of performance: number and percentage of correct responses during instruction, same-day tests, next-day tests (see Figure A), maintenance tests given 2 weeks after instruction, and words read in sentences.

The error correction episode should end with the student making the correct response. Instead of providing or showing the correct response and then asking the student, "Now do you understand?" have the student repeat the correct response (e.g., T: "No. This word is *circus.* What is this word?" S: "Circus." T: "Good.").

Although much remains to be learned about how teachers should respond when students make mistakes during instruction, the combined results of experimental studies conducted to date provide some guidance for teachers. This research suggests that error correction will be more effective and efficient when it is immediate, direct, quick, and ends with the student making the correct response.

Evaluate the Effects of Error Correction

As with any instructional method or technique, teachers should evaluate the error correction procedures they use. Two questions should be addressed in evaluating an error correction procedure. First, what is the procedure's *effectiveness* in helping students respond correctly in the future? This can be directly and simply determined by observing how the

FIGURE A

Number of sight words read correctly by primary students with developmental disabilities 1 day after instruction. Yellow data points show performance on words taught with ASR error correction; red data points show performance on words taught with NR error correction. Breaks in data paths separate word sets.

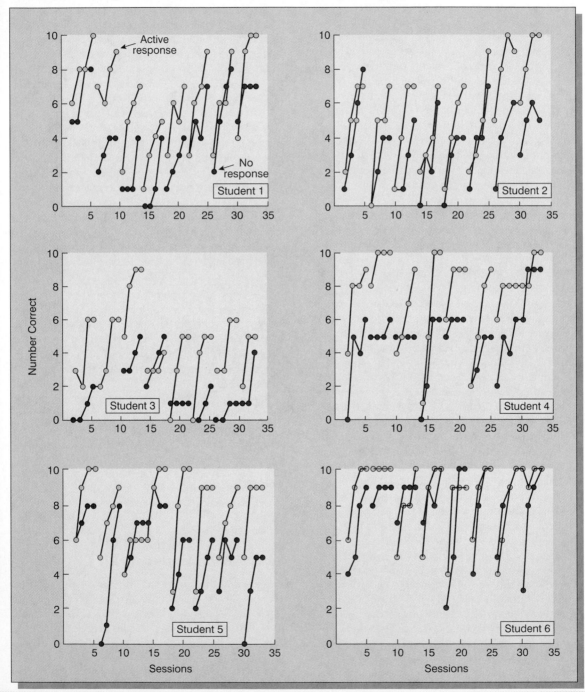

student responds to the same item or task situation the next time it is presented. Teachers should also consider the *efficiency* of the error correction procedures they use. A complex and time-consuming error correction procedure may be effective (the student responds correctly in the future) but too inefficient because it limits the total number of learning trials experienced by the learner during the lesson. Like most questions concerning effective instructional practices, the question of how much time should be spent in error correction is an empirical one. Its answer is to be found in the performance of students.

Figure Source: From "Effects of Active Student Response During Error Correction on the Acquisition, Maintenance, and Generalization of Sight Words by Students with Developmental Disabilities" by P. M. Barbetta, T. E. Heron, & W. L. Heward, *Journal of Applied Behavior Analysis, 26,* p. 116. Reprinted by permission.

- *Aim for naturally occurring contingencies of reinforcement.* The most basic of all strategies for promoting generalization and maintenance is to increase the probability that a student's new behavior/skill will be reinforced by those in his or her natural environment (e.g., the regular classroom, the playground, the community, recreational and work settings) (Baer & Wolf, 1970; Hendrickson, Strain, Tremlay, & Shores, 1982; Kohler & Greenwood, 1986). This can be accomplished by (a) teaching only functional skills that will be needed and are likely to be valued by people in the natural environment and (b) teaching students to perform the new skills with enough accuracy and fluency to produce reinforcement in the natural environment.
- *Use a general case strategy to select teaching examples.* Instructional examples that systematically represent the response requirements and stimulus variations found in the natural environment should be selected and incorporated into lessons (Horner, Sprague, & Wilcox, 1982; Horner, Williams, & Steveley, 1987; Sprague & Horner, 1984). Incorporating negative teaching examples—situations in which the student should not perform the behavior—can also improve the student's success in the natural environment (Horner, Eberhard, & Sheehan, 1986).
- *Program common stimuli.* If the generalization setting (e.g., the regular classroom) differs greatly from the setting in which teaching takes place, the student may not perform the new behavior. Programming common stimuli is accomplished by (a) incorporating into the teaching situation as many typical features of the generalization setting as possible and/or (b) creating a new common stimulus that the student learns to use in the teaching setting and that is transportable to the generalization setting, where it prompts or assists performance of the target skill (Anderson-Inman, Walker, & Purcell, 1984; Trask-Tyler, Grossi, & Heward, 1994; van den Pol et al., 1981).
- *Teach self-management skills.* The only person who is with the learner at all times and in all places is the learner's own self. Students can use self-management to promote the generalization and maintenance of their new knowledge and skills (Ackerman & Shapiro, 1984; Agran, Fodor-Davis, Moore, & Deer, 1989; Hughes, 1994; Rhode, Morgan, & Young, 1983; Sowers, Verdi, Bourbeau, & Sheehan, 1985).

✻ *Educational Placement Alternatives*

Although the regular public schools are changing their ways of providing services to students with mental retardation, they are doing so slowly. Traditionally, the student

Community-based instruction provides these secondary students with mental retardation an opportunity to acquire employment skills in a real work setting.

During the 1992–93 school year, only 5% of students with mental retardation were educated in the regular classroom, with 25% being served in resource room programs and 59% in separate classes (U.S. Department of Education, 1994). See Polloway (1984) for a comprehensive review of the history and research concerning the most effective classroom placement for students with mild retardation.

with mild mental retardation (EMR) was educated in a self-contained classroom with 12 to 18 other EMR students. Children with moderate and severe mental retardation were usually excluded from the local public school and placed into a special school for children with disabilities or into an institution.

For many students today, the label of mental retardation still results in a placement decision, and more often than not that placement is a separate class. Even though the IDEA mandates that children with disabilities be educated with their nondisabled peers to the greatest extent possible, only about one third of students with mental retardation are spending all or part of the school day in the regular classroom, with supplemental instruction provided by a resource teacher.

But, as we saw in Chapter 2, simply putting a child with disabilities into a regular classroom does not necessarily mean that student will be accepted socially or receive the most appropriate and needed instructional programming. Many special and regular educators, however, are developing programs and methods for integrating the instruction of students with mental retardation with that of their nondisabled peers. Systematically planning for the students' inclusion in the classroom through team games and group investigation projects and directly training all students in specific skills for interacting with one another are just some of the methods for increasing the chances of a successful regular class placement (Gottlieb & Leyser, 1981; Stainback, Stainback, Raschke, & Anderson, 1981; Strain, Guralnick, & Walker, 1986).

Peer tutoring programs have also proven effective in promoting the instructional and social inclusion of students with mental retardation into regular classrooms (Delquadri, Greenwood, Whorton, Carta, & Hall, 1986; Osguthorpe & Scruggs, 1986). For example, Cooke et al. (1982) implemented a classwide peer tutoring system in a first-grade classroom in which a student with Down syndrome participated. During the course of this 5-month study, she not only interacted directly and positively with her peer tutor but also learned more than 40 sight words from her classmate.

The relative appropriateness of inclusion in the regular classroom may change for some students as they move from the elementary grades to the secondary level when opportunities for community-based instruction in vocational and life skills are critical. The extent to which students with mental retardation, like all students with disabilities, are educated in general education classrooms must be determined by the student's individual needs.

> Students with mental retardation often benefit from similar programs for students who are not disabled. During the early elementary grades, students with mental retardation, as well as their chronological age peers, need instruction in basic academic skills. Reading, mathematical calculations, and writing are core curricular areas that should be included in programs for all students. During this period, many students with mental retardation can also benefit from full or partial inclusion in regular classroom settings.
>
> As students get older, their needs begin to differ and thus curricular differentiation becomes an important consideration. . . . Rather than being integrated into a world history class, many students with mental retardation may be better served by learning the necessary functional skills for independent living. Skills such as job readiness, how to use leisure time, how to budget and shop, how to cook and how to maintain a household are important. While all individuals must learn these skills in order to be independent, most students learn them on their own, without specific instructional activities that focus on these areas. Students with mental retardation, on the other hand, often need structured learning experiences in order to learn these skills. (Smith & Hilton, 1994, pp. 6–7)

About 10% of students with mental retardation continue to attend special schools or residential facilities. Sometimes a number of small neighboring school districts pool their resources to offer a special school program for students with moderate/severe/profound mental retardation. Many special educators today believe, however, that schools prohibit students from obtaining an education in the least restrictive environment and that all children should attend their local neighborhood schools regardless of the type or severity of their disability (e.g., Brown et al., 1989a).

See the January, 1995, issue of *Educational Leadership*.

In Chapter 11 we examine the case for educating children with severe disabilities in their neighborhood schools.

✳ *Current Issues and Future Trends*

In 1961 John F. Kennedy created the first President's Committee on Mental Retardation. The committee was charged with conducting an intensive study of mental retardation and making recommendations for national policy. A year later, results of the many task forces, public hearings, visits to facilities, and extensive interviews with professionals, parents, and persons with mental retardation were compiled into the committee's report (Mayo, 1962). The report contained specific recommendations related to human and legal rights, prevention, research, education, and medical and other services for individuals with mental retardation. Many of the committee's recommendations set the stage for much of what took place during the next two decades, particularly in the areas of research and legislation confirming the rights of retarded citizens.

How Many Can You Do in 1 Minute?

....

Using Daily Time Trials to Help Students with Mental Retardation Add and Subtract with Fluency

The conventional wisdom goes something like this: Students with mental retardation can learn, but because they learn at a slower rate than students without disabilities, they should be given more time to complete their work. Although it is generally true that children with mental retardation acquire new skills more slowly, teachers may be doing students with disabilities a disservice by always providing plenty of time for them to do their work. Accuracy measures alone do not provide a complete picture of learning. For instance, whereas two students might each complete a page of math problems with 100% accuracy, the one who finishes in 2 minutes is more accomplished than the one who needs 5 minutes to answer the same problems. To be functional, many of the skills we use every day in the home, community, or workplace must be performed at a certain rate of speed.

Providing students with practice to build fluency is an important part of teaching. After the initial *acquisition stage* of learning, when a student learns *how* to perform the skill correctly, the student progresses to the *practice stage* of learning, in which the focus should shift to building **fluency**. "The teacher does not push fluency when the student cannot yet work the problems correctly. Similarly, when teaching a student to be fluent, techniques used to promote accuracy are not used. During fluency instruction, elaborate explanations and corrections are not needed; in fact, they might even slow the student down. Instead, the teacher talks about and rewards fluency" (Howell & Lorson-Howell, 1990, p. 21).

Daily time trials (giving students the opportunity to perform a skill as many times as they can in a brief period) are an excellent tactic for building fluency. Several studies have shown that both general and special education students not only benefit from time trials but also like to be timed (see Van Houten, 1980). For example, 11 students with mental retarda-

tion participated in a study evaluating the effects of 1-minute time trials on the rate and accuracy of answering single-digit math facts (Miller, Hall, & Heward, in press). During the first 2 weeks of the study, when they were told to complete as many problems as they could during an untimed 10-minute work period, the students answered correctly an average of 8.4 problems per minute (see Figure A). During the next phase, in which a series of seven 1-minute time trials was conducted with a 20-second rest period between each time trial (equaling a total of 10 minutes, as in the first phase), the students' correct rate increased to 13.2 per minute. Fluency improved to 16 problems per minute during a final phase, when immediate feedback and self-correction were conducted immediately after each of two consecutive time trials.

Did working faster harm the students' accuracy? Not at all: The students answered correctly 85% of all the problems they attempted during the 10-minute work period, but their accuracy improved to 89% when time trials were used. When asked which method they preferred, 10 of the 11 students indicated they liked time trials better than the untimed work period.

Fluency training in the form of 1-minute time trials or counting periods has been used successfully to help individuals with disabilities improve a wide range of academic, vocational, and other skills (e.g., Johnson & Layng, 1994; McCuin & Cooper, 1994; Possi, 1994; Stump et al., 1992; Weinstein & Cooke, 1992).

Guidelines for Conducting Time Trials

- Keep the time for each trial *short*. One minute is sufficient for most academic skills.
- Do time trials *every day*. For example, a series of two or three 1-minute oral reading time trials could be conducted at the end of each day's lesson.
- Make time trials *fun*. Time trials should not be presented as a test; they are a learning activity that can be approached like a game.

Mean number of math facts answered correctly by 11 elementary students with mental retardation during a daily 10-minute math period. Four of the students participated only 3 days per week due to mainstreaming.

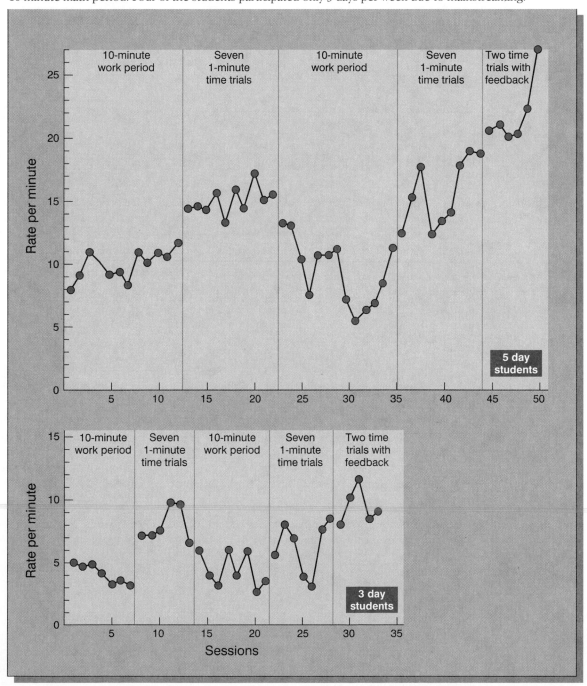

- Use time trials only during the *practice stage of learning,* after students have learned how to do the skill correctly.
- Follow time trials with a more *relaxed activity.*
- Feedback to students should *emphasize proficiency* (total number correct), not simply accuracy (percentage correct).
- Have each student try to *beat his or her own best score.*

- Have students *keep track of their progress* by self-graphing.
- Consider using a *performance feedback chart* to provide both individual and group feedback during a time trial program (Van Houten, 1980, 1984).

Adapted from A. D. Miller and W. L. Heward, (1992), "Do Your Students Really Know Their Math Facts? Using Daily Time Trials to Build Fluency," *Intervention in School and Clinic, 28,* pp. 98–104. Used by permission.

Figure Source: From "Effects of Sequential 1-Minute Time Trials with and Without Inter-trial Feedback and Self-Correction on General and Special Education Students' Fluency with Math Facts," by A. D. Miller, S. W. Hall, & W. L. Heward, *Journal of Behavioral Education,* in press. Used by permission.

Subsequent presidents have reconvened the Committe on Mental Retardation to track the accomplishment of earlier goals and to attempt to predict future needs. In its 1976 report *Mental Retardation: Century of Decision*, the committee outlined the country's major objectives in the Field of mental retardation through the year 2000.

1. Attainment of citizenship status in law and in fact for all mentally retarded individuals in the United States, exercised to the fullest degree possible under the conditions of disability
2. Reduction of the incidence of mental retardation from biomedical causes by at least 50% by the year 2000.
3. Reduction of the incidence and prevalence of mental retardation associated with social disadvantage to the lowest level possible by the end of this century.
4. Adequate and humane service systems for all persons with mental retardation in need of them
5. Attainment of a high and stable level of international relations in the cooperative resolution of the universal human problems of preventing and ameliorating mental retardation
6. Achievement of a firm and deep public acceptance of persons with mental retardation as members in common of the social community and as citizens in their own right

Although a great deal remains to be done to realize these goals, some accomplishments have been made in each of the areas. We will briefly describe some recent accomplishments and current activities in three related areas: human and legal rights, prevention, and normalization.

Rights of Citizens with Mental Retardation

We have come a long way since the time when people with mental retardation were exterminated, ridiculed, or employed as court jesters, but we still have a long way to go. Of all the goals of the first President's Committee on Mental Retardation, we have the most concrete evidence of having accomplished the goal of legal rights for persons with mental retardation.

Numerous court decisions have advanced the position that a person with mental retardation has and should be able to exercise, with assistance from society if necessary, the same rights and freedoms as a nondisabled citizen. More than 20 years ago, the AAMR advocated the following rights of persons with mental retardation.

Basic Rights

I. The basic rights include, but are not limited to, those implied in "life, liberty, and the pursuit of happiness," and those specified in detail in the various documents that provide the basis for governing democratic nations. Specific rights of persons with mental retardation include but are not limited to these:

 A. The right to freedom of choice within the individual's capacity to make decisions and within the limitations imposed on all persons

 B. The right to live in the least restrictive individually appropriate environment

 C. The right to gainful employment and to a fair day's pay for a fair day's labor

 D. The right to be part of a family

 E. The right to marry and have a family of his or her own

 F. The right to freedom of movement, hence not to be interned without just cause and due process of law, including the right not to be permanently deprived of liberty by institutionalization in lieu of imprisonment

 G. The rights to speak openly and fully without fear of undue punishment, to privacy, to the practice of a religion (or the practice of no religion), and to interaction with peers

Specific Extensions

II. Specific extensions of and additions to these basic rights, which are due persons with mental retardation because of their special needs include but are not limited to:

 A. The right to a publicly supported and administered comprehensive and integrated set of rehabilitative programs and services

 B. The right to a publicly supported and administered program of training and education including, but not restricted to, basic academic and interpersonal skills

 C. The right, beyond those implicit in the right to education described above, to a publicly administered and supported program of training toward the goal of maximum gainful employment

 D. The right to protection against exploitation, demeaning treatment, or abuse

 E. The right, when participating in research, to be safeguarded from violations of human dignity and to be protected from physical and psychological harm

 F. The right, for an individual who may not be able to act effectively in his or her own behalf, to have a responsible, impartial guardian or advocate appointed by the society to protect and effect the exercise and enjoyment of these foregoing rights

Many states have organized citizen advocacy programs to aid individuals with mental retardation. An advocate is a volunteer committed to becoming personally involved with the welfare of a person with mental retardation and to becoming knowledgeable about the services available for that person. In a sense, an advocate is an informed friend who can legally take a stand to see that his or her friend's rights are not abused and that the necessary educational and other services are in fact delivered. Being an advocate can be an excellent way to serve a citizen with mental retardation and in the process learn much about the field. Persons with disabilities are increasingly using self-advocacy as a means of improving their quality of life.

To learn how you might go about getting to know an adult with disabilities, see the Teaching & Learning box, "A Friendship Program for Future Special Education Teachers," in Chapter 15.

Prevention of Mental Retardation

Each week in this country, more than 2,000 babies are born who are or at some point will be diagnosed with mental retardation. As scientific research, both medical and

The December 1992 issue of the journal *Mental Retardation* is devoted to articles on prevention.

behavioral, has generated new knowledge about the causes of mental retardation, procedures and programs designed to prevent its occurrence have increased.

Probably the biggest single preventive strike against mental retardation (and many other disabling conditions, including blindness and deafness) was the development of an effective rubella vaccine in 1962. When rubella (German measles) is contracted by mothers during the first 3 months of pregnancy, it causes severe damage in 10% to 40% of the unborn children (Krim, 1969). Fortunately, this cause of mental retardation can be eliminated if women are vaccinated for rubella before becoming pregnant.

Phenylketonuria (PKU) is a genetically inherited condition in which a child is born without an important enzyme needed to break down the amino acid phenylalanine, which is found in many common foods. Failure to break down this amino acid causes brain damage that results in severe mental retardation. By analyzing the concentration of phenylalanine in a newborn's blood plasma, doctors can diagnose PKU and treat it with a special diet. Most children with PKU who receive a phenylalanine-restricted diet early enough have normal intellectual development (Berman & Ford, 1970).

Toxic exposure through maternal substance abuse and environmental pollutants (e.g., lead poisoning) are two major causes of preventable mental retardation that can be combated with education and training (Shroeder, 1987).

Advances in medical science have enabled doctors to identify certain genetic influences strongly associated with mental retardation. One approach to prevention offered by many health service organizations is **genetic counseling,** a discussion between a specially trained medical counselor and prospective parents about the possibilities that they may give birth to a child with disabilities on the basis of the parents' genetic backgrounds.

For a discussion of the ethical and legal issues involved in genetic counseling, see Pueschel (1991).

Amniocentesis is a procedure in which a sample of fluid is withdrawn from the amniotic sac surrounding the fetus during the second trimester of pregnancy (usually about the 14th to 17th week). Fetal cells are removed from the amniotic fluid and grown in a cell culture for about 2 weeks. At that time, a chromosome and enzyme analysis is performed to identify the presence of about 80 specific genetic disorders prior to birth. Many of these disorders, such as Down syndrome (O'Brien, 1971), are associated with mental retardation.

A new technique for prenatal diagnosis that may eventually replace amniocentesis is **chorion villus sampling** (CVS). With CVS, a small amount of chorionic tissue (a fetal component of the developing placenta) is removed and tested. The most significant advantage of CVS is that it can be performed earlier than amniocentesis (during the 8th to 10th week of pregnancy), and because fetal cells exist in relatively large numbers in the chorion, they can be analyzed immediately without waiting for them to grow for 2 to 3 weeks. Although CVS is being used increasingly, it has been associated with a miscarriage rate of about 10 in 1,000 (compared with 2.5 in 1,000 with amniocentesis) and is still considered experimental. The relative safety and risks of CVS are discussed by Rhoads et al. (1989).

Medical advances such as these have noticeably reduced the incidence of mental retardation caused by some of the known biological factors, but huge advancements in research are needed to reach the goal of lowering the incidence of biomedical mental retardation by 50% by the year 2000.

As we saw earlier, most children with mental retardation are in the mild range, and their developmental delays have no clear-cut etiology. These are the children whose mental retardation is thought to be primarily the result of a poor environment during their early years. The poor environment may be a result of parental neglect, poverty, disease, bad diet, and other factors—many of which are completely out of the hands of the child's parents.

Two of the most well known and long-running research and intervention programs aimed at reducing the incidence of developmental retardation are the Milwaukee Project and the Juniper Gardens Children's Project. The Milwaukee Project involved early identification of infants considered to be high risk (children living in conditions associated with psychosocial disadvantage). During a 15-year period, education and family support services were provided to the children and their mothers. A book on this longitudinal study reports improvements in the children's cognitive and language development abilities (Garber, 1988).

For nearly three decades, the Juniper Gardens Children's Project has addressed the problems of psychosocial retardation by developing and evaluating home, school, and community-based interventions based on applied behavior analysis (Greenwood, Carta, Hart, Thurston, & Hall, 1989; Greenwood et al., 1994).

Although measuring the effects of programs that aim to prevent psychosocial retardation is much more difficult than measuring the decreased number of children suffering from a disease like PKU, the preliminary results of these projects are encouraging, and some models of effective early intervention have been identified (Ramey & Landesman Ramey, 1992).

Normalization

The principle of **normalization** refers to the use of progressively more normal settings and procedures "to establish and/or maintain personal behaviors which are as culturally normal as possible" (Wolfensberger, 1972, p. 28). Normalization is not a single technique or set of procedures but rather an overriding philosophy. That philosophy says that persons with mental retardation should, to the greatest extent possible, be both physically and socially integrated into the mainstream of society regardless of the degree or type of disability.

As the belief in normalization grows among both professionals and the public, the time draws nearer when all persons with mental retardation will experience the benefits of humane and effective treatment and educational, residential, and vocational opportunities.

> The November 1989 issue of *Education & Treatment of Children* reviews various research programs by the Juniper Gardens Children's Project. See Chapter 14 for more on intervention programs for young children at risk for developmental disabilities.

> Wolf Wolfensberger (1983), the most well known champion of the normalization principle, has proposed the term *social role valorization* to replace *normalization.* He writes, "The most explicit and highest goal of normalization must be the creation, support, and defense of valued social roles for people who are at risk of social devaluation" (p. 234).

. . . .

Summary

Defining Mental Retardation

- The definition incorporated into the IDEA states that mental retardation involves both significantly subaverage general intellectual functioning and deficits in adaptive behavior manifested between birth and 18 years of age. Intellectual functioning is usually measured with a

standardized intelligence test and adaptive behavior with an observation checklist or scale.

- The most recent AAMR definition of mental retardation, the "1992 System," represents a shift away from conceptualizations of mental retardation as an inherent trait or permanent state of being to a description of the individual's present functioning and the environmental supports needed to improve it.

Classification of Mental Retardation

- There are four degrees of mental retardation as classified by IQ score: mild, moderate, severe, and profound.

- Children with mild mental retardation may experience substantial performance deficits only in school. Their social and communication skills may be normal or nearly so. They are likely to become independent or semi-independent adults.

- Most children with moderate mental retardation show significant developmental delays during their preschool years. Most school children with moderate mental retardation are educated in self-contained classrooms, and most live and work in the community as adults if individualized programs of support are available.

- Most persons with severe and profound mental retardation are identified in infancy. Some adults with severe and profound mental retardation can be semi-independent; others need 24-hour supports throughout their lives.

- Classification in the 1992 System is based on four levels and intensities of supports needed to improve functioning in the environments in which the individual lives: intermittent, limited, extensive, and pervasive.

Causes of Mental Retardation

- All of the more than 250 known causes of mental retardation are biological.

- Etiology is unknown for most individuals with mild mental retardation. Increasing evidence, however, suggests that psychosocial disadvantage in early childhood is a major cause of mild mental retardation.

Prevalence

- Theoretically, 2.3% of the population would score two standard deviations below the norm on IQ tests, but this does not account for adaptive behavior, the other criterion for diagnosis of mental retardation. Many experts now cite an incidence figure of approximately 1% of the total population.

- During the 1992–93 school year, approximately 1% of the total school enrollment received special education services under the disability category of mental retardation.

Historical Background

- Primitive people left individuals with mental retardation and other disabilities to die. Later, people with mental retardation became objects of superstition and ridicule.

- The first attempts to educate children with mental retardation came during the early 19th century in Europe and spread to the United States. Later in the century, however, large state institutions, which came to be seen as custodial rather than educational, became the primary means of service.

- The movement today is away from institutions and segregation and toward education in the least restrictive integrated environment.

Educational Approaches

- Curriculum should focus on functional skills that will help the student be successful in self-care, vocational, domestic, community, and leisure domains.

- Applied behavior analysis is widely used in teaching students with mental retardation. Effective techniques include task analysis, direct and frequent measurement, repeated opportunities to respond, systematic feedback, transfer of stimulus control from teacher-provided cues and prompts to natural stimuli, and programming for generalization and maintenance.

Educational Placement Alternatives

- Although some children with mental retardation attend special schools, most are being educated in their neighborhood schools—either in special classes or in regular classes where they receive special help or attend a resource room for part of the day.

- Many children with mild retardation are educated in regular classrooms, with extra help provided as needed. They can generally master standard academic skills up to about a sixth-grade level.

- Students with moderate mental retardation are usually taught communication, self-help and daily living skills, and vocational skills, along with limited academics. Most children with moderate mental retardation are educated in self-contained classrooms.

- Despite their severe disabilities, people with severe and profound mental retardation can learn. Curricula stress functional communication and self-help skills.

Current Issues and Future Trends

- Recent laws, including PL 94–103, the IDEA, and the Americans with Disabilities Act, have extended and affirmed the rights of persons with mental retardation. Advocates can help protect the rights of individuals with mental retardation.

- Recent scientific advances—including genetic counseling, amniocentesis, chorion villus sampling (CVS), virus vaccines, and early screening tests—are helping reduce the incidence of clinical or biologically caused retardation.

- Although early identification and intensive educational services to high-risk infants show promise, there is still no widely used technique to decrease the incidence of mental retardation caused by psychosocial disadvantage.

- The current goal is to make the lives of people with mental retardation—at home, in school, and at work—as normal as possible. With this in mind, institutions are necessarily inappropriate. Thus, we must develop normalized and effective training and transition programs and community services for individuals with mental retardation and work to change public attitudes.

For More Information

Journals

American Journal on Mental Retardation. Published bimonthly by the American Association on Mental Retardation, 1719 Kalorama Road, NW, Washington, DC 20009. Publishes empirical studies, reviews of research, and theoretical articles dealing with the behavioral, social, and biological aspects of mental retardation.

Education and Training in Mental Retardation and Developmental Disabilities. Published four times per school year by the Division on Mental Retardation of the Council for Exceptional Children, 1920 Association Drive, Reston, VA 22091-1589. Publishes experimental studies and discussion articles dealing with the education of individuals with mental retardation.

Mental Retardation. Published bimonthly by the American Association on Mental Retardation, 1719 Kalorama Road, NW, Washington, DC 20009. Concerned with new approaches to methodology, critical summaries, essays, program descriptions, and research studies dealing with all aspects of mental retardation.

Research in Developmental Disabilities. Published quarterly by Pergamon Press, Maxwell House, Fairview Park, Elmsford, New York. Publishes original behavioral research and theory on severe and pervasive developmental disabilities, as well as coverage of the legal and ethical aspects of applying treatment procedures to children and adults with mental retardation.

Books

Mental Retardation

Beirne-Smith, M., Patton, J. R., & Ittenbach, R. (1994). *Mental retardation* (4th ed.). Englewood Cliffs, NJ: Merrill/Prentice Hall.

Blatt, B. (1987). *The conquest of mental retardation.* Austin, TX: Pro-Ed.

MacMillan, D. L. (1982). *Mental retardation in school and society* (2nd ed.). Boston: Little, Brown.

Mulick, J. A., & Antonak, R. (Eds.). (1985–1994). *Transitions in mental retardation* (Vols. 1–5). Norwood, NJ: Ablex.

Robinson, G. A., Patton, J. R., Polloway, E. A., & Sargent, L. R. (Eds.). (1989). *Best practices in mild mental disabilities.* Reston, VA: Council for Exceptional Children.

Smith, J. D. (1995). *Pieces of purgatory: Mental retardation in and out of institutions.* Pacific Grove, CA: Brooks/Cole.

Applied Behavior Analysis and Behavioral Teaching Methods

Alberto, P. A., & Troutman, A. C. (1995). *Applied behavior analysis for teachers* (4th ed.). Englewood Cliffs, NJ: Prentice-Hall/Merrill.

Cipani, E., & Spooner, F. H. (1993). *Teaching students with severe disabilities.* Needham Heights, MA: Allyn & Bacon.

Lovitt, T. C. (1995). *Tactics for teaching* (2nd ed.). Engle-wood Cliffs, NJ: Prentice-Hall/Merrill.

Rusch, F. R., Rose, T., & Greenwood, C. R. (1988). *Introduction to behavior analysis in special education.* Englewood Cliffs, NJ: Prentice-Hall.

Schloss, P. J., & Smith, M. A. (1994). *Applied behavior analysis in the classroom.* Needham Heights, MA: Allyn & Bacon.

Snell, M. E. (1993). *Instruction of students with severe disabilities* (4th ed.). New York: Macmillan.

Sulzer-Azaroff, B., & Mayer, G. R. (1991). *Behavior analysis for lasting change.* New York: Holt, Rinehart & Winston.

Wolery, M., Ault, M. J., & Doyle, P. M. (1992). *Teaching students with moderate to severe disabilities.* New York: Longman.

Wolery, M., Bailey, D. B., & Sugai, G. M. (1988). *Effective teaching: Principles and procedures of applied behavior analysis.* Needham Heights, MA: Allyn & Bacon.

Organizations

American Association on Mental Retardation (AAMR), 5201 Connecticut Avenue, NW, Washington, DC 20015. Primarily includes researchers, teacher educators, and psychologists interested in mental retardation.

Association for Retarded Citizens, 2709 Avenue E East, Arlington, TX 76011. An advocacy organization including parents and professionals, with active local chapters in most states.

The Arc (formerly the Association for Retarded Citizens). An advocacy organization consisting primarily of parents and family members. The Arc promotes the general welfare of individuals with mental retardation of all ages and in all settings. P.O. Box 6109, Arlington, TX 76005.

Division on Mental Retardation and Developmental Disabilities (MRDD), Council for Exceptional Children, 1920 Association Drive, Reston, VA 22091. With more than 7,500 members, MRDD works to promote professional growth and research to advance programs for persons with mental retardation and developmental disabilities.

CHAPTER

5

Students with Learning Disabilities

* Why has the concept of learning disabilities proven so difficult to define?

* Do most students who are identified as learning disabled have a "true" disability, or are they just low achievers?

* Why does the area of learning disabilities continue to be so vulnerable to outlandish treatment programs?

* What are the most important skills for students with learning disabilities to master?

* Should all students with learning disabilities be educated in the regular classroom?

No area of special education has experienced as much rapid growth, extreme interest, and frantic activity as learning disabilities. This statement is as true today as it was a decade ago. The number of children identified as learning disabled has increased greatly in recent years, making this category the largest in special education. The increase has helped fuel an ongoing debate over the very nature of the learning disability concept. Some believe the increase in the number of children identified as learning disabled indicates the true extent of the disability. Others contend that too many low achievers—children without a disability who are simply doing poorly in school—have been improperly identified as learning disabled, placing a severe strain on the limited resources available to serve those students challenged by true learning disabilities.

Learning disabilities has also been the focus of much public attention and interest, as demonstrated by countless newspaper stories, magazine articles, and television documentaries (e.g., "Does Your Child Have a Learning Disability?"). Learning disabilities, more than any other area of special education, seems to create misunderstanding and controversy. There is considerable confusion and disagreement, not just on the part of the general public but among professionals and parents as well, on such basic questions as What is a learning disability? and How should students with learning disabilities be taught? In some ways, learning disabilities brings out both the worst and the best that special education has to offer. Learning disabilities has served as a breeding ground for fads and miracle treatments ("New Vitamin and Diet Regimen Cures Learning Disabilities!"). At the same time, some of the most innovative teachers and scholars in special education have devoted their careers to learning disabilities. Methods of assessment and instruction first developed for students with learning disabilities have influenced and benefited the entire field of education.

✳ *Defining Learning Disabilities*

From its very beginning as a category of special education, controversy has raged over how learning disabilities should be defined. More than 40 definitions for learning disabilities have been proposed (Bennett & Ragosta, 1984), but none has been universally accepted. The definition that has had the most impact was first written in 1968, when the National Advisory Committee on Handicapped Children of the U.S. Office of Education drafted a definition that was eventually published, with only minor changes in wording, as the federal definition of learning disabilities in the IDEA. It reads:

> "Specific learning disability" means a disorder in one or more of the basic psychological processes involved in understanding or in using language, spoken or written, which may manifest itself in an imperfect ability to listen, think, speak, read, write, spell, or to do mathematical calculations. The term includes such conditions as perceptual handicaps, brain injury, minimal brain dysfunction, dyslexia, and developmental aphasia. The term does not include children who have learning problems

which are primarily the result of visual, hearing or motor handicaps, of mental retardation, or of environmental, cultural, or economic disadvantages. (U.S. Office of Education, 1977b, p. 65083)

When operationalizing the definition of learning disabilities, most states and school districts require that three criteria be met:

1. A discrepancy between the child's potential and actual achievement
2. An exclusion criterion
3. The need for special education services

A closer look at each of these criteria will show why it has been so difficult to come up with a definitive definition of learning disabilities.

Discrepancy

Children who are having minor or temporary difficulties in learning should not be identified as learning disabled. The term is meant to identify children with a true disability, which, according to federal guidelines, is evidenced by a "severe discrepancy between achievement and intellectual ability" (U.S. Office of Education, 1977, p. 65083). Intellectual ability is most often measured by an IQ test, and achievement by a standardized achievement test. Learning disabilities is characterized by an "unexpected" difference between general ability and achievement—a discrepancy that would not be predicted by the student's general intellectual ability and opportunities to learn.

The federal government proposed several formulas for determining a severe discrepancy. These formulas involved mathematical computations using the student's IQ with chronological age (CA) or number of years in school to reach an expected grade equivalency (EGE). Three of these formulas were as follows:

$$EGE = \text{number of years in school} \times IQ/100 + 1.0$$
$$EGE = IQ \times CA/100 - 5$$
$$\text{Severe discrepancy} = CA \ (IQ/300 + 0.17) = 2.5$$

"The various additions, subtractions, divisions, and ratios generated by these formulas were essentially meaningless and, in all cases, misleading" (Reynolds, 1992, p. 4). All of the proposed formulas were eventually rejected, and the final rules and regulations for the IDEA published by the federal government did not contain a specific definition of and formula for determining a severe discrepancy. This failing left states to find their own criteria for implementing the definition of learning disabilities. Confusion and disagreement over exactly how a severe discrepancy should be determined have led to widely differing procedures for identifying and classifying students as learning disabled (C. R. Reynolds, 1992; Stanovich, 1991). For example, the Ohio Department of Education uses the following rule for determining when a severe discrepancy criterion exists:

Each child shall have a severe discrepancy between achievement and ability which adversely affects his or her educational performance to such a degree that special

---

The term *learning disabilities* did not exist before 1963. Later in the chapter, we look at the historic background of the disability category that now includes half of all students who receive special education services.

In a survey in all 50 states and the District of Columbia, however, Mercer, King-Sears, and Mercer (1990) found that most states were using a definition of learning disabilities containing the key components found in the federal definition.

Finlan (1992) attributes the large differences in the percentage of the total school population identified as learning disabled—ranging across states from 2.19% to 8.66%—to the different methods the states use to determine a severe discrepancy.

education and related services are required. The basis for making the determination shall be:

(i) Evidence of a discrepancy score of two or greater than two between intellectual ability and achievement in one or more of the following seven areas:

    (a) Oral expression,

    (b) Listening comprehension,

    (c) Written expression,

    (d) Basic reading skills,

    (e) Reading comprehension,

    (f) Mathematics calculation, or

    (g) Mathematics reasoning.

(ii) The following formula shall be used in computing the discrepancy score:

    (a) From:

        (i) The score obtained for the measure of intellectual ability,

        (ii) Minus the mean of the measure of intellectual ability,

        (iii) Divided by the standard deviation of the measure of intellectual ability.

    (b) Subtract:

        (i) The score obtained for the measure of achievement,

        (ii) Minus the mean of the measure of achievement,

        (iii) Divided by the standard deviation of the measure of achievement.

    (c) The result of this computation equals the discrepancy score. If the discrepancy score is two or greater than two, a severe discrepancy exists. (Rules for the Education of Handicapped Children, effective July 1, 1982, p. 69)

See the winter 1987 issue of *Learning Disabilities Research* for detailed discussion of the discrepancy concept.

The Council for Learning Disabilities (CLD; 1986) published a position statement citing eight reasons for opposing the use of discrepancy formulas. The CLD position statement also included these recommendations: (a) that discrepancy formulas be phased out as required procedure for identifying individuals with learning disabilities; (b) that when discrepancy formulas must be used, they be used with extreme caution; and (c) that the results of discrepancy formulas should never be used to dictate whether an individual has a learning disability. In lieu of discrepancy formulas, CLD recommends improved comprehensive multidisciplinary assessment of all areas of learning disabilities identified by federal rules and regulations (oral expression, listening comprehension, and writing expression, in addition to reading and mathematics). After conducting two experiments evaluating the dependability of formula-based identification of students with learning disabilities, Macmann et al. (1989) conclude, "It appears that the severe discrepancy concept has outlived its usefulness as a viable model for service allocation" (p. 144)

Exclusion

The concept of learning disabilities is meant to identify students with significant learning problems that cannot be explained by mental retardation, sensory impairment, emotional disturbance, or lack of opportunity to learn. Kirk (1963) used the term *specific learning disabilities* to differentiate students with learning disabilities from the much larger group of children who are low achievers.

Several noted special educators have criticized the exclusion clause in the federal definition of learning disabilities because it says that children with other disabilities cannot be considered learning disabled as well. For example, some children whose primary diagnosis is mental retardation do not achieve up to their expected potential (Wallace & McLoughlin, 1979). Hammill (1976) challenges the notion that

Students with learning disabilities experience significant learning difficulties that cannot be explained by mental retardation, sensory impairment, emotional disturbance, or lack of educational opportunity.

only children with IQ scores in the normal range can be identified as learning disabled. He rests his criticism on two arguments. First, most IQ tests are made up of items that measure past learning. If a child with a learning disability has not learned enough of the information included on the IQ test, he will score at a level associated with mental retardation. Second, too many sources of measurement error are involved in intelligence testing to make clear-cut differential diagnosis statements such as "This student's learning difficulties are the result of mild mental retardation, but the problems experienced by this student stem from learning disabilities."

Special Education

A student with learning disabilities needs special education that "should involve practices that are unique, uncommon, of unusual quality and that, in particular, supplement the organizational and instructional procedures used with the majority of children" (Ames, 1977, p. 328). This criterion is meant to keep children who have not had the opportunity to learn from being identified as learning disabled. These children should progress normally as soon as they receive typically effective instruction at a curricular level appropriate to their current skills. Students with learning disabilities are those who show specific and severe learning problems despite normal educational efforts and therefore need special educational services to help remediate their achievement deficiencies.

The NJCLD-Proposed Definition

The National Joint Committee on Learning Disabilities (NJCLD) is a group composed of official representatives from 10 professional organizations involved with students with learning disabilities. The NJCLD believed that the federal definition of learning disabilities had served the educational community reasonably well but had several inherent weaknesses (Hammill, Leigh, McNutt, & Larsen, 1981). Myers and Hammill (1990) identify those elements of the IDEA definition with which the NJCLD was not satisfied:

The IQ scores and academic performance of inner-city students who are classified as learning disabled today suggest that many may have been identified and served under the category of educable mental retardation (EMR) 25 years ago (Gottlieb, Alter, Gottlieb, & Wishner, 1994). The spring 1990 issue of *Learning Disability Quarterly* discusses whether IQ scores should be considered in the concept of learning disabilities.

More than 250,000 individuals are members of the 10 organizations represented by NJCLD.

To see how learning disabilities are defined from the perspectives of adults with learning disabilities, see Reiff, Gerber, and Ginsburg (1993). The August/September 1992 issue of *Journal of Learning Disabilities* and the summer, 1993 issue of *Learning Disability Quarterly* are devoted to issues and programs concerning adults with learning disabilities.

1. *Exclusion of adults.* Since enactment of the federal law, there has been major interest in understanding the special needs of and developing programs for adolescents and adults with learning disabilities (e.g., Alley & Deshler, 1979; Mangrum & Strichart, 1988; Patton & Polloway, 1993). The IDEA definition of learning disabilities refers only to school-age children, which thereby eliminates adults from consideration.

2. *Reference to basic psychological processes.* Members of the NJCLD maintain that use of the phrase "basic psychological processes" has generated extensive and perhaps unnecessary debate over how to teach students with learning disabilities but that how to teach is a curricular issue, not a definitional one. The NJCLD believes the intent of the original phrase was only to show that a learning disability is intrinsic to the person affected.

3. *Inclusion of spelling as a learning disability.* Because spelling can be integrated with other areas of functioning—namely, written expression—it is redundant and should be eliminated from the definition.

4. *Inclusion of obsolete terms.* The NJCLD believes that inclusion of terms such as *dyslexia, minimal brain dysfunction, perceptual impairments,* and *developmental aphasia,* which historically have proven difficult to define, only adds confusion to the definition of learning disability.

5. *The exclusion clause.* The wording of the final clause in the IDEA definition has led to the belief that learning disabilities cannot occur along with other disabilities. A more accurate statement, according to the NJCLD, is that a person may have a learning disability along with another disability, but not *because of* another disability. In other words, a learning disability should be considered a disability in its own right.

In response to these problems with the federal definition, the NJCLD proposed a definition of learning disabilities in 1981 and revised it slightly in 1989:

> Learning disabilities is a generic term that refers to a heterogeneous group of disorders manifested by significant difficulties in the acquisition and use of listening, speaking, reading, writing, reasoning, or mathematical abilities. These disorders are intrinsic to the individual and presumed to be due to central nervous system dysfunction, and may appear across the life span. Problems in self-regulatory behaviors, social perception, and social interaction may exist with learning disabilities but do not themselves constitute a learning disability. Although learning disabilities may occur concomitantly with other handicapping conditions (for example, sensory impairment, mental retardation, serious emotional disturbance) or with extrinsic influences (such as cultural differences, insufficient or inappropriate instruction), they are not the result of those conditions or influences. (National Joint Committee on Learning Disabilities, 1989, p. 1)

The NJCLD's requirement that the disorder is "intrinsic to the individual and presumed to be due to central nervous system dysfunction" can be seen as an effort to limit the use of the term *learning disabilities* to the "hard-core" or severely learning disabled. For additional rationale and discussion of the NJCLD definition, see Hammill (1990) and Myers and Hammill (1990).

After comparing and contrasting 11 definitions of learning disabilities, Hammill (1990), one of the prime contributors to the NJCLD definition, thinks that consensus is near:

> The NJCLD never intended to write the perfect definition, only a better one. A study of the definitions discussed in this paper suggests that the committee was successful in its efforts. The NJCLD definition has obtained a high level of acceptance among multiple national associations and individuals and is arguably the best one that is presently available. None of the NJCLD members believes that their definition has settled the issue for all time. Political realities are such that the NJCLD definition may

never replace the 1977 USOE definition in law. But this may not be important. What is important, however, is that professionals and parents unite around one definition so that we can say with assurance, "This is what we mean when we say *learning disabilities.*" (p. 83)

The Debate Continues

The field of learning disabilities continues to struggle with defining the very nature of the "unexpected" learning problems it was created to study and treat. Some prominent special educators believe there is little or no difference between students identified as having learning disabilities and those who are low achievers. Algozzine and Ysseldyke (1983) argue that despite attempts to create a sophisticated category, learning disabilities is merely a "subset of school failure" and that the concept has little meaning beyond signifying poor achievement in school.

> Since its inception, the classification of learning disabilities has been an ill-defined, poorly conceptualized, incredibly popular idea. There are millions of children who perform poorly in reading, writing, mathematics, listening, speaking, and other academic areas; significant numbers of students are failing to profit from their education experiences, but no defendable system exists for classifying or categorizing these students; there are no defensible inclusionary and exclusionary principles. (Ysseldyke, Algozzine, & Epps, 1983, p. 165)

Although virtually everyone in education recognizes that present definitions of learning disabilities are inadequate, finding a definition that provides clear-cut criteria for identification and serves as a standard by which to interpret and assess research findings has "proven easier said than done" (Conte & Andrews, 1993, p. 149). In the words of Kavale, Forness, and Lorsbach (1991), the "definitional problem in LD is fraught with many complexities making it difficult to achieve closure" (p. 263). They suggest that current definitions not be looked on as real in the sense of providing the "essence" of learning disabilities in a matter that can be judged either true or false. Instead, definitions should be viewed as operational definitions representing the information that certain groups have agreed on. The following points should be kept in mind:

- Present definitions are neither "good" or "bad," only useful. In promulgating the LD field, existing definitions have to be viewed as successful (perhaps too successful).
- Present definitions tell us relatively little about LD in any scientific sense. Instead, the definitions are convenient descriptive renderings of what LD is generally perceived to be.
- Additions or deletions to definitions, like the addition of social skills to the list of LD deficits, make little difference. Contentious debate about the appropriateness of any addition or deletion is futile because it simply represents one group's stipulation as opposed to another's.
- It is easy to understand why the problem of defining LD seems interminable. As long as a particular group can achieve consensus, its definition is as good as any other. The lack of absolute criteria makes all arguments relative.
- Present definitions should be accepted for what they are: a global rendering appropriate for program development. (adapted from Kavale et al., 1991, p. 263)

Kavale, Fuchs, and Scruggs (1994), however, analyzed the same data that have been used as evidence for suggesting no difference exists between students with learning disabilities and low achievers. They concluded that students with learning disabilities can be "clearly differentiated" from low achievers on measures of intellectual ability and achievement.

We close this discussion of the difficulties in defining learning disabilities by recognizing a central truth: Labeling does not cause disabilities, and neither will the removal of a label cure them (Lerner, 1993). From an educator's standpoint, the most important issue should not revolve around whether to consider the academic deficiencies exhibited by a student as evidence of learning disabilities. Instead, we should focus our resources and energies on determining how to go about assessing and effectively remediating the specific academic and social skill deficits in each student's repertoire.

✴ *Characteristics of Students with Learning Disabilities*

In describing the various categories of exceptionality, a list of the physical and psychological characteristics often exhibited by the individuals who make up that group is typically presented. The inherent danger in such lists is the tendency to assume, or at least to look for, *each* of those characteristics in *all* of the children considered to be in the category. This danger is especially troublesome with learning disabilities.

A national task force found 99 separate characteristics of children with learning disabilities described in the literature (Clements, 1966). The first four characteristics on Clements's list were hyperactivity, perceptual-motor impairments, emotional ups and downs, and general coordination deficits. Specific academic difficulty, the fundamental defining characteristic of learning disabilities today, was ranked only eighth on the Clements list.

Since Clements's report, several major studies of the characteristics of students with learning disabilities have been published (Cone, Wilson, Bradley, & Reese, 1985; Kavale & Reese, 1992; Kirk & Elkins, 1975; McLeskey, 1992; Norman & Zigmond, 1980; Sheppard & Smith, 1983). The results of two studies are representative of this body of research. McLeskey (1992) examined the demographic, intellectual, achievement, and placement data for 790 students enrolled in K–12 learning disabilities programs in Indiana. Cone et al. (1985) reported similar information for 1,839 students with learning disabilities in Iowa. Some of the findings from these two studies are presented here:

- Three fourths of the students in both studies were initially identified as learning disabled in the elementary grades.
- In both studies, males outnumbered females by a 3-to-1 ratio across primary, elementary, and secondary age levels.
- The mean IQ score for the entire sample in each study was 94 (McLeskey) and 95 (Cone et al.).
- Students with more severe discrepancies tended to be identified at the primary level; discrepancies became less severe in higher grade levels (McLeskey).
- The students exhibited more academic deficiencies in reading and spelling than in mathematics (Cone et al.).
- Students' relative level of academic achievement decreased progressively as their grade level increased (Cone et al.).
- Before being identified with a learning disability, 58% of the sample had been retained in a grade (McLeskey).

Individuals with learning disabilities are an extremely heterogeneous group. Mercer (1991) writes that more than 500,000 combinations of cognitive or socioemotional problems associated with learning disabilities are theoretically possible. The extreme heterogeneity between students both within and across studies has hampered the interpretability and utility of research in learning disabilities (Durrant, 1994).

Numerical reasoning and computation pose major problems for many students with learning disabilities. See Bley and Thornton (1994) for specific suggestions on teaching math to students with learning disabilities.

- The percentage of students with behavioral problems (15%) remained consistent across grade levels (McLeskey).

Kavale and Reese (1992) concluded their study of 917 students with learning disabilities in Iowa with this profile of "the average LD student":

> a 13-year-old male in the middle of the sixth grade who has an IQ of 96. This student attends a multicategorical resource program and receives speech/language support service in a public school for 78 minutes per day. The initial staffing takes place at the end of the third grade, mostly due to teacher referral for poor academic performance—most often in reading. At its lowest level, reading performance is depressed by almost four years and mathematics by three years, making for a significant discrepancy between expected and actual achievement. The IEP emphasizes reading goals, with reading instruction delivered exclusively in special education and the remaining academic subjects in regular education. The three-year placement in special education improves reading performance by almost two years, mathematics by 1 1/2years. There are no plans to change placement. (p. 89)

Social Acceptance

Other researchers have investigated the social acceptance of students with learning disabilities, their classroom deportment, and their ability to attend to a task. The results of this research are far from conclusive, perhaps partly because of the heterogeneous nature of learning disabilities and partly because of the lack of agreement in and inconsistent application of identification criteria.

Most researchers who have investigated the social status of students with learning disabilities have concluded, for example, that low social acceptance is common (Bryan & Bryan, 1978; Gresham, 1982). After reviewing the published studies on the social status of learning disabled individuals, however, Dudley-Marling and Edmiaston (1985) concluded that, as a group, learning disabled individuals may be at greater risk for attaining low social status but that some students with learning disabilities are, in fact, popular. Two subsequent studies continued the contradictory findings on peer acceptance. Gresham and Reschly (1986) found significant deficits in the social skills and peer acceptance of 100 mainstreamed students with learning disabilities when compared with 100 students without disabilities. But in the same issue of the same journal, Sabornie and Kauffman (1986) reported more optimistic findings of no significant difference in the sociometric standing of 46 mainstreamed learning disabled high school students and 46 peers without disabilities. Moreover, they discovered that some of the students with learning disabilities enjoyed socially rewarding experiences in the mainstream classrooms.

One reason for the lack of congruence between studies investigating the social competence of students with learning disabilities may be their focus on comparing students with learning disabilities with their nondisabled peers at specific points in time. Speculating that social skills and acceptance of individual students may change over time, Vaughn and Hogan (1994) conducted a within-individual longitudinal analysis of the social competence of 10 children with learning disabilities during a 6-year period. Their results showed that the social skill scores of individual children can change, sometimes dramatically, between kindergarten and fifth grade. They concluded that an examination of social competence at any one time, particularly for boys, does not provide a good indicator of an individual student's social competence over time.

One interpretation of these studies is that social acceptance is not a characteristic of learning disabilities, but rather an outcome of the different social climates created by teachers, peers, parents, and others with whom students with learning disabilities interact. This interpretation is supported by the authors of a study of 210 students with and without learning disabilities in grades 3 to 10 who found that students with learning disabilities in classes where they are accepted by their teachers were not less well liked or less well known by their classmates than students from other achievement groups (Vaughn, McIntosh, Schumm, Haager, & Callwood, 1993). In fact, Vaughn et al. found that approximately 90% of the students in their study had a mutual "best friend," which was slightly better than either low-achieving or high-achieving students. Toward that end, researchers have begun to identify the types of problems experienced by children with learning disabilities who are ranked low in social acceptance and to discover instructional arrangements that promote the social status of students with learning disabilities in the regular classroom.

An interesting study by Coleman and Minnett (1992) of 146 children with and without learning disabilities in grades 3 through 6 suggests that social competence may be related to a child's social status among peers, and not to disability, as is often assumed. Rather than simply comparing the social competence (e.g., positive and negative interactions with peers, number of friends) and self-concept of students with learning disabilities against those of children without disabilities, the researchers first separated both groups of students into three levels of social status. Social status—popular, neglected, or rejected—was determined by a peer nomination procedure in which students circled the names of three classmates they would "most like to play with" and put an X next to the three names they "did not like to play with." Although the children with learning disabilities differed from children without disabilities on "virtually all indexes of academic competence regardless of social status" (p. 234), some of the children with learning disabilities were popular and shared many characteristics of popular children without disabilities. In fact, many of the students with learning disabilities actually had higher levels of self-concept than their nondisabled peers of equal social status. Coleman and Minnett concluded that although children with learning disabilities are often rejected by their peers, rejection is not an inevitable outcome.

> We must learn more about these children who, despite their academic difficulties, appear capable of succeeding in the social mainstream of public elementary education. It seems unlikely that we will be able to completely eliminate the academic difficulties encountered by children with LD; but studying children who are socially successful despite limited academic success seems a profitable avenue for identifying social skills that may be useful to other children with LD. (p. 244)

For discussion and debate over a proposed definition of learning disabilities that includes social skills deficits as a primary subtype of learning disability, see Conte and Andrews (1993); Gresham (1993); and Gresham and Elliott (1989).

Attention Problems and Hyperactivity

Attention deficit (the inability to attend to a task) and hyperactivity (high rates of purposeless movement) are frequently cited as characteristics of children with learning disabilities. The term currently used to describe this combination of behavioral traits is **attention-deficit disorder,** or **ADD.** Children are diagnosed as having ADD according to criteria found in the *Diagnostic and Statistical Manual of Mental Disorders* (*DSM-IV*) (American Psychiatric Association [APA], 1994), which refers to the condition as *attention-deficit/hyperactivity disorder,* or ADHD. "The essential feature of attention-deficit/hyperactivity disorder is a persistent pattern of inattention and/or hyperactivity-impulsivity that is more frequent and severe than is typically observed in individuals at a comparable level of development" (APA, 1994, p. 78). To diagnose ADD, a physician must determine that a child consistently displays six or more symptoms of either inattention or hyperactivity-impulsivity for a period of at least 6 months (see Table 5.1).

The diagnostic criteria for ADD are so diverse and subjective (e.g., is often "on the go") that a child who is not diagnosed by one physician may very well be by the next doctor his parents take him to. Parents have been known to engage in "physician shopping," taking their child from one doctor to another until a diagnosis of ADD is made, sometimes on the basis of the physician's "idiosyncratic criteria" or even without seeing the child (Reid, Maag, & Vasa, 1993). After their review of 48 articles and books written on ADD by leading authorities revealed that 69 characteristics and 38 different causes of ADD had been proposed, Goodman and Poillion (1992) concluded that ADD was an acronym for "*Any Dysfunction or Difficulty.*" They go on to remark:

> The problems in researching the ADD label are reminiscent of the research encountered in the 1960s with the MBI and MBD labels. A proliferation of symptoms, or characteristics, was attached to the label, but no cause-effect relationship was ever established between symptoms and brain injury/dysfunction. Research efforts proved futile, and the terminology gave way to the learning disability label. The learning disability label seems to be suffering a similar fate. If a child is of normal intelligence and below grade level in school achievement, he or she can be labeled LD with any number of secondary characteristics diagnosed. . . . As professionals have become disenchanted with the term, they are turning increasingly to ADD as an explanation of the wide variety of children's problems in school. . . . Without specific characteristics and causes identified for this disorder, ADD may share the same fate as MBI, MBD, and LD. As a result, the children who are identified as having this disorder will fall victim to the ineffective cycles and spirals in America's educational system. (pp. 53–54)

Estimates of the prevalence of ADD range from 3% to 10% of all school-age children (Wender, 1987). These figures suggest that the typical classroom will have from one to three children either diagnosed as ADD or presenting the problems typically associated with ADD (DuPaul, Stoner, Tilly, & Putnam, 1991). A random national sample of family practitioners found that approximately 5% of all elementary students screened received a diagnosis of ADD (Wolraich et al., 1990).

It is important to stress that ADD is not the same as a learning disability. Although some children with learning disabilities are hyperactive and inattentive, many are calm and work hard at learning tasks (Samuels & Miller, 1985). Many children without learning disabilities also have trouble attending and sitting still. Likewise, numerous children who display impulsivity, inattention, and/or hyperactivity do well in school. ADD is not a disability category recognized by the IDEA. However, the Office of Special Education and Rehabilitation Services (OSERS) of the U.S. Department of Education issued a policy memorandum stating that although children with ADD are not *automatically* mandated to receive special education services, they can be served under the "other health impaired" category if limited alertness negatively affects academic performance or another disability area (e.g., learning disabilities) if the child meets eligibility criteria (Davila, Williams, & MacDonald, 1991).

Drug Therapy with Children with ADD

The most commonly prescribed treatment for ADD is drug therapy. Methylphenidate, a member of the amphetamine family sold under the trade name

See the Teaching & Learning box "Signaling for Help" in Chapter 1 to find out how one learning disabilities resource room teacher helps her students stay on task while working at their desks.

See Reid, Maag, and Vasa (1993) for a critique of ADD as a new disability category. The October/November 1993 issue of *Exceptional Children* is devoted to matters pertaining to the education of children with attention deficit disorder.

TABLE 5.1
Diagnostic criteria for attention-deficit/hyperactive disorder (ADHD)

■ **Diagnostic Criteria for Attention-Deficit/Hyperactivity Disorder**

A. Either (1) or (2):

(1) six (or more) of the following symptoms of **inattention** have persisted for at least 6 months to a degree that is maladaptive and inconsistent with developmental level:

Inattention

(a) often fails to give close attention to details or makes careless mistakes in schoolwork, work, or other activities

(b) often has difficulty sustaining attention in tasks or play activities

(c) often does not seem to listen when spoken to directly

(d) often does not follow through on instructions and fails to finish schoolwork, chores, or duties in the workplace (not due to oppositional behavior or failure to understand instructions)

(e) often has difficulty organizing tasks and activities

(f) often avoids, dislikes, or is reluctant to engage in tasks that require sustained mental effort (such as schoolwork or homework)

(g) often loses things necessary for tasks or activities (e.g., toys, school assignments, pencils, books, or tools)

(h) is often easily distracted by extraneous stimuli

(i) is often forgetful in daily activities

(2) six (or more) of the following symptoms of **hyperactivity-impulsivity** have persisted for at least 6 months to a degree that is maladaptive and inconsistent with developmental level:

Hyperactivity

(a) often fidgets with hands or feet or squirms in seat

(b) often leaves seat in classroom or in other situations in which remaining seated is expected

(c) often runs about or climbs excessively in situations in which it is inappropriate (in adolescents or adults, may be limited to subjective feelings of restlessness)

Ritalin, is the most prescribed medication. Although amphetamines are stimulants that normally increase a person's activity level, they produce a paradoxical effect in many children; that is, a reduced level of activity typically follows ingestion of the drug.

The number of children on stimulant medication has increased tremendously in recent years. A survey by the Baltimore, Maryland, County Health Department found that 5.96% of all elementary-age schoolchildren were receiving drug treatment for hyperactivity/inattentiveness (Safer & Krager, 1988). Given the results of nine previous biannual surveys, this figure represents a doubling of the rate of medication treatment for hyperactive/inattentive students every 4 to 7 years. Singh and Ellis

TABLE 5.1 *(continued)*

(d) often has difficulty playing or engaging in leisure activities quietly

(e) is often "on the go" or often acts as if "driven by a motor"

(f) often talks excessively

Impulsivity

(g) often blurts out answers before questions have been completed

(h) often has difficulty awaiting turn

(i) often interrupts or intrudes on others (e.g. butts into conversations or games)

B. Some hyperactive-impulsive or inattentive symptoms that caused impairment were present before age 7 years.

C. Some impairment from the symptoms is present in two or more settings (e.g., at school [or work] and at home).

D. There must be clear evidence of clinically significant impairment in social, academic, or occupational functioning.

E. The symptoms do not occur exclusively during the course of a Pervasive Developmental Disorder, Schizophrenia, or other Psychotic Disorder and are not better accounted for by another mental disorder (e.g., Mood Disorder, Anxiety Disorder, Dissociative Disorder, or a Personality Disorder).

Code based on type:

314.01 Attention-Deficit/Hyperactivity Disorder, Combined Type: if both Criteria A1 and A2 are met for the past 6 months

314.00 Attention-Deficit/Hyperactivity Disorder, Predominantly Inattentive Type: if Criterion A1 is met but Criterion A2 is not met for the past 6 months

314.01 Attention-Deficit/Hyperactivity Disorder, Predominantly Hyperactive-Impulsive Type: if Criterion A2 is met but Criterion A1 is not met for the past 6 months

Coding note: For individuals (especially adolescents and adults) who currently have symptoms that no longer meet full criteria, "In Partial Remission" should be specified.

Source: American Psychiatric Association: *Diagnostic and Statistical Manual of Mental Disorders,* Fourth Edition. Washington, DC: American Psychiatric Association, 1994.

(1993) estimate that more than 1 million U.S. schoolchildren are given daily doses of stimulant medication in an effort to control hyperactivity and attention deficits.

Although many physicians, parents, and teachers report positive results with stimulant therapy for children with learning disabilities or ADD, results of controlled research are mixed (Gadow, 1986; Swanson et al., 1993). After examining 341 published reviews of research on the effects of stimulant medication on children with ADD, Swanson et al. (1993) reported these generalizations about what should be expected:

An extended discussion of the use of psychotropic medication (behavior- and/or mood-altering drugs) is beyond the scope of this text. Gadow's (1986) book is an excellent source of information on this important topic for educators. The most common alternative to the use of drugs to treat hyperactivity is behavioral interventions. See Houlihan and Van Houten (1989) and O'Leary (1980) for reviews of these methods.

It is difficult to predict the effects of Ritalin in an individual child. The child's age, size, or weight cannot be used to determine the optimum dosage in terms of the desired effects on hyperactivity and safety. Direct and daily measurement of a student's performance on curricular materials is one promising technique for evaluating the effects of drugs and determining appropriate dosage levels (e.g., Stoner, Carey, Martin, & Shinn, 1994).

- Temporary management of overactivity, inattention, and impulsivity
- Temporary improvement of deportment, aggression, and increased academic output
- No improvement in long-term adjustment (academic achievement, arrest rate)
- Side effects such as increases in tics, disruptions in eating and sleeping patterns, possible negative effects on cognition

Given the questionable benefits of drug therapy with children and the fact that undesirable side effects are sometimes noted (e.g., insomnia, decreased appetite, headaches, disruption of normal growth patterns, irritability, reduced emotional affect, increased blood pressure), some professionals now view drug treatment as an inappropriate "easy way out" that might produce short-term improvements in behavior but result in long-term harm. "When stimulants work in the short-term, pharmacological intervention may be used as a crutch and may postpone or prevent the use of non-pharmacological interventions, which may be more effective in the long run" (Swanson et al., 1993, p. 158).

Kohn (1989) questions the use of drugs not only with children with ADD but also with children who do not conform to expected standards of behavior in the classroom or at home. He believes the use of Ritalin "may have much greater relevance for stress reduction in caregivers than intrinsic value to the child" (p. 98).

Behavioral Problems

Regardless of the interrelationships of these characteristics, teachers and other caregivers responsible for planning educational programs for students with learning disabilities need skills in dealing with social and behavioral difficulties as well as academic deficits. We examine some of these important teaching skills in Chapter 6.

The type and incidence of classroom behavioral problems exhibited by children with learning disabilities have been the subject of considerable research. Epstein and Cullinan have conducted a series of studies that reveal a higher-than-normal rate of behavioral problems among students with learning disabilities (Epstein, Bursuck, & Cullinan, 1985; Epstein, Cullinan, & Lloyd, 1986; Epstein, Cullinan, & Rosemier, 1983). They point out that although their data definitely show increased behavioral problems among children with learning disabilities, the relationships between the students' problem behavior and academic difficulty are not known. In other words, it cannot be said that either the academic deficits or the behavioral problems cause the other difficulty. Also, the data from these studies summarize large groups of students. Many children with learning disabilities exhibit no behavioral problems at all.

Learning Disabilities Subtypes?

Because of the many learning and behavioral characteristics associated with learning disabilities and the inability to create an accurate profile of characteristics for persons labeled learning disabled, some professionals are suggesting that distinct subtypes of learning disability exist and should be classified. McKinney (1985) states that the literature collectively argues against a "single syndrome" theory of learning disability and that it is feasible to create more homogeneous diagnostic subgroups within this presently broad and ill-defined category of exceptional children. It is much too early to predict whether the search for subgroups among individuals with learning disabilities will have any legitimate implications for education and treatment.

Life-Span Perspective

Another perspective on the characteristics of individuals with learning disabilities is the life-span view. Table 5.2 presents Mercer's (1992) summary of the major problem areas most likely to occur, the purposes of assessment and treatment, and the treatments most recommended during five different age spans.

It is important to remember that the fundamental characteristic of students with learning disabilities is a specific and significant achievement deficiency in the presence of adequate overall intelligence. Some children with learning disabilities are also hyperactive (or any of the other characteristics cited in this section), and some are not. And children who display any of these other characteristics but who do not also have deficits in achievement should not be considered learning disabled.

✳ *Causes of Learning Disabilities*

In almost every case, the exact cause of a child's learning disability is unknown; however, a wide variety of causes have been proposed. Three major categories of etiologic factors are brain damage, biochemical imbalance, and environmental factors.

Brain Damage

Some individuals with learning disabilities show definite signs of brain damage, which may well be the cause of their learning problems (Duffy & McAnulty, 1985; Geshwind & Galaburda, 1987). Spivak (1986) has estimated that as many as 20% of children with learning disabilities have sustained a prior brain injury, either before (prenatal), during (perinatal), or after (postnatal) birth. Some professionals believe that all children with learning disabilities suffer from some type of brain injury or dysfunction of the central nervous system. Indeed, this belief is inherent in the NJCLD definition of learning disabilities that states that learning disorders are "presumed to be due to central nervous system dysfunction." The brain damage is not considered extensive enough to cause a generalized and severe learning problem across all kinds of intellectual development, so the individual may be referred to as minimally brain damaged.

The ingestion of alcohol and other drugs by women during pregnancy often causes brain damage and learning problems. These causes of learning and other disabilities are discussed in Chapter 14.

Learning to read is the most common academic problem experienced by students with learning disabilities.

TABLE 5.2 A life-span view of learning disabilities across five different age levels, summarizing likely problem areas, purposes of assessment and treatment, and the treatments most recommended

	PRESCHOOL	GRADES K–1	GRADES 2–6	GRADES 7–12	ADULT
Problem areas	Achievement of developmental milestones (e.g., walking) Receptive language Expressive language Visual perception Auditory perception Short attention span Hyperactivity Self-regulation Social skills Concept formation	Academic readiness skills (e.g., alphabet knowledge, quantitative concepts, directional concepts, etc.) Receptive language Expressive language Visual perception Auditory perception Reasoning Motor development Attention Hyperactivity Social skills	Reading skills Arithmetic skills Written expression Verbal expression Receptive language Attention span Hyperactivity Social-emotional Reasoning	Reading skills Arithmetic skills Written expression Verbal expression Listening skills Study skills Metacognition Social-emotional-delinquency	Reading skills Arithmetic skills Written expression Verbal expression Listening skills Study skills Social-emotional Metacognition
Assessment	Prediction of high risk for later learning problems	Prediction of high risk for later learning problems	Identification of learning disabilities	Identification of learning disabilities	Identification of learning disabilities
Treatment types	Preventative	Preventative	Remedial Corrective	Remedial Corrective Compensatory Learning strategies	Remedial Corrective Compensatory Learning strategies
Treatments with most research and/or expert support	Direct instruction in language skills Behavioral management Parent training	Direct instruction in academic and language areas Behavioral management Parent training	Direct instruction in academic areas Behavioral management Parent training Metacognitive training	Direct instruction in academic areas Tutoring in subject areas Direct instruction in learning strategies (study skills) Self-control training Curriculum alternatives Metacognitive training	Direct instruction in academic areas Tutoring in subject (college) or job area Compensatory instruction (i.e., using aids such as tape recorder, calculator, computer) Direct instruction in learning strategies

Source: From Students with Learning Disabilities (4th ed.) (p. 50) by C. D. Mercer, 1992, New York: Merrill/Macmillan. Reprinted by permission.

Somos Todos Ayudantes y Estudiantes!

....

Two years of foreign language study is an entrance requirement for many 4-year colleges, and approximately half of all colleges require second-language skills for graduation (Ganschow & Sparks, 1987). To deny a student access to foreign language study or to fail to provide a student the opportunity to experience successful language study may unnecessarily limit his or her future educational choices. Failure to provide successful foreign language study not only limits a student's participation in the educational mainstream but also denies him or her the opportunity to experience the cultural benefits that accrue from skills in a second language. Yet students with learning disabilities are frequently discouraged from attempting a foreign language in high school. Students with learning disabilities are already experiencing academic difficulties, some people believe, so why enroll them in a course likely to be especially difficult?

Wiig and Semel (1984) state that foreign language learning presents one of the greatest barriers to the academic career of students with learning disabilities. They cite the basic vocabulary and grammatical rules of a foreign language emphasized from the beginning, as well as the more abstract vocabulary and complex syntactic structures taught as study progresses. Unless special instructional modifications are made, most students with learning disabilities find study of a foreign language an unsuccessful struggle. Although the literature of special education in general, and learning disabilities in particular, contains many examples of methods for successfully mainstreaming students with disabilities into most areas of the school curriculum, procedures for providing successful foreign language instruction for students with learning problems are virtually nonexistent. Recently, several foreign-language educators have suggested methods for helping the learner with special needs (Barnett, 1989; DiGiandomenico & Carey, 1988).

The key features of systematic peer tutoring systems—many opportunities to actively respond, immediate feedback, lots of praise and encouragement, progressing at each student's rate, mastery learning with maintenance—are consistent with recommendations for teaching foreign language. Peer tutoring may be especially well suited for helping students with learning disabilities acquire and maintain the large amounts of vocabulary they encounter from the beginning of foreign language study.

The Peer Tutoring System

A reciprocal, classwide peer tutoring system was implemented within a second-year, "modified" Spanish class in an urban high school. The class was designed to provide an opportunity to study Spanish at a somewhat slower pace and focused on the most useful, practical aspects of the language for 6 students with learning disabilities and 10 students who were considered at risk for failing a foreign language class. The program was adapted from a classwide peer tutoring model devised at Ohio State University (Cooke, Heron, & Heward, 1983; Miller, Barbetta, & Heron, 1994).

Students worked in pairs, each tutoring the other for 5 minutes per day on a set of eight *palabras para aprender* (words to learn). Students both said and wrote the Spanish translation of words and phrases presented pictorially on flash cards and received praise or corrective feedback from their tutors after each response. When a student correctly wrote an item for 2 consecutive days on the tutor-administered test at the end of each day's session, that item went into the *palabras para repasar* (words to review) pocket in his or her peer-tutoring folder. All words in that pocket were tested on a weekly maintenance test given by the teacher.

Results

All of the students learned Spanish vocabulary words almost as fast as the system allowed. The six students with learning disabilities demonstrated an average rate of learning ranging from 7.0 to 7.9 new words every 2 days (the maximum rate of progress was 8 words every 2 days). To assess whether the students could learn words even faster, three tutoring pairs

Folder and flash cards used by high school students with learning disabilities for Spanish peer-tutoring program

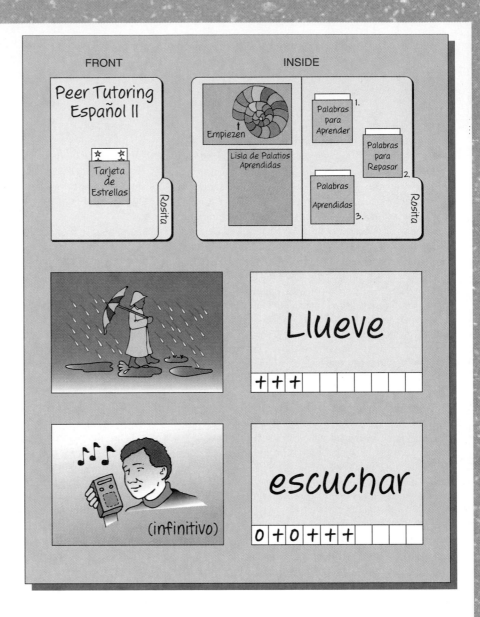

worked with sets of 12 words during the study's final 2 weeks. They learned new words at an average rate of 11.3 to 11.7 words every 2 days.

The students not only taught each other new Spanish vocabulary but also remembered what they learned. As a group, the students averaged 87% of all words correct on the weekly tests of maintenance. When asked their opinions of the peer-tutoring program, 15 of the 16 students said they would like to use it again for studying Spanish, and 14 said they wished peer tutoring was used in their other academic classes. These three comments sum up the students' opinions about the program:

"This was about the most helpful thing I can remember for learning things you usually don't want to. The program was excellent!"

"I think this is a program that should be used in the classroom. It causes the kids to get involved in their learning instead of just having the teacher dictate to you all day."

"Boy, if we'd been doing this all year, I'd be acing this course!"

Based on Wright, J. E., Cavanaugh, R. A., Sainato, D. M., & Heward, W. L. (in press). Teaching each other Spanish: Evaluation of a classwide reciprocal peer tutoring program for learning disabled and at-risk high school students. *Education and Treatment of Children*.

In cases in which actual evidence of brain damage cannot be shown (and this is the situation with the majority of children with learning disabilities), the term *minimal brain dysfunction* is sometimes used, especially by physicians. This wording implies brain damage by asserting that the child's brain does not function well.

Most educators place little value on brain dysfunction as an explanation of the difficulties experienced by most students with learning disabilities. As Smith and Robinson (1986) state, "The evidence linking behavioral characteristics to brain dysfunction is circumstantial, speculative, and in most cases clearly not documentable. Identifying brain damage does not lead to sets of instructional or remediation strategies that produce guaranteed or uniform results" (p. 223).

Current etiologic theories linking learning disabilities to brain damage pose two major problems. The first problem is lack of evidence. Not all children with learning disabilities display clinical (medical) evidence of brain damage, and not all children with brain damage have learning disabilities. Boshes and Myklebust (1964) reported the results of EEG readings given to 200 normal children and 200 children with learning disabilities. Results showed that 29% of the normal children and 42% of the children with learning disabilities displayed abnormal brain wave patterns. Even though more children with learning disabilities were rated abnormal, certainly these results show no direct, one-to-one relationship between brain injury and learning disability.

The second problem with the brain-damage assumption is that it can serve as a powerful built-in excuse for failure to teach the student. If a student does not learn, it is thought to be no one's fault; after all, she has a brain injury that "prevents" her from learning. The concern that teachers do not let diagnoses of real or suspected neurological problems sway their educational judgments is shared by virtually all professionals in learning disabilities, even those who believe that a true learning disability is caused by central nervous system damage or dysfunction. Myers and Hammill (1990) conclude their discussion of etiology with these cautionary words:

> For the teacher or clinician who is not engaged in systematic research, the primary concerns are to handle the correlative symptoms . . . to teach the children to read, speak, write, and so on. Whether learning disabilities in an individual case are symptoms that result from brain injury or developmental delay will not essentially alter the methods of teaching the student. . . . Isolation of definite or presumed etiologies for the observed disabilities is of only tangential interest and value to the teacher-clinician and plays a minor role in the preparation of instructional programs. (p. 22)

Assessment of brain damage is often done with an **electroencephalograph (EEG)**, which measures and makes a graph of brain waves. Brain damage is inferred from the presence of abnormal brain waves.

Biochemical Imbalance

Some researchers claim that biochemical disturbances within a child's body are the cause of learning disabilities. Feingold (1975a, 1975b, 1976) received much publicity for his claims that artificial colorings and flavorings in many of the foods children eat can cause learning disabilities and hyperactivity. He recommended a treatment for learning disabilities that consisted of a diet with no foods containing synthetic colors or flavors. A number of research studies were conducted to test the Feingold diet, some claiming positive results (Connors, Goyette, Southwick, Lees, & Andrulonis, 1976; Cook & Woodhill, 1976). In a comprehensive review of diet-related studies, however, Spring and Sandoval (1976) concluded that very little evidence supported Feingold's theory. Many of the studies were poorly conducted, and the few experiments that were scientifically sound concluded that only a small portion of hyperactive children might be helped by the special diet.

In response to the controversy over diet treatments, the American Council on Science and Health (1979) issued the following statement:

> Hyperactivity will continue to be a frustrating problem until research resolves the questions of its cause, or causes, and develops an effective treatment. The reality is that we still have a great deal to learn about this condition. We do know now, however, that diet is not the answer. It is clear that the symptoms of the vast majority of the children labeled "hyperactive" are not related to salicylates, artificial food colors, or artificial flavors. The Feingold diet creates extra work for the homemakers and changes the family lifestyle . . . but it doesn't cure hyperactivity. (p. 5)

Cott (1972) hypothesized that learning disabilities can be caused by the inability of a child's bloodstream to synthesize a normal amount of vitamins. On the basis of his contention, some physicians began megavitamin therapy with children with learning disabilities. Megavitamin treatment consists of massive daily doses of vitamins in an effort to overcome the suspected vitamin deficiencies.

Two studies designed to test the effects of megavitamin treatment with learning disabled and hyperkinetic children found that huge doses of vitamins did not improve the children's performance (Arnold, Christopher, Huestis, & Smeltzer, 1978; Kershner, Hawks, & Grekin, 1977). And several researchers have cautioned against the potential risks of large doses of vitamins. Toxic effects such as scurvy, cardiac arrhythmia, headaches, and abnormalities of the liver may result, especially from megadoses of certain B vitamins (Eastman, 1978; Golden, 1980).

Although it is possible, or even probable, that biochemistry may affect a student's behavior and learning in the classroom, no scientific evidence exists today to reveal the nature or extent of that influence. It is understandable that claims of cure create a great deal of excitement and interest among both professionals and parents. Rooney (1991), who reviewed and critiqued a number of "controversial therapies" claiming to cure or remediate the learning and/or behavioral problems experienced by children with disabilities, suggests that we "read the fine print" before accepting a discovery.

> Vitamin therapy has also been recommended for children with mental retardation; some studies claim increases in IQ and improvements in behavior as a result of large doses of vitamin-mineral supplements (e.g., Harrell, Capp, Davis, Peerless, & Ravitz, 1981). After reviewing the Harrell et al. study and others, however, Pruess, Fewell, and Bennett (1989) concluded that "vitamin therapy is clearly not useful for young children with Down syndrome" (p. 340).

Environmental Factors

Lovitt (1978) cites three types of environmental influences that he believes are related to children's learning problems: emotional disturbance, lack of motivation, and poor instruction. Many children with learning problems have behavioral disorders as well. Whether one causes the other or whether both are caused by some other factor(s) is uncertain. In addition, it is difficult to identify reinforcing activities for some students with learning disabilities; they may not be interested in many of the things other children like. Some studies have shown that finding a key to the child's motivational problem can sometimes solve the learning problem as well (Lovitt, 1977).

One variable that is likely to be a major contributor to children's learning problems is the quality of instruction. Lovitt (1978) states it this way:

> [A] condition which might contribute to a learning disability is poor instruction. Although many children are able to learn in spite of poor teachers and inadequate techniques, others are less fortunate. Some youngsters who have experienced poor instruction in the early grades never catch up with their peers. (p. 169)

Engelmann (1977) is even more direct:

> Perhaps 90 percent or more of the children who are labeled "learning disabled" exhibit a disability not because of anything wrong with their perception, synapses, or memory, but because they have been seriously mistaught. Learning disabilities are made, not born. (pp. 46–47)

Lovitt and Engelmann are among a growing number of special educators who believe that the best way to help a student with learning problems is to emphasize the assessment and training of those specific behaviors (e.g., reading and math skills) that are troublesome for that particular student. Mounting evidence indicates that many students' learning problems can be remediated by direct, systematic instruction. It would be naive to think, however, that the learning problems of all children stem from inadequate instruction. Perhaps Engelmann's other 10% are those children whose learning disability is caused by a malfunctioning central nervous system. In any event, from an educational perspective, good systematic instruction should be the treatment of first choice for all students with learning disabilities.

At present there is much more speculation than hard evidence about the etiology of learning disabilities, but the search for the real causes of children's learning problems must go on. Only when positive identification of the causes of learning disabilities has been made can prevention become a realistic alternative.

✳ *Identification and Assessment*

In education the word *assessment* is synonymous with testing. Literally hundreds of tests have been developed to measure virtually every motor, social, or academic response children make (Mitchell, 1985). Much of the testing in education is conducted primarily for the purpose of identifying children for certain special education categories and placement.

> At some point along the continuum of services provided by the school, there must be a cutoff that dictates which children will be served by special education and which will remain totally the responsibility of the general education program. Obviously, the vast majority of children who have trouble in school will have to stay in regular classes. In any event, the type of assessment that deals with identification is of the utmost importance in states where laws, policies, or traditions make it mandatory that children be classified according to type of handicap before they can qualify for special services. (Myers & Hammill, 1990, p. 66)

Because of the complex way that learning disabilities is defined, the task of identifying the true student with learning disabilities guarantees that a battery of

For a critical examination of how assessment of children with learning disabilities is conducted, see Lovitt (1986) and Ysseldyke et al. (1983), who contend that too many tests are administered that produce too little useful data for planning instruction. These authors make a strong case for spending less time and fewer resources on assessment for classification and diagnosis and more resources on instruction.

Three texts that describe special education assessment practices in detail and examine many widely used tests are McLoughlin and Lewis (1994); Salvia and Ysseldyke (1991); and Venn (1994). For excellent discussions of systematic assessment for instructional planning—that is, for using assessment to determine what to teach and how to teach—see Howell, Fox, and Morehead (1993) and Zigmond and Miller (1986).

tests will be administered. One study of 14 school districts in Michigan found that, on the average, three to five different tests were given to each student referred for learning disabilities (Perlmutter & Parus, 1983). When Shepard and Smith (1981) examined how the determination of a learning disability was made in 1,000 individual cases in Colorado, they discovered that half of the school district funds available for services to students with learning disabilities were expended on identification alone. As a result of these assessment practices, children with learning disabilities have been called the "most diagnosed" of all exceptional children (Lovitt, 1982).

Even though identification and placement are appropriate and important functions of educational testing, assessment has a much more important purpose: to provide information for planning and implementing an instructional program for the child.

At least five types of tests or methods are commonly used in assessing learning disabilities: norm-referenced tests, process tests, informal reading inventories, criterion-referenced tests, and direct daily measurement. Of these five types, norm-referenced tests and process tests are indirect assessment devices; that is, the child's general ability along various dimensions is measured. Informal reading inventories, criterion-referenced tests, and direct daily measurement can be classified as direct assessment techniques. Direct assessment measures the specific skills and behaviors that a child is to be taught. The choice between direct and indirect assessment is largely determined by the approach to instructional remediation taken by a given school program, which is discussed later in this chapter.

Norm-Referenced Tests

Norm-referenced tests are designed so that one student's score can be compared with those of other students of the same age who have taken the same test. Because a deficit in academic achievement is the major characteristic of students with learning disabilities, standardized achievement tests are commonly used. Some standardized achievement tests—such as the *Iowa Tests of Basic Skills* (Hieronymus & Lindquist, 1978), the *Peabody Individual Achievement Test* (Dunn & Markwardt, 1970), the *Woodcock-Johnson Psychoeducational Battery* (Woodcock, 1978), and the *Wide Range Achievement Test* (WRAT) (Jastak & Jastak, 1965)—are designed to measure a student's overall academic achievement. Scores on these tests are reported by grade level; a score of 3.5, for example, means that the student's score equaled the average score by those students in the norm group who were halfway through the third grade.

A recent statewide study in Iowa found that the Woodcock-Johnson Psychoeducational Battery was used to measure academic achievement of students tested for learning disabilities more than twice as often as the WRAT, which had been the predominant test of achievement in a previous study (Kavale & Reese, 1992).

Other norm-referenced tests measure achievement in certain academic areas. Some of the frequently administered reading achievement tests are the *Durrell Analysis of Reading Difficulty* (Durrell, 1955), the *Gates-McKillop Reading Diagnostic Test* (Gates & McKillop, 1962), the *Gray Oral Reading Tests* (Gray, 1963), the *Spache Diagnostic Reading Scales* (Spache, 1963), and the *Woodcock Reading Mastery Tests* (Woodcock, 1974). The *KeyMath Diagnostic Arithmetic Test* (Connolly, Natchman, & Pritchett, 1973) and the *Stanford Diagnostic Arithmetic Test* (Beatty, Madden, & Gardner, 1966) are often used to test arithmetic achievement.

Process Tests

The concept of process, or ability, testing grew out of the belief that learning disabilities are caused by a basic underlying difficulty of the child to process, or use, environmental stimuli in the same way that children without disabilities do. These general abilities are categorized under headings such as visual perception, auditory perception, and visual-motor coordination. The developers and users of these tests believe that if the child's specific perceptual problems can be identified, treatment programs can then be designed to improve those problems, and the child's learning disability will be remediated. Two of the most widely used process tests used for diagnosing and assessing learning disabilities are the *Illinois Test of Psycholinguistic Abilities* (ITPA) (Kirk, McCarthy, & Kirk, 1968) and the *Marianne Frostig Developmental Test of Visual Perception* (Frostig, Lefever, & Whittlesey, 1964).

ITPA

First published in 1961 and later revised in 1968, the ITPA consists of 12 subtests, each designed to measure some aspect of psycholinguistic ability that Kirk and his colleagues considered central to learning. Results of the test are graphically depicted on a profile showing in which of the 12 areas a child demonstrates weaknesses. Many remedial education programs and activities for children with learning disabilities have been based on the psycholinguistic or information-processing model. Although research on the effectiveness of these training programs has not validated their effectiveness, one major contribution of the ITPA to educational assessment cannot be denied: The ITPA was developed and has been used as an assessment tool for gathering data that can be translated directly into an educational program designed to meet the individual needs of a specific child.

> For reviews of this research, see Hammill and Larsen (1974, 1978).

The Frostig

The *Marianne Frostig Developmental Test of Visual Perception* (Frostig et al., 1964) was developed by Frostig and her colleagues to measure certain dimensions of visual perception they considered crucial to a child's ability to learn to read. The Frostig test comprises five subtests designed to pinpoint the kinds of perceptual difficulties a child has. The five areas are visual-motor coordination, figure-ground discrimination, constancy of shape, position of objects in space, and spatial relationships.

Informal Reading Inventories

Teachers' growing awareness of the inability of formal achievement tests and process tests to provide truly useful information for planning instruction has led to greater use of teacher-developed and -administered tests, particularly in the area of reading. An informal reading inventory usually consists of a series of progressively more difficult sentences and paragraphs that a student is asked to read aloud. By directly observing and recording aspects of the student's reading skills—such as mispronounced vowels or consonants, omissions, reversals, substitutions, and comprehension—the teacher can determine the level of reading material that is most suitable for the child and the specific reading skills that require remediation.

> For a list of children's literature recommended for students with learning disabilities, see Higbee Mandlebaum (1992).

Criterion-Referenced Tests

Criterion-referenced tests differ from norm-referenced tests in that a child's score on a criterion-referenced test is compared with a predetermined criterion, or mastery level, rather than with normed scores of other students. The value of criterion-referenced tests is that they identify the specific skills the child has already learned and the skills that require instruction. A criterion-referenced test widely used by special educators is the *BRIGANCE Diagnostic Inventory of Basic Skills* (Brigance, 1983), which includes 140 skill sequences in four subscales: readiness, reading, language arts, and math. Some commercially distributed curricula now include criterion-referenced test items for use both as a pretest and posttest. The pretest assesses the student's entry level to determine which aspects of the program he or she is ready to learn; the posttest evaluates the effectiveness of the program. Criterion-referenced tests can be, and often are, informally developed by classroom teachers.

Direct Daily Measurement

Direct daily measurement means observing and recording, every day, a child's performance on the specific skill being taught. In a program teaching multiplication facts, for example, the student's performance of multiplication facts would be assessed each day that multiplication was taught. Measures such as correct rate (number of facts stated or written correctly per minute), error rate, and percentage correct are often recorded.

See Bushell and Baer (1994) for a powerful argument in support of making direct and frequent measurement of student performance an integral part of educational practice.

Two advantages of direct daily measurement are clear. First, it gives information about the child's performance on the skill under instruction. Second, this information is available on a continuous basis so that the teacher can adjust the child's program according to changing (or perhaps unchanging) performance, not because of intuition, guesswork, or the results of a test that measures something else. Direct and frequent measurement is the cornerstone of the behavioral approach to education introduced in Chapter 4 and is becoming an increasingly popular assessment and evaluation technique in all areas of special education. One teaching approach

Self-recording and self-graphing daily measures of academic performance is an excellent way to motivate and involve students in their own learning.

used by some learning disabilities teachers, based entirely on direct daily measurement, is precision teaching.

Precision Teaching

Precision teaching is a system of direct daily measurement of student performance originated by Ogden R. Lindsley. Lindsley, who had worked with B. F. Skinner at Harvard, translated much of the traditional operant (behavioral) terminology into language that sounded more natural in the schools. Thus, precision teachers look at behavior as movement, at antecedent and consequent events as events before and after the child's movement, at reinforcement schedules as arrangements of the events that follow a movement, and so on. Then Lindsley developed a set of simple but effective procedures that teachers can follow to identify, monitor, and make decisions about critical movements children need to make to succeed in school. Finally, on the basis of data suggesting that children take bigger and bigger steps as they become more proficient at a movement, Lindsley devised the Standard Behavior Chart (Figure 5.1) to graphically show the student's progress from day to day.

Since its inception, precision teaching has been refined and improved by many teachers and researchers. As presently practiced, precision teaching consists of the steps summarized here and illustrated in Figure 5.1:

1. Precisely pinpoint the movement the child must make to learn the skill required—writing digits, saying words, and so on.
2. Next, observe the child's performance of the movement, noting both accuracy and fluency (speed), and chart the results.
3. Using the information from a few days' observation, set an aim (objective) for the child, in terms of both accuracy and fluency, and note it on the chart.
4. Connect the average performance from the first few days with this aim, producing a line on the chart that represents the minimum progress the child must make each day to reach the aim in the time available.
5. As the days and weeks pass, continue to measure the child's performances every day, charting the information every day.
6. Paying careful attention to the chart, follow certain decision rules that tell when the program should be changed—to prevent the child from slipping below the line of minimum progress.
7. Whenever a program change (phase change) is needed, note the change on the chart, draw a new aim and a new minimum progress line, and begin again—before the child has had a chance to fail.

Precision teaching is neither a specific method of teaching nor a curriculum but a way of evaluating the effects of instruction and making instructional decisions. As such, it has potential as a technological partner for all other methods of measurably effective instruction (Potts et al., 1993). For example, over a 2-year period Stump et al. (1992) taught precision teaching to 36 general and special education teachers as part of an inservice training program that included study guides and SAFMEDS as activities to increase students' vocabulary knowledge. The teachers, in turn, introduced the approach to 694 students, 125 of whom were students with learning disabilities. All but one teacher who received training implemented the approach; the majority of students, whether general or special education students in self-contained or mainstreamed classrooms, increased their accuracy and fluency on timed vocabu-

For more information about precision teaching, see Johnston and Layng (1994); Lindsley (1972); McGreevy (1983); Potts, Eshleman, and Cooper (1993); White (1986); White and Haring (1980); and the *Journal of Precision Teaching*.

SAFMEDS (*Say All Fast, a Minute Every Day, Shuffled*) is a fluency-building procedure in which a student orally states the answers to as many facts printed on flash cards as he or she can in 1 minute. Each fact or vocabulary term is printed on one side of the flash card and its definition on the other side. For more explanation and examples of SAFMEDS, see Eshleman (1985) and Potts et al. (1993).

FIGURE 5.1 A standard behavior chart used in precision teaching

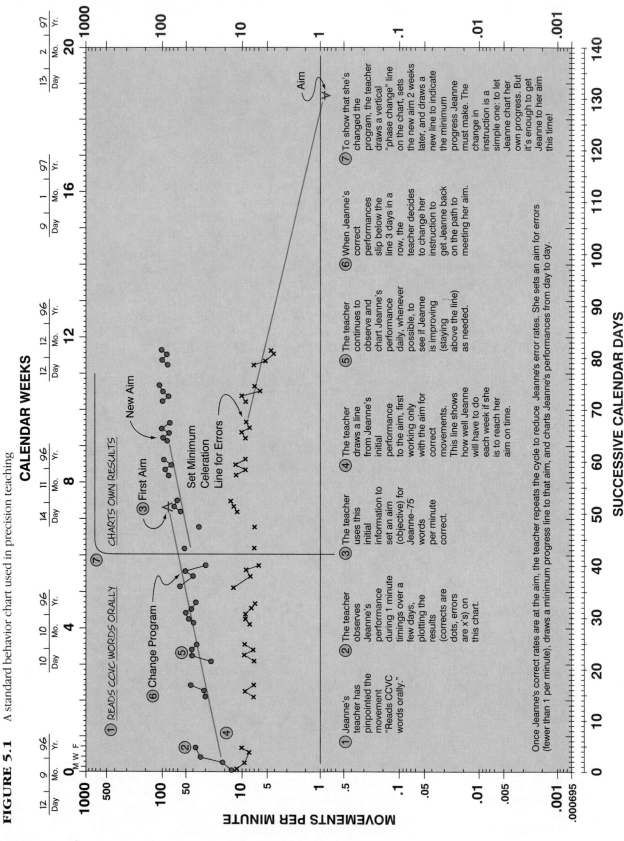

Source: Adapted from Exceptional Teaching (p. 276) by O. White and N. Haring, 1976, New York: Merrill/Macmillan. Reprinted by permission.

lary quizzes; and most teachers and students found the approach worthwhile and enjoyable.

Ecological Assessment

Results obtained from normative and criterion-referenced assessments are sufficient to determine instructional objectives and teaching procedures for most students. Some students' learning problems are complex enough, however, to warrant a more thorough assessment approach, known as *ecological assessment.* Ecological assessment encompasses two related perspectives. First, the student with learning disabilities is seen as possessing a "behavioral ecology" in the sense that changes in one behavior may affect other behaviors. Second, behavior is viewed within an environmental context whereby changes in one environmental condition may produce changes in other conditions, which, in turn, affect the child's performance (Rogers-Warren & Warren, 1977). Thus, an ecological assessment takes into account both the student and the various environments in which he or she lives.

Heron and Heward (1988) describe six factors to consider in an ecological assessment: (a) physiological factors (medications, health); (b) physical aspects of the environment (e.g., amount of space provided to student, seating arrangements, lighting, noise); (c) student-student interaction (how other children behave toward the child with learning disabilities); (d) teacher-student interaction (effects that various teacher behaviors have on the child); (e) home environment; and (f) the student's reinforcement history. Ecological assessment data are obtained through a wide range of sources, including student records, interviews with parents and other caregivers, tests, academic products, direct observations, and behavioral checklists.

Although one can obtain a rich, descriptive database about a student from an ecological assessment, teachers must weigh the costs and benefits of the approach.

> The key to using an ecological assessment is to know when to use it. Full-scale ecological assessments for their own sake are not recommendable for LD teachers charged with imparting a great number of important skills to many children in a limited amount of time. In most cases, the time and effort spent conducting an exhaustive ecological assessment would be better used in direct instruction. While the results of an ecological assessment might prove interesting, they do not always change the course of a planned intervention. Under what conditions then will an ecological assessment yield data that will significantly affect the course of treatment? Herein lies the challenge. Educators must become keen discriminators of: (1) situations in which a planned intervention has the potential for affecting student behaviors other than the behavior of concern; and (2) situations in which an intervention, estimated to be effective if the target behavior is viewed in isolation, may be ineffective because other ecological variables come into play. (Heron & Heward, 1988, p. 231)

Recommendations for Assessment

The number of tests and assessment approaches available for students with learning disabilities is staggering. Children with learning disabilities are probably subjected to more testing sessions with more types of tests than any other exceptional children. It is no wonder many teachers, parents, and students become confused with the com-

All of the assessment approaches described in this chapter are often used with other exceptional children, as well as with students in general education.

plexity of the assessment process. Lovitt (1989) offers the following recommendations for assessment:

- *Assess directly.* In many instances, it is more sensible for teachers to measure something they are teaching than to gather inappropriate data from standardized tests. Many of the items on standardized tests are not the ones being taught.
- *Assess frequently.* If teachers want to know how a student is doing on a certain skill or behavior, it is important to gather pertinent data frequently, rather than rely on standardized tests, which are generally given only once or twice a year.
- *Assess the most important and most critical behaviors most often.* Teachers should decide which behaviors are most in need of change and then gather as much data as possible on them.
- *Inform pupils about the assessment process.* Teachers can help pupils by explaining not only the reasons for various measurements, but also, in many cases, the meaning of the results.
- *Conduct assessments in the students' classrooms or homes under normal circumstances.* When pupils are taken to testing chambers outside their familiar surroundings, they are generally not at ease, even if efforts have been made to establish rapport.
- *Assess skills and behaviors that are part of the pupils' IEPs.* It makes sense for teachers to rely on the students' IEPs for guidance on instruction and measurement. Too often, items included in IEPS are overlooked in instruction.
- *Become familiar with the techniques for conducting ecological assessments.* If detailed reports about certain pupils are desired, the ideas from that approach, coupled with ongoing data, blend together quite nicely.
- *Communicate with parents and other interested caregivers frequently and directly about the progress of their children.* Be open to suggestions from them about behaviors that should be assessed that are not being monitored.[1]

✳ *Prevalence*

Learning disabilities is by far the largest of all special education categories. During the 1992–93 school year, 2.37 million children ages 6 to 21 were identified as learning disabled and received special education services (U.S. Department of Education, 1994). This figure represents 4.1% of the total school enrollment in the U.S. during the 1992–93 school year and 52% of all children with disabilities served in the United States (U.S. Department of Education, 1994). The number of students with learning disabilities has grown tremendously since the passage of the IDEA. The 1992–93 number is 5.4% higher than that of just 1 year earlier and represents almost three times the number of children with learning disabilities who received special education in 1976–77, the first year the federal government reported such data. Among the reasons cited by the government for the growth in the number of children with learning disabilities are "eligibility criteria that permit children with a wide range of learning problems to be classified as learning disabled; social acceptance and/or preference for the learning disabled classification; the reclassification of some mentally retarded children as learning disabled; and the lack of general education alternatives for children who are experiencing learning problems in regular classes" (U.S. Department of Education, 1986, p. 5).

During this same period, the percentage of students ages 6 through 21 receiving special education services under the category of mental retardation dropped from approximately 1 in every 4 students in 1976–77 to 1 in 10 students in 1992–93.

---

[1]From Thomas C. Lovitt, "Introduction to Learning Disabilities." Copyright © 1989 by Allyn and Bacon. Reprinted/Adapted by permission.

Many educators and professionals in special education are alarmed by the rising prevalence figures for learning disabilities. They believe that the ever-increasing numbers of students classified as learning disabled are the result of overidentification and misdiagnosis of low-achieving students, which thus reduces the resources available to serve the student who is "truly" learning disabled. Hallahan (1992), however, believes that the current numbers of students being served as learning disabled may not be a gross overestimate of the actual number and may be closer to the truth than most have previously thought. He suggests two reasons for the increase in prevalence figures: the newness of the field of learning disabilities and social/cultural changes in society.

> We have been engaged in the formal study of learning disabilities for only 20 to 30 years. Although 20 to 30 years may seem like a long time to a culture obsessed with youth, it is not much more than an eye blink to scientists engaged in serious study of a phenomenon as complex as learning disabilities, or to educators grappling to come up with the best ways to identify and educate these children. . . . The dramatic increase in students served as learning disabled may not be due to identification procedures run amok, as critics would have us believe. Instead, the increase may be, in part, a reflection of professionals' and parents' growing recognition of the condition of learning disabilities and how to deal with it. . . . I hypothesize that social/cultural changes over the past 20 to 40 years may have led to an increase in the prevalence of learning disabilities in two ways. First, social/cultural changes [e.g., poverty, substance abuse by pregnant women] have put the development of children's central nervous systems at increasing risks of disruption. Second, they have placed an increasing degree of psychological stress on children and their families. . . . Exactly what proportion of the increase represents bogus cases of learning disabilities is open for speculation and future research. In the meantime, we should be open to the idea that at least some of the increase represents students who are in very real need of learning disabilities services.[2]

✳ *Historical Background*

By the 1950s, most public schools had established special education programs (or at least offered some type of special service) for students with mental retardation, physical disabilities, behavioral disorders, and vision or hearing impairments. But a group of children remained who were having serious learning problems at school yet did not fit into any of the existing categories of exceptionality. They did not "look" disabled; that is, the children seemed physically intact, yet they experienced extreme difficulty in learning certain basic skills and subjects at school. In searching for help with their children's problems (remember, the public schools had no programs for these children), parents turned to other professionals—notably doctors, psychologists, and speech and language specialists. Understandably, these professionals viewed the children from the perspectives of their respective disciplines. As a result, terms such as *brain damage, minimal brain dysfunction, neurological impairment, perceptual handicap, dyslexia,* and *aphasia* were often used to describe or account for the various problems. Some of these terms are still used today, as a variety of disciplines have been and continue to be influential in the area of learning disabilities.

Early in this century, the term *word blindness* was used in conjunction with individuals who had extreme difficulty learning to read (Hinshelwood, 1895; Orton, 1925).

For more detailed presentations on the history of learning disabilities, see Lovitt (1989); Mercer (1992); and Myers and Hammill (1990).

[2]From "Some thoughts on why the prevalence of learning disabilities has increased," by Hallahan, D. P., 1992, *Journal of Learning Disabilities, 25*(9), 523–528. Copyright © 1992 by PRO-ED, Inc. Reprinted by permission.

Although coining of the term *learning disabilities* and the focused attention to this area of special education were phenomena of the 1960s, the area is closely related to research conducted with brain-injured children with mental retardation in the 1940s and 1950s by Strauss, Werner, Lehtinen, and Kephart. The study of neuropsychological (brain-behavior) functions by several 19th-century German scientists provided a knowledge base on which Strauss and other early pioneers in the field of learning disabilities would build (Opp, 1994).

Origins

Most historians of special education place the official beginning of the learning disabilities movement in 1963, when Dr. Samuel Kirk delivered an address to a group of parents who were meeting in Chicago to form a national organization. The children of these parents were experiencing serious difficulties in learning to read, were hyperactive, or could not solve math problems. The parents did not believe that their children's learning problems were the result of mental retardation or emotional disturbance, nor were they satisfied with the labels most often applied to their children. Kirk (1963) said, "Recently, I have used the term 'learning disabilities' to describe a group of children who have disorders in development in language, speech, reading, and associated communication skills" (n.p.). The parents liked the term and, that very evening, voted to form the Association for Children with Learning Disabilities (ACLD).

Milestones

In 1968, three more milestones were reached. First, the National Advisory Committee on Handicapped Children drafted and presented to Congress a definition of learning disabilities that would later be incorporated into the IDEA as the definition used to govern the dispersal of federal funds for support of services to children with learning disabilities. Second, the Council for Exceptional Children (CEC), the largest organization of special educators and other professionals serving exceptional children, established the Division for Children with Learning Disabilities (DCLD). Third, Lloyd Dunn published his article "Special Education for the Mildly Retarded—Is Much of It Justifiable?" (Dunn, 1968). Dunn argued that the proliferation of self-contained classrooms at that time was not supported by evidence of their effectiveness and that the evaluation and placement procedures typically used with children with mild disabilities were questionable on many grounds. This article led many special educators to a much closer self-examination of all of their practices, including those involving learning disabilities.

Legislative Support

Largely because of the intense lobbying efforts of the ACLD and DCLD, legislators were made aware of children with learning disabilities who were not covered under any previous legislation providing educational support for students with disabilities. As a result, the Children with Learning Disabilities Act (part of PL 91–230) was passed by Congress in 1969. This legislation authorized a 5-year program of federal funds for teacher training and the establishment of model demonstration programs for stu-

Today, the organization's name is the **Learning Disabilities Association of America (LDA)**. It is a powerful advocacy group of more than 50,000 members dedicated to the support of services and programs for persons with learning disabilities. Most LDA members are parents, although many teachers and other professionals are also members.

In 1982 the membership of DCLD left CEC to form an independent organization, the Council for Learning Disabilities (CLD). In that same year, a new Division for Learning Disabilities (DLD) was created within CEC. Many learning disabilities professionals maintain membership in both CLD and DLD.

dents with learning disabilities. In 1975, learning disabilities was one of the disability categories included in the IDEA.

✳ *Educational Approaches*

Most learning disabilities specialists believe in a diagnostic-prescriptive approach, in which the results of diagnosis (assessment) lead directly to a prescription (plan) for teaching. Ysseldyke and Salvia (1974) outline two major models of instructional remediation within the overall framework of the diagnostic-prescriptive approach: the ability training (or process) model and the skill training (or task-analysis) model. Although there are many variations and versions within each approach, fundamental differences exist between the two models.

Ability Training

Ability trainers believe that a child's observed performance deficit (learning problem) results from weakness in a particular ability thought necessary to perform a given task. (That is, a particular child may have failed to learn to read because of a visual-perceptual disorder.) These abilities are usually classified as perceptual-motor, sensory, or psycholinguistic. Educational remediation involves testing the child (e.g., with the ITPA or Frostig tests) to determine disabilities and then prescribing instructional activities for remediating those disabilities. If deficits in basic abilities cause the child's learning problem, remediating those deficits should result in improved achievement. The logic is sound.

The three most widely known ability-training approaches have been *psycholinguistic training,* based on the ITPA; the *visual-perceptual approach,* based on the Frostig Developmental Test of Visual Perception (Frostig & Horne, 1973); and the *perceptual-motor approach* (Kephart, 1971). According to Kephart, motor development precedes visual development; he believes that the lack of proper perceptual-motor development, such as eye-hand coordination, is often a cause of reading difficulty. Kephart's program teaches four areas of motor development: balance and posture, locomotion, contact, and receipt and propulsion.

Another approach to teaching children with learning disabilities is the *multisensory approach.* Although teachers are more likely to work directly on academic skills, this approach is still based primarily on an information-processing model. As its name suggests, the multisensory approach employs as many of the child's senses as possible in an effort to help him or her learn.

The most notable multisensory programs are those developed by Fernald (1943) and Slingerland (1971). Fernald's method is known as the VAKT technique. To learn a new letter, for example, the child would see the letter (visual), hear the letter (auditory), and trace the letter (kinesthetic and tactile). Little scientific research has been conducted on the multisensory method.

Effectiveness of Ability Training

Little research evidence supports the effectiveness of ability training. Hammill, Goodman, and Wiederholt (1974) reviewed the results of studies conducted on the Kephart and Frostig approaches. They concluded that 13 of the 14 studies evaluating the Frostig reading materials produced unimpressive results. Of 15 studies using

See Sleeter (1986) for an interesting perspective on the history of learning disabilities that is quite different from that provided by most textbooks. She contends that the category of learning disabilities was originally created to explain the failures of White middle-class children when U.S. school achievement standards were raised following the Soviet Union's launching of *Sputnik.*

Kephart's perceptual-motor training program, only 6 reported significant improvements (intelligence, school achievement, and language functioning were measured in these studies). In addition, only 4 of 11 studies measuring visual-motor functioning reported that the training significantly improved visual-motor performance. In another review, Myers and Hammill (1976) found that, in general, the Frostig materials improved children's scores on the Frostig Developmental Test of Visual Perception (Frostig et al., 1964) but that it was questionable as to whether reading achievement improved.

Two more comprehensive reviews have also found the effectiveness of the perceptual-motor approach wanting. Kavale and Mattison (1983) reanalyzed 180 studies that investigated the effectiveness of the perceptual-motor approach and concluded that it is "not effective and should be questioned as a feasible intervention technique for exceptional children" (p. 165). After reviewing the results of 85 perceptual-motor training studies, Myers and Hammill (1990) stated:

> Unlike 25 years ago, when research on the topic was sparse, one can no longer assume that these kinds of activities will be beneficial to the children who engage in them. In fact, in the long run they may even be somewhat harmful because (a) they may waste valuable time and money and (b) they may provide a child with a placebo program when the child's problems require a real remedial effort. We would suggest that when these programs are implemented in the schools, they be considered as highly experimental, nonvalidated services that require very careful scrutiny and monitoring. (p. 448)

In a major review of 38 studies of ITPA-based psycholinguistic training, Hammill and Larsen (1974, 1978) concluded that "the overwhelming consensus of research evidence concerning the effectiveness of psycholinguistic training is that it remains essentially nonvalidated" (1978, p. 412). Critics of Hammill and Larsen's ITPA review (e.g., Lund, Foster, & McCall-Perez, 1978) claim they were not justified in their conclusions because many of the original studies were poorly controlled. Minskoff (1975) suggests that the earlier psycholinguistic research was not a good basis on which to evaluate the approach because it tended to be incomplete and methodologically inadequate. She goes on to specify criteria for future psycholinguistic research, presumably so that its effectiveness will be more clearly understood.

Sowell, Packer, Poplin, and Larsen (1979) followed Minskoff's criteria in a study designed to evaluate the effectiveness of psycholinguistic training with 63 first graders. They found the psycholinguistic training program to be unsuccessful and concluded their study with this comment:

> At best, psycholinguistic training should be viewed as experimental and not be employed extensively until its usefulness can be effectively demonstrated. In reality, the onus of documenting the value of psycholinguistic training procedures falls primarily to those individuals who produce and/or advocate them. Until such time as experimental validation for this approach is forthcoming, educators are well advised to utilize other strategies in attempting to stimulate academic and/or language skills in children under their care. (p. 76)

Skill Training

Skill trainers believe that a student's demonstrated performance deficit is the problem. For example, if a student has not learned a complex skill (e.g., reading a sen-

---

The CLD has published a position statement opposing the measurement and training of perceptual and perceptual-motor functions as part of educational services for individuals with learning disabilities (see *Learning Disability Quarterly,* summer 1986, p. 247). The organization cites lack of scientific evidence in support of the claimed benefits of perceptual and perceptual-motor training.

Tim's daily session in the "writing room" is spent practicing, self-evaluating, and self-editing the specific writing skills he needs to master.

tence) and has had sufficient opportunity and wants to succeed, a skill trainer would conclude that the student does not have the necessary prerequisite skills in his or her repertoire (e.g., reading letter sounds, reading single words) and would provide direct instruction focused on those prerequisite skills.

Skill trainers use the following approaches:

1. Precise, operational definitions of the specific behaviors they intend to teach
2. Task analysis to break down complex skills into smaller units, or subskills, requiring the learner to master only one component of the task at a time
3. Direct teaching methods that require the learner to practice the new skill many times
4. Direct and frequent measurement to monitor the student's progress and evaluate instruction

Applied behavior analysis, direct instruction, and precision teaching are all associated with skill-training approaches. All are closely related to one another, and all systematically manipulate aspects of the student's instructional environment (e.g., materials, prompts or cues, feedback) in an attempt to facilitate the acquisition, retention, and generalization of new skills.

Direct Instruction

The most widely researched and highly developed skill-training teaching program is the Direct Instruction Model derived from research by Siegfried Engelmann and Wesley Becker and their colleagues at the University of Oregon. Two major rules underlie the Direct Instruction Model: "Teach more in less time," and "Control the details of the curriculum."

Teaching "more in less time" recognizes that even if students with disabilities are taught by an effective program that enables them to progress at the *same rate* as their nondisabled peers, they will always remain behind. Only by teaching at a *faster rate* can the achievement gap be reduced. The design of the details of the curriculum—the selection and sequencing of instructional examples—is at the heart of the Direct Instruction Model.

Carnine and Kameenui (1992) provide detailed explanations and examples of how principles of systematic curriculum design are used to promote higher-order thinking by mainstreamed students with disabilities. To learn about the theoretical base underlying Direct Instruction, see Engelmann and Carnine's *Theory of Instruction* (1982).

221

Direct Instruction curriculum materials in reading (e.g., Engelmann & Bruner, 1988), mathematics (e.g., Engelmann & Carnine, 1991), and language arts (Engelmann & Silbert, 1993) are available from Science Research Associates. The author of this book has first-hand experience with the effectiveness of Direct Instruction. When they were preschoolers, both of his children learned to read from their mother with the help of *Teach Your Child to Read in 100 Easy Lessons* (Engelmann, Haddox, & Bruner, 1983).

> Direct Instruction is an intensive intervention designed to increase not only the amount of learning but also its quality by systematically developing important background knowledge and explicitly applying it and linking it to new knowledge. Direct Instruction designs activities that carefully control the background knowledge that is required so that all students can "build hierarchies of understanding," not just those students who come to school with the appropriate background knowledge. In the process, mechanistic skills evolve into flexible strategies, concepts combine into schemata, and success in highly structured situations develops into successful performance in naturalistic, unpredictable, complex environments. (Carnine, Grossen, & Silbert, in press)

In addition to explicit curriculum design, Direct Instruction involves certain teaching procedures. *Scripted lessons* indicate what the teacher should do and say for each item or task presented in the lesson. Scripted lessons ensure consistent, quality instruction. Direct Instruction is typically conducted with *small groups* of children (5 to 10), which has been found to be more efficient than one-to-one instruction and allows more teacher attention and feedback and individualization than large group instruction. High rates of active student response are generated by having students *chorally respond* in unison to a *rapidly paced* series of teacher-presented items (Carnine, 1976; Heward, Courson, & Narayan, 1989). To help both the pacing and the simultaneous participation by all students, the teacher uses signals (e.g., hand movements, claps) to cue the student when to respond. Correct responses are *praised,* and *corrective feedback* is provided for incorrect responses.

Follow Through is a nationwide, comprehensive educational program for economically disadvantaged children, kindergarten through third grade. Many Head Start children enter Follow Through programs. See Chapter 14.

Direct Instruction is supported by an impressive body of research demonstrating its effectiveness. An evaluation of the Direct Instruction Model conducted by the nationwide Follow Through program and involving more than 8,000 children in 20 communities showed that children made significant gains in academic achievement (Gersten, Carnine, & White, 1984; Watkins, 1988). These children caught up to or even surpassed the national norms on several arithmetic, reading, and language skills as measured by the Wide Range Achievement Test (Jastak & Wilkinson, 1984) and the Metropolitan Achievement Tests (Balow, Farr, Hogan, & Prescott, 1978). On other skills, such as spelling, the Direct Instruction students finished a little below the national norm but still showed significant gains. None of the other educational approaches evaluated by the Follow Through program was as effective as Direct Instruction. For more information on the effectiveness of Direct Instruction, see Becker (1992) and Weisberg (1994).

Learning Strategies Instruction

Dixon and Rossi (1995) describe a three-phase process for teaching students with learning disabilities a question-asking and discussion strategy to improve reading comprehension.

Teaching specific academic skills to students with learning disabilities may not be enough because they often fail to use their acquired knowledge and skills appropriately in novel situations. A major development during the past decade has been the emphasis on teaching students with learning disabilities how to learn. These *learning strategies* are viewed as skills in their own right and are taught in a direct, systematic fashion. Some of the initial research on the learning strategies was conducted by Deshler and Schumaker and their colleagues at the University of Kansas Research Institute on Learning Disabilities (Deshler, Schumaker, & Lenz, 1984; Schumaker, Deshler, Alley, & Warner, 1983). They have developed, field-tested, and validated a learning strategies curriculum for adolescents with learning disabilities.

Task-specific strategies help students guide themselves successfully through a learning task. The Sentence Writing Strategy (Schumaker & Sheldon, 1985), for example, provides students with a set of steps for using a variety of formulas when writing sentences. Case, Harris, and Graham (1992) taught four fifth- and sixth-grade students with learning disabilities to use a 5-step self-instructional strategy to solve addition and subtraction word problems. The students learned to (a) read the problem aloud, (b) look for important words and circle them (e.g., *how many left, how much more*), (c) draw pictures to help tell what is happening, (d) write down the math sentence, and (e) write down the answer. In a related study, nine elementary students with learning disabilities used tape-recorded cues with their own voices reminding them of a 10-step problem solving strategy for math problems (Wood, Rosenberg, & Carran, 1993). The students continued to use the self-instructional strategy to solve problems when the tape-recorded cues were withdrawn in the study's final phase.

The June/July 1993 issue of the *Journal of Learning Disabilities* is devoted to articles on learning strategies instruction. See the January 1995 issue of *Educational Leadership*, pp 50–51.

Content Enhancements

Educating students with learning disabilities at the secondary level is particularly difficult. Poor listening, note-taking, reading, and study skills limit the ability of students with learning disabilities to obtain needed information from lectures, reading, and homework assignments. *Content enhancement* is the general name given to a wide range of techniques used to help students organize, comprehend, and retain critical curriculum content (Lenz, Bulgren, & Hudson, 1990). Content enhancements include advance organizers, visual displays, study guides, guided notes, mnemonic devices, computer-assisted instruction, and peer mediation activities such as collaborative learning or peer tutoring (Crank & Bulgren, 1993; Heward 1994; Hudson, Lignugaris-Kraft, & Miller, 1993; Miller, Barbetta, & Heron, 1994).

Lovitt and his colleagues at the University of Washington have conducted research on how textbooks and other classroom materials can be modified to promote the success of students with mild disabilities in mainstream classrooms. *Graphic organizers*—visuospatial arrangements of information containing words or statements connected graphically to show meaningful relationships—is one of the methods they have found effective (see Figure 5.2) (Horton & Lovitt, 1989; Horton, Lovitt, & Bergerud, 1990). The *framed outline* technique is a study guide procedure that provides students with guided, active response during independent seatwork or homework (Lovitt, Rudsit, Jenkins, Pious, & Benedetti, 1986). *Guided notes* is a method for organizing and enhancing curriculum content and providing students with a means of actively responding during a lecture (Heward, 1994).

Recent studies have demonstrated *mnemonic instruction* (use of memory-enhancing) strategies as a promising method for improving students' recall of specific academic content. For example, Nagel, Schumaker, and Deshler (1986) used a first-letter mnemonic strategy, TEENS, to help students remember the five sense organs: *t*ongue, *e*ars, *e*yes, *n*ose, and *s*kin. Scruggs and Mastropieri (1992) reported that 19 middle school students with learning disabilities performed better on delayed-recall tests when life science facts were taught with mnemonic pictures that symbolically represented those facts. The students also learned to successfully generate and apply their own mnemonic strategies to novel content.

Guided notes and mnemonic instruction are described further in Teaching & Learning features later in this chapter.

FIGURE 5.2

A graphic organizer presenting rearranged content information from an 8-page sequence in a middle school science text

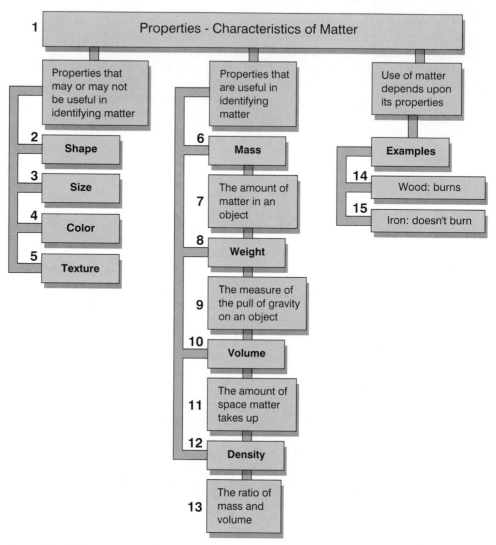

Source: From "Construction and Implementation of Graphic Organizers for Academically Handicapped and Regular Secondary Students" by S. V. Horton and T. C. Lovitt, 1989, *Academic Therapy*, Vol. 24, p. 630. Copyright © 1989 by PRO-ED, Inc. Reprinted by permission.

Positive Focus

With its unending stream of claims, counterclaims, and controversy, the area of learning disabilities at times seems to lose sight of its fundamental goals and some common-sense truths. Fortunately, the work of a number of leaders in learning disabilities provides a standard of good sense. Tom Lovitt, a professor of special education at the University of Washington, is one of those people. Although everyone in special education may not agree with him, Lovitt's views are backed by more than 25 years of classroom-based research on virtually every aspect of the education of children with learning disabilities: assessment, teaching techniques, and adapting curriculum materials, for example. He once wrote that, all things being equal, a teacher who imparts many skills to many children is good, and one who does not is not (Lovitt, 1977). After all, teaching is helping children learn new things. He believes that the primary purpose for teachers and students coming together is the development of children's academic and social skills and that teachers should work directly and systematically toward that end.

There are many strategies and techniques for remediating skill deficits and reducing the frequency of behavioral problems. But we should not become so concerned with fixing everything we believe is wrong with the student that we forget about building upon all that is positive. Here, Lovitt (1989) reminds us of the importance of maintaining a positive focus for students with learning disabilities:

> Although we don't know how to really define LD youngsters (and heaven knows we've tried), we do know that they don't do as well as their non-LD mates in oral and silent reading, reading comprehension, spelling, mathematics, history, science, geography, industrial arts, music, or family living. Because of these many deficits and deviations, we teachers, in all good faith, set out to remediate as many of the "shortfalls" as possible so that learning disabled youth will be as normal and wonderful as we are. We should reconsider this total remedial approach to learning disabilities. One reason for considering an alternative might be obvious if we thought of a day in the life of an LD youth. First, the teacher sets out to remediate his reading, then his math, and then his language, social skills, and soccer playing. Toward the end of the day, she attempts to remediate his metacognitive deficits. That lad is in a remediation mode throughout the day. Is it any wonder that the self-concepts, self-images, self-esteems, and attributions of these youngsters are out of whack?
>
> We should spend some time concentrating on these youngsters' positive qualities. If, for example, a girl is inclined toward mechanics, or a boy to being a chef, we teachers should nurture those skills. And if an LD child doesn't have a negotiable behavior, we should locate one and promote it. I can't help but think that if every youngster, LD or otherwise, had at least one art, trade, skill, or technique about which he or she was fairly competent, that would do more for that youngster's adjustment than would the many hours of remediation to which the child is subjected. Perhaps that accent on the positive would go a long way toward actually helping the remediation process. If children knew they could excel in something, that might help them become competent in other areas as well. (p. 477)

✳ *Educational Service Alternatives*
The Regular Classroom

The IDEA requires that students with disabilities be educated with their nondisabled peers to the maximum extent possible and that they be removed from the regular classroom only to the extent that their disability necessitates. During the 1992–93 school year, 25% of students with learning disabilities were served in the regular classroom; most of the remaining 75% were there for only certain periods or activities (U.S. Department of Education, 1994). According to a survey conducted of 60 school districts in 18 states, 100% of students with learning disabilities spend at least some of each school day in the regular classroom—on the average, 2.1 hours (35%) per day (U.S. Department of Education, 1989). A number of methods can be used singly or in combination to help make the regular classroom an effective learning environment for many students with learning disabilities. For example, adapting curricular materials (Hudson et al., 1993), modifying testing procedures (Garjía, Salend, & Henrick, 1994), increasing the frequency of active student response (Heward, 1994), using mastery learning (Gusky, Passaro, & Wheeler, 1995), and employing

See the January, 1995, issue of *Educational Leadership*, pp. 13–17.

Mnemonic Instruction
....
by Margo A. Mastropieri and Thomas E. Scruggs

Success in school is strongly associated with the ability to learn and remember verbal information. For example, students are frequently expected to remember such things as states and their capitals, multiplication facts, U.S. presidents, science vocabulary, and mathematical formulas. Students who have particular difficulty remembering this type of information typically have great difficulty succeeding in school.

Unfortunately, many students with mild cognitive disabilities exhibit difficulty remembering verbal information. Deficits in semantic memory have been clearly documented in students with learning disabilities and mild mental retardation. Some researchers have linked these problems to difficulties in effectively using appropriate learning strategies to help improve recall by more effectively encoding, storing, and finally retrieving important information.

During the past several years, we have been studying *mnemonic* (memory-enhancing) strategies and evaluating their effectiveness with students who have difficulty remembering academic information. We primarily have studied the use of these strategies by students with learning disabilities; however, we have also found that they can be useful for students with mild mental retardation, behavioral disorders, as well as for normally achieving and gifted students.

A variety of types of mnemonic strategies can be useful, depending on the type of information that needs to be remembered. We will describe the keyword method and its variations, the pegword method, and letter strategies.

The Keyword Method

The keyword method is one of the most versatile mnemonic strategies. It is useful when linking a new, unfamiliar word with familiar information. For example, to remember that the Italian word *mela* [may-la] means "apple," first construct a keyword for *mela*. A keyword is a word that sounds like the new word (*mela*) but is familiar and easy to picture. In this case, "mailbox" would be a good keyword for mela because it sounds like *mela* and is easy to picture.

Next, you draw (or ask students to imagine) a picture of the keyword and its referent doing something together. In this case, it could be a picture of a mailbox with an apple in it. Finally, students study the picture and are told, when asked for the meaning of *mela,* to think of the keyword *mailbox,* remember the picture with the mailbox in it, remember *what else* was in the picture, and retrieve the correct answer, *apple.* Although there are several steps to successful retrieval, research has shown that students with learning difficulties can easily use the keyword method and remember far more information when they do so.

To help remember that George M. Cohan wrote the patriotic song "Over There" during World War I, students could use the picture shown in Figure A. In this picture, (ice cream) *cone* is the keyword for Cohan. When one child asks, "Where did you get the cone?" the other child points and sings, "Over there." Students who have studied the picture and its mnemonic strategy can then remember the answer to the question "Who was George M. Cohan?"

Sometimes two keywords can be used. For example, to teach that Annapolis is the capital of Maryland, construct keywords of both Annapolis ("an apple") and Maryland ("marry") and show a picture of apples getting married.

Sometimes keywords are not necessary because the words are already familiar. Sometimes pictures can be *mimetic,* or direct representations. For example, to show that sponges attach themselves to the ocean floor, a mimetic picture can be shown in which sponges are shown attached to the ocean floor. Sometimes *symbolic* pictures are needed, as when the information is familiar but abstract. For example, to show that birds are *warm blooded,* a picture can be shown of a bird sitting in the warm sunshine. In this case, the sun is a symbol for warm blooded. In contrast, fish and reptiles can be pictured in *cold* scenes, as a symbol for cold blooded. This method of using mimetic, symbolic, or acoustic (keyword) reconstructions has been called *reconstructive elaborations,* and it can be used to adapt a wide variety of content information.

FIGURE A Mnemonic picture for remembering that George M. Cohan wrote the song "Over There." Source: Reprinted with permission from M. A. Mastropieri and T. E. Scruggs (1991), Teaching Students Ways to Remember: Strategies for Learning Mnemonically, p. 49 (Cambridge, MA: Brookline Books).

The Pegword Method

The pegword method employs rhyming words for numbers (*one* is *bun, two* is *shoe, three* is *tree,* etc.) when information to be remembered is numbered or ordered. For example, to remember that an example of a *third-class* lever is a *rake,* create a picture of a rake leaning against a tree (three). To remember that insects have *six* legs, create a picture of insects on *sticks* (pegword for *six*). To remember that Newton's first (or, number one) law of motion is that objects at rest tend to stay at rest, show a picture of a *bun* (pegword for *one*) resting.

Pegwords can be combined with keywords. For example, to remember that the mineral *rhodochrosite* is number 4 on the Mohs' hardness scale, show a picture of a *road* (keyword for *rhodochrosite*) going through a *door* (pegword for 4).

Letter Strategies

Most individuals can remember using letter strategies at one time or other to remember information. For example, most people can remember using the acronym HOMES to remember the names of the Great Lakes: Huron, Ontario, Michigan, Erie, and Superior. However, this strategy will only be effective if students are familiar with the names of the Great Lakes because they will only have the first letters as a prompt. Another helpful letter strategy is the acronym FARM-B to remember the classes of vertebrates: fish, amphibians, reptiles, mammals, birds.

Acrostics and related strategies can also be helpful. For example, the sentence "My very educated mother just served us nine pizzas" can be used to remember the planets in order: Mercury, Venus, Earth, Mars, Jupiter, Saturn, Uranus, Neptune, Pluto.

Letter strategies can also be combined with keywords. For example, the countries of the Central Powers in World War I included Turkey, Austria-Hungary, and Germany. These countries can be represented by the acronym TAG, which in Figure B is pictured being played in Central Park, keyword for *Central Powers.*

Recommendations

Here are some recommendations for incorporating mnemonic strategies into classroom teaching for students with learning difficulties:

1. *Teach just a small number of strategies at first.* Explain every step of the strategy very carefully

Central Powers (Central Park)   **T**urkey, **A**ustria, **G**ermany

FIGURE B   Mnemonic picture for remembering the names of the countries in the Central Powers during World War I: Turkey, Austria-Hungary, and Germany. Source: Reprinted with permission from M. A. Mastropieri and T. E. Scruggs (1991), Teaching Students Ways to Remember: Strategies for Learning Mnemonically, p. 119 (Cambridge, MA: Brookline Books).

and be sure to monitor for understanding. When students begin to show facility in using the method, more strategies can be included.

2. *Monitor for comprehension.* Students need to be made aware that they are learning two things: important content information and the strategies for remembering that information. This can be prompted by asking for each separately: "What is the capital of New Hampshire, Mary?" "Good. How did you remember that?" Additionally, students should not be taught to remember information they do not understand. Ensure comprehension of the information before applying memory strategies.

3. *Mnemonic pictures do not need to be great works of art.* They simply need to portray the relevant strategic information clearly. However, if you are certain that you cannot draw at all, try the following: Use stick figures, use cut-outs from magazines, employ a student "artist," ask students to draw their own pictures, or promote student use of imagery.

4. *Teach students to generalize mnemonic strategies to their own independent use.* However, they should first be well acquainted with a variety of teacher-developed mnemonic strategies. Teachers can promote group brainstorming of possible keywords and interactive pictures and carefully explain the steps to construction of mnemonic strategies. Finally, prompt strategy construction and provide feedback.

For further information, see M. A. Mastropieri and T. E. Scruggs (1991), *Teaching Students Ways to Remember: Strategies for Learning Mnemonically* (Cambridge, MA: Brookline Books).

Margo A. Mastropieri and Thomas E. Scruggs are professors in the Department of Educational Studies, Purdue University. They are coeditors of the journal *Learning Disabilities: Research and Practice.*

classwide peer-tutoring programs (Miller et al., 1994; Simmons et al., 1994) have all been shown to increase the academic success of students with learning disabilities in the regular classroom. In addition, school districts are providing teachers with more inservice training programs focusing on the identification, assessment, and remediation of children's learning problems.

Success in the regular class-room is enhanced when students follow directions, show interest in the subject matter, and work cooperatively in groups.

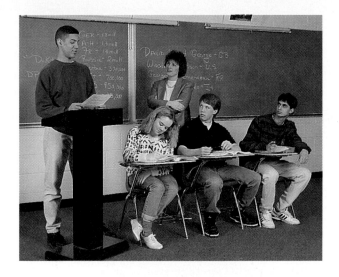

Ellet (1993) asked 89 regular education high school teachers to rate those student skills and behaviors they believed were most important for success in the regular education classroom. The 10 things those teachers thought were most important for success are shown in Table 5.3. This list helps identify at least some of the skills special educators must help students who have learning disabilities learn in order to help them succeed in the regular classroom: organizational skills and how to use their time wisely (Shields & Heron, 1989), note taking (Suritsky & Hughes, 1991), study skills (Hoover, 1989), completing their homework on time (Cavanaugh, 1990; Trammel, Schloss, & Alper, 1994), and getting along with others (Cartledge & Milburn, 1995).

TABLE 5.3
The 10 most important things a student with learning disabilities should do to achieve success in the regular education classroom

STUDENT SKILL/BEHAVIOR	MEAN RATING*
Follows directions in class	3.72
Comes to class prepared with materials	3.48
Uses class time wisely	3.48
Makes up assignments and tests	3.43
Treats teachers and peers with courtesy	3.40
Completes and turns in homework on time	3.37
Works cooperatively in student groups	3.19
Completes tests with a passing grade	3.19
Appears interested in subject	2.90
Takes notes in class	2.88

*Skills are ordered from most to least important as ranked by teachers; 4 is the highest possible score.

Source: From "Instructional Practices in Mainstreamed Secondary Classrooms" by Linda Ellet, 1993, *Journal of Learning Disabilities,* Vol. 26, p. 59. Copyright © 1993 by PRO-ED, Inc. Reprinted by permission.

Guided Notes
························

Helping Students with Learning Disabilities (and Their Classmates) Succeed in the Regular Classroom

The lecture is widely used in middle and high school classrooms to present academic content to students. The teacher talks, and students are held responsible for obtaining, remembering, and using the information at a later time (usually on a quiz or test). Most successful students take notes during teacher lectures that they study later. Students who take good notes and study them later consistently receive higher test scores than students who only listen to the lecture and read the text (Baker & Lombardi, 1985; Carrier, 1983).

Although various strategies and formats for effective note taking have been identified, they are seldom taught to students (Saski, Swicegood, & Carter, 1983). The listening, language, and, in some cases, motor-skill deficits of many students with learning disabilities make it extremely difficult for them to identify what is important and write it down correctly and quickly enough during a lecture. While trying to choose and write one concept in a notebook, the student with learning disabilities might miss the next two points. When teachers develop guided notes (GN) to accompany their presentations, both mainstreamed students with disabilities and their regular classroom peers benefit.

What Are Guided Notes?

Guided notes are teacher-prepared handouts that "guide" a student through a lecture with standard cues and specific space in which to write key facts, concepts, and/or relationships (see sample in Figure A). Guided notes take advantage of one of the most consistent and important findings in recent educational research: *Students who make frequent, relevant responses during a lesson learn more than students who are passive observers.*

Initial Research

Carol Kline's (1986) master's thesis was the first of an ongoing series of experimental evaluations of GN conducted at Ohio State University. Carol was unhappy with the results of her efforts to teach U.S. history to secondary students with learning disabilities. Although she used a high-interest, low-reading-level text developed for students with poor reading skills such as hers and followed up each reading assignment with lectures and class discussions, most of Carol's students failed miserably when they were tested over the content she had worked so hard to cover. As a means of increasing each student's active participation during class and, hopefully, to improve their success with the content, we decided to try GN. At the beginning of every class session throughout the study—sometimes the students took their own notes, sometimes they completed GN—Carol encouraged her students to take good notes. All 10 students in the class earned higher scores on quizzes administered after lectures with GN than when they took their own notes. In fact, if letter grades had been assigned according to quiz scores, the average grade in the class would have been an A– when GN were used, compared with a D when students took their own notes.

As encouraging as the results of the first study were, students usually must maintain important lesson content for more than a few minutes after class. In the following two studies, next-day quizzes were used to measure achievement. All 5 mainstreamed students with learning disabilities and 17 of the 18 nondisabled students in a middle school science class earned higher scores on next-day oceanography quizzes following GN lectures (Yang, 1988). Pados (1989) also used next-day quizzes to evaluate the effects of guided notes in teaching U.S. history in a fifth-grade classroom (Figure A). Not only did the 2 students with learning disabilities who were mainstreamed into the class and all 11 general education students obtain higher quiz scores with GN, but so did 6 of the 7 students in the class who were

American History Guided Notes   Name _____

Road to Revolution II

A. *New Problems and New Troubles*

    1. The French and Indian War _____

        a. The British thought the colonists _____

        b. Britain also thought the colonists _____

    2. In 1764, Parliament decided to _____ the colonists to help pay the bills for the war.

        a. Colonists had to pay a tax on _____

          and _____

        b. _____ collected the taxes.

    3. _____ — the British lawmaking group.

    4. _____ — the people who collected the taxes. They were allowed to keep part of the taxes themselves.

B. *The Stamp Act (1765)*

    1. Under this law, colonists had to buy _____ for all kinds of paper products.

        a.

        b.

        c.

C. *"Taxation without Representation"*

    1. "Taxation without Representation" means _____

      _____ by a lawmaking group in which you have no representation.

        a. Colonists could not _____

        b. Colonists also could not _____

    2. James Otis, a young lawyer from Massachusetts, referred to the Stamp Act as _____

D. *Protest and Repeal*

    1. _____ — a group of colonists formed to protest the taxes.

        a. It was founded by _____

        b.

        c.

        d.

    2. In 1766, the British Parliament *repealed* the Stamp Act (tax).

        a. Repeal—means _____

    3. The colonists thought _____

FIGURE A   Example of guided notes used by fifth-grade students learning U.S. history. Source: From G. E. Pados, 1989, "A Comparison of the Effects of Students' Own Notes and Guided Notes on the Daily Quiz Performance of Fifth-Grade Students." Unpublished master's thesis, The Ohio State University, Columbus, Ohio. Used by permission.

enrolled in the district's program for gifted and talented children.

Because research has shown that successful students take more accurate notes than unsuccessful students (e.g., Norton & Hartley, 1986), it was also important to determine whether and to what extent GN help students produce a more accurate record of the lecture than when taking their own notes. Pados (1989) measured the accuracy of note taking by calculating the percentage of key concepts/facts presented in the lecture that were accurately recorded in the students' notes. The two mainstreamed students with learning disabilities correctly recorded a mean of only 18% of all lecture facts/concepts when taking their own notes, compared with an overall accuracy of 89% when using GN. GN also resulted in large improvements in the accuracy of the lecture notes taken by both the general education students (own notes, 34%; GN, 97%) and by the students in the gifted program (own notes, 38%; GN, 97%).

Resource Room Help

For some students, taking accurate lecture notes may not be enough to ensure success on subsequent tests. Additional contingencies may be necessary to increase the probability that the student studies and reviews those notes. Even though all five of the special education students in the Yang (1988) study earned higher next-day quiz scores with GN than when they took their own notes, the improved scores for four of the students were still below a passing grade. A procedure was implemented in the study's final phase in which the special education students took the GN they had completed in science class to the resource room later in the day for several minutes of review and study supervised by the resource room teacher. The quiz scores for all five students with learning disabilities were higher during the GN-with-review phase than during the first GN phase when no review in the resource room was conducted.

Pados (1989) included a supervised review of lecture notes in the resource room as part of the general procedure for the two students with learning disabilities throughout all phases of her study. The

resource room teacher only reviewed with each student the information included in the student's notes; the special education teacher supplied no additional information or content. The mean quiz score for the LD students was 93% during the combined GN phases with resource room review, compared with 64% when they took their own notes to the resource room for review. Lazarus (1991, 1993) replicated the resource room review procedure and found improved test scores over and above the use of GN alone.

Short Form or Long Form?

Fran Courson's (1989) doctoral dissertation evaluated the effectiveness of two different GN formats during a social studies unit in a special classroom of 19 seventh graders who had learning disabilities or were academically at risk. With "short-form GN," students filled in blanks with single words or short phrases, whereas the "long-form GN" required students to write sentences or phrases in the open space following asterisked (*) cues. Every student in the class earned higher next-day quiz scores with either GN format than they did when taking their own notes, but no difference was found between the two GN formats. Figure B shows the next-day quiz scores earned by one student throughout the study and is representative of the basic pattern of results found across students. Similar results were obtained on 2-week review tests: Students performed better on items that had been instructed with either GN format (80% vs. 43%), but neither format produced significantly better maintenance. Short-form GN produced slightly higher note-taking accuracy (97%), compared with the long-form GN (94%), but note-taking accuracy with either GN format was much greater than when students took their own notes (19%).

Better on Their Own

Donna White (1991), a teacher of high school students with learning disabilities, assessed the extent to which using GN might improve the accuracy of her students' own note taking. Following a baseline in which they took their own notes for the entire lecture on U.S. history, eight secondary students with learning disabilities used GN for half of each day's lecture and took their own notes during the other half of the lecture. Each of the eight students improved the accuracy of note taking during the study, from a group mean of 17% during baseline to 84% during the study's final phase when GN were no longer used.

The results of White's study suggest a whole new program of thematic research exploring how GN might be used, not only to help students succeed in their current content academic subjects but also to help students improve their own note-taking skills. A great amount of research on GN remains to be done: At this time, the range of curricular areas, student characteristics, and formats for which GN can be effective is largely unknown. Nevertheless, the research conducted to date has produced results strong enough and consistent enough to suggest some advantages of GN and recommendations for their use.

Advantages of GN

In addition to the data showing superior test performance by students when they use GN, research suggests the following advantages to their use:

- Students must actively respond to and interact with the lesson's content.

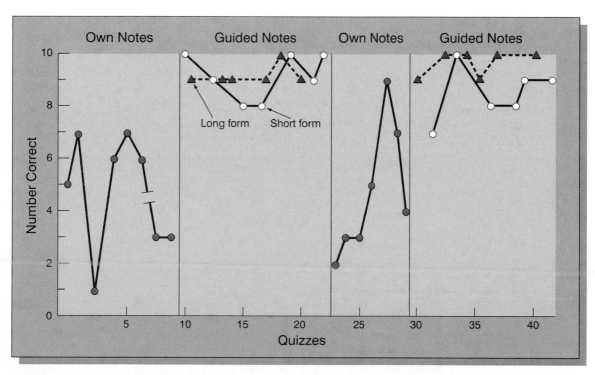

FIGURE B   Number of correct answers on social studies quizzes given 1 day after teacher lectures. Source: From F. H. Courson, 1989, Differential Effects of Short- and Long-Form Guided Notes on Test Scores and Accuracy of Note Taking by Learning Disabled and At-Risk Seventh Graders during Social Studies Instruction. Unpublished doctoral dissertation, The Ohio State University, Columbus, Ohio. Used by permission.

- Key concepts, facts, and relationships are cued/highlighted.
- Students are better able to determine whether they are "getting it" and are more likely to ask the teacher to clarify.
- Students produce a standard and accurate set of notes for study and review.
- Teachers are more likely to stay on task with content and sequence of lecture.
- Teachers must plan the lesson or lecture carefully.

You may be wondering whether providing GN for students is spoon-feeding them or making it too easy to learn. If so, consider this: Students who are using GN are actively responding and interacting with the curriculum content. That is not making it "too easy"—that is helping them learn. By contrast, we may make it "too easy" for our students when we allow them to sit quietly and passively attend to ongoing instruction.

Suggestions for Using GN in the Classroom

- Include background information so that students' note taking focuses on the important facts, concepts, and relationships they need to learn.

- Provide consistent cues (e.g., asterisks, lines, bullets) so that students will know where, when, and how many concepts they should record.
- Do not use a simple fill-in-the-blank format in which students need only listen or look up now and then to copy down a word.
- Do not require students to write too much or else the lesson will bog down.
- Include all critical facts, concepts, and relationships that students are expected to learn.
- Produce GN on a word processor so that changes and updates can be easily made.
- Consider gradually fading the use of GN to help students learn to take notes in classes in which GN are not used.
- Provide follow-up activities to ensure that students complete and study their notes. Giving a daily quiz is one way to do this and provide additional opportunities to respond at the same time.

Based on "Three 'Low-Tech' Strategies for Increasing the Frequency of Active Student Response during Group Instruction" by William L. Heward. In R. Gardner III, D. M. Sainato, J. O. Cooper, T. E. Heron, W. L. Heward, J. Eshleman, & T. A. Grossi (Eds.), 1994, *Behavior Analysis in Education: Focus on Measurably Superior Instruction* (pp. 283–320). Pacific Grove, CA: Brooks/Cole.

The Consultant Teacher

A consultant teacher provides support to regular classroom teachers and other school staff who work directly with students with learning disabilities. The consultant teacher helps the regular teacher select assessment devices, curriculum materials, and instructional activities. The consultant may even demonstrate teaching methods or behavior management strategies. A major advantage of this model is that the consultant teacher can work with several teachers and thus indirectly provide special education services to many children. The major drawback is that the consultant has little or no direct contact with the children. Heron and Harris (1993) describe procedures consultant teachers can use to increase their effectiveness in supporting mainstreamed children.

The Resource Room

The resource room is the most common service delivery model for educating children with learning disabilities. A resource room is a specially staffed and equipped classroom where students with learning disabilities come for one or several periods during the school day to receive individualized instruction. A resource room was the primary educational placement for 54% of all students with learning disabilities during the 1992–93 school year (U.S. Department of Education, 1994).

The resource teacher is a certified learning disabilities specialist whose primary role is to teach needed academic skills, social skills, and learning strategies to the students who are referred to the resource room. Most of the students are in their regular classrooms for part of the school day and come to the resource room only for specialized instruction in the academic skills, usually reading or mathematics, or social skills they need to smooth their integration into the regular classroom. Other students may receive all of their academic instruction in the resource room and attend the regular classroom only for such periods as art, music, and social studies. In addition to teaching students with learning disabilities, the resource teacher also works closely with each student's regular teacher to suggest and help plan each student's program in the regular classroom.

Ronni Hochman (1994), a middle school learning disabilities resource room teacher, offers these suggestions for placing a child with learning disabilities into the regular classroom:

> I think a key to a resource room is identifying where the child's successes are and initially putting him back into the regular classroom only in the areas in which he can

> The federal government defines a resource room as a setting outside the regular class in which a student receives special education and related services for at least 21% and not more than 60% of the school day.

A resource room program can provide students with learning disabilities with intense, individualized instruction on the academic and social skills they need for success in the mainstream.

experience a great amount of success. I use the child's time in the resource room to build those skills he needs to learn to be completely integrated into the regular classroom—whether it's learning to read better or learning to complete a task. (personal communication)

Some advantages of the resource room model are that (a) students do not lose their identity with their peer group, which reduces the chance they will be stigmatized as "special"; (b) students can receive the intense, individualized instruction they need every day, which might be impossible for the regular teacher to provide; and (c) flexible scheduling allows the resource room to serve a fairly large number of students (Wiederholt, Hammill, & Brown, 1983). A typical resource room teacher serves an average of 20 students (U.S. Department of Education, 1989).

A survey of resource room teachers found that their biggest concerns were unclear role descriptions; variable expectations of administrators and regular classroom teachers; and insufficient time for planning, consulting, and observing students (McLoughlin & Kelly, 1982). Lieberman (1982) points out several disadvantages of pull-out programs such as resource rooms: They require students to spend time traveling between classrooms; they may result in inconsistent instructional approaches between settings; and they make it difficult to determine whether students should be held accountable for what they missed while out of the regular classroom.

Although the resource room concept remains popular, its success depends on the skills of the resource teacher and the school's administrative practices. In particular, procedures must be determined that will help the child with learning disabilities generalize the skills learned in the resource room to the regular classroom (Anderson-Inman, Walker, & Purcell, 1984).

The Self-Contained Classroom

During the 1992–93 school year, 20% of students with learning disabilities were served in self-contained classrooms (U.S. Department of Education, 1994).

In a self-contained classroom, the learning disabilities teacher is responsible for all educational programming for a group of about 8 to 12 students with learning disabilities. The academic achievement deficiencies of some children with learning disabilities are so severe that they need full-time placement in a learning setting with a specially trained teacher. In addition, poor work habits and inappropriate social behaviors make some students with learning disabilities candidates for the self-contained classroom, where distractions can be minimized and individual attention stressed. It is important, however, that placement in a self-contained (separate) class not be considered permanent. Students should be placed in a self-contained class only after unsuccessful attempts to serve them adequately in other less restrictive environments.

Only 1% of students with learning disabilities are served in separate schools (U.S. Department of Education, 1994).

Although the effectiveness and appropriateness of the self-contained classroom have been the subject of much debate, some students appear to benefit from full-time separate class instruction. For example, a follow-up study of 10 high school students 5 to 6 years after they had been enrolled for a year in a self-contained learning disabilities program showed them to be performing as well as nondisabled students in a comparison group (Leone, Lovitt, & Hansen, 1981). Even though the students' performances varied considerably, their oral reading ability, free-time and occupational interests, and general success in high school were within the normal range. The results of this study suggest that placement in a self-contained special class because of significant academic deficits in the elementary grades does not preclude success in high school.

✳ *Current Issues and Future Trends*

Learning disabilities is such a dynamic and controversial area that an entire book could easily be devoted to a discussion of current issues. Some of these issues include what terminology to use (is a "reading disability" the same as a "learning disability"?), the concern for the special needs of adults with learning disabilities, what kind of training learning disabilities teachers should receive, how federal and state funds should be appropriated, and what to do about the proliferation of controversial "cures" for learning disabilities. We will briefly discuss two issues: the continuing debate over defining and identifying the "true nature" of learning disabilities and where students with learning disabilities should be taught (full inclusion).

Will the Real Student with Learning Disabilities Please Stand Up?

The widely differing findings of prevalence studies (from 5% to 30% of the school-age population) illustrate the lack of a standard operational definition of learning disabilities. Some prominent special educators believe that the trend toward expanding the learning disabilities classification to include more and more children indicates a misunderstanding of the concept and only detracts from and weakens services to children who have severe learning problems. Myers and Hammill (1990), for example, believe that far too many students are identified as learning disabled:

> A number of teachers will note readily that many, possibly most, of the "learning disabled" students enrolled in their programs do not satisfy either the 1977 USOE or the NJCLD definition. This is because, in many school districts, all students who are thought to be able to profit from tutoring or remedial education are arbitrarily called learning disabled. As a consequence of such definitional liberality, the learning disability programs have become glutted with underachieving students, culturally different students, and poorly taught students. (p. 13)

To Tell the Truth was a popular TV game show in the 1960s. A panel of celebrities would ask questions of three contestants, only one of whom was actually the person all were pretending to be. In some respects, the search to find the "truly" learning disabled from among the many students who do poorly in school is like that TV game show. Many questions (in the form of achievement tests, intelligence tests, and more tests) are given to the contestants (students) whose answers are judged by a panel of experts (teachers, school psychologists, and administrators) charged with picking out the "real" students with learning disabilities from the "pretenders." The differences, of course, are significant too. On the game show, the consequences for a wrong answer were no more serious than a loud buzzer and ending up with a consolation prize; but in the game of identifying students with learning disabilities, mistakes can be costly. A "No, he's not learning disabled" answer can be devastating for the student who truly needs specially designed instruction to meet his individual learning needs. If the team of selection experts concludes "Yes, there is one" when the student's achievement deficits are simply because he has not had sufficient contact with an appropriate general education curriculum, then the resources available to help students with learning disabilities are stretched further.

> When it comes to finding the definition of learning disabilities, we should forget about it, at least for now. Far too much time, money, and space in textbooks and journals have been taken up by this futile mission. Those concerned with this goal have sought the answer by administering one test after another, giving multiple tests, and like

There is no consensus among the "experts" regarding who is learning disabled. Two studies have shown that educators will identify some children as learning disabled even when all of their evaluative data are in the normal range and that the single most reliable variable predicting whether a student will be identified is the *amount* of information presented on the student (the more information, the more likely the student will be identified), rather than the type of information or its relationship to usual identification criteria (Algozzine & Ysseldyke, 1981; Ysseldyke, Algozzine, Richey, & Graden, 1982).

alchemists of old, carefully selecting and combining subtests and items from many tests. The thinking is, apparently, that if the proper battery of tests, subtests, or items can be blended and then administered and if the proper multivariate analysis is employed, then we will be able to tell who is really learning disabled and who isn't (the pretenders!). And further, if our tests and measurements are highly sophisticated, we will know about the many subtypes of learning disabilities. Wrong! (Lovitt, 1989, p. 473)

The discussion of what constitutes a true learning disability is likely to go on for some time. What a child's learning problem is called is not so important; what is important is that schools provide an educational program responsive to the individual needs of all children who have difficulty learning.

Should All Students with Learning Disabilities Be Educated in the Regular Classroom?

The IDEA mandates that all students with disabilities receive a program of special education services planned to meet their individual needs in the least restrictive environment. For the majority of students with learning disabilities, the least restrictive environment for all or most of the school day is the regular education classroom of their same-age peers. The currently popular movement toward full inclusion of all students with disabilities in regular classrooms, however, has many professionals and advocates for students with learning disabilities worried. They think that although the full inclusion movement is based on strong beliefs and has the best intentions of children with disabilities at heart, little research supports it (Division for Learning Disabilities, 1993; Kauffman & Hallahan, 1994; Martin, 1993; Silver, 1993). They fear that the special education services for students with learning disabilities guaranteed by the IDEA—particularly the meaningful development and implementation of IEPs and the identification of the least restrictive environment for each student along a continuum of placement options—will be lost if full inclusion becomes reality. They wonder how, for example, a middle school student with learning disabilities who spends the entire school day in regular education subject matter classes will receive the individualized reading instruction at the second grade level that he or she needs. With full inclusion into the general education classroom comes the general education curriculum (Pugach & Warger, 1993). The regular education classroom for some students with learning disabilities may actually be more restrictive than a resource room or special class placement when the instructional needs of the student are considered—and remember that academic deficit is the primary characteristic and remedial need of students with learning disabilities (Adelman, 1992; Poplin, 1981).

All of the major professional and advocacy associations concerned with the education of children with learning disabilities have published position papers against full inclusion (see Table 5.4) (CLD, 1993; DLD, 1993; LDA, 1993; NJCLD; 1994). Each group recognizes and supports the placement of students with learning disabilities in regular classrooms to the maximum extent possible, given that the instructional and related services required to meet each student's individualized educational needs are provided, but they strongly oppose the policies that mandate the same placement and instruction for all students with learning disabilities. Each group believes that special education for students with learning disabilities requires a continuum of service options that includes the possibility of some or even all instruction taking place outside the regular classroom.

See "A Case for Special Classroom Placements" by Douglas Fuchs and Lynn Fuchs in Chapter 2, and the January, 1995, issue of *Educational Leadership*, pp. 22–25.

TABLE 5.4   *(continues on next page)*
How two major professional and advocacy groups for learning disabilities view full inclusion

---

Council for Learning Disabilities

CLD SUPPORTS school reform efforts that enhance the education of all students, including those with learning disabilities (LD). The Council SUPPORTS the education of students with LD in general education classrooms *when deemed appropriate* by the Individual Education Program (IEP) team. Such inclusion efforts require the provision of needed support services in order to be successful. One policy that the Council CANNOT SUPPORT is the indiscriminate full-time placement of ALL students with LD in the regular classroom, a policy often referred to as "full inclusion." CLD has grave concerns about any placement policy that ignores a critical component of special education service delivery: Program placement of each student should be based on an evaluation of that student's individual needs. The Council CANNOT SUPPORT any policy that minimizes or eliminates service options designed to enhance the education of students with LD and that are guaranteed by the Individuals with Disabilities Education Act.

Learning Disabilities Association of America

"Full inclusion," "full integration," "unified system," "inclusive education" are terms used to describe a popular policy/practice in which all students with disabilities, regardless of the nature or severity of their disability and need for related services, receive their total education with the regular education classroom in their home school. The Learning Disabilities Association of America does not support "full inclusion" or any policies that mandate the same placement, instruction, or treatment of ALL students with learning disabilities. Many students with learning disabilities benefit from being served in the regular education classroom. However, the regular education classroom is not the appropriate placement for a number of students with learning disabilities who may need alternative instructional environments, teaching strategies, and/or materials that cannot or will not be provided with the context of a regular classroom placement.

Some authors are so concerned about recent trends such as considering learning disabilities to be a *mild* disability in every case, not wanting to identify and label a student's disability, and the full inclusion movement, that they fear for the very existence of the learning disability field.

> Presently, the learning disabilities field as we know it is in danger of extinction. At a recent conference presentation, a group of school psychologists and educators expressed their belief that within 5 years the category would no longer exist. Even if we abandon the categorical label, children with learning disabilities will still be there. . . . We have a moral and legal obligation to provide individuals with learning disabilities with appropriate services. We must make concerted efforts to preserve the service delivery system for the individuals for whom it was originally created, rather than wholeheartedly embrace current trends. (Mather & Roberts, 1994, p. 56)

••

Summary

Defining Learning Disabilities

• There is no one, universally agreed-on definition of learning disabilities. Most definitions, however, incorporate three criteria that must be met. The student with learning disabilities must (a) have a severe discrepancy between potential or ability and actual achievement, (b) have learning problems that cannot be attributed to

TABLE 5.4 *(continued)*

LDA believes that decisions regarding educational placement of students with learning disabilities must be based on the needs of each individual student rather than administrative convenience or budgetary considerations and must be the result of a cooperative effort involving educators, parents, and the student when appropriate.

LDA strongly supports the Individuals with Disabilities Act (IDEA) which mandates:

♦ a free and appropriate public education in the least restrictive environment appropriate for the student's specific learning needs

♦ a team-approved Individualized Education Program (IEP)

♦ a placement decision must be made on an individual basis and considered only after the development of the IEP

♦ a continuum of alternative placements to meet the needs of students with disabilities for special education and related services

♦ a system for the continuing education of regular and special education and related services personnel to enable these personnel to meet the needs of children with disabilities

LDA believes that the placement of ALL children with disabilities in the regular classroom is as great a violation of IDEA as is the placement of ALL children in separate classrooms on the basis of their type of disability.

LDA URGES THE U.S. DEPARTMENT OF EDUCATION AND EACH STATE TO MOVE DELIBERATELY AND REFLECTIVELY IN SCHOOL RESTRUCTURING, USING THE INDIVIDUALS WITH DISABILITIES ACT AS A FOUNDATION – MINDFUL OF THE BEST INTERESTS OF ALL CHILDREN WITH DISABILITIES.

Sources: Excerpt from "Concerns About 'Full Inclusion' of Students with Learning Disabilities in Regular Education Classrooms," *Learning Disability Quarterly,* Spring, 1993, Vol. 16, p. 126. Reprinted by permission, Council for Learning Disabilities. Excerpt from "Position Paper on Full Inclusion of All Students with Learning Disabilities in the Regular Classroom," *LDA Newsbrief,* March/April, 1993, Vol. 28, No. 2. Copyright (c) 1993 by the Learning Disabilities of America Association.

other disabilities, such as blindness or mental retardation, and (c) need special educational services to succeed in school.

• No matter which definition is used, educators should focus on each student's specific skill deficiencies for assessment and instruction.

Three-fourths are identified for learning disabilities services in the elementary grades.

Severe discrepancies in reading are most frequently followed by problems in mathematics.

• The single defining characteristic is a specific and significant achievement deficiency in the presence of adequate overall intelligence.

Characteristics of Learning Disabilities

• Students with learning disabilities are an extremely heterogeneous group:

Boys outnumber girls 3 to 1.

Causes of Learning Disabilities

• Although the actual cause of a specific learning disability is seldom known, the suspected causes are grouped into three categories: brain damage, biochemical imbalance, and environmental factors such as poor instruction.

Identification and Assessment

- Most learning disabilities professionals take a diagnostic-prescriptive approach to assessment; that is, results of assessment should lead directly to a plan for classroom instruction.
- Norm-referenced tests compare a child's score with the scores of other age-mates who have taken the same test.
- Process tests are designed to measure a child's ability in different perceptual or psycholinguistic areas.
- Teachers use informal reading inventories to observe directly and record a child's reading skills.
- Criterion-referenced tests compare a child's score with a predetermined mastery level.
- Direct and daily measurement involves regularly assessing a child on a specific skill each time it is taught. Precision teaching is one system for assessing student progress and for making instructional decisions based on direct and daily measurement.

Prevalence

- Because of the varied assessment procedures used, wide differences are evident from state to state in the percentage of the school-age population identified as having learning disabilities.
- Learning disabilities is the largest category in special education. Students with learning disabilities represent about 4.1% of the total school enrollment in the United States and about half of all students receiving special education.

Historic Background

- Learning disabilities is a relatively new, rapidly growing field in special education.
- The term *learning disabilities* was first used in 1963 by S. A. Kirk to describe children who have serious learning problems in school but no other obvious disabilities.
- During the late 1960s, two organizations—LDA and DLD (CEC)—helped bring about federal legislation providing funds for learning disabilities programs.

Educational Approaches

- Ability training involves prescribing instructional activities designed to remediate a student's presumed weakness in underlying basic abilities. Psycholinguistic training, the visual-perceptual approach, the perceptual-motor approach, and the multisensory approach are all types of ability training. Little research supports the effectiveness of ability training.
- Skill training is based on the belief that a student's performance deficit is the problem, not a sign of an underlying disability. In skill training, remediation is based on the direct instruction of precisely defined skills, many opportunities to practice, and the direct measurement of a student's progress. Research has shown the skill-training approach—including applied behavior analysis, Direct Instruction, and precision teaching—to be effective.
- Learning strategies help students guide themselves successfully through specific tasks or general problems.
- Content enhancements, such as graphic organizers, mnemonic instruction, study guides, and guided notes, help make curriculum content more accessible to students with learning disabilities.

Educational Service Alternatives

- Most students with learning disabilities spend at least part of each school day in the regular classroom.
- In some schools, a consultant teacher helps regular classroom teachers work with children with learning disabilities.
- In the resource room, a specially trained teacher works with the children on particular skill deficits for one or more periods per day.
- A few children with learning disabilities attend separate, self-contained classes. This placement option, however, should be used only after attempts to serve the child in a less restrictive setting have failed, and it should not be considered permanent.

Current Issues and Future Trends

- The discussion and debate over what constitutes a true learning disability are likely to continue. It is most important for schools to respond to the individual needs of all children who have difficulty learning.
- Most professionals and advocates for students with learning disabilities do not support "full inclusion," which would eliminate the continuum of service delivery options.

For More Information

Journals

Intervention in School and Clinic. Published five times a year by PRO-ED, 8700 Shoal Creek Boulevard, Austin, TX 78758-6897. An interdisciplinary journal directed to teachers, parents, educational therapists, and specialists in all fields who deal with the day-to-day aspects of special and remedial education.

Journal of Learning Disabilities. Published 10 times a year by PRO-ED, 8700 Shoal Creek Boulevard, Austin, TX 78758-6897. Publishes research and theoretical articles relating to learning disabilities.

Journal of Precision Teaching. Published by the Center for Individualized Instruction, Jacksonville State University, Jacksonville, AL 36265. A multidisciplinary journal dedicated to a science of human behavior that includes direct, continuous, and standard measurement. Publishes both formal and informal articles describing precision teaching projects.

Learning Disabilities Research and Practice. Published four times a year by the Division for Learning Disabilities, Council for Exceptional Children, 1920 Association Drive, Reston, VA 22091.

Learning Disability Quarterly. Published four times a year by the Council for Learning Disabilities. Emphasizes practical implications of research and applied research dealing with learning disability populations and settings.

Books

Ariel, A. (1992). *Education of children and adolescents with learning disabilities.* New York: Macmillan.

Bley, N. S., & Thornton, C. A. (1994). *Teaching mathematics to students with learning disabilities* (3rd ed.). Austin, TX: PRO-ED.

DuPaul, G. J., & Stoner, G. (1994). *ADHD in the schools: Assessment and intervention strategies.* New York: Guilford Press.

Harris, W. J., & Schutz, P. N. B. (1986). *The special education resource room: Rationale and implementation.* New York: Merrill/Macmillan.

Lerner, J. W. (1993). *Learning disabilities: Theories, diagnosis, and teaching strategies* (6th ed.). Boston: Houghton Mifflin.

Lerner, J. W., Lowenthal, B., & Lerner, S. R. (1995). *Attention deficit disorders: Assessment and teaching.* Pacific Grove, CA: Brooks/Cole.

Lewis, R. B., & Doorlag, D. H. (1995). *Teaching special students in the mainstream* (4th ed.). Englewood Cliffs, NJ: Prentice-Hall/Merrill.

Lovitt, T. C. (1989). *Introduction to learning disabilities.* Needham Heights, MA: Allyn & Bacon.

Mercer, C. D. (1992). *Students with learning disabilities* (4th ed.). New York: Macmillan.

Myers, P. I., & Hammill, D. D. (1990). *Learning disabilities: Basic concepts, assessment practices, and instructional strategies* (4th ed.). Austin, TX: PRO-ED.

Organizations

Learning Disabilities Association of America (LDA), 4156 Library Road, Pittsburgh, PA 15234. Founded in 1963, LDA is a large, active organization of parents and educators that advocates for services to children with learning disabilities.

Council for Learning Disabilities (CLD), P.O. Box 40303, Overland Park, KS 66204. An independent organization of professionals who work with individuals with learning disabilities. Publishes *Learning Disabilities Quarterly,* holds semiannual conferences to disseminate research and information, and promotes standards for learning disabilities professionals.

Division for Learning Disabilities (DLD), Council for Exceptional Children, 1920 Association Drive, Reston, VA 22091. Includes teachers, teacher educators, researchers, and other members of CEC who work with or on behalf of individuals with learning disabilities.

Students with Emotional and Behavioral Disorders

* Why should a child who behaves badly be considered disabled?

* If the law requires that all students with disabilities receive special education services, why do some experts claims that many students with emotional and behavioral disorders are not being served?

* How are behavior problems and academic performance interrelated?

* Who is more severely disabled: the acting-out, aggressive child or the withdrawn child?

* What are the most important skills for teachers of students with emotional and behavioral disorders?

Childhood should be a happy time, a time for playing, growing, learning, and making friends—and for most children it is. But some children's lives are a constant turmoil. Some strike out at others, sometimes with disastrous consequences. Others are so shy and withdrawn that they seem to be in their own worlds. In either case, playing with others, making friends, and learning all the things a child must learn are extremely difficult for these children. They are children with emotional and behavioral disorders. These children are referred to with a variety of terms: *emotionally disturbed, socially maladjusted, psychologically disordered, emotionally handicapped,* or even *psychotic* if their behavior is extremely abnormal or bizarre.

Many children with emotional and behavioral disorders are seldom really liked by anyone—their peers, teachers, siblings, even parents. Sadder still, they often do not even like themselves. The child with behavioral disorders is difficult to be around, and attempts to befriend him—most are boys—may lead only to rejection, verbal abuse, or even physical attack. With some emotionally withdrawn children, overtures or approaches seem to fall on deaf ears, and yet these children are not deaf.

Although most children with emotional and behavioral disorders are of sound mind and body, their noxious or withdrawn behavior is as serious an impediment to their functioning and learning as the physical and developmental disabilities that challenge other children with disabilities. Children with emotional and behavioral disorders make up a significant portion of students who need special education.

✳ *Defining Emotional and Behavioral Disorders*

There is no generally agreed-on definition of behavioral disorders. Like their colleagues in mental retardation and learning disabilities, special educators in the area of emotional and behavioral disorders have been struggling to reach consensus on a definition. A definition should provide unambiguous guidance for the reliable identification of students who need special education services because of the disability in question. Definitions that appear "theoretically sound" or "legally defensible" on paper are often found wanting in practice.

A clear definition of behavioral disorders is lacking for numerous reasons. First, disordered behavior is a social construct; there is no clear agreement about what constitutes good mental health. Second, different theories of emotional disturbance use concepts and terminology that do little to promote meaning from one definition to another. Third, measuring and interpreting disordered behavior across time and settings is a difficult, exact, and costly endeavor. Cultural influence is another problem; expectations and norms for appropriate behavior are often quite different across ethnic and cultural groups. In addition, frequency and intensity are concerns. All children behave inappropriately at times—how often and with how much intensity must a student engage in a particular behavior before he is considered disabled because of the behavior? Finally, disordered behavior sometimes occurs in conjunction with other disabilities (most notably mental retardation and learning disabilities), making it difficult to tell whether one condition is the result or the cause of the other.

Many children without disabilities sometimes act in the same ways as children with emotional and behavioral disorders, but not as often or with such intensity. And, of course, many children with emotional and behavioral disorders are likable.

McIntyre (1992a, 1993) has written extensively on the influence of cultural differences on behavioral norms and expectations.

246

Although numerous definitions have been proposed, the one first written in 1957 by Eli Bower (1960) has had the most impact on special education. Bower's definition, with only a few changes, was adopted by the U.S. Department of Education as the definition of seriously emotionally disturbed children, one of the disability categories covered by the IDEA.

Seriously emotionally disturbed is defined as follows:

(i) The term means a condition exhibiting one or more of the following characteristics over a long period of time and to a marked degree, which adversely affects educational performance.

(a) An inability to learn which cannot be explained by intellectual, sensory, and health factors;

(b) An inability to build or maintain satisfactory interpersonal relationships with peers and teachers;

(c) Inappropriate types of behavior or feelings under normal circumstances;

(d) A general pervasive mood of unhappiness or depression; or

(e) A tendency to develop physical symptoms or fears associated with personal or school problems.

(ii) The term includes children who are schizophrenic [or autistic]. The term does not include children who are socially maladjusted unless it is determined that they are seriously emotionally disturbed. (45 CFR 121a.5[b][8][1978])

This definition may seem straightforward enough at first. It specifies three conditions that must be met: *chronicity* ("over a long period of time"), *severity* ("to a marked degree"), and *difficulty in school* ("adversely affects educational performance"); and it lists five types of problems that qualify. But in fact, the definition is extremely vague and leaves much to the subjective opinion of the authorities (usually teachers) who surround the child. How does one operationalize such terms as *satisfactory interpersonal relationships, normal, inappropriate,* and *pervasive?*

And how does one determine that some behavior problems represent social maladjustment, whereas others are indicative of true emotional disturbance? This determination is critical because children who are socially maladjusted are not considered disabled and are therefore ineligible for special education services under the IDEA. Bower's original definition did not include any mention of social maladjustment, and the inclusion in the federal definition of this seemingly illogical criterion for ineligibility has been heavily criticized (Center, 1990; Cline, 1990; Kauffman, 1993b; Peterson, Benson, Edwards, Rosell, & White, 1986). Bower (1982) never intended a distinction between emotional disturbance and social maladjustment; the five components of the definition were, in fact, meant to be indicators of social maladjustment. It is difficult to conceive of a child who is sufficiently socially maladjusted to have received that label but who does not display one or more of the five characteristics (especially b) included in the federal definition. As written, the definition seemingly excludes children on the same basis for which they are included.

A harsh critic of federal policy toward the education of children with emotional and behavioral disorders, Kauffman has written, "The federal definition is, if not claptrap, at least dangerously close to nonsense" (1982, p. 4). Indeed, the definition appears to have offered little direction to states and local school districts. Mack (1980) found that only 12 states included all of the federal criteria in their definitions and that the percentages of school-age children identified varies widely from state to state.

The Council for Children with Behavioral Disorders (CCBD), the major professional organization of special educators concerned with children with emotional and behavioral disorders, has contributed to a new proposed definition to replace the definition of serious emotional disturbance in the IDEA. This definition, developed

The federal definition was later revised to exclude children with autism from the category of seriously emotionally disturbed. Autism was added as a new disability category in the 1990 amendments to PL 92–142. Autism is discussed in Chapter 11.

by the National Mental Health and Special Education Coalition, a group composed of some 30 professional mental health and education associations, describes emotional and behavioral disorders as a disability characterized by

> (i) behavioral or emotional responses in school programs so different from appropriate age, cultural, or ethnic norms that they adversely affect educational performance. Educational performance includes the development and demonstration of academic, social, vocational, and personal skills. Such a disability is
>> (a) more than a temporary, expected response to stressful events in the environment;
>> (b) is consistently exhibited in two different settings, at least one of which is school-related; and
>> (c) is unresponsive to direct intervention in general education or the child's condition is such that general education interventions would be insufficient.
> (ii) Emotional and behavioral disorders can co-exist with other disabilities.
> (iii) This category may include children or youth with schizophrenic disorders, affective disorders, anxiety disorders, or other sustained disturbances of conduct or adjustment when they adversely affect educational performance in accordance with section (i). (Forness & Knitzer, 1992, p. 13)

The proposed definition specifies the functional educational dimensions of this disability category, does not contain reference to the exclusion of students with social maladjustment, and focuses on the sources of data needed to determine whether a student is behaviorally disordered (CCBD, 1989). Numerous other definitions of behavioral disorders have been proposed (Kauffman, 1977; Ross, 1974). Although each definition differs somewhat, all agree that a child's behavior, to be considered disordered, must differ markedly (extremely) and chronically (over time) from current social or cultural norms. As we show throughout this chapter, special education for students with emotional and behavioral disorders is most effective when it focuses on what they actually do and what the environmental conditions are when they misbehave, rather than attempts to define and classify some inner disturbance.

The Role of Teacher Tolerance in Defining Children's Emotional and Behavioral Disorders

Even though no definition of behavioral disorders proposed so far has provided a consistent, universally agreed-on standard for identification, diagnosis, communication, and research, they all place the concept of behavioral disorders in a "conceptual ballpark" (Hewett & Taylor, 1980). And teacher tolerance is a major player in that ballpark. A number of studies show that a student's identification as behaviorally disordered is largely a function of the teacher's notion of children's expected or acceptable behavior. In a **longitudinal study,** Rubin and Balow (1978) found that 59% of all children who had received three or more annual ratings had been identified as behaviorally disordered by at least one teacher at some time between kindergarten and sixth grade. Of course, this study suggests another important conclusion as well—that a great many children do experience some type of behavior problem during their early school years. Although most of these problems do go away, teachers identify problems at the time as an indication of emotional disturbance.

The role of teacher tolerance in identifying children as behaviorally disturbed is significant. Algozzine (1980) found that, as a group, regular classroom teachers rated

---

Sidebar:

CCBD has officially adopted the position that the term *behaviorally disordered* is more appropriate than the term *seriously emotionally disturbed*. The CCBD endorses use of the term *behaviorally disordered* because (a) it does not suggest any particular theory of causation or set of intervention techniques, (b) it is more representative of the students who are disabled by their behavior and are being served under the IDEA, and (c) it is less stigmatizing (Huntze, 1985). Two studies have shown that the label *behaviorally disordered* implies less negative dimensions to teachers than does the term *emotionally disturbed* (Feldman, Kinnison, Jay, & Harth, 1983; Lloyd, Kauffman, & Gansneder, 1987). Both preservice and inservice teachers indicated they thought children labeled behaviorally disordered were more teachable and likely to be successful in a regular classroom than were children identified as emotionally disturbed.

A *longitudinal study* follows the development of the same subjects over a period of years.

certain behaviors as more disturbing than did a comparison group of special education teachers. In a subsequent study, Curran and Algozzine (1980) found that teachers with varying levels of tolerance for immature or defiant behaviors differentially
rated a hypothetical child's likelihood of success in the regular classroom. These
studies suggest that "emotional disturbance is a function of the perceiver. . . . What is
disturbance to one teacher may not be to another" (Whelan, 1981, pp. 4–5).

Classification of Emotional and Behavioral Disorders

As mentioned in Chapter 1, classification of the observed phenomena within a given
field is an important scientific task. A reliable and valid classification system for
behavioral disorders would foster accurate communication among researchers, diag-
nosticians, and teachers. Better communication could result, most importantly, in a
child's receiving the educational placement and treatment that have been proven
most effective for his or her specific behavior problem. Unfortunately, such a workable classification system has yet to be developed in the area of behavioral disorders.

The DSM-IV

One system for classifying behavioral disorders is the *Diagnostic and Statistical
Manual of Mental Disorders* (*DSM-IV*), developed by the American Psychiatric Association (1994). The *DSM-IV* is an elaborate and vast classification system consisting of
230 separate diagnostic categories, or labels, to identify the various types of disordered behavior noted in clinical practice. Because of its more precise language, its
use of more examples, and the greater amount of information it requires about the
person being diagnosed, the *DSM-IV* represents an improvement in clinical classification over earlier versions.

    The *DSM-IV* classification system is used regularly in the mental health profes-
sions; however, it suffers from a lack of reliability. Even with the more precise language, it is not uncommon for one psychiatrist or psychologist to classify a child into
one category and a second examiner to place the same child into a completely different category.

> Teachers' tolerance for deviant behavior and their expectations for classroom performance are major factors to consider in plans to integrate children with disabilities into regular classrooms. Excellent discussions of this issue are found in Anderson-Inman et al. (1984); Braaten et al. (1988); and Kauffman, Wong, Lloyd, Hung, and Pullen (1991).

Teachers' expectations of acceptable behavior and tolerance of immature and deviant behavior play a significant role in the identification of children with emotional and behavioral disorders.

But an even greater problem is that putting a child into a given category provides no guidelines for education and treatment. Knowing that a child has been diagnosed as fitting a certain category in the *DSM-IV* provides a teacher with virtually no useful information on what intervention or therapy is needed.

Quay's Statistical Classification

Another well-known classification system was developed by Quay and his coworkers (Quay, 1975, 1986). Quay collected a wide range of data—including behavior ratings by parents and teachers, life histories, and children's responses on questionnaires—for hundreds of children with emotional and behavioral disorders. When Quay analyzed all of this information statistically, he found that children's behavioral disorders tend to appear in groups, or clusters. Children who showed some of the behaviors in a given cluster had a higher than chance likelihood of also showing the other traits and behaviors in that cluster. Quay calls the four clusters conduct disorder, anxiety-withdrawal, immaturity, and socialized aggression.

Children described as having a *conduct disorder* are likely to be disobedient and/or disruptive, get into fights, be bossy, and have temper tantrums. *Anxiety-withdrawal* (sometimes called *personality disorder*) in children is identified by social withdrawal, anxiety, depression, feelings of inferiority, guilt, shyness, and unhappiness. *Immaturity* is characterized by a short attention span, extreme passivity, daydreaming, preference for younger playmates, and clumsiness. *Socialized aggression* is marked by truancy, gang membership, theft, and a feeling of pride in belonging to a delinquent subculture. Although Quay's system has proven quite reliable—the same four clusters of behavioral and personality traits have been found in many samples of children with emotional and behavioral disorders (Quay, 1986)—it does not provide treatment information. Therefore, its usefulness is limited primarily to describing the major types of children's behavioral disorders for purposes of research and communication.

Direct Observation and Measurement

Another approach to classifying children's emotional and behavioral disorders is through direct observation and measurement. What about the behavior of children with emotional and behavioral disorders does one measure? What dimensions of their behavior are different from those of their normal peers? Behavior can be measured and classified along several dimensions: frequency, duration, topography, and magnitude.

Frequency.   *Frequency* refers to how often a particular behavior is performed. Almost all children cry, get into fights with other children, and sulk from time to time; yet we are not apt to label them emotionally disturbed. The primary difference between children with emotional and behavioral disorders and normal children is the **rate** at which these kinds of undesirable activities occur. Although disturbed children may not do anything that nondisabled peers do not do, they do certain undesirable things much more often (e.g., crying, hitting others) and/or engage in desirable behaviors too infrequently (e.g., playing with others).

Duration.   Closely related to frequency is duration. **Duration** is a measure of how long a child engages in a given activity. Again, even though normal children and

When a group of special education teachers was asked to rate the behavior problems exhibited most often by 244 students identified as seriously emotionally disturbed, 7 of the 12 most prevalent problems were conduct disorders (Pullis, 1991).

For a detailed explanation of procedures for direct and frequent measurement of behavior, see Alberto and Troutman (1995) and Cooper et al. (1987).

those with emotional and behavioral disorders may do the same things, the amount of time the behaviorally disordered child spends in certain activities is often markedly different—either longer or shorter—from that of the other children. For example, many young children have temper tantrums, but the tantrums generally last no more than a few minutes. A child with emotional and behavioral disorders may tantrum for more than an hour at a time. Sometimes the problem is one of too short a duration, as with paying attention or working independently. Some children with emotional and behavioral disorders cannot stick to one task for more than several seconds at a time.

Topography.   **Topography** refers to the physical shape or form of behavior. For instance, throwing a baseball and rolling a bowling ball involve different topographies. Although both involve the arm, each activity requires a different movement. Some of the responses emitted by a child with emotional and behavioral disorders are seldom, if ever, seen in normal children. These behaviors may be maladaptive, bizarre, or dangerous to the child or others.

Magnitude.   Finally, behavior can be classified by its magnitude or intensity. The **magnitude** of a child's responses may be too little (e.g., talking in a volume so low that he or she cannot be heard) or too much (e.g., slamming the door).

Stimulus Control.   Children with emotional and behavioral disorders also have difficulty discriminating when and where certain behaviors are appropriate. Learning that kind of stimulus control is a major task of growing up, which most children master naturally through socialization. They pick it up from friends, siblings, parents, and other adults. Some children with emotional and behavioral disorders, however, often appear unaware of their surroundings. They do not learn the proper time and place for many actions without being carefully instructed.

Advantages of Behavioral Dimensions.   The advantage of defining and classifying emotional and behavioral disorders in terms of these behavioral dimensions is that identification, instructional strategies, and evaluation of the effects of treatment can all revolve around objective measurement. This approach leads to a direct focus on the child's problem—the inappropriate behavior—and ways of dealing with it, as opposed to concentrating on some problem within the child. If the child can learn new socially acceptable ways to behave, he or she need no longer be considered behaviorally disordered (CCBD, 1989; Sugai & Maheady, 1988).

Degree of Severity

Children's emotional and behavioral disorders can also be classified by degree of severity (Clarizio, 1990). Although children have sometimes been referred to as displaying mild, moderate, and severe behavior problems, at least one study suggests that this three-level distinction is not supported in practice. Olson, Algozzine, and Schmid (1980) found that teachers of students with emotional and behavioral disorders regularly identified only two levels, or degrees, of behavioral disturbance: mild and severe. Students who were viewed as mildly emotionally disturbed were those who could respond to interventions provided in regular classrooms by regular class teachers with the support of guidance counselors or consulting teachers. Students who needed intense treatment programs and residential placement were considered to have severe emotional and behavioral disorders.

Classification by degree of severity, however, is primarily after the fact. Important decisions as to type of educational programming and placement should be based on an objective assessment of the child's individual needs, rather than on someone's opinion that the child is either mildly or severely disturbed.

✳ *Characteristics of Children with Emotional and Behavioral Disorders*

Intelligence and Achievement

Contrary to one popular myth, most children with emotional and behavioral disorders are not bright, intellectually above-average children who are simply bored with their surroundings. Many more children with emotional and behavioral disorders score in the slow learner or mildly retarded range on IQ tests than do normal children. Two surveys that used national samples reported average IQ scores for students with emotional and behavioral disorders. Valdes, Williamson, and Wagner (1990) reported a mean IQ of 86, with about half of their sample scoring between 71 and 90. The students in a study by Cullinan, Epstein, and Sabornie (1992) had an average mean IQ score of 92.6. Cullinan et al. concluded that the higher IQ scores in their study were because the students spent more time in regular classrooms and had been in special education for fewer years than the students in the Valdes et al. survey.

Whether children with emotional and behavioral disorders actually have any less real intelligence than normal children is difficult to say. An IQ test measures only how well a child performs certain tasks. It is possible that the disturbed child's inappropriate behavior has interfered with past opportunities to learn the tasks included on the test but that the child really has the necessary intelligence to learn them. In any event, IQ tests are good indicators of school achievement, and children with emotional and behavioral disorders are noted for their problems with learning and academic achievement. On the basis of his review of research related to the intelligence of children with emotional and behavioral disorders, Kauffman (1993b) concluded:

> We have accumulated enough research on these students' intelligence to draw this conclusion: although the majority fall only slightly below average in IQ, a disproportionate number, compared to the normal distribution, score in the dull normal and mildly retarded range, and relatively few fall in the upper ranges. (p. 227)

Even when IQ scores are taken into account, however, children with emotional and behavioral disorders achieve below the levels suggested by their scores. Overall, it is estimated that only 30% of students with behavioral disorders are performing at or above grade level (Knitzer, Sternberg, & Fleisch, 1990). Recent reports based on nationwide studies (Chesapeake Institute, 1994; Valdes et al., 1990) report the following academic outcomes for students with emotional and behavioral disorders:

- Two thirds could not pass competency exams for their grade level.
- These children have the lowest grade point average of any group of students with disabilities.

See Chapter 4 for a discussion of IQ tests.

- Forty-four percent failed one or more courses in their most recent school year.
- They have a higher absenteeism rate than any other disability category (missing an average of 18 days of school per year).
- Forty-eight percent drop out of high school, compared with 30% of all students with disabilities and 24% of all high school students.
- Over 50% are not employed within 2 years of exiting school.

Social Skills and Interpersonal Relationships

The ability to develop and maintain interpersonal relationships during childhood and adolescence is an important predictor of present and future adjustment. Many students with emotional and behavioral disorders often experience great difficulty in making and keeping friends (Cartledge & Milburn, 1995). A study comparing the social relationships of secondary students who have behavioral disorders with those of same-age peers who do not have behavioral disorders reported lower levels of empathy toward others, participation in fewer curricular activities, less frequent contacts with friends, and lower quality relationships for the adolescents with behavioral disorders (Schonert-Reichl, 1993).

Antisocial Behavior

The most common pattern of behavior exhibited by children with emotional and behavioral disorders is one of antisocial behavior, sometimes called *externalizing* behavioral disorders. Approximately two thirds of the children placed in special education programs for students with emotional and behavioral disorders exhibit antisocial behavioral patterns (Valdes et al., 1990). Antisocial children commonly display behaviors like these in the classroom (Walker, Colvin, & Ramsey, 1995): is out of seat, runs around the room, disturbs peers, hits or fights, ignores the teacher, complains excessively, steals, destroys property, does not comply with directions, argues and talks back, distorts the truth, has temper tantrums, does not complete assignments. Clearly, an ongoing pattern of such behavior presents a major challenge for teachers of antisocial children.

Even though all children sometimes cry, hit others, and refuse to comply with requests of parents and teachers, children with emotional and behavioral disorders do so frequently. Also, the antisocial behavior of children with emotional and behavioral disorders often occurs with little or no provocation. Aggression takes many forms—verbal abuse toward adults and other children, destructiveness and vandalism, and physical attacks on others. These children seem to be in continuous conflict with those around them. Their own aggressive outbursts often cause others to strike back in attempts to punish them. It is no wonder that children with emotional and behavioral disorders are seldom liked by others and find it difficult to establish friendships.

Many believe that most children who exhibit deviant behavioral patterns will grow out of them with time and become normally functioning adults. Although this popular wisdom holds true for many children who exhibit such problems as withdrawal, fears, and speech impairments (Rutter, 1976), research indicates that it is not so for children who display consistent patterns of aggressive, coercive, antisocial, and/or delinquent behavior (Patterson, Cipaldi, & Bank, 1991; Robins, 1979; Wahler & Dumas, 1986; Walker et al., 1995). Robins (1966) conducted a follow-up study of more than 500 adults who as children had been seen by a clinic staff because of

For an interesting article on how puppetry can help students with emotional and behavioral disorders develop social and affective awareness and social skills, see Caputo (1993). Storytelling can also be an effective means for helping students learn to understand and express their emotions (Bauer & Balius, 1995).

Aggression and acting out are the major characteristics of Quay's (1975) conduct disorder and socialized aggression categories.

A pattern of antisocial behavior early in a child's school career is the best single predictor of delinquency in adolescence (Walker et al., 1995).

Everyone Participates in This Science Class

·······················

Using Response Cards to Increase Achievement

Rashawn had raised his hand for the last time. He had wanted to answer several of his teacher's questions, especially when she asked whether anyone could name the clouds that look like wispy, spun cotton. But it just wasn't his day to get called on. Rashawn tried to follow along, but after a while he lost interest and laid his head on his desk.

Dean did get called on once, but he didn't raise his hand too often. It was a lot easier just to sit there. If he could just be quiet and still like Rashawn over there, then he wouldn't have to think about learning all this weather stuff. Then it got too hard for Dean to just sit, so he started acting out. This got his teacher's attention several times.

"Dean, please pay attention."

"Stop that, Dean!"

"Dean, how do you expect to learn this material for tomorrow's test if you're not part of the group?"

The next day, both Rashawn and Dean did poorly on the test of meteorology concepts. But because Rashawn and Dean each had a long history of poor school achievement, terms such as *inattentiveness, slow learner, attention deficit disorder, learning disabilities,* and *behavioral disorders* were sometimes used by teachers as "explanations" for their lack of academic success. But another explanation for the two boys' low test scores is also possible. Perhaps their poor scores—as well as their chronic under-achievement in school—were directly influenced by the instruction they typically received.

Neither boy had actively participated during the previous day's lesson. Instead of being active learners who made frequent responses to the lesson's content, both boys were, at best, passive observers. Educational research has made one finding very clear: *Students who respond actively and often usually learn more than students who passively attend to ongoing instruction.* (For reviews of this research, see Fisher and Berliner [1985] and Greenwood, Delquadri, and Hall [1984].) Although most teachers

recognize the importance of active student participation, it is difficult to accomplish during group instruction. A common strategy during whole class instruction is for the teacher to pose a question or problem to the entire class and then to call on one student to answer. This technique often results in more frequent responses by high-achieving students and few or no responses by low-achieving students such as Rashawn and Dean (Maheady, Mallete, Harper, & Saca, 1991). Response cards are one alternative to the traditional hand raising (HR) and one-student-participating-at-a-time method of group instruction.

Response Cards

Response cards (RCs) are cards, signs, or items that are simultaneously held up by all students to display their responses to a question or problem presented by the teacher. Although response cards can take many forms, they are of two basic types: preprinted and write-on. When using *preprinted response cards,* each student selects from a personal set of cards the card with the answer he or she wishes to display. Examples of preprinted RCs include *Yes/True* and *No/False* cards, numbers, colors, traffic signs, molecular structures, and parts of speech. Instead of a set of different cards, a single preprinted RC with multiple answers can be given to each student (e.g., a card with clearly marked sections identified as proteins, fat, carbohydrate, vitamins, and minerals for use in a lesson on healthful eating habits). In its humblest version, the preprinted card with multiple responses is a "pinch card" because the student responds by simply holding up the cards with thumb and forefinger and "pinches" or points to the part of the card displaying his or her answer. Brightly colored plastic clothespins make excellent "pinching" tools; students simply clip the pin on the selected part of the response card and hold the cards overhead. Preprinted RCs may also have built-in, movable devices for displaying answers, such as a cardboard clock with movable hour and minute hands.

Preprinted response cards can be developed for any curriculum area or lesson content.

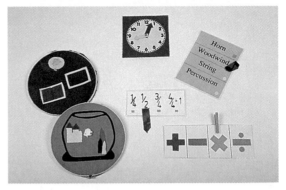

The movable parts on these response cards let students select or create different answers.

When using *write-on response cards,* students mark or write their answers to each instructional item on blank cards or boards that are erased between learning trials. A set of 40 durable write-on response cards can be obtained by purchasing a 4 foot by 8 foot sheet of white laminated "bathroom" board sold in most builders' supply stores and lumberyards. The cost is generally less than $20, including the charge for cutting the sheet into individual 9 inch by 12 inch response cards. Markers can be obtained through most office and art supply stores. Use "dry erase" markers (one good brand is EXPO) or china markers. Paper towels or facial tissues will easily wipe clear the dry erase markers. If china markers are used, a bit more "elbow grease" is required to erase answers; old cloth towels work better.

Students can also use small chalkboards as write-on response cards, but students' responses may be difficult for the teacher to see in a full-size classroom. Write-on response cards can also be custom-made to provide background or organizing structure for students' responses. For example, music students might mark notes on a response card with permanent treble and bass clef scales, and students in a driver's education class could draw where their car should go on response cards on which various traffic and street intersections are permanently shown.

Research on Response Cards

Response cards have been developed and evaluated through a series of studies conducted in both regular and special education classrooms at the elementary, middle, and secondary levels (see Heward, 1994). In an experiment representative of this group of studies, Gardner, Heward, and Grossi (1994) compared the use of write-on RCs with HR during whole-class science lessons in an inner-city fifth-grade classroom. The study produced three major findings.

First, students responded to teacher-posed questions an average of 21.8 times per 30-minute session when RCs were used, compared with a mean of only 1.5 academic responses when the teacher called on individual students to respond orally. (Look at the accompanying figure and think of Student 3 as Rashawn and Student 4 as Dean.) The higher partic-

With write-on response cards, each student in the class can answer every question his or her teacher asks about the story just read.

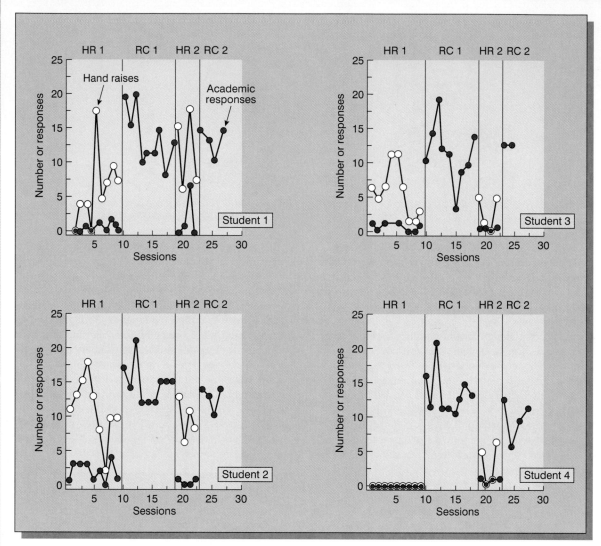

Number of academic responses to teacher-posed questions and hand raises by four fifth-grade students during whole-class science lessons in which students participated by hand raising (HR) or response cards (RC). Source: From "Effects of Response Cards on Student Participation and Academic Achievement: A Systematic Replication with Inner-City Students during Whole-class Science Instruction" by R. Gardner, III, W. L. Heward, & T. A. Grossi. Journal of Applied Behavior Analysis, 1994, Vol. 27, p. 67. Reprinted by permission.

ipation rate achieved with RCs takes on additional significance when its cumulative effect is calculated over the course of a 180-day school year. On the basis of the results of this study, if RCs were used instead of HR for just 30 minutes per day, each student would make more than 3,700 additional academic responses during the school year.

Second, all 22 students scored higher on next-day quizzes and on 2-week review tests that followed lessons with RCs than they did on quizzes and tests that followed lessons with HR.

Third, all but one student preferred RCs over raising their hands to be called on.

Suggestions for Using Response Cards in the Classroom

- Model several question-and-answer trials and provide students with practice on how to use them.
- Maintain a lively pace throughout the lesson (keep the intervals between trials short).
- Give clear cues when students are to hold up and put down their cards.
- Provide feedback based on the "majority response" (see Heward, Courson, & Narayan [1989] for suggestions on how to do this).
- Remember that students can benefit and learn from watching others; do not let students think it is cheating to look at classmates' response cards.

Specific Suggestions for Using Preprinted Response Cards

- Design and construct the cards to be as easy to see as possible (e.g., consider size, print type, color codes).
- Make the cards easy for students to manipulate and display (e.g., put answers on both sides of the cards so that students can see what they are showing the teacher, attach a group of related cards to a ring).
- Begin instruction on new content with a small set of fact/concept cards (perhaps only two), gradually adding additional cards as students' skills improve.

Specific Suggestions for Using Write-On Response Cards

- Limit language-based responses to one or two words.
- Keep a few extra markers on hand.
- Be sure students do not hesitate to respond because they are concerned about making spelling mistakes: you might (a) provide several practice trials with new words or terms before the lesson begins; (b) write new words or important technical terms on the chalkboard or overhead projector and tell students to refer to them during the lesson; or (c) use the "don't worry" technique, telling students to try their best but that misspellings will not be counted against them.
- Students enjoy doodling on their response cards. After a good lesson, let students draw on the cards a few minutes.

behavior problems. Robins used structured interviews to gather such information as work history, alcohol and drug use, performance in the armed services, arrest, social relationships, and marital history. A control group of 100 adults who grew up in the same communities as the subjects was used for comparison. The results were significant. Of those adults who had been referred to a clinic for behavior problems as children, 45% had five or more antisocial traits. Only 4% of those in the control group showed that many antisocial characteristics. In analyzing the results further, Robins found that those who as children had been referred to the clinic for antisocial behavior—theft, fighting, discipline problems in school, truancy, and the like—had the most difficulty adjusting as adults. Furthermore, as adults, they tended to raise children who had a higher incidence of problem behaviors than normal, thus continuing the cycle. As Walker et al. note:

> Preschool children, particularly boys, engage in oppositional, overly active, pestering, random, and unfocused forms of behavior that do not seem serious at this developmental level. However, the manifestations of this behavior pattern in adolescence are *very* different and have great salience and impact. . . . It is very important to note that preschoolers who show the early signs of antisocial behavior patterns do not grow out of them. Rather, as they move throughout their school careers, they grow *into* these unfortunate patterns with disastrous results to themselves and oth-

ers. This myth that preschoolers will outgrow antisocial behavior is pervasive among many teachers and early educators and is very dangerous because it leads professionals to do nothing early on when the problem can be effectively addressed. (p. 47)

Withdrawn Behavior

Some children with emotional and behavioral disorders are anything but aggressive. Their problem is the opposite—too little social interaction with others. They are said to have *internalizing* behavioral disorders. Although children who consistently act immature and withdrawn do not present the threat to others that antisocial children do, their behavior creates a serious impediment to their development. These children seldom play with others their own age. They usually do not have the necessary social skills to make friends and have fun, and they often retreat into daydreams and fantasies. Some are fearful of things without reason, frequently complain of being sick or hurt, and go into deep bouts of depression. Obviously, such behavioral patterns limit the child's chances to take part in and learn from the school and leisure activities in which normal children participate.

Because children with internalizing problems may be less disturbing to others, there is the danger of their not being identified. Happily, the outlook is fairly good for the child with mild or moderate degrees of withdrawn and immature behavior who is fortunate enough to have competent teachers and other school professionals responsible for his or her development. Carefully outlining the social skills the child should learn and gradually and systematically arranging opportunities for and rewarding those behaviors often prove successful.

> These children make up Quay's (1975) personality disorder and immaturity dimensions.

> Social skills training is discussed later in this chapter.

✴ Causes of Emotional and Behavioral Disorders

Several theories and conceptual models have been proposed to explain abnormal behavior. Regardless of the conceptual model from which behavioral disorders are viewed, the suggested causes of disordered behavior can be grouped into two major categories: biological and environmental.

Biological Factors

For the vast majority of children with emotional and behavioral disorders, there is no evidence of organic injury or disease; that is, they appear to be physically healthy and sound. Some experts believe that all children are born with a biologically determined temperament. Although a child's inborn temperament may not in itself cause a behavior problem, it may predispose the child to problems. Thus, certain events that might not produce abnormal behavior in a child with an easy-going temperament might result in disordered behavior by the child with a difficult temperament (Thomas & Chess, 1984; Thomas, Chess, & Birch, 1968). Even when a clear biological impairment exists, however, no one has been able to say with certainty whether the physiological abnormality actually causes the behavior problem or is just associated with it in some unknown way.

Environmental Factors

Environmental factors involve events in the child's life that affect the way he or she acts. Environmental factors are considered important in the development of emotional and behavioral disorders in all conceptual models (except within a strict biological stance, which few subscribe to). Which events are important and how they are analyzed, however, are viewed differently by professionals with different approaches (e.g., a behavior analyst and a cognitive psychologist).

Dodge (1993) has identified three primary causal factors that contribute to the development of conduct disorder and antisocial behavior: (a) an adverse early rearing environment, (b) an aggressive pattern of behavior displayed on entering school, and (c) social rejection by peers. Considerable research evidence supports Dodge's contention that these causal factors operate in temporal sequence (Patterson, Reid, & Dishion, 1992; Wahler & Dumas, 1986). The two major settings in which these events take place are home and school.

The Influence of Home

The relationship that children have with their parents, particularly during the early years, is critical to the way they learn to act. Observation and analysis of parent-child interaction patterns show that parents who treat their children with love, are sensitive to their children's needs, and provide praise and attention for desired behaviors tend to have normal children with positive behavioral characteristics. Antisocial children often come from homes in which parents are inconsistent disciplinarians, use harsh and excessive punishment, and show little love and affection for good behavior (Becker, 1964; Walker et al., 1995). In a longitudinal study examining the behavior and school performance of seventh-grade boys as a correlate of various factors present during the fourth grade, ineffective discipline and infrequent parental involvement with the child proved the best predictor of delinquency in the seventh grade (Walker, Stieber, Ramsey, & O'Neill, 1991).

Because of the research on the relationship between parental child-rearing practices and behavior problems, some mental health professionals have been quick to pin the blame for children's behavior problems on parents. But the relationship between parent and child is dynamic and reciprocal; in other words, the behavior of the child affects the behavior of the parents just as much as the parents' actions affect the child's actions (Patterson, 1980, 1982, 1986; Sameroff & Chandler, 1975). Therefore, it is not practical, at the least, and wrong, at the worst, to place the blame for abnormal behavior in young children on their parents. Instead, professionals must work with parents to help them systematically change certain aspects of the parent-child relationship in an effort to prevent and modify these problems.

See Chapter 13 for an in-depth discussion of working with parents.

The Influence of School

School is where children spend the largest portion of their time outside the home. Therefore, it makes sense to carefully observe what takes place in schools in an effort to identify other events that may cause problem behavior. Also, because most children with emotional and behavioral disorders are not identified as such until they are in school, it seems reasonable to question whether the school actually contributes to the incidence of behavioral disorders. Some professionals have gone further than simply questioning; they think that schooling is the major cause of children's emotional and behavioral disorders. There is no evidence, however, to support this contention. As with physiological or family causes, we cannot say for sure whether a child's school experiences are the lone cause of the behavior problems, but we can identify ways the school can influence or contribute to the child's emotional disturbance (e.g., through inappropriate expectations or inconsistent management).

Several studies have demonstrated that what takes place in the classroom can maintain and actually strengthen deviant behavioral patterns even though the teacher is trying to help the child (Bostow & Bailey, 1969; Thomas, Becker, & Armstrong, 1968; Walker & Buckley, 1973). Walker (1979) concluded:

> It is apparent that a child's behavior pattern at school is the result of a complex interaction of (1) the behavior pattern the child has been taught at home, including attitudes toward school, (2) the experiences the child has had with different teachers in the school setting, and (3) the relationship between the child and his/her current teacher(s). Trying to determine in what proportion the child's behavior pattern is attributable to each of these learning sources is an impossible and unnecessary task. Deviant child behavior can be changed very effectively without knowing the original causes for its acquisition and development. (p. 7)

✳ *Identification and Assessment*

As was stressed in the discussion of learning disabilities (Chapter 5), the primary purpose of assessment is not to determine whether the child *has something* called an emotional and behavioral disorder, but to see whether the child's behavior is *different enough to warrant special services* and, if so, to indicate what those services should be.

Many school districts do not use any systematic method for identifying children with emotional and behavioral disorders. Why? Because most children with emotional and behavioral disorders identify themselves. They stand out. This does not mean, however, that identification is always a sure thing. Identification of emotional disturbance is always more difficult with younger children because the behavior of all young children changes quickly and often. Also, some withdrawn children go undetected because their problems do not draw the attention of parents and teachers. Antisocial children, on the other hand, seldom go unnoticed.

Some have speculated that systematic screening and identification methods are not used because the schools would identify many more children than they could serve (Kauffman, 1993b). If only a portion of the children with behavior problems can be served, those children with the most obvious and severe disturbances will receive the services, and they are clearly identifiable without formal methods.

Screening Tests

Assessment of emotional and behavioral disorders, as with all disabilities, answers four basic questions concerning special education services: (a) Who might need help? (b) Who really does need help (who is eligible)? (c) What kind of help is needed? and (d) Is the help benefiting the student? The first question is answered through **screening,** a process of eliminating children who are not likely to be disabled and of identifying those who either show signs of behavioral disturbance or seem to be at risk for developing behavior problems. Children identified via the screening process then undergo more thorough assessment to determine their eligibility for special education and their specific educational needs.

Children who display patterns of antisocial behavior on entering school run the risk of developing more serious and long-standing behavior problems as they progress through school and life (Patterson, Cipaldi, & Bank, 1991; Welby, Dodge, & Valente, 1993). Walker et al. (1995) stress the importance of systematically screening and identifying as early as possible those children who are at risk for developing serious patterns of antisocial behavior. But before a problem can be addressed, it must be recognized. Walker et al. recommend the following guidelines for early screening and identification of students at risk for antisocial behavioral patterns:

- A proactive rather than a reactive process should be used.
- To obtain the broadest possible perspective on the target student's at-risk status, a multiagent (teacher, parent, observer) and multisetting (classroom, playground, home) approach to screening should be employed.
- At-risk students should be screened as early as possible—ideally at the preschool and kindergarten levels.
- Teacher nominations and rankings or ratings should be used in the early stages of screening and supplemented later in the process by direct observations, school records, peer and parent ratings, and other sources.

Most screening devices consist of behavior checklists that are completed by teachers, parents, peers, and/or children themselves. One widely used screening test for emotional and behavioral disorders is *A Process for In-School Screening of Children with Emotional Handicaps* (Bower & Lambert, 1962). This device employs ratings of the child's behavior by his or her teacher and peers and the child. If the child is rated negatively by the teacher and classmates or by him- or herself, it is suggested that the child be evaluated further. The instrument has three forms: one with rating scales and questions appropriate for kindergarten through 3rd grade, one for 4th through 7th grade, and one for 8th through 12th grade.

The *Achenbach Behavior Checklist* is a screening instrument that can be used by teachers or parents of children aged 6 to 16 (Achenbach, 1991). The teacher's form includes 112 behaviors (e.g., "cries a lot," "not liked by other pupils") on a 3-point scale: "Not True," "Somewhat or Sometimes True," or "Very True or Often True." The *Revised Behavior Problem Checklist* (Quay & Peterson, 1987) consists of 89 items designed to identify and classify children's behavior problems across six dimensions: Quay's (1975) original four of conduct disorder, anxiety-withdrawal, immaturity, and socialized aggression—plus *psychotic behavior* (repetitive speech, expresses strange ideas) and *motor excess* (restlessness).

Research on the use of behavior checklists has generally found low **interrater agreement** (e.g., Simpson, 1991; Simpson & Halpin, 1986). Simpson (1991) concluded that

> rating the behavior of children remains an extremely subjective activity. Even when the same type of raters (i.e., regular education teachers) rate the same child in the same behavioral context (i.e., the school situation), one can still expect marked differences in the ratings.... [T]he recommendation is obvious, ... clinicians should collect behavior ratings from as many raters as possible before reaching diagnostic conclusions about a child. (p. 71)

A recently developed and promising screening instrument is the *Systematic Screening for Behavioral Disorders* (SSBD) (Walker & Severson, 1990). The SSBD, which was normed and field-tested in school districts throughout the country, identifies students who may have increased risk for behavioral disorders (Walker et al., 1988). The SSBD employs a 3-step **multiple-gating screening** process for narrow-

Many districts now require an intermediate step between screening and full-scale assessment. This step consists of interventions in the regular classroom designed to maintain the child in the regular classroom and to prevent a suspected or developing problem from getting worse.

Interrater agreement (also called *interobserver agreement*) is the extent to which the data recorded by two persons who have observed the same events, or in this case completed the same checklist for the same child, match or agree with one another.

ing down the number of children suspected of having serious behavior problems. In Stage I of the SSBD, classroom teachers rank-order every student in their classrooms according to behavioral profiles on two dimensions: externalizing problems (antisocial behavior, acting out, aggression) and internalizing problems (withdrawal, anxiety, little interaction with peers). Only the top three students on each list progress to Stage II, the Critical Events Index.

> Critical events are behavioral pinpoints of high salience and intensity that do not depend on frequency to define their severity. Any occurrence of these target behaviors is viewed as an indicator of major disruption of social-behavioral adjustment processes in school. Critical events have been characterized as analogous to "behavioral earthquakes" in terms of their ecological disruptiveness and severity. Because of their salience and low base rates of occurrence, critical events are viewed as indicative of serious behavioral pathology and may strongly reinforce negative peer and teacher social perception biases toward students who exhibit them. (Todis, Severson, & Walker, 1990, pp. 75–76)

The 33 items that make up the Critical Events Index were developed from previous research on teachers' standards and behavioral expectations (Walker & Rankin, 1983). They include such externalizing behaviors as "is physically aggressive with other students" and "makes lewd or obscene gestures" and such internalizing behaviors as "vomits after eating" and "has auditory or visual hallucinations." Students who exceed normative criteria on the Critical Events Index advance to Stage III of the SSBD, which consists of direct and repeated observations during independent seatwork periods in the classroom and on the playground during recess. Children who meet or exceed cutoff criteria for either or both observational measures are referred to child study teams for further evaluation.

The SSBD is the most systematic, fully developed instrument presently available for screening children for possible emotional and behavioral disorders. Several adaptations of the SSBD have been developed and field-tested for use with preschool children (Feil & Becker, 1993; Sinclair, Del-Homme, & Gonzalez, 1993; Walker, Severson, & Feil, 1994).

Projective Tests

A **projective test** consists of ambiguous stimuli (e.g., "What does this inkblot look like to you?") or open-ended tasks (e.g., "Complete this sentence for me: 'Most girls . . . '"). It is assumed the subject's responses to such items that have no right or wrong answer will reveal true personality characteristics. The most famous projective test is the *Rorschach Test* (Rorschach, 1942), which consists of a set of 10 cards, each containing an inkblot, the left and right halves being mirror images of each other. The subject is shown one card at a time and told, "Tell me what you see, what it might be for you. There are no right or wrong answers." Another well-known projective test is the *Thematic Apperception Test* (TAT) (Morgan & Murray, 1935). A person taking the TAT is shown a series of pictures and is asked to make up a story about each picture, telling who the people are; what they are doing, thinking, and feeling; and how it will turn out.

A projective test specifically developed for screening children with emotional disorders is the *Draw a Person: Screening Procedure for Emotional Disturbance,* in which the child is asked to draw three pictures: a man, a woman, and him- or herself (Naglieri, McNeish, & Bardos, 1991). Studies have shown that children in programs for students with emotional and behavior problems include in their drawings a statistically higher frequency of signs (e.g., distorted body parts, frowning mouth) associated with emotional disturbance than do nondisabled children (McNeish & Naglieri, 1993; Naglieri & Pfeiffer, 1992).

Although interesting, the results of projective tests have proven to be of minimal value in prescribing appropriate intervention. Children often do not respond in a testing or interview situation in the same way they do in the classroom or at home. Also, these assessment procedures test an indirect and extremely limited sample of a child's behavioral repertoire, and just as important, they do not assess how the child typically acts over a period of time. One-time measures are not sufficient as a basis for either identifying the presence of an emotional or behavioral disorder or planning education and treatment.

Direct Observation and Measurement of Behavior

In recent years, direct and frequent measurement has been increasingly used for assessing children with emotional and behavioral disorders. With this method, the actual behaviors that cause a child to be considered disturbed in the first place are clearly specified and observed in the settings where they normally occur every day (e.g., in the classroom, on the playground). Precise statements can then be made about what problem behaviors must be weakened and what prosocial and adaptive behaviors should occur with greater frequency. In addition to providing specific information on the frequency of occurrence of the behaviors targeted for intervention, direct and repeated measurement also enables the teacher to observe systematically and note what events typically occur before and after the behavior(s) of concern (Cooper, Heron, & Heward, 1987; Sulzer-Azaroff & Mayer, 1991). This information can be very helpful in designing effective interventions for changing behavior.

Direct and frequent observation of student behavior enables precise identification of what behaviors are most in need of change and whether our educational efforts are working.

Kauffman (1993b) makes a strong case for direct and frequent measurement with children with emotional and behavioral disorders.

> The intractability of defining and classifying youngsters' *disorders* does not, fortunately, preclude useful definition and measurement of behavior. . . . Indeed, the teacher who cannot or will not pinpoint and measure the relevant behaviors of the students he or she is teaching is probably not going to be very effective. . . . Not to define precisely and to measure these behavioral excesses and deficiencies, then, is a fundamental error; it is akin to the malpractice of a nurse who decides not to measure vital signs (heart rate, respiration rate, temperature, and blood pressure), perhaps arguing that he or she is too busy, that subjective estimates of vital signs are quite adequate, that vital signs are only superficial estimates of the patient's health, or that vital signs do not signify the nature of the underlying pathology. The teaching profession is dedicated to the task of changing behavior—changing behavior demonstrably for the better. What can one say, then, of educational practice that does not include precise definition and reliable measurement of the behavioral change induced by the teacher's methodology? *It is indefensible.* (pp. 491–492)

✳ *Prevalence*

Estimates vary tremendously as to how many children have emotional and behavioral disorders, from 0.5% to 20% or more of the school-age population. On the basis of his survey of California schools, Bower (1981) concluded that two or three children in the average classroom (about 10%) can be expected to show signs of emotional disturbance. In a longitudinal study by Rubin and Balow (1978), 7.4% of the 1,586 children in the sample were considered to have a behavior problem by every teacher who rated them during the 3-year period.

With such widely varying estimates, people obviously are using different criteria to decide whether a child is behaviorally disordered. The difference in prevalence figures stems as much from how the figures are collected as from the use of different definitions (Kauffman, 1993b). Most surveys ask teachers to identify students in their classes who display behavior problems at that point in time. Many children exhibit inappropriate behavior for short periods, and such one-shot screening procedures will identify them, as in the Rubin and Balow (1978) study in which more than half of all students were identified as having behavior problems by at least one teacher at some time during their elementary school careers. As Hewett and Taylor (1980) observe:

> In our experience, when you walk into any elementary classroom, you can usually pick out two or three children who are "not with it" and who are visible enough to stand out from other members of the class in terms of their problem behavior. And if you stay long enough, you can usually determine if they "fit" within the teacher's range of tolerance for behavioral differences. Whether they would be the same children a week or semester later is debatable. Thus, we get almost no meaning from incidence figures. (p. 42)

A major study of education for children with emotional and behavioral disorders that investigated 26 programs in 13 states during the 1987–89 school years supports the "two or three students per classroom" figure: "Estimates suggest 10% of the child population has behavior problems serious or sustained enough to warrant intervention, [and] 3% to 5% are judged to be seriously emotionally disturbed"

(Knitzer, Steinberg, & Fleisch, 1990, n.p.). Surveys suggest that the prevalence of conduct disorder varies between 2% and 6% of the general school-age population, which translates into a total figure ranging from 1.3 to 3.8 million cases (Kazdin, 1993).

Annual reports from the federal government, however, show far fewer children being served. The 402,668 children aged 6 to 21 who received special education under the seriously emotionally disturbed category during the 1992–93 school year under the IDEA represented only about 0.7% of the school-age population (U.S. Department of Education, 1994). Although this figure marked the greatest number of children with emotional and behavioral disorders ever served and ranked emotional disturbance as the fourth largest category of special education, it means that only 20% to 30% of children with emotional and behavioral disorders are being served.

The number of children being served represents less than half of the 2% estimate the federal government has traditionally used in its estimates of funding and personnel needs for students with emotional and behavioral disorders. Kauffman (1993b) believes that social policy and economic factors caused the government to first reduce (from 2% to 1.2%) its estimate of the prevalence of behavioral disorders and then to stop publishing an estimate altogether. "The government obviously prefers not to allow wide discrepancies between prevalence estimates and the actual number of children served. It is easier to cut prevalence estimates than to serve more students" (p. 50).

Regardless of what prevalence study one turns to, it is evident there are many thousands of school children whose disordered behavior is handicapping their educational progress but who are not presently receiving the special education they need. Although the IDEA clearly mandates that all children with disabilities receive individualized special education services, the definition included in the law may be partially responsible for the great disparity between the estimated prevalence of children with emotional and behavioral disorders and the number of such children receiving special education (Bower, 1982; Kauffman, 1986, 1993b; Knitzer, 1982; Wood, 1985). The uncertain meaning of many aspects of the definition allows determination of whether a child is behaviorally disordered to be more a function of a school district's available resources (its ability to provide the needed services) than a function of the child's actual needs for such services.

> Faced with a shortage of adequately trained personnel and insurmountable budget problems, what can we expect of school officials? They cannot risk litigation and loss of federal funds by identifying students they cannot serve. . . . The social policy mandate changes the question, at least for those who manage budgets, from "how many students with emotional and behavioral disorders are there in our schools?" to "how many can we afford to serve?" And to save face and try to abide by the law, it is tempting to conclude that there are, indeed, just as many students with emotional and behavioral disorders as one is able to serve. (Kauffman, 1993b, p. 51)

Gender

Boys are much more likely than girls to be identified as emotionally and behaviorally disordered. Surveys of school-age children with behavioral disorders have found a male-to-female ratio of approximately 4:1 (Cullinan, Epstein, & Kauffman, 1984; Cullinan, Epstein, & Sabornie, 1992). Boys identified as emotionally and behaviorally disordered are likely to have externalizing disorders and to exhibit antisocial, aggressive behavior. Girls with emotional and behavioral disorders are more likely to show internalizing disorders such as anxiety and social withdrawal.

Juvenile Delinquency

Although the word *delinquent* is a legal term, the offenses an adolescent commits to be labeled delinquent constitute a behavioral disorder. In 1988 there were more than 1.6 million arrests of children under the age of 18 (U.S. Department of Commerce, 1990). The rate and seriousness of crimes committed by juveniles have been increasing. Snarr and Wolford (1985) point out that 40% of all violent crimes are committed by juveniles but that this age group comprises only about 20% of the total population. Persons under the age of 18 accounted for 16.1% of all arrests in 1988, but the same age group represented 28.2% of all arrests for serious crimes. Arrest rates for juveniles increase sharply during the junior high years. This pattern probably reflects both the greater harm adolescents can cause to society as a result of their inappropriate behavior and the fact that younger children are often not arrested (and therefore do not show up on the records) for committing the same acts that lead to the arrest of an older child.

Younger children, however, are being arrested; in 1988 more than 600,000 arrests of children under age 15 were made. And younger children are committing more serious and violent crimes than in the past (Cavan & Ferdinand, 1975). Children under the age of 15 account for 5.2% of all arrests, but they are responsible for 11.1% of all arrests for serious crimes (U.S. Department of Commerce, 1990a). Although boys have generally committed crimes involving aggression (e.g., assault, burglary) and girls have been associated with sex-related offenses (e.g., prostitution), more and more violent offenses are being committed by girls (Siegel & Senna, 1991). Offenses involving the use of illegal drugs have also increased tremendously in recent years.

About half of all juvenile delinquents are *recidivists* (repeat offenders). Recidivists are more likely to begin their criminal careers at an early age (usually by age 12), commit more serious crimes, and continue a pattern of repeated antisocial behavior as adults (Tolan, 1987). The total number of criminal offenses committed by youths against others and property is, of course, impossible to determine. Many crimes go unreported or unsolved, which leaves identification of the perpetrators unknown; however, Table 6.1 indicates the possible extent of the problem and the many crimes often committed by individual juvenile offenders. Originally intended to show the ability of positive peer-culture counseling groups to provide confidentiality and to generate a feeling of trust among the youths and their adult leader, this table gives further information on the characteristics of juvenile offenders.

✳ *Educational Approaches*

Several different approaches to educating emotionally disturbed children are used, each with its own definitions, purposes of treatment, and types of intervention.

Theoretical and Conceptual Models

On the basis of the work of Rhodes and his colleagues (Rhodes & Head, 1974; Rhodes & Tracy, 1972a, 1972b), Kauffman (1993b) identifies six conceptual models

TABLE 6.1
Reported and unreported crimes by juvenile offenders

OFFENSES KNOWN TO COURT	OFFENSES NOT KNOWN TO COURT DISCUSSED IN GROUP
Student A Petty larceny; brutality (holding 9-year-old boy over burning trash barrel).	Auto theft; breaking and entering.
Student B Beyond control of parent; sexual intercourse with 12-year-old sister.	Auto theft; attempted rape; stealing; shoplifting; breaking and entering; vandalism; sexual acts with animals; incest with mother.
Student C Shoplifting; disorderly conduct; grand larceny; breaking and entering; destroying private property; truancy.	Habituation to drugs; grand larceny; petty larceny; arson; auto theft; carrying concealed weapons.
Student D Curfew violation; auto theft; breaking and entering; public intoxication; operating motor vehicle without license.	Carrying deadly weapon; robbery; arson; auto theft; multiple breaking and entering; three instances of assault and battery.
Student E Truancy; runaway; obtaining merchandise under false pretenses.	Habituation to drugs; shoplifting; auto theft; vandalism; "rolling queers" for money (assault, battery, robbery).
Student F Petty larceny; contempt of court; curfew violation; breaking and entering.	Malicious cutting and wounding; housebreaking; stealing; forgery; shoplifting.
Student G Breaking and entering; attempted safe burglary; safe burglary.	Carrying a deadly weapon; malicious cutting and wounding; burglary; concealing stolen property; fraud; stealing from automobiles.
Student H Shoplifting; runaway; violation of probation.	Breaking and entering; stealing.
Student I Public intoxication; petty larceny; carrying concealed deadly weapon; burglary; attempted safecracking.	Shoplifting; driving without license; breaking and entering.

Source: Reprinted with permission from Vorrath, Harry H., and Larry K. Brendtro. *Positive Peer Culture.* 2nd Ed. (New York: Aldine de Gruyter). Copyright © 1985 by Harry H. Vorrath and Larry K. Brendtro, p. 84.

for understanding and treating emotional and behavioral disorders. Let's take a brief look at each one in the following subsections.

Biogenic

The biogenic model suggests that deviant behavior is a physical disorder with genetic or medical causes. It implies that these causes must be cured to treat the emotional disturbance. Treatment may be medical or nutritional.

Psychodynamic

Based on the idea that a disordered personality develops out of the interaction of experience and internal mental processes (ego, id, and superego) that are out of balancc, a psychodynamic model relies on psychotherapy and creative projects for the child (and often the parents), rather than academic remediation.

Psychoeducational

For a description of life-space interviewing and suggestions on how to use it, see Wood and Long (1991); for a debate over its effectiveness, see Gardner (1990a, 1990b) and Long (1990).

The psychoeducational model is concerned with "unconscious motivations and underlying conflicts (hallmarks of psychodynamic models) yet also stresses the realistic demands of everyday functioning in school, home, and community" (Kauffman, 1993b, p. 105). Intervention focuses on therapeutic discussions, such as *life-space interviews,* to allow children to understand their behavior rationally and to plan to change it (Rich, Beck, & Coleman, 1982).

Humanistic

The humanistic model suggests that the child with emotional and behavioral disorders is not in touch with his or her own feelings and cannot find self-fulfillment in traditional educational settings. Treatment takes place in an open, personalized setting where the teacher serves as a nondirective, nonauthoritarian "resource and catalyst" for the child's learning.

Ecological

The ecological model stresses the interaction of the child with the people around him or her and with social institutions. Treatment involves teaching the child to function within the family, school, neighborhood, and larger community.

Behavioral

Applied behavior analysis was introduced in Chapter 4.

The behavioral model assumes that the child's inappropriate and maladaptive behavior has been learned from his or her history of interactions with the environment. The behaviorally oriented educator uses applied behavior analysis techniques to help the child learn new, appropriate responses and eliminate inappropriate ones.

Few programs or teachers use only the techniques suggested by one model; most programs and teachers employ an *eclectic* approach, which means they combine a number of theories, philosophies, and methods in their work with students with emotional and behavioral disorders (Beare, 1991). The models themselves are not entirely discrete; they overlap in certain areas. Sometimes the difference is mostly a matter of wording; the actual classroom practices of teachers using the different models may be quite similar.

Our main purpose here is to make you aware of these different approaches. It is beyond the scope of this text to do justice to a description of each model and to compare and contrast them. We will say, however, that little empirical evidence attests to the effectiveness of treatment approaches based on the psychodynamic model of underlying subconscious causes of children's problems (Levitt, 1957, 1963). Cullinan, Epstein, and Lloyd (1991) compared the psychoeducational, behavioral, and ecological models. With respect to the effectiveness with which each model can cause desired improvements in behavior at the time and place of intervention, they judged that there was weak scientific support for the psychoeducational model and too little research available on which to evaluate the ecological model. "In contrast, there is a substantial body of good research demonstrating that many behavioral interventions can bring about swift, fairly reliable, and often dramatic improvements in problem behaviors" (pp. 153–154).

For examples of research on behavioral interventions, see the journals *Behavioral Disorders* and the *Journal of Applied Behavior Analysis.*

Cullinan et al. (1991) concluded that none of the models provides complete guidance on how behavioral disorders come about and how to treat them. "In theory and in practice, what is known about behavioral disorders is far less than what is not known. To change this imbalance must be a major activity of our profession" (p. 155).

Focusing on Alterable Variables

The twofold task of the teacher of children with emotional and behavioral disorders is to help students replace antisocial and maladaptive behaviors with more socially appropriate behaviors. The frequent displays of antisocial behavior, the absence of appropriate social skills, and the academic deficits exhibited by many students with emotional and behavioral disorders make this a staggering teaching challenge. This challenge is made all the more difficult because the teacher seldom, if ever, can control or even know all of the factors affecting a student's behavior. There is typically a host of contributing factors over which the teacher can exert little or no control (e.g., the delinquent friends with whom the student associates before and after school). But it does little good to bemoan the student's past (which no one can alter) or to use all of the things in the student's current life that cannot be changed as an excuse for failing to help the student in the classroom. Special educators should focus their attention and efforts on those aspects of a student's life that they can effectively control. This philosophy might be called "focusing on alterable variables."

> The focus of the special educator's concern should be on the contributing factors that the teacher can alter. Factors over which the teacher has no control may determine how the child or youth is approached initially, but the teacher is called upon to begin working with specific pupils after disorders have appeared. The special educator has two primary responsibilities: first, to make sure that he or she does no further disservice to the student; and second, to manipulate the student's present environment to foster development of more appropriate behavior in spite of unalterable past and present circumstances. Emphasis must be on the present and future, not the past. And although other environments may be important, the teacher's focus

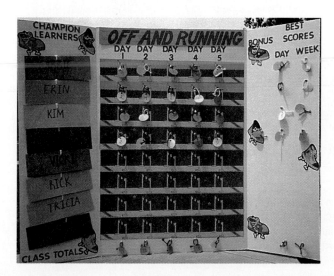

Two powerful instructional variables that teachers can control are the amount and quality of feedback that students receive for their efforts.

must be on the classroom environment. Certainly teachers may profitably extend their influence beyond the classroom, perhaps working with parents to improve the home environment or using community resources for the child's benefit. But talk of influence beyond the classroom, including such high-sounding phrases as ecological management, is patent nonsense until the teacher has demonstrated that he or she can make the classroom environment productive of improved behavior. (Kauffman, 1993b, pp. 490–491)

Teaching Social Skills

Most students with emotional and behavioral disorders show significant deficits in social skills. They often have difficulty expressing their feelings, participating in group activities, and responding to failure or criticism in positive and constructive ways. Understandably, a large part of special education for students with emotional and behavioral disorders consists of social skills instruction.

For detailed information on how to teach social skills, see Cartledge and Milburn (1995); Rutherford, Chipman, DiGangi, and Anderson (1992); and Serna (1993). For a review of 27 studies that examine specific social skills interventions and their effects on students with behavior problems, see Zaragoza, Vaughn, and McIntosh (1991).

TABLE 6.2
Social skills curricula

Some of the many social skills training programs available from commercial publishers are listed here. Most social skills curricula include scripted lesson plans, roleplaying activities, follow-up assignments and activities, suggestions for motivating students, and checklists, rating scales, and/or other methods for assessing student progress. Some programs include videotapes illustrating appropriate and inappropriate behaviors. See Schumaker, Pederson, Hazel, and Meyen (1983) for guidelines and suggestions for evaluating and choosing a social skills training program.

CLASS: Contingencies for Learning Academic and Social Skills (Hops & Walker, 1988). Published by Educational Achievement Systems, Seattle, WA.

Getting Along with Others (Jackson, Jackson, & Monroe, 1983). Includes 32 lessons across 17 social skills areas such as following directions, handling name calling and teasing, and offering to help. Available from Research Press, Dept. 95, P.O. Box 9177, Champaign, IL 61826.

I Can Problem Solve (Shure, 1992). Designed to help children learn to resolve interpersonal problems and prevent antisocial behavior. Available in three age/developmental levels: preschool, K–primary grades, and intermediate elementary grades. Available from Research Press.

RECESS: A Program for Reducing Negative Aggressive Behavior (Walker, Hops, & Greenwood, 1993). Educational Achievement Systems.

Social Skills for Daily Living (Schumaker, Hazel, & Pederson, 1989). Available from American Guidance Service, Publishers Building, 4201 Woodland Road, Circle Pines, MN 55014.

Skillstreaming the Adolescent: A Structured Learning Approach to Teaching Prosocial Skills (Goldstein et al., 1980). Activities designed to increase self-esteem and develop competence in dealing with peers, family, and authority figures. *Skillstreaming* programs for elementary and preschool children are also available. Available from Research Press.

Stephens (1992) has developed an inventory of 132 specific social skills for school-age children grouped into 30 subcategories under four major areas. An assessment device and suggested teaching activities for each skill are included. The four major categories and representative subcategories of Stephens's social skills curriculum are as follows:

1. *Self-related behaviors:* accepting consequences, ethical behavior, expressing feelings, positive attitude toward self
2. *Task-related behaviors:* attending behavior, following directions, performing before others, quality of work
3. *Environmental behaviors:* care for the environment, dealing with emergencies, lunchroom behavior
4. *Interpersonal behaviors:* accepting authority, gaining attention, helping others, making conversations

A large number of social skills curricula and training programs have been developed, field-tested, and made available to educators. Several of the most well known and validated social skills curricula and training programs are shown in Table 6.2.

Values clarification—activities that help students identify their own beliefs and values and how they affect their choices and behavior—can contribute to the overall effectiveness of a social skills training program (Abrams, 1992).

TABLE 6.2 *(continued)*

Social Skills in the Classroom (Stephens, 1992). An inventory of 132 specific social skills grouped in four categories: self-rated behaviors, task-related behaviors, environmental behaviors, and interpersonal behaviors. Available from Psychological Assessment Resources, Odessa, FL.

Taking Part: Introducing Social Skills to Children (Cartledge & Kleefeld, 1991). Helps students in preschool classrooms through third grade learn social skills in six units: making conversation, communicating feelings, expressing oneself, cooperating with peers, playing with peers, and responding to aggression and conflict. Published by American Guidance Service.

The Prepare Curriculum: Teaching Prosocial Competencies (Goldstein, 1988). Activities and materials for middle and high school students in 10 areas, such as problem solving, anger control, stress management, and cooperation. Published by Research Press.

The Walker Social Skills Curriculum Includes *ACCEPTS: A Curriculum for Children's Effective Peer and Teacher Skills* (Walker et al., 1983), designed for children grades K–6, and *ACCESS: Adolescent Curriculum for Communication and Effective Social Skills* (Walker, Todis, Holmes, & Horton, 1988) for students at the middle and high school levels. Available from PRO-ED, 8700 Shoal Creek Blvd., Austin, TX 78757.

Working Together (Cartledge & Kleefeld, 1994). Incorporates stories and activities based on folk literature to teach social skills to students in grades three through six and older students with special needs. Published by American Guidance Service.

Alternative Responses

Students with emotional and behavioral disorders often get into fights and altercations because they lack the social skills needed to handle or defuse provocative incidents. The slightest snub, bump, or misunderstood request—which would be laughed off or ignored by most children—can precipitate an aggressive attack on the part of some students. Knapczyk (1992) taught four secondary students with behavioral disorders positive alternative responses to situations that previously had precipitated aggressive outbursts (see Table 6.3). Instruction consisted of individualized videotape modeling and behavioral rehearsal. Two male students who were leaders in the school served as actors for the videotapes—one playing the role of the subject, simulating his usual reactions to provoking situations and demonstrating appropriate alternative responses, the other acting out the usual reactions of classmates. After watching the videotapes, the subject students discussed the circumstances of the incidents with their special class teacher and practiced specific alternative responses. Not only did treatment result in a decreased frequency of aggressive acts by all four students across several settings, but a concurrent decrease in the number of provoking antecedent events was also noted.

TABLE 6.3
Examples of alternative behaviors a student can learn to emit in response to provoking antecedent events

ANTECEDENT EVENTS	ALTERNATIVE RESPONSES
Participant initiates a greeting and is ignored or called a name	1. Repeat the greeting 2. Greet another person 3. Walk away without saying anything else.
Participant requests an object and request is denied	1. Make request of another person 2. Work on another activity that does not require object
Participant reaches for an object and person tries to retain it	1. Ask politely for object 2. Ask someone else for object 3. Work on another activity until person finishes using object
Participant asks person to engage in an activity and the request is turned down	1. Suggest another activity 2. Ask someone else 3. Start an activity that does not involve another person
Participant touches another person and is pushed or hit by the person	1. Ignore the incident 2. Say "Excuse me" to person 3. Engage person in a conversation or appropriate activity

Source: From "Effects of Developing Alternative Responses on the Aggressive Behavior of Adolescents" by Dennis R. Knapczyk, *Behavioral Disorders,* 1992, Vol. 17, p. 249. Reprinted by permission.

Self-Management: Learning Responsibility and Self-Direction

An increasing amount of research has been conducted on teaching self-control or self-management skills to children, and the results of much of this work are encouraging (Clark & McKenzie, 1989; Rhode, Morgan, & Young, 1983). Many children with emotional and behavioral disorders think they have little control over their lives. Things just seem to happen to them, and being disruptive is their means of reacting to a world that is inconsistent and frustrating. Children who learn self-management skills find out that they can have some control over their own behaviors and, as a result, over their environment.

Self-management strategies are also appealing from the standpoint of generalizing treatment gains from one setting to another. An external control agent (e.g., special education teacher in the resource room) cannot go with the student to all of the settings in which the child needs to exhibit newly learned behavior (e.g., staying in his seat and completing a whole workbook page). But the one person who is always with the student is the student's own self (Baer & Fowler, 1984).

When children learn to observe and record their own behavior, they can see for themselves the effects of various events on their performance. They can also be taught to influence certain events themselves. In one of the first self-management studies with students with emotional and behavioral disorders, Drabman, Spitalnik, and O'Leary (1973) taught a group of eight 9- and 10-year-olds to evaluate and record their social and academic work behaviors. Initially, the students were rewarded with tokens when their own evaluations matched those of the teacher; then, just teacher praise was given for accurate evaluations; finally, the students rated themselves and decided how many tokens they had earned during the day. A classroom token economy was operating during this study. Spot checks showed that the children evaluated themselves accurately and honestly. Disruptive behavior decreased, and academic achievement increased.

Numerous research studies have since demonstrated that children with behavior problems can effectively use **self-monitoring** to help regulate their behavior. Self-monitoring can be aided by a prompt to record the target behavior; for example,

> Self-management research with students with emotional and behavioral disorders is reviewed by Nelson, Smith, Young, and Dodd (1991).

Andy's academic work and social interactions with others have improved since he began self-monitoring and evaluating his own behavior.

For a review of research on self-monitoring as a behavior management technique see Webber, Scheuerman, McCall, and Coleman (1993).

a prerecorded tone from a cassette tape player might serve as the cue to monitor and record one's behavior (Blick & Test, 1987). Lovitt (1995) describes the use of "countoons," which remind children not only what behavior to record but also what consequence they are to self-deliver. Figure 6.1 shows a countoon that was taped to an elementary student's desk, showing her what behavior to monitor (finger snapping), how to record it (by putting an X through the next number on the countoon), and what her self-delivered consequence would be each time (solving 25 arithmetic problems).

An impressive study demonstrating the potential of self-management techniques for the generalization of improved behavior across classroom settings was conducted by Rhode, Morgan, and Young (1983). Six students with emotional and behavioral disorders learned to bring their highly disruptive and off-task behaviors under control in a resource room with a combination of techniques that featured self-evaluation. Initially, the teacher rated each student and awarded points at 15-minute intervals on a scale from 5 (*great*) to 0 (*poor*) for classroom behavior and academic work. Then the students began to evaluate their own behavior with the same rating system (Figure 6.2 shows the card the students used). The teacher continued to rate each student.

The Rhode et al. (1983) study was a **systematic replication** and extension of the earlier research by Drabman et al. (1973). It serves as an excellent example of how the special education knowledge base can progress through an ongoing line of scientific research.

Teacher and students compared their ratings: If the student's rating was within one point of the teacher's, he received the number of points he had given himself. If teacher and student matched exactly, the student earned an additional bonus point. The teacher then began to fade the number of times she also rated the students. After the students were behaving at acceptable levels and accurately self-evaluating their behavior, they began to self-evaluate once every 30 minutes in the regular classroom. Eventually, the self-evaluation cards and point system were withdrawn, and students were encouraged to continue to self-evaluate themselves "privately." Figure 6.3 shows the results of the students' behavior in both the resource room and the regular classroom.

Self-management can also be taught as a social skill in its own right consisting of five elements: (a) selecting and defining the target behavior, (b) observing and

FIGURE 6.1

A countoon that can be taped to a student's desk as a reminder of the target behavior, the need to self-record it, and the self-delivered consequence

Source: "From Tactics for Teaching" (Second Edition) (p. 329) by T. C. Lovitt, 1995, Englewood Cliffs, NJ: Prentice-Hall/Merrill. Reprinted by permission.

FIGURE 6.2
Card used for self-evaluation by students

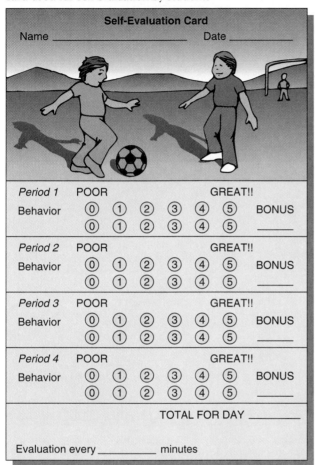

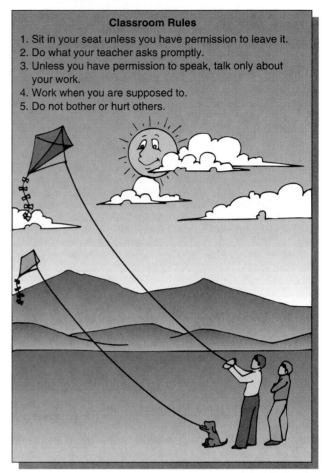

Front of Card   Back of Card

Source: From *Generalization and Maintenance of Treatment Gains on Behaviorally/Emotionally Handicapped Students from Resource Rooms to Regular Classrooms Using Self-Evaluation Procedures* (p. 157) by Ginger Rhode. Unpublished doctoral dissertation, Utah State University, 1981. Reprinted by permission.

recording the target behavior, (c) specifying the procedures for changing the behavior, (d) implementing those procedures, and (e) evaluating the self-management effort (Cooper, Heron, & Heward, 1987). Carter (1993) details a 9-step procedure for helping students plan and carry out a self-management project. Although much more research is needed, teaching students with emotional and behavioral disorders to have some control over their own lives by giving them the skills to make changes in their behavior is a promising approach.

Classroom Management

Managing the classroom environment for students with emotional and behavioral disorders requires a great deal of knowledge and skill. Teachers must know when and how to use behavioral strategies such as **positive reinforcement**, *shaping,*

Adolescents in special education, especially those with emotional and behavioral disorders or learning disabilities, are a high-risk group for alcohol and drug abuse (Kress & Elias, 1993). Self-management training programs might help reduce substance abuse by helping students learn how to avoid and deal with stress and peer pressure.

FIGURE 6.3

Appropriate behavior for six students with emotional and behavioral disorders and randomly selected nondisabled peers

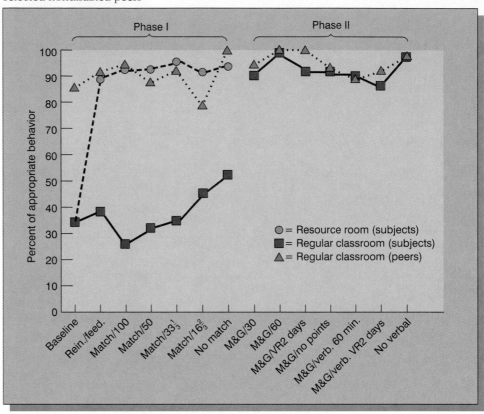

Source: From "Generalization and Maintenance of Treatment Gains on Behaviorally Handicapped Students from Resource Rooms to Regular Classrooms Using Self-Evaluation Procedures" by G. Rhode, D. P. Morgan, and K. R. Young, 1983, *Journal of Applied Behavior Analysis,* Vol. 16, p. 184. Reprinted by permission.

An explanation of these techniques is beyond the scope of this book. See Justen and Howerton (1993) for an explanation and clarification of eight behavior management terms commonly found in the special education literature. A number of excellent books are available for the teacher who wishes to learn more about classroom and behavior management (e.g., Alberto and Troutman, 1995; Epanchin, Townsend, & Stoddard, 1994; Kameenui & Darch, 1995; Kerr & Nelson, 1989; Rhode, Jensen, & Reavis, 1993; Smith & Rivera, 1993; Walker & Shea, 1995).

contingency contracting, **extinction** (ignoring disruptive behavior), **differential reinforcement of other behavior** (reinforcing any behavior except the undesirable response), *response cost,* **time-out** (restricting students' access to reinforcement for a brief time following an inappropriate behavior), and **overcorrection** (requiring restitution beyond the damaging effects of the antisocial behavior, as when a child who takes another child's cookie must return it plus one of her own). These are just some of the behavior management skills needed by a competent teacher of students with emotional and behavioral disorders.

These behavior change techniques should not be implemented as isolated events, but rather incorporated into an overall instructional and classroom management plan that might include a **token economy** and/or a *level system* to help each student learn greater independence and earn more privileges (Barbetta, 1990a, 1990b; Smith & Farrell, 1993).

When designing and implementing classroom management strategies, teachers of students with emotional and behavioral disorders must be careful not to create an environment in which coercion is the primary means by which students are moti-

In a level system, students earn greater independence and more privileges as their behavior improves.

vated to participate and follow rules. Coercive environments, in addition to promoting escape and avoidance behavior by those being coerced, do not teach what to do as much as they focus on what not to do (Sidman, 1989). Teachers of students with emotional and behavioral disorders must strive to design classroom environments that not only are effective in decreasing antisocial behavior but also increase the frequency of positive teacher-student interactions (Gunter, Denny, Jack, Shores, & Nelson, 1993; Shores, Gunter, & Jack, 1993).

Interventions should be selected and matched to the nature of the problem they are designed to solve. Figure 6.4 shows the "intervention ladder" developed by Smith and Rivera (1993) to illustrate a hierarchy of classroom management and disciplinary measures.

> Prevention is the foundation of the ladder, based on the notion that educators should first try to prevent conduct problems. . . . If direct intervention becomes necessary, educators should select interventions on the lower rungs of the ladder before resorting to those found higher up. This requires a sensitive match between infractions and the intervention procedures that educators select. This process requires teachers to continually evaluate the learning environment they have created, monitor their own actions, seek to prevent conduct problems, and intervene purposefully and systematically when the need arises. The selection of interventions aimed at reducing or eliminating violations of conduct codes should reflect a sensitivity to the seriousness of the infractions and the outcome of those measures tried earlier. (pp. 16–17)

The effective teacher of children with emotional and behavioral disorders must have skills beyond arranging environmental variables and measuring behavior. With children who have emotional and behavioral disorders, the way assignments, expectations, and consequences for behavior are communicated to the child can be as important as the consequences themselves. Rothman (1977) stresses the importance of avoiding a win-lose situation, in which the teacher gains status by dominating the child. Rather, a win-win arrangement is the goal—when the child wins, the teacher wins.

Group Process

The "power" of the peer group can be an effective means of producing positive changes in students with behavioral disorders (Barbetta, 1990a; Coleman & Webber, 1988). Implementing a *group process* model, however, is much more complicated than bringing together a group of children and hoping they will benefit from positive

Walker and Shea (1995) describe an 11-step process for designing level systems. West et al. (1995) describe how to use a "musical clock light" to encourage positive classroom behavior.

What similarities do you see between the intervention ladder and the continuum of services discussed in Chapter 2?

FIGURE 6.4
The intervention ladder

Source: From "Effective Discipline" by Deborah Deutsch Smith and Diane M. Rivera, 1993, p. 17. Published by PRO-ED, Austin, TX. Used by permission.

Specific strategies for teaching peers to help one another decrease inappropriate behavior include *peer monitoring*—a student is taught to observe and record a peer's behavior and to provide the peer with feedback (Fowler, Dougherty, Kirby, & Kohler, 1986; Smith & Fowler, 1984) and *peer confrontation*—peers are trained to confront one another when inappropriate behavior occurs or is about to occur, explaining why the behavior is a problem and suggesting or modeling an appropriate alternative response (Salend, Jantzen, & Giek, 1992; Sandler, Arnold, Gable, & Strain, 1987).

peer influence. Most children with emotional and behavioral disorders have not been members of successfully functioning peer groups in which appropriate behavior is valued, nor have many such children learned to accept responsibility for their actions. The teacher's first and most formidable challenge is helping promote group cohesiveness. Barbetta (1991) recommends some basic rules for fostering the development of group cohesiveness:

- Every child is an equal member of the group and, as such, is accountable and responsible to the group.
- The group "moves" as often as possible as one.
- The group works out all major decisions and problems together.
- All major rewards are earned and shared by the group.
- Only in rare instances is a student "removed" from the group (no longer accountable to the group for his or her behavior).
- The teacher functions as a member of the group but has veto power when necessary.

Although group process treatment programs take many forms, most incorporate group meetings and **group-oriented contingencies.** Two types of group meetings are usually held daily. A planning meeting is held each morning in which the group reviews the daily schedule, each group member states a behavioral goal for the day, peers provide support and suggestions to one another for meeting their goals, and a group goal for the day is agreed on. An evaluation meeting is held at the end of each day to discuss how well the individual and group goals were met, and each group member must give and receive positive peer comments. Problem-solving meetings are held whenever any group member, including the teacher, feels the need to discuss a problem. The group identifies the problem, generates several solutions, discusses the likely consequences of each solution, develops a plan for the best solution, and makes verbal commitments to carry out the plan. Group-oriented contingencies specify certain rewards and privileges that are enjoyed by the group if their behavior meets certain criteria (Barbetta, 1990a). The criteria for earning the rewards, as well as the rewards themselves, are determined by the group.

For one teacher's personal reflections on teaching students with emotional and behavioral disorders with a group process approach see "My Return Voyage" later in this chapter.

Teaching Academic Skills

A continuing concern in the field of emotional and behavioral disorders is poor academic achievement. Although students with emotional and behavioral disorders require the help of a specially trained teacher to work on their specific behavior problems, academic instruction cannot be neglected. Most children with emotional and behavioral disorders are already achieving at a rate below that of their nondisabled peers; ignoring the three Rs only puts them further behind. Reading, writing, and arithmetic are as important to children with emotional and behavioral disorders as they are to any child who hopes to function successfully in our society.

Fortunately, most students with emotional and behavioral disorders learn when presented with direct, systematic instruction. Despite the widely recognized and significant deficits in academic achievement experienced by students with emotional and behavioral disorders, a recent review of the literature turned up only 12 research articles specifically investigating academic skill improvement for such students (Ruhl & Berlinghoff, 1992). Clearly, our field has much work ahead.

Students with emotional and behavioral disorders can sometimes learn better social and affective skills in the process of learning how to participate in collaborative learning activities and serving as academic tutors for one another (Cartledge & Cochran, 1993; Cochran, Feng, Cartledge, & Hamilton, 1993).

Affective Traits of a Good Teacher

In addition to academic and behavior management skills, the teacher of children with emotional and behavioral disorders must be able to establish healthy child-teacher relationships. Morse (1976) believes that teachers need two important affective characteristics to relate effectively and positively to emotionally disturbed children. He calls these traits differential acceptance and an empathetic relationship.

Differential acceptance means the teacher can receive and witness frequent and often extreme acts of anger, hate, and aggression from children without responding similarly. Of course, this is much easier said than done. But the teacher of students with emotional and behavioral disorders must view disruptive behavior for what it is—behavior that reflects the student's past frustrations and conflicts with himself and those around him—and try to help the child learn better ways of behaving. Acceptance should not be confused with approving or condoning antisocial behavior; the child must learn that he is responding inappropriately. Instead, this concept calls for understanding without condemning.

Most effective teachers of students with emotional and behavioral disorders are expert at recognizing and using nonverbal cues that are part of every teacher-student interaction. See Banbury and Hebert (1992) for a discussion of body language and gestures in classroom interactions.

Having an *empathetic relationship* with a child refers to a teacher's ability to recognize and understand the many nonverbal cues that often are the keys to understanding the individual needs of emotionally disturbed children.

Kauffman (1993b) stresses the importance of teachers' communicating directly and honestly with behaviorally troubled children. Many of these children have already had experience with supposedly helpful adults who have not been completely honest with them. Children with emotional and behavioral disorders can quickly detect someone who is not genuinely interested in their welfare.

The teacher of children with emotional and behavioral disorders must also realize that his or her actions serve as a powerful model. Therefore, it is critical that the teacher's actions and attitudes be mature and demonstrate self-control. Hobbs (1966) describes the kind of person he believes would make a good teacher and model for students with emotional and behavioral disorders:

> A decent adult; educated, well trained; able to give and receive affection, to live relaxed, and to be firm; a person with private resources for the nourishment and refreshment of his own life; not an itinerant worker but a professional through and through; a person with a sense of the significance of time; of the usefulness of today and the promise of tomorrow; a person of hope, quiet confidence, and joy; one who has committed himself to children and to the proposition that children who are emotionally disturbed can be helped by the process of reeducation. (pp. 1106–1107)

The academic development of students with behavior disorders must not be ignored.

✳ *Educational Placement Alternatives*

During the 1992–93 school year, 37% of school-age children with emotional and behavioral disorders were served in a self-contained classroom, 28% in a resource room, 16% in a regular classroom with consultation, 14% in a special public school, and 5% in a residential or homebound placement (U.S. Department of Education, 1994). In a national survey, Cullinan et al. (1992) found that students with emotional and behavioral disorders who were mainstreamed spent an average of 2.6 hours per day in regular classrooms. Nearly 50% of the students in the study spent up to half of the school day in regular classrooms, with only 19% spending no time in the mainstream. By contrast, an earlier study found that just 17% of students with emotional and behavioral disorders spent up to half of the school day in regular classrooms, and 44% had no mainstream time (Kauffman, Cullinan, & Epstein, 1987). The results of the more recent survey may reveal an increasing willingness on the part of regular classroom teachers to accept students with emotional and behavioral disorders into their classrooms. However, direct comparison of the results from the two studies cannot be done because the earlier survey was conducted in two Midwestern states.

A study comparing middle school students who spent the entire school day in self-contained classrooms with students who were mainstreamed into various classes in regular classrooms for at least 1 hour per day found that the mainstreamed students had better academic records and better work habits than the students who spent the entire day in a special class (Meadows, Neel, Scott, & Parker, 1994). Although these results would seem to support the contention by some that all students with emotional and behavioral disorders should be included in regular classrooms, the authors point out that the mainstreamed students did not exhibit the extreme aggression, lack of self-control, or degree of withdrawal as did the students who stayed in the special class. They also noted that placement in general education classrooms typically represents "a major reduction, . . . not complete cessation, of differential programming" (p. 178). That is, the general education teachers did not make instructional or management accommodations to meet the needs of the mainstreamed students. Thus, it is hard to imagine how students with severe emotional and behavioral disorders would receive an appropriate education in the regular classroom.

See the January, 1995, issue of *Educational Leadership*, pp. 7–11 and 22–25.

A similar conclusion has been drawn by Schneider and Leroux (1994), who reviewed 25 studies comparing the progress of students with emotional and behavioral disorders in different educational placements. Acknowledging the difficulties in comparing and collapsing the results of studies done with different students and with different methodologies, they report that special programs (which included resource rooms, self-contained classrooms, special schools, and treatment centers) appear to be more effective in promoting academic achievement, but comparisons between types of special programs are inconclusive. Better gains in children's self-concept are noted for less restrictive settings. Discussing the least restrictive alternative for students with emotional and behavioral disorders, Schneider and Leroux write:

> The first conclusion we can draw is that youngsters with behavioral disorders require more support than is available to the regular classroom teacher unassisted by at least resource room personnel. Second, it would appear that most youngsters with behavioral disorders will require ongoing support for a number of years. . . . For these

My Return Voyage

By Patricia M. Barbetta

The "power" of the peer group can be an effective means of producing positive changes in children with emotional and behavioral disorders. Patty Barbetta, now a member of the special education faculty at Florida International University in Miami, spent 11 years as a teacher, teacher supervisor, and education director at the Pressley Ridge School, a special school for children and adolescents with severe emotional and behavioral disorders in Pittsburgh, Pennsylvania. Here Patty describes some of her experiences implementing a behavior analytic group process model.

What was I doing? What could I possibly be thinking—returning to a frontline position in a classroom for children with emotional and behavioral disorders after 5 years as a program supervisor? These were the questions my coworkers, friends, and family asked, and for very good reasons. They recalled my early teaching experiences with these children: the hours I spent restraining Jeremy, who never thought twice before hitting me and hitting hard; the day the fire chief threatened to fine me when Sam falsely set off the alarm "just one too many times"; the time I developed a behavioral contract for Connie to follow her mother's directions, only to have her run away from home. And my biannual trips to the emergency room for a tetanus shot necessitated by student bites.

Reasons for Returning

My reasons for returning to the classroom were many, but I will mention just two. First was the progress we had made during my first year of teaching. Don't get me wrong. We still had behavior problems right through the last day of school. But by the end of the year, the problems were less frequent and typically were resolved quickly. In our second year (we virtually had the same group), we managed to function well enough to earn money for a field trip to Washington, D.C.—a 3-day trip that, despite the time the entire group had to take a time-out at Arlington Cemetery, went off without major incident. We were by far the best-behaved group at the Smithsonian (much better than some of the general education groups). Witnessing our hard-earned gains was very rewarding.

Second, I had an interest in directly implementing group process techniques as a new component of the treatment program at Pressley Ridge. I admit I didn't readily buy into the group model at first. The idea of handing over "control" to a group of students with behavioral disorders scared me. These students working together as a group? I simply couldn't imagine it. Most of them had never been part of a successfully functioning peer group. When they did participate as a group, it was usually in antisocial activities like shoplifting, hanging out on the street corner harassing passersby, or picking on timid students in the school cafeteria.

"That's His Problem, Not Mine"

As I had feared, things did not go well when I first tried a group approach. The students, accustomed to individualized, teacher-designed and -directed classroom management systems, resented being asked to be involved in their own treatment. And they especially resented being held accountable to each other. The students were simply not very good at working together, problem solving, or encouraging each other to behave appropriately. More to the point, they were *terrible* at these skills. Most did everything they could to undermine the group effort by intentionally losing points needed to earn group activities. They often refused to get involved in each other's problems: "That's his problem, Miss, not mine." Furthermore, many of them intentionally encouraged inappropriate behaviors by laughing at and providing their off-task friends with even more creative ways for misbehaving. As for us teachers, we thought it was much simpler to "just do things ourselves." There were many very unhappy students and teachers in that early transition period, but we since have learned how we could have made that transition much smoother.

Three Important Lessons

I learned three very important lessons during the transition to a group programming model. First, implementing a successful group process program is much more complicated than simply bringing together a group of students. Teachers and students alike have to work very hard to develop well-functioning groups. Second, the peer group is an extremely powerful resource—one that we cannot afford to waste. When the groups at our school started to "gel," we observed some positive and very powerful group pressure at work. I remember watching Danaire, a young man with a history of acting-out problems, calmly and effectively de-escalating Louie (a new group member) on many occasions when he was about to assault a staff person. And I recall the first time Rico, a tough inner-city kid, shook Chad's hand when he finally learned his multiplication facts. Why was this so amazing? You see, Chad was pretty much the "class nerd," and it took several weeks for Rico to even recognize his existence. The two never became best friends, but they were able to help each other out on occasion. And finally, and maybe most importantly, I learned that involving the students in their treatment was not giving up "control." As teachers, we sometimes kid ourselves into thinking we are in "control." Every student in the room contributes to each other's behaviors;

their influence already existed. The effective use of group process program strategies helped us guide this peer influence.

So, what was my return to the classroom like? Frustrating, exciting, challenging, exhausting, and rewarding are a few descriptors that come to mind. You might think that after 8 years in the field it would have been simple. Working with students with behavioral disorders is often rewarding, but it is never simple. The Voyagers (my group that return year) reminded me of this.

The Voyagers

Who were the Voyagers? Well, they were 12 very different 13- to 15-year-old boys who were referred to our program for a variety of behavior problems. Why did they decide to call themselves the Voyagers? They said it was because they would be "voyaging smoothly through their year to return quickly to their public schools." Well, not quite. Things did start out great (commonly referred to as the "honeymoon period"), but we quickly hit a few "meteor storms."

Just a few examples. Eric, who referred to himself as "The King of Going Off"—or the "Go-Off Master," for short—was very big for his age. He enjoyed staring down, shoving, and hitting students and staff, and he did so often. Then there was Mark, the class thief, who stole anything that wasn't tied down. Then he would hide the stolen item in a fellow Voyager's desk to try to get him in trouble. Gary lived in a rough neighborhood and lived with his alcoholic mother. He often came to school tired and angry. On a bad day, even the simplest request would set him off. What did he do when he was "off"? Usually, he threw his desk across the room. Russell, the class clown, occasionally felt the need to run out into the woods, gather sticks and leaves, attach them to his

clothes, and come back into the classroom acting like "Rambo." This was sometimes funny, but hardly appropriate. And don't let me forget James, whose favorite activity was hanging and swinging from the doorway while making funny noises combined with the most creative combinations of swear words you could imagine. Remember, I've just described only 5 of the 12 Voyagers.

Were we ever able to function as a group? Yes, we were on many occasions, but only after many disappointing moments, terribly difficult days, and many opportunities to practice pulling it together as a group. We spent many days with restricted privileges because of poor group performances, but no group was more pleased to earn top-level privileges. We may not have made it to the Halloween party, but we did win the Christmas door-decorating contest. And it might have taken us 55 minutes to walk back into school after we lost an intramural football game in the fall, but no group could touch us at the tug-of-war during Spring Field Day.

Was I crazy to go back into the classroom? Probably. Was I sorry I did? No way. I learned more that year about effective strategies for working with students with emotional and behavioral disorders than ever before. And along the way I managed to help a few troubled kids. It was a rough return voyage, but a very rewarding one. ✳

youngsters, the least restrictive setting *possible* would appear to be a well-equipped resource room in a regular school. However, not enough research has been conducted on the capabilities of resource rooms to manage various problematic behaviors. Pending more conclusive data, one might speculate that some pupils may display behaviors too disruptive to be managed in this type of setting. On the other hand, there are clear drawbacks to more self-contained special settings, especially with regard to children's self-concept. (pp. 201, 203)

Epstein, Foley, and Cullinan (1992) conducted a national survey of programs for adolescents with emotional and behavioral disorders. On the basis of teachers' descriptions of their programs, Epstein et al. report five types of programs for students with emotional and behavioral disorders in grades 7 through 12. Characteristic features of those five program types, and the percentage of teachers in the survey who identified those descriptions as best describing their own programs, are as follows:

- *Mainstreaming* (34%): Primary importance is placed on increasing students' time spent in the regular classroom; academic curriculum and activities parallel the regular classroom; the student-teacher ratio is low; students with other high-incidence disabilities often are part of program.
- *Classroom structure* (30%): Students are taught to be respectful to one another in a positive, supportive, and nonthreatening atmosphere; classroom rules and consequences are explicitly communicated and enforced; daily activities follow a predictable routine; one-to-one academic instruction is designed to meet individual needs.
- *Social and school survival skills* (16%): Emphasis is on how to get along with others, manage their own thoughts and feelings, use problem-solving skills, and demonstrate responsibility for self; students are taught study skills, learning strategies, and time management; life-space interviewing, reality therapy, and crisis interventions are used; academics are addressed through tutoring.
- *Instruction in nontraditional content* (12%): Interpersonal and school-coping skills are approached through an affective curriculum of vocational, career, outdoor, and/or leisure educational experiences; academics emphasize functional skills for independent living; team teaching and multidisciplinary student evaluations are used.
- *Individualized communication and instruction* (8%): Comprehensive diagnostic assessment is used to develop an individualized treatment program for each student; considerable communication is done with parents and mainstream teachers; counseling is provided for such areas as psychological, vocational, and substance abuse problems; consequences for inappropriate behavior may include in-school and out-of-school suspensions.

✳ Current Issues and Future Trends

The field of special education for students with emotional and behavioral disorders faces a number of critical and ongoing issues. Foremost among the concerns of many experts is revising the federal definition of this disability so that all children with emotional and behavioral disorders will be eligible for special education. The major problem with the current federal definition of "seriously emotionally disturbed" is that it attempts to distinguish between students who exhibit "true" emotional disturbance (considered a disability covered under the IDEA) and those whose disordered and antisocial behaviors are thought to be the result of social maladjustment. Socially maladjusted children and youths are not eligible for special education. A related concern is ensuring that traditionally underserved groups of children and youths not be denied services for emotional and behavioral disorders, particularly those who are poor, from historically oppressed minorities, and homosexual (McIntyre, 1993a).

Development of an effective system of special education services for school-age youths with disabilities in correctional institutions, an increasing number of whom have emotional and behavioral disorders, will become an increasingly important challenge; 20% of students with emotional and behavioral disorders are arrested at least once before they leave school, compared with 9% for all students with disabilities and 6% of all students (Chesapeake Institute, 1994). At present, about 450,000 delinquent youths are placed in detention centers or training schools each year in the United States, with another 300,000 sent to adult jails (Leone, Rutherford, & Nelson, 1991). The educational outlook is bleak for juveniles with disabilities who find themselves in jails and detention centers. Although it can be argued that adjudicated delinquents are, by virtue of the behaviors that precipitated their arrest, behaviorally disordered, most juvenile offenders receive few or no special education services (McIntyre, 1993b). Those incarcerated youths who do receive special education services typically receive substandard services (Leone, 1994).

See Nelson, Rutherford, and Wolford's (1987) book *Special Education in the Criminal Justice System*.

Although the challenges faced by those who work with students with emotional and behavioral disorders appear daunting and unrelenting, the field has also experienced significant advancements and successes. Recently, a group of nationally known leaders in the field of emotional and behavioral disorders met to review the field's knowledge base and to make recommendations for the improvement of policy and practice (The Peacock Hill Working Group, 1991). In addition to identifying and describing the key characteristics of a number of successful intervention programs from around the country, the group cited the following strategies that, when used in combination, are likely to result in successful programming for students with emotional and behavioral disorders:

- *Systematic, data-based interventions.* It is critical that interventions be selected and evaluated on the basis of data regarding their effectiveness.
- *Continuous assessment and monitoring of progress.* Curriculum-based assessment and direct, daily measurement are two strategies for attaining the level of measurement required for success.
- *Provision for practice of new skills.* Skills taught in isolation, without provision for practicing them in everyday situations, are unlikely to be retained.
- *Treatment matched with the problem.* A student whose primary problem is getting along with others needs intensive instruction in social skills, not an exclusive focus on academics or the suppression of a particular noxious behavior. Treatment must also address the relevant settings in the student's life and not be confined to the school setting alone.
- *Multicomponent treatment.* The *additive* effects of different classroom interventions and related treatment modalities are often critical to successful outcomes. For some disorders, long-term outcome has been measurably better when combinations of instructional, behavior, psychopharmacological, and/or family treatments are systematically coordinated.

- *Programming for transfer and maintenance.* Interventions must include strategies for the maintenance and transfer of treatment gains to new settings.
- *Commitment to sustained intervention.* Some disorders of emotion and behavior may require interventions over the individual's life span. One-shot cures simply are not now available, nor are they likely to be developed in the future. Programs should provide follow-up and continued intervention as needed.

Summary

Defining Emotional and Behavioral Disorders

- There is no single, widely used definition of emotional and behavioral disorders. Most definitions require a child's behavior, in order to be considered disordered, to differ markedly (extremely) and chronically (over time) from current social or cultural norms.

- Many leaders in the field of emotional and behavioral disorders do not like the federal definition of *seriously emotionally disturbed* found in the IDEA because students who are "socially maladjusted" are not eligible for special education services.

- The CCBD and the National Mental Health and Special Education Coalition have proposed a definition of *emotional and behavioral disorders* as a disability characterized by "behavioral or emotional responses in school programs so different from appropriate age, cultural, or ethnic norms that they adversely affect educational performance."

- Teacher tolerance and expectations for behavior contribute to a child's identification as behaviorally disordered.

- No widely accepted system for classifying behavioral disorders exists.

- The *DSM-IV* classifies children's emotional and behavior problems across 230 diagnostic categories noted in clinical practice.

- Quay's classification system describes four clusters of behavior problems: conduct disorders, anxiety-withdrawal, immaturity, and socialized delinquency.

- Behavioral disorders can be described and classified in terms of their frequency, duration, topography, and magnitude. Improper stimulus control is also a problem for many children with emotional and behavioral disorders.

- Most children with emotional and behavioral disorders have mild to moderate problems that can be treated effectively in the regular classroom and at home. Children with severe emotional and behavioral disorders require intensive programming, often in a more restrictive setting.

Characteristics of Children with Emotional and Behavioral Disorders

- On the average, students with emotional and behavioral disorders score somewhat below normal on IQ tests and achieve academically below what their scores would predict.

- Many students with emotional and behavioral disorders have difficulty developing and maintaining interpersonal relationships.

- There are two general types of emotional and behavioral disorders, often referred to as externalizing and internalizing problems.

- Children with externalizing problems frequently exhibit antisocial behavior; many become delinquents as adolescents.

- Children with internalizing problems are overly withdrawn and lack social skills needed to interact effectively with others.

Causes of Emotional and Behavioral Disorders

- The two groups of causes suggested for behavioral disorders are biological and environmental.

- Because of its central role in a child's life, the school can also be an important contributing factor to a behavior problem.

Identification and Assessment

- Although several screening tests have been developed, many school districts do not use any systematic method for identifying children with emotional and behavioral disorders.

- Whereas antisocial children stand out, withdrawn children may go unnoticed.

- Screening should be conducted as early as possible and include information from multiple agents and multiple settings.

- Projective tests often yield interesting results, but they are rarely useful in planning and implementing interventions.

- Direct and continuous observation and measurement of specific problem behaviors within the classroom is an assessment technique that indicates directly whether and for which behaviors intervention is needed.

Prevalence

- Although the U.S. Department of Education has traditionally estimated that children with emotional and behavioral disorders comprise 2% of the school-age population, the number of children served is less than half of the 2% estimate.

- The ratio of boys to girls in programs for students with emotional and behavioral disorders is approximately 4:1. Although there are many exceptions, boys are likely to have externalizing problems and girls are more likely to have internalizing problems.

Educational Approaches

- Six conceptual models of children's emotional and behavioral disorders have been proposed: biogenic, psychodynamic, psychoeducational, humanistic, ecological, and behavioral. Although each approach has a distinct theoretical basis and suggests types of treatment, many teachers use techniques from more than one of the models.

- Research supports the behavioral and ecological models, which analyze and modify the ways a child interacts with the environment.

- Teachers should concentrate their resources and energies on alterable variables—those things in a student's environment the teacher can influence.

- Many students with emotional and behavioral disorders benefit from systematic social skills training.

- Self-management skills can help students develop a sense of control over their environment, responsibility for their actions, and self-direction.

- A good classroom management system creates a positive, supportive, and noncoercive environment that promotes prosocial behavior and academic achievement.

- Group process approaches use the power of the peer group to help students with emotional and behavioral disorders learn to behave appropriately.

- Two important affective traits for teachers of students with emotional and behavioral disorders are differential acceptance and empathetic relationship.

Educational Placement Alternatives

- The greatest percentage of students with emotional and behavioral disorders are served in self-contained classrooms.

- Nearly 50% of the students with emotional and behavioral disorders spend up to half of the school day in regular classrooms; only about 1 in 5 spend no time in the mainstream.

- Comparing the behavioral and academic progress of students with emotional and behavioral disorders in different educational placements in an effort to determine which setting is the best is difficult because students with milder disabilities are mainstreamed first and more often, whereas those students who exhibit more severe behavioral disturbances tend to remain in special classes.

Current Issues and Future Trends

- Special education services are needed for the many incarcerated adolescents with emotional and behavioral disorders in correctional institutions.

- Successful programs for students with emotional and behavioral disorders are characterized by systematic, data-based interventions; continuous assessment and monitoring of student progress; provision for practice of new skills; matching treatment with the problem; multicomponent treatments; programming for transfer and maintenance of newly learned skills; and their commitment to follow-up and continued intervention as needed.

. . . .

For More Information

Journals

Behavior Therapy. Published five times a year by Academic Press for the Association for the Advancement of Behavior Therapy.

Behavioral Disorders. Published quarterly by the Council for Children with Behavioral Disorders, Council for Exceptional Children. Publishes research and discussion articles dealing with behavioral disorders in children.

Beyond Behavior. The subtitle of this provocative and interesting journal is *A Magazine for Exploring Behavior in Our Schools.* Published three times a year by CCBD, *Beyond Behavior* presents commentary, essays, and first-person accounts related to understanding and working with students with emotional and behavioral disorders.

Education & Treatment of Children. Published quarterly by Pressley Ridge School, Pittsburgh, Pennsylvania. Includes experimental studies, discussion articles, literature reviews, and book reviews covering a wide range of education and treatment issues with children.

Journal of Applied Behavior Analysis. Published quarterly by the Society for the Experimental Analysis of Behavior, Lawrence, Kansas. Publishes original experimental studies demonstrating improvement of socially significant behaviors. Many studies involve children with emotional and behavioral disorders as subjects.

Journal of Emotional and Behavioral Disorders. A multi-disciplinary journal featuring articles on research, practice, and theory. Published quarterly by PRO-ED, Austin, Texas.

Nelson, C. M., Rutherford, R. B., & Wolford, B. I. (Eds.). (1987). *Special education and the criminal justice system.* New York: Merrill/Macmillan.

Rhode, G., Jensen, W. R., & Reavis, H. K. (1993). *The tough kid book: Practical classroom management strategies.* Longmont, CO: Sopris West.

Shapiro, E. S., & Cole, C. L. (1994). *Behavior change in the classroom: Self-management interventions.* New York: Guilford Press.

Smith, D. D., & Rivera, D. M. (1993). *Effective discipline* (2nd ed.). Austin, TX: PRO-ED.

Walker, H. M., Colvin, G., & Ramsey, E. (1995). *Antisocial behavior in schools: Strategies and best practices.* Pacific Grove, CA: Brooks/Cole.

Walker, J. E., & Shea, T. M. (1995). *Behavior management: A practical approach for educators.* Pacific Grove, CA: Brooks/Cole.

Books

Cartledge, G., & Milburn, J. F. (1995). *Teaching social skills to children and youth: Innovative approaches.* Needham Heights, MA: Allyn & Bacon.

Epanchin, B. C., Townsend, B., & Stoddard, K. (1994). *Constructive classroom management: Strategies for creating positive learning environments.* Pacific Grove, CA: Brooks/Cole.

Kameenui, E. J., & Darch, C. B. (1995). *Instructional classroom management: A proactive approach to behavior management.* White Plains, NY: Longman.

Kauffman, J. M. (1993). *Characteristics of emotional and behavioral disorders of children and youth* (5th ed.). Englewood Cliffs, NJ: Merrill/Prentice Hall.

Kerr, M. M., & Nelson, C. M. (1989). *Strategies for managing behavior problems in the classroom* (2nd ed.). Englewood Cliffs, NJ: Merrill/Prentice Hall.

Organizations

American Association for the Advancement of Behavior Therapy, 15 West 36th Street, New York, NY 10018. Includes psychologists, educational researchers, and educators (primarily at the university level).

Council for Children with Behavioral Disorders (CCBD), Council for Exceptional Children, 1920 Association Drive, Reston, VA 22091. With more than 8,500 members, CCBD is the second largest of CEC's 17 divisions. Includes teachers, teacher educators, and researchers interested in promoting the general welfare and education of children with emotional and behavioral disorders.

The Federation of Families for Children's Mental Health. A national parent-run organization focused on the needs of children and youths with emotional, behavioral, or mental disorders and their families. 1021 Prince Street, Alexandria, VA 22314-2071.

Students with Communication Disorders

- How can a true communication disorder be differentiated from a communication difference?

- How can the severity of a communication disorder change from one situation to another?

- How have changes in the assessment and treatment of communication disorders paralleled other changes in special education?

- When should an alternative and augmentative communication system be developed for a student?

- Why are professional teamwork and parent involvement especially critical in treating communication disorders?

*I*magine trying to go through an entire day without speaking. How would you make contact with other people? You would be frustrated when others did not understand your needs and feelings. By the end of the day, besides feeling exhausted from trying to make yourself understood, you might even be starting to question your ability to function adequately in the world.

Although relatively few people with communication disorders are completely unable to express themselves, an exercise such as the one just described would increase your awareness of some of the problems and frustrations faced every day by children and adults who cannot communicate effectively. Language—"the most powerful, fascinating skill that humans possess" (Reed, 1994, p. v)—is central to human existence. Children who cannot absorb information through listening and reading and/or who cannot express their thoughts in spoken words are virtually certain to encounter difficulties in their schools and communities. When communication disorders persist, it may be hard for children to learn, to develop, and to form satisfying relationships with other people.

✳ *Communication, Language, and Speech*

Before specific types of communication disorders and their effects on learning are discussed, some definitions of basic terms will be helpful.

Communication

Communication is the exchange of information and ideas. It involves encoding, transmitting, and decoding messages. It is an interactive process requiring at least two parties, each playing the dual roles of sender and receiver. We take part in literally thousands of communicative interactions every day. An infant cries, and her mother picks her up. A dog barks, and its owner lets it out of the house. A teacher smiles, and his student knows that an assignment has been accomplished well. Each of these interactions includes three elements needed to qualify as communication: (a) a message, (b) a sender who expresses the message, and (c) a receiver who responds to the message.

Although speech and language comprise the message system most often used in human communication, spoken or written words are not necessary for true communication to occur. Both paralinguistic behaviors and nonlinguistic cues are used in human communication. *Paralinguistic behaviors* are nonlanguage sounds (e.g., *oohh,* laugh) and speech modifications (e.g., variations in pitch, intonation, rate of delivery, pauses) that change the form and meaning of the message. *Nonlinguistic* cues include body posture, facial expressions, gestures, eye contact, head and body movement, and physical proximity.

Lindfors (1987) has enumerated several important functions that communication serves, particularly between teachers and children:

The study of non-linguistic behaviors that augment language is called **kinesics.**

1. *Narrating.* Children need to be able to tell (or follow the telling of) a "story"—that is, a sequence of related events connected in an orderly, clear, and interesting manner. Five-year-old Cindy tells her teacher, "I had a birthday party. I wore a funny hat. Mommy made a cake and Daddy took pictures." Fourteen-year-old David tells the class about the events leading up to Christopher Columbus's first voyage to America.

2. *Explaining/informing.* Teachers expect children to interpret the explanations of others in speech and in writing and also to put what they understand into words so that their listeners or readers will be able to understand it too. In a typical classroom, children must respond frequently to teachers' questions: "Which number is larger?" "How do you suppose the story will end?" "Why do you think George Washington was a great president?"

3. *Expressing.* It is important for children to express their personal feelings and opinions and to respond to the feelings of others. Speech and language can convey joy, fear, frustration, humor, sympathy, anger. A child writes, "I have just moved. And it is hard to find a friend because I am shy." Another tells her classmates, "Guess what? I have a new baby brother!" Through such communicative interactions, children gradually develop a sense of self and an awareness of other people.

Language

Language is a system used by a group of people for giving meaning to sounds, words, gestures, and other symbols to enable communication with one another. Lahey (1988) defines language as "a code whereby ideas about the world are expressed through a conventional system of arbitrary signals for communication" (p. 2). A child may learn to identify a familiar object, for example, by hearing the spoken word *tree,* by seeing the printed word *tree,* by viewing the sign language gesture for *tree,* or by encountering a combination of these signals. When we hear, speak, read, or write with language, we transmit information.

The symbols and the rules governing their use are essentially arbitrary in all languages, and spoken English is no exception. The arbitrariness of language means there is usually no logical, natural, or required relationship between a set of sounds and the object, concept, or action it represents. The word *whale,* for example, brings to mind a large mammal that lives in the sea, but the sound of the word has no apparent connection with the creature. *Whale* is merely a symbol we use for this particular mammal. A small number of onomatopoeic words—such as *tinkle, buzz,* and *hiss*—are considered to sound like what they represent, but most words have no such relationship. Likewise, some hand positions or movements in sign language, called *iconic signs,* look like the object or event they represent (e.g., tipping an imaginary cup to one's lips is the manual sign for *drink*). Remember, language is used to express descriptions of and relations between objects and events; it does not reproduce those objects and events.

Dimensions of Language

Language is often described along five dimensions: phonology, morphology, syntax, semantics, and pragmatics. **Phonology** is the study of the linguistic rules governing a language's sound system. Phonological rules describe how sounds can be sequenced and combined. The English language uses approximately 45 different sound elements, called **phonemes.** Only the initial phoneme prevents the words *pear* and *bear* from being identical, for example; yet in one case we think of a fruit, and in the other a large animal.

The **morphology** of a language governs how the basic units of meaning are combined into words. Phonemes, the individual sounds, do not carry meaning. A **morpheme** is the smallest element of language that carries meaning. The word *baseball,* for example, consists of two morphemes: *base* and *ball.* The *-s* added to make *baseballs* would be a third morpheme.

Syntax is the system of rules governing the meaningful arrangement of words into sentences. If morphemes could be strung together in any order, language would be an unintelligible tangle of words. Syntactical rules are language-specific (e.g., Japanese and English have different rules), and they specify relations among the subject, verb, and object. For example, "Help my chicken eat" conveys a meaning much different from "Help eat my chicken."

Semantics is a system of rules that relate phonology and syntax to meaning; that is, semantics describes how people use language to convey meaning.

Finally, **pragmatics** is a set of rules governing how language is used. Lahey (1988) describes three kinds of pragmatic skills: (a) using language to achieve various communicative functions and goals, (b) using information from the conversational context (e.g., modifying one's message according to listener reactions), and (c) knowing how to use conversational skills effectively (e.g., beginning and ending a conversation, turn taking). "To ignore pragmatics is to concentrate on language structure and to remove language from its communicative context" (Owens, 1994, p. 50).

One model of language, developed by Bloom and Lahey (1978), describes three components of language—form, content, and use—that make up an integrated system. The *form* of the language is its surface structure that connects sound and meaning (phonology, morphology, syntax). The *content* is based on knowledge of the world and our feelings about it. Thus, the form of language allows us to express and understand content (semantics). The *use* of language refers to the ways language functions in communication (pragmatics). It includes both our purposes in communicating and how we choose a specific form to express a particular message.

Speech

Speech is the actual behavior of producing a language code by making appropriate vocal sound patterns (Hubbell, 1985). Although it is not the only possible vehicle for expressing language (gestures, manual signing, pictures, and written symbols can also be used), speech is a most effective and efficient method. Speech is also one of the most complex and difficult human endeavors. Speech sounds are the product of four separate but related processes (Hulit & Howard, 1993): **respiration** (breathing provides the power supply for speech), **phonation** (the production of sound when the vocal folds of the larynx are drawn together by the contraction of specific muscles, causing the air to vibrate), **resonation** (the sound quality of the vibrating air is shaped as it passes through the throat, mouth, and sometimes nasal cavities), and **articulation** (the formation of specific, recognizable speech sounds by the tongue, lips, teeth, and mouth). Figure 7.1 shows the normal speech organs.

Most languages start out in oral form, developed by people speaking with each other. Reading and writing are secondary language forms that represent the oral

---

Phonemes are represented by letters or other symbols between slashes. For example, the phoneme /n/ represents the "ng" sound in *sing;* /i/ represents the long "e" as in *see.*

This model can be helpful in understanding and treating a child's communication disorder.

FIGURE 7.1
The normal speech organs

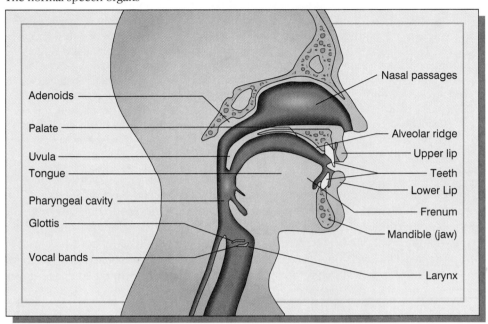

Adenoids

Palate

Uvula

Tongue

Pharyngeal cavity

Glottis

Vocal bands

Nasal passages

Alveolar ridge

Upper lip

Teeth

Lower Lip

Frenum

Mandible (jaw)

Larynx

form. There is no one-to-one correspondence, however, between *graphemes* (print symbols or letters) and phonemes.

Normal Language Development

Despite the complexity of our language system, most children, without any formal instruction, learn to understand language and then to speak during the first few years of life. They integrate form, content, and use to communicate. The process of learning language is a remarkable one that is not fully understood. Parents, teachers,

Good communicators use nonlinguistic cues such as body posture and gestures and pragmatic conversational skills such as turn taking.

and scholars for centuries have been fascinated by the phenomenon of language acquisition in children.

> Whether a child grows up in a "traditional" society or in a "technological" one; whether in a large extended family or in a small nuclear one; whether on a Pacific island, in an urban ghetto, or in a tribal farm compound; whether in a villa, a straw hut, an apartment, or a tent; whether with or without formal schooling; whether in a wet, dry, hot, or cold climate—the child will acquire the language of his community. Humans vary in which languages and dialects they acquire, in how rapidly they acquire them . . . in how talkative they are, in what they use language for, and in how effectively they express themselves in speech and/or writing. But virtually all of them acquire at least one linguistic system for relating meanings. . . . Further, there is striking similarity in how all children learn their language. (Lindfors, 1987, p. 91)

Children with hearing impairments have a special set of problems in learning language. See Chapter 8.

Understanding how young, normally developing children acquire language is helpful to the teacher or specialist working with children who have delayed or disordered communication. Knowledge of normal language development can help the specialist determine whether a particular child is simply developing language at a slower-than-normal rate or whether the child shows an abnormal pattern of language development. Table 7.1 identifies some of the key features of speech and language development of a typically developing child. As we consider normal language development, remember that the ages at which a normal child acquires certain speech and language skills are not rigid and inflexible. Children's abilities and early environments vary widely, and all of these factors affect language development. Nevertheless, most children follow a relatively predictable sequence in development of speech and language.

As the descriptions in Table 7.1 indicate, children's words and sentences often differ from adult forms while the children are learning language. Lindfors (1987) points out that children who use such structures as "All gone sticky" and "Where he is going?" or pronunciations like "cwackers" and "twuck" or word forms like "comed," "goed," or "sheeps" gradually learn to replace them with acceptable adult forms. The early developmental forms drop out as the child matures, usually without any special drilling or direct instruction.

It is also worth noting that children often produce speech sounds inconsistently. The clarity of a sound may vary according to such factors as where the sound occurs in a word and how familiar the word is to the child. Although speech sounds generally become clearer as the child grows older, there are exceptions to this rule of gradual progress. Kenney and Prather (1986), for example, found that 3½-year-old children made fewer errors on the /s/ sound than did children aged 4 to 5½. The reasons for these reversals in accuracy are not clear.

✳ *Defining Communication Disorders*

As already noted, the development of speech and language is a highly individual process. No child conforms exactly to precise developmental norms; some are advanced, some are delayed, and some acquire language in an unusual sequence. Unfortunately, some children deviate from the normal to such an extent that they have serious difficulties in learning and interpersonal relations. Children who are not able to make themselves understood or who cannot comprehend ideas that are spoken to them by others are likely to be greatly handicapped in virtually all aspects of education and personal adjustment.

When does a communication difference become a communication disorder? In making such judgments, Emerick and Haynes (1986) emphasize the impact that a communication pattern has on one's life. A communication difference would be considered a disability, they note, when any one of these criteria is met:

- The transmission and/or perception of messages is faulty
- The person is placed at an economic disadvantage
- The person is placed at a learning disadvantage
- The person is placed at a social disadvantage
- There is a negative impact on the person's emotional growth
- The problem causes physical damage or endangers the health of the person (pp. 6–7)

To be considered eligible for special education services, a child's communication disorders must have an adverse effect on learning. The definition of the "speech or language impaired" category of disability in the IDEA reads: "a communication disorder, such as stuttering, impaired articulation, a language impairment, or voice impairment which adversely affects . . . educational performance" (U.S. General Accounting Office, 1981, p. 36).

Most specialists in the field of communication disorders make a distinction between speech disorders and language disorders. Children with *impaired speech* have difficulty producing sounds properly, maintaining an appropriate flow or rhythm in speech, or using the voice effectively. Speech disorders are impairments in language form. Children with *impaired language* have problems in understanding or using the symbols and rules people use to communicate with each other. A child may have difficulty with language form, content, and/or use. Speech and language are obviously closely related to each other. Some people find it helpful to view speech as the means by which language is most often conveyed. A child may have a speech impairment, a language disorder, or both.

Speech Disorders

A child's speech is considered impaired if it is unintelligible, abuses the speech mechanism, or is culturally or personally unsatisfactory (Perkins, 1977). The most widely quoted definition of speech impairment is probably that of Van Riper, who states, "Speech is abnormal when it deviates so far from the speech of other people that it calls attention to itself, interferes with communication, or causes the speaker or his listeners to be distressed" (Van Riper & Emerick, 1984, p. 34). A general goal of specialists in communication disorders is to help the child speak as clearly and pleasantly as possible so that a listener's attention will focus on what the child says, rather than how he or she says it.

It is always important to keep the speaker's age, education, and cultural background in mind when determining whether speech is impaired. A 4-year-old girl who says, "Pwease weave the woom" would not be considered to have a speech impairment, but a 40-year-old woman would surely draw attention to herself with that pronunciation because it differs markedly from the speech of most adults. A traveler unable to articulate the /l/ sound would not be clearly understood in trying to buy a bus ticket to Lake Charles, Louisiana. A male high school student with an extremely high-pitched voice might be reluctant to speak in class for fear of being mimicked and ridiculed by his classmates.

The three basic types of speech disorders are articulation, voice, and fluency. Each type is discussed later in the chapter.

TABLE 7.1

Overview of normal language development

Birth to 6 Months
- Infant first communicates by crying, which produces a reliable consequence in the form of parental attention.
- Different types of crying develop — a parent can often tell from the baby's cry whether she is wet, tired, or hungry.
- Comfort sounds—coos, gurgles, and sighs—contain some vowels and consonants.
- Comfort sounds develop into babbling, sounds that in the beginning are apparently made for the enjoyment of feeling and hearing them.
- Vowel sounds, such as /i/ (pronounced "ee") and /e/ (pronounced "uh"), are produced earlier than consonants, such as /m/, /b/, and /f/.
- Infant does not attach meaning to words she hears from others, but may react differently to loud and soft voices.
- Turns eyes and head in the direction of a sound.

6 to 12 Months
- Babbling becomes differentiated before the end of the first year and contains some of the same phonetic elements as the meaningful speech of 2-year-olds.
- Baby develops **inflection**—her voice rises and falls.
- May respond appropriately to "no," "bye-bye," or her own name and may perform an action, such as clapping her hands, when told to.
- Will repeat simple sounds and words, such as "mama."

12 to 18 Months
- By 18 months, most children have learned to say several words with appropriate meaning.
- Pronunciation is far from perfect; baby may say "tup" when you point to a cup or "goggie" when she sees a dog.
- Communicates by pointing and perhaps saying a word or two.
- Responds to simple commands such as "Give me the cup" and "Open your mouth."

18 to 24 Months
- Most children go through a stage of **echolalia**, in which they repeat, or echo, the speech they hear. Echolalia is a normal phase of language development, and most children outgrow it by about the age of 2½.
- Great spurt in acquisition and use of speech; begins to combine words into short sentences, such as "Daddy bye-bye" and "Want cookie."
- Receptive vocabulary grows even more rapidly; at 2 years of age may understand more than 1,000 words.
- Understands such concepts as "soon" and "later" and makes more subtle distinctions between objects such as cats and dogs, and knives, forks, and spoons.

Language Disorders

Some children have serious difficulties in understanding language or in expressing themselves through language. A child with a *receptive language disorder* may be unable to learn the days of the week in proper order or may find it impossible to follow a sequence of commands, such as "Pick up the paint brushes, wash them in the sink, and then put them on a paper towel to dry." A child with an *expressive lan-*

TABLE 7.1 *(continued)*

2 to 3 Years

- The 2-year-old child talks; saying sentences like, "I won't tell you" and asking questions like, "Where my daddy go?"
- May have an expressive vocabulary of up to 900 different words, averaging three to four words per sentence.
- Participates in conversations.
- Identifies colors, uses plurals, and tells simple stories about her experiences.
- Able to follow compound commands such as "Pick up the doll and bring it to me."
- Uses most vowel sounds and some consonant sounds correctly.

3 to 4 Years

- The normal 3-year-old has lots to say, speaks rapidly, and asks many questions.
- Sentences are longer and more varied: "Cindy's playing in water"; "Mommy went to work"; "The cat is hungry."
- Uses speech to request, protest, agree, and make jokes.
- Understands children's stories, grasps such concepts as *funny, bigger,* and *secret*; and can complete simple analogies such as "In the daytime it is light; at night it is... "
- Substitutes certain sounds, perhaps saying "baf" for "bath" or "yike" for "like."
- Many 3-year-olds repeat sounds or words ("b-b-ball," "l-l-little"). These repetitions and hesitations are normal and do not indicate that the child will develop a habit of stuttering.

4 to 5 Years

- Has a vocabulary of over 1,500 words and uses sentences averaging five words in length.
- Begins to modify her speech for the listener; for example, uses longer and more complex sentences when talking to her mother than when addressing a baby or a doll.
- Can define words like *hat, stove*, and *policeman* and can ask questions like "How did you do that?" or "Who made this?"
- Uses conjunctions such as *if, when*, and *because*.
- Recites poems and sings songs from memory.
- May still have difficulty with such consonant sounds as /r/, /s/, and /z/ or with blends like "tr," "gl," "sk," and "str."

After 5 Years

- Language continues to develop steadily, though less dramatically, after age 5.
- Typical 6-year-old uses most of the complex forms of adult English.
- Some consonant sounds and blends are not mastered until age 7 or 8.
- Grammar and speech patterns of child in first grade usually match those of her family, neighborhood, and region.

guage disorder may have a limited vocabulary for his age, be confused about the order of sounds or words (e.g., "hostipal," "aminal," "wipe shield winders"), and use tenses and plurals incorrectly (e.g., "Them throwed a balls"). Children with difficulty in expressive language may or may not also have difficulty in receptive language. For instance, a child may be able to count out six pennies when asked and shown the symbol *6,* but he may not be able to say the word *six* when shown the symbol. In that case, the child has an expressive difficulty but his receptive language is adequate. He may or may not have other disorders of speech or hearing.

The American Speech-Language-Hearing Association (ASHA) defines a language disorder as "the impairment or deviant development of comprehension and/or use of a spoken, written, and/or other symbol system. The disorder may involve (1) the form of language (phonologic, morphologic, and syntactic systems), (2) the content of language (semantic system), and/or (3) the function of language in communication (pragmatic system) in any combination" (1982, p. 949).

Leonard (1986) has noted that children with impaired language frequently play a passive role in communication. They may show little tendency to initiate conversations. When language-disordered children are asked questions, "their replies rarely provide new information related to the topic" (p. 114).

Children with serious language disorders are likely to have problems in school and social development. It is often difficult to detect children with language disorders; their performance may lead people to mistakenly classify them with disability labels such as mental retardation, hearing impairment, or emotional disturbance, when in fact these descriptions are neither accurate nor appropriate. For example, an 11-year-old girl with a neurological impairment that affected her speech and language production was perceived by her fifth- and sixth-grade peers as "frightened, nervous, tense, and unlovable." These perceptions "obviously could have a negative impact on her self-concept" (Gies-Zaborowski & Silverman, 1986, p. 143).

A child may also be markedly delayed in language development. Even though a relatively wide range of language patterns and age milestones is considered normal, some children do not acquire speech or the ability to understand language until much later than normally expected. We would regard a 6-year-old child who cannot use such pronouns as *I, you,* and *me* as having a serious delay in language development. In rare cases, children who have no other impairment may even fail to speak at all.

> Language is so important to academic performance that it can be impossible to differentiate a learning disability from a language disorder. Again, the emphasis should be on remediating a child's skill deficits, rather than on labeling them.

Dialects and Differences

> *Myth:* A speech-language pathologist accepts a position in a Head-start facility on a Native American reservation. On his first day, he notices that all of the children appear to be uncommunicative. They do not initiate conversation, and they do not respond to direct questions such as "What is your name?" He reports to the director that the children are severely language delayed.
>
> *Reality:* The speech-language pathologist is unaware of many of the cultural rules of communication for the community. The children's behavior is normal for communication with a stranger or outsider. In addition, cultural rules dictate that members do not speak their own names.
>
> *Myth:* A 15-year-old black female from suburban Cleveland omits some final consonants and reduces final consonant clusters. She should not be considered for therapy since these are features of Black English Vernacular.
>
> *Reality:* After consideration of the child's speech community, it is not likely that Black English Vernacular features are a part of her middle income, highly educated environment. A possible articulation disorder or hearing loss should be considered. (Taylor & Payne, 1994, p. 137)

The way children speak reflects their culture. Before entering school, most children have learned patterns of speech and language appropriate to their families and neighborhoods. Every language contains a variety of forms, called *dialects,* that result from historic, geographical, and social factors. The English language, for example, includes such variations as Standard American English (as used by most teachers, employers, and public speakers), Black English, Appalachian English, Southern English, a New York dialect, and Spanish-influenced English. A child who uses these variations should not be treated as having a communication disorder.

It is certainly possible, however, for a child to have a communication disorder within his or her dialect. The American Speech-Language-Hearing Association (1983) considers it essential for a specialist to be able to "distinguish between dialectal differences and communicative disorders" and to "treat only those features or characteristics that are true errors and not attributable to the dialect" (p. 24). A speech or language difference from the majority of children, then, is not necessarily a communication disorder in need of treatment. Some major factors in creating speech and language differences are race and ethnicity, social class, education, occupation, geographical region, and peer group identification (Taylor & Payne, 1994). Problems may arise in the classroom and in parent-teacher communication if the teacher does not accept natural communication differences among children and mistakenly assumes that a speech or language impairment is present (Bankson, 1982; Reed, 1994).

> For children whose native language is not English, the distinction between a language difference and a communication disorder is critical. Chapter 3 offers guidelines for assessing learners from culturally and linguistically diverse backgrounds.

✳ *Types and Causes of Communication Disorders*

Many types of communication disorders and numerous possible causes are recognized. A speech impairment may be *organic*—that is, attributable to a specific physical cause. Examples of physical factors that frequently result in communication disorders are cleft palate, paralysis of the speech muscles, absence of teeth, craniofacial abnormalities, enlarged adenoids, and neurological impairments. Organic speech impairments may be a child's primary disability or may be secondary to other disabilities, such as delayed intellectual development, impaired hearing, and cerebral palsy.

Most communication disorders are not considered organic but are classified as functional. A *functional* communication disorder cannot be ascribed to a specific physical condition, and its origin is not clearly known. McReynolds (1990) points out that decades of research on the causes of many speech and language impairments have produced few answers. A child's surroundings provide many opportunities to learn appropriate and inappropriate communication skills; some specialists believe that functional communication disorders derive mainly from environmental influences. It is also possible that some speech impairments are caused by disturbances in the motor control system and are not fully understood.

Regardless of whether a communication disorder is considered organic or functional, a child with speech or language substantially different from that of others in the same age and cultural group requires special training procedures to correct or improve the impairment.

Articulation Disorders

Articulation disorders are the most prevalent type of speech impairment among school-age children. The correct articulation, or utterance, of speech sounds requires us to activate a complicated system of muscles, nerves, and organs. Haycock (1933), who compiled a classic manual on teaching speech, describes how the speech organs are manipulated into a variety of shapes and patterns, how the breath

TEACHING & LEARNING

Developing Language and Leadership

···········

Young children with impaired speech or language are often frustrated by the difficulty they experience in asking questions, expressing their needs, or conveying their wishes to other people. When unable to make themselves understood, some children may resort to physical communication (e.g., pulling, pushing, or hitting classmates), whereas others become so frustrated that they stop trying to communicate.

Judith Hurvitz, Sarah Pickert, and Donna Rilla believe that teachers can help children develop language skills by encouraging them to assume leadership roles in the classroom. Activities that carry responsibility, power, and prestige, they maintain, are useful in promoting language and social interaction. Here are some suggestions developed for Karen, a hypothetical 5-year-old with a communication disorder:

- Ask Karen to sit on a chair while the rest of the children are seated on the floor.
- Allow Karen to wear a special hat or badge.
- Give Karen the authority to distribute rewards, such as stars or tokens, to other children.
- Let Karen lead circle-time activities by taking attendance, directing group songs, and greeting others ("Hi, Judy").
- Allow Karen to assign daily classroom jobs to other children ("Barry, mats." "Ron, get snack.").
- Have Karen act as class messenger, especially when the recipient of the message is familiar with the meaning to be conveyed (she might say to the librarian, "Need book.").

- Permit Karen to choose how class members will participate in a particular activity; for example, designating whether boys or girls will go first in line ("Boys first.").
- Give Karen a picture to hold up and ask her to call on a child to describe the picture ("Donna, what this?").
- Let Karen lead the group in a movement activity by calling out actions ("March!" "Walk!" "Sit!").
- Suggest words that Karen can use to solve a problem herself when she asks for teacher intervention. Say, "Go to Anthony and tell him, 'I want my block'" or "Take your puzzle to Glen and say, 'Help me.'"
- Encourage Karen to work with another child in such tasks as cleaning up after snack time or moving a bulky table.
- Invite Karen to talk with a classmate by using a pair of toy telephones (this often generates enthusiasm).

Activities such as these can help children use language more effectively and with greater variety. They also enable children to experience the pleasure and power of using language to control their environments.

From "Promoting Children's Language Interaction" by J. A. Hurvitz, S. M. Pickert, and D. C. Rilla, 1987, *Teaching Exceptional Children, 19*(3), pp. 12-15. Reston, VA: Council for Exceptional Children. Adapted by permission.

---

and voice must be "molded to form words." For example, here is Haycock's description of how the /v/ sound is correctly produced:

> The lower lip must be drawn upwards and slightly inwards, so that the upper front teeth rest lightly on the lip. Breath must be freely emitted between the teeth and over the lower lip, and voice must be added to the breath. (n.p.)

Should any part of this process function imperfectly, a child will have difficulty articulating the /v/. Clearly, in such a complicated process, many types of errors are possible.

Articulation errors are of four basic kinds: substitution, distortion, omission, and addition. Children may *substitute* one sound for another, as in saying "train" for *crane* or "doze" for *those.* Children with this problem are often certain they have said the correct word and may resist correction. Substitution of sounds can cause considerable confusion for the listener. Children may *distort* certain speech sounds while attempting to produce them accurately. The /s/ sound, for example, is relatively difficult to produce; children may produce the word *sleep* as "schleep," "zleep," or "thleep." Some speakers have a lisp; others a whistling /s/. Distortions can cause misunderstanding, though parents and teachers often become accustomed to them. Children may *omit* certain sounds, as in saying "cool" for *school.* They may drop consonants from the ends of words, as in "pos" for *post.* Most of us leave out sounds at times, but an extensive omission problem can make speech impossible to understand. Children may also *add* extra sounds, making comprehension difficult. They may say "buhrown" for *brown* or "hamber" for *hammer.*

Dysarthria and *apraxia* refer to two groups of articulation disorders caused by neuromuscular impairments. Lack of precise motor control needed to produce and sequence sounds causes distorted and repeated sounds.

Degree of Severity

Like all communication disorders, articulation problems vary in degree of severity. Many children have mild or moderate articulation disorders. Usually their speech can be understood, but they may mispronounce certain sounds or use immature speech, like that of younger children. These problems often disappear as a child matures. If a mild or moderate articulation problem does not seem to be improving over an extended period or if it appears to have a negative effect on the child's interaction with others, referral to a communication disorders specialist is indicated.

A severe articulation disorder is present when a child pronounces many sounds so poorly that his speech is unintelligible most of the time. In that case, even the child's parents, teachers, and peers cannot easily understand him. The child with a severe articulation disorder may "chatter away and sound as though he or she is talking gibberish" (Liebergott, Favors, von Hippel, & Needleman, 1978, p. 17). He may say, "Yeh me yuh a wido," instead of, "Let me look out the window," or perhaps, "Do foop is dood" for "That soup is good." The fact that articulation disorders are prevalent does not mean that teachers, parents, and specialists should regard them as simple or unimportant. On the contrary, as Emerick and Haynes (1986) observe,

Although Austin's physical disabilities make it difficult for him to articulate speech sounds well enough to be understood, he is discovering a whole new world of communication possibilities by learning to use a computerized speech synthesizer.

"An articulation disorder severe enough to interfere significantly with intelligibility is . . . as debilitating a communication problem as many other disorders. . . . articulation disorders are not simple at all, and they are not necessarily easy to diagnose effectively" (p. 153).

Voice Disorders

Voice disorders occur when quality, loudness, or pitch is inappropriate or abnormal. Such disorders are far less common in children than in adults. Considering how often some children shout and yell without any apparent harm to their voices, it is evident that the vocal cords can withstand heavy use. In some cases, however, a child's voice may be difficult to understand or may be considered unpleasant. As Moore (1982) observes, a person's voice may be considered disordered if it differs markedly from what is customary in the voices of others of the same age, gender, and cultural background. Moore uses the term *dysphonia* to describe any condition of poor or unpleasant voice quality and notes that a voice—whether good, poor, or in between—is closely identified with the person who uses it.

The two basic types of voice disorders involve phonation and resonance. A *phonation disorder* causes the voice to sound breathy, hoarse, husky, or strained most of the time. In severe cases, there is no voice at all. Phonation disorders can have organic causes, such as growths or irritations on the vocal cords, but hoarseness most frequently comes from chronic vocal abuse, such as yelling, imitating noises, or habitually talking while under tension. A breathy voice is unpleasant because it is low in volume and fails to make adequate use of the vocal cords.

A voice with a *resonance disorder* suffers from either too many sounds coming out through the air passages of the nose (*hypernasality*) or, conversely, not enough resonance of the nasal passages (*hyponasality*). The hypernasal speaker may be perceived as talking through her nose or having an unpleasant twang. A child with hypernasality has speech that is excessively nasal, neutral, or central-sounding, rather than oral, clear, and forward-sounding (Cole & Paterson, 1986). A child with hyponasality (sometimes called *denasality*) may sound as though he constantly has a cold or a stuffed nose, even when he does not. As with other voice disorders, the causes of nasality may be either organic (e.g., cleft palate, swollen nasal tissues, hearing impairment) or functional (perhaps resulting from learned speech patterns or behavior problems).

Fluency Disorders

Normal speech makes use of rhythm and timing. Words and phrases flow easily, with certain variations in speed, stress, and appropriate pauses. **Fluency disorders** interrupt the natural, smooth flow of speech with inappropriate pauses, hesitations, or repetitions. One type of fluency disorder is known as *cluttering,* a condition in which speech is very rapid, with extra sounds or mispronounced sounds. The clutterer's speech is garbled to the point of unintelligibility.

The best-known (and probably least understood) fluency disorder, however, is **stuttering.** This condition is marked by "rapid-fire repetitions of consonant or vowel sounds, especially at the beginning of words; and complete verbal blocks" (Jonas, 1976, p. 7). The cause of stuttering remains unknown, although the condition has been studied extensively with some interesting results. Stuttering is far more common among males than females, and it occurs more frequently among twins. The prevalence of stuttering is about the same in all Western countries: Regardless of what language is spoken, about 1% of the general population has a stuttering problem. Stuttering is much more commonly reported among children than adults; prevalence estimates in school-age populations are around 5% (Ham, 1986; Martin & Lindamood, 1986). Stuttering is considered a disorder of childhood; it rarely begins past the age of 6 (Emerick & Haynes, 1986). According to Jonas (1976), stuttering typically makes its first appearance between the ages of 3 and 5, "*after* the child has already made great strides toward fluency. . . . The trouble comes later, just as speech is becoming less of a feat and more of a habit" (p. 11).

All children experience some dysfluencies—repetitions and interruptions—in the course of developing normal speech patterns. It is important not to overreact to dysfluencies and to insist on perfect speech; some specialists believe that stuttering can be caused by pressures placed on a child when parents and teachers react to normal hesitations and repetitions by labeling the child a stutterer. Lingwell (1982) explains that stuttering is not just one specific disorder but many, which may be why there are several conflicting theories about its cause. According to Lingwell, stuttering can be caused by neurological, psychological, or allergic factors or can result from rhythmic control or faulty learning patterns.

Stuttering is situational; that is, it appears to be related to the setting or circumstances of speech. A child may be likely to stutter when talking with the people whose opinions matter most to him, such as parents and teachers, and in situations like being called on to speak in front of the class. Most people who stutter are fluent about 95% of the time; a child with a fluency disorder may not stutter at all when singing, talking to a pet dog, or reciting a poem in unison with others. Reactions and expectations of parents, teachers, and peers clearly have an important effect on any child's personal and communicative development.

Several researchers and clinicians have explored the effects of social pressures on stuttering by examining its incidence in cultures other than our own. Gerald Jonas, who himself was affected by stuttering, derives insights from a comparison of American Indian tribes. He observes that certain tribes, such as the Utes and the Bannocks of the Rocky Mountain region, have an unusually permissive attitude toward children's speech and have virtually no stuttering problems. Other tribes, such as the Cowichans of the Pacific Northwest, are highly competitive, expecting children to take part in complicated rituals at a young age, and have a high incidence of stuttering. Jonas (1976) suggests that the reason the Ute and Bannock children do not stutter may be that no one ever tries to "make them speak correctly." But he acknowledges that this theory fails to explain "why in so many other cultures some children of nagging parents turn into stutterers while others do not" (p. 14).

Van Riper (1972) reflects on the importance of cultural attitudes toward stuttering in the following passage:

> Once, on Fiji in the South Pacific, we found a whole family of stutterers. As our guide and translator phrased it: "Mama kaka; papa kaka; and kaka, kaka, kaka, kaka." All six persons in that family showed marked repetitions and prolongations in their speech; but they were happy people, not at all troubled by their stuttering. It was just the way they talked. We could not help but contrast their attitudes and the simplicity of their stuttering with those which would have been shown by a similar family in our own land, where the pace of living is so much faster, where defective communication is rejected, where stutterers get penalized all their lives. To possess a marked speech

disorder in our society is almost as handicapping as to be a physical cripple in a nomadic tribe that exists by hunting. (p. 4)

Language Disorders

Language disorders are usually classified as either receptive or expressive. As described earlier, a receptive language disorder interferes with the understanding of language. A child may, for example, be unable to comprehend spoken sentences or to follow a sequence of directions. An expressive language disorder interferes with production of language. The child may have a very limited vocabulary, may use incorrect words and phrases, or may not even speak at all, communicating only through gestures. A child may have good receptive language when an expressive disorder is present or may have both expressive and receptive disorders in combination.

To say that a child has a language delay does not necessarily mean that the child has a language disorder. As Reed (1994) explains, a language delay implies that a child is slow to develop linguistic skills but acquires them in the same sequence as normal children. Generally, all features of language are delayed at about the same rate. A language disorder, however, suggests a disruption in the usual rate and sequence of specific emerging language skills. A child who consistently has difficulty in responding to who, what, and where questions but who otherwise displays language skills appropriate for his or her age would likely be considered to have a language disorder.

Chaney and Frodyma (1982) list several factors that can contribute to spoken language disorders in children:

- Cognitive limitations or mental retardation
- Environmental deprivation
- Hearing impairments
- Emotional deprivation or behavioral disorders
- Structural abnormalities of the speech mechanism

Environmental influences are thought to play an important part in delayed, disordered, or absent language. Some children are rewarded for their communication efforts; others, unfortunately, are punished for talking, gesturing, or otherwise attempting to communicate. A child who has little stimulation at home and few chances to speak, listen, explore, and interact with others will probably have little motivation for communication and may well develop disordered patterns of language. Children who have had little exposure to words and experiences may need the teacher's help in encouraging communication. Active participation in experiences gives children the opportunity to learn and use appropriate vocabulary.

Aphasia

Some severe disorders in expressive and receptive language result from impairments of the brain. The term **aphasia** is frequently used to describe a "breakdown in the ability to formulate, or to retrieve, and to decode the arbitrary symbols of language" (Holland & Reinmuth, 1982, p. 428). Aphasia is one of the most prevalent causes of language disorders in adults, most often occurring suddenly, following a cardiovascular event (stroke). Aphasia can also occur in children, however, as either a congenital or an acquired condition. Head injury is considered a significant cause of aphasia in children. Aphasia may be either expressive or, less commonly, receptive.

> Some professionals view learning disabilities (see Chapter 5) and autism (see Chapter 11) primarily as language disorders.

Children with mild aphasia have language patterns that are close to normal but may have difficulty retrieving certain words and tend to need more time than usual to communicate (Linebaugh, 1986). Children with severe aphasia, however, are likely to have a markedly reduced storehouse of words and language forms. They may not be able to "use language for successful communicative interchange" (Horner, 1986, p. 892).

✳ *Identification and Assessment*

"Don't worry, she'll grow out of it."
"Speech therapists can't help a child who doesn't talk."
"He'll be all right once he starts school."

These "misguided and inaccurate remarks" indicate widely held attitudes toward communication disorders (Thompson, 1984). Thompson contends that such attitudes are "at best worrying and annoying, at worst positively destructive to the child's social, emotional, and intellectual development" (p. 86).

To avoid the consequences of unrecognized or untreated speech and language disorders, it is especially important for children to receive professional assessment and evaluation services. When assessing or diagnosing a child suspected of having a communication disorder, the specialist seeks to meet the following objectives:

1. *To describe the problem.* What are the dimensions of the communicative disturbance with respect to voice, fluency, language, and articulation?
2. *To estimate its severity.* How large a problem is it?
3. *To identify factors that are related to the problem.* What are the antecedents and consequences of it?
4. *To estimate prospects for improvement.* What estimate can we make of the extent of possible recovery and the time frame of treatment?
5. *To derive a plan of treatment.* What are the specific targets for therapy, and how can the client best be approached? (Emerick & Haynes, 1986, p. 50)

Case History and Examination

Most professional speech and language assessments begin with the creation of a case history about the child. This typically involves completing a biographical form that includes such diverse information as the child's birth and developmental history, illness, medications taken, scores on achievement and intelligence tests, and adjustment to school. The parents may be asked when the child first crawled, walked, and uttered words. Social skills, such as playing readily with other children, may also be considered.

The specialist carefully examines the child's mouth, noting any irregularities in the tongue, lips, teeth, palate, or other structures that may affect speech production. If the child has an organic speech problem, the child is referred for possible medical intervention.

Evaluation Components

Testing procedures vary according to the suspected type of disorder. Often the specialist conducts broad screenings to detect areas of concern and then moves to more detailed testing in those areas. A comprehensive evaluation to detect the presence of a communication disorder would likely include the following components.

Articulation Test

The speech errors the child is making are assessed. A record is kept of the sounds that are defective, how they are being mispronounced, and the number of errors. Examples of articulation tests include the *Photo Articulation Test* (Pendergast, Dickey, Selmar, & Soder, 1984), the *Test of Minimal Articulation Competence* (Secord, 1981), and the *Goldman-Fristoe Test of Articulation* (Goldman & Fristoe, 1986).

Hearing Test

Hearing is usually tested to determine whether a hearing problem is causing the speech disorder.

Audiometry, a formal procedure for testing hearing, is discussed in Chapter 8.

Auditory Discrimination Test

This test is given to determine whether the child is hearing sounds correctly. If unable to recognize the specific characteristics of a given sound, the child will not have a good model to imitate. The *Auditory Discrimination Test* (Wepman, 1973) and the *Test of Auditory Discrimination* (Goldman, Fristoe, & Woodcock, 1990) are two examples.

Language Development Test

This test is administered to help determine the amount of vocabulary the child has acquired, because vocabulary is generally a good indication of intelligence. Frequently used tests of language development include the *Peabody Picture Vocabulary Test* (Dunn, 1965) and the *Tests of Language Development* (Newcomber & Hammill, 1988).

Another form of evaluation used more and more frequently is an overall language test, which assesses the child's understanding and production of language structures (e.g., important syntactical elements like conjunctions showing causal relationships). An example is the *Clinical Evaluation of Language Functions* (Semel & Wiig, 1980).

Language Samples

An important part of any evaluation procedure is obtaining a language sample, an accurate example of the child's expressive speech and language. The effective exam-

A comprehensive assessment of communication disorders includes articulation, auditory discrimination, vocabulary tests, and a language sample.

iner does not ask merely, "Does the child talk?" but rather, "How does the child communicate?" (Ulrey, 1982, p. 123). The examiner considers such factors as intelligibility and fluency of speech, voice quality, and use of vocabulary and grammar. Some speech-language pathologists use structured tasks to evoke language samples. They may, for example, ask a child to describe a picture, tell a story, or answer a list of questions. Most specialists, however, use informal conversation as their preferred procedure to obtain language samples (Atkins & Cartwright, 1982). They believe that the child's language sample will be more representative if the examiner uses natural conversation, rather than highly structured tasks. Emerick and Haynes (1986) advise examiners to tape-record language samples instead of take notes, which can be distracting to the child. Open-ended questions, such as, "Tell me about your family," are suggested, rather than yes-no questions or questions that can be answered with one word, such as, "What color is your car?"

Behavioral observation is becoming increasingly important in assessing communication disorders. Objective recording of children's language competence in social contexts has added much to our knowledge of language acquisition. It is imperative that the observer have experience in reliably recording speech and language and sample the child's communication behavior across various settings, rather than limiting it to a clinic or examining room. A parent-child observation is frequently arranged for young children. The specialist provides appropriate toys and activities and requests the parent to interact normally with the child.

McCormick and Schiefelbusch (1990) note that assessment and evaluation of intervention efforts increasingly emphasize the importance of gathering data on both the child's and the adult's behavior in the language interaction. The extent to which the child learns and uses language effectively in the classroom depends to a large extent on the teacher's language behavior. Observational data can be used to suggest and guide needed changes in the adult's behavior (Blank, 1988).

Arena Assessment

When multiple members of a transdisciplinary team are involved in planning and carrying out an intervention for a child with a communication disorder, a strategy known as *arena assessment* may prove beneficial. Arena assessment is a group assessment procedure in which parents, teachers, speech-language pathologists, and other involved participants seat themselves in a circle or semicircle around the child. Wolery and Dyk (1984) suggest five advantages for the arena assessment approach. First, because many similar or even identical test items appear on the tests given by different specialists, redundancy is eliminated, and both the child and parents are spared responding repeatedly to the same item. Second, unnecessary handling of the child by various professionals is reduced. Third, team members observe the child perform across a wider range of performance domains and end up with a more holistic view of the child. Fourth, team members have an opportunity to observe and learn from one another. Finally, consensus regarding the child's status and intervention needs is more likely because each team member observes the same set of child behaviors.

After the assessment procedures have been completed, the speech-language pathologist reviews the results of the case history, formal and informal tests, language samples, behavioral observations, medical records, and other available data. A treatment plan is then developed in cooperation with the child's parents and teachers to set up realistic communication objectives and to determine the methods that will be used. Kelly and Rice (1986) suggest giving parents an opportunity to question and react to the recommendations and to discuss their willingness to follow through with the treatment plans. It is also appropriate, they note, to inform parents of the frequency of therapy, the costs involved, and the availability of resources in the community.

✻ *Prevalence*

Estimates of the prevalence of communication disorders in children vary widely. Reliable figures are hard to come by because investigators often employ different definitions of speech and language disorders and sample different populations. Fein (1983) reviewed various prevalence studies of school-age populations and concluded that speech impairments serious enough to warrant special attention are present in approximately 4.2% of children. This represents a large population, compared with other categories of exceptional children. A 4.2% prevalence rate would mean that between 2 million and 3 million children in the United States have communication disorders. In the 1992–93 school year, 1,000,154 children aged 6 to 21 received special education services under the IDEA category of "speech or language impairments." This number represents about 1.7% of the resident population and 21.6% of all students receiving special education services, which makes speech or language impairments the second largest category after learning disabilities.

Fein (1983) reports that speech impairments tend to be more prevalent among males than females and about the same in each of the major geographical regions of the United States. Similarly, the National Center for Health Statistics (1981) states that approximately twice as many boys as girls have speech impairments.

Figures on the prevalence of language disorders are less reliable. Reed (1994) notes that about 1% of school-age children are considered to have language disorders. Because definitions of learning disabilities emphasize understanding and use of spoken and written language (see Chapter 5), however, a sizable percentage of children who are served in special education programs for students with learning disabilities could also be regarded as having language disorders.

Some figures are available on the incidence and prevalence of specific types of communication disorders. In the past, articulation disorders were by far the most common type of speech problem found in children. The American Speech-Language-Hearing Association (ASHA) estimated in 1961 that 80% of the school-age population with communication disorders had articulation disorders. Changing emphasis and improved assessment techniques, however, have led to changes in the relative number of children treated for speech and language disorders. A 1982 ASHA survey indicated that "54% of speech-language pathologists' clients were primarily exhibiting language impairments" (cited in Fein, 1983, p. 37).

The prevalence of communication disorders does not remain the same throughout the life span. The percentage of children with speech and language disorders, though rather high, decreases significantly from the earlier to the later school grades. For example, Hull, Mielke, Willeford, and Timmons (1976) found that about 7% of all 1st-grade boys were reported as having "extreme articulation deviations," but only 1% of 3rd-grade boys and 0.5% of 12th-grade boys fell into that category. Culton (1986) studied more than 30,000 college freshmen who had undergone screening tests during a 13-year period and found that 2.4% exhibited speech disorders, with an additional 2.3% reporting they had recovered from earlier speech disorders. The largest part of the population with speech-language impairments is composed of young children with articulation problems. Many of these disorders (e.g., saying "wabbit" for *rabbit* or "thith" for *this*), though significant enough to merit professional attention, are apparently not severe enough to persist into adulthood. They respond favorably to intervention and/or maturation.

✳ *Historical Background*

Although there have always been people with speech and language disorders, special education and treatment for this population are relatively recent developments. The first special class for "speech defective" children in the United States was established in New York in 1908 (Hewett & Forness, 1977), whereas special education for other groups of children with disabilities—those with hearing or visual impairments or challenged by mental retardation—was begun much earlier, which suggests that communication disorders have historically been considered less severe and less easily recognized than other disabilities.

During the 19th century, some treatment was provided at clinics and hospitals for people with communication disorders. The earliest specialists were college and university professors who, in the course of their study of normal speech processes, became interested in people with irregular patterns of speech, particularly stuttering and articulation disorders. Although U.S. therapists concentrated primarily on the correction of speech defects, prior to World War II European specialists (largely physicians) had developed a considerable body of scientific knowledge about communication disorders (Boone, 1977). The postwar years saw a proliferation of clinical services and research efforts. Many speech pathologists became especially interested in the rehabilitation of military personnel who had developed communication disorders because of damage to the brain or to the physical speech mechanisms. Speech and hearing clinics and centers were established in many cities, often operating in cooperation with hospitals or universities.

In recent years, services in the regular public schools to children with speech and language disorders have expanded noticeably. Professionals who provide remedial services to children with communication disorders are today usually called *speech language pathologists or communication disorders specialists*, rather than speech therapists. In 1978, the name of the major professional organization involved with communication disorders was changed to the American Speech-Language-Hearing Association (though it is still abbreviated as ASHA). These changes in terminology reflect awareness of the interrelationships among speech, language, and other aspects of learning, communication, and behavior. Speech is no longer viewed as a narrow specialty concerned with disorders to be corrected in isolation. Increasingly, speech-language pathologists who work in school settings now function as team members concerned with children's overall education and development. The trend is increasingly for remedial procedures to be carried out in the regular classroom, rather than in a special speech room, and the speech-language pathologist often provides training and consultation for the regular classroom teacher, who may do much of the direct work with a child with communication disorders.

Through the mid-1900s, the professional titles *speech teacher* and *speech correctionist* were popular, reflecting an emphasis on correcting articulation, fluency, and voice disorders.

✳ *Educational Approaches*

Various approaches are employed in the treatment of speech and language disorders. The profession of speech-language pathology addresses both organic and functional causes and encompasses practitioners with numerous points of view and a wide range of accepted intervention techniques. Medical, dental, and surgical procedures can help many children whose speech problems result from organic causes. Some specialists employ structured exercises and drills to correct speech sounds; others emphasize speech production in natural language contexts. Some prefer to work with children in individual therapy sessions; others believe that group sessions are advantageous for language modeling and peer support. Some encourage children to imitate the therapist's speech; others prefer to have the child listen to tapes of his or her own speech. Some specialists follow a structured, teacher-directed approach, in which targeted speech and language behaviors are precisely prompted, recorded, and reinforced; others favor less structured methods. Some speech-language therapists focus exclusively on a child's expressive and receptive communication; others devote attention to other aspects of the child's behavior and environment, such as self-confidence and interactions with parents and classmates. Clearly, many possible options may be explored in devising an appropriate treatment plan.

Articulation Disorders

Speech-language pathologists, according to Bernthal and Bankson (1986), feel more comfortable and competent when dealing with articulation disorders than with other types of speech and language impairments. This response is probably attributable, they note, to the fact that articulation disorders can be broken down into identifiable segments more readily than can disorders of voice, fluency, or language. Also, a child can logically progress from articulating simple sounds in isolation to syllables, words, phrases, sentences, and sustained conversation. A large percentage of functional articulation disorders either are treated successfully or simply fade away as the child matures.

Treatment Models

Four models of treatment are widely used for articulation disorders (Bernthal & Bankson, 1986; Creaghead, Newman, & Secord, 1989). In the *discrimination model,* emphasis is on developing the child's ability to listen carefully and detect the differences between similar sounds (e.g., the *t* in *take* and the *c* in *cake*). The child learns to match speech to that of a standard model by using auditory, visual, and tactual feedback.

The *phonologic model* seeks to identify the pattern of sound production and to teach the child to produce gradually more acceptable sounds. A child who tends to omit final consonants, for example, might be taught to recognize the difference between word pairs—for example, *two* and *tooth*—and then to produce them more accurately.

The *sensorimotor model* emphasizes the repetitive production of sounds in various contexts, with special attention to the motor skills involved in articulation; frequent exercises are employed to produce sounds with differing stress patterns.

The *operant conditioning model* seeks to define antecedent events, present specific stimuli, and shape articulatory responses by providing reinforcing consequences. These four models to the remediation of articulation disorders are not mutually exclusive of one another. The interventions planned by many speech-language pathologists involve a combination of the four approaches.

A generally consistent relationship exists between children's ability to recognize sounds and their ability to articulate them correctly (Creaghead et al., 1989). Whatever treatment model(s) are used, the specialist may have the child carefully watch how sounds are produced and then use a mirror to monitor his or her own speech production. Children are expected to accurately produce problematic sounds in syllables, words, sentences, and stories. They may tape-record their own speech and listen carefully for errors. It is sometimes helpful for children to learn to recognize the difference between the way they produce a sound and the way other people produce it. As in all communication training, it is important for the teacher, parent, or specialist to provide a good language model, to reward the child's positive performance, and to encourage the child to talk.

Voice Disorders

When a child has a voice disorder, a medical examination should always be sought. Organic causes often respond to surgery or medical treatment. In addition, communication disorders specialists sometimes recommend environmental modifications; a person who is consistently required to speak in a noisy setting, for example, may benefit from the use of a small microphone to reduce vocal straining and shouting (Moore & Hicks, 1994). Most remedial techniques, however, offer direct vocal rehabilitation, which helps the child with a voice disorder gradually learn to produce more acceptable and efficient speech. Depending on the type of voice disorder and the child's overall circumstances, vocal rehabilitation may include such activities as exercises to increase breathing capacity, relaxation techniques to reduce tension, or procedures to increase or decrease the loudness of speech.

Applied behavior analysis has had a major impact on the treatment of voice disorders in recent years (Johnson, 1986). Because many voice problems are directly attributable to vocal abuse, behavioral principles are frequently used to shape and modify abusive vocal behaviors. Many children and adults have thus been able to break habitual patterns of vocal misuse. Computer technology has also been successfully applied in the treatment of voice disorders. Some instruments enable speakers to see visual representations of their voice patterns on a screen or printout; speakers are thus able to monitor their own vocalizations visually as well as auditorily and to develop new patterns of using their voices more naturally and efficiently (Bull & Rushakoff, 1987).

Visi-pitch is an example of a visual speech display. It can be used with Apple and IBM computers.

Fluency Disorders

The treatment of stuttering and other fluency disorders varies widely according to the orientation of the client and the therapist. Throughout history, people who stutter have been subjected to countless treatments—some of them unusual, to say the least. Past treatments included holding pebbles in the mouth, sticking fingers into a light socket, talking out of one side of the mouth, eating raw oysters, speaking with the teeth clenched, taking alternating hot and cold baths, and speaking on inhaled rather than exhaled air (Ham, 1986). For many years, it was widely thought that stuttering was caused by a tongue that was unable to function properly in the mouth. It was not uncommon for early physicians to prescribe ointments to blister or numb the tongue or even to remove portions of the tongue through surgery!

Today's treatment methods tend to emphasize one of two general approaches (Ham, 1986). One approach might be termed "symptom modification." Using various techniques, the therapist takes aim at the stuttering itself and/or the stutterer's underlying emotional dimensions. The principal goal of such therapy is to develop the person's ability to control the stuttering in situations in which communication is required. The other prevalent approach could be labeled "fluency reinforcement." A therapist using this methodology would regard stuttering as a learned response and seek to eliminate it by establishing and encouraging fluent speech.

Application of behavioral principles has strongly influenced recent practices in the treatment of fluency disorders. Hegde (1986) observes that punishing stuttering is socially undesirable as well as ineffective and tends to generate emotional side effects, but the "positive reinforcement of nonstuttered utterances can be an attractive alternative" (p. 521). Children may learn to manage their stuttering by deliberately prolonging certain sounds or by speaking slowly to get through a "block." They may increase their confidence and fluency by speaking in groups, where pressure is minimized and successful speech is positively reinforced. They may learn to monitor their own speech and to reward themselves for periods of fluency. They may learn to speak to a rhythmic beat or with the aid of devices that mask or delay their ability to hear their own speech. Tape recorders are often used for drills, simulated conversations, and documenting progress.

Effective treatment programs do not focus on only one aspect of stuttering, but instead identify and alter its communicative, behavioral, and emotional components (Emerick & Haynes, 1986). Hegde (1993) emphasizes the importance of generalization of the targeted speech behaviors to natural settings—that is, outside the clinic. A therapist, for example, might go with the stutterer to a store or restaurant and conduct the treatment in an unobtrusive manner. Parents, teachers, siblings, and peers may be invited to the treatment sessions and trained to reinforce stutter-free patterns of speech at home or school.

When interacting with a child who stutters, it is recommended that a teacher pay primary attention to what the child is saying, rather than to the difficulties in saying it. This focus helps the child develop a more positive attitude toward him- or herself and communication with others. When the child experiences a verbal block, the teacher should be patient and calm, say nothing, and maintain eye contact with the child until he or she finishes speaking.

Children often learn to control their stuttering and produce increasingly fluent speech as they mature. No single method of treatment has been recognized as most effective. Stuttering frequently decreases when children enter adolescence, regardless of which treatment method was used. In some cases, the problem even disappears with no treatment at all. Martin and Lindamood (1986) studied the phenomenon of spontaneous recovery from stuttering and concluded that approximately 40% to 45% of children diagnosed as stutterers apparently outgrow or get over their dysfluencies without formal intervention.

For some specific suggestions for how classroom teachers can help children with speech dysfluencies, see "Helping the Child Who Stutters" later in this chapter.

Language Disorders

Treatments for language disorders are also extremely varied. Some programs focus on precommunication activities that encourage the child to explore and that make the environment conducive to the development of receptive and expressive language. Clearly, children must have something they want to communicate. And because children learn through imitation, it is important for the teacher or specialist to talk clearly, use correct inflections, and provide a rich variety of words and sentences.

Chaney and Frodyma (1982) describe two methods to encourage language development in preschool children with disabilities: the precision method and the experiential method. In the *precision method,* children are placed into groups according to their ability levels in each of several areas, such as language, cognition, motor skills, self-help skills, and social skills. Group lessons and activities, each about 20 minutes long, emphasize language through tasks a child has not yet learned, and extensive data on each child's performance are maintained. The *experiential method* uses groups of children with varying levels of language ability; children with higher language skills serve as models for those whose language is less well developed. Different demands and expectations are placed on each child, and each day's activities are presented around a unified theme or experience. Activities for one day, for example, might revolve around clothing. The children might discuss what clothes they are wearing, paste clothes on paper dolls, wash clothes, and learn concepts of size and color by using articles of clothing.

Some specialists in language disorders do a great deal of written and verbal labeling to help the child develop language content—that is, attach meaning to important objects in the environment. In many instances, children's language skills improve when they become better able to pay attention. The specialist may reinforce the child for imitating facial expressions or body movements or simply for maintaining eye contact. Some speech-language pathologists emphasize pairing actions with words, teaching the natural gestures that go along with such expressions as "up," "look," and "good-bye." D'Angelo (1981) recommends wordless picture books as a means of building vocabulary, conversational skills, and positive attitudes in children with language disorders. A parent or teacher can use questions such as "What is happening in the picture?" and "What things do you see?" to initiate conversations with a child.

Speech-language specialists are increasingly employing naturalistic interventions to help children develop and use language skills. *Naturalistic interventions* occur in real or simulated activities that naturally occur in the home, school, or community environments in which a child normally functions. Goldstein, Kaczmarek, & Hepting (1994) offers this definition of and rationale for the development and use of naturalistic interventions:

> The term **milieu teaching** is also used to refer to naturalistic interventions.

> Naturalistic interventions vary in the extent to which they depart from the didactic teaching strategies historically implemented in "pull-out" models of treatment for communications disorders. Typically, naturalistic interventions are characterized by their use of dispersed learning trials, attempts to base teaching on the child's attentional lead within the context of normal conversational interchanges, and orientation toward teaching the form and content of language in the context of normal use. Didactic intervention approaches, on the other hand, have been conducted using substitute stimuli (e.g., pictures, puppets) or simulation settings that are amenable to teaching specific skills using mass trials. Naturalistic approaches were developed as an alternative to didactic language intervention, because children often experienced difficulties in generalizing new skills to everyday contexts where they were needed. (p. 102)

Kaiser (1993) recommends that naturalistic, or *milieu teaching strategies,* be

- brief and positive in nature,
- carried out in the natural environment as opportunities for teaching functional communication occur, and
- occasioned by student interest in the topic. (p. 349)

Helping the Child Who Stutters

Suggestions for Classroom Teachers

There is no easy treatment for stuttering because the causation, type, and severity of nonfluencies vary from child to child. In addition, some children are unaware of their nonfluencies. Although others are aware, they are comfortable with their speech and enjoy participating in classroom discussion. Many are self-conscious at a very early age and fear speaking aloud. Despite this variability, teachers can significantly help a child who stutters by enhancing the child's fluency. This can be accomplished by providing a good speech model, improving the child's self-esteem, and creating a good speech environment.

Provide a Good Speech Model

1. *Reduce your rate of speech.* Young children often imitate the speech rate of their parents and other significant adults. This rate may be inappropriately fast for the child's motoric and linguistic competencies. Slower speech provides the child the time needed to organize thoughts, choose vocabulary and grammatical form, and plan the speech act motorically.
2. *Create silences in your interactions.* Pauses placed at appropriate places in conversation help create a relaxed communication environment, slower rate of speech, and a more natural speech cadence. Pause for 2 to 3 seconds before responding to a child's questions and statements.
3. *Model simple vocabulary and grammatical forms.* Stuttering is more likely to occur in longer words, words that are used less frequently, and more grammatically complex sentences.
4. *Model normal nonfluencies.* If you are highly fluent, you may need to make a conscious effort to use normal nonfluencies, such as interjections ("um" or "ah"), or an occasional whole-word repetition, phrase repetition, or pause. Children should be aware that even fluent speech contains nonflu-

encies. This knowledge will help them accept nonfluencies and reduce the fear of speaking.

Improve the Child's Self-Esteem

1. *Disregard moments of nonfluency.* Create a positive communication environment by reinforcing moments of fluency and ignoring nonfluencies. Do not give instructions on how to be fluent. Saying "Slow down," "Take a deep breath," or "Stop and start over" implies that the child is not doing enough. This might increase guilt and diminish self-confidence.
2. *Show acceptance of what the child expresses, rather than how it is said.* Ask the child to repeat only the parts of the utterance that were not understood, rather than those that were nonfluent. This request indicates that you did listen and that it is the message that is important.
3. *Treat the child who stutters like any other child in the class.* Do not reduce your expectations because of the nonfluencies.
4. *Acknowledge nonfluencies without labeling them.* Do not refer to the problem of stuttering. Instead, use words that the child uses to describe his or her speech, such as "bumpy" or "hard." Assure the child that it is okay to have dysfluencies—everyone does.
5. *Help the child feel in control of speech.* Follow the child's lead in conversation. Speech will more likely be fluent if the child can talk about areas of interest.
6. *Accept nonfluencies.* Be aware of negative bias—being overly concerned about normal nonfluencies because you see the child as a stutterer. Maintain eye contact and remain patient.

Create a Good Speech Environment

1. *Establish good conversational rules.* Interruptions may distract the child and increase the nonfluencies. Ensure that no one interrupts and that everyone gets a chance to talk.

2. *Listen attentively.* Listen to the child's speech and avoid absentminded "uh-huhs." Active listening lets the child know that content is important. Use naturalistic comments (e.g., "Yes, Johnny, that is a large blue truck.") in place of generic statements (e.g., "Good talking!").

3. *Suggest that the child cease other activities while speaking.* It is sometimes difficult to perform two different motoric acts, such as coloring and talking, simultaneously. Asking the child to stop other activities while speaking may improve fluency.

4. *Prepare the child for upcoming events.* The emotionality of birthdays, holidays, field trips, and changes in the daily schedule may cause apprehension and increase stuttering. Discussing upcoming events can reduce fear associated with the unknown and should enhance the child's fluency.

A speech-language pathologist should be contacted when a child exhibits signs of stuttering or when the parents are concerned about speech fluency. Seek this referral immediately; waiting to see whether or not the child will "outgrow" the stuttering is seldom beneficial. Although some children who stutter get better without help, many do not. Early intervention may prevent the child from developing a severe stutter. In its initial stages, stuttering can almost always be treated successfully by teachers, parents, and speech-language pathologist working together.

From "Stuttering: The Role of the Classroom Teacher" by G. R. LaBlance, K. F. Steckol, & V. L. Smith, *Teaching Exceptional Children,* 1994, *26*(2), 10–12. Used by permission.

Naturalistic interventions involve *structuring the environment* to create numerous opportunities for the desired child responses (e.g., holding up a toy and asking, "What do you want?") and *structuring adult responses* to a child's communication (e.g., the child points outside and says, "Go wifth me," and the teacher says, "OK, I'll go with you."). Good milieu teaching should "more closely resemble a conversation than a rote instructional episode" (Kaiser, 1993, p. 350). But good naturalistic teaching does not mean the teacher should wait patiently to see whether and when opportunities for meaningful and interesting language use by children occur. Environments in which language teaching takes place should be designed to catch students' interest and increase the likelihood of communicative interactions that can be used for teaching purposes. Kaiser (1993) describes six strategies for arranging environments that create naturally occurring language teaching opportunities (see Table 7.2).

No matter what the approach to treatment, clearly children with language disorders need to be around children and adults with something interesting to talk about. As Reed (1994) points out, it was assumed for many years that a one-to-one setting was the most effective format for language intervention. Emphasis was on eliminating distracting stimuli and focusing a child's attention on the desired communication task. Today, however, the importance of language as an interactive, interpersonal behavior is generally recognized, and naturally occurring intervention formats can expose children with language disorders to "a variety of stimuli, experiences, contexts, and people that are not available in one-to-one situations" (Reed, 1986, p. 276).

Whatever intervention methods they use, effective speech-language pathologists establish specific goals and objectives, keep precise records of their students' behaviors, and arrange the learning environment so that each child's efforts at communication will be rewarded and enjoyable.

TABLE 7.2
Six strategies for increasing natural opportunities for language teaching

1. **Interesting materials**. Students are likely to communicate when things or activities in the environment interest them. *Example:* James lay quietly on the rug, with his head resting on his arms. Ms. Davis sat at one end of the rug and rolled a big yellow ball right past James. James lifted his head and looked around for the ball.

2. **Out of reach.** Students are likely to communicate when they want something that they cannot reach. *Example:* Mr. Norris lifted a drum off the shelf and placed it on the floor between Judy and Annette, who were both in wheelchairs. Mr. Norris hit the drum three times and then waited, looking at his two students. Judy watched and clapped her hands together. Then, she reached for the drum with both arms outstretched.

3. **Inadequate portions.** Students are likely to communicate when they do not have the necessary materials to carry out an instruction. *Example:* Mr. Robinson passed out paints and water to the four children at the art table. He handed a paintbrush to each of the children except Mary. "Now, let's all paint a beautiful picture," he said and smiled at Mary. "Brush!" exclaimed Mary. "Need brush."

4. **Choice making.** Students are likely to communicate when they are given a choice. *Example:* Peggy's favorite pastime is listening to tapes on her tape recorder. On Saturday morning, Peggy's father said to her, "We could listen to your tapes" (pointing to the picture of the tape recorder on Peggy's communication board) "or we could go for a ride in the car" (pointing to the picture of the car). "What would you like to do?" Peggy pointed to the picture of the tape recorder. "OK, let's listen to this new tape you like," her father said as he put the tape in and turned on the machine.

5. **Assistance.** Students are likely to communicate when they need assistance in operating or manipulating materials. *Example:* Tammy's mother placed a small windup car on the table, turned the key, and let it race toward Tammy. Tammy clapped her hands and grabbed the little toy as it slowed to a stop. She fidgeted with the key for a few moments and then, with a worried look, held the toy car toward her mother. "Help," she said.

6. **Silly situations.** Students are likely to communicate when something happens that they don't expect. *Example:* Ms. Esser was helping Kathy put on her socks and shoes after rest time. After assisting with the socks, Ms. Esser put one of the shoes on her own foot. Kathy stared at the shoe for a moment and then looked up at her teacher, who was smiling. "No," laughed Kathy, "my shoe."

Source: Reprinted with the permission of Simon & Schuster, Inc. from the Merrill/Prentice Hall text *Instruction of Students with Severe Disabilities* 4/e by Martha E. Snell. Copyright 1993 by Merrill/Prentice Hall.

Augmentative and Alternative Communication

Augmentative and alternative communication (AAC) refers to a diverse set of strategies and methods to assist individuals who are unable to meet their communication needs through speech or writing. AAC can be viewed as a model with three components (Lloyd, Quist, & Windsor, 1990):

1. A representational symbol set, or vocabulary
2. A means for selecting the symbols
3. A means for transmitting the symbols

Each of the three components of AAC may be unaided and aided. *Unaided techniques* do not require a physical aid or device (Lloyd & Kangas, 1994). They include oral speech, gestures, facial expressions, general body posture, and manual signs. Of course, individuals without disabilities use a wide range of unaided augmentative communication techniques. *Aided techniques* of communication involve an external device or piece of equipment. Table 7.3 presents a comparison of unaided and aided methods of AAC in terms of some advantages and disadvantages to both the user and the listener.

The Crestwood Company publishes a catalog of AAC devices for children and adults. See "For More Information" at the end of this chapter.

Symbol Sets and Symbol Systems

Individuals who do not speak so that others can understand must have access to vocabulary that matches as nearly as possible the language they would use and generate in various situations if they could speak. Beukelman (1988) suggests that decisions about what items to include in a student's augmentative vocabulary should be based on

- vocabulary that peers in similar situations and settings use
- what communication partners (e.g., teachers, parents) think will be needed
- vocabulary the student is already using in all modalities
- contextual demands of specific situations

After selecting the vocabulary for an augmentative communication system, one needs to choose or develop a collection of symbols in which each symbol represents

Joshua and his friend use his communication board for many purposes.

TABLE 7.3

Some advantages and disadvantages of unaided and aided methods for alternative and augmentative communication (AAC)

AIDED[1]	UNAIDED[2]
Advantages	**Advantages**
Highly adaptable to motoric and sensory needs.	No difficulty with portability.
Human-aided scanning can increase social closeness.	Message can be sent quickly.
Suitable for persons who have problems processing temporal, transient stimuli.	May enhance eye contact and general interaction because total attention of listener required.
	Can be used to teach grammatical structures.
	Some evidence that signing can improve receptive language.
Disadvantages	**Disadvantages**
Problems with portability.	ASL signs require good motor control.
Listener must usually concentrate on display rather than on message sender.	Research indicates little true use of signs by persons who have severe cognitive disabilities.
Efficiency is dependent on transient motor state (e.g., fatigue, excitement).	Signing is unintelligible to most people in integrated settings.
Vocabulary expansion can be difficult.	
Grammatically complete messages are improbable due to vocabulary, time, or motoric constraints.	
Can be forgotten, lost, or ruined.	

[1] e.g., pictures, books, electronic displays, etc
[2] e.g., signing, gestures, nonsymbolic behaviors

Source: Reprinted with the permission of Simon & Schuster, Inc. from the Merrill/Prentice Hall text *Instruction of Students with Severe Disabilities* 4/e by Martha E. Snell. Copyright 1993 by Merrill/Prentice Hall.

one or more specified meanings. There are numerous commercially available *symbol sets,* a collection of pictures or drawings in which each symbol has one or more specified meaning, from which a person's AAC vocabulary might be constructed. Symbol sets—such as *The Oakland Picture Dictionary* (Kirsten, 1981), the *Picture Communication Symbols* (Mayer-Johnson, 1986), and the *Pictogram Ideogram Communication* symbols (Johnson, 1985)—are graphic, which means that the symbols "look like" the object or concept they represent as much as possible.

In contrast to symbol sets, *symbol systems* are structured around an internal set of rules that govern how new symbols are added to the system. One of the most well known symbol systems is *Blissymbolics.* Bliss symbols were developed in the 1940s by Austrian chemical engineer Charles Bliss as a graphic symbol system for international communication and adapted by the Easter Seal Communication Institute in Toronto, Canada, in the early 1970s for use by nonspeaking persons with physical disabilities (McDonald, 1980). Bliss symbols represent concepts through a combination of geometric shapes. The user of Blissymbolics combines multiple symbols to create new meanings (e.g., *school* is communicated by selecting the symbols *house-gives-knowledge*). The system offers a means of greatly expanded communication to the nonspeaking individual who can learn the new language of Blissymbolics. Because many of the Blissymbolics are abstract, however, and do not look like the concept they represent, some individuals have difficulty learning the system. In one study, adolescents with severe physical disabilities quickly learned to use graphic line drawings that directly represented vocabulary objects but developed little functional use of the Bliss symbols (Hurlbut, Iwata, & Green, 1982).

Figure 7.2 shows how seven different symbol sets represent some common concrete and abstract referents. Symbol sets may also be "homemade," consisting of photos, pictures, and perhaps words and the alphabet.

Selecting the Symbols

Symbols are selected in augmentative communication by direct selection, scanning, or encoding responses (Lloyd & Kangas, 1994). *Direct selection* involves pointing to the symbol one wishes to express with a finger or fist, or sometimes with a wand attached to the head or chin. With a limited number of selections widely spaced from one another, the user can select symbols by "eye pointing." *Scanning* techniques present choices to the user one at a time, and the user makes a response at the proper time to indicate which item or group of selections he or she wants to communicate. Scanning can be machine or listener assisted (e.g., the listener may point to symbols one at a time while watching for the user's eye-blink that signals selection). *Encoding* involves giving multiple signals to indicate the location of the symbol or item to be selected. Usually, the user makes a pair of responses that direct the listener to a specific printed message on a reference list. Encoding can be particularly useful for a student whose severe physical impairments prohibit reliable selection by pointing to an item, unless there are very few symbols and they are widely spaced. In a display in which symbols are organized by color and number, for example, a student can first touch one card (to select the "red" group of messages) and then make a second pointing response to indicate which number message in the red group is intended.

Transmitting the Symbols

Once vocabulary and a symbol set have been selected, a method of transmitting the symbols must be determined. The most common tool for augmentative communication display and transmission is the *communication board*, a flat area (often a tray or table attached to a wheelchair) on which the symbols are arranged for the user to select. A student may have a basic communication board of common words, phrases, numbers, and so forth for use across many situations and various situational boards, or miniboards, with specific vocabulary for certain situations (e.g., at a restaurant, in science class). Symbols can also be transported and displayed in a wallet or photo album.

Recent technological advances have resulted in several electronic devices that offer a wide range of alternatives for transmitting communication symbols. Dedicated communication aids—such as the Prentke Romich Intro Talker, the Prentke Romich Liberator, DECtalk by Digital Equipment Company, and Sentinent System's Dynavok—offer computerized speech selection and transmission.

See Table 7.4 for suggestions on how to communicate with a person who uses AAC. More ideas for being a good communication partner can be found in the Teaching & Learning box at the end of this chapter.

World-renowned physicist Stephen W. Hawking explains how he uses a computerized speech synthesizer in "My Communication System" later in this chapter.

FIGURE 7.2

Examples of symbols used to represent several relatively common concrete and abstract referents from some widely used graphic symbol sets. PCS = Picture Communication Symbols, PIC = Pictogram Ideogram Communication.

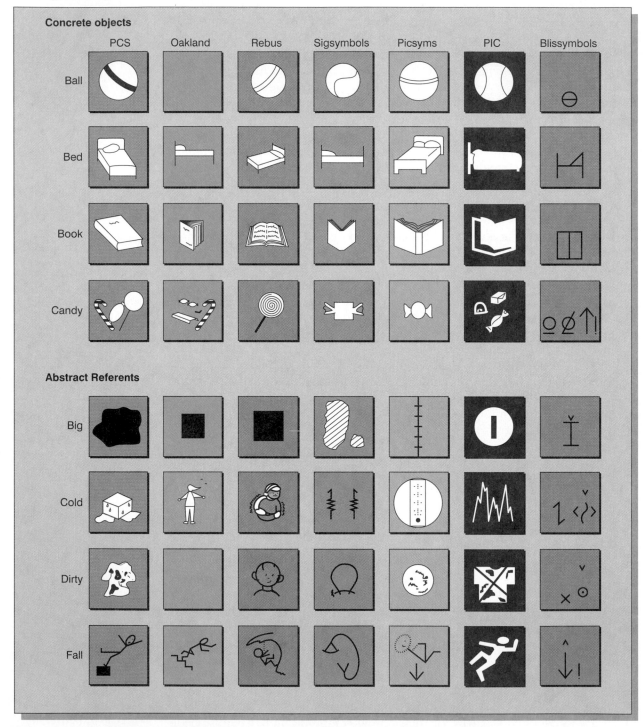

Source: From "Non-Speech Modes and Systems" by G. C. Vanderheiden and L. L. Lloyd. In S. W. Blackstone (Ed.), 1986, *Augmentative communication* (ff. 49–161). Rockville, MD: American Speech-Language-Hearing Association. Used by permission.

TABLE 7.4
How to talk with a person who uses AAC

Communicating with someone who does not speak can be a challenging, even unnerving, experience for many natural speakers. Here are 10 suggestions for those who use speech to communicate that will help improve the quality of their conversations with people who use ACC:

- Introduce yourself.
- Ask the person to show you how the communication system works.
- Pause to let the person construct a message. Be patient; it might take a while.
- Relax and give yourself a chance to get used to a slower rhythm of communication. Don't feel like you have to fill all the silent spaces by talking all the time.
- Be sure to give your new friend a chance to ask you questions or to make comments.
- Even though you might guess what's coming next from context, don't finish the person's sentences unless given permission or prompted to do so.
- Interact at eye-to-eye level if you can. If the person's in a wheelchair, you might grab a chair and sit across from her.
- Pay attention to facial expressions and gestures, just as you would with someone who communicates by speech.
- Don't be afraid to say you don't understand something and to ask to have it repeated.
- Talk directly to the person; don't communicate with her through someone else.

Source: Adapted from "Beyond Public Awareness: The Road to Involvement!" by S. W. Blackstone, 1991, *Augmentative Communication News, 4*(2), p. 6. Published by Augmentative Communication, Inc., Monterey, CA. Used by permission.

Facilitated Communication

Facilitated communication (FC) is a type of augmentative communication in which a "facilitator" provides assistance to someone in typing or pointing to vocabulary symbols. Facilitated communication, first developed in Australia for use with persons with cerebral palsy (Crossley, 1988; Crossley & Remington-Guerney, 1992), was brought to the United States and used primarily with persons with autism and mental retardation by Biklen (1990), who describes it like this:

> In facilitation a parent, friend, teacher, speech language clinician or other communication partner provides physical and emotional support as the person with a communication disability tries to point in order to communicate. The method can involve pointing at pictures or letters. The physical support may include: assistance in isolating the index finger; stabilizing the arm to overcome tremor; backward resistance on the arm to slow the pace of pointing or to overcome impulsiveness; a touch of the forearm, elbow or shoulder to help the person initiate typing; or pulling back on the arm or wrist to help the person not strike a target repetitively. Emotional support involves providing encouragement but not direction. It is important that the person look at the target. Also, the facilitator must work to avoid influencing the person's selections. . . . Fading physical support causes the typists to pay better attention to looking at the keyboard. (*The Syracuse Record,* November 1, 1993, n.p.)

FC typically involves an alphanumeric keyboard on which the user types out his message one letter at a time. Advocates have reported that FC has produced dra-

This communication device transmits the user's selections visually and via synthesized speech.

matically more sophisticated language than the user is able to produce by speech, signing, or gestures (Biklen, 1990, 1992; Crossley, 1988), which has led to speculations of average intelligence by individuals previously thought to have severe or profound intellectual disabilities. FC generated a tremendous amount of attention in both the special education literature and the popular press. State education and mental retardation agencies and school districts hired FC experts and sent their teachers to be trained in the new technique. Many children and adults with disabilities were "facilitated" on a daily basis. All of this was done in the absence of any objective, scientific evaluation of FC.

Although some educators and many parents raised questions from the beginning over the efficacy and appropriateness of FC, asking for some "data" supporting its use, many more were too excited about the promises of this new wonder therapy to ask too many questions. FC just seemed too good to be true. But as the uniformly negative results of carefully controlled empirical studies on FC have grown (e.g., Oswald, 1994; Wheeler, Jacobson, Paglieri, & Schwartz, 1993), more are questioning its use. Research designed to validate FC has repeatedly demonstrated either facilitator influence (correct or meaningful language is produced only when the facilitator "knows" what should be communicated) or no unexpected language competence compared with the participants' measured IQ or a standard language assessment. Green (1992), who reviewed 15 studies in which FC was experimentally evaluated with 138 individuals, concluded that "none of the 138 participants was shown to be the source of the assisted communications. In fact, there is strong evidence in several [studies] that the communications were controlled *entirely* by the assistants" (p. 9).

Facilitated communication is examined further in Chapter 11.

❋ *Educational Service Alternatives*

Although some self-contained special classes are specifically designed for children with speech or language impairments, the regular classroom is by far the most prevalent setting for school-age children with communication disorders. During the 1992–93 school year, approximately 85% of children with speech or language impairments were served in the regular classroom, 9% in resource rooms, and 4% in separate classes (U.S. Department of Education, 1994). There is an increasing tendency for communication disorders specialists to serve as consultants for regular and special education teachers (and parents), rather than spend most of their time providing direct services to individual children. The specialist concentrates on assessing communication disorders, evaluating progress, and providing materials and techniques. Teachers and parents are encouraged to follow the specialist's guidelines.

Surveys of members of the American Speech-Language-Hearing Association (Mansour, 1985; Shewan, 1986) have found that speech-language pathologists are employed in a wide variety of settings, with the largest single group—about 37%—working in schools. Other settings include hospitals, speech and hearing clinics, nursing homes, physicians' offices, and private practices. The caseloads of these professionals vary widely according to the setting and the types and severity of communication disorders among their clients. The most prevalent pattern of service delivery in schools is a specialist who works with a child for two sessions each week. The most prevalent communication disorders among children served by school speech-language pathologists are, in order of frequency, language disorders (52.2% of a typical caseload), articulation disorders (34.8%), hearing impairments (4.5%), fluency disorders (4.1%), and voice disorders (2.4%) (Shewan, 1986).

Sometimes the specialist visits schools according to a regular schedule and gives individual or group therapy to the children, but this approach is becoming somewhat less common. Communication is seen as occurring most appropriately in the natural environment, rather than in the clinical setting. Integrated therapy is provided in the natural environment (classroom or home) in the context of ongoing routines. Some professionals believe it is impossible to adequately serve the child with a speech or language disorder with an isolated therapy approach (two or three 30-minute sessions each week with a specialist). In fact, this approach has been described as a futile attempt to "sweep back a river with a broom" (Hatten & Hatten, 1975).

> ASHA can provide further information about the training, qualifications, and responsibilities of speech-language pathologists. The address of ASHA appears in the listing of resources at the end of this chapter.

❋ *Current Issues and Future Trends*

The future will probably find specialists in communication disorders functioning even more indirectly than they do today. They will continue to work as professional team members, assisting teachers, parents, physicians, and other specialists in recognizing potential communication disorders and in facilitating communication skills. Inservice training will become an ever more important aspect of the specialist's responsibilities.

My Communication System

By Stephen W. Hawking

Stephen W. Hawking is Lucasian Professor of Mathematics and Theoretical Physics at The University of Cambridge. He has amyotrophic lateral sclerosis (ALS). Sometimes called Lou Gehrig's disease, after one of its most famous victims, ALS is a motor neuron disease of middle or late life that involves progressive degeneration of nerve cells that control voluntary motor functions. Initial symptoms usually entail difficulty walking, clumsiness of the hands, slurred speech, and an inability to swallow normally. The muscles of the arms and legs waste away; eventually, walking is impossible and control of the hands is lost, although sensation remains normal. There is no known cause or cure for ALS. Professor Hawking responded to our request to describe the augmentative communication system he uses by writing the following story.

I am quite often asked, "How do you feel about having ALS?" The answer is, "Not a lot." I try to lead as normal a life as possible and not think about my condition or regret the things it prevents me from doing, which are not that many. It was a great shock to me to discover that I had motor neuron disease. I had never been very well coordinated, physically, as a child. I was not good at ball games, and my handwriting was the despair of my teachers. But things seemed to change when I went to Oxford at the age of 17. I took up coxing and rowing. I was not Boat Race standard, but I got by at the level of intercollege competition.

In my third year at Oxford, however, I noticed that I seemed to be getting clumsier, and I fell over once or twice for no apparent reason. Shortly after my 21st birthday, I went into the hospital for tests. I was in for 2 weeks,

Physicist Stephen W. Hawking

during which I had a wide variety of tests. After all that, they didn't tell me what I had, except that it was not multiple sclerosis and that I was an atypical case. I didn't feel like asking for more details because they were obviously bad.

The realization that I had an incurable disease that was likely to kill me in a few years was a bit of a shock. How could something like that happen to me? Why should I be cut off like this? Not knowing what was going to happen to me or how rapidly the disease would progress, I was at loose ends. The doctors told me to go back to Cambridge and carry on with the research I had just started, in general relativity and cosmology. But I was not making much progress with the research, and, anyway, I might not live long enough to finish my Ph.D. I felt like a tragic character. I took to listening to Wagner, but reports in magazines that I drank heavily are an exaggeration.

Before my condition had been diagnosed, I had been very bored with life. There had not seemed to be anything worth doing. But after I came out of the hospital, I dreamt several times that I would sacrifice my life to save others. After all, if I were going to die anyway, it might as well do some good.

But I didn't die. In fact, although there was a cloud hanging over my future, I found, to my surprise, that I was enjoying life in the present more than before. I began to make progress with my research, and I got engaged to Jane Wilde, a girl I had met just about the time my condition was diagnosed. Our engagement changed my life. It gave me something to live for. But it also meant that I had to get a job, if we were to get married.

Up to 1974, I was able to feed myself and get in and out of bed. Jane managed to help me and bring up two children without outside help. However, things were getting more difficult, so we took to having one of my research students live with us. In return for free accommodation and a lot of my attention, [the student] helped me get up and go to bed. In 1980 we changed to a system of community and private nurses, who came in for an hour or two in the morning and evening. This lasted until I caught pneumonia in 1985 and had to have a tracheotomy operation. After this, I had to have 24-hour nursing care, which was made possible by grants from several foundations.

Before the operation, my speech had been getting more slurred, so only a few people who knew me well could understand me. But at least I could communicate. I wrote scientific papers by dictating to a secretary, and I gave seminars through an interpreter, who repeated my words more clearly. However, the tracheotomy removed my ability to speak altogether. For a time, the only way I could communicate was to spell out words letter by letter, by raising my eyebrows when someone pointed to the right letter on a spelling card. It is pretty difficult to carry on a conversation like that, let alone write a scientific paper.

Today, I communicate with a computer system. A computer expert in California, Walter Woltosz, sent me a program he had written called Equalizer. This program allowed me to select words from a series of menus on the screen by pressing a switch in my hand. The program could also be controlled by a switch operated by head or eye movement. When I have built up what I want to say, I can send it to a speech synthesizer. At first, I just ran the Equalizer program through a desktop computer. However, David Mason, of Cambridge Adaptive Communications, who is also the husband of one of my nurses, put together the system I now use. I have a Datavue 25 computer mounted to the back of my wheelchair that runs from a battery under the chair's seat. The screen is mounted where I can see it, though you have to view it from the right angle. I run a program called Living Center, written by a company called Words Plus of Sunnyvale, California. A cursor moves across the upper part of the screen. I can stop it by pressing a switch in my hand. In this way, I can select words that are printed on the lower part of the screen. This system allows me to communicate much better than I could before; I can manage up to 15 words a minute. I can either speak what I have written or save it on a disk. I can then print it out or call it back and speak it sentence by sentence, like I'm doing now. Using this system, I have written a book and a dozen scientific papers. I have also given a number of scientific and popular talks. They have been well received. I think that is in large part due to the quality of my speech synthesizer, made by Speech Plus, also of Sunnyvale, California.

One's voice is very important. If you have a slurred voice, people are likely to treat you as mentally deficient: "Does he take sugar?" This synthesizer is by far the best I have heard because it varies the intonation and doesn't speak like a Dalek. The only trouble is that it gives me an American accent; however, the company is working on a British version.

I have had motor neuron disease for practically all my adult life. Yet it has not prevented me from having a very attractive family and being successful in my work. This is thanks to the help I have received from my wife, my children, and a large number of other people and organizations. I have been lucky, in that my condition has progressed more slowly than is often the case. But it shows that one need not lose hope. ✷

Changing Populations

Speech-language pathologists who work in schools are likely to find themselves working with an increasing percentage of children with severe and multiple disabilities who previously did not receive specialized services from communication disorders specialists. Caseloads are already growing in many school districts, and financial restrictions make it virtually impossible for all students with communication disorders to receive adequate services from the relatively few specialists who are employed. Even though all students with disabilities are supposed to receive all of the special services they need, the schools' financial problems necessitate difficult decisions at the local level. Some programs may choose to provide special services only to those students with the most severe speech and language impairments. Others may concentrate their professional resources on higher-functioning students who are considered to have the best potential for developing communication skills. Parents, advocates, and professional organizations will play an instrumental role in determining which children are to receive specialized speech and language services.

Paraprofessional personnel may, in the future, be more widely trained to work directly with children who have speech and language disorders, while professionals concentrate on diagnosis, prescriptive programming, evaluation, and the use of technology. Peer tutoring or therapy approaches using students without disabilities as language models are likely to become more prevalent. These approaches may allow more students to receive specialized help.

Currently, speech and language intervention programs are heavily oriented toward the preschool and school-age population. Although early detection and intervention will clearly remain a high priority among communication disorders specialists, there is a need for long-term studies to document the effectiveness of early intervention on later speech and language development. Professionals are also becoming increasingly aware of the special speech and language needs of adolescents and adults, many of whom have untreated communication problems. The future will likely see greater attention to the assessment and treatment of speech and language disorders caused by the aging process.

Across-the-Day Interventions

The traditional role of the speech-language pathologist will probably continue to change, from that of offering direct therapy to students to "facilitating the implementation of communication interventions in the classroom environment" (Goldstein et al., 1994, p. 106). As previously discussed, naturalistic interventions that take place in the actual environments in which children use language are gradually becoming the norm.

But "naturalness" is no guarantee of effectiveness. As Goldstein et al. (1994) point out, the real challenge lies in designing and implementing "across-the-day" interventions that can be used effectively by teachers and other significant persons in the child's life. The most effective communication disorders specialist of the future will be expert not only in designing interventions that can be implemented in the classroom and home but also in training and supporting teachers and parents in carrying out those interventions.

Communication Partners

·····················

Strategies for Opening Doors to Communication

Effective communication requires two parties—two people who work as partners in the communication act. When one of the partners has little or no understandable speech, communication is often limited and frustrating for both. If the two persons work together and the normally speaking person learns to employ several strategies for systematic communication, however, significant information can be exchanged. June Bigge (1991) describes nine strategies that communication partners can use that will open doors to help individuals with severe speech impairments enjoy increased communication effectiveness.

Establish and Use Yes, No, and Other Fundamental Signals

A primary goal is to have the student use, or at least approximate, the spoken words or traditional head signals for *yes* and *no*. If necessary, signals may be given by using the head in a nontraditional way. An upward glance can mean *yes;* a glance to the side, *no;* a drop of the head or a shrug of shoulders might signify *I don't know.* If a student's technique is not obvious, ask for a demonstration: "Please show me how you say yes/no." This type of unaided communication system can go anywhere with the student. Aided signals may consist of a smiling face symbol or the word *yes* printed on one arm of a wheelchair and a frowning face or the word *no* on the opposite arm. Likewise, the teacher may write *yes* on one end of the chalkboard and *no* on the other end. To respond, the student looks at one end of the board or the other. Once reliable signals for indicating *yes, no,* and *I don't know* messages have been established, post them and tell others.

Use of *yes, no,* and *I don't know* responses should accompany other components of a student's communication system; they should not be the only components. Each student must have access to communication components that also allow access to the language he or she would know how to use if able to speak. Until this happens, students will not be in a position to generate their own language and must always remain in a somewhat dependent and passive role.

Provide Opportunities for Initiation

When attempting to interact with individuals with physical and speech differences, people tend to quickly take over leadership in the interaction. They inadvertently fail to wait long enough for the person to initiate requests and other communications. This failure leads to learned helplessness or passivity on the part of the person with the disability. Instead of anticipating students' needs and providing fillers for silence in communicative interactions, set up potential communicative opportunities and *wait* for the student to initiate.

Present a Range of Choices and Then Repeat Them One at a Time

To avoid ambiguity in asking questions, use this important listener-assisted auditory scanning strategy. Present the range of choices: "Do you want a drink of water or milk?" Then repeat each question separately: "Water?" "Milk?" Adding the option "neither of these" to any list of choices is a more advanced strategy for partners to use and is very helpful to the nonspeaking person.

Wait for the Expression and Expansion of Ideas

Allow students with physical and speech disabilities time to think about the content of what they want to convey, time to make the necessary motor movements to relay their message, and time after their first response to add more information. The motor response itself may be very slow for some children.

They may need time to think of ways to change the direction of the conversation to more nearly reflect their original intent or to add information.

Narrow the Options to Find the Category About Which the Person Has Something to Say

Sometimes it is not clear what an individual is trying to tell or ask. What is the quickest way to find out? Use listener-assisted auditory scanning and first narrow the options by finding a category. Ask, "Are you thinking of telling something? Or asking something?" "Telling?" "Asking?" Once that is decided, ask, "Do you want to talk about somebody, some place, some things, or feelings, or none of these?" If the answer is a place, for example, you could narrow the options by asking, "Is it about home, or school, or some place else?" Then repeat each category one at a time to allow the individual to indicate a choice.

Clarify and Verify to Assure That Messages Are Received Correctly

Effectiveness of communication interactions limited to *yes* and *no* responses hinge on a communication partner's use of the clarification strategy. It is a great temptation to ask an individual only dead-end and fact-level yes-and-no questions when that person does not speak intelligibly. But speakers with unclear speech have ideas, feelings, and reactions to share with those who will listen. And these kinds of message exchanges depend very much on clarification strategies of communication partners. To clarify and verify, communication partners repeat the perceived messages in their entirety or by segments to see whether the message was received correctly. The strategy involves stating first what they think has been communicated so far. If the message was received correctly and verified by a positive answer to the question "Is this exactly right?" then the conversation may move on. If the message is not verified as correct, then more clarification is necessary. The strategy now involves repeating the message in segments and asking questions like these after each segment: "Am I close?" "Is there more to it than that?" "Do you want to change part of what I said?" "Is this too specific or too general?"

Talk "Up To" Not "Down To" the Person

It is tempting to "talk down to" a person who has an obvious disability. Be aware of your own behavior in this respect. Attempt to stimulate the student's intellect and not bore him or her or fill in communication silences with just anything. Finding out a student's needs, feelings, interests, and problems is an important skill. Too often, individuals who do not speak so that others can understand find themselves answering questions over and over on the same topics: age, family, school, and pets. How dull and frustrating it must be to be denied the opportunity for variety and depth in conversations! Regardless of age, do the student a favor and allow him or her to try to experience higher levels of understanding and a greater variety of messages and information in the conversation.

Recognize Deadlocks

In conversations with students who do not speak clearly, partners often meet barriers. But partners can learn to recognize and correct barriers. In communication breakdowns, communication partners can use conversational repair strategies (Blackstone, Cassatt-James, & Bruskin, 1988). For example, the student may wish to say something, but a partner does not reflect the correct message. Sometimes the student may realize that a block has been reached over an unimportant topic and would rather drop the subject than waste time pursuing it. The opposite may also be true; the message is very important. The partner can help the speaker by saying, "I'm really stuck. Do you want to go on trying?" Be certain the student does not feel pressured into changing topics. Partners should persist if the student indicates it is important to do so. If the conversation must be terminated before both partners are satisfied, they can keep the communication open by saying, "I have to leave, but I'll think about it. You think too, and maybe you'll find another way of telling me."

Teach These Strategies to Other Communication Partners

Teachers and communication specialists should provide opportunities for persons to expand their conversational interactions to include new people both inside and outside school. Signs and signals must be taught to others so that consistent procedures are used. It is advisable for parents to teach baby-sitters, family friends, relatives, and the neighborhood children. Teachers must teach schoolmates, classroom aides, and other teachers.

Responsibility for opening doors to communication does not lie only with communication partners. Individuals with communication disorders must learn to cue prospective communication partners, includ-ing those in the community at large. Nonspeaking students can learn to direct communication partners to the location of brief and easily accessible written cues for effecting satisfying communications for both parties.

From *Teaching Students with Physical Disabilities* (3rd ed.) (pp. 231–244) by J. Bigge, 1991, Englewood Cliffs, NJ: Merrill/Prentice Hall. Adapted by permission.

Summary

Communication, Language, and Speech

- Communication is any interaction that transmits information. Narrating, explaining, informing, and expressing are major communicative functions.

- A language is an arbitrary symbol system that enables a group of people to communicate; each language has rules of phonology, morphology, syntax, and semantics that describe how users put sounds together to convey meaning.

- Speech is the vocal response mode of language and the basis on which language develops.

- Normal language development follows a relatively predictable sequence. Most children learn to use language without direct instruction, and by the time most children enter first grade, their grammar and speech patterns match those of the adults around them.

Defining Communication Disorders

- A child has a speech disorder if his or her speech draws unfavorable attention to itself, interferes with the ability to communicate, or causes social or interpersonal problems.

- Some children have trouble understanding language (receptive language disorders); others have trouble using language to communicate (expressive language disorders); still other children have language delays.

- Speech or language differences based on cultural dialects are not communication disorders; however, children with dialects may also have speech or language disorders.

Types and Causes of Communication Disorders

- Although some speech disorders have physical (organic) causes, most are functional disorders that cannot be directly attributed to physical conditions.

- Types of communication disorders include articulation, voice, fluency, and language disorders.

- Stuttering is the most common fluency disorder.

Identification and Assessment

- Assessment of a suspected communication disorder may include some or all of the following components:

  Case history

  Physical examination

  Articulation test

  Hearing test

  Auditory discrimination test

  Language development test

  Overall language test

  Conversation with the child or language sample

  Behavioral observations of child's language competence in social contexts

Prevalence

- As many as 5% of school-age children may have speech impairments serious enough to warrant attention.

- Nearly twice as many boys as girls have speech impairments.

- Children with articulation problems represent the largest category of speech-language impairments.

Historical Background

- Communication disorders have historically been considered less severe and have been less easily recognized than other disabilities.
- Regular public schools have recently expanded services to children with speech and language disorders.
- Speech is no longer a narrow specialty concerned with correcting isolated disorders; remedial procedures are often carried out in the regular classroom.

Educational Approaches

- The different types of communication disorders call for different approaches to remediation; behavioral approaches are frequently used.
- Articulation disorders may be treated by one of four common models: the discrimination model, the phonological model, the sensorimotor model, or the operant conditioning model.
- Voice disorders can sometimes be treated medically or surgically if there is an organic cause, but the most common remediation is direct vocal rehabilitation.
- Treatment of fluency disorders emphasizes either symptom modification or fluency reinforcement.
- Language disorders are treated by either individual or group approaches.

- Alternative and augmentative communication (AAC) may be necessary in severe situations. AAC may be unaided or aided and consists of three components:

    A representational symbol set, or vocabulary

    A means for selecting the symbols

    A means for transmitting the symbols

Educational Service Alternatives

- Most children with speech and language problems attend regular classes.

Current Issues and Future Trends

- In the future, communication disorders specialists will probably provide largely consultative services and inservice training, rather than direct one-to-one therapy. They will help train parents, teachers, and paraprofessionals to work with most children, while they concentrate on diagnosis, programming, and direct intensive services to a few children with special needs.
- Further service needs to be directed toward older youths and adults with untreated speech and language problems.
- Use of special devices to help individuals with communication disorders will expand. Electronic devices are now widely used to analyze children's speech and language and to provide instruction.
- Efforts to develop and implement across-the-day interventions programs for children with communication disorders will increase in the future.

For More Information

Journals

Augmentative and Alternative Communication. Published by the International Society for Augmentative and Alternative Communication, P.O. Box 1762, Station R, Toronto, Ontario M4G 4A3, Canada.

Communication Outlook. Emphasizes the use of augmentative communication techniques and technology. Published quarterly by Artificial Language Laboratory, Computer Science Department, Michigan State University, East Lansing, MI 48824.

Journal of Childhood Communication Disorders. Published twice yearly by CEC's Division for Children with Communication Disorders (DCCD). (See description given under "Organizations.")

Journal of Speech and Hearing Disorders. Published quarterly by the American Speech-Language-Hearing Association (ASHA). Includes articles dealing with the nature, assessment, and treatment of communication disorders.

Language, Speech, and Hearing Services in the Schools. Also published quarterly by ASHA; focuses on practical applications of speech and language training and provides activities for teachers and specialists consistent with current research and theory.

Books

Baumgart, D., Johnson, J., & Helmstetter, E. (1990). *Augmentative and alternative communication systems for persons with moderate and severe disabilities.* Baltimore: Paul H. Brookes.

Bernstein, D. K., & Tiegerman, E. (1993). *Language and communication disorders in children* (3rd ed.). New York: Macmillan.

Blackstone, S. W. (Ed.). (1989). *Augmentative communication: Implementation strategies.* Rockville, MD: American Speech-Language-Hearing Association.

Hegde, M. N. (1993). *Treatment procedures in communicative disorders.* Austin, TX: PRO-ED.

Hulit, L. M., & Howard, M. R. (1993). *Born to talk: An introduction to speech and language development.* New York: Macmillan.

Kent, R. D. (1994). *Reference manual for communicative sciences and disorders.* Austin, TX: PRO-ED.

Love, R. J. (1992). *Childhood motor speech disability.* New York: Macmillan.

Luterman, D. M. (1991). *Counseling the communicatively disordered and their families.* Austin, TX: PRO-ED.

McCormick, L., & Schiefelbusch, R. L. (1990). *Early language intervention: An introduction* (2nd ed.). New York: Merrill/Macmillan.

Owens, R. E. (1991). *Language disorders: A functional approach to assessment and intervention.* New York: Macmillan.

Reed, V. A. (1994). *An introduction to children with language disorders* (2nd ed.). New York: Macmillan.

Shames, G. H., Wiig, E. H., & Secord, W. A. (1994). *Human communication disorders* (4th ed.). New York: Macmillan.

Wallach, G. P., & Butler, K. G. (1994). *Language learning disabilities in school-age children and adolescents.* New York: Macmillan.

Organizations

American Speech-Language-Hearing Association, 10801 Rockville Pike, Rockville, MD 20852. The major professional organization concerned with speech and language. Serves as a certifying agency for professionals who provide speech, language, and hearing services. Publishes several journals, sponsors research in communication disorders, and provides a comprehensive *Guide to Professional Services,* which also includes information on accredited training programs. Also sponsors the National Student Speech, Language, Hearing Association, which has chapters on many college and university campuses.

Crestwood Company, 6625 North Sidney Place, Milwaukee, WI 53209-3259; (414) 352-5678. Publishes a catalog featuring a wide range of augmentative and alternative communication devices for children and adults.

Division for Children with Communication Disorders (DCCD), Council for Exceptional Children, 1920 Association Drive, Reston, VA 22091. Includes teachers and communication disorders specialists who work with exceptional children. Sponsors sessions at state, provincial, and national conferences.

Students Who Are Deaf or Hard-of-Hearing

* In what important ways do the child who is deaf and the child who is hard-of-hearing differ?

* Why can reading not simply replace hearing speech as a means of learning and understanding language?

* How do advocates of oral and total communication approaches to educating students who are deaf differ in philosophies and teaching methods?

* Why do you think American Sign Language (ASL) has not been fully accepted as the language of instruction in school programs for children who are deaf?

* Is the inability to hear a disability in Deaf culture?

Nature attaches an overwhelming importance to hearing. As unborns we hear before we can see. Even in deep comas, people often hear what is going on around them. For most of us, when we die, the sense of hearing is the last to leave the body. (Walker, 1986, p. 165)

As Lou Ann Walker, the child of deaf parents, observes in her autobiography, people who have normal hearing usually find it difficult to fully appreciate the enormous importance of the auditory sense in human development and learning. Many of us have simulated blindness by closing our eyes or donning a blindfold, but it is virtually impossible to switch off our hearing voluntarily.

From the moment of birth, children learn a great deal by using their hearing. Newborns are able to respond to sounds by startling or blinking. At a few weeks of age, infants with normal hearing can listen to quiet sounds, recognize their parents' voices, and pay attention to their own gurgling and cooing sounds. Within the first year of life, babies acquire much information by listening; they discriminate meaningful sound from background noise and localize and imitate sounds (Lowell & Pollack, 1974).

As hearing children grow, they develop language by constantly hearing people talk and by associating these sounds with innumerable activities and events. They attach meaning to sound, quickly learning that people convey information and exchange their thoughts and feelings by speaking and hearing. By the time the typical hearing child enters school, he or she is likely to have a vocabulary of more than 5,000 words. And that child has already had perhaps 100 million meaningful contacts with language (Napierkowski, 1981).

As we saw in Chapter 7, language acquisition and development, though complex, occur naturally and spontaneously in most children. Most children with hearing impairments, however, are not able to participate in this process without special help. They may acquire a good deal of information about the world but have few symbols or patterns available to help them send and receive messages. They miss out on many early and critical opportunities for developing basic communication skills. Hans Furth (1973), a psychologist who devoted much of his career to studying the language development of people with hearing impairments, suggests that a good way to approximate the experience of a child who is deaf from birth or early childhood is to watch a television program in which a foreign language is being spoken—with the sound on the TV set turned off. You would face the double problem of being unable to read lips and understand an unfamiliar language.

Hearing is vital to every aspect of our daily existence. If you were unable to hear, you would, at best, find it difficult to participate fully in the activities of your school or college, your job, your neighborhood, and even your own family unless some special adaptations were made. At worst, you might find that society's great reliance on speech and hearing as avenues of communication made it virtually impossible for you to function effectively.

Today, many children with impaired hearing are identified in early childhood. They are often helped to hear better through the use of hearing aids or surgery. They may learn to communicate with their families and friends by using speech,

This woman's "hearing dog" wakes her when the alarm rings.

speechreading, sign language, or other techniques. Although many people with hearing impairments achieve the highest levels of educational, professional, and personal success, it is impossible to truly compensate for the loss of hearing. The information and understanding that come through the auditory channel can never be fully replaced.

As Paul and Quigley (1990, 1994) point out, however, the educational, vocational, and social development of an individual with a hearing impairment is influenced by many factors in addition to the type and degree of hearing loss. These include the age at which the hearing impairment began, the attitudes of the child's parents and siblings, the opportunities available for the child to develop oral and manual communication skills, and the presence or absence of other disabilities. A child's potential for learning can certainly not be predicted from the results of a hearing test alone.

✸ *Defining Hearing Impairments*

When we speak of a person with normal hearing, we generally mean that he or she has enough hearing to understand speech. Assuming that listening conditions are adequate, a person with normal hearing can interpret speech in everyday situations without relying on any special device or technique. A person who is **deaf** is not able to use hearing to understand speech, although he or she may perceive some sounds. Even with a hearing aid, the hearing loss is too great to allow a deaf person to understand speech through the ears alone. A deaf person has a profound hearing impairment and is dependent on vision for language and communication, even with the use of amplification systems (Paul & Quigley, 1990).

A person who is **hard-of-hearing** has a significant hearing loss that makes some special adaptations necessary. As Berg (1986) points out, however, it is possible for a hard-of-hearing child to respond to speech and other auditory stimuli. "Communicatively, the hard-of-hearing child is more like the normal hearing child than like the deaf child, because both use audition rather than vision as the primary mode for speech and language development" (p. 3). In other words, the hard-of-hearing child's speech and language skills, though they may be delayed or deficient, are developed mainly through the auditory channel. Children who are hard-of-hearing are able to use their hearing to understand speech, generally with the help of a hearing aid.

Hearing impairment is a generic term that includes hearing disabilities ranging from mild to profound, thus encompassing children who are deaf and those who are hard-of-hearing. When used by educators, the term *hearing impairment* indicates an auditory disability for which special services are needed. Most children who receive special education for a hearing impairment have some degree of **residual hearing.**

A hearing impairment may also be described in terms of *age of onset.* It is important to consider whether a hearing loss is **congenital** (present at birth) or **adventitious** (acquired later in life). The terms *prelingual hearing impairment* and *postlingual hearing impairment* refer to whether a hearing loss is sustained before or after the development of spoken language. A child who, from birth or soon after, is unable to hear the speech of other people will not learn speech and language spontaneously, as do children with normal hearing. A child who acquires a hearing impairment after speech and language are well established, usually after age 2, has educational needs very different from the prelinguistically hearing-impaired child. The educational program for a child who is prelingually deaf usually focuses on acquisition of language and communication, whereas that of a child who is postlingually deaf usually emphasizes the maintenance of intelligible speech and appropriate language patterns.

How We Hear

Audition, the act or sense of hearing, is a complex and not completely understood process. The function of the ear is to gather sounds (acoustical energy) from the environment and to transform that energy into a form (neural energy) that can be interpreted by the brain (Harris, 1986).

Figure 8.1 shows the major parts of the human ear. The *outer ear* consists of the external ear and the auditory canal. The part of the ear we see, the **auricle,** functions to collect sound waves into the **auditory canal (external acoustic meatus).** When sound waves enter the auditory canal, they are slightly amplified as they move toward the middle ear. Sounds enter the *middle ear* through the Eustachian tube, where they meet the **tympanic membrane (eardrum),** which moves in and out in response to variations in sound pressure. These movements of the eardrum change the acoustical energy into mechanical energy, which is transferred to three tiny bones (the *hammer, anvil,* and *stirrup*). The base (called the *footplate*) of the third bone in the sequence, the stirrup, rests in an opening called the *oval window,* the path through which sound energy enters the inner ear. The vibrations of the three

---

When a hearing impairment goes undetected, some students who are hard-of-hearing are mistakenly thought to have learning disabilities or behavioral disorders.

Even very slight levels of residual hearing can be useful.

A person without external ears could still hear quite well, losing perhaps only 5 to 7 decibels in sound volume. The intensity or loudness of sound is measured in **decibels (dB).**

bones (together called the **ossicles**) transmit energy from the middle ear to the inner ear with little loss. The most critical and complex part of the entire hearing apparatus is the *inner ear,* which is covered by the temporal bone, the hardest bone in the entire body. The inner ear contains the **cochlea,** the main receptor organ for hearing, and the semicircular canals, which control the sense of balance. The cochlea, which resembles the coiled shell of a snail, consists of two fluid-filled cavities. When energy is transmitted by the ossicles, the fluid in the cochlea moves. Tiny hairs within the cochlea change the motion of the fluid into neural impulses that are transmitted along the auditory nerve to the brain.

The Nature of Sound

Sound is measured in units that describe its intensity (measured in **decibels [dB]**) and frequency. Both are important in considering the needs of a child with impaired hearing. Zero dB represents the smallest sound a person with normal hearing can perceive, which is called the *zero hearing-threshold level* (HTL), or **audiometric zero.** Larger dB numbers represent increasingly louder sounds. A low whisper 5 feet away registers about 10 dB, a running automobile about 65 dB, and Niagara Falls about 90 dB. Conversational speech 10 to 20 feet away registers about 30 to 65 dB. A sound of about 125 dB or louder will cause pain to the average person. A person may have a loss of up to 25 dB (not be able to hear any sound of less than 25 dB) and still

> Also within the inner ear is the **vestibular mechanism,** which controls the sense of balance by movement-sensitive fluid in the semicircular canals. For more detailed discussions of the anatomy of the ear and the physiology of hearing, see Harris (1986) or Schneiderman (1984).

FIGURE 8.1

Parts of the human ear. The external part of the ear and the auditory canal make up the outer ear. The middle ear includes the eardrum, hammer, anvil, and stirrup. The inner ear includes the round window, the oval window, the semicircular canals, and the cochlea. Damage to any part can cause a hearing loss.

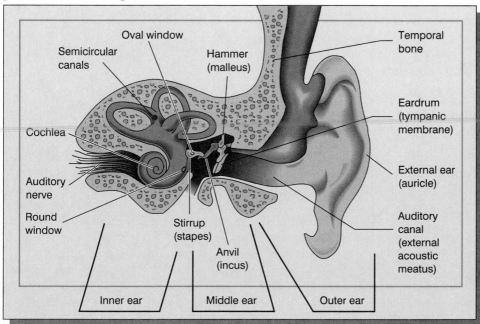

Heather Whitestone, Miss America 1995, is deaf. She won the talent competition with a dance routine set to music she could not hear. Whitestone counted the beats in her head and synchronized her dance moves to reflect changes in the music.

be considered to have hearing within the normal range (Davis & Silverman, 1978). The 25-dB level is often used in screening school children for hearing loss, although, as Berg (1986) warns, such one-shot tests may fail to identify a sizable percentage of hard-of-hearing children.

In addition to dB loss, it is important to consider the listening environment. Northern and Lemme (1982) observe that speech needs to be only 10 to 15 dB louder than background noise for normally hearing adults to listen and understand comfortably. For children with impaired hearing, speech may need to be significantly louder than background noise for them to be able to attend to the message being transmitted.

The frequency, or pitch, of sounds is measured in cycles per second, or **hertz (Hz);** 1 hertz equals 1 cycle per second. The lowest note on a piano has a frequency of about 30 Hz, middle C about 250 Hz, and the highest note about 4,000 Hz. Human beings are able to hear frequencies ranging from about 20 to 20,000 Hz (Davis & Silverman, 1978), but many of these audible sounds are outside the speech range, the frequency range in which ordinary conversation takes place. Although a person who cannot hear very low sounds (e.g., a foghorn) or very high sounds (e.g., a piccolo) may suffer some inconvenience, he or she will encounter no significant problems in the classroom or everyday life. A person with a serious hearing loss in the speech range, however, is at a great disadvantage in communication.

The frequency range generally considered most important for hearing spoken language is 500 to 2,000 Hz. The sounds of English speech vary in their frequency level. For example, the /s/ phoneme (as in the word *sat*) is a high-frequency sound, typically occurring between 4,000 and 8,000 Hz (Northern & Lemme, 1982). A student whose hearing loss is more severe at the higher frequencies will thus have particular difficulty in discriminating the /s/ sound. Conversely, phonemes such as /dj/ (the sound of the *j* in *jump*) and /m/ occur at low frequencies and will be more problematic for a student with a low-frequency hearing impairment. As you might expect, a student with a high-frequency impairment tends to hear men's voices more easily than women's voices.

❋ *Types and Causes of Hearing Impairment*

Conductive and Sensorineural Hearing Impairments

The two main types of hearing impairments are conductive and sensorineural. A **conductive hearing loss** results from abnormalities or complications of the outer or middle ear. A buildup of excessive wax in the auditory canal can cause a conductive hearing loss, as can a disease that leaves fluid or debris. Some children are born with incomplete or malformed auditory canals. A hearing loss can also be caused if the eardrum or ossicles do not move properly. As its name implies, a conductive hearing impairment involves a problem with conducting, or transmitting, sound vibrations to the inner ear. Because the rest of the auditory system is generally intact, conductive hearing losses can often be corrected through surgical or medical treatment. Hearing aids are usually beneficial to persons with conductive impairments.

A **sensorineural hearing loss** refers to damage to the auditory nerve fibers or other sensitive mechanisms in the inner ear. The cochlea converts the physical characteristics of sound into corresponding neural information that the brain can process and interpret (Berg, 1986); impairment of the cochlea may mean that sound is delivered to the brain in a distorted fashion or is not delivered at all. Amplification—making the source of sound louder—may or may not help the person with a sensorineural hearing impairment. Unfortunately, most sensorineural hearing impairments cannot be corrected by surgery or medication. The combination of both conductive and sensorineural impairments is called a *mixed hearing loss.*

Hearing impairment is also described in terms of being *unilateral* (present in one ear only) or *bilateral* (present in both ears). Most students who receive special programs for hearing impairments have bilateral losses, although the degree of impairment may not be the same in both ears. Children with unilateral hearing impairments generally learn speech and language without major difficulties, although they tend to have problems localizing sounds and listening in noisy or distracting settings. Some evidence suggests, however, that children with unilateral hearing impairments may be at a disadvantage in acquiring certain academic skills (Keller & Bundy, 1980).

Causes of Hearing Impairment

The causes of hearing impairment are usually classified as exogenous or endogenous. *Exogenous* causes stem from factors outside the body (e.g., disease, toxicity, injury) and reduce the auditory system's ability to receive and transmit sounds. *Endogenous* hearing impairments are inherited from the parents' genes. Although several hundred causes of hearing impairment have been identified, for about 30% of children with hearing impairments the exact cause is listed as "unknown" (Moores, 1987).

According to S. C. Brown (1986), four prevalent causes of deafness and severe hearing impairment in children warrant special attention:

1. *Maternal rubella.* Although rubella (also known as German measles) has relatively mild symptoms, it has been shown to cause deafness, visual impairment, heart disorders, and a variety of other serious disabilities in the developing child when it affects a pregnant woman, particularly during the first trimester. A major epidemic of rubella that took place in the United States and Canada between 1963 and 1965 accounted for more than 50% of the students with hearing impairments in special education programs in the 1970s and 1980s.

2. *Heredity.* With the exception of periods of rubella epidemics, the leading cause of deafness is genetic factors (Vernon, 1987). There is strong evidence that congenital hearing impairment runs in some families. A tendency toward certain types of adventitious hearing loss may also be inherited. Even though 90% of children who are deaf are born to hearing parents, about 30% of the school-age population of students who are deaf have relatives with hearing impairments (Moores, 1987). More than 200 types of hereditary or genetic deafness have been identified.

3. *Prematurity and complications of pregnancy.* These factors appear to increase the risk of deafness and other disabilities. It is difficult to precisely evaluate the effects of prematurity on hearing impairment, but early delivery and low birth weight have been found to be more common among children who are deaf than among the general population. Complications of pregnancy arise from a variety of causes.

> Maternal rubella continues to be a significant cause of hearing impairment. An effective vaccination for rubella is available, and all women of childbearing age should receive it.

4. *Meningitis.* The leading cause of adventitious hearing impairment is meningitis. It is a bacterial or viral infection that can, among its other effects, destroy the sensitive acoustic apparatus of the inner ear. Difficulties in balance may also be present. Brown (1986) reports that children whose deafness is caused by meningitis generally have profound hearing losses but are not likely to have additional disabilities.

Another significant cause of hearing impairment is *otitis media,* an infection or inflammation of the middle ear. If untreated, otitis media can result in a buildup of fluid and a ruptured eardrum, which causes permanent conductive hearing impairment.

Causes of hearing impairment that appear to have declined in recent years because of improved medical treatment include blood (Rh) incompatibility between mother and child, mumps, and measles. On the other hand, the percentages of students with deafness caused by meningitis, heredity, and otitis media appear to be increasing. In addition, some factors related to people's environments and activities are regarded as growing causes of hearing loss. Noise pollution—repeated exposure to loud sounds, such as industrial noise, jet aircraft, guns, and amplified music—is increasingly a cause of hearing impairment. Damage to hearing can also result from frequent deep-sea diving; Edmonds (1985) found that more than 70% of professional divers had evidence of sensorineural high-frequency deafness.

Hearing impairment occurs at a higher-than-usual incidence rate among certain groups of individuals with other disabilities. Down syndrome often involves irregularities in the auditory canal and a tendency for fluid to accumulate in the middle ear; as many as 75% of children with Down syndrome may also have significant hearing impairments (Northern & Lemme, 1982). Among children with cerebral palsy, there is also a substantially higher-than-normal incidence of hearing impairment. It is always advisable to test the hearing of any child who is referred for special education services.

> See Chapter 11 for more information on children with multiple disabilities.

Effects of Hearing Impairment

The effects of hearing impairment—especially a prelinguistic loss of 90 dB or greater—are complex and pervasive. It is perhaps impossible for a person with normal hearing to fully comprehend the immense difficulties a deaf child faces trying to learn language. Hearing children typically acquire a large vocabulary and a knowledge of grammar, word order, idiomatic expressions, fine shades of meaning, and many other aspects of verbal expression by listening to others and to themselves from early infancy. A child with a hearing impairment, however, is exposed to verbal communication only partially or not at all.

Language Skills

Children with hearing impairments—even those with superior intelligence and abilities—are at a great disadvantage in acquiring language skills. As Norris (1975) points out, the grammar and structure of English often do not follow logical rules, and a person with prelingual hearing impairment must exert a great deal of effort to read and write with acceptable form and meaning. For example, if the past tense of *talk* is *talked,* then why doesn't *go* become *goed?* If the plural of *man* is *men,* then shouldn't the plural of *pan* be *pen?* It is far from easy to explain the difference between the expressions "He's beat" (tired) and "He was beaten" to a person who has never had normal hearing.

When standard measures of reading and writing achievement are used with students who are deaf, examiners typically find that the students' vocabularies are smaller and their sentence structures are simpler and more rigid than those of hearing children of the same age or grade level (Meadow, 1980). Many students who are deaf tend to write sentences that are short, incomplete, or improperly arranged. They may omit endings of words, such as the plural *-s, -ed,* or *-ing.* They may have difficulty in differentiating questions from statements. The following excerpts from papers written by high school students who are deaf illustrate some language problems directly attributable to impaired hearing:

> She is good at sewing than she is at cooking.
>
> Many things find in Arkansas.
>
> To his disappointed, his wife disgusted of what he made.
>
> I was happy to kiss my parents because they letted my playing football. (Fusfeld, 1958, cited in Meadow, 1980, p. 33)

Academic Performance

Not counting the obvious effects of the amount, type, and quality of instruction, five variables appear to be closely correlated with the academic achievement of students with hearing impairments (Moores, 1985; Paul & Quigley, 1990):

1. *The severity of the hearing impairment.* The greater the hearing loss, the more likely the child will experience difficulty in learning language and academic skills. Even a slight hearing impairment, however, has been shown to have adverse effects on academic achievement (Paul & Quigley, 1987).
2. *The age at the onset of the hearing loss.* A child who loses hearing before acquiring speech and language (usually before age 2) is at a much greater disadvantage than a child with a postlingual hearing impairment.
3. *Intelligence test scores.* As with hearing children, higher scores on standardized tests of intelligence are correlated with greater amounts of academic success.
4. *The socioeconomic status of the family.* A child with hearing impairments whose parents are affluent and college educated is more likely to achieve academic success than a child from a low-income, less educated family.
5. *The hearing status of the parents.* A deaf child of deaf parents is considered to have better chances for academic success than a deaf child with normally hearing parents—particularly if the parents are highly educated.

Studies assessing the academic achievement of students with hearing impairments have routinely found them to lag far behind their hearing peers. Several national surveys of the academic achievement of students with hearing impairments have been carried out and reported by the Center for Assessment and Demographic Studies (CADS) at Gallaudet University. The first three studies (involving 12,000, 17,000, and 7,000 students, respectively) used a version of the Standard Achievement Test adapted for students with hearing impairment (DiFrancesca, 1972; Gentile & DiFrancesca, 1969; Trybus & Karchmer, 1977). The results were essentially the same: Students with severe and profound hearing impairments (students who were deaf) were reading at about a fourth-grade level or lower, and their mathematics performance was around the fifth-grade level. Growth in reading achievement was between 0.2 and 0.3 grade levels per year of schooling. The most recent CADS survey repeated the findings of the earlier studies (Allen, 1986). For the oldest group of students (16 to 18 years), the median grade level for reading comprehension ranged from 2.9 to 3.2; for arithmetic computation, it ranged from 7.0 to 7.5.

Geers (1985) notes that the relatively poor performance of students who are deaf, especially on tests normed on hearing students, has led teachers to expect too little of these students. For many students who are deaf, "it is more informative to define their strengths and weaknesses in relation to other children with hearing impairments than in relation to their age-mates with normal hearing" (Geers, 1985, p. 57). Several educators have warned that achievement tests, including the adapted version of the SAT, measure a severely or profoundly hearing-impaired student's competence with the English language rather than overall academic achievement (Moores, 1987; Quigley & Paul, 1986).

We must not, however, equate academic performance with intelligence. Most children who are deaf have normal intellectual capacity, and it has been repeatedly demonstrated that their scores on nonverbal intelligence tests are approximately the same as those of the general population. Deafness "imposes no limitations" on the cognitive capabilities of individuals (Moores, 1987, n.p.). The problems that students who are deaf often experience in education and adjustment may be largely attributable to a bad fit between their perceptual abilities and the demands of spoken and written English (Hoemann & Briga, 1981). Command of English is only one indicator of a person's intelligence and ability.

Sign language is the first language for many persons who are deaf. It is a visual-spatial language. Attempting to assess the intelligence of a Deaf individual by his or her understanding and use of English—a phonologically based second language to which this person has had limited access because of its phonological base—is just as inappropriate as using an English language assessment battery to classify a Hispanic child.

> Many persons who are deaf do not view their hearing impairment as a disability. Like other cultural groups, these members of the Deaf community (who spell *Deaf* with a capital *D*) share a common language and social practices.

It may be impossible for a person with normal hearing to fully comprehend the immense difficulties a prelingually deaf child faces trying to learn language.

Social and Psychological Factors

Impaired hearing can also influence a child's behavior and socioemotional development. Research has not provided clear insights into the effects of hearing impairment on behavior; however, it appears that the extent to which a child with hearing impairment successfully interacts with family members, friends, and people in the community depends largely on others' attitudes and the child's ability to communicate in some mutually acceptable way. Children who are deaf and of Deaf parents are thought to have higher levels of social maturity, adjustment to deafness, and behavioral self-control than do children who are deaf of hearing parents, largely because of the early use of manual communication between parent and child that is typical in homes with Deaf parents. In the opinion of Schlesinger (1985) and other psychologists, "Most deaf parents welcome their children who are deaf and are not rendered powerless or helpless by them" (p. 108).

Persons with hearing impairments frequently express feelings of depression, withdrawal, and isolation, particularly those who experience adventitious loss of hearing (Meadow-Orlans, 1985). A study of more than 1,000 deaf adolescents who were considered disruptive in the classroom (Kluwin, 1985) found that the most frequently related factor was reading ability; that is, students who were poorer readers were more likely to exhibit problem behaviors in school. A number of children who are deaf do have serious behavioral disorders that require treatment; unfortunately, relatively few specialists in the identification and treatment of behavioral disorders are able to communicate easily and directly with students who are deaf, so the special needs of this population remain largely unmet.

Many individuals who are deaf tend to associate primarily with other Deaf people; this may be mistakenly viewed as clannishness. Certainly, communication plays a major role in anyone's adjustment. Most individuals with hearing impairments are fully capable of developing positive relationships with their hearing peers when a satisfactory method of communication can be used.

Generalizations about how people who are deaf are supposed to act and feel should be viewed with extreme caution. Lane (1988), for example, makes a strong case against the existence of the so-called psychology of the deaf. He shows the similarity of the traits attributed to deaf people in the professional literature to traits attributed to African people in the literature of colonialism and suggests that those traits do not "reflect the characteristics of deaf people but the paternalistic posture of the hearing experts making these attributions" (p. 8). In addition, he argues that the scientific literature on the "psychology of the deaf" is flawed in terms of test administration, test language, test scoring, test content and norms, and its description of subject populations, arguments that have been noted by other researchers as well (Moores, 1987; Paul & Quigley, 1990).

To read more from and about Deaf culture, see the three Profiles and Perspectives features later in this chapter.

✷ Identification and Assessment

The earlier a hearing impairment is identified, the better a child's chances are for receiving treatment and thus developing good communication ability, which is essential for learning both academic and social skills. If a child's hearing impairment goes unnoticed until the age of 5 or 6, when children usually enter school, countless opportunities for learning will surely have been lost. The science of **audiology** has made many advances in recent years. The development of sophisticated instruments

"Deaf President Now"

A Student Protest Heard Around the World

Gallaudet University in Washington, DC, is the world's only university dedicated exclusively to the education of deaf students (students with normal hearing are admitted into some of its programs). A federally funded institution chartered by Congress in 1864, Gallaudet had never had a deaf president.

When a presidential vacancy occurred in 1988, many Gallaudet students, faculty, and alumni expected that a deaf person would be appointed; however, an educator with normal hearing, who was unable to use sign language, was initially selected for the position. A week of turbulent protests and demonstrations ensued, calling for a "Deaf President Now" and focusing national and international attention on Gallaudet. We asked Bridgetta Bourne and Jerry Covell, two of the protest's four primary student leaders, to tell us the dramatic story.

Bridgetta Bourne

When I identify myself as a deaf person, it's much like a Black person identifying herself as Black. All members of minority groups face certain challenges, and for us—the deaf—the challenge is communication. As a deaf person, I feel disabled, even among groups that include people with other disabilities. I still can't communicate with them without an interpreter.

There was recently a march from the White House to the Capitol, in support of the Americans with Disabilities Act. There were many people with disabilities, but I didn't really feel like part of that community. Without an interpreter, I was basically lost. So the concept of oppression is one in which people in power are making decisions for me—about my life, about what I should do. Oppressed people have no voice.

Oppression is dangerous and pervasive. We even had it at Gallaudet, our own institution. Obviously, we should have a hand in running our own

Bridgetta Bourne

Jerry Covell

school, and that's why the Deaf President Now protest happened and why it was so successful. There had been so many years of struggle, so many years of deaf people being told they could not make decisions for themselves. You either have to release your anger at this oppression or just hold it in, as so many deaf people did in the past.

Jerry Covell

Prior to the Deaf President Now movement, Gallaudet had gone through six presidents, all of them hearing men. These hearing presidents served useful purposes, such as founding the college, expanding programs and services, creating new educational fields, and changing Gallaudet from college to university status. When the sixth president resigned and the board of trustees began a search for a new one, we all felt that the time was definitely right for a deaf president.

Gallaudet is universally recognized and respected for its leadership in educating the deaf. Now we needed a deaf person to truly represent Gallaudet and the Deaf community. We needed a deaf person who could prove to hearing people that he or she is capable of carrying out the duties and responsibilities of a university president; this would open the door to further opportunities for deaf people. There were qualified deaf people out there, with good backgrounds of education and experience. All but 4 of the 21 members of the board of trustees were hearing people. Many of them had good backgrounds in business, fund-raising, and public relations, and they contributed to Gallaudet in that way, but they had little or no understanding of deafness and Deaf culture. They needed to be convinced! So we held rallies. We got letters of support from many well-known people, including [U.S.] presidential candidates and senators. Public awareness grew. We felt confident, especially after the

three finalists in the presidential search were announced: two deaf men and a hearing woman. Then the final selection was announced by means of a press release: "Gallaudet University Appoints First Woman President." We couldn't believe our eyes! We were shocked and extremely upset. Please keep in mind, we didn't see this as a gender issue at all. It was strictly a hearing-deaf issue; a deaf woman president would have been great.

Bridgetta

We marched downtown to the hotel where the chairman of the board of trustees was staying. We wanted a personal explanation of why they'd selected a hearing person over a deaf person. There was a reception going on inside the hotel, to introduce the new president of Gallaudet. We hadn't planned a demonstration or a sit-in, but people were just so angry! Our sitting in the street was all spontaneous. We didn't have a permit or anything; we just marched. The police came out with police cars, barriers, and bullhorns, to try to stop us. Signs and banners appeared. I remember a deaf couple who had a dog wearing a sign: "I understand sign language better than the new president of Gallaudet."

Jerry

It was late at night by the time we got to the hotel, chanting and cheering. I remember seeing lights being turned on all over the hotel and people looking out the windows, wondering what was going on. Finally, the chairman came out. She couldn't understand sign language, either. She said, "We felt this was the best decision for Gallaudet." We went round and round asking questions. We asked, "When will a deaf person get the chance to be president of Gallaudet?" "When will you allow this?" Eventually the chairman said, "Deaf people are not ready to

function in a hearing world." Ooooh, that hurt! Everyone was stunned—even the interpreter. We were ready for real action after that. The infamous quote really pulled us together; it lit a flame under us. So in a way, we should thank the chairman.

We set out to shut Gallaudet down. On Monday morning, we put kryptonite bike locks on the campus gates and parked cars in front of them. Students told everyone—administrators, faculty, staff, even board of trustees members—"Don't come in today. Go home. The campus is closed." When we took control of the campus, it showed how serious we were about the board's selection and the chairman's statement. The news media came in, and of course we took advantage of that.

Bridgetta

As Jerry says, the protest brought people together. Before the protest, it seemed that Gallaudet consisted of many different groups of deaf people. We came from various backgrounds. Some were interested in academics, others in sports, politics, or whatever. Some had gone to mainstream schools and others to deaf schools. Some were oral and others signed. But all rallied around the Deaf President Now movement, and our efforts were truly coordinated.

Jerry

Our chants, in sign and speech, were important to the Deaf President Now movement. One of our chants was "Four! Four! Four!" We had four demands before we would release the university back: First, the hearing president had to be replaced by a deaf person. Second, the chairman of the board of trustees had to resign because of her statement. Third, a majority of the board of trustees had to consist of deaf people. And fourth, there had to be no reprisals against faculty, staff, or students who were involved in the protest.

Toward the end of the week of protest, the new president resigned or "stepped aside," as she put it. But she hadn't yet been replaced. So we changed our chant to "Three and a half! Three and a half!" That kept the motivation alive. We also chanted "Deaf and Proud!" and "Deaf Power!" We adapted that last one from the Black Power movement. We made the chant by putting one hand over an ear and raising the fist high in the air.

The media began to call us "the deaf civil rights movement." Deaf peo-

ple came in from all over the country. There was a large crowd, perhaps as many as 7,000. We marched toward the Capitol to try to have Congress recognize our movement. As we marched, we chanted: "We are—standing tall! United, strong, and walking proud to be deaf! Shouting to the world—time is now!"

The rest is history. Dr. I. King Jordan, a deaf man, was appointed president of Gallaudet. The chairman of the board of trustees was replaced by a deaf person. With those two demands met, we accepted a verbal agreement that the board of trustees would have a deaf majority within 5 years and that there would be no reprisals. So we

released the university. We changed our chant from "Deaf President Now" to "Deaf President Forever!" And when Dr. Jordan first appeared before a huge crowd, we chanted, "King! King! King!" It was the most inspirational and the best thing that ever happened to us when King Jordan said, "Deaf people can do anything—except hear."

Bridgetta

What happened at Gallaudet has had an international impact. And with your help, things are going to continue to get better and better for deaf people. ✸

The passage of PL 99-457 in 1986 has led to greater emphasis on serving infants and preschoolers with disabilities (see Chapter 14).

and techniques has enabled audiologists to detect and describe hearing impairments with increasing precision. Most instruments used to test hearing now incorporate computers into their design (Kelly, 1987).

Despite modern audiological techniques, hearing impairment still goes undetected in many children. All infants, hearing and deaf alike, babble, coo, and smile. Later on, children who are deaf tend to stop babbling and vocalizing because they cannot hear themselves or their parents, but a baby's silence may be mistakenly attributed to other causes. Unfortunately, many children with hearing impairments have been erroneously labeled mentally retarded or emotionally disturbed. Some have even spent years inappropriately placed in institutions because nobody realized their problem was deafness rather than mental retardation or emotional disturbance. To avoid such misplacements in the future, efforts are continually made to conduct screening tests for hearing impairment and to educate doctors, teachers, and parents to recognize the signs of hearing loss in children. Table 8.1 offers a guide to auditory behaviors that should be present in infants with normal hearing. Failure to demonstrate these responses may mean that an infant's hearing is impaired.

Pure-Tone Audiometry

An **audiologist** specializes in the evaluation of hearing ability and the treatment of impaired hearing. An **otologist** is a physician who specializes in the diagnosis and treatment of diseases of the ear.

Hearing is formally assessed by a testing procedure called *pure-tone audiometry*. The examiner uses an **audiometer,** an electronic device that generates sounds at different levels of intensity and frequency. The child, who receives the sound either through earphones (air conduction) or through a bone vibrator (bone conduction), is instructed to hold up a finger when he hears a sound and to lower it when he hears no sound. The test seeks to determine how loud sounds at various frequencies must be before the child is able to hear them. Most audiometers deliver tones in 5-dB increments from 0 to 120 dB, with each dB level presented in various frequencies

TABLE 8.1
Expected auditory behaviors

In determining whether an infant has a hearing impairment, it is helpful for parents and teachers to have knowledge of the normal sequence of auditory development. Audiologist Linda Cleeland has provided the following guide to behaviors that may be expected at certain ages. If a young child is not displaying these behaviors, it is advisable to have the child's hearing professionally tested.

1 Month

- Will jump or startle in response to loud noises
- Will begin to make gurgling sounds

3 Months

- Will make babbling sounds
- Will be aware of voices
- May quiet down to familiar voices close to ear
- Stirs or awakens from sleep when there is a loud sound relatively close

6 Months

- Makes vocal sounds when alone
- Turns head toward sounds out of sight or when name is called and speaker is not visible
- Vocalizes when spoken to directly

9 Months

- Responds differently to a cheerful versus angry voice
- Tries to copy the speech sounds of others

12 Months

- Can locate a sound source by turning head (whether the sound is at the side, above, or below level)
- Ceases activity when parent's voice is heard
- Recognizes own name
- Uses single words correctly
- Vocalizes emotions
- Laughs spontaneously
- Disturbed by nearby noise when sleeping
- Attempts imitation of sounds and words
- Understands some familiar phrases or words
- Responds to music or singing
- Increases babbling in type and amount

24 Months

- Has more than 50 words in vocabulary
- Uses two words together
- Responds to rhythm of music
- Uses voice for a specific purpose
- Shows understanding of many phrases used daily in life
- Plays with sound-making object
- Uses well-inflected vocalization
- Refers to himself/herself by name

Source: From "The Function of the Auditory System in Speech and Language Development," by L. K. Cleeland, 1984, *The Hearing-Impaired Child in School,* pp. 15–16 by R. K. Hull and K. I. Dilka (Eds.). Orlando, FL: Grune & Stratton. Reprinted by permission.

usually starting at 125 Hz and increasing in octave intervals (doubling in frequency) to 8,000 Hz. The results of the test are plotted on a chart called an **audiogram.**

To obtain a hearing level on an audiogram, the child must be able to detect a sound at that level at least 50% of the time. A child with a hearing impairment does not begin to detect sounds until a high level of loudness is reached. For example, a

An audiometer generates tones of precise intensity and frequency.

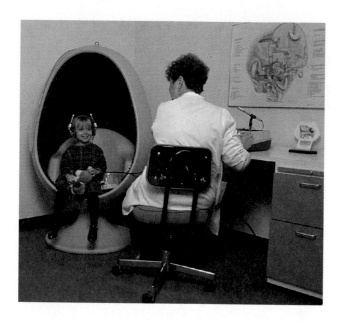

child who has a 60-dB hearing loss cannot begin to detect a sound until it is at least 60-dB loud, in contrast to a child with normal hearing, who would detect that same sound at a level between 0 and 10 dB.

Speech Audiometry

Speech audiometry tests a person's detection and understanding of speech. A list of two-syllable words is presented at different dB levels. The **speech reception threshold (SRT),** the dB level at which the individual can understand half of the words, is measured and recorded for each ear.

Alternative Audiometric Techniques

Alternative techniques have been developed for testing the hearing of very young children and individuals with severe disabilities who are not able to understand and follow conventional audiometry procedures (Roeser & Yellin, 1987). In **play audiometry,** the child is taught to perform simple but distinct activities, such as picking up a toy or putting a ball in a cup, whenever she hears the signal, either pure tones or speech. A similar procedure is **operant conditioning audiometry,** in which the child is reinforced with a token or small candy when he or she pushes a lever in the presence of a light paired with a sound. No reinforcer is given for pushing the lever when the light and sound are off. Next, the sound is presented without the light. If the child pushes the lever in response to the sound alone, the examiner knows the child can hear that sound. The intensity and frequency of the sound are then varied to determine which levels of sound the child can hear (Lloyd, Spradlin, & Reid, 1968). **Behavior observation audiometry** is a passive assessment procedure in which the child is not conditioned to make a specific response. Instead, the child's reactions to sounds are observed. A sound is presented at an increasing level of intensity until a response, such as head turning, eye blinking, or cessation of play, is reliably observed.

Two other techniques rely on physiological reactions to assess hearing. **Evoked-response audiometry** uses electrodes to sense slight electric signals that the auditory nerve generates in response to sound stimulation. Thus, the audiologist can detect hearing impairments in infants or others who may not respond to conventional testing because a voluntary response is not required. **Impedance audiometry** tests a child's middle ear function by inserting a small probe and pump to detect sound reflected by the eardrum. It is especially useful in detecting middle ear problems that can result in temporary or permanent conductive hearing loss (MacCarthy & Connell, 1984).

Degrees of Hearing Impairment

An individual's hearing impairment is usually described by the terms *slight, mild, moderate, severe,* and *profound,* depending on the average hearing level, in decibels, throughout the frequencies most important for understanding speech (500 to 2,000 Hz). Table 8.2 lists the decibel levels associated with these degrees of hearing impairment, some likely effects of each level of hearing impairment on children's speech and language development, and some considerations for educational programs.

No two children have exactly the same pattern of hearing, even if their responses on a hearing test are similar. Just as a single intelligence test cannot provide sufficient information to plan a child's educational program, the needs of a child with hearing impairment cannot be determined from an audiometric test alone. Success in communication and school achievement cannot be predicted simply by looking at an audiogram. Children hear sounds with differing degrees of clarity, and the same child's hearing ability may vary from day to day. Some children with very low levels of measurable hearing are able to benefit from hearing aids and can learn to speak. On the other hand, some children with less apparent hearing loss are not able to function well through the auditory channel and must rely on vision as their primary means of communication.

The level of hearing loss required for children to be considered deaf for educational placement purposes has changed considerably over the past decades (Connor, 1986). In the 1960s, many children with average hearing losses of 50, 60, or 70 dB were routinely enrolled in special schools and classes for children who are deaf. Today, however, those children are regarded as hard-of-hearing, rather than deaf, thanks to improved methods of testing, amplification, and teaching.

Mild Loss

Figure 8.2 shows the audiogram of Vicki, a child with a mild hearing impairment. Vicki is able to understand face-to-face conversation with little difficulty but misses much of the discussion that goes on in her classroom—particularly if several children are speaking at once or if she cannot see the speaker clearly. Many of her friends are unaware that she has a hearing impairment. Vicki benefits from wearing a hearing aid and receives occasional speech and language assistance from a speech-language pathologist.

Moderate Loss

Figure 8.3 shows the audiogram of Raymond, a child with a moderate hearing impairment. Without his hearing aid, Raymond can hear conversation only if it is

TABLE 8.2

Effects of different degrees of hearing loss on speech and language and probable educational needs

FAINTEST SOUND HEARD	EFFECTS ON UNDERSTANDING LANGUAGE AND SPEECH	PROBABLE EDUCATIONAL NEEDS AND PROGRAMS
27 to 40 dB (slight loss)	• May have difficulty hearing faint or distant speech • Will not usually have difficulty in school situations	• May benefit from a hearing aid as loss approaches 40 dB • Attention to vocabulary development • Needs favorable seating and lighting • May need speechreading instruction • May need speech correction
41 to 55 dB (mild loss)	• Understands conversational speech at a distance of 3 to 5 feet (face to face) • May miss as much as 50% of class discussions if voices are faint or not in line of vision • May have limited vocabulary and speech irregularities	• Should be referred for special education evaluation and educational follow-up • May benefit from individual hearing aid and training in its use • Favorable seating and possible special education supports, especially for primary-age children • Attention to vocabulary and reading • May need speechreading instruction • Speech conservation and correction, if indicated
56 to 70 dB (moderate loss)	• Can understand loud conversation only • Will have increasing difficulty with group discussions • Is likely to have impaired speech • Is likely to have difficulty in language use and comprehension • Probably will have limited vocabulary	• Likely to need resource teacher or special class • Should have special help in language skills, vocabulary development, usage, reading, writing, grammar, etc. • Can benefit from individual hearing aid through evaluation and auditory training • Speechreading instruction • Speech conservation and speech correction

loud and clear. He finds male voices easier to hear than female voices because his loss is less pronounced in the lower frequencies. Raymond's teacher attempts to arrange favorable seating for him, but most class discussions are impossible for him to follow. Raymond attends a part-time special class for children with hearing impairments and is in a regular classroom for part of the day.

Severe Loss

Figure 8.4 shows the audiogram of Brenda, a child with a severe hearing impairment. Brenda can hear voices only if they are very loud and 1 foot or less from her ear. She wears a hearing aid, but it is uncertain how much she is gaining from it. She can distinguish most vowel sounds but hears only a few consonants. She can hear a door

TABLE 8.2   *(continued)*

FAINTEST SOUND HEARD	EFFECTS ON UNDERSTANDING LANGUAGE AND SPEECH	PROBABLE EDUCATIONAL NEEDS AND PROGRAMS
71 to 90 dB (severe loss)	• May hear loud voices about 1 foot from the ear • May be able to identify environmental sounds • May be able to discriminate vowels but not all consonants • Speech and language likely to be impaired or to deteriorate • Speech and language unlikely to develop spontaneously if loss is present before 1 year of age	• Likely to need a special education program for hearing-impaired children, with emphasis on all language skills, concept development, speechreading, and speech • Needs specialized program supervision and comprehensive supporting services • Can benefit from individual hearing evaluation • Auditory training on individual and group aids • Part-time regular class placement as profitable for student
91 dB or more (profound loss)	• May hear some loud sounds but senses vibrations more than tonal pattern • Relies on vision rather than hearing as primary avenue for communication • Speech and language likely to be impaired or to deteriorate • Speech and language unlikely to develop spontaneously if loss is prelingual	• Will need a special education program for children who are deaf, with emphasis on all language skills, concept development, speechreading, and speech • Needs specialized program supervision and comprehensive support services • Continuous appraisal of needs in regard to oral or manual communication • Auditory training on individual and group aids • Part-time regular class placement may be feasible

slamming, a vacuum cleaner, and an airplane flying overhead. She must always pay close visual attention to a person speaking with her. Brenda attends a full-time special class for children with hearing impairments in a regular public school.

Profound Loss

Figure 8.5 shows the audiogram for Steve, a child with a profound hearing impairment. Steve cannot hear conversational speech at all. His hearing aid seems to help him be aware of certain loud sounds, such as a fire alarm or a bass drum. Steve is congenitally deaf and has not developed intelligible speech. He attends a residential school for children who are deaf and uses sign language as his principal means of communication.

✳ Prevalence

About 20 million Americans experience some difficulty in receiving and processing aural communication. It is estimated that about 1% of the general population have

FIGURE 8.2

Audiogram for Vicki, who has a mild hearing impairment

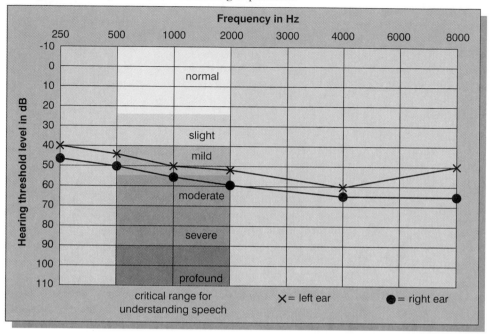

FIGURE 8.3

Audiogram for Raymond, who has a moderate hearing impairment

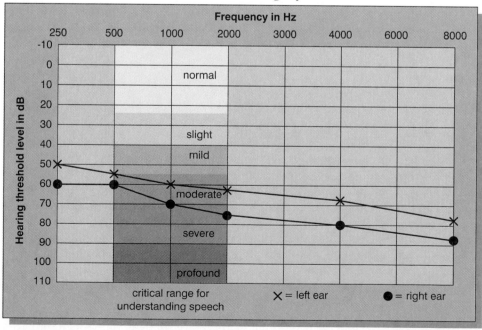

FIGURE 8.4
Audiogram for Brenda, who has a severe hearing impairment

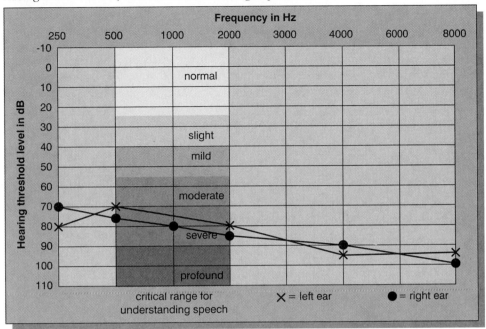

FIGURE 8.5
Audiogram for Steve, who has a profound hearing impairment

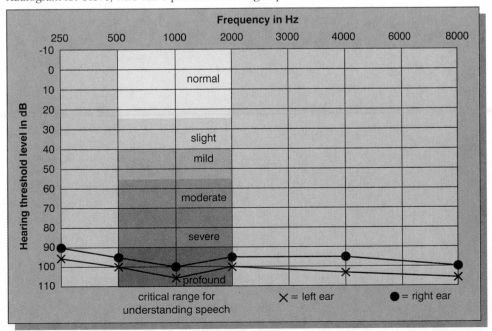

severe to profound hearing impairments. The incidence of hearing impairment in adults increases with age; Stein (1988) estimates that almost 40% of persons over age 75 experience some limitations in hearing.

Like other disabilities, estimates of incidence and prevalence of hearing impairment within the school-age population vary considerably. Stein (1988) states that less than 2% of children from birth through age 14 have impaired hearing, yet other authorities have concluded that approximately 5% of all school-age children have hearing impairments (Bensberg & Sigelman, 1976; Davis & Silverman, 1970). Many of these impairments, however, are not considered severe enough to require special education services. Hoemann and Briga (1981) estimate that only about 0.2% of the school-age population (1 child in 500) have a severe or profound hearing impairment. A 1986 report estimated 129,000 school-age children in the United States who could "at best hear and understand shouted speech" and included among these 22,000 who "could not hear and understand any speech" (Ries, 1986, p. 8). Males, African American students, and children aged 6 to 11 were found to be somewhat overrepresented in the hearing-impaired group in comparison with their proportions in the general population.

The U.S. Department of Education (1994) reports that during the 1992–93 school year, 60,896 students, or 1.3% of all students aged 6 to 21 who received special education services, were served under the hearing impairments disability category. Of the students with hearing impairments receiving special education services, approximately 90% have prelingual hearing loss (Commission on Education of the Deaf, 1988).

For every child identified as deaf, there are probably six or seven children who are hard-of-hearing and who may need certain special education services. Surveys suggest that although over 90% of the children in the United States identified as deaf are receiving special services, the percentage of hard-of-hearing children receiving special services may be only 20% or less (Berg, 1986; Moores, 1987). It is likely, then, that a significant number of students with hearing impairments in regular classes may not be receiving the special assistance they need for effective learning and adjustment. One educator describes the hard-of-hearing child as "the most neglected exceptional child in our public day school system other than the gifted" (Gonzales, 1980, p. 20).

✸ *Historical Background*

Plann (1992) writes an interesting story of Roberto Fransico Pradez, Spain's first deaf teacher of deaf students, whom she credits as being the founding father of deaf education.

Children and adults who are deaf have long been a source of fascination and interest. In the late 16th century, one of the first educational programs for exceptional children of any kind—a school for the children who were deaf of noble families—was established in Spain by Pedro Ponce de León (1520–1584), an Augustinian monk and scholar. At that time, for children to be recognized as persons under the law—and therefore eligible to inherit their families' titles and fortunes—it was necessary for them to be able to speak and read. Ponce de León reportedly achieved success in teaching speech, writing, reading, arithmetic, and foreign languages to some of his students (Sacks, 1986). During the 18th century, schools for children who were deaf were set up in England, France, Germany, Holland, and Scotland. Both oral and manual methods of instruction were used.

Nineteenth-Century Opportunities in the United States

Children with hearing impairments were among the first groups of individuals with disabilities to receive special education in the United States. The American Asylum for the Education of the Deaf and Dumb opened in Hartford, Connecticut, in 1817. The original name of this institution indicates the prevailing philosophy of the early 19th century, when persons who were deaf were viewed as incapable of benefiting from oral instruction. At that time, students who were deaf were considered most appropriately served in asylums, special sanctuaries removed from normal society. Many of the private, public, and parochial schools for students who were deaf founded in the 19th century were, in fact, located in small towns, away from major centers of population. For the most part, these were residential institutions.

During the second half of the 19th century, instruction in speech and speechreading became widely available to students who were deaf throughout the United States. In fact, oral approaches to educating students with hearing impairments came to dominate professional thought to such a great degree that the use of sign language in schools was officially prohibited at an international conference held in 1880.

A particularly influential figure during this era was Alexander Graham Bell, the inventor of the telephone, who had a lifelong interest in deafness. His mother was deaf, and his father and grandfather were teachers of speech and articulation. Bell himself married Mabel Hubbard, a deaf student whom he had tutored.

Before the end of the 19th century, several day schools for students who were deaf were established. In general, however, the late 19th century brought about an "increasing isolation of children who are deaf from their families and from society at large" (Moores & Kluwin, 1986, p. 106). And it was not until many years later that most schools relaxed their restrictions against the use of sign language.

Recent Educational Opportunities

Educational opportunities for children who are deaf in regular public schools have only recently become widespread. In most areas of the United States, in accordance with the least restrictive environment concept, parents now have the option of choosing between local public school programs and residential school placement. Today, about 80% of children who are deaf in the United States attend local school programs, and nearly one half of these children are integrated into regular classrooms at least part of the time (U.S. Department of Education, 1994). Of the 11.5% of students with hearing impairments who attend residential schools, about one third do so as day students (Schildroth, 1986); that is, they live at home with their families while attending the special school program.

Today, increasing attention is given to the needs of students with hearing impairments with additional disabilities such as mental retardation, learning disabilities, behavioral disorders, visual impairments, and physical disabilities. Around 30% of the children currently enrolled in schools and classes for students with hearing impairments have other disabilities (Orlansky, 1986b; Schildroth, 1986). Many programs also seek to meet the needs of the sizable population of children with hearing impairments from culturally diverse backgrounds. The challenge of teaching English communication skills to a deaf child when a language other than English is spoken in the home is particularly complex.

This school, now more than 175 years old, is known today as the American School for the Deaf.

Decibel, the unit of measure for the intensity of sound, is named for Alexander Graham Bell.

Chapter 3 contains further information about children with disabilities from non-English and bilingual backgrounds.

Over the years, many special methods and materials have been developed for and used with children with hearing impairments, and much research has been conducted. Techniques, theories, and controversies have proliferated, often with passionate proponents. Yet we still do not fully understand the effects of hearing impairment on learning, communication, and personality, nor have we solved the most difficult problem inherent in educating students who are deaf: *teaching spoken language to children who cannot hear.*

Many students who are deaf leave school unable to read and write English proficiently. According to Paul and Quigley (1990):

> No general improvement in achievement in most students who are severely to profoundly hearing-impaired has been observed since the . . . early years of the 20th century. The average student completing a secondary education program is still reading and writing at a level commensurate with the average 9- to 10-year-old hearing student. Achievement in mathematics is about one or two grades higher. Since the beginning of formal achievement testing, two enduring patterns above been reported: *low levels* and *small gains* in achievement despite 12 to 13 years of education. (p. 227)

Many students who are deaf are not able to communicate effectively, sometimes not even with normal-hearing schoolmates or members of their own families. Parents are often given confusing, contradictory information and advice when it is discovered their child has a hearing impairment; identification of a deaf child is often devastating for parents. The rate of unemployment and underemployment among deaf adults is shockingly high, and their wages are lower than those of the hearing population.

In response to these problems, Congress established the Commission on Education of the Deaf with the Education of the Deaf Act of 1986. After studying the field, the commission began its report to Congress with these words:

> The present state of education for persons who are deaf in the United States is unsatisfactory. Unacceptably so. This is the primary and inescapable conclusion of the Commission on Education of the Deaf. (1988, p. viii)

The commission went on to make 52 recommendations for improving the education of students with hearing impairments. Many questions remain unanswered, and many challenges remain in educating children with hearing impairments.

✳ *Educational Approaches*
Amplification and Auditory Training and Learning

Deafness is often mistaken to be a total lack of hearing. In years past, it was assumed that individuals who were deaf simply did not hear at all. This view was incorrect. Hearing loss occurs in many degrees and patterns. Nearly all children who are deaf have some amount of residual hearing. With help, they need not grow up in a "silent world."

Modern methods of testing hearing and improved electronic technology for the amplification of sound enable many children with hearing impairments today to use their residual hearing productively. Even children with severe and profound hearing impairments can benefit from hearing aids in the classroom, home, and community, regardless of whether they communicate primarily in an oral or manual mode. Ross (1986) considers residual hearing to be the "biologic birthright" of every hearing-impaired child, one that "should be used and depended on to whatever extent possible" (p. 51). It is important for teachers and audiologists to cooperate with each other in reaching this goal.

Amplification Instruments

A hearing aid is an amplification instrument; that is, it functions to make sounds louder. Levitt (1985) describes the hearing aid as "the most widely used technological aid of all. . . . a low cost, acoustic amplification system that can be programmed to best match the needs of each user" (pp. 120–121). There are dozens of kinds of hearing aids; they can be worn behind the ear, in the ear, on the body, or in eyeglasses. Children can wear hearing aids in one or both ears (monaural or binaural aids). Today's hearing aids are generally smaller and lighter than older models, yet they are also more powerful and versatile. Whatever its shape, power, or size, a hearing aid picks up sound, magnifies its energy, and delivers this louder sound to the user's ear and brain. In many ways, the hearing aid is like a miniature public address system, with a microphone, an amplifier, and controls to adjust volume and tone (Clarke & Leslie, 1980). One study found that the academic performance of students with hearing impairments was positively correlated with the length of time they had worn their hearing aids (Blair, Peterson, & Viehweg, 1985).

Hearing aids can be helpful to many children in increasing their awareness of sound. The aids make sounds louder, but not necessarily clearer. Thus, children who hear sounds with distortion will still experience distortion with hearing aids. The effect is similar to turning up the volume on an old transistor radio: You can make the music louder, but you cannot make the words clearer. And even the most powerful hearing aids generally cannot enable children with severe and profound hearing losses to hear speech sounds beyond a distance of a few feet. No hearing aid can cure a hearing loss or by itself enable a child who is deaf to function normally in a regular classroom. In all cases, it is the wearer of the hearing aid, not the aid itself, who does most of the work in interpreting conversation.

Teachers should check daily to see that a child's hearing aid is functioning properly. The Ling Five Sound Test is a quick and easy way to determine whether a child can detect the basic speech sounds (Ling, 1976). With the child's back to the teacher (to ensure that visual clues do not confound the results), the child repeats each of five sounds spoken by the teacher: /a/, /oo/, /e/, /sh/, and /s/. Ling states that these five sounds are representative of the speech energy in every English phoneme and that a child who can detect these five sounds should be able to detect every English speech sound. Absent or abnormal hearing aid function should be checked immediately; most breakdowns are due to problems with the battery.

The earlier in life a child can be fitted with an appropriate hearing aid, the more effectively he or she will learn to use hearing for communication and awareness. Today, it is not at all unusual to see hearing aids on infants and preschool children; the improved listening conditions become an important part of the young child's speech and language development. A worthwhile goal is to provide for a child a sense of hearing that is "integrated into the personality" (Lowell & Pollack, 1974, n.p.). To derive the maximum benefit from a hearing aid, a child should wear it

Financial assistance from local or state agencies is often available for the purchase and maintenance of hearing aids.

throughout the day. Residual hearing cannot be effectively developed if the aid is removed or turned off outside the classroom. It is important for the child to hear sounds while eating breakfast, shopping in the supermarket, and riding the school bus.

In the classroom, problems of distance, room reverberation, and background noise often interfere with a student's ability to discriminate the desired auditory signal with a personal hearing aid (Berg, 1986). When the signal-to-noise ratio is poor, the hearing-impaired child may find the auditory signal audible but not "intelligible" (Boothroyd, 1978). Group assistive listening devices can solve the problems of distance, noise, and reverberation in the classroom. They do not replace the child's personal hearing aid but augment it in group listening situations (Zelski & Zelski, 1985). In most systems, a radio link is established between the teacher and the children with hearing impairments, with the teacher wearing a small microphone-transmitter (often on the lapel, near the lips) and each child wearing a receiver that doubles as a personal hearing aid (Ross, 1986). An FM radio frequency is usually employed, and wires are not required, so teacher and students can move freely around the classroom area. The FM device creates a listening situation comparable to the teacher's "being only 6 inches away from the child's ear at all times" (Ireland, Wray, & Flexer, 1988, p. 17). Classroom amplification systems are used in both special classes and mainstream settings where students with hearing impairments are integrated with nonimpaired students.

Auditory Learning

Auditory training/learning programs help children make better use of residual hearing. All children with hearing impairments, regardless of whether their preferred method of communication is oral (speech) or manual (signs), should participate in lessons and activities that help them improve their listening ability. Many children with hearing impairments have much more auditory potential than they actually use, and their residual hearing can be most effectively developed in the context of actual communication and daily experiences (Ross, 1981). An auditory training program should not be limited to artificial exercises in the classroom.

A traditional **auditory training** program for young children with hearing impairments begins by teaching awareness of sound. Parents might direct their

---

Ho (1991) describes the Easy Listener Freefield Sound System, which functions as a specialized portable PA system to increase auditory attention for all students, and the Easy Listener Personal FM System, in which students with mild hearing impairments wear a receiver and headphones.

The combination of amplification and auditory training can help a hearing impaired child make the most of his residual hearing.

child's attention to such sounds as a doorbell ringing or water running. They might then focus on localization of sound—for example, by hiding a radio somewhere in the room and encouraging the child to look for it. Discrimination of sounds is another important part of auditory training; a child might learn to notice the differences between a man's voice and a woman's voice, between a fast song and a slow song, or between the words *rack* and *rug.* Identification of sounds comes when a child is able to recognize a sound, word, or sentence through listening.

The focus today is on *auditory learning*—that is, teaching the child to "learn to listen" and to "learn by listening," instead of simply "learning to hear" (Ling, 1986). Advocates of auditory learning contend that the first three levels of auditory training—detecting, discriminating, and identifying sounds—are important but insufficient for developing the student's residual hearing. Auditory learning emphasizes a fourth and highest level of listening skills—the comprehension of meaningful sounds.

Some teachers find it helpful to conduct formal auditory training/learning sessions in which a child is required to use only hearing—he or she would have to recognize sounds and words without looking at the speaker. In actual practice, however, the student gains useful information from vision and the other senses to supplement the information received from hearing. Consequently, all senses should be effectively developed and constantly used.

> Teachers should help parents recognize and take advantage of the many opportunities for auditory training and learning around the house.

Speechreading

Speechreading is the process of understanding a spoken message by observing the speaker's face. Children with hearing impairments, whether they have much or little residual hearing and whether they communicate primarily through oral or manual means, use their vision to help them understand speech. Some sounds are readily distinguished by watching the speaker's lips. For example, the word *pail* begins with the lips in a shut position, whereas the lips are somewhat drawn together and puckered at the corners for the word *rail.* Paying careful attention to a speaker's lips may help an individual with hearing impairment derive important clues—particularly if he or she is also able to gain some information through residual hearing, signs or gestures, facial expressions, and familiarity with the context or situation.

> Speechreading was traditionally called *lipreading,* but understanding speech from visual clues involves more than simply looking at the lips.

Speechreading, however, is extremely difficult and has many limitations. About half of all English words have some other word(s) that appear the same in pronunciation; that is, although they sound quite different, they look alike on the lips. Words such as *bat, mat,* and *pat,* for example, look exactly alike and simply cannot be discriminated by watching the speaker's lips. To complicate matters, the visual clues may be blocked by a hand or a pencil, chewing gum, or a mustache. Many speakers are virtually unintelligible through speechreading; they may seem not to move their lips at all. In addition, it is extremely tiring to watch lips for a long time, and it may be impossible to do so at a distance, such as during a lecture.

Walker (1986) estimates that even the best speechreaders detect only about 25% of what is said through visual clues alone; "the rest is contextual piecing together of ideas and expected constructions" (p. 19). The average deaf child might accurately speechread only about 5% of what is said (Vernon & Koh, 1970).

The frustrations of speechreading are graphically described in this passage by Shanny Mow (1973), a teacher who is deaf:

> Like the whorls on his fingertips, each person's lips are different and move in a peculiar way of their own. When young, you build confidence as you guess correctly

"ball," "fish," and "shoe" on your teacher's lips. This confidence doesn't last. As soon as you discover there are more than four words in the dictionary, it evaporates. Seventy percent of the words when appearing on the lips are no more than blurs. Lipreading is a precarious and cruel art which rewards a few who have mastered it and tortures the many who have tried and failed. (pp. 21–22)

> The September 1988 issue of *The Volta Review* contains several articles on speechreading.

Despite the problems inherent in speechreading, it can be a valuable adjunct in the communication of a hearing-impaired person. According to Moores (1987), few new techniques have been developed recently, and little research has been done into the most effective ways of teaching speechreading. Although speechreading cannot take the place of hearing, improved methods might well enable many people with hearing impairments to make better use of their vision in decoding messages.

Oral Approaches

Educational programs with an oral emphasis view speech as essential if students who are deaf are to function in the hearing world. Training in producing and understanding speech and language is incorporated into virtually all aspects of the child's education. Currently, about one third of the educational programs for students who are deaf in the United States use a predominantly oral approach (Reagan, 1985). Connor (1986) observes that the use of speech and the development of oral receptive skills have declined markedly in recent years as more and more educational programs for students with hearing impairments rely on sign language systems to transmit instructional information.

A child who attends a program with an oral emphasis typically uses several means to develop residual hearing and the ability to speak as intelligibly as possible. Auditory, visual, and tactile methods of input are frequently used. Much attention is given to amplification, auditory training, speechreading, the use of technological aids, and above all, talking. Oral education tends to emphasize parent and family involvement. A few schools and classes maintain a purely oral environment and may even prohibit children from pointing, using gestures, or spelling out words to communicate. Children in these programs must express themselves and learn to understand others through speech alone. Other programs also emphasize speech but are more flexible. They may use a variety of approaches to help students produce and understand spoken language.

Cued Speech

Cued speech is a method of supplementing oral communication. It seeks to supply a visual representation of spoken language by adding cues, in the form of hand signals near the chin, to assist the deaf person in identifying sounds that cannot be distinguished through speechreading. The hand signals must be used in conjunction with speech; they are neither signs nor manual alphabet letters and cannot be read alone. Eight hand shapes are used to identify consonant sounds, and four locations identify vowel sounds. A hand shape coupled with a location gives a visual indication of a syllable. See Figure 8.6 for a representation of cued speech.

According to Cornett (1974), who developed the system, cued speech can clarify the patterns of spoken English and give intensive language input to young children. It does not disrupt the natural rhythm of speech. Of course, the child's parents and teachers and preferably peers as well must learn the cues. Reportedly, cued

Focus on Intervention

Tips for Facilitating Communication

People with hearing impairments are increasingly participating in community life. It is not unusual for a businessperson, bank teller, student, police officer, or anyone else to have the opportunity to communicate with a person who is deaf. Yet many people with normal hearing are unsure of themselves. As a result, they may avoid deaf people altogether or use ineffective and frustrating strategies when they do attempt to communicate.

The following tips for facilitating communication were suggested by the Community Services for the Deaf program in Akron, Ohio. These tips provide basic information about three common ways that persons who are deaf communicate: through speechreading, with sign language or the assistance of an interpreter, and by written communication. Usually, the person will indicate the approach he or she is most comfortable with. If the person relies mainly on speechreading (lipreading), here are things you can do to help.

- Face the person and stand or sit no more than 4 feet away.
- The room should have adequate illumination, but don't seat yourself in front of a strong or glaring light.
- Try to keep your whole face visible.
- Speak clearly and naturally, and not too fast.
- Don't exaggerate your mouth movements.
- Don't raise the level of your voice.
- Some words are more easily read on the lips than others. If you are having a problem being understood, try substituting different words.
- It may take a while to become used to the deaf person's speech. If at first you can't understand what he or she is saying, don't give up.
- Don't hesitate to write down any important words that are missed.

If the deaf person communicates best through sign language (and you do not), it will probably be necessary to use an interpreter. Here are some considerations to keep in mind:

- The role of the interpreter is to facilitate communication between you and the person who is deaf. The interpreter should not be asked to give opinions, advice, or personal feelings.
- Maintain eye contact with the deaf person and speak directly to him or her. The deaf person should not be made to take a back seat in the conversation. For example, say, "How are you today?" instead of "Ask her how she is today."
- Remain face-to-face with the deaf person. The best place for the interpreter is behind you and a little to the side of you. Again, avoid strong or glaring light.
- Remember, it is the interpreter's job to communicate everything that you and the deaf person say. Don't say anything that you don't want interpreted.

Written messages can be helpful in exchanging information. Consider the following:

- Avoid the temptation to abbreviate your communication.
- Write in simple, direct language.
- The deaf person's written English may not be grammatically correct, but you will probably be able to understand it. One deaf person, for example, wrote "Pay off yesterday, finish me" to convey the message "I paid that loan off yesterday."
- Use visual aids, such as pictures, diagrams, and business cards.
- Don't be afraid to supplement your written messages with gestures and facial expressions.
- Written communication has limitations, but it is often more effective than no communication at all.

Remember that English is not the first language of many deaf people. They are deprived of a great deal of information because they cannot hear. Skills of spoken and written English are not an accurate reflection of a deaf person's intelligence or ability to function independently.

FIGURE 8.6
Hand shapes and locations used in cued speech

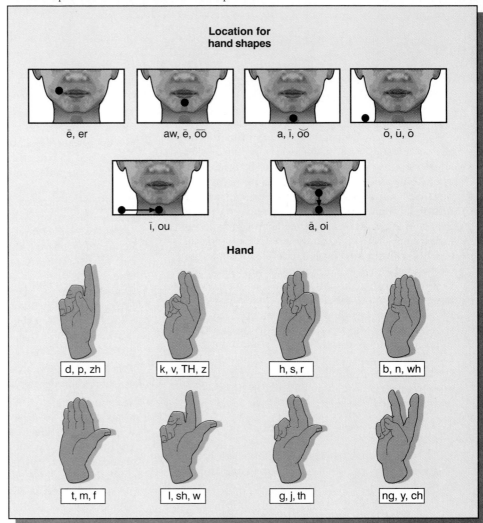

speech can be learned in 10 to 20 hours of instruction. Although cued speech is advocated by a number of active parent groups and is widely used in educational programs for children with hearing impairments in Australia, the system has not become popular in the United States (Calvert, 1986).

Benefits of Oral Approaches

Educators who use an oral approach acknowledge that teaching speech to children who are deaf is difficult, demanding, and time-consuming for the teacher, the parents, and—most of all—the student. Speech comes hard to the deaf child, and no recent development has made the task any easier.

> There has been neither a clear record of steady improvement in teaching methods nor significant breakthroughs that have either markedly reduced the level of effort or significantly increased the quality of the result for 400 years. (Calvert, 1986, p. 167)

The rewards of successful oral communication, however, are thought to be worth all the effort. And indeed, most students with hearing losses no worse than severe can learn speech well enough to communicate effectively with hearing people. Paul and Quigley (1990) point out that the best results are obtained with students with hearing impairments who are enrolled in indisputably comprehensive oral programs or who are integrated most of the school day into regular education programs. They note also that most students with severe hearing impairments who develop good speech represent a select group of students who are deaf: They typically have above-average IQs, have parents who are highly involved in their education, and come from above-average socioeconomic status families (Geers & Moog, 1989).

Total Communication

Educational programs with an emphasis on **total communication** advocate the use of a variety of forms of communication to teach language to students with hearing impairments. Practitioners of total communication maintain that simultaneous presentation of manual communication (by signs and fingerspelling) and speech (through speechreading and residual hearing) makes it possible for children to use either one or both types of communication (Ling, 1984). Since its introduction as a teaching philosophy in the 1960s, total communication has become "the predominant method of instruction in schools for the deaf" (Luterman, 1986, p. 263). A survey found that the percentage of deaf students who both speak and sign (62.2%) is far greater than that who only speak (21.1%) or who only sign (16.7%) (Wolk & Schildroth, 1986).

> Roy Holcomb, a deaf graduate of the Texas School for the Deaf and Gallaudet University, coined the term and is credited as the father of total communication (Gannon, 1981).

Sign Language

Sign language uses gestures to represent words, ideas, and concepts. Some signs are *iconic;* that is, they convey meaning through hand shapes or motions that look like or appear to imitate or act out their message. In making the *cat* sign, for example,

Total communication requires the simultaneous use of signs and speech.

the signer seems to be stroking feline whiskers on his or her face; in the sign for *eat,* the hand moves back and forth into an open mouth. Most signs, however, have little or no iconicity; they do not resemble the objects or actions they represent. If sign language were simply a form of pantomime, then most nonsigners would be able to understand it with relatively little effort. But several studies have shown that the majority of signs cannot be guessed by people who are unfamiliar with that particular sign language (Klima & Bellugi, 1979).

Teachers who practice total communication generally speak as they sign and make a special effort to follow the form and structure of spoken English as closely as possible. Several sign language systems have been designed primarily for educational purposes, with the intention of facilitating the development of reading, writing, and other language skills in students with hearing impairments. *Manually Coded English* is the term applied to several educationally oriented sign systems, such as *Seeing Essential English* (Anthony, 1971), *Signing Exact English* (Gustason, Pfetzing, & Zawolkow, 1980), and *Signed English* (Bornstein, 1974). These sign systems incorporate many features of American Sign Language and also seek to follow correct English usage and word order. Students with hearing impairments often must use two or more sign language systems, depending on the person with whom they are communicating.

Some signs, such as cat *(left) and* eat *(right) are iconic; they look like the objects or actions they represent.*

Fingerspelling

Fingerspelling (dactylology) is often used in conjunction with other methods of communication. Fingerspelling, or the manual alphabet, consists of 26 distinct hand positions, one for each English letter. A one-hand manual alphabet is used in the United States and Canada (Figure 8.7). Some manual letters—such as *C, L,* and *W*—resemble the shape of printed English letters, whereas others—such as *A, E,* and *S*—have no apparent similarity. As in typewriting, each word is spelled out letter by letter.

A user of sign language relies on fingerspelling to spell out proper names for which no signs exist and to clarify meanings. The *Rochester Method* uses a combination of oral communication and fingerspelling but does not use sign language. The teacher fingerspells every letter of every word as he or she speaks, and the hearing-impaired student learns to use the same means of expression. The Rochester Method also emphasizes reading and writing; its advocates believe that this approach facilitates the acquisition of correct language patterns.

Supporters of total communication methods believe that this approach is the best way to provide a "reliable receptive-expressive symbol system," especially in the preschool years when communication between parent and child is vitally important

Fingerspelling is also used by many people who are both deaf and visually impaired. The manual alphabet can be used at close distances or felt with the hand if a person is totally blind.

FIGURE 8.7
The manual alphabet used to fingerspell English in North America

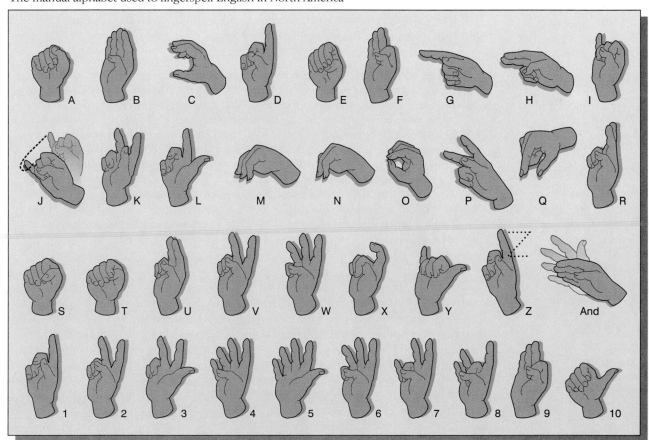

(Denton, 1972, n.p.). Several researchers have found that children as young as 5 months of age are able to produce and understand signs effectively (e.g., Maestas y Moores & Moores, 1980; Orlansky & Bonvillian, 1985; Prinz & Prinz, 1979).

Although there is no firm evidence that the use of sign language by children who are deaf inhibits acquisition of speech (Moores, 1987; Rooney, 1982; Sacks, 1986), some specialists contend that it is difficult for children with hearing impairments to process signs and speech when they are presented together. "Even for experts it is not easy to combine signs and speech effectively," writes Ling (1984, p. 11), noting that they are usually produced at different rates of speed. In Ling's view, the simultaneous use of signs and speech is likely to impair the quality of speech, signs, and/or language. It may be better, he suggests, for children to learn oral and manual skills separately, rather than at the same time.

Total communication has gained wide acceptance in educational programs for students with hearing impairments. Signs are used in over 75% of educational programs for students with severe and profound hearing impairments (Gallaudet Research Institute, 1985). Luterman (1986), however, regards the effects of the movement toward total communication as unproven. Many educators consider total communication to have facilitated parent-child and teacher-child communication and to have enhanced children's self-esteem, but these supposed gains cannot be easily documented. Luterman (1986) further observes that "total communication has not made any substantial changes in the depressingly low academic achievement of children who are deaf" (p. 263).

Some educators have expressed concern over the consistency and quality of signing that occurs in many total communication classrooms. Stewart (1992), who argues for increased pre- and inservice sign training for teachers, writes:

> Having ridden a wave of popularity to become the most prominent communication approach in the field, total communication appears to be advancing to its own judgment day. Programs that advocate the use of signs have been characterized by linguistic inconsistency in the signing behavior of teachers . . . whereas English, and to a lesser extent American Sign Language (ASL), might be promoted as the primary language base in total communication programs, Pidgin English (PSE) best described the way most teachers tend to sign. . . . Most teachers of the deaf have spent the first 20 years of their lives using only speech and English skills as their primary means of communication. Then after a couple of sign courses, several field experiences, and limited background information on the pedagogical implications of signing, these teachers are given classrooms and expected to become effective as instructors in what is essentially a foreign medium of communication. (pp. 69, 82)

American Sign Language (ASL)

American Sign Language (often referred to as ASL or Ameslan) is the language of the Deaf culture in the United States and Canada. Although the sign languages used by native deaf speakers were once thought to be nonlanguages (alinguistic), ASL is now viewed as a legitimate language in its own right, rather than as an imperfect variation of spoken English. ASL is a visual-gestural language with its own rules of syntax, semantics, and pragmatics (Wilbur, 1987). In ASL the shape, location, and movement pattern of the hands, the intensity of motions, and the signer's facial expressions all communicate meaning and content. As Paul and Quigley (1990) point out:

American Sign Language (ASL) is a legitimate language with its own vocabulary, syntax, and grammatical rules; it does not correspond to spoken or written English.

ASL is particularly structured to accommodate the eye and motor capabilities of the body. The grammatical structure of ASL is spatially based. Space and movement play important linguistic roles. (p. 128)

Because ASL has its own vocabulary, syntax, and grammatical rules, it does not correspond to spoken or written English. Articles, prepositions, tenses, plurals, and the word order are often expressed differently from those of standard English. It is difficult to make precise word-for-word translations between ASL and English, just as it is difficult to translate many foreign languages into English word for word.

Most children who are deaf do not learn ASL at home; only about 12% of children who are deaf have deaf parents (Reagan, 1985). It is often passed from children to other children (usually in residential schools), rather than from parents to children. ASL is seldom used within a total communication program. Although the manual communication that total communication teachers use often borrows individual signs from ASL, those signs are presented according to English syntax, resulting in a kind of "Pidgin Sign English."

Lane (1988) views hearing educators' insistence on imposing a manual form of English on students who are deaf as another sign of the ethnocentrism and paternalism often displayed by the hearing establishment toward students who are deaf.

Deaf of Deaf is the term used by those in the Deaf community to refer to children who are deaf and have deaf parents.

> This ethnocentric misunderstanding about the nature and status of sign language leads teachers to "fix up" the children's "arbitrary gestures" to make them more like English. New signs are invented by hearing people for English function words and suffixes that have no place, of course, in American Sign Language, and the grammatical order of the signs is scrambled in an attempt to duplicate English word order. No deaf child has ever learned such a system as a native language and indeed could not, for it violates the principles of the manual-visual channel of communication. No deaf adult uses such ways of communicating. But the system is widely used in classrooms with the claim that it assists the deaf child in learning English. (p. 10)

Many members of the Deaf community and some educators are calling for recognition of ASL as the deaf child's first language. They believe that English might be better learned in the context of a bilingual education approach after the child has mastered his or her native or first language (ASL). Among this group are Paul and Quigley (1990), who criticize the current use of various forms of manually coded English in total communication programs because (a) the codes have been contrived by a small group of persons; (b) they are not widely used outside a specific educational environment; (c) practitioners often use signs from various systems, so it is difficult for students with hearing impairments to form reliable hypotheses about the rules of English; and (d) after more than 15 years of use, there is little evidence of improvements in the English literacy or academic achievement of students who are deaf.

Language Instruction

Numerous techniques and materials have been developed to help children with hearing impairments acquire and use written language. The relationship between written and spoken expression is obviously close, but there is no exact correspondence between the type of communication method a child uses (oral only or total communication) and the method of language instruction that a particular school or class employs.

Instructional programs in language for students with hearing impairments are generally classified as either structured or natural. Advocates of a structured approach believe that students with hearing impairments do not acquire English naturally—they must learn the language by analyzing and categorizing its grammatical rules and relationships. A well-known structured method, developed more than 65 years ago but still widely used, is the Fitzgerald Key (Fitzgerald, 1929). This method provides several labeled categories, such as who, what, where, and when. The child learns to generate correct sentences by placing words into the proper categories.

Proponents of the natural approach believe that if students are exposed to a language-rich environment, they will naturally discover the rules and principles of English. Neither grammar nor parts of speech, for example, are taught directly. An example of a natural method is Natural Language for Children who are Deaf (Groht, 1958). This method emphasizes language development through modeling and conversation; games and activities are preferred to formal drills and exercises.

Moores and Maestas y Moores (1981) provide a helpful review of methods of language instruction, noting that virtually no research has been conducted to evaluate the advantages of one approach over the other and that most educational programs today tend to use a combination of structured and natural methods.

Controversy and Choices

Educators, scientists, philosophers, and parents—both hearing and deaf—have for many years debated the most appropriate instructional methods for children who are deaf. Today, this controversy is as lively as ever. The fundamental disagreement concerns the extent to which children who are deaf should express themselves through speech and perceive the communication of others through speechreading and residual hearing. Research has yet to provide (and perhaps never will provide) a definitive answer to the question of which communication method is best. There is general agreement, however, that our educational programs for students who are deaf leave much room for improvement.

Different children communicate in different ways. Some children with hearing impairments, unfortunately, have experienced deep frustration and failure because of rigid adherence to an oral-only program. They have left oral programs without having developed a usable avenue of communication. Equally unfortunate is the fact that other children with hearing impairments have not been given an adequate opportunity to develop their auditory and oral skills because they were placed in educational programs that did not provide good oral instruction. In both cases, children have been unfairly penalized. Every hearing-impaired child should have access to an educational program that uses a communication method appropriate to his or her unique abilities and needs.

✳ *Educational Service Alternatives*
Placement

Educational programs for children with hearing impairments are available in residential schools, special day schools, and regular public schools. Schildroth (1986) notes that enrollment in the more than 60 public residential schools for children with hearing impairments in the United States has declined sharply as public school programs have become more widely available and as the majority of students whose deafness was caused by the rubella epidemics of the mid-1960s have departed from the school-age population. About 40% of students with hearing impairments who attend residential schools commute (Paul & Quigley, 1990). Over 90% of the students currently enrolled in residential schools have severe and profound prelingual hearing impairments. Nearly one third of the students with hearing impairments served in residential schools have additional disabilities.

Educational programs for children with hearing impairments in local public schools have expanded in response to federal legislation, improvements in hearing aids and other technology, and an increased demand by parents and deaf citizens for services at the local level (Davis, 1986). Children with hearing impairments in regular schools may attend self-contained classes or may be integrated into general education classrooms for all or part of the school day. Fewer than 50% of students with hearing impairments are integrated into regular classrooms to some degree and that most of those who are mainstreamed have hearing losses of less than 90 dB Karchmer (1984).

According to Davis (1986), the most important ingredients for the hearing-impaired child's success in the regular classroom are (a) good oral communication skills, (b) strong parental support, (c) average or above-average intelligence, (d) self-confidence and other personal qualities, and (e) adequate support services, such as tutoring, audiological consultation, and speech therapy. As with all learners, we should never overlook the most fundamental factor in determining how successful a student will be in the regular classroom (or any other placement): *quality of instruction.* After studying the math achievement of 215 secondary students with hearing impairments who were either in self-contained classrooms or mainstreamed into regular classes with or without an interpreter, Kluwin and Moores (1989) concluded, "Quality of instruction is the prime determinant of achievement, regardless of placement" (p. 327).

Several publications provide helpful guidelines, practical suggestions, and descriptions of programs that have successfully integrated students with hearing impairments into regular classes (Dale, 1984; Kampfe, 1984; Lynas, 1986; Orlansky, 1979; Webster & Ellwood, 1985).

Writer's Workshop

·························

Writing Process Teaching with Students Who Are Deaf

By Barbara R. Schirmer

Reading and writing are so integral to educational success, social interaction, and economic opportunities that it is hard to imagine what it would be like to struggle with written language. For students who are deaf, reading and writing present tremendous challenges. Regardless of how effectively the deaf child can communicate about complex issues person to person, reading and writing about these issues require that the child be able to manipulate the surface structure of English. This is a daunting task for children who are not fluent in oral English.

Reading and writing are interrelated processes involving the construction of meaning through text. Educators of children who are deaf have typically focused more of their instructional time on reading than writing. However, the whole language movement has provided an impetus for teachers to provide rich linguistic environments that offer a balance of classroom opportunities for reading, writing, and face-to-face language (signing, speaking, receiving sign, and listening).

Traditional approaches for teaching writing emphasized student learning of writing skills and rules, frequent practice in mastering techniques, and evaluation methods that promoted error-free compositions as the goal of writing instruction (Luetke-Stahlman & Luckner, 1991; McAnally, Rose, & Quigley, 1994). These approaches have been widely viewed as unsuccessful in helping students who are deaf become motivated writers who can effectively use writing to interact with others, communicate feelings, explore ideas, give and ask for help, direct the behavior of others, provide information, and create imaginative worlds (Schirmer, 1994).

Current approaches to teaching writing have been labeled "process writing" because they emphasize what individuals think about and do from inception of idea to finished product. Many teachers believe that stressing process over product allows children to develop as writers in much the same way as they develop as speakers and signers.

Writer's Workshop is a teaching model based on the principles of writing process teaching. The model can be implemented just as effectively in small self-contained classrooms with a relatively homogeneous group of students who are deaf as in large heterogeneous general education classrooms with one or a few students who are deaf. It has worked successfully with students who are deaf in kindergarten through high school (Andrews & Gonzalez, 1992; Johnson, 1992; Kluwin & Kelly, 1992; Luckner & Isaacson, 1990; Sturdivant, 1992).

The following qualities characterize the learning environment of Writer's Workshop:

- *Choice.* In Writer's Workshop, students have complete freedom to make decisions about their compositions, from topic to genre, vocabulary to sentence structures, voice to organization, and even whether to complete or not complete any given piece of writing.
- *Audience.* Students in Writer's Workshop classes know that their writing will reach individuals who are genuinely interested in reading and responding to their in-progress and completed pieces.
- *Time.* Writer's Workshop periods are substantial enough for students to engage in sustained effort without interruptions and are important enough to be regularly scheduled within each school week.
- *Stages in the writing process.* In Writer's Workshop, students are taught and encouraged to apply the stages in the writing process that researchers had observed in skilled writers: planning, writing, and revising (see Figure A).

Guidelines for Implementation

- Set aside 30 to 45 minutes for each Writer's Workshop period and don't allow interruptions. It is better to have three 35-minute periods each week than five 20-minute periods.
- Use 5- to 10-minute mini-lessons at the opening of each Writer's Workshop period to provide direct instruction in a skill or concept with which the

FIGURE A   This illustration was drawn by a high school student in response to the assignment "Illustrate the steps you go through when you write."

children have been grappling in their writing. Mini-lessons can cover the stages of the writing process, how to choose a topic, questions to ask and the kinds of comments that are helpful during conferences with the teacher and conferences with peers, techniques for planning one's writing, strategies for revising, how to edit, qualities of good writing, and how to decide which pieces to publish. For children who are deaf in general education classrooms, the educational interpreter or classroom teacher of children who are deaf can interpret the presentation.

- Teach the children how to use conferences for helping them make decisions about their writing. These conferences should be directed by the children and should support them in answering questions such as these: What do I want to write about? What do I already know about this topic, and what do I need to find out? Who is my audience? What have I done to get my ideas figured out, and what should I do next? How does it sound, or look, so far? What should I change? How will my reader feel as he or she reads this? What will my reader think about? What can I do to make it clearer? In classrooms with hearing children, conferences with children who are deaf who communicate through sign can be facilitated with the assistance of a sign language interpreter or teacher of children who are deaf who circulates around the class.
- Provide an author's folder for each child to keep as a portfolio. The author's folder should contain a list of topic ideas that the child has generated, drafts of writing-in-progress, list of revision suggestions, editing checklist, names and dates of completed pieces, and rules of the Writer's Workshop class period.
- Keep revision for ideas separate from revision for English sentences structures and mechanics. Because of the difficulty that children who are deaf have with English syntax, their written language tends to look nongrammatical. The writing of children who are deaf whose native language is ASL often follows the word order of ASL (a word order significantly different from that in English), and English morphemes are either left out or used inappropriately. If the teacher focuses all of the deaf child's attention on syntax, the child will see writing as a negative and even hopeless activity. But if syntax is placed in the context of editing, the final step of revision, the child can be guided to use English syntax as a model for written language.

Barbara R. Schirmer trains teachers of the deaf at Lewis and Clark College, Portland, Oregon. She is the author of *Language and Literacy Development in Children Who Are Deaf* (Merrill/Prentice Hall, 1994).

There is much debate over where students who are deaf should be educated, with some research evidence—and much strong opinion—to support both residential and mainstream placement. With the increased emphasis on inclusion, many question the effectiveness and appropriateness of residential placements for any student. Research, however, has not demonstrated that residential schools may contribute to academic or social deficits in students who are deaf. Some studies, on the contrary, suggest that residential schooling may be the most effective placement for some students. For example, Braden, Maller, and Paquin (1993) report that the performance IQs of children with hearing impairments who were educated in residential schools increased over a 3- to 4-year time period but that the scores of similar students in regular school day programs did not.

> The results of this study clearly disprove the belief that placement in residential, segregated programs invariably inhibits cognitive abilities. The assumption that children with hearing impairments are best served in mainstream settings should be suspended until additional information is available regarding placement effects on such children's cognitive, social and academic development. (p. 432)

In a study of the effects of mainstreaming on the academic achievement of high school students who are deaf, Kluwin (1993) reported that although those students who were mainstreamed into more regular classrooms for academic content fared better on achievement measures than students who spent all or most of the day in a separate class, the difference may have been the result of curriculum programming and class selection, not the actual placement where instruction took place. In discussing his findings, Kluwin writes:

See the January, 1995, issue of *Educational Leadership*.

> The conclusion we would reach is that for some deaf students, mainstreaming is a good education option; but for others, special classes are more appropriate. . . . Ultimately, we can neither condemn nor support any one type of education placement for deaf students because multiple factors enter into a complex constellation of relationships. We are, in fact, thrown back to the very basis for special education, that is, the individual consideration of each child and each situation. (pp. 79, 80)

Educational Interpreters

Interpreting—signing the speech of a teacher or other speaker for a person who is deaf—began as a profession in 1964 with the establishment of a professional organization called the Registry of Interpreters for the Deaf (RID). Many states have programs for training interpreters, who must meet certain standards of competence to be certified by the RID. The organization was initially comprised primarily of *freelance interpreters,* who interpret primarily for deaf adults in situations such as legal or medical interactions.

Sign language interpreting is demanding, physical work. In fact, a survey found that 87% of interpreters experience symptoms of repetitive stress injury or carpal tunnel syndrome in their wrists (Stedt, 1992).

The role of the *educational interpreter* (sometimes referred to as an *educational transliterator*) has made it possible for many students with hearing impairments to enroll in and successfully complete postsecondary programs. There has also been greater use of educational interpreters in elementary and secondary classrooms (Gustason, 1985). Duties of interpreters vary across schools; they are likely to perform such tasks as tutoring, assisting regular and special education teachers, keeping records, and supervising students with hearing impairments (Salend, & Longo, 1994; Zawolkow & DeFiore, 1986).

An educational interpreter makes it possible for Kristin, who is deaf, to succeed in the regular classroom.

I Am Not Disabled—I'm Just Deaf

Jesse Thomas was 15 years old when he testified before the National Council on Disabilities. He explained his views on the use of American Sign Language and mainstreaming. Excerpts from his testimony follow:

I think I have to explain that I am not disabled—I'm just deaf. Deaf persons are a minority group. They use American Sign Language (ASL) and are part of the Deaf Culture. One of the main reasons that mainstreaming is not good is because mainstreaming lacks Deaf Culture and ASL. I can't really explain Deaf Culture. I do know that Deaf Culture makes me proud of who I am—DEAF.

Here are reasons why I think Deaf schools should be favored over the mainstream:

- Learning through an interpreter is very hard. It is pretty tiring for me to keep my eyes on one "place" all day long. After watching an interpreter all morning, I find myself not paying attention in the afternoon.
- It is bad socially in the mainstream situation. I communicate in SIGN, and my peers in my hearing school SPEAK.
- You are ALWAYS outnumbered. There are basically 25 kids in my classes—all hearing but me. That's a ratio of 25:1!
- You don't feel like it's YOUR school; it's like you're along for the ride. I was in one school for sixth grade and got to know some kids, and the junior high was in another town, and I knew nobody there.
- You never know Deaf adults. Once in a while, there is someone who is deaf but thinks hearing, not a Deaf person who is proud to be deaf.
- You don't belong. There are still a lot of people whose faces show sympathy at the word *deaf* and gasp at the thought of a world devoid of hearing. Those people think, "My God, deaf people CAN'T HEAR, there must be something terribly astray with them!"
- You don't feel comfortable as a deaf person. I don't think there should be such a thing as "overcoming deafness." This implies that a person should push being deaf aside and be more hearing. That is absolutely ridiculous. Don't you think that a person should be what he is? I am Deaf; I will succeed as a Deaf person.

I've experienced BOTH kinds of social and educational situations, mainstream and deaf school, and I'll have to say that I favor Deaf schools over mainstreaming. In Deaf schools, the social situation and education is much more normal for Deaf people than in hearing schools. ✺

From "Not Disabled—Just Deaf," 1991, *Let's Talk, 33*(2), p. 30. Published by the American Speech-Language-Hearing Association. Reprinted by permission.

Postsecondary Education

Gallaudet also has programs to train teachers of deaf children. Both deaf and hearing students are accepted into these programs.

A growing number of educational opportunities are available to students with hearing impairments after completion of a program at high school level. The oldest and best known is Gallaudet University in Washington, DC, which offers a wide range of undergraduate and graduate programs in the liberal arts, sciences, education, business, and other fields. Students with hearing impairments from throughout the United States, Canada, and other countries compete for admission. Classes at Gallaudet are taught in simultaneous communication, through speech and sign language. The National Technical Institute for the Deaf (NTID), located at the Rochester (New York) Institute of Technology, provides wide-ranging programs in technical, vocational, and business-related fields such as computer science, hotel management, photography, and medical technology. Both Gallaudet and NTID are supported by the federal government, and each enrolls approximately 1,500 students with hearing impairments.

More than 150 other institutions of higher education have developed special programs of supportive services for students with hearing impairments. Among these are four regional postsecondary programs that enroll substantial numbers of students with hearing impairments: St. Paul (Minnesota) Technical-Vocational Institute, Seattle (Washington) Central Community College, the Postsecondary Education Consortium at the University of Tennessee, and California State University at Northridge.

The percentage of students with hearing impairments who attend postsecondary educational programs has risen dramatically in the past 20 years. About 40% of all students with hearing impairments go on to receive higher education (Connor, 1986). Enrollment has increased most sharply in areas of study related to business and office careers (Rawlings & King, 1986). It is hoped that the increase in postsecondary programs will expand vocational and professional opportunities for deaf adults.

✳ *Current Issues and Future Trends*

As more children with hearing impairments are educated in regular public school settings, it appears likely that oral methods of instruction will continue to be extremely important. Speech, after all, is the most widely used form of communication among teachers and students in regular classes. Manual communication, especially ASL, however, will probably become more familiar to the general public. Training in sign language is already offered to children with normal hearing in some schools, and an increasing number of people who contact the public in the course of their jobs—such as police officers, firefighters, flight attendants, and bank tellers—will learn to communicate manually with individuals who have hearing impairments. Television programs, films, concerts, and other media using interpreters or printed captions are becoming more widely available. It is no longer unusual to see a sign language interpreter standing next to a public speaker or performer.

Despite the recent expansion of postsecondary programs of education and training, many adults with hearing impairments still find limited opportunities for appropriate employment and economic advancement. Recent court decisions regarding the rights of students with hearing impairments have had mixed results. In one case (*Barnes v. Converse College,* 1977), a court ordered a private college to provide, at its own expense, an interpreter for a deaf student. In another case (*Southeastern Community College v. Davis,* 1979), the U.S. Supreme Court decided that a college could not be compelled to admit a hearing-impaired student into its nursing program. A widely publicized Supreme Court case (*Board of Education of the Hendrick Hudson Central School District v. Rowley,* 1982) resulted in a local school district's not being required to provide, at its expense, a sign language interpreter for a deaf child who was performing adequately without one in the regular classroom. Similar cases are certain to arise in the future, as hearing-impaired people become increasingly aware of their civil rights and seek access to education, employment, and other rights.

The central role that ASL plays in the Deaf culture, combined with the growing recognition that ASL is the deaf child's first language, will probably heighten the

> The *Rowley* case is discussed in Chapter 2. It was the first Supreme Court case to be argued by a lawyer who is deaf.

intensity of the long-standing debate over how language should be taught to children with hearing impairments. As an illustration of the intensity with which many people who are deaf view this issue, 85 students at the Tennessee School for the Deaf were suspended when they resisted a decree by the school that they sign in English word order instead of being allowed to communicate in ASL (McCracken, 1987).

Technological advances are already having a significant impact on the lives of many individuals with hearing impairments. In addition to the sophisticated techniques now used to detect hearing losses and to make use of even slight amounts of residual hearing, a number of devices known as speech production aids help persons who are deaf monitor and improve their own speech (Calvert, 1986). Cochlear implants have been successful in enabling even some persons with profound sensorineural hearing impairments to make use of residual hearing (Karmody, 1986; Miller & Pfingst, 1984; Yaremko, 1993). Microcomputers are also being increasingly used in language and academic instruction of students with hearing impairments. Prinz and Nelson (1985), for example, describe a successful microcomputer program that uses pictures and representations of ASL signs to improve the reading and writing skills of children who are deaf.

Among the most intriguing concepts is the possibility that an automatic speech recognition system may someday be perfected. Such a system could enable a deaf person to instantly decipher the speech of other people, perhaps through a small portable printout device that would be activated by the speaker's voice. The research required to develop a speech recognition system is highly complex, as human speech patterns differ immensely. Nevertheless, improvements in technology, coupled with a concern for individual needs and rights, will enable people with impaired hearing to participate more fully in a broad range of educational, vocational, social, and recreational activities in their schools and communities.

Continual progress in electronics and computer technology is making the telephone and television more accessible to people with hearing impairments. The telephone has long served as a barrier to deaf people in employment and social interaction, but acoustic couplers now make it possible to send immediate messages over conventional telephone lines in typed or digital form. Telecommunication devices (called *TTY* or *TDD systems*) are now widely used and relatively inexpensive. Similarly, closed captioning is used on more and more television programs; thus, a hearing-impaired person who has a special decoding device is able to read captions or subtitles on the television screen. Another recent form of technology, known as *real-time graphic display,* facilitates rapid captioning of live presentations, such as public lectures.

Deafness: Disability or Culture?

We close this chapter with two Profiles and Perspectives features on the Deaf culture. Many leaders in the Deaf community are strong advocates against the development and use of technology designed to "cure" deafness, particularly the use of cochlear implants with deaf children. The story by Andrew Soloman effectively presents their case. In the other feature, Bonnie Tucker looks at the issue from the perspective of society's responsibility to provide services for individuals with disabilities.

Defiantly Deaf

Deaf People Live, Proudly, in Another Culture, But Not a Lesser One

By Andrew Soloman

The protest at the Lexington Center, which includes New York's oldest Deaf school, is an important stage in the Deaf struggle for civil rights, and on April 25, the first day of student demonstrations, I ask an African-American from the 11th grade whether she has also demonstrated for race rights. "I'm too busy being Deaf right now," she signs. "My two older brothers aren't Deaf, so they're taking care of being black. Maybe if I have time I'll get to that later."

Another student intercedes. "I am black and Deaf and proud and I don't want to be white or hearing or different in any way from who I am." Her signs are pretty big and clear. The first student repeats the sign "proud"—her thumb, pointing in, rises up her chest—and then suddenly they are overcome with giggles and go back to join the picket line.

This principle is still new to me, but it has been brewing in the Deaf community for some time: while some deaf people feel cut off from the hearing world, or disabled, for others, being Deaf is a culture and a source of pride. ("Deaf" denotes culture, as distinct from "deaf," which is used to describe a pathology.) A steadily increasing number of deaf people have said that they would not choose to be hearing. To them, the word "cure"—indeed the whole notion of deafness as pathology—is anathema.

The Deaf debates are all language debates. "When I communicate in A.S.L., my native language," M. J. Bienvenu, a political activist, said to me, "I am living my culture. I don't define myself in terms of 'not hearing' or of 'not' anything else." A founder of the Bicultural Center (a sort of Deaf think tank), M. J. is gracious, but also famously terrifying: brilliant, striking-looking and self-possessed, with signing so swift, crisp and perfectly controlled that she seems to be rearranging the air in front of her into a more acceptable shape. Deaf of Deaf, with Deaf sisters, she manifests, like many other activists, a pleasure in American Sign Language that only poets feel for English. "When our language was acknowledged," she says, "we gained our freedom." In her hands "freedom"—clenched hands are crossed before the body, then swing apart and face out—is like an explosion.

A "Family" Gathering

I attended the National Association of the Deaf convention in Knoxville, Tennessee, with almost 2,000 Deaf participants. At Lexington, I saw Deaf people stand up to the hearing world. I learned how a TTY works, met pet dogs who understood sign, talked about mainstreaming and oralism and the integrity of visual language. I became accustomed to doorbells that flashed lights instead of ringing. But none of this could have prepared me for the immersion that is the NAD convention, where the brightest, most politicized, most committed Deaf gather for political focus and social exchange. There, it is not a question of whether the hearing will accept the existence of Deaf culture, but of whether Deaf culture will accept the hearing.

I arrive the night of the president's reception. There are 1,000 people in the grand ballroom of the Hyatt Regency, the lights turned up because these people are unable to communicate in darkness. The crowd is nearly soundless; you hear the claps that are part of the articulation of A.S.L., the clicks and puffing noises the deaf make when they sign, and occasionally their big uncontrolled laughter. People greet each other as if they have been waiting forever for these encounters—the Deaf community is close, closed and affectionate.

Deaf people touch each other far more than the hearing, and everyone here hugs friends. I, too, find myself hugging people as if I have known them forever. Yet I must be careful of the difference between a friendly and a forward embrace; how you touch communicates a world of meaning in Deaf circles. I must be careful of looking abstractly at people signing; they will think I am eavesdropping. I do not know any of the etiquette of these new circumstances. "Good luck with the culture shock," more than one person says to me, and I get many helpful hints.

As I look across the room it seems as if some strange human sea is breaking into waves and glinting in the light, as thousands of hands move at stunning speed, describing a spatial grammar with sharply individual voices and accents. The association is host to the Miss Deaf America pageant, and the young beauties, dressed to the nines and sporting their state sashes, are objects of considerable attention. "Look how beautifully she expresses herself," says someone, pointing to one contestant, and then, of another: "Can you believe that blurry Southern signing? I didn't think anyone really signed like that!" (Regional variations of sign can be dangerous: the sign that in New York slang means "cake" in some Southern states means "sanitary napkin.")

The luminaries of the Deaf world—activists, actors, professors—mix comfortably with the beauty queens. I am one of perhaps a dozen hearing people at this party. I have heard Deaf people talk about how their "family" is the Deaf community. Rejected in so many instances by parents with whom they cannot communicate, united by their struggle with a world that is seldom understanding of them, they have formed inviolable bonds of love of a kind that are rare in hearing culture. At the National Association of the Deaf, they are unmistakable. Disconcerting though it may sound, it is impossible, here, not to wish you were Deaf. I had known that Deaf culture existed, but I had not guessed how heady it is.

The Association members are a tiny minority, less than 10 percent of the nation's Deaf; most deaf people are what the Deaf call "grass roots." The week after the convention, the national Deaf bowling championships in Baltimore will attract a much larger crowd, people who go to Deaf clubs, play cards and work in blue-collar jobs. Below them in the Deaf status structure are the peddlers (the Deaf word for the mendicants who "sell" cards with the manual alphabet on subways—the established Deaf community tried as early as the 40's to get them off the streets).

At the V.I.P. party after the radiant Miss Deaf Maryland has won, I am talking to Alec Naiman, a world traveler who was one of the pilots at this year's Deaf fly-in at the Knoxville airport. We are discussing a trip he made to China. "I met some Deaf Chinese people my first day, and went to stay with them. Deaf people never need hotels; you can always stay with other Deaf people. We spoke different signed languages, but we could make ourselves understood. Though we came from different countries, Deaf culture held us together. By the end of the evening we'd talked about Deaf life in China, and about Chinese politics, and we'd understood each other linguistically and culturally. No hearing American could do that in China," he says. "So who's disabled then?"

Making the Irregular Regular

How to reconcile this Deaf experience with the rest of the world? Should it be reconciled at all? M. J. Bienvenu has been one of the most vocal and articu-

This Wizard's Dorothy communicates in American Sign Language.

late opponents of the language of disability. "I am Deaf," she says to me in Knoxville, drawing out the sign for "Deaf," the index finger moving from chin to ear, as though she is tracing a broad smile. Considerably gentler now than in her extremist heyday in the early 80's, she acknowledges that "for some deaf people, being deaf is a disability. Those who learn forced English while being denied sign emerge semilingual rather than bilingual, and they are disabled people. But for the rest of us, it is no more a disability than being Japanese would be."

I have heard of a couple who opted for an abortion when they heard that their child was hearing, so strong a view did they hold on the superiority of Deaf ways. But I also met many Deaf individuals who objected to the way that the Deaf leadership (focused around the National Association of the Deaf) have presumed to speak for all the deaf people of America. There were plenty who said that being deaf is of course a disability, and that anything you could do about it would be welcome. They were righteously indignant at the thought of a politically correct group suggesting that their problems weren't problems.

It is tempting in the end, to say that there is no such thing as a disability. Equally, one might admit that almost everything is a disability. There are as many arguments for correcting everything as there are for correcting nothing. Perhaps it would be most accurate to say that "disability" and "culture" are really matters of degree. Being Deaf is a disability and a culture in modern America; so is being gay, so is being black; so is being female; so even, increasingly, is being a straight white male. So is being paraplegic, or having Down syndrome. What is at issue is which things are so "cultural" that you wouldn't think of "curing" them, and which things so "disabling" that you must "cure" them—and the reality is that for some people each of these experiences is primarily a disability experience while for others it is primarily a cultural one. ✳

Summary

Definitions, Types, and Measurement

- There are many different levels of hearing ability. A deaf person is not able to understand speech through the ears alone. A hard-of-hearing person is able to use hearing to understand speech, generally with the help of a hearing aid.
- Hearing impairments can be classified in several ways: A congenital hearing impairment is present at birth; an adventitious hearing impairment is acquired later in life.
- A prelingual hearing impairment occurs before the child has developed speech and language; a postlingual hearing impairment occurs after that time.
- A hearing impairment can be conductive or sensorineural, depending on the type and location of the impairment.
- A hearing impairment can be unilateral (in one ear) or bilateral (in both ears).

Identification and Assessment

- A formal hearing test generates an audiogram, which graphically shows the intensity of the faintest sound an individual can hear at various frequencies.
- Hearing impairments are classified as slight, mild, moderate, severe, or profound, depending on the degree of hearing loss.

- Generally, for educational placement purposes, only children with hearing losses greater than 90 dB are considered deaf.

Prevalence

- Students with hearing impairments represent just over 1% of all school-age students receiving special education.
- About 5% of all school-age children have some form of hearing impairment, but most do not require special education.
- Although most children who are deaf participate in special education programs, only about 20% of hard-of-hearing children receive special services.

Causes of Hearing Impairment

- The four most common causes of hearing impairment are maternal rubella, heredity, prematurity and complications of pregnancy, and meningitis.

Historic Background

- Children who were deaf were one of the first groups of exceptional children to receive special education.

Deafness

1993–2013—
The Dilemma

By Bonnie Tucker

During the last twenty years, technological advances to assist people with hearing impairments surpassed the expectation of many. Hearing aids improved tremendously, both with respect to quality and aesthetics. The newer aids block out background noise and emphasize sound in the speech range, which has enabled some severely hearing-impaired people to benefit from aids for the first time. . . . Cochlear implants have enabled some profoundly deaf people, both children and adults, to understand speech without having to rely on speechreading or interpreters; some cochlear implantees are able to converse on the voice telephone with strangers.

Twenty years ago I, for one, did not foresee these almost Orwellian transformations. Today, however, my vision for the future is unlimited. Given the rapidly advancing state of technology in this area, it is not unrealistic to assume that twenty years hence the technological advances of the past two decades will seem outmoded, even ancient. It is not unrealistic to assume that in twenty years cochlear implants will enable profoundly deaf people to understand speech in most circumstances, including on the telephone. We are not there yet, but we are on our way.

Many members of the Deaf community, including leaders of the National Association of the Deaf (NAD) . . . do not *want* cochlear implants. They do not *want* to hear. They want their children to be Deaf, and to be a part of the Deaf world. "We like being Deaf," they state. "We are proud of our Deafness." . . . They claim the *right* to their own "ethnicity, with our own language and culture, the same way that Native Americans or Italians bond together"; they claim the right to "personal diversity," which is "something to be cherished rather than fixed and erased. And they *strongly* protest the practice of placing cochlear implants in children. . . . These same individuals, however, are among the strongest advocates for laws and special programs to protect and assist people with hearing impairments. They argue fiercely for the need for interpreters, TTYs, telephone relay services, specially funded educational programs, and close-captioning, at no cost to themselves. On the one hand, therefore, they claim that deafness is not a disability, but a state of being, a "right" that should not be altered. On the other hand, they claim that deafness *is* a disability that society should compensate for by providing and paying for services to allow deaf people to function in society. . . .

Do Deaf people have the right to refuse to accept new technology, to refuse to "fix" their Deafness if such repair becomes possible? Yes, absolutely. They *do* have the right, if they wish to exercise that right, to cherish their Deaf culture, their Deaf ethnicity, their "visually oriented" personal diversity. They have *every* right to choose *not* to fix their Deafness. . . . Do Deaf people have the right to demand that society pay for the resulting cost of that choice, however? No, I do not believe they do.

By way of analogy, suppose that blindness and quadriplegia were "curable" due to advanced technology. Blind people could be made to "see" via artificial means such as surgical implantation or three-dimensional eyeglasses; quadriplegic individuals could be made to "walk" and use their arms via artificial means such as surgical nerve implantation or specially built devices. Oh, the blind people might not see as perfectly as sighted people—they might still miss some of the fine print. And the quadriplegic individuals might walk with a limp or move their arms in a jerky fashion. But, for the most part, they would require little special assistance.

Suppose that 10 blind people chose not to make use of available technology for the reason that blindness is not a "disability," not something to be fixed, but that blind people are simply "auditory oriented," and 20 quadriplegic people chose not to make use of available technology for the reason that quadriplegics are simply "out-of-body oriented." How long will society agree to pay for readers, attendants, and other services and devices to assist those blind and quadriplegic individuals who have exercised their right to be diverse? More important, how long *should* society be asked to pay for such services and devices?

When technology advances to the extent that profoundly deaf people could choose to "hear"—which, eventually, it surely will—Deaf people will have to resolve the dilemma, both for reasons of practicality *and* morality. . . . Deaf people will have to decide whether to accept hearing or to remain Deaf. They have every right to choose the latter course. If they do so, however, they must assume responsibility for that choice and bear the resultant cost, rather than thrust that responsibility upon society. . . . As our grandparents used to say, "You can't have your cake and eat it too." ✸

Bonnie Tucker is a professor of Law at Arizona State University. From "Deafness: 1993–2013—The Dilemma" by Bonnie Tucker, *The Volta Review, 95,* (1993), pp. 105-108. Used by permission.

- Oral approaches dominated deaf education in the early years.
- Traditionally, most deaf children were educated in residential schools; today, about 80% attend local public schools.

Amplification and Auditory Training and Learning

- Amplification and auditory training seek to enable students with hearing impairments to use their residual hearing more effectively.
- Speechreading can provide useful visual information but has many limitations. Most English sounds cannot be distinguished through vision alone.

Educational Approaches

- Some educators use a primarily oral approach to the education of students with hearing impairments, emphasizing the development of speech and related skills.
- Other educators use a total communication approach, using sign language and fingerspelling simultaneously with speech.

Educational Services Alternatives

- About one fifth of students with hearing impairments are educated in separate schools or residential facilities.
- Most of the nearly one half of students with hearing impairments who are educated in regular classrooms or resource rooms have hearing losses of less than 90 dB.
- A growing number of postsecondary educational opportunities are available. About 40% of all students with hearing impairments go on to other educational programs after high school.

Current Issues and Future Trends

- An increasing awareness of the rights of hearing-impaired individuals is positively affecting education, employment, and economic opportunities.
- Technology holds much promise for addressing the communication problems faced by deaf persons.
- Many leaders of the Deaf culture do not view deafness as a disability and oppose efforts to "cure" it or make them more like the mainstream hearing culture.

For More Information

Journals

American Annals of the Deaf. Published by the Conference of Educational Administrators Serving the Deaf and the Convention of American Instructors of the Deaf, 814 Thayer Avenue, Silver Spring, MD 20910. Presents articles dealing with education of deaf students and those with hearing impairments.

Journal of the American Deafness and Rehabilitation Association (Formerly *Journal of Rehabilitation of the Deaf*), P.O. Box 251554, Little Rock, AR 72225. Focuses on research, innovations, patterns of service, and other topics related to deaf adults.

Sign Language Studies. Published quarterly by Linstok Press, 9306 Mintwood Street, Silver Spring, MD 20901. Contains research and practical articles related to sign language and manual communication.

The Volta Review. Published nine times a year by the Alexander Graham Bell Association for the Deaf, 3417 Volta Place, NW, Washington, DC 20007. Encourages teaching of speech, speechreading, and use of residual hearing to deaf persons. Advocates oral approaches.

Books

Luetke-Stahlman, B., & Luckner, J. (1991). *Effectively educating students with hearing impairments.* New York: Longman.

Luterman, D. M. (Ed.). (1986). *Deafness in perspective.* San Diego: College-Hill.

Luterman, D. M. (Ed.). (1987). *Deafness in the family.* Boston: Little, Brown.

McAnally, P. L., Rose, S., & Quigley, S. P. (1994). *Language learning practices with children who are deaf* (2nd ed.). Austin, TX: PRO-ED.

Mindel, E. D., & Vernon, M. (1986). *They grow in silence: Understanding deaf children and adults* (2nd ed.). San Diego: College-Hill.

Moores, D. F. (1987). *Educating the deaf: Psychology, principles, and practices* (3rd ed.). Boston: Houghton Mifflin.

Moores, D. F., & Meadows-Orlans, K. P. (Eds.). (1990). *Educational and developmental aspects of deafness.* Washington, DC: Gallaudet.

Paul, P. V., & Jackson, D. W. (1993). *Toward a psychology of deafness: Theoretical and empirical perspectives.* Needham Heights, MA: Allyn & Bacon.

Paul, P. V., & Quigley, S. P. (1990). *Education and deafness.* New York: Longman.

Paul, P. V., & Quigley, S. P. (1994). *Language and deafness* (2nd ed.). San Diego: College-Hill.

Ross, M. (Ed.). (1990). *Hearing-impaired children in the mainstream.* Monkton, MD: York Press.

Schirmer, B. R. (1994). *Language and literacy development in children who are deaf.* Englewood Cliffs, NJ: Merrill/Prentice Hall.

Van Cleve, J. V. (Ed.). (1986). *Gallaudet encyclopedia of deaf people and deafness.* New York: McGraw-Hill.

Vernon, M., & Andrews, J. F. (1990). *The psychology of deafness.* New York: Longman.

Walker, L. A. (1986). *A loss for words: The story of deafness in a family.* New York: Harper & Row.

Organizations

Alexander Graham Bell Association for the Deaf, 3417 Volta Place, NW, Washington, DC 20007 (voice/TDD: 202-237-5220). Provides brochures, books, software, audiovisual materials, and other information on hearing impairment, with an auditory-oral emphasis. Publishes *The Volta Review* for professionals, *Our Kids Magazine* for parents, and *Newsounds* newsletter. Sponsors organizations for teachers, parents, researchers, and oral deaf adults.

Gallaudet University, 800 Florida Avenue, NE, Washington, DC 20002. Its bookstore has one of the most complete collections of professional and popular literature about hearing impairment, communication, education, psychology, and related topics. Also has children's sign language books that appeal to many readers. Provides free catalogs of book lists; arranges tours of the Gallaudet campus for visitors.

National Association of the Deaf, 814 Thayer Avenue, Silver Spring, MD 20910. A clearinghouse for information about education, employment, legal issues, communication, technological aids, and other topics. Sponsors activities for Deaf adults, children, and parents (voice/TDD: 301-587-1788).

National Center for Law and the Deaf, Gallaudet University, 800 Florida Avenue, NE, Washington, DC 20002 (voice/TDD: 202-651-5373).

National Cued Speech Association, P.O. Box 31345, Raleigh, NC 27622. Provides information, training, and publications on the cued speech system of identifying sounds and supplementing speechreading skills.

National Information Center on Deafness, Gallaudet University, 800 Florida Avenue, NE, Washington, DC 20002 (voice/TDD: 800-672-6720).

Students Who Are Blind or Have Low Vision

- In what ways does loss of vision affect learning?

- How does the age at which vision is lost impact the student?

- Normally sighted children enter school with a great deal of knowledge about trees. How can a teacher help the young child who is congenitally blind learn about trees?

- What compensatory skills do students with visual impairment need?

- How do the educational goals and instructional methods for children with low vision differ from those for children who are blind?

ixteen-year-old Maria is a bright, college-bound student who has been totally blind since birth. She recently took a series of intellectual and psychological tests and performed well, scoring at about her expected age and grade level. Something unusual happened, however, on one of the test items. The examiner handed Maria an unpeeled banana and asked, "What is this?" Maria held the banana and took several guesses but could not answer correctly. The examiner was astonished, as were Maria's teachers and parents. After all, this section of the test was intended for young children. Even though Maria had eaten bananas many times, she had missed out on one important aspect of the banana experience: she had never held and peeled a banana by herself.

This true story (adapted from Swallow, 1978) illustrates the tremendous importance of vision in obtaining accurate and thorough information about the world in which we live. Many of the concepts that children with normal vision seem to acquire almost effortlessly may not be learned at all by children with visual impairments—or may be learned incorrectly—unless someone deliberately teaches the concepts to them. Teachers who work with children with visual impairments find it necessary to plan and present a great many firsthand experiences. Often, the best teachers are those who enable children with visual impairments to learn by doing things for themselves.

Even when information is deliberately presented to children with visual impairments, they may not learn it in exactly the same way that children with normal vision would. Students with visual impairments may learn to make good use of their other senses; hearing, touch, smell, and taste can be useful channels of sensory input, but they do not totally compensate for loss of vision. Touch and taste cannot tell children much about things that are far away—or even just beyond their arms' length. Hearing can tell them a good deal about the near and distant environment, but it seldom provides information that is as complete, continuous, or exact as the information people obtain from seeing their surroundings.

Students with visual impairments display a wide range of visual abilities—from total blindness to relatively good residual (remaining) vision. The one characteristic these students share is "a visual restriction of sufficient severity that it interferes with normal progress in a regular educational program without modifications" (Scholl, 1986a, p. 29). The classroom is one important setting in which vision plays a critical role in learning. In school, normally sighted children are routinely expected to exercise several important visual skills. They must be able to see clearly; they must focus on different objects, shifting from near to far as needed; they must have good eye-hand coordination; they must be able to remember what they have seen; they must discriminate colors accurately; they must be able to see and interpret many things simultaneously; they must be able to maintain visual concentration. Children with visual impairments have deficits in one or more of these abilities. As a result, they need special equipment and/or adaptation in instructional procedures or materials to function effectively in school.

People who are blind are not gifted with an extraordinary sense of hearing or touch. They may learn to be more sensitive, however, to the information about the environment that they gain from their nonvisual senses.

✳ *Defining Visual Impairment*

Visual impairment has both legal and educational definitions. The legal definition of blindness relies heavily on measurements of **visual acuity,** which is the ability to clearly distinguish forms or discriminate details at a specified distance. Most frequently, visual acuity is measured by reading letters, numbers, or other symbols from a chart 20 feet away. The familiar phrase "20/20 vision" does not, as some people think, mean "perfect vision"; it simply indicates that at a distance of 20 feet, the eye can see what a normally seeing eye should be able to see at that distance. As the bottom number increases, visual acuity decreases.

Legal Blindness

If a person's visual acuity is 20/200 or less in the better eye *after the best possible correction* with glasses or contact lenses, then one is considered **legally blind.** If Jane has 20/200 vision while wearing her glasses, she needs to stand at a distance of 20 feet to see what most people can see from 200 feet away. In other words, Jane must get much closer than normal to see things clearly. Her legal blindness means that Jane will likely find it difficult to use her vision in many everyday situations. But many children with 20/200, or even 20/400, visual acuity succeed in the regular classroom with special help. Some students' visual acuity is so poor they are unable to perceive fine details at any distance, even while wearing glasses or contact lenses.

A person may also be considered legally blind if his or her **field of vision** is extremely restricted. When gazing straight ahead, a normal eye is able to see objects within a range of approximately 180 degrees. If David's field of vision is only 10 degrees, he is able to see only a limited area at any one time (even though his visual acuity within that small area may be quite good). Some people with limited fields of vision describe their perceptions as viewing the world through a narrow tube or tunnel; they may have good central vision but poor **peripheral vision** at the outer ranges of the visual field. Conversely, some eye conditions make it impossible for people to see things clearly in the central visual field but allow relatively good peripheral vision.

Whether the visual field impairment is central or peripheral, a person is considered legally blind if he or she is restricted to an area of 20 degrees or less from the normal 180-degree field. It is common for the visual field to decrease slowly over a period of years and for the decrease to go undetected in children and adults. A thorough visual examination should always include measurement of the visual field, as well as visual acuity.

Children who are legally blind are eligible to receive a wide variety of educational services, materials, and benefits from governmental agencies. They may, for example, obtain records (known as "Talking Books"), tapes, and record players from the Library of Congress. Their schools may be able to buy books and educational materials from the American Printing House for the Blind because the federal quota system allots states and local school districts a certain financial allowance for each legally blind student (Chase, 1986b). A person who is legally blind is also entitled to vocational training, free U.S. mail service, and an additional income tax exemption.

Even though these services and benefits are important to know about, the legal definition of blindness is not especially useful to teachers. Some children who do not

Some people, with or without correction, have visual acuity that is better than 20/20. If the vision in one of your eyes is rated as 20/10, for example, you can see from 20 feet what the "20/20" eye must be within 10 feet in order to see.

meet the criteria for legal blindness have visual impairments severe enough to require special educational techniques and materials. Other students, whose visual impairments qualify them as legally blind, find little or no use for many of these special education services. Educators differentiate between students who are blind and students with low vision. This distinction does not rely on precise measurements of visual acuity or visual field, but instead considers the extent to which a child's visual impairment affects learning and makes special methods or materials necessary.

Low Vision

A child who is **blind** is totally without sight or has so little vision that he or she learns primarily through the other senses. Most children who are blind, for example, use their sense of touch to read **braille.** A child with **low vision,** on the other hand, is able to learn through the visual channel and generally learns to read print. Although there is no universally agreed-on definition of low vision, the definition Corn (1989) offers stresses the functional use of vision:

> Low vision is a level of vision that with standard correction hinders an individual in the visual planning and execution of tasks, but which permits enhancements of the functional vision through the use of optical or nonoptical aids and environmental modifications and/or techniques. (p. 28)

Today, the great majority of children who receive special education services for visual impairments have useful vision; students with low vision comprise between 75% and 80% of the school-age visually impaired population (Bryan & Jeffrey, 1982).

The terms **visual efficiency** (Barraga, 1983) and *functional vision* (Corn, 1989) denote how well a person uses whatever vision he or she has. Functional

Braille is a system of representing letters, numbers, and other symbols with combinations (patterns) of six raised dots. We examine braille later in the chapter.

A child who has been blind since birth has a background of learning through hearing, touch, and the other nonvisual senses.

vision is the "visual ability sufficient for utilizing visual information in the planning and execution of a task" (Corn, 1989, p. 28). Functional vision cannot be determined by measuring a child's visual acuity or visual field, nor can it be predicted. Some children with severe visual impairments use what vision they have very capably. Other children with relatively minor visual impairments are unable to function as visual learners; they may even behave as though they were blind. Barraga and her colleagues have shown that systematic training in visual recognition and discrimination can help many children with visual impairments use their remaining vision more efficiently.

Age at Onset

Like other disabilities, visual impairment can be congenital (present at birth) or adventitious (acquired). It is useful for a teacher to know the age at which a student acquired a visual impairment. A child who has been blind since birth naturally has quite a different perception of the world than does a child who lost vision at age 12. The first child has a background of learning through hearing, touch, and the other nonvisual senses, whereas the second child has a background of visual experiences on which to draw. Most people who are adventitiously blind retain a visual memory of things they formerly saw. This memory can be helpful in a child's education; an adventitiously blind child may, for instance, remember the appearance of colors, maps, and printed letters. At the same time, however, the need for emotional support and acceptance may be greater than that of the congenitally blind child, who does not have to make a sudden adjustment to the loss of vision.

Many persons who have lost their sight report that the biggest difficulty in adapting is dealing with the attitudes and behavior of those around them. Some of those attitudes and behaviors are no doubt influenced by the beliefs, superstitions, and mythology that comprise "the folklore of blindness."

> The influence of the folklore of blindness generally is expressed in attitudes towards (and by) blind people that sound absurd but are genuinely felt. . . . One finds that folk beliefs are divided into two groups. On the negative side of this dichotomy are the beliefs that blind people are either helpless and pathetic or evil and contagious and probably deserve their fate. On the more positive side are the beliefs that blind people have special or even magical abilities, special powers of perception, and deserve special attention. . . . All of us are greatly influenced by what we believe. Irrational beliefs are especially important for a counselor to understand, because they are carried in an idiosyncratic way by each client. An appreciation of superstition and folklore gives the professional a great advantage in understanding the irrational beliefs in both the client and the people he or she must deal with in adapting to the loss of vision. (Wagner-Lampl & Oliver, 1994, pp. 267–268)

✳ *Types and Causes of Visual Impairment*

The basic function of the eye is to collect visual information from the environment and transmit it to the brain. A simplified diagram of the eye appears in Figure 9.1. The eye is stimulated by light rays reflected from objects in the visual field. In the normal eye, these light rays come to a clear focus on the central part of the **retina.** This multilayered sheet of nerve tissue at the back of the eye has been likened to the

FIGURE 9.1
The human eye

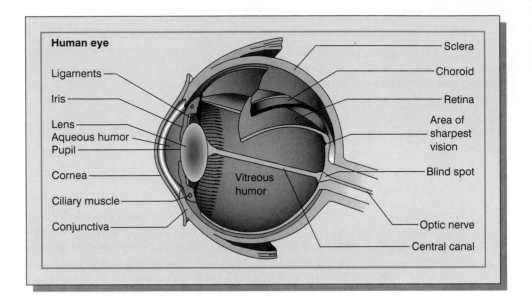

film in a camera: For a clear image to be transmitted to the brain, the light rays must come to a precise focus on the retina. The optic nerve is connected to the retina. It conducts visual images to the brain.

In the process of vision, light rays must pass through several structures and substances in the eye itself. Each of these bends the light a little bit to produce the ideal image on the retina. The light first hits the **cornea,** the curved transparent membrane that protects the eye (much as an outer crystal protects a watch face). It then passes through the **aqueous humor,** a watery liquid that fills the front chamber of the eye. Next, the light passes through the **pupil,** a circular hole in the center of the colored **iris;** the pupil contracts or expands to regulate the amount of light entering the eye. The light then passes through the **lens,** a transparent, elastic structure suspended by tiny muscles that adjust its thickness so that both the near and far objects can be brought into sharp focus. Finally, the light passes through the **vitreous humor,** a jellylike substance that fills most of the eye's interior. Disturbances of any of these structures can prevent the clear focusing of an image on the retina.

Refractive Errors

An **optometrist** specializes in the evaluation and optical correction of refractive errors. An **ophthalmologist** is a physician who specializes in the diagnosis and treatment of eye diseases and conditions.

Refraction is the process of bending light rays when they pass from one transparent structure into another. As just described, the normal eye refracts light rays so that a clear image is perceived on the retina; no special help is needed. However, for many people—perhaps half the general population (Miller, 1979)—the size and shape of the eye prevent refraction from being perfect. That is, the light rays do not focus clearly on the retina. **Refractive errors** can usually be corrected by glasses or contact lenses, but if severe enough, they can cause permanent visual impairment.

In **myopia,** or *nearsightedness,* the eye is larger than normal from front to back. The image conducted to the retina is thus somewhat out of focus. A child with myopia can see near objects clearly, but more distant objects, such as a chalkboard or a movie, are blurred or not seen at all. The opposite of myopia is **hyperopia,** commonly called *farsightedness.* The hyperopic eye is shorter than normal, preventing the light rays from converging on the retina. A child with hyperopia has difficulty seeing near objects clearly but is able to focus well on more distant objects. **Astigmatism** refers to distorted or blurred vision caused by irregularities in the cornea or other surfaces of the eye; both near and distant objects may be out of focus. Glasses or contact lenses can correct many refractive errors by changing the course of light rays to produce as clear a focus as possible.

Other Types and Causes of Visual Impairment

Although the most frequently mentioned visual impairments are in visual acuity and field of vision, one's vision may be impaired in several other significant ways. **Ocular motility,** the eye's ability to move, may be hampered. This impairment can cause problems in binocular vision, which is the ability of the two eyes to focus on one object and fuse the two images into a single clear image (Ward, 1986). **Binocular vision** is actually a complicated process, requiring good vision in each eye, normal eye muscles, and smooth functioning of the coordinating centers of the brain (Miller, 1979).

Several conditions make it difficult or impossible for a child to use the eyes together effectively. **Strabismus** describes an inability to focus on the same object with both eyes because of an inward or outward deviation of one or both eyes. If left untreated, strabismus and other disorders of ocular motility can lead to permanent loss of vision. When the two eyes cannot focus simultaneously, the brain avoids a double image by suppressing the visual input from one eye. Thus, the weaker eye (usually the one that turns inward or outward) can actually lose its ability to see. **Amblyopia** refers to this reduction in or loss of vision in the weaker eye from lack of use even though no disease is present. The usual treatment for amblyopia is to place a patch over the stronger eye so that the weaker eye is forced to develop better vision through training and experience. This treatment is most effective if started in early childhood. Eye muscle surgery may also help correct the muscle imbalance and prevent further loss of vision in the weaker eye (Batshaw & Perret, 1992).

Other kinds of visual impairments include problems in **accommodation,** in which the eye cannot adjust properly for seeing at different distances. A child with difficulty in accommodation may have trouble shifting from reading a book to looking at the chalkboard and back again. Some children with visual impairments have a condition known as **nystagmus,** a rapid, involuntary back-and-forth movement of the eyes in a lateral, vertical, or rotary direction. Nystagmus is generally not discernible by the person with the impairment (Chase, 1986b). Severe nystagmus can cause problems in focusing and reading.

Approximately 18,000 people in the United States are affected by **albinism,** the lack of pigmentation in the eyes, skin, and hair. Albinism results in moderate to severe visual impairment by reducing visual acuity and causing nystagmus (Ashley & Cates, 1992). Children with albinism almost always have **photophobia,** a condition in which one's eyes are extremely sensitive to light. A child with albinism needs to avoid areas of strong light or glare, but tinted glasses, caps, and sunscreens usually enable safe enjoyment of most outdoor activities.

Color vision can also be impaired. A child with deficient color vision is not actually color-blind; that is, he or she does not see only in black and white. The child may

How do people who cannot discriminate the colors red and green drive safely? They learn to look at the position of the light on the traffic signal: Red ("Stop") is always at the top; green ("Go") is always on the bottom.

find it difficult to distinguish certain colors, however; red-green confusion is most common, occurring in about 8% of males and 0.4% of females (Ward, 1986). Deficient color vision does not get better or worse as a child gets older, and it is usually not considered an educationally significant visual impairment.

A **cataract** is a cloudiness in the lens of the eye that blocks the light necessary for seeing clearly. Vision may be blurred, distorted, or incomplete. Some people with cataracts liken their vision to looking through a dirty windshield. If the cataract is extremely cloudy or dense, a person may be unable to perceive any details at all. Cataracts are common in older people but may also occur in children. Most children born with cataracts have their cloudy lenses surgically removed. They must then wear special postcataract eyeglasses or contact lenses and usually need to wear bifocals or have one pair of glasses for distance vision and another pair for reading because the glasses or contact lenses cannot change focus as a natural lens does. A permanent lens is sometimes implanted into the eye after cataract surgery, but this procedure is not yet universally accepted by ophthalmologists.

Glaucoma is a prevalent disease marked by abnormally high pressure within the eye. The various types of glaucoma are all related to disturbances or blockages of the fluids that normally circulate within the eye. Central and peripheral vision are impaired or lost entirely when the increased pressure damages the optic nerve. Although glaucoma can be extremely painful in its advanced phase, it frequently goes undetected for long periods, and children may not even be aware of the small, gradual changes in their vision. If detected in its early stages, glaucoma can often be treated successfully with medication or surgery. Figure 9.2 shows how the world might look to someone with cataracts or glaucoma.

Several important causes of visual impairment and blindness involve damage to the retina, the light-sensitive tissue that is so critical for clear vision. The retina is rich in blood vessels and can be affected by disorders of the circulatory system. Children and adults with diabetes frequently have impaired vision as a result of hemorrhages and the growth of new blood vessels in the area of the retina. This condition, known as **diabetic retinopathy,** is the leading cause of blindness for people between 20 and 64 years of age. Laser surgery has been helpful in some instances, but there is no effective treatment as yet. The American Academy of Ophthalmology (1985) advises, however, that up to half of all cases of diabetic retinopathy could be prevented through early diagnosis and treatment. All children and adults with diabetes should receive regular detailed eye examinations.

Chapter 10 includes further information on diabetes in children.

Retinitis pigmentosa (RP) is the most common of all inherited retinal disorders. This disease causes gradual degeneration of the retina. The first symptom is usually difficulty in seeing at night, followed by loss of peripheral vision. A small amount of central vision may be maintained. In most cases, RP is not treatable, although recent research has helped identify families at high risk of having affected children (Kaiser-Kupfer & Morris, 1985). RP sometimes occurs in people who are congenitally deaf. The unfortunate combination of congenital deafness and gradual retinitis pigmentosa is known as **Usher's syndrome,** a significant cause of deaf-blindness among adolescents and adults.

Macular degeneration is a condition in which the central area of the retina (the macular area) gradually deteriorates. In contrast with retinitis pigmentosa, the individual with macular degeneration usually retains peripheral vision but loses the ability to see clearly in the center of the visual field. Early warning signs are a slight blurring of vision in one eye, usually followed by a hole or blind spot in the area of

FIGURE 9.2

(a) Charts used to record field of vision. Shaded area indicates normal field of vision. Dark spot near center is the macula, or area of sharpest central vision. (b) The same street scene as it might be viewed by a person with normal vision, cataracts, or advanced glaucoma.

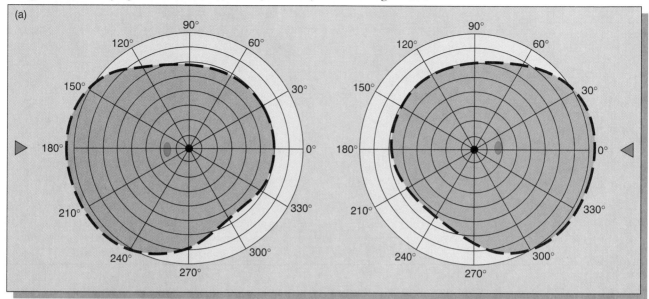

(a)

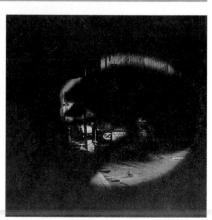

(b)

Source: The Lighthouse, New York Association for the Blind, New York. Reprinted by permission.

greatest visual acuity (Chalifoux, 1991). Although total blindness is rare, visual loss can progress to a state of legal blindness, making tasks such as reading difficult. Macular degeneration is common in older adults (about 1 in every 4 persons past age 75) but fairly rare in children.

Detached retinas result when the retina becomes partially or totally separated from the outer layers of tissue in the eye. This condition may accompany several diseases of the eye or can result from trauma. Detached or torn retinas can frequently be repaired by surgery.

Retinopathy of prematurity (ROP), formerly referred to as *retrolental fibroplasia,* can result from placing low-birthweight babies in incubators and administering high levels of oxygen. When the infants are later removed from the oxygen-rich incubators, the change in oxygen levels can produce an abnormally dense growth of blood vessels and scar tissue in the eyes, leading to various degrees of visual impairment and often total blindness from retinal detachment. During the 1940s, premature infants were routinely given high doses of oxygen, and approximately 25% were diagnosed with ROP. By 1952, ROP had reached epidemic proportions and was the largest single cause of childhood blindness (Newell, 1982). The amount of oxygen given to premature infants was greatly reduced in the 1950s, and the incidence of ROP decreased. It has been estimated that for each case of blindness prevented, however, 16 infants may have died because of insufficient oxygen (Lucey & Dangman, 1984).

ROP is one example of how medical technology can have both positive and negative outcomes.

> Since the mid-1960s, the incidence of milder ROP has risen again. Among the factors leading to this rise are modern medical techniques that allow pediatricians to save low birthweight, high-risk infants. . . . In the early 1980s, there was a resurgence of ROP. An estimated 2,100 infants were reported with some degree of ROP annually. Of these infants, approximately 23 percent became seriously visually impaired or blind. This rate was similar to that of the 1943–1953 "epidemic" years (Phelps, 1981). The birthweight of children with ROP has progressively declined. Most would have died if they had been born in earlier decades. ROP now primarily affects babies with a birthweight of less than 1,000 grams (about 2.2 pounds). (Trief, Duckman, Morse, & Silberman, 1989, p. 500)

An educator seldom needs detailed knowledge concerning the etiology and medical status of a child's visual impairment, but familiarity with how a student's particular visual impairment affects classroom performance is important. It is useful to know, for example, that Linda has difficulty reading under strong lights, that Ahmad has only a small amount of central vision in his right eye, or that Yoko sometimes experiences eye pain. Basic knowledge of the conditions described here can help a teacher understand some aspects of a child's learning and behavior and decide when to refer a child for professional vision care.

✳ *Prevalence*

Children with visual impairments constitute a small percentage of the school-age population—about 1 child in 1,000. During the 1992–93 school year, the federal government reported that 23,811 children aged 6 to 21 received special education services under the IDEA within the category of visual impairments (U.S. Department of Education, 1994). The federal government figure includes children with low vision who require special education but do not meet the criteria of legal blindness. The actual number of students with visual impairments is probably somewhat higher than the government figures because some students with visual impairments are counted under other disability categories such as deaf-blindness and multiple disabilities. Still, it is doubtful that students with visual impairments exceed 0.1% of the entire school-age population.

Surveys of the reading methods that students with visual impairments use give some insight into the heterogeneity and changing nature of this population. The 1987 American Printing House census of students who are legally blind in grades K through 12 identified 33% of students with visual impairments as visual readers, who primarily use regular or large-print materials. The next largest group included auditory readers (17%), who use recorded or taped materials or are read to aloud, followed by braille readers (12%). Nonreaders and prereaders comprise the remaining 38%. These figures are consistent with the observation that a sizable percentage of blind and students with visual impairments have other significant disabilities. According to Scholl (1986a), recent reports from the field indicate that approximately one third of the school-age population of students with visual impairments have at least one additional disability.

The prevalence of children with visual impairments within the population of children receiving special education services is also small—only 0.5% of all school-age children with disabilities in 1992–93. Educators and parents of children with visual impairments frequently express concern about this low prevalence because they fear that when financial resources are limited, students with visual impairments may not receive adequate services from specially trained teachers. It may be particularly difficult for a local public school to provide comprehensive services for a child with visual impairment who resides in a rural area. Small school districts often cooperate with each other in employing special teachers for students with visual impairments.

Nonreaders, as used here, refers to students with visual impairments with additional severe disabilities; *prereaders* are children with visual impairments who are expected to follow an academic program and learn to read.

✳ *Historical Background*

People with visual impairments, although not a large population, have been a conspicuous group throughout history. In most countries, the education of children who are blind is a high priority; schools and other special programs for children who are blind have historically been established before those for other groups of disabled children. Today, more than 1,000 separate organizations provide special services to people with visual impairments in the United States. There are so many resources, in fact, that it is advisable for a person who is blind to take a special course in how to identify and use the most appropriate services, products, and information available (Winer, 1978).

In contrast, programs for individuals with less visible disabilities, such as learning disabilities, have a comparatively short history.

Several explanations are possible for the special attention given to people who are blind or visually impaired. Blindness is usually readily apparent to the observer and often evokes feelings of pity and sympathy. It is perhaps the most feared of any disability (Wagner-Lampl & Oliver, 1994). There are also many widely held stereotypes and misconceptions about blind people. One study found that sighted people considered people who are blind to have "nice," "sweet," and "charming" personalities (Klinghammer, 1964). Other old but persistent assumptions are that children who are blind are naturally gifted in music, that they have a sixth sense enabling them to detect obstacles, that they have better-than-normal hearing, and that they have superior memory skills.

For an interesting discussion of the "folklore of blindness" and its effects on both individuals who are blind and those around them, see Wagner-Lampl and Oliver (1994).

Valentin Hauy (1745–1822) is given credit for starting the first school for children who are blind, the *Institution des Jeunes Aveugles* in Paris, which opened in 1784. Hauy had been shocked at seeing people who were blind performing as jesters and beggars on the streets of Paris and resolved to teach them more dignified ways of earning a living. The subjects taught at Hauy's school included reading and writing (using embossed print), music, and vocational skills. The competence demonstrated by Hauy's students impressed citizens in France and elsewhere in Europe. By the early 19th century, residential schools for children who were blind had been established in several other countries, including England, Scotland, Austria, Germany, and Russia (Koestler, 1976; Roberts, 1986).

Influenced by the European schools, Dr. Samuel Gridley Howe founded the Perkins School for the Blind in Watertown, Massachusetts, one of the oldest and best-known residential schools for students who are blind (Bledsoe, 1993). The most famous teacher-student pair in U.S. history, Anne Sullivan and Helen Keller, spent several years at Perkins. Within the next few decades, most states had opened public residential schools for children with visual impairments. Such schools continued to educate the great majority of children with visual impairments until the mid-20th century (Koestler, 1976).

The first public school class in the United States totally for children who were blind opened in Chicago in 1900; the first class for children with low vision began in Cleveland in 1909; and the first itinerant teaching program for children with visual impairments attending regular classes was implemented in Oakland, California, in 1938 (Ward, 1979). Mainstreaming of children with visual impairments thus has a relatively long and successful history.

Sight-Saving Classes

This trend parallels the emphasis on teaching children with hearing impairments to use their residual hearing as much as possible (see Chapter 8).

For a good part of this century, many children with low vision were educated in special sight-saving classes in both regular public schools and residential schools for the blind. It was generally believed that a child's remaining vision should be conserved by not using it too much. In extreme instances, children with impaired but useful vision were even blindfolded or educated in dark rooms so that their precious vision would not be used up or lost. Today, a dramatically different approach prevails. Eye specialists agree that vision, even if imperfect, *benefits* from use; thus, educational programs for children with visual impairments concentrate on helping them develop and use their visual abilities as much as possible.

A Wave of Children with Visual Impairments

As mentioned, thousands of infants became blind or severely visually impaired because of retinopathy of prematurity in the 1940s and 1950s. This unfortunate medical occurrence, however, had a beneficial side effect in expanding the educational opportunities available to children with visual impairments. Because the residential schools then in existence were unable to accommodate the large sudden influx of children affected by ROP and because many parents did not want their children to attend distant residential schools, educational programs and services for students with visual impairments became much more widely available in the regular public schools during the 1950s and 1960s. Although the majority of children blinded by ROP are now adults, public school programs for children with visual impairments have continued to develop and diversify. Today, in most regions of the United States and Canada, parents may choose between public and residential school education for a child with visual impairments.

✳ *Educational Approaches*

When we think of teachers of children with visual impairments, we often think of specialized equipment and materials, such as braille, canes, tape recorders, and magnifying devices. Although media and materials do play an important role in the education of children with impaired vision, the effective teacher must know a great deal more than how to use these special devices. Because they are frequently called on to teach skills and concepts that most children acquire through vision, teachers of students with visual impairments must be knowledgeable, competent, and creative. They must plan and carry out activities that will help their students gain as much information as possible through the nonvisual senses and by participation in active, practical experiences.

Many educators and psychologists have described the obstacles to learning imposed by blindness or severe visual impairment. Lowenfeld (1973), for example, observes that a blind child may hear a bird singing but get no concrete idea of the bird itself from this sound alone. A teacher interested in teaching such a student about birds (to follow up on Lowenfeld's example) might plan a series of activities that would have the student touch birds of various species and manipulate related objects such as eggs, nests, and feathers. The student might assume the responsibility for feeding a pet bird at home or in the classroom. Perhaps a field trip to a poultry farm could be arranged. Through experiences such as these, children with visual impairments can gradually obtain a more thorough and accurate knowledge of birds than they could if their education were limited to reading books about birds, memorizing vocabulary, or feeling plastic models.

There are virtually no limits on the extent to which a child with visual impairments may participate in a full, well-rounded school program. Educators should ensure that a visually impaired student's IEP "includes the full range of instructional areas: those studied with nonhandicapped peers, those that require special instruction, and those outside of the school curriculum that are essential to enable them to compete with their nonhandicapped peers when they move into the adult world" (Scholl, 1987, p. 36). Successfully accomplishing this goal, however, requires that special educators provide support, consultation, and materials to regular teachers with students with visual impairments in their classes.

To find out how individuals who are blind can learn to identify birds, see "Listen to the Birds" on the next page.

There are virtually no limits to the kinds of activities in which students with visual impairments can participate. This spelunker is totally blind.

Listen to the Birds
· ·
By Eileen Koper Bender

*B*irding (sometimes called bird-watching) is an absorbing hobby of learning to identify birds. Hundreds of species exist in the bird world and can be identified by their appearance, behavior, surroundings, and—importantly, for our purposes—by their calls and songs. "Birders" are those persons who engage in this activity. They can be recognized by the upturned posture of their heads, ears cocked in the direction of even the faintest bird call, field glasses (or telescopic low-vision aids) at the ready. An avid blind birder often carries a minirecorder to tape bird calls for later comparison with bird song identification field guide cassettes.

Our birding program began as a portion of the leisure-time instructional program at the Greater Pittsburgh Guild for the Blind. Leisure-time instruction involves an examination of an individual's leisure preferences, instruction in adapting the materials and methods necessary for resumption of a specific activity, practice in those skills required to use the adapted materials and methods, and attention to the development of attitudes of leisure well-being. Interestingly, birding is rarely mentioned as an activity of choice when participants who are adventitiously blind think about activities they enjoyed before blindness, analyze why they enjoyed them, and begin to develop the goals they feel they can attain in the leisure-time program. When I mentioned the idea of birding to him, one young tough growled, "Birds are for nerds!" Yet the familiar structure of the Pennsylvania meadows and stands of tall trees, coupled with the high probability of attaining a new skill, made the activity magnetic for many trainees, even the reluctant young man.

The fact that 80% of birds are identified by sound, not sight, diminishes the impact of blindness on this activity. On the trail, I notice that those of us who are sighted are all *listening* as hard as we can, not looking. Birds, although noisiest in spring, are always present, everywhere. Whether the new birder returns home to an urban, suburban, or rural setting, there are birds to be heard. How impressive to be able to identify the visitor who is singing in the spruce tree on the corner!

These 12 steps have worked for us in initiating individuals with visual impairments to birding:

1. *You can! You can! You know you can!* Introduce the idea of birding as an activity that just about anyone can do. Most nature sounds are in the mid-frequency range, so even the elderly with high-frequency hearing losses can hear most birds.

2. *Take me to your leader!* Invite a knowledgeable person to discuss birds with your group. You can find a leader through a local Audubon Society, nature center, or a parks and recreation department.

3. *Pleased to meet you!* Sit in a circle with your leader to discuss birds. This need not be a high-powered scientific lecture, but factual information should emerge. Answer such questions as What are birds? What is a feather? How can one identify a wing feather? How does preening work? What is the largest bird? the smallest? How big is a condor's wing span? Why do peacock feathers look as they do? Information about nests, mating habits, and migrations can be discussed. Allow time for questions and conversation. This session should leave you feeling that you have *so* much more to discover. Stop when all are anxious for the promised walk to hear bird songs.

4. *The promise.* Have your walk scheduled and announce the time at the meeting. You promised the possibility of hearing "Peter, Peter, Peter," "Purty, purty, I'm so purty!" "Cheer up! Cheer-a-lee!" and "Drink a tea!" Word phrases are enormously helpful in identifying and remembering bird calls and songs.

5. *How big? So-o-o-o big.* Establish size comparison so that when your leader speaks of a robin-sized bird or a sparrow-sized bird or a hummingbird as big as the first joint on your thumb, all will have a specific idea of the size of the bird.

6. *Lucky you!* You are in luck if you have a copy of the *Birdsong Tutor,* the birdsong tutorial cassettes for persons who are visually impaired, developed by the Cornell Laboratory of Ornithology (see the resource list cited later). The tutorial

is divided into four sections. The first is an introduction to the diversity of natural sounds. The second focuses on habitat exploration. The third expands on the theme of using natural sounds as habitat indicators that help listeners form mental pictures of their surroundings, and the fourth is a motivational section for further study of natural sounds.

7. *On the trail.* Choose a setting for your birdwalk suitable for your group. We have a favorite trail with a cedar-chip cover that makes for easy access after rains; has nicely spaced uphills and downhills that are not too steep; passes through stands of tall trees, around a large meadow, and through stands of brush; and passes by tree-rich suburban backyards. The variety of habitats at this site ensures that trainees will hear natural sounds common to their home locales.

8. *Beat off the volunteers.* Just kidding! Make sure you have sighted guides for those who need them. You will find that this activity becomes popular with volunteers who will remain enthusiastic about this new activity and become regulars. Your leader will undoubtedly know nature lovers who will be glad to add nice touches in the form of information about plants and wildlife as you are immersed in your natural surroundings.

9. *He's a bird dog!* Now and then the question comes up: "Will a guide dog disturb the birds?" "Not any more than two dozen people," our leader says.

10. *Kissing and "pishing" birds are curious and territorial.* If you don't have fancy birchwood Audubon bird calls (complete with rosin capsules), practice a few high-pitched smooches on the thumb-forefinger curled side of your tunneled fist or "pish" (with teeth together exhale as you whisper "pish, pish, pish, pish!"). The birds will answer those strange two-legged creatures making those silly sounds in their yards.

11. *Tack on an owl prowl.* It is confidence building, eerie, and wonderful to be on the trail at dusk to dark. As night falls, the birds become silent. Our leader plays a few seconds of the tape of a screech owl call. Very shortly we hear the answering call. He plays the call again, and our curious visitor (sometimes more than one) comes closer and closer until the melodies of the warbling *who-o-o*'s tossed back and forth from trees to tape fill us with awe. Especially at this breathless

time, seeing the delight of the faces of each person there, our basic philosophy is reaffirmed. Leisure is more than time spent, more than activity. It is a state of mind. Next time, we must do a woodcock stalk!

12. *Be a mocking bird.* Repeat, repeat, and repeat the activity. You can follow up the walks with a list of the birds that have been heard. One of our volunteers kept a list of the 26 birds encountered on our last walk. During our next leisure-time instruction class, we relistened to those birds on the tapes, remembering the "word phrases" that helped us identify the birds and relating them to the birds that trainees know are in their home territories. You won't be bored. Migrations ensure new bird visitors as well as familiar favorites each time you walk, even if you choose the same trails. (Important! Counsel novices to concentrate on one call at a time while enjoying the surroundings.)

Few animal sounds are as lovely as birdsongs. Hearing the clear fluting of a wood thrush in the tall trees or a whippoorwill throwing the boomerang of its voice across a summer marsh makes listening a thrill, a privilege, and an utterly engaging immersion into the grand tour of the world around us.

Some Helpful Resources

Cornell Laboratory of Ornithology. (1989). *A birdsong tutor for visually handicapped individuals* (Cassette recording). Available from Library of Natural sounds, 159 Sapsucker Woods Road, Ithaca, NY 15480.

National Library Service for the Blind and Physically Handicapped. *Birding: Introduction to ornithological delights for blind and visually handicapped individuals.* Available from the Library of Congress, CMLS, P.O. Box 9150, Melbourne, FL 32902.

Peterson Field Guides. (1989). *Birding by ear.* (Eastern/central cassette guides to birdsong identification). Boston: Houghton Mifflin.

Adapted from "A Birding Program for the Blind" by E. K. Bender, *RE:view, 26,* 92–96, 1994. Reprinted with permission of the Helen Dwight Reid Educational Foundation. Published by Holdref Publications, 1319 Eighteenth St., N.W., Washington, D.C. 20036-1802. Copyright (c) 1994.

Special Adaptations for Students Who Are Blind

Braille is the primary means of literacy for persons who are blind (Schroeder, 1989). Braille is a system of reading and writing in which letters, words, numbers, and other systems are made from arrangements of raised dots. The system was developed around 1830 by Louis Braille, a young Frenchman who was blind. Although the braille system is more than 165 years old, it is by far the most efficient approach to reading by touch and is still an essential skill for people who have too little vision to read print. Students who are blind can read braille much more rapidly than they could the raised letters of the standard alphabet.

The braille system is complex. Figure 9.3 shows the braille alphabet and numerals. In many ways, it is like the shorthand that secretaries use. Abbreviations, called *contractions*, help save space and permit faster reading and writing. For example, when the letter *r* stands by itself, it means "rather." The word *myself* in braille is written *myf*. Frequently used words, such as *the, and, with,* and *for,* have their own special contractions. For example, the *and* symbol ⠿ appears four times in the following sentence:

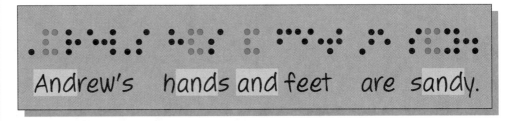

Many similar abbreviations assist in the more efficient reading and writing of braille. Mathematics, music, foreign languages, and scientific formulas all can be put into braille. When children who are blind attend regular public school classes, a specially trained teacher provides individual instruction in braille reading and writing.

> Chinese braille is a sound-based system that assigns a six-dot braille cell to each of 21 consonants, 16 vowels, and 5 tones. But in Chinese there is no link between the thousands of written characters and their sounds, so part of the language cannot be shared by braille readers. Wu (1993) has proposed refinements she believes will improve Chinese braille.

FIGURE 9.3

The braille system for representing numbers and letters

The six dots of the Braille cell are arranged and numbered thus: 1●●4 2●●5 3●●6	1 a	2 b	3 c	4 d	5 e	6 f	7 g	8 h	9 i	0 j
The capital sign, dot 6, placed before a letter makes it a capital. The number sign, dots 3, 4, 5, 6, placed before a character, makes it a figure and not a letter.	k	l	m	n	o	p	q	r	s	t
	u	v	w	x	y	z	Capital Sign	Number Sign	Period	Comma

Source: From the Division for the Blind and Physically Handicapped, Library of Congress, Washington, DC 20542.

Cooperative planning with the regular classroom teacher is critical so that books can be ordered or prepared in advance. The regular classroom teacher is not usually expected to learn braille, but some teachers find it helpful and interesting to do so. The braille system is not as difficult to learn as it first appears.

Most children who are blind are introduced to braille at about the first-grade level. The majority of teachers introduce contractions early in the program, rather than have the child learn to write out every word, letter by letter, and later unlearn this approach. Of course, it is important for the child who is blind to know the full and correct spelling of words even if every letter does not appear separately in braille. It usually takes several years for children to become thoroughly familiar with the system and its rules. The speed of braille reading varies a great deal from student to student, but it is almost always much slower than the speed of print reading. Pester (1993) makes recommendations for braille instruction for individuals who are blind adventitiously.

Young children generally learn to write braille by using a *brailler,* a six-keyed device that somewhat resembles a typewriter. Older students are usually introduced to the slate and stylus, in which the braille dots are punched out one at a time by hand, from right to left. The slate-and-stylus method has certain advantages in note taking; it is much smaller and quieter than the brailler.

> There is some evidence of a nationwide decline in braille literacy (Wittenstein, 1993).

Technology and Other Special Aids

Typically, braille books are large, expensive, and cumbersome. It can be difficult for students who are blind to retrieve information quickly when they must tactually review many pages of braille books or notes. Recent technological developments are making braille more efficient, thus enabling many students who are blind to function more independently in regular classrooms, universities, and employment settings (Kelly, 1987; Todd, 1986).

Written Communication

One system, known as VersaBraille II+ (Telesensory System, Inc.), is a portable laptop computer on which students who are blind can take notes and tests in class and

The brailler is a six-keyed device that punches the raised braille dots in special paper.

prepare assignments and papers at home. The keyboard has six keys that correspond to the dots in a braille cell, a numeric keypad, and a joystick. Students can check their work by reading a dynamic tactile display on the top of the VersaBraille II+ consisting of 20 braille cells, each made up of small pins that move up and down as the text progresses. Students store their work on a 3.5-inch floppy disk that can be used with a talking word-processing program such as the BRAILLE-EDIT Xpress (BEX) or to produce standard English print copies for teachers to read. A printer by Ohtsuki produces pages with both braille and print formats, enabling both blind and sighted readers to use the same copy.

Typewriting is an important means of communication between children who are blind and their sighted classmates and teachers and is also a useful skill for further education and employment. Instruction in typing should begin as early as feasible in the child's school program. Today, handwriting is less widely taught to students who are totally blind, with the noteworthy exception that it is necessary for children to learn to sign their own names so that they can assume such responsibilities as maintaining a bank account, registering to vote, and applying for a job.

A wide range of specialized materials and devices has been specially developed or modified for the instruction of students who are blind. Most of these educational materials are available from state instructional materials centers for the visually impaired or from the American Printing House for the Blind.

Manipulatives and Tactile Aids

Manipulatives are generally recognized as effective tools in teaching beginning mathematics skills to elementary students (Parham, 1983). When using most manipulatives, such as Cuisenaire rods, however, sighted students use length and color to distinguish the various numerical values of the rods. Belcastro (1989) has developed a set of rods that enables students who are blind to quickly identify different values by feeling the lengths and tactile markings associated with each number.

Another mathematical aid for students who are blind is the Cranmer Abacus. The abacus, long used in Japan, has been adapted to assist students who are blind in

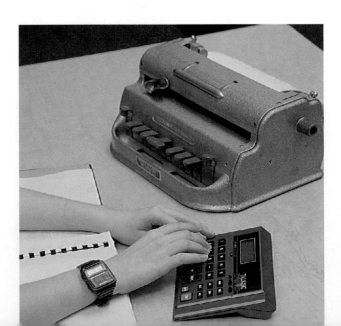

A talking calculator and watch.

learning number concepts and making calculations. Manipulation of the abacus beads is particularly useful in counting, adding, and subtracting.

For more advanced mathematical functions, the student is likely to use the Speech-Plus talking calculator, a small electronic instrument that performs most of the operations of any standard calculator. It "talks" by voicing entries and results aloud and also presents them visually in digital form. This is only one of many instances in which the recent development of synthetic speech technology has helpful implications for people who are blind. Talking clocks and spelling aids are also available.

In the sciences and social studies, several adaptations encourage students who are blind to use their tactile and auditory senses for firsthand manipulation and discovery. Examples are embossed relief maps and diagrams, three-dimensional models, and electronic probes that give an audible signal in response to light. Curriculum modification projects, such as MAVIS (Materials Adaptation for Students with Visual Impairments in the Social Studies) and SAVI (Science Activities for the Visually Impaired), emphasize how students with visual impairments can, with some modifications, participate in learning activities along with normally sighted students.

> Further information about these programs is available from the organizations listed at the end of the chapter.

Technological Aids

The Optacon (optical-to-tactile converter) is a small electronic device that converts regular print into a readable vibrating form for blind people. The Optacon does not convert print into braille but into a configuration of raised "pins" representing the letter the camera is viewing. When the tiny camera of the Optacon is held over a printed *E,* for example, the user feels on the tip of one finger a vertical line and three horizontal lines. Although extensive training and practice are required, many children and adults who are blind are able to read regular print effectively with the aid of the Optacon. It can allow students to work with typewriters, calculators, computer terminals, and small print.

The Kurzweil Personal Reader is another technological development with exciting implications for individuals with visual impairments and other disabilities. This sophisticated computer is an *optical character recognition* (OCR) system that scans and reads via a synthetic voice typeset and other printed matter. The reader can regulate the speed (up to 350 words per minute) and tone of the voice and can even have the machine spell out words letter by letter if desired. The "intelligence" of the Kurzweil Personal Reader is constantly being improved, and the machines are currently in use at most residential schools and also in many public school programs, public libraries, rehabilitation centers, and colleges and universities. The first Kurzweil machine weighed more than 300 pounds and cost $50,000, but the current model is much smaller and sells for about $8,000.

> Although the cost of some assistive technology, such as the Kurzweil Personal Reader, is prohibitive for many people, low-interest loans and financial assistance can sometimes be arranged (Uslan, 1992).

Computer Access

Assistive technology that provides access to personal computers offers tremendous opportunities for education, employment, communication, and leisure enjoyment for individuals with visual impairments. These devices fall into two basic categories (Schreier, Leventhal, & Uslan, 1991): (a) devices that magnify screen images through specialized hardware or software and (b) computer screen-access systems that use speech recognition software to enable the user to "tell" the computer what to do.

Brandon can adjust the speed and pitch of the Kurzweil Reading Machine's "voice."

Special Adaptations for Students with Low Vision

As noted, the great majority of children enrolled in educational programs for the visually impaired have some potentially useful vision. Their learning need not be restricted to touch, hearing, and other nonvisual senses. Currently, there is great emphasis on developing children's abilities to use their vision as effectively as possible. Recent research has shown that structured programs of visual assessment, training, and evaluation can dramatically improve these abilities; the earlier in life that such programs begin, the more likely they are to be successful (Corn, 1986; Fellows, Leguire, Rogers, & Bremer, 1986; Ferrell, 1985).

Corn (1989) believes that professionals must understand some basic premises about low vision and its effects on a person to guide curriculum development and instructional planning:

- *Those with congenital low vision view themselves as "whole"; they do not have remaining or residual vision.* Although it may be proper to speak of "residual vision" in reference to those who experience adventitious low vision, those with congenital low vision do not have a "normal" vision reference. They view the world with all of the vision they have ever had.
- *Those with low vision generally view the environment as "stationary" and "clear."* Although there are exceptions, this premise tries to dispel the misconception that people with low vision live in an impressionistic world in which they are continuously wanting to "clear" the image.
- *Low vision offers a different aesthetic experience.* Low vision may alter an aesthetic experience but does not necessarily produce a lesser one.
- *20/20 acuity is not needed for visual function for most tasks or for orientation and mobility within most environments.*

- *Clinical measurements do not dictate visual functioning.* Such measurements provide a "ballpark" in which to anticipate visual functioning.
- *Those with low vision can enhance visual functioning through the use of optical aids, nonoptical aids, environmental modifications, and/or techniques.*
- *The use of low vision is not in all circumstances the most efficient or preferred method of functioning.* For some individuals or tasks, the use of vision alone or in combination with other senses may reduce one's ability to perform. For example, using vision while pouring salt on food may not be the most efficient method for determining how much salt has been poured.
- *Low vision has unique psychological aspects.* Those with low vision have life experiences not encountered by those without such a condition. Much can be learned about the adjusting processes for those who are visually impaired congenitally and adventitiously.
- *Those who have low vision may develop a sense of visual beauty, enjoy their visual abilities, and use vision to learn.*[1]

Visual Functioning

The current emphasis on use of low vision is largely attributable to the influential work of Natalie Barraga (1964, 1970, 1980, 1983). She demonstrated that children, even those with extremely limited visual acuity or visual field, could be helped to improve their visual functioning dramatically. Visual efficiency, as defined by Barraga, includes such skills as controlling eye movements, adapting to the visual environment, paying attention to visual stimuli, and processing visual information rapidly. The fundamental premise in developing visual efficiency is that children learn to see and must be actively involved in using their own vision. Merely furnishing a classroom with attractive things for children to see is not sufficient. A child with low vision may, without training, be unable to derive much meaningful information through vision. Forms may be perceived as vague masses and shapeless, indistinct blobs. Training has helped many children learn to use their visual impressions intelligently and effectively, to make sense out of what they see.

Barraga's *Program to Develop Efficiency in Visual Functioning,* including a helpful *Source Book on Low Vision* (which can be purchased separately), is available from the American Printing House for the Blind.

Downing and Bailey (1990) stress the importance of teaching the basic visual skills of attending, localizing, tracking, shifting gaze, scanning, and reaching (moving) toward an object within functional activities for the individual. For example, instead of having the child with low vision practice his visual skills by sorting miscellaneous junk objects, he could use those skills while learning to make a fruit and ice cream drink.

Corn (1989) suggests four goals around which to base instructional activities in a program in the use of low vision. Her four goals respond to the question For what purposes do we use vision?

- *To gain information from directed visual experience.* A 4-year-old child may be asked to count the number of egg yolks in a bowl to see if more are needed to follow a recipe, or a 3-year-old may be asked to repeat a dance step that has been demonstrated.

---

[1]Adapted from Corn, A. L. "Instruction in the use of vision for children and adults with low vision: A proposed program model," *RE:view, 21,* 26–38, 1989. Reprinted with permission of the Helen Dwight Reid Educational Foundation. Published by Holdref Publications, 1319 Eighteenth St., N.W., Washington, D.C. 22036-1802. Copyright (c) 1989.

- *To gain information from incidental visual experiences.* A 12-year-old may notice the symbol of a plumbing company on a truck outside a friend's home and infer that there may be a plumbing problem in the house.
- *To gain an appreciation of visual experiences.* A child may select a video game to play for the enjoyment of watching the target move about the screen.
- *To utilize vision for the planning or execution of a task.* An adult may observe visually a narrow passage and determine whether it will be necessary to turn his or her body sideways to go through the opening. Through instruction, the individual may be able to enhance his or her ability to use visual observations to plan or execute the task.[2]

Optical Devices

Many children with low vision are able to benefit from special optical devices. These may include glasses and contact lenses, small hand-held telescopes, and magnifiers placed on top of printed pages. Such aids cannot give normal vision to children with visual impairments but may help them perform better at certain tasks, such as reading small print or seeing distant objects.

Optical aids are usually specialized, rather than all-purpose. Juanita might, for example, use her glasses for reading large print, a magnifier stand for reading smaller print, and a monocular (one-eye) telescope for viewing the chalkboard. A usual disadvantage of corrective lenses and magnifiers is that the more powerful they are, the more they tend to distort or restrict the peripheral field of vision. Some field-widening lenses and devices are now available for students with limited visual fields. These include prisms and fish-eye lenses, designed to make objects appear smaller so that a greater area can be perceived on the unimpaired portions of a student's visual field. Instruction in vision use should not be taught only in isolated time blocks, but rather incorporated into all parts of the low-vision student's curriculum (Corn, 1986). For example, a child learning daily living skills might be encouraged to use his vision to identify and reach for his toothbrush.

Today, many ophthalmologists, optometrists, and clinical facilities specialize in the assessment and treatment of low vision. A professional examination can help determine which types of optical aids, if any, are appropriate for a particular student. It is usually a good idea to furnish optical aids on a trial or loan basis so that the student can gradually learn to use and evaluate them in natural settings. A follow-up session should then be scheduled.

Reading Print Materials

Students with low vision use three basic approaches for reading print: (a) *approach magnification* (reducing the distance between the eye and the page of print from 40 cm to 5 cm results in 8× magnification) (Jose, 1983), (b) *lenses* (optical devices), and (c) *large type* (Corn & Ryser, 1989). Large type was first introduced in the Cleveland Public Schools in 1913 in the form of 36-point "clear face" type (Eakin & McFarland, 1960).

> Children whose vision is extremely limited are more likely to use monocular (one-eye) than binocular (two-eye) aids, especially for seeing things at a distance. See "Helping the Student with Low Vision" later in the chapter for suggestions to help children become accustomed to their optical aids.

---

[2]Adapted from Corn, A. L. "Instruction in the use of vision for children and adults with low vision: A proposed program model," *RE:view, 21,* 26–38, 1989. Reprinted with permission of the Helen Dwight Reid Educational Foundation. Published by Holdref Publications, 1319 Eighteenth St., N.W., Washington, D.C. 22036-1802. Copyright (c) 1989.

Most optical aids are designed for special purposes. Brock uses his monocular telescope for distance viewing.

Many books and other materials are available in large print for children with low vision. The American Printing House for the Blind produces books in 18-point type. Some states and other organizations produce large-type materials, but the size and style of the print fonts, spacing, paper, and quality of production vary widely. This book is set in 10-point type. Following are four examples of different large-print type sizes.

This is 14 point type.

This is 18 point type.

This is 20 point type.

This is 24 point type.

Large-print materials have certain disadvantages. Making print very large sharply reduces the number of letters and words that can be seen at one time; it thus becomes more difficult for a student to read smoothly, with a natural sweep of eye movements. It is generally agreed that a child with visual impairments should use the smallest print size that he or she can read comfortably. A child may be able to transfer from large print to smaller print as reading efficiency increases, just as most normally sighted children do.

A significant number of children with low vision are able to learn to read using regular-sized print with or without the use of optical aids. Stokes (1976) believes that "large type should not be recommended by a doctor or used by a teacher unless a thorough comparison with regular type is made" (p. 346). This approach permits a much wider variety of materials and eliminates the added cost of obtaining large-print books or enlarging texts with special duplicating machines. Although print size is an important variable, other equally important factors to consider are the quality

Some students with low vision who read print are also taught to read braille, especially if their visual acuity is expected to decrease because of a degenerative eye condition (Holbrook & Koenig, 1992).

These students with visual impairments at a state-run residential school are reading print materials in various large-size type.

of the printed material, the contrast between print and page, the spacing between lines, and the illumination of the setting in which the child reads.

Table 9.1 presents a comparison of advantages and disadvantages of large-print materials and optical devices. Corn and Ryser (1989) obtained information from the teachers of 399 students with low vision on such variables as reading speed and achievement, fatigue, and access to various materials. They concluded that, in most instances, reading regular print with an optical device is preferable to large-print materials:

> The use of optical devices (for those who can benefit from them) should be viewed as the least restrictive approach to gain access to all regular-print materials for near and distance tasks. The receipt of a prescription for a telescopic device gives the student access to chalkboards, signs, and events in the distance. . . . [O]ptical devices are individualized educational tools and are just as important to a child with a low vision as is a brace to a child with a physical handicap or a hearing aid to a hearing-impaired child. (pp. 348–349)

Some educational programs use closed-circuit television systems to enable students with low vision to read regular-sized printed materials. These systems usually include a sliding table on which a book is placed, a television camera with a zoom lens mounted above the book, and a television monitor nearby. The student is able to adjust the size, brightness, and contrast of the material and can select either an ordinary black-on-white image or a negative white-on-black image, which many students prefer. The teacher may also have a television monitor that lets him or her see the student's work without making repeated trips to the student's desk. A disadvantage of closed-circuit television systems (in addition to cost) is that they are usually not portable, so the student who uses television as a primary reading medium is largely restricted to the specially equipped classroom or library.

Other Classroom Modifications

Other classroom adaptations for students with low vision are often minor but can be very important. Many students benefit from desks with adjustable or tilting tops so that they can read and write at close range without constantly bending over and casting a shadow. Most regular classrooms have adequate lighting, but special lamps may

TABLE 9.1
Advantages and disadvantages of large-print materials

OPTICAL DEVICES	LARGE-TYPE MATERIALS
Advantages	**Advantages**
• Access to materials of various sizes, such as regular texts, newspapers, menus, and maps.	• Little or no instruction is needed to use a large-type book or other materials.
• Lower cost per child than large-type materials.	• Quota-account funds are available for large-type books.
• Lighter weight and more portable than large-type materials.	• A low vision clinical evaluation is not needed.
• No ordering or waiting time for production or availability.	• Students carry large-type "books" like other students in their classes.
• Access to distant print and objects, such as chalkboards, signs, and people.	• Funds for large-type books come from school districts that may require parental or other funding for optical devices.
Disadvantages	**Disadvantages**
• A low vision clinical evaluation must be obtained for the prescription of optical devices.	• Enlarging print by photocopy emphasizes imperfect letters.
• Funding for clinical evaluation and optical devices must be obtained.	• Pictures are in black, white, and shades of gray.
• Instruction in the use of the optical devices is needed.	• Fractions, labels on diagrams, maps, and so forth are enlarged only to a print size smaller than 18-point type.
• The cosmetics of optical devices may cause self-consciousness.	• The size and weight of large-type texts are difficult to handle.
• Optical problems associated with the optics of devices need to be tolerated.	• Large-type materials are not readily available after the school years, and students may be nonfunctional readers with regular type.

still be helpful for some children. Writing paper should have a dull finish to reduce glare; an off-white color such as buff or ivory is generally better than white. Some teachers have found it helpful to give students with low vision chairs with wheels so that they can easily move around the chalkboard area or other places in the classroom where instruction is taking place without constantly getting up and down. Dittoed worksheets in light purple or other poorly contrasting colors are difficult for most students with low vision to use; an aide or classmate could first go over the worksheet with a dark pen or marker. A teacher can make many other modifications, using common sense and considering the needs of the individual student with low vision.

Gellhaus and Olson (1993) offer numerous suggestions for using color and contrast to improve the educational environment of students with visual impairments with multiple disabilities.

Listening

Children with visual impairments—both those who are totally blind and those with low vision—must obtain an enormous amount of information through the sense of hearing. A great deal of time in school is devoted to speaking and listening to others. Students with visual impairments also make frequent use of recorded materials, particularly in high school. Recorded books and magazines and the equipment to use them can be obtained through the Library of Congress, the American Printing House for the Blind, the Canadian National Institute for the Blind, Recordings for the Blind, and various other organizations, usually on a free-loan basis. Each state has a designated library that provides books and materials for blind readers.

Helping the Student with Low Vision

• •

What does a child with low vision actually see? It is difficult for us to know. We can try to obtain some idea of total blindness by wearing a blindfold, but the majority of children with visual impairments are not totally blind. Even when two children share the same cause of visual impairment, it is unlikely that they see things in exactly the same way. And each child may see things differently at different times. We asked a few people with low vision to describe how they see. Here are some excerpts from what they told us.

> Have you ever been out camping in a strange place? When it's dark and you're trying to find your way from the tent to the bathroom, and you can't wear your glasses or contact lenses—that's like the way I see. I'm pretty much nearsighted. I can see a far object, I mean I know the image is there, but I can't distinguish it. I can see a house. It is just a white blob out there. I couldn't tell you what color is the roof trim, or where the windows are.*

> Put on a pair of sunglasses. Then rub Vaseline all around the central part of each lens. Now try reading a book. Or crossing a street. I never see blackness. . . . If I am looking at a picture, it's not like I see a hole in the middle. I fill something in there, but it wouldn't necessarily be what is really there. That's how I describe it to people—take a newspaper, hold it up, and look straight ahead. Now describe what you see here, off to the side . . . that's what I see all the time.*

Suggestions for Teachers

The following suggestions for teachers of students with low vision are from the Vision Team, a group of specialists in visual impairment who work with regular class teachers in 13 school districts in Hennepin County, Minnesota.

• Using the eyes does not harm them. The more children use their eyes, the greater their efficiency will be.

• Holding printed material close to the eyes may be the child with low vision's way of seeing best. It will not harm the eyes.

• Although eyes cannot be strained from use, a child with low vision's eyes may tire more quickly. A change of focus or activity helps.

• Copying is often a problem for children with low vision. The child may need a shortened assignment or more time to do classwork.

• It is helpful if the teacher verbalizes as much as possible while writing on the chalkboard or using the overhead projector.

• Some children with low vision use large-print books, but many do not. As the child learns to use vision, it becomes more efficient, and the student can generally read smaller print.

• Dittoes can be difficult for the child with low vision to read. Giving that child one of the first copies or the original from which the ditto was made can be helpful.

• The term *legally blind* does not mean educationally blind. Most children who are legally blind function educationally as sighted children.

• Contrast, print style, and spacing can be more important than the size of the print.

• One of the most important things a child with low vision learns in school is to accept the responsibility of seeking help when necessary, rather than waiting for someone to offer help.

• In evaluating quality of work and applying discipline, the teacher best helps the child with low vision by using the same standards that are used with other children.

Perhaps most important of all, an attitude of understanding and acceptance can help the student with low vision succeed in the regular classroom.

Using Low-Vision Aids

Children who have low-vision aids, such as special eyeglasses, magnifiers, and telescopes, may need instruction and assistance in learning how to use them most effectively. Here are some tips written especially for children to help them become accustomed to low-vision aids:†

Low vision aids should be portable and easy to use.

- *Low-vision aids take time to get used to.* At first, it seems like just a lot more things to take care of and carry around, but each aid you have will help you with a special job of seeing. You will get better with practice. In time, reaching for your telescope to read the chalkboard will seem as natural as picking up a pencil or pen to write. It's all a matter of practice.
- *Lighting is very important.* Always work with the most effective light for you. It makes a big difference in how clear things will look. Some magnifiers come with a built-in light, but most times you will have to use another light. A desk lamp is best. (The overhead light casts a shadow on your book or paper as you get close enough to see it.) Be sure the light is along your side, coming over your shoulder.
- *Be sure to keep your aids clean.* Dust, dirt, and fingerprints are hard to see through. Clean the lenses with a clean, soft cloth (never paper). If you have contact lenses, clean them with a special solution, following your doctor's instructions carefully. Always be sure your hands are clean to begin.
- *Keep your aids in their cases when you are not using them.* They will be more protected and always ready for you to take with you wherever you go.
- *Carry your low-vision aids with you.* Most of them are small and lightweight. In that way, you will have them when you need them. If you have aids you use only at school, you may want to ask your teacher to keep them for you in a safe place.
- *Experiment in new situations.* Can you see the menu at McDonald's? Watch the football game? See prices on toys? Find your friend's house number? The more often you use your low-vision aid, the better you will get at using it.
- *Try out different combinations of aids with and without your glasses or contact lenses.* In this way, you will find the combination that works best for you.

---

*From *Voices: Interviews with Handicapped People* by M. D. Orlansky and W. L. Heward, 1981, Columbus, OH: Merrill. †From *A Closer Look at Low Vision Aids* by Marybeth Dean with illustrations by Gail Feld. Available from the Connecticut State Board of Education and Services for the Blind, Division of Children's Services, 170 Ridge Road, Wethersfield, CT 06109.

When talking with a person who is blind, don't be afraid to use words such as *look* and *see.* Individuals with visual impairments use these words too.

Because many students with visual impairments are able to process auditory information at a faster rate than that of average conversational speech, devices are available to increase the playback rate of tapes without significantly distorting the quality of the speech. The ever-increasing use of synthetic speech equipment probably means that listening skills will become even more important in the future to students with visual impairments. Rhyne (1982) investigated the ability of students who are blind to comprehend synthetic speech; he found that the aural (listening) mode was a generally efficient way to learn and that students' comprehension increased as they gained more experience listening to synthetic speech.

Because there are so many useful opportunities for learning through listening, an important component of the educational program of virtually every child with visual impairments is the systematic development of listening skills. Children do not automatically develop the ability to listen effectively simply by being placed in a regular classroom, nor are students with visual impairments necessarily better listeners than normally sighted students.

Birding can be an enjoyable and educational way to practice and develop listening skills. See "Listening to the Birds" earlier in this chapter.

Listening involves several components, including attention to and awareness of sounds, discrimination, and assignment of meaning to sound (Heinze, 1986). Good listening skills tend to broaden a student's vocabulary and to support the development of speaking, reading, and writing abilities. Learning-to-listen approaches can take an almost unlimited variety of forms. Young children, for example, might learn to discriminate between sounds that are near and far, loud and soft, high-pitched and low-pitched. A teacher might introduce a new word into a sentence and ask the child to identify it. Older students might learn to listen for important details while there are distracting background noises, to differentiate between factual and fictional material, or to respond to verbal analogy questions. Some structured programs for developing listening skills have been developed (Alber, 1974; Stocker, 1973; Swallow & Conner, 1982). Instruction in this area can be among the most useful parts of a visually impaired student's curriculum.

Practical Living and Social Skills

Richardson (1993) describes three classes of change—in the work, in the workplace, and in the worker's activity—that can improve the performance of daily living skills by persons with visual impairments. Tape-recorded instructions can be used as self-help devices by individuals who are blind. See "I Made It Myself, and It's Good!" later in this chapter.

Some educators of students with visual impairments suggest that academic achievement has traditionally been overemphasized at the expense of important basic living skills. Hatlen (1976), for example, calls for giving "the most urgent attention" to such areas as cooking, grooming, shopping, financial management, decision making, recreational activities, personal hygiene, and social behavior. Specific instruction in these skills can facilitate a student's eventual independence as an adult. The specially trained teacher, the regular class teacher, other specialists, the parents, and the student should all participate in planning and providing instruction that will be practical and relevant to the student's needs and future objectives.

Hatlen (1978) further recommends, if necessary, teaching students with visual impairments how to deal with strangers, how to interpret and explain their visual impairments to other people, and how to make socially acceptable gestures in conversation. It is also important for students to be aware of the range of career opportunities available to them and to be informed about services, resources, and responsibilities in their communities.

Some individuals with visual impairments engage in repetitive body movements or other behaviors, such as body rocking, eye rubbing, hand waving, and head weaving. These behaviors were traditionally referred to in the visual impairment literature as "blindisms" or "blind mannerisms." **Stereotypic behavior** (or *stereotypy*) is a more clearly defined term that subsumes "blindisms" and "mannerisms"; it is also a more appropriate term in that such behaviors are also exhibited by other children and do not occur across all children with blindness (Gense & Gense, 1994).

Although not necessarily harmful, stereotypic behavior can place a person with visual impairments at a social disadvantage because these actions are conspicuous and may call negative attention to the person. It is not known why many children with visual impairments engage in stereotypic behaviors. However, various behavioral interventions have been used to help individuals with visual impairments reduce stereotypic behaviors such as repetitive body rocking (McAdam, O'Cleirigh, & Cuvo, 1993), head drooping during conversation (Raver, 1984), and off-task behaviors that interfere with learning (Barton & LaGrow, 1985).

Reviews of the literature on social skills of children with visual impairments indicate that, compared with children with normal sight, they interact less during free time and are often delayed in the development of social skills (Erin, Dignan, & Brown, 1991; Skellenger, Hill, & Hill, 1992). One explanation of these differences may be that children with visual impairments are not able to see the social signals given by others and as a result are less likely to engage in reciprocal interactions (Rugow, 1984).

Huebner (1986) provides an excellent set of guidelines for teaching social skills. She emphasizes the importance of developing socially acceptable behaviors, which in turn facilitate independence, self-confidence, and acceptance by others in school, community, and employment settings. Even though a child with visual impairment may perform a task safely and independently, he or she may not do so in a traditional, socially acceptable manner—for example, the child who likes to eat oatmeal by scooping it up to her mouth with her fingers!

Human Sexuality

Sighted children typically learn a great deal about human sexuality through vision. They see people establish social and sexual relationships with each other; they can see their own and others' bodies. Children who are blind, however, may grow up with serious knowledge gaps or misconceptions about sexuality and reproduction, particularly if parents and teachers fail to provide information and explanations. "I know girls have breasts," an adolescent who is blind told his counselor, "but I don't know where they are!" (Elliott, 1979).

Modesty makes it difficult for children who are blind to learn by touching others' bodies, and it is sometimes mistakenly assumed that people who are blind are uninterested in sex. In some European countries, live human models are used to familiarize students who are blind with anatomy and sexuality, but this practice has not been widely adopted in North America. In addition to providing accurate biological information, instructional programs should also consider the emotional aspects of sexual experience and the possible genetic implications, as some kinds of visual impairment can be passed from parents to children.

Issues in Assessment

There is a continuing concern about the use (and possible misuse) of intelligence tests with children with visual impairments. Intelligence tests, standardized on

Some young children with sensory impairments experience difficulty in receiving and expressing affection, behaviors that have been shown to facilitate future development in other areas of social competence (Compton & Niemeyer, 1994). The development of affection represents an important area for research and instruction.

Pava (1994) conducted a national survey of 161 women and men with visual impairments to assess their perceived vulnerability to sexual and physical assault. Although women respondents perceived themselves to be at more risk for assault than men, 1 in 3 of all the respondents reported having been targets of attempted or actual assault at some point in their lives. A curriculum of rape prevention and self-defense training has been developed for women with visual impairments (Pava, Bateman, Appleton, & Glascock, 1991).

"I Made It Myself, and It's Good!"

....

Students with Developmental Disabilities and Visual Impairments Learn to Use Tape-Recorded Recipes

*I*f special education is to contribute to meaningful lifestyle changes for students, it must focus on the instruction of functional skills for postschool environments. Being able to prepare one's own food is a critical skill for independent living. Steve, Lisa, and Carl were 17 to 21 years old and enrolled in a class for students with multiple disabilities at a residential school for the blind. They were living in an on-campus apartment used to teach daily living skills. Several unsuccessful attempts had been made to teach basic cooking skills to the three students. None of the students possessed any functional vision or braille skills, and their IQ scores ranged from 64 to 72 on the Perkins Binet Test of Intelligence for the Blind.

To learn new skills, especially those involving long chains of responses such as food preparation, students like Steve, Lisa, and Carl require intensive instruction over many trials. Once a particular skill sequence is learned, its generalization to other settings and situations (e.g., to another recipe) and maintenance across time (2 weeks later the student has "forgotten") is often lacking. The challenge was to discover a method for teaching cooking skills to the three students that not only was effective initially but also enabled the students to successfully prepare recipes on which they had not received direct instruction and that resulted in long-term maintenance of their new skills.

A "Walkman Cookbook"

Because the three students were blind, it was not possible to use picture cookbooks or color-coded recipes that have been used successfully with learners with mental retardation and other disabilities (Bergstrom, Pattavina, Martella, & Marchand-Martella,

in press; Book, Paul, Gwalla-Ogisi, & Test, 1990; Johnson & Cuvo, 1981). Instead, tape-recorded recipes were used. Students wore a cooking apron on which two pockets had been sewn. One pocket at the waist held a small audiocassette recorder; the second pocket, located at the chest, held a switch (sold as a foot switch and available for about $5 in any electronics store) that the students pushed to turn the tape player on and off. Each step from the task-analyzed recipes was prerecorded in sequence on a cassette tape ("Open the bag of cake mix by tearing it at the tab."). A beep signaled the end of each direction.

Performance Measures

The number of steps from each of the recipes that each student independently completed was measured during preinstruction (baseline), instruction, and maintenance phases. To assess generalization, probes were also conducted on two classes of recipes on which the students received no training. *Simple generality* items could be prepared with the same set of cooking skills learned in a related trained item. *Complex generality* recipes required the use of skills learned in two different trained items. The relationship between the trained recipes and the two types of recipes used to assess generality is shown in the accompanying table. As a measure of social validity, each trial was also scored as to whether the food prepared was edible.

Baseline

To objectively assess whether learning has occurred, student performance must be measured before any instruction has begun. The first baseline trial was conducted without the tape-recorded recipes to determine which food preparation steps, if any, each student could already perform without any assistance or adaptive equipment. It was then necessary to find out whether the students could successfully prepare the food items if they were simply given the tape-recorded recipes. After showing the students how to operate the tape recorder to play the prerecorded

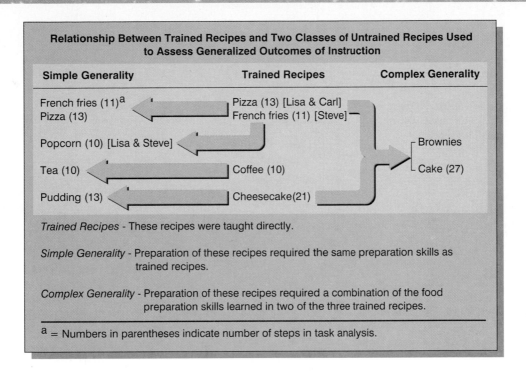

Relationship Between Trained Recipes and Two Classes of Untrained Recipes Used to Assess Generalized Outcomes of Instruction

Simple Generality	Trained Recipes	Complex Generality

French fries (11)[a]
Pizza (13)

Popcorn (10) [Lisa & Steve]

Tea (10)

Pudding (13)

Pizza (13) [Lisa & Carl]
French fries (11) [Steve]

Coffee (10)

Cheesecake(21)

Brownies

Cake (27)

Trained Recipes - These recipes were taught directly.

Simple Generality - Preparation of these recipes required the same preparation skills as trained recipes.

Complex Generality - Preparation of these recipes required a combination of the food preparation skills learned in two of the three trained recipes.

[a] = Numbers in parentheses indicate number of steps in task analysis.

instructions, students were asked to prepare each recipe but were given no other prompts, assistance, or feedback.

Instruction

Students were told that the taped recipes told them exactly what to do and where to find the food items and utensils. They practiced using the remote switch to control the rate of instructions by stopping the tape each time they heard a beep. Training for each step of the task analysis consisted of a three component least-to-most prompt hierarchy (verbal, physical, and hand-over-hand guidance) following errors and verbal praise for correct responses. Training on each food item continued until a student correctly performed all steps on two consecutive trials over two sessions.

Results

All three students learned to prepare the trained food items with the tape-recorded recipes. A total of 12, 19, and 35 instructional trials were needed to teach Lisa, Carl, and Steve to prepare three different recipes. (The high number of trials required for Steve to master the coffee and cheesecake recipes was caused by repeated mishaps when pouring liquids. This problem was solved by teaching Steve to use his fingers to feel where and how much liquid he was pouring.) Even more important, without any direct training on those items, each student was able to prepare both the simple and the complex generality food items with tape-recorded recipes after they had mastered the trained items.

The accompanying graphs show Steve's performance on the trained recipes and on the complex generality recipes that required a combination of cooking skills from the french fries and cheesecake recipes. But lines on a graph showing how many steps were correctly performed can be misleading with a complex skill like cooking. A mistake on any one of several crucial steps in the 27-step task analysis for making microwave cake (e.g., not stirring the egg into the batter) would result in a cake no one would want to eat. Before training, none of Steve's 13 attempts to make any of the trained items could be eaten, whereas all 6 of his posttraining attempts were

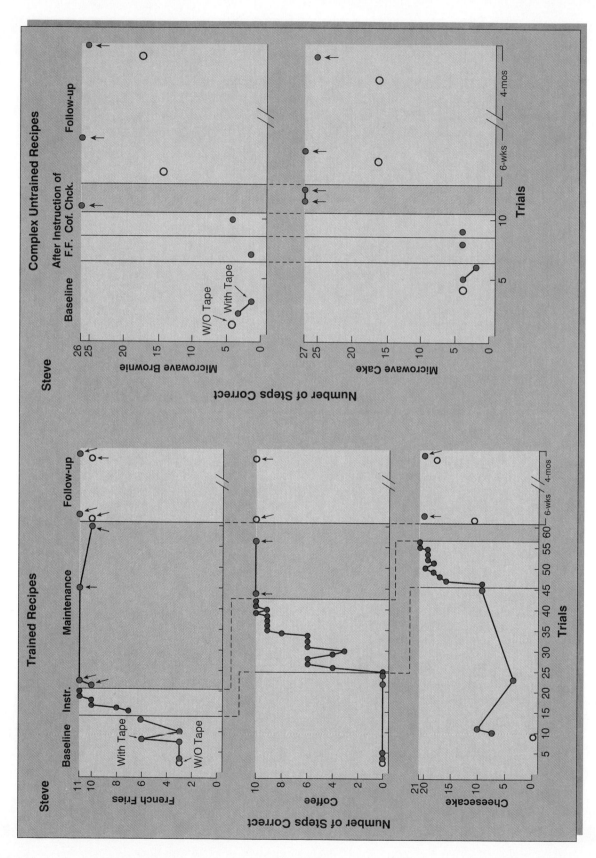

418

Steve has learned to accurately pour and measure the milk for his cake by placing his fingers in the bowl.

edible. Before he learned how to prepare the related items, Steve was unsuccessful in all 20 of his attempts to make the simple generality recipes and on each of 4 attempts to prepare the complex generality recipes. After learning how to make the related items, he was able to follow tape-recorded recipes to successfully prepare the recipes for which he had received no direct training: on 82% of the trials (9 out of 11) with the simple generality recipes and on all 3 trials with the complex generality recipes. In follow-up probes conducted at 6 weeks and 4 months after the study ended, Steve was still able to prepare each of the food items successfully. Lisa and Carl showed similar gains in their ability to prepare food for themselves.

A self-operated audio prompting system such as the one used in this and other studies (Briggs et al., 1990; Davis, Brady, Williams, & Burta, 1992) offers several advantages. First, audio prompts can be tailored to the individual skills and curriculum needs of each student. Tape-recorded instructions can be as precise or as general as demanded by the known or probable tasks and environments to be faced by the learner. Vocabulary can be modified, the pacing of instructions speeded up or slowed down, and instructions for particularly difficult steps repeated or given in more detail. (To see how preschoolers with disabilities can use a self-operated auditory prompting device, see "The Idea Bunny" in Chapter 14.) A self-management feature, in which the student self-records or self-evaluates the performance of each step before activating the tape for the next step, could easily be added. The student might use his or her own voice to record special prompts or reminders relevant to certain steps of the task (e.g., "Have I checked for spills?"). Verbal praise and encouragement from teachers, parents, friends, or the student him- or herself could also be included in the tape-recorded instructions.

Second, individuals with disabilities are currently using a variety of prosthetic devices to increase their independence in domestic, community, and employment settings. Some assistive devices, however, may not be used by the learner in the natural setting. A student in a crowded restaurant, for example, may be hesitant to remove a laminated ordering card from her pocket or purse because it marks her as different. By contrast, the tremendous popularity of Walkman-type personal stereos enables the wearer of audio headphones to go unnoticed. The use of an audio prompting system allows the person with disabilities to listen to a series of self-delivered prompts in a private, unobtrusive, and normalized manner that does not impose on or bother others. The self-operated feature of the system places the student in a position of control over the environment, thereby increasing the probability of independent functioning. As Carl remarked when sharing with his girlfriend the microwave cake he had just made, "I made it myself, and it's good!"

Adapted from "Teaching Young Adults with Developmental Disabilities and Visual Impairments to Use Tape-Recorded Recipes: Acquisition, Generalization, and Maintenance of Cooking Skills" by S. A. Trask-Tyler, T. A. Grossi, & W. L. Heward, 1994, *Journal of Behavioral Education, 4,* pp. 283–311. Used by permission.

sighted children, are often based largely on visual concepts. They may include questions such as "Why do people have hedges around their homes?" or "What should you do if you see a train approaching a broken track?" The results of these tests may well give an inaccurate picture of the abilities and needs of a child with visual impairments. Regrettably, many children with visual impairments have been placed in inappropriate educational programs because of strict reliance on standardized test performance.

Helpful reviews of assessment procedures and guidelines for appropriate use of tests with children with visual impairments have been provided by Bradley-Johnson and Harris (1990); Chase (1986a, 1986b); and Hall, Scholl, and Swallow (1986). A number of instruments, though not specifically designed for students with visual impairments, may nevertheless be useful in assessing certain aspects of performance. In gathering information that will be helpful in developing educational goals for a child with visual impairment, a variety of formal and informal procedures should be used. The results of developmental or intelligence tests should always be supplemented by careful observations of the child's behavior in school and play situations. Teachers and parents are usually in the best position to observe the child's communication, exploration, and social interaction over an extended period. Their contributions should play a major part in planning the educational program of a child with visual impairments.

Orientation and Mobility

The educational program of a child with visual impairment could hardly be considered complete or appropriate if it failed to include instruction in orientation and mobility. **Orientation** is the ability to establish one's position in relation to the environment through the use of the remaining senses. **Mobility** is the ability to move safely and efficiently from one point to another (Lowenfeld, 1973). For most students, more time and effort is spent in orientation training than in learning specific mobility techniques. It is extremely important that, from an early age, children with visual impairments be taught basic concepts that will familiarize them with their own bodies and their surroundings. For example, they must be taught that the place where the leg bends is called a *knee* and that rooms have walls, doors, windows, corners, and ceilings.

Orientation and mobility (O&M) instruction is a well-developed subspecialty in the education and rehabilitation of individuals who are blind and visually impaired. Many specific techniques are involved in teaching students with visual impairments to understand their environment and maneuver through it effectively. Training in such skills should be given by qualified *O&M specialists*. The Association for Education and Rehabilitation of the Blind and Visually Impaired (AER), the professional organization that certifies O&M specialists, also recognizes the important role of O&M assistants (Wiener et al., 1990). The O&M assistant is a paid employee who provides selected O&M services under the direction and supervision of a certified O&M specialist.

The long cane is the most widely used device for adults with severe visual impairments who travel independently (Jacobson, 1993). The traveler does not "tap" the cane but sweeps it lightly in an arc while walking to gain information about the path ahead. Properly used, the cane serves as both a *bumper* and a *probe*. The cane acts as a bumper by protecting the body from obstacles such as

O&M specialists are called *peripatologists* in some states.

parking meters and doors; it is also a probe to detect in advance such things as drop-offs or changes in travel surface (e.g., from grass to concrete or from a rug to a wooden floor).

Even though mastery of cane skills can do much to increase a person's independence and self-esteem, cane use poses certain disadvantages (Tuttle, 1984). The cane cannot detect overhanging obstacles such as tree branches and provides only fragmentary information about the environment, particularly if the person who is blind is in new or unfamiliar surroundings. Unfortunately, many adventitiously blinded persons do not begin learning cane travel skills until 1 to 2 years after losing their sight; they mention concern about acceptance by others and the negative stigmas they believe are associated with the cane (Wainapel, 1989).

Until recently, formal O&M instruction, especially for cane use, was seldom given to children younger than about 12 years of age; however, the importance of early development of travel skills and related concepts is now generally recognized (Pogrund & Rosen, 1989). Today, it is not at all unusual for preschool children to benefit from the services of an O&M specialist, but there is disagreement over which, if any, mobility device is most suitable for initial use by very young children (Dykes, 1992). Professionals recognize the long cane's benefits of increased protection and confidence while traveling but question whether preschoolers can handle the motor and conceptual demands of long cane use. These concerns have led to the development of a variety of alternative mobility devices, including modified and smaller canes such as the Connecticut precane (Foy, Von Scheden, & Waiculonis, 1992) and the "kiddy cane" (Pogrund, Fazzi, & Schreier, 1993).

Although the long cane is a relatively simple and sturdy piece of equipment, it takes a beating during training and everyday use. In anticipation of "the inevitable need to repair canes," O&M specialist Tom Langham (1993) always carries a tool kit that includes such items as pliers, hacksaw, pipe cutter, Allen wrenches, red and white reflective tape, wax, and a bent coat hanger.

Under the watchful eyes of an orientation and mobility specialist, Matthew is learning how to gain information about the path ahead by sweeping his cane in an arc.

In a sophisticated experimental comparison of long cane and precane use by preschoolers, Clarke, Sainato, and Ward (1994) found that the children "were capable of learning to use the long cane . . . for protection with a respectable degree of skill" (p. 29) but that all four children used the precane device more appropriately overall. This study demonstrates the importance of providing young children with direct, systematic instruction in cane skills. The authors also note that although the precane has been touted by some as requiring little or no instruction for use (Foy et al., 1992), before training, the children in the study showed little understanding of the function or use of the device: They would drag it behind them, bang it up and down on the floor, or wear it looped around their necks.

A small percentage of people with visual impairments (about 1% to 3%) travel with the aid of guide dogs (Hill & Jacobson, 1985). Like the cane traveler, the guide dog user must have good O&M skills to select a route and to be aware of the environment. The dog wears a special harness and has been trained to follow several basic verbal commands, to avoid obstacles, and to ensure the traveler's safety. Several weeks of intensive training at special guide dog agencies are required before the person and dog can work together effectively. Misunderstandings sometimes arise if people with guide dogs are refused entry into restaurants, hotels, airplanes, or other places that normally do not permit animals; state and local regulations permit guide dogs to have access to these places. Guide dogs are especially helpful when a person must travel over complicated or unpredictable routes, as in large cities. They are not usually available to children under 16 years of age or to people with multiple disabilities.

In the area of mobility, most people with visual impairments find it necessary to rely occasionally on the assistance of others. The *sighted guide technique* is a simple method of helping a person with visual impairments to travel:

- When offering assistance to a person who is blind, speak in a normal tone of voice and ask directly, "May I help you?" This helps the person locate you.
- Do not grab the arm or body of the person who is blind. Permit him or her to take your arm.
- The person with visual impairment should lightly grasp the sighted person's arm just above the elbow and walk half a step behind in a natural manner.
- The sighted person should walk at a normal pace, describing curbs or other obstacles and hesitating slightly before going up or down. Never pull or push a person who is blind when you are serving as a sighted guide.
- Do not try to push a person who is blind into a chair. Simply place his or her hand on the back of the chair, and the person will seat him- or herself.

When students with visual impairments attend regular classes, it may be a good idea for one of the students and the O&M specialist to demonstrate the sighted guide technique to classmates. To promote independent travel, however, overreliance on the sighted guide technique should be discouraged once the student has learned to get around the classroom and school.

Several recently developed electronic travel aids may facilitate orientation and independent travel for individuals with visual impairments. These include a laser beam cane, which emits a sound to signal objects in the traveler's path, as well as hazards overhead and drop-offs below. Other devices, designed for use in conjunction with a standard cane or guide dog, send out sound waves to bounce off objects and give the trained traveler information about the environment through auditory or tactual channels. Electronic travel aids have even been used with blind infants as young as 6 months in an attempt to enhance their early learning and awareness by enabling them to explore their environment more thoroughly and independently (Ferrell, 1984). Disadvantages of electronic travel aids include high cost, the extensive training required, and possible problems in adverse weather conditions. Hill and Jacobson (1985) note that users of electronic travel aids found them helpful in orienting themselves to new settings but tended to use the aids less after they had become familiar with the environment.

Whatever the preferred method of travel, most students with visual impairments can generally learn to negotiate familiar places, such as school and home, on their own. Many students with visual impairments can benefit from learning to use a systematic method for obtaining travel information and assistance with street crossing (Florence & LaGrow, 1989; LaGrow & Mulder, 1989). Good orientation and mobility skills have many positive effects. A child with visual impairment who can travel independently is likely to develop more physical and social skills and more self-confidence than a child who must continually depend on other people to get around. Good travel skills also expand a student's opportunities for employment and independent living.

✳ *Educational Service Alternatives*
Public Schools

In the past, most children with severe visual impairments were educated in residential schools for children who are blind. Today, however, 60% of the children with visual impairments are educated in regular school classrooms for at least part of the school day (U.S. Department of Education, 1994). Supportive help is usually given by *itinerant teacher-consultants,* sometimes called *vision specialists.* These specially trained teachers may be employed by a residential school, school district, regional education agency, or state or province. Their roles and caseloads vary widely from program to program (Flener, 1993; Willoughby & Duffy, 1989). In general, however, the itinerant teacher-consultant may be expected to assume some or all of the following responsibilities:

- Collaboratively develop with the regular classroom teacher curricular and instructional modifications according to the child's individual needs.
- Provide direct instruction on compensatory skills to the student with visual impairments (e.g., listening, typing skills).
- Obtain or prepare specialized learning materials.
- Adapt reading assignments and other materials into braille, large-print, or tape-recorded form or arrange for readers.
- Make referrals for low-vision aids services; train students in the use and care of low-vision aids.
- Interpret information about the child's visual impairment and visual functioning to other educators and parents.
- Help plan the child's educational goals, initiate and maintain contact with various agencies, and keep records of services provided.
- Consult with the child's parents and other teachers.

The itinerant teacher-consultant may or may not provide instruction in orientation and mobility. Some programs, particularly in rural areas, employ dually certified teachers who are also orientation and mobility specialists. Other programs employ one teacher for educational support and another for orientation and mobility training. Students on an itinerant teacher's caseload may range from infants to young adults and may include children who are blind or those with low vision or multiple disabilities. In rural areas, the itinerant teacher often spends a great deal of time on the road to visit and work with each student and has many challenging responsibilities.

Some public school programs have special resource rooms for students with visual impairments. In contrast with the itinerant teacher-consultant, who travels from school to school, the resource room teacher remains in one specially equipped location and serves students with visual impairments for part of the school day. Usually, only large school districts have resource rooms for students with visual impairments.

The amount of time the itinerant teacher-consultant or resource room teacher spends with a visually impaired student who attends regular classes varies considerably. Some students may be seen every day because they require a great deal of specialized assistance. Others may be seen weekly, monthly, or even less frequently because they are able to function well in the regular class with less support.

Public school education for children with visual impairments has many advocates. McIntire (1985) writes that "the least restrictive environment for children who are blind is in the local public school regular classroom with nonhandicapped children" (p. 163); Cruickshank (1986) maintains that "the blind child is perhaps the eas-

Patrick is getting along fine in the regular classroom—thanks to the instructional adaptations jointly planned by his itinerant vision specialist and his classroom teacher.

iest exceptional child to integrate into a regular grade in the public schools" (p. 104). To make this integration successful, however, a full program of appropriate educational and related services must be provided (Curry & Hatlen, 1988). As Griffing (1986) observes, "No category of handicap requires greater coordination and cooperation among resources than the area of the blind and visually impaired" (p. 5). The key person in the program for a child with visual impairments is the regular classroom teacher. An extensive study of the elements of successful mainstreaming of children with visual impairments in public school classes found that the single most important factor was the regular classroom teacher's flexibility (Bishop, 1986). Other aspects of the school situation found to be highly important were peer acceptance and interaction, availability of support personnel, and adequate access to special supplies and equipment.

Residential Schools

Residential schools continue to meet the needs of a sizable number of children with visual impairments. There are 52 such schools operating in the United States today. The current population of residential schools consists largely of children with visual impairments with additional disabilities, such as mental retardation, hearing impairment, behavioral disorders, and cerebral palsy. Some parents are not able to care for their children adequately at home; others prefer the greater concentration of specialized personnel, facilities, and services that the residential school usually offers.

Parents and educators who support residential school education for children with visual impairments frequently point to the leadership that such schools have provided over a long period, with their "wealth and broad range of expertise" (Miller, 1985, p. 160). These supporters argue that a residential school can be the least restrictive environment for many students with visual impairments and multiple disabilities. A follow-up study of students with visual impairments at a state school for the blind found that parents, local education agencies, and the students themselves generally considered the residential school placement to have been appropriate and beneficial (Livingston-White, Utter, & Woodard, 1985). Among the advantages cited were specialized curriculum and equipment, participation in extracurricular activities, individualized instruction, small classes, and improved self-esteem.

Placement in a residential school program need not be regarded as permanent. Many children with visual impairments move from residential schools into public schools (or vice versa) as their needs change. Some students in residential schools attend nearby public schools for all or part of their school day. Most residential schools encourage parent involvement and have recreational programs that bring students with visual impairments into contact with sighted peers. Independent living skills and vocational training are important parts of the program at virtually all residential schools.

In several states and provinces, there is close cooperation between public school and residential school programs that serve children with visual impairments. Thurman (1978), for example, reports that the residential school in Canada's Atlantic provinces employs a network of itinerant teacher-consultants who provide instruction, materials, and assistance to children with visual impairments attending regular public schools. These professionals offer regular consultation to the various teachers who also work with students with visual impairments. It is expected that most children with visual impairments in this region will gradually be integrated into their

About 10% of students with visual impairments attend residential schools (U.S. Department of Education, 1994). See Chapter 11 for information on children with multiple disabilities, including those who are deaf-blind.

The June 1993 issue of the *Journal of Visual Impairment and Blindness* is devoted to current issues and concerns regarding residential schools.

local public schools and that the residential school will serve mainly students with multiple disabilities and young children with visual impairments who require training in basic skills.

A residential school for students who are blind has an opportunity to work closely with consumers, parents, professionals, and funding agencies in developing a wide array of community-based services. Cooperative working relationships and creative short- and long-term planning efforts have the potential to generate positive and reality-based services that respond to present-day needs within the context of community integration. Residential schools—primarily because of the expertise of their staff but also because of their location, centralization of resources, and availability of facilities—have the potential to become responsive resource centers on regional and state levels.

Residential schools have long played an important role in training teachers of children with visual impairments on both a preservice and inservice basis. The residential school is usually well equipped to serve as a resource center for instructional materials and as a place where students with visual impairments can receive specialized evaluation services. An increasing number of residential schools now offer short-term training to students with visual impairments who attend regular public schools. One example is a summer workshop emphasizing braille, mobility, and vocational training.

✳ *Current Issues and Future Trends*

As we have noted, children with visual impairments constitute a small portion of the school-age population, but they have many unique needs. Although the current trend toward full inclusion of children with visual impairments into regular public school classrooms is generally welcomed, some educators caution against wholesale placement of children with visual impairments in regular schools without adequate support. Many vision professionals tend to resist noncategorical special education programs for students with visual impairments. It is unrealistic, they argue, to expect regular teachers or teachers trained in other areas of special education to be competent in such specialized techniques as braille, mobility, and visual efficiency.

Specialization of Services

Although financial restrictions may require some public school and residential school programs for children with visual impairments to close down or to consolidate with programs for children with other disabilities, strong support exists for the continuation of highly specialized services. It is likely that both public school and state-run residential programs for children with visual impairments will continue to operate well into the future, occasionally challenging each other for the privilege of serving the relatively small number of available students. The results of this competition may well prove favorable if both types of schools are encouraged to improve the quality of their educational services.

As more infants and preschool children with visual impairments are identified, greater emphasis will be placed on specialized programs of early intervention (Ferrell, 1986). Older students must receive more systematic instruction in skills related to employment and independent living, and continuing efforts will be made to improve coordination of services between educational programs and postschool rehabilitation agencies. The current interest in children with low vision will extend beyond the area of vision use and into many other aspects of education and development. Some evidence suggests that children with low vision may have a more difficult time than children who are totally blind in gaining social acceptance by sighted children in public schools (Corn, 1986; Spenciner, 1972); thus, new programs will be designed to address the psychosocial needs of children with low vision.

Technology and Research

New technological and biomedical developments will continue to aid students with visual impairments, particularly in the areas of mobility, communication, and use of low vision. In the future, it may even be possible to provide a form of artificial sight to some people who are totally blind, by implanting electrodes into the brain and connecting them to a miniature television camera built into an artificial eye (Dobelle, 1977; Marbach, 1982). Research in artificial sight is in the early experimental stages but suggests much promise. Other systems of electronic vision substitution rely on tactile images projected onto an area of the body, such as the back or abdomen, which enables the person who is blind to perceive a visionlike sensation.

Fighting Discrimination

Like other groups of individuals with disabilities, people with visual impairments are becoming increasingly aware of their rights as citizens and consumers and are fighting discrimination based on their disabilities. As Willoughby (1980) observes, many people—even some who work with students with visual impairments—tend to underestimate their students' capacities and to deny them a full range of occupational and personal choices. The future will probably bring a gradual shift away from some of the vocational settings in which people with visual impairments have traditionally worked (e.g., piano tuning, sheltered workshops, rehabilitation counseling) in favor of a more varied range of employment opportunities. These and other trends will be appropriately reflected in future programs of education and training for children with visual impairments.

Summary

Defining Visual Impairment

• Vision is a critical sense that children use to obtain information about the world. Without it, they need special materials and attention to enable them to learn and develop to their full potential.

• Visual impairment has both legal and educational definitions.

• An educational definition considers the extent to which a visual impairment makes special education materials or methods necessary.

• Children with low vision can learn through the visual channel, and many learn to read print.

• Besides impairments in visual acuity and field of vision, a child may have problems with ocular motility or visual accommodation, photophobia, or defective color vision.

• The age at onset of a visual impairment affects a child's educational and emotional needs.

Types and Causes of Visual Impairment

• The eye collects light reflected from objects, focuses the objects' image on the retina, and transmits the image to the brain. Difficulty with any part of this process can cause vision problems. Common types of visual impairment include

Myopia (nearsightedness)

Hyperopia (farsightedness)

Astigmatism (blurred vision caused by irregularities in the cornea or other eye surfaces)

Cataract (blurred or distorted vision caused by cloudiness in the lens)

Glaucoma (loss of vision caused by high pressure within the eye)

Diabetic retinopathy, retinitis pigmentosa, macular degeneration, and retinal detachment (all caused by problems with the retina)

Retinopathy of prematurity (retrolental fibroplasia) (caused by administration and withdrawal of high doses of oxygen to premature infants in incubators)

Prevalence

- Visual impairment is a low-incidence disability, affecting less than 0.1% of the school-age population. About one third of all students with visual impairments have additional disabilities.

Historical Background

- Educating students who are blind is one of the oldest fields of special education.

- Hauy started the first school for children who are blind in Paris in 1784; by the early 19th century, several other European countries had started residential schools for children who are blind.

- The first schools in the United States for children who are blind were private residential schools, established around 1830, and were soon followed by public residential schools.

- Until recently, children with low vision were not encouraged to use their sight so as to conserve it; today, they are taught to concentrate on developing and using their vision as much as possible.

- The influx of children whose blindness was caused by retinopathy of prematurity led to expansion of regular public school programs for children with visual impairments in the 1950s and 1960s.

- Most parents can choose between public day and residential schools for their children with visual impairments. Neither placement need be considered permanent.

Educational Approaches

- Teachers of children with visual impairments need specialized skills, along with knowledge, competence, and creativity.

- Most children who are blind learn to read braille and write with a brailler and a slate and stylus. They may also learn to type and use special equipment for mathematics, social studies, and listening to or feeling regular print.

- Children with low vision should learn to use their residual vision as efficiently as possible. Many use optical aids and large print to read regular type.

- All children with visual impairments need to develop their listening skills.

- Most students with visual impairments also need special instruction in practical daily living skills, interpersonal skills, and human sexuality.

- Some children with visual impairments need help in reducing or eliminating stereotypic behaviors.

- The teacher must use direct observation and a variety of informal and formal procedures to assess children with visual impairments. Standardized intelligence tests are often inappropriate.

- Orientation and mobility (O&M) instruction is a must for individuals who are blind or have severe visual impairments.

Educational Service Alternatives

- Most children with visual impairments spend at least part of each school day in regular classes with sighted peers.

- In many districts, a specially trained itinerant vision specialist provides extra help for students and regular class teachers.

- Some programs also have separate orientation and mobility instructors or separate resource rooms for students with visual impairments.

- About 10% of the children with visual impairments, especially those with other disabilities, attend residential schools.

Current Issues and Future Trends

- Children with visual impairments are likely to receive specialized services in the future in both regular and residential schools.

- Greater emphasis will be placed on intervention with visually impaired infants and young children and on training older students for independence.

- Children with low vision will receive more attention in the coming years, and it is hoped that all people with visual impairments will benefit from new technological

and biomedical developments. Artificial sight may be possible in the future.

- Career opportunities for persons with visual impairments will likely expand as these individuals become more aware of their legal and human rights.

For More Information

Journals

Journal of Visual Impairment and Blindness. Published 10 times per year by the American Foundation for the Blind, 15 West 16th Street, New York, NY 10011. An interdisciplinary journal for practitioners and researchers concerned with the education and rehabilitation of children or adults who are blind or have visual impairments. Includes regular updates on technological and legislative developments.

RE:view (formerly *Education of the Visually Handicapped*). Published quarterly by the Association for Education and Rehabilitation of the Blind and Visually Impaired, 206 North Washington Street, Room 320, Alexandria, VA 22314. Includes practical articles, research studies, interviews, and other features relevant to teachers of students with visual impairments, orientation and mobility specialists, rehabilitation workers, administrators, and parents. Twice per year *RE:view* publishes its *Semi-Annual Listing of Current Literature: Blindness, Visual Impairment, Deaf-Blindness,* an annotated bibliographic listing of articles, books, and other publications designed to "provide a fairly complete and coordinated compilation of professional literature related to serious visual impairment."

The Sight-Saving Review. Published quarterly by the National Society to Prevent Blindness, 500 East Remington Road, Schaumburg, IL 60173. Emphasizes new developments in the assessment and treatment of visual impairments, low-vision aids, eye safety, and health education.

Books

Barraga, N. C., & Erin, J. N. (1992). *Visual handicaps and learning* (3rd ed.). Austin, TX: PRO-ED.

Best, A. B. (1991). *Teaching children with visual impairments.* Philadelphia: Open University Press.

Jose, R. (1983). *Understanding low vision.* New York: American Foundation for the Blind.

Rugow, S. M. (1988). *Helping the child with visual impairments with developmental problems: Effective practice in home, school, and community.* New York: Teachers College Press.

Scholl, G. T. (Ed.). (1986). *Foundations of education for blind and visually handicapped children and youth: Theory and practice.* New York: American Foundation for the Blind.

Torres, I., & Corn, A. L. (1990). *When you have a visually impaired student in your classroom: Suggestions for teachers.* New York: American Foundation for the Blind.

Organizations

American Foundation for the Blind, 15 West 16th Street, New York, NY 10011. Provides many publications and films about blindness. Distributes aids and appliances for people with impaired vision. Publishes the *Journal of Visual Impairment and Blindness* and *Directory of Agencies Serving the Visually Handicapped in the United States.*

American Printing House for the Blind, 1839 Frankfort Avenue, Louisville, KY 40206. Provides books, magazines, and many other publications in braille, large-print, and recorded form. Distributes educational materials and aids specially designed for the blind and helpful publications for teachers. Attempts to register all U.S. children who are legally blind through state departments of education or residential schools. Also provides recordings and computer materials.

Association for Education and Rehabilitation of the Blind and Visually Impaired, 206 North Washington Street, Alexandria, VA 22314. Emphasizes educational, orientation, mobility, and rehabilitation services. Holds regional and national conferences in the United States and Canada. Publishes *RE:view* and a yearbook compiling recent literature in this field.

Canadian National Institute for the Blind, 1921 Bayview Avenue, Toronto, Ontario M4G 3E8, Canada. The central agency for information, materials, and supportive services for people with visual impairments in Canada. Maintains regional and local offices in all provinces. Effectively depicts the growth and development of a young blind child in a film, Shelley.

Division on Visual Handicaps (DVH), Council for Exceptional Children, 1920 Association Drive, Reston, VA 22091. DVH, with more than 1,000 members, has promoted appropriate education programs for individuals who have visual disabilities since 1954.

National Association for Parents of the Visually Impaired, 2011 Hardy Circle, Austin, TX 78756. Provides practical information for parents. Sponsors parent groups in several areas. Holds conferences and workshops for parents and teachers.

National Federation of the Blind, 1800 Johnson Street, Baltimore, MD 21230. The largest organization of blind people in the United States, with many state and local chapters. Provides publications and films that emphasize the rights and capabilities of people who are blind. Seeks to involve blind people in education and employment and to avoid discrimination. Also sponsors activities and publications for parents of children who are blind.

Students with Physical and Health Impairments

- How can the type and degree of disability experienced by a child with a physical or health impairment vary from one environment to another?

- How might the visibility of a physical or health impairment affect a child?

- How do the nature and severity of a child's physical disability affect IEP goals and objectives?

- To what extent should the classroom environment be modified to accommodate students with physical and health impairments?

- How can an adaptive or assistive device be a hindrance as well as a help?

hildren with physical and health impairments are an extremely varied population. Describing all of them with a single set of characteristics would be impossible, even if we used very general terms. Their physical disabilities may be mild, moderate, or severe. Their intellectual functioning may be normal, below normal, or above normal. Children may have a single impairment or a combination of impairments. They may have lived with the physical or health impairment since birth or have suddenly acquired it. The students whose special education needs we consider in this chapter have a great many individual differences; there is no typical case of anything. Although we can make general statements about some physical and health-related conditions, numerous variations occur in the degree and severity of the conditions and how they may affect a child and his or her educational needs.

Many students with physical and health impairments adjust to their conditions well. They present no unusual behavior problems and are fully capable of learning in the regular classroom and interacting successfully with their nondisabled peers. The sophistication of today's medical treatments enables many children with physical and health impairments to attend school regularly. Hospital stays tend to be shorter, physical therapy and many routine medical regimens can be provided in school settings, and surgery can often be scheduled during vacation periods.

Most children with physical and health impairments are generally included in educational programs on the basis of their particular learning needs, not according to their specific disability or disease. It is important for teachers (and often for other students as well) to understand how a particular condition may affect a child's learning, development, and behavior. Linda, for example, has undergone long periods of hospitalization and finds it difficult to keep up with her academic work. Gary takes medication that controls his seizures most of the time, but it also tends to make him drowsy in the classroom.

Physical and health problems can give rise to special needs in the school setting. Because of their disabilities or illnesses, children with physical and health impairments may require modifications in the physical environment, in teaching techniques, in communication, or in other aspects of their educational programs. In defining the population of children with disabilities according to the IDEA, the federal government emphasizes that a child's educational performance must be adversely affected by severe orthopedic impairments (including those caused by cerebral palsy, amputations, fractures, and burns) or by other serious or long-standing health problems that limit the child's strength, vitality, or alertness (e.g., muscular dystrophy, hemophilia).

Some children with physical and health impairments are extremely restricted in their activities and intellectual functioning; others have no major limitations on what they can do and learn. Some appear entirely normal; others have highly visible disabilities. Some children must use special devices or equipment that call attention to the disability; others display behaviors that are not under voluntary control. Some disabilities are always present; others occur only from time to time. Over an extended period, the degree of disability may increase, decrease, or remain about the same.

The special problems that children with physical and health impairments encounter in school also vary in kind and degree. Brian, who uses a wheelchair for mobility, is disappointed that he is unable to compete with his classmates in football, baseball, and track. Yet he participates fully in all other aspects of his high school program with no special modifications other than the addition of a few ramps in the building and a newly accessible washroom. Most of Brian's teachers and friends, in fact, do not think of him as needing special education at all. Janice becomes tired easily and attends school for only 3 hours per day. Kenneth uses a specially designed chair so that he can sit more comfortably in the classroom. Special modifications or alterations should not, however, be any more restrictive than necessary. A bright child who uses a wheelchair should not be removed from the regular school program and placed in a class where he or she can interact only with other students with mental retardation or other learning problems.

Some physical and health impairments may cause possible complications or emergencies to arise in the classroom; it is important for the teacher to know how to manage the situation effectively and when and how to seek help. Thus, general information and suggested guidelines shape our basic approach to the topic of children with physical and health impairments.

✳ *Defining Physical and Health Impairments*

Literally hundreds of physical and health impairments can affect children's educational performance. Here we address only those that are encountered most fre-

With a little help from a classmate, another musician joins the marching band.

quently in school-age children. Some conditions are *congenital,* meaning present at birth; other conditions are acquired during the child's development as a result of illness, accident, or unknown cause.

Orthopedic and Neurological Impairments

An **orthopedic impairment** involves the skeletal system—bones, joints, limbs, and associated muscles. A **neurological impairment** involves the nervous system, affecting the ability to move, use, feel, or control certain parts of the body. Orthopedic and neurological impairments are two distinct and separate types of disabilities, but they may cause similar limitations in movement. Many of the same educational, therapeutic, and recreational activities are likely to be appropriate for students with orthopedic and neurological impairments (Bigge, 1991; Shivers & Fait, 1985). And there is a close relationship between the two types: For example, a child who is unable to move his legs because of damage to the central nervous system (neurological impairment) may also develop disorders in the bones and muscles of the legs (orthopedic impairment), especially if he does not receive proper therapy and equipment.

Whatever their cause, orthopedic and neurological impairments are frequently described in terms of the affected parts of the body. The term *plegia* (from the Greek "to strike") is often used in combination to indicate the location of limb involvement:

> **Quadriplegia.** All four limbs (both arms and legs) are affected; movement of the trunk and face may also be impaired.
>
> **Paraplegia.** Motor impairment of the legs only.
>
> **Hemiplegia.** Only one side of the body is affected; for example, the left arm and the left leg may be impaired.
>
> **Diplegia.** Major involvement of the legs, with less severe involvement of the arms.

Less common forms of involvement include the following:

> **Monoplegia.** Only one limb is affected.
>
> **Triplegia.** Three limbs are affected.
>
> **Double hemiplegia.** Major involvement of the arms, with less severe involvement of the legs.

It is difficult to establish precise criteria for describing the degree or extent of motor involvement in orthopedic and neurological impairments. Children's difficulties in performing motor-related tasks may vary from time to time, depending on such factors as positioning, fatigue, and medication. The terms *mild, moderate,* and *severe* are often used to describe the functioning of children with a wide variety of physical and health impairments. The criteria in Table 10.1 provide guidelines for determining level of impairment, but the chart should not be interpreted too rigidly.

Cerebral Palsy

Cerebral palsy is one of the most prevalent physical impairments in children of school age. It is a long-term condition resulting from a lesion to the brain or an

TABLE 10.1

Guidelines for determining level of impairment

Severe Disability
1. Total dependence in meeting physical needs.
2. Poor head control.
3. Deformities, present or potential, that limit function or produce pain.
4. Perceptual and/or sensory-integrative deficits that prevent achievement of academic and age-appropriate motor skills.

Moderate Disability
1. Some independence in meeting physical needs.
2. Functional head control.
3. Deformities, present or potential, that limit independent function or produce pain.
4. Perceptual and/or sensory-integrative deficits that interfere with achievement of academic and age-appropriate motor skills.

Mild Disability
1. Independence in meeting physical needs.
2. Potential to improve quality of motor and/or perceptual skills with therapy intervention.
3. Potential for regression in quality of motor and perceptual skills without intervention.

Source: From *Occupational and Physical Therapy Services in School-Based Programs: Organizational Manual* (p. 24) by McKee et al., 1983, Houston, TX: Psychological Services Division, Harris County Department of Education. Adapted by permission.

abnormality of brain growth that causes a variety of disorders of movement and posture. Many diseases can affect the developing brain and lead to cerebral palsy (Batshaw & Perret, 1992). Cerebral palsy can be treated but not cured; the impairment usually does not get progressively worse as a child ages. Cerebral palsy is not fatal, not contagious, and in the great majority of cases, not inherited.

Children with cerebral palsy have disturbances of voluntary motor functions that may include paralysis, extreme weakness, lack of coordination, involuntary convulsions, and other motor disorders. They may have little or no control over their arms, legs, or speech, depending on the type and degree of impairment. They may also have impaired vision or hearing.

Intellectual impairments may accompany cerebral palsy. Nelson and Ellenberg (1986) found that 41% of the children with cerebral palsy in their study scored below 70 on a standardized IQ test. The probability of mental retardation appears greater when a convulsive disorder is also present (Smith, 1984). Other surveys have estimated that about one third of children with cerebral palsy have intelligence within or above the normal range (e.g., Verhaaren & Connor, 1981). Such estimates should be interpreted cautiously, however. As Levine (1986) points out, students with cerebral palsy often have motor and/or speech impairments that limit the appropriateness of standardized intelligence tests; thus, an IQ score should never serve as the sole descriptor of a child's actual or potential ability. It is also important to bear in mind that no clear relationship exists between the degree of motor impairment and the degree of intellectual impairment (if any) in children with cerebral palsy (or other physical disabilities). A student with only mild motor impairment may experience severe developmental delays, whereas a student with severe motor impairments may be intellectually gifted.

Convulsive disorders are described later in this chapter.

See the story by theoretical physicist Stephen W. Hawking later in this chapter.

The causes of cerebral palsy are varied and not clearly known. It has often been attributed to the occurrence of injuries, accidents, or illnesses that are *prenatal* (before birth), *perinatal* (at or near the time of birth), or *postnatal* (soon after birth). Recent improvements in obstetrical delivery and neonatal care, however, have not decreased the incidence of cerebral palsy, which has remained steady during the past 20 years or so at about 1.5 in every 1,000 live births (Kudrjavcev et al., 1983). An extensive study of children with cerebral palsy (Nelson & Ellenberg, 1986) found that the factors most likely to be associated with cerebral palsy were mental retardation of the mother, premature birth (gestational age of 32 weeks or less), low birth weight, and a delay of 5 minutes or more before the baby's first cry. The researchers concluded that cerebral palsy does not appear to be caused by a single factor and that complications of labor and delivery are not so important in causing cerebral palsy as was previously thought. Prevention of cerebral palsy, then, is likely to prove extremely difficult.

Types of Cerebral Palsy.   Cerebral palsy is divided into several categories according to muscle tone (hypertonia or hypotonia) and quality of motor involvement (athetosis or ataxia) (Blackburn, 1987; Gillham, 1986). Children may also be described as having mixed cerebral palsy, consisting of more than one of these types, particularly if their impairments are severe.

Approximately 60% of all individuals with cerebral palsy have **hypertonia** (commonly called *spasticity*), which is characterized by tense, contracted muscles. Their movements may be jerky, exaggerated, and poorly coordinated. They may be unable to grasp objects with their fingers. When they try to control their movements, they may become even more jerky. If they are able to walk, it may be with a scissors gait, standing on the toes with knees bent and pointed inward. Deformities of the spine, hip dislocation, and contractures of the hand, elbow, foot, and knee are common.

Most infants born with cerebral palsy have **hypotonia,** or weak, floppy muscles, particularly in the neck and trunk. When hypotonia persists throughout the child's first year without being replaced with spasticity or athetoid involvement, the condition is called *generalized hypotonia.* Hypotonic children typically have low levels of motor activity, are slow to make balancing responses, and may not walk until 30 months of age (Bleck, 1987). Severely hypotonic children must use external support to achieve and maintain an upright position.

Athetosis occurs in about 20% of all cases of cerebral palsy. Children with athetoid cerebral palsy make large, irregular, twisting movements they cannot control. When they are at rest or asleep, there is little or no abnormal motion. An effort to pick up a pencil, however, may result in wildly waving arms, facial grimaces, and extension of the tongue. These children may not be able to control the muscles of their lips, tongue, and throat and may drool. They may also seem to stumble and lurch awkwardly as they walk. At times their muscles may be tense and rigid; at other times, they may be loose and flaccid. Extreme difficulty in expressive oral language, mobility, and activities of daily living often accompanies this form of cerebral palsy.

Ataxia is noted as the primary type of involvement in only 1% of cases of cerebral palsy (Blackburn, 1987). Children with ataxic cerebral palsy have a poor sense of balance and hand use. They may appear to be dizzy while walking and may fall easily if not supported. Their movements tend to be jumpy and unsteady, with exaggerated motion patterns that often "overshoot" the intended objects. They seem to be constantly attempting to overcome the effect of gravity and stabilize their bodies.

The motor impairment of children with cerebral palsy often makes it frustrating, if not impossible, for them to play with toys. See "Adapting Toys for Children with Cerebral Palsy" later in this chapter.

Rigidity and **tremor** are additional but much less common types of cerebral palsy. Children with the rare rigidity type of cerebral palsy display extreme stiffness in the affected limbs; they may be fixed and immobile for long periods. Tremor cerebral palsy, also rare, is marked by rhythmic, uncontrollable movements; the tremors may actually increase when the children attempt to control their actions.

The more severe forms of cerebral palsy are often identified in the first few months of life, but in many other cases, cerebral palsy is not detected or diagnosed until later in childhood. Parents may be the first to notice that their child is having difficulty crawling, balancing, or standing. According to Bleck (1979), about 80% of children with cerebral palsy are capable of learning to walk although many need to use wheelchairs, braces, and other assistive devices, particularly for moving around outside the home.

Complications.   Infants and children with cerebral palsy may experience feeding problems. They may at first be unable to suck or swallow and may choke on food or regurgitate it. Such difficulties can be overcome with early physical therapy; the therapist can show parents how best to position the child and how to give the appropriate types and amounts of food. In this and various other areas, therapy and parent education should begin as early as possible. Muscle tension can sometimes be partially controlled by medications, braces, and special adaptive equipment. Orthopedic surgery may increase a child's range of motion or obviate such complications as hip dislocations and permanent muscle contractions.

Gillham (1986) describes cerebral palsy as the result of "not just a brain with a bit missing, but a reorganized brain, working to its own rules" (p. 64). Because cerebral palsy is such a complex condition, it is most effectively managed through the cooperative involvement of physicians, teachers, physical therapists, occupational therapists, communication specialists, counselors, and others who work directly with children and families. Regular exercise and careful positioning in school settings help the child with cerebral palsy move as fully and comfortably as possible and prevent or minimize progressive damage to muscles and limbs.

Spina Bifida

About 1 in 2,000 infants is born with **spina bifida,** a congenital defect in the vertebrae that enclose the spinal cord. As a result, a portion of the spinal cord and the nerves that normally control muscles and feeling in the lower part of the body fail to develop normally. Of the three types of spina bifida, the mildest form is **spina bifida occulta,** in which only a few vertebrae are malformed, usually in the low spine. The defect is often not visible externally. If the flexible casing (*meninges*) that surrounds the spinal cord bulges through an opening in the infant's back at birth, the condition is called **meningocele.** These two forms do not usually cause any loss of function for the child. However, in the most common form of spina bifida—**myelomeningocele**—the spinal lining, spinal cord, and nerve roots all protrude. The protruding spinal cord and nerves are usually tucked back into the spinal column shortly after birth. This is the most serious condition, carrying a high risk of paralysis and infection. In general, the higher the location of the lesion on the spine, the greater the effect on the body and its functioning (Pieper, 1983). The term *neural tube defect* is sometimes used to describe spina bifida and similar impairments.

About 80% to 90% of children born with spina bifida develop *hydrocephalus,* the accumulation of cerebrospinal fluid in tissues surrounding the brain (Mitchell,

Adapting Toys for Children with Cerebral Palsy

· ·

Spontaneous and independent use of commercially available toys is not possible for many children with cerebral palsy. The toys often require more coordination or strength than these youngsters have. Children with uncontrolled movements may push toys out of reach or knock them over. This inability to manipulate the environment is frustrating for both children and their teachers and parents.

Lack of play experience can have a devastating effect upon a child. Continuous inability to engage in physical activity and gain mastery over the environment may cause the child to lose motivation and become passive. Because playing is an integral part of intellectual, social, perceptual, and physical development, growth in these areas may be limited when the child cannot actively play.

Toys can be adapted to make them more accessible to children with physical disabilities. Five types of modifications are most effective in promoting active, independent use of play materials. Although most of the adaptations are simple, they can make the difference between success and failure for a child.

Stabilization

Stabilizing a toy enhances its function in two ways. First, stabilizing prevents the child's uncontrolled movements and difficulty directing the hand to desired locations from moving objects out of reach or knocking them over. Second, many children with cerebral palsy have difficulty performing tasks that require holding an object with one hand while manipulating it in some way with the other hand. Toys with a base can be clamped to a table. Masking tape is an inexpensive and effective way to secure many toys. Velcro is another excellent material for stabilizing toys, by placing the hook side of the Velcro on the toy and mounting the loop side on a clean surface. Suction cups can also stabilize a toy for a short time on a clean, non-wood surface.

Boundaries

Restricting the movement of toys such as cars or trains makes it easier for some children to use and retrieve them if pushed out of reach. Boundaries can be created in various ways depending upon how the object is to be moved. For example, push toys can be placed in the top of a cardboard box or on a tray with edges to create a restricted area. Pull toys can be placed on a track, and items that require a banging motion, such as a tambourine, can be held in a wood frame with springs.

Grasping Aids

Many children with cerebral palsy have difficulty grasping objects and are therefore unable to hold and feel things independently. The ability to hold objects can be facilitated in a variety of ways. A Velcro strap can be placed around the child's hand with Velcro also placed on the materials to be held, thus creating a bond between the hand and the object. A universal cuff can be used for holding sticklike objects such as crayons or pointers. Simply enlarging an item by wrapping foam or tape around it may make it easier to hold.

Manipulation Aids

Some toys require isolated finger movements, use of a pincer grasp, and controlled movements of the wrist, which are too difficult for a child with physical disabilities. Various adaptations can help compensate for deficits in these movements. Extending and widening pieces of the toy will make swiping and pushing easier. Flat extensions, knobs, or dowels can be used to increase the surface area. A crossbar or dowel, placed appropriately, can compensate for an inability to rotate the wrist.

Switches

Some children have such limited hand function that they can operate only toys that are activated by a

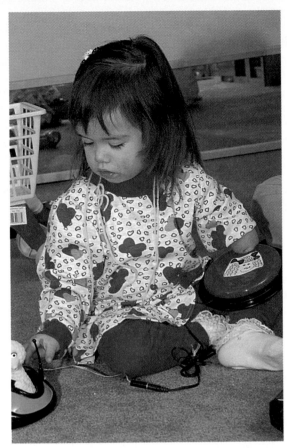

An adapted switch makes battery operated toys accessible and fun for Madelyn.

switch. Commercially available, battery-operated toys can be modified to operate by adapted switches. Teachers can make and adapt their own switches and toys (Burkhardt, 1981; Wright & Momari, 1985) or purchase them from a number of firms that serve persons with disabilities. After determining some physical action—such as moving a knee laterally, lifting a shoulder, or making a sound—that the child can perform consistently and with minimum effort, one selects the type of switch best suited to that movement. The switch is always positioned in the same place, which facilitates automatic switch activation and allows the child to give full attention to the play activity rather than concentrating on using the switch.

General Considerations

Positioning should be considered when children with cerebral palsy play with toys. Good positioning will maximize freedom of movement, improve the ability to look at a toy, and facilitate controlled, relaxed movement. An occupational or physical therapist should determine the special positioning needs of each child. Placement of the toy is crucial. It should be within easy reach and require a minimum of effort to manipulate. The child should not become easily fatigued or have to struggle. The child must be able to look at the toy while playing. Activities should be interesting and facilitate cognitive growth yet not be beyond the child's conceptual capabilities. Toys should be sturdy and durable. Avoid toys with sharp edges or small pieces that can be swallowed.

These principles for adapting toys can be applied to other devices, such as communication aids, computers, environmental controls, and household items, to make them easier to use. Making an educational environment more accessible gives children with physical disabilities greater control of their surroundings and the opportunity to expand the scope of their learning experiences.

From "Making Toys Accessible for Children with Cerebral Palsy" by Carol Schaeffler, Spring 1988, *Teaching Exceptional Children, 20,* pp. 26–28. Used by permission.

1983). Left untreated, this condition can lead to head enlargement and severe brain damage. Hydrocephalus is treated by the surgical insertion of a **shunt,** a one-way valve that diverts the cerebrospinal fluid away from the brain and into the bloodstream. Replacements of the shunt are usually necessary as a child grows older. Teachers who work with children who have shunts should be aware that blockage, disconnection, or infection of the shunt may result in increased intracranial pressure. Warning signs such as drowsiness, vomiting, headache, irritability, and squinting should be heeded because a blocked shunt can be life-threatening (Charney, 1992). Shunts have become safer and more reliable in recent years and can be removed in many school-age children when the production and absorption of cerebrospinal fluid are brought into balance (Gillham, 1986).

Usually children with spina bifida have some degree of paralysis of the lower limbs and lack full control of bladder and bowel functions. In most cases, these children have good use of their arms and upper body (although some children experience fine-motor problems). Children with spina bifida usually walk with braces, crutches, or walkers; they may use wheelchairs for longer distances. Some children need special help in dressing and toileting; others are able to manage these tasks on their own. Most children with spina bifida need to use a **catheter** (tube) or bag to collect their urine. **Clean intermittent catheterization** (CIC) is taught to children with urinary complications so that they can empty their bladders at convenient times (Tarnowski & Drabman, 1987). According to Pieper (1983), this technique is effective with both boys and girls, works best if used every 3 to 4 hours, and does not require an absolutely sterile environment.

Muscular Dystrophy

Muscular dystrophy refers to a group of long-term diseases that progressively weaken and waste away the body's muscles. The most common form is *Duchenne muscular dystrophy,* which affects boys (1 in 3,500) much more frequently than girls. The child appears normal at birth, but muscle weakness is usually evident between the ages of 2 and 6, when the child begins to experience difficulty in running or climbing stairs. The child may walk with an unusual gait, showing a protruding stomach and hollow back. The calf muscles of a child with muscular dystrophy may appear unusually large because the degenerated muscle has been replaced by fatty tissue.

Children with muscular dystrophy often have difficulty getting to their feet after lying down or playing on the floor. They may fall easily. By age 10 to 14, the child loses the ability to walk; the small muscles of the hands and fingers are usually the last to be affected. Some doctors and therapists recommend the early use of electrically powered wheelchairs; others suggest employing special braces and other devices to prolong walking as long as possible.

Unfortunately, there is no known cure for most cases of muscular dystrophy, and the disease is often fatal. A good deal of independence can be maintained, however, by regular physical therapy, exercise, and the use of appropriate aids and appliances. In school a teacher should be careful not to lift a child with muscular dystrophy by the arms: Even a gentle pull may dislocate the child's limbs. The teacher may also need to help the child deal with the gradual loss of physical abilities and the possibility of death.

Osteogenesis Imperfecta

Osteogenesis imperfecta is a rare (1 in 20,000 births) inherited condition marked by extremely brittle bones. The skeletal system does not grow normally, and the bones are easily fractured. Children with osteogenesis imperfecta are fragile and must be protected. Wheelchairs are usually necessary, although the children may be able to walk for short distances with the aid of braces, crutches, and protective equipment. Like other children with orthopedic impairments, the child with osteogenesis imperfecta may have frequent hospitalizations for treatment and surgery. Some children, understandably, are reluctant to be touched or handled. Usually chil-

See "Using Dolls to Teach Self-catheterization Skills to Children with Spina Bifida" later in this chapter.

Telethons and other fund-raising activities on behalf of persons with disabilities have become controversial in recent years. Some self-advocacy groups and professionals believe they perpetuate negative stereotypes and portray people with disabilities as objects of pity (see the November 1993 issue of the *TASH Newsletter*).

dren with osteogenesis imperfecta have adequate use of their hands and can participate in most classroom activities if they receive appropriate physical support and protection. As the children mature, their bones may become less brittle, and they may require less attention.

Spinal Cord Injuries

Spinal cord injuries usually stem from accidents. Injury to the spinal column is generally described by letters and numbers indicating the site of the damage; for example, a C5-6 injury means the damage has occurred at the level of the fifth and sixth cervical vertebrae, a flexible area of the neck susceptible to injury from whiplash and diving or trampoline accidents. A T12 injury refers to the twelfth thoracic (chest) vertebra, and an L3 to the third lumbar (lower back) area. In general, paralysis and loss of sensation occur below the level of the injury. The higher the injury on the spine and the more the injury (lesion) cuts through the entire cord, the greater the paralysis (Gilgoff, 1983). Automobile accidents and falls are the most frequent causes of spinal cord injury to children.

Students who have sustained spinal cord injuries usually use wheelchairs for mobility. Motorized wheelchairs, though expensive, are recommended for those with quadriplegia, whereas children with paraplegia can use self-propelled wheelchairs. Children with quadriplegia may have severe breathing problems because the muscles of the chest, which normally govern respiration, are affected. In most cases, children with spinal cord injuries lack bladder and bowel control and need to follow a careful management program to maintain personal hygiene and avoid infection and skin irritation.

Rehabilitation programs for children and adolescents who have sustained spinal cord injuries usually involve physical therapy, the use of adaptive devices for mobility and independent living, and psychological support to help them adjust to a sudden disability. With supportive teachers and peers, students with paralysis can participate fully in school programs. Adolescents and adults are often particularly concerned about sexual function. Even though most spinal cord injuries do affect sexuality, with understanding partners and positive attitudes toward themselves, many individuals with spinal cord injuries are able to enjoy satisfying sexual relationships. Some counselors now specialize in addressing the sexual concerns of people with paralysis due to physical disabilities, spinal cord injury, or other conditions.

Maria Serrao, who has paraplegia and has used a wheelchair since age 5, has created a fitness video oriented to people with disabilities (*Everyone Can Exercise!* by Brentwood Home Video). A photo of Ms. Serrao can be found in Chapter 15.

Traumatic Brain Injury

Injuries to the head are common in children and adolescents. It is predicted that each year 1 in 500 school-age children will be hospitalized with traumatic head injuries (Kraus, Fife, & Conroy, 1987). Significant causes of head trauma include automobile, motorcycle, and bicycle accidents; falls; assaults; gunshot wounds; and child abuse. Severe head trauma often results in a *coma,* an abnormal deep stupor from which it may be impossible to arouse the affected individual by external stimuli for an extended period (Michaud & Duhaine, 1992). Temporary or lasting symptoms may include cognitive and language deficits, memory loss, seizures, and perceptual disorders. Victims may display inappropriate or exaggerated behaviors ranging from extreme aggressiveness to apathy. Children may also have difficulty paying attention and retaining new information. The educational and lifelong needs of students with head injuries are likely to require comprehensive programs of academic, psychologi-

Each year about 65,000 children and adults are treated in hospital emergency rooms for head injuries as a result of bicycle accidents. Most of those injuries would be avoided if riders wore an approved safety helmet (Raskin, 1990). If you know anyone who rides a bicycle, do not let him or her ride without a helmet.

cal, and family support (Savage & Wolcott, 1994). Although few educational programs have been specifically designed for this population, educators have recognized that many of these children need special education services.

When it was originally passed, the IDEA did not specifically mention the needs of children who have experienced head trauma and/or coma; however, when the law was amended in 1990 (PL 101–476), traumatic brain injury was added as a new disability category. Because many children with head injury have other ongoing health problems such as paralysis, chronic fatigue, headaches, and seizures, they are often served under the category "Other Health Impaired." Although research on the educational effects of head trauma is limited, we do know that many children who have suffered serious head injury experience subsequent problems in learning, behavior, and adjustment (Gerring & Carney, 1992).

Students with head injuries reenter school with deficits from their injuries compounded by an extended absence from school. Ylvisaker (1986) recommends that the child with a head injury return to school when he or she is physically capable, can respond to instructions, and can sustain attention for 10 to 15 minutes. Tyler and Mira (1993) suggest a number of modifications that school programs can make to assist the student with a head injury during the reentry period:

For more information about students with head injuries and recommendations for successful school reentry, see Bigler (1990), Steensma (1992), and Tucker and Colson (1992).

- A shortened school day, concentrating academic instruction during peak performance periods, frequent breaks, and a reduced class load may be necessitated by the chronic fatigue that some students with head injury experience for a year or more.
- A special resource period at the beginning and end of each school day when a teacher, counselor, or aide helps the student plan or review the day's schedule, keep track of assignments, and monitor progress may be required because of problems with loss of memory and organization.
- Modifications such as an extra set of textbooks at home, a peer to help the student move efficiently from class to class, and early dismissal from class to allow time to get to the next room can help the student who has difficulties with mobility, balance, or coordination (adaptive physical education is often indicated).
- Behavior management and/or counseling interventions may be needed to help with problems such as poor judgment, impulsiveness, overactivity, aggression, destructiveness, and socially uninhibited behavior often experienced by students with head injury.
- Modifications of instruction and testing procedures such as tape-recording lectures, assigning a note taker, and allowing extra time to take tests may be needed.
- IEP goals and objectives may need to be reviewed and modified as often as every 30 days because of the dramatic changes in behavior and performance by some children during the early stages of recovery.

Limb Deficiency

Limb deficiency is the absence or partial loss of an arm or leg. Congenital limb deficiency is rare, occurring in about 1 in every 20,000 births. Acquired limb deficiency (amputations) may be the result of surgery or accident. A **prosthesis** (artificial limb) is often used to facilitate balance, enable the child to participate in a variety of tasks, and create a more normal appearance. Some students or their parents, however, prefer not to use artificial limbs. Most children become quite proficient at using their remaining limbs. Some children who are missing both arms, for example, learn to write, eat, and perform vocational tasks with their feet. They have a much greater feeling of being in contact with objects and people than they would if they used prosthetic limbs. Unless children have other impairments in addition to the absence of limbs, they should be able to function in a regular classroom without major modifications.

Chronic Illness and Other Health-Related Conditions

Many conditions can affect a child's health, whether permanently, temporarily, or intermittently. In general, the conditions we discuss in this section are *chronic;* that is, they are present over long periods and tend not to get better or disappear. Children with chronic illnesses are not usually confined to beds or hospitals except during occasional flare-ups of their diseases, but "even with good control and years of remission, the threat of a recurrent crisis is ever present" (Kleinberg, 1982, p. 5).

The usual and proper course of action for children and families affected by chronic health-related conditions is to seek medical treatment. In many instances, however, an illness or health impairment can significantly affect school performance and social acceptance; consequently, it is important for a teacher to be aware of it. Although chronic illnesses and other health-related conditions are generally less visible than orthopedic and neurological impairments, their effects on a child may be just as great.

An *acute* illness, in contrast, is severe but of limited duration.

Convulsive Disorders (Epilepsy)

Theoretically, anyone can have a *seizure,* a disturbance of movement, sensation, behavior, and/or consciousness caused by abnormal electrical activity in the brain. It

This special educator does not allow Jamika's chronic illness to prevent her from participating in developmentally appropriate play activities.

is not uncommon for seizures to occur if someone has a high fever, drinks excessive alcohol, or experiences a blow to the head. When seizures occur chronically and repeatedly, however, the condition is known as a **convulsive disorder** or, more commonly, **epilepsy.** With proper medical treatment and the support of parents, teachers, and peers, most students with convulsive disorders lead full and normal lives. Epilepsy itself constitutes a disorder only while a seizure is actually in progress. Most students with epilepsy have normal intelligence.

Epileptic seizures may be largely or wholly controlled by anticonvulsant medications. Some children require such heavy doses of medication that their learning and behavior are adversely affected, and some medications have undesirable side effects, such as drowsiness, nausea, weight gain, and thickening of the gums.

The specific causes of epilepsy are not clearly known. It is believed that people become seizure-prone when a particular area of the brain becomes electrically unstable. This condition may result from an underlying lesion caused by scar tissue from a head injury, a tumor, or an interruption in blood supply to the brain (Gillham, 1986). In many cases, the origin of seizure activity cannot be traced to a particular incident. A convulsive disorder can occur at any stage of life but most frequently begins in childhood. A wide variety of psychological, physical, and sensory factors are thought to trigger seizures in susceptible persons—for example, fatigue, excitement, anger, surprise, hyperventilation, hormonal changes (as in menstruation or pregnancy), withdrawal from drugs or alcohol, and exposure to certain patterns of light, sound, or touch.

During a seizure, a dysfunction in the electrochemical activity of the brain causes a person to lose control of the muscles temporarily. Between seizures (that is, most of the time), the brain functions normally. Many unfortunate misconceptions about epilepsy have circulated in the past and are still prevalent even today. Negative public attitudes, in fact, have probably been more harmful to people with epilepsy than has the condition itself.

Teachers, school health care personnel, and perhaps classmates need to be aware that a child is affected by a convulsive disorder so that they can be prepared to deal with a seizure if one should occur in school. There are several types of seizures, three of which are relatively common. The **generalized tonic-clonic seizure** (formerly called *grand mal*) is the most conspicuous and serious type of convulsive seizure. A generalized tonic-clonic seizure can be disturbing and frightening to someone who has never seen one. The affected child has little or no warning that a seizure is about to occur; the muscles become stiff, and the child loses consciousness and falls to the floor. Then the entire body shakes violently as the muscles alternately contract and relax. Saliva may be forced from the mouth; legs and arms may jerk; and the bladder and bowels may be emptied. After about 2 to 5 minutes, the contractions diminish, and the child either goes to sleep or regains consciousness in a confused or drowsy state. Generalized tonic-clonic seizures may occur as often as several times a day or as seldom as once a year. They are more likely to occur during the day than at night. (See Figure 10.1 for procedures for handling seizures in the classroom.)

The **absence seizure** (previously called *petit mal*) is far less severe than the generalized tonic-clonic seizure but may occur much more frequently—as often as 100 times per day in some children. Usually there is a brief loss of consciousness, lasting anywhere from a few seconds to half a minute or so. The child may stare blankly, flutter or blink his eyes, grow pale, or drop whatever he is holding. He may

FIGURE 10.1

Procedures for handling generalized tonic-clonic seizures

The typical seizure is not a medical emergency, but knowledgeable handling of the situation is important. When a child experiences a generalized tonic-clonic seizure in the classroom, the teacher should follow these procedures:

- Keep calm. Reassure the other students that the child will be fine in a minute.

- Ease the child to the floor and clear the area around him of anything that could hurt him.

- Put something flat and soft (like a folded coat) under his head so it will not bang on the floor as his body jerks.

- You cannot stop the seizure. Let it run its course. Do not try to revive the child and do not interfere with his movements.

- Turn him gently onto his side. This keeps his airway clear and allows saliva to drain away.

  DON'T try to force his mouth open.

  DON'T try to hold on to his tongue.

  DON'T put anything in his mouth.

- When the jerking movements stop, let the child rest until he regains consciousness.

- Breathing may be shallow during the seizure, and may even stop briefly. In the unlikely event that breathing does not begin again, check the child's airway for obstruction and give artificial respiration.

Some students recover quickly after this type of seizure; others need more time. A short period of rest is usually advised. If the student is able to remain in the classroom afterwards, however, he should be encouraged to do so. Staying in the classroom (or returning to it as soon as possible) allows for continued participation in classroom activity and is psychologically less difficult for the student. If a student has frequent seizures, handling them can become routine once teacher and classmates learn what to expect. If a seizure of this type continues for longer than five minutes, call for emergency assistance.

Source: From *Epilepsy School Alert* by The Epilepsy Foundation of America, 1987, Washington, DC: Author.

be mistakenly viewed as daydreaming or not listening. The child may or may not be aware that he has had a seizure, and no special first aid is necessary. The teacher should keep the child's parents advised of seizure activity and may also find it helpful to explain it to the child's classmates.

A **complex partial seizure** (also called *psychomotor seizure*) may appear as a brief period of inappropriate or purposeless activity. The child may smack her lips, walk around aimlessly, or shout. She may appear to be conscious but is not actually aware of her unusual behavior. Complex partial seizures usually last from 2 to 5 minutes, after which the child has amnesia about the entire episode. Some children may respond to spoken directions during a complex partial seizure.

A **simple partial seizure** is characterized by sudden jerking motions with no loss of consciousness. Partial seizures may occur weekly, monthly, or only once or twice a year. The teacher should keep dangerous objects out of the child's way and, except in emergencies, should not try to physically restrain him or her.

Many children experience a warning sensation, known as an *aura,* a short time before a seizure. The aura takes different forms in different people; distinctive feelings, sights, sounds, tastes, and even smells have been described. The aura can be a useful safety valve enabling the child to leave the class or group before the seizure actually occurs. Some children report that the warning provided by the aura helps them feel more secure and comfortable about themselves.

In some children, absence and partial seizures can go undetected for long periods. An observant teacher can be instrumental in detecting the presence of a seizure disorder and in referring the child for appropriate medical help. The teacher can also assist parents and physicians by noting both the effectiveness and the side effects of any medication the child takes. Today, the majority of children with convulsive disorders can be helped with medication. Drugs can sharply reduce or even eliminate seizures in many cases. All children with convulsive disorders benefit from a realistic understanding of their condition and accepting attitudes on the part of teachers and classmates.

Diabetes

Juvenile diabetes mellitus is a disorder of metabolism; that is, it affects the way the body absorbs and breaks down the sugars and starches in foods. Diabetes is a common childhood disease, affecting about 1 in 600 school-age children, so it is likely that most teachers will encounter students with diabetes at one time or another (Winter, 1983). Without proper medical management, the diabetic child's system is not able to obtain and retain adequate energy from food. Not only does the child lack energy, but many important parts of the body—particularly the eyes and the kidneys—can be affected by untreated diabetes. Early symptoms of diabetes include thirst, headaches, weight loss (despite a good appetite), frequent urination, and cuts that are slow to heal.

Children with diabetes have insufficient insulin, a hormone normally produced by the pancreas necessary for proper metabolism and digestion of foods. To regulate the condition, insulin must be injected daily under the skin. Most children with diabetes learn to inject their own insulin—in some cases as frequently as four times per day—and to determine the amount of insulin they need by testing the level of sugar and other substances in their urine. Children with diabetes must follow a specific and regular diet prescribed by a physician or nutrition specialist. A regular exercise program is also usually suggested.

Teachers should be aware of the symptoms of insulin reaction, also called *diabetic shock.* It can result from taking too much insulin, unusually strenuous exercise, or a missed or delayed meal (the blood sugar level is lowered by insulin and exercise and raised by food). Symptoms of insulin reaction include faintness, dizziness, blurred vision, drowsiness, and nausea. The child may appear irritable or have a marked personality change. In most cases, giving the child some form of concentrated sugar (e.g., a sugar cube, a glass of fruit juice, a candy bar) ends the insulin reaction within a few minutes. The child's doctor or parents should inform the teacher and school health personnel of the appropriate foods to give in case of insulin reaction.

A *diabetic coma* is more serious. A coma indicates that too little insulin is present; that is, the diabetes is not under control. Its onset is gradual rather than sudden. The symptoms of diabetic coma include fatigue; thirst; dry, hot skin; deep, labored breathing; excessive urination; and fruity-smelling breath. A doctor or nurse should be contacted immediately if a child displays such symptoms.

A form that teachers can use to monitor and record seizures is shown in Figure 10.2. For more information about record keeping and what to observe before, during, and after a seizure, see Michael (1992).

Diabetic retinopathy is a leading cause of blindness in adults.

FIGURE 10.2

A sample seizure documentation recording form

SEIZURE MONITORING FORM

Name: _____   **Date:** _____

Seizure medication: _____   **Time of last administration:** _____

Careful observation and documentation will allow you to describe three possible components of the seizure: 1) antecedent events—activities preceding the seizure; 2) seizure activity—motoric behavior during the seizure; and 3) post-ictal state—behavior following the seizure. For each of the following descriptors, note the occurrence/nonoccurrence and indicate by numbering if there was a sequence evident.

Antecedent Events

Classroom activity preceding seizure: _____

Change in student's behavior: _____

Time of onset: _____

Seizure Activity

face _____   R arm _____   L arm _____

trunk _____   R leg _____   L leg _____

Motor tone: limp _____   rigid _____   alternating limb movements _____

Position of eyes: rolled back _____   turned to R _____   turned L _____

Breathing: beginning of seizure: normal _____   interrupted _____

                        middle of seizure: normal _____   interrupted _____

                        end of seizure: normal _____   interrupted _____

Skin color: pale _____   blue _____   red _____   other _____

Incontinence: bladder _____   bowel _____

Post-Ictal Activity

Time seizure ended: _____

Duration of seizure: _____

Behavior immediately following seizure: _____   drowsy _____   asleep _____

awake inactive _____   awake active _____

crying/agitated _____

Source: From "Special Health Care Procedures" by M. M. Ault, J. C. Graff, and J. P. Rues. Reprinted with the permission of Simon & Schuster, Inc. from the Merrill/Prentice Hall text *Instruction of Students with Severe Disabilities* by Martha E. Snell. Copyright 1993 by Merrill/Prentice Hall.

Asthma

Asthma is a chronic lung disease characterized by episodic bouts of wheezing, coughing, and difficulty breathing. "Asthma is a complex disease in which inflammation of the airways is both the cause and effect of the problem" (Kraemer & Bierman,

1983, p. 160). An asthmatic attack is usually triggered by allergens (e.g., pollen, certain foods, pets), irritants (e.g., cigarette smoke, smog), exercise, or emotional stress, which results in a narrowing of the airways in the lungs. This reaction increases the resistance to the airflow in and out of the lungs, making it harder for the individual to breathe. The severity of asthma varies greatly: The child may experience only a period of mild coughing or extreme difficulty in breathing that requires emergency treatment. Many asthmatic children experience normal lung functioning between episodes.

Asthma is the most common lung disease of children; estimates of its prevalence range from 3% to as high as 10% of school-age children (Aaronson & Rosenberg, 1985; Kraemer & Bierman, 1983). More boys than girls are affected. The causes of asthma are not completely known. Symptoms generally begin in early childhood but sometimes do not develop until late childhood or adolescence. Asthma tends to run in families, which suggests that an allergic intolerance to some stimulus may be inherited. Symptoms of asthma might also first appear following a viral infection of the respiratory system.

Primary treatment for asthma begins with a systematic effort to identify the stimuli and environmental situations that provoke attacks. The number of potential allergens and irritants is virtually limitless, and in some cases it can be extremely difficult to determine the combination of factors that results in an asthmatic episode. Changes in temperature, humidity, and season (attacks are especially common in autumn) are also related to the frequency of asthmatic symptoms. Rigorous physical exercise produces asthmatic episodes in some children. Asthma can be controlled effectively in most children with a combination of medications and limiting exposure to known allergens. Most children whose breathing attacks are induced by physical exercise can still enjoy physical exercise and sports through careful selection of activities (e.g., swimming generally provokes less exercise-induced asthma than running) and/or taking certain medications prior to rigorous exercise.

A clear interrelationship also exists between emotional stress and asthma. Periods of psychological stress increase the likelihood of asthmatic attacks, and asthmatic episodes produce more stress. Treatment often involves counseling or an asthma teaching program (Kraemer & Bierman, 1983), in which children and their families are taught ways to reduce and cope with emotional stress.

Asthma is one of the most frequently cited reasons for missing school. Chronic absenteeism makes it difficult for the child with asthma to maintain performance at grade level, and homebound instructional services may be necessary. The majority of children with asthma who receive medical and psychological support, however, successfully complete school and lead normal lives. By working cooperatively with parents and medical personnel to minimize the child's contact with provoking factors, the classroom teacher can play an important role in reducing the impact of asthma.

Cystic Fibrosis

Cystic fibrosis is a genetically transmitted disease of children and adolescents. The body's exocrine glands excrete a thick mucus that can block the lungs and parts of the digestive system. Children with cystic fibrosis often have difficulty breathing and are susceptible to pulmonary disease (lung infections). Malnutrition and poor growth are common characteristics of children with cystic fibrosis because of pancreatic insufficiency that causes inadequate digestion and malabsorption of nutrients, especially fats. They often have large and frequent bowel movements because food passes through the system only partially digested. A study found that 40% of children with cystic fibrosis were below the 5th percentile weight for their age (Cystic Fibrosis Foundation, 1992). With current treatment, the average life expectancy of individuals with cystic fibrosis is 29 years (Cystic Fibrosis Foundation, 1992).

Medications prescribed for children with cystic fibrosis include enzymes to facilitate digestion and solutions to thin and loosen the mucus in the lungs. During vigorous physical exercises, some children may need help from teachers, aides, or classmates to clear their lungs and air passages.

Cystic fibrosis is a hereditary disease that affects 1 in 2,500 live Caucasian births. Medical research has not determined exactly how cystic fibrosis functions. The symptoms may result from a missing chemical or substance in the body, but no reliable cure for cystic fibrosis has yet been found. Nonetheless, many children and young adults with this condition are able to lead active lives. With continued research and treatment techniques, the long-range outlook for children affected by cystic fibrosis is improving.

Hemophilia

Hemophilia is a rare hereditary disorder in which the blood does not clot as quickly as it should. The most serious consequences are usually internal, rather than external, bleeding; contrary to popular opinion, minor cuts and scrapes do not usually pose a serious problem. Internal bleeding, however, can cause swelling, pain, and permanent damage to joints, tissues, and internal organs and may necessitate hospitalization for blood transfusions. It is thought that emotional stress may intensify episodes of bleeding (Verhaaren & Connor, 1981). A student with hemophilia may need to be excused from some physical activities and may use a wheelchair during periods of susceptibility. As with most children who have health-related impairments, however, good physical condition is important for development and well-being, so the restrictions on activities should not be any greater than necessary.

Burns

Burns are a leading type of injury in childhood. Most often, burns result from household accidents, but sometimes they are caused by child abuse. As Yurt and Pruitt (1983) point out, the skin is the largest organ of the human body and one of the most important; serious burns can cause complications in other organs, long-term physical limitations, and psychological difficulties. Children with serious burn injuries usually experience pain, scarring, limitations of motion, lengthy hospitalizations, and repeated surgery. Some children with severe burns on their faces and other areas wear sterilized elastic masks to protect and soften the skin.

The disfigurement caused by severe burns can affect a child's behavior and self-image, especially if teachers and peers react negatively. When a child is returning to class after prolonged absence resulting from an extensive burn injury, it may be advisable for the teacher, parents, or other involved person (e.g., a social worker, physical therapist) to explain to classmates the nature of the child's injury and appearance (Yurt & Pruitt, 1983).

Acquired Immune Deficiency Syndrome (AIDS)

Persons with **acquired immune deficiency syndrome (AIDS)** are not able to resist and fight off infections because of a breakdown in the immune system. In 1983

Getting children with cystic fibrosis to consume enough calories is critical to their health and development. Stark et al. (1993) used a behaviorally based treatment intervention that included nutrition education, rewards for meeting gradually increasing calorie goals, and relaxation training to successfully increase calorie consumption and growth rates of three children with cystic fibrosis. Increased calorie consumption was maintained at a 2-year follow-up.

The most up-to-date data and recommendations for prevention and treatment can be obtained from the National AIDS Information Clearinghouse (1-800-458-5231).

Students receiving special education services may be more prone to contracting the HIV because of a lack of knowledge about the disease. For recommendations on developing and implementing an HIV/AIDS prevention and education curriculum for students with disabilities, see Colson and Carlson (1993), Kelker, Hecimovic, & LeRoy (1994), and Lerro (1994).

the virus that causes AIDS was isolated and given the name **human immunodeficiency virus (HIV).** AIDS is contracted when the HIV is passed from a carrier (not all persons who have the HIV get AIDS) to another person through sexual contact or through the blood (via intravenous drug use with shared needles, transfusions of unscreened contaminated blood). Pregnant women can transmit the HIV to their unborn children. There is no known cure or vaccine for the disease, which is fatal. It is estimated that between 1 and 1.5 million people in the United States are infected with the HIV. The incidence rate for AIDS has increased alarmingly, and projections of the number of people who may contract the disease and die are staggering.

Although only a small number of young children diagnosed with AIDS have survived to school age, the continuing development of drug treatments to counter or slow the progression of the disease means it is likely that increasing numbers of children with HIV infection and AIDS will be in the classroom. Children with HIV infection and AIDS are afforded legal protection and the right to a public education under Section 504 of the Rehabilitation Act of 1973, which states that "no otherwise qualified individual with handicaps . . . shall solely by reason of his handicap be excluded from the participation in, be denied the benefits of, or be subjected to discrimination under any program or activity receiving Federal financial assistance."

A 1990 memorandum from the Office of Civil Rights clarified that a child with AIDS "generally will be considered 'handicapped' under Section 504 due to the substantial limitation on a major life activity caused by either physical impairment or the reaction of others to the perceived disease."

Significant neurological complications and developmental delays have been noted in children with AIDS (Barnes, 1986; Epstein, Sharer, & Goudsmit, 1988), but we do not yet know what the special education needs of these children might encompass. On the basis of current knowledge about AIDS, Byers (1989) suggests the following implications and recommendations:

1. We certainly must continue with an AIDS curriculum in grades K–12 in an effort to prevent the disease from further infiltrating the pre-adolescent and adolescent populations.
2. Children harboring the virus cannot legally be excluded from schools unless they are deemed a direct health risk for other children (e.g., exhibit biting behavior, open sores). Consequently, chronic illness specialists, school psychologists, counselors, and teachers will need to make AIDS a priority issue, and be active in facilitating school/peer acceptance and the social adjustment of a child with AIDS.
3. Teachers, counselors, and other specialists will also need to be prepared to provide family therapy and broad-based support groups for parents and/or children within the school setting.
4. Pediatric AIDS patients present a particular challenge for special education professionals, due to the erratic course of neurological deterioration. The child may be stable for a number of months and then deteriorate rapidly over a period of weeks (Epstein et al., 1988), and thus require regular monitoring of his or her educational needs.
5. Specific educational treatments for children infected with HIV await further research, and this appears to be the ultimate challenge for special educators. (p. 13)[1]

---

[1]From "AIDS in Children: Effects on neurological development and implications for the future," by J. Byers, 1989, *The Journal of Special Education, 23*(1), 5–16. Copyright (c) 1989 by PRO-ED, Inc. Reprinted by permission.

Other Health Problems and Related Concerns

Of course, many other significant physical and health-related conditions can influence a child's learning and behavior at school. Heart disease, cancer, and juvenile rheumatoid arthritis are conditions that generally do not require special teaching techniques or adaptive equipment. Yet they may cause variations in a child's performance as a direct result of not only the condition itself but also the child's frequent absences from school and the effects of medication, fatigue, and pain.

Children with a physical or health impairment may be afraid of going to the hospital and being separated from their parents. They may look and feel different from their classmates. An older student may resent medication, therapy, prohibitions on activities, and other restrictions that limit independence and may worry about an uncertain future. The family of a child with a physical or health impairment often encounters many demands on time and energy, as well as financial problems from long-term medical care and equipment costs, which are often not covered by insurance. A teacher's concern and familiarity with a student's physical or health impairment can do much to improve the quality of the child's school experience.

Important Variables to Consider

In assessing the effects of a physical or health impairment on a child's development and behavior, many factors should be taken into consideration. Important among these are the severity and visibility of the impairment and the age at which the disabling condition was first acquired.

Severity

Most children learn by exploring their surroundings, interacting with other people, and having a wide variety of experiences in their homes, neighborhoods, schools, and communities. A minor or transient physical or health impairment, such as those most children experience while growing up, is not likely to have lasting effects; but a severe, long-standing impairment can greatly limit a child's range of experiences. Many such disabling conditions seriously restrict a child's mobility and independence, much as a severe visual or hearing impairment would. The child may not be able to travel alone at all and may have few opportunities to explore the environment by seeing, hearing, touching, smelling, or tasting things. Some children may spend most of the time at home or in a hospital. Some are in virtually constant pain or become tired after any sort of physical exertion. Some take medications that decrease their alertness and responsiveness. Some may be physically fragile and afraid of injury or death.

Visibility

Some physical impairments are highly visible and conspicuous. How children think about themselves and the degree to which they are accepted by others often are affected by the visibility of a condition. Some children need to rely on a variety of special orthopedic appliances, such as wheelchairs, braces, crutches, and adaptive tables. They may ride to school on a specially equipped bus or van. In school they may need assistance using the toilet or may wear helmets. Although such special devices and adaptations do help children meet important needs, they often have the

The severity, visibility, and age of acquisition of a physical or health impairment all affect an individual's adaptation and development.

unfortunate side effect of making the physical impairment more visible, thus making the child look even more different from nondisabled peers. Many people with disabilities report that their hardware (wheelchairs, artificial limbs, communication devices, and other apparatus) creates a great deal of curiosity and leads to frequent, repetitive questions from strangers. For many children, learning to explain their disabilities and respond to questions can be an appropriate component of their educational programs. They may also benefit from discussing such concerns as when to ask for help from others and when to decline offers of assistance.

Age at Acquisition

As with virtually all disabilities, it is important for the teacher to be aware of the child's age at the time he or she acquired the physical or health impairment. A child who has not had the use of his or her legs since birth may have missed out on some important developmental experiences, particularly if early intervention services were not provided. In contrast, a teenager who suddenly loses the use of his or her legs in an accident has likely had a normal range of experiences throughout childhood but may need considerable support from parents, teachers, specialists, and peers in making a successful adaptation to life with this newly acquired disability.

✺ Prevalence

Because there are numerous different physical and health impairments and no universally accepted definition of this population, it is difficult to obtain accurate and meaningful prevalence statistics. Physical and health impairments often occur in combination with other disabilities, so children may be counted under other categories, such as learning disabilities, speech impairment, or mental retardation. For special education placement purposes, a diagnosis of mental retardation usually takes precedence over a diagnosis of physical impairment. Also, because of improved medical and surgical treatment or the results of successful early intervention programs (Grove, 1982), many of the approximately 250,000 children born each year with significant birth defects are not considered disabled in terms of needing special education services by the time they reach school age.

During the 1992–93 school year, 46,498 children with orthopedic impairments and 63,982 children with other health impairments between the ages of 6 and 21 were served in special education programs (U.S. Department of Education, 1994). Together, these categories represent about 2.4% of all children receiving special education services; however, as noted earlier, the number of children with physical and health impairments included under other special education categories is not known but is probably sizable.

The children most frequently placed in special education programs for physical, orthopedic, or health impairments are those with cerebral palsy. In some programs, half or more of the students considered to have physical or health impairments have cerebral palsy. Spina bifida and muscular dystrophy also account for relatively high percentages of the students who receive such services.

Current Incidence Trends

The causes of physical disabilities and health impairments have changed somewhat over the years. Medical detection, genetic counseling, and vaccination programs have significantly reduced the incidence of numerous diseases that formerly affected many children. Additionally, it is now possible to correct or control a variety of orthopedic, neurological, and health impairments—through early surgery, physical therapy, medication, and the use of artificial internal or external body parts—to the point where many conditions formerly regarded as crippling, disabling, or disfiguring are no longer so.

However, medical and technological advances (particularly in neonatal and emergency care) mean more infants and children with serious physical and health impairments are surviving. Many of these children require special education services. The number of children and young adults who suffer physical and health impairments as the result of motor vehicle accidents, child abuse and neglect, and drug and alcohol abuse is also increasing. Many individuals and families affected by these factors are likely to need specialized educational and emotional support.

✳ *Historical Background*

Perhaps because so many types of physical and health impairments exist, it is difficult to trace the development of services for this population with any precision. Before there were public school educational opportunities, which began around the turn of this century, most children with severe physical disabilities were kept at home, in hospitals, or in institutions. If local public schools were willing to accept them and make any necessary modifications, some children with mild to moderate physical disabilities probably attended regular classes, especially if their intellectual functioning was not impaired.

The first special public school class for children with physical disabilities in the United States was established in Chicago around 1900. Two American physicians, Winthrop Phelps and Earl Carlson, made noteworthy contributions to the understanding and acceptance of children with physical disabilities. Phelps demonstrated that children could be helped through physical therapy and the effective use of braces; Carlson (who himself had cerebral palsy) was a strong advocate of developing the intellectual potential of children with physical disabilities through appropriate education (Hewett & Forness, 1977).

As the 20th century progressed, the educational needs of children with physical and health impairments were gradually recognized. A dual system of special education prevailed for most children with disabilities throughout most of this century; that is, virtually all children with disabilities such as blindness, deafness, and mental retardation were served either in state-run residential schools or in separate classes in local schools. This system, however, did not apply to children with physical impairments; hardly any state residential schools were established for them. Instead, emphasis has long been placed on making services available at the community level. Children who were kept at home or in hospitals for reasons of health or accessibility were served by homebound or hospital teachers, who traveled from place to place. Special self-contained classes for children with physical and health impairments were set up in many regular public schools. Large school districts sometimes operated special schools solely for children with physical disabilities. These special classes or schools typically had modifications such as ramps, adapted toilets, special gymnasiums, and space for wheelchairs in school cafeterias.

See Chapter 1 for a description of these laws.

Many special classes and schools still exist for children with physical and health impairments. Today, however, the trend is toward greater integration of students with physical and health impairments into regular public school classes. The implementation of the IDEA and Section 504 of the Rehabilitation Act of 1973—as well as numerous court cases requiring architectural accessibility, appropriate educational programs for children in the least restrictive environment, and an end to discrimination against persons with disabilities—have had a positive impact on this integration. No longer may a child be denied the right to attend the local public school simply because there is a flight of stairs at the entrance, or bathroom or locker facilities are not suitable, or school buses are not equipped to transport wheelchairs. The local public school district now has the responsibility of providing suitable programs, facilities, and services to meet each child's educational needs. Today, many thousands of children with physical and health impairments are successfully attending regular classes.

✳ *Educational Implications and Interventions*

The Interdisciplinary Approach

Children with physical and health impairments usually come into contact with a great many teachers, physicians, therapists, and other specialists, both in and out of school. It is important that both regular and special educators make informed decisions about each child's needs, in cooperation with parents and other professionals. Members of an interdisciplinary team have many opportunities to share information about a child from their individual vantage points. The team approach has special relevance to a child with a physical or health impairment. The medical, educational, therapeutic, vocational, and social needs of students with physical and health impairments are often complex and frequently affect each other. Communication and cooperation among educational and health care personnel are crucial if the student's diverse needs are to be met. For example, in devising appropriate toileting procedures for Riccardo, a pediatrician may recommend a diet based on a medical examination of bowel and bladder functioning, a biomedical technician may then design an adaptive device to facilitate Riccardo's transfer from wheelchair to toilet, and a physical therapist may help him use the device, while demonstrating proper bracing and muscle-strengthening techniques to Riccardo's parents and teachers.

Sirvis and Heintz Caldwell (1995) suggest that an interdisciplinary team of professionals and parents should work toward achieving five general goals in the educational program of a student with a physical or health impairment:

1. Physical independence, including mastery of daily living skills
2. Self-awareness and social maturation
3. Communication
4. Academic growth
5. Career education and life skills training

Two particularly important specialists for many children with physical and health impairments are the physical therapist and the occupational therapist. Each is a licensed health professional who must complete a specialized training program and meet rigorous standards.

Physical therapists (PTs) use specialized knowledge to plan and oversee a child's program in making correct and useful movements. They may prescribe specific exercises to help a child increase control of muscles and use specialized equipment, such as braces, effectively. Massage and prescriptive exercises are perhaps the most frequently applied procedures, but physical therapy can also include swimming, heat treatment, special positioning for feeding and toileting, and other techniques. PTs encourage children to be as motorically independent as possible; help develop muscular function; and reduce pain, discomfort, or long-term physical damage. They may also suggest dos and don'ts for sitting positions and activities in the

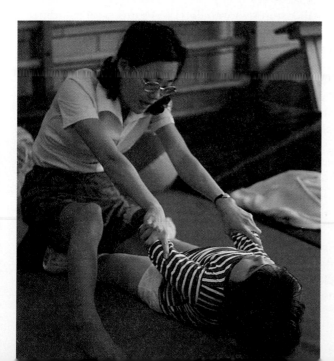

A physical therapist has prescribed specific exercises to increase Tamara's muscular control and range of movement.

classroom and may devise exercise or play programs that children with and without disabilities can enjoy together.

Occupational therapists (OTs) are concerned with a child's participation in activities, especially those that will be useful in self-help, employment, recreation, communication, and other aspects of daily living. They may help a child learn (or relearn) such diverse motor behaviors as drinking from a modified cup, buttoning clothes, tying shoes, pouring liquids, cooking, and typing on a computer keyboard. These activities can enhance a child's physical development, independence, vocational potential, and self-concept. OTs conduct specialized assessments and make recommendations to parents and teachers regarding the effective use of appliances, materials, and activities at home and school. Many OTs also work with vocational rehabilitation specialists in helping students find opportunities for work and independent living after completion of an educational program.

> PTs and OTs provide three types of school-based services: Indirect treatment consisting of consultation, inservice education, and monitoring; in-class management where the therapist facilitates the student's performance during class activities; and direct treatment in which the student's attention is diverted from classroom activities to those that comprise a therapy session. (Cusick, 1991, p. 18)

Additional specialists who frequently offer services to children with physical and health impairments include *prosthetists,* who make and fit artificial limbs; *orthotists,* who design and fit braces and other assistive devices; *biomedical engineers,* who develop or adapt technology to meet a student's specialized needs; and *medical social workers,* who assist students and families in adjusting to disabilities.

Horn (1991) provides an example of the importance of professionals working together and sharing the expertise derived from research in their respective disciplines. She reviewed the published research on teaching motor skills to children with physical disabilities instruction and found that the various methods used represented four basic approaches:

- *Neurodevelopmental approach.* Designed to provide the sensation of normalized postures and movement; emphasizes normalization of postural tone and reflex mechanisms underlying normal postures, movements, and patterns of coordination (Bobath, 1980). Intervention consists of changing and improving motor functioning by inhibiting abnormal patterns, normalizing muscle tone, and facilitating equilibrium (e.g., the therapist gently rocks a child back and forth on a large ball).
- *Sensory integration techniques.* Designed to integrate sensory systems (e.g., balance, touch, movement, olfactory, auditory, visual) through controlled sensory inputs from multiple modalities and self-initiated stipulations (Ayres, 1972). The lower sensory systems of balance, touch, and movement receive primary emphasis (e.g., using a vibrator to stimulate a weak muscle group).
- *Naturalistic context.* Designed to stimulate motor skills in the context of the natural environment within normal daily activities (Campbell, McInerney, & Cooper, 1984).
- *Behavioral programming.* Designed to bring about motor behavior changes through the application of applied behavior analysis (e.g., shaping new motor behaviors through systematic use of antecedent prompts and feedback).

After analyzing the results of experimental evaluations of the effectiveness of each approach, Horn concludes that (a) the data on the neurodevelopmental approach are inconclusive, neither supporting nor refuting its effectiveness because of problems of inconsistent measurement and implementation across the studies; (b) only four studies of the sensory integration approach were found, each focusing on an isolated technique, which prohibits statements about the effectiveness of the approach; (c) no experimental studies of the naturalistic approach had yet been conducted, which makes the theoretically logical conclusions about its effectiveness only speculative; and (d) behavioral programming had the strongest empirical base for its effectiveness. She also notes that although behavioral programming provides specific technology of *how* to train motor skills, it does not indicate *what* skills should be trained.

> Teachers and therapists daily face the questions of what to teach and how to teach. Unfortunately, too often they are left to rely on their assumptions and intuitions, rather than research findings. There is widespread acceptance among practitioners of neuromotor and sensory stimulation therapies, which have evolved from a medical tradition. Thus, behavioral programming typically has been overlooked or underemphasized despite its relatively strong empirical base. Physical, speech, and occupational therapies should examine this approach and develop procedures for incorporating behavioral techniques into their intervention programs. Multidisciplinary teams may facilitate this process. Special educators and psychologists often have backgrounds in behavioral approaches. Physical and occupational therapists could provide information on what to teach as well as some specific techniques, whereas educators could provide the how to teach procedures. (Horn, 1991, p. 193)

Health Care Objectives

Many students with orthopedic and physical disabilities have health care needs that require specialized procedures such as taking prescribed medication (Harchik, 1994), clean intermittent catheterization (CIC), tracheostomy care, ventilator/respirator care (Lehr & Macurdy, 1994), and managing special nutrition and dietary needs (Harvey Smith, 1994). Students who learn to perform all or part of their daily health care needs increase their ability to function independently in normal environments and lessen their dependence on caregivers. Figure 10.3 provides examples of possible IEP objectives related to health-care procedures.

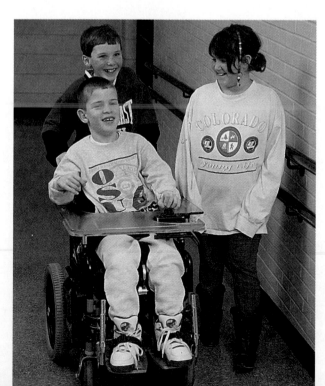

The barrier-free architecture in Troy's neighborhood school makes it easy and natural for all students to interact with one another.

FIGURE 10.3
Sample IEP objectives related to special health-care procedures

Tube feeding:

- Student will explain (orally, in writing, or through other means) reasons for alternative eating method.
- Student will describe steps necessary in implementing the procedure.
- Student will indicate desire to eat.
- Student will measure feeding liquid to be placed in feeding bag or syringe.
- Student will pour food in feeding bag or syringe.
- Student will direct cleaning of feeding equipment.
- Student will clean equipment.
- Student will feed self.

Tracheostomy suctioning:

- Student will indicate need to be suctioned.
- Student will turn on suction machine.
- Student will hold suction tube while procedure is being implemented.
- Student will describe steps necessary to suction.
- Student will explain to others the indicators of need for suctioning.

Catheterization:

- Student will indicate time to be catheterized.
- Student will self-catheterize.
- Student will describe steps in implementing the process.
- Student will wash materials necessary.
- Student will assemble materials necessary.
- Student will hold catheter steady during procedure.
- Student will describe indicators of problems related to catheterization.

Source: From "Meeting Special Health Care Needs of Students" by D. H. Lehr and S. Macurdy in *Promoting Health and Safety: Skills for Independent Living* by M. Agran, N. E. Marchand-Martella, and R. C. Martella, 1994, p. 82. Pacific Grove, CA: Brooks/Cole. Used by permission.

Environmental Modifications

Teachers frequently find it necessary to modify the environment to enable a student with physical and health impairments to participate more fully in the classroom. An environmental modification may involve adapting the equipment or materials used for a given task or changing the manner in which the task is done (Sowers, Jenkins, & Powers, 1988). Wright and Bigge (1991) describe four types of environmental modifications: (a) changes in location of materials and equipment, (b) work surface modifications, (c) object modifications, and (d) manipulation aids.

Although barrier-free architecture is the most publicly visible type of environmental modification for making community buildings and services more accessible, some of the most functional adaptations require little or no cost. Consider, for example, the following guidelines:

- Changing desk- and tabletops to appropriate heights for students who are very short or who use wheelchairs
- Providing a wooden pointer to enable a student to reach the upper buttons on an elevator control panel
- Installing paper cup dispensers near water fountains so that they can be used by students in wheelchairs
- Moving a class or an activity to an accessible part of a school building so that a student with a physical impairment can be included

Positioning, Seating, and Lifting

Importance of Positioning and Seating

Proper positioning, seating, and regular movement are critically important for children with physical disabilities. Proper positioning and movement encourage the development of muscles and bones and help maintain healthy skin. In addition to the health-related issues, positioning can influence how a child with physical disabilities is perceived and accepted by others. Simple adjustments can contribute to improved appearance and greater comfort and increased health for the child with physical disabilities (Wright & Bigge, 1991):

- Good positioning results in alignment and proximal support of the body.
- Stability positively affects use of the upper body.
- Stability promotes feelings of physical security and safety.
- Good positioning can reduce deformity.
- Positions must be changed frequently.

Proper seating helps combat poor circulation, muscle tightness, and pressure sores, and it contributes to proper digestion, respiration, and physical development. Be attentive to the following:

- Pelvic position: hips as far back in the chair as possible and weight distributed evenly on both sides of the buttocks.
- Foot support: both feet level and supported on the floor or wheelchair pedals.
- Shoulder/upper trunk support: seat belt, pummel or leg separator, and/or shoulder and chest straps may be necessary for upright positions.

Lifting and Transferring Students

To prevent the development of pressure sores and help students maintain proper seating and positioning, teachers must know how to move and transfer students with physical disabilities. Routines for lifting, transferring, and repositioning children with physical disabilities should be developed for each child and entail standard procedures for (a) making contact with the child, (b) communicating what is going to happen in a manner the child can understand, (c) preparing the child physically for the transfer, and (d) requiring the child to participate in the routine as much as possible (Stremel et al., 1990). Figure 10.4 shows an example of an individualized rou-

Incidentally, a student should not be described as being "confined to a wheelchair." This expression suggests that the person is restrained or even imprisoned. Actually, most students who use wheelchairs leave them from time to time to exercise or to lie down. It is preferable to say that a student "has a wheelchair" or "uses a wheelchair to get around." A working knowledge of techniques associated with wheelchair use can be helpful to a teacher in reducing problems and making classrooms and school buildings accessible (Venn, Morganstern, & Dykes, 1979).

Guidelines for shifting the position of students in their wheelchairs and for moving students to and from a wheelchair to toilets and to the classroom floor are provided by Parette and Hourcade (1986).

Using Dolls to Teach Self-Catheterization Skills to Children with Spina Bifida

························

Persons with physical and health impairments often require regular medical regimens ranging from simple procedures (such as taking prescribed oral medications) to more complex routines (injection of insulin to control diabetes). The ability to self-administer needed medical routines increases the individual's independence to function in normal environments and eliminates reliance on a caretaker. When complex procedures must be performed by children or persons with learning problems, direct systematic instruction is indicated. If the procedures involve invading the body or errors during practice are potentially hazardous, simulation training can be used. This program evaluated the effectiveness of simulation training with a doll.

Children and Setting

Cathy and Teresa, ages 4 and 8, two girls with spina bifida whose urinary functions were managed by intermittent catheterization performed by their parents, participated in the training program. Both girls were scheduled to attend regular schools during the fall (preschool and second grade), and their parents had requested they learn self-catheterization to promote independent functioning and adaptation in the classroom.

Task Analysis and Measurement

A task analysis of self-catheterization yielded four basic skill components, each with multiple steps: preparation (6 steps); placing and adjusting a compact magnifying mirror (6 steps); catheter insertion and removal (11 steps); and cleanup (9 steps). The children's performance on each step in the task analysis on the doll and then on themselves was observed and recorded during measurement probes before and after training of each of the four skill components. During each doll probe, the child was asked to show how to catheterize the doll; no help or feedback was given. In vivo (self-) probes were conducted after each doll probe to determine if training with the doll generalized to self-administration of the procedure. The child was asked to show how to catheterize herself and to do the best she could but to stop whenever she wished.

Simulation Training

Each child was taught to perform each step of the procedure on a plastic doll with female genitalia and movable arms and legs. The children were told that they were going to learn to catheterize themselves but that a doll with the same urinary problems needed their help first. The trainer described and modeled on the doll the steps in the skill component under instruction. The child was then asked to demonstrate and verbalize the steps for that component ("Show me how you can help the doll with her catheter, and tell her what you're doing"). To simulate the performance of self-catheterization, the doll was manipulated from a sitting position on the child's lap, facing forward. If the child made an error or performed a step out of sequence, the trainer provided verbal prompts ("Where does that end of the catheter go?"), visual prompts (pointing), and manual guidance as necessary. Correct responses were praised.

Results and Discussion

The number of correct responses performed by each child on both doll and self-probes across each skill component is shown in Figure A. During baseline (before training), the children performed few of the steps correctly on either the doll or themselves. After training and practice with the doll, their performance improved both on the doll and on themselves. Cathy required training on herself for several steps of the catheterization insertion and removal component, which she performed correctly on the doll but had trouble with on herself. Follow-up reports from the parents indicated both children were catheterizing themselves independently.

Doll training appears to offer several advantages for teaching children how to self-administer medical procedures. First, because they associated dolls with

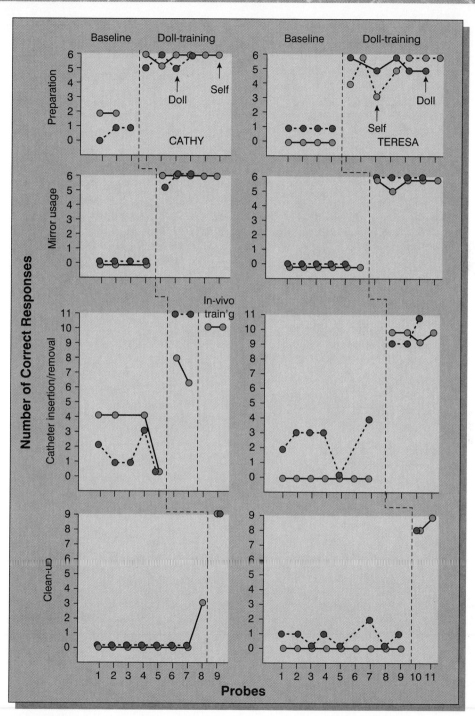

FIGURE A
Number of correct responses within skill components on simulation (doll) and in vivo (self-) probes for each participant

play activities, children's interest and willingness to participate in training might be increased. Second, children may be reluctant to perform an unfamiliar and intrusive procedure on themselves. Allowing children to achieve mastery on a doll before self-application may desensitize them to the process and decrease the likelihood of making potentially harmful errors while practicing on themselves. Finally, using a doll enables many more opportunities for practice than does the child's normal catheterization schedule. The use of dolls appears to be an efficient means of training. Across a 9-day period, total training time was 4 hours and 30 minutes for Cathy and 2 hours and 45 minutes for Teresa.

From "Teaching Self-Catheterization Skills to Children with Neurogenic Bladder Complications" by N. A. Neef, J. M. Parrish, K. F. Hannigan, T. J. Page, and B. A. Iwata, Fall 1990, *Journal of Applied Behavior Analysis, 22,* pp. 237–243. Adapted with permission.

tine for lifting and carrying a preschool child with physical disabilities and severe auditory impairments. Posting charts and photos of recommended positions for individual students can help remind teachers, paraprofessionals, and other staff to use proper transferring and positioning techniques (Rikhye, Gothelf, & Appell, 1989).

Skin care is a major concern for many children with physical disabilities. The skin underneath braces or splints should be checked daily to identify persistent red spots that indicate an improper fit. A health care professional should be contacted if any spot does not fade within 20 minutes after the pressure is relieved (Campbell, 1993).

Assistive Technology

Although the word *technology* often conjures up images of sophisticated computers and other "hardware," technology includes any systematic method for accomplishing a practical task or purpose based on scientific principles. **Assistive technology** is defined in the IDEA as "any item, piece of equipment, or product system, whether acquired commercially off the shelf, modified, or customized, that is used to increase, maintain, or improve functional capabilities of individuals with disabilities." Individuals with physical disabilities use assistive technology devices for a variety of purposes, but especially for increasing mobility, performing daily life skills, improved environmental manipulation and control, better communication, access to computers, and enhanced learning (Butler, 1988; Lewis, 1993).

Both low-technology adaptive devices and high-technology assistive equipment are used by individuals with physical and health impairments in many everyday activities. Special eating utensils, such as forks and spoons with custom-designed handles or straps, may enable children to feed themselves more independently. Simple switches are common parts of homemade environmental control systems to enable persons with disabilities to operate electric appliances such as a television, stereo, computer, or electric wheelchair (Levin & Scherfenberg, 1987; Wright & Momari, 1985).

Many students are unable to move freely from place to place without the assistance of a mobility device. Clarke (1988) describes and compares a variety of mobility devices and suggests that they be selected with the following variables in mind:

- Child's motor capabilities
- Child's physical strength and endurance
- Cost of the device

For a list of catalogs and sources for assistive technology devices, see "For More Information" at the end of this chapter.

FIGURE 10.4

Example of a routine for lifting and carrying a child with physical disabilities

Name: Lisa _____ Date: 9/16/96 _____

Lifting and Carrying Routine

Follow these steps each time you pick Lisa up from the floor, move her from one piece of equipment to another, or move her in the classroom from one location or activity to another.

Step	Activity	Desired Response
Contact	Touch Lisa gently. Tell her you are going to move her.	Wait for Lisa to relax.
Communication	Use the appropriate sign to tell Lisa where you are going (i.e., sign toilet for going to the bathroom area).	Wait for Lisa to sign for 3 seconds. If she doesn't make the sign, help her by physically guiding her to make the sign.
Preparation	Make sure Lisa's tone is not stiff before you move her. Use deep pressure and repositioning to attain alignment and reduce tone.	Wait for Lisa's body to come into alignment and for her tone to relax.
Lifting	Place Lisa in a sitting position if she is lying on the floor. She will be lifted from a standing position if in the stander. Tell Lisa that you are going to lift her. Use the sign for lift.	Wait for Lisa to move her arms forward toward you. If she does not reach forward, use facilitation to move her arms forward.
	Place your arms around Lisa's back and under her knees to lift her into your arms.	
Carrying	Turn Lisa away from you so that she is facing away and can see where you are moving. Lean her back against your body to provide support, and hold her with one arm under her pelvis and hips, with her legs in front. If her legs become stiff, use your other arm to hold her legs apart by coming under one leg and between the two legs to hold them gently apart.	Lisa will be able to watch where she is going.
Repositioning	Place Lisa on the floor or in another piece of equipment. Tell her what you are doing by using the correct sign (i.e., sit; stand) and the sign for the activity (i.e., toilet for bathroom).	Lisa will be ready to participate in the next activity.

Source: From "Special Health Care Procedures" by M. M. Ault, J. C. Graff, and J. P. Rues. Reprinted with the permission of Simon & Schuster, Inc. from the Merrill/Prentice Hall text *Instruction of Students with Severe Disabilities* by Martha E. Snell. Copyright 1993 by Merrill/Prentice Hall.

- Physical layout of the home, school, and community
- Educational and therapy goals

Advances in wheelchair design have made manual chairs lighter and stronger, powered chairs have been adapted for use in rural areas, and new environmental controls have put the wheelchair user in contact with both immediate and distant parts of their world.

New technological aids for communication are used increasingly with children whose physical impairments prevent them from speaking clearly. For students who

See the section on alternative and augmentative communication in Chapter 7.

"Gottcha!" When properly matched to the unique needs of a student with physical disabilities, assistive technology can open up whole new worlds of instructional, communication, and entertainment opportunities.

are able to speak but have limited motor function, voice input/output products enable them to access computers (Esposito & Campbell, 1987). Such developments allow students with physical impairments to communicate expressively and receptively with others and to take part in a wide range of instructional programs.

Telecommunications technology is used by many individuals with physical disabilities to expand their world, to gain access to information and services, and to meet new people. Electronic mail (E-mail) (Gandel & Laufer, 1993) and amateur (ham) radio are used by many adults with disabilities to communicate with others, to make new friends, and to build and maintain relationships.

Technology can seldom be pulled "off the shelf" and serve a student with disabilities with maximum effectiveness. Before purchasing and training a child to use a technological device, teachers should carefully consider certain characteristics of the child and of the potential technologies (Parette, Hourcade, & VanBiervliet, 1993). An assessment of the child's academic skills, social skills, and physical capabilities should help identify the goals and objectives for the technology, as well as narrow down the kinds of devices that may be effective. The child's preferences for certain types of technology should also be determined. At that point, the characteristics of potentially appropriate technologies should be considered, including availability, simplicity of operation, initial and ongoing cost, adaptability to meet the changing needs of the child, and the reliability and repair record of the device.

> Handi-Hams is an international organization of people with and without disabilities who help people with physical disabilities expand their world through amateur radio. To find out about this organization and other sources for adaptive devices and assistive technology, see "For More Information" at the end of this chapter.

Attitudes

How parents, teachers, classmates, and others react to a child with physical disabilities is at least as important as the disability itself. Many children with disabilities suffer from excessive pity, sympathy, and overprotection; others are cruelly rejected, stared at, teased, and excluded from participation in activities with nondisabled children. All children, whether or not they face the challenges presented by a disability, need to develop respect for themselves and to feel that they have a rightful place in their families, schools, and communities.

Children with physical disabilities should have chances to participate in activities and to experience success and accomplishment. Effective teachers accept these children as worthwhile individuals, rather than as disability cases. They encourage the children to develop a positive, realistic view of themselves and their physical

> Parette, Hofman, and VanBiervliet (1994) offer specific suggestions for how professionals can document the need for and seek funding for assistive technology for infants and toddlers with disabilities.

conditions. They expect the children to meet reasonable standards of performance and behavior. They help the children cope with disabilities wherever possible and realize that, beyond their physical impairments, these children have many qualities that make them unique individuals.

✳ *Educational Service Alternatives*

Children with physical and health impairments are served in a wide variety of educational settings as diverse as regular classrooms and homes and hospitals. About one third of all school-age students under both disability categories in the IDEA concerning physical disabilities—Orthopedic Impairments and Other Health Impairments—are served in the regular classroom.

The regular public school classroom, in which the school-age child with physical and health impairments is educated along with classmates without disabilities, is the educational setting that most parents and educators prefer. As Pieper (1983) observes, "Just as the concept that children with disabilities should be dependent on charity for their education is fast giving way, so too are we questioning the belief that medical settings and medically oriented staff are appropriate to foster academic learning, life skills or social behaviors" (p. 21). The amount of supportive help that may be required to enable a student with physical disabilities to function effectively in a regular class varies greatly, according to each child's condition, needs, and level of functioning. Many children with physical and health impairments require only minor modifications, such as ramps and altered seating arrangements, whereas some need special equipment and considerable assistance in moving around, eating, using the toilet, administering medication, and performing other daily activities. An effective program in an integrated school setting can encourage independence, communication, and social development and can make nondisabled students more aware of their peers with disabilities.

For most children with chronic illnesses, the regular classroom with home or hospital tutoring offered as needed on a time-limited basis through the regular education system is all that is needed; for others, a full array of special education services may be necessary. Lynch, Lewis, and Murphy (1993) stress the importance of matching the individual needs of students with chronic illness to the service delivery system:

> Although the extended procedures and potentially stigmatizing effects of the special education system argue against it as the system most appropriate for *all* students who have chronic illnesses, there are several features that are advantageous. The accountability built into services and their evaluation, the partnership between parents and teachers, the procedural safeguards, and the assignment of authority are all characteristics of [special education] programs that make sense for children with chronic illness. (p. 218)

Some students with chronic illnesses are absent from school for extended periods because of flare-ups or scheduled medical treatment. Successful reentry of children who have missed extended periods of school because of illness or the contraction of a disease requires preparation of the child, his or her parents, classmates, and school personnel (Sexson & Madan-Swain, 1993). A classroom presentation aimed at preparing classmates might be conducted a week or two prior to the child's reentry. Children should be given information and encouraged to ask questions about the child and the disease. Questions that peers often ask about a child with a health problem are shown in Table 10.2.

Teachers are typically not well informed about the educational implications of chronic illness. Lynch et al. (1993) recommend two approaches for meeting the

To find out the percentage of school-age students with orthopedic impairments and other health impairments served in six different educational environments during the 1992–93 school year, see Table 1.2 in Chapter 1.

Peckham (1993) provides a lesson plan answering the questions and concerns of classmates of a student with cancer.

TABLE 10.2
Questions that peers often ask about a child's illness or disease

---

- Is the disease contagious?
- Will _____ die from it?
- Will he/she lose any more limbs?
- Can _____ still play, visit me at home, drive, date, etc.?
- Should we talk about _____'s illness or should we ignore it?
- What will other kids think if I'm still friends with _____?
- What's wrong with _____?
- Will _____ be different (look funny, bleed, faint, cough, vomit) when he comes back?

Source: From "School reentry for the child with chronic illness" by S. B. Saxson and A. Madan-Swain, 1993, *Journal of Learning Disabilities, 26*(2), 115–125, 137. Copyright (c) 1993 by PRO-ED, Inc. Reprinted by permission.

informational needs of teachers and other school personnel. First, short information packets about each of the most common chronic illnesses should be developed. These packets would include information on the educational and social complications along with suggestions for instructing and interacting with the child. The appropriate packet would be given to everyone in the school in contact with the child, from teachers to psychologists to bus drivers to cafeteria workers. Second, teachers and staff should attend roundtables addressing the chronic illnesses most prevalent in the school district. These roundtables would provide forums for accurate, up-to-date information and the opportunity for open, uncensored questioning and discussion. Medical professionals, parents, a teacher experienced in educational issues related to the illness, and a student or adult with the illness should be included. Videotaping the roundtables would provide a supplemental resource to the information packets.

There is a need for improved programs of education and counseling for students with terminal illnesses. These programs should give realistic support to the child and family in dealing with death and in making the best possible use of the time available. When a child dies, teachers and classmates may also be seriously affected, and their needs should also be considered and talked about.

Many people without disabilities tend to feel uncomfortable in the presence of a person with a visible disability and react with tension and withdrawal (Allsop, 1980). This response is probably attributable to lack of previous contact with individuals with disabilities: People may fear that they will say or do the wrong thing. A study by Belgrave and Mills (1981) found that when people with physical disabilities specifically mentioned their disabilities in connection with a request for help ("Would you mind sharpening my pencil for me? There are just some things a person can't do from a wheelchair."), they were perceived more favorably than they were when no mention was made of the disability.

The classroom can be a useful place to discuss disabilities and to encourage understanding and acceptance of a child with a physical or health impairment. Some teachers find that simulation or role-playing activities are helpful. Classmates might, for example, have the opportunity to use wheelchairs, braces, or crutches to expand

For a discussion of ways that classroom teachers can help themselves, classmates, and parents deal with the death of a student, see Thornton and Krajewski (1993).

their awareness of some barriers a classmate with physical disabilities faces. Pieper (1983) notes that most children with physical and health impairments are "neither saintly creatures nor pitiable objects" (p. 8). She suggests that teachers emphasize cooperation rather than competition by choosing tasks that require students to work together. It is important to give praise when earned but not to make the child with a physical impairment a teacher's pet who will be resented by other students. Factual information can also help build a general understanding of an impairment. Classmates should learn to use accurate terminology and offer the correct kind of assistance when needed.

Special classes for children with physical disabilities are also offered in many public schools. Some districts have entire schools designed or adapted especially for students with physical disabilities, whereas in others self-contained special classrooms are housed within regular elementary or secondary school buildings. Special classes usually provide smaller class size, more adapted equipment, and easier access to the services of professionals such as physicians, physical and occupational therapists, and specialists in communication disorders and therapeutic recreation.

Homebound or hospital education programs are available to children with severe physical and health impairments. If a child's medical condition necessitates hospitalization or treatment at home for a lengthy period (generally 30 days or more), the local school district is obligated to develop an IEP and to provide appropriate educational services to the child through a qualified teacher. Some children need home- or hospital-based instruction because their life-support equipment cannot be made portable. Such *technologically assisted students* are in need of "both a medical device to compensate for the loss of a vital body function and substantial and ongoing nursing care to avoid death or further disability" (Office of Technology Assessment, 1987, p. 3). This is usually regarded as the most restrictive level of special education service because little or no interaction with nondisabled students is possible in a home or hospital setting. Most large hospitals and medical centers employ educational specialists who cooperate with the hospitalized student's home school district in planning and delivering instruction. Homebound children are visited regularly by itinerant teachers or tutors hired by the school district. Some school programs use a closed-circuit TV system to enable children to see, hear, and participate in class discussions and demonstrations from their beds (Kleinberg, 1984).

✸ *Current Issues and Future Trends*

Children with physical and health impairments are being integrated into regular educational programs as much as possible today. No longer is it believed that the regular classroom is an inappropriate environment for a child with physical limitations. Although architectural and attitudinal barriers still exist in some areas, integrated public school programs are gradually becoming the norm instead of the exception.

Related Services

Integrating students with physical and health impairments, however, has raised several controversial issues. Many questions center on the extent of responsibility properly assumed by teachers and schools in caring for a child's physical and health needs. In a well-publicized case (*Irving Independent School District v. Tatro,* 1984),

---

A person should *never* be equated with a disability label, as in "He's a C.P." or "She's an epileptic."

The continuum of educational services, as described in Chapter 2, is especially applicable to children with physical and health impairments.

The term *medically fragile* is also used to refer to students who are dependent on life-support medical technology. Wadsworth, Knight, and Balser (1993) propose 15 guidelines for placing a child who is medically fragile into the school environment.

the U.S. Supreme Court decided that a school district was obligated to provide inter-mittent catheterization service to a young child with spina bifida. The Court consid-ered catheterization to be a related service, necessary for the child to remain in the least restrictive educational setting and able to be performed by a trained layperson. Some educators and school administrators believe that services such as catheteriza-tion are more medical than educational and should not be the school's responsibil-ity. The expense of such services and the availability of insurance pose potential problems for school personnel. Nevertheless, the *Tatro* case means that "handi-capped children with medical problems who were once excluded from school pro-grams may now be provided access since certain medical services can be provided by qualified personnel who are not physicians" (Vitello, 1986, p. 356). Similar questions have been raised with regard to the equipment and special services that children with physical or health impairments may need in regular schools. For example, who should bear the cost of an expensive computerized communication system for a child with cerebral palsy—the parents, the school, both, or some other agency?

We will likely see a continuation of the present trend to serve children with physical and health impairments in regular classrooms as much as possible. Thera-pists and other support personnel will come into the classroom to assist the teacher, child, and classmates. This appears to be a more effective and economical use of pro-fessional time and skill than removing a child with disabilities from the classroom in order to provide services in an isolated setting.

See the January, 1995, issue of *Educational Leadership*, pp. 18–22, and pp. 42–44.

New and Emerging Technologies for Persons with Severe Physical Disabilities

Recent developments in technology and biomedical engineering hold exciting impli-cations for many individuals with physical disabilities. People with paralysis resulting from spinal cord injury and other causes are already benefiting from sophisticated microcomputers that can stimulate paralyzed muscles by bypassing damaged nerves. In 1982 Nan Davis became the first human being to walk with permanently paralyzed

Schools are required to pro-vide related health care ser-vices, such as tube feeding, so that children with disabilities can be educated in the least restrictive environment.

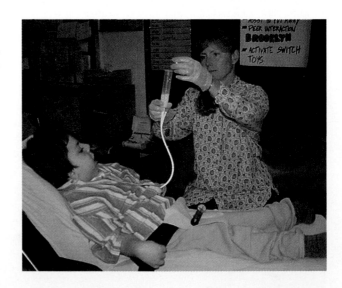

muscles; she was able to control a computer with her brain and transmit impulses to sensors placed on her paralyzed muscles. Such systems will become more efficient and widespread in the future, helping many people with various kinds of physical impairments. Improved medical treatment will also alleviate some physical and health-related conditions.

Animal Assistance

Using animals to assist people with physical disabilities has also generated much recent interest. Animals can help children and adults with disabilities in many ways. Nearly everyone is familiar with guide dogs, which can help people who are blind travel independently, and some agencies train hearing dogs to assist people who are deaf by alerting them to sounds. Another recent and promising approach to the use of animals by people with disabilities is that of a "helper" or "service dog." Depending on a person's needs, dogs can be trained to carry books and other objects (in saddlebags), pick up telephone receivers, turn light switches on or off, and open doors. Dogs can also be used for balance and support—for example, to help a person propel a wheelchair up a steep ramp or to help a person stand up from a seated position. And dogs can be trained to contact family members or neighbors in an emergency.

Monkeys have been trained to perform such complex tasks as preparing food, operating record and tape players, and turning the pages of books (MacFadyen, 1986). Sometimes technological and animal assistance are combined, as when a person uses a laser beam (emitted from a mouth-held device) to show a monkey which light switch to turn on.

In addition to providing practical assistance and enhancing the independence of people with disabilities, animals also appear to have social value as companions.

To learn how researchers are developing robots to assist students with physical disabilities in the classroom, see "Grasping the Future" which begins on the next page.

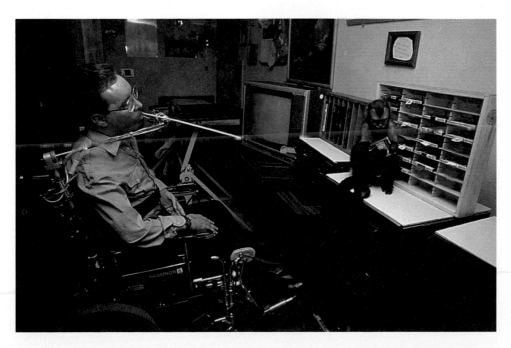

Helper monkeys have been trained to assist with many daily living and work-related tasks.

Grasping the Future

Robotic Aids in the Classroom

by Richard D. Howell

One of the most exciting areas of technological innovation in special education is in the development of new assistive tools for persons with severe physical disabilities. The augmentation or enhancement of human capabilities in the areas of communication, mobility, and manipulation is of increasing interest to a new generation of rehabilitation engineers and technologists in the schools. In the area of communication, the advances of computer-based augmentative communication devices have provided a much-needed capability to interact with others outside the person's immediate environment. In the area of mobility, new advances in wheelchair design have made manual chairs lighter and stronger, powered chairs have been adapted for use in rural areas, and new environmental controls have put the wheelchair user in contact with both immediate and distant parts of their world. Another area that has received minimal but growing attention is the use of robots to increase the manipulation potential of persons with severe physical disabilities.

Just What Is a Robot?

Most people think they know what robots are, but they usually attribute many more capabilities to robots than they actually possess. For instance, they are still not "intelligent" or even very flexible tools—that is, able to learn, plan, and work on information

in unique ways. The word *robot* is derived from a Czech word that means "forced labor," defined in the dictionary as "any mechanical device operated automatically, especially by remote control, to perform in a seemingly human way" (*Webster's New World Dictionary of the American Language,* 1986, p. 1231)—clearly, machines of a whole new order! In fact, robots are currently being used in medical surgeries in several countries, have come to be associated with state-of-the-art manufacturing techniques, and are now entering the area of human services, including rehabilitation and education.

Robots have great potential as assistive tools for students with disabilities. First, robots can provide students with disabilities opportunities for *independent manipulation.* Given the inherent problems with both human and nonhuman personal aides, the robot provides a device under the exclusive control of the human operator. Second, when properly designed, robots can provide increased *educational access and opportunities* for students with and without disabilities. Given the national trends toward inclusive education, which will place regular and special education students in the same room for most of the day, we must attempt to design systems that have a broader viability for all students. To be successful, however, every tool must be justified in its usage and able to stand on its own. Personal robotic devices must eventually meet the same demands as other general-purpose tools, including functionality, viability, reliability, and cost effectiveness.

Robots as New Instructional Tools

Once a student has had an educational robotic system properly fitted to her individual capabilities and has received the proper training to establish what the

environment is and how it works, she is prepared to address a variety of educational experiences, including physical manipulations of instructional materials. An analysis of academic content areas where robots may be applicable revealed that science education provides the content area with the greatest potential for developing a manipulation-rich environment. The key to the increased learning that takes place in an activity-based approach is that students who actively and frequently respond to the science materials will be more engaged and more motivated than students who must try to imagine what the results of a particular set of experiments might look like and mean. Several studies have attempted to compare the use of textbook-based learning approaches with activity-based, inquiry-oriented approaches in the teaching of science to students with disabilities. Some of these studies have found that more dynamic, activity-oriented approaches facilitate the learning of science concepts and factual information by students with disabilities (e.g., Mastropieri & Scruggs, 1992; Morocco, Dalton, & Tivnan, 1990; Scruggs, Mastropieri, Bakken, & Brigham, 1993; Shymansky, Kyle, & Alport, 1983). It seemed reasonable to hypothesize that a robot might be able to be integrated into a dynamic science activity in order to enhance and expand the manipulation capabilities of students with disabilities.

The story of Troy's use of an educational robot is derived from direct observations during a 4-month period in a local public school setting. As you read the vignette, you may want to refer to the accompanying diagram of the robotic system components to imagine what it is like to use this unique system.

Troy's Story: Grasping His World

Some children are so bound up within their own bodies that they cannot

Which object weighs the most? As his skills at controlling the robot increase, Troy comes into contact with ever more complex and exciting learning experiences.

direct the most basic of hand movements or communicate their needs. Such a child is Troy, a handsome and willful 10-year-old with severe physical involvement due to cerebral palsy. Troy is obviously bright and as social as he can be without understandable language. He cannot pick up and hold a block or a ball, and when he does manage to grasp an object, he soon drops it involuntarily or squeezes it unmercifully tight in a hand that will not bend or twist at any angle. Without the use of fully functioning hands, his ability to work, learn, play, and take care of himself is so limited that he is almost totally dependent on others.

When Troy heads down the hall at the school to work with the robot, he is expectant and speeds up the motor on his powered wheelchair, forcing us to hustle just to keep up with him. As he moves into place at the table with the robot and science materials, he becomes more powerful in an obvious manner. The power is all the more precious because it has been earned. Troy

had to work and concentrate hard in order to learn how to use his new tool effectively, and he knows that new, interesting learning experiences await him.

The robot that Troy is using is actually a light industrial system typically used to test electronic parts and do relatively fine manipulations. It is strong enough to move objects that weigh several pounds and has been adapted for use in many different educational and rehabilitation settings around the world. At the current time, only two or three robotic devices have been developed specifically for use by persons with disabilities.

Troy uses a guarded 5-switch adaptive input device to control the software that runs the robot (see Figure A). When Troy was first introduced to the robot, he approached it with an unfettered frenzy, pressing switches constantly and randomly. He liked watching the robot move but was unable to understand the linked sequences of actions required to make

the robot move purposefully through space, grasp an object, and then present it to Troy for investigation.

The robot moves rather slowly and deliberately as Troy uses both preprogrammed and directed movements as he grasps and moves objects through the structured science activities. The software and computer system that Troy uses to control the robot is positioned such that he can easily see the computer screen displaying a brightly colored control screen display. The software gives Troy discrete control over six joint motors which move the robot in the X, Y, and Z vectors (three-dimensional space), which allows him to move the robot arm to any place within the robot's working space. He also can move the robot to six preprogrammed locations.

Even though the movements are still slow and laborious, Troy uses his new tool with growing confidence and independence. He has learned that he can control his environment, albeit more purposefully and slowly than you

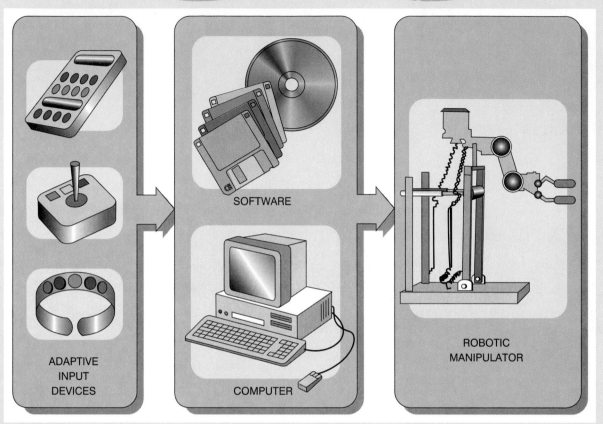

FIGURE A
Components of an educational robotic system

or I might like—but it is his, and his alone, to command.

Robots in Your Future?

The future of personal robotics is not yet clear. Before robots become common in educational and rehabilitation settings, a number of simultaneous developments in both the hardware and software must occur: a standard control software that runs the same programs across robot systems, a well-defined set of criteria and procedures for ensuring the user's safety, robots that have been specifically developed for use by humans for their personal needs, and a cost-effective system.

Research and development activities funded by the National Institute on Disability and Rehabilitation Research (NIDRR), The Ohio State University, and the Center for Applied Science Rehabilitation and Engineering in rehabilitation A. I. duPont Institute are contributing to those advances. Scientists and educators are working toward the goal of integrating science materials, accessible instruments, software tools, and robots into a complete science laboratory environment. This setting will someday enable both students with disabilities and nondisabled learners to work together within a powerful laboratory-based science setting incorporating the best tools and instructional strategies available.

We are still some distance from being able to advocate the use of robotic devices as they currently exist as being an "answer" to manipulation deficits. But advances in the design, precision, and control of new robots, especially those designed specifically for use with persons having disabilities, promise that research and development efforts will go forward in this area.

Who knows? There might be a robot in your closet someday. So keep checking. . . .

Richard Howell is a member of the special education faculty and the Biomedical Engineering Center at The Ohio State University. His research focuses on the development of assistive devices and educational robots for persons with severe physical disabilities and sensory impairments. Dick can usually be found in a corner of his office (which doubles as laboratory), pulling out his hair over a piece of hardware or software that is not doing what it is supposed to do.

People frequently report that their helper animals serve as ice-breakers in opening up conversations and contacts with nondisabled people in the school and community. In addition, the responsibilities of caring for an animal are a worthwhile and rewarding experience for many people, with or without disabilities.

Students with physical limitations should be encouraged to develop as much independence as possible. Often, well-meaning teachers, classmates, and parents tend to do too much for a child with a physical or health impairment. It may be difficult, frustrating, and/or time-consuming for the child to learn to care for his or her own needs, but the confidence and skills gained from independent functioning are well worth the effort in the long run. Nevertheless, most persons with physical disabilities find it necessary to rely on others for assistance at certain times, in certain situations. Effective teachers can help students cope with their disabilities, set realistic expectations, and accept help gracefully when it is needed.

Employment and Life Skills

A major area of concern is employment, one of the most critical aspects of adult life. Many studies show that successful and remunerative work is among the most important variables in enabling people with disabilities to lead satisfying, productive, and independent lives. Yet negative attitudes persist on the part of many employers. Vocational and professional opportunities must be expanded to include individuals with disabilities more equitably. While children are in school, their education should help them investigate practical avenues of future employment, and there should be ongoing contact between educators and vocational rehabilitation specialists.

> The employment and lifestyles of adults with disabilities are examined in detail in Chapter 15.

There are many self-help groups for people with disabilities. These groups can help provide information and support to children affected by similar disabilities. It is usually encouraging for a child and parent to meet and observe capable, independent adults who have disabilities, and worthwhile helping relationships can be established. Some groups operate centers for independent living, which emphasize adaptive devices, financial benefits, access to jobs, and provision of personal care attendants. Other groups are active as advocates for social change, countering instances in which people with disabilities are excluded from meaningful participation in society.

We must work to improve the quality of education, increase physical access to public buildings, improve public attitudes, and provide greater support for parents and families. As these needs are met, the opportunity to participate fully in all facets of everyday community life will be open to all people with physical disabilities and health impairments.

Summary

Defining Physical and Health Impairments

- Children with physical and health impairments are a widely varied population. Some are extremely restricted in activities; others have few limitations.

- An orthopedic impairment involves the skeletal system; a neurological impairment involves the nervous system.

- Physical impairments are described in terms of type of limb involvement.

- Cerebral palsy is a long-term condition arising from impairment to the brain and causing disturbances in voluntary motor functions.

- Spina bifida is a congenital condition that may cause loss of sensation and severe muscle weakness in the lower part of the body. Children with spina bifida can usually participate in most classroom activities but need assistance in toileting.

- Muscular dystrophy is a long-term condition; most children gradually lose the ability to walk independently.

- Other conditions that can affect a child's classroom performance include osteogenesis imperfecta, spinal cord injuries, and amputations or missing limbs.

- Head injuries are a significant cause of neurological impairments and learning problems.

- Seizure disorders produce disturbances of movement, sensation, behavior, and/or consciousness.

- Diabetes is a disorder of metabolism that can often be controlled with injections of insulin.

- Children with cystic fibrosis, asthma, hemophilia, severe burns, or other chronic health conditions may need modifications in their education or activities or other special services, such as counseling.

- Important variables to consider in providing appropriate services include severity, visibility, and age at acquisition of a physical or health impairment.

Prevalence

- There is no universal definition of the physically and health-impaired population, and many children counted under other disability categories also have physical or health impairments.

- In 1992–93, 2.4% of all school-age students who received special education services were reported under the orthopedic impairments and other health-impaired categories.

- Cerebral palsy accounts for the largest single group of children with physical impairments.

Historical Background

- Public school programs for children with physical disabilities began around the turn of the century.

Educational Implications and Intervention

- Children with physical and health impairments typically require services from an interdisciplinary team of professionals.

- Physical therapists (PTs) use specialized knowledge to plan and oversee a child's program in making correct and useful movements. Occupational therapists (OTs) are concerned with a child's participation in activities, especially those that will be useful in self-help, employment, recreation, communication, and other aspects of daily living.

- Students with physical and health impairments can increase their independence by learning to take care of their personal health-care routines such as clean intermittent catheterization and self-administration of medication.

- Adaptations to the physical environment and to classroom activities can enable students with physical and health impairments to participate more fully in the school program.

- Proper positioning and seating is important for children with physical disabilities. A standard routine for lifting and moving a child with physical disabilities should be followed by all teachers and other staff.

- Assistive technology is any piece of equipment or device used to increase, maintain, or improve functional capabilities of individuals with disabilities.

- How parents, teachers, classmates, and others react to a child with physical disabilities is at least as important as the disability itself.

Educational Service Alternatives

- About one third of students with physical and health impairments are served in regular classrooms.

- The amount of supportive help that may be required to enable a student with physical disabilities to function effectively in a regular class varies greatly, according to each child's condition, needs, and level of functioning.

- Successful reentry of children who have missed extended periods of school because of illness or the contraction of a disease requires preparation of the child, his or her parents, classmates, and school personnel.

- Special classes usually provide smaller class size, more adapted equipment, and easier access to the services of professionals such as physicians, physical and occupational therapists, and specialists in communication disorders and therapeutic recreation.

- Some technologically assisted children require home- or hospital-based instruction because their life-support equipment cannot be made portable.

Current Issues and Future Trends

- The education of students with physical and health impairments in regular classrooms has raised several controversial issues, especially with regard to the provision of medically related procedures and services in the classroom.

- New and emerging technologies such as bionic body parts and robot assistants offer exciting possibilities for the future.

- Animals, particularly dogs and monkeys, can assist people with physical disabilities in various ways.

- Helping individuals with physical disabilities gain and keep meaningful employment is a major challenge to special education, employers, and self-advocacy groups.

For More Information

Journals

ACCENT on Living, P.O. Box 700, Bloomington, IL 61701. A quarterly journal of practical information, with articles on varied topics, including employment, aids to independent living, architectural barriers, and family concerns. Primarily written by and about people with physical and health impairments. Also sponsors an extensive catalog of assistive devices and a computerized information retrieval system.

Assistive Technology, RESNA, 1101 Connecticut Avenue NW, Suite 700, Washington, DC 20036. Information about technology for individuals with disabilities.

The Disability Rag, P.O. Box 145, Louisville, KY 40201. Described as "a spicy, irreverent journal." A bimonthly publication tackling controversial issues affecting people with disabilities and serving as a forum for opinion and debate. Features articles on such topics as telethons, legal battles, sexuality, and media portrayals of people with disabilities.

Disability Studies Quarterly. Published by the Department of Sociology, Brandeis University, Waltham, MA 02254. Regularly prints abstracts of current research projects, book reviews, announcements of conferences, resources, and grants. Focuses on social and psychological issues, as well as advocacy, economics, and attitudes of and toward persons with physical and other disabilities.

Disabled USA. Published quarterly by the President's Committee on Employment of the Handicapped, 1111 20th Street, NW, Suite 600, Washington, DC 20036. Reports on current developments in employment, rehabilitation, and independent living. Seeks to document progress in employment and to encourage new opportunities for workers with disabilities.

Rehabilitation Literature. Published monthly by the National Easter Seal Society, 2023 West Ogden Avenue, Chicago, IL 60612. An interdisciplinary publication containing abstracts of current research and practice, with an emphasis on children and adults with orthopedic, neurological, and other physical and health-related impairments. Regularly features reviews of recent books.

Books

Batshaw, M. L., & Perret, Y. M. (1992). *Children with disabilities: A medical primer* (3rd ed.). Baltimore: Paul H. Brookes.

Bigge, J. L. (1991). *Teaching individuals with physical and multiple disabilities* (3rd ed.). New York: Merrill/Macmillan.

Bleck, E. E., & Nagel, D. A. (Eds.). (1981). *Physically handicapped children: A medical atlas for teachers* (2nd ed.). Orlando, FL: Grune & Stratton.

Gerring, J. P., & Carney, J. M. (1992). *Head trauma: Strategies for educational reintegration.* San Diego, CA: Singular.

Goldfarb, L. A., Brotherson, M. J., Summers, J. A., & Turnbull, A. P. (1986). *Meeting the challenge of disability or chronic illness: A family guide.* Baltimore: Paul H. Brookes.

Hanson, M. J., & Harris, S. R. (1986). *Teaching the young child with motor delays: A guide for parents and professionals.* Austin, TX: PRO-ED.

Pieper, E. (1983). *The teacher and the child with spina bifida* (2nd ed.). Rockville, MD: Spina Bifida Association of America.

Savage, R. C., & Wolcott, G. F. (Eds.). (1994). *Educational dimensions of acquired brain injury.* Austin, TX: PRO-ED.

Sowers, J., & Powers, L. (1991). *Vocational preparation and employment of students with physical and multiple disabilities.* Baltimore: Paul H. Brookes.

Organizations

Division for Physical and Health Disabilities (DPHD), Council for Exceptional Children, 1920 Association Drive, Reston, VA 22091-1589.

Many national agencies and organizations provide information, educational programs, and community services to children and adults with specific physical and health impairments and to their parents and teachers. Many of these have state and local chapters. Listed here are some of the largest organizations that disseminate publications and encourage research into the causes and treatment of physical and health impairments.

Cystic Fibrosis Foundation, 6000 Executive Boulevard, Rockville, MD 20852

Epilepsy Foundation of America, 4531 Garden City Drive, Landover, MD 20785

Juvenile Diabetes Association, 23 East 26th Street, New York, NY 10010

Muscular Dystrophy Association, 810 Seventh Avenue, New York, NY 10019

National Easter Seal Society, 2023 West Ogden Avenue, Chicago, IL 60612

Spina Bifida Association of America, 343 South Dearborn Street, Chicago, IL 60604

United Cerebral Palsy Associations, Inc., 66 East 34th Street, New York, NY 10016

Sources for Assistive Technology Devices and Other Information

Assistive Technology Sourcebook, RESNA, 1101 Connecticut Avenue NW, Suite 700, Washington, DC 20036

Handi-Ham System, Courage HANDI-HAM System (WOZSW), Courage Center, 3915 Golden Valley Road, Golden Valley, MN 55422. An international organization of persons with and without disabilities who help people with disabilities expand their world through amateur radio. The System matches students with one-to-one helpers, provides instruction, and loans radio equipment.

Into the Mainstream: A Syllabus for a Barrier-Free Environment, United States Rehabilitation Services Administration, Superintendent of Documents, Washington, DC 20402.

The Disability Bookshop Catalog, Twin Peaks Press, P.O. Box 129, Vancouver, WA 98666 (Phone: (800) 637-2256). Information on hundreds of books, tapes, and videos of interest to people with disabilities.

The Illustrated Directory of Handicapped Products, Trio Publications, Inc., 3600 West Timber Court, Lawrence, KS 66049. Annually updated descriptions of mobility devices, environmental control devices, adapted sports equipment, clothing, and eating devices.

Trace ResourceBook, Trace Research and Development Center, University of Wisconsin, S-151 Waisman Center, 1500 Highland Avenue, Madison, WI 53705. Describes technologies for environmental control and computer access.

Students with Severe Disabilities

* Why is a curriculum based on typical developmental stages inappropriate for students with severe disabilities?

* How can the principle of partial participation contribute to the quality of life of a student with severe disabilities?

* Can teaching with structure and precision make it more difficult for students with severe disabilities to make choices and express their individuality?

* What are the benefits for students with severe disabilities who are educated in regular, integrated schools?

* What are the likely effects on students who are not disabled when they share a regular classroom with peers with severe disabilities?

ive-year-old Zack is learning to feed himself with a spoon. A teacher shows 13-year-old Toni that it is more appropriate to shake hands than to hug a person when first introduced. Martha, who is 20, is learning to ride a city bus to her afternoon job at a cafeteria, where she clears tables and sorts silverware. Zack, Toni, and Martha have severe disabilities. But except for their general need for ongoing supports from others and for instruction in skills that children without disabilities usually acquire at a younger age, they have little in common. The skills and needs of students with severe disabilities are highly diverse.

Because of their intense intellectual, physical, and/or behavioral limitations, children with severe disabilities learn much more slowly than any other group of children (including other children with disabilities). Indeed, without direct and systematic instruction, many individuals with severe disabilities are not able to perform the most basic, everyday tasks we take for granted, such as eating, toileting, and communicating our needs and feelings to others.

Students with severe disabilities often have combinations of obvious and not-so-obvious disabilities that require special additions or adaptations in their education. But a severe disability does not preclude meaningful achievements. Despite the severity and multiplicity of their disabilities, students with severe disabilities can and do learn.

However, large-scale efforts to develop effective methods of instruction for students with severe disabilities are relatively recent phenomena. In the not-too-distant past, individuals with the most severe disabilities were a neglected population; it was widely believed that they were incapable of learning useful skills. They usually were placed in institutions as infants or young children and were considered beyond the responsibility of the public educational system. They often received no education or training at all and were provided with only basic, custodial-level care.

Although students with severe disabilities were excluded from educational programs—and from mainstream society in general—in the past, a philosophy of inclusion now prevails. Laws requiring free, appropriate programs of public education for all students with disabilities; the ever growing body of evidence demonstrating that individuals with severe disabilities can learn and function effectively in integrated school, work, and community settings; and the belief that inclusion is the "right thing to do" all support the new philosophy.

✳ *Defining Severe Disabilities*

No single, widely accepted definition of *severe disabilities* has yet emerged. Most definitions are based on tests of intellectual functioning, developmental progress, or the extent of educational need. According to the system of classifying levels of mental retardation previously used by the American Association on Mental Retardation, persons receiving IQ scores of 35 to 40 and below would be considered to have severe mental retardation; scores of 20 to 25 and below result in a classification of profound mental retardation. In practice, however, the term *severe disabilities* often includes many individuals who score in the moderate level of mental retardation (IQ scores of 40 to 55) (Wolery & Haring, 1994).

Traditional methods of intelligence testing, however, are virtually useless with children whose disabilities are profound. If tested, they tend to be assigned IQ scores at the extreme lower end of the continuum. Knowing that a particular student has an IQ of 25, however, is of no value in designing an appropriate educational program. Educators of students with severe and profound disabilities tend to focus on the specific skills a child needs to learn, rather than on intellectual level.

It was once common to take a developmental approach to the definition of severe disabilities. Justen (1976), for example, proposed that individuals with severe disabilities are "those individuals age 21 and younger who are functioning at a general developmental level of half or less than the level which would be expected on the basis of chronological age" (p. 5). Most educators now maintain that developmental levels have little relevance to this population and instead emphasize that a student with **severe disabilities**—regardless of age—is one who needs instruction in basic skills, such as getting from place to place independently, communicating with others, controlling bowel and bladder functions, and self-feeding. Most children without disabilities are able to acquire these basic skills in the first 5 years of life, but the student with severe disabilities needs special instruction to do so. The basic-skills definition makes it clear that education for students with severe disabilities must not focus on traditional academic instruction.

The definition of severe disabilities used by the U.S. Department of Education refers to the need for educational and related services that go "beyond" what is typically available in regular and special education programs.

> The term "severely handicapped children and youth" refers to handicapped children who, because of the intensity of their physical, mental, or emotional problems, or a combination of such problems, need highly specialized educational, social, psychological, and medical services beyond those which are traditionally offered by regular and special education programs, in order to maximize their potential for useful and meaningful participation in society and for self-fulfillment.
>
> The term includes those children and youth who are classified as seriously emotionally disturbed (including children and youth who are schizophrenic), autistic, profoundly and severely mentally retarded, and those with two or more serious handicapping conditions such as deaf-blind, mentally retarded-blind, and cerebral palsied-deaf.
>
> Severely handicapped children and youth may experience severe speech, language, and/or perceptual-cognitive deprivations and evidence abnormal behavior such as failure to respond to pronounced social stimuli; self-mutilations; self-stimulation; manifestation of intense and prolonged temper tantrums; absence of rudimentary forms of verbal control; and may also have extremely fragile physiological conditions. (*Federal Register,* 1988, p. 118)

The inclusion of extremely challenging behavioral problems, such as self-injurious behavior, in the federal definition is not intended to imply that all children with severe disabilities exhibit such characteristics—most do not. The inclusion of such examples in the federal regulations, however, makes it clear that every child is entitled to a free public education in the least restrictive environment no matter how complicated or challenging the learning, behavioral, or medical problems (Wolery & Haring, 1994).

The term *severe disabilities* generally encompasses individuals with severe and profound disabilities in intellectual, physical, and social functioning. An increasing

See Chapter 4 for discussion of IQ testing and classification of intellectual functioning. Imagine the difficulty, as well as the inappropriateness, of giving an IQ test to a student who cannot hold his head up or point, let alone talk.

Some educators question whether children with profound disabilities can benefit from education. See "Are All Children Educable" later in this chapter. Readers wishing to learn more about the educability debate are referred to these additional references: Baer (1981b, 1984); Kauffman (1981); Noonan, Brown, Mulligan, and Rettig (1982); Orelove (1984); Tawney (1984); and Ulicny, Thompson, Favell, and Thompson (1985).

number of professionals, however, are making a distinction between individuals with profound disabilities and those with severe disabilities. Sternberg (1994) believes that a distinction between severe and profound disabilities is necessary because the "expectations and implications for each are different. These differences are related not only to one's capability for independent functioning but also to the utility of specific educational or training models and methods" (p. 7). According to Sternberg, an individual with **profound disabilities** is one who

> exhibits profound developmental disabilities in all five of the following behavioral-content areas: cognition, communication, social skills development, motor-mobility, and activities of daily living (self-help skills); and requires a service structure with continuous monitoring and observation. . . . This definition also posits a ceiling of 2 years of age for each area of functioning (6 years of age for those classified as severely disabled). If the individual functions above that level, the individual cannot be classified as profoundly disabled. (p. 6)

Thus, an individual with profound disabilities, according to Sternberg, functions at a level no higher than that of a typically developing 2-year-old in all five areas (whereas the functioning of a student with severe disabilities in one or more of these areas may be less delayed, up to the level of a typical 6-year-old).

The Association for Persons with Severe Disabilities (TASH) defines severe disabilities as

> individuals of all ages who require extensive ongoing support in more than one major life activity in order to participate in integrated community settings and to enjoy a quality of life that is available to citizens with fewer or no disabilities. Support may be required for life activities such as mobility, communication, self-care, and learning, as necessary for independent living, employment and self-sufficiency. (Lindley, 1990, p. 1)

Information on TASH can be found at the end of this chapter. The organization's journal, *Journal of the Association for Persons with Severe Disabilities* (*JASH*), is a primary source for the latest research and conceptual developments in educating learners who are challenged by severe disabilities.

The TASH definition not only refers to the level, duration, and focus of support needed by persons with severe disabilities but also specifies the goals and expected outcomes of that support.

Compared with some other areas of special education—mental retardation, learning disabilities, and behavioral disorders in particular—there have been less concern and debate over the definition of severe disabilities. This is not an indication that professionals are not interested in defining the population of students they serve, but rather a reflection of two features inherent in severe disabilities. First, there is little need for a definition that precisely describes who is and who is not to be identified by the term *severe disabilities*. Although the specific criteria a school district uses to define learning disabilities have major impact on who will be eligible for special education services, whether or not special education is needed by any student who is even being considered severely disabled is never an issue. Second, because of the tremendous diversity of learning and physical challenges experienced by such students, any single descriptor such as "severe disabilities" is inadequate. Statements that specify the particular educational goals and support needs of individual students are more meaningful.

✳ *Characteristics of Students with Severe Disabilities*

Throughout this book, it has been pointed out how definitions and lists of characteristics used to describe a disability category have limited meaning at the level of the individual student. And, of course, it is at the level of the individual student where special education takes place, where decisions about what and how to teach are made. As various physical, behavioral, and learning characteristics associated with severe disabilities are described, keep in mind that students with severe disabilities constitute the most heterogeneous group of all exceptional children. As Guess and Mulligan (1982) point out, the differences among students with severe disabilities are greater than their similarities.

Students with severe disabilities exhibit extreme deficits in intellectual functioning and also may need special services and supports because of motor impediments; communication, visual, and auditory impairments; and medical conditions such as seizure disorders. Many have medical and physical problems that require frequent attention. Many students with severe disabilities have more than one disability. Even with the best available methods of diagnosis and assessment, it is often difficult to identify the nature and intensity of a child's multiple disabilities or to determine how combinations of disabilities affect a child's behavior. Some children, for example, do not respond in any observable way to visual stimuli, such as bright lights or moving objects. Is this because the child is blind as a result of eye damage, or is the child unresponsive because of profound mental retardation due to brain damage (Orlansky, 1981)? Such questions arise frequently in planning educational programs for students with severe disabilities.

The one defining characteristic of students with severe disabilities is that they exhibit obvious deficits in multiple life-skill or developmental areas (Sailor & Guess, 1983). No specific set of behaviors is common to all individuals with severe disabilities. Each student presents a unique combination of physical, intellectual, and social characteristics. Educators generally agree, however, that the following behaviors and skill deficits frequently are observed in students with severe disabilities (Brown et al., 1991; Wolery & Haring, 1994).

> For information on what teachers should know about the special health care needs of students with the most severe and profound disabilities, see Ault, Graff, and Rues (1994).

1. *Slow acquisition rates for learning new skills.* Compared with students with disabilities in general, students with severe disabilities learn at a slower rate, require more instructional trials to learn a given skill, learn fewer skills in total, have difficulty learning abstract skills or relationships, and without practice, often forget quickly what they learn (Brown et al., 1991).
2. *Difficulty in generalizing and maintaining newly learned skills. Generalization* refers to the performance of skills under conditions different from those in which they initially were learned. *Maintenance* refers to the continued use of a new skill after instruction is terminated. Poor generalization and maintenance of new knowledge and skills are fundamental characteristics of all students with disabilities. For students with severe disabilities, however, generalization and maintenance seldom occur without instruction that is meticulously planned to facilitate it.
3. *Severe deficits in communication skills.* Almost all students with severe and multiple disabilities are limited in their abilities to express themselves and to understand others. They communicate at a low rate and typically receive fewer opportunities to communicate with other persons in their environment (Rowland, 1990). Many cannot talk or gesture meaningfully; they might not respond when communication is attempted. Of course, this makes education and social interaction extremely difficult; some children are not able to follow even the simplest requests.
4. *Impaired physical and motor development.* Most children with severe disabilities have limited physical mobility. Many cannot walk; some cannot stand or sit up without support. They are slow to perform such basic tasks as rolling over, grasp-

ing objects, and holding up their heads. Physical deformities are common and may worsen without consistent physical therapy.

5. *Deficits in self-help skills.* Some children with severe disabilities are unable to independently care for their most basic needs, such as dressing, eating, exercising bowel and bladder control, and maintaining personal hygiene. They usually require special training involving prosthetic devices and/or adapted skill sequences to learn these basic skills.

6. *Infrequent constructive behavior and interaction.* Nondisabled children and those whose disabilities are less severe typically play with other children, interact with adults, and seek out information about their surroundings. Many children with severe disabilities do not. They may appear to be completely out of touch with reality and may not show normal human emotions. It may be difficult to capture the attention of or evoke any observable response from a child with profound disabilities.

7. *Frequent inappropriate behavior.* Many children with severe disabilities do things that appear to have no constructive purpose. These activities may take the form of ritualistic (e.g., rocking back and forth, waving fingers in front of the face, twirling the body), self-stimulatory (e.g., grinding the teeth, patting the body), and/or self-injurious behaviors (e.g., head banging, hair pulling, eye poking, hitting or scratching or biting oneself). Although some of these behaviors may not be considered abnormal in and of themselves, the high frequency with which some children perform these activities is a serious concern because they interfere with learning more adaptive behaviors and with acceptance and functioning in integrated settings.

Joey's enthusiasm and determination are evident each time his teacher uses music in a lesson.

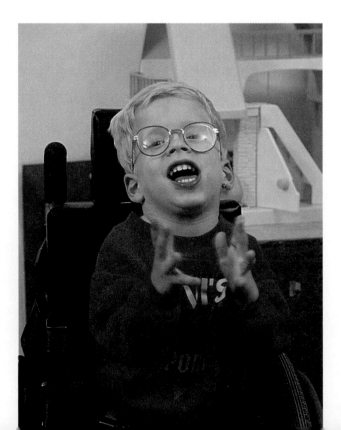

Descriptions of behavioral characteristics, such as those just mentioned, can easily give an overly negative impression. Despite the intense challenges their disabilities impose on them, many students with severe disabilities exhibit warmth, persistence, determination, a sense of humor, sociability, and various other desirable traits (Forest & Lusthaus, 1990; Stainback & Stainback, 1991). Many teachers find great satisfaction in working with students who have severe disabilities and in observing their progress in school, home, and community settings.

Students with Dual Sensory Impairments

A particularly challenging group of students with severe disabilities includes those with dual sensory impairments. "There is perhaps no condition as disabling as deaf-blindness, the loss of part or all of one's vision and hearing" (Bullis & Otos, 1988, p. 110). Many of the several thousand children in the United States and Canada who are deaf-blind were born with visual, hearing, and other impairments after an epidemic of rubella affected thousands of pregnant women in the mid-1960s. Students with dual sensory impairments were the first group of exceptional children to receive special education under federal mandate when the government established a special network of regional and state centers in 1968. When the IDEA was passed in 1975, it included a section on students with dual sensory impairments, defined as those who have

> both auditory and visual disabilities, the combination of which causes such severe communication and other developmental and educational problems that they cannot properly be accommodated in special education programs solely for the hearing handicapped child or for the visually handicapped child. (U.S. Office of Education, 1977a, p. 42478)

An educational program for children who are deaf is often inappropriate for a child who also has limited vision because, on the one hand, many methods of instruction and communication rely heavily on the use of sight. On the other hand, programs for visually impaired students usually require good hearing because much instruction is auditory. Although 94% of individuals labeled deaf-blind have some functional hearing and/or vision (Fredericks & Baldwin, 1987), the combined effects of the dual impairments severely impede the development of communication and social skills, especially when mental retardation also is involved.

The intellectual level of students with dual sensory impairments ranges from giftedness (as in the famous case of Helen Keller, who lost her sight and hearing at about 16 months of age) to profound mental retardation. The majority of children who have both visual and hearing impairments at birth experience major difficulties in acquiring communication and motor skills, mobility, and appropriate social behavior.

> Because these individuals do not receive clear and consistent information from either sensory modality, a tendency exists to turn inward to obtain the desired level of stimulation. The individual therefore may appear passive, nonresponsive, and/or noncompliant. Students with dual sensory impairments may not respond to or initiate appropriate interactions with others and often exhibit behavior that is considered socially inappropriate (e.g., hand flapping, finger flicking, head rocking). (Downing & Eichinger, 1990, pp. 98–99)

Educational programs for students with dual sensory impairments who require instruction in basic skills are generally similar to those for other students with severe

Learning to perform a simple task that would be taken for granted by a person who is not disabled can have tremendous impact on the life of a child with severe disabilities. See the Profiles & Perspectives box "Little Changes with Big Impacts" at the end of this chapter.

It is difficult to assess accurately the degree of sensory impairments in most students who are deaf-blind because additional disabilities or other barriers to communication limit the students' responses to typical testing procedures (Wolf, Delk, & Schein, 1982).

Teaching techniques involving the sense of touch are used to provide and supplement instructional stimuli for students with dual sensory impairments.

Curricula for assessing and teaching functional communication skills to students who are deaf-blind have been developed by the Perkins School for the Blind (1978) and the Alabama Institute for the Deaf-Blind (1989).

disabilities. Although most students with dual sensory impairments can make use of information presented in visual and auditory modalities, when used in instruction these stimuli must be enhanced and the students' attention directed toward them. Tactile teaching techniques involving the sense of touch are used to supplement the information obtained through visual and auditory modes.

Helen Keller (1903) once said that blindness separates one from things but that deafness separates one from people. Communication is achieved only with great difficulty by persons who are deaf-blind and requires greater effort on the part of communication partners (Tedder, Warden, & Sikka, 1993). The use of dual communication boards can help students who are deaf-blind discriminate the receptive or expressive functions of responses from a communication partner (Heller, Ware, Allgood, & Castelle, 1994). When a communication partner points to pictures or symbols on his or her board, a receptive message is provided to the student, requiring a response from the student on her board. The communication partner can point to the student's board and provide imitative prompts or corrective feedback to help the student make expressive messages.

Robert Smithdas (1981), a man who is deaf-blind, vividly describes the importance of supplementing information about the world with other sensory modes.

> The senses of sight and hearing are unquestionably the two primary avenues by which information and knowledge are absorbed by an individual, providing a direct access to the world in which he lives. . . . When these senses are lost or severely limited, the individual is drastically limited to a very small area of concepts, most of which must come to him through his secondary senses or through indirect information supplied by others. The world literally shrinks; it is only as large as he can reach with his fingertips or by using his severely limited sight and hearing, and it is only when he learns to use his remaining secondary senses of touch, taste, smell, and kinesthetic awareness that he can broaden his field of information and gain additional knowledge. (p. 38)

In 1968, fewer than 100 students with dual sensory impairments were being served in specialized educational programs, virtually all of which were located at residential schools for children who are blind. Today, about 6,000 students with dual sensory impairments are being educated in the United States in hundreds of different programs, including those located at schools for children who are deaf, early childhood developmental centers, vocational training centers, and regular public schools

(Zambone & Huebner, 1992). Students who are deaf-blind who progress to high school and postsecondary levels usually are integrated into educational programs for students with other disabilities or into programs for nondisabled students, with supportive assistance provided by special teachers, intervenors, interpreters, or tutors. Downing and Eichinger (1990) describe instructional strategies to support the education of students with dual sensory impairments in regular classrooms.

Persons with dual sensory impairments have the potential to achieve success and enjoyment in employment and independent living, but they need systematic instruction to facilitate communication, generalization of skills, and development of appropriate social behaviors (Bullis & Bull, 1986).

Students with Autism

Autism is a condition marked by severe impairment of intellectual, social, and emotional functioning. According to the widely used definition endorsed by the Autism Society of America, the essential features of the condition typically appear prior to 30 months of age and consist of disturbances of (a) developmental rates and/or sequences; (b) responses to sensory stimuli; (c) speech, language, and cognitive capacities; and (d) capacities to relate to people, events, and objects (Ritvo & Freeman, 1978). It is estimated that autism occurs in approximately 5 of every 10,000 children (Matson, 1994). Although autism is quite rare, it is actually more common than blindness in children (Lotter, 1966; Rutter, 1965).

Lovaas and Newsom (1976) provide a graphic description of six frequently observed characteristics of children with autism.

> Although the precise cause of autism is unknown, it almost certainly is of biological or organic origin (Rutter & Schopler, 1987; Smith, 1993).

1. *Apparent sensory deficit.* We may move directly in front of the child, smile, and talk to him, yet he will act as if no one is there. We may not feel that the child is avoiding or ignoring us, but rather that he simply does not seem to see or hear. The mother also reports that she did, in fact, incorrectly suspect the child to be blind or deaf. . . . As we get to know the child better, we become aware of the great variability in this obliviousness to stimulation. For example, although the child may give no visible reaction to a loud noise, such as a clapping of hands directly behind his ears, he may orient to the crinkle of a candy wrapper or respond fearfully to a distant and barely audible siren.

2. *Severe affect isolation.* Another characteristic that we frequently notice is that attempts to love and cuddle and show affection to the child encounter a profound lack of interest on the child's part. Again, the parents relate that the child seems not to know or care whether he is alone or in the company of others.

3. *Self-stimulation.* A most striking kind of behavior in these children centers on very repetitive stereotyped acts, such as rocking their bodies when in a sitting position, twirling around, flapping their hands at the wrists, or humming a set of three or four notes over and over again. The parents often report that their child has spent entire days gazing at his cupped hands, staring at lights, spinning objects, etc.

4. *Tantrums and self-mutilatory behavior.* Although the child may not engage in self-mutilation when we first meet him, often the parents report that the child sometimes bites himself so severely that he bleeds, or that he beats his head against walls or sharp pieces of furniture so forcefully that large lumps rise and his skin turns black and blue. He may beat his face with his fists. . . . Sometimes the child's aggression will be directed outward against his parents or teachers in the most primitive form of biting, scratching, and kicking. Some of these children absolutely tyrannize their parents by staying awake and making noises all night, tearing curtains off the

window, spilling flour in the kitchen, etc., and the parents are often at a complete loss as to how to cope with these behaviors.

5. *Echolalic and psychotic speech.* Most of these children are mute; they do not speak, but they may hum or occasionally utter simple sounds. The speech of those who do talk may be echoes of other people's attempts to talk to them. For example, if we address a child with the question, "What is your name?" the child is likely to answer, "What is your name?" (preserving, perhaps, the exact intonation of the one who spoke to him). At other times the echolalia is not immediate but delayed; the child may repeat statements he has heard that morning or on the preceding day, or he may repeat TV commercials or other such announcements.

6. *Behavior deficiencies.* Although the presence of the behaviors sketched above is rather striking, it is equally striking to take note of many behaviors that the autistic child does not have. At the age of 5 or 10, he may, in many ways, show the behavioral repertoire of a 1-year-old child. He has few if any self-help skills but needs to be fed and dressed by others. He may not play with toys, but put them in his mouth, or tap them repetitively with his fingers. He shows no understanding of common dangers. (From "Behavior Modification with Psychotic Children" by O. I. Lovaas and C. D. Newsom, 1976, in *Handbook of Behavior Modification and Behavior Therapy* by Harold Leitenberg (Ed.). (pp. 308–309). Englewood Cliffs, NJ: Prentice-Hall. Reprinted by permission.)

Clearly, children who behave as Lovaas and Newsom describe are profoundly disturbed. Their prognosis generally is considered to be extremely poor, with problems persisting into adulthood for over 95% of cases (Lotter, 1978; Rutter, 1970). Their education and treatment require intensive behavioral programming to reduce the frequency of self-injurious and/or self-stimulatory behaviors (Simeionson, Olley, & Rosenthal, 1987).

On the brighter side, however, a great deal of exciting and promising research may lead to better futures for children with autism (Koegel & Frea, 1993; Valcante, 1986). For example, the work of Ivar Lovaas and his colleagues at the University of California at Los Angeles indicates the tremendous potential of early intervention with autistic children. Lovaas (1987) provided a group of 19 children with autism with an intensive early intervention program of one-to-one behavioral treatment for more than 40 hours per week for a period of 2 years or more before reaching the age of 4. Intervention also included parent training and mainstreaming into a regular, preschool environment. When compared with a control group of 19 similar children at age 7, children in the early intervention group had gained 20 IQ points and had made major advancements in educational achievement. Nine of the children were able to advance from first to second grade in a regular classroom and were considered by their teachers to be well adjusted.

Follow-up evaluations of the same group of 19 children several years later at the average age of 11.5 years showed that the children had maintained their gains (McEachin, Smith, & Lovaas, 1993). In particular, 8 of the 9 "best outcome" children were considered to be "indistinguishable from average children on tests of intelligence and adaptive behavior" (p. 359). In discussing the outcomes of this research, Lovaas (1994) states:

> After 1 year of intensive intervention, fifty percent of the children can be integrated into regular kindergarten classrooms. Then, we have them repeat kindergarten to get a head start on first grade. Successful passing of first grade is the key. Those that pass first grade are likely to obtain normal IQ scores and normal functioning. The children who don't make it into first grade are likely to need intensive supports for their entire life.

Facilitated communication, a controversial method of assisting persons with autism and other nonverbal individuals to communicate, was introduced in Chapter 6 and is discussed later in this chapter.

For a description of this intensive, home-based training program, see Lovaas (1981). Other excellent sources of information on the assessment and education of children with autism are Harris and Handleman (1994); Koegel and Kern Koegel (1995); and Matson (1994).

Only 4.7% of school-age children with autism were served in regular classrooms during the 1991–92 school year (U.S. Department of Education, 1994).

The work of Lovaas and his colleagues represents a landmark accomplishment in the education and treatment of children with autism. First, they have discovered and validated at least some of the factors that can be controlled to help children with autism achieve normal functioning in a regular classroom. Second, the successful results offer real hope and encouragement for the many teachers and parents working to learn more about helping children with autism.

> As is shown in Chapter 14, to be most effective, early intervention must begin as early as possible in a child's life and be intensive, systematic, and of long duration.

✳ *Prevalence*

Because there is no universally accepted definition of severe disabilities, there are no accurate and uniform figures on prevalence. Estimates of the prevalence of severe disabilities range from 0.1% to 1% of the population (Ludlow & Sobsey, 1984). Brown (1990) considers students with severe disabilities to be those who function intellectually in the lowest functioning 1% of the school-age population.

The number of students with severe disabilities who receive special education services under the IDEA cannot be determined from data supplied by the U.S. Department of Education because severe disabilities is not one of the disability categories under which the states make their annual report. Students who have severe disabilities are counted among other categories of exceptionality, including mental retardation, multihandicapped, other health impaired, and deaf-blind.

The difficulty in obtaining accurate prevalence figures indicates the current uncertainties surrounding the definition and classification of students with severe disabilities. The available information, however, shows that this is neither a small nor an isolated population; in fact, individuals with severe disabilities comprise several different subgroups of students, whose needs are not always the same.

✳ *Historical Background*

Little is known about the treatment of individuals with severe disabilities throughout most of history. Because severe disabilities so often occur in conjunction with medical and physical disabilities, many of these children did not live past infancy or early childhood. In many early societies, abandonment or deliberate killing of children with severe impairments is thought to have been a common practice (Anderson, Greer, & Rich, 1982). Even today, a philosophy of "survival of the fittest" continues to prevail in some parts of the world.

To say that humane treatment and education of individuals with severe disabilities did not begin until the 20th century would be an oversimplification. As Scheerenberger's (1984) comprehensive review points out, efforts were made throughout history to understand the causes of severe disabilities and, at times, to provide care and training. In the 19th century, physicians Jean Itard, Edouard Seguin, and Samuel Gridley Howe achieved notable advances in systematically teaching communication and self-help skills to children with severe disabilities. Certainly, many other dedicated teachers, parents, and caregivers sought to help people with severe disabilities; unfortunately, their names are lost in history.

During the second half of the 19th century, hundreds of state-operated residential institutions were established in the United States. An optimistic philosophy prevailed at the outset, and some individuals with severe disabilities were, in fact,

Are All Children Educable?

Some educators, other professionals, and citizens question the wisdom of spending large amounts of money, time, and human resources attempting to train children who have such serious and profound disabilities that they may never be able to function independently. Some would prefer to see resources spent on children with higher apparent potential—especially when economic conditions limit the quality of educational services for all children in the public schools. "Why bother with children who fail to make meaningful progress?" they ask.

> Accelerating a response rate may indeed be a worthy first goal in an educational program if there is reasonable hope of shaping the response into a meaningful skill. Nevertheless, after concerted and appropriate effort by highly trained behavior therapists, for a reasonable period of time, a child's failure to make significant progress toward acquisition of a meaningful skill could reasonably be taken as an indication that the child is ineducable. . . . Granted, all children probably are educable if education is defined as acceleration of any operant response. But such a definition trivializes the meaning of the term *education* and, even without consideration of benefit, moots the question of educability. Formulating consensual definitions of education, meaningful skill, and significant progress will be difficult, but it is a task we cannot avoid. . . . We suggest that public response to the questions "What is education?" "What skills are meaningful?" "What rate of progress is significant?" and "What cost/benefit ratios are acceptable?" sampled with sufficient care, could be invaluable in deciding who is educable and who is not. (Kauffman & Krouse, 1981, pp. 55–56)

A special educator who is also the parent of a daughter with severe disabilities disagrees.

> If anyone were to be the judge of whether a particular behavior change is "meaningful," it should certainly not be only the general taxpayer, who has no idea how rewarding it is to see your retarded 19-year-old acquire the skill of toilet flushing on command or pointing to food when she wants a second helping. I suspect that the average taxpayer would not consider it "meaningful" to him or her for Karrie to acquire such skills. But in truth, it is "meaningful" to that taxpayer whether he recognizes it or not, in the sense that it is saving him or her the cost of Karrie's being institutionalized, which she certainly would have been by now if she never showed any progress; thus it is functional for the taxpayer even though his or her answer to the question "Is this meaningful?" might well be "No" or "Not enough to pay for."
>
> The complexity, cost, and hopelessness of evaluating fairly the "meaningfulness" of various behavior changes leads me to conclude that

successfully educated and returned to their home communities (Wolfensberger, 1976).

At first, many institutional programs were called asylums for the feebleminded. They later came to be called hospitals, state schools, or training centers. But under whatever name, education and training were usually not provided to those residents with the most severe disabilities. Many observers commented on the bleak, unstimulating environments, the lack of adequate care, and the prevailing attitude of pessimism in most large, residential institutions. And once placed in an institution, a child with severe disabilities was unlikely ever to leave it. Unless parents were able to provide care and training at home or to afford an expensive private school education, children with severe disabilities had virtually no opportunities to learn useful skills or to lead satisfying lives.

During the last 20 years or so, several judicial decisions and new laws have had important effects on the development of educational services for children with severe disabilities. Particularly significant was the case of *Pennsylvania Association for Retarded Children (PARC) v. Commonwealth of Pennsylvania* (1972). Before the PARC case, many states had laws allowing public schools to deny educational services no one should be denied an education. . . . I would be very resistant to the idea that we should now, at this infant stage of the science and technology of education for severely retarded students, give up intensive skill training for anyone. (Hawkins, 1984, p. 285)

In many ways, our knowledge of the learning and developmental processes of children with severe disabilities is still primitive and incomplete. We do know, however, that children with severe disabilities are capable of benefiting significantly from appropriate and carefully implemented educational programs. Even in cases in which little or no progress has been observed, it would be wrong to conclude that the student is incapable of learning. It may instead be that our teaching methods are imperfect and that the future will bring improved methods and materials to enable that student to learn useful skills (Baer, 1981b). Children, no matter how severe their disabilities, have the right to the best possible public education and training society can offer them.

Virtually every parent of a child with severe disabilities has heard a host of negative predictions from educators, doctors, and concerned friends and family. Parents often are offered such discouraging forecasts as "Your child will never talk" or "Your child will never be toilet-trained." Yet in many instances those children make gains that far exceed the professionals' original predictions. Despite predictions to the contrary, many children have learned to walk, talk, toilet themselves, and perform other "impossible" tasks.

There are still many unanswered questions in the education of children whose disabilities are complex and pervasive (Sailor, Gee, Goetz, & Graham, 1988). Even though their opportunities for education and training are expanding rapidly, nobody really knows their true learning potential or the extent to which they can be successfully integrated into the nondisabled population. What we do know is that students with the most severe disabilities will go no farther than we let them; it is up to us to open doors and to raise our sights, not to create additional barriers.

Don Baer, professor of human development at the University of Kansas and a pioneer in the development of effective teaching methods for persons with severe disabilities, offers this wise perspective on the question of educability.

Some of us have ignored both the thesis that all retarded persons are educable and the thesis that some retarded persons are ineducable, and instead have experimented with ways to teach some previously unteachable people. Over a few centuries, those experiments have steadily reduced the size of the apparently ineducable group relative to the obviously educable group. Clearly, we have not finished that adventure. Why predict its outcome, when we could simply pursue it, and just as well without a prediction? Why not pursue it to see if there comes a day when there is such a small class of apparently ineducable persons left that it consists of one elderly institution resident who is put forward as ineducable. If it comes, that will be a very nice day, and the next day will be even better. (Baer, 1984, p. 299) ✳

to children with severe disabilities because they were considered ineducable. In the PARC case, the court decided against exclusion and noted that education could be useful to severely handicapped individuals

Without exception, expert opinion indicates that all mentally retarded persons are capable of benefiting from a program of education. . . . The vast majority are capable of achieving self-sufficiency and the remaining few, with such education and training, are capable of achieving some degree of self-care; that the earlier such education and training begins, the more thoroughly and more efficiently a mentally retarded person will benefit from it and, whether begun early or not, that a mentally retarded person can benefit at any point in his life and development from a program of education. (*Pennsylvania Association for Retarded Children (PARC) v. Commonwealth of Pennsylvania*, 1972)

Many other cases—including *Wyatt v. Stickney* (1971); *Pennhurst State School and Hospital v. Halderman* (1981); *Armstrong v. Kline* (1979); *Irving Independent School District v. Tatro* (1984); and *Homeward Bound, Inc. v. Hissom Memorial Center* (1988)—have since upheld the right of students with severe disabilities to receive a free, appropriate program of education at public expense. The provisions

H. R. Turnbull (1993), an attorney and the father of a son with severe disabilities, provides a thorough overview of federal laws and major court cases related to the education of children with disabilities.

An extended school year is used to meet the requirements of a free, appropriate public education for some students with severe disabilities. To learn about the legal requirements, judicial rulings, and practical guidelines for educators concerning the extended school year, see Rapport and Thomas (1993).

of the IDEA fully apply to children with severe disabilities: They must have access to an educational program in the least restrictive setting possible, and their parents or guardians must be involved in the development of an appropriate IEP. These legal and judicial developments, coupled with an awareness of the potential of students with severe disabilities brought about by advances in teaching methods, have produced a dramatic expansion of educational programs in public schools, vocational facilities, and other community-based settings in recent years.

Even though the courts and the IDEA mandated the right to a free, appropriate public education for all students, many questioned the "educability" of those with severe disabilities.

> Those who advocated on behalf of persons with severe disabilities could not point to irrefutable success stories during the 1970s that would convince others that *all* children would indeed benefit. Thus, we had to insist upon being given the opportunity to show what could be done, and in the meantime, special education for students with the most severe disabilities had to be a question of values. We would provide a free and appropriate education for these young people, not because of past demonstrations of remarkable progress supported by empirical data, but because it was right and just to do so—and long overdue. (Meyer, 1991, p. 287)

The year 1975 marks the beginning of the modern era in the education of persons with severe disabilities, not only because the IDEA became law that year but also because that was when a group of 30 people, led by founding President Norris Haring of the University of Washington, created the American Association for the Education of the Severely/Profoundly Handicapped. The organization later changed its name to the Association for Persons with Severe Disabilities (TASH). Today, TASH has a membership of more than 9,000 educators, parents, and other individuals who are concerned with improving the quality of life for individuals of all ages who have severe disabilities. TASH membership includes many highly creative and productive researchers and teachers who have played leading roles in developing effective educational practices for students with severe disabilities.

The organization's journal, the *Journal of the Association for Persons with Severe Disabilities (JASH)*, is a primary source for research and theoretical developments related to educating learners who are challenged by severe/profound disabilities.

In recent years, a dramatic increase has occurred in the number of books, research studies, curricula, and other materials designed to help children and adults with severe disabilities function in integrated settings. In the 20 years since individuals with the most severe disabilities began their "odyssey into the public schools and the community, the movement has grown far beyond what its advocates might have imagined" (Meyer, 1991, p. 287). Although much has been accomplished, much remains to be done. A strong case can be made that the education of students with severe disabilities is the most exciting and dynamic area in all of special education today.

✳ *Causes of Severe Disabilities*

For a list and discussion of "classic" articles considered by experts to have greatly influenced the education of persons with severe disabilities, see Spooner, Enright, Haney, and Heller (1993).

Severe intellectual disabilities can be caused by a wide variety of conditions, largely biological, that may occur before (prenatal), during (perinatal), or after birth (postnatal). In almost every case, a brain disorder is involved. Brain disorders are the result of either *brain dysgenesis* (abnormal brain development) or *brain damage* (caused by influences that alter the structure or function of a brain that had been developing normally up to that point). From a review of 10 epidemiological studies (McLaren & Bryson, 1987), Coulter (1994) estimated that prenatal brain dysgenesis accounts for most cases of severe cognitive limitations and that perinatal and postnatal brain damage account for a minority of cases.

A significant percentage of children with severe disabilities are born with chromosomal abnormalities, such as Down syndrome, or with genetic or metabolic disorders that can cause serious problems in physical or intellectual development. Complications of pregnancy—including prematurity, Rh incompatibility, and infectious diseases contracted by the mother—can cause or contribute to severe disabilities. A pregnant woman who uses drugs, drinks alcohol excessively, or is poorly nourished has a greater risk of giving birth to a child with severe disabilities. Because their disabilities tend to be more extreme and more readily observable, children with severe disabilities are more frequently identified at or shortly after birth than are children with mild disabilities.

The birth process itself involves certain hazards and complications: Infants are particularly vulnerable to oxygen deprivation and brain injury during delivery. Severe disabilities also may develop later in life from head trauma caused by automobile and bicycle accidents, falls, assaults, or abuse. Malnutrition, neglect, ingestion of poisonous substances, and certain diseases that affect the brain (e.g., meningitis, encephalitis) also can cause severe disabilities.

Although hundreds of medically related causes of severe disabilities have been identified, in about one sixth of all cases, the cause cannot be clearly determined (Coulter, 1994).

> Coulter (1994) states that a brain disorder is "the only condition that will account for the existence of profound disabilities" (p. 41).

> Severe disabilities can be caused by most of the conditions known to be potential causes of mental retardation (see Table 4.4 in Chapter 4).

✳ *Educational Approaches*

How does one go about teaching students with severe disabilities? To answer this question, three fundamental and interrelated questions must be considered:

> What skills should be taught?

> What methods of instruction should be employed?

> Where should instruction take place?

Of course, each of these three questions must be asked for all students, but when the learner is a student with severe disabilities, the answers take on enormous importance. During the past 15 years, major changes and advancements in the education of students with severe disabilities have led to new responses to the questions of curriculum, teaching methods, and placement.

Curriculum: What Should Be Taught to Students with Severe Disabilities?

Not long ago, educators focused on the so-called mental or developmental ages of their students. Although this approach may be helpful in identifying what skills a student can and cannot perform, it also may detract from the most effective use of instructional time because it "assumes that those sequences of behavior typical of nonhandicapped students are relevant for the student with severe or profound disabilities" (Brown, 1987, p. 43). Strict reliance on a developmental approach may lead to an emphasis on teaching prerequisite skills that are not really essential for later steps (Ludlow & Sobsey, 1984) and that may contribute to the perception of students with severe disabilities as eternal children (Bellamy & Wilcox, 1982). Today, most educators of individuals with severe disabilities consider it important to be familiar with the normal sequences of child development, but they recognize that their students often do not acquire skills in the same way that nondisabled students do and that developmental guides should not be the primary basis for determining teaching procedures. For example, a 16-year-old student who is just learning to feed and toilet herself should not be taught in the same way or with the same materials as a nondisabled 2-year-old who is just learning to feed and toilet herself. The past experiences, present environments, and future prospects of the two individuals are, of course, quite different even though their ability to perform certain skills may be similar. Freagon (1982) offers a thoughtful critique of the developmental sequencing strategy.

> When the developmental curricular strategy is employed, severely handicapped students have considerable impediments to achieving a postschool adult life-style that is similar to those of nonhandicapped persons. In the first place, when instructional activities are based on mental, language and social, and gross and fine motor ages, severely handicapped students rarely, if ever, gain more than 1 or 2 developmental years over the entire course of their educational experience. Therefore, 18-year-old students are relegated to performing infant or preschool or elementary nonhandicapped student activities. They are never seen as ready to engage in 18-year-old activities. In the second place, little, if any, empirical evidence exists to support the notion that severely handicapped students need to learn and grow along the same lines and growth patterns as do nonhandicapped students in order to achieve the same goal of education. (p. 10)

Learning to operate a photo-copy machine is one of the functional vocational skills identified by Sheila's IEP team.

Contemporary curriculum content for students with severe disabilities is characterized by its focus on functional skills that can be used in immediate and future domestic, vocational, community, and recreational/leisure environments. Educational programs are future oriented in their efforts to teach skills that will enable students with severe disabilities to participate in integrated settings as meaningfully and independently as possible after they leave school.

Functionality

A *functional skill* is one that is immediately useful to a student and that is frequently demanded in his or her natural environment. Placing pegs into a pegboard or sorting wooden blocks by color would not be considered functional because these tasks are not required in most people's natural environment. Learning to dress oneself (McKelvey, Sisson, Van Hasselt, & Hersen, 1992), ride a public bus (Robinson, Griffith, McComish, & Swasbrook, 1984), and purchase items from coin-operated vending machines (Sprague & Horner, 1984) are examples of functional skills. Functional instructional activities employ real materials in a meaningful activity. Table 11.1 provides additional examples of functional and nonfunctional materials and activities.

Chronological Age-Appropriateness

Wherever possible, students with severe disabilities should participate in activities that are appropriate for same-age peers without disabilities. Adolescents with severe disabilities should not use the same materials as young, nondisabled children; in fact, having teenagers sit on the floor and play clap-your-hands games or cutting and pasting cardboard snowmen highlights their differences and discourages integration. It is more appropriate to teach recreational skills, such as bowling and tape recorder operation, or to engage the students in holiday projects, such as printing greeting cards. Teachers of adolescent students with severe disabilities should avoid decorating classroom walls with child-oriented characters such as Big Bird or Mickey Mouse and should not refer to their students as "boys," "girls," or "kids" when "young men," "young women," or "students" is clearly more age appropriate.

It is critically important to build an IEP for a student with severe disabilities around functional and age-appropriate skills. Because nonschool settings demand such skills and because nondisabled peers exhibit them, functional and age-appropriate behaviors are more likely to be reinforced in the natural environment and, as a result, to be maintained in the student's repertoire (Horner, Dunlap, & Koegel, 1988; Stokes & Baer, 1977).

Making Choices

Imagine going through an entire day without being able to make a choice, any choice at all. Someone else will decide what you will wear, what you will do next, what you will eat for lunch, whom you will sit next to, and so on throughout the day, every day. In the past, students with severe disabilities were given few opportunities to make choices and decisions or to express preferences; the emphasis was on establishing instructional control over students. Traditionally, persons with severe disabilities have simply been cared for and taught to be compliant.

> Some caregivers might feel that to complete tasks for persons with disabilities is easier and faster than allowing them to do it for themselves; while others may have the attitude that the person already has enough problems coping with his or her disabil-

Several excellent and comprehensive curriculum guides of functional skills and related instructional activities for students with severe disabilities are available (e.g., Falvey, 1989; Ford et al., 1989; Fredericks et al., 1980a, 1980b; Giangreco, Cloninger, & Iverson, 1993; Neel & Billingsley, 1989; Wilcox & Bellamy, 1987).

For an excellent comparison of functional and nonfunctional learning tasks, see "My Brother Darryl" in Chapter 4.

TABLE 11.1

Examples of functional and nonfunctional tasks, activities, and materials for secondary students with severe disabilities

SKILL DOMAIN	FUNCTIONAL TASK	NONFUNCTIONAL BECAUSE OF MATERIALS	NONFUNCTIONAL BECAUSE OF ACTIVITY
Domestic/Self-help	Student attending to instructions of how to put on her winter hat	Student attending to instructions of how to put on a play police chief's hat	Student attending to instructions to look at a magazine picture of a woman putting on a hat
Leisure	Student being manually guided in operating a video game	Student being manually guided in operating a play video game made from a milk carton	Student being manually guided in putting toy pegs in a pegboard[1]
Vocational	Student following instructions to sort like-size nuts and bolts into a package	Student following instructions to sort plastic, toy nuts and bolts into slots on a form board	Student following instructions to fill up egg cartons with cotton balls
Community living	Student attending to teacher demonstration of counting out 50¢ in change	Student attending to teacher demonstration of counting toy coins	Student attending to teacher demonstration of matching a real coin to a magazine picture of a coin
Social/Communication	Student being manually guided in signing "Hi" when first greeted by the teacher	Student being manually guided in holding up a cartoon of "Smokey the Bear" waving "Hi"	Student being manually guided in drawing a picture of someone signing "Hi"

[1] In this example the activity *and* the materials would be nonfunctional.

Source: From D. H. Reid et al., 1985, "Providing a More Appropriate Education for Severely Handicapped Persons: Increasing and Validating Functional Classroom Tasks," *Journal of Applied Behavior Analysis, 18,* p. 292. Reprinted by permission.

ity. Regardless of the underlying intention, the result can be to overprotect, to encourage learned helplessness, and to deprive the individual of potentially valuable life experiences. (Guess, Benson, & Siegel-Causey, 1985, p. 83)

Special educators are recognizing the importance of choice making as a means of making activities meaningful and as an indicator of quality of life for students with severe disabilities (Brown & Lehr, 1993; Newton, Horner, & Lund, 1991). Increasing efforts are being made to help students with severe disabilities express their preferences and make decisions about matters that will affect them, such as the types of settings in which they will live and work, what foods they will eat, the partners they will socialize with, and whether or not they want to participate in daily routines and activities (Bannerman, Sheldon, Sherman, & Harchik, 1990).

Parsons, McCarn, and Reid (1993) describe a choice provision program that was successful in helping adults with severe disabilities make mealtime choices. Gothelf, Crimmins, Mercer, and Finocchiaro (1994) describe a 10-step method for teaching choice making to students who are deaf-blind. Wacker, Wiggins, Fowler, and Berg (1988) reported the results of three experiments in which students with profound disabilities used preprogrammed microswitches to demonstrate preferences for toys and types of social attention, as well as to make requests. In another study, adults with moderate mental retardation learned to choose self-directed leisure activities by electing and placing picture cards into a sequenced activity book (Bambara & Ager, 1992).

Shevin and Klein (1984) offer several suggestions for incorporating choice-making activities into the classroom programs of students with severe disabilities. For example, a child might be presented with pictures of two activities and asked to point to the one she would rather engage in. Another child might be asked, "Whom would you like for your partner?" Or the teacher might say, "Should we do this again?" Of course, in presenting such choices, the teacher must be prepared to accept whichever alternative the student selects and to follow through accordingly.

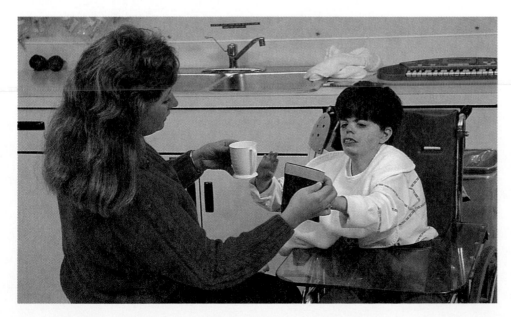

Since learning to make choices and express her preferences, Kimberly's quality of life has improved greatly.

Communication Skills

The fall 1993 issue of the *Journal of the Association for Persons with Severe Handicaps* is devoted to articles on enhancing communication with individuals with severe disabilities.

Effective communication is essential to our quality of life, enabling us to express our desires and choices, to obtain and give information, and most important, to form and maintain relationships with others (Chadsey-Rusch, Drasgow, Reinoehl, Halle, & Collet-Klingenberg, 1993; Ferguson, 1994; Kaiser, 1993). Early research and training in communication for persons with severe disabilities focused on remediation of specific forms of communication, such as the production of speech sounds, words, and descriptive phrases (Kaiser & Goetz, 1993). However, the focus of and methods used to teach communication skills to students with severe disabilities have undergone significant changes during the past 20 years. Two assumptions or changes in perspective regarding the nature of communication are shaping contemporary research and instructional practices in communication for persons with severe disabilities: (a) Communication is independent of the specific mode that is used as a channel for communication, and (b) communication occurs when communication partners establish shared meanings (Ferguson, 1994; Kaiser & Goetz, 1993).

Rowland and Schweigert (1993) have developed an environmental inventory of 52 items that enables teachers to analyze the extent to which specific activity encourages functional communication for a particular student. Reichle and Keogh (1986) discuss rules for decision making in selecting the most appropriate methods of communication for students with severe disabilities.

To restate the first assumption, communication must be functional. As with all other skill domains, instruction and supports in the area of communication for persons with severe disabilities have focused increasingly on the development of functional communication. To be functional, communication must "work"; that is, it must influence the behavior of others to "bring about effects that are appropriate and natural in a given social context" (Calculator & Jorgensen, 1991, p. 204)

Implicit in the second assumption is a new understanding that the responsibility for successful communication rests with both communication partners. Shared meaning is more likely when the communication partner who is relatively more skilled uses the principles of "responsive interaction," such as following the lead of the less skilled speaker, balancing turns between conversation partners, and responding with interest and affect (Blackstone, 1981; Fox & Westling, 1991).

A good deal of research also has been done on specialized methods of teaching communication skills to children and youths with severe disabilities. Many students with severe disabilities are able to learn to understand and produce spoken language; speech is always a desirable goal, of course, for those who can attain it. A student who can communicate verbally is likely to have a wider range of educational, employment, residential, and recreational opportunities than a student who is unable to speak.

For specific suggestions on being a good communication partner, see the Teaching & Learning box "Communication Partners" at the end of Chapter 7.

Ferguson (1994) believes that research and communication training for individuals with severe disabilities eventually will evolve to another level, at which it will be recognized that

> what we really seek is not "socially effective communication repertoires" at all, but *membership,* specifically participatory, socially valued, image-enhancing membership. The purpose of all of our interventions, programs, indeed, schooling in general, is *to enable all students to actively participate in their communities so that others care enough about what happens to them to look for ways to include them as part of that community.* (p. 10)

Augmentative and Alternative Communication (AAC).   Because of sensory, motor, cognitive, or behavioral limitations, some students with severe disabilities may not learn to speak intelligibly even after extensive training. Many systems of augmentative and alternative communication (AAC) have proven useful—including gestures, various sign language systems, pictorial communication boards, symbol systems, and electronic communication aids. Although the specialized forms of communication used by some individuals with severe disabilities limit the number of people with whom they can communicate because the contrived and idiosyncratic nature of their systems requires specialized knowledge by their communication partner (Heller et al., 1994), they do enable many students with severe disabilities to receive and express basic information, feelings, needs, and wants. Sign language and other communication systems also can be learned by a student's teachers, peers, parents, and employers, thus encouraging use outside the classroom. Some students—after learning basic communication skills through sign language, communication boards, or other strategies—later are able to acquire speech skills. Researchers are working to develop "partner friendly" forms of communication.

Facilitated Communication.   Facilitated communication (FC) is a process by which a communication partner, called a facilitator (most often a teacher, sometimes a friend or parent), provides physical support (typically by placing a hand on the individual's elbow, forearm, or hand) to assist an individual who cannot speak or whose speech is limited to type on a keyboard or to point at pictures, words, or other symbols on a communication board. A basic premise of FC is that people with autism and moderate or severe mental retardation have an "undisclosed literacy" consistent with "normal intellectual functioning."

FC has produced tremendous interest and controversy, both in the professional literature and in the popular media. Claims of meaningful and extensive communication and vocabulary use by individuals with autism or mental retardation whose use of language had previously been nonexistent or extremely limited generated understandable excitement that a powerful and widely effective new treatment might have been discovered. Even though little or no scientific evidence was available to support these claims, FC was soon being widely implemented in special education and adult human services programs serving individuals with disabilities.

Numerous studies have been conducted in an attempt to validate the authorship of communication generated by FC. After reviewing all 25 scientific evaluations of FC that at the time had been accepted for publication by peer-reviewed professional journals or presented at professional meetings, Shane and Green (1994) concluded that "FC is neither a generally valid nor reliable means for people with disabilities to communicate themselves and that facilitators cannot judge accurately and reliably how much they control FC productions" (p. 157). Proponents, however, claim that conducting objective "tests" of FC is inherently confrontational and creates an atmosphere of "distrust" in which the process cannot work (Biklen, 1993; Borthwick, Morton, Crossley, & Biklen, 1992). These same proponents, however, "have been quick to take at face value the few (and questionable) reports of controlled tests that seemed to produce evidence supporting FC's validity" (Green & Shane, 1994, p. 158).

In the light of the overwhelming weight of the scientific evidence showing that the communication attributed to individuals with severe disabilities during FC was influenced by the facilitator (Rimland, 1993), several prominent professional organizations recently have passed resolutions or position statements cautioning that FC is unproven and that no important decisions should be made regarding a student's or client's life that are based on the process unless authorship can be confirmed (e.g., AAMR, see Figure 11.1; American Psychological Association [APA]).

Baumgart, Johnson, and Helmstetter (1990) and Blackstone (1989) describe AAC systems and their use by students with severe disabilities. For more information on AAC, see Chapter 7; for specific suggestions on how to communicate with a person who uses AAC, see Table 7.4 in Chapter 7.

FC was introduced in Chapter 6.

For comprehensive reviews of experimental research on FC, see Green and Shane (1994) and Jacobson (1994).

FIGURE 11.1

American Association on Mental Retardation policy on facilitated communication

A substantial number of objective clinical evaluations and well-controlled studies indicate that Facilitated Communication, a technique of physically assisting people with autism or mental retardation to communicate through type or communication boards, has not been shown to result in valid messages from the person being facilitated.

Therefore, be it resolved that the Board of Directors of the American Association on Mental Retardation does not support the use of this technique as the basis for making any important decisions relevant to the individual being facilitated without clear, objective evidence as to the authorship of such messages. *Adopted June 1994*

Source: Reprinted from AAMR *News & Notes,* September/October, 1994, Vol. 7(5), p. 1. Reprinted by permission.

Advocates of FC contend that objective evaluation of FC is not important because the benefits are potentially large and the procedure carries little risk (e.g., Haskew & Donnellan, 1992). Unfortunately, use of FC has not been without risks; there have been criminal investigations of parents, family members, or other caretakers falsely accused of mistreatment or abuse via FC-produced communications (Johnson, 1994).

In contrast to the AAMR and APA, TASH contends that FC can be an effective means of communication for some individuals with disabilities and believes that limiting its use could violate the individual's right to communicate. The TASH Resolution on Facilitated Communication states that FC can be a viable alternative means of expression for some individuals; encourages "careful, reflective use" of the technique; and recognizes the importance of finding ways to confirm communication competence or authorship (see Figure 11.2).

Rob Horner (1994), one of the most productive researchers and respected leaders in the field of severe disabilities, offers these comments on the continuing FC controversy:

> It is important to remember the need to bring this debate home to the families, teachers, and clinicians who wish above all else to communicate well with their children/students/co-workers. For those of us who need to know what we are to do tomorrow, there is great conflict . . . I do not believe there is sufficient documentation to argue that all FC should be avoided. We need more careful, rigorous research (both experimental and phenomenological) to understand if, when and why FC is effective. At the same time, I believe there is sufficient evidence from *both* experimental and phenomenological writings to suggest that FC should *always* be used in the context of regular opportunities to test the role of the facilitator. Serendipitous reports are not adequate . . . authorship is not just one important issue in FC—it is the central, *first* issue to be resolved. . . . when coherent communication occurs when the facilitator is knowledgeable and does not occur when the facilitator is not knowledgeable, the issue of authorship is paramount. (p. 186)

For extensive discussion and debate by both proponents and critics of FC, see the August 1994 issue of *Mental Retardation* and the fall 1994 issue of *JASH*.

Recreational and Leisure Skills

Most children develop the ability to play and, later, to occupy themselves constructively and pleasurably during their free time. But children with severe disabilities may not learn appropriate and satisfying recreational skills unless they are specifically taught. Teaching appropriate leisure and recreational skills helps individuals with severe disabilities to interact socially, maintain their physical skills, and become more

FIGURE 11.2

Resolution on facilitated communication by TASH: The Association for Persons with Severe Handicaps

---

THEREFORE BE IT RESOLVED THAT:

TASH regards access to alternative means of expression an individual right.

TASH encourages its membership to become informed about the complexities of facilitated communication training and practice and to stay informed of new research and practice throughout the facilitated communication training process.

TASH encourages people who decide to become facilitators to seek training in the method.

TASH encourages careful, reflective use of facilitated communication.

TASH encourages facilitators to work in collaboration with individuals with severe disabilities to find ways of confirming communication competence when using facilitation. To this end, TASH encourages use of multiple strategies, including, for example: controlled designs; portfolio analysis; and transitioning to independent typing.

TASH urges that when allegations of abuse or other sensitive communication occur, facilitators and others seek clarification of the communication and work to ensure that users of facilitation

are given the same access to legal and other systems that are available to persons without disabilities. It is important not to silence those who could prove their communication competence while using facilitation or any other method of expression.

TASH expresses its appreciation to individuals who have disabilities and who have learned to communicate through facilitation and who have been instrumental in discovering ways for themselves and others to demonstrate their communication competence.

Source: Reprinted from "TASH Resolutions" in *TASH Newsletter,* December 1994/January 1995, *20/21,* p. 7. Reprinted by permission.

involved in community activities. A survey by Pancsofar and Blackwell (1986) found that many persons with severe disabilities do not use their unstructured time appropriately; rather than participate in enjoyable pursuits, they may spend excessive time sitting, wandering, or looking at television. A variety of programs to teach recreational and leisure skills have recently been developed; this area is now generally acknowledged as an important part of the curriculum for students with severe disabilities.

Horst, Wehman, Hill, and Bailey (1981) describe how several students with severe disabilities, aged 10 to 21, were taught age-appropriate leisure skills. The activities were selected "largely on the basis that many nonhandicapped peers regularly engage in these types of activities" (p. 11). Precise teaching procedures were followed in the assessment and teaching of throwing and catching a Frisbee, operating a cassette tape recorder, and playing an electronic bowling game. All students were able to increase their skills in these activities.

An integrated aerobic conditioning program was enjoyed by 14 children 6 to 13 years old with moderate to severe disabilities and by 25 fifth- and sixth-grade peers without disabilities (Halle, Gabler-Halle, & Bemben, 1989). Datillo and Mirenda (1987) developed a computerized procedure that enables nonspeaking students with severe disabilities to indicate their preferences and to control access to leisure-time activities (e.g., music, action video, slides).

For information and guidelines for selecting and teaching community-based recreational and leisure activities, see Moon (1994); Moon and Bunker (1987); Schlein, Meyer, Heyne, and Brandt (1995; Schleien and Ray (1988); and Wehman, Renzaglia, and Bates (1985).

Modifying the rules by which some team games are played can provide enough supports to enable an individual with severe disabilities to participate (Krebs & Coultier, 1992). For example, Table 11.2 presents how the rules of a girls' fast-pitch softball league were modified to accommodate the skill limitations of Katie, a player with severe disabilities (Bernabe & Block, 1994).

Prioritizing and Selecting Instructional Targets

Teachers must learn good choice-making skills too. Students with severe disabilities present numerous skill deficits often compounded by the presence of challenging

TABLE 11.2
Rule modifications that enabled a player with severe disabilities to participate meaningfully in a girls' softball league

MODIFICATIONS FOR KATIE

1. Defensively, it was decided to place Katie in center field. This was more of a safety decision than a modification because Katie could not field a hit ball. Children at this age have a tendency to make contact with the ball either too early or too late, resulting in more balls being hit toward the left and right fields and fewer to center field. Also, there would be three other outfielders (natural supports) who could back-up and overshadow Katie's position in front, to her left and right (in softball there are four outfield positions: left field, center field, right field, and short center). Thus, the chances of Katie's being hit by the ball would be minimized if she were put into a position where balls are less likely to be hit.

2. Katie is slow and deliberate when she fields the ball, and she rarely stops balls even when they are hit directly to her. Therefore, out of fairness to Katie and her team, the offense could only advance two bases if the ball were hit directly to her. It should be noted that this particular modification was suggested by the coaches and approved by 87% of the players without disabilities.

3. Offensively, it was decided to allow Katie to hit a ball off a tee because she could not hit a pitched ball. Katie was allowed three attempts to hit the ball from the tee. The possibility, therefore, for a base on balls and being hit by a pitch did not exist for her. If she did not hit the ball in three attempts she was called "out." When Katie hit the ball, she ran unassisted to first base.

4. For baserunning, the distance to first base was shortened to account for Katie's running ability. Prior to the beginning of the season, some of Katie's teammates were timed on how fast they could run to first base, and an average time was computed. Using this average time as a standard, Katie was asked to run toward first base. While her teammates could make it all the way to first base in the given time, Katie only made it about halfway. Thus, the distance to first base for Katie was approximately half the distance to regular first base.

5. In consideration of Katie's safety and out of fairness to Katie's hitting and running ability, the defense had to play at normal depths. If Katie made contact with the ball and the ball was in fair territory, the fielder had to throw the ball to the first baseman positioned at regulation first base. If the fielder threw the ball to regulation first base before Katie stepped on her modified first base, Katie was called out. Otherwise, she was called "safe." As a result of a safe call, a pinch runner took Katie's place at regulation first base. At this point, Katie was taken back to the dugout.

Source: From E. A. Bernabe and M. E. Block, 1994, "Modifying Rules of a Regular Girls Softball League to Facilitate the Inclusion of a Child with Severe Disabilities." *Journal of the Association for Persons with Severe Handicaps, 19,* p. 26. Reprinted by permission.

behaviors, and each of those *could* (but not necessarily *should*) be targeted as an IEP goal or instructional objective. It is seldom, if ever, possible, however, to design and implement a teaching program to deal simultaneously with all of the learning needs and challenging behaviors presented by an individual with severe disabilities. (In the rare instance in which the resources to do so might be available, such an all-at-once approach would not be recommended anyway.) One of the greatest responsibilities a special educator undertakes in his or her role as a member of an IEP team is the selection of instructional objectives.

Judgments about how much a particular skill ultimately will contribute to a student's overall quality of life are difficult to make. In many cases, we simply do not know how useful or functional a behavioral change will prove to be (Baer, 1981). Whichever skills are chosen for instruction, they ultimately must be meaningful for the learner and his or her family.

Several methods have been devised to help IEP team members prioritize the relative significance of suggested skills or learning activities (e.g., Dardig & Heward, 1981; Giangreco et al., 1993). Each member of the IEP team might rate those activities along a variety of criteria or items such as those shown in Figure 11.3. Such prioritization of IEP skills and objectives, of course, is not only important for students with severe disabilities but also can be used in the development of all IEPs.

Instructional Methods: How Should Students with Severe Disabilities Be Taught?

Care and concern for the well-being of students with severe disabilities and assurance that they have access to educational programs are important. By themselves, however, care and access are not enough. To learn effectively, students with severe disabilities need more than love, care, and classroom placement. They seldom acquire complex skills through imitation and observation alone; they are not likely to blossom on their own.

The learning and behavioral problems of students with severe disabilities are so extreme and so significant that instruction must be carefully planned and executed. "Precise behavioral objectives, task analysis, and other individualized instructional techniques combine to form a powerful teaching process" for students with severe disabilities (Ludlow & Sobsey, 1984, p. 22). Indeed, structure and precision are essential. The teacher must know what skill to teach, why it is important to teach it, how to teach it, and how to recognize that the student has achieved or performed the skill.

An effective teacher of students with severe disabilities learns to use task analysis (described in Chapter 4), in which skills are broken down into a series of specific, observable steps, and the student's performance of each step is carefully monitored. Table 11.3 presents a breakdown of an important self-care skill—washing one's hands—into small precise steps. Some students may require even more specific steps than the 19 listed here; others might need fewer steps. Before any instruction begins, the teacher needs to accurately assess a student's performance of the task. Judy might be able to perform all of the steps up to Step 15 (turning off the water), whereas Sam might not even be able to demonstrate Step 1 (going to the sink). Such assessment helps the teacher determine where to begin instruction. He or she can gradually teach each required step, in order, until the student can accomplish the entire task independently. Without this sort of structure and precision in teaching, a great deal of time is likely to be wasted.

Several recent texts provide excellent and detailed descriptions of how to plan, conduct, and evaluate instruction for students with severe and profound disabilities (Cipani & Spooner, 1994; Snell, 1993; Sternberg, 1994; Westling & Fox, 1995).

FIGURE 11.3
A method for prioritizing possible instructional activities

Criteria	Activity											
	1	2	3	4	5	6	7	8	9	10	11	12
1. Can be used in current environments	—	—	—	—	—	—	—	—	—	—	—	—
2. Can be used in future environments	—	—	—	—	—	—	—	—	—	—	—	—
3. Can be used in four or more different environments	—	—	—	—	—	—	—	—	—	—	—	—
4. Affords daily opportunities for interaction with non-disabled persons	—	—	—	—	—	—	—	—	—	—	—	—
5. Increases student independence	—	—	—	—	—	—	—	—	—	—	—	—
6. Helps maintain student in, or promotes movement to the least restrictive environment	—	—	—	—	—	—	—	—	—	—	—	—
7. Is chronologically age-appropriate	—	—	—	—	—	—	—	—	—	—	—	—
8. Student will acquire in 1 year the necessary skills to participate in the activity	—	—	—	—	—	—	—	—	—	—	—	—
9. Parents rate as a high priority	—	—	—	—	—	—	—	—	—	—	—	—
10. Promotes a positive view of the individual	—	—	—	—	—	—	—	—	—	—	—	—
11. Meets a medical need	—	—	—	—	—	—	—	—	—	—	—	—
12. Improves student's health or fitness	—	—	—	—	—	—	—	—	—	—	—	—
13. If able, student would select	—	—	—	—	—	—	—	—	—	—	—	—
14. Student shows positive response to activity	—	—	—	—	—	—	—	—	—	—	—	—
15. Advocacy, training, and other support can be arranged so that student can participate in the activity in the absence of educational services	—	—	—	—	—	—	—	—	—	—	—	—
16. Related service staff support selection of activity	—	—	—	—	—	—	—	—	—	—	—	—
17. Transportation is no barrier	—	—	—	—	—	—	—	—	—	—	—	—
18. Cost is no barrier	—	—	—	—	—	—	—	—	—	—	—	—
19. Staffing is no barrier	—	—	—	—	—	—	—	—	—	—	—	—
20. Environments are physically accessible	—	—	—	—	—	—	—	—	—	—	—	—
TOTAL												

(Rating of: 3 = strongly agree with statement, 2 = agree somewhat with statement, 1 = disagree somewhat with statement, 0 = disagree strongly with statement for 12 different activities)

Source: Adapted from J. C. Dardig and W. L. Heward, 1981, "A Systematic Procedure for Prioritizing IEP Goals." *The Directive Teacher, 3,* pp. 6–7. Adapted by E. Helmstetter, 1989, "Curriculum for School-Age Students: The Ecological Model" in F. Brown and D. Lehr (Eds.), *Persons with Profound Disabilities: Issues and Practices* (p. 254). Baltimore: Paul H. Brookes. Reprinted by permission.

TABLE 11.3
Task analysis for hand-washing

1.   Go to bathroom sink.
2.   Grasp the cold water faucet.
3.   Turn on the water.
4.   Wet your hands.
5.   Pick up the soap (with the dominant hand).
6.   Rub the soap on the other hand.
7.   Put the soap down.
8.   Rub palms together.
9.   Rub back of hand (with palm of opposite hand).
10. Rub back of other hand (with palm of opposite hand).
11. Put hands under water.
12. Rinse palm of hands (until all visible suds removed).
13. Rinse back of hands (until all visible suds removed).
14. Grasp the cold water faucet.
15. Turn off the water.
16. Pick up towel.
17. Dry your palms.
18. Dry the back of your hands.
19. Hang towel over rack.

Source: From *Systematic Instruction of Persons with Severe Handicaps* (3rd ed.) (p. 75) by M. E. Snell (Ed.), 1987, New York: Merrill/Macmillan. Reprinted by permission.

Careful attention should be given to the following components of an instructional program for a student with severe disabilities.

The student's current level of performance must be precisely assessed. Is Keeshia able to hold her head up without support? For how many seconds? Under what conditions? In response to what verbal or physical signal? Unlike traditional assessment procedures, which may rely heavily on standardized scores and developmental levels, assessment of children with severe disabilities emphasizes each learner's ability to perform specific, observable behaviors. Assessment should not be a one-shot procedure, but should take place at different times, in different settings, and with different persons. The fact that a student with a severe disability does not demonstrate a skill at one particular time or place does not mean that he or she is incapable of demonstrating that skill. Precise assessment of current performance is valuable in determining which skills to teach and at what level the instruction may start.

The skill to be taught must be defined clearly. "Carlos will feed himself" is too broad a goal for many students with severe disabilities. A more appropriate statement might be "When applesauce is applied to Carlos's right index finger, he will move the finger to his mouth within 5 seconds." A clear statement like this enables the teacher and other observers to determine whether Carlos attains this objective. If, after repeated trials, he has not, a different method of instruction should be tried.

The skills must be ordered in an appropriate sequence. The teacher must be able to arrange "a relationship between the student and his environment which results in positive experiences for the student and small positive changes in skill acquisition" (Sailor & Haring, 1977, p. 73). This does not imply that students with severe disabilities will always acquire skills in exactly the same order as students without disabilities, but it is useful to consider that some skills logically come before others and that some groups of skills are naturally taught at the same time.

The teacher must provide a clear prompt or cue to the child. It is important for the child to know what action or response is expected of him or her. A cue can be verbal; the teacher might say, "Bev, say *apple,*" to indicate what Bev must do before she will receive an apple. Or a cue can be physical; the teacher might point to a light switch to indicate that Bev should turn on the light. It also may be necessary for the teacher to demonstrate an activity many times and to physically guide the child through some or all of the tasks required in the activity.

The child must receive feedback and reinforcement from the teacher. Students with severe disabilities must receive clear information about their performance, and they are more likely to repeat an action if it is followed immediately by a reinforcing consequence. Unfortunately, it can be quite difficult and time-consuming to determine what items or events a noncommunicative child finds rewarding. Many teachers devote extensive efforts to reinforcer sampling; that is, they attempt to find out which items and activities are reinforcing to a particular child, and they keep careful records of what is and is not effective. Spradlin and Spradlin (1976) describe how a teacher worked with a child with severe disabilities for more than 2 years to find an effective reinforcer he could use in an instructional program. A total of 57 different items were tried as reinforcers, including praise, hugs, drinks, food, candy, toys, and audio and visual stimuli.

Strategies that promote generalization of learning must be used. It is well known and documented that students with severe disabilities have difficulty in gen-

For a review of research on methods of delivering and fading instructional prompts to students with severe disabilities, see Doyle, Wolery, Ault, and Gast (1988) and Wolery, Ault, and Doyle (1992).

Chris's teacher will gradually fade out the use of response prompts and physical guidance as Chris's ability to respond independently increases.

eralizing the skills they learn. As Horner, McDonnell, and Bellamy (1986) note, "Education for students with severe disabilities is relevant only to the extent that the knowledge and behaviors that the students acquire become part of their daily routine" (p. 289). Thus, an effective teacher has students perform tasks in different settings and with different instructors, cues, and materials before concluding with confidence that the student has acquired and generalized a skill.

The student's performance must be carefully measured and evaluated. Because students with severe disabilities often make progress in very small steps, it is important to measure performance precisely. Careful measurement helps the teacher plan instruction that will be appropriate to the child's needs and evaluate the program's effectiveness. Change in performance is shown most clearly when data on the child's efforts are collected every day. When working on dressing skills, for example, a teacher might measure the number of seconds it takes a child to remove a sock from her right foot when given the cue "Chandra, take off your sock." Over a period of time, Chandra should perform the task more rapidly. If she does not, some aspect of the instructional program may have to be changed. Accurate information about a child's performance helps the teacher design an appropriate educational program. Some programs keep videotaped records of students' performance on specific tasks. This record can add an important dimension to documenting behavioral changes over extended periods.

Partial Participation

The principle of **partial participation,** first described by Baumgart et al. (1982), acknowledges that even though some individuals with severe disabilities are not able to independently perform all steps of a given task or activity, they often can be taught to perform selected components or an adapted version of the task. A nonverbal student, for example, may be able to point to pictures of menu items on a laminated card to place an order at a fast-food restaurant. Snell, Lewis, and Houghton (1989) taught three elementary-age students with cerebral palsy and mental retardation to perform selected task analysis components of toothbrushing while the teacher performed the steps the students could not do. Both teachers and parents of two of the three students rated the students' partial participation in the toothbrushing activity as "meaningful" in that they appeared "happier and less likely to fuss" when they were participating in dental care, rather than having their teeth brushed for them. Follow-up data indicated that the toothbrushing skills generalized into the home and were maintained for 19 months following training.

Partial participation can be used to help the learner be more active in a task, make more choices in how the task will be carried out, and provide more control over the activity. Figure 11.4 is an example of how partial participation could be used within each step of a task analysis for making a blender drink.

Ferguson and Baumgart (1991) describe and offer suggestions for avoiding four types of errors or common misapplications of partial participation: (a) *passive participation*—the learner is present but not actively participating; (b) *myopic participation*—the student's participation is limited to only some parts of the activity that are chosen more for the convenience of others; (c) *piecemeal participation*—partial participation and the accompanying concepts of functional, activity-based, age-appropriate curriculum activities are only used part of the time; and (d) *missed participation*—in trying to help students become independent, the point of partial participation is missed altogether.

Several principles and guidelines for facilitating generalization are discussed in Chapter 4. More detailed information can be found in Baer (1981a); Browder and Snell (1993); Cooper, Heron, and Heward (1987); Haring (1988); and Horner, Dunlap, and Koegel (1988).

An excellent booklet by Farlow and Snell (1994) shows teachers how to use student performance data to make instruction more effective and efficient.

FIGURE 11.4

Example of how partial participation could be used within each step of a task analysis for making a blender drink

Task: Making a blender drink **Teacher's Assistance**	*Learner:* Saundra **Learner's Participation**	**Goal**
1. Announces activity	Lifts her head to listen	Active
2. Wheels Saundra to the cabinet	—	—
3. Gets out the utensils	Grasps a spoon	Active
4. Wheels Saundra to the table	Releases the spoon on the table	Active
5. Shows fruits	Selects one fruit by grasping it and pushing it to the teacher	Choice
6. Shows beverages	Selects one beverage by grasping it and pushing it to the teacher	Choice
7. Puts the ingredients in the blender	Operates the blender with a switch when the chosen ingredients are in	Control
8. Spoons the blender drink into a glass	Indicates if ready to drink	Control
9. Holds out a straw	Places the straw in the glass and drinks	Active Control

Key: Partial participation may have the goal of encouraging the learner to be more active in the routine (Active), to make more choices (Choice), or to have more control of the routine (Control). These goals are shown for each step of the task analysis.

Source: From D. M. Browder and M. E. Snell, 1993, "Daily Living and Community Skills." Reprinted with the permission of Simon & Schuster, Inc. from the Merrill/Prentice Hall text *Instructiona of Students with Severe Disabilities*, 4/e by Martha E. Snell. Copyright 1993 by Merrill/Prentice Hall.

Challenging Behavior

As students with severe disabilities are increasingly served in integrated school and community settings, notable changes have occurred in how teachers manage disruptive, aggressive, or socially unacceptable behaviors. In the recent past, a student who displayed "excess" behaviors, such as stereotypic head-weaving, may have been subjected to some unpleasant and undignified procedure, such as having his or her head restrained or perhaps having a teacher manipulate his or her head up and down for several minutes (Gast & Wolery, 1987). Some maladaptive behaviors of students with severe disabilities were routinely "treated" with the application of aversive consequences (e.g., being sprayed with water mist) or with an extended time-out from instruction. These were "modes of intervention which most people would reject as absolutely unacceptable if they were used with a person who does not have disabilities" (Center on Human Policy, 1986, p. 4).

With today's emphasis on respect for the individual student and on preparation for independent living, a growing number of educational programs deal with challenging, excessive, or unacceptable behaviors in more functional and dignified ways. Specifically, they attempt to (a) understand the meaning that a behavior has for a student, (b) offer the student a positive alternative behavior, (c) use nonintrusive intervention techniques, and (d) use strategies that have been validated and are intended for use in integrated community settings (Center on Human Policy, 1986).

Carr et al. (1994); LaVigna and Donnellan (1987); and Meyer and Evans (1989) provide detailed descriptions and guidelines on the use of such "nonaversive" treatment strategies.

Gentle teaching is a philosophy and an approach for treating problem behaviors by individuals with disabilites that relies on "valuing" the person and "giving warm assistance and protection when necessary" (McGee & Gonzalez, 1990, p. 244). Neither aversive stimulation nor contingent reinforcement is reported to be part of the approach. McGee (1992), the major proponent of gentle teaching, claims, "Behavior problems will evaporate like the morning dew if we express unconditional valuing" (McGee & Menolascino, 1992, p. 109). Although gentle teaching sounds wonderful, examination of the claims made in its behalf yields little evidence of effectiveness (Bailey, 1992; Jones & McCaughey, 1992). Mudford's (1995) review of independent studies of gentle teaching found it unsuccessful with seven of nine individuals, which led him to conclude that gentle teaching "cannot be considered an ethically defensible treatment alternative" (p. 345).

Aggression, acting out, noncompliance, and other problem behaviors during instruction sometimes can be reduced by relatively simple modifications of the instructional task or the way it is presented. For example, providing students with a choice of tasks (Dunlap, Kern-Dunlap, Clark, & Robbins, 1991), interspersing easy or high-probability tasks or requests with more difficult items or low-probability requests (Harchik & Putzier, 1990; Horner, Day, Sprague, O'Brien, & Heathfield, 1991), maintaining a rapid pace of instruction (Carnine, 1976; Dunlap, Dyer, & Koegel, 1983), and reducing task difficulty or errors (Carr & Durand, 1985; Weeks & Gaylord-Ross, 1981) have all been shown to reduce the frequency of problem behavior during instruction.

Functional analysis refers to a variety of behavior assessment methodologies for determining the environmental variables that are setting the occasion for and maintaining challenging behaviors such as self-injury (Iwata et al., 1994). By identifying which conditions or sources of reinforcement are significant for an individual, appropriate and effective treatment programs then can be developed. Recent research and applications of functional analysis can be found in the summer 1994 issue of the *Journal of Applied Behavior Analysis*.

Individual or Group Instruction?

Some educational programs for students with severe disabilities conduct instruction almost entirely on a one-to-one basis; that is, a teacher works with one student at a time. For many years, most professionals believed that one-to-one instruction was the only effective teaching arrangement for students with severe disabilities; about 90% of the articles about teaching or modifying the behavior of students with severe disabilities described a one-to-one approach (Favell, Favell, & McGimsey, 1978). The rationale was that one-to-one teaching minimized distractions and increased the likelihood of the student responding only to the teacher.

One-to-one instruction, however, has a number of disadvantages (Snell & Brown, 1993):

For a review of research on the relationship between instructional variables and problem behavior, see Munk and Repp (1994).

- Skills learned in one-to-one settings often do not generalize to larger groups of students.
- When a student is taught alone, he or she is isolated from other students, thereby missing opportunities for social interaction and peer reinforcement.
- One-to-one instruction provides no opportunities for incidental or observation learning from other students.
- One-to-one instruction is not a cost-effective use of the teacher's time.

Research investigating the effectiveness of small-group teaching with students who have severe disabilities has produced encouraging results. Alberto, Jobes, Sizemore, and Dorn (1980) found a group instructional arrangement to be at least as

For reviews of research on group instruction, see Keel and Gast (1992); Polloway, Cronin, and Patton (1986); and Reid and Favell (1984).

effective as individual instruction and noted appropriate peer interactions. Brown, Holvoet, Guess, and Mulligan (1980) found greater generalization of skills learned in group instruction. Curran (1983) and Orelove (1982) found that students with severe disabilities were capable of incidental learning of vocabulary; that is, when words were presented to a certain student in a small group, other students in the group could also learn to understand them. Westling, Ferrell, and Swanson (1982) found that group instruction resulted in much more efficient use of teacher time.

Edwards (1986) advocates the use of heterogeneous groupings because the needs of students who require high levels of caretaking are "more easily handled when their presence is in smaller numbers in a classroom" (p. 10). According to Snell and Brown (1993), the effectiveness of group instruction is enhanced when teachers do the following:

Choral responding and response cards can be used to enable every student in the group to respond to each item or question (see Chapter 6).

- Encourage students to listen and watch other group members and then praise them for doing so.
- Keep instruction interesting by keeping turns short, giving all members turns, giving turns contingent on attending, and using demonstrations and a variety of materials that can be handled.
- Involve all members by using multilevel instruction to individualize to each student's targeted skills and mode of response.
- Use partial participation and material adaptation to enable all students to respond.
- Keep waiting time to a minimum by controlling the group size and limiting the amount of teacher talk and the amount/length of student response in a single turn.
- Promote cooperation among group members.

Where Should Students with Severe Disabilities Be Taught?

The Benefits of the Home School

What is the least restrictive and most appropriate educational setting for a student with severe disabilities? This question continues to be the subject of much debate and discussion. Some special educators are calling for the abolition of all separate placements for students with severe disabilities (Brown et al., 1989a; Sailor et al., 1989; Stainback & Stainback, 1991). Lou Brown—who has long advocated for the inclusion of persons with severe disabilities in integrated school, vocational, and community settings—and his colleagues at the University of Wisconsin make a strong case for why students with severe disabilities should attend their "home school" (the same school a student would attend if he or she were not disabled).

> The environments in which students with severe intellectual disabilities receive instructional services have critical effects on where and how they spend their postschool lives. Segregation begets segregation. We believe that when children with intellectual disabilities attend separate schools, they are denied opportunities to demonstrate to the rest of the community that they can function in integrated environments and activities; their nondisabled peers do not know or understand them and too often think negatively of them; their parents become afraid to risk allowing them opportunities to learn to function in integrated environments later in life; and taxpayers assume they need to be sequestered in segregated group homes, enclaves,

work crews, activity centers, sheltered workshops, institutions, and nursing homes. (Brown et al., 1989a, p. 1)

Brown and his colleagues offer four reasons why they believe home schools should replace segregated and clustered schools. They define a clustered school as "a regular school attended by an unnaturally large proportion of students with intellectual disabilities, but it is not the one any or most would attend if they were not labeled disabled" (1989a, p. 1). First, when students without disabilities go to an integrated school with peers who are disabled, they are more likely to function responsibly as adults in a pluralistic society. Second, various sources of information support integrated schools as more meaningful instructional environments. (Hunt, Goetz, and Anderson [1986], for example, compared the IEP objectives for students with severe disabilities who were taught at integrated versus segregated schools. They found the quality of IEP objectives—in terms of age-appropriateness, functionality, and the potential for generalization of what was being taught to other environments—was higher for the students educated in integrated schools.) Third, parents and families have greater access to school activities when children are attending their home schools. Further, and perhaps most convincing, is the argument that there are greater opportunities to develop a wide range of social relationships with nondisabled peers when attending one's home school. Table 11.4 presents examples of 11 kinds of social relationships that might develop between students. Table 11.5 presents an assessment of the likelihood that each type of relationship will develop in a home school or in a clustered school.

For a discussion of 10 challenging issues concerning whether students with severe disabilities should be served in regular or special education classrooms in home schools, see Brown et al. (1989b).

See the January, 1995, issue of *Educational Leadership*, pp. 42–46.

Social Contacts

Although research has shown that simply placing students with disabilities into regular schools and classrooms does not necessarily lead to increased positive social interactions (Gresham, 1982), regular class participation can provide additional opportunities for positive social contacts. Kennedy and Itkonen (1994) described the effects of regular class participation on the social contacts with peers without disabil-

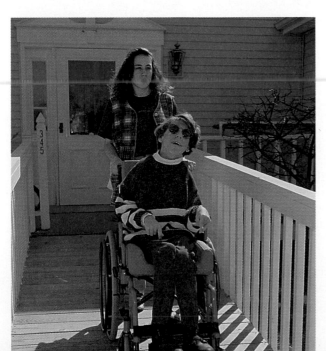

Friendships and after-school relationships between students with disabilities and their nondisabled peers are more likely to develop when all students attend their home school.

TABLE 11.4
Social relationships that can develop between students with severe disabilities and their
nondisabled peers when they attend the same school

SOCIAL RELATIONSHIP	EXAMPLE
Peer tutor	Leigh role-plays social introductions with Margo, providing feedback and praise for Margo's performance.
Eating companion	Jennifer and Rick eat lunch with Linda in the cafeteria and talk about their favorite music groups.
Art, home economics, industrial arts, music, physical education companion	In art class, students were instructed to paint a sunset. Tom sat next to Dan and offered suggestions and guidance about the best colors to use and how to complete the task.
Regular class companion	A fifth-grade class is doing a "Know Your Town" lesson in social studies. Ben helps Karen plan a trip through their neighborhood.
During-school companion	"Hangs out" and interacts on social level: After lunch and before the bell for class rang, Molly and Phyllis went to the student lounge for a soda.
Friend	David, a member of the varsity basketball team, invites Ralph, a student with severe disabilities, to his house to watch a game on TV.
Extracurricular companion	Sarah and Winona prepare their articles for the school newspaper together and then work on the layout in the journalism lab.
After-school-project companion	The sophomore class decided to build a float for the homecoming parade. Joan worked on it with Maria, a nondisabled companion, after school and on weekends in Joan's garage.
After-school companion	On Saturday afternoon, Mike, who is not disabled, and Bill go to the shopping mall.
Travel companion	David walks with Ralph when he wheels from last-period class to the gym, where Ralph helps the basketball team as a student manager.
Neighbor	Interacts with student in everyday environments and activities. Parents of nondisabled students in the neighborhood regularly exchange greetings with Mary when they are at school, around the neighborhood, at local stores, at the mall, at the grocery.

Source: From "The Home School: Why Students with Severe Disabilities Must Attend the Schools of Their Brothers, Sisters, Friends, and Neighbors" by L. Brown et al., 1989, *Journal of the Association for Persons with Severe Handicaps, 14,* p. 4. Adapted by permission.

ities for three high school students with severe and multiple disabilities. Don was 18 years old and classified as having severe intellectual retardation, along with paraplegia, cerebral palsy, and visual impairments. He used a wheelchair, which he moved himself for short distances, and lived in a 50-person facility for people with multiple disabilities and intensive health-care needs. Manny was also 18 years old and classified as having severe retardation. He communicated with two- or three-word sentences and had a 10-year history of hitting and pinching others. Ann was 19 years old with moderate mental retardation. Her communications ranged from a few words to elaborate sentences. She was receiving instruction regarding appropriate topics of conversation and maintaining physical distance when interacting with others. Ann received medication for generalized tonic-clonic seizures and would often yell, run away, and hit others during transitions from one class or activity to another. Contin-

TABLE 11.5

Feasibility and likelihood of developing and maintaining 11 kinds of social relationships between students with and without disabilities in home and clustered schools

SOCIAL RELATIONSHIP	HOME SCHOOL				CLUSTERED SCHOOL			
	DEVELOPMENT		LONGITUDINAL		DEVELOPMENT		LONGITUDINAL	
	FEASIBLE	LIKELY	FEASIBLE	LIKELY	FEASIBLE	LIKELY	FEASIBLE	LIKELY
Peer tutor	Yes	Yes	Yes	Yes	Yes	Yes	No	No
Eating companion	Yes	Yes	Yes	Yes	Yes	Yes	No	No
Art, home economics, industrial arts, music, or physical companion	Yes	Yes	Yes	Yes	Yes	Yes	No	No
Regular class companion	Yes	Yes	Yes	Yes	Yes	Yes	No	No
During-school companion	Yes	Yes	Yes	Yes	Yes	Yes	No	No
Friend	Yes	Yes	Yes	Yes	Yes	Yes	No	No
Extracurricular companion	Yes	Yes	Yes	Yes	Yes	No	No	No
After-school-project companion	Yes	Yes	Yes	Yes	Yes	No	No	No
After-school companion	Yes	Yes	Yes	Yes	No	No	No	No
Travel companion	Yes	Yes	Yes	Yes	No	No	No	No
Neighbor	Yes	Yes	Yes	Yes	No	No	No	No

Note. *Social relationship* refers to a positive personal interaction between a student with severe intellectual disabilities and a peer or other person who is not disabled.

Longitudinal refers to positive personal interactions between a student with severe intellectual disabilities and a peer or others who are not disabled that are developed, maintained, and enhanced across elementary, middle, and high school years.

Home school is the school a student with intellectual disabilities would attend if he or she were not disabled.

Clustered school is a regular school attended by an unnaturally large proportion of students with intellectual disabilities, but it is not the one any or most would attend if they were not disabled.

Feasible refers to a situation in which all of the structural resources necessary for a particular kind of social relationship to develop are present.

Likely refers to the probability of a particular kind of social relationship occurring, given the reasonable efforts of parents, guardians, professionals, and others.

Companion is a nondisabled person who accompanies, associates with, or assists a student who is severely intellectually disabled.

Source: From "The Home School: Why Students with Severe Disabilities Must Attend the Schools of Their Brothers, Sisters, Friends, and Neighbors" by L. Brown et al., 1989, *Journal of the Association for Persons with Severe Handicaps, 14,* p. 5. Adapted by permission.

gency contracts were in effect for both Manny and Ann as a preventive behavior management procedure; they could earn privileges for not engaging in problem behaviors.

A *social contact* was defined as a student with disabilities interacting with a peer(s) within the context of a meaningful activity (e.g., eating lunch, conducting a science project) for a minimum of 15 minutes. Each of the three students participated in a different regular classroom (average size, 25 students) for one period each school day, 5 days per week. Figure 11.5 shows the number of social contacts and the number of peers without disabilities included in those contacts.

Several aspects of this study deserve special comment. First, regular class participation increased the number of social contacts for each student even though ongoing opportunities to contact nondisabled peers were provided through "friendship" and peer tutoring programs during those weeks when the students were not in the regular classroom (shown as *baseline* in the figure). Second, the increases in social contacts were the result of participation for only one class period per day. It might be presumed that additional participation (e.g., two or three periods per day) would result in even more frequent contacts. Third, the increased social contacts were obtained without an elaborate training program or intensive intervention. Each student simply began participating in the regular classroom after a "circle of friends" introduction by the special education teacher to the regular class peers that stressed the similarities among all students, the need for students to support one another, and the importance of social relationships (O'Brien, Forest, Snow, & Hasbury, 1989).

A wide variety of strategies for promoting desired social relationships has been developed. One strategy is to provide the student with disabilities a skill for initiating and maintaining interaction. For example, two nonverbal boys with severe and profound mental retardation and multiple physical disabilities learned to initiate play activities with nondisabled peers by showing badges with photographs of activities (Jolly, Test, & Spooner, 1993). Other strategies focus on the behavior of peers without disabilities, such as cooperative learning activities (Eichinger, 1990; Putnam, 1993). Still other approaches involve changes in the roles and responsibilities of instructional faculty, such as teaching teams (Ferguson, Meyer, Jeanchild, Juniper, & Zingo, 1992; Giangreco, 1991; Thousand & Villa, 1990). Many of these strategies for facilitating the regular classroom inclusion of students with severe disabilities are compatible with one another, and it is typical for a program to incorporate multiple, concurrent methods for identifying and providing supports for students, their teachers, and their peers.

> Increased social contacts and positive social acceptance with peers without disabilities as a result of inclusion have been reported by a number of other researchers as well (e.g., Cole & Meyer, 1991; Evans, Salisbury, Palombaro, Berryman, & Hollowood, 1992; Hanline, 1993; Hunt, Farron-Davis, Beckstead, Curtis, & Goetz, 1994; Romer & Haring, 1994). To learn about a method for building social supports for students with disabilities in regular classrooms, see "Everyone Belongs" later in this chapter. The winter 1994 issue of *JASH* is devoted to the impact of inclusion on students with severe disabilities and their peers without disabilites.

Experiences and Transformations of General Education Teachers

To find out how regular education teachers reacted to having a student with severe disabilities placed in their classrooms, Giangreco, Dennis, Cloninger, Edelman, and Shattman (1993) interviewed 19 general education teachers in grades kindergarten through ninth grade. They found that regardless of how the child with severe disabilities was placed in the general education classroom, most teachers initially described the placement in cautious or negative terms (e.g., "reluctant," "nervous," "unqualified," "angry"). Despite their initial negative reactions, 17 of the teachers experienced "increased ownership and involvement" with the child with severe disabilities as the school year progressed. Giangreco et al. refer to this process of changing attitude and perspective as *transformation*.

FIGURE 11.5

Frequency of social contacts by three high school students with severe disabilities. Each data point represents the mean frequency of contacts per day across the 35 weeks of the study.

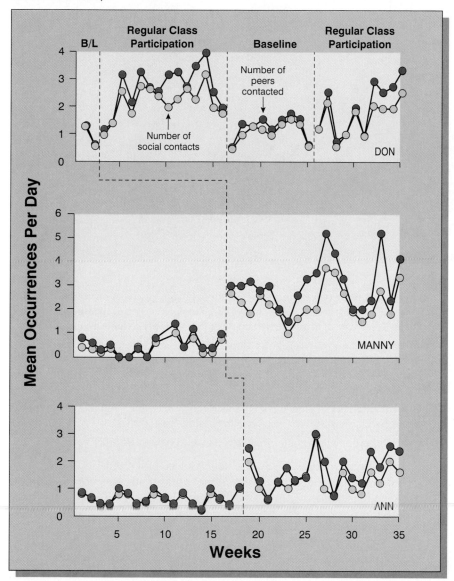

Source: From "Some Effects of Regular Class Participation on the Social Contacts and Social Networks of High School Students with Severe Disabilities," 1994, by C. H. Kennedy and T. Itkonen, *Journal of the Association for Persons with Severe Handicaps, 19,* p. 6. Reprinted by permission.

Transformations were gradual and progressive, rather than discrete and abrupt. . . . A number of teachers who had these experiences reportedly came to the realization they *could* be successful and that including the student was not as difficult as they had originally imagined. . . . The following quotes typify the comments of teachers who underwent significant transformation.

"I started seeing him as a little boy. I started feeling that he's a person too. He's a student. Why should I not teach him? He's in my class. That's my responsibility. I'm a teacher!"

In the end, the best inclusion facilitators are the students themselves.

For detailed information about administrative, curricular, and instructional strategies designed to support the education of students with severe disabilities in regular schools, see Sailor et al. (1989); Stainback and Stainback (1991, 1992); and Thousand, Villa, and Nevin (1994).

"I made the full swing of fighting against having Bobbi Sue placed in my room to fighting for her to be in a mainstream classroom working with kids in the way that she had worked with them all year long. I'm a perfect example of how you have to have an open mind."

"I started watching my own regular classroom students. They didn't treat him any differently. They went about their business like everything was normal. So I said, 'If they can do it, I can do it.' He's not getting in their way. They're treating him like everybody else."

"They were always letting me know when I forgot something. 'You didn't remember to include Sarah.' So they were very good at letting me know."

"The kids help you figure it out." (Giangreco et al., 1993, pp. 365–366)[*]

According to Ferguson et al. (1992), the key to successful regular classroom participation for students with severe disabilities is the work of an *inclusion facilitator.* An effective inclusion facilitator—who is often but not necessarily the special education teacher—plays three roles: (a) a *broker,* who locates resources and matches them to the student's needs, (b) an *adapter,* who develops and suggests changes in lesson plans and activities to better accommodate the student with disabilities, and (c) a *collaborator,* who works effectively with other adults toward shared goals.

How Much Time in the Regular Classroom?

Although the social benefits of regular class participation for students with disabilities—as well as for their peers without disabilities—have been clearly shown, the effects of inclusion on the attainment of IEP goals and objectives is not yet known.

---

[*]From Giangreco, M. F., Dennis, R., Cloninger, C., Edelman, S., & Schattman, R. (1993). "I've counted Jon": Transformational experiences of teachers educating students with disabilities. *Exceptional Children*, *59*, 359–372, copyright (1993) by the Council for Exceptional Children. Reprinted by permission.

The functional IEP goals and objectives for students with severe disabilities are seldom reflected in the academic curriculum of the regular classroom (especially at secondary level). Available instruction time is especially valuable to students who by definition require direct, intensive, and long-term instruction to acquire basic skills that students without disabilities learn without instruction. A major challenge for both special and general educators is to develop models and strategies for including students with severe disabilities in regular classroom activities without sacrificing their opportunities to acquire, practice, and generalize the functional skills they need most.

The question of how much time students with severe disabilities should spend in the regular classroom is an important one. Although a few full inclusion advocates might argue that every student with disabilities should have a full-time regular class placement regardless of the nature of his or her educational needs, most special educators probably would agree with Brown et al. (1991), who argue that students with severe intellectual disabilities should be based in the same schools and classrooms they would attend if they were not disabled but that they should also spend some time elsewhere.

> There are substantial differences between being *based in* and *confined to* regular education classrooms. "Based in" refers to "being a member of a real class," "where and with whom you start the school day" "you may not spend all your time with your class, but it is still your group and everyone knows it." . . . It is our position that it is unacceptable for students with severe disabilities to spend either 0% or 100% of their time in regular education classrooms. . . . How much time should be spent in regular classes? Enough to ensure that the student is a member, not a visitor. A lot, if the student is engaged in meaningful activities. Quite a bit if she is young, but less as she approaches 21. There is still a lot we do not know. (pp. 40, 46)

✳ *The Challenge and Rewards of Teaching Students with Severe Disabilities*

The current extension of public education and community-based services to individuals with severe disabilities is a tremendously important and challenging development. Teachers—both special and general educators—who are providing instruction to students with severe disabilities can rightfully be called pioneers on an exciting new frontier of education. Professionals who are involved in educating students with severe disabilities "can look back with pride, and even awe, at the advances they have made. In a relatively brief period, educators, psychologists, and other professionals have advocated vigorously for additional legislation and funds, extended the service delivery model into the public schools and community, and developed a training technology" (Orelove, 1984, p. 271).

Future research will increase our understanding of the ways students with severe disabilities acquire, maintain, and generalize functional skills. Better techniques of measuring and changing behavior are constantly being developed; these are balanced with a growing concern for the personal rights and dignity of individuals with severe disabilities.

Teaching students with severe disabilities is difficult and demanding. The teacher must be well organized, firm, and consistent. He or she must be able to man-

Billingsley and Kelley (1994) reported that 39 of 51 instructional methods considered to be "best practice" for educating students with severe disabilities are considered acceptable and appropriate for use in general education classrooms.

See the January, 1995, issue of *Educational Leadership*, pp. 7–11 and pp. 22–25.

Everyone Belongs
....

Building the Vision with MAPS, the McGill Action Planning System

by Marsha Forest and
Jack Pearpoint, Directors

Centre for Integrated Education and Community, Toronto, Canada

A shared vision has caught the imagination of parents and educators across Canada: a vision of all children—including those with severe disabilities—being educated in regular classrooms alongside their brothers and sisters, friends and neighbors. The movement to integrate children with disabilities into ordinary classrooms is founded on a simple yet profound philosophy: Everyone belongs. MAPS, the McGill Action Planning System, is a systems approach to problem solving that has helped many schools turn vision into reality. MAPS was designed by a team of educators who were searching for ways to help welcome children with disabilities back into regular schools and classrooms. The original MAPS team consisted of the two authors plus Judith Snow, Evelyn Lusthaus, and John O'Brien.

Assumptions of the MAPS Process

1. All people are valuable and can contribute to life on this globe.
2. All people have abilities, talents, and gifts.
3. All people can learn!
4. Disability is a social construct. People are not disabled; systems disable people.
5. There is a real need for support, services, and educators who will reach out and nurture the potential of every child.
6. The only label we recommend is a person's name. Labels hide the fact that we really don't know what to do. After that, we suggest adopting a problem-solving mode that creatively figures out what to do for each unique individual.

7. Common sense is the most important and least common sense.

Who Goes to a MAP?—Friends!

The size of the group that gathers for a MAP session can vary from two to two dozen. The key ingredients for participants are intimate and personal contact with the individual being mapped. A grandmother or neighbor, a friend—all are on equal footing with professionals, who are welcomed and needed, but as individuals, not as "therapists." Parents and family members usually have the most to offer, if asked. Their perspectives are all welcome in a MAP.

Peer participation is critical. Class-/age-mates have enormous untapped energy and creative capacity. Their "straight talk" often empowers teachers with new ideas. Adults must be careful not to constrain or downgrade the participation of peers: They are critical and equal partners in the MAPS process.

The delicate question is whether or not the individual who is being "mapped" should be present. It is a judgment call; it works both ways. We hedge toward full participation. People understand an enormous amount, more than we think. Also, a MAP is an "upper," a real boost for an individual who previously has been excluded. Full participation also saves time in trying to explain it all later.

What Happens at a MAP?

How does it work?

"Mapping" is a collaborative problem-solving process aided by a two-person team of facilitator and recorder. The facilitator, positioned at the open end of a half-circle formed by the participants, presents eight key questions to the group. The facilitator must be skilled in group process and have a problem-solving orientation. Most important, the facilitator must be committed to building an integrated school community. The information and ideas generated during the session are marked on a large piece of chart paper by the recorder. Public charting is vital to the

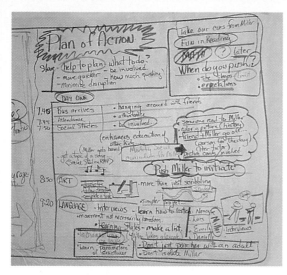

A portion of Miller's MAP.

MAPS process: It generates "images" that help participants visualize the relationships between and among people and actions, thus promoting the creation of additional problem-solving strategies. It also serves as a permanent record of the plans and commitments made by the group. The recorder need not be an artist, but it is vital that the MAP be printed or written clearly, using the participants' words. The chart should include contributions from everyone in the group.

MAPS planning typically occurs in one or two sessions, and approximately 3 hours are required to fully address these questions.

1. *What's a MAP?* The facilitator begins the MAPS process by asking participants, "What is a map?" A recent group gave these answers:

   • Something that gives direction
   • A thing that helps you get somewhere
   • Routes to different places
   • A way to find a new way
   • Stops you from getting lost

2. *What is the individual's history?* The participants most intimate with the child being mapped—usually parents and family members—are asked to give a 10- to 15-minute history focusing on key milestones and events in the individual's life.

3. *What is your dream for the individual?* This question is intended to get people, especially parents, to imagine their vision for the child's future. Many parents of children with disabilities have lost their ability to dream about what they really want for their child. The vision of the future should not be limited by money or current realities. This question helps the group focus on the direction in which the individual is now heading and encourages concrete action plans for realizing the vision.

4. *What is your nightmare?* This question is the hardest to ask but is very important to get on the table. We must understand the nightmare in order to prevent it. No parent has ever said, "I'm worried that my child won't attend a university, won't get an A on the next test, or won't learn to spell." Instead, the nightmare question brings out what is in the heart of virtually every parent of a child with a severe disability: "We're afraid our child will end up in an institution, work in a sheltered workshop, and have no one to care for her when we die." The MAPS planning must reflect an understanding of the nightmare; preventing the nightmare is one measure of its success.

5. *Who is the individual?* With this question, the MAPS process shifts into a no-holds-barred brainstorming mode. Participants are asked to give words or phrases that describe the person being mapped. The rule is no jargon, no labels; just describe how you see the person. The image of a unique and distinct personality should emerge. Here are examples from a recent MAP for Miller, a 14-year-old who, to some, is "severely handicapped and mentally retarded."

   • She has a brother.
   • She gets around in a wheelchair.
   • She's lots of fun.
   • She's active like crazy.
   • She's radical/bad (really means good).
   • She's temperamental.
   • She likes to touch.
   • She wants to be involved.
   • She looks at you.
   • She can talk some.

6. *What are the individual's strengths, abilities, gifts, and talents?* All too often, we focus on the things a child with a disability cannot do. It is vital to build upon strengths and abilities. This can be a difficult question for parents, who have been struggling with negatives for so long. This question also is intended to produce a brainstormed list from the entire group. Here is part of the list generated for Miller.

- She can make us laugh.
- She moves her arms, can throw a ball.
- She likes to listen to music.
- She's persistent, tries real hard.
- She can count and remember numbers.
- She enjoys stories and movies.

7. *What are the individual's needs?* This, too, is a brainstorm. Don't let people stop each other, but don't get bogged down either. Keep it short and record people's words and perceptions. Parents, teachers, and peers often have different perceptions about needs. For Miller, it was decided that what she needed most of all was

   a communication system that lets her express her wants and feelings

   more independence with dressing and other self-care skills

   to be with her own age-group

   places to go and things to do after school

   teenage clothes

8. *What is the plan of action?* This is the final and most important question of all. The MAPS planning group imagines what the individual's ideal day at school would look like and what must be done to make it a reality. Step by step, the MAPS group goes through an entire day, envisioning the various environments and activities the individual will experience and what kinds of resources, supports, and adaptations can be created to make the day successful. For example, a peer volunteers to meet the taxi that brings Miller to school each morning and to walk with her to the classroom; during language arts period, a classmate will help Miller practice with her communication board; and the principle of partial participation will be used on the playground when Miller bats in the softball game and a teammate runs the bases for her.

In addition to describing what a MAP is, we believe it's important to emphasize what MAPS is not:

1. *A MAP is not a trick, a gimmick, or a quick-fix solution to complex human problems.* MAPS is not a one-shot session that will provide the magic bullet to blast a vulnerable person into the everyday life and fabric of school and community. MAPS is a problem-solving process; the plans for action are not set in stone, but must be reviewed and changed as often as needed.

2. *A MAP is not a replacement for an Individualized Education Plan (IEP).* A MAP session may help provide useful information for an IEP, but it is not a substitute for the IEP process and must not be treated as such. A MAPS participant must be personally and/or professionally involved in the individual's life, not simply someone who has tested or given intermittent therapy to the individual.

3. *A MAP is not controlled by experts in order to design a neat program package.* The outcome of a MAP must meet three criteria: (a) The plan must be a personalized plan of action, a one-of-a-kind MAP tailor-made for the person; (b) the person is at the heart of every aspect of the MAP; and (c) the plan brings the person closer and closer into the daily life of the school and community.

4. *A MAP is not a tool to make any segregated setting better.* MAPS was designed to liberate people from segregated settings; it is only for people and organizations figuring out together how to get a person fully included in life.

5. *A MAP is not an academic exercise.* It is a genuine, personal approach to problem solving with and on behalf of real individuals who are vulnerable. A MAP produces outcomes that have real implications for how the person will live his or her life.

Miller and friends.

6. *MAPS is not just talk.* MAPS is talk and action. A MAP gives clear directions and action steps for inclusion.

The metaphor for MAPS is a kaleidoscope, a beautiful instrument whose design changes constantly. We see the kaleidoscope as the outcome of each MAP. It is a medley of people working together to make something unique and better happen. It is more than anyone can do alone.

For additional information and training materials on MAPS, write the Centre for Integrated Education and Community, 24 Thome Crescent, Toronto, Ontario, Canada, M6H 2S5. Two journal articles describing the MAPS approach are Forest and Lusthaus (1990) and Vandercook, York, and Forest (1989).

---

age a complex educational operation, which usually involves supervising paraprofessional aides, student teachers, peer tutors, and volunteers. The teacher must be knowledgeable about one-to-one and group instruction formats and be able to work cooperatively with other professionals, such as physicians, psychologists, physical therapists, social workers, and language specialists. He or she must maintain accurate records and be constantly planning for the future needs of the students. Effective communication with parents, school administrators, vocational rehabilitation personnel, and community agencies is also vital.

Students with the most severe disabilities sometimes give little or no apparent response, so their teachers must be sensitive to small changes in student behavior. The effective teacher is consistent in designing and implementing strategies to improve learning and behavior (even if some of the students' previous teachers were not). The effective teacher should not be too quick to remove difficult tasks or requests that result in noncompliance or misbehavior. It is better to teach students to request assistance (Durand, 1986) and to intersperse tasks that are easy for the student to perform (Munk & Repp, 1994; Sprague & Horner, 1990).

There is a difference between either expecting miracles or being passively patient and simply working each day at the job of designing, implementing, and evaluating systematic instruction and supports. As Lovaas (1981) writes, it can be a mistake to expect a miracle:

> We were expecting a sudden step forward, that possibly somehow we would hit upon some central cognitive, emotional, or social event inside the child's mind that would help him make a sudden and major leap ahead. . . . Such a leap would have been so gratifying, and it would have made our work so much easier. It never happened. Instead, progress followed slow, step-by-step upward progression, with only a few and minor spurts ahead. We learned to settle down for hard work. (p. x)

Some might consider it undesirable to work with students with severe disabilities because of their serious and multiple disabilities. Yet working with students who require instruction at its very best can offer many highly rewarding teaching experiences. Much satisfaction can be felt in teaching a child to feed and dress herself independently, helping a student make friends with nondisabled peers, and supporting a young adult's efforts to live, travel, and work as independently as possible in the community. Both the challenge and the potential rewards of teaching students with severe disabilities are great.

Little Changes with Big Impacts

Reactions to Progress by Students with Severe Disabilities

by Michael F. Giangreco

Teachers and therapists are people who want to make a difference, people who hope that what they do will improve the quality of life for the students and families with whom they work. Laura is one such teacher. During the past few years, Laura has been working with a heterogeneous group of students with challenging needs at East Middle School. One aspect of its educational program is to teach skills that will allow students to participate more fully in the community with nondisabled individuals. Laura sometimes has gotten discouraged because the rates of progress seemed low for some of her students with the most severe disabilities. She started asking, "Am I really helping? Am I really making a difference?"

Then one day Laura received the following letter from a parent regarding her daughter, Jackie, a 13-year-old girl with Down syndrome who functioned in the range of severe mental retardation and was diagnosed as legally blind.

Dear Laura,

After school we went grocery shopping, me, Jackie, and Sheldon (the baby). On our way home, Jackie said, "Mom, you forgot Italian bread." She was right. I said we would have to go without—I was not hauling the baby out of the car again. Jackie said, "I can buy it myself at P & C." I said, "I don't know, Jackie." "Yes, Mom, my teacher helped me." She was so sure she could do it that I didn't want to defeat her—so off to P & C. I pulled up in front with mounting panic. Jackie was still positive she could do it. I explained that the bread was back by the meat and bakery—we had bought it here before, but not recently. Jackie said, "I know—it has a light." I then gave Jackie $2 and let her go. Four minutes later (it seemed like 2 hours), she was back at the car with her Italian bread in a shopping bag and her change tight in her hand. I couldn't believe it—talk about the taste of success—I think that was the *best* bread we have ever had! Be proud, teacher—Mom is!

When Laura shared the letter with me, it was clear that this seemingly small achievement had a big impact. It reminded me of a similar experience I had had as a teacher. Tom was one of the most challenging students I had ever encountered. Several years earlier, he had suffered a severe brain stem injury in a bicycle-auto accident. The injury left Tom with profound mental retardation, severe physical disabilities, and blind. Tom was nonverbal and nonambulatory and had no functional use of his limbs or hands. He slept a lot and seemed alert for only short periods during the day. For a few years after his accident, Tom was fed through a plastic tube inserted into his stomach. Tom's family had worked very hard to teach him to eat by mouth again. When I met Tom, he was able to be fed pureed foods by mouth, but he still had the gastrostomy tube in his stomach as a precaution because he was prone to dehydration during the summer.

In a meeting with Tom's parents to plan his IEP, his dad said, "We'd like him to learn something, anything, so we know that he can learn." We agreed that one goal would be to try to teach Tom to follow a simple direction, "Open up," so that he could be fed, have his teeth brushed, and accept medicine. With an instructional procedure called time-delay, Tom began responding to the direction. Although this tiny achievement did little for Tom directly, it had a major impact on the quality of his life indirectly. For the first time in a long time, people at home and at school were encouraged because Tom had learned. This hopeful experience resulted in Tom's receiving more frequent and positive interaction from others.

Seemingly small accomplishments hold the potential for tremendous positive impact. Professionals in schools can make a difference when they work collaboratively with families to select and teach meaningful skills to enhance a student's quality of life at home, at school, and in the community. ✳

Michael F. Giangreco is Research Assistant Professor, Center for Developmental Disabilities, University of Vermont. He is a national leader in the movement to provide meaningful education services and outcomes to students with severe disabilities in inclusive classrooms and is coauthor of the widely used COACH curriculum (Giangreco, Cloninger, & Iverson, 1993).

Summary

Defining Severe Disabilities

- The student with severe disabilities needs instruction in many of basic skills that most children without disabilities acquire without instruction in the first 5 years of life.

- Students with profound disabilities have pervasive delays in all domains of functioning at a developmental level no higher than 2 years.

- TASH defines persons with severe disabilities as "individuals of all ages who require extensive ongoing support in more than one major life activity in order to participate in integrated community settings and to enjoy a quality of life that is available to citizens with fewer or no disabilities."

Characteristics of Students with Severe Disabilities

- Students with severe disabilities frequently have multiple disabilities, including physical problems, and usually look and act markedly different from children without disabilities.

- Children with severe disabilities frequently show some or all of the following behaviors or skill deficits:

  Slow acquisition rates for learning new skills

  Difficulty in generalizing and maintaining newly learned skills

  Severe deficits in communication skills

  Impaired physical and motor development

  Deficits in self-help skills

  Infrequent constructive behavior and interaction

  Frequent inappropriate behavior

- Despite their intense challenges, students with severe disabilities often exhibit many positive characteristics, such as warmth, humor, sociability, and persistence.

- Students with dual sensory impairments cannot be accommodated in special education programs designed solely for students with hearing or visual impairments. Although the vast majority of children labeled deaf-blind have some functional hearing and/or vision, the dual impairments severely impede learning of communication and social skills.

- The essential features of autism typically appear prior to 30 months of age and consist of disturbances of (a) developmental rates and/or sequences; (b) responses to sensory stimuli; (c) speech, language, and cognitive capacities; and (d) capacities to relate to people, events, and objects.

- Although the prognosis for children with autism has traditionally been poor, some children have achieved normal functioning by the primary grades as a result of an intensive, behaviorally oriented program of early intervention and preschool mainstreaming.

- Despite their limitations, children with severe disabilities can and do learn.

Prevalence

- Students with severe and multiple disabilities are served and counted under several disability categories, making prevalence figures hard to determine.

- Estimates of the prevalence of severe disabilities range from 0.1% to 1% of the population.

Historical Background

- Throughout most of history, many children with severe disabilities probably died in infancy.

- State-run custodial institutions were established during the 19th century but offered little in the way of education and training for individuals with the most severe disabilities.

- Within the last 20 years, numerous court cases and laws have mandated free public education for all children, regardless of the nature or severity of their disabilities.

Causes of Severe Disabilities

- Brain disorders, which are involved in most cases of severe intellectual disabilities, are the result of either *brain dysgenesis* (abnormal brain development) or *brain damage* (caused by influences that alter the structure or function of a brain that had been developing normally up to that point).

- Severe and profound disabilities most often have biological causes, including

  Chromosomal abnormalities

  Genetic and metabolic disorders

  Complications of pregnancy and prenatal care

  Birth trauma

  Later brain damage

- In about one sixth of all cases of severe disabilities, the cause cannot be clearly determined.

Educational Approaches

- A curriculum based on typical developmental milestones is inappropriate for most students with severe disabilities.

- Students with severe disabilities must be taught skills that are functional, age appropriate, and directed toward the community. Interaction with nondisabled students should occur regularly.

- Students with severe disabilities should be taught choice-making skills.

- The emphasis of research and training in communication for persons with severe disabilities has shifted from the remediation of specific forms of communication to a focus on functional communication of any mode that enables communication partners to establish shared meanings.

- Effective instruction requires structure and precision. Skills must be broken down into small steps; current performance must be precisely assessed; the target skill must be stated clearly; and skills must be taught in an appropriate sequence.

- Some students with severe disabilities use augmentative and alternative systems of communication (AAC), such as gestures, various sign language systems, pictorial communication boards, symbol systems, and electronic communication aids.

- Facilitated communication (FC) is a process by which a communication partner, called a facilitator, provides physical support to assist an individual who cannot speak or whose speech is limited to typing on a keyboard or to pointing at pictures, words, or other symbols on a communication board.

- Although proponents claim that FC enables some people with autism and moderate or severe mental retardation to display an "undisclosed literacy" consistent with "normal intellectual functioning," scientific research to date has not confirmed those claims.

- Students with severe disabilities should also be taught age-appropriate recreation and leisure skills.

- Because each student with severe disabilities has many learning needs, teachers must carefully prioritize and choose IEP objectives and learning activities that will be of most benefit to the student and his or her family.

- Effective instruction of students with severe disabilities is characterized by these elements:

  The student's current level of performance must be precisely assessed.

  The skill to be taught must be defined clearly.

  The skills must be ordered in an appropriate sequence.

  The teacher must provide a clear prompt or cue to the student.

  The student must receive immediate feedback and reinforcement from the teacher.

  Strategies that promote generalization of learning must be used.

  The student's performance must be carefully measured and evaluated.

- Partial participation is both a philosophy for selecting activities and a method for adapting activities and supports to enable students with severe disabilities to actively participate in meaningful tasks they are not able to perform independently.

- The teacher of students with severe disabilities must be skilled in positive, instructionally relevant strategies for assessing and dealing with challenging and problem behaviors.

- Research and practice are providing increasing support for the use of integrated group instruction arrangements with students with severe disabilities.

- Students with severe disabilities are more likely to develop and maintain social relationships with students without disabilities if they attend their home school and participate at least part of the time in the regular classroom.

- Although the initial reactions and feelings of many general education teachers who have a student with severe disabilities placed in their classrooms are negative, those apprehensions and concerns over how to treat the student often transform into positive experiences as the student becomes a regular member of their classroom.

- Working with students who require instruction at its very best can offer many highly rewarding teaching experiences.

For More Information

Journals

Focus on Autistic Behavior. A journal for practitioners who work with individuals with autism and pervasive developmental disabilities. Articles deal with assessment, behavior management, curriculum, instruction, related services, and vocational training. Published bimonthly by PRO-ED, Austin, TX.

Journal of Autism and Developmental Disorders. A quarterly journal that publishes multidisciplinary research on all severe psychopathologies in childhood.

Research in Developmental Disabilities. Published quarterly by Pergamon Press, Elmsford, NY 10523. Includes articles on theory and behavioral research related to people "who suffer from severe and pervasive developmental disabilities."

Journal of the Association for Persons with Severe Disabilities (JASH). Published quarterly by the Association for Persons with Severe Disabilities, 7010 Roosevelt Way N.E., Seattle, WA 98115. Publishes articles reporting original research, reviews of the literature, and conceptual or position papers that offer new directions for service delivery and program development and effective assessment and intervention methodologies.

Books

Browder, D. M. (1991). *Assessment of individuals with severe disabilities: An applied behavioral approach to life skills assessment* (2nd ed.). Baltimore: Paul H. Brookes.

Brown, F., & Lehr, D. H. (1989). *Persons with profound disabilities: Issues and practices.* Baltimore: Paul H. Brookes.

Cipani, E. C., & Spooner, F. (Eds.). (1994). *Curricular and instructional approaches for persons with severe disabilities.* Boston: Allyn & Bacon.

Goetz, L., Guess, D., & Stremel-Campbell, K. (Eds.). (1987). *Innovative program design for individuals with dual sensory impairments.* Baltimore: Paul H. Brookes.

Harris, S. L., & Handleman, J. S. (Eds.). (1994). *Preschool programs for children with autism.* Austin, TX: PRO-ED.

Horner, R. H., Meyer, L. H., & Fredericks, H. D. B. (Eds.). (1986). *Education of learners with severe disabilities: Exemplary service strategies.* Baltimore: Paul H. Brookes.

Koegel, R. L., & Koegel, L. (1995). *Teaching children with autism.* Baltimore: Paul H. Brookes.

Lovaas, O. I. (1981). *Teaching developmentally disabled children: The ME book.* Austin, TX: PRO-ED.

Matson, J. L. (Ed.). (1994). *Autism in children and adults: Etiology, assessment, and intervention.* Pacific Grove, CA: Brooks/Cole.

Meyer, L., Peck, C., & Brown, L. (Eds.). (1990). *Critical issues in the lives of people with severe disabilities.* Baltimore: Paul H. Brookes.

Orelove, F. P., & Sobsey, D. (1987). *Educating children with multiple disabilities: A transdisciplinary approach.* Baltimore: Paul H. Brookes.

Snell, M. E. (Ed.). (1993). *Instruction of students with severe disabilities* (4th ed.). Englewood Cliffs, NJ: Merrill/Prentice Hall.

Sternberg, L. (Ed.). (1994). *Individuals with profound disabilities: Instructional and assistive strategies* (3rd ed.). Austin, TX: PRO-ED.

Westling, D. L., & Fox, L. (1995). *Teaching persons with severe disabilities.* Englewood Cliffs, NJ: Merrill/Prentice-Hall.

Wilcox, B., & Bellamy, G. T. (1987). *The activities catalog: An alternative curriculum for youth and adults with severe disabilities.* Baltimore: Paul H. Brookes.

Wolery, M., Ault, M. J., & Doyle, P. M. (1992). *Teaching students with moderate to severe disabilities.* New York: Longman.

Organizations

ABLENET, 360 Hoover Street N.E., Minneapolis, MN 55413. Offers information and publications on the use of automated learning devices, microswitches, and other technology with persons who have severe disabilities. Has available for purchase a book by Jackie Levin and Lynn Scherfenberg, *Breaking Barriers: How Children and Adults with Severe Disabilities Can Access the World Through Simple Technology.*

The Association for Persons with Severe Disabilities (TASH), 7010 Roosevelt Way N.E., Seattle, WA 98115. "TASH is an organization of professionals in partnership with people with disabilities, their families and others who are dedicated to education, research and advocacy on behalf of individuals of any age who have severe intellectual disabilities and their families, so that these persons may live, learn, work and enjoy life and relationships with dignity, respect and individualized support" (Association for Persons with Severe Disabilities, 1990, p. 1).

Through its journal and monthly newsletter, disseminates a wide variety of useful information to teachers, parents, administrators, researchers, and others. Through its annual convention, provides a major professional forum for the exchange of new developments relating to the education of persons with severe disabilities. Through its many state and local chapters, also sponsors conferences and activities.

Center on Human Policy, 724 Comstock Avenue, Syracuse, NY 13244. Provides reports and other resources on the integration of people with severe disabilities into community life. Also distributes materials encouraging the development of positive attitudes about persons with disabilities in schools and the media.

Department of Specialized Educational Services, Madison Metropolitan School District, 545 West Dayton Street, Madison, WI 53703. In cooperation with the Department of Studies in Behavioral Disabilities at the University of Wisconsin, has been especially active in developing programs of instruction for children with severe disabilities and in

seeking to facilitate integration with nondisabled individuals. Has available for purchase a number of curriculum guides and other materials.

Helen Keller National Center for Deaf-Blind Youths and Adults, 111 Middle Neck Road, Sands Point, NY 11050. Offers training programs for persons with impaired vision and hearing and consultation to agencies providing services to this population. Publishes *Directory of Agencies and Organizations Serving Deaf-Blind Individuals,* curriculum manuals, and other informational materials about deaf-blindness.

Autism Society of America, 8601 Georgia Avenue, Suite 503, Silver Spring, MD 20910. An organization of family members and professionals dedicated to the education and welfare of children and adults with severe disorders of communication and behavior.

Gifted and Talented Students

by Richard D. Howell, William L. Heward, and Raymond H. Swassing

* Why do students who are very bright need specialized education?

* How has the evolving definition of giftedness changed the ways in which students are identified and served?

* How can the regular classroom teacher provide instruction at the pace and depth needed by gifted and talented students while at the same time meeting the needs of other students in the classroom?

* Should gifted students be educated with their same-age peers or with older students who share the same intellectual and academic talents and interests?

* What provisions should be made to accurately identify students with outstanding talents who are from diverse cultural groups or have disabilities?

*J*anie has just completed her report on the solar system and is word-processing it for class tomorrow. She looks out her bedroom window and wonders what might be happening on the countless planets that circle all of those stars. And she thinks about the circumstances that made life possible on the third planet from the star called Sol. What Janie is doing may not seem special—after all, most students type school reports and wonder about extraterrestrial life—until we learn that she is just 6 years old. Janie is functioning years ahead of her age-mates. She writes in complete sentences, expresses herself exceptionally well, and has a powerful urge to know the answers to many and varied problems.

Toney Jojola saunters down a dusty back road near his home in the Southwest. Toney is excited because today his mentor and great-aunt has promised to teach him the process of applying the rich charcoal slip to the pottery he is making. His people have been making pottery for hundreds of years, but somehow it seems to take on multiple meanings in his hands. He notices and uses small variations in color and texture to embed symbolism into his pieces. Perhaps this one will have the winged serpent that he favors so much, reminding everyone that an immense trade network existed in prehistoric America that reached from Canada to South America. Toney sees much in his pottery, in his ancestors who have inspired him, in the beauty that is the earth made functional, and in a desire for continuity in his life. Toney does not say much in school or express himself very well in writing, but he understands everything that is being said and talked about. He is very patient and seems tentative in his behavior, not wanting to create a disturbance that would draw attention to himself. During class he dreams of the pottery designs he will someday create in the studio that he will inherit from his great-aunt.

Malcolm, a ninth grader, runs from school to the bus stop for the bus that will take him to the local university, where he is taking his second course in creative writing. He is excited about showing his latest short story to the professor. Malcolm's prose brings into focus all of the pain he sees around him, critically analyzing the leadership of his community and nation. He believes he has a message that must be heard; he is powerfully moved to reach out to the disaffected, the disenfranchised, as well as the ambivalent of all races. He has many ideas for changing what he believes is wrong with his government. He believes deeply in his vision and knows he can make a difference once he learns how to communicate his message as effectively as possible. Bursting with energy and desire, Malcolm struggles to sit still while the bus moves him ever closer to his training ground for the future.

Our study of exceptional children thus far has focused on students with intellectual, behavioral, or physical disabilities—children who require specially tailored programs of education in order to benefit from education. Gifted and talented children represent the other end on the continuum of academic, artistic, social, and scientific abilities. Gifted and talented children may also find that a traditional curriculum is inappropriate; it may not provide the advanced and unique challenges they require to learn most effectively. They, too, need special educational opportunities if they are to reach their potential.

It may seem hard to imagine that students like Janie, Toney, or Malcolm need special education. However, the impressive performance by these students is, in part, a product of special modifications in their education programs that were made to enhance and develop their individual talents. Janie's precocious academic skills benefited from early identification and accelerated schooling; Toney's creative talents have been nurtured and pushed under the tutelage of his mentor and a nationally famous artist. Malcolm's exceptional literary and analytical abilities blossomed once he began taking college classes. But they may not have been able to meet their potential if they had not received additional assistance, including specialized instruction and other curricular options.

Who are these precocious youngsters—the scientists, artists, and writers, the dancers, inventors, and leaders of the future? What are their special abilities and talents? How can they be identified? What kinds of curricular modifications and educational approaches will help them achieve their maximum potential? In this chapter, we review one of the most important areas in all of education: special education for students with exceptional abilities and talents.

✳ *Defining Giftedness and Talent*

Intelligence, creativity, and talent have been central to the various definitions of giftedness that have been proposed over the years. Lewis Terman (1925), one of the pioneers in the field, defined the gifted as those who score in the top 2% on standardized tests of intelligence. Guilford (1959) believed that creativity was the key to the solutions and innovations by the most gifted scientists and inventors. Witty (1951), recognizing the value of including special skills and talents, described gifted and talented children as those "whose performance is consistently remarkable in any potentially valuable area" (p. 62). These three concepts continue to be reflected in the current and still-evolving definitions of gifted and talented children.

Federal Definition

According to the Gifted and Talented Children's Act of 1978, gifted and talented children are those

> possessing demonstrated or potential abilities that give evidence of high performance capability in such areas as intellectual, creative, specific academic or leadership ability, or in the performing or visual arts, and who by reason thereof require services or activities not ordinarily provided by the school. (PL 95–561, Title IX, sec. 902)

The areas in which a child can show outstanding performance or unusual potential cover almost the full range of human endeavor. Intellectual ability and specific academic aptitude are only two areas. *General intellectual ability* refers to overall performance on intelligence or achievement tests. Children who meet this criterion usually do or can perform well in most academic areas. Children with *specific academic aptitude* have outstanding ability in one or two areas. For example, Malcolm, who has specific academic aptitude, performs extremely well in English, literature, and history; his work in mathematics and science, however, is no better than that of most of his same-age peers.

Psychomotor ability—high performance in gross- and fine-motor development (e.g., diving, gymnastics)—was included as a sixth area of giftedness in an earlier federal definition (PL 91–230). But Congress believed that schools' existing athletic programs serve such students adequately.

The federal definition has received fairly widespread acceptance, and most states have used it as a basis for their efforts to identify and serve gifted and talented students (Passow & Rudnitski, 1994). Most states limit their definition of giftedness, however, to the three areas of general intellectual ability, creativity, and leadership (Sisk, 1987).

A New Proposed Definition of Outstanding Talent

In the recent report *National Excellence: A Case for Developing America's Talent,* the U.S. Department of Education (1993) has proposed a new definition of students with exceptional talent, based on new research on cognition and assessment "reflecting today's knowledge and thinking" (p. 3).

> Children and youth with outstanding talent perform or show the potential for performing at remarkably high levels of accomplishment when compared with others of their age, experience, or environment. These children and youth exhibit high performance capability in intellectual, creative, and/or artistic areas, possess an unusual leadership capacity, or excel in specific academic fields. They require services or activities not ordinarily provided by the schools. Outstanding talents are present in children and youth from all cultural groups, across all economic strata, and in all areas of human endeavor.
>
> To put this definition into practice, schools must develop a system to identify gifted and talented students that:
>
> 1. *Seeks variety* - looks throughout a range of disciplines for students with diverse talents;
> 2. *Uses many assessment measures* - uses a variety of appraisals so that schools can find students in different talent areas and at different ages;
> 3. *Is free of bias* - provides students of all backgrounds with equal access to appropriate opportunities;
> 4. *Is fluid* - uses assessment procedures that can accommodate students who develop at different rates and whose interests may change as they mature;
> 5. *Identifies potential* - discovers talents that are not readily apparent in students, as well as those that are obvious; and

Malcolm's exceptional writing abilities blossomed once he began college courses.

6. *Assesses motivation* - takes into account the drive and passion that play a key role in accomplishment. (p. 26)

This definition does not use the term *gifted,* which "connotes a mature power rather than a developing ability, and, therefore, is antithetical to recent research findings about children" (p. 26). The definition implies that environmental factors are at least as critical to the presence of outstanding talent as are genetic predispositions and that these talents are to be found across all cultural and socioeconomic groups and other areas of human endeavor. By embracing the terms *outstanding talent* and *exceptional talent,* the framers of this definition avoid the negative commentary and implications of labeling a child as gifted and bring it into line with school programs that are changing their names and focus from the IQ-derived label of "gifted" to talent development (Piirto, personal communication, 1994).

This definition presents a new conception of gifted children that radically departs from previous definitions by broadening the understanding of talents, reducing the focus on the IQ, and focusing on certain environmental and personality areas, as well as on specific talents. In addition it puts forward the challenge that the nation should "raise the expectations for all students in America, including those with outstanding talent" (Piirto, 1994, p. 3).

Renzulli's Three-Trait Definition

Renzulli's (1978) definition of giftedness is based on an interaction among three basic clusters of human traits: (a) above-average general abilities, (b) a high level of task commitment, and (c) creativity. Gifted and talented children are those

> possessing or capable of developing this composite set of traits and applying them to any potentially valuable area of human performance. Children who manifest or are capable of developing an interaction among the three clusters require a wide variety of educational opportunities and services that are not ordinarily provided through regular instructional programs. (p. 184)

Figure 12.1 illustrates how the three components of ability (actual or potential), task commitment, and creative expression are jointly applied to a valuable area of human endeavor. Like the federal definition, Renzulli's provides a great deal of freedom in determining who is considered gifted and talented, depending on the interpretation of "valuable" human performance.

An Emerging Paradigm: From Intelligence to Talent

Feldhusen (1992a) concludes, "There is no psychological, genetic, or neurological justification for a diagnostic category called 'gifted.' The very term, of course, implies hereditary transmission, for how else could a 'gift' be placed in a child" (p. 3). Feldhusen has proposed a new conception of "giftedness" that does not use the term *gifted:*

> Talented youth are those who have especially high aptitude, ability, or potential in any worthwhile area of human endeavor as determined by tests, rating scales, behavioral observations, or assessment of past performance in authentic learning activities and in comparison with a normative peer group. (Feldhusen & Moon, 1995, p. 104)

FIGURE 12.1

Renzulli's three-component definition of giftedness

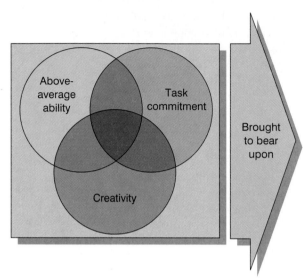

General Performance Areas

Mathematics • Visual Arts • Physical Sciences • Philosophy • Social Sciences • Law • Religion • Language Arts • Music • Life Sciences • Movement Arts

Specific Performance Areas

Cartooning • Astronomy • Public Opinion Polling • Jewelry Design • Map Making • Choreography • Biography • Film Making • Statistics • Local History • Electronics • Musical Composition • Landscape Architecture • Chemistry • Demography • Microphotography • City Planning • Pollution Control • Poetry • Fashion Design • Weaving • Play Writing • Advertising • Costume Design • Meteorology • Puppetry • Marketing • Game Design • Journalism • Electronic Music • Child Care • Consumer Protection • Cooking • Ornithology • Furniture Design • Navigation • Genealogy • Sculpture • Wildlife Management • Set Design • Agricultural Research • Animal Learning • Film Criticism • etc.

Source: From "What Makes Giftedness? Reexamining a Definition" by J. S. Renzulli, 1978 *Phi Delta Kappan, 60,* p. 184. Reprinted by permission.

> A *paradigm* is an overall model or view of a concept or phenomenon.

Feldman (1992) describes a new "emerging paradigm" of giftedness (see Figure 12.2). This perspective emphasizes *talent* as the primary defining characteristic of giftedness and focuses on the identification of special talents and aptitudes. This focus is partly in response to the definitional controversy driven by public perceptions of elitism that come with calling anyone *gifted* and the narrowly restrictive societal perspective on intellectualism (Ring & Shaughnessy, 1993). This new conception of giftedness represents the growing recognition of the importance of balancing theoretical with practical definitions of giftedness that emphasize situated problem solving (Sternberg, 1988), talents that are context and domain related, and the importance of sustained, deliberate practice on the realization of the person's talent (Ericsson & Charness, 1994).

Piirto's Pyramid of Talent Development

A recent definition consistent with the new paradigm is by Piirto (1994), who defines the gifted as

> those individuals who, by way of learning characteristics such as superior memory, observational powers, curiosity, creativity, and the ability to learn school-related subject matters rapidly and accurately with a minimum of drill and repetition, have a right to an education that is differentiated according to those characteristics. These children become apparent early and should be served throughout their educational lives, from preschool through college. They may or may not become producers of knowledge or makers of novelty, but their education should be such that it would give them the background to become adults who do produce knowledge or make new artistic and social products. (p. 34)

FIGURE 12.2
The emerging paradigm of giftedness

Old	New
Giftedness Is High IQ	Many Types of Giftedness
Trait-Based	Qualities-Based
Subgroup Elitism	Individual Excellence
Innate, "In There"	Based on Context
Test-Driven	Achievement-Driven, "What You Do" Is Gifted
Authoritarian, "You Are or Are Not Gifted"	Collaborative, Determined by Consultation
School-Oriented	Field- and Domain-Oriented
Ethnocentric	Diverse

Source: From "Has There Been a Paradigm Shift in Gifted Education?" by D. H. Feldman, 1992. In N. Colangelo, S. G. Assouline, and D. L. Ambroson (Eds.), *Talented Development: Proceedings from the 1991 Henry and Jocelyn Wallace National Research Symposium on Talent Development.* Unionville, New York: Trillium. Reprinted by permission.

Piirto believes that the purpose of special education for gifted and talented students is to develop their talent in specific domains of achievement. Figure 12.3 illustrates Piirto's conception of talent development as a three-tiered pyramid that requires

1. certain aspects of personality that are already present or that must be cultivated (e.g., curiosity, self-discipline, imagination)
2. a minimum IQ threshold that is different for different types of talent; the highest levels of IQ are not required for most domains of adult talent
3. specific talent manifested in physical or mental ways in a specific domain (e.g., science, literature, art, music, mathematics)

The "lucky stars" above the pyramid in Piirto's model represent the significant role that chance plays in the realization of giftedness. A child with great potential who is born into poverty will probably not have that potential recognized and developed; however, the potentially gifted child fortunate enough to be born and raised in a family and community that recognizes and supports that potential at home and at school will probably develop into a talented adult.

> This is a sobering fact, and it should provide the impetus for the schools to find, and help, those children whose "luck" may not have permitted them to be born into an environment that will nurture their great potential. In all cases, the school is merely an environmental factor in the development of giftedness, but the school can either be a powerful shaper or a deterrent to that development. (Piirto, 1994, p. 37)

✳ *Characteristics of Students Who Are Gifted and Talented*

The stereotype of the gifted student as a little adult with taped glasses, a pocket protector to hold pens and calculator, and arms laden with volumes of Homer, Plato,

FIGURE 12.3
Piirto's pyramid of talent development

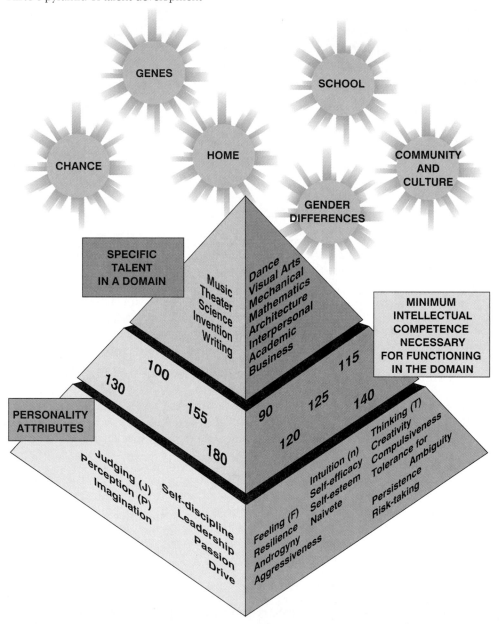

Source: Reprinted with the permission of Simon & Schuster, Inc. from the Merrill/Prentice Hall College text *Talented Children and Adults: Their Development and Education* by Jane Piirto. © 1994 by Merrill/Prentice Hall.

and Einstein is not based in reality. Physically, gifted students as a group do not differ substantially from other children their age. Any one gifted child may be taller or shorter than her age-mates. The child may weigh more, about the same, or less than her peers. In other words, a gifted and talented student would not be easily identifiable on a class picnic.

Giftedness is a complex concept covering a wide range of abilities and traits. Some students have special talents. They may not be outstanding in academics, but they may have special abilities in such areas as music, dance, art, or leadership. Other children may have intellectual abilities found only in 1 child in 1,000 or 1 child in 10,000. Learning and intellectual characteristics in those persons who are considered to be gifted and talented include (Clark, 1992; Gallagher & Gallagher, 1994; Maker, 1993; Piirto, 1994):

- The ability to rapidly acquire, retain, and use large amounts of information
- The ability to relate one idea to another
- The ability to make sound judgments
- The ability to perceive the operation of larger systems of knowledge that may not be recognized by the ordinary citizen
- The ability to acquire and manipulate abstract symbol systems
- The ability to solve problems by reframing the question and creating novel solutions

Silverman (1995) identifies the following characteristics for the "highly gifted," or children with IQ scores at least three standard deviations above the mean (IQ > 145):

- Intense intellectual curiosity
- Fascination with words and ideas
- Perfectionism
- Need for precision
- Learning in great intuitive leaps
- Intense need for mental stimulation
- Difficulty conforming to the thinking of others
- Early moral and existential concern
- Tendency toward introversion (pp. 220-221)

We must remember that the characteristics mentioned here are generalizations about the population of gifted and talented students, not the description of any single individual. We may meet a gifted child who does not neatly match these characteristics. It may be the child's giftedness that makes him or her unique, and the uniqueness may defy any attempt to categorize it into a neat, well-ordered compartment. We must also realize that many lists of gifted characteristics portray gifted children as having only virtues and no flaws (Gallagher, 1975). The very attributes by which we identify gifted children, however, can cause some problems. High verbal ability, for example, may prompt gifted students to talk themselves out of troublesome situations or to dominate class discussions. High curiosity may give them the appearance of being aggressive or snoopy as they pursue anything that comes to their attention. The two lists in Table 12.1 describe both positive and not-so-positive aspects of intellectual giftedness. List A describes the positive side; List B identifies some of the problems that may occur as a result of these positive traits.

Awareness of individual differences is also important in understanding gifted students. Like other children, gifted children show both interindividual and intraindividual differences. For example, if two students are given the same reading achievement test and each obtains a different score, we can speak of interindividual differences in reading achievement. If a student who obtains a high reading achievement score obtains a much lower score on an arithmetic achievement test, we say the stu-

The ability to manipulate symbol systems is a key indicator of intellectual giftedness. Although the most common symbol system is language, there are numerous other symbol systems, such as scientific notation, music and dance notation, mathematics, and engineering symbols. These systems can be incorporated into creative endeavors, as well as academic and intellectual areas.

See "Making the Earth a Better Place" later in this chapter.

For information on the affective dimensions of giftedness, see Swassing (1994).

TABLE 12.1
Two sides to the behavior of gifted and talented students

LIST A: POSITIVE ASPECTS	LIST B: NOT-SO-POSITIVE ASPECTS
1. Expresses ideas and feelings well	1. May be glib, making fluent statements based on little or no knowledge or understanding
2. Can move at a rapid pace	
3. Works conscientiously	2. May dominate discussions
4. Wants to learn, explore, and seek more information	3. May be impatient to proceed to next level or task
5. Develops broad knowledge and an extensive store of vicarious experiences	4. May be considered nosey
	5. May choose reading at the expense of active participation in social, creative, or physical activities
6. Is sensitive to the feelings and rights of others	
7. Makes steady progress	6. May struggle against rules, regulations, and standardized procedures
8. Makes original and stimulating contributions to discussions	7. May lead discussions "off the track"
9. Sees relationships easily	8. May be frustrated by the apparent absence of logic in activities and daily events
10. Learns material quickly	
11. Is able to use reading skills to obtain new information	9. May become bored by repetitions
	10. May use humor to manipulate
12. Contributes to enjoyment of life for self and others	11. May resist a schedule based on time, rather than task
13. Completes assigned tasks	
14. Requires little drill for learning	12. May lose interest quickly

Most highly gifted children experience *asynchronous development,* in which mental, physical, emotional, and social development occur at dramatically different rates. Their cognitive and intellectual abilities usually develop far ahead of their physical development.

dent has an intraindividual difference across the two areas of performance. A graph of any student's abilities would reveal some high points and some lower points; scores would not be the same across all dimensions. The gifted student's *pattern* of performance, however, may be well above the average for that grade and/or age, as we see in Figure 12.4. Leslie's and Jackie's overall abilities are similar. Leslie performs higher in vocabulary and social studies than Jackie, however, and Jackie shows higher performance in science and mathematics than Leslie. These are *interindividual* differences. Each student also has *intraindividual* differences in scores. For example, Leslie has the vocabulary of an 11th grader but scores only at a 7th-grade equivalent in mathematics; Jackie earned grade equivalents of 10th grade in science and mathematics and 7th grade in writing.

Creativity

To many, creative ability is central to the definition of giftedness. Clark (1986) calls creativity "the highest expression of giftedness" (p. 45), and Sternberg (1988) suggests that

FIGURE 12.4

Profiles of two gifted and talented children, both of whom are 10 years old and in the fifth grade

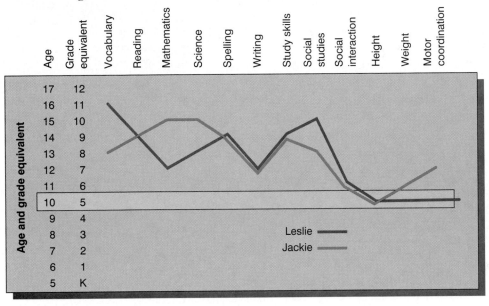

those gifted individuals who make the greatest long-range contributions to society are probably those whose gifts involve coping with novelty—specifically, in the area of insight. Creative and insightful individuals are those who make discoveries and devise the inventions that ultimately change society. (p. 74)

Although we all profess to know "it" when we see "it," there is no universally accepted definition of creativity. Guilford (1987), who studied the emergence of creativity as one aspect of his overall theorizing concerning human intelligence, describes these dimensions of creative behavior:

- *Fluency*—the creative person is capable of producing many ideas per unit of time.
- *Flexibility*—a wide variety of ideas, unusual ideas, and alternative solutions are offered.
- *Novelty/Originality*—low probability, unique words, and responses are used; the creative person has novel ideas.
- *Elaboration*—the ability to provide details is evidenced.
- *Synthesizing ability*—the person has the ability to put unlikely ideas together.
- *Analyzing ability*—the person has the ability to organize ideas into larger, inclusive patterns. Symbolic structures must often be broken down before they can be reformed into new ones.
- *Ability to reorganize or redefine existing ideas*—the ability to transform an existing object into one of different design, function, or use is evident.
- *Complexity*—the ability to manipulate many interrelated ideas at the same time is shown. (adapted from Guilford, 1987, pp. 42-47)

Maker (1993) contends that the three areas that appear most often within the various definitions of the gifted and talented involve high intelligence, high creativity, and excellent problem-solving skills. She states, "Such an individual is capable of:

PROFILES & PERSPECTIVES

Making the Earth a Better Place

Who Said It?

Who do you think made each of these observations? Check your selections with the correct answers found at the bottom.

1. After the strife of war begins the strife of peace.
   A. Napoleon Bonaparte
   B. Carl Sandburg
   C. Dwight Eisenhower
   D. Matthew O'Brien
   E. Abraham Lincoln

2. Global peace is a powerful weapon. If we have it, we can use it to make the earth a better place.
   A. Tom Brokaw
   B. Winston Churchill
   C. Henry David Thoreau
   D. Robert Campbell
   E. Mahatma Gandhi

3. The truth is more important than the facts.
   A. Frank Lloyd Wright
   B. Oscar Wilde
   C. Alyce Jaspers
   D. Albert Einstein
   E. Golda Meir

4. Cooperation is a crucial part of survival. Cooperation is key in human life because humans' needs are so diverse, requiring for their fulfillment more skills, more talents, and more learning than any one individual can possess or acquire.
   A. Lester Brown
   B. Buckminster Fuller
   C. Polao Salori
   D. Andrea Goldberg
   E. John Nesbit

5. The only way for earth to even come near perfection is for the people in our society who are in the best position to create a perfect earth to become somewhat competent.
   A. John F. Kennedy
   B. Margaret Mead
   C. John Lennon
   D. Nelson Mandela
   E. Peter Bret Lamphere

6. After much deep thinking and evaluation of those thoughts, I have come to the realization that, without a shadow of a doubt, the most crucial global issue today, and for years to come, is arms reduction.
   A. Edward Kennedy
   B. Mikhail Gorbachev
   C. Roy Stoner
   D. Jimmy Carter
   E. George Bush

7. Change lately has given us humans quite a stir. Berlin wall down, democracy up; Noriega down, taxes up. What a fast changing world we live in.
   A. Barbara Walters
   B. Peter Jennings
   C. Walter Cronkite
   D. Connie Chung
   E. Robert Campbell

8. People should feel obligated to leave the world a little better than they found it.
   A. Pippa Bowde
   B. Carl Sagan
   C. Robert Redford
   D. Teddy Roosevelt
   E. Mother Teresa

9. Death in the rain forest used to be a natural part of life. The message was simple: Death was the beginning of a new generation. Now that man has entered the picture, death has come to have a new meaning: An end to birth.
   A. Barry Lopez
   B. Andrea Goldberg
   C. Carl Sagan
   D. Manuel Lujan
   E. Abbie Hoffman

10. If there is no personal concern, nothing happens.
   A. Martin Luther King
   B. Carl Rogers
   C. Benjamin Spock
   D. Thomas Jefferson
   E. Danielle Eckert ✳

Answers: (1) Carl Sandburg; (2) Robert Campbell, age 10; (3) Frank Lloyd Wright; (4) Andrea Goldberg, age 9; (5) Peter Bret Lamphere, age 9; (6) Roy Stoner, age 9; (7) Robert Campbell, age 10; (8) Pippa Bowde, age 11; (9) Andrea Goldberg, age 9; (10) Danielle Eckert, age 9. All of the statements above, other than Nos. 1 and 3, were written by gifted students. We are grateful to Sandy Lethem and Dennis Higgins, Facilitators for the Gifted at the Zuni Elementary Magnet School, Albuquerque, New Mexico, for sharing their students' thoughts on the environment.

a) creating a new or more clear definition of an existing problem, b) devising new and more efficient or effective methods, c) reaching solutions that may be different from the usual, but are recognized as being effective, perhaps more effective, than previous solutions." This dynamic perspective characterizes a gifted person as "a problem solver—one who enjoys the challenge of complexity and persists until the problem is solved in a satisfying way" (Maker, 1993, p. 71).

Piirto (1992) studied creative individuals in a variety of areas and summarized the characteristics of highly creative individuals within their field of creativity, thus linking their high abilities to a particular area of expertise. She reports that (a) each of these fields has specific predictive behaviors in childhood, (b) there is developmental process in the emergence of talents in various domains, and (c) the IQ should be minimized in importance and subsumed into a more contextual view of children performing tasks within specific domains.

Torrance (1993) attempted to summarized the abilities and achievements of a group of highly creative individuals who were followed for 30 years in a longitudinal study of creativity. He formulated a list of the 10 most common characteristics across the group of high-ability adults who were judged to have achieved far beyond their peers in creative areas. The list includes a number of characteristics that do not typically appear in the literature:

1. Delight in deep thinking
2. Tolerance of mistakes
3. Love of one's work
4. Clear purpose
5. Enjoyment in one's work
6. Feeling comfortable as a minority of one
7. Being different
8. Not being well rounded
9. A sense of mission
10. The courage to be creative

Torrance summarized his analysis of this group of persons he called Beyonders by stating, "Forces, such as love of one's work, persistence, purpose in life, love of challenge, diversity of experience, high energy level, a sense of mission, and other Beyonder characteristics are dominating over creative ability, intelligence, and high school achievement" (p. 135). He concluded by asserting that the predictive ability of the commonly held measures of creativity is insufficient to predict reliably the emergence of highly creative individuals in later life.

Piirto (1994) reminds us that although many gifted and talented students do become scientists, physicians, inventors, and great artists and performers, they have no obligation to do so and that providing them the differentiated education they need should not be predicated on an expectation that they "owe society."

> These children have no greater obligation than any other children to be future leaders or world class geniuses. They should just be given a chance to be themselves, children who might like to classify their collection of baseball cards by the middle initial of the players, or who might like to spend endless afternoon hours in dreamy reading of novels, and to have an education that appreciates and serves these behaviors. (p. 34)

It is often difficult to differentiate between the concepts of talent and creativity, perhaps because they may exist on a continuum, rather than as separate entities. If we examine the life of a highly talented individual, such as the famous dancer Martha Graham, we can see the duality of creativity and talent. Her creativity is evident in her pioneering modern dance techniques and her innovative methods of expression in the choreography of the dance. However, her great talent as a dancer as seen in her eloquent movements is equally impressive and serves notice that not only was she a talented dancer, but she could also create new dances with great meaning and impact on the viewer.

To meet one of Torrance's Beyonders, see the Profiles & Perspectives box on the next page.

Gifted and talented children are most often identified by creativity, talent, and/or extreme intellectual ability that is atypical for their age. See "Precocity as a Hallmark of Giftedness" later in this chapter.

There Is No Such Thing as "Typically Gifted"

The Story of a Beyonder

Paul Torrance has been tracking and reporting on the progress of a group of highly gifted and creative students since they graduated from high school in 1959 (Torrance, 1969, 1977). His most recent report in this ongoing longitudinal study is a 30-year follow-up of a group of 26 scholars, writers, inventors, executives, teachers, and other innovators he calls "Beyonders." "In the financial world, we call them billionaires. In sociometry, we call them sociometric stars. In the workplace, we call them rate busters or workaholics. In creative achievement, I have coined the word 'Beyonders.' As a group, they write inordinate numbers of books or articles, they invent scores of innovative devices, paint hundreds of masterpieces, or produce hundreds of films" (Torrance, 1992, p. 131).

Luann Metz is a Beyonder. Luann's high school scores on creativity measures and sociometrics indicated that she was highly gifted, and many of her peers and teachers predicted meteoric success for her. And she certainly has achieved in a number of different and important ways, but her path was by no means linear or predictable. She even described herself as a "gypsy—collecting unemployment" until late into her 20s as evidence of her intermittent relationship with the formal world of careers, families, and responsibility. She held a number of interesting jobs during this period, including medical secretary, freelance writer, photographer, trekking guide to the Andes, and a teacher for USAID in Ecuador. Although never having engaged in any typical patterns of employment, she reported that she always seemed to be working at several different jobs at the same time.

When Luann was contacted 30 years later, she was in the second year of her doctoral program in anthropology. She reported to interviewers that she had written approximately 30 published feature stories, many unpublished works, and two published books, with two others in preparation. She had received five grants for scientific, literary, or art projects, had developed many inservice training projects, and had edited and ghost-written a monthly column. She had also conceived, planned, and led six expeditions to the Andes. Probably her best known book grew out of this activity and was described by the *New York Times* as "a practical guide to Peru, Bolivia, Ecuador, and Colombia." And the list goes on and on, a wide-ranging exhibition of talent and ability displayed in anything but a predictable pattern. When asked to talk about her own concept of creativity, she responded in typically candid fashion:

> I think everyone walking the earth is creative, so the question is meaningless. Are you looking for public products? Some of the people with the most unusual perspectives and most creative minds I know are not "creative" in this public sense, but make the world immeasurably richer through their effect on the people around them. I think it is typical of our culture to associate creativity with specific products and individual achievement. Produce, produce—ego, ego! I would like to see some cross-cultural studies of cooperative creative efforts. What about morality and ethics in terms of products? Many people consider advertising to be a highly creative field, but I find the ethics of promoting (some) dubious products or encouraging people to buy when they might not have the money, or packaging political candidates and whitewashing their records to be highly unethical or at least ethically and morally questionable. We certainly know where unbridled consumerism is leading us in terms of the environment and the national debt. True creativity should involve questioning the premises of our consumer culture and working on other, more deeply satisfying ways for people to live. ✳

From "The Beyonders in a thirty year longitudinal study of creative achievement" by E. Paul Torrance. Reprinted by permission of the *Roeper Review*, Volume 15, Number 3, © 1992, February/March, 1993. *Roeper Review* P. O. Box 329, Bloomfield Hills, MI 48303.

✳ Prevalence

The Marland Report of 1972 originally included a minimum estimate of gifted and talented students at 3% to 5% of the total school-age population in the United States at that time. This estimate was derived from the predicted number of highly talented individuals one would expect to find at the "high end" of the normal curve, or about

The concept of giftedness includes many talents that enrich our quality of life.

two standard deviations above the mean. Because most of the states that have begun programs for the gifted and talented base them on the Marland Report, they have also accepted as guidelines for identification those estimates of the prevalence of giftedness within the population. If we consider those students regarded as highly talented, estimates for the occurrence of giftedness range as high as 10% to 15% of the total school-age population (Renzulli, 1978).

By 1990, 38 states reported serving more than 2 million students in K-12 gifted programs (U.S. Department of Education, 1993). This number ranks gifted and talented students as the second largest group of exceptional children receiving special education services. The number and percentage of students identified as gifted and talented vary from state to state; for instance, four states identify more than 10% of the student population as gifted and talented; 21 states identify less than 5% as such (U.S. Department of Education, 1993).

On the basis of an estimate that gifted and talented children comprise 5% of the school-age population, approximately 2.5 million additional gifted and talented children may need special education (Clark, 1992). This discrepancy between need and the level of service may make gifted and talented children the most underserved group of exceptional children.

The remaining states did not report the numbers of children served. Unlike students with disabilities, states are not required to provide special services to gifted and talented students or to report the number of children served.

✳ *Historical Background*

Two major themes in the history of gifted and talented education are (a) the development of theories of intelligence and its measurement and (b) the schools' provision of differentiated curriculum experiences for gifted students.

Precocity as a Hallmark of Giftedness

Four Scenarios Based on Actual Stories

by Jane Piirto

Four-year-old Maria has been waiting and waiting to go to school. She plays school all the time. She is the teacher, and her dolls are the students. At her day-care center, she is the one who always leads the other kids in games because she is the only one who can read. The other kids look up to her, except when she tries to make them do things they really don't want to do, such as count by twos. The day-care center teacher told Maria's mother that Maria was very bright. When Maria went for her preschool screening, the district recommended that she be tested by the school psychologist. The school psychologist told Maria's mother that Maria had an IQ of 145 on the Stanford-Binet Intelligence Scale, a score that put her in the 99th percentile. This score would qualify her for the district's program for the academically talented, which started at the third grade, although they did have enrichment lessons in first and second grade.

Finally, it is the first day of school; Maria turned 5 in August. She has her new dress and new shoes on. Her mother braids her hair and fastens it with new barrettes. When she gets to school, she is anxious for her mother to leave, yet still she feels shy, with all of these children here. Half of them are crying as their parents leave them. Maria looks around the room and sees a shelf of books. She always reads when she doesn't know what else to do, so she goes over to the shelf and waits for things to calm down. After all of the parents have gone, the teacher tells the children to sit on a line painted on the floor. As the children have come into the room, they have been given large name tags. The teacher sits on a small chair with the children in a semicircle around her and says, "My name is Mrs. Miller, boys and girls. Welcome to kindergarten. In kindergarten, we will learn our letters and our numbers so that we can learn to read in first grade."

"I can read already," Maria says, jumping up.

"That's nice," says Mrs. Miller. "Maria, when we want to talk, first we must stand, and then we must wait until Mrs. Miller calls on us."

"But I can read already!" Maria's voice gets petulant, and tears form in the corners of her eyes.

"Maria, that's nice," said Mrs. Miller. "But in kindergarten, we will learn how to read right. Please sit down now."

Maria is chagrined. Feeling shame and embarrassment, she sits down. She has taken the first step to under-achievement. Underachievement is the prevailing situation in the education of academically talented young children in most schools today. By the time she has been socialized into the kindergarten milieu, Maria will have learned to keep quiet about her abilities and even to suppress that she can read. In first grade, she will comply with the reading tasks in order to fit in. By second grade, even though she will be getting all of her work right, she will have learned that she doesn't have to put forth any effort in school in order to be the best student. By third grade, she will have learned that boredom—as long as she's quietly bored—and waiting—as long as she's not disruptive while she's waiting—are what the school seems to expect of her. By fourth grade, when she gets into a pull-out program for academically talented students, she will resent it when the teacher of the academically talented tries to challenge her, and in challenging her, stretches her capabilities. Maria's story, unfortunately, is typical of many young academically talented children who enter the public school system.

Maria is *precocious* in her abilities; that is, she can easily do things typically seen only in older children. She is

Theories of Intelligence

Historically, the development and delivery of services to students who are gifted and talented have been based on the prevailing conceptions of intelligence. The perception of "intelligence" has evolved rapidly after a long period of relative stability in which intelligence was viewed as a central, or unitary, concept. Socrates provided one of the earliest written descriptions of the characteristics of gifted individuals by saying that they possessed "gifts of nature." Unfortunately, this early belief that a person who evidenced great talent, skill, or creativity was *given* a gift from some greater not alone. In fact, the main way to recognize talented students is by their precocity. Even without special testing, their talents, resembling the achievements of older children, can be spotted by teachers who are sensitive to the concept of *precocity*.

Philip is also in kindergarten. He is given letters and numbers to color and to recognize. He always is the last to finish because he spends his time elaborating on the drawings that go with the letters. His detailed drawings resemble those of children in third or fourth grade. Philip draws whenever and wherever he can, and eventually his teacher complains to his parents that Philip never finishes his work because he is always drawing.

His drawing passion gives way to a love for other artistic media. He may not like crayons because they don't allow him the shading details he wants to achieve. He may want to mold and sculpt in the Play-Doh and may build figures that are quite realistic. His cars, horses, and fighting characters are praised by his classmates. He may not be a good academic student, but his talent in art is recognized. He is asked to do the bulletin boards, and students may even pay him a few cents to draw them a realistic-looking horse. Philip's precocious talent needs to be developed.

When Mrs. Samuelson brings in the books from the library for the science unit, Kathleen and Mike fight over the book about paleontology. Even though

the book contains many big words, both children get the idea of what the words mean through context. After they have read the book on paleontology, they move to others. When Mrs. Samuelson teaches them through fiction, they say they don't like the story because fiction is "lies," and they continue to read the nonfiction books about science and nature that she occasionally brings. The characteristic of liking nonfiction, and especially nonfiction about science and nature, indicates their precocity in science, and soon the consultant teacher has set up a learning center with many nonfiction materials written on a high level.

Kathleen and Mike continue to "eat the 'hard' material up," asking for more and more. In the hands-on science unit, if the activities are too easy, the two appear bored, finish early, and may be disruptive because they know the lesson already. Mrs. Samuelson is a wise teacher, and she and the talent development consultant teacher have provided extension lessons for such precocious children.

When Matt was a small boy, his mother took a picture of him, sitting on the stool next to the fireplace, reading while the family opened their Christmas gifts. The party was loud and getting long, and Matt was tired. What was he reading? The telephone book. Matt just loved numbers. When his mother read to him, Matt would always notice the numbers of the pages. When they would drive to the store to

shop, he would remember that the sale prices had changed, and he even inquired what a percent sign meant. When he had a chance, later on in school, he ran for treasurer of the clubs, and in high school he was statistician for the sports teams.

Matt has always been precocious in mathematics, even though he had to wait for years and years until the mathematics got challenging enough for him. Sometimes he even dreams in numbers and calculations. Once, he had a chance to join a math club after school. Everyone in the club was precocious. They formed a team and went to the state Math Counts competition, and they placed. Matt was glad that his teachers recognized his extreme interest in numbers and provided him extension and enrichment activities that built on his mathematical talents.

These four scenarios indicate the types of precocious behavior talented students might display when their abilities are great. I call these behaviors *predictive behaviors*. These children are often difficult to locate because they might wish to "fit in" and not to create disturbances, but their talents can be found by teachers, parents, and educators who look closely. ✳

Jane Piirto is on the education faculty at Ashland University, in Ashland, Ohio. She is the author of the text *Talented Children and Adults* (Merrill/Prentice Hall, 1994).

being such as a god, or nature itself, became the basis for popular views of giftedness for many centuries to come.

Early 19th-century works, including a classic study by Sir Francis Galton (1869/1936), focused on the concept of genius. Galton was the first to offer a definition of genius that used observable characteristics or outcomes. His study was based on famous adults, however, and contributed little to the identification and nurturing of potential in children. Furthermore, Galton thought that the largest proportion of human intelligence was fixed and immutable. This view eventually came to be enshrined as the theory of fixed intelligence, wherein people believed they were born and died with the same amount of intelligence regardless of their life experiences.

Two events in the early 1900s cemented the marriage of the theory of fixed intelligence to a method of measuring it. First, in 1905 the French government commissioned two psychologists, Alfred Binet and Theophile Simon, to develop a means of separating groups of slow learners from other children in order to provide them appropriate educational services. Second, these scales were translated into English and refined by Lewis Terman at Stanford University in 1916 for the U.S. government to use in sorting soldiers for a variety of duties in World War I. Known as the Stanford-Binet Intelligence Scale, it was published in 1916 and was most recently revised in 1986 (Thorndike, Hagen, & Sattler, 1986). It has become the scale against which all other measures of intelligence are compared.

The result of these events was the emergence of a single number, the "intelligence quotient" or "IQ," which came to represent the overall intellectual abilities of a person. IQ tests and related tools became the dominant process for determining the intellectual differences among human beings and continues to be used widely today.

Terman was also known for initiating one of the most famous longitudinal studies of gifted individuals; it was published in a 5-volume series, *Genetic Studies of Genius.* This study, which lasted from 1925 through 1959, reported on the lives of approximately 1,500 gifted individuals as they advanced from childhood into their adult lives. Terman's colleagues and students also developed numerous articles and papers, including two that reported on the life satisfaction of some of Terman's original subjects (P. S. Sears, 1979; R. R. Sears, 1977).

For inclusion in the Terman study, a child had to have an IQ of 140 or above as measured by the 1916 Stanford-Binet. Measures were taken in a number of areas, including social and physical development, achievement, character traits, books read, and play interests. This study did much to refute popular misconceptions about gifted individuals, including "early ripe, early rot," "genius and insanity go hand in hand," and the stereotype of the gifted child as a little adult.

Leta S. Hollingworth, an educational psychologist, became aware of the needs of the highly gifted when she tested a child with a score of more than 180 on the Stanford-Binet. This was the beginning of a series of case studies Hollingworth conducted with children of extremely high intelligence. In *Children Above IQ 180* (1942, 1975), Hollingworth reported the histories of 12 such children from the New York City area. The children's school histories varied considerably. One factor that differentiated the successful from the unsuccessful in school was early recognition of their superior talents and the willingness of parents and school personnel to act on that awareness. Some of the case studies revealed that these gifted children were frustrated and felt stifled by regular school procedures. Early identification, guidance, personal interest in the children, and special programs contributed to helping the youngsters adjust and accept learning as a rewarding challenge (Hollingworth, 1975). Hollingworth was an early advocate for testing above grade level and for developing differentiated curriculum; she was also an active feminist (Benjamin, 1990).

Although certain myths were dispelled by the early studies, problems were also evident. A narrow view of giftedness, dominated by IQ score, prevailed for many years. Because of this, it is probable that many children with special gifts and talents were not recognized or given the opportunity to develop fully. IQ score came to be relied on excessively as an identification tool and as a predictor of success in life (Witty, 1940, 1951). Giftedness was restricted to high IQ scores and came to be associated with only White, urban, middle- and upper-class segments of society (Witty,

For more information on Leta Hollingworth, who herself was highly gifted, see Peters (1994).

1940). In the early 1950s, Guilford, a psychologist noted for his work on analyzing and categorizing mental processes, challenged the field to look beyond traditional conceptions of intelligence and to view the IQ score as a small sample of mental abilities (Guilford, 1956). Since that challenge, the concept of giftedness has developed in several directions to involve many forms of intellectual activity.

After the apparent success of these early attempts at using intelligence tests, the test results came to be used more broadly for educational planning and decision making. In fact, as Clark (1992) asserts, "During this period, the test became the ultimate authority" (p. 14). This slavish attachment to the results of intelligence testing went unexamined and untested until a disparate group of scholars such as Piaget, Skinner, and Vygotsky proposed new theoretical challenges to the conception of intelligence and its measurement and development. Even today, the vast majority of the population believe that such extraordinary performances by individuals must be largely, if not entirely, the result of innate predispositions, rather than the result of environmental factors, such as (a) parental support; (b) access to learning materials, tools, and opportunities to use them; (c) active and repeated practice responding to learning phenomena; and (d) motivating contingencies.

The traditional method of identifying gifted and talented students has relied on measures of general intellectual abilities using IQ test results, which have been shown to be highly correlated with school success. But it is now broadly accepted that the abilities measured by IQ tests are only one aspect of the overall talents and abilities that an individual possesses. The proponents of competing theories of intelligence have been characterized as being either "lumpers" or "splitters" (Weinberg, 1989). The defining points involve whether theorists view intelligence as a unitary concept, thus "lumping" all characteristics into a single concept (e.g. Terman, 1925), or whether a number of interactive factors determine overall intelligence, wherein intelligence is "split" into a number of interactive but different traits (e.g. Gardner, 1983; Guilford, 1967; Sternberg, 1988).

Gardner's theory of multiple intelligences (1983) offers an expanded definition of intelligence by including seven separate domains that operate somewhat independently of one another but that still interact at other levels when a person is engaged in active problem solving. In each of the domains, people use their prior knowledge, experiences, and ability to analyze and synthesize information in order to solve a wide range of problems. Gardner's theory of intelligence has gained widespread acceptance by many educators because of its intuitive attractiveness and ability to account for varying types of giftedness beyond intellectual and academic achievement. His theory also acknowledges the contributions of both genetics and environment to intellectual functioning.

> A national survey found that 73% of school districts use the IQ and achievement tests as the primary tool for identifying the only category of gifted student that they serve: students with high general intelligence (U.S. Department of Education, 1993).

> For example, a growing body of evidence from studies across a variety of fields suggests powerfully positive benefits attributable to deliberate and focused practice in the field of endeavor (Ericcson & Charness, 1994).

> In Gardner's (1983) theory, seven distinct intelligences—linguistic, musical, logical-mathematical, spatial, bodily-kinesthetic, interpersonal, and intrapersonal—function relatively independent of one another.

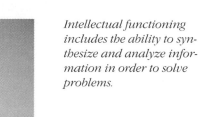

Intellectual functioning includes the ability to synthesize and analyze information in order to solve problems.

Sternberg's (1985) triarchic theory of intelligence involves an interaction among three basic kinds of information-processing components in humans: metacomponents, performance components, and knowledge-acquisition components. He asserts that three types of giftedness may be occurring at three levels—internal, experiential, and applied—after which Sternberg named three corresponding types of giftedness:

- *Analytically gifted.* A person who is strong in planning strategies for solving problems, information representation, allocating resources in order to solve problems, and in monitoring one's resources
- *Creatively gifted.* A person who is good at generating new ideas and reformulating problems, able to go beyond the current problem definitions, and able to automatize information in specialized domains, such as dance, music, languages, or sports
- *Practically gifted.* A person who has strengths and talents in the application of his or her intelligence to real-world problems; particularly adept at the areas of adaptation to new problem states, the shaping of inquiry in his or her field of endeavor, and the appropriate and timely selection of a working environment

During the 1960s, attention turned to creativity and other alternatives to the traditional IQ score for identifying gifted and talented children. Some efforts were initiated to identify and develop talent among the culturally diverse; this movement continued to expand during the 1970s (Torrance, 1977). Also during the 1970s, the need to identify gifted and talented individuals among females and students with disabilities came to be more widely recognized.

Other theorists, including Sternberg (1985) and Naglieri and Das (1987), stress problem-solving and processing capabilities as being critical to the understanding and assessment of human intellectual functioning. The result of these new philosophical perspectives has been the questioning of traditional assessment practices, including intelligence testing. In addition, a movement toward alternative, or "authentic," means of determining the learning of students has resulted in the use of more student-produced documents and products.

Current definitions have grown out of the awareness that IQ alone does not define all of the possible areas of giftedness. Some people have advanced talents in socially valued endeavors that cannot be measured by intelligence tests; intelligence tests are, as Guilford suggested, only a small sample of intellectual activity in limited areas of human endeavor. The concept of giftedness has expanded to include many talents that contribute substantially to the quality of life—for both the individual and society.

School Programs and National Agendas

Early promotion and rapid advancement classes are two methods of *acceleration*, a method for providing special education to gifted students that we examine later in this chapter.

The provision of educational services to students identified as gifted and talented has a long but sporadic history. The first special education services aimed at accommodating students thought to be gifted and talented were initiated in St. Louis in 1868 and involved a plan for flexible promotion. Around 1900, rapid advancement classes were established, in which children could complete 2 years worth of academic work in 1 year, or 3 years worth of work in 2. This and other "acceleration" strategies, such as multiple tracking options and advanced coursework, were practiced as the primary intervention strategies until the early 1900s.

The Progressive Education Movement in the 1920s advocated a new approach called "enrichment," which involved more in-depth instruction and ability grouping as the appropriate interventions for students who were gifted and talented. One of the earliest enrichment programs for gifted children began in the early 1920s in Cleveland, Ohio. In 1922, a group of "publicly spirited" women organized to promote classes for gifted students (Goddard, 1928). The Cleveland program remains one of the longest running, continuous programs for gifted children in the United States.

The enrichment of academic content generally occurred in the regular classroom for the next 30 years, until the Soviet Union launched a small satellite called *Sputnik* into space. This event precipitated a questioning of the academic and scientific capabilities of Americans and resulted in the National Defense Education Act of 1958, which funded a nationwide revival of mathematics, science, and foreign language studies. After a relatively brief period of interest, the needs of gifted and talented students were generally ignored for another 20 years, until the publication of the Marland Report in 1972. In 1975, gifted and talented students were passed over for inclusion in the IDEA (PL 94–142), but they received recognition and funding from the Title IV-C Grants program in 1977. In 1982, the Office of the Gifted and Talented in the U.S. Department of Education was closed after being in existence for just 6 years. The next formal recognition of the needs of the gifted and talented involved the enactment of the *Jacob Javits Gifted and Talented Students Education Act* (1988), which supports research, teacher preparation, and service delivery concerns. This moderately funded act (under $10 million in 1992) provides federal money for special projects, a national research center, and a position within the U.S. Department of Education with responsibility for the gifted. Twenty-eight projects were funded for 1990, and 13 for 1991.

The National Research Center on the Gifted and Talented (NRC/GT), located at the University of Connecticut, is a collaborative effort of four universities: Connecticut, Georgia, Virginia, and Yale. The center also involves state departments of education and collaborating school districts. Its mission for the first year included program evaluation, applying theory to identification, teaching and evaluation, giftedness among the economically disadvantaged, and identifying future research needs.

The latest document detailing the impact of neglecting our "best and brightest" is *National Excellence: A Case for Developing America's Talent* (U.S. Department of Education, 1993). The report is an all-too-familiar call to Americans that we are falling behind on almost all measures of academic performance when compared with our students' past performance and with that of our global competition. In the foreword to the report, Secretary of Education Richard Riley calls this general and ongoing lack of support "a quiet crisis" and predicts, "Our neglect of these students makes it impossible for Americans to compete in a global economy demanding their skills" (p. iii).

✳ *Identification and Assessment*

Although the use of IQ as the sole criterion for giftedness has been out of favor for many years, it is important to remember that Binet and Simon made a significant contribution to the education of gifted children by developing the first instrument that could predict school success. A standardized objective measure, however crude, makes it possible to identify some children with above-average academic potential. Intelligence tests offered the first means of locating bright children, and plans for meeting their special needs could then be developed.

Intelligence tests may be part of the identification process, but no single index or procedure can identify all gifted and talented children. Current best practice calls for a multifactored assessment approach that uses information from a variety of sources, including:

• Intelligence tests

Only 2 cents of every $100 spent on elementary and secondary education in the United States supports gifted and talented education (U.S. Department of Education, 1993).

The address of the NRC/GT is provided in "For More Information" at the end of this chapter.

For a comparison of various intelligence tests and suggestions for their use in identifying gifted children, see Bireley (1995) and Silverman (1995).

- Creativity measures
- Achievement tests
- Portfolios of student works
- Teacher nomination based on reports of student behavior in the classroom
- Parent nomination
- Self-nomination
- Peer nomination

"We can find outstanding talent by observing students at work in rich and varied educational settings. Providing opportunities and observing performance give the best information on children's strengths" (*National Excellence: A Case for Developing America's Talent*, pp. 25-26).

Feldhusen (1992a) has pressed for the abandonment of attempts to identify "gifted students" and instead suggests concentrating on (a) searching for talents in all students, (b) searching for those with very high levels of talent or precocity in a "worthwhile area" of human endeavor, and (c) attempting to use the best instructional methods in order that students would develop their talent to their highest degrees. Feldhusen and Moon (1995) suggest that all identification efforts should aim to identify talent that represents both *precocity* and *potential*. "The student's performance is far ahead of age peers and exhibits potential for continued superior achievements. That momentum is best sustained by continuing opportunities to surge ahead, to develop the talents to the highest degree through accelerated and enriched learning experiences that maintain academic challenge and motivation to achieve" (p. 104).

Richert, Alvino, and McDonnel (1981) contend that the identification of gifted and talented students must take into account six basic principles:

1. *Advocacy.* The identification procedures should be for the benefit of all students.
2. *Defensibility.* The best research should be used.
3. *Equity.* The civil rights of all students should be safeguarded, and disadvantaged talented students should be identified.
4. *Pluralism.* A broad definition of talent should be used.
5. *Comprehensiveness.* Various kinds of talented students should be identified and served.
6. *Pragmatism.* The district should be permitted to make local modifications of the guidelines and tools.

To accurately and equitably locate students who require specialized services for their talents, Clark (1992) presented a definitive approach that is both extensive and comprehensive. This model identification procedure is a progressive filtering process that refines the potential pool of students to an identified and served group of students (see Figure 12.5). The process is time-consuming and thorough, beginning with the development of a large pool of potentially gifted students in the initial stages (Searching and Screening); testing, consulting, and analyzing data (Development of Profile and Case Study); identification decisions and placement (Committee Meeting for Consideration, Placement in Gifted Program); and finally the development of an appropriate educational program for the child.

We can demonstrate how this process would work with a student thought to have great potential—say, the little girl Janie described at the beginning of this chapter. First, Janie's highly refined intellectual behaviors would have to be noticed by a teacher, parent, her peers, or another person who would then forward a nomination for additional screening. Table 12.2 shows questions that Janie's teacher might ask.

Multidimensional screening involves a rigorous examination of teacher reports, family history, student inventories, and work samples, and perhaps the administra-

FIGURE 12.5

A model for identifying gifted and talented students

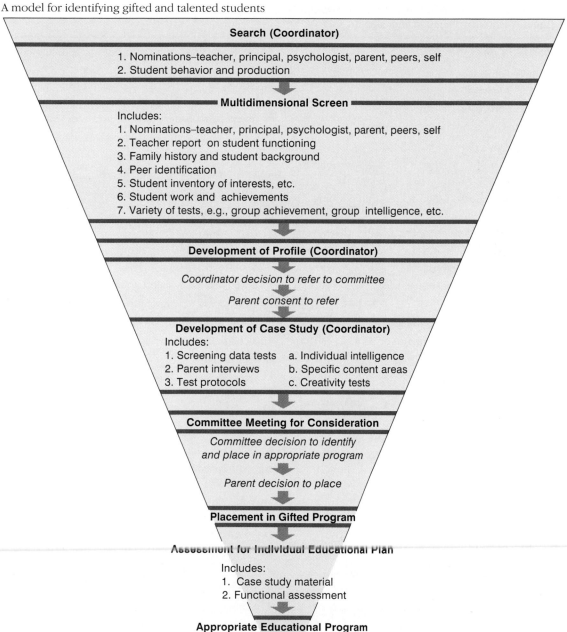

Search (Coordinator)

1. Nominations–teacher, principal, psychologist, parent, peers, self
2. Student behavior and production

Multidimensional Screen

Includes:

1. Nominations–teacher, principal, psychologist, parent, peers, self
2. Teacher report on student functioning
3. Family history and student background
4. Peer identification
5. Student inventory of interests, etc.
6. Student work and achievements
7. Variety of tests, e.g., group achievement, group intelligence, etc.

Development of Profile (Coordinator)

Coordinator decision to refer to committee

Parent consent to refer

Development of Case Study (Coordinator)

Includes:

1. Screening data tests   a. Individual intelligence
2. Parent interviews   b. Specific content areas
3. Test protocols   c. Creativity tests

Committee Meeting for Consideration

*Committee decision to identify
and place in appropriate program*

Parent decision to place

Placement in Gifted Program

Assessment for Individual Educational Plan

Includes:

1. Case study material
2. Functional assessment

Appropriate Educational Program

Source: Reprinted with the permission of Simon & Schuster, Inc. from the Merrill/Prentice Hall College text *Growing Up Gifted* 4/e by Barbara Clark. Copyright 1992 by Merrill/Prentice Hall.

TABLE 12.2
Questions about classroom behavior that can guide a teacher's efforts to identify and nominate students who may be gifted and talented

In the classroom does the child

- Ask a lot of questions?
- Show a lot of interest in progress?
- Have lots of information on many things?
- Want to know why or how something is so?
- Become unusually upset at injustices?
- Seem interested and concerned about social or political problems?
- Often have a better reason than you do for not doing what you want done?
- Refuse to drill on spelling, math facts, flash cards, or handwriting?
- Criticize others for dumb ideas?
- Become impatient if work is not "perfect"?
- Seem to be a loner?
- Seem bored and often have nothing to do?
- Complete only part of an assignment or project and then take off in a new direction?
- Stick to a subject long after the class has gone on to other things?
- Seem restless, out of seat often?
- Daydream?
- Seem to understand easily?
- Like solving puzzles and problems?
- Have his or her own idea about how something should be done? And stay with it?
- Talk a lot?
- Love metaphors and abstract ideas?
- Love debating issues?

This child may be showing giftedness cognitively.

Does the child

- Show unusual ability in some area? Maybe reading or math?
- Show fascination with one field of interest? And manage to include this interest in all discussion topics?
- Enjoy meeting or talking with experts in this field?

- Get math answers correct, but find it difficult to tell you how?
- Enjoy graphing everything? Seem obsessed with probabilities?
- Invent new obscure systems and codes?

This child may be showing giftedness academically.

Does the child

- Try to do things in different, unusual, imaginative ways?
- Have a really zany sense of humor?
- Enjoy new routines or spontaneous activities?
- Love variety and novelty?
- Create problems with no apparent solutions? And enjoy asking you to solve them?
- Love controversial and unusual questions?
- Have a vivid imagination?
- Seem never to proceed sequentially?

This child may be showing giftedness creatively.

Does the child

- Organize and lead group activities? Sometimes take over?
- Enjoy taking risks?
- Seem cocky, self-assured?
- Enjoy decision making? Stay with that decision?
- Synthesize ideas and information from a lot of different sources?

This child may be showing giftedness through leadership ability.

Does the child

- Seem to pick up skills in the arts—music, dance, drama, painting, etc.—without instruction?
- Invent new techniques? Experiment?
- See minute detail in products or performances?
- Have high sensory sensitivity?

This child may be showing giftedness through visual or performing arts ability.

Source: Reprinted with the permission of Simon & Schuster, Inc. from the Merrill/Prentice Hall College text *Growing Up Gifted* 4/e by Barbara Clark. Copyright 1992 by Merrill/Prentice Hall, Inc.

tion of group achievement or group intelligence tests. The coordinator of gifted services at the school or district level would review this information and determine whether the results indicate a potential for giftedness and justify the referral of the case to a placement committee. If the coordinator believed there was sufficient evidence to continue, the parents would be asked if they would like to refer Janie for more extensive testing to determine whether she qualifies for gifted services. The coordinator then would manage the development of a case study that includes screening data, parent interviews, test protocols, individual intelligence test, creativity tests, and tests in specific content areas. These data then would be compiled, organized, and presented to the placement committee for consideration. The committee would determine whether Janie qualified for services and what type of program would be best suited for her particular pattern of giftedness. The parents would be an integral part of this meeting and would have to agree with the results and placement decisions that are developed in committee. Janie would then be placed into a gifted program, and the development of her IEP would be initiated by the special education teacher or person in charge of the program. This level of assessment would be more focused and use all of the previous case study materials and other functional assessments to determine where Janie should start in the program and the overall focus of the special education services she would receive. At this point, Janie would begin her new and more appropriate educational program, which would provide exciting and innovative experiences designed to increase her intellectual and creative capabilities.

Multicultural Assessments

To effectively serve talented students from different cultural backgrounds, we must first individually, and then as a society, deal with thorny philosophical issues that involve the priorities of dominant cultures' relations with minority cultural groups. This dichotomy in power has evolved two distinct approaches toward the accommodation of minority cultures: cultural assimilation and cultural pluralism (Kitano, 1991). For many years, the integration of minority groups was based on the "melting pot" theory of cultural assimilation, which had the effect of downplaying the minority culture as a precondition of entry into the dominant culture. Recently, however, widespread dissatisfaction with this philosophy and practice has led to a reconceptualization of acculturation as being a "tossed salad," in effect a place where we all meet and congregate but with each person retaining his or her original identity and cultural characteristics.

> **These concepts were presented in Chapter 3.**

Many people believe that we must first work on our own attitudes before we can accept and appropriately deal with culturally different children in our schools. Plummer (1995) believes that everyone involved in the education of a child must develop a "multicultural identity," which involves forming a new awareness of cultural diversity, and an acceptance of one's own cultural identity. This perspective requires a teacher to develop "a repertoire of culturally appropriate skills and [use] a variety of culturally appropriate interventions in servicing the needs of all gifted and talented children" (p. 286).

Biases inherent in the identification process are primarily to blame for the underrepresentation of students from minority groups such as African Americans, Latinos, and Native Americans in gifted programs nationally (Plummer, 1995; Van Tassel-Baska, Patton, & Prillaman, 1991). In addition, minorities are not entering many important fields in mathematics and science. For example, African Americans make up 12% of the population yet earn just 5% of the bachelor's degrees awarded each year in mathematics and science, receive only 1% of the doctoral degrees, and make up just 2% of all employed scientists and engineers in this country. Hispanics make up 9% of the population but represent just 3% of the bachelor's degrees in science and mathematics, 2% of the doctoral degrees, and 2% of all employed scientists in this country (U. S. Department of Education, 1991). In response to the prevailing reliance on intelligence testing and the desire to identify underserved and minority students, Feldhusen (1992b) asserts that

> most current identification systems call for multiple measures which are added up to a single composite index of giftedness. Many youth from special populations have not had the broad opportunities to develop such a broad pattern of giftedness, but they have often developed special talent within a particular domain. The identification process should be designed to find the special talent. Subsequent educational service should focus on facilitating growth in this talent area. (p. 123).

Current "best practices" for identifying gifted and talented students from diverse cultural groups involve a multifactored assessment process that meets these criteria (Frasier, 1987; Gay, 1978; Maker, 1994; Ortiz & Gonzales, 1991; Plummer, 1995; Tonemah, 1987; Woliver & Woliver, 1991):

- Identification should have a goal of inclusion, rather than exclusion.
- Data should be gathered from multiple sources providing both objective and subjective data (e.g., parent interviews, individual intelligence testing, performance on group problem-solving tasks, motivational and behavioral factors, individual conferences with candidates).
- A combination of formal and informal testing techniques, including teacher referrals, the results of intelligence tests, and individual achievement tests, should be used.
- A generally greater sensitivity to aspects of "acculturation" and "assimilation" that allows for multiple perspectives to be identified and honored should be demonstrated.
- Identification procedures should begin as early as possible—before children are exposed to prejudice and stereotyping—and be continuous.
- Unconventional measures involving arts and aesthetic expression such as, dance, music, creative writing, and crafts should be used.
- Information gathered during the identification process should be used to help determine the curriculum.

Maker (1994) developed a procedure called DISCOVER, which has been used to assess children from diverse cultural groups and females in an equitable fashion. Based on Gardner's theoretical framework of multiple intelligences, the DISCOVER assessment process involves a series of five progressively more complex problems that provide children with various ways to demonstrate their problem-solving competence by interacting with the content and with one another.

> Problem Types I and II require convergent thinking and are most similar to the types of question found on standardized intelligence and achievement tests. Type I problems are highly structured. The solver knows the solution method and must recall or derive the correct answer and involve convergent thinking. Type II problems also are highly structured, but the solver must decide on the correct method to use. . . . Type III problems are clearly structured, but a range of methods can be used to solve them and they have a range of acceptable answers. Type IV and V problems are more open ended, less structured, and require much more divergent thinking. . . . Type IV problems are commonly found in tests of creativity. Type V problems are extremely ill

Assessment of young children's abilities to solve mathematical-spatial problems might include the time used to complete puzzles, the number of puzzles completed, and the particular problem-solving strategies used by the child.

structured. The solver must explore the possibilities, identify the questions to be answered, and determine the criteria by which an effective solution will be recognized. (Maker, Neilson, & Rogers, 1994, p. 7)

Figure 12.6 shows an example of DISCOVER problem-solving activities for four types of intelligences for children in grades K-2. Children use a Pablo© kit, a 21-piece set of tangrams (geometric shapes), to demonstrate their problem-solving abilities with mathematical-spatial problems. Observers record the time used to complete the puzzles, the number of puzzles completed, and particular problem-solving strategies used by the child. A different bag of toys provides the material for assessing the child's linguistic (storytelling) skills.

Maker et al. (1994) report positive results from using the DISCOVER model to assess the problem-solving abilities of students from African American, Navajo, Tohono O'Odham, and Mexican American cultural groups: (a) the children identified by the process closely resemble the cultural characteristics of the communities from which they come; (b) equitable percentages of children from various ethnic, cultural, linguistic, and economic groups are identified; (c) the process is equally effective with boys and girls; and (d) students identified through the process make gains equal to or greater than those of students who were identified by traditional standardized tests when placed in special enrichment programs.

Gifted and Talented Girls

Some of the key issues that appear in the literature concerning the identification and education of females who are gifted and talented involve (a) conflicts concerning role definitions (McCormick & Wolf, 1993), (b) extreme stress related to a lack of self-esteem (Genshaft, Greenbaum, & Borovosky, 1995), (c) poor course selection based on academic choices made in middle school and high school (Clark, 1992), and (d) a lack of parental and general community support for female achievements (Hollinger, 1995).

Cultural barriers, test and social biases, organizational reward systems, sex-role stereotyping, and conflicts between career and marriage and family all act as external impediments to the advancement of gifted and talented women (Kerr, 1985). In reviewing the topic of gifted women, Silverman (1986) points out that the history of genius and women's roles has been contradictory (eminent contributions cannot be made from a subservient status) and that identification procedures reflect masculine (product-oriented) versus feminine (development-oriented) concepts of giftedness.

FIGURE 12.6

Activities and Intelligences	Problem Type				
	Type I	**Type II**	**Type III**	**Type IV**	**Type V**
Spatial	Find a piece shaped like a ____. (Teacher shows a shape.)	Find pieces that look like a rainbow. (Observer shows pictures.)	Find pieces and make mountains. (Observer shows pictures.)	Make any animal with as many pieces as you need. Tell about your animal if you want. (Observer provides connectors.)	Make anything you want to make. Tell about it if you wish.
Mathematical-Spatial	Complete simple tangram puzzles with a one-to-one correspondence between the tangram pieces and the puzzles.	Complete simple tangram puzzles with more than one solution that works.	Complete complex tangram puzzles with multiple solutions.	Make a square with as many tangram pieces as you can.	Make a design or a pattern with the pieces.
Mathematical	Complete one- and two-digit addition and subtraction problems.	Complete magic squares using addition and subtraction.	Write correct number sentences using numbers given (in any order).	Write as many correct number problems as you can with an answer of 10.	None
Linguistic	Provide a label for toys given.	Make groups of toys and tell how items in the group are alike. (Some are obvious.)	Make different groups of toys and tell how items in each group are alike. (Encourage going beyond the obvious.)	Tell a story that includes all your toys.	Write a story about a personal experience, something you made up, or anything you wish.

Source: From C. J. Maker, A. B. Nielson, & J. A. Rogers "Giftedness, Diversity, and Problem-Solving."
Teaching Exceptional Children, 1994, *27,* p. 9. Copyright (1994) by the Council for Exceptional Children.
Reprinted by permission.

The journal *Gifted Education International* published a special issue on gifted and talented girls and women (1994, Vol. 9, No. 3).

Programs serving gifted and talented females should strive to (a) alter attitudes toward nontraditional career choices, (b) influence the attitudes and behavior of significant others in the girls' environment, (c) change sex-biased instructional practices in the schools, and (d) change the image of math and science to a gender-free domain (Fox, Brody, & Tobin, 1980). Silverman (1986, 1989) makes these recommendations for improving the special education of gifted girls:

- Hold high expectations for girls.
- Believe in their logical and mathematical abilities.
- Expose both boys and girls to female role models.
- Actively recruit girls for advanced placement math and science classes.
- Encourage and deal with girls' multiple interests and talents.
- Use nonsexist texts, language, and communication.

The intellectual abilities and talents of children with disabilities can be fostered by providing daily opportunities for practicing superior abilities and for enjoying feelings of success.

- Form support groups for girls.
- Encourage independence.

Gifted and Talented Students with Disabilities

Especially troubling are stories of young students with disabilities who fail inside the walls of the school and succeed outside them later in life. What would we think if we saw Thomas Edison sitting in a remedial reading group or Helen Keller being left alone in the back of the room as instruction swirled around her? These now-famous persons and many others have had some type of disabling condition and have triumphed over its handicapping effects to distinguish themselves in the world.

Maker (1977) investigated students with visual, hearing, and physical disabilities and found wide individual differences in intellectual capacity, cognitive development, and self-concept. No single pattern, or set, of characteristics would help identify individual students as gifted and talented. Whitmore and Maker (1985) conducted the most detailed examination of the needs and accomplishments of gifted and talented students with physical disabilities. On the basis of five case studies involving students with visual, hearing, physical, and learning disabilities, they concluded that teachers and parents can foster the intellectual and talent development of children with disabilities by

- Keeping perceptions of the individual's physical limitations open-ended
- Conveying positive, realistic expectations
- Encouraging the development of increasing levels of independence
- Helping the child formulate a positive, attainable goal for the future
- Guiding the child's development of self-understanding and constructive coping strategies
- Providing daily opportunities for the child to build inherent superior abilities and to enjoy feelings of success
- Advocating for appropriate educational opportunities
- Pursuing positive social experiences for the child (pp. 231-234)

World-famous theoretical physicist Stephen W. Hawking talks about his views of the Big Bang singularity and quantum mechanics beginning on the following page.

I Was Thinking About Black Holes

by Stephen W. Hawking

Stephen W. Hawking is Lucasian Professor of Mathematics and Theoretical Physics at the University of Cambridge in England. He is considered by many to be the foremost theoretical physicist in the world today. His goal is to develop a "grand unifying theory" of the entire universe. Such a theory would encompass all known laws of science and describe how the universe began. While a student in college, he was diagnosed with amyotrophic lateral sclerosis (ALS), a degenerative disease of the nervous system sometimes called Lou Gehrig's disease. He uses a wheelchair for mobility and a computer-assisted synthetic speech

Stephen W. Hawking

generator to communicate (see "My Communication System" in Chapter 10). We asked Professor Hawking to describe a short history of his interests and work as a student and scientist.

I was born on January the 8th, 1942, exactly 300 years after the death of Galileo. However, I estimate that about 200,000 other babies were also born that day; I don't know whether any of them were later interested in astronomy.

We lived in Highgate, North London. During World War II, our house was damaged by a V2 rocket, which landed a few doors away. Fortunately, we were not there at the time. In 1950, we moved to the cathedral city of Saint Albans, 20 miles north of London. My father wanted me to go to Westminster School, one of the main "public," that is to say, private, schools. He himself had gone to a minor public school. He thought that this, and his parents' poverty, had held him back and had led to his being passed over in favor of people with less ability but more social graces. However, I was ill at the time of the scholarship exam and so did not go to Westminster. Instead, I went to the local school, Saint Albans School, where I got an education that was as good as, if not better than, that I would have had at Westminster. I have never found that my lack of social graces has been a hindrance.

I was a fairly normal small boy, slow to learn to read, and very interested in how things worked. I was never more than about halfway up the class at school (it was a very bright class). When I was 12, one of my friends bet another friend a bag of sweets that I would never come to anything. I don't know if this bet was ever settled, and, if so, which way it was decided.

My father would have liked me to do medicine. However, I thought that biology was too descriptive and not sufficiently fundamental. Maybe I would have thought differently if I had been aware of molecular biology, but that was not generally known about at the time. Instead, I wanted to do mathematics, more mathematics, and physics. My father thought, however, that there would not be any jobs in mathematics, apart from teaching. He therefore made me do chemistry, physics, and only a small amount of mathematics. Another reason against mathematics was that he wanted me to go to his old College, University College, Oxford, and they did not do mathematics at that time. I duly went to University College in 1959 to do physics, which was the subject that interested me most, because it governs how the universe behaves. To me, mathematics is just a tool with which to do physics.

Most of the other students in my year had done military service and were a lot older. I felt rather lonely during my first year and part of the second. It was only in my third year that I really felt happy at Oxford. The prevailing attitude at Oxford at that time was very anti-work. You were supposed to either be brilliant without effort or to accept your limitations and get a fourth-class degree. To work hard to get a better class of degree was regarded as the mark of a gray man, the worst epithet in the Oxford vocabulary.

At that time, the physics course at Oxford was arranged in a way that made it particularly easy to avoid work. I did one exam before I went up and then had 3 years at Oxford, with just the final exam at the end. I once calculated that I did about 1,000 hours of work in the 3 years I was at Oxford, an average of an hour a day. I'm not proud of this lack of work, I'm just describing my attitude of complete boredom and feeling that nothing was worth making an effort for. One result of my illness has been to change all that; when you are faced with the possibility of an early death, it makes one realize that life is worth living and that there are lots of things you want to do.

Because of my lack of work, I had planned to get through the final exam by doing problems in theoretical physics and avoiding any questions that required factual knowledge. However, I didn't sleep the night before the exam because of nervous tension. So I didn't do very well. I was on the borderline between a first- and second-class degree, and I had to be interviewed by the examiners to determine which I should get. In the interview, they asked me about my future plans. I replied I wanted to do research. If they gave me a first, I would go to Cambridge. If I only got a second, I would stay in Oxford. They gave me a first.

I thought there were two possible areas of theoretical physics that were fundamental and in which I might do research. One was cosmology, the study of the very large. The other was elementary particles, the study of the very small. However, I thought that elementary particles were less attractive because, although scientists were finding lots of new particles, there was no proper theory of elementary particles. All they could do was arrange the particles in families, like in botany. In cosmology, on the other hand, there was a well-defined theory, Einstein's General Theory of Relativity.

I had not done much mathematics at school or at Oxford, so I found General Relativity very difficult at first and did not make much progress. Also, during my last year at Oxford, I had noticed that I was getting rather clumsy in my movements. Soon after I went to Cambridge, I was diagnosed as having ALS, amyotrophic lateral sclerosis, or motor neuronic disease, as it is known in England. The doctors could offer no cure or assurance that it

would not get worse. The only consolation they could give me was that I was not a typical case.

At first the disease seemed to progress fairly rapidly. There did not seem much point in working at my research because I didn't expect to live long enough to finish my Ph.D. However, as time went by, the disease seemed to slow down. I also began to understand General Relativity and to make progress with my work. However, what really made the difference was that I got engaged to a girl named Jane Wilde, whom I had met about the time I was diagnosed with ALS. This gave me something to live for.

If I were to get married, I had to get a job. And to get a job, I had to finish my Ph.D. I therefore started working hard for the first time in my life. To my surprise, I found I liked it. Maybe it is not really fair to call it work.

I applied for a research fellowship at Caius College, pronounced "keys." I was hoping that Jane would type my application, but when she came to visit me in Cambridge, she had her arm in plaster, having broken it. I must admit that I was less sympathetic than I should have been. However, it was her left arm, so she was able to write out my application to my dictation, and I got someone else to type it.

I got the fellowship and have been a fellow of Caius College ever since.

Having got a fellowship, I knew we could get married, which we did in July 1965.

My research up to 1970 was in cosmology, the study of the universe on a large scale. My most important work in this period was on singularities. Observations of distant galaxies indicate that they are moving away from us: The universe is expanding. This implies that the galaxies must have been closer together in the past. The question then arises: Was there a time in the past when all of the galaxies were on top of

each other and the density of the universe was infinite? Or was there a previous contracting phase, in which the galaxies managed to avoid hitting each other? Maybe they flew past each other and started to move away from each other. To answer this question required new mathematical techniques. These were developed between 1965 and 1970, mainly by Roger Penrose and myself. Penrose was then at Birkbeck College, London. Now he is at Oxford. We used these techniques to show that there must have been a state of infinite density in the past, if the General Theory of Relativity was correct.

This state of infinite density is called the Big Bang singularity. It would be the beginning of the universe. All of the known laws of science would break down at a singularity. This would mean that science would not be able to predict how the universe would begin, if General Relativity is correct. However, my more recent work indicates that it is possible to predict how the universe would begin if one takes into account the theory of quantum mechanics, the theory of the very small.

General Relativity also predicts that massive stars will collapse in on themselves when they have exhausted their nuclear fuel. The work that Penrose and I had done showed that they would continue to collapse until they reached a singularity of infinite density. This singularity would be an end of time, at least for the star and anything on it. The gravitational field of the singularity would be so strong that light could not escape from a region around it, but would be dragged back by the gravitational field. The region from which it is not possible to escape is called a black hole, and its boundary is called the event horizon. Anything or anyone who falls into the black hole through the event horizon will come to an end of time at the singularity.

I was thinking about black holes as I got into bed one night in 1970, shortly after the birth of my daughter, Lucy. Suddenly, I realized that many of the techniques that Penrose and I had developed to prove singularities could be applied to black holes. In particular, the area of the event horizon, the boundary of the black hole, could not decrease with time. And when two black holes collided and joined together to form a single hole, the area of the horizon of the final hole would be greater than the sum of the areas of the horizons of the original black holes. This placed an important limit on the amount of energy that could be emitted in the collision. I was so excited that I did not get much sleep that night.

From 1970 to 1974, I worked mainly on black holes. But in 1974, I made perhaps my most surprising discovery: Black holes are not completely black! When one takes the small-scale behavior of matter into account, particles and radiation can leak out of a black hole. The black hole emits radiation as if it were a hot body.

Since 1974, I have been working on combining General Relativity and quantum mechanics into a consistent theory. One result of that has been a proposal I made in 1983 with Jim Hartle, of Santa Barbara: that both space and time are finite in extent but they don't have any boundary or edge. They would be like the surface of the Earth, but with two more dimensions. The Earth's surface is finite in area, but it doesn't have any boundary. In all of my travels, I have not managed to fall off the edge of the world.

If this proposal is correct, there would be no singularities, and the laws of science would hold everywhere, including at the beginning of the universe. The way the universe began would be determined by the laws of science. I would have succeeded in my ambition to discover how the universe began. But I still don't know why it began. ✳

Bireley (1995) optimistically predicts, "One of the most positive outcomes of the current movement toward inclusion may be increased appropriate service to such children who need accommodation for their widely disparate abilities" (p. 202). Clark (1992) admonishes educators to remember that students who are gifted with disabilities face daunting odds: "The learning disability will always be there, and the child must learn how to compensate for it. The struggle will always be there; the frustration will always be there. Compensatory skills such as learning how to touch type, learning word processing, using calculators and recorders, and learning organizational skills should be taught to the learning disabled child. Behavior modification techniques often used in special education may also be tried" (p. 563).

✳ *Educational Approaches*
Curricular Goals

The overall goal of educational programs for gifted and talented students should be the fullest possible development of every child's actual and potential abilities. In the broadest terms, the educational goals for these youngsters are no different from those for all children. Feelings of self-worth, self-sufficiency, civic responsibility, and vocational and avocational competence are important for everyone. However, some additional specific educational outcomes are especially desirable for gifted and talented students.

Gallagher (1981) has classified the educational objectives of programs for gifted students into two areas: (a) mastering the knowledge structure of disciplines and (b) heuristic skills. Knowledge structures include both basic principles and systems of knowledge; heuristic skills include problem solving, creativity, and use of the scientific method. In other words, gifted students need both content knowledge and the abilities to use and develop that knowledge effectively.

For gifted and talented students, the three R's alone do not comprise the basics. Gifted students are about to enter a world where information is transmitted and processed at amazing rates and where international travel and business will require them to have a wide range of social and language skills in addition to their specialty or profession. Research skills, keyboarding and computer usage, speed reading, at least one foreign language, and interpersonal and affective development should be systematically taught as part of the curriculum. The skills of systematic investigation are fundamental abilities that gifted students use throughout a lifetime of learning. These skills include the use of references, the use of the library, the gathering of information (data), and the reporting of findings in a variety of ways. These skills may ultimately be used in diverse settings, such as law and medical libraries, museums, chemical and electrical laboratories, theatrical archives, and national parks.

Most authors and teachers agree that the most important concern in developing appropriate curriculum is to match the students' specific needs with a *qualitatively different* curricular intervention. According to Kaplan (1988), the differentiated curriculum should

1. be responsive to the needs of the gifted student as both a member of the gifted population and as a member of the general population.
2. include or subsume aspects of the regular curriculum.
3. provide gifted students with opportunities to exhibit those characteristics that were instrumental in their identification as gifted individuals.
4. not academically or socially isolate these students from their peers.
5. not be used as either a reward or a punishment for gifted students. (p. 170)

Feldhusen and Moon (1995) advocate the development of an individualized "growth plan" designed to develop a broad program of services for gifted and talented students. The growth plan differs from special education's IEP along several important dimensions: (a) It is not a requirement for services to be provided, (b) it is more flexible, having no time restrictions, reporting requirements, or physical boundaries, and (c) it is primarily collaboratively planned but essentially student directed. The growth plan should include assessment information, student-generated goals (in consultation with others), and the recommended activities for accomplishing these goals. A key feature of this approach is that the student is guided toward the establishment of his or her own goals and is an active participant in all instructional and evaluative activities. This method is consistent with Maker's (1994) contention that "one of the most important goals of these [gifted] programs is to increase the individual learner's control of the learning process and opportunities for decision making in situations involving both learning and other aspects of living" (p. 18).

Piirto (1994) recommends that curriculum and instruction for gifted and talented students

- *Be based on learning characteristics of academically talented children.* These characteristics include "their ability to learn at a faster rate; their ability to think abstractly about content that is challenging; their ability to think productively, critically, creatively, and analytically; and their ability to increase constantly and rapidly their store knowledge . . . of both facts and of processes and procedures" (p. 384).
- *Possess academic rigor.* The widespread abuse of grading practices, the "dumbing down" of the curriculum, and the lowered expectations of teachers have all sapped curriculum of its strength and rigor. There is a distinct need to increase

the relevance, discipline, and depth of current curriculum, primarily within the regular education setting where most gifted students are for most of the day.

- *Be interdisciplinary.* Academically talented students should be exposed to the structures, terminologies, and methodologies of various disciplines.

Curriculum Organization and Delivery Methods

Gifted and talented students need exposure to a challenging and conceptually rich curriculum. Far too many gifted children are "languishing in the regular classroom, unable to focus their attention on material that was mastered long ago, is unbearably simplistic, and has been reiterated beyond their tolerance level" (Silverman, 1995, p. 220). Because gifted students learn at a faster rate than most students and can absorb and reconfigure more concepts, they benefit from a differentiated curriculum that is modified in both its pace and depth (Piirto, 1994). *Acceleration* is the general term for modifying the pace at which the student moves through the curriculum; *enrichment* means probing or studying a subject at a greater depth than would occur in the regular curriculum.

Acceleration

Acceleration means providing a student with opportunities to move through required curriculum at a faster pace. The many acceleration options include

- Early admission to school
- Grade skipping/advancement
- Content acceleration in one or two subjects while remaining with age peers
- Testing out of courses
- Curriculum compacting or telescoping
- Concurrent enrollment in both high school and college
- Advanced placement tests
- Early admission to college

Silverman (1995) believes that acceleration is a "necessary response to a highly gifted student's faster pace of learning" (p. 229). Research indicates that when acceleration is practiced wisely, students benefit by having increased interest in school, attaining higher levels of academic achievement, receiving recognition of accomplishment, and completing higher levels of education in less time, which provides increased time for pursuing careers at the end of schooling (Kulick & Kulick, 1984; Robinson & Noble, 1991; Southern & Jones, 1991). Finally, one of the practical benefits of acceleration is that it is both time- and cost-effective for school personnel to implement (Swiatek & Benbow, 1991).

A commonly heard concern is that early admission and grade skipping will lead to social or emotional problems because the child will be in a classroom with older students who are more advanced physically and emotionally. Feldhusen and Moon (1995) state that "ridiculous myths . . . circulate among school personnel" (p. 105) that talented students will suffer from the "pressure" to achieve at higher levels and will "burn out" or become "social misfits." Although this concern is understandable, research shows that if acceleration is done properly, few, if any, socioemotional problems result (Robinson & Noble, 1991; Southern & Jones, 1991). After reviewing a

Technology can be used to provide both acceleration and enrichment opportunities for gifted students. See "New and Emerging Technologies for Gifted and Talented Students" later in this chapter.

For specific guidelines for teachers and parents who are considering early admission or grade advancement, see Feldhusen (1992b) and Feldhusen, Proctor, and Black, 1986. The March/April, 1992 issue of *The Gifted Child Today* contains 11 articles on acceleration.

decade of longitudinal research on the academic acceleration of mathematically precocious youths, Swiatek (1993) found no evidence that acceleration harms willing students either academically or socially/emotionally. Feldhusen (1992c)—a strong advocate for acceleration who believes it is "the most powerful educational service we can offer to gifted and talented youth" (n.p.)—writes:

> A more salient question to ask is what are the risks of *not* advancing the children. The excruciating daily boredom (Feldhusen & Kolloff, 1985), the problems of dealing with peers who are less mature intellectually, and the learning to get by may produce serious emotional problems. For some highly gifted students there can be clear social ostracism because of the child's advanced interests and precocious verbal behaviors. . . . Thus, for a number of reasons the problems of social and/or emotional adjustment for the gifted child may be greater in the age-grade placement than in an advanced grade. (p. 46)

Curriculum Compacting

Many gifted and talented students have already mastered much of the content of the regular curriculum when the school year begins. In fact, one study found that 60% of *all* fourth graders in a certain school district were able to attain a score of 80% correct or higher on a test of mathematics content before they had even opened their books in September (EPIE, 1980). The finding of one national survey that teachers usually make only minor, if any, changes in curricular content for gifted students is not encouraging in this respect (Archambault et al., 1993). In a related study, the same researchers found that in over 84% of the instructional activities, gifted and talented children were not provided with any meaningful instructional or curricular differentiation (Westberg, Archambault, Dobyns & Slavin, 1993).

Curriculum compacting—compressing the instructional content and materials so that academically able students have more time to work on more challenging materials—is one of the major techniques for adapting and developing curriculum for talented students in the regular classroom. Curriculum compacting has been shown to be an effective way to ensure that gifted and talented students cover the important information and materials within the regular education curriculum and are then able to move beyond it to meet their special instructional needs. To be effective, however, teachers must have a deep understanding of the curricular content and be able not only to condense the material but also to modify its presentation and evaluate the outcomes of the instruction.

It appears that regular education teachers will need systematic professional development activities in order to develop and use the skills needed to successfully engage in curriculum compacting. A series of studies on the impact of a progressive staff development program showed some promise in terms of teaching teachers how to adapt their curricula (Reis, 1995). The intervention involved three steps to facilitate curriculum compacting: (a) assess the target content areas, (b) determine the content to be eliminated, and (c) substitute the more appropriate content. The researchers found that the 436 teachers who participated in the study successfully eliminated 40% to 50% of the curricular content without detrimental effects on the academic performance of 783 gifted and talented students. In addition, the gifted and talented students scored significantly higher on tests of mathematics and science concepts after the content was altered.

Teachers must avoid the temptation and ease of providing gifted students the MOTS curriculum (More of The Same)—repetitious and unnecessary drill and practice of the same kinds of items or problems the students have already mastered. MOTS activities do not represent differentiated curriculum for gifted and talented students and may be one reason that some students underachieve (Clark, 1992).

Enrichment

Enrichment experiences let students investigate topics of interest in greater detail than is ordinarily possible with the standard school curriculum. Topics of investigation may be based on the ongoing activities of the classroom but may permit students to go beyond the limits of the day-to-day instructional offerings. However, by allowing the students to help define the area of interest and independently access a variety of information and materials, the teacher can learn to facilitate the development of gifted and talented students' competencies and skills.

Enriching the content of instruction to include more innovation, novelty, and sophistication is the most common method of differentiating curriculum for academically talented students. The use of new teaching techniques is also advocated, including the use of new technologies for the organization, manipulation, and presentation of student products. Enriching the curriculum generally involves adding new and different information from a variety of disciplines outside the traditional curriculum. This is the strategy of choice by most regular education teachers when attempting to provide additional opportunities for gifted and talented students in their classrooms. It is important to remember that enrichment is meant to be thoughtfully and systematically applied to the educational program of targeted students.

Enrichment is not a "do-your-own-thing" approach with no structure or guidance. Children involved in enrichment experiences should not be released to do a random, haphazard (and thus inefficient) project. A basic framework that defines limits and sets outcomes is necessary. Projects should have purpose, direction, and specified outcomes. A teacher should provide guidance where necessary—and to the degree that is necessary—to keep the youngsters efficient.

Ideally, the teacher provides enrichment opportunities for all students, but it is often beyond the abilities of teachers to do this for an entire class. Reis (1995) recommends that schools hire *enrichment specialists,* who would provide direct services to high-ability students half of the time and "serve as a catalyst for all types of enrichment services to the entire school the rest of the time" (p. 383). She believes that such schoolwide enrichment activities would provide benefits to all students (see Table 12.3).

Suggestions for Curriculum Differentiation Outside the Classroom

For some students with outstanding talents, the things that take place outside the classroom may be more important and rewarding than many of the things that take place within it. The teacher should always attempt to connect with both human and physical resources that are available within the community. Much more flexibility is offered by outside learning environments because of the relaxed scheduling and the lack of physical barriers they offer to students. The options for learning outside the school generally fall into two categories: (a) special courses offered by educational agencies and (b) community-based learning opportunities (Piirto, 1994).

- *Internships and mentor programs.* The value and power of a viable mentor to the realization of talent or creativity have been recognized since the Middle Ages. The importance of mentors cannot be underestimated in certain artistic and scientific fields where the development of both conceptual and performance skills is critical to success. These opportunities allow students with exceptional talents to be exposed to one of the most powerful and proven educational strategies—the modeling, practice, and direct feedback and reinforcement of important behaviors within a real-world setting.

What's more important for gifted and talented students—acceleration or enrichment? "The question of acceleration versus enrichment is irrelevant, because this group of students needs both. They learn at a very accelerated pace, and they need high-level conceptual material outside the regular curriculum" (Silverman, 1995, p. 229).

Do gifted and talented students benefit the most by participating in acceleration and enrichment programs with peers who show similar intellectual abilities? See the National Association for Gifted Children's position statement on ability grouping (Figure 12.7).

FIGURE 12.7
Position statement on ability grouping by the National Association for Gifted Children

---

NATIONAL ASSOCIATION FOR GIFTED CHILDREN
POSITION PAPER

Ability Grouping

The National Association for Gifted Children (NAGS)periodically issues policy statements that deal with issues, policies, and practices that have an impact on the education of gifted and talented students. Policy statements represent the official convictions of the organization.

All policy statements approved by the NAGC Board of Directors are consistent with the organization's belief that education in a democracy must respect the uniqueness of all individuals, the broad range of cultural diversity present in our society, and the similarities and differences in learning characteristics that can be found within any group of students. NAGC is fully committed to national goals that advocate both excellence and equity for all students, and we believe that the best way to achieve these goals is through *differentiated* educational opportunities, resources, and encouragement for all students.

The practice of grouping, enabling students with advanced abilities and/or performance to be grouped together to receive appropriately challenging instruction, has recently come under attack. NAGC wishes to reaffirm the importance of grouping for instruction of gifted students. Grouping allows for more appropriate, rapid, and advanced instruction, which matches the rapidly developing skills and capabilities of gifted students.

Special attention should be given to the identification of gifted and talented students who may not be identified through traditional assessment methods (including economically disadvantaged individuals, individuals of limited English proficiency, and individuals with handicaps), to help them participate effectively in special grouping programs.

Strong research evidence supports the effectiveness of ability grouping for gifted students in accelerated classes, enrichment programs, advanced placement programs, etc. Ability and performance grouping has been used extensively in programs for musically and artistically gifted students, and for athletically talented students with little argument. Grouping is a necessary component of every graduate and professional preparation program, such as law, medicine, and the sciences. It is an accepted practice that is used extensively in the education programs in almost every country in the western world.

NAGC does not endorse a tracking system that sorts all children into fixed layers in the school system with little attention to particular content, student motivation, past accomplishment, or present potential.

To abandon the proven instructional strategy of grouping students for instruction at a time of educational crisis in the U.S. will further damage our already poor competitive position with the rest of the world, and will renege on our promise to provide an appropriate education for all children.

Source: The National Association for Gifted Children, Washington, DC. Adopted November, 1991.
Reprinted by permission.

- *Special courses.* Many specialized courses are offered within most communities, including courses at local colleges and universities, and arts and cultural events, museums, and workshops at recreation centers. These courses may or may not have high school or college continuing education credits attached to them. They form a rich variety of additional opportunities for students to encounter mentors, new friends, and expansive concepts that may not be available in the confines of the school curriculum.
- *Odyssey of the Mind.* This is an international program designed to bring together children from every country in a cooperative problem-solving environment. Teams are formed in three age divisions: grades K-5, grades 6-8, and grades 9-12. The process begins at the school level and advances through regional, state,

TABLE 12.3
Benefits to all students of a schoolwide enrichment program

1. Enrichment experiences (assemblies, performances, speakers) are often organized by the enrichment specialist.

2. Mini-courses and advanced training opportunities are often scheduled for a wider range of students than are normally identified in the enrichment program.

3. Curriculum materials, computer software, and equipment are often supplied to classroom teachers by the enrichment specialist to provide exciting work opportunities for all students in the classroom.

4. Staff development for classroom teachers is often provided by the enrichment specialist to benefit all students in areas such as creative thinking skills, research techniques, and critical thinking.

5. Model lessons in a variety of areas (creativity training, thinking skills) that benefit both teachers and students are often taught in classrooms by enrichment specialists.

6. Enrichment specialists encourage high-ability students to present to classrooms the products they have developed in the program. After seeing these products, other students often become interested in pursuing similar work under the supervision of the classroom teacher.

7. When enrichment programs such as Future Problem Solving and Odyssey of the Mind are introduced by the enrichment specialist, other students and teachers often become involved.

8. When classroom teachers learn to modify regular curriculum (including eliminating curriculum that students already know) for high-ability students, other students benefit.

9. Classroom teachers are often encouraged to use more challenging work to meet the needs of high-ability students, and the challenge often benefits other students.

10. Textbooks with more advanced content are often advocated by enrichment specialists. These books offer more appropriate challenges to all students.

11. A philosophical belief may emerge, because of the presence of the program, that one major goal of education is the identification and development of talent in all children.

Source: From S. M. Reis, "What Gifted Education Can Offer the Reform Movement: Talent Development." In J. L. Genshaft, M. Bireley, and C. L. Hollinger (Eds.), *Serving Gifted and Talented Students,* 1995, p. 384. PRO-ED Publishers: Austin, TX. Reprinted with permission.

Addresses for Odyssey of the Mind, Junior Great Books, and the Future Problem Solving programs are provided in "For More Information" at the end of the chapter.

national, and, finally, international levels of competition. Each of the teams is given three types of problems to solve, some that take months to solve, others that require only days, and some that must be solved spontaneously. The problems require a unique blend of creativity, basic knowledge, and cooperative problem solving in order to distinguish team processes and products from each other.

• *Junior Great Books.* This is a highly structured educational program that involves students reading selections from a number of areas, including classical, philosophical, fiction, and poetry, and then discussing their meaning with teachers. The teachers must undergo special training and use specific questioning techniques designed to elicit high-quality responses from the students.

• *Summer programs.* Many summer programs are available to gifted and talented students that offer educational experiences as diverse as environmental studies and space and aeronautical studies. A number of new program offerings have been aimed at gifted minority students at the state and local levels. Summer pro-

A good mentor provides students with exceptional talents opportunities to develop both their conceptual and performance skills in a real-world setting.

grams are usually relatively brief but intense learning experiences that concentrate on specific areas of intellectual, artistic, or cultural affairs.

- *International curricular experiences.* New Zealanders have a cultural rite of passage they refer to as "the trek," wherein they pack their bags and travel in modest fashion to the far reaches of the planet. It is an eye-opening experience for people from a tiny Pacific island and one that gives them an exceptional opportunity to see and touch the world in an intimate fashion. An international curricular experience can merge this act of exploration with the demands of a structured learning experience such as the International Baccalaureate Program. Numerous international programs offer academic credits for study at participating educational agencies around the world. They are excellent opportunities to develop global interactional skills with academically rigorous studies.

Instructional Models and Methods

The Schoolwide Enrichment Triad Model

The Schoolwide Enrichment Triad Model not only attempts to meet the needs of the gifted and talented students within the regular classroom setting but also is meant to be used with the other students in the classroom (Renzulli & Reis, 1986). The model has undergone several revisions since it was first introduced and now provides new identification procedures, the inclusion of all students in the planned activities, and even more extensive follow-up activities. The process involves first identifying a "talent pool" of high-ability students (usually about 15% to 20% of the school's enrollment) by using a multifactored assessment approach, including achievement tests, teacher and peer nominations, and creativity assessments. Once the students are identified, they are able to take part in specialized services, many of which are also available and appropriate for other learners in the same classroom. Reis (1995) discusses some of the relevant features of this instructional approach:

1. Interest and learning styles assessments are used with talent pool students. Informal and formal methods are used to create and/or identify individual students' interests and to encourage students to further develop and pursue their interests in various ways.

New and Emerging Technologies for Gifted and Talented Students

....

Teachers of gifted students must deal with both conceptual and practical issues as they plan for the integration of technology into their classroom instruction. They must first have a clear idea of their own curricular focus and which aspects of technology they wish to use if they are to enhance the understanding and use of this information. This is primarily a matching process between the conceptual information and the best manner of presenting and manipulating this information by using a technological tool. The results of this process should be (a) a conceptual framework in which instruction will take place and (b) the identification of the technological methods and tools to be used in instructional delivery.

Integrating technology into a classroom is a dynamic and flexible merger of known concepts and skills with the unknown capabilities and liabilities that accompany new technologies. The constant interaction and friction within this lively environment results in the particular technology-use scenario that each teacher eventually develops. These scenarios can be as minimal as simple word-processing or computer-assisted instruction or as sophisticated as a fully integrated multimedia, telecommunications, and simulation development capability in the classroom.

Software Selection and Acquisition

The identification of appropriate software for a gifted student is dependent on the curricular goals developed by the teacher for a particular student. If the curricular demand is to build research and scientific inquiry skills, then the best software might be simulations, database systems, interactive videodisc programs, and possibly spreadsheets. If the curriculum focuses on expressive writing, then the use of word-processing, desktop publishing, and graphics software would be appropriate.

Perry (1989) provides several selection criteria that he believes should be applied when previewing educational software for use in gifted education. These criteria include (a) the provision for differing levels of ability, (b) branching capabilities, (c)

reusability—that is, students can profit from using the software more than one time, (d) an evaluation component, (e) a challenge for students, and (f) accurate and up-to-date content. See Table A for suggested software.

Intelligent Computer-Assisted-Instruction (ICAI)

ICAI software analyzes and interprets student responses and presents new information to the learner, modeled on the student's own cognitive strengths and weaknesses. The critical difference between ICAI and traditional CAI programs is in their ability to collect diagnostic information and act on it; basically, it "learns" from the user's responses. In addition, these programs are able to modify their instructional strategies on the basis of patterns of information they gather from student responses.

An example of an ICAI program is a math tutor that initially presents to a student a group of mathematics problems at a defined difficulty level. After responding to the initial set of problems, the program analyzes the response patterns and sets a starting point within a sequenced set of problems for the learner. The student then begins working on this first set, with the ICAI program analyzing the correct solutions and the types and patterns of errors the student makes. The program uses these error patterns to create "expert models" that will progressively guide the student through problem solution, providing hints and directional cues on student errors. The program thus monitors, evaluates, and constructs problem solutions for each individual student user.

Virtual Reality

These new three-dimensional simulations will provide opportunities for creative development and the exploration of both real and imaginary environments. Virtual reality will help "concretize" formerly highly abstract concepts (Papert, 1980) and thus allow for earlier and more powerful instructional interventions with gifted students. An example of an educational application of virtual reality is a social studies simulation of a medieval village. The student would access the virtual "medieval world" through the computer-based simulation and a helmet that transmits the sounds and images to the user. A data-glove or joystick allows a limited response capability in order to manipulate "objects" in the village/world. The student can walk through the streets up to the castle, enter the castle, and take part in a grand feast in the main hall. The food, entertainment, and interactions can all be modeled in the virtual world to closely approximate those revealed in historic documents and paintings. The student can come to know and

TABLE A
Suggested software for gifted students

CURRICULAR AREA	SOFTWARE TITLE	GRADES	PRODUCER
Reading	Reader Rabbit	K–1	Learning Company
	The Playroom	K–1	Brøderbund Software
	Talking Classroom	K–2	Orange Cherry Software
	Expanded Books (Series)	All ages	Voyager Company
	Silwa Literature Series	9+	Queue, Inc.
	Review of American Literature	10–college	Queue, Inc.
Writing and desktop publishing	Bilingual Writing Center	2+	Learning Company
	Children's Writing and Publishing Center	2+	Learning Company
	Kidworks	K–4	Davidson and Associates
	Pagemaker	4+	MacWarehouse
Mathematics	In the Neighborhood	2+	Critical Thinking Press
	Math Blaster Mystery	1+	Davidson and Associates
	NumberMazes	K–6	Great Wave Software
	Operation Neptune	4+	Learning Company
	The King's Rule	4+	Wings for Learning
	Excel	6+	MacWarehouse
	Lotus 1, 2, 3	6+	MacWarehouse
Science	All About Science (series)	4–8	Ventura Educational
	Destination: MARS!	5–12	Compu-Teach
	McGraw-Hill Science and Technical Reference Set	9+	McGraw-Hill
Fine arts	Kid Pix	K–6	Brøderbund Software
	Fractal Design Painter	4+	Fractal Design
	Intervals, Melodies, Chord Qualities, Harmonies, Rhythms	6+	University of Delaware

TABLE A (continued)

CURRICULAR AREA	SOFTWARE TITLE	GRADES	PRODUCER
Multimedia Tools	HyperCard 2.2	4+	Claris
	Adobe Premier	6+	MacWarehouse
	Director 3.1	6+	MacWarehouse

Key to Companies

Brøderbund Software
PO Box 12947
San Rafael, CA 94913-2947

Claris Corporation
440 Clyde Avenue
Mountain View, CA 94943

Compu-Teach
78 Olive Street
New Haven, CT 06511

Critical Thinking Press & Software
PO Box 448
Pacific Grove, CA 93950

Davidson and Associates, Inc.
19840 Pioneer Avenue
Torrance, CA 90503

Fractal Design
335 Spreckels Drive, Suite F
Aptos, CA 95001-2380

Great Wave Software
5353 Scotts Valley Drive
Scotts Valley, CA 95066

The Learning Company
6493 Kaiser Drive
Fremont, CA 94555

MacWarehouse
PO Box 3013
1690 Oak Street
Lakewood, NJ 08701-3013

McGraw-Hill Publishing Company
11 W. 19th Street
New York, NY 10011

Orange Cherry Software
Box 390 Westchester Avenue
Pound Ridge, NY 10576-0390

Queue, Inc.
338 Commerce Drive
Fairfield, CT 06430

Ventura Educational Systems
3440 Brokenhill Street
Newbury Park, CA 91320

Voyager Company
1351 Pacific Coast Highway
Santa Monica, CA 90401

University of Delaware
Office of Computer Based Instruction
Willard Hall Education Building
Newark, DE 19716

Wings for Learning
1600 Green Hills Road
PO Box 660002
Scotts Valley, CA 95607-0002

experience the reality of medieval life in a manner that is both exciting and educational.

However, there may also be a "dark side" to virtual reality that has not been fully articulated in the rush to bring this technology into the recreational and entertainment marketplaces. Access to a variety of virtual worlds has the potential to be so engrossing that students would reject other types of learning or play experiences. The potential danger is that chil-dren might become isolated within these mental environments that are so easily molded to meet their desires and forsake the somewhat "messy" real world, where one must work at relationships and life.

Electronic Communities

Developments in telecommunications will allow for greater interactions and sharing among gifted students from across the world. The distant interactions will provide new impetus for students to continue their studies and perhaps to reach out and assist in the process of globalizing education for the future. A number of distance learning projects have already been initiated throughout the United States, linking students from across town to across the world with one another. The curricular focus of these projects is as diverse as second language learning and social studies and language arts. Their most important contribution to learning, however, may be in the areas of cultural understanding and interpersonal communications. Students may be able to more fully realize and deal with the realities of a global community through such learning opportunities. The world grows smaller through such contacts, and an understanding of different cultures and peoples will serve to prepare them better to deal with both global competition and cooperation as they mature into adulthood.

Source: Adapted from R. D. Howell "Technological Innovations in the Education of Gifted and Talented Students" in *Serving Gifted and Talented Students* by J. L. Genshaft, M. Bireley, and C. L. Hollinger (Eds.), 1994, pp. 155-171. PRO-ED Publishers: Austin, TX. Reprinted with permission.

2. Curriculum compacting is offered to all eligible students. The regular curriculum of the classroom is modified by eliminating redundant or repetitious information and materials.
3. Three types of enrichment activities are offered to students: Type I, general exploratory experiences; Type II, purposefully designed instructional methods and materials; and Type III, advanced-level studies with greater depth and complexity.

Reis and Cellerino (1983) use a "revolving door" identification model (Renzulli, Reis, & Smith, 1981) that allows all children in the talent pool to participate in Type I and Type II enrichment activities. Only students who show serious interest in a specific topic evolve into Type III investigators. Students are never compelled to begin Type III investigations; it remains an open option for them.

When a student indicates a particular area of interest, the teacher must determine whether the interest is serious enough to warrant launching an in-depth investigation or whether it is only a temporary, superficial interest. Reis and Cellerino (1983) interviewed Michael, a second-grade student in their gifted program, who, as a result of Type I and Type II activities, expressed a strong interest in Tchaikovsky. They asked Michael these questions:

1. Michael, will you tell me a little about Tchaikovsky and how you became interested in knowing more about him?
2. Have you read any books about him and his music?
3. How long have you been interested in studying about Tchaikovsky?
4. Do you like looking in different books to find information?
5. Do you have any ideas about what you would like to do with the information you find? (p. 137)

Michael's responses showed his interest in Tchaikovsky to be genuine. After specifying objectives for his research, Michael's teachers helped him set up a management plan for his investigation. Potential sources of information were identified, and a timeline was developed. Then Michael was encouraged to generate a specific idea for a product of his investigation and to consider an audience for his product. Michael's product, a children's book of 30 typed pages and an audio-taped version that plays selections of Tchaikovsky's music, is now part of both his school's and his local public library's collection. On the first page of his book, Michael wrote,

> Some of you may wonder why a second grader would want to write a book about Tchaikovsky. People get interested in different things for different reasons. For example, I got interested in Tchaikovsky because I like his music. I play the piano and have a whole book of his music. At Christmas I saw the ballet of the Nutcracker Suite. His music can be both cheerful and sad at the same time. I wondered how music can be both happy and sad at the same time so I decided to learn about Tchaikovsky's life.
>
> I wondered if when he was sad he wrote sad music, and if when he was happy he wrote happy music. In this book you will get to know a little bit more about Tchaikovsky, how he lived and about the music he wrote. (Reis & Cellerino, 1983, p. 139)[*]

Responsive Learning Environment

The Responsive Learning Environment (RLE), developed by Clark (1986), is a flexibly structured learning environment designed to turn the classroom into a "laboratory for learning" that is closely related to the real world of people and ideas. The teacher's role is critical to the establishment of the classroom and community-based experiences. Basically, the teacher assists students in defining their personal and group goals and helps them maintain their motivation for learning. Students are encouraged to shift roles according to the definition of their problem, with a minimum of time limitations for their investigations. "The teacher, the parent, and the student are seen to be a team in achieving effective learning" (Clark, 1992, p. 280).

Clark (1992) describes the following as important characteristics of the RLE:

- There is an open, respectful, and cooperative relationship among teachers, students, and parents that includes planning, implementing, and evaluating the learning experience.
- The environment is more like a laboratory or workshop that is rich in materials with simultaneous access to many learning activities. The emphasis is on experimentation and involvement.
- The curriculum is responsive, flexible, and integrative. The needs and interests of the students provide the base from which the curriculum develops.
- There is a minimum of total group lessons. Most instruction is in small groups among individuals.
- The student is an active participant in the learning process. Movement, decision making, self-directed learning, invention, and inquiry are encouraged.
- Assessment, contracting, and evaluation are all used as tools to aid in the growth of the students.
- The physical placement of the furniture, seating of the students, and traffic patterns are planned to support learning.
- There is evidence of student work and input in the physical appearance of the room. (pp. 280-281)

The RLE focuses its attention on the development of a dynamic physical environment both within and without the school walls and a supportive social and emotional environment among peers and students. An example of the RLE in action is

---

[*]Excerpt from Reis, S.M., & Cellerino, M. (1983). Guiding gifted students through independent study. *Teaching Exceptional Children*, *15*, 136–139. © (1983) by The Council for Exceptional Children. Reprinted by permission.

the "school within a school" model that allows for small teams of teachers to interact with students in a common undertaking in academic, creative, or artistic areas. Students in this type of program get a rare opportunity to interact with cooperating faculty in a relatively cooperative and open environment while still within the school walls. Students can attend the regular classroom for the bulk of their day and visit the "common areas" at different times throughout the day to continue their investigations and relationships with their extended educational "family."

Maker's Integrated Curriculum Model

Maker (1993) builds her curricular interventions around a theoretical conception of the gifted person as "a problem solver—one who enjoys the challenge of complexity and persists until the problem is solved in a satisfying way" (p. 7). The role of the teacher, then, is to facilitate and arrange the intellectual, emotional, and physical environment to make it possible for high achievement and creativity to take place. Formerly, this differentiation was thought to require a special teacher, a special classroom, and special materials; however, the current realities of fiscal and intellectual retrenchment have modified the demand for such accommodations.

Many authors are advocating that a more collaborative stance be taken between gifted coordinators and advocates and the regular classroom teachers with whom the students have always spent the majority of their time. In addition, it is important to remember that studies of regular education teachers indicate they do not normally modify the curriculum, make differentiated assignments, or provide specialized opportunities for students who are highly capable or talented (Archambault et al., 1993; Westberg, Archambault, Dobyns, & Slavin, 1993). This finding means that substantive initial education, training, and support should precede the initiative to meet the needs of gifted and talented students in the regular classroom. The demands of modifying and individualizing curriculum should not be underestimated, given the multitude of other pressing concerns that comprise the day-to-day life in the regular classroom. Maker (1982) proposes a process by which the key elements of content, process, products, and the environment of a child's learning situation can be modified.

- *Content modifications.* The content of a curriculum is the type of subject matter being taught. In general, the goal is to develop content that is more advanced, complex, innovative, and original than what is usually encountered in the classroom.
- *Process modifications.* The strategies and methods used in delivering the content to learners are key features of instruction. The goal is to provide students with many opportunities to actively respond to the content, including independent research, cooperative learning, peer coaching, simulations, and apprenticeships.
- *Product modifications.* The products of learning are the outcomes associated with instruction. The goal is to encourage a variety of ways that students can present their thoughts, ideas, and results.
- *Environment modifications.* The learning environment is both the physical characteristics of the setting(s) and the ambiance created by the teachers or facilitators. The goal is first to establish a positive working environment and then to rearrange the layout. Such ideas as peer tutoring, learning centers, management sheets, and learning packets can help students take more active control and interest over their learning.

One teacher who uses Maker's model of curriculum design and delivery is Shirly Begay, a high school teacher of English at the Rock Point Community School in Rock Point, Arizona. She discusses the way she integrates the various aspects of the curriculum with the underlying theory of multiple intelligences and problem-solving emphases.

We follow a problem-solving model. When I presented the first lesson, I wanted the students to become familiar with what I was talking about, so I used illustrations. I said, "You can't be hasty about solving a problem, or you'll be considered a sloppy problem solver. You'll come up with sloppy solutions, sloppy alternatives, and sloppy options." I wanted them to spend plenty of time gathering ideas and thinking about the answers to the questionnaires they sent out.

Most of the time when we introduce problem solving to children, we want them to imagine and make up problems, but this time I wanted them to think of the problems faced by teenagers in this remote area. They brainstormed and then selected problems they didn't want their children to have. We are hoping to remedy some of these problems. I know we can't do away with most of them, but we can lessen the pressure of some, especially if we look at them in different ways. I don't want the students' ideas to stop in the classroom. I want them to write the results for publication in the school's newspaper or to read them to the chapter presidents, chapter officers, or the school board.

For this problem-solving experience, I wanted the students to create a "before" picture and another after they found solutions and remedied the problem. Most Navajo students like to incorporate artwork into whatever they do. I allow them to do artwork and visual/imaginative things with whatever they have read. Most of the students who are gifted hate to write, but a few of them love to write poems and essays, so I encourage them to use both language and visual art. (cited by Maker, Nielson, & Rogers, 1994, p. 16)[*]

The Autonomous Learner Model

The Autonomous Learner Model (ALM) was developed by Betts (1985) to meet the cognitive, social, and emotional needs of gifted students. The guiding philosophy of the approach originated in the work of Tannenbaum (1983), who advocated that instruction should go beyond the prescribed role of students as "consumers" of information to that of "producers" of knowledge. The ALM was designed to be done in a special class setting by a specially trained teacher, with a great deal of community involvement and support. The program has five sequential steps that move the students from an initial state of awareness to the complete (autonomous) control over their learning within a 2½- to 3-year period. The five dimensions of the ALM are as follows:

1. *Orientation* provides a foundation in aspects of the model and expectations for students, educators, parents, and community members.
2. *Individual development* gives students the appropriate skills, concepts, and attitudes for life-long learning as they become autonomous learners.
3. *Enrichment activities* develop "student-based content," as opposed to "prescribed content," by teachers and other adults. Students explore new content and are given the opportunity to decide what they want to study and how they want to study the problem(s).

---

[*]Excerpt from C. J. Maker, A. B. Nielson, & J. A. Rogers "Giftedness, Diversity, and Problem Solving." *Teaching Exceptional Children*, 1994, *27.* © 1994 by the Council for Exceptional Children. Reprinted by permission.

Letting students choose the kinds of problems they wish to study and how they will go about their investigations is one method for differentiating curriculum for students with outstanding academic abilities.

4. *Seminars* emphasize the "production" of ideas and topics. Learners work together in small groups and develop a "seminar" that they use to present their ideas and findings.
5. *In-depth study* allows the students long-term opportunities to pursue topics of their choice either alone or in small groups.

The ALM is a combination in-and-out-of-school model that attempts to provide a saturated learning environment for gifted and talented students. Because the model is designed specifically for gifted and talented students, teachers are able to engage in both highly individualized activities and collaborative group enrichment activities out in the community. A unique feature of this program is the non-negotiable requirement that students engage in "service" activities in which they must contribute their time and effort for direct involvement with people who need help. This service includes such activities as volunteering at a hospital or clinic for AIDS patients, providing food and other supplies for homeless or disadvantaged families, and tutoring children with learning problems.

Teachers of the Gifted

No instructional theory or approach is more important than the teacher who implements it. A question many people ask is whether the teacher must be gifted to teach gifted children effectively. The answer is "not necessarily"—in the sense of giftedness as used in this chapter. All teachers should be gifted, regardless of whom they teach, and teachers should be gifted in different ways to teach different children. Nonetheless, teachers of gifted children do need some particular qualities; they must (Clark, 1992; Lindsey, 1980; Piirto, 1994; Story, 1985)

- Be willing to accept unusual and diverse questions, answers, and projects
- Be intellectually curious

- Be systematic and businesslike
- Have a variety of interests
- Appreciate achievement
- Demonstrate both quality and quantity in verbal interactions with students
- Be flexible in scheduling time to meet students' needs
- Be process oriented, with children's creative productivity the ultimate goal
- Be flexible and open to new ideas
- Understand, accept, respect, trust, and like self
- Have literary and cultural intellectual interests
- Tolerate ambiguity
- Be well prepared in instructional techniques
- Be well prepared in content area
- Want to teach gifted students
- Share enthusiasm, love of learning, and joy of living
- Realize that they may not know as much about some topics as the children do and be comfortable with that situation

✹ _Current Issues and Future Trends_

The current ethos surrounding the development and provision of special education services to gifted and talented students involves movement on several fronts:

- The conceptual and definitional nature of "giftedness" is being more intensively questioned
- The possibility that almost all services for gifted and talented students will originate with the regular teacher from within the regular classroom
- The increased pressure to identify and serve students from several underserved populations, including different cultural groups, females, students with disabilities, and children from disadvantaged environments

First, advocates and writers in the field are growing increasingly wary of the word _gifted,_ realizing that in some ways it is a conceptually loaded term that perpetuates the myth that talent is predetermined and not the result of extensive effort on the part of students, teachers, parents, and communities. It simply makes it too easy for society as a whole to ignore these students' needs and to ascribe their growth and development (or lack thereof) to uncontrollable, unseen forces beyond the reach of our instructional interventions. An unintended result is that both individuals and societal institutions can assert that because these students can easily "make it on their own," they need no extra help from society. If only the misconception that all of these students "make it" despite the neglect were true. The available data indicate that large numbers of students who would qualify for gifted and talented services drop out of school and that many more students who are culturally different, disabled, or economically disadvantaged are never even identified. Estimates of this group of underachieving gifted students range from 10% to 20% of all high school dropouts (Davis & Rimm, 1989), and an even more shocking finding is that 40% of the top 5% of the high school graduates do not complete college (DeLeon, 1989).

Second, there is a growing awareness that gifted advocates will need to conceptualize the special services to gifted and talented students in a different manner than the "traditional" model of a gifted teacher in a pull-out gifted classroom. Most of the newer instructional models (e.g., Renzulli's Schoolwide Enrichment Model, Maker's Integrated Curriculum Model) occur within the regular classroom and depend heavily on interactions within the community, with few requiring a special teacher or classroom. There are obvious and important impacts on teacher training, classroom management, and curriculum if these events become the dominant pattern of educational service delivery in the schools. In addition, there will be an emphasis on collaboration, rather than on independent instruction. This emphasis means that teachers of the gifted and other advocates will have to work closely with regular educators to get services to gifted and talented students. Finally, the increasingly sophisticated use of technological tools and related methods will provide gifted students with greater "connectivity" and independence in the future. In some cases, this ability to communicate with persons from distant and differing cultures and languages will provide new avenues of expression for gifted and talented students. In addition, the ability to explore topics in greater depth through the use of global databases and to create interactive presentations about their discoveries will allow gifted and talented students to become more independent and exert greater control over their own learning.

See the January, 1995, issue of *Educational Leadership*, pp. 64–70.

Third, increasing numbers of persons are advocating more accurate identification procedures that will provide access to special educational services for gifted students who are members of several underserved populations. Persons who have high ability or talent comprise a very different group of exceptional learners, but it is important to remember that all talent, including exceptional talent, can suffer from a lack of quality educational experiences, informative feedback, and emotional support. Students who exhibit high ability and talent are susceptible to the same fears and frustrations that come with a lack of interest or understanding of their needs and abilities regardless of race, gender, socioeconomic status, and disability status. Maker (1989) summarizes the most recent recommendations for curricula and teaching strategies for culturally diverse gifted students.

1. Identify student's strengths and plan a curriculum to develop these abilities.
2. Provide for development of basic skills and other abilities students lack.
3. Regard differences as positive, rather than negative, attributes.
4. Provide for involvement of parents, the community, and mentors or role models.
5. Create and maintain classrooms with a multicultural emphasis. (p. 301)

In addition, there is a pressing need to provide counseling services to gifted and talented students. Gallagher (1990) points out that our "track record" of understanding and then facilitating the emotional growth of gifted and talented students is weak to nonexistent. As with all children and adults, a number of predictable and unpredictable crises will occur throughout our lives. With their heightened sense of social justice and greater awareness of the needs of others, students who are gifted and talented often experience the confusion and estrangement with more depth than their age-mates.

For information on counseling gifted and talented students, see Delisle (1992); Genshaft, Bireley, and Hollinger (1995); Silverman (1993); and Van Tassel-Baska (1990).

Gifted and talented students need our assistance; they need specialized curriculum, instructional strategies, materials, and experiences that allow them to realize their potential. As we face increasingly complex problems in the global village of the future, we will need as much help as we can get from our citizenry. There are new approaches and perspectives concerning the manner in which students are identified and services are delivered that reflect insights into the way humans learn and create. These innovations promise to provide not only students with high ability and talents a brighter learning future but also the country and world in which they live.

Dumbing Down

Pretending That All Students Are Equal Doesn't Make It So

by Robin Marantz Henig

Last summer, I ran into my neighbor when I dropped by the pool for an evening swim. She was sitting in the slanting sunshine, a closed paperback on her lap, and she and the other swim-team mothers waited for practice to end.

I asked how her sons were enjoying the summer and she told me how well they were doing on the team. She even told me their best lap times, in seconds, down to the hundredths. This was not bragging—simply the way things are around here. Yet when she asked about my daughters, I didn't tell her that both had been accepted for the highly selective academic programs in their respective schools. This was also the way things are around here.

My neighbor and I are both products of our national ambivalence about ability: it's O.K. to extol athletic excellence, but there's something elitist, or at least unseemly, about even acknowledging intellectual excellence.

The notion of intellectual accomplishment, as opposed to performance in other spheres, must be uniquely threatening to the American egalitarian spirit. How else to explain the offensive attitude of many public schools—the very places where academic achievement should be cultivated and celebrated—toward our brightest children?

School officials seem to make decisions based on the belief that no child is smarter than any other child. But of course some are smarter, just as some are better athletes or musicians. The school system's lie hurts everyone, but especially the kids with the greatest intellectual promise.

When the boy across the street asked for harder work in sixth-grade math, he was told he couldn't get too far ahead of the rest of the class—it would run counter to the school's group-oriented philosophy. Yet he was capable of working at an eighth-grade level or higher, while some kids in his class were still mastering third-grade skills.

What perverse logic would force him to tread water for an entire year so as not to outdistance the others? If he were a 12-year-old Michael Jordan, would his coach caution him not to make too many baskets so the others would have a chance to score?

Very bright kids are victims of the trend toward "heterogeneous classrooms," which lump together children who perform at, above, and below grade level. And though experts say high achievers are a good influence on slower kids and though teachers may intend to offer "differentiated instruction," in practice this rarely happens. Sometimes simple logistics make it impossible. Sometimes accelerating an individual goes against some inexplicable educational philosophy.

My own daughters, who are now 10 and 14, wasted a lot of time in heterogeneous classrooms while the lesson was repeated again and again until everyone got it.

When my younger one was in third grade, the teacher said she wouldn't call on her when she raised her hand because the teacher knew she knew the answer. So my daughter sat quietly, trying hard to focus on the lesson even though she couldn't participate. Expecting her to blossom intellectually in such a setting is like expecting the young Jordan to get better at basketball just by showing up at a gym.

My older daughter suffered similarly until in fifth grade she moved to a homogeneous class, one of the few our school system still grudgingly offers. Finally, she could learn something each day that she didn't already know. "It's perfect—I love it—everyone's like me," she said after her first day. They weren't, really; they were white and black and Indian and Chinese and Hispanic and Sri Lankan.

By spending all day with intellectual peers, my daughter and her classmates have learned that their brainpower is not only admirable but something to revel in. This is a rare and wonderful lesson in a community that hands out trophies for sports but not for schoolwork. So is the corollary: that intelligence, like the muscles of a powerful swimmer, can be exercised and stretched, so that all kids can achieve their personal best. ✳

Summary

Defining Giftedness and Talent

- The federal government defines gifted and talented children as exhibiting high performance capability in intellectual, creative, and/or artistic areas, possessing an unusual leadership capacity, or excelling in specific academic fields.

- Renzulli's definition of giftedness is based on the traits of above-average general abilities, high level of task commitment, and creativity.

- Feldhusen's definition of giftedness emphasizes talent as the primary defining characteristic.

- Piirto defines the gifted as having superior memory, observational powers, curiosity, creativity, and ability to learn.

Characteristics of Students Who Are Gifted and Talented

- Learning and intellectual characteristics of gifted and talented students include the ability to

  Rapidly acquire, retain, and use large amounts of information

  Relate one idea to another

  Make sound judgments

  Perceive the operation of larger systems of knowledge that may not be recognized by the ordinary citizen

  Acquire and manipulate abstract symbol systems

  Solve problems by reframing the question and creating novel solutions

- Gifted children are by no means perfect, and their unusual talents and abilities may make them either withdrawn or difficult to manage in the classroom.

- Gifted students need both basic and advanced content knowledge and the abilities to use and develop that knowledge effectively.

- Many gifted children are creative. Although there is no universally accepted definition of creativity, we know that creative children have knowledge, examine it in a variety of ways, critically analyze the outcomes, and communicate their ideas.

- Guilford includes dimensions of fluency, flexibility, originality, and elaboration in his definition of creativity.

Prevalence

- Gifted students make up about 5% of the school-age population.

Historical Background

- Standardized intelligence tests, beginning with the Stanford-Binet, have been used during most of this century to predict school success and to identify unusually bright children. Reliance on these tests has tended to restrict giftedness to students with high IQ scores, resulting in a very narrow range of students being placed in contemporary programs.

- The concept of giftedness has expanded in recent years to include creativity and other alternatives to traditional IQ scores. We have also come to recognize giftedness among the culturally diverse, among females, and among children with disabilities.

Identification and Assessment

- IQ tests are the initial, but not necessarily the best, means for locating high-ability students.

- The usual means of identification include a combination of IQ scores; creativity and achievement measures; teacher, parent, and peer nominations; and self-nomination.

- Maker's DISCOVER procedure can be used to identify gifted students from diverse cultural groups and females in an equitable fashion.

- Teachers and parents can foster the intellectual and talent development of children with disabilities by conveying positive, realistic expectations; encouraging independence; guiding constructive coping strategies; providing daily opportunities to build abilities and enjoy success; and pursuing positive social experiences for the child.

Educational Approaches

- Three common approaches to educating gifted and talented students are ability grouping, enrichment, and acceleration.

- Four models for teaching gifted students are Renzulli's Schoolwide Enrichment Triad Model, Clark's Responsive Learning Environment, Maker's Integrated Curriculum Model, and Betts's Autonomous Learner Model.

- Teachers of the gifted must be flexible, curious, tolerant, competent, and self-confident.

Current Issues and Future Trends

- The conceptual and definitional nature of "giftedness" is being more intensively questioned.
- The likely possibility is that most services for gifted and talented students will originate from the regular teacher within the regular classroom.

- The importance of identifying gifted and talented students among females, individuals with disabilities, and diverse cultural groups is now being recognized. We need better procedures for identifying, assessing, teaching, and encouraging these children.
- As we have seen with other exceptional children, we must improve society's attitudes toward gifted and talented children if we are to improve their futures.

For More Information

Journals

Gifted Child Quarterly. Published four times per year by the National Association for Gifted Children, 1155 15th Street N.W., #1002, Washington, DC 20005. Publishes articles by both parents and teachers of gifted children.

Gifted Child Today (formerly G/C/T). Published six times per year by GCT, Inc., 350 Weinacker Avenue, Mobile, AL 36604. Publishes articles with ideas aimed at parents and teachers of gifted, talented, and creative youngsters.

Gifted International. Published semiannually by the World Council for Gifted and Talented Children, Dr. Dorothy Sisk, Secretariat, Lamar University, College of Education, P.O. Box 10034, Beaumont, TX 77710. Devoted to international communication among educators, researchers, and parents.

Journal for the Education of the Gifted. Published quarterly by the Association for the Gifted (TAG), Council for Exceptional Children, 1920 Association Drive, Reston, VA 22091. Presents theoretical, descriptive, and research articles presenting diverse ideas and different points of view on the education of gifted and talented students.

Journal of Creative Behavior. Published by Creative Educational Foundation, Inc., State University College, 1300 Elmwood Avenue, Buffalo, NY 14222. Devoted to research reports and program suggestions and designed to understand and enhance creative behavior in children and adults.

Roeper Review. Published quarterly by the Roeper City and Country Schools, 2190 North Woodward, Bloomfield Hills, MI 48013. Publishes articles by teachers, researchers, and students in gifted education.

Books

Berger, S. L. (1994). *College planning for gifted students* (2nd ed.). Reston, VA: Council for Exceptional Children.

Clark, B. (1992). *Growing up gifted: Developing the potential of children at home and at school* (4th ed.). Englewood Cliffs, NJ: Merrill/Prentice Hall..

Colangelo, N., & Davis, G. A. (Eds.). (1991). *Handbook of gifted education.* Needham Heights, MA: Allyn & Bacon.

Gallagher, J. J., & Gallagher, S. (1994). *Teaching the gifted child* (4th ed.). Needham Heights, MA: Allyn & Bacon.

Genshaft, J. L., Bireley, M., & Hollinger, C. L. (Eds.). (1995). *Serving gifted and talented students: A resource for school personnel.* Austin, TX: PRO-ED.

Heller, K. A., Monks, F. J., & Passow, A. H. (Eds.), (1993). *International handbook of research and development of giftedness and talent.* Tarrytown, NY: Pergamon.

Maker, C. J. (1989). *Critical issues in gifted education: Defensible programs for cultural and ethnic minorities.* Austin, TX: PRO-ED.

Parke, B. N. (1989). *Gifted students in regular classrooms.* Boston, MA: Allyn & Bacon.

Piirto, J. (1994). *Talented children and adults: Their development and education.* Englewood Cliffs, NJ: Merrill/Prentice Hall.

Silverman, L. K. (Ed.). (1993). *Counseling the gifted and talented.* Denver, CO: Love.

Sisk, D. (1987). *Creative teaching of the gifted.* New York: McGraw-Hill.

Renzulli, J. S. (1994). *Schools for talent development: A practical plan for total school improvement.* Reston, VA: Council for Exceptional Children.

Van Tassel-Baska, J. (Ed.). (1990). *A practical guide to counseling the gifted in a school setting* (2nd ed.). Reston, VA: Council for Exceptional Children.

Van Tassel-Baska, J. (Ed.). (1994). *Comprehensive curriculum for gifted learners* (2nd ed.). Needham Heights, MA: Allyn & Bacon.

Organizations

American Creativity Association, P.O. Box 26068, St. Paul, MN 55126. A new organization that promotes creativity in business, education, the arts, sciences, and social and political decision making.

The Association for the Gifted (TAG), Council for Exceptional Children, 1920 Association Drive, Reston, VA 22091. A growing division of CEC that includes teachers, teacher educators, administrators, and others interested in gifted and talented children.

Future Problem Solving, Future Problem Solving International, 315 West Huron, Suite 140B, Ann Arbor, MI 48103-4203.

Gifted Child Society, Suite 6, 190 Rock Road, Glen Rock, NJ 07452. An organization for parents, also offers information and inservice training for educators.

Junior Great Books, Junior Great Books Foundation, 40 East Huron, Chicago, IL 60611.

National Association for Gifted Children, 1155 15th Street N.W. #1002, Washington, DC 20005. An organization for parents, professionals, and others interested in gifted and talented children.

National Research Center on the Gifted and Talented (NRC/GT), University of Connecticut, Stoors, CT 06269-2002.

Odyssey of the Mind, OM Association, P.O. Box 547, Glassboro, NJ 08028.

World Council for Gifted and Talented Children, Lamar University, P.O. Box 10034, Beaumont, TX 77710. The organization's purpose is to promote worldwide communication on issues related to the education and development of gifted children.

PART III

Family and Life-Span Issues ....

Working with Parents and Families

- What can a teacher learn from the parents and families of students with disabilities?

- What information or assistance should the teacher provide to parents and families?

- Does the nature or severity of a student's disability change the importance or objectives of parental and family involvement?

- How meaningful can IEP/IFSP goals and objectives be if the student's family does not participate in developing them?

- At what point are legitimate needs of parents not the proper focus of the special educator's efforts?

A parent is a child's first teacher, the person who is always there giving encouragement, prompts, praise, and corrective feedback. Parents are responsible for helping the young child learn literally hundreds of skills. No one ever knows as much about a child as a parent does. And no one else has as much vested interest in that child. These are safe statements, obviously true for the vast majority of parent-child relationships. Yet only recently have special educators begun to understand these fundamental truths.

For years, many educators viewed parents as either troublesome (if they asked too many questions or, worse, offered suggestions about their child's education) or uncaring (if they did not jump to attention whenever the professional determined the parent needed something—which usually was advice from the professional). Parents, too, have often seen professionals as adversaries. But more recently, parent involvement has received a great deal of attention in special education. Parents and teachers have developed better ways to communicate and work with each other for the common benefit of the child with special educational needs.

We will explore some of the reasons the parent-teacher relationship has not always been positive and some examples of the progress that has been made. To better understand a parent's perspective, we will look at some of the ways a child's disabilities affect the family and the roles and responsibilities of parents and siblings. As we describe some of the techniques for communicating with and involving parents in their children's education, you will see that working with parents and families of exceptional children is among the most important and rewarding skills a teacher can develop.

✳ *The Parent-Teacher Partnership*
Benefits of Parent-Teacher Partnership

Parents and teachers who work actively and effectively with one another make a powerful team. A strong parent-teacher partnership is beneficial to the professional, the parent, and the child. A productive parent-professional relationship provides professionals with the following:

- Greater understanding of the overall needs of the child and the needs and desires of the parent.
- Data for more meaningful selection of target behaviors that are important to the child in his or her world outside the school.
- Access to a wider range of social and activity reinforcers provided by parents.
- Increased opportunities to reinforce appropriate behaviors in both school and home settings.
- Feedback from parents as to changes in behavior that can be used to improve programs being implemented by professionals and parents.
- The ability to comply with legislation mandating continuing parental input to the educational process.

A productive parent-professional relationship provides parents with the following:

- Greater understanding of the needs of their child and the objectives of the teacher.
- Information on their rights and responsibilities as parents of an exceptional child.
- Specific information about their child's school program and how they can become involved.
- Specific ways to extend the positive effects of school programming into the home.
- Increased skills to help their child learn functional behaviors that are appropriate for the home environment.
- Access to additional important resources (current and future) for their child.

And, of most importance, a productive parent-professional relationship provides the child with the following:

- Greater consistency in his or her two most important environments.
- More opportunities for learning and growth.
- Access to expanded resources and services. (Heward et al., 1979, p. 226)

Barriers to Effective Parent-Teacher Interaction

Let's face it—parents and teachers do not always cooperate. They may sometimes even seem to be on opposite sides, battling over what each thinks is best for the child. The child, unfortunately, never wins that battle. She needs to have the people who are responsible for the two places where she spends most of her life—home and school—work together to make those environments consistent. Both home and school must be supportive of her job of learning. Some parents and teachers make assumptions and hold attitudes toward one another that are counterproductive. Parents may complain of professionals who are negative, unavailable, or patronizing. Teachers may complain that parents are uninterested, uncooperative, or hostile.

Roos (1980), a special educator who is also the father of a child with mental retardation, blames much of parents' hostility and negative attitudes on what he calls "professional mishandling." Many professionals hold negative stereotypes and false assumptions about what parents of children with disabilities face and need (Donnel-

A parent is a child's first teacher.

lan & Mirenda, 1984). These attitudes have often led to poor relationships between parents and professionals.

Sonnenschein (1981) describes several attitudes and behaviors of professionals that create roadblocks to effective partnerships.

The Parent as Vulnerable Client

Professionals who see parents only as helpless souls in need of assistance make a grave mistake. Teachers need parents and what they have to offer as much as parents need teachers.

Professional Distance

Most professionals in human services develop some degree of professional distance to avoid getting too involved with a client—supposedly to maintain objectivity and credibility. But aloofness or coldness in the name of professionalism has hindered or terminated many a parent-teacher relationship. Parents must believe that the professional really cares about them (Murray, 1990).

The Parent as Patient

Some professionals make the faulty assumption that having a child with disabilities causes the parent to need therapy. Roos (1985) writes, "I had suddenly been demoted from the role of a professional to that of parent as patient and had experienced the common assumption of many professionals that parents of a problem child are emotionally maladjusted and are prime candidates for counseling, psychotherapy, or tranquilizers" (p. 246).

The Parent as Responsible for the Child's Condition

Some parents do feel responsible for their child's disability and, with a little encouragement from a professional, can be made to feel completely guilty. A productive parent-professional relationship focuses on collaborative problem solving, not on laying blame.

The Parent as Less Intelligent

Parents' information and suggestions are given little recognition. Parents are considered too biased, too involved, or too unskilled to make useful observations. Some professionals concede that parents have access to needed information but contend that parents are not able to, or should not, make any decisions based on what they know.

The Parent as Adversary

Some teachers expect the worst whenever they interact with parents. Even if that attitude can be partially explained by previous unpleasant encounters with unreasonable parents, it is at best a negative influence on new relationships.

Tendency to Label Parents

As with the students they teach, some educators seem eager to label parents. If parents disagree with a diagnosis or seek another opinion, they are *denying;* if they refuse a suggested treatment, they are *resistant;* and if parents insist that something is wrong with their child despite test evidence to the contrary, they are called *anxious.* The professional who believes that a parent's perception may be the correct one is rare—yet parents often do know best.

Of course, we must be just as careful in generalizing about professionals' behavior as we are with parents. Most teachers do not act in such negative ways toward parents. To the extent that teachers and other special educators believe and behave in these ways, however, it is understandable that parents may feel intimidated, confused, angry, or hostile. But the factors working against positive parent-teacher relationships cannot all be attributed to professional mishandling. Some parents are genuinely difficult to work with or unreasonable.

> The attitudes and behaviors of the parents have also contributed to negative interactions. There is no easy way to tell a mother and father that their child is substantially handicapped. Some parents want to hear the hard truth; others want to be eased into it. Professionals may carefully choose their words with the greatest sensitivity, yet still offend the parents. Sometimes parents are unforgiving and do not realize the difficult position of the professional. They may vent their anger at the professional and discuss the professional's "gross lack of sensitivity" with family and friends. (Turnbull, 1983, p. 19)

> There are situations in which parents fight long and hard for services for their child. After the services are found and the child is receiving an appropriate education, the parents continue their intense advocacy until minor issues with professionals become major confrontations. As one mother stated, "For years I have scrapped and fought for services. Now I come on like gangbusters over issues that are really not that important. I don't like what has happened to me. I've ended up to be an aggressive, angry person." This posture leads to unproductive interactions between parents and professionals. (Bronicki & Turnbull, 1987, p. 10)

The purpose of examining factors that cause friction between parents and teachers is not to determine fault, but to identify factors we can change and improve. Professionals who recognize that some of their own behaviors may diminish the potential for productive relationships with parents are in a better position to change their actions and obtain the benefits that such relationships can provide. Perhaps the first and most important step for the teacher is to avoid sweeping generalizations about parents of exceptional children and to treat them with respect as individuals. After all, isn't that how teachers want to be treated?

Breaking Down Barriers to Effective Parent-Teacher Interaction

Negative interactions between parents and teachers can be related to a mutual lack of awareness and understanding of each other's roles and responsibilities. During recent years, a number of forces have come together to focus national attention on the importance of a parent-teacher partnership based on mutual respect and participation in decision making (Turnbull & Morningstar, 1993). Although many things have contributed to the greater involvement of parents in the education of their exceptional children, three groups are primarily responsible: parents, educators, and legislators.

Parents: Advocates for Change

An *advocate* is someone who speaks for or pleads the case of another. Parents of exceptional children have played that role for many years, but recently they have done so with impressive effectiveness. The first parent group organized for children with disabilities was the National Society for Crippled Children, which began in 1921. The National Association for Retarded Citizens (now called The Arc), organized in 1950, and the United Cerebral Palsy Association, organized in 1948, are two national parent organizations that have been largely responsible for making the public aware of their children's needs. The Learning Disabilities Association of America (LDA), another group organized by and consisting mostly of parents, has been instrumental in bringing about educational reform. As we saw in Chapters 1 and 2, parents have played the primary role in bringing about litigation and legislation establishing the right to a free and appropriate public education for children with disabilities.

More than any other group, parents themselves have been responsible for their greater involvement in special education. They have formed effective organizations that have been the impetus for much educational reform. As individuals, they are learning more about their children's educational needs and are seeing the potential benefits of an effective parent-teacher partnership.

Educators: Striving for Greater Impact

Educators have recognized the necessity of expanding the traditional role of the classroom teacher to meet the special needs of children with disabilities. This expanded role demands a view of teaching as more than delivering the three R's. Teachers now realize that self-care, social, vocational, and leisure skills are critical to the successful functioning of a student with disabilities. Special educators attach high priority to developing and maintaining the functional skills that will enable an individual with disabilities to be successful in school, home, work, and community settings.

Implementation of this new priority has implications and applications outside the classroom, and teachers have begun to look outside the school for assistance and support. Parents are a natural and needed ally for expanding educational services to the home and community. At the very least, teachers benefit from information that parents provide about their children's success with specific skills outside the classroom.

But parents do much more than just report on behavioral change. They can tell what skills their children need to learn and, just as important, which skills they have already acquired. Parents can work with teachers to provide needed extra practice of skills at home and even to teach their children new skills. Research shows that parents can enhance the development of children with disabilities by teaching them at home (e.g., Baker, 1989; Snell & Beckman-Brindley, 1984; Wedel & Fowler, 1984). Research attesting to the positive outcomes of early intervention with preschoolers with disabilities also supports the focus on working cooperatively with parents (e.g., Bailey & Wolery, 1992; Greenwood et al., 1994; Odom & Karnes, 1988; Smith & Strain, 1984).

> We examine the effects and methods of early intervention in Chapter 14.

In short, special educators have given up the old notions that parents should not be too involved in their children's educational programs or that they should not try to teach their children for fear of doing something wrong. Teachers now realize that parents are a powerful and necessary ally. Only through an effective parent-teacher partnership can everyone's goals—teacher's, parent's, and child's—be fulfilled.

Legislators: Mandates for Involvement

As we have seen, the IDEA mandates parent involvement in the education of children with disabilities. Federal law provides statutory guidelines for parent-professional interaction in regard to a free and appropriate education, referral, testing, placement, and program planning. In addition, the law provides due process procedures if parents believe that their child's needs are not being met. Although some educators initially viewed the IDEA as "the parents' law" and were threatened by the new role it specified for parents, most understand that it represents sound educational practice and welcome the parent involvement it encourages.

In sum, we can attribute special educators' interest in working effectively with parents and families of children with disabilities to three related factors:

1. Many parents want to be involved.
2. Research and practice have shown repeatedly and convincingly that educational effectiveness can be greatly enhanced with the assistance and involvement of parents.
3. The law requires it.

For a discussion of the IDEA as it relates to the parent-professional relationship, see Turnbull and Turnbull (1990).

✳ *Effects of a Child's Disabilities on Parents and Family*

The special educator usually interacts with parents and families of children with disabilities for two primary reasons: (a) to obtain information and suggestions that can help the teacher do a better job in the classroom and (b) to provide information and assistance to parents for working with their children outside the classroom. The teacher who wants to both seek and provide assistance must be able to communicate effectively with parents. Effective communication is more likely when the educator understands and respects the responsibilities and challenges that parents and families of children with disabilities face.

> All I wanted was a baby and now I've got doctors' appointments, therapy appointments, surgeries, medical bills, a strained marriage, no more free time. . . . When you have a handicapped child, you don't just have to deal with the child and the fact that he's handicapped. You have to adjust to a whole new way of life. It's a double whammy. (Simon, 1987, p. 15)

Parental Reactions to a Child with Disabilities

A great deal has been written about parents' reactions to the birth of a child with disabilities or to the discovery that their child has a learning problem or a physical disability. Reviewing the literature describing parental responses to the birth of a child with disabilities, Blacher (1984) found a consistent theme suggesting three stages of adjustment. First, parents are said to experience a period of emotional crisis characterized by shock, denial, and disbelief. This initial reaction is followed by a period of emotional disorganization that includes alternating feelings of anger, guilt, depression, shame, lowered self-esteem, rejection of the child, and overprotectiveness. Finally, it is presumed that parents eventually reach a third stage in which they accept their child.

The birth of a baby with disabilities or the discovery that a child has a disability is an intense and traumatic event. And evidence suggests that many parents of children with disabilities experience similar reactions and emotional responses and that most go through an adjustment process, trying to work through their feelings (Eden-

On the basis of observations of 130 participants in two parent support groups over a period of several years, Anderegg, Vergason, and Smith (1992) developed a revised model of Blacher's work they call the "grief cycle," which consists of three stages: confronting, adjusting, and adapting.

Piercy, Blacher, & Eyman, 1986; Featherstone, 1980). But emphasizing stages of adjustment as the basis for planning or delivering family services poses two potential problems. First, it is easy to assume that all parents must pass through a similar sequence of stages and that time is the most important variable in adjustment. In fact, parents react to the arrival of a child with disabilities in many ways (Allen & Affleck, 1985). For some parents, years may pass and they still are not comfortable with their child; others report that having a child with disabilities has strengthened their life or marriage (Bradley, Knoll, & Agosta, 1992; Schell, 1981). The sequence and time needed for adjustment are different for every parent. The one common thread is that almost all parents and families can be helped during their adjustment by sensitive and supportive friends and professionals (Schlesinger & Meadow, 1976; Turnbull, 1983).

A second concern is that the various stages of adjustment have a distinct psychiatric flavor, and professionals may mistakenly assume that parents must be maladjusted in some way. As Roos (1985) notes, some educators seem to assume that all parents of children with disabilities need counseling.

> It may be that many parents do respond in ways that are well-described by the stage model. But it is dangerous to impose this model on all parents. Those who exhibit different response patterns might be inappropriately judged as "deviant." Parents who do not progress as rapidly through the "stages" might be considered slow to adjust. And those who exhibit emotions in a different sequence might be thought of as regressing. (Allen & Affleck, 1985, p. 201)

As Farber (1975) points out, it is a mistake to think of parents of children with disabilities as psychological curiosities; they are more like the parents of normal children than they are different. Parenting any child is a tremendous challenge that produces emotional responses and requires adjustment. Parents of children with disabilities, like the parents of all children, must sometimes operate under financial, physical, emotional, and marital stress. Parents of children with disabilities, however, must also deal with the additional tasks of securing and relating to the special services their children need.

Blackstone (1981), himself the parent of a child with disabilities, gives examples of how parents of exceptional children are often viewed and treated differently from other parents:

> The parent of the normal child skips monthly PTA meetings, and his behavior is considered normal. The parent of the exceptional child skips monthly meetings, and he is said to be uncaring and hard to reach.
>
> A couple with normal children divorce. They are said to be incompatible. The couple with an exceptional child divorce, and it is said that the child ruined the marriage.
>
> The parents of a normal child are told that because their child is having reading difficulties, it would be "nice" if they could work with her at home. The parents of the exceptional child are told that if they do not work with their child, she will not learn! (pp. 29–30)

The Many Roles of the Exceptional Parent

Parenthood is an awesome responsibility; parents of children with disabilities face even greater responsibility. Educators who are not parents of a child with disabilities

Turnbull and Turnbull (1985) offer a collection of moving personal stories by parents of children with disabilities.

Singer and Powers (1993) describe a variety of interventions to help families cope with everyday challenges of having a family member with disabilities.

cannot know the 24-hour reality of being the parent of a child with disabilities or chronic illness. Nonetheless, they should strive for an awareness of the varied and demanding roles these parents must fulfill. Seven major challenges that parents of exceptional children face are discussed next (Heward et al., 1979).

Teaching

Even though all parents are their children's first teachers, most children acquire a great many skills without their parents' trying to teach them. Children with disabilities, however, often do not learn many important skills as naturally or as independently as their peers. In addition to systematic teaching techniques, some parents must learn to use, and/or teach their children to use, special equipment and assistive devices such as hearing aids, braces, wheelchairs, and adapted eating utensils.

Counseling

All parents are counselors in the sense that they deal with their developing children's changing emotions, feelings, and attitudes. But in addition to all of the normal joys and pains of raising a child, parents of a child with disabilities must deal with the feelings their child has as a result of his particular disability. "Will I still be deaf when I grow up?" "I'm not playing outside anymore—they always tease me." "Why can't I go swimming like the other kids?" Parents play an important role in how the child with disabilities comes to feel about himself. Their interactions can help develop an active, outgoing child who confidently tries many new things or contribute to a withdrawn child with negative attitudes toward himself and others.

Managing Behavior

Even though all children act out from time to time, the range and severity of challenging behaviors exhibited by some children with disabilities demand specialized and consistent treatment. Some parents must learn to use behavior management techniques in order to have a good relationship with their children (Snell & Beckman-Brindley, 1984).

Parenting Siblings Without Disabilities

Children are deeply affected by having a brother or sister with special needs (Powell & Ogle, 1985; Wilson, Blacher, & Baker, 1989). Brothers and sisters of a child with disabilities often have concerns about their sibling's disability: uncertainty regarding the cause of the disability and its effect on them, uneasiness over the reactions of their friends, a feeling of being left out or of being required to do too much for the child with disabilities (Dyson, Edgar, & Crnic, 1989).

> For suggestions on how to conduct a support group for siblings of children with disabilities, see Summers, Bridge, and Summers (1991).

Maintaining the Parent-to-Parent Relationship

Having a child with disabilities often puts stress on the relationship between husband and wife (Frey, Greenberg, & Fewell, 1989). Particular stress can be as diverse as arguing over whose fault the child's disability is, disagreeing over what expectations should be made for the child's behavior, and spending so much time, money, and energy on the child with disabilities that little is left for each other (Cohen, Agosta, Cohen, & Warren, 1989).

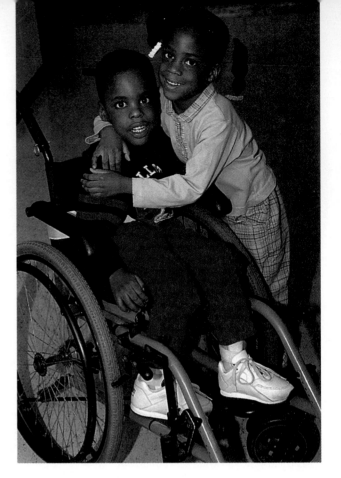

Nondisabled brothers and sisters often have special needs and concerns because of their sibling's disability.

Educating Significant Others

George (1988) describes a group therapy program designed to help grandparents and extended family of children with disabilities develop positive and supportive roles toward the child and parents.

Grandparents, aunts and uncles, neighbors, and even the school bus driver can have an important effect on the development of a child with disabilities. Whereas the parents of a child without disabilities can reasonably expect their child to receive certain kinds of treatment from significant others, parents of children with disabilities know they cannot necessarily depend on appropriate interactions. Parents of a child with disabilities must try to ensure that, as much as possible, other people interact with their child in a way that facilitates acquisition and maintenance of adaptive behaviors. Schulz (1985) describes her response to anyone who stares at her son with Down syndrome: She looks the person squarely in the eye and says, "You seem interested in my son. Would you like to meet him?" (p. 6). This usually ends the staring and often creates an opportunity to provide information or begin a friendship.

Relating to the School and Community

Although the IDEA describes specific rights of parents of children with disabilities, it also implies certain responsibilities. Although some involvement in the educational process is desirable for all parents, it is a must for parents of children with disabilities. They need to acquire special knowledge (e.g., understanding what a criterion-referenced test is) and to learn special skills (e.g., participating effectively in an IEP planning meeting). In addition, parents of children with disabilities often have other concerns over and above those of most parents; for example, whereas all parents may be concerned about having adequate playgrounds, the parents of a child who uses a wheelchair may also find themselves having to advocate for an accessible playground.

Another way to understand how a child's disability affects family members is to examine the likely impact of the child's special needs at various ages. Turnbull et al. (1990) describe the possible issues and concerns that parents and siblings face during four life-cycle stages. Table 13.1 outlines their analysis. A study by Wikler (1986) lends support to the concept that parents and siblings face different challenges at different life-cycle stages of the child with disabilities. Wikler's study of 60 families found higher levels of family stress at the onset of adolescence and at the onset of adulthood.

Parents of children with disabilities face many and varied challenges, but in the end, they adjust and strive to simply "have a family life." A research team that asked families of young children with developmental delays to "tell their story" in terms of "how is it going for you," wrote:

> Many issues concern these parents. What concerns them most is something beyond specific problems, something more comprehensive. This more general adaptive problem appears again and again in parents' accounts of living with a child who exhibits developmental delays early in life: The creation of a sustainable and meaningful daily routine of family life. (Gallimore, Weisner, Bernheimer, Guthrie, & Nihira, 1993, p. 186)

These authors use the term *family accommodation* to describe the various ways families respond to the challenges and sometimes conflicting circumstances that often result from having a child with disabilities. Gallimore et al. (1993) found that the 102 families they interviewed used a total of 680 different accommodations or proactive efforts in order to create and sustain a family environment and daily routine. These accommodations ranged across 10 different domains or areas, such as family sustenance and financial base, home convenience and safety, child care, and marital relationship.

Abuse and Neglect of Children with Disabilities

Child abuse and neglect occur with alarming frequency. In 1992 more than 2.7 million cases of child abuse were reported, and it is believed that the true incidence is much higher (Child Help USA, 1994). Because the majority of child abuse and neglect cases are never reported—some professionals think the number of actual cases is at least twice the number of reported cases (Straus, Gelles, & Steinmetz, 1980)—it is impossible to know the true extent of the problem. Estimates vary considerably, but Harrison and Edwards (1983) think that as many as 20% of all children may be neglected or physically, sexually, or emotionally abused.

Although the incidence of parental abuse and neglect of children with disabilities is also unknown, Kurtz and Kurtz (1987) state that "a growing body of evidence establishes a convincing connection between child maltreatment and handicapped children" (p. 216). Zirpoli (1987) found that not only were children with disabilities overrepresented in child abuse samples but they also were more likely to be abused for a longer period.

> Whereas the infant with colic may increase family stress for a limited period, the child with cerebral palsy, or any other long-term or permanent handicap, presents a potential long-term family crisis. As a result, children with handicaps are not only at greater risk for abuse, but for longer periods of time. It is no wonder, then, that children with handicaps are disproportionately represented in child abuse samples. (p. 44)

Cutler (1993) explains the intricacies of special education to parents and offers step-by-step advice on how to make the "system work" on behalf of their children with disabilities.

To read firsthand accounts from parents about the challenges of raising a child with disabilities, see "Being a Family" later in this chapter.

TABLE 13.1
Possible issues encountered by parents and siblings at different life-cycle stages of an individual with disabilities

Life-Cycle Stage	Parents	Siblings
Early Childhood, ages 0–5	• Obtaining an accurate diagnosis • Informing siblings and relatives • Locating services • Seeking to find meaning in the exceptionality • Clarifying a personal ideology to guide decisions • Addressing issues of stigma • Identifying positive contributions of exceptionality • Setting great expectations	• Less parental time and energy for sibling needs • Feelings of jealousy over less attention • Fears associated with misunderstandings of exceptionality

Life-Cycle Stage	Parents	Siblings
School Age, ages 6–12	• Establishing routines to carry out family functions • Adjusting emotionally to educational implications • Clarifying issues of mainstreaming vs. special class placement • Participating in IEP conferences • Locating community resources • Arranging for extracurricular activities	• Division of responsibility for any physical care needs • Oldest female sibling may be at risk • Limited family resources for recreation and leisure • Informing friends and teachers • Possible concern over younger sibling surpassing older • Issues of "mainstreaming" into same school • Need for basic information on exceptionality

Is a child's disability the reason he or she is abused and neglected, as some studies suggest (Fontana, 1971; Milner & Wimberley, 1980)? Or do abuse and neglect produce a disability in an otherwise normally developing child (Brandwein, 1973; Elmer, 1977)?

> In many cases, to ask the question of whether children are abused because they are handicapped, or handicapped because they are abused, is something akin to the old question of which came first—the chicken or the egg. We know this much for certain: some children are abused because they are handicapped, and some children are handicapped because they are abused. (Morgan, 1987, p. 45)

In most instances, however, it would be a mistake to say simply that a child's disability caused the abuse and neglect. Researchers have concluded that child abuse and neglect have no single cause but are the product of the complex interactions of numerous variables, only one of which concerns the child's characteristics (Kurtz &

TABLE 13.1 *(continued)*

Life-Cycle Stage	Parents	Siblings
Adolescence, ages 12–21	• Adjusting emotionally to possible chronicity of exceptionality • Identifying issues of emerging sexuality • Addressing possible peer isolation and rejection • Planning for career/vocational development • Arranging for leisure-time activities • Dealing with physical and emotional change of puberty • Planning for postsecondary education	• Overidentification with sibling • Greater understanding of differences in people • Influence of exceptionality on career choice • Dealing with possible stigma and embarrassment • Participation in sibling training programs • Opportunity for sibling support groups
Life-Cycle Stage	**Parents**	**Siblings**
Adulthood, ages 21–	• Planning for possible need for guardianship • Addressing the need for appropriate adult residence • Adjusting emotionally to any adult implications of dependency • Addressing the need for socialization opportunities outside the family • Initiating career choice or vocational program	• Possible issues of responsibility for financial support • Addressing concerns regarding genetic implications • Introducing new in-laws to exceptionality • Need for information on career/living options • Clarify role of sibling advocacy • Possible issues of guardianship

Source: From *Families, Professionals, and Exceptionality: A Special Partnership* (Second Edition) by A. P. Turnbull and H. R. Turnbull, 1990, pp. 134–135. Englewood Cliffs, NJ: Merrill/Prentice Hall. Used by permission.

Kurtz, 1987; Zirpoli, 1987, 1990). Just a few of the many factors that have been found to correlate with a higher incidence of child abuse are the parent's own abuse as a child, alcohol or drug dependency, unemployment, poverty, and marital discord. But again, it is important to stress that seldom is any one of these factors the lone cause of child abuse. For example, even though it is true that the lower a family's income, the greater the probability that child abuse and neglect will occur, many children from poor families receive loving and nurturing care. Likewise, the great majority of parents of children with disabilities provide a loving and nurturing environment.

There is a need for greater awareness of the problem of child abuse and neglect throughout society, but especially among professionals who work with children and families. Because teachers see children on a daily basis for most of the year,

Being a Family

The Experience of Raising a Child with a Disability or Chronic Illness

Having a child with disabilities has profound effects on all aspects of family life. Bradley, Knoll, and Agosta (1992) conducted detailed interviews with the parents of 92 children with disabilities or severe chronic illness to learn about the challenges faced by these families. The excerpts from those interviews that follow offer a glimpse of the level of care that families must provide for their children with disabilities, the added expense of having a child with disabilities, and the ongoing constant struggle to obtain needed services.

Taking Care of the Child

Most children with severe disabilities and chronic health problems need extensive and ongoing assistance which places parents and other family members in the role of caregiver. These comments by parents offer a glimpse at the day-to-day demands care requires:

- Mike sleeps when he wants to, mostly during the day. He sleeps with a heart monitor which alarms several times per night, because he stops breathing frequently. Usually I'm up by 8:00 and often cannot go to bed until 12:00 or 1:00 because of Mike's feedings and medication. It's hard to fit all of this into a day and still have time for sleep.

- He can aspirate, so meals must be organized. Two months ago he was yelling and he choked on rice. He went out and I had to bag him and change his trach. When I did, there was a rice plug, and a new law of quiet and calm was set down for meal times.

- There is a monitor when Jacob is in the bathtub to see that he doesn't slip and fall which could start bleeding. Or if he does, so that they will know what to do immediately. Usually pressure and ice are applied. If bleeding continues, an injection of "Factor 8," which controls bleeding, is given. He must be monitored where he plays; e.g., no glass, sharp edges on things, etc. Any kind of cut or fall could affect Jacob's condition. All furniture has been built or rebuilt by the father to have rounded edges. The parents state they didn't take training wheels off Jacob's bicycle for one year after he had the bike for fear he might fall off. The mother states that when he rides it now she watches him. The doctor says the main thing is to protect his head. Any head injury could result in bleeding and you wouldn't always know this.

- We're used to it all—we got routines down. The longer we do it, the smoother things go. . . . Only one scary time so far—Douglas's tube caught on the door handle and his trach came out. I panicked, but Douglas's father was home and he "simply" reinserted the trach and reattached the tube to the ventilator machine. Douglas meanwhile had turned gray, then blue for just a minute or less. I was crying as he began breathing again and his color came back. Douglas said to me, "Are you OK, Mom?" I don't think he has a recollection of what's happened at those moments when his breathing stopped.

Trying to Just Be a Family

The major challenge confronting most families was how to meet the complex care needs of their child with a disability or chronic health problem and still function as a family. Each family has a unique story.

- We moved from Burnsville to Bloomington because of the school district—lost friends—didn't go to church for several years—wouldn't let him stay in church nursery—would choke and gag—people were afraid. Couldn't drive on freeway—he couldn't stay in car seat—had to take back roads and stop all the time. Didn't have baby-sitters—went from being socially active to hermits—lost a whole lot emotionally. My husband was offered a job and turned it down—we didn't dare leave. Couldn't take a vacation—lost freedom to make some choices in our life.

- I [Dad] can write a book on it—you lose all flexibility. The brother didn't have a normal 3rd and 4th year of childhood. He spent it in the hospital with his brother and he is very sensitive. The parents try to compensate. The family gets separated because they can't just get in the van and go. No spontaneity.

Paying the Bills

Taking care of a child with physical disabilities, especially chronic health problems, is very expensive.

- We had to find another place to live with first floor bedroom, widened doorways, enlarged front porch, central air, ramp, van, washer and dryer. House renovation: $10,000. Van: $18,500. Air: $1,450. Porch: $1,400. Ramp: $1,000. Washer and dryer: $1,100. Furnishings to accommodate supplies: $800. We've got the following equipment: Suction machine, portable suction machine, generator for emergency power, hospital bed, air pressure mattress, wheelchair, room monitor, humidifier, bath chair, oxygen, air cleaner, gastronomy tube pump, breathing treatment machine. And all the following expenses have gone up: formula, diapers, appliances, utility bills, medications.

- They won't cover a wheelchair— that will lead to larger medical problems later on. Can't get correctional shoes. Can't get things to make Suzie's life easier and more functional that we can't afford. Can't buy better bed to help her sleep. Suzie was sleeping on waterbed which helped but had to sell. Can't buy adaptive toys (for example, one toy costs $39.95). Can't buy standing board, side-line chair, corner chair.

Battling the System

Many parents of children with disabilities share a similar fate: having to do constant battle with the very system and professionals in charge of the supports the family needs.

- It isn't the child or young person that makes you crazy—it is the system. . . . I don't understand why it is necessary to call on outside advocates to intervene to get these issues resolved. Why are our services always dependent on the good will of a particular social worker when the family assumes they are doing their job? Why do you have to monitor people who are supposed to be helping you?
- As Colin got worse, both parents ended up unemployed. DSHS commented, "White middle class folks looking for something for nothing." Because initial reports were that Colin would live only 2 years,

they have been refused. Governor's aide recommended getting a divorce so they could get help through state.

- I don't understand why they fight us tooth and nail for every little thing and would not ask us a single question if we left and abandoned him to an institution. Our newest battle is now the school system. We are now in court at great expense to our family so that Jim can get the nursing he needs at school. I am a little tired of being a pioneer. We are fighting like this to get him into BOCES (a special school program for students with disabilities)—can you imagine what it is going to be like to get him into elementary school?
- Dad sits on a lot of statewide coalitions and even with his visibility things are a struggle. Both parents are tired and would love to go back to just being a family.

Positive Outcomes

No family exposed to the complex care needs, daily crises, and effects on family lifestyle associated with caring for a child with disabilities can avoid profound stress and major changes. In spite of these powerful forces, many families report positive outcomes and a measure of increased strength and togetherness as a result of their decision to care for their child in the home.

- I grew up—learned and developed patience, tolerance. Now I have a different outlook on life—to face each day, whatever it brings with it. Mary and I have gone through some real crises and that has brought us closer.
- Most stress and dissatisfaction come from outside sources. Pete has been a joy (despite his problems), and I have never regretted my decision to adopt him. I have learned a lot (and

I am still learning) from him every day. Pete's excitement about life and learning, despite his severe problems, despite his past, is remarkable. His achievements, emotionally, academically, artistically over the past 3 years are amazing, considering his hospitalization in the ICU for $4\frac{1}{2}$ years. Best of all Pete is a funny, bright, loving child who gets into lots of mischief to keep me busy, but who constantly makes me laugh (often at ourselves). Pete has enriched our family in a way that no one else could and each of us has learned something about ourselves through him. Not one of us would trade a single hour with Pete for a winning lottery ticket. We're all very proud of him. Pete is the most loved member of his immediate and his extended family.

- *Dad:* Biggest thing is becoming acquainted with entirely different set of folks who share similar things. . . . Now I better appreciate the normal development of our other child. Lots of intangible goods that come out of seeing a DD child develop.
- *Mom:* Robbie is truly a blessing. People in our lives because of Robbie are people we learn from, are inspired by: teachers, medical people, other professionals, parents. . . . None of this could be possible if he was placed out of home. Expanded our connection to community around us. Have had to reach outside of ourselves. ✸

Adapted from "Emerging Issues in Family Support" by V. J. Bradley, J. Knoll, & J. M. Agosta, 1992, American Association on Mental Retardation, Washington, DC. Used by permission.

Information on detecting signs of child abuse and neglect can be obtained from the Child Help USA. Anyone can and should report a suspected case of child abuse; reports can be filed anonymously. If you do not know the appropriate local agency to contact, call the toll-free number of the Child Help USA Hotline: (800) 422-4453.

they are in the best position to identify and report suspected cases of abuse. All 50 states require that teachers and other professionals who frequently come into contact with children report suspected cases of child abuse and neglect (Meddin & Rosen, 1986). Indeed, many state laws require any citizen who suspects child abuse and neglect to report it, and most states impose criminal penalties for failure to do so. People who, in good faith, report suspected cases are immune from civil or criminal liability. All educators should become familiar with the child abuse laws in their states and learn how to recognize and report indicators of child abuse and neglect.

> Educators must be willing to get involved. Unfortunately, they and other professionals are frequently unwilling to file a report even when child abuse is highly suspected. Indeed, it may be very difficult for a person to make a child abuse report even anonymously. However, one must consider the possible consequences of not reporting suspected abuse. (Zirpoli, 1987, p. 46)

Ecobehavioral Treatment of Families with Histories of Child Abuse and Neglect

Another empirically tested program for helping abusive and neglectful parents is the Active Parenting Program, developed by the UCLA Project for Developmentally Disabled Children and Children's Institute International (Ambrose, Hazzard, & Haworth, 1980).

One of the most successful programs for preventing and treating child abuse and neglect is Project 12-Ways, developed at the University of Southern Illinois. The guiding philosophy of Project 12-Ways is that family problems can be eased by eliminating stress-producing factors, such as unemployment, and by teaching both children and parents the skills necessary for getting along together without abuse and neglect. Recognizing the multidimensional factors that lead to abuse and neglect and that the entire family must be understood and treated as a dynamic system, the project employs an ecobehavioral approach to treatment (Lutzker & Campbell, 1994). That is, rather than prescribe a standard treatment regimen consisting of one or two components, a thorough assessment of the family's needs and resources is conducted. Following the assessment, the family and a project counselor jointly determine goals. An individualized program of family support services is then implemented; it typically consists of several of the following facets:

- *Parent-child training.* Parents are helped to understand their children's behavior and are taught positive, nonpunitive forms of child management. Both parents and children are taught how to be more affectionate to one another.
- *Basic skills training.* Parents are given hands-on assistance in learning how to deal with important child development areas, such as toilet training, bed-wetting, dressing, and language/conversational skills.
- *Health maintenance and nutrition.* Behaviors that can cause health problems are addressed. Parents are helped to find medical care for themselves and their family.
- *Stress reduction.* Many family conflicts result from a parent's stresses and anxieties. Parents are taught systematic relaxation techniques to control stress.
- *Home safety and cleanliness.* Parents are taught to eliminate safety hazards and to improve home cleanliness and personal hygiene.
- *New parent.* New parents receive training and counseling in preparation for childbirth and infant care. Instruction includes health care during pregnancy, infant development, safety, family planning, and use of leisure time.
- *Family activities.* Families learn to spend free time together, engaging in inexpensive activities designed to develop family cohesiveness and positive relations.

- *Problem solving.* Family members are instructed in problem solving, negotiation training, and communication skills as appropriate means of resolving conflicts.
- *Money management..* Training is provided in basic money management, such as saving and budgeting for essential goods and services. Families are also taught how to resolve debts.
- *Self-control.* Parents learn behavioral self-control techniques to control their tempers and to meet personal goals, such as losing weight or stopping smoking.
- *Self-esteem training.* Self-esteem and assertiveness training gives parents tools for resolving conflicts and for asserting their positions within the family without being destructive to others.
- *Job finding.* Unemployed and underemployed parents are given assistance with job-related skills, such as interviewing and resumé preparation.

✳ *Parent-Teacher Communication*

Regular two-way communication with parents is the foundation of an effective parent-teacher partnership. Without open, honest communication between teacher and parent, many of the positive outcomes cannot be achieved. The three most-used methods of communication between parents and teachers are conferences, written messages, and the telephone.

> Turnbull and Turnbull (1990) recommend asking parents what methods of home-school communication they prefer.

Parent-Teacher Conferences

Although parent-teacher conferences are as common to school as recess and homework and have been with us for just about as long, conferences are not always the effective vehicle for communication that they should be. Too often, parent conferences turn out to be stiff, formal affairs, with teachers anxious and parents wondering what bad news they will hear this time. In fact, Bensky et al. (1980) found that teachers ranked communication with parents as a major source of job stress. Fortunately, recognition of the critical role that parents play in their child's education and greater parent participation in the schools as a result of IEP planning meetings have enhanced parent-teacher communication skills; parents and teachers are learning to talk with one another in more productive ways.

In a face-to-face meeting, parents and teachers can exchange information and coordinate their efforts to assist the child with disabilities at home and in school. Conferences should not be limited to the beginning and end of the school year, but scheduled regularly. Special educators should view the parent-teacher conference as a method for planning and evaluating jointly initiated teaching programs.

> Suggestions for interacting with angry parents and resolving conflicts and disagreements are provided by Fish (1990) and Margolis and Brannigan (1990).

Preparing for the Conference

Preparation is the key to effective parent-teacher conferences. Stephens, Blackhurst, and Magliocca (1982) recommend establishing specific objectives for the conference, reviewing the student's cumulative progress, preparing examples of the student's work along with a graph or chart showing specific performance, and preparing an agenda for the meeting. Figure 13.1 shows an outline for preparing a parent-teacher conference agenda. After planning the conference agenda, the teacher might examine alternative ways to present delicate issues, perhaps getting feedback from others on her style and manner of speaking (Roberds-Baxter, 1984).

By showing parents specific examples of their children's progress, teachers set the occasion for parental praise and approval of student effort.

Conducting the Conference

Parent-teacher conferences should usually be held in the child's classroom because (a) the teacher feels comfortable in familiar surroundings; (b) the teacher has ready access to student files and instructional materials; (c) the classroom itself serves as a reminder to the teacher of things the child has done; and (d) the classroom, with its desks, chairs, and teaching materials, reminds the teacher and parents that the purpose of the conference is their mutual concern for improving the child's education (Bennett & Hensen, 1977). When conducting parent conferences in their classrooms, however, teachers should not make the mistake of hiding behind their desks, creating a barrier between themselves and the parents, or of seating parents in undersized chairs meant for students.

Stephens and Wolf (1980) recommend a 4-step sequence for parent-teacher conferences:

1. *Build rapport.* Establishing mutual trust and the belief that the teacher really cares about the student is important to a good parent-teacher conference. A few minutes should be devoted to relevant small talk. The teacher might begin with something positive about the child or family, rather than a superficial statement about weather or traffic.

2. *Obtain information.* Parents can provide teachers with important information for improving instruction. Teachers should use open-ended questions that cannot be answered with a simple yes or no; for example, "Which activities in school has Felix mentioned lately?" is better than "Has Felix told you what we are doing now in school?" The first question encourages the parent to provide more information—the teacher is trying to build conversation, not preside over a question-and-answer session. Throughout the conference, the teacher should show genuine interest in listening to the parents' concerns, avoid dominating the conversation, and refrain from using comments that judge, threaten, or function as verbal roadblocks to communication (see Table 13.2).

3. *Provide information.* The teacher should give parents concrete information about their child in jargon-free language. The teacher should share examples of schoolwork and data on student performance—what has already been learned and what needs to be learned next. When the student's progress has not been as great as was hoped for, parents and teacher should look together for ways to improve it.

4. *Summarize and follow up.* The conference should end with a summary of what was said. The teacher should review strategies agreed on during the conference

Turnbull and Turnbull (1990) offer guidelines for holding conferences in parents' homes.

For detailed descriptions of how to plan and conduct parent conferences, see Simpson (1990) and Turnbull and Turnbull (1990).

FIGURE 13.1

Parent-teacher conference outline

Conference Outline

Date _____ 2-14-96 _____   Time _____ 4:30 - 5:00 _____

Student's Name _____ Jeremy Wright _____
Parents' Name(s) _____ Barbara and Tom _____
Teacher's Name _____ Tim G. _____
Other Staff present _____ None _____

Objectives for Conference: (1) Show graph of J's reading progress, (2) find out about spelling program,
   (3) get parents' ideas: intervention for difficulties on playground/in gym, (4) share list of books of leisure reading

Student's Strengths   •good worker academically, wants to learn
                        •excited about progress in reading fluency

Area(s) Where Improvement is Needed: •continue w/spelling @ home
                                         • arguments & fighting w/other kids

Questions to Ask Parents: •Interactions w/friends while playing in neighborhood?
                              •How would they feel about f'dback from classmate re: playground/gym behavior?
                              •Consequences?

Parent's Responses/Comments: •very pleased w/reading - want to build on it.
                                 •wondering how long w/in-home spelling?
                                 •willing to give rewards @ home: playground/gym

Examples of Student's Work/Interactions: •graph of corrects/errors per min.: reading
                                             •weekly pre- & post test scores: spelling.

Current Programs and Strategies Used by Teacher: •reading: silent read, two 1-min. time trials, self-charting
                                                         comprehension practice
                                                     •spelling: practice w/tape recorder, self-checking

Suggestions for Parents: •continue spelling games (invite friends)
                             •Show interest in/play fantasy games (Dung. & Dragons) W/J

Suggestions from Parents: •Try using some high-interest spelling words (e.g., joust, castle)
                              •Matt & Amin could help with playground/gym program

Follow-up Activities: (Agreed to in conf)
     Parents: •Continue to play spelling game 2 nights per week
                  •Take J to library for adventure books

     Teacher: •Ask J for high-interest words & use 3-4 in his weekly list.
                  •Develop peer intervention strategy w/Matt, Amin & J (group contingency?)

Date Called for Follow-up and Outcome:
                  Feb. 28 (Friday)

Source: Adapted from *Working with Parents of Handicapped Children* (p. 233) by W. L. Heward, J. C. Dardig, and A. Rossett, 1979, Englewood Cliffs, NJ: Merrill/Prentice Hall, Inc. Adapted by permission.

and indicate the follow-up activities that either party will do to help carry out those strategies. Some teachers use carbon paper and make a duplicate copy of their conference notes so that parents will also have a record of what was said or agreed on.

Written Messages

Even though much can be accomplished in parent-teacher conferences, the amount of time they require suggests that conferences should not be the sole means of maintaining parent-teacher communication. Ammer and Littleton (1983) asked 217 parents of exceptional children to check in which methods they most preferred to receive regular information from school. Letters from school was checked by 69% of the parents, more than any other method of communication. Some teachers use frequent written messages to communicate with parents. Although the report card that most schools send parents every grading period is a written message, its infrequency and standardized format limit its usefulness as a means of communication.

Many teachers regularly send "happy-grams" home with their students, specifying something positive the student has accomplished and giving parents an opportunity to praise the child at home and stay abreast of activities in the classroom. A book by Kelly (1990) includes school-home notes that can be duplicated and used for a variety of communication purposes.

> Parents in this study indicated that their next two preferred vehicles for receiving information from their children's schools were parent-teacher conferences (51%) and telephone calls from teachers (45%). Home visits (19%) ranked as the least preferred method of establishing or improving home-school communication.

TABLE 13.2

Communication roadblocks that educators should avoid in their interactions with parents

Moralizing:	"You should . . . " "You ought . . . " "It is your responsibility to . . . "
Lecturing:	"I told you . . . " "Do you realize . . . " "One of these days . . . "
Judging/criticizing:	"You're wrong . . . " "One of your problems is . . . " "That was a mistake . . . "
Prying:	"Why?" "How?" "When?" "Who?"
Providing answers prematurely:	"Here's what you do . . . " "I suggest . . . "
Threatening:	"If you do that I'll . . . " "Unless you take my advice . . . "
Ordering:	"You must . . . " "You will . . . " "You have to . . . "
Consoling/excusing:	"You'll be just fine . . . " "You didn't know any better . . . "
Diagnosing/analyzing:	"You're just going through the stage of . . . " "You're behaving that way because . . . "
Using sarcasm/cynicism:	"You think you've got it bad . . . " "Life's just a barrel of laughs . . . "
Overusing clichés/phrases:	"You know . . . " "I mean . . . " "That's neat . . . " "Far out . . . "

Source: From *Families, Professionals, and Exceptionality: A Special Partnership* (p. 150) by A. P. Turnbull and H. R. Turnbull, 1986. Englewood Cliffs, NJ: Merrill/Prentice Hall. Reprinted by permission.

A two-way parent-teacher communication system can be built around a reporting form the child carries between home and school. The form should be simple to use and read, with space to circle or check responses or to write short notes. Such an interactive reporting system can be used on either a daily or weekly basis, depending on the behaviors involved (Sicley, 1993).

A daily report card system was used with three junior high school boys having serious academic and behavior problems (Schumaker, Hovell, & Sherman, 1977). Different teachers marked a card for each boy in each of six classes. Parents provided privileges (e.g., snacks, television time, staying up an extra half-hour before bed) based on the teachers' ratings of their child's school performance. All three students improved their adherence to classroom rules and their academic performance. An ongoing communication system, such as the one shown in Figure 13.2, can be used to provide parents with information about homework assignments, as well as about their child's work and behavior in class.

A home-school contract is a behavioral contract that specifies parent-delivered rewards contingent on completion of classroom tasks; for example, for each page of the reading workbook completed, the student might earn a quarter to be used to buy a model airplane (Heward & Dardig, 1978). Home-school contracts use parent-controlled rewards, build in parent recognition and praise of the child's accomplishments, and involve the teacher and parents together in a positive program to support the child's learning.

The class newsletter is another method some teachers use to increase parent-teacher communication. Even though putting together a class newsletter requires a lot of work, in many cases it is worth the effort. Most teachers have access to a word processor, and a 1- to 3-page monthly newsletter can give parents who do not attend meetings or open houses information that is too long or detailed to give over the telephone. A newsletter is also an excellent way to recognize those parents who participate in various activities. By making the newsletter a class project, the teacher can include student-written stories and news items and can create an enjoyable learning activity for the entire class.

To find out how important regular home-school communication was to the partnership between one student's family and his teacher, see "The Way It's Supposed to Work" later in this chapter.

Watching a movie with her sister and friends is one of the rewards Christine chose for her homework contract.

FIGURE 13.2

A home-school communication sheet for monitoring homework assignments and in-school behavior

Assignment Monitoring Sheet

Name _____   Date: _____

PERIOD	ASSIGNMENT	FEEDBACK			COMMENT	SIGNATURE
1		HWC HWNC	CWC CWNC	AB UB		
2		HWC HWNC	CWC CWNC	AB UB		
3		HWC HWNC	CWC CWNC	AB UB		
4		HWC HWNC	CWC CWNC	AB UB		
5		HWC HWNC	CWC CWNC	AB UB		
6		HWC HWNC	CWC CWNC	AB UB		
7		HWC HWNC	CWC CWNC	AB UB		

KEY:
HWC = HomeWork Completed   HWNC = HomeWork Not Completed
CWC = ClassWork Completed   CWNC = ClassWork Not Completed
AB   = Acceptable Behavior   UB   = Unacceptable Behavior

****

Parent Feedback/Assistance Request

Feedback or Issue of Concern:

_____

_____

_____

Action Requested: phone conference   _____
                           conference at school   _____
                           none   _____

Best day/time to contact: day: _____
                                 time: _____

Parent Signature: _____   Phone: _____

Source: From "Home-school partnerships: A cooperative approach to intervention," by M. E. Cronin, D. L. Slade, C. Bechtel, and P. Anderson, 1992, *Intervention in School and Clinic, 27*(5), 286–292. Copyright (c) 1992 by PRO-ED, Inc. Reprinted by permission.

Although not used for regular or interactive communication with parents, school handbooks and special-purpose handouts describing policies and procedures, identifying personnel, suggesting parenting tips, and so on, are another means of using written materials to provide information to parents (Jensen & Potter, 1990).

The Telephone

A brief, pleasant telephone conversation can be an excellent way to maintain communication with parents. Regular telephone calls that focus on a child's positive accomplishments let parents and teachers share in the child's success and recognize each other's contributions. Teachers should set aside time on a regular basis so that each child's parent receives a call once every 2 or 3 weeks. Of course, teachers need to find out what times are convenient for parents to receive calls. Keeping a log of the calls helps maintain the schedule and reminds teachers of any necessary follow-up.

Another way teachers can use the telephone is to organize a class "telephone tree." Telephone trees can be an efficient way to get information to all parents associated with a class. The teacher calls only two or three parents, each of whom calls two or three more, and so on. And a telephone tree gives parents a way to get actively involved and perhaps to get to know some of the other parents.

Heward and Chapman (1981) used daily recorded telephone messages as a way to increase parent-teacher communication. The teacher of a primary learning disabilities class recorded brief messages on an automatic telephone answering machine. Parents could call five nights per week from 5:00 p.m. until 7:00 a.m. the next morning and hear a recorded message like this one:

> Good evening. The children worked very hard today. We are discussing transportation. They enjoyed talking about the airport and all the different kinds of airplanes. The spelling words for tomorrow are train, t-r-a-i-n; plane, p-l-a-n-e; truck, t-r-u-c-k; automobile, a-u-t-o-m-o-b-i-l-e; and ship, s-h-i-p. Thank you for calling. (p. 13)

The number of telephone calls the teacher received from the parents of the six children in the class each week was recorded for the entire school year. The teacher received a total of only 5 calls for the 32 weeks when the recorded messages were not available (0.16 calls per week), compared with 112 calls during the 6 weeks the message system was in operation (18.7 per week). During the nonmessage portions of the study, the next day's spelling list was sent home with the children each day, and parents were asked to help their children with the words. Nonetheless, scores on the daily five-word spelling tests improved for all six students when the recorded messages were available.

Recorded telephone messages can be used to provide schoolwide and classroom-by-classroom information, good news (e.g., Citizen of the Month), and suggestions for working with children at home (Heward, Heron, Gardner, & Prayzer, 1991; Minner, Beane, & Prater, 1986; Test, Cooke, Weiss, Heward, & Heron, 1986). Parent callers can also leave messages for the teacher (e.g., a question or a report on how a home-based instructional program is going), enabling the system to be used for two-way communication.

Teacher-recorded telephone messages can also be used to provide parents with the information and encouragement they need to successfully implement home-based tutoring programs. For an example of how this can be done, see "The Telephone" on the following page.

The Telephone

·······················

An Underused Method of Home-School Communication

Virtually all parents and educators agree on the importance of regular communication between home and school. How to manage parent-teacher communication most effectively is the question. A face-to-face conference can accomplish much, but parent-teacher conferences demand a great deal of time from both parties and, realistically, can be held only from time to time. Written notes from the teacher; daily, two-way home-school notes; and class newsletters can all be excellent means of communication. The time required to prepare and reproduce daily notes or a class newsletter, however, coupled with the uncertainty of student delivery, can make written communication a labor-intensive and sometimes unreliable method of parent-teacher communication—at least in terms of communicating with a number of parents on a regular, sustained basis.

Somewhat surprisingly in this era of high technology, the telephone—everyday technology that has been with us for decades—has been a relatively unexploited means of parent-teacher communication. Of course, if used in typical fashion, the time required to call and speak individually with the parents of all 20 students enrolled in a resource room program, for example, would place the telephone in the same category as conferences and written messages for regular, sustained communication: a weekly call perhaps, but daily communication would most likely be out of the question. Recently, however, teachers have begun to use the telephone in a different way. By recording daily messages on a telephone-answering machine, teachers can provide a great deal of information to parents at relatively little cost. Parents can call the given number and listen at their convenience, literally 24 hours a day. Parents can also leave messages on the recorder, posing a question, offering a suggestion, and so on.

In addition to information exchange, some studies have begun to explore ways in which teachers can use recorded messages to help parents carry out home-based instruction. One junior high learning disabilities teacher used a telephone-answering machine to manage a summer writing program. Parents of several of her students had indicated their desire to try to help their children maintain or extend some of their academic skills over the summer months. Each day during the 9-week program, the teacher recorded instructions for the session and a story-starter idea. One story starter went like this:

> *Danger on Shore—You are going up the river in a boat. You feel safe because the unfriendly natives are on the far shore. Suddenly you notice a leak. . . .*

Parent and student called together, the student wrote for 10 minutes on that day's topic, and the parent scored the student's writing according to criteria provided by the teacher. The parents rewarded their children for progress and reported the results after the next day's message. Every few days, parents mailed the stories to the teacher.

To get an idea of the results of the program, compare the following stories. Story 8 was written by James before his parents started the program to help him write more action words and adjectives. Story 33 was the sixth story written after his parents began to reward adjectives.

From "A Telephone-Managed, Home-Based Summer Writing Program for LD Adolescents" by M. E. Hassett, C. Engler, N. L. Cooke, D. W. Test, A. B. Weiss, W. L. Heward, and T. E. Heron in *Focus on Behavior Analysis in Education,* pp. 89–103, by W. L. Heward, T. E. Heron, D. S. Hill, and J. Trap-Porter (Eds.), 1984, Columbus, OH: Merrill. Adapted by permission.

8

July 7   James D

First I would go to candy, allways thinking of my self. Later I would go to the meat department. After the meat department I wrul go to wine department

Aug 12 #33 Talking with a Star   James D

I look up from my salad, thick chocolate milk shake, hot golden crisp french fries, and delicious Big Mac with extra pickles.

I glance through shiney, clear glass and see a small, brown creature with a glowing red chest, short legs, long arms, and a large head with big greenish-blue eyes and a smashed-in nose.

I grab a white napkin and rush up to him. With the tip of his glowing right index finger he writes...

E.T.

Two stories written by a 13-year-old boy with learning disabilities during an in-home summer program. Story 8 was written during baseline; Story 33, when his parents were rewarding the use of adjectives

✳ *Parent Involvement*

Parents and the Individualized Education Program

IFSPs are discussed Chapter 14.

As discussed in Chapter 2, an individualized education program (IEP) or an individualized family services plan (IFSP) must be developed for every child with disabilities. This requirement of the IDEA is intended to ensure that every child with disabilities receives special educational services suited to his or her individual needs. Parents are required to be members of the IEP planning team, although they may waive this right by signing a document stating they do not wish to participate.

> The IEP meeting serves as a communication vehicle between parents and school personnel, and enables them as equal participants, to jointly decide what the child's needs are, what services will be provided to meet those needs, and what the anticipated outcomes will be. (Federal Register, 1981, p. 5462)

Giangreco, Cloninger, and Iverson (1993), the developers of *COACH,* a highly regarded program for planning and implementing inclusive educational programs for students with disabilities, believe that active family involvement is the "cornerstone of relevant and longitudinal" educational planning. They present five powerful arguments to support that case:

- *Families know certain aspects of their children better than anyone else.* Although teachers and other school staff observe students throughout a 5- to 6-hour school day, this is only a fraction of a student's entire day. As educators, we must remind ourselves that we spend only about half the days of the year with our students, seeing them less than a third of each of those days. Nonschool time may provide key information that has educational implications, such as the nature of the student's interests, motivations, habits, fears, routines, pressures, needs, and health. By listening to parents, educators can gain a more complete understanding of the student's life outside school.
- *Families have the greatest vested interest in seeing their children learn.* In our professional eagerness to help children learn, we sometimes convey a message to parents that teachers care more about their children than they do. Of course, this is rarely the case. It can be dangerous to make assumptions about a parent's intentions.
- *The family is likely to be the only group of adults involved with a child's educational program throughout his or her entire school career.* Over the course of a school career, a student with special educational needs will encounter so many professionals that it will be difficult for the family to remember all the names. Some of these professionals will work with the child for years, others for a year or less. Eventually, even the most caring of them will depart because they are professionals who are paid to be part of the student's life. While such diversity can be healthy if it is well coordinated, the varying input of professionals could prove harmful if it is so random and chaotic that it offers no real form of direction. Professionals must build upon a family-centered vision for the child, rather than re-invent a student's educational program each year.
- *Families have the ability to influence positively the quality of educational services provided in their community.* Historically, families have been responsible for improving access to educational and community-based opportunities for their children with disabilities. Undoubtedly, families will continue to play a vital role in improving educational services.
- *Families must live with the outcomes of decisions made by education teams all day, every day.* People rarely appreciate someone else making decisions that will

affect their lives, without including them in the decision-making. When families do not do what professionals have prescribed, this may be an indication that the family was inadequately involved in the decision-making process. As professionals, when we make decisions we must constantly remind ourselves that they are likely to affect other people besides the child and have an effect outside of school. In our experience, when given the opportunity to participate in educational planning, families can play an invaluable role in determining appropriate educational experiences and can do an excellent job of pinpointing priorities.[1]

Despite these compelling arguments for the advantages of family involvement, research on parents' attitudes about and participation in IEP conferences is mixed. In interviews conducted with 32 mothers of preschool children with disabilities, Winton and Turnbull (1981) found that, when asked to rank the characteristics of an ideal preschool, the mothers identified parent involvement as the least important factor; the most important factor to the mothers was competent, expert teachers. Lusthaus, Lusthaus, and Gibbs (1981) compiled questionnaire results from 98 parents of students enrolled in self-contained classrooms and resource rooms in eight elementary schools in a middle-class suburban school district. More than half of the parents said they wanted to participate in IEP planning conferences at the level of providing information. The majority were content to let professionals make most decisions. When decisions were to be made about what kinds of records should be kept on their children, what medical services were to be provided, or whether their children would be transferred to other schools, however, more parents wanted to have control over the decisions. Polifka (1981) concluded from a parent survey that parents do want to play an active role in IEP planning.

Studies on what actually happens during IEP meetings are more conclusive. Parent attendance (mostly mothers) at IEP conferences varies widely across school districts, from less than 50% to as high as 95% (Singer & Butler, 1987). Numerous studies have found that the level of parental participation is more often passive than active (Goldstein, Strickland, Turnbull, & Curry, 1980; Lynch & Stein, 1982; Scanlon, Arick, & Phelps, 1981; Vaughn, Bos, Harrell, & Lasky, 1988). In a survey of almost 2,300 parents from all over the United States, slightly more than half (52%) of the parents indicated that their children's IEP had been completely written before the meeting (National Committee for Citizens in Education, 1979). Goldstein et al. (1980) observed IEP meetings for elementary students with mild disabilities and found similar results: The average meeting lasted only 36 minutes and consisted mainly of the special education teacher's explaining an already-written IEP to the parent. In another study, observation of 47 IEP conferences revealed the following: (a) In only 6 of the conferences did both mother and father attend, with only mothers attending all others; (b) 28 of the conferences consisted of the special education teacher explaining an already-completed IEP to the parent(s); (c) approximately one third of the responses by parents consisted of passive contributions (e.g., head nodding); and (d) the average duration of the meetings was 25 minutes (Vacc et al., 1985).

> Given the extended families in which many children with disabilities live and the variety of caretakers with whom they interact, Adelman (1994) suggests that the term *home involvement* better describes the nature and need for family support services than terms such as *parent involvement* and *family involvement.*

---

[1]Excerpted from Giangreco, M. F., Cloninger, C. J., & Iverson, V. S. (1993), *Choosing Options and Accommodations for Children (COACH),* pp. 6–7, Baltimore, MD, Paul H. Brookes. Reprinted by permission of the author.

The research supports what was stated earlier: We should not rely on generalizations assumed to be true for all parents of children with disabilities. Furthermore, this research must be viewed with the understanding that, for years, most parents were not asked (and in some instances have not wanted) to participate in their children's education; then almost overnight, they are expected or even virtually required to do so. It is not surprising that parents have mixed feelings about how much their participation is really desired and how much they really can or should contribute.

Many parents do take advantage of the IEP meeting to offer significant input into their children's education programs. In one IEP conference

> the mother of a moderately retarded child questioned why her son was being taught to label prehistoric animals verbally. The parent asked the teachers what type of job they expected the child to have as an adult. The teachers replied that they had never really considered job opportunities for the child, since he was only 10. To the teachers, 10 seemed young; to the parents, 10 meant that almost half his formal education was completed. As the meeting progressed, it was clear that the parents were specifying objectives related to independence as an adult (telling time, reading survival words, sex education) that were different from the more traditional curriculum proposed by the teachers. Through sharing evaluation data, goals for the child, and special problems, all parties involved created a curriculum that met everyone's approval. (Turnbull, 1983, p. 22)

Parents and professionals are working together to increase the level of parent participation in IEP team meetings. In one innovative strategy that Goldstein and Turnbull (1982) investigated, school counselors attended the IEP conferences with the parents and served as advocates by introducing the parents, clarifying jargon, directing questions to parents, verbally praising parents for contributing, and summarizing the decisions made at the meeting. The counselors received no formal training; they were simply given a sheet of instructions outlining their five functions. Parents who were accompanied by a counselor-advocate made more contributions. Turnbull and Morningstar (1993) provide more than 50 suggestions that school personnel can take before and during the IEP conference to facilitate parent involvement (see Table 13.3).

Parents also have a responsibility to make an effort to improve their knowledge and skills for active and effective participation in IEP/IFSP conferences. Strickland and Turnbull (1993) describe group training sessions in which parents learn what goes into an IEP and how to participate more actively in developing it. A group of parents of children with disabilities recommends that parents use the following checklist of questions to determine whether they are contributing as a productive member of the IEP or IFSP:

- Am I honest with team members about my child's abilities and skill level?
- Do I share information about my child and family that will help determine the services we need?
- Am I committed to the plan as outlined . . . that is, will I take responsibility for some of the strategies?
- Am I contributing to the plan in any way? (Equipment, ideas, time, decisions?)
- When I disagree or am disappointed, do I talk to the team about it, instead of to other people who are not involved?
- Do I ask for clarification, additional information, or help in making difficult decisions or choices?

The process for prioritizing IEP goals and objectives shown in Chapter 11 (Figure 11.3) is one technique for systematically recognizing and incorporating parents' and family members' input.

- Am I effective in persuading team members of the importance of my family's priorities and values—can I negotiate some compromises without demanding?
- Do I respect the knowledge, skill and experiences of other team members, and also respect their time, schedules and priorities?[1]

Parents as Teachers

All parents are responsible for their children's learning many skills. But typically developing children learn many skills from their parents that children with disabilities do not learn without systematic instruction. For some children with disabilities, the casual routines of everyday home life may not provide enough practice and feedback to teach them important skills. Many parents have responded by systematically teaching their children needed self-help and daily-living skills or by providing home-tutoring sessions to supplement classroom academic instruction.

Not all educators agree on the role that parents should play when it comes to teaching children with disabilities. Some professionals give a variety of reasons why parents should not tutor their children: Parents do not have the teaching skills required for effective tutoring; home tutoring is likely to end in frustration for both parent and child; most teachers do not have the time to guide and support parents' efforts; and home tutoring may give children little rest from instruction. Each of these concerns may represent a legitimate problem in individual situations.

The other perspective—that parents can serve as effective teachers for their children—is supported by numerous reports of research studies and parent involvement projects in which parents have successfully taught their children at home (e.g., Barbetta & Heron, 1991; Sandler & Coren, 1981; Thurston & Dasta, 1990). The majority of parents who have participated in these home-tutoring programs considered it a positive experience for both the parents and children. Feedback from parents and children who participated in a summer home reading program in which remedial readers read to their parents included these positive comments (Brown & Moore, 1992):

> One mother commented, "This was a family affair. It was good for us to sit and listen to our child read."
> A father said, "We're going to continue reading at home throughout the year. It's not that difficult to do, and I know my son profits from the practice."
> One little boy said, "I really like reading at home with my parents, especially when I know I'm going to get a pizza!" (p. 20)

In most instances in which parents wish to tutor their children at home, they can and should be helped to do so. Properly conducted, home-based parent teaching strengthens a child's educational program and gives enjoyment to both child and parent. It is important, however, for professionals to examine carefully to what extent parent tutoring is appropriate. Not all parents want to teach their children at home or have the time to learn and use the necessary teaching skills—and professionals must not interpret that situation as an indication that the parents do not care enough about their children.

Bristor (1987) and Thurston (1989) describe techniques that teachers can use to help parents who wish to tutor their children at home. For suggestions on how teachers can help parents work with their children at home to improve study skills and personal responsibility, see Hoover (1993) and Luckner (1994).

---

[1]From Stoner, G., Hunt, M., Cornelius, P., Leventhal, P., Miller, P., & Murray, T. (1994). Parents on the team. *TASH Newsletter, 20*(5), 9–11. Originally from the booklet "Into Our Lives," reprinted by permission of the Family Child Learning Center, Tallmadge, OH.

TABLE 13.3

Suggestions for increasing parent involvement in the IEP conference

Preconference Preparation

- Appoint a service coordinator to coordinate all aspects of the IEP conference.
- Solicit information from the family members about their preferences and needs regarding the conference.
- Discuss the meeting with the student and consider his or her preferences concerning the conference.
- Decide who should attend the conference and include the student if appropriate. Encourage the family to consider inviting extended family members, friends, and advocates who might provide valuable insights.
- Arrange a convenient time and location for the meeting.
- Assist the family with logistical needs such as transportation and child care.
- Without educational jargon, inform the family verbally or in writing of the following:
    1. The purpose of the meeting.
    2. The time and location of the conference.
    3. The names of the participants.
- Share information the family wants before the conference. This may include a draft of the proposed IEP.
- Encourage the student, family members, and their advocates to visit the proposed placements for the student prior to the conference.
- Facilitate communication between the student and family members about the conference.
- Encourage the family members to share information and discuss concerns with the participants prior to the conference.
- Gather needed information from school personnel.
- Prepare an agenda to cover the remaining components of the IEP conference.
- Provide the family with samples of the MAPS process and encourage them to complete one at home before the meeting *or* hold a MAPS with them.

Initial Conference Proceedings

- Greet the student, the family, and their advocates.
- Provide a list of all participants or use name tags.
- Introduce each participant with a brief description of his or her role in the conference.
- State the purpose, review the agenda, and ask for additional issues to be covered.
- Determine the amount of time that the participants have available for the conference and share the option of rescheduling if needed to complete the agenda.
- Ask if the family members desire clarification of their legal rights.

Review of Formal Evaluation and Current Levels of Performance

- Provide the family members with a written copy of evaluation results if desired.
- Avoid educational jargon as much as possible and clarify diagnostic terminology throughout the conference.
- If a separate evaluation conference has not been scheduled, ask the diagnostic personnel to report the following:
    1. The tests administered.
    2. The results of each.
    3. The options based on the evaluation.
- Summarize the findings, including strengths, gifts, abilities, and needs.
- Identify implications of test results for planning purposes.
- Ask the family members for areas of agreement and disagreement with corresponding reasons.
- Review the student's developmental progress and current levels of performance in each class.

TABLE 13.3 *(continued)*

- Ask the family members if they agree or disagree with the stated progress and levels.
- Strive to resolve the disagreement with student work samples and solicit information from the family members about collecting further samples.
- Proceed with the IEP only when you and the family members agree about the student's exceptionality and current levels of performance.

Development of Goals and Objectives

- Encourage the student, family members, and advocates to share their dream for the student's participation in the home, school, and community.
- Collaboratively generate appropriate goals and objectives for all subject areas requiring special instruction consistent with dream.
- Discuss goals and objectives for future educational and vocational options.
- Identify objectives to expand the positive contributions that the student can make to the family, friends, and the community.
- Prioritize all goals and objectives in light of the student preferences and needs.
- Clarify the manner in which responsibility for teaching the objectives will be shared among the student's teachers.
- Ask the family members and advocates if they would like to share in the responsibility for teaching some of the objectives at home or in the community.
- Determine how and when each identified goal and objective will be assessed.
- Explain to the family members and advocates that the IEP is not a guarantee that the student will attain the goals; rather, it represents that school personnel will teach these goals and objectives.

Determination of Placement and Related Services

- Include the student, family members, and advocates in a discussion of the benefits and drawbacks of viable placement options.
- Select a placement option that allows the student to be involved with peers without exceptionalities as much as possible.
- Agree on a tentative placement until the family members can visit and confirm its appropriateness.
- Discuss the benefits and drawbacks of modes of delivery for related services that the student needs.
- Specify the dates for initiating related services and anticipated duration.
- Share the names and qualifications of all personnel who will provide services with the family members and advocates.

Conclusion of the Conference

- Assign follow-up responsibility for any task requiring attention.
- Review with the student, family members, and advocates any responsibilities they have agreed to assume.
- Summarize orally and on paper the major decisions and follow-up responsibilities of all participants.
- Set a tentative date for reviewing the IEP document.
- Identify strategies for ongoing communication with the student, family members, and advocates.
- Express appreciation to the student, family members, and advocates for their help in the decision-making process.
- Allow time for the family to provide feedback and comments about the meeting. This may require follow-up contacts.
- Schedule additional meetings if necessary to complete the agenda or follow-up activities and tasks generated during the meeting.

Source: Reprinted with permission of Simon & Schuster, Inc. From "Family and Professional Interaction," by A. P. Turnbull & M. E. Morningstar, 1993. In M. E. Snell, *Instruction of Students with Severe Disabilities* (4th ed.) (pp. 44–45). Englewood Cliffs, NJ: Merrill/Prentice Hall, Inc.

There are also other circumstances in which parent tutoring is probably ill-advised:

- If parents disagree over whether the child should be tutored
- If no quiet, nondistracting place is available in the home
- If tutoring might result in neglecting needs of other family members
- If either parent resents the time spent tutoring or feels guilty if tutoring sessions are skipped or cut short
- If tutoring time deprives the child of opportunities to make friends with other children or develop necessary social skills (Maddux & Cummings, 1983, p. 31)

Commenting on the appropriateness of parents teaching a child with severe disabilities at home, Hawkins and Hawkins (1981) write:

Training and motivating parents to carry out a small number of teaching tasks each day does seem appropriate. These should be tasks that have most of the following characteristics: (1) they are brief, usually requiring no more than three or four minutes each; (2) the ultimate value of them to the parent is obvious (thus self-dressing, but perhaps not block-stacking); (3) they fit the daily routine almost automatically, not requiring a special, noticeable training "session" (thus self-bathing, but not basic communication-board training); (4) they are tasks that cannot be accomplished readily at school alone, either because the opportunities are infrequent or absent (getting up in the morning, toileting), or because training must occur at every opportunity if it is to achieve its objective (mealtime behaviors, walking appropriately with family). (pp. 17–18)

Lovitt (1977, 1982) offers four guidelines for parent tutoring:

1. *Establish a specific time each day for the tutoring sessions.*
2. *Keep sessions short.* Brief 5- to 10-minute sessions held daily are more likely to be effective than 30- to 40-minute periods, which can produce frustration or will tend to be skipped altogether.
3. *Keep responses to the child consistent.* Lovitt believes that it is particularly important for parents to respond to their child's errors in a consistent, matter-of-fact way. By praising the child's successful responses (materials and activities at the child's appropriate instructional level are a must) and providing a consistent, unemotional response to errors (e.g., "Let's read that word again, together"), par-

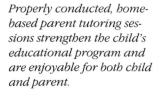

For a review of research documenting the results of using family members in home-based teaching programs with children with severe disabilities, see Snell and Beckman-Brindley (1984).

Properly conducted, home-based parent tutoring sessions strengthen the child's educational program and are enjoyable for both child and parent.

ents can avoid the frustration and negative results that can occur when home tutoring is mishandled.

4. *Keep a record.* Parents, just like classroom teachers, can never know the exact effects of their teaching unless they keep records. A daily record enables both parents and child to see gradual progress that might be missed if subjective opinion is the only basis for evaluation. Most children do make progress under guided instruction. A record documents that progress, perhaps providing the parent with an opportunity to see the child in a new and positive light.

Parent Education and Support Groups

Education for parenting is not new; educational programs for parents date back to the early 1800s. But as a result of greater parent involvement in the education of children with disabilities, many more programs are offered for and by parents. Parent groups can serve a variety of purposes—from one-time-only dissemination of information on a new school policy, to make-it-and-take-it workshops in which parents make an instructional material to use at home (e.g., a math facts practice game), to multiple-session programs on participation in IEP/IFSP planning or child behavior management. Just a few of the many topics that parent education and support groups address are listed in Table 13.4. Parent groups serve a variety of purposes, but most are designed to accomplish one or more of these (Miller & Hudson, 1994):

1. To disseminate information and suggestions to assist parents in the challenge of raising a child with disabilities
2. To provide a forum for parents to share information with and support one another
3. To exchange information from parents that will enhance their child's education program

There is consistent agreement in the parent education literature on the importance of involving parents in planning and, whenever possible, actually conducting parent groups (Baker, 1989; Kroth, 1981; Turnbull & Turnbull, 1990). To determine what parents want from a parent program, both open and closed needs assessment procedures should be used. An open-ended needs assessment consists of questions like these:

1. The best family time for my child is when we _____.
2. I will never forget the time that my child and I _____.
3. When I take my child to the store, I am concerned that he/she will _____.
4. People think my child is unable to _____.
5. I'm worrying about making a decision about my child's _____.
6. Sometimes I think my child will never _____.
7. My child is especially difficult around the house when he/she _____.
8. I give my child a hug when he/she _____.
9. The hardest thing about having a special child is _____.
10. I wish I knew more about _____. (Heward et al., 1979, p. 240)

Parents' responses to open-ended questions can provide a tremendous amount of information about what kinds of parent training programs might be needed and appreciated.

A closed needs assessment asks parents to indicate, from a list of possibilities, items they would like to learn more about. For example, parents might be asked to

Espe-Sherwindt and Crable (1993) discuss considerations in providing support to parents with mental retardation. For a review of the literature on parent education programs and research, see Dangle and Polster (1984).

Baker (1989) describes a 10-session "parents as teachers" training program in which parents of children with mental retardation and other disabilities learn behaviorally based teaching principles for teaching self-help skills, play skills, and decreasing behavior problems. Books such as *Steps to Independence: A Skills Training Guide for Parents and Teachers of Children with Special Needs* (Baker & Brightman, 1989) and classic parenting manuals such as *Parents Are Teachers* (Becker, 1971) and *Living with Children* (Patterson, 1979) are excellent resources for "parents as teachers" training programs.

The Way It's Supposed to Work

A Family and Teacher Partnership in Support of Jay

Ann P. Turnbull and Mary E. Morningstar

Ann, the parent, and Mary, the teacher, share some of the ways that they collaborated to support Ann's son, Jay, and why their partnership was such a success.

Ann's Perspective

Jay was in Mary's class for the last year of his high school program, and it was a very positive experience for him and our entire family. The first evening that our family met Mary, we were impressed with her energy, state-of-the-art knowledge, and obvious commitment to her students. Mary quickly earned our confidence in terms of the programming that she was doing, and we were totally together in our values for integration, productivity, and independence.

Mary organized an inservice program that allowed teachers and parents to work together and to share information about disabilities with the typical students in the school to help prepare them for positive interactions. It gave us a chance to go to classes, meet students and teachers, and feel like "part of the school." Right away, Mary got Jay established as a manager of the football team, helped facilitate relationships between Jay and typical students (an opportunity he had never really had before), and helped him dress "cool," walk "cool," and generally fit into the school.

In terms of family contact, Mary treated us, Jay's parents and sisters, with respect and dignity. There have been times in the past that I have felt judged by teachers, and often, it made me feel defensive. To the contrary, I always felt that Mary was able to see my strengths and to value how conscientiously our family was trying to support Jay.

We exchanged a notebook back and forth, and I always looked forward to reading Mary's positive messages. It was a great source of connection and camaraderie for all of us. It was as if we had a visit each day.

I also remember how wonderful it was for Mary to bring Jay and his classmates to our house a couple of days a week for their domestic training. It was a bonus for Jay to be able to learn domestic skills in his own setting, and it was certainly a bonus for our family to have assistance in housekeeping.

One of the confidences that I had throughout the entire year was that Jay was in a quality program and that Mary knew exactly what she was doing. It was an incredible relief for our family to not feel that we had to advocate during every spare minute to ensure opportunities for Jay. We knew that Mary was doing a good job, and we could relax and spend time in family recreation rather than in evening advocacy meetings. What a relief from previous years!

Mary's Perspective

The most crucial part of my school program always started during that first meeting with the family. I have always preferred that my first visit take place in the family's home. This puts the

put one check mark by any item of the following topics that is something of a problem and two check marks by any area that is of major interest:

___ Bedtime behavior

___ Eating behavior

___ Interactions with sibling(s)

___ Personal cleanliness (dressing, toileting)

___ Interactions with strangers

___ Compliance with parental requests

___ Interactions with opposite sex

___ Home chores

___ On-task behavior

___ Leisure activities

family more at ease, lets me get a feel for how the family lives, and lets me meet the brothers and sisters.

As with all of my families, my first visit with Ann, Rud, Jay, Kate, and Amy included completing a parent inventory and a skills preference checklist. The inventory included such items as Jay's daily schedule: What did he do each day? What did he need help with? What was important to him and to his family? I also identified his level of performance and past experiences with certain functional activities, such as grocery shopping, domestic chores, riding a public bus, and having a job. Finally, it looked at future goals: Where did Jay want to work? Where was he going to live? Who would be his friends?

From this inventory, we moved to the preference checklist. On the basis of Jay's activities and skill levels, we figured out what Jay should spend his time learning while in school. Once all of this was done, we picked specific goals and objectives to work on for that year and plugged them into a weekly schedule. What seemed to me to be "just doing my job as a special education teacher" often had a profound effect on families. I remember

Ann and Rud's being awed by this process. As parents of a young man with disabilities, they greatly valued the opportunity to work with the schools to tailor a program for their son. Their enthusiasm and excitement with Jay's program helped sustain me through some of the more trying school days.

Continued communication with the family is critical to the success of any school program. As did all of my students, Jay carried his home-school communication notebook back and forth with him each day. This was my lifeline with the family. Any issues, problems, great ideas, changes in schedule, or good things that happened were written down in that notebook. In fact, it was such an important chronicle of our school year that when Jay graduated, we fought over who would keep the notebook! Our compromise was to make a copy for me as a keepsake.

Parent-professional partnerships require give-and-take on both sides. What was most important to me in my relationship with the Turnbulls was their willingness to support me and follow through with Jay's program at home. Ann mentioned that Jay was the manager of the football team, but what

she left out was that Rud and Kate enthusiastically attended just about every game, both home and away. They were there not only to cheer the Whitman Vikings but also to support Jay, and through Jay, me and my program.

Knowing that Ann and Rud were there to support my efforts was the most critical component of Jay's successful year. Their involvement provided me with the sustenance to continue my efforts and to continue to improve my program. A school- and community-based program requires more than an 8-hour day. It touches the lives of not only the student and teacher but also the family, school friends, neighbors, employers, store workers, bus drivers, and all who come in contact with that student and family. Establishing a positive and mutually beneficial family-professional partnership requires much effort and skill, but the outcomes of such a relationship far outweigh the efforts.

Reprinted with the permission of Simon & Schuster, Inc. Adapted from "Family and Professional Interaction" by A. P. Turnbull & M. E. Morningstar, 1993. In M. E. Snell, *Instruction of Students with Severe Disabilities* (4th ed) (pp. 31–32). Englewood Cliffs, NJ: Merrill/Prentice Hall, Inc.

____ Employability skills

____ Study habits

____ Making friends

____ Planning for the future

____ Other _____

Bailey and Simeonsson (1988a) have developed the Family Needs Survey, consisting of 35 items organized into six categories (e.g., needs for information, support, financial needs, family functioning). Because they have obtained different profiles of responses for mothers and fathers, they recommend that both mothers and fathers complete the needs survey. Bailey and Simeonsson also recommend combining open-ended questions with an overall assessment of family needs. They simply ask parents to list on a piece of paper their "five greatest needs as a family." By examining the results of needs assessment questionnaires, parents and professionals together can plan parent education groups that are responsive to parents' real needs.

TABLE 13.4
Possible topics for parent education and support groups

1. Self-help skills (dressing, brushing teeth, etc.)	22. Bicycle safety
2. Leisure-time activities	23. Interpretation of test results
3. Participation in IEP process	24. How to help your mainstreamed child adjust/succeed in the regular class
4. Summer reading program	
5. Teaching your child responsibility and organization	25. Dealing with sibling rivalry
6. Interacting with peers	26. Reading to your child at home
7. Preparing for the family vacation	27. Dealing effectively with significant others
8. Developing and implementing family rules	28. Program for grandparents
9. Safety in the home	29. Fathers-only program
10. Recreation/physical education activities to do at home	30. Organizing morning activities
	31. Home fire safety and escape
11. Gardening with a child with disabilities	32. Helping your child make friends
12. Adapting your home for a wheelchair	33. Setting up a parent-run resource room
13. Adapting your home for child who is blind	34. Organizing a summer odd-job program for children
14. Community resources for parents of children with disabilities	35. Organizing a parent-run respite care exchange system
15. Eating/mealtime behaviors	36. Acceptance and use of prosthetic equipment
16. Shopping skills	37. Preparing for your child's future
17. How to choose/train a baby-sitter	38. Dealing with professionals
18. Making a home study carrel	39. Selection and care of pets for children with disabilities
19. Cooking skills/activities	
20. Speech activities/games	40. Developing a parent-to-parent support group
21. Home-school communication systems (notes, telephone)	

How Much Parent Involvement?

It is easy for educators to get carried away with a concept, especially one like parent involvement, that has so much promise for positive outcome. But teachers and everyone else involved in providing special education services to children with disabilities should not take a one-sided view of parent involvement. Sometimes the time and energy required for parents to participate in home treatment programs or parent education groups cause stress among family members or guilt if the parents cannot fulfill teachers' expectations (Doernberg, 1978; Winton & Turnbull, 1981). The time required to provide additional help to a child with disabilities may take too much time and attention away from other family members (Kroth, 1981; Turnbull & Turnbull, 1982).

When helping families assess their strengths and needs, professionals must not overlook the importance of leisure time.

Kroth (1981) and his colleagues have developed a model guide for parent involvement—the Mirror Model for Parental Involvement—that recognizes that parents have a great deal to offer, as well as a need to receive services from special educators. The model assumes that not all parents need everything that professionals have to offer and that no parent should be expected to provide everything. The Mirror Model attempts to give parents an equal part in deciding what services they need and what services they might provide to professionals or other parents. The top half of the model, as illustrated in Figure 13.3, assumes that professionals have certain information, knowledge, and skills that should be shared with parents to help them with their children. The bottom half of the model assumes that parents have information, knowledge, and skills that can help professionals be more effective in assisting children.

Cone, Delawyer, and Wolfe (1985) developed the Parent/Family Involvement Index to objectively measure 12 types of parent involvement in a special education program.

✳ *Guidelines for Working with Parents and Families of Children with Disabilities*

No single approach or set of techniques will be effective or even appropriate with every parent and family. The following suggestions, however, can serve as valuable guidelines for professionals in their interactions with parents.

- *Do not assume that you know more about the child, his or her needs, and how those needs should be met than do the parents.* If you make this assumption, you

FIGURE 13.3
Mirror model for parent involvement in public schools

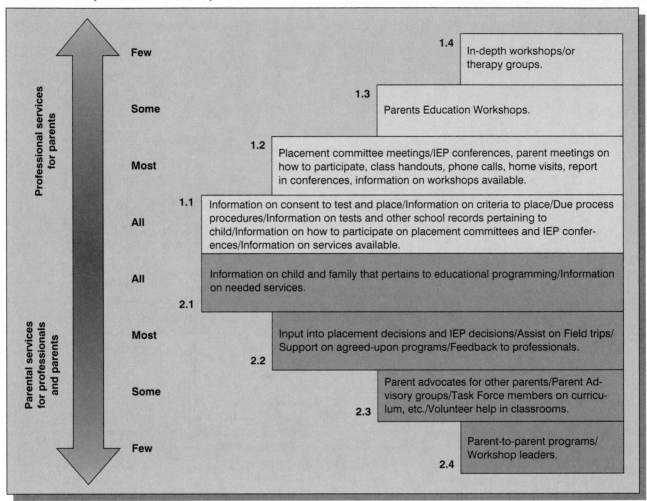

Source: From "Involvement with Parents of Behaviorally Disordered Adolescents" by R. Kroth, in *Educating Adolescents with Behavior Disorders* (p. 129) by G. Brown, R. L. McDowell, and J. Smith (Eds.), 1981, Columbus, OH: Merrill. Reprinted by permission.

will often be wrong and, worse, will miss opportunities to get and provide meaningful information.

- *Speak in plain, everyday language.* Using educationese does not help a professional communicate effectively with parents (or anyone else, for that matter). Lovitt (1982), a strong believer that we must "junk our jargon," gives us this example from a student's official folder:

    Art shows apraxia due to a vestibular-based deficit. He has laterality, proprioceptive, and sensorimotor dysfunction. Postural ocular deficits are present. He prefers to use right hand but his left hand is more accurate in kinesthesia and proprioception. Nystagmus is depressed during vestibular stimulation. Motor planning activities are difficult for him. (p. 303)

Such a description is of little value to Art's teachers and parents. It would be much better to state clearly what things Art can do now, and what specific things he needs to learn to do.

- *Do not let generalizations about parents of children with disabilities guide your efforts.* If you are genuinely interested in what a father or mother feels or needs, ask. Do not assume a parent is in the x, y, or z stage and therefore needs a, b, or c.

- *Do not be defensive toward or intimidated by parents.* No, you cannot really know what being the parent of a child with disabilities is like unless you are one. But as a trained teacher, you know a great deal about how to help children with disabilities learn; you do it every day, with lots of children. Offer the knowledge and skills you have without apology, and welcome parents' input.

- *Maintain primary concern for the child.* If you are a child's teacher, you interact with parents and families in an effort to improve the child's educational program. In that role, you are not a marriage counselor or therapist. If a parent or family member indicates the need for non-special-education services, offer to refer him or her to professionals trained and qualified to provide those services.

- *Help parents strive for realistic optimism.* Children with disabilities and their families benefit little from professionals who either are doom-and-gloom types or minimize the significance of a disability. Professionals should help parents analyze and prepare for their child's future (Giangreco et al., 1993; Turnbull & Turnbull, 1990).

- *Start with something parents can be successful with.* Involvement in their child's educational program is a new experience for many parents. Do not punish parents who show an interest in helping their child at home by setting them up to fail by giving them complicated materials, complex instructions, and a heavy schedule of nightly tutoring. Begin with something simple that is likely to be rewarding to the parent.

- *Do not be afraid to say, "I don't know."* Sometimes parents ask questions that you cannot answer or need services that you cannot provide. It is okay to say, "I don't know." The mark of a real professional is knowing when you need help, and parents will think more highly of you (Giangreco, Cloninger, Mueller, Yuan, & Ashworth, 1990).

✳ *Current Issues and Future Trends*

Special educators and families of children with disabilities will continue to develop more effective ways of working together. These efforts will probably be increasingly driven by values such as those suggested by the Syracuse University Center on Human Policy (1987): (a) Families should receive the supports necessary to maintain their children at home, (b) family services should support the entire family, and (c) family supports should maximize the family's control over the services and supports they receive. Thus, we predict that family preservation and family empowerment will increasingly become the goals of working with families with children with disabilities. Family-centered services are predicated on the belief that the child is part of a family system and that effective change for the child (who is one part of the system) cannot be achieved without helping the entire family (the whole system) (Turnbull & Turnbull, 1990). The rationale for family empowerment is based on the belief that families are the primary and most effective social institution, that families cannot be replaced, that parents are and should remain in charge of their families, and that the role of professionals is to help parents in their capacity as family leaders (Callister, Mitchell, & Talley, 1986).

The changing demographics of our society mean that educators will increasingly work with families from culturally and linguistically diverse backgrounds (Lynch & Hanson, 1992). The information needs and support services desired by families from different cultural and ethnic groups may vary, and majority educators must work to be sensitive to those differences (Sontag & Schacht, 1994). Thomas, Correa, & Morsink (1995) stress the importance of majority educators and minority families working collaboratively:

> The role of the professional working with the culturally diverse family is multifaceted. Professionals must first assess their own biases toward different ethnic groups. Second, they must make an effort to understand the family. At the same time, the minority family must be helped to understand and participate in the traditional Anglo mainstream culture. Acculturation into school life is a two-way process in which professionals and families collaborate. (p. 263)

Correa (1989) recommends strategies professionals can use:

- Empowering families with skills for adapting to and coping with a school system different from what they are used to
- Providing written and oral information in ways family members can understand
- Assisting families through the transition from the native culture to the mainstream school culture
- Serving as *cultural brokers* between the majority and minority culture
- Serving as a mediator and advocate for the minority group
- Removing linguistic and communication differences to enhance interaction
- Assessing the family in terms of experiences in their native country; the role and expectations of extended family members and siblings; the types and amount of community support available; religious, spiritual, and/or cultural beliefs related to parenting practices

Wayman, Lynch, and Hanson (1990) provide guidelines for professionals making home visits to families from diverse cultural backgrounds.

Professionals and parents are working to develop and provide a wide range of supportive services for families of children with disabilities. Programs are being implemented to help parents plan effectively for the future, develop problem-solving skills, and acquire competence in financial planning, coping with stress, locating and using community services, and finding time to relax and enjoy life, to name just a few areas of emphasis. In addition, the development and provision of quality respite care services have become major issues in many communities. Simply defined, *respite care* is the temporary care of a disabled individual for the purpose of providing relief to the parent and guardian (Salisbury & Intaglia, 1986). Many parents of children with severe disabilities identify the availability of reliable, high-quality respite care as their single most pressing need (Grant & McGrath, 1990; Rimmerman, 1989). Fortunately, because of the efforts of parent advocacy groups and concerned professionals, respite services are becoming more and more available throughout the country.

Parents and family are the most important people in a child's life. Good teachers should be next in importance. Working together, teachers, parents, and families can and do make a difference.

"We were really getting worn down. During the first 4 years of Ben's life, we averaged 4 hours of sleep a night. We were wearing ourselves out; I have no doubt we would have completely fallen apart," said Ben's mother, Rebecca Arnett. Ben was born with a neurological condition that produces frequent seizures and extreme hyperactivity. "My husband, Roger, used his vacations for sleeping in. The respite program came along just in time for us.

"It was hard at first. There's an overwhelming guilt that you shouldn't leave your child. We didn't feel like anyone else could understand Ben's problems. But we had to get away. Our church gave us some money, with orders to take a vacation. It was the first time Roger and I and our 12-year-old daughter, Stacy, had really been together since Ben was born. I was upset at first, calling twice a day to see if everything was all right. But it was wonderful, for everybody."

"Cleo, the respite care worker who stayed with Ben that first time and many times since, is something else. She takes him to McDonald's, shopping, all over. When Ben knows she's coming, he runs for his jacket. He loves her. We've had five or six different respite workers stay with Ben during the year we've used the program, and he likes them all.

"Once parents get over that initial period of letting go, they realize that it's OK to have a life of your own apart from your handicapped child. For us it was a real lifesaver."

Ed Harper, director of Residential and Family Services for Franklin County, Ohio, explains: "Respite gives families a chance for a more natural lifestyle. Some of the families we serve have gone years without a real break of any kind. Once they try our program and find that a responsible, trained adult can care for their child, it's like a new lease on life.

"At present we are serving about 300 families. Each respite worker completes a 40-hour training program covering feeding techniques, first aid, use of adaptive equipment, leisure-time activities, and so on. We conduct an initial home visit to explain the program and determine the family's spe-cial needs. Our workers can be scheduled for any length of time, from 4 hours up to 2 weeks of continuous care. Our respite care is conducted in the family's home or at a respite facility. A sliding-fee scale determines the hourly cost according to income and family size."

Respite care can benefit the family member with disabilities as well. Susan Clark told of the time she stayed with Stephanie, a 25-year-old woman with mental retardation, so that her mother, who had not had a vacation since her daughter's birth, could go to Florida. "Stephanie and I went everywhere—to the movies, the county fair, out to eat. She did things she had never done in her life. That week was a vacation for her, too."

Another parent, Jean Williams, describes the program this way: "Our son Tom's autism has meant a lot of restrictions in our family life for the past 25 years, bringing with it many problems and much resentment. At last we have been given a no-strings-attached, low-cost way to loosen some of those restrictions. Funny thing is, our Tom is such a nice guy—it's sure good to be able to get far enough away every so often to be able to see that."

Summary

The Parent-Teacher Partnership

- A successful parent-teacher partnership provides benefits for the professional, the parents, and—most important—the child.

- Actions of parents, concerned educators, and legislators have all helped increase parent participation in the special education process.

Effects of a Child's Disabilities on Parents and Family

- All parents and family members must adjust to the birth of a child with disabilities or the discovery that a child has a disability. This adjustment process is different for each parent, and educators should not make assumptions about an individual parent's stage of adjustment.

- A family member's disability is likely to affect parents and siblings without disabilities in different ways during the different stages of the life cycle.
- Parents face extra challenges and responsibilities in raising children with disabilities, including teaching and counseling the child, managing behavior, dealing with their other children and other significant people, maintaining the parent-to-parent relationship, and relating to the school and community.
- Children with disabilities are overrepresented among reported cases of child abuse and neglect. The presence of a disability, however, is just one of a complex set of variables related to child abuse. Most parents of children with disabilities provide a loving and supportive home.

Parent-Teacher Communication

- Regular two-way communication is critical to effective parent-teacher partnerships.
- Conferences, written messages, and telephone calls are three ways to maintain communication.

Parent Involvement

- The extent to which individual parents participate in IEP and IFSP meetings varies, but educators can use many strategies to increase participation.
- Many parents can and should learn to help teach their child with disabilities.

- Parents and professionals should work together in planning and conducting parent education groups.

Guidelines for Working with Parents and Families of Children with Disabilities

- Do not assume you know more about a child than do the parents.
- Speak in plain, everyday language.
- Do not use generalizations or assumptions.
- Do not be defensive toward or intimidated by parents.
- Keep concern for the child at the forefront.
- Help parents strive for realistic optimism.
- Start with something with which parents can be successful.
- Do not be afraid to say, "I don't know."

Current Issues and Future Trends

- Professionals who work with parents should value family needs and support families in maintaining control over the services and supports they receive.
- Educators must learn to respect cultural and ethnic differences when working with families.
- Respite care—the temporary care of an individual with disabilities by nonfamily members—is a critical support for many families with children with severe disabilities.

For More Information

Journal

The Exceptional Parent. Mission is to empower mothers and fathers of children with disabilities by providing practical information and emotional support. Contains articles for parents and professionals on subjects such as improving parent-professional relationships, maintaining family relationships, and managing financial resources. Published six times per year by the Psy-Ed Corporation, P.O. Box 3000, Dept. EP, Denville, NJ 07834.

Books

Baker, B. L. (1989). *Parent training and developmental disabilities.* Washington, DC: American Association on Mental Retardation.

Cutler, B. C. (1993). *You, your child, and "special" education: A guide to making the system work.* Baltimore: Paul H. Brookes.

Gartner, A., Lipsky, D. K., & Turnbull, A. P. (1990). *Supporting families with a child with a disability.* Baltimore: Paul H. Brookes.

Kroth, R. (1985). *Communicating with parents of exceptional children* (2nd ed.). Denver: Love.

Lutzker, J. R., & Campbell, R. (1994). *Ecobehavioral family interventions in developmental disabilities.* Pacific Grove, CA: Brooks/Cole.

Mullins, J. (1987). Authentic voices from parents of exceptional children. *Family Relations, 36,* 30–33. (This journal article contains a list of 60 books written by parents of children with various disabilities.)

Salisbury, C. L., & Intaglia, J. (1986). *Respite care support for persons with developmental disabilities and their families.* Baltimore: Paul H. Brookes.

Shea, T. M., & Bauer, A. M. (1993). *Parents and teachers of children with exceptionalities.* Needham Heights, MA: Allyn & Bacon.

Simpson, R. L. (1990). *Conferencing parents of exceptional children* (2nd ed.). Austin, TX: PRO-ED.

Singer, G. H. S., & Powers, L. E. (Eds.). (1993). *Families, disability, and empowerment: Active coping skills and strategies for family interventions.* Baltimore: Paul H. Brookes.

Stewart, J. C. (1986). *Counseling parents of exceptional children* (2nd ed.). New York: Merrill/Macmillan.

Turnbull, A. P., & Turnbull, H. R., III (1990). *Families, professionals, and exceptionality: A special partnership* (2nd ed.). New York: Macmillan.

Turnbull, H. R., III, & Turnbull, A. P. (1985). *Parents speak out: Then and now* (2nd ed.). New York: Merrill/Macmillan.

Organizations

National Center on Child Abuse and Neglect, U.S. Department of Health and Human Services, P. O. Box 1182, Washington, DC 20013. Offers Child Help USA Hotline with a toll-free number: (800) 422-4453.

National Parent Network on Disabilities, 1600 Prince Street, #115, Alexandria, VA 22314. (Phone V-TDD: 703-684-6763). A consortium and clearinghouse of information about parent training and information centers, parent groups, and professional organizations with interest in parent and family issues.

National Parent CHAIN, 515 West Giles Lane, Peoria, IL 61614. A volunteer organization to establish a national information and education network for citizens with disabilities and their families.

Pacer (Parent Advocacy Coalition for Educational Rights) Center, 4701 Chicago Avenue South, Minneapolis, MN 55407.

Parents Educational Advocacy Center, 116 West Jones Street, Raleigh, NC 27611.

PEP (Parents Educating Parents) Project, Georgia Association for Retarded Citizens, 1851 Ram Runway, Suite 104, College Park, GA 30337.

The Federation of Families for Children's Mental Health, 1021 Prince Street, Alexandria, VA, 22314-2071. A national parent-run organization focused on the needs of children and youths with emotional, behavioral, or mental disorders and their families.

Early Childhood Special Education

- Why is it so difficult to measure the effectiveness of early intervention programs?

- How can we provide early intervention services for a child whose disability is not yet present?

- Why are developmentally appropriate practices not always sufficient for a young child who is exhibiting significant developmental delays?

- Which of the many goals of early childhood special education do you think are most important?

- Why is a multidisciplinary team so critical to effective early intervention?

*M*ost children experience a phenomenal amount of learning from the time they are born until they enter school. They grow and develop in orderly, predictable ways, learning to move about their world, communicate, and play. As their ability to manipulate their environment increases, so does their level of independence. Normal rates and patterns of child development contrast sharply with the progress experienced by most children with disabilities. If they are to master the basic skills that most children acquire naturally, many preschoolers with disabilities need carefully planned and implemented instruction.

Not too many years ago, parents who were concerned about deficits in their child's development were told, "Don't worry. Wait and see. She'll probably grow out of it." As a result, many children with disabilities fell further and further behind their typically developing peers. Only recently have educators become convinced of the need for early identification and intervention. From a virtual absence of educational programs for young children with disabilities 25 years ago, early childhood special education is today one of the most prominent and fastest growing components in all of education. Virtually every special educator now recognizes the importance of early intervention services not only for infants, toddlers, and preschoolers with disabilities but also for young children who are at risk for developing a disability. Indeed, developing an effective system of early intervention services has become a national priority.

✴ *Effects of Early Intervention*
A Definition of Early Intervention

Literally hundreds of studies have attempted to determine the effects of early intervention. Before looking at a few of them, we will consider a definition of early intervention.

Early intervention consists of a wide variety of educational, nutritional, childcare, and family supports, all designed to reduce the effects of disabilities or prevent the occurrence of learning and developmental problems later in life for children presumed to be at risk for such problems. McConnell (1994) provides an excellent definition of early intervention:

> Early intervention can be defined as a loosely structured confederation of publicly and privately funded home- and classroom-based efforts that provide (1) compensatory or preventative services for children who are assumed to be at risk for learning and behavior problems later in life, particularly during the elementary school years, and (2) remedial services for problems or deficits already encountered. . . . Simply put, early intervention must provide early identification and provision of services to reduce or eliminate the effects of disabilities or to prevent the development of other problems, so that the need for subsequent special services is reduced. (pp. 75, 78)

Early Studies

Skeels and Dye (1939) reported the earliest and one of the most dramatic demonstrations of the critical importance of early intervention. Because there was no room at an orphanage, two "hopeless" baby girls, aged 13 and 16 months, had been transferred from an orphanage to a ward of adult women in an institution for persons with mental retardation. "The youngsters were pitiful little creatures. They were tearful, had runny noses, and coarse, stringy, and colorless hair; they were emaciated, undersized, and lacked muscle tone or responsiveness. Sad and inactive, the two spent their days rocking and whining" (Skeels, 1966, p. 5). At the time of their transfer, the two children had IQs estimated between 35 and 46, which classified them in the moderate to severe range of mental retardation. After living with the older women for 6 months, the girls' IQs were measured at 77 and 87, and a few months later, both had IQs in the mid-90s. Such regular intelligence testing was not a common procedure, but because of their unusual placement, the two children were observed closely.

After hearing of the girls' remarkable improvement, Skeels and Dye looked for possible causes. They learned that the children had received an unusual amount of attention and stimulation. Ward attendants had purchased toys and books for the girls, and residents had played and talked with them continuously. Excited by the possibilities, Skeels and Dye convinced the state authorities to permit a most unusual experiment. They selected 13 additional 1- to 2-year-old children. All but two were classified as mentally retarded (average IQ of 64) and, because of a prevailing state law, were judged unsuitable for adoption. The children in this experimental group were removed from the unstimulating orphanage and placed in the one-to-one care of teenage girls with mental retardation who lived at the institution. Each adolescent "mother" was taught how to provide basic care and attention for her baby—how to hold, feed, talk to, and stimulate the child. The children also attended a half-morning kindergarten program at the institution.

A group of 12 children, also under 3 years of age, remained in the orphanage. Children in this contrast group received adequate medical and health services but no individual attention. The children in the contrast group had an average IQ of 86 at the beginning of the study; only two were classified as mentally retarded.

Two years later, the children in both groups were retested. The experimental group showed an average *gain* of 27.5 IQ points, enough for 11 of the 13 children to become eligible for adoption and be placed in good homes. The children in the contrast group who stayed in the orphanage had *lost* an average of 26 IQ points.

Twenty-five years later, Skeels (1966) located all of the subjects in the original study. What he discovered was even more impressive than the IQ gains originally reported. Of the 13 children in the experimental group, 11 had married; the marriages had produced nine children, all of normal intelligence, and only one of the marriages had ended in divorce. The experimental group's median level of education was the 12th grade, and four had attended college. All were either homemakers or employed outside the home, in jobs ranging from professional and business work to domestic service (for the two who had not been adopted). The story for the 12 children who had remained in the orphanage was less positive. Four were still institutionalized in 1965, and all but one of the noninstitutionalized subjects who were employed were working as unskilled laborers. The median level of education for the contrast group was the third grade. Skeels (1966) concluded his follow-up study with these words:

> It seems obvious that under present-day conditions there are still countless infants with sound biological constitutions and potentialities for development well within the normal range who will become retarded and noncontributing members of society unless appropriate intervention occurs. It is suggested by the findings of this

Access to developmentally appropriate toys provides tremendous benefits to young children with disabilities. All of the toys included in the *Toy Guide for Differently-Abled Kids!* published by Toys "Я" Us have been tested with preschoolers with disabilities and are identified according to their likelihood of promoting growth in 1 or more of 10 developmental or skill areas. The catalog is endorsed by the National Parent Network on Disabilities.

study and others published in the past 20 years that sufficient knowledge is available to design programs of intervention to counteract the devastating effects of poverty, sociocultural, and maternal deprivation. . . . The unanswered questions of this study could form the basis for many life-long research projects. If the tragic fate of the twelve contrast group children provokes even a single crucial study that will help prevent such a fate for others, their lives will not have been in vain. (p. 109)

Although the Skeels and Dye study can be criticized for its lack of tight experimental methodology, it provided a major challenge to the belief that intelligence was fixed and that, therefore, little could be expected from intervention efforts. This classic study served as the foundation and catalyst for many subsequent investigations into the effects of early intervention.

Kirk (1958) reported another often-cited study highlighting the importance of early intervention. This study measured the effects of 2 years of preschool training on the social and cognitive development of 43 children with mental retardation (IQs ranging from 40 to 85). Fifteen of the children in the experimental group lived in an institution and attended a nursery school; 28 children lived at home and attended a preschool program. Children in the control group—12 in an institution and 26 living at home—did not receive the preschool training. The children who received early intervention gained between 10 and 30 IQ points; the IQ scores of the control group children declined. The differences between the groups were maintained over a period of years.

The Milwaukee Project

The Milwaukee Project is another widely cited effort in early intervention (Garber & Heber, 1973; Heber & Garber, 1971; Strickland, 1971). The project's goal was to reduce the incidence of mental retardation through a program of parent education and infant stimulation for children considered to have a high potential for retarded

A stimulating, language-rich environment enhances the social and cognitive development of all young children.

development because of their mothers' levels of intelligence and conditions of poverty. Mothers with IQs of 70 or less and their high-risk infants were chosen as subjects. The mothers received training in child care and were taught how to interact with and stimulate their children. Beginning before the age of 6 months, the children also participated in an infant stimulation program conducted by trained teachers. By the age of 3½, the experimental children tested an average of 33 IQ points higher than a control group of children who did not participate in the program.

Hailed by the popular media as the "Miracle in Milwaukee," this study is sometimes offered as proof that a program of maternal education and early infant stimulation can reduce the incidence of mental retardation caused by psychosocial disadvantage. The Milwaukee Project has, however, been criticized for its research methods. Page (1972), for example, questions whether bias in sampling and testing was adequately controlled. Nevertheless, according to Garber and Heber (1973):

> Infant testing difficulties notwithstanding, the present standardized test data, when considered along with performance on learning tasks and language tests, indicate an unquestionably superior present level of cognitive development on the part of the experimental group. Also, the first wave of our children are now in public schools. None have been assigned to classes for the retarded. (p. 114)

Recent Demonstrations of the Effectiveness of Intensive Early Intervention

Two variables that appear highly related to outcome effectiveness of early intervention are the intensity of the intervention and the level of participation. Ramey and Ramey (1992) summarize the results of three early intervention projects that show strong evidence that children at risk for developmental delays and poor school outcomes respond favorably to intensive, systematic early intervention. The Abecedarian Project was an experiment to test whether mental retardation caused by psychosocial disadvantage could be prevented by intensive, early education preschool programs (in conjunction with medical and nutritional supports) beginning shortly after birth and continuing until the children entered kindergarten (Martin, Ramey, & Ramey, 1990). Children in the Abecedarian Project received early intervention that was both intensive and of long duration: a full-day preschool program, 5 days per week, 50 weeks per year. Compared with children in a control group who received supplemental medical, nutritional, and social services but did *not* receive daily early educational intervention services, children in the early intervention group made positive gains in IQ scores by age 3, were 50% less likely to fail a grade, and scored higher on IQ and reading and mathematics achievement tests at age 12.

A related finding was that children of low-IQ mothers benefited the most from early intervention. The authors report that at age 3, for the mothers with IQs below 70 who were in the control condition, all but one of their children had IQs in the mentally retarded or borderline intelligence range. In contrast, all of the children in the early intervention group tested in the normal range of intelligence (>85) by age 3.

> This new finding is consistent with a selection principle identified as *targeted intervention,* which indicates that primary prevention of childhood disorders is more likely for certain subgroups than for others (Landesman & Ramey, 1989). Because the majority of children with mild and moderate mental retardation come from families with extremely low resources and with parents who have limited intellectual resources themselves, these families are the ones that are most in need of early

During a period of 15 years, the Milwaukee Project continued to provide education and family support services to children born of low-IQ mothers. A book by Garber (1988), the coordinator of the project's research team, claims significant improvements in intelligence, language performance, and academic achievement for the children who received services, compared with a control group of disadvantaged children from mothers of average intelligence.

Weisburg (1994) describes a successful early intervention prevention program in which preschoolers from low-income backgrounds received 2 years of intensive reading instruction based on the Direct Instruction model and materials (see Chapter 5) before they entered kindergarten.

intervention and are those that benefit the most in terms of outcomes valued by society. (Ramey & Ramey, 1992, p. 338)

Project CARE, the second study reported by Ramey and Ramey (1992), compared the effectiveness of home-based early intervention in which mothers learned how to provide developmental stimulation for their infants and toddlers with center-based early intervention like that provided in the Abecedarian Project (Wasik, Ramey, Bryant, & Sparling, 1990). Children who received the full-day, center-based preschool program 5 days per week, supplemented by home visits, showed gains in the intellectual functioning "almost identical" to those found in the Abecedarian Project. A "disappointing finding" was that the intellectual functioning of children in the home-based-only treatment group did not improve. Ramey and Ramey suggest, "One plausible interpretation of these results is that the home-based treatment was not sufficiently intensive, on a day-to-day basis, to produce the same benefits that occur when a more formally organized and monitored center-based program is provided year round" (1992, p. 339).

The Infant Health and Development Program extended the early intervention techniques developed in the first two studies to infants who were born prematurely and at low birth weight (<2,500 g, or about 5½ pounds), two conditions that place children at risk for developmental delays (Ramey et al., 1992). This large-scale study involved nearly 1,000 children and their families in eight locations throughout the United States. Home visits were conducted from shortly after birth through age 3. Because of health problems associated with prematurity and low birth weight, the children did not begin attending the center-based early education program until 12 months of age and continued until age 3. Improvements in intellectual functioning were noted, with babies of comparatively higher birth weight showing increases similar in magnitude to those found in the Abecedarian Project and Project CARE.

Of particular interest was the finding concerning the relation between how much children and their families participated in the early intervention and the intellectual development of the children. Figure 14.1 shows the percentage of children in the control group and in low, medium, and high levels of participation. Levels of participation describe how actively the family participated in the project's three major components: (a) number of scheduled home visits completed, (b) number of group parent meetings attended, and (c) the child's attendance at the center preschool program. The percentages of children whose IQ scores fell in the range associated with mental retardation based on IQ tests administered at age 3 for each of the groups were 17% for the control group, 13% of the low participation, 4% of the medium participation, and less than 2% of the high participation. The most active participants had an almost ninefold reduction in the incidence of mental retardation compared to the control group.

Together, the results of these three studies summarized by Ramey and Ramey (1992) "support the proposition that intensive early educational intervention can produce long-lasting benefits in both intellectual performance and school achievement" (p. 342).

Many other studies have attempted to measure early intervention outcomes. White, Bush, and Casto (1986) conducted a "review of reviews" and found that 94% of a sample of 52 previous reviews of the literature concluded that early intervention resulted in substantial immediate benefits for children with disabilities, those at risk, and those living in impoverished environments. The immediate benefits included improved cognitive, language, social-emotional, and motor growth and better rela-

Male children are usually more vulnerable to physical impairments and developmental delay as a result of prenatal anomalies, birth injury, low birth weight, and childhood disease (Jaklin, 1989). A longitudinal study of children in a Swedish community, however, found that low-birth-weight girls suffered greater relative impairments in IQ scores and school achievement at ages 10 and 13 than did low-birth-weight boys (Lagerström, Bremme, Eneroth, & Magnusson, 1991).

FIGURE 14.1

Percentage of low-birth-weight children at age 3 with IQ scores indicative of intellectual performance at the borderline (≤ 85) and mild (≤ 70) levels of mental retardation within a control group (pediatric follow-up) and three levels of participation in an early intervention program

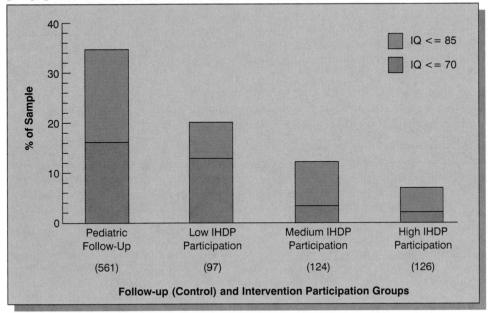

Source: From "Effective Early Intervention" by C. T. Ramey and S. L. Ramey, *Mental Retardation,* 1992, *30,* p. 341. Used by permission.

tionships and functioning with parents and siblings. Analyzing the long-term effects of early intervention, Lazar and Darlington (1982) pooled the data from 12 follow-up studies of children who had participated in preschool programs for socioeconomically disadvantaged children. At the time of the follow-up studies, the children who had participated in the preschool programs were in the 3rd to 12th grades. Fewer of the early intervention children had been placed in special education classes (14% vs. 29%), and fewer had been held back to repeat a school year (26% vs. 37%).

Questions About the Research Base

Although the results reported on the long-term efficacy of early intervention are generally positive, numerous methodological problems make it difficult to conduct this kind of research in a scientifically sound manner (Bricker, 1986; Dunst, 1986; Strain & Smith, 1986). Among the problems are the difficulties in selecting meaningful and reliable outcome measures; the wide disparity among children in the developmental effects of their disabilities; the tremendous variation across early intervention programs in curriculum focus, teaching strategies, length, and intensity; and the ethical concerns of withholding early intervention from some children so that they may form a control group for comparison purposes (Bailey & Wolery, 1992; Casto, 1988; Guralnick, 1988).

In a meta-analysis of 74 studies investigating the efficacy of early intervention with preschool children with disabilities, Casto and Mastropieri (1986) conclude that early intervention produces positive effects and that longer, more intensive pro-

Reviews of the efficacy of early intervention can be found in Bailey and Wolery (1992); Bricker (1986); Dunst, Snyder, and Mankinen (1986); Guralnick (1991); Odom and Karnes (1988); and Smith and Strain (1984).

grams are generally more effective. They did not, however, find support for two conclusions common to the majority of previous reviews of the literature: They found no evidence that early intervention programs are more effective when begun at an earlier age, as opposed to a later age, and they disagreed with previous reviewers who concluded that greater levels of parental involvement are associated with greater effectiveness. Casto and Mastropieri's paper has drawn heavy criticism from other experts on early intervention research, who claim the analysis suffers from conceptual and methodological weaknesses (e.g., Dunst & Snyder, 1986; Strain & Smith, 1986).

In concluding their critique of the Casto and Mastropieri analysis, Strain and Smith (1986), for example, comment on the large but admittedly scientifically questionable body of research that generally indicates positive outcomes of early intervention:

> What do we do then with a data base that is flawed or that offers conflicting results? First, we do not need to apologize for lack of rigor. The methodological weaknesses do not so much reflect poor science or scientists as the reality of field research on complicated questions. The unassailable educational experiment that proves causality once and for all is a myth. Yet, we should not stop trying, with scientific methods, to understand the complexity. . . . Experiments principally designed to determine whether or not early intervention is effective lose their vitality and usefulness. If it looks like a pig, roots, and snorts, it probably is a pig. Similarly, if it looks like we get effects, some weak, some strong, some ambiguous, there probably is a relation between intervention and child outcomes. . . . Policy and program developers have a professional imperative to proceed using the least dangerous assumption that providing appropriate early intervention services is beneficial to handicapped infants, preschoolers, and their families. (pp. 263–264)

Most special educators agree with this position and believe that early intervention and preschool services can accomplish the following benefits for children with disabilities, those who are at risk for developmental delays, and their families:

- Help produce gains in physical development, cognitive development, language and speech development, social competence, and self-help skills
- Help prevent the development of secondary disabilities
- Reduce family stress and help parents and families support the development of a young child with disabilities
- Reduce the need for special education services or placement in special classrooms once the child reaches school age
- Save society the costs of higher levels of educational and social services that will be needed later in life if early intervention is not provided (see Wood, 1981)
- Reduce the likelihood of social dependence in adulthood

Donnellan (1984) suggests that teachers, policy planners, and other human service providers use the *criterion of the least dangerous assumption* when objective data are not available to indicate clearly which placement, program, or procedure is the best or most appropriate. In these instances, decision makers should consider which option will do the least harm to children and their families.

❋ *Legislative Support for Early Childhood Special Education*

Early Education Program for Children with Disabilities

The development and implementation of early intervention services for young children with disabilities have been aided by federal legislation. The first federal law

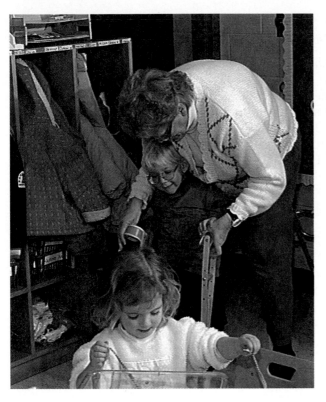

In addition to helping young children with disabilities make developmental gains, early intervention can help prevent secondary disabilities, provide needed support for parents and families, and reduce the need for special education services when children reach school age.

written exclusively for preschoolers with disabilities, the Handicapped Children's Early Childhood Assistance Act (PL 90–538), was passed in 1968. This bill created the Early Education Program for Children with Disabilities (EEPCD), the purpose of which is to develop model early intervention programs for children with disabilities from birth through age 8. Since it began, with 24 funded programs in 1969, EEPCD has funded more than 600 projects in all 50 states and several U.S. territories.

EEPCD model projects have collectively developed thousands of print and audiovisual products on early childhood special education, such as screening and assessment devices, curriculum guides, and parent training materials. Many of the products have been purchased and distributed by commercial publishers. Directors of EEPCD model demonstration projects that have been evaluated rigorously and proven worthy of replication can apply for outreach funds to help others set up similar programs elsewhere.

Head Start

In 1972 Head Start (a nationwide program begun in 1965 to provide preschool services to children from low-income families) was required by law to reserve at least 10% of its enrollment capacity for children with disabilities. Today, 13.4% of the 500,000 children enrolled in Head Start programs across the country are children with disabilities—a total of 36,133 children (Sinclair, 1993).

The EEPCD was originally called the Handicapped Children's Early Education Program (HCEEP). A *model program* evaluates the effectiveness of new assessment, curriculum, instructional procedures, and/or service delivery arrangements (or, as is often the case, a new combination of old techniques) with the hope that if the model proves effective, it can serve as the basis for developing other similar programs. See Karnes and Stayton (1988) for a review of 96 different EEPCD model programs for infants and toddlers. Suarez, Hurth, and Prestridge (1988) analyzed the characteristics of all 131 EEPCD programs funded during 1982–1986.

The Individuals with Disabilities Education Act (PL 94–142)

In 1973 the Division for Early Childhood (DEC) was established within the Council for Exceptional Children. With more than 7,000 members, DEC is the fourth largest division of CEC. For a chronology of federal legislation and support of early childhood special education, see Hebbeler, Smith, and Black (1991).

The Individuals with Disabilities Education Act (IDEA) of 1975 (PL 94–142), which mandated a free, appropriate public education for all school-age children with disabilities, also included a section on preschool special education. The law required that all children aged 3 to 5 with disabilities receive special education services if state law or practice already provided general public education for children in that age-group. To stimulate other states to begin programs for preschoolers with disabilities, the IDEA included an incentive grant program that provided funds for establishing or improving preschool programs for children with disabilities. The preschool incentive grants were distributed on the basis of the number of children identified in the state. Although the professionals, parents, and legislators who drafted the IDEA clearly endorsed the concept of early childhood special education, the incentive grant program was insufficient. By the 1980–81 school year, only 16 states provided special education services for the full 3- to 5-year-old range, and an additional 22 states required services for preschoolers with disabilities at the age of 4 or 5 (U.S. Comptroller General, 1981).

PL 99–457: The Federal Mandate for Early Childhood Special Education

Since 1975, Congress has enacted three bills reauthorizing and amending PL 94–142. The second of the bills—PL 99–457, the Education of the Handicapped Act Amendments of 1986—has been called "the most important legislation ever enacted for developmentally variable children" (Shonkoff & Meisels, 1990, p. 19).

PL 99–457 contains two major provisions concerning the early education of preschoolers with disabilities. Before passage of this law, Congress estimated that states were serving about 70% of children with disabilities aged 3 to 5 years under the voluntary provisions of PL 94–142; 31 states and territories did not require special education for at least part of that age-group (Koppelman, 1986). For infants and

The IDEA requires that special education be provided for all children with disabilities ages 3 to 5 years.

toddlers with disabilities from birth through age 2, systematic early intervention ser-vices were scarce or nonexistent in many states. PL 99–457 includes a mandatory preschool component for children 3 to 5 years old and a voluntary incentive grant program for early intervention services to infants and toddlers and their families.

Preschool Services for 3- to 5-Year-Olds

PL 99–457 requires states to provide preschool services to all children with disabili-ties aged 3 to 5 years. The regulations governing these programs are similar to those for PL 94–142, with these major exceptions:

1. Children do not have to be identified and reported under existing disability cate-gories (e.g., mental retardation, learning disabilities) in order to receive services.
2. IEPs must include a section with instructions and information for parents.
3. Local education agencies may elect to use a variety of service delivery options (home-based, center-based, or combination programs), and the length of the school day and school year may vary.
4. Preschool special education programs must be administered by the state educa-tion agency; however, services from other agencies may be contracted to meet the requirement of a full range of services.

Early Intervention for Infants and Toddlers

The second major change brought about by the passage of PL 99–457 was the provi-sion of incentive grants to give states 5 years in which to develop and implement "statewide, comprehensive, coordinated, multidisciplinary, interagency" services of early intervention for infants and toddlers with disabilities and their families. The law covers individuals from birth through age 2, inclusive, who need early intervention services because they

> (a) are experiencing developmental delays, as measured by appropriate diagnostic instruments and procedures in one or more of the following areas: Cognitive devel-opment, physical development, language and speech development, psychosocial development, or self-help skills, or (b) have a diagnosed physical or mental condi-tion which has a high probability of resulting in developmental delay.
>
> Such terms may also include, at a State's discretion, individuals from birth to age 2, inclusive, who are at risk of having substantial delay if early intervention services are not provided. (Section 672)

These federal regulations provide states with three categories of eligibility under which they can provide early intervention services to infants and toddlers: developmental delay, established conditions, and documented risk (Shonkoff & Meisels, 1991). *Developmental delay* includes children with significant delays or atypical patterns of development. Each state's definition of developmental delay must be broad enough to include all disability categories covered by the IDEA, but children do not need to be classified or labeled according to those categories in order to receive early intervention services. *Established conditions* include children with a diagnosed physical or medical condition that almost always results in develop-mental delay or disability. Examples of established conditions are Down syndrome, fragile-X syndrome or other conditions associated with mental retardation, brain or spinal cord damage, sensory impairments, fetal alcohol syndrome (FAS), and mater-nal acquired immune deficiency syndrome (AIDS).

By 1993, 41 states and jurisdictions were in full implementation sta-tus under PL 99–457 for the provision of early intervention services to infants and toddlers who have disabilities or are at risk and to their families; all but 1 of the remaining states had received an extended year of funding to bring their programs into compliance (U.S. Department of Educa-tion, 1994).

FAS is described later in this chapter.

Although they are not required to do so, states may also use funds provided by PL 99–457 to provide early intervention for infants and toddlers who fall under two types of *documented risk*. Children considered *biologically at risk* have a greater than usual probability of developmental delay or disability because of their pediatric histories or current biological conditions (e.g., significantly premature birth, low birth weight). Children may be considered *environmentally at risk* for developmental delay because of factors such as extreme poverty, parental substance abuse, homelessness, abuse or neglect, or parental intellectual impairment.

Individualized Family Services Plan

PL 99–457 represents a major shift in the focus of educational services. Consistent with current research and understanding of child learning and development, the legislation does not view children as isolated service recipients (Meisels & Provence, 1989). Instead, the law prescribes family-focused early intervention services, delivered according to an *Individualized Family Services Plan (IFSP)*. The IFSP is developed by a multidisciplinary team that includes the child's parents and family. Each IFSP must contain the following elements:

- A statement of the child's present level of functioning in cognitive, speech and language, psychosocial, motor, and self-help skills
- A statement of the family's strengths and needs relating to the child's development
- A statement of the major expected outcomes to be achieved for the child and family, including criteria, procedures, and time lines for evaluating progress
- A description of the specific early intervention services necessary to meet the unique needs of the child and family, including frequency, intensity, and method of delivering the services
- The projected dates for initiation and expected duration of services
- The name of the case manager from the profession most immediately relevant to the infant's, toddler's, or family's needs who will be responsible for implementation of the plan
- The steps to be taken to support a successful transition from early intervention (infant) services to the preschool program

The IFSP must be evaluated once a year and reviewed with the family at 6-month intervals. Recognizing the critical importance of time for the infant with disabilities, the law allows for initiation of early intervention services before the IFSP is completed, if the parents give their consent. "The IFSP effectively redefines the service recipient as being the family (rather than the child alone)" (Krauss, 1990, p. 388). These are examples of items that have been included as family goals on IFSPs:

- Family will locate reading materials about child's condition.
- Grandmother will learn handling techniques with child.
- Dad will learn to simplify activities that he enjoys so child can participate.
- Parents will make a 2-month medical appointment with the physicians.
- Family will integrate the child's developmental goals into the family's daily living activities.
- Staff will provide ongoing parent education programs.
- Mother will increase time for herself.
- Respite care: 5 days, 20 hours provided per month.
- Parents will assist child with crawling using reciprocal motion for 10 feet once daily by the end of 8 weeks.

- Using "Let's Talk" cards, mother will spend 10 minutes each day talking and playing with child. (Bailey, Winton, Rouse, & Turnbull, 1990, p. 18)

The enactment of PL 99–457 formalizes society's recognition of the importance of early intervention for both children who are experiencing disabilities and those who are at risk for substantial developmental delays in the future. But before early intervention services can begin, the children must be identified.

✳ *Identification and Assessment*

Early childhood experts agree that the earlier intervention is begun, the better. Child development expert Burton White, who has conducted years of research with normally developing infants and preschoolers at Harvard University's Pre-School Project, believes that the period from 8 months to 3 years is critical to cognitive and social development. Discussing the development and learning by nondisabled children, White (1975) says that "to begin to look at a child's educational development when he is 2 years of age is already much too late" (p. 4).

Smith and Strain (1984) argue that research supports beginning intervention as early as possible in a child's life. If the first years of life are the most important for children without disabilities, they are even more critical for the child with disabilities, who, with each passing month, risks falling even further behind nondisabled agemates. Hayden and Pious (1979) contend that some interventions may even need to begin at or before birth.

> It is simply never too early to intervene, and . . . from the data base we now have, it seems clear that urgently needed interventions should occur long before a child is born. Once a child has arrived, the work necessarily shifts into amelioration, away from prevention—always a second choice for intervention. . . . Beginning at birth is not too soon. (p. 273)

Prenatal Risk Factors

We know more today than ever before about conditions associated with increased probability of the birth of a baby with disabilities. We know, for example, that a history of certain disabilities in a family should make us watch for similar risks to any future children. We know that malnutrition during pregnancy can produce severe developmental problems in the baby. And we know that diseases during pregnancy, particularly rubella, can cause serious disabilities in the newborn. Other signs of an at-risk pregnancy include

In the United States, 3 of every 100 babies are born with major birth defects.

- Birth of a previous child with a chromosomal abnormality
- Alcohol or drug use during pregnancy
- Age of the mother over 35 (although women over 35 have only 7% of the babies born, they give birth to more than 33% of all babies with Down syndrome)
- Two or more congenital malformations in the parents
- Mental retardation in the mother
- Absence of secondary sex characteristics in the mother
- History of several miscarriages for the mother

With widespread genetic counseling, along with greater public awareness of these conditions as predictors of disabilities, many parents or prospective parents

Smoking during pregnancy and inadequate prenatal care increase the risk of *sudden infant death syndrome* (SIDS), the leading cause of death in the United States for infants from 1 month to 1 year old. Sleep position is also a risk factor. The incidence of SIDS has dropped sharply in countries that advocate back or side sleeping. The U.S. Department of Health has begun a campaign to encourage parents of infants to put their baby to sleep on its back or side. The "Back to Sleep" Program to increase SIDS prevention and awareness has a toll-free hotline: (800) 505-CRIB.

Carmichael Olson (1994) provides an excellent overview of FAS and offers guidelines for early intervention.

can make better decisions, based on more information, about having a child. Likewise, better prenatal care can reduce the incidence of prematurity and low birth weight, both of which are also associated with a higher frequency of disabilities. Even with 10-fold improvements in public awareness, prenatal care, and early education, however, the possibility of eliminating most disabilities is not likely to be realized in this century. Thus, the need for effective early intervention programs will continue to challenge us.

Fetal Alcohol Syndrome

We know that drug and alcohol use by pregnant women can have devastating effects on the fetus that result in developmental delays and other disabilities. Fetal alcohol syndrome (FAS), caused by excessive alcohol use during pregnancy, often produces serious physical defects and developmental delays. FAS is diagnosed when the child has two or more craniofacial malformations and growth is below the 10th percentile for height and weight (Griesbach & Polloway, 1990). Children who have some but not all of the diagnostic criteria for FAS and a history of prenatal alcohol exposure are sometimes labeled **fetal alcohol effects (FAE).** The incidence of FAS is estimated at 1 to 3 per 1,000 live births; however, FAS birth rates among alcoholic women are about 25 per 1,000 (Burd & Martsolf, 1989).

FAS is one of the leading known causes of mental retardation and has an incidence figure higher than Down syndrome, cerebral palsy, and spina bifida (Streissguth et al., 1991). In addition to physical problems, many children with FAS have neurological damage that contributes to cognitive and language delays. Other problems in learning and behavior often exhibited by children with FAS include sleep disturbances, motor dysfunctions, hyperirritability, challenging behaviors such as aggression and conduct problems, and poor academic achievement (Burgess & Streissguth, 1992; Howard, Williams, & McLaughlin, 1994).

Despite the rising awareness of the hazards of alcohol during pregnancy, each year several thousand children are born in the United States with birth defects caused by prenatal alcohol exposure. Although research has shown that the fetus is most vulnerable to the effects of alcohol or other toxins during the first trimester and that children with FAS are usually born to mothers who are heavy drinkers, research has determined no safe level of drinking during pregnancy. *Women who are pregnant or anticipating pregnancy should abstain from drinking alcohol in any amount.*

Prenatal Exposure to Cocaine

Use of illegal drugs during pregnancy, especially cocaine, has reached epidemic proportions and is reported at all economic and educational levels. The president's National Drug Control Strategy Report estimates that 100,000 babies are born to cocaine-using women each year (Kusserow, 1990). Miller (1989) reports that, through written surveys, hospitals found 17% of women used cocaine during pregnancy; shocking as this figure is, self-reported use of an illegal substance is almost certain to produce an underestimation. Indeed, Frank et al. (1988) found that 24% of the pregnant women they interviewed failed to report cocaine use that was later verified by urine tests. Hospitals that conduct urine tests on newborns are finding 10% to 15% positive for cocaine (Miller, 1989), yet presence of the drug in the urine of newborns only indicates cocaine use within 48 hours prior to delivery. Cocaine-exposed infants project distress signals such as increased respiration and movement and high-pitched crying, and they often show little ability to interact with caretakers or respond to comforting (Williams & Howard, 1993).

Sensationalized reports in the popular media suggested that the schools were soon to be invaded by tens of thousands of "cocaine babies" possessing a heretofore unseen "type" of disability. Direct, objective observation by early childhood professionals, however, does not support this scenario (Schutter & Brinker, 1992). Although it has been estimated that about one third of children prenatally exposed to cocaine experience delays in language and/or problems with attention and self-regulation (Griffith, 1992), these problems may also be the result of other causes. Whatever the long-term effects of prenatal exposure to cocaine on learning and development may be, they are likely to be compounded, if not overshadowed, by the debilitating effects of the combination of poor prenatal care, poverty, and impoverished learning environments that the majority of these children also experience (Williams & Howard, 1993).

See "Perspectives on Educating Young Children Prenatally Exposed to Illegal Drugs" on the following pages. For an analysis of behavioral interventions with children prenatally exposed to alcohol and cocaine, see Howard, Williams, and McLaughlin (1994).

Screening

As a general rule, the more severe a disability, the earlier it can be detected. In the delivery room, medical staff can identify certain disabilities, such as microcephaly, cleft palate, and other physical deformities, as well as most instances of Down syndrome. Within a few days after birth, analysis of a newborn's blood and urine can detect metabolic disorders that will usually result in mental retardation if not treated within 4 to 12 weeks. Within the first few weeks, other physical characteristics such as coma, paralysis, seizures, or rapidly increasing head size can signal possible disabilities. Within the first months, delays in the development of various critical behaviors can tell a trained observer that an infant is at risk of developing a disability.

Some disabilities, such as learning disabilities or mild mental retardation, do not show up until a child is in school and his or her performance in academic subjects is clearly behind that of peers. But even in those cases, if the child is enrolled in a preschool staffed by competent and experienced professionals, it is possible to note learning problems or lags early.

Even though many measures have been developed to screen for high-risk infants and children, use of the measures is still far from universal. One national effort is the Early and Periodic Screening, Diagnosis, and Treatment (EPSDT) provision of the Social Security Amendments of 1967. Required since 1972, EPSDT was set up to increase the early identification of child health problems and to connect children from low-income families with medical and other related services. But EPSDT has drawn criticism for failing both to reach more of the children it should serve and to provide as much information as it could (Margolis & Meisels, 1987). At its best, however, EPSDT is empowered to screen only children who receive Medicaid; no such screening program is even recommended by the federal or state governments for other children.

Nonetheless, there are promising developments for early identification of infants with disabilities. For example, the SKI*HI Project at Utah State University, in conjunction with the Utah State Health Department, has developed a statewide screening procedure to detect hearing impairment (Finch, 1985). The procedure involves revisions of Utah's birth certificate format to include indicators associated

For descriptions of other statewide systems for screening and tracking infants with disabilities and at-risk factors, see Meisels and Provence (1989).

Perspectives on Educating Young Children Prenatally Exposed to Illegal Drugs

by Judith J. Carta

About 5 years ago, several of my colleagues from the Juniper Gardens Children's Project began to be aware of the issue of young children entering our local preschool and child care settings who had been identified as having been prenatally exposed to drugs, especially cocaine. Media reports were just beginning to publish articles in which they described "a new population" of children who were entering schools who were like no others previously seen in classrooms. They were described as out of control, with no ability to focus attention, lacking in affect, and born without the sense to tell the difference between right and wrong. As a result, teachers felt afraid and unequipped to handle this onslaught of children about whom they had no knowledge and experience. Potential foster and adoptive parents became hesitant to open their homes and families to them.

These fears have been based on several myths about children who may have been prenatally exposed to drugs. These misconceptions are conveyed in some of the questions we are most frequently asked about children prenatally exposed to drugs.

Do they all have behavior problems or learning difficulties?

Children whose prenatal histories include their mothers' use of drugs are not a homogeneous group, but one that represents a very wide range of abilities. Some of these children have physical and mental disabilities; others appear to be unaffected. Some children are passive and socially withdrawn; others are aggressive. Some children are "unattached"; others are constantly seeking attention and affection. No profile or set of characteristics appears to define this group; they do not appear to have an easily identifi-

able "syndrome." Some group studies of these children have reported that approximately 30% perform at a lower level than typically developing children. This average figure for children with a history of prenatal drug exposure fails to account for variation in how individual children may be affected and all the other factors from their prenatal or postnatal environments that may account for their developmental outcomes.

So, what accounts for the growing number of children in inner-city classrooms with significant behavior and learning problems? Aren't these problems caused by their mothers' drug use?

It is interesting that only behavior problems in inner-city schools are being linked to prenatal drug use. Such a conclusion suggests that only mothers in the inner city are using drugs. In reality, the problem of prenatal drug use is not unique to the inner city or to any particular racial or ethnic group. No one group "owns" the problem of prenatal substance exposure. It is as likely to occur in rural areas as in urban areas or the suburbs.

But how can we make sense of the rising tide of behavior problems of children in the inner city? What accounts for some children's sudden episodes of violence, difficulties in attention, lack of social skills, or the other types of difficulties that are appearing more often in our classrooms?

Although prenatal substance exposure may be a factor in explaining the wide-ranging types of problems occurring with greater frequency in our schools, many risk factors associated with living in poverty and less-than-adequate caregiving may also be responsible. For example, two factors associated with living in a drug-using lifestyle in poverty are violence and drug trafficking. Violence is a fact of life in communities where drug trafficking occurs. A large percentage of children in these neighborhoods witness violence in their neighborhoods as well as in their homes. Mothers of these children are often the victims of abuse, as are the children themselves. A growing body of research on the effects of exposure to violence or maltreatment of children points to many of the same behavioral symptoms we have seen attributed to prenatal drug exposure.

Another factor associated with children's behavioral and learning difficulties is the quality of caregiving they receive in a substance-using lifestyle. Unfortunately, substance abuse often results in behaviors that are in conflict with high-quality, nurturing caregiving. Persons who are substance abusers are often inconsistent parents and caregivers, behaving one way toward their children when they are straight, another way when they are high or coming down. Attempting to get straight often requires a period of separation from children because many residential treatment centers do not allow children. These parents are often socially isolated and lack a network of friends or family. They have difficulty getting the things they need for themselves and their children, accessing services, child care, jobs, and educational opportunities. The lack of support, resources, and sometimes the bare necessities poses severe challenges to providing quality caregiving for any parent.

These risk factors and many others can act in combination with prenatal exposure to drugs, as well as with each other, to produce the behavior and learning problems we see. These factors can threaten a child's developmental and educational outcomes and pose challenges to teachers, caregivers, and parents that, in turn, affect a child's development and educational success.

Will children prenatally exposed to drugs require specialized interventions that have not yet been developed?

No evidence currently exists to suggest that these children exhibit a unique set of problems requiring a special curriculum or set of educational or caregiving procedures. As previously mentioned, all of these children do not have problems, and when they do, their difficulties are ones that are exhibited by other children. Some children who are prenatally exposed may have language or social problems; others may have cognitive, motor, or adaptive deficits. Interventions are available that have been documented as effective in improving skills in each of these areas. These interventions are designed to be implemented by special educators, regular classrooms teachers, parents, and a wide range of professionals. We expect that these interventions will be as effective for children with a history of prenatal exposure to illegal drugs as they have been for other children. What is noteworthy, however, is that we do not need a curriculum or intervention aimed at the population of children who have been drug exposed; what we do need is a set of instructional procedures to address any of the problem behaviors and skill deficiencies exhibited by these children. Therefore, our suggested approach to deter-

mining interventions for children who are prenatally exposed to illegal drugs is identical to the approach we use for all children: Identify specific behaviors that require remediation, determine specific interventions that address those behaviors, systematically implement those interventions, and monitor the effects of the interventions on the specified behaviors.

What will require special attention, however, are the numerous risks these children face growing up within drug-using lifestyles. Until we begin to address in a comprehensive and intensive manner many of the risks associated with living in concentrated poverty, our efforts to provide interventions for these children will have little chance of producing lasting effects. ✳

Judith J. Carta, Ph.D., is a principal investigator at the Early Childhood Research Institute on Substance Abuse, a research consortium among the University of Kansas, the University of Minnesota, and the University of South Dakota. The institute's goal is to develop interventions for children who are at risk for developmental delays because of prenatal exposure to alcohol or other drugs.

with hearing loss. The project coordinates follow-up home visits to every infant in the state who is discovered to be at risk for hearing loss.

The Apgar Scale

The Apgar scale is a screening test for newborn infants. Developed in 1952 by Dr. Virginia Apgar, an anesthesiologist, the scale measures the degree of prenatal asphyxia (oxygen deprivation) an infant experiences during birth. The screening is administered to virtually 100% of the babies born in U.S. hospitals. According to Dr. Frank Bowen, former director of neonatology at Children's Hospital in Columbus, Ohio, "Every delivery should have a person whose primary interest is the newborn," and it is this person—nurse, nurse anesthesiologist, or pediatrician—who administers the Apgar.

The test administrator evaluates the infant twice on five physiological measures: heart rate, respiratory effort, response to stimulation, muscle tone, and skin color. On each measure, the child is given a score of 0, 1, or 2 (see Figure 14.2). The scoring form describes the specific characteristics of each measure so that the results are as objective as possible.

If the newborn receives a low score on the first administration of the test, which is conducted 60 seconds after birth, the delivery room staff takes immediate resuscitation action. The staff's role is to help the infant complete the transition to the world outside the mother's body by establishing strong respiration. This first test measures how the baby fared during the birth process.

The scale is given again 5 minutes after birth. At that point a total score of 0 to 3 (out of a possible 10) indicates severe asphyxia; 4 to 6, moderate asphyxia; and 7 to 10, mild asphyxia. "Some stress is assumed on all births," according to Dr. Bowen.

FIGURE 14.2
The Apgar evaluation scale

			60. sec.	5 min.
Heart rate	Absent Less than 100 100 to 140	(0) (1) (2)	 1	 2
Respiratory effort	Apneic Shallow, irregular Lusty cry and breathing	(0) (1) (2)	 1	 1
Response to catheter stimulation	No response Grimace Cough or sneeze	(0) (1) (2)	 1	 2
Muscle tone	Flaccid Some flexion of extremities Flexion resisting extension	(0) (1) (2)	 1	 2
Color	Pale, blue Body pink, extremities blue Pink all over	(0) (1) (2)	 0	 1
	Total		4	8

The 5-minute score measures how successful any resuscitation efforts were. Again, a low score calls for continuing action to help the infant.

"A 5-minute score of 6 or less deserves follow-up," says Dr. Bowen, "to determine what is causing the problem and what its long-term consequences will be." The Apgar has been shown to identify high-risk infants—those who have a greater than normal chance of developing later problems. Research has shown that oxygen deprivation at birth contributes to neurological impairment, and the 5-minute Apgar score correlates well with eventual neurological outcomes.

Developmental Screening Tests

The most widely used screening instrument for developmental delays is the *Denver Developmental Screening Test* (DDST) (Frankenburg, Dodds, & Fandal, 1975). The DDST can be administered in 15 to 20 minutes and used with children from 2 weeks to 6 years of age. It assesses 107 skills arranged in four developmental areas: gross motor, language, fine motor–adaptive, and personal-social. Each test item is represented on the scoring form by a bar showing at what ages 25%, 50%, 75%, and 90% of normally developing children can perform that skill. The child is allowed up to three trials per item. A delay is noted when the child cannot perform a skill that 90% of younger children can perform. A child's performance is considered abnormal if two of the developmental areas contain two or more delayed items. The child would then be referred for further detailed assessment of his or her abilities.

The recently published *Denver II* is a revision and restandardization of the DDST based on the performance of over 2,000 children representing a cross section of the Colorado population (Frankenburg, Dodds, Archer, Shapiro, & Bresnick, 1990). The Denver II differs from the DDST in several ways: (a) The number of items has been increased to 125, most of the new items in the area of language development; (b) DDST items that had proven difficult to administer and/or interpret were eliminated or modified; (c) items on which there were significant differences in the performance of children from different ethnic groups, maternal education, and/or place of residence (rural, urban, semirural) are identified in the *Denver II Technical Manual* so that the diagnostician can determine whether a delay may be due to sociocultural differences; and (d) the test form was modified to fit the schedule of health maintenance visits recommended by the American Academy of Pediatrics. A child's performance on each item is scored as "pass" or "fail" and then interpreted as representing "advanced," "OK," "caution," or "delayed" performance by comparing the child's performance with those of the same age in the standardized population. Figure 14.3 shows the test form for the Denver II.

Many other screening measures are available. The *Battelle Developmental Inventory Screening Test* (BDIST) (Newborg, Stock, Wnek, Guidubaldi, & Suinicki, 1989) can be administered to children with and without disabilities, aged birth through 8 years. The Battelle has adapted testing procedures for use with children with different disabilities. The *Developmental Profile-II* (DP-II) is normed for children from birth to 9½ years old and consists of five subtests: Physical, Self-Help, Social, Academic, and Communication (Alpern, Boll, & Shearer, 1986). The DP-II relies entirely on parent report.

Glascoe and Bryne (1993) compared the accuracy—the percentage of children with and without problems who are correctly detected—of the DP-II, the BDIST, and the Denver II. The results of each of the three developmental screening tests were

Although most newborns are evaluated in terms of gestational weight and age and are screened for certain specific disorders, the Apgar scale is at present the only screening test universally used with infants. Another widely practiced screening procedure is the analysis of newborn blood and urine samples to detect metabolic disorders, such as PKU, that produce mental retardation. Many hospitals also routinely analyze newborn blood and urine samples to detect the presence of illegal drugs and other toxins.

FIGURE 14.3 Test form for the Denver II

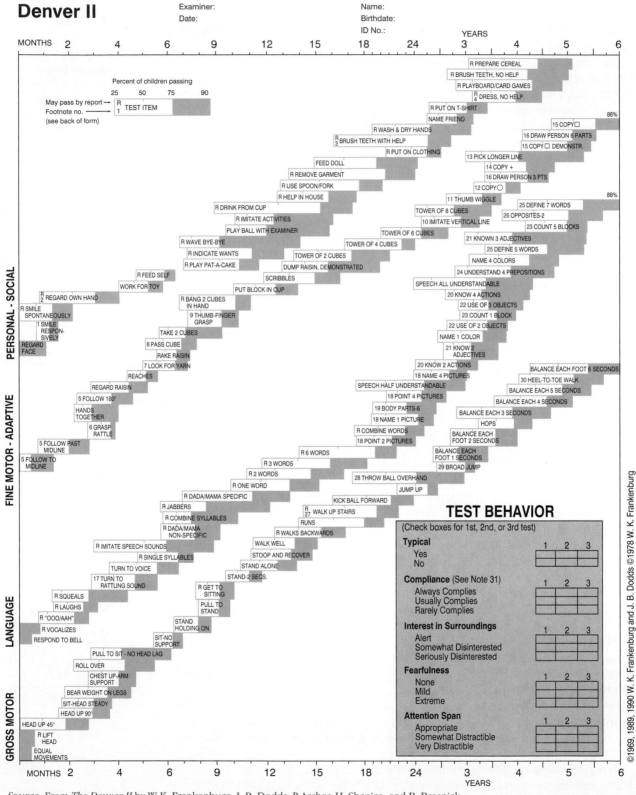

Source: From *The Denver II* by W. K. Frankenburg, J. B. Dodds, P. Archer, H. Shapiro, and B. Bresnick, 1990, Denver: Denver Developmental Materials, Inc.

compared with the results from a battery of intelligence, adaptive, language, and achievement tests that showed 20% of the 89 infants, toddlers, and preschoolers in the study actually had developmental delays or other disabilities. The DP-II identified fewer than 1 in 4 of the children with developmental problems. The Denver II detected the majority of children with difficulties, but most children without problems also failed the test. The BDIST proved to be the most accurate screening test, correctly classifying 72% of the children with difficulties and 76% of the children without diagnoses.

Several early childhood screening tests are based on the *Gesell Developmental Schedules* (Gesell et al., 1940; Knobloch & Pasamanick, 1974), which describe normal motor development, adaptive behavior, language, and personal-social behavior in infants and young children. The *Bayley Scales of Infant Development* (Bayley, 1969), which evaluate an infant's development from 2 to 30 months, are standardized adaptations of the Gesell schedules. The *Developmental Screening Inventory* (Knobloch, Pasamanick, & Sherard, 1966), also based on the Gesell schedules, was designed for pediatricians to use in assessing developmental delays in children between 1 and 18 months of age. The *Brazelton Neonatal Assessment Scale* (Brazelton, 1973) is a more detailed assessment of the newborn.

None of these measures or practices, however, adds up to any kind of truly systematic effort to screen all young children. Most state and local screening programs are aimed at older children, especially those about to start school. It is insufficient to screen children only once during their early years. Developmental screening should occur on multiple occasions between birth and age 6 and should be available throughout the year (Bailey & Wolery, 1989). And it is critical that screening involve multiple sources of information (Meisels & Provence, 1989). For example, a longitudinal study of 268 adolescents with disabilities and an equal number of control group students without disabilities found that, in children from birth to 3 years of age, parental traits such as maternal level of education were more accurate predictors of later involvement in special education than were variables such as the child's rating on developmental screening scales (Kochanek, Kabacoff, & Lipsitt, 1990). Conversely, results from the same study showed that, for children from 4 to 17 years of age, child-centered measures such as developmental competence were more predictive of later problems. Kochanek et al. (1990) conclude:

> Early identification models that focus solely on developmental delay or adverse medical events from birth to 3 years of age are inadequate in fully identifying children eventually judged to be handicapped. While such models will identify youngsters with established conditions, they will ultimately identify only a small segment of the total handicapped population. (p. 535)

Identifying high-risk infants and young children most often depends on the experience and concern of the adults who deal with them. Chief among those adults are pediatricians and nurses, social workers, day-care staff, preschool teachers, and most of all, the child's parents. One study has shown that mothers' estimates of their preschool children's levels of development correlate highly with those that professionals produce by using standardized scales (Gradel, Thompson, & Sheehan, 1981). More important, parental involvement in screening has been found to reduce the number of misclassifications (Henderson & Meisels, 1994).

Screening tests have also been developed for the early detection of behavioral disorders and autism. See Chapter 6 for a description of *Systematic Screening for Behavior Disorders* (SSBD), which has been adapted for use with preschoolers (Sinclair, Del'Homme, & Gonzales, 1993; Walker, Severson, & Feil, 1994). Two widely used screening instruments for autism are the *Autism Behavior Checklist* (ABC) (Krug, Arick, & Almond, 1980) and the *Childhood Autism Rating Scale* (CARS) (Schopler, Reichler, & Renner, 1988).

For a review of research on the use of parental input during screening and assessment of young children, see Diamond and Squires (1993).

Screening Kindergarten Children

Several assessment devices attempt to measure a child's readiness for academic learning, with specific tasks related to early reading and math skills. Other tests are designed to measure a child's readiness for school, such as the *BRIGANCE K and 1 Screen for Kindergarten and First Grade* (Brigance, 1982) and the *Metropolitan Readiness Tests* (Nurss & McGauvran, 1986). Readiness tests usually include items to assess a child's prereading and premath skills, as well as socioemotional development, gross- and fine-motor performance, and general cognitive development.

Although too late to result in early intervention, increasing efforts are being made to screen kindergarten children to identify those who may be at risk for special education placement in later years. One approach to kindergarten screening is the *Early Prevention of School Failure* (EPSF), which consists of a battery of five tests assessing language development, fine- and gross-motor skills, and visual-motor skills (e.g., copying geometric forms). Roth, McCaul, and Barnes (1993) evaluated the accuracy of predictions of whether a child will be retained at the same grade, referred for special education assessment, and/or placed in special education on the basis of results of EPSF screening administered when the child enters kindergarten. Using the data from one school district that conducted EPSF screening with all 161 children who entered kindergarten over a 2-year period, Roth et al. calculated that EPSF screening was approximately 83% accurate in classifying which children would be retained in grade level, 82% correct in predicting referral, and 80% accurate in identifying which children would be placed in special education by the end of the third grade.

The *Rating Inventory for Screening Kindergartners* (RISK) is a 34-item rating scale with which kindergarten teachers use a 1-to-6 rating scale to estimate a child's abilities in several domains and to judge how often certain behaviors occur in relation to other children in the class (Coleman & Dover, 1989). The RISK is completed during the child's second semester in kindergarten. Coleman and Dover (1993) report that the RISK scale accurately predicted the eventual placement in regular or special education in grades 3 through 6 for 94% of more than 1,100 children in two school districts during a 4-year period.

Not all children who are screened as high risk will necessarily have disabilities. Some grow up to live normal lives, without any special help. The goal of early screening is to identify a possible or likely disability before it can take its full toll on the child's future. For those who are identified, screening is only the first step. The next step is a careful and detailed assessment of all critical areas of development.

Assessing Developmental Domains

A wide variety of assessment devices are available, including both formal standardized measures and less formal checklists and rating scales based on observations. Bailey and Wolery (1989) describe and compare numerous formal evaluation instruments for identifying and assessing delayed or abnormal progress in intellectual development, auditory perception, or affective and social development.

As more and more intervention programs for young children with disabilities are started, the number of informal observation checklists, rating scales, and other assessment devices also grows. Most have been developed by federally funded model programs or locally sponsored centers for young children with disabilities. In general, assessment tools seek to measure a child's development in six key areas:

For further discussion of screening and assessment of infants and preschoolers, see Bailey and Simeonsson (1988a); Bailey and Wolery (1989); Fewell (1991); Henderson and Meisels (1994); and Meisels (1989).

1. *Cognitive skills.* Children use cognitive skills when they attend to stimuli, perform preacademic skills such as sorting or counting, remember things they have done in the past, plan and make decisions about what they will do in the future, integrate newly learned information with previously learned knowledge and skills, solve problems, and generate novel ideas.
2. *Motor skills.* The ability to move one's body and manipulate objects within the environment provides a critical foundation for all types of learning. Motor development involves improvements in general strength, flexibility, endurance, and eye-hand coordination and includes large-muscle movement and mobility such as walking, running, throwing and small-muscle, fine-motor control like that needed to pick up a toy, write, or tie a shoe.
3. *Communication and language skills.* Communication involves the transmission of messages, information about needs, feelings, knowledge, desires, and so forth. Children use communication and language skills when they receive information from others, share information with other individuals, and use language to mediate their actions and to effectively control the environment. This domain encompasses all forms of communication development, including a child's ability to respond nonverbally with gestures, smiles, or actions, and the acquisition of spoken language—sounds, words, phrases, sentences, and so on.
4. *Social and play skills.* Children who have developed competence in social skills with one another share toys and take turns, cooperate with others, and resolve conflicts.
5. *Affective and emotional development.* Children should feel good about themselves and know how to express their emotions and feelings.
6. *Self-care and adaptive skills.* As young children develop self-care and adaptive skills such as dressing/undressing, eating, toileting, toothbrushing, and handwashing, their ability to function independently across multiple environments increases, which provides and enhances opportunities for additional kinds of learning.

Fine motor control and social skills are two important areas of child development.

Generally, these six areas are broken down into specific, observable tasks and sequenced developmentally—that is, in the order in which most children learn them. Sometimes each task is tied to a specific age at which a child should normally be able to perform it. This arrangement allows the observer to note significant delays or gaps, as well as other unusual patterns, in a high-risk child's development. These developmental domains are not mutually exclusive. There is considerable overlap between domains as well as across subskills within a specific domain. Most activities by children in everyday settings involve skills from multiple domains. For example, playing marbles typically involves skills from the cognitive, motor, communication, and social domains.

Early childhood special educators must be knowledgeable about the typical development of children without disabilities. Normal development is useful as a guide for intervention and a yardstick against which to measure each child's individual needs and progress. A curriculum may try to give a child with disabilities instruction in all of the processes or skills that a normal child might develop without specific teaching. Or it might try to measure all of the skills the child has already learned and then teach only those that are missing. In both instances, the ultimate goal is to help the child develop as many of the behaviors of a normal child of the same age as possible.

Curriculum-Based Assessment

See Bagnato, Neisworth, and Capone (1986) for a description and rationale of curriculum-based assessment, as well as a review of 21 assessment measures useful for curriculum-based assessment in early childhood special education programs.

A growing number of early intervention programs are moving away from assessments based entirely on developmental milestones and are incorporating curriculum-based assessment. Each item in a curriculum-based assessment relates directly to a skill in the program's curriculum, thereby providing a direct link among testing, teaching, and progress evaluation. But, as Notari and Bricker (1990) note, "Although theoretically more appealing, many curriculum-based assessments in fact are drawn from items on standardized tests, thus decreasing their relevance to intervention programming" (p. 118).

For further descriptions of the EPS-I and research on its utility, reliability, and validity, see Bricker, Bailey, and Slentz (1990) and Notari and Bricker (1990).

An empirically tested curriculum-based assessment device intended to facilitate the link among assessment, intervention, and evaluation is the *Evaluation and Programming System: For Infants and Young Children* (EPS-I) (Bricker, Gentry, & Bailey, 1985). Designed for use with children ranging in age from 1 month to 6 years, the EPS-I is divided into six domains: fine motor, gross motor, self-care, cognitive, social-communication, and social. Each domain is divided into strands that group related behaviors and skills considered essential for infants and young children to function independently. All skills selected for inclusion in the EPS-I meet five instructional characteristics:

1. They are functional, in that they enhance the child's ability to cope with daily environmental demands.
2. They are generic, allowing for modifications and adaptations for infants and children with disabilities.
3. They are easily integrated within the classroom or home by teacher or parent.
4. They are observable and measurable, enabling objective determination of performance and progress.
5. They are organized by long- and short-range goals, rather than according to typical developmental sequences.

Guidelines for the Assessment of Young Children

The accuracy and usefulness of assessment information depend not just on the kind of device or method used. The experience and training of the observer, the number of observations, the settings in which the child is observed, and the care with which the data are interpreted all affect the validity and reliability of an assessment. Assessment of young children with special needs should be viewed as an ongoing, multifaceted effort to obtain information that will help make decisions. The kinds of decisions that typically must be made and the function of assessment designed to help answer those questions have been identified by Wolery, Strain, and Bailey (1992):

- whether to refer the child for additional assessment (screening)
- whether the child has a developmental delay or disability (diagnostic)
- whether the child is eligible for services (eligibility)
- what the child should be taught (curricular planning)
- where the child should receive services (placement)
- whether the child is making adequate progress in learning important skills (monitoring of instructional program)
- whether the desired outcomes were achieved (program evaluation) (pp. 96–97)

Each type of decision requires that different questions be asked and different measurements and procedures be used. Although professionals from various disciplines are typically involved in assessment of infants, toddlers, and preschoolers with special needs, teachers should be "intimately involved in assessing children to decide what to teach" (Wolery et al., 1992, p. 97). Table 14.1 illustrates assessment for curricular planning for Scott, a 5-year-old with moderate mental retardation, communication disorders, a suspected hearing impairment, and some motor weaknesses. Scott is currently enrolled in an integrated kindergarten and has been in early intervention for several years.

Assessment of young children should be guided by a number of criteria (Bailey & Wolery, 1989; Fewell, 1991; McLoughlin & Lewis, 1994; Meisels & Provence, 1989):

- Assessments should be conducted in a child's natural environment in a nonthreatening way.
- Direct observation of behavior is necessary to accurately determine the child's abilities. Checklists and rating scales, although sufficient for targeting general areas of strength and weakness, usually do not pinpoint the specific behaviors that define those areas.
- Assessments should be repeated over time. It is dangerous to decide that a disability does or does not exist on the basis of one test or observation. Young children's behavior is simply too variable, and the consequences of being wrong too great, to base a decision on one assessment session, no matter how extensive it is.
- Eligibility for services should not be determined by single or limited criteria, but rather by an assessment process that obtains multiple sources of information. For example, Meisels and Provence (1989) describe a 5-month-old infant with Down syndrome who scored in the average range on the Bayley and Vineland Scales used by the early intervention agency to determine eligibility. Because the agency used multiple eligibility criteria (including the diagnosis of Down syndrome, a condition of established risk), the child and his family qualified for services despite the test score in the normal range.
- A multidisciplinary assessment should be conducted. It is important that the members of a multidisciplinary assessment team cooperate to determine their

TABLE 14.1

Characteristics and examples of assessment for curricular planning

CHARACTERISTIC	DESCRIPTION	EXAMPLE
Assessment should include a variety of measures in a variety of settings.	The assessment procedures include the use of curriculum-referenced tests, teacher-devised and informal tests, direct observation in natural settings (home and classroom), and interviews with people who know the child.	The teacher uses developmental scales to assess Scott's communication, motor, and cognitive development. She devises some testing situations to determine how he does particular skills. She observes him during play sessions with other children to note his social interaction, play, and language skills. She observes him at lunch and in the bathroom to identify his self-care skills. She interviews his parents, former teachers, and therapists to secure additional information.
Assessment results should provide a detailed description of the child's functioning.	The results include a description of (a) the child's developmental skills across all relevant areas, (b) what the child can and cannot do, and (c) what factors influence the child's skills/abilities.	The teacher analyzes the results of her assessment activities, summarizes what Scott can and cannot do in each area, and describes what factors appear to influence his performance (e.g., what toys he appears to like, which children he interacts with, what help he needs on different tasks, and what appears to motivate his behavior).
Assessment activities should involve the child's family.	The family should fulfill the following roles: receive information from professionals, observe the assessment activities, provide information about the child's development and needs, gather new information, and validate the assessment results.	The teacher plans the assessment with the family. She asks them about how Scott does different skills, how he spends his time, and what concerns and goals they have for him. She allows them to observe the testing. She asks them to gather information on some skills at home. She reviews the results with them and asks them to confirm, modify, qualify, and – if necessary – refute the findings.
Assessment activities should be conducted by professionals from different disciplines.	Frequently, assessment from the following disciplines is needed: speech/language therapy, physical therapy, occupational therapy, audiology, social work, health professionals (nurses and physicians), psychology, nutrition, special education, and possibly others.	The teacher coordinates the assessment activities of the team. Because of Scott's communication delays, a speech and language pathologist assesses him. An audiologist assesses his hearing, a physical therapist and an occupational therapist assess his motor skills, and the special education teacher assists the kindergarten teacher in assessing his social and cognitive skills.
Assessment activities should result in a list of high-priority objectives.	Assessment activities will identify more skills than are possible to teach; therefore, those of most value are identified. All team members, including the family, are involved in this decision. Skills are selected to be focused on if they are useful to the child, have long-term benefits, and/or are important to the family.	After the results have been analyzed, the team (including the parents) meets to review the findings. They discuss which skills Scott needs to learn, which ones will be most useful, which will result in long-term benefit, and which are most important to his family. The most important skills are listed as goals on his Individualized Educational Program (IEP).

Source: From "Reaching Potentials of Children with Special Needs" by M. Wolery, P. S. Strain, and D. B. Bailey, Jr. In S. Bredekamp and T. Rosegrant (Eds.), *Reaching Potentials: Appropriate Curriculum and Assessment for Young Children* (Vol. 1), 1992, p. 100. Copyright (c) 1992 by the National Association for the Education of Young Children, Washington, DC. Reprinted by permission.

respective roles before assessment begins. Intentional overlapping in role assignments helps eliminate gaps in the assessment process.

- The assessment process should involve parents and family. Information gathered from interviews with parents and observations of parent-child interactions is extremely important in determining meaningful instructional targets. Not only is the information from parents necessary for a complete assessment, but their cooperation and involvement as active partners throughout the assessment process are also desired because parents play a critical role in most early intervention programs (Winton, 1986; Winton & Bailey, 1988). Vincent and her colleagues developed the Parent Inventory of Child Development in Nonschool Environments, which helps identify skills important to parents and the home (Vincent et al., 1983).

- The child should be kept motivated during administration of assessment items, and testing should not continue if the child's attention or performance declines after a time.

- Test items and administration should be modified if necessary to allow a child with a disability to perform at his or her highest ability level. Bailey and Wolery (1989) recommend that "after following standard administration procedures, assessors should 'test the limits' of children's performance" (p. 61). For example, changing the way a test item is presented (perhaps repeating it and using gestural cues) or even partially assisting a child in responding may provide significantly more useful information about the child's current level of functioning than can be gained by simply marking a score of zero and proceeding to the next item. Although this suggestion goes against the rules of administering standardized tests, the information acquired about the child's abilities and its usefulness in determining appropriate instructional targets are often more important than calculation of a test score.

Proceed with Caution

DuBose (1981) has noted the particular difficulty posed by evaluating children with severe disabilities. Because there are so few reliable assessment instruments for use with children who are severely impaired, professionals often must adapt standardized tests and devise informal assessment tasks. DuBose warns that when adaptations must be made, they must be carefully noted and results interpreted with care. The examiner must know why a particular test was given, what it is meant to tap, and what the child's test performances indicate.

Serious dangers can arise from errors in screening or assessment. Children with disabilities or at risk for developmental delays who are not identified may miss

Assessment should be conducted in natural, nonthreatening environments with the child motivated to do her best.

crucial opportunities for early intervention and the special services they and their families need; as a result, their problems may get worse. However, referring children without disabilities for early intervention raises the cost of providing such services, creates anxiety for parents and families, and may cause the child to suffer the stigma of an erroneous label. As we saw in Chapter 1, teachers may have lower expectations for children with disability labels and as a result may provide fewer opportunities to learn. Early intervention personnel in one study, for example, were asked to rate the behavioral functioning of two 24-month-old children shown on videotape segments. Children were rated less favorably when the observers were told they had been prenatally exposed to cocaine (Thruman, Brobeil, Ducette, & Hurt, 1994).

Most early childhood special educators are against the use of disability categories with preschoolers, noting the unreliability of psychometric testing, the fact that such labels have little utility for program planning, and the possible negative effects of labeling young children (Haring et al., 1992; McLean, Smith, McCormick, Schakel, & McEvoy, 1991; Meisels & Shonkoff, 1990). Categorical labels (e.g., learning disabilities, behavioral disorders, mental retardation) do little to direct appropriate services, especially for the majority of children who experience mild to moderate developmental delays. Noncategorical diagnosis and noncategorical service delivery are legal and philosophical features of early intervention (Neisworth & Bagnato, 1992). Because federal legislation does not require the use of specific disability labels, early intervention programs can serve preschoolers under the general "at-risk" category, thereby avoiding the possible disadvantages of labeling.

> Many early childhood special educators are against the use of intelligence testing in early intervention. The use of IQ tests with young children is put "on trial" by Neisworth and Bagnato (1992).

✳ *Curriculum in Early Childhood Special Education Programs*

Child Development

What is the purpose of early intervention programs for children with special needs? A good basic answer to that question would go something like this: Early childhood special education programs, like all early childhood education programs, should promote the development of infants and young children. But what is child development, and what is it exactly that develops? If we tried to answer this question on the basis of reading early intervention outcomes research, we might erroneously come away with the idea that development "is synonymous with the acquisition of cognitive or intellectual skills, since scores on IQ tests have served as the primary outcome measure in much of the research" (Bailey & Wolery, 1992, p. 43). Cognitive ability—whether evaluated by IQ tests or more direct measures—is a critically important area of development, but it is just one of several areas in which a child's interactions with the environment progressively advance in complexity and maturity. Bailey and Wolery (1992) offer the following definition of development and clarify the primary objective of those who wish to promote children's development:

> [W]e define development broadly as including changes in behavior, thoughts, and feelings, and in competence in multiple areas of functioning. Development occurs in part from maturation and in part from interactions with the social and physical envi-

ronment. The task of the teacher, parent, or other specialist is to design an environ-ment and provide activities that maximize children's meaningful interactions with the environment and thereby promote their development. (p. 43)

Early intervention services provided by programs for infants and young chil-dren with special needs are typically organized and delivered to facilitate children's development within the six major domains or skills areas described earlier (e.g., cog-nitive, communication, self-help).

Developmentally Appropriate Practice

Most early childhood educators share a common philosophy that learning environ-ments, teaching practices, and other components of programs that serve young chil-dren should be based on what is typically expected of and experienced by children of different ages and developmental stages. This philosophy and the guidelines for practice based on it are called *developmentally appropriate practice* (DAP) and are described in widely disseminated materials published by the National Association for the Education of Young Children (NAEYC) (Bredekamp, 1987; Bredekamp & Roseg-rant, 1992). The DAP guidelines were created partially in response to concerns that too many early childhood programs were focusing too much on academic prepared-ness and not providing young children with enough opportunities to engage in the less structured play and other activities that typify early childhood. "For example, some people considered it developmentally appropriate for 4- and 5-year olds to do an hour of seatwork, toddlers to sit in high chairs with dittos, or babies in infant seats to 'do' the calendar" (Bredekamp, 1993, p. 261).

DAP recommends the following guidelines for early childhood education pro-grams:

(a) activities should be integrated across developmental domains
(b) children's interests and progress should be identified through teacher observation
(c) teachers should arrange the environment to facilitate children's active exploration and interaction
(d) learning activities and materials should be real, concrete and relevant to the young child's life
(e) a wide range of interesting activities should be provided
(f) the complexity and challenges of activities should increase as the children under-stand the skills involved (adapted from Bredekamp, 1987)

Most early childhood special educators view the DAP guidelines as providing a foundation or context within which to provide early intervention for children with special needs; but by themselves the DAP guidelines are inadequate to ensure the individualized intervention that such children need. Wolery et al. (1992) suggest four reasons that a curriculum based entirely on DAP may not be sufficient for young chil-dren with disabilities:

1. Many children with special needs have delays or disabilities that make them depen-dent upon others.
2. Many children with special needs have delays or disabilities that keep them from learning well on their own.
3. Many children with special needs develop more slowly than their typically develop-ing peers.
4. Many children with special needs have disabilities that interfere with how they interact, and, as a result, they often acquire additional handicaps. (adapted from pp. 101–102)

For a discussion and debate concerning the role of the NAEYC's developmentally appro-priate practice (DAP) for early childhood spe-cial education, see Bre-dekamp (1993); Carta, Atwater, Schwartz, and McConnell (1993); and Johnson and Johnson (1993). For a list of explicit practices rec-ommended by leaders in early childhood spe-cial education, see *DEC Recommended Prac-tices* (DEC, 1993).

Goals of Early Education for Children with Special Needs

Early childhood special education programs should be designed and evaluated with respect to the following outcomes or goals (Bailey & Wolery, 1992; *DEC Recommended Practices*, 1993; Wolery & Sainato, 1993, in press):

1. *Support families in achieving their own goals.* Although the child with special needs is undoubtedly the focal point of early intervention, a major function of early intervention is helping families achieve the goals most important to them (Bailey, 1994; Dunst et al., 1994). Professionals realize that families function as a system and that separating the child from the system results in limited and fragmented outcomes. The development and provision of responsive family-centered services, especially for children from birth to age 36 months, have become so important that some early childhood special educators argue that the family is the primary client and family support the primary goal of early intervention (Bailey, 1994; Dunst et al., 1994).

2. *Promote child engagement, independence, and mastery.* Early childhood special education seeks to minimize the extent to which children are dependent on others and different from their age-mates. Intervention strategies should "promote active engagement (participation), initiative (choice making, self-directed behavior), autonomy (individuality and self-sufficiency) and age-appropriate abilities in many normalized contexts and situations" (Wolery & Sainato, 1993, p. 53). In situations in which independence is not safe, possible, or practical, support and assistance should be provided to enable the child to participate as much as he or she can. "For example, in getting ready for a bath, a 3-year-old child should not be expected to adjust the water to the appropriate temperature, but could be expected to help get ready for the bath (e.g., getting bath toys, assisting in taking off clothing)" (Wolery & Sainato, 1993, p. 53).

To read how preschoolers with disabilities can learn to be more independent, see the "Idea Bunny" later in this chapter.

3. *Promote development in all important domains.* Successful early intervention programs help children make progress in each of the key areas of development described earlier (e.g., cognitive, motor, communication, social). Because young children with disabilities are already behind their typically developing age-mates, Wolery and Sainato (1993, in press) suggest that early childhood special educators should only use instructional strategies that lead to rapid learning. Instructional strategies that produce rapid learning help the child with disabilities by saving time for other goals and moving closer to normal developmental levels.

4. *Build and support social competence.* Social skills, such as learning to get along with others and making friends, are among the most important skills anyone can learn. Most children learn such skills naturally, but many children with disabilities do not learn to interact effectively and properly simply by playing with others (McEvoy & Yodel, 1993). In fact, one leader in the field of early childhood special education suggests that "understanding and promoting the social competence of young handicapped children may well be the most important challenge to the field of early intervention in the decade of the 1990s" (Guralnick, 1990, p. 3).

5. *Facilitate the generalized use of skills.* As effortlessly as most typically developing children seem to generalize what they learn at one time in one setting or situation to another place and time, many children with disabilities have extreme difficulty in remembering and using previously learned skills in other settings and

situations. "Early interventionists should not be satisfied if children learn new skills; they should only be satisfied if children use those skills when and wherever they are appropriate" (Wolery & Sainato, 1993, p. 54).

6. *Prepare and assist children for normalized life experiences with their families, in school, and in their communities.* Early intervention should be characterized by the principle of normalization; that is, services should be provided in settings that are as much like the typical settings in which young children without disabilities play and learn as is possible. A large and growing body of published research literature demonstrates the benefits of integrated early intervention to children with disabilities and their families and suggests strategies for effective mainstreaming programs (Miller et al., 1992; Peck, Odom, & Bricker, 1993; Sainato & Strain, 1993; Wolery & Wilbers, 1994).

7. *Help children and their families make smooth transitions.* A transition occurs when a child and his or her family move from one early intervention program or service delivery mode to another. For example, program transitions typically occur at age 3 when a child with disabilities moves from a home-based early intervention program to an early childhood special education classroom, and again at age 5 when the child moves from a preschool classroom to a regular kindergarten classroom. Preparing and assisting children and their families for smooth transitions ensures the continuity of services, minimizes disruptions to the family system, and is another important way for promoting the success of young children with disabilities as they move into more normalized environments (Carta, Atwater, Schwartz, & Miller, 1990; Fowler, Schwartz, & Atwater, 1991; Hanline, 1993). Cooperative planning and supports for transitions must come from the professionals in both the sending and the receiving programs (Chandler, 1993).

8. *Prevent or minimize the development of future problems or disabilities.* Prevention of future problems is a major goal of early intervention. Indeed, early intervention programs that serve at-risk infants and toddlers are designed entirely with prevention as their primary goal.

Selecting IEP/IFSP Objectives

Many early childhood special education programs employ a developmentally based curriculum; that is, the typical gains that children without disabilities make in the various developmental domains are used as a basis for sequencing instructional objectives and evaluating child progress. The developmental curriculum is not the most appropriate for all young children with disabilities. Bailey and Wolery (1984) remind us:

> The purposes of the early intervention curriculum are to accelerate children's developmental progress and to maximize independent functioning. With some children (e.g., mildly and moderately handicapped children) the primary emphasis is on accelerating developmental progress. With more severely handicapped children, the emphasis is on maximizing independent functioning. (p. 17)

For preschoolers with severe disabilities and/or sensory impairments, the objectives suggested by a developmentally based curriculum may be inappropriate. A functionally based curriculum, focusing on skills that will enable immediate improvement in interaction with their environments, may be more appropriate. Laura, for example, is a 5-year-old with multiple disabilities who is unable to dress herself. Because dressing oneself is a functional skill that promotes independent functioning,

Early childhood special educators employ the same strategies for promoting the generalization and maintenance of learning described in Chapter 4.

As noted earlier, preventative efforts are most effective when intervention services are begun early, conducted in a systematic and intensive fashion, and provided over a significant period of time (McEachin, Smith, & Lovaas, 1993; Ramey & Ramey, 1992).

it might be chosen as an appropriate objective for Laura in a functionally based curriculum. Careful assessment determines what specific steps in dressing that Laura cannot perform, and direct instruction in those steps would follow. By contrast, a curriculum that follows typical developmental sequences would focus on the developmental prerequisites to getting dressed—such as grasping objects and using various gross- and fine-motor movements.

Early childhood special educators do not have to choose between a strict developmental or functional approach. Many early intervention programs for children with disabilities use a combination of the two approaches, relying on a normal sequence of development as a general guide to the curriculum but applying functional considerations to select specific instructional targets for each child.

The breadth of developmental domains and many activities that young children typically engage in provide an almost unlimited number of possibilities for instructional objectives. Notari-Syverson and Shuster (1995) recommend that potential IEP/IFSP objectives for infants and young children be evaluated by five criteria:

1. *Functionality.* A functional skill (1) increases the child's ability to interact with people and objects in his or her daily environment and (2) may have to be performed by someone else if the child cannot do it.
2. *Generality.* In this context, a skill has generality if it (1) represents a general concept as opposed to a particular task, (2) can be adapted and modified to meet the child's disability, and (3) can be used across different settings, with various materials, and with different people.
3. *Instructional context.* The skill should be easily integrated into the child's daily routines and taught in a meaningful way that represents naturalistic use of the skill.
4. *Measurability.* A skill is measurable if its performance or a product produced by its performance can be seen and/or heard. Measurable skills can be counted or timed and enable objective determination of learning progress.
5. *Relation between short-term and long-range goals.* Short-term objectives should be hierarchically related; the achievement of short-term objectives should contribute directly to the attainment of long-term goals.

Figure 14.4 shows 11 questions that can be used to assess potential IEP/IFSP objectives according to these five criteria.

> For an informative and interesting discussion of what is *not* known about curriculum and instruction in early childhood special education, see Wolery (1991).

✸ *Intervention Strategies in Early Childhood Special Education*

> For a description of general curriculum and intervention strategies used in early childhood special education, see Bailey and Wolery (1992) and Wolery and Sainato (in press).

Like their colleagues who work with elementary and secondary students with disabilities, early childhood special educators are, first and foremost, teachers. As teachers, they must be skilled in using a wide range of instructional strategies and tactics. In this section, we briefly look at three instructional challenges that all early childhood special educators must deal with: promoting the communication and language skills of young children, increasing children's social competence, and planning an activity schedule.

Developing Language in Preschoolers with Disabilities

Learning the native language of their community is a major developmental task of children. Most children learn to speak and communicate effectively with little or no formal teaching. By the time they enter school, most children have essentially mastered their native tongue. But children with disabilities often do not acquire language in the spontaneous, seemingly effortless manner of their peers without disabilities (Barney & Landis, 1987). And as children with disabilities slip further and further behind their peers, their language deficits make social and academic development even more difficult. Preschoolers with disabilities need opportunities and activities directed at language use and development throughout the day (Goldstein, Kaczmarek, & Hepting, 1994).

Eileen Allen and Jane Rieke are two language specialists who, like most of their colleagues, believe that teachers of preschool children must use strategies to help children develop language skills all day long, throughout a total program. They also believe that the basic measure of success of a language intervention should be how much the child talks. Research has shown that the more a child talks, the better the child talks (Hart & Risley, 1975; Rieke, Lynch, & Soltman, 1977). K. E. Allen (1980a) says that good teachers do three things to ensure effective intervention for language-delayed children:

1. They arrange the environment in ways that are conducive to promoting language: by providing interesting learning centers (blocks, housekeeping and dramatic play, creative and manipulative materials); by balancing child-initiated and teacher-structured activities; and by presenting materials and activities that children enjoy.
2. They manage their interactions with children so as to maximize effective communication on the part of each language-impaired child and use every opportunity to teach "on the fly."
3. They monitor the appropriateness of environmental arrangements, their own behavior, and that of the children in order to validate child progress and thus program effectiveness.

Two models or approaches that teachers can use for systematically encouraging and developing language use throughout the school day are the *incidental teaching model* (Hart & Risley, 1968, 1975) and the *mand model* (Rogers-Warren & Warren, 1980; Warren, McQuarter, & Rogers-Warren, 1984). The essential feature of the incidental teaching model is that when the child wants something from the teacher—help, approval, information, food, or drink—the teacher takes the opportunity to promote language use. In other words, whenever the child initiates an interaction with the teacher, the teacher uses that opportunity to get the best possible language from the child. Allen (1980b) offers the following example of an incidental teaching episode described by Hart:

> A four-year-old girl with delayed language stands in front of the teacher with a paint apron in her hand. The teacher says, "What do you need?" (Teacher does not anticipate the child's need by putting the apron on the child at the moment.)
>
> If the child does not answer, the teacher tells her and gives her a prompt: "It's an apron. Can you say 'apron'?" If the child says "apron," the teacher ties it while giving descriptive praise, "You said it right. It is an apron. I am tying your apron on you." The teacher's last sentence models the next verbal behavior, "Tie my apron," that the teacher will expect once the child has learned to say "apron."
>
> If the child does not say "apron," the teacher ties the apron. No further comments are made at this time. The teacher must not coax, nag or pressure the child. If each episode is kept brief and pleasant, the child will contact the teacher frequently. Thus, the teacher will have many opportunities for incidental teaching. If the teacher pressures the child, such incidental learning opportunities will be lost. Some chil-

For a rationale and instructional guidelines for using signing to increase the communication and language abilities of young children in integrated preschool programs, see Zeece and Wolda (1995).

Creating sociodramatic play scripts that require children to interact with one another (e.g., customer and clerk at a shoe store or hamburger stand) can be effective in promoting communication skills (Goldstein, 1993).

FIGURE 14.4
Five criteria for evaluating IEP/IFSP objectives for infants, toddlers, and preschoolers with disabilities

FUNCTIONALITY

1. **Will the skill increase the child's ability to interact with people and objects within the daily environment?**
   The child needs to perform the skill in all or most of the environments in which he or she interacts.
   Skill: Places object into container.
   Opportunities: Home – Places sweater in drawer, cookie in paper bag.
   School – Places lunch box in cubbyhole, trash in trash bin.
   Community – Places milk carton in grocery cart, rocks and soil in flower pot.

2. **Will the skill have to be performed by someone else if the child cannot do it?**
   The skill is a behavior or event that is critical for completion of daily routines.
   Skill: Looks for object in usual location.
   Opportunities: Finds coat on coat rack, gets food from cupboard.

GENERALITY

3. **Does the skill represent a general concept or class of responses? The skill emphasizes a generic process, rather than a particular instance.**
   Skill: Fits objects into defined spaces.
   Opportunities: Puts mail in mailbox, places crayon in box, puts cutlery into sorter.

4. **Can the skill be adapted or modified for a variety of disabling conditions?**
   The child's sensory impairment should interfere as little as possible with the performance.
   Skill: Correctly activates simple toy.
   Opportunities: Motor impairments – Activates light, easy-to-move toys (e.g., balls, rocking horse, toys on wheels, roly-poly toys).
   Visual impairments – Activates large, bright, noise-making toys (e.g., bells, drums, large rattles).

5. **Can the skill be generalized across a variety of settings, materials, and/or people?**
   The child can perform the skill with interesting materials and in meaningful situations.
   Skill: Manipulates two small objects simultaneously.
   Opportunities: Home – Builds with small interlocking blocks, threads laces on shoes.
   School – Sharpens pencil with pencil sharpener.
   Community – Takes coin out of small wallet.

INSTRUCTIONAL CONTEXT

6. **Can the skill be taught in a way that reflects the manner in which the skill will be used in daily environments?**
   The skill can occur in a naturalistic manner.
   Skill: Uses object to obtain another object.
   Opportunities: Uses fork to obtain food, broom to rake toy; steps on stool to reach toy on shelf.

7. **Can the skill be elicited easily by the teacher/parent within classroom/home activities?**
   The skill can be initiated easily by the child as part of daily routines.
   Skill: Stacks objects.
   Opportunities: Stacks books, cups/plates, wooden logs.

MEASURABILITY

8. **Can the skill be seen and/or heard?**
   Different observers must be able to identify the same behavior.
   Measurable skill: Gains attention and refers to object, person, and/or event.
   Nonmeasurable skill: Experiences a sense of self-importance

dren may learn to avoid the teacher—they will simply do without; other children may learn inappropriate ways, such as whining and crying, to get what they want. (unpaged)

Through repeated interactions of this type, children learn that language is important; it can get them what they want, and teachers listen when they speak and want to hear more about things of interest to them. An important guideline in inci-

FIGURE 14.4 *(continued)*

9. **Can the skill be directly counted (e.g., by frequency, duration, distance measures)?**
    The skill represents a well-defined behavior or activity.
    Measurable skill: Grasps pea-sized object.
    Nonmeasurable skill: Has mobility in all fingers.

10. **Does the skill contain or lend itself to determination of performance criteria?**
    The extent and/or degree of accuracy of the skill can be evaluated.
    Measurable skill: Follows one-step directions with contextual cues.
    Nonmeasurable skill: Will increase receptive language skills.

HIERARCHICAL RELATION BETWEEN LONG-RANGE GOAL AND SHORT-TERM OBJECTIVE

11. **Is the short-term objective a developmental subskill or step thought to be critical to the achievement of the long-range goal?**
    Appropriate: Short-Term Objective – Releases object with each hand.
    Long-Range-Goal – Places and releases object balanced on top of another object.

Inappropriate: 1. The Short-Term Objective is a restatement of the same skill as the Long-Range-Goal, with the addition of an instructional prompt (e.g., Short-Term Objective – Activates mechanical toy with physical prompt. Long-Range-Goal – Independently activates mechanical toy) or a quantitative limitation to the extent of the skill (e.g., Short-Term Objective – Stacks 5 1-inch blocks; Long-Range-Goal – Stacks 10 1-inch blocks).

2. The Short-Term Objective is not conceptually or functionally related to the Long-Range Goal (e.g., Short-Term Objective – Releases object voluntarily; Long-Range Goal – Pokes with index finger).

Source: From A. R. Notari-Syverson and S. L. Shuster, "Putting Real-Life Skills into IEP/IFSPs for Infants and Young Children," 1995, *Teaching Exceptional Children, 27*(2), p. 31. Used by permission.

dental teaching is to keep interactions brief and pleasant so that there will be many more opportunities. The child should never be interrogated or put on the spot (K. E. Allen, 1980a).

Warren and Gazdag (1990) combined incidental teaching and mand-model techniques into a *milieu instructional approach* to teach two 3-year-olds with developmental delays various language forms during naturalistic play. The authors describe the differences between the two complementary techniques.

> The distinction between the two procedures centers on who (trainer or child) initiates the instructional interaction. With the mand-model the teacher is in the role of facilitator, initiating the interaction by "manding" a target response, typically by asking a target probe question about the event or activity to which the child is attending. In the incidental teaching procedure, the child initiates the interaction either verbally or nonverbally. The trainer then elicits the target response by prompting a more elaborate response. (p. 70)

Mothers of preschoolers with language impairments can learn to use milieu language training procedures at home with their children (Alpert & Kaiser, 1992).

Table 14.2 shows examples of instructional episodes using incidental teaching and mand-model techniques. The methods have much in common. Both view the teacher as (a) an astute and systematic observer and recorder of children's language, (b) a sensitive and willing listener, and (c) a systematic responder who helps the child "say it better" through differential feedback (K. E. Allen, 1980a).

Promoting the Social Competence of Preschoolers with Disabilities

In addition to any deficits in cognitive, motor, language, and other developmental areas, many young children with disabilities exhibit problems in social skills (Odom, McConnell, & McEvoy, 1992). When placed in mainstreamed settings, many preschoolers with disabilities interact infrequently and incompetently with other children. Strain and his colleagues (Sainato, Goldstein, & Strain, 1992; Strain, 1981; Strain & Odom, 1986) have investigated the use of peer social initiations as a means of increasing the social competence of preschoolers with disabilities. The procedure involves teaching nondisabled peers to direct social overtures to their classmates

TABLE 14.2
Examples of language-prompting episodes using mand-model and incidental teaching procedures

EXAMPLE 1	EXAMPLE 2
Mand Model	
Context: Child is scooping beans with a ladle and pouring them into a pot. Trainer: "What are you doing?" (target probe question) Child: No response. Trainer: "Tell me." (mand) Child: "Beans." Trainer: "Say, *pour beans.*"(model) Child: "Pour beans." Trainer: "That's right, you're pouring beans into the pot." (verbal acknowledgement + expansion)	Context: Trainer gives each child a turn to blow bubbles. Trainer: (holds the wand up to the child's mouth) "What do you want to do?" (target probe question) Child: "Bubbles." Trainer: "*Blow* bubbles." (model) Child: "Blow bubbles." Trainer: "OK, you want to blow bubbles. Here you go." (verbal acknowledgement + expansion + activity participation)
Incidental Teaching	
Context: Making pudding activity. Trainer gives peer a turn at stirring the pudding as the subject looks on. Child: "Me!" (child initiates) and reaches for ladle. Trainer: "Stir pudding." (model) Child: "Stir pudding." Trainer: "All right. You stir the pudding, too." (verbal acknowledgement + expansion + activity participation)	Context: Trainer and subject are washing dishes together in a parallel fashion. Child: "Wash." (Child initiates with an action-verb, partial target response) Trainer: "Wash what?" (elaborative question) Child: "Wash" (incorrect response). Trainer: "Wash *what*?" (elaborative question) Child: "Wash cups." Trainer: "That's right. We're washing cups." (verbal acknowledgement + expansion)

Source: From "Facilitating Basic Vocabulary Acquisition with Milieu Teaching Procedures" by S. F. Warren, *Journal of Early Intervention,* 1992, *16,* p. 242. Reprinted by permission.

with disabilities. Strain and Odom (1986) recommend that peer intervention agents be taught to make initiations to children with disabilities in the form of (a) play opportunities, (b) offers to share, (c) physical assistance, and (d) affection. These initiations are recommended on the basis of naturalistic studies of the social interactions of both preschoolers with and without disabilities; the studies showed that such initiations were followed by a positive response more than 50% of the time and that responding to the social bids of others increased a child's social acceptability.

The strategy requires careful arrangement of the classroom environment to encourage greater social interaction. For example, the probability of social interaction can be increased by limiting the number of toys so that, to participate, children must share and by requiring the children to play within a confined area. The key feature of the procedure, however, is the careful training of the peers who are chosen to serve as "confederates." Training sessions usually take between 20 and 25 minutes and incorporate teacher modeling and both teacher and confederate role-playing of the desired social initiation. Figure 14.5 shows a sample script for an initial training session in which children learn how to initiate sharing. Training is followed by daily intervention sessions, in which the teacher arranges an activity for the children that is conducive to social interaction and then prompts and verbally reinforces the confederate for being a good teacher and the target child with disabilities for being a good player.

Positive results have been documented using the peer initiation intervention with preschool children with mental retardation, autism, and behavioral disorders (Goldstein, Kaczmarek, Pennington, & Shafer, 1992). The outcomes include more positive social responses by all target children, more social initiations by some target children, longer social exchanges by target children, and generalization of social interactions by target children to other integrated preschool settings.

Developing a Preschool Activity Schedule

Teachers in preschool programs for children with disabilities face the challenge of organizing the program day into a schedule that meets each child's individual learning needs. The schedule should include free play, one-to-one and small-group instruction; provide each child with many learning opportunities to explore the envi-

To learn about a social skills training program to teach preschoolers with developmental delays how to make friends, see Kohler and Strain (1993).

McConnell, McEvoy, and Odom (1992) identify 49 interventions for increasing social interaction skills of young children with disabilities.

The systematic arrangement of play activities and the use of peer "confederates" can be used to increase the social competence and language skills of children with disabilities.

FIGURE 14.5

Sample script for an initial training session in which children learn how to initiate sharing

TEACHER: "Today you are going to learn how to be a good teacher. Sometimes your friends in your class do not know how to play with other children. You are going to learn how to teach them to play. What are you going to do?"

CHILD RESPONSE: "Teach them to play."

TEACHER: "One way you get your friend to play with you is to share. How do you get your friend to play with you?"

CHILD RESPONSE: "Share."

TEACHER: "Right! You share. When you share, you look at your friend and say. 'Here,' and put a toy in his hand. What do you do?" (Repeat this exercise until the child can repeat these three steps.)

CHILD RESPONSE: "Look at friend and say, 'Here,' and put the toy in his hand."

ADULT MODEL WITH ROLE-PLAYER: "Now, watch me, I am going to share with _____. Tell me if I do it right." (Demonstrate sharing.) "Did I share with _____? What did I do?"

CHILD RESPONSE: "Yea! _____ looked at _____, said 'Here _____' and put a toy in his hand."

ADULT: "Right. I looked at _____ and said, 'Here _____' and put a toy in his hand. Now watch me. See if I share with _____." (Move to the next activity in the classroom. This time provide a negative example of sharing by leaving out the "put in hand" component. Put the toy beside the role-player.) "Did I share?" (Correct if necessary and repeat this example if child got it wrong.) "Why not?"

CHILD RESPONSE: "No. You did not put the toy in _____'s hand."

ADULT: "That's right. I did not put the toy in _____'s hand. When I share, I have to look at _____ and say, 'Here _____' and put the toy in his hand." (Give the child two more positive and two more negative examples of sharing. When the child answers incorrectly about sharing, repeat the example. Vary the negative examples by leaving out different components: looking, saying 'Here,' and putting in hand.)

CHILD PRACTICE WITH ADULTS: "Now _____, I want you to get _____ to share with you. What do you do when you share?"

CHILD RESPONSE: "Look at _____ and say. 'Here _____,' and put a toy in his hand."

ADULT: "Now, go get _____ to play with you." (For those practice examples, the role-playing adult should be responsive to the child's sharing.) (To the other confederates:) "Did _____ share with _____? What did she/he do?"

CHILD RESPONSE: "Yes/No. Looked at _____ and said, 'Here _____' and put a toy in his hand."

ADULT: (Move to the next activity.) "Now, _____, I want you to share with _____."

Introduce Persistence

TEACHER: "Sometimes when I play with _____, he/she does not want to play back. I have to keep on trying. What do I have to do?"

CHILD RESPONSE: "Keep on trying."

TEACHER: "Right, I have to keep trying. Watch me. I am going to share with _____. Now I want you to see if I keep on trying." (Role-player will be initially unresponsive.) (Teacher should be persistent until child finally responds.) "Did I get _____ to play with me?" **CHILD:** "Yes." **TEACHER:** "Did he want to play?" **CHILD:** "No." **TEACHER:** "What did I do?" **CHILD:** "Keep on trying. No?" **TEACHER:** "Right, I kept on trying. Watch. See if I can get _____ to play with me this time." (Again, the role-player should be unresponsive at first. Repeat above questions and correct if necessary. Repeat the example until the child responds correctly.)

Source: From "Peer Social Interactions: Effective Intervention for Social Skills Development of Exceptional Children" by P. S. Strain and S. L. Odom, 1986, *Exceptional Children,* Vol. 52, p. 547. Reprinted by permission.

ronment and communicate with others throughout the day; and allow easy transition from activity to activity. In short, the schedule should provide a framework for maximizing instruction while remaining manageable and flexible. In addition, how activities are scheduled and organized in integrated programs has considerable effect on the frequency and type of interaction that occurs between children with and without disabilities (Burstein, 1986; Harris & Handleman, 1994) and on the extent to which the mainstreamed children benefit from instruction (O'Connell, 1986).

Lund and Bos (1981) suggest that teachers begin planning a preschool schedule by determining the basic activities and time blocks. The next steps in constructing the schedule are filling in the approximate amount of time to spend on each activity each day, sequencing the components, scheduling children for individual and group instruction, and assigning staff (teachers, aides, and volunteers). Table 14.3 shows sample daily schedules for three preschoolers with disabilities.

The physical arrangement of the classroom itself must support the planned activities. Figure 14.6 shows an example of a preschool classroom layout. Lund and Bos (1981) make the following suggestions for setting up a preschool classroom:

> O'Connell (1986) offers suggestions for structuring the physical arrangement of small-group learning activities in mainstreamed preschool classrooms.

TABLE 14.3
Sample activity schedules for three preschoolers with disabilities

	CHILD		
TIME	**HEATHER**	**DUNCAN**	**JUSTIN**
8:50	Photographic activity schedule	Handwriting	Answering questions
9:10	Expressive language (nouns)	Verbal imitation of words	Expressive language (nouns)
9:30	Following complex directions	Conversation skills	Number-object correspondence
9:45	Receptive language (nouns)	Verbal imitation of words	Counting to a number
10:00	Edmark Reading	Following complex directions	Using playground equipment
10:15	Undressing	Using construction toys	Riding a tricycle
10:30	Using playground equipment	Using playground equipment	Edmark Prereading
10:45	Social initiations	Social initiations	Edmark Prereading
11:00	Providing personal information	Reading (computer software)	Photographic activity schedule
11:15	Following complex directions	Following complex directions	
11:30	Lunch	Lunch	Lunch
12:00	Verbal imitation of words	Verbal imitation of words	Motor imitation
12:15	Story (expressive language)	Story (expressive language)	Expressive language (nouns)
12:40	Receptive language (nouns)	Receptive language (nouns)	Pre-handwriting
1:00	Receptive language (verbs)	Receptive language (verbs)	Using construction toys
1:25	Alphabet letter identification	Expressive language (nouns)	Matching skills (computer software)
1:45	Pre-handwriting	Dressing	
2:00			Pre-handwriting (computer software)

Source: From "The Princeton Child Development Institute" by L. McClannahan and P. J. Krantz. In S. L. Harris and J. S. Handleman, *Preschool Programs for Children with Autism,* 1994, p. 113. Austin, TX: PRO-ED. Used by permission.

FIGURE 14.6

Example of a preschool classroom layout

Preschool Classroom - Millbrook

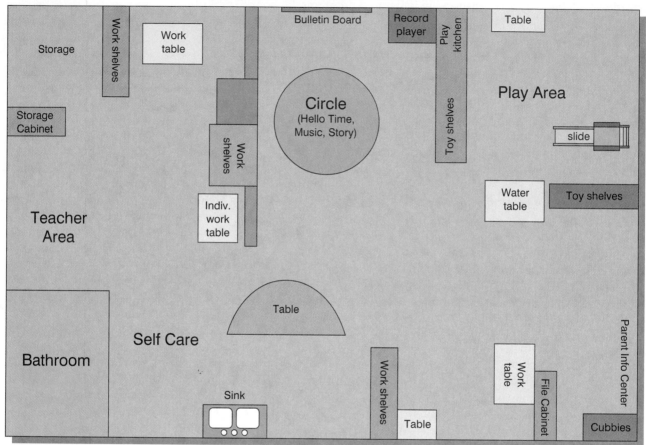

Source: From "TEACCH Services for Preschool Children" by C. Lord and E. Shopler. In S. L. Harris and J. S. Handleman, *Preschool Programs for Children with Autism,* 1994, p. 95. Austin, TX: PRO-ED. Used by permission.

- Place individual work areas and quiet activities together, away from avenues of traffic, to encourage attending behavior.
- Provide a stable area, such as an activity table and rug, where a variety of group programs can be conducted.
- Place the activity table within easy access of storage so that materials are readily obtainable.
- Place materials used most often close together for accessibility (e.g., clipboard, individual program materials).
- Label or color-code all storage areas so that aides and volunteers can easily find needed materials.
- Arrange equipment and group areas so that the students can move easily from one activity to another. Picture or color codes can be applied to various work areas.
- Provide lockers or cubbies for students so they know where to find their belongings. Again, add picture cues to help the students identify their lockers.

✳ *Service Delivery Alternatives for Early Intervention*

Where early intervention takes place varies, depending on the age of the child and the special supports he or she and the family need. Early intervention services for infants and newborns with significant disabilities are often provided in hospital settings. Most early childhood special education services, however, are provided in the child's home, in a center- or school-based facility, or in a combination of both settings.

Hospital-Based Programs

Increasingly, early intervention services are being provided to hospitalized newborns and their families. Low-birth-weight and other high-risk newborns who require specialized health care are placed in neonatal intensive care units (NICUs). Many NICUs now include a variety of professionals, such as neonatologists who provide medical care for infants with special needs, nurses who provide ongoing medical assistance, social workers or psychologists who help parents and families with emotional and financial concerns, and infant education specialists who promote interactions between parents and infants (Brown, Thurman, & Pearl, 1993; Flynn & McCollum, 1989).

Home-Based Programs

As the name suggests, a home-based program depends heavily on parental training and cooperation. The parents assume the primary responsibility of caregivers and teachers for their child with disabilities. Parent training is usually provided by a teacher or trainer who visits the home regularly to guide the parents, act as a consultant, evaluate the success of intervention, and regularly assess the child's progress. Home visitors (or home teachers or home advisors, as they are often called) in some programs are specially trained paraprofessionals. They may visit as frequently as several times a week but probably no less than a few times a month. They sometimes carry the results of their in-home evaluations back to other professionals, who may recommend changes in the program.

Perhaps the best-known home-based program is the nationally validated Portage Project (Shearer & Shearer, 1972). Operated by a consortium of 23 school districts in south-central Wisconsin, the Portage Project has produced its own assessment materials and teaching activities, *The Portage Guide to Early Education*. The program is based on 450 behaviors, sequenced developmentally and classified into self-help, cognition, socialization, language, and motor skills. A project teacher normally visits the home 1 day each week to review the child's progress during the previous week, describe activities for the upcoming week, demonstrate to the parents how to carry out the activities with the child, observe the parent and child interacting and offer suggestions and advice as needed, and summarize where the program stands and indicate what records parents should keep during the next week. The Portage Project has been replicated in hundreds of locations around the country (Shearer & Snider, 1981). A review of outcome studies on the Portage Project states that there is evidence of developmental acceleration in mildly delayed children (Sturmey & Crisp, 1986).

Idea Bunny

....

Helping Preschoolers Be More Independent

by Diane M. Sainato, Marie C. Ward, Jamie Brandt, Jill McQuaid, and Tamara C. Timko

After the initial flurry of the children's arrival at the preschool had subsided, their teacher gathered the children together for the morning's opening circle time. They sang the "Good Morning" song, charted the weather, and handed out jobs for the day. Just before circle time ended, the teacher said, "Today during our center time we have many fun things to do. Please remember only a few children at a time are to be at each center. When you take an activity off the shelf, be sure to return it to the same place. Now everyone find something to do. I will be here to help you."

Most of the children made immediate choices regarding the activities available. The teacher had to remind some children of the rules regarding "waiting your turn" and using "inside voices." Most of the children were quietly engaged during the 15-minute center time; however, Sally, who chose a matching and sorting task, dumped the variety of colored bears onto the table and promptly forgot what she was to do next. She was quickly frustrated with waiting for the teacher to notice her and wandered off without completing the task. When the teacher noticed Sally, she took her hand and brought her back to the table where her bears had been left. The teacher reminded Sally what to do, showed her an example, and moved to help another child. This time Sally matched several bears by color, then, growing bored with the task, carried the bucket of bears over to the water table and proceeded to dump them into the water. This time the teacher sternly said, "Sally, what are you supposed to be doing?" Sally replied, "I don't know."

Sally's teacher has the expectation that children in her preschool will be able to listen to directions, choose tasks, handle materials, engage in those tasks in an independent fashion, and, after completing the task, return the materials to their proper place. Young children such as Sally, who may or may not

have been identified as having special needs, often have not had the opportunity to learn skills which would enable them to engage the environment in the absence of teacher direction. Learning to perform tasks independent of teacher direction is a skill necessary for successful transition and inclusion into many typical classrooms. These skills are not only necessary in the kindergarten classroom but throughout the child's years of education (Sainato & Lyon, 1989).

The Idea Bunny

To help preschool children develop independent performance skills, we built upon the work of other researchers who had successfully used auditory prompting systems with older students with disabilities (Alberto, Sharpton, Briggs, & Stright, 1986; Trask-Tyler, Grossi, & Heward, 1994). In previous studies, students used a foot pedal or hand-operated switch to operate a Walkman-type tape recorder in order to play prerecorded instructions to perform various components of tasks such as meal preparation (see "I Made It Myself and It's Good!" in Chapter 9). We adapted the auditory prompting system to make it more appropriate for preschool children and called it the Idea Bunny, a soft stuffed-bunny toy with a miniature cassette recorder sewn inside. A foot pedal was attached to the cassette recorder through a small opening in the bunny's underside. The Idea Bunny was placed on a table close to a bookshelf that held a variety of tasks. Prior to beginning the study, we developed an analysis of each task to determine the component steps. For example, the steps of a picture completion task are as follows:

1. Pick the basket containing picture pieces from the shelf.
2. Take the basket to the table.
3. Place the pieces on the table to show the picture.
4. Choose one piece and find another to make a picture.
5. Put the picture at the top of the table.
6. Put the pieces back into the basket.
7. Return the basket to the shelf.

We then created a script of instructions that included the steps for each learning task. The Idea Bunny "said" one step when the child pressed the foot pedal. Children were taught to use the Idea Bunny to help them complete steps in the table-time activity. A beep sounded to signal the end of a specific step. At the end of the task, the Idea Bunny asked the child to stick his ears together to signal the teacher that the child was finished. The bunny's script for the picture completion task is described in the next section.

Picture Completion

"Hello! I'm happy you came to see Idea Bunny today. I have a great idea for you to try. Today we are going to complete pictures together. Go to the shelf and find the basket of pictures that are cut in half. Bring the basket back to the table [beep]. Take all of the pieces out of the basket and turn them around so that you can see the picture on each piece [beep]. Choose one piece and pick another piece so that it makes a picture. Match the two pieces together and put them at the top of the table [beep]. Keep on matching the pieces together until they have all been matched to make pictures [beep]. Great job! Now that you are finished matching the pieces, pick them up and place them in the basket [beep]. Take the basket of picture pieces back to the shelf where you found them [beep]. Now, put my ears together so the teacher knows you have finished your work. We had a great time today! Let's play again tomorrow [beep]."

"Hello! I'm happy you came to see Idea Bunny. Today we are going to complete pictures together."

FIGURE A

Percentage of intervals in which active engagement and teacher prompts were recorded while three preschoolers with disabilities participated in a tabletop learning activity before and after being trained to use the Idea Bunny

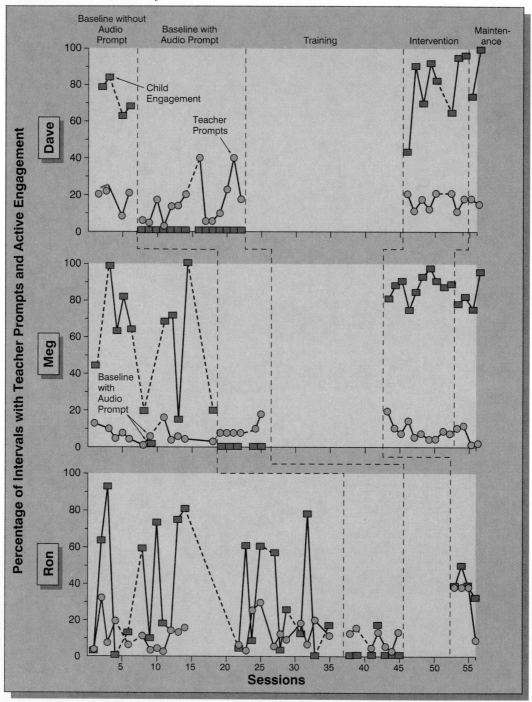

Figure source: From "Idea Puppy: Teaching Preschool Age Children with Disabilities to Build Independent Work Skills with the Use of a Self-Operated Audio Prompt Device" by J. Stemley, 1993. Unpublished master's thesis, The Ohio State University. Used by permission.

Results of Research

To date we have conducted three studies using the Idea Bunny as an auditory prompting device in preschool classrooms for young children with developmental disabilities (Brandt, 1992; Stemley, 1993; Ward, 1994). The studies' results show that even though children are initially able to do the tasks, they require a great deal of teacher direction. Children have to be taught to use the Idea Bunny. At first, the children in our studies often played the whole tape just to listen to the bunny "talk." Then they forgot what the bunny had first told them to do. Figure A shows a typical pattern of responding for two preschool children using the Idea Bunny. We find that in the baseline without Idea Bunny condition, the children are engaged in the task but require a high rate of teacher prompts to keep on task. When the teacher steps out of the situation (baseline with Idea Bunny) and leaves children alone with the Idea Bunny without training, they show very little task engagement. We then trained each child to use the Idea Bunny in a one-to-one situation with the teacher. During the intervention phase, we noted that children were much more engaged with the task and the rate of teacher prompts was low and stable.

The results of this study showed that preschoolers with developmental disabilities were able to learn to use the auditory prompt device. Children's independent engagement increased and, most importantly, maintained following the removal of the prompt device (Stemley, 1993). Children appeared to enjoy the Idea Bunny and often patted him on the head and kissed him before they left the center. Sometimes they would talk back to the Bunny. One day when the bunny said, "Good morning, I'm glad you came to see me today," a child replied, "Hi, Bunny, I'm so happy to see you, too."

Suggestions for Using the Idea Bunny in the Classroom

1. Begin with skills that are in the child's repertoire. This activity should be for practice, not introducing new skills.
2. Design a space for the center away from the general play areas of the classroom.
3. Create a task analysis for each activity and develop scripts to match.
4. Try out the scripts first to see whether the steps are too long.
5. Teach the children to use the prompting device.
6. Monitor children to see that they understand the task.
7. Place all of the materials needed to complete the task in close proximity to the children.

Diane M. Sainato is a faculty member in the special education program at The Ohio State University, where she directs a master's degree personnel training program in early childhood education and conducts research on the Idea Bunny and other ways to increase young children's independence. Marie C. Ward teaches at Illinois State University; Jamie Brandt and Jill McQuaid are early childhood special education teachers. Tamara Timko is a doctoral student at The Ohio State University.

The Transactional Family Systems Model (TFSM) at the University of Washington provides home-based intervention to infants who are medically fragile from birth to 2 years and their families (Hedlund, 1989). The program's primary goal is to foster positive interactions between parents and their babies. The TFSM home visitor helps parents become sensitive to their infant's behavioral repertoire and adjust their interactions to match the baby's needs. Videotaping helps parents learn about the significance of the fleeting and subtle cues these babies often express with their body language. Once parents become sensitive to their babies' behavioral cues, the home visitor helps them adjust their own communication styles accordingly. Parents receive guided practice and encouragement in interactions with their baby. TFSM staff highlight small increments of developmental progress. The ultimate goal of the TFSM program is to give parents a sense of competence and to help them see their child as a developing individual despite a disability or medical condition.

For suggestions for developing IFSP/IEPs for children who are medically fragile, see Prendergast (1995).

An early intervention program based in the home has several advantages, especially if the home is the child's own.

- The home is the child's natural environment, and parents have been the child's first teachers.
- Other family members—siblings and perhaps even grandparents—have more opportunity to interact with the child, for both instruction and social contact. These significant others can play an important role in the child's growth and development.
- Home learning activities and materials are more likely to be natural and appropriate. And it is often true that a parent can give more time and attention to the child than even the most adequately staffed center or school.
- Parents who are actively involved in helping their child learn and develop clearly have an advantage over parents who feel guilt, frustration, or defeat at their seeming inability to help their child. (Of course, this does not imply that parents of a child in a center-based program cannot or do not take an active role in their child's learning and growth.)
- In sparsely populated regions, a home-based program allows a child to live at home while receiving an intensive education, without totally disrupting the family's life.
- Home-based programs can also be less costly to operate without the expenses of maintaining a facility and equipment and transporting children to and from the center (Bailey & Bricker, 1985).

Home-based programs, however, are not without disadvantages:

- Because the programs place so much responsibility on parents, they are not effective with all families. Not all parents are able or willing to spend the time required to teach their children, and some who try are not effective teachers.
- Early childhood special education programs must learn to more effectively serve the large and growing number of young children who do not reside in the traditional two-parent family—especially the many thousands of children with teenage mothers who are single, uneducated, and poor. Many of these infants and preschoolers are at risk for developmental delays because of the impoverished conditions in which they live, and it is unlikely that a parent struggling with the realities of day-to-day survival will be able to meet the added demands of involvement in an early intervention program (Turnbull & Turnbull, 1990).
- Because the parent—usually the mother—is the primary service provider, children in home-based programs may not receive as wide a range of services as they would in a center-based program, where they can be seen by a variety of professionals. (It should be noted, however, that the services of professionals such as physical therapists, occupational therapists, or speech therapists can be, and sometimes are, provided in the home.)
- The child may not receive sufficient opportunity for social interaction with peers.

Center-Based Programs

Center-based programs provide early intervention services in a special educational setting outside the home. The setting may be part of a hospital complex, a special day-care center, or a preschool. Some children may attend a specially designed developmental center or training center that offers a wide range of services for children with varying types and degrees of disabilities. One program's setting was an outdoor playground specially built on a New York City rooftop (Jones, 1977). Wherever they are, these centers offer the combined services of many professionals and paraprofessionals, often from several different fields.

Most center-based programs encourage social interaction, and some try to integrate children with disabilities and typically developing children in day-care or preschool classes. Some children attend a center each weekday, for all or most of the day; others may come less frequently, although most centers expect to see each child at least once a week. Parents are sometimes given roles as classroom aides or encouraged to act as their child's primary teacher. A few programs allow parents to spend time with other professionals or take training while their child is somewhere else in the center. Virtually all EEPCD model programs and most other effective programs for young children with disabilities recognize the critical need to involve the parents, and they welcome parents in every aspect of the program.

A good example of a center-based program is the PEECH (Precise Early Education of Children with Handicaps) project originally developed at the University of Illinois. Designed for children aged 3 to 5 with mild to moderate disabilities, PEECH combines classroom instruction for up to 10 children with disabilities and 5 nondisabled children. A team approach to intervention and parental involvement includes a classroom teacher and a paraprofessional aide, a psychologist, a speech-language pathologist, and a social worker. Children spend 2 or 3 hours in class each day, with some time in large and small groups and individualized activities. Parents are included in all stages of the intervention, including policy making. The project offers a lending library and toy library for parents to use, as well as a parent newsletter. The project's ultimate goal is to successfully integrate youngsters with disabilities into regular classes whenever possible. Early childhood special educators at 200 replication sites in 36 states have received training in various components of the PEECH program (Karnes, Beauchamp, & Pfaus, 1993).

The Carousel Preschool Program is a center-based early childhood program operated in conjunction with the University of South Florida. The Carousel program operates two integrated preschool classrooms, one serving 4- to 5-year-old children with severe behavioral disorders and one serving children considered at risk for developing severe behavior problems in the future. Both classrooms provide a regular preschool curriculum to 16 children, half of whom are same-age peers without behavior problems. Classroom teachers work to engage all students—those with disabilities, those at risk, and nondisabled children—in the same activities. To ensure the transition to integrated, least restrictive settings, Carousel staff provide a follow-up program and inservice training to the teachers and aides in the children's new schools.

Center-based programs generally offer three advantages that are difficult to build into home-based efforts:

• Increased opportunity for a team of specialists from different fields—education, physical and occupational therapy, speech and language pathology, medicine, and others—to observe each child and cooperate in intervention and continued assessment. Some special educators feel that the intensive instruction and related services that can be provided in a center-based program are especially important for children with severe disabilities (Rose & Calhoun, 1990). Many centers hold

The curricula, teaching methods, daily activity schedule, approaches to integration, methods of parent involvement, and transition planning used by 10 different preschool programs for children with autism are described by Harris and Handleman (1994).

regular meetings (perhaps once a month) at which all those involved with the child sit down to discuss his progress, his response to the strategies used, and new or revised objectives for him.

- The opportunity for contact with typically developing peers makes center programs especially appealing for some children.
- Parents involved in center programs no doubt feel some relief at the support they get from the professionals who work with their child and from other parents with children at the same center.

Disadvantages of a center-based program include the expense of transportation, the cost and maintenance of the center itself, and the probability of less parent involvement than in home-based programs.

Combined Home-Center Programs

Many early intervention programs combine center-based activities and home visitation. Few center programs take children for more than a few hours a day, for up to 5 days per week. But because young children with disabilities require more intervention than a few hours a day, many programs combine the intensive help of a variety of professionals in a center with the continuous attention and sensitive care of parents at home. Intervention that carries over from center to home clearly offers many of the advantages of the two types of programs and negates some of their disadvantages.

The Charlotte Circle Project is a combination home- and center-based early intervention program for infants and toddlers with severe/profound disabilities (Rose & Calhoun, 1990). The project is based on the social reciprocity model, which views the child's behavior as affecting the parent, whose behavior in turn affects the behavior of the child—hence the "circle" in the project's name. Nonresponsiveness, nonvocal behavior, irritability, lack of imitation responses, and the need for special

> Bailey and Simeonsson (1988b) provide a detailed discussion of the relative advantages and disadvantages of home-based versus center-based early intervention.

Programs like the Charlotte Circle Project in North Carolina teach parents to identify and increase the frequency of positive behaviors by their infants such as smiling or imitating.

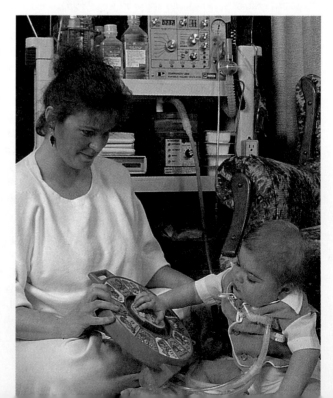

health-care routines (e.g., tube feeding, suctioning) all present special challenges to normal infant-parent interactions; behaviors associated with these problems are often viewed negatively. The Charlotte Circle Project attempts to identify and increase the frequency of alternative positive behaviors that will cause parents to want to continue their interactions with their child (Rose & Calhoun, 1990; Rose, Calhoun, & Ladage, 1989).

The center-based component of the project's classroom instruction occurs from 9:00 A.M. to 1:00 P.M. throughout the year. Parents can enroll their children for either a 3- or 5-day week. The home-based/family services component entails monthly home visits; the visits include family-focused assessment and planning, demonstrations of instructional techniques, and provision of information and other support. Between regularly scheduled home visits, ongoing individualized consultation and collaboration with parents and families are available as needed.

In a survey of 67 EEPCD model programs serving infants and toddlers with disabilities, Karnes and Stayton (1988) found that 70% of the programs offered a home-center combination option, 13% offered home-based services only, and 12% were center-based only. In practice, however, most children (52%) are actually served in centers, compared with 27% who receive all services at home and 15% who participate in a home-center combination. It is probably best to view these choices—home, center, or combined programs—as more alike than different. In fact, they do seem to have more in common than not: carefully sequenced curricula, strong parent involvement, explicit goals and frequent assessment of progress, integration of children with and without disabilities whenever possible, and staff teams that consist of specialists in several fields.

> The most frequently used sites for the provision of early childhood special education services during 1992–93 were the child's home (34%), followed by early intervention classroom (33%), and an outpatient center (29%) (U.S. Department of Education, 1994).

❋ *Who Can Help?*
Physicians and Other Health Professionals

The success of efforts to prevent disabilities in children and to identify, assess, and intervene with children who have special needs as early as possible requires the training and experience of a wide range of professionals. Current "best practice" guidelines for early childhood services call for a transdisciplinary approach to the delivery of related services in which parents and professionals work together in assessing needs, developing the IFSP, providing services, and evaluating outcomes (DEC Recommended Practices, 1993; McDonnell & Hardman, 1900).

No other professional has as great an opportunity to prevent certain disabilities as the obstetrician. Knowing many of the conditions that predict possible disabilities, the obstetrician can examine the family history and recommend genetic counseling if there appears to be a significant risk. Because this physician sees an expectant mother several times during pregnancy, he or she can monitor any possible problems that arise, perform or refer her for amniocentesis if necessary, and generally ensure the kind of prenatal care that reduces the risk of problems at birth. In the delivery room, the doctor's concern for possible birth trauma can contribute to preventing problems or identifying them early.

In the same way, the pediatrician (or perhaps the family doctor) has the chance to see the infant soon after birth and then regularly during the first months of life. His or her attention to the Apgar ratings and an immediate postnatal examination of the infant can help prevent problems or identify high-risk infants. Because most

> See McCollum and Hughes (1988) and Woodruff and McGonigel (1988) for discussions of different team models used in early childhood programs. PL 99–457 requires that each IFSP must identify a case manager who will be responsible for seeing that the plan is implemented and coordinating the delivery of services with other agencies and professionals. See Bailey (1989) for a discussion of issues related to case management in early childhood services.

moderate to severe disabilities and sensory impairments are recognizable at birth or soon afterward, the pediatrician's role is critical. Other conditions, such as parental neglect or abuse, may also be evident to the attentive physician. For the same reasons, nurses and nurse practitioners can be of enormous help in noting and questioning possible disabilities or conditions in the home that might lead to a disability.

Later, other health professionals also contribute to identification, assessment, or treatment of specific problems that can cause disabilities. An ophthalmologist can detect early vision problems and can fit a child with corrective lenses (as can an optometrist). An audiologist can assess a child's hearing and prescribe a hearing aid or other treatment if there is a loss.

Other Early Intervention Specialists

Increasingly, early intervention services are being provided to hospitalized newborns and their families. NICUs now include a variety of professionals, such as neonatologists who provide medical care for infants with special needs, nurses who provide ongoing medical assistance, social workers or psychologists who help parents and families with emotional and financial concerns, and infant education specialists who promote interaction between parents and infant (Flynn & McCollum, 1989).

A psychologist can evaluate a child's socioemotional skills and cognitive development. Psychologists often participate in a child's initial assessments and frequently administer standardized tests. Staff psychologists often participate in team planning for a child. Although school psychologists have traditionally been trained to provide standardized assessments for school-age students and consultation to classroom teachers, their participation in preschool programs for children with disabilities is likely to increase as the public schools provide more early childhood special education services (Widerstrom, Mowder, & Willis, 1989).

Because so large a portion of mild disabilities is based in social and cultural factors, a social worker can be instrumental in helping children receive much needed services. It is often the social worker who is admitted to many homes in low socioeconomic areas, which correlate with higher incidences of mild retardation and learning problems. The case worker can observe young children whose behavior suggests future problems and refer them for assessment and possible treatment. Later, the social worker may help explain, monitor, or evaluate the progress of a home-based intervention.

A speech-language pathologist is an important part of almost every intervention team. Speech and language specialists usually assess every child referred for services, and they participate in the intervention plans for many children.

For children who have physical or multiple disabilities, a physical therapist is important. Physical therapy can help prevent further deterioration of muscles; it can also be applied to teaching a child gross- and fine-motor coordination. Likewise, an occupational therapist contributes to the intervention program for children with physical, multiple, or other severe impairments. He or she provides instruction in movement, self-help skills, and the use of adaptive equipment.

Early Childhood Educators

Teachers and other staff in regular preschools and day-care centers may be the first to identify certain delays in development or other problems like mild sensory impair-

The inattentiveness, developmental delays, and mild learning disabilities of some young children is due to lead poisoning. Needleman (1992) reported that up to 16% of children in the United States have blood lead levels high enough to place them at risk for neurological damage and impaired functioning. Most children exposed to lead poisoning are African Americans living in poverty.

ments, socioemotional problems, learning difficulties, or language problems. Prompt referral for special education services can often get these children with mild disabilities the help they need before they fall significantly behind their peers. As more and more children with disabilities are integrated into regular preschools, the role of general education teachers and paraprofessionals in these settings has become even more critical. Regular preschool and kindergarten teachers also play important roles in supporting a child's transition into a mainstream setting.

The actual delivery of services, whether in a home or center program, is most often the province of the special teacher, regardless of what title that person has. The special teacher must be the most knowledgeable about a child's instructional goals and objectives, the specific strategies and activities that will accomplish them, and the child's day-to-day progress. That teacher must be well trained in observing, analyzing, selecting, and sequencing learning tasks so that the child overcomes delays rather than falls further behind. The teacher must be imaginative and willing to try new things but patient enough to give a program a chance once it is begun. The teacher must be able not only to find what motivates and reinforces a child but also to relate to all of the other individuals involved in the child's program. In a home-based program, the home teacher or visitor must be able to train parents to take primary responsibility for teaching their child. Even in center-based programs, a large share of the center's parent-training efforts may fall to the special teacher.

The combined expertise and talents of all of these professionals have little chance of providing maximum benefit for the child and family unless they can work together as an effective multidisciplinary team. One of the first tasks for team members is to delineate their respective roles in terms of providing direct service and serving as an effective and cooperative team member (Chase, Thomas, & Correa, 1995). Table 14.4 shows examples of typical service providers and team member roles for 12 professionals who often work with infants, toddlers, and preschoolers with disabilities.

> The Division for Early Childhood recommends specific training and certification requirements for early childhood special educators (DEC, 1993; McCollum, McLean, McCartan, & Kaiser, 1989).

> For guidelines and suggestions for the effective use of paraprofessionals, see Cook, Tessier, and Klein (1992) and Courson and Heward (1988).

Parents—Most Important of All

Of all the people needed to make early intervention work, parents are the most important. Given enough information, parents can help prevent many risks and causes of disabilities—before pregnancy, before birth, and certainly before a child has gone months or years without help. Given the chance, parents can become active in determining their children's educational needs and goals. And given some guidance, training, and support many parents can teach their children at home and even at school.

It is no wonder, then, that the most successful intervention programs for young children with disabilities take great care to involve parents (Harris & Handleman, 1994). Parents in early intervention programs for children with disabilities frequently assume roles as members of advisory councils for the programs, consumers who inform others, staff members, primary teachers, recruiters, curriculum developers, counselors, assessment personnel, and evaluators and record keepers.

Parents are the most frequent and constant observers of their children's behavior. They usually know better than anyone else what their children need, and they can help educators set realistic goals. They can report on events in the home that outsiders might never see—for instance, how a child responds to other family members. They can monitor and report on their children's progress at home, beyond the more controlled environment of the center or preschool. In short, they can con-

TABLE 14.4

Direct service and team member roles of professionals involved in early intervention with infants, toddlers, and preschoolers with disabilities (adapted from Bailey, 1988)

PERSONNEL	DIRECT SERVICE PROVIDER	TEAM MEMBER
Audiologists	• Determine auditory function and characteristic of hearing losses • Assess and monitor middle ear infections • Determine relationship of auditory function and communication development • Recommend appropriate amplification or assistive devices	• Interpret all auditory function reports to family and professionals • Provide team members with instruction on hearing loss and use of amplification or assistive devices
Early childhood special educators	• Conduct screening and child-find programs • Assess children's developmental competence • Develop an individualized IFSP or IEP for each child and family • Assess family needs and strengths • Implement family support services or parent education • Evaluate program effectiveness • Advocate for children and families	• Coordinate interdisciplinary services • Integrate and implement interdisciplinary team recommendations • Coordinate services from multiple agencies • Provide consultation to other professionals, families, and other caregivers • Support inclusive early intervention by serving as itinerant/consultant to the early childhood educators
Early childhood general educators	• Develop learning environments and activities that promote DAP philosophy. • Develop learning environments and activities that promote social interactions of children with and without disabilities. • Integrate multicultural education into all aspects of program. • Provide families with information and support related to enhancing the development of the child. • Evaluate program effectiveness • Advocate for children and families	• Integrate interdisciplinary team recommendations • Collaborate with ECSE on instructional strategies and social integration for children with disabilities • Provide consultation to other professionals, families, and other caregivers
Nutritionists	• Develop nutrition care plans through assessments of nutritional status, food intake, eating behavior, and feeding skills	• Coordinate nutrition services • Provide consultation and technical assistance to parents and team members • Provide preventive nutrition information, services, guidance • Make referrals to community resources

tribute to their children's programs at every stage—assessment, planning, classroom activities, and evaluation. Many parents even work in classrooms as teachers, teacher aides, volunteers, or other staff members.

    Most early intervention programs focus on the home as the best and most natural learning environment and on the parent as the best and most natural teacher for

TABLE 14.4 *(continued)*

PERSONNEL	DIRECT SERVICE PROVIDER	TEAM MEMBER
Nurses	• Assess physiological, psychological, and developmental characteristics of the child and family • Plan and implement interventions to improve the child's health and developmental status • Develop medical plans to treat underlying causes of medical or developmental problems • Administer medications, treatments, and regimens prescribed by a licensed physician • Monitor complex medical procedures (tracheotomy suctioning, catheterization procedures, G-tube feeding, mechanical ventilation, etc.)	• Collaborate with caregivers and team members to meet basic health and daily-care needs of the child • Assist in interpreting all medical information and reports • Make referrals to community resources
Occupational therapists	• Assess children's developmental levels, functional performance, sensory processing, and adaptive responses • Assess family-infant interactions • Recommend, select, design, and fabricate assistive seating and orthotic devices • Prevent secondary impairments	• Provide consultation to other professionals on the child's functioning and integrate therapy recommendations • Consult with caregivers and team members on adaptive or assistive devices
Physicians	• Provide services to the child, including assessment, provision of a "medical home," comprehensive medical care, diagnosis, treatment, and referral	• Provide consultation and instruction to parents and team members • Consult with community service settings on child's diagnosis and treatment
Psychologists	• Administer psychological and developmental tests and other assessment procedures • Plan a program of psychological services, including family counseling, parent training, and child development	• Integrate and interpret assessment information to parents and team members • Coordinate psychological services • Collaborate with team members on family needs and strengths

the child. Even center-based programs rely heavily on parents as teachers who carry the center program into the home. But in our efforts to involve parents, we should heed this warning:

> Early childhood professionals, in their zeal to attain those all-important early developmental gains, should not push parents to the point of burn-out. Early childhood professionals will pass the child on to new programs; their task will be finished when the child reaches school age. But the family will only be beginning a lifetime of

TABLE 14.4 *(continued)*

PERSONNEL	DIRECT SERVICE PROVIDER	TEAM MEMBER
Physical therapists	• Assess for motor skills, neuromotor, neuro-musculoskeletal, cardiopulmonary, oral motor, and feeding • Implement environmental modifications and recommend adaptive equipment and mobility devices	• Provide consultation to teach handling, positioning, and movement techniques to facilitate motor functioning and posture • Collaborate on methods for integrating therapy into the child's program
Social workers	• Make home visits to evaluate a child's living conditions and patterns of parent-child interaction • Assess psychosocial development of the child within the family context • Provide individual or group counseling for family members	• Build partnerships with the family • Consult with team members on family needs and strengths • Coordinate community services • Consult with team members on the impact of culture on the family, and how to provide culturally competent intervention
Speech-language pathologists	• Assess communication and oral-motor abilities • Plan and implement appropriate therapeutic programs • Design augmentative communication systems including manual sign language, computerized communication devices, or picture/symbol systems	• Provide consultation to caregivers and team members regarding communication and oral-motor therapy programs • Refer children to medical or other professional services necessary
Vision specialists	• Conduct assessment of functional vision • Determine the relationship of development and visual loss • Provide early orientation and mobility programs • Recommend assistive or low-vision devices	• Interpret visual functioning to caregivers and team members • Consult and refer children to medical or other professional services necessary • Collaborate on designing environments that accommodate the child's visual loss • Teach caregivers and team members sighted-guide techniques • Assist caregivers and team members with pre-braille or low-vision instruction

Source: From *Interactive Teaming: Consultation and Collaboration in Special Programs* by C. C. Thomas, V. I. Correa, and C. V. Morsink, 1995, pp. 322–324. Englewood Cliffs, NJ: Prentice-Hall/Merrill. Used by permission.

responsibility. For early childhood programs, a task equally as important as the achievement of developmental gains is the preparation of families for the long haul. Families must learn to pace themselves, to relax and take time to meet everyone's needs. They must learn that the responsibility of meeting an exceptional child's needs is not a 100-yard dash to be completed in one intensive burst of effort. It is more like a marathon, where slow and steady pacing wins the race (Weyhing, 1983). (Turnbull et al., 1986, p. 93)

Of all the people needed to make early intervention effective, parents are the most important.

And finally, Hutinger, Marshall, and McCartan (1983), the authors of the curriculum developed by the Macomb 0-3 Project, an early intervention program in Macomb, Illinois, remind us that, when all is said and done, we must not forget that early childhood is supposed to be a fun, happy time for children and for the adults who are fortunate enough to work with them.

> Even though the children for whom this curriculum is intended demonstrate behaviors and conditions that may very well make life difficult for them as well as for their families, please do not forget the importance of play, joy and emotional well-being in interactions with these young children. We as professionals who work with young handicapped children sometimes are so serious about the magnitude of our mission that any element of fun, humor or pleasure is absent in our work with both children and their families.
>
> Part of our mission as professionals in the field of early childhood special education is to possess an art of enjoyment ourselves and to help instill it in the young children and families with whom we work.
>
> Early childhood comes but once in a lifetime. . . . Let's make it count!

Summary

Effects of Early Intervention

- Research has documented that early intervention can provide both intermediate and long-term benefits for young children with disabilities and those at risk for developmental delay. Benefits of early intervention include
  gains in physical development, cognitive development, language and speech development, social competence, and self-help skills
  prevention of secondary disabilities conditions
  reduction of family stress
  reduced need for special education services or placement during the school year

savings to society of the costs of additional educational and social services that would be needed later in life if early intervention was not provided

reduced likelihood of social dependence in adulthood

- The effectiveness of early intervention is increased when it begins early in the child's life, is intensive, and conducted for a long time.

Legislative Support for Early Childhood Special Education

- The first federal legislation written exclusively for preschoolers with disabilities—the Handicapped Children's Early Childhood Assistance Act (PL 90–538), passed in 1968—provided funding for diverse and innovative approaches to early intervention.
- Since 1972, Head Start programs have been required to reserve at least 10% of their enrollment capacity for children with disabilities.
- PL 99–457, the Education of the Handicapped Act Amendments of 1986, requires states to provide special education services (via IEPs) to all preschool children with disabilities, aged 3 through 5, and early intervention services (via IFSPs) to all infants and toddlers from birth to 36 months with disabilities.
- States may also service infants and toddlers who, because of established conditions or documented biological or environmental risks, are at risk for developmental delays.

Identification and Assessment

- More genetic counseling, better prenatal care, wider screening for metabolic disorders, and public education can help prevent disabilities.
- Certain disabilities and conditions that often result in disabilities can be detected during pregnancy, in the delivery room, or soon after birth.
- As a rule, the more severe the disability, the earlier it can be detected.
- There is no universal system to screen all infants.
- Most newborns receive an Apgar rating and a screening for certain metabolic disorders.
- Other screening tests based on normal child development are used only when a concerned adult feels an evaluation is necessary.
- Many formal and informal assessment tools are available for assessing a child's development across various domains: cognitive skills, motor skills, communication

and language skills, social and play skills, affective and emotional development, self-care and adaptive skills.

- Normal development is useful as a guide for intervention and as a yardstick against which to measure each child's individual needs and progress.
- Programs are moving away from assessments based entirely on developmental milestones and are incorporating curriculum-based assessment, in which each item relates directly to a skill included in the program's curriculum, which thereby provides a direct link among testing, teaching, and progress evaluation.

Curriculum in Early Childhood Special Education Programs

- Developmentally appropriate practices (DAP) provide a foundation or context within which to provide early intervention for children with special needs, but by themselves the DAP guidelines are inadequate to ensure the individualized intervention such children need.
- Early intervention and education programs for children with special needs should be designed and evaluated according to these outcomes or goals:

Support families in achieving their own goals.

Promote child engagement, independence, and mastery.

Promote development in all important domains.

Build and support social competence.

Facilitate the generalized use of skills.

Prepare and assist children for normalized life experiences with their families, in school, and in their communities.

Help children and their families make smooth transitions.

Prevent or minimize the development of future problems or disabilities.

- IEP/IFSP objectives for infants and young children can be evaluated according to their functionality, generality, instructional context, measurability, and relation between short- and long-range goals.

Intervention Strategies in Early Childhood Special Education

- Promoting language development—helping children learn to talk—is a primary curriculum goal for preschoolers with disabilities. The incidental teaching model and the mand-model procedure are two methods for encouraging and developing language use throughout the school day.

- Many young children with special needs require instruction to develop social competence.

Service Delivery Alternatives for Early Intervention

- In home-based programs, a child's parents act as the primary teachers, with regular training and guidance from a teacher or specially trained paraprofessional who visits the home.

- In center-based programs, a child comes to the center for direct instruction, although the parents are usually involved. Center programs allow a team of specialists to work with the child and enable the child to meet and interact with other children.

- Many programs offer the advantages of both models by combining home visits with center-based programming.

Who Can Help?

- A wide range of professionals should be involved in a team that works with young children with disabilities, including obstetricians, pediatricians, nurses, psychologists, social workers, and teachers.

- Parents are the most important people in an early intervention program. They can act as advocates, participate in educational planning, observe their children's behavior, help set realistic goals, work in the classroom, and teach their children at home.

• •

For More Information

Journals

Day Care and Early Education. Published bimonthly by Behavioral Publications, 72 Fifth Avenue, New York, NY 10016. Directed at day-care personnel; focuses on innovative ideas for educating preschool children.

Infants and Young Children. Published quarterly by Aspen Publishers, 7201 McKinney Circle, Frederick, MD 21701.

Journal of Early Intervention. Published by the Division for Early Childhood, Council for Exceptional Children, 1920 Association Drive, Reston, VA 22091.

Topics in Early Childhood Special Education. Published quarterly by PRO-ED, 5341 Industrial Oaks Boulevard, Austin, TX 78735.

Young Children. Published bimonthly by the National Association for the Education of Young Children, 1834 Connecticut Avenue, NW, Washington, DC 20009. Spotlights current projects, theory, and research in early childhood education as well as practical teaching ideas.

Books

Anastasiow, N. J., & Harel, S. (1993). *At-risk infants: Interventions, families, and research.* Baltimore: Paul H. Brookes.

Bailey, D. B., & Simeonsson, R. J. (1988). *Family assessment in early intervention.* New York: Merrill/Macmillan.

Bailey, D. B., & Wolery, M. (1989). *Assessing infants and preschoolers with disabilities.* New York: Merrill/Macmillan.

Bailey, D. B., & Wolery, M. (1992). *Teaching infants and preschoolers with disabilities* (2nd ed.). New York: Macmillan.

Brown, W., Thurman, S. K., & Pearl, L. W. (1993). *Family-centered intervention with infants and toddlers: Innovative cross-disciplinary approaches.* Baltimore: Paul H. Brookes.

Cook, R. E., Tessier, A., & Klein, M. D. (1992). *Adapting early childhood curricula for children with special needs* (3rd ed.). New York: Macmillan.

Guralnick, M. J., & Bennett, F. C. (Eds.). (1987). *The effectiveness of early intervention for at-risk and disabled children.* New York: Academic Press.

Harris, S. L., & Handleman, J. S. (Eds.). (1994). *Preschool programs for children with autism.* Austin, TX: PRO-ED.

Johnson, L. J., Gallagher, R. J., LaMontagne, M. J., Jordan, J. B., Gallagher, J. J., Hutinger, P. L., & Karnes, M. B. (Eds.). (1994). *Meeting early intervention challenges: Issues from birth to three.* Reston, VA: Council for Exceptional Children.

Krajicek, M., & Thompkins, R. (1993). *The medically fragile infant.* Austin, TX: PRO-ED.

Meisels, S. J., & Shonkoff, J. P. (1990). *Handbook of early childhood intervention.* New York: Cambridge University Press.

Neisworth, J. T., & Bagnato, S. J. (1987). *The young exceptional child: Early development and education.* New York: Macmillan.

Noonan, M. J., & McCormick, L. (1993). *Early intervention in natural environments.* Pacific Grove, CA: Brooks/Cole.

Odom, S. L., & Karnes, M. B. (Eds.). (1988). *Early intervention for infants & children with disabilities.* Baltimore: Paul H. Brookes.

Odom, S. L., McConnell, S. R., & McEvoy, M. A. (Eds.). (1992). *Social competence of young children with disabilities: Nature, development, and intervention.* Baltimore: Paul H. Brookes.

Peck, C. A., Odom, S. L., & Bricker, D. D. (1993). *Integrating young children with disabilities into community programs.* Baltimore: Paul H. Brookes.

Raver, S. A. (1991). *Strategies for teaching at-risk and handicapped infants and toddlers: A transdisciplinary approach.* New York: Macmillan.

Rosenkoetter, S. E., Hains, A. H., & Fowler, S. (1994). *Bridging early services for children with special needs and their families.* Baltimore: Paul H. Brookes.

Thurman, S. K., & Widerstrom, A. H. (1990). *Young children with special needs: A developmental and ecological approach* (2nd ed.). Baltimore: Paul H. Brookes.

Wolery, M., & Wilbers, J. S. (Eds.). (1994). *Including young children with special needs in early childhood programs.* Washington, DC: National Association for the Education of Young Children.

Zirpoli, T. J. (1995). *Understanding and affecting the behavior of young children.* Englewood Cliffs, NJ: Prentice-Hall/Merrill.

Organizations

The Division for Early Childhood (DEC), Council for Exceptional Children, 1920 Association Drive, Reston, VA 22091.

National Association for the Education of Young Children (NAEYC), 1834 Connecticut Avenue, NW, Washington, DC 20009-5786.

National Center for Clinical Infant Programs (NCCIP), 2000 14th Street North, Suite 380, Arlington, VA 22201-2500; (703) 528-4300.

National Early Childhood Technical Assistance System (NEC-TAS), Suite 500, NCBC Plaza, Chapel Hill, NC 27514; (919) 962-2001.

National Head Start Resource Access Program Administration for Children, Youth, and Families, Office of Human Development Services, P.O. Box 1182, Washington, DC 20013.

Transitions to Adulthood

* Should special educators in the schools be responsible for the successes and failures of adults with disabilities?

* How can services such as sheltered employment programs, that are designed and intended to help adults with disabilities, also limit their participation in life activities?

* Does it make sense for society to provide the ongoing supports a person with severe disabilities needs in order to work in the community?

* Will any large state-operated institutions be available for persons with severe disabilities 10 years from now? Should there be?

* Why must quality of life be the ultimate outcome measure for special education?

What happens to youth with disabilities when they leave school and enter the adult world? Do graduates of special education programs find work? Where do they live? How do the social, recreational, and leisure activities of adults with disabilities compare with the expectations and experiences of most citizens? How do adults with disabilities rate their quality of life—Are they happy? How can special education programs for school-age children with disabilities prepare them for adjustment and successful integration into the adult community? What are the most appropriate and effective programs and services for supporting adults with disabilities in their efforts to find and keep meaningful work, to locate a home, or to use community recreation centers? How can special education interrelate its goals and services with those of other human service agencies, such as vocational education and rehabilitation, residential services, and community recreation programs?

Many special educators today see finding answers to questions like these as their highest priority. We begin by taking a look at the results of several studies that have focused on what is perhaps the most important question of all regarding the ultimate effectiveness of special education: What happens to students with disabilities after they leave school?

✳ *How Do Former Special Education Students Fare as Adults?*

More than 40 studies of graduates and leavers of secondary special education programs provide enlightening, if not encouraging, information. The research methodology used to determine postschool outcomes for young adults with disabilities consists primarily of *follow-up* and *follow-along* studies that obtain information via interviews, surveys, or direct observation with former students, their parents, and/or employers. Here are some of the results of those studies:

Employment Status

- Two follow-up studies of young adults who had left secondary special education programs in Vermont school districts found employment rates of 55% and 62%, with just two thirds of those working in full-time positions, compared with an employment rate of 82% for youths without disabilities (Hasazi, Gordon, & Roe, 1985; Hasazi, Johnson, Hasazi, Gordon, & Hull, 1989).
- Employment prospects were worse for young women: only 23% of female former special education students were employed 2 years after leaving school, as compared with a statewide employment rate of 71% for females without disabilities (Hasazi et al., 1989). A recent analysis of postschool outcomes for graduates from three school districts in Washington State found few significant differences between genders for youths with learning disabilities and mild mental retardation (Levine & Edgar, 1995).

Spending time with an adult with disabilities is an excellent way for the prospective special educator to begin to answer these questions. See "A Friendship Program" later in this chapter.

A *follow-up study* collects information at a single point in time (e.g., 1 year or 2 years after a student's graduating class leaves school) and gives a "snapshot" of adult adjustment; a *follow-along study* collects information on postschool outcomes at multiple points in time. Follow-along studies enable the measurement of progress over time (Darrow & Clark, 1992). A list of 24 follow-up studies of former special education students conducted since 1984 can be found in Johnson and Rusch (1993).

- Sixty-nine percent of 234 young adults had jobs 4 years after they left secondary special education programs in Colorado, but only one third were employed full time (Mithaug, Horiuchi, & Fanning, 1985).
- Young adults with learning disabilities have found employment rates ranging from 72% to 80%, with about half of those employed working full-time (deBettencourt, Zigmond, & Thornton, 1989; Scuccimarra & Speece, 1990; Sitlington & Frank, 1990; Sitlington, Frank, & Carson, 1993; Zigmond & Thornton, 1985).
- When compared with other high school graduates with "mild disabilities," youths with behavioral disorders have lower employment rates (Sitlington, Frank, & Carson, 1993).
- Parent interviews concerning the employment status of 300 young adults with mental retardation who had left public school special education programs in Virginia revealed an employment rate of 42%, with three fourths of those employed earning less than $500 per month (Wehman, Kregel, & Seyfarth, 1985a).
- Although the employment outcomes for all youth with disabilities are poor when compared with those of the population in general, the outlook is much worse for those whose disabilities are severe. The 117 young adults with moderate, severe, or profound mental retardation in the Virginia study had an *unemployment* rate of 78.6% (Wehman, Kregel, & Seyfarth, 1985b). Of the 25 who were working, just 14 had found paid work in the community, 11 were working in sheltered workshops, and only 8 earned more than $100 per month.
- One study found that only 39% of adults with mental retardation and related developmental disabilities were working for pay, and of that group, 77% worked in segregated facilities such as sheltered workshops and work activity centers (Lakin, Hill, Chen, & Stephens, 1989).
- From a 10-year follow-up of former students of a state-operated residential school, it was estimated that 69% of adults with visual impairments are unemployed (Heiden, 1989).
- Between 50% and 75% of all adults with disabilities are unemployed, "depending on which survey you choose to review" (Wehman, 1992, p. 112).

> Bullis and Gaylord-Ross (1991) describe a transition program for youths with behavioral disorders.

> Sheltered workshops and work activity centers are discussed later in the chapter.

Wages and Benefits

- Median hourly wage for all youth with disabilities was $5.72, less than $12,000 per year for full-time, year-round employment *(National Longitudinal Transition Study)*.
- Less than half of employed youth with mental retardation received health insurance, sick leave, or vacation benefits (Frank & Sitlington, 1993).
- The incomes of many individuals with disabilities hover near the poverty level (Mithaug et al., 1985; Scuccimarra & Speece, 1990).
- A follow-up study of young adults with learning disabilities or behavioral disorders conducted 1 year after they had graduated from public school special education programs or had left because they were too old to meet eligibility requirements found that 77% had jobs but that only 27% of those who were working were earning minimum wage or above (Will, 1986).
- The average hourly pay for individuals with mental retardation who were working in sheltered workshops 3 years after graduating from high school was $1.59 (Frank & Sitlington, 1993).

> The *National Longitudinal Transition Study* (NLTS) is an ongoing effort to assess and monitor changes in the adult adjustment of youth with disabilities after they leave secondary special education programs. NLTS has tracked 8,700 youths with disabilities who left U.S. secondary special education programs in 1985-87. Several major reports of NLTS findings have been issued (Wagner, 1991; Wagner, D'Amico, Marder, Newman, & Blackorby, 1993; Wagner et al., 1991).

Living Arrangement and Community Participation

A disability affects more than a person's likelihood of obtaining work. Adults with disabilities face numerous obstacles in day-to-day living that affect where and how they live, how well they can use community resources, and their opportunities for social interaction. Unlike their nondisabled peers, a disproportionate number of young adults with disabilities live with their parents, and many report a high degree of social isolation.

• Two years after high school, 83% of youth with disabilities lived with their parents; 3 years later, 55% still lived with their parents (NLTS).
• Thirty-seven percent of youth with disabilities who have been out of high school for 3 to 5 years were living independently (alone, with a spouse or roommate, in a college dormitory or military housing, not as a dependent), compared with 60% of the general population (NLTS).
• Twenty-five percent of young adults with learning disabilities indicated they were "dissatisfied" with their social life 2 years after leaving high school (Scuccimarra & Speece, 1990).
• After being out of high school for 3 to 5 years, 51% of young adults with disabilities were registered to vote, compared with 66% of the general population.
• A survey conducted by Louis Harris and Associates and reported to the U.S. Congress in 1986 found that 56% of adults said their disabilities prevented them from moving about the community, attending cultural or sporting events, and socializing with friends outside their homes.

Postsecondary Education

The percentage of first-time, full-time freshmen enrolled in college who indicate they have a disability has increased significantly in recent years (Henderson, 1992). The majority are students with learning disabilities. For information on promoting the success of postsecondary education for students with learning disabilities, see Brinckerhoff, Shaw, and McGuire (1993).

Participation in and completion of postsecondary college and vocational programs greatly increase the likelihood of obtaining employment and generally experiencing "success" as an adult. Compared with their peers without disabilities, fewer former special education students pursue postsecondary education.

• Three years following graduation, 66% of the young adults with mental retardation who were interviewed by Frank and Sitlington (1993) reported they had participated in no postsecondary training of any kind.
• A follow-up of 1,242 youths who had been out of school for 1 year found that 15% had taken at least one postsecondary course (at a vocation training school, 2-year community college, or 4-year college), compared with 56% of youth without disabilities (Fairweather & Shaver, 1991).
• When only high school graduates in the same study were compared, 21.2% of youths with disabilities and 64.3% of youths without disabilities had participated in postsecondary education (Fairweather & Shaver, 1991).
• The NLTS found that 37% of young adults who had graduated from high school had enrolled in postsecondary education programs within 3 to 5 years, compared with 68% of the general same-age population (Wagner et al., 1993).

Drop-Outs

Students who do not complete secondary schooling are likely to face more difficulties in adult adjustment than those who do. Special education students who do not

The percentage of first-time, full-time freshmen enrolled in college who indicate that they have a disability has increased significantly in recent years. Most are students with learning disabilities.

complete school are more likely to have lower levels of employment and wages and higher rates of problems with the criminal justice system than those who finish (Lichtenstein, 1993; Wagner, Blackorby, Cameto, & Newman, 1993). Only 58% of the more than 220,000 teenagers and young adults with disabilities who exited from the public schools during the 1991–92 school year graduated with a diploma or received a certificate of completion, and it is estimated that 30% of students with disabilities who enroll in high school drop out before they finish (U.S. Department of Education, 1994). Factors found to reduce the probability that a student with disabilities will drop out include low absenteeism, job-specific vocational experience, receiving individual attention such as tutoring or counseling, socializing with other students outside school, and joining extracurricular activities (Wagner, 1991). Strategies for combating dropouts among students with disabilities can be found in Cohen and deBettencourt (1991); Diem and Katims (1991); and Lovitt (1991). Data from the NLTS have revealed an encouraging note concerning dropouts with disabilities: 27% had enrolled in a program to earn a high school diploma within 3 to 5 years after they had dropped out (Wagner, 1991).

Overall "Success"

Although useful, isolated statistics cannot provide a complete picture of the overall adjustment to adult life experienced by young people with disabilities. "The fabric of

The case studies of four young adults with learning disabilities who had dropped out of high school "cast doubt on the prevailing opinion that school dropouts are 'losers' and 'failures'" (Lichtenstein, 1993, p. 336). Their personal stories reveal both the shortfalls and inadequacies of the secondary special education and transition services they had received and the "considerable resiliency" in the former students' efforts to seek out jobs, develop friendships, gain alternative education credentials, and pursue career ambitions. Case studies describing the transition experiences of four young adults with mental retardation can be found in Lichtenstein and Michaelides (1993).

youths' lives is a complex interweaving of their activities and experiences with work, school, family, friends, and living arrangements" (U.S. Department of Education, 1993, p. 88). Being a successful adult involves much more than holding a job; it is achieving status as an independent and active member of society. Independence for an adult has been defined as the "ability to participate in society, to work, have a home, raise a family, and share the joys and responsibilities of community life" (Stoddard, 1978, quoted in Fisher, 1989, p. 94).

Halpern (1985) recommends that a composite set of variables is needed to identify "successful" transition to adulthood. Two follow-up studies of former special education students operationalized Halpern's concept of the "successful" young adult by these criteria: (a) employed (full- or part-time) in a competitive job, a homemaker, a full-time student, or in a job-training program; (b) buying a home, living independently, or living with a friend or spouse; (c) paying at least a portion of one's living expenses; and (d) being involved in more than three different leisure activities.

In a statewide follow-up study of graduates of secondary special education programs in Iowa, Sitlington, Frank, and Carson (1993) found only 5.8% of 737 students with learning disabilities, 5 of 142 students with mental retardation (3.5%), and just 1 of 59 students with behavioral disorders could be judged as having made a "successful adult adjustment" (p. 230) 1 year after they had completed high school. Frank and Sitlington (1993) reported that 3.9% of more than 300 young adults with mental retardation met a standard for "high success" (requiring full-time employment, living on their own or in a supervised apartment and paying more than half of one's living expenses), while the postschool adjustment status of an additional 18.5% met their composite criteria for "low success" (at least half-time employment, living on their own or in a group home, paying at least a portion of their expenses, and involvement in at least one leisure activity).

Most of the transition follow-up research has focused on the first year or two after youth leave school. The ongoing NLTS has developed a measure of adult adjustment that includes independent functioning in three domains: (a) employment (competitively employed in a full-time job or engaged in job training or post-secondary education), (b) residential arrangements (living alone or with a spouse or roommate), and (c) social activities (having friends, belonging to social groups). When assessed at a period less than 2 years out of school, only 6.4% of all youth with disabilities met these three criteria. When the same measures are assessed after individuals have been out of school for 3 to 5 years, however, 20% were judged to be independent in all three domains (Wagner et al., 1993). Even with this significant increase, four out of every five former special education students had still not achieved the status of independent adulthood after being out of high school for up to 5 years.

Findings such as these have focused attention on what has become perhaps the dominant issue in special education today—the transition from school to adult life in the community. No longer can special educators be satisfied with evaluation data that show improved performance on classroom-related tasks. We must work equally hard to ensure that the preparation that students receive during their school years plays a direct and positive role in helping them adjust to successful life in the adult community.

It is important to note that the very small percentage of young adults who met the criteria for "successful" transition to adult life in both of these studies had *graduated* from secondary special education programs. Young adults who leave secondary programs by routes other than graduation do not fare as well as those who do complete school with a diploma or certificate (Wagner, et al., 1993).

In addition to leaving school with poor academic, work-related, social, and daily living skills, many young adults with disabilities face the "demands of adult life with a debilitating lack of self-confidence and self-esteem" (Fourqurean & LaCourt, 1991, p. 21).

✳ *Transition from School to Adult Life*
Transition and the IDEA

In response to the growing concern over the failure of so many young adults with disabilities in the job market and community living, Congress included funds to support the improvement of secondary special education programs when it amended the IDEA in 1983 (PL 98-199).

Will's "Bridges" Model of School-to-Work Transition

PL 98-199 authorized federal funding for "Secondary Education and Transitional Services for Youth with Disabilities" (Sec. 626). The Office of Special Education and Rehabilitation Services (within the U.S. Department of Education) proposed a model of transition services that encompassed three levels of service, each conceptualized as a "bridge" between the secondary special education curriculum and adult employment (Will, 1986). Each of the three levels differs in terms of the nature and extent of the services an individual with disabilities needs to make a successful transition from school to work. At the first level are students who require no special transition services. On graduation from an appropriate secondary special education curriculum, these young adults, presumably those with mild disabilities, would make use of the *generic employment services* already available to people without disabilities in the community (e.g., job placement agencies). At the second level are persons with disabilities who require the *time-limited transitional services* offered by vocational rehabilitation or adult service agencies that are specially designed to help individuals with disabilities gain competitive, independent employment. The third level of transitional services consists of *ongoing employment services* that are necessary to enable persons with severe disabilities to enjoy the benefits of meaningful, paid work.

For a history of the transition movement in special education see Halpern (1992); Rusch, DeStefano, Chadsey-Rusch, Phelps, and Szymanski (1992); and Wehman (1992).

Halpern's Three-Dimensional Model

Because it showed the federal government's recognition of the need to improve the employment outcomes for special education students, Will's bridges model for school-to-work transition was viewed as a move in the right direction. Many special educators, however, thought that it offered a too-limited perspective on transition. In a paper representative of this view, Halpern (1985) wrote that it is a mistake to focus on adult employment as the sole purpose and outcome of transition services: "Living successfully in one's community should be the primary target of transitional services" (p. 480). Halpern proposed a transition model that directed Will's generic, time-limited, and ongoing support services toward helping students with disabilities adjust to adult life in the community in three domains: (a) the quality of residential environment, (b) adequacy of social and interpersonal network, and (c) meaningful employment (see Figure 15.1).

This broader view that transition must focus on all domains of adult functioning characterizes the field today and serves as the basis for the design, delivery, and evaluation of secondary special education programming. The 1990 amendments to the IDEA (PL 101-476) detailed the process by which transition services would be provided by (a) defining transition services as aimed at more than employment,

A Friendship Program for Future Special Education Teachers

························

by Jill C. Dardig

Scott and Ted, both big sports fans, attended several local basketball and baseball games together. They cheered for the Pickerington High School Lady Tigers in the state tournament and scarfed frank after frank on "Dime-a-Dog Night" at a Columbus Clippers game. Kelly and Kami went out to dinner at several of their favorite restaurants. They also spent some quiet nights at home baking brownies, looking at family pictures, and just talking. Paula and Todd attended a concert, went to the mall, and spent an evening with popcorn and a video at Todd's apartment.

Scott, Kelly, and Paula, all college students learning to become special education teachers, were doing their fieldwork for a required course entitled Focus on Adults with Disabilities. Each student in this class is paired with an adult with developmental disabilities living in a group home, family home, or supported living apartment in the community. Each student spends time getting to know his or her new friend on an informal and personal basis and planning some at-home and community-based activities they can enjoy together during the semester. Students do not function as teachers, but in the role of a friend or companion. In this way, students are able to look at their special friends in a different light—not as a school-age child, but as a similar-aged peer who is learning to be an independent adult.

After meeting with his or her friend (and sometimes group home or supported living staff) to determine what the friend might enjoy doing, each college student designs a clear and attractive calendar or schedule to record planned activities. The schedule may be written, but if the friend cannot read, the scheduled activities are illustrated by photos, pictures, symbols, or objects (e.g., a menu from Bob Evans, a K-Mart ad, a puzzle piece, or a page from *TV Guide*). This schedule allows the friend to anticipate and prepare for each activity and provides cues for their friends, family, and caregivers to ask questions and discuss the person's weekly activities.

We Both Had a Good Time

Students also keep a journal. They record and reflect on their activities and pay special attention to identifying which skills their friend is lacking that he or she could have learned in school to enable the person to become more independent in the home and community settings when he or she reaches adulthood. Here are some journal entries of a recent class, detailing a variety of activities:

> Norma Bernstein recalled: "We visited the Northland Mall, where we wandered in and out of stores. Mary and I tried on a pair of high heels, and we both had a good time laughing as we attempted to walk."
>
> Scott Martin wrote: "Upon returning to his apartment, Ted was very happy, almost ecstatic. He acted out dribbling and shooting a basketball, to let everyone know that he and his 'Special Friend' had gone to a game. This made me feel fantastic, and I could sense that we were starting to bond."

Scott included Ted in some everyday activities like gassing up and washing his car—both by hand and in an automatic car wash. Ted was thrilled; he had never participated in these activities with a friend before.

> Dean Scheiderer said: "I did not know what to expect on my first 'date' with Jack. Nothing had been planned, and I expected to stay around the home so that we would have a chance to get acquainted. Jack must have seen me pull in because he was waiting outside with his hat and jacket on. He wanted to see my truck. I don't just mean looking at my truck, I mean getting in, listening to the radio, and examining everything. It was a good ice-breaker, and we sat outside for some time."
>
> After a later meeting, Dean wrote: "At the bowling alley we rented a lane and our shoes. After finding our bowling balls, we were ready to bowl a couple of 300 games. Neither of us reached that goal, and I learned that I didn't know how to keep score manually, so we just threw our balls down the alley. Jack had good form, although his balls had a hard time reaching the end of the lane.

Week 1	Week 2	Week 3	Week 4	Week 5
-Talk -Get to know each other -Watch a T.V. program	**REVCO** -Go to Revco -Buy nail polish -Do nails	-Talk -Make blueberry muffins	-Take Bonnie to have her hair done	-Take Bonnie to the mall -Mall walking -Window shopping
Week 6	**Week 7**	**Week 8**	**Week 9**	**Week 10**
-Take Bonnie & Mary out for dinner and bowling	-Take Bonnie to see a movie	-Have Bonnie help me with my grocery shopping	-Take Bonnie shopping at the **KMART**	-Make cookies -Watch a movie

Shannon Griffith and her new friend Bonnie prepared this schedule of their upcoming activities.

Once his ball even rolled almost back to us. We both got a kick out of it and laughed for several minutes."

Kelly Byers commented: "After dinner, Kami and I went shopping at the Target department store. Kami picked out a card for her brother's birthday and helped me choose a present for my newborn nephew. After Target, we went to a pet store, since she loves animals."

Karen Watson wrote: "Lou and I went to the Racquet Club of Columbus to watch indoor tennis. Prior to going into the building, Lou told me that he knew you had to be quiet when watching tennis. He was very quiet and, in fact, told me to "Shhh!" a few times. We watched for an hour or so and then went to Antrim Park and walked around the lake. We talked about a lot of different topics—conversation does not lack with Lou. This was a very pleasant evening."

If Edna Could Re-Do Her Education

Aside from having a good time, students completing this field placement gained many valuable insights. Their most frequent observation and strongest recommendation had to do with many of their friends' lack of social skills. Several students noticed that basic social skills, such as saying "please" when requesting items, greeting the student when he or she arrived, and shaking hands and saying "thank you" at the end of the evening, were lacking. Students thought that many of these important skills could have been acquired easily and naturally if their friends had experienced early inclusion with their nondisabled peers while participating in informal school and community activities.

Barbara Miller illustrated and explained her feelings about this issue:

> "Edna and I spent a lot of our time at the City Center Mall—an activity she had expressed an interest in. It turned out to be quite an experience. Edna had a difficult time navigating her way around people; she seemed to just 'bulldoze' ahead without going around people or other obstacles. I finally resorted to keeping her close to me so that she wouldn't run anyone down. We browsed in many stores and had pizza there too, and Edna had a great time. As soon as we got back to her home, however, she vanished without a word. . . . Later, during a trip to the movies and out to dinner, Edna spoke very loudly and annoyed other customers, despite my reminders to speak quietly. Edna can be such a pleasant and nice young woman, but she seems oblivious to others around her. I can't help but think this would not be the case if she had spent some time with her nondisabled peers more while growing up. . . . If Edna could re-do her education, I think she would have benefited from spending time, both in and outside school, with her nondisabled peers. She could have learned two-sided conversation, age-appropriate and varied leisure time options, consideration for others' needs and desires, and better mobility skills.

> Scott concurred: "Inclusion early-on would have been an excellent help with Ted's verbal and social skills."

> Paula Kruer stated: "Todd definitely could have learned social skills earlier in his life. I believe teachers need to take a look at their students and give a lot of thought as to what skills will be needed not only while they are in school but also during their adult life. This is so important, and this placement has given me the opportunity to realize this."

Another critical skill that many of the friends lacked was the ability to make a choice of movie, food, activity, and so on.

> Kelly said: "Today, Kami and I went to dinner at Pizza Hut. We continued to talk about our families and our work. I noticed Kami waits for me to do everything. Open the door, serve the food, anything that requires a decision."

> Scott had a similar reaction: "A really big difference was that (in spending time with Ted) I always took the lead with decision making. I had to be sure to wait and prompt responses from him or else I would not have known which store he wanted to visit or what flavor of ice cream he preferred."

Future teachers can keep this in mind and give students repeated opportunities to make choices of things like snacks, books, and leisure time activities.

Appropriate affect and expression of feelings were other areas in which many adults had some difficulty.

> Paula Kruer noted: "Todd lacks a sense of humor. I usually associate with people who like to have fun and laugh. It was very hard for me to relate to Todd, who hardly ever laughed or seemed to want to have a good time."

Many students observed that their adult friends, even if they were quite verbal, did not have adequate conversation skills. Some adults could answer questions, but did not ask questions of the students or initiate conversation.

> Barbara Miller said: "Edna apparently has little or no concept of friendship. Her life experiences have provided her with the model that adults are 'providers.' She has learned ways to manipulate adults into gaining whatever it is she deems important . . . She never asked me when she would see me again. Our conversation was usually one-sided, with me asking her a lot of questions, but rarely was the reverse true."

Money handling skills were also identified as critically important in making a person more adept in the community, and many of the adults experienced difficulty paying for items independently.

> Looking back, Beth Wahl stated: "Ben could have been taught basic skills that would have been helpful in integrating him into society. Handling money transactions and telling time could have prevented the need for someone to keep track of Ben's every move in stores and restaurants."

Another area in which some of the adults were weak were self-care skills.

> Norma observed: "I believe that Mary could have been taught basic hygiene, housekeeping, and social skills during her school years so that she could enjoy more independence and less frustration as she deals with these issues now."

> As Beth noted: "This placement helped me realize the need for an emphasis in schools to be placed on daily living skills, skills that students will need when they become adults living in the community. It will be helpful to remember this when I become a teacher."

The Importance of Being Future Oriented

Although the students who take this course will be certified to teach students in grades K through 12, spending time with an adult will help them as teachers to become more future oriented in their instruction—to think beyond the day's activities or the week's goals for a particular child with a disability. This experience will help teachers select and teach functional skills to their school-age students so that eventually they will be as fully integrated into the community as possible.

> As Barbara stated: "This experience gave me a different perspective of being a friend to an adult rather than a teacher. Now I have a much greater resolve in seeing inclusion successfully take place in my classes. I am also much more keenly aware of how the public feels when encountering someone like Edna in the community."

> Janet Fleming said: "This experience will enable me to visualize students as adults and thus to think ahead to behaviors that may or may not be appropriate when my student is 22 years old and beyond. No matter what grade level I teach, I will have a much clearer view of which skills are functional, which are

not, and which will allow my students to take full advantage of the world around them."

An unanticipated benefit of this course has been that several students have chosen careers working with adults with disabilities in the residential and vocational areas, two growing fields with good employment prospects.

If your teacher-training program does not offer a course such as this one, you can arrange to get to know a special friend as a volunteer through a local group home or an advocacy agency like The Arc. Developing a special friendship with an adult with disabilities will help you become a more responsive and effective teacher of children and youths with special needs.

Jill C. Dardig is Professor of Education at Ohio Dominican College in Columbus, Ohio, where she trains special education teachers.

(b) specifying how transition services would be incorporated into a student's IEP, and (c) indicating the schools' primary responsibility for monitoring the provision of transition services (DeStefano & Wermuth, 1992).

Definition of Transition Services

Transition services are defined in the IDEA as

> a coordinated set of activities for a student, designed within an outcome-oriented process, which promotes movement from school to postschool activities, including postsecondary education, vocational training, integrated employment (including supported employment), continuing and adult education, adult services, independent living, and/or community participation. (20 U.S.C. 1401 (a) (19)

Supported employment is defined and discussed later in the chapter.

Individualized Transition Plan

When a student reaches the age of 16, an *individualized transition plan* (ITP) is written. Developed and included as part of the IEP process, a student's ITP outlines actions, events, and resources that will affect and support his or her move from school to adulthood. A well-written ITP details the types of supports and curricular programming that will be required to enable a smooth and successful transition to postschool residential, community, and vocational settings. The student's IEP/ITP team specifies postgraduation outcomes and goals and then develops an individualized program of instruction and activities designed to reach those outcomes. Postschool outcomes should drive the secondary programming for every student with disabilites over the age of 16. Transition plans can take many formats, but every ITP must include all required information and be clear to the parties involved. "The

The IDEA specifies that an ITP may be written beginning at age 14 or younger if the IEP team determines it appropriate for an individual student.

FIGURE 15.1

Halpern's three-dimensional conceptualization of transition.

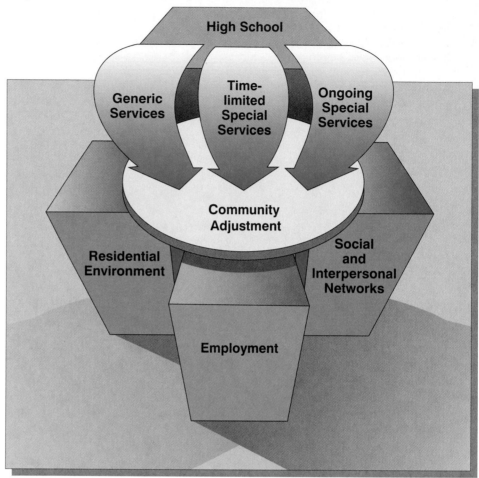

Source: From "Transition: A Look at the Foundation," by A. S. Halpern, 1985, *Exceptional Children, 51,* p. 481. Reprinted by permission.

For examples of ITP formats and transition planning and support activities, see Clark and Kolstoe (1995); Gajar, Goodman, and McAfee (1993); Udvari-Solner, Jorgenson, and Courchane (1992); Wehman (1992); and West et al. (1992). Additional sources are listed in the For More Information section at the end of the chapter.

plan should include annual goals and short-term objectives which reflect skills required to function on the job, at home, and in the community. Transition services should also be specified, including referral to appropriate agencies, job placement, and on-the-job follow-up" (Wehman, Kregel, & Barcus, 1985, p. 30). Figure 15.2 is an example of an ITP designed to solicit and encourage the student's input, choices, and decision.

After graduation, the ITP can be incorporated into an *individual rehabilitation plan* if the young adult is served by vocational rehabilitation, or made part of an *individualized habilitation plan* if the young adult is served by a community adult services agency (e.g., a county program for people with developmental disabilities). A well-written transition plan ensures that parents are aware of available adult services and employment options in the community, improves the chances that adult services will be available with few disruptions to the graduating student, and provides school and adult-service personnel with a set of procedures and timelines to follow.

FIGURE 15.2

Example of a format used to write an individualized transition plan (ITP).

Name of Individual Participants		Age _____ Date _____

Transition Issues If yes $\boxed{X}$	What is your current situation?	What is your future goal? What is the Supportive Educational Goal (IEP)?	What agency will be involved in reaching goal?	Who will be responsible?	When: Start Finish
Recreation/Leisure: Will you need help in finding community recreation and/or leisure activities? ☐					
Financial/Income: Will you need help supporting yourself? ☐					
Advocacy/Legal: Will you need assistance and support in linking to adult services or long-term planning? ☐					
Medical/Health: Will you need help in addressing medical needs? Will you need health insurance? ☐					
Counseling/Other: Will you need support from community counseling services? ☐					
Employment/ Cont. Education: Will you need help in finding a job or continuing your education? ☐					
Transportation: Will you need help in traveling to and from your home, work or community services? ☐					
Residential/Personal Independence: Will you need help in living arrangements or personal independence? ☐					

Note: This ITP was developed by the Monroe #1 Board of Cooperative Educational Services, NY.

Source: From "Vocational Preparation and Transition" by M. S. Moon and K. Inge, 1993. Reprinted with the permission of Simon & Schuster, Inc. from the Merrill/Prentice Hall text *Instruction of Students with Severe Disabilities* 4/e by Martha E. Snell. © 1993 by Merrill/Prentice Hall, Inc.

The School's Responsibility

For recommendations on how transition services can be made more relevant and effective for students and families from culturally diverse backgrounds, see Atkins (1992) and Boone (1992). Cooperation and communication are keys to effective transition planning. See "What Were We Really Saying?" later in this chapter.

Transition is also viewed as a process involving the coordination, delivery, and transfer of services from the secondary school program to receiving agencies (e.g., employers, postsecondary education and vocational training programs, residential service providers; Edgar, 1987). Although work-study and vocational training programs for special education students and vocational rehabilitation services for adults with disabilities have existed in every state for a long time, systematic coordination of and communication between schools and community-based adult services have not typically occurred. Although interagency cooperation is critical to the success of transition, the PL 101-476 amendments to the IDEA "made it clear that the initial and ultimately most significant transition responsibilities lie with schools" (Moon & Inge, 1993, p. 583).

Beginning Career Development and Transition Activities Early

DCDT publishes the journal *Career Development of Exceptional Individuals.*

The Council for Exceptional Children's Division on Career Development and Transition (DCDT) believes that career development and transition services should begin in the elementary grades for all children with disabilities. Three basic principles underlying the provision of career education and transition services from DCDT's position statement are:

An excellent career education curriculum is Brolin's *Life-Centered Career Education* (1993, 1995).

1. *Education for career development and transition is for individuals with disabilities of all ages.* [A]nyone in our society with a disability that is severe enough to qualify for special education programming or services is much more likely to encounter significant adult adjustment and employment assistance demands after leaving school. The nature of these demands vary, but *every* disability categorical group has problems in employment, independent living, and person-social relationships . . . The defensibility for earlier intervention in the areas of career development and transition skills is as strong as the longstanding position of special educators for the importance of early educational intervention with children who are at risk or who have identifiable disabilities.

2. *Career development is a process begun at birth and continues throughout life.* Career development, from the broad perspective of fostering life-long career competencies in the work world, independent living skills in the community, and personal-social relationships at home and in the community, is actually only different terminology for what some disciplines refer to as normal human growth and development.

Szymanski (1994), another advocate of transition as a life-long process, describes several principles for ensuring that transition interventions are maximally under the control of the student, promote independence and autonomy, are least intrusive, and are most natural for the chosen environment.

3. *Early career development is essential for making satisfactory choices later.* A frequent criticism of secondary employment training programs is that there are too few choices and that professionals too often end up making those choices for students . . . The best way to prepare individuals for self-knowledge (interests, abilities, limiting barriers) and decision-making is to begin the process of self-awareness and choice-making as early as possible. (Clark, Carlson, Fisher, Cook, & D'Lonzo, 1991, pp. 115-116.)

Figure 15.3 shows the career development and transition model developed by Clark and Kolstoe (1995). This model focuses on obtaining work after one leaves school but gives equal importance to competencies that are critical for life as an adult. The four mutually important elements of the model—(a) values, attitudes, and habits; (b) human relationships; (c) occupational information; and (d) acquisition of job

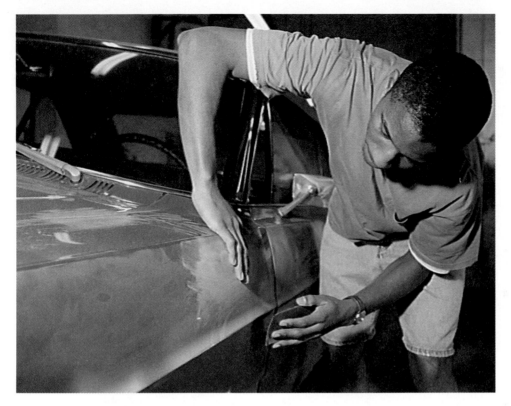

Secondary school programs can facilitate the successful transition to the adult world of work by providing functional curricula and real work experiences in integrated community job sites.

and daily living skills—are superimposed over vertical lines that extend upward, undergirding the high school, postsecondary, and adult options for education and training. The relative emphasis of the four elements changes as a student progresses through the elementary and middle school grades and moves into high school and postsecondary education or vocational training opportunities and as individual needs and career goals change.

Developing career awareness and vocational skills during the elementary years does not mean, of course, that 6-year-old children should be placed on job sites for training. Appropriate transition-related objectives should be selected at each age level (Freagon et al., 1906, Wehman, 1985). For example, elementary students might sample different types of jobs through classroom responsibilities such as watering plants, cleaning chalkboards, or taking messages to the office. Young children with disabilities might also visit community work sites where adults with disabilities are employed. In addition, assessment and teaching of job performance skills can be accomplished with elementary-age special education students through prevocational work samples, which provide practice on skills (e.g., counting, packaging, following directions) and which are related to a variety of potentially available jobs in the community (Scott, Ebbert, & Price, 1986). Middle school students should begin to spend time at actual community job sites, with an increasing amount of in-school instruction devoted to the development of associated work skills, such as being on time, staying on task, and using interpersonal skills (Egan, Fredericks, & Hendrickson, 1985; Sulzbacher, Haines, Peterson, & Swatman, 1987). Secondary students should spend an increasing amount of time receiving instruction at actual community job

Numerous models for conceptualizing and guiding the delivery of transition services have been developed. All stress the importance of providing career education at an early age, a functional secondary school curriculum that provides work experience in integrated community job sites, systematic coordination between the school and adult service providers, parental involvement and support, and a written ITP to guide the entire process. For descriptions of various transition education approaches, see Clark and Kolstoe, 1995; Freagon et al. (1986); Hutchins and Renzaglia (1990); McDonnell, Hardman, and Hightower (1989); Rusch et al. (1987); Siegel et al. (1993); and Wehman (1992).

FIGURE 15.3
A school-based career development and transition education model

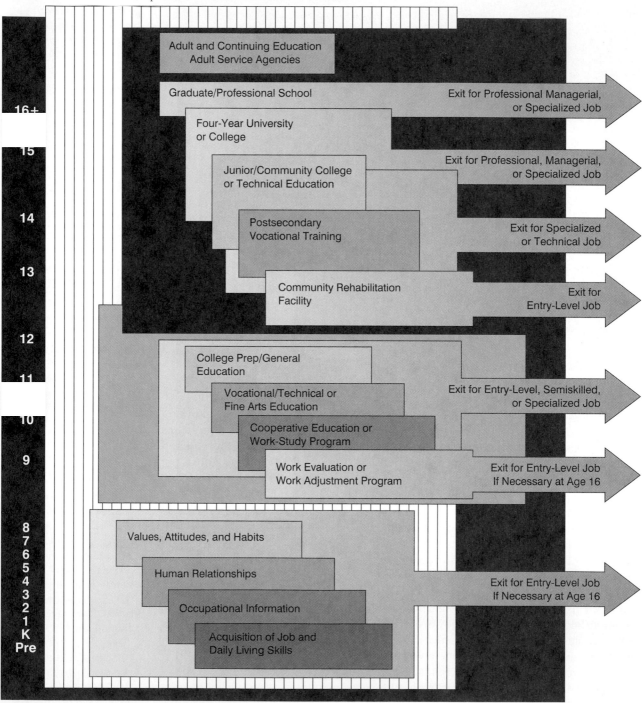

Source: From *Career Development & Transition Education for Adolescents with Disabilities* (2nd ed.) by G. M. Clark and O. P. Kolstoe, 1995, p. 46. Needham Heights, MA: Allyn & Bacon. Used by permission.

sites. For example, Test, Grossi, and Keul (1988) describe a procedure for systematically teaching a 19-year-old student with mental retardation janitorial skills in a competitive work setting. The remaining hours of in-school instruction should focus on acquisition of functional skills needed in the adult work, domestic, community, and recreational/leisure environments toward which the student is headed (Brown et al., 1979). Examples of curriculum activities in the domestic, community, leisure, and vocational domains that might be incorporated into a student's IEP are shown in Table 15.1.

✳ *Employment*

Work can be defined as using one's physical and/or mental energies to accomplish something productive. Our society is based on a work ethic; we place a high value on work and on people who contribute. Besides providing economic support, work offers opportunities for social interaction and a chance to use and enhance skills in a chosen area. Work generates the respect of others, and it can be a source of pride and self-satisfaction (Terkel, 1974).

All young adults face important questions about what to do with their lives—whether to attend college or technical school, whether to work as a bricklayer or an accountant—but for the person without disabilities, the difficulty involves choosing from a number of options. By contrast, the young adult with disabilities too often has few, if any, options from which to choose. Occupational choices decrease if the person with disabilities has limited skills; they may decrease further due to the nature of the disability; and, needlessly, choices and opportunities are still further limited because of employers' prejudices and misconceptions about people with disabilities. For most adults with disabilities, obtaining and holding a job is the major rehabilitation goal.

Competitive Employment

A person who is competitively employed performs work valued by an employer, functions in an integrated setting with nondisabled co-workers, and earns at or above the federal minimum wage (Rusch, Chadsey-Rusch, & Lagomarino, 1987). Wehman and Hill (1985) further specify that a person who is truly competitively employed receives no subsidized wages of any kind. Virtually all special educators who have studied the transition of students with disabilities from school to adult life believe that only through significant revision of the public school curriculum and improved coordination of school and adult vocational habilitation services can the prospect of competitive employment be enhanced for young adults with disabilities (e.g., Bellamy & Horner, 1987; Clark & Kolstoe, 1995; Wehman et al., 1985). Wehman et al. (1985) consider three characteristics critical to good secondary school programs. First, the curriculum must stress functional skills; that is, students must learn vocational skills that they will actually need and use in local employment situations. Second, school-based instruction must be carried out in integrated settings as much as possible. Students with disabilities must be given ample opportunities to learn the interpersonal skills necessary to work effectively with co-workers in integrated work sites. Third, community-based instruction should begin as early as about age 12 for students with severe disabilities and must be used for progressively extended periods as students near graduation. While on work sites in the community, students

Giving students the responsibility of directing and managing their own IEP is an excellent way to help them learn self-determination and independence (Martin, Marshall, & Maxson, 1993; Martin, Marshall, Maxson, & Jerman, 1993).

When the parents of 163 high school students with severe disabilities were asked what they perceived to be the most important adult services their children would need after graduation and at 5 years and 10 years thereafter, they ranked a secure vocational placement that offered meaningful work as the first priority for all three points in time (McDonnell, Wilcox, Boles, & Bellamy, 1985).

Several follow-up studies have found a positive correlation between paid work experiences during high school, and postschool employment (e.g., D'Amico, 1991; Hasazi et al., 1985, 1989; Kohler, 1994; Scuccimarra & Speece, 1990). The NLTS, however, found that only 39% of young adults with disabilities had been enrolled in work experience programs during high school. The Career Ladder Program (CLP) is a comprehensive transition program for youths with mild disabilities that includes real work experience during the senior year. (Siegel et al., 1993).

TABLE 15.1

Examples of transition-related curriculum activities in four domains that might be included in a student's IEP

DOMESTIC	COMMUNITY	LEISURE	VOCATIONAL
Elementary			
Picking up toys/belongings	Eating meals in a restaurant	Climbing on monkey bars	Picking up plate, silverware, and
Washing dishes with family	Using restroom in a local	Playing board games	glass after a meal
Making bed	restaurant	Playing tag with neighbors	Returning toys/belongings to
Dressing	Putting trash into container	Scouts	appropriate storage space
Grooming	Choosing correct change to	Coloring	Cleaning the room at the end
Eating skills	ride city bus	Playing kickball	of the day
Toileting skills	Giving the clerk money to	Croquet	Working on a task for a desig-
Sorting clothing	purchase an item	Riding bicycles	nated period (10–15 minutes)
Vacuuming	Responding appropriately to	Playing with dolls and other	Wiping tables after meals
Setting the table at mealtime	pedestrian safety signs	age-appropriate toys	Following 2– to 4–step instruc-
	Going to neighbor's house	Community soccer league	tions
	for lunch	Nintendo	Answering the telephone
			Emptying trash
			Taking messages to people
Middle School			
Washing clothes	Crossing streets safely	Playing volleyball	Mopping/waxing floors
Cooking a simple hot meal	Purchasing an item from a	Taking aerobic classes	Cleaning windows
(soup, salad, and sandwich)	department store	Playing checkers with a	Filling lawn mower with gas
Keeping bedroom clean	Purchasing a meal at a restau-	friend	Hanging and bagging clothes
Making snacks	rant	Playing miniature golf	Busing tables
Mowing lawn	Using local transportation	Cycling	Working for 1–2 hours with
Raking leaves	system to get to and from		family on weekends
	recreational facilities		

Light, Dumlao, and Stecker (1993) describe how students with severe disabilities can make and use video résumés to effectively present themselves to potential employers.

should receive direct instruction in areas such as specific job skills, ways to increase production rates, and transportation to and from employment sites.

> Students should train and work in the community whenever possible. This is not only to expose them to the community and work expectations, but to expose future employers and co-workers to their potential as reliable employees. (Wehman et al., 1985, p. 29)

Training students with disabilities for successful employment is more than a philosophical notion or philanthropic deed; it is a pragmatic concept that meets the needs of students and society as the changing nature of the workforce evolves and produces more of the kinds of jobs for which persons with disabilities can compete.

> Without question there will be increasing demand for a *diversified* labor force as we come into the 21st Century. Work opportunities will abound in selected areas such as entry service occupations in the hotel and restaurant industries, inventory management, and clerical support. These are all areas where people with disabilities, if sufficiently trained and exposed to the work environment, will make a contribution to society, to business and industry, and will at the same time better their lives. (Wehman, 1992, p. 115)

TABLE 15.1 *(continued)*

DOMESTIC	COMMUNITY	LEISURE	VOCATIONAL
Making a grocery list	Participating in local scout troop	Attending high school or local college basketball games	Cleaning sinks, bathtubs, and fixtures
Purchasing items from a list			Operating machinery (such as dishwasher, buffer)
Vacuuming and dusting	Going to a neighbor's house for lunch on Saturday	Hanging out at local mall	Internship with school janitor
Setting an alarm clock at night and turning it off when waking	Riding the city bus with family or school friends	Swimming	Internship with school office staff
Using deodorant		Attending crafts class at city recreation center	Following a daily schedule
High School			
Cleaning all rooms in place of residence	Utilizing bus system to move about the community	Jogging	Performing required janitorial duties at J. C. Penney
Developing a weekly budget	Depositing checks into bank account	Boating	Performing housekeeping duties at Days Inn
Cooking meals		Watching college basketball	
Operating thermostat to regulate heat or air	Using community department stores	Video games	Performing grounds keeping duties at local college campus
		Card games	
Doing yard maintenance	Using community grocery stores	YMCA swim class	Performing food service at mall cafeteria
Maintaining personal needs		Gardening	
Caring for and maintaining clothing	Using community health facilities (physician, pharmacist)	Going on a vacation	Performing laundry duties at local laundromat
		Collecting tapes or CDs	
Taking care of menstrual needs		Reading magazines or comics	Performing photography at local bank
		Hanging out/sleeping over with friends	Performing food-stocking duties at large grocery store
			Performing messenger/reception duties at local business

From P. Wehman, M. S. Moon, J. M. Wood, and M. Barcus, Transition from School to Work: New Challenges for Youth with Severe Disabilities, 1988, pp. 140–141. Paul H. Brookes Publishing Co., P.O. Box 10624, Baltimore, MD 21285-0624. Reprinted by permission of the publisher and author.

Supported Employment

For adults with disabilities, especially those with severe intellectual and/or physical disabilities, the opportunity to earn real wages for real work has been almost nonexistent in this country. This situation has continued to exist despite numerous demonstrations that persons with severe disabilities can learn meaningful vocational tasks when provided with systematic training and on-the-job support (e.g., Bellamy et al., 1979; Gaylord-Ross et al., 1991; Gold, 1976; Rusch, 1990). A new type of vocational opportunity has emerged that is aimed at helping individuals with severe disabilities who have historically been unemployed or restricted to sheltered settings. Supported employment enables persons with severe disabilities to participate successfully in integrated work environments.

The supported employment or supported work movement recognizes that many adults with severe disabilities require ongoing, often intensive support to obtain, learn, and hold a job. The incorporation of supported employment into PL 99-506, the Rehabilitation Act Amendments of 1986, has led to a proliferation of fed-

To learn how one vocational training program prepares individuals with disabilities for competitive employment in the restaurant industry, see Touchstone Cafe later on in this chapter.

erally assisted supported employment programs throughout the country. **Supported employment** is

- competitive work in integrated work settings;
- for persons with the most severe disabilities;
- for whom competitive employment has not traditionally occurred;
- or for whom competitive employment has been interrupted or intermittent as a result of a severe disability; and
- who, because of the severity of their disability, need intensive support services; or
- extended services in order to perform such work. (PL 102–569 [sec. 635(b)(6)(c)(iii)])

Types of Supported Employment

Four distinct placement models have been developed and widely reported in the supported employment literature:

- individual placement (job coach model)
- work enclaves (workstation model)
- mobile work crew
- small business enterprises (entrepreneurial model)

Although other supported employment models have been used and proposed, a national survey found that over 90% of the nearly 75,000 individuals participating in supported employment programs in 42 states/territories are served by one of these four models (Revell et al., 1994). This same survey found a national mean average weekly wage for supported employment participants of $111.44, which reflected an increase of 500% over the average weekly salary earned by these individuals before supported employment. Persons with various types and degrees of disabilities obtained significant increases in earnings, and the individual placement model resulted in the highest hourly and monthly wages.

Wehman and Kregel (1985) describe an *individual placement* model for supported employment that consists of four components:

1. A comprehensive approach to job placement
2. Intensive job-site training and advocacy
3. Ongoing monitoring of client performance
4. A systematic approach to long-term job retention and follow-up

The supported employment specialist is the key to making a supported work program effective. The supported employment specialist, sometimes called a job coach, is a community-based professional who works in a nonprofit job placement program, a public vocational or adult services program, or a secondary special education program. Table 15.2 identifies the major activities and responsibilities of a supported employment specialist in each component of the supported work model. Effective job coaching requires many skills, flexibility, and hard work, and the success of supported employment placement often hinges on the job coach's abilities and problem-solving creativity. As important as job coaches are, they are generally undertrained and underpaid.

Although all participants in supported employment continue to receive support and services as needed, the amount of direct on-the-job assistance the supported employment specialist provides is gradually reduced as the new employee acquires greater competence in completing the job requirements independently (Kregel, Hill, Hill & Banks, 1988; Wehman, Hill, Brooke, Pendleton, & Britt, 1985).

An *integrated work setting* requires regular contact with nondisabled co-workers. In 1986, 9,633 individuals were working in federally assisted Supported Employment Demonstration Projects in 20 states. Just 2 years later, the supported employment movement had grown to a total of 32,342 participants nationally, and the cumulative wages these workers earned grew from $1.4 million to $12.4 million in the 15 states that reported earnings data (Wehman, Kregel, Shafer, & West, 1989). By 1991, it was estimated that approximately 90,000 persons with disabilities were working through supported employment (Revell, Wehman, Kregel, West, & Rayfield, 1994).

For details on developing supported employment programs, see Bellamy, Rhodes, Mank, and Albin (1988) and Rusch (1990). The winter 1989 issue of the *Journal of Applied Behavior Analysis* is devoted to research on supported employment.

TABLE 15.2

Responsibilities of a supported employment specialist during each component of the supported work model proposed by Wehman and Kregel (1985)

COMPONENT	ACTIVITIES
Job placement	Structured efforts to find jobs for client and matching client strengths to job needs
	Planning of transportation arrangements and/or travel training
	Active involvement with parents to identify appropriate job for client
	Communication with Social Security Administration
Job site training and advocacy	Trained staff provides behavior skill training to improve client's work performance
	Trained staff provides necessary social skill training at job site
	Staff works with employers and co-workers in helping client
Ongoing monitoring	Provides for regular written feedback from employer on client progress
	Utilizes behavioral data related to client work speed, proficiency, need for staff assistance, etc.
Follow-up and retention	Implements periodic client and parent satisfaction questionnaires
	Implements planned effort to reduce staff intervention at job site
	Provides follow-up to employer in form of phone calls and visits to job sites as needed
	Communicates to employer regarding staff accessibility as needed
	Helps client relocate or find new job if necessary

Source: From "A Supported Work Approach to Competitive Employment of Individuals with Moderate and Severe Handicaps" by P. Wehman and J. Kregel, 1985, *Journal of the Association for Persons with Severe Handicaps, 10,* p. 5. Reprinted by permission.

Wehman, Hill, et al. (1985) report the employment status of 167 adults who were placed in part- and full-time paid jobs with the supported work model. The clients ranged in age from 18 to 66 years old and had a median IQ score of 49.

> The great majority (86%) were receiving regular financial aid from the government at the time of placement. In fact, 81% earned under $200 as an annual salary the year prior to placement, which indicates the level of economic independence exhibited by these individuals prior to intervention. A total of 71% lived with their parents or family and 90% lacked skills to use public transportation at the time of their initial placement. (p. 275)

A total of 252 job placements, most in entry-level minimum-wage positions, were made with more than 100 employers, representing primarily service occupations, such as cleaning and custodial work in hotels, restaurants, and hospitals. The average length of employment for all 167 of the persons in the study was 19 months. At the time of the report, 72 clients were still employed. The authors note that the 8.1 months of employment during their clients' first year on the job compares favorably with the results of a study by the National Hotel and Restaurant Association (1983) that found more than 2,300 individuals without disabilities had retained their comparable entry-level positions for an average of only 5 months. They also point out that the average total cost of $5,255 per client for the supported work program, which resulted in an average of 19 months of paid employment per client, compares favorably with the average annual cost of $4,000 per year for adult day programs

A national survey of 308 job coaches in 20 states found that half were provided with 8 hours or less training before beginning work and were usually paid less than $17,000 per year (Agosta, Brown, & Melda, 1993). To learn about strategies for hiring, training, and managing job coaches, see Grossi, Test, and Keul (1991).

What Were We Really Saying?

Removing Transition Hurdles with Effective Communication

by Sue Brewster and Lyn Doll

Let us introduce ourselves: Sue is a job-training coordinator and transition specialist for an urban school system; Lyn is the mother of Karen, a young adult with a disability. We would like to share what we learned about helping young adults with disabilities transition from school to adult life from our experience with a transition-planning meeting for Karen.

Karen

Karen, challenged by mental retardation, epilepsy, and osteoporosis, which requires her to use a wheelchair, was in her last year of high school. Throughout high school, Karen had participated in a variety of work experiences in the community, such as at a restaurant, child care facility, two different nursing homes, and a large general department store. Karen's strengths include her desire to work in the community, social skills, and quality of work. Staying on task, poor productivity, and short-term memory were areas of difficulty.

Karen and her family were feeling the many stresses that occur with leaving high school and moving into the adult world. The county board of mental retardation and developmental disabilities (MR/DD), which provides vocational, residential, recreation, and other services to individuals with dis-

abilities, had presented Karen and her family with two options: community-based employment or a sheltered workshop environment. At the time, community-based employment was only an option for persons who could work at least 20 hours per week with minimal support, such as a job coach stopping in every week or so. Individuals whose disabilities prevented them from working the required hours or who needed more support were automatically placed on the waiting list for the sheltered workshop. Karen's seizure disorder and physical disability made it difficult for her to meet the required working hours for community placement, yet she had frequently expressed her desire to work in the community.

To help prepare Karen for community placement, Sue had found Karen a nonpaying work experience at a restaurant on a nearby university campus. Karen's duties were to bus tables and clean off trays. Grant funds to increase transition services for youths with disabilities were used to provide transportation to and from the job site and for a maximum of 100 job-coaching hours. Karen and her job coach, Chris, began working at the restaurant for 8 hours per week. It was hoped that this nonpaid work experience would lead to paid employment and possibly additional working hours after graduation.

As the 100 hours of grant-funded job coaching neared completion, Chris thought that Karen would continue to need support services on the job. Lyn preferred that Karen work in the community, but she had many questions concerning the feasibility of community work. Sue, who had visited Karen at the job site, thought that things were going pretty well, and the restaurant manager had indicated the "possibility" of offering Karen competitive employment. Sue was also concerned that the grant funding might be lost for

other students if this placement failed. At this point, Sue arranged a transition-planning meeting for all interested parties in an effort to determine what support services Karen would need after graduation and to try to solidify the employment placement.

Karen's Transition Meeting

The meeting was held at the restaurant with all interested parties present: Karen; Lyn and Bill, Karen's parents; Mark, Karen's older brother; Sue, the job training coordinator; Chris, the job coach; Jim, the restaurant manager; two people from the county MR/DD program; and a representative from the Bureau of Vocational Rehabilitation (BVR).

After all had introduced themselves, Sue began the meeting by asking Chris, "How is Karen doing since you've been with her for 6 weeks on the job?" Knowing what the stakes were and who was present around the table (parents and restaurant manager), Chris hesitated and then said something positive while admitting that Karen had some "slow days." When Bill, Karen's father, asked Jim, the restaurant manager, whether he would have to hire somebody else to do the job if Karen didn't get it, he sounded as if he didn't really expect that Karen would ever work in the community.

Throughout the meeting, it seemed that people were saying one thing and meaning another. Everyone seemed to be communicating at cross purposes, to have his or her own agenda and objective. The meeting ended with everyone feeling very negative, exhausted, and perplexed. Most important, the meeting ended without a community job for Karen.

Bubble Heads

Two months after the meeting, Sue, feeling as though she had failed, met with Lyn to figure out what went

Karen's ITP meeting: What people said and what they were really thinking

wrong at the meeting. They decided to ask each participant to remember what he or she was thinking during the meeting and to compare that with the statements they had actually said. After talking with the participants and comparing what was said with what they "were really saying," Sue and Lyn learned some important lessons about effective communication during transition planning. The figure shows actual statements made by members of the planning team; the bubbles show what each person was really thinking.

Communication Breakdown

- The seating arrangement is important. The meeting had been conducted at a long, narrow table. A round table would have helped ensure that each team member had equal opportunity to talk and be heard by everyone and to see and hear the person speaking.
- Too many people hampers effective communication. Both the family and the employer expressed the feeling of being overwhelmed by the number of people (10) who were present at the meeting.
- Listen to what people are saying they want and need, even if their request differs from what you think should occur. For example, Lyn was saying to Sue that she would like to see Karen working in the community, rather than in a sheltered workshop. At the same time, her husband and son were voicing skepticism and were being "protective" of Karen. Sue did not consider the interactions between the family members and only considered what she thought would be best for Karen. Sue should have met with the family prior to the transition meeting to help the family sort out

and determine what they wanted.
- Because Lyn was surrounded with negative beliefs about Karen's ability to work in the community, she left the meeting thinking that perhaps her husband and son had been right all along. The family gave up hope of community work for Karen. This made it easy for the business to not offer Karen the job.
- Sue may not have been "really listening" to the family because of her job-placement requirement. She may have been more concerned with meeting her "placement quota" than with the concerns of the family.
- Not once during the meeting did anyone ask Karen where she wanted to work and what she thought her strengths, weaknesses, and support needs were. Service providers have to "step outside their realm" and place the individual with a disability in the center of the planning to ensure that his or her requests and desires are addressed.

Professionals Sometimes Build Their Own Hurdles

- Even though they want to do the right thing, service providers often get trapped by their own rules and regulations and their "usual" way of doing business. The agencies (BVR and MR/DD) gave up by stating that they could not provide services to Karen if she was not going to get paid at least minimum wage or work at least 20 hours per week.
- Potential employers will avoid getting involved when they deal with too many professionals, bureaucratic tangles, or "turf fighting" between agencies.

Karen's New Job

Everyone except Karen seemed to have given up after that fateful meeting. But Karen persisted in expressing her interest in a job in the community. Sue brought the transition team together again to address the requests and needs of Karen and her family. By being flexible and creative, Sue has worked during the last 2 years to create jobs for Karen and others with significant challenges. Karen is now doing meaningful work in an integrated job in the community. Karen is currently working at Anderson's General Store in a group placement (enclave) with three other individuals with significant challenges. Her job entails moving and facing items to the front of the shelves. Karen works 3 days per week for 3 hours per day with the support of a job coach. To help alleviate the family's concerns about Karen struggling in the community, Sue arranged for them to observe Karen at work.

Karen's production rate currently keeps her from earning minimum wage, but she has the opportunity to do meaningful work for pay and to interact with nondisabled peers. In the last year, Karen has made another transition. She has moved from her parents' home to a group home with four other adults with disabilities. With her supports and effective communication among service providers and the family, Karen is continuing her "transition" to independence. ✺

Sue Brewster is a job training coordinator for the Toledo Public School System in Toledo, Ohio. Lyn Doll, coordinator for the Local Interagency Transition Team and a parent mentor for adult issues, ensures that services for individuals with disabilities are family driven.

The supported employment movement is enabling tens of thousands of individuals like Paul to experience, for the first time in their lives, the benefits of real work for real wages.

For a thought-provoking examination and debate of the issues concerning whether adults with severe disabilities should be permitted to perform meaningful work without pay in community-based integrated work sites while undergoing extended training, see Bellamy et al. (1984) and Brown et al. (1984).

(sheltered workshops and work activity centers). This comparison is especially favorable when one takes into account the total client wages earned and income taxes contributed.

In the *enclave* or *workstation model* of supported employment, a small group of no more than eight persons with disabilities performs work with special training or job supports within a normal business or industry. The work enclave provides a useful alternative to traditional, segregated sheltered employment, offering many of the benefits of community-based integrated employment, as well as the ongoing support necessary for long-term job success.

Rhodes and Valenta (1985) report the preliminary results of a work enclave that resulted in the employment of six persons with severe disabilities. They established a working agreement with Physio Control Corporation of Redmond, Washington, to create a separate production line within the company to employ persons with severe disabilities. Physio Control employs 900 people in its Redmond facility, where it manufactures biomedical equipment, primarily heart defibrillators. A nonprofit organization called Trillium Employment Services was created to provide the employment training and ongoing support the workers with severe disabilities needed. The work enclave employees have become part of a production line that does subassemblies of defibrillator components, such as chest paddles and wire harnesses. As much as possible, tasks are selected that are of the same type performed by other employees of the company. The work enclave employees are supervised by Physio Control, although legal employment responsibility rests with the support organization (Trillium) until an individual's 3-month productivity averages 65% of the productivity of other Physio Control employees. At that time, the individual is hired as a Physio Control employee. Work enclave employees receive wages commensurate with their productivity rates. Training and supervision procedures use a behavioral model, incorporating task analysis and direct instruction of specific job skills as well as arrangement of the physical and social aspects of the work environment to encourage improved work rates (Bellamy et al., 1979).

At the end of 1 year, all of the enclave employees were producing at or above 50% of the productivity standard of other Physio Control employees. Total wages earned by all program employees for the first year were $20,207, including $2,425

The success of supported employment depends in large part on *job development,* the identification and creation of community-based employment opportunities for individuals with disabilities. For suggestions on how job developers can improve their "sales pitch" to the business community, see Fabian, Luecking, and Tilson (1994); Hagner and Daning (1993); and Nietupski, Verstegen and Hamre-Nietupski (1992).

The individual placement (job coach) model is the most widely used supported employment approach (79.7%), followed by work enclaves (14.5%), mobile work crews (5.3%), and small business enterprises (0.1%) (Revell et al., 1994).

Strategies for evaluating job performance and measuring on-the-job social integration for supported employees at a workstation are described by Test, Keul, Williams, Slaughter, and Allen (1992).

paid by the employees in federal income tax. Total public costs for the program were $15,945 for the first year, with the majority of those costs incurred during the first 5 months of the program. With respect to interaction with nondisabled co-workers, Rhodes and Valenta (1985) report:

> Managers and supervisors within the assembly area report frequent daily contact between enclave and other employees. These occur within the work environment as well as during breaks and lunch. Contacts are said to be overwhelmingly positive. Social contacts have also occurred through company-sponsored events such as picnics, dinners, and dances, and through privately initiated events between managers and employees. (p. 15)

In their conclusion, however, the authors warn that

> for program developers and industrial managers contemplating this alternative, it will be necessary to insure that employees not become segregated from the rest of the working community (much like the "handicapped wing" of a public school). A balance must be attained in providing the structure to support training interventions, to address low productivity, and insure adaptability to changing work demands, without sacrificing the advantages of a normal industrial environment. (p. 18)

The *mobile work crew model* of supported employment is organized around a small single-purpose business, such as building or grounds maintenance. Like the enclave model, a mobile work crew involves the ongoing supervision of a small group of supported employees in an integrated community employment setting. A general manager may be responsible for finding and coordinating the work of several small crews of three to eight individuals, with each crew supervised by a supported employment specialist. Mobile work crews are organized as not-for-profit corporations; the extra costs the organizations incur because their employees do not work at full productivity levels are covered by public funds. Such costs are usually less than would be needed to support the work crew employees in activity centers, which provide little or no real work or reimbursement.

The *small business enterprise model* provides supported employment for persons with disabilities by establishing a business that takes advantage of existing commercial opportunities within a community. The business hires a small number of individuals with severe disabilities, as well as several employees without disabilities. One example of the entrepreneurial model is the Port Townsend Baking Company, a commercial bakery in Port Townsend, Washington.

Although measures such as the number of persons placed, hours worked, wages earned, and taxes paid are important outcomes in evaluating supported employment programs, so too is job satisfaction. When 34 supported employees were interviewed (22 who were in individual placements and 12 in the workstation model), the majority said they (a) liked their jobs, (b) were satisfied with the supports they received from their job coach, (c) had had input in selecting their jobs, (d) would rather work in the community than in a sheltered workshop, and (e) had friends at work (Test, Hinson, Solow, & Keul, 1993).

Using Natural Supports to Learn Independence and Adaptability on the Job

The complexity of competitive and supported work environments requires persons with disabilities to use a wide range of vocational and social skills. Consider the many behaviors covered by this list of work performance measures that can be used to evaluate the independent performance of employees with disabilities.

Performance measures

1. Works independently
2. Completes all assigned tasks
3. Attends to job tasks consistently

4. Meets company standards for quality of work
5. Meets company standards for rate of work performance
6. Follows company procedures
7. Maintains good attendance and punctuality
8. Takes care of equipment and materials
9. Maintains acceptable appearance

Adaptability measures

1. Obtains/returns materials for tasks
2. Adjusts rate of performance according to job demands
3. Works safely
4. Follows a schedule
5. Manages time properly
6. Is able to adjust to changes in routine
7. Solves work-related problems independently

Social skills measures

1. Follows directions
2. Accepts criticism
3. Asks for assistance when necessary
4. Gets along with fellow workers
5. Interacts appropriately with customers (Lagomarcino, Hughes, & Rusch, 1989, p. 143)

To earn high marks for most of these measures, an employee must display some degree of independence and adaptability in the workplace. Successful employees independently solve minor problems (e.g., clear off an obstructed work area before beginning) instead of calling their supervisor. Successful employees are sensitive to cues in the work setting that signal changing demands, and they adjust their performance accordingly.

Traditional methods of "job coaching" have relied on direct instruction by an outside agent to teach targeted job tasks or social skills in response to the employer's current standards and expectations. The employment specialist returns to provide more training and intervention whenever the supported employee's productivity slips, the criteria for successful performance on the job change, or other problems arise on the job. Mithaug, Martin, Agran, and Rusch (1988) point out that this approach fosters too much dependence on the job coach, working against the supported employee's learning how to solve problems on the job and assuming responsibility for his or her own management. The always-on-call job coach may also prevent the employer and co-workers from figuring out and implementing natural solutions to problems.

Natural Supports

The role of the employment specialist/job coach is evolving from one of primary supporter for the employee with disabilities to one who works with the employer and co-workers to create innovative and natural support networks. In general, *natural support* occurs when:

- Services (implementation, training and support) for employees with disabilities are consistent with the culture of the workplace.

Johnson and Rusch (1990) found that the actual number of hours of direct training by employment specialists did not decline over time in clustered or mobile crew supported employment programs, as had been noted with individual placements. They suggest that clustered and mobile crew approaches have been marketed to employers with the promise that the employment specialists will always be present, which may increase the likelihood of unnecessary supervision and inhibit the development of employee independence.

- Workers experience typical employment status.
- Supports are varied, flexible, individualized, and extend beyond the workplace.
- Employers and co-workers have ownership of support-related decisions and problem solving.
- Professionals are seen as external agents. Their role is to help identify, develop, and facilitate the typical or indigenous supports of the workplace. (Mank et al., 1993, p. 3)

The Importance of Co-workers

Social interaction is a natural feature of the workplace. Social interaction provides an important source of support for any employee, with or without disabilities, and it is associated with job performance and job satisfaction (Nisbet & Hagner, 1988). Because of their consistent presence in the work environment, co-workers can be a potentially powerful source of natural support for workers with disabilities (Rusch & Minch, 1988). Rusch, Hughes, McNair, and Wilson (1990) define a co-worker as an employee who works in the proximity of the supported employee, performs the same or similar duties, and/or takes breaks or eats meals in the same area as the supported employee. Six types of co-worker involvement beneficial to supported employees are described in Table 15.3. McNair and Rusch (1992) have developed and field-tested the *Co-worker Involvement Instrument,* a 10-item assessment device for measuring co-worker involvement with supported employees.

In a typical supported employment program, the employment specialist provides direct, on-site job training to the employee with disabilities and serves as the primary source of support and assistance to the supported employee. Although the job coach gradually reduces the time spent in direct, on-site training and support as the supported employee becomes acclimated to the job, this model of "outside assistance" has several inherent drawbacks (Curl, 1990; Hughes et al., 1990). First, the arrival and presence of the job coach can be disruptive to the natural work setting. Second, the supported employee may perform differently in the presence of his or her job coach. Third, it is difficult for the employment specialist to be sensitive to the changing demands of the job over time and to provide continued support and training consistent with those changes. Fourth, the cost of providing training and support by an employment specialist who must travel to the job site is higher and the efficiency of the approach is lower than one that takes advantage of the natural interactions of co-workers. Fifth, and perhaps most important, the supported employee may become too dependent on the job coach, thereby missing the opportunity to develop independence and flexibility. A skilled and friendly co-worker can provide information, answer questions, demonstrate job tasks, provide assistance and repeat instructions as needed, give social praise and feedback for performance, and serve as an important contact point for the supported employee's entry into the social fabric of the workplace (Baumgart & Askvig, 1992).

Although some co-workers provide support naturally, observations in the workplace indicate that some formal training is usually necessary to make co-workers' "help" effective in maintaining successful employment by the disabled worker. For example, one study found that co-workers typically presented more than 100 instructions in the first 2 hours of employment training (Curl, Lignugaris/Kraft, Pawley, & Salzberg, 1988)—a frequency likely to overwhelm a newly hired employee with disabilities. Several approaches for co-worker training have been developed recently.

Rusch, Johnson, and Hughes (1990) found fairly extensive involvement with nondisabled co-workers by supported employees working in individual or workstation placements regardless of the supported employees' level of disability. Supported employees working in mobile work crews, however, experienced far less co-worker involvement. When combined with data showing significantly lower earnings for supported employees working in mobile work crews as compared with those in individual or clustered placements, these results raise the question of whether the mobile work crew should continue to be considered an appropriate supported employment model (Kregel et al., 1989).

TABLE 15.3
Types of co-worker involvement

Advocating. A co-worker advocates for a supported employee by *optimizing, backing,* and *supporting* a supported employee's employment status. *Optimizing* refers to encouraging a supervisor to assign high-status and relevant tasks to a supported employee; *backing* refers to supporting a supported employee's rights, for example, by attempting to prevent practical jokes aimed at a supported employee. It also includes speaking up for a supported employee or offering explanations during differences of opinion. *Supporting* relates to providing emotional support to a supported employee in the form of friendship, association, etc.

Associating. A co-worker interacts socially with a supported employee at the workplace.

Befriending. A co-worker interacts socially with a supported employee outside the workplace.

Collecting Data. A co-worker collects data by observing and recording social and/or work performance.

Evaluating. A co-worker appraises a supported employee's work performance and provides (written/oral) feedback to him or her.

Training. A co-worker supports a supported employee by providing on-the-job skill training.

Source: From *Co-worker Involvement Scoring Manual and Index* by F. R. Rusch, C. Hughes, J. McNair, and P. G. Wilson, 1990, Champagne, IL: University of Illinois. Used by permission.

Co-workers can be taught how to provide support during brief, 15- to 20-minute sessions during breaks or before or after work. Curl (1990) has developed a program in which co-workers learn to use a simple 4-step procedure in which they provide instructions, demonstrate the job task, observe the supported employee performing the same task, and deliver praise and evaluative feedback on the trainee's performance.

Self-Management

The belief that employees with disabilities should be taught independence in the workplace has gained widespread acceptance among supported employment professionals and has spawned an exciting and promising area of research. Hughes, Rusch, and Curl (1990) suggest identifying natural cues in the work environment that can be used to promote independent performance. For example, clocks or whistles may signal going to a job station; co-workers stopping work and leaving the job station might be the prompt for break time; and a growing pile of dirty dishes should be the cue to increase the rate of dish washing. The job specialist's role expands from training the employee how to perform various vocational and social skills to teaching the supported employee how to respond independently to the cues that occur naturally in the workplace. When naturally occurring cues are insufficient to cue the desired behavior, the supported employee can be taught to respond to contrived cues, such as picture prompts depicting individual steps in a multiple-step task (Wilson, Schepis, & Mason-Main, 1987) or prerecorded verbal prompts interspersed between and within favorite music that the employee listens to on a Walkman-type cassette player (Grossi, 1995; West, Rayfield, Clements, Unger, Thornton, 1994).

Self-monitoring, which has proven so successful in the classroom, can also be effectively used in employment training. Research has shown that employees with disabilities can use self-monitoring—observing, counting, and recording one's per-

A study by Likins, Salzberg, Stowitschek, Lignugaris/Kraft, and Curl (1989) demonstrates the potential of co-workers as job trainers for supported employees. Three women with mental retardation who were employed in the food preparation area of a self-service cafeteria were taught a 19-step sequence by co-workers for preparing a chef salad and how to conduct quality-control checks of their salads.

Mithaug, Martin, and Agran (1987) describe an approach they call the *adaptability model* designed to help students learn independence in the workplace. Instructional activities are designed to foster four kinds of skills inherent in self-determination: decision making, independent performance, self-evaluation, and making adjustments the next time they perform the task.

Additional information on how to increase the independence and adaptability of employees with disabilities can be found in Rusch (1990).

Agran and Moore (1994) provide training scripts and monitoring forms for teaching self-instruction of job skills to students with mental retardation.

formance—to increase their job productivity and independence (Ackerman & Shapiro, 1984; Grossi, 1991; Wheeler, Bates, Marshall, & Miller, 1988). For example, Allen, White, and Test (1992) developed a picture/symbol form that employees with disabilities can use to self-monitor their performance on the job (see Figure 15.4).

Employees with disabilities can also learn to self-manage their work performance by providing their own verbal prompts and instructions. Salend, Ellis, and Reynolds (1989) used a self-instructional strategy to teach four adults with severe mental retardation to "talk while you work." Productivity increased dramatically and error rates decreased when the women verbalized to themselves, "Comb up, Comb down, Comb in bag, Bag in box" while packaging combs in plastic bags. Hughes and Rusch (1989) taught two supported employees working at a janitorial supply company how to solve problems by using a self-instructional procedure consisting of four statements:

1. Statement of the problem (e.g., "Tape empty")
2. Statement of the response needed to solve the problem (e.g., "Need more tape")
3. Self-report (e.g., "Fixed it")
4. Self-reinforcement (e.g., "Good")

Sheltered Employment

The **sheltered workshop** is the most common type of vocational setting for adults with disabilities. Sheltered workshops serve individuals with a wide variety of disabilities, although about half are persons with mental retardation. Sheltered workshops can be classified as providing one or more of three types of programs: (a) evaluation and training for competitive employment in the community (commonly referred to as transitional workshops), (b) extended or long-term employment, and (c) work activities.

Many sheltered workshops offer both transitional and extended employment situations within the same building. Transitional workshops continually try to place their employees in community-based jobs. Extended employment workshops are operated to provide whatever training and support services are necessary to enable individuals with severe disabilities to work productively within the sheltered environment. The Wage and Hour Division of the U.S. Department of Labor requires that persons working in an extended sheltered workshop receive at least 50% of the minimum wage; they may be paid an hourly wage or a piecework rate.

All sheltered workshops have at least two elements in common. First, they offer rehabilitation, training, and—in some instances—full employment. Second, to provide meaningful work for clients, a sheltered workshop must operate as a business. Sheltered workshops—especially extended workshops striving to provide steady, meaningful, paid employment—generally engage in one of three types of business ventures: contracting, prime manufacturing, or reclamation.

Contracting is the major source of work in most workshops. A contract is an agreement that a sheltered workshop will complete a specified job (e.g., assembling and packaging a company's product) within a specified time for a given price. Most sheltered workshops have one or more professional staff members, called contractors or contract procurement persons, whose sole job is to obtain and negotiate contracts with businesses and industries in the community. Contracts do not come to sheltered workshops as a form of charity or community service. Workshops must bid competitively for each job and therefore must carefully take into account not only

FIGURE 15.4

A picture/symbol form that a student or employee with disabilities could use to self-monitor job performance

Task Sheet					
Student: _____ Week of: _____ Observer: _____					
	M	T	W	Th	Comments
1. Job needs (e.g., name tag, lunch).					
2. Get work assignment.					
3. Get cart.					
4. Find and enter room.					
5. Check drapes.					
6. Check TV.					
7. Make bed.					
8. Dust.					
9. Stock amenities.					
10. Empty wastebaskets.					
11. Clean bathroom.					
12. Vacuum.					
13. Fill out hotel checklist					

Source: From "Using a Picture/Symbol Form for Self-monitoring within a Community-based Training Program," by C. P. Allen, J. White, and D. W. Test, 1992, *Teaching Exceptional Children, 24*(2), p. 55. Used by permission.

Touchstone Cafe

Vocational Training with a Flavor

On July 10, 1990, Touchstone Cafe opened its doors for business in Columbus, Ohio. This in itself is nothing new in a city where every week new restaurants open amid fanfare and high hopes while recently-opened restaurants quietly go under. What makes Touchstone Cafe different from the more than 600 restaurants in Columbus is its primary purpose—preparing adults with disabilities for jobs in the food service industry.

Trainers with Experience

Touchstone Cafe is a full-service restaurant featuring moderately priced lunch and dinner menus of American cuisine. The restaurant is staffed by 20 to 25 trainees, each of whom works 15 to 30 hours per week, and 10 to 12 trainers. Trainers know exactly what it is like in the "real world" of restaurant work because they either have worked or still do work in local restaurants as servers, cooks, dishwashers, cashiers, and so on. The trainees, who range in age from 18 to 55 years old, all have developmental disabilities or psychiatric disorders and no recent history of successful competitive employment.

Trainees spend approximately 6 months at Touchstone, where they receive training on a minimum of three different restaurant jobs and instruction on employment-related areas such as transportation, interviewing, social skills, and money management as specified by an individual vocational plan.

Touchstone Cafe's Restaurant Advisory Board includes 20 restaurant professionals who represent more than 150 local restaurants, ranging from fast-food chains (Wendy's, White Castle), family-style restaurants (Bob Evans, Tee Jaye's Country Place), and up-scale, white-tablecloth establishments (Rigsby's, Lindey's). They have made commitments to provide employment opportunities to graduates of the program. Mark Emerson, Vice President of Operations for Max & Erma's Restaurants: "The Touchstone concept is long overdue. For us in the restaurant industry, it's a welcome approach. We like the idea of hiring workers with the training and experience people at Touchstone receive." But although Emerson and other professionals support the concept and have given their time and expertise to help Touchstone get started, the businesses they represent will not hire or keep someone from the program who cannot do the job. Touchstone trainees are not guaranteed employment by the participating restaurants. After developing specific job skills, each trainee must interview and be selected for a job. Then he or she must keep that job just like any other worker—through reliable and satisfactory performance.

Meeting Competitive Standards

Teresa Grossi, who was Touchstone's first director of training, says that trainees begin working toward the goal of competitive employment in another restaurant from their first day at Touchstone. "Productivity is a must in the restaurant business, whether you work in the front or the back of the house. When things are hopping during peak hours, an employee can't bus tables like he's got all day or decide he'll take a break at the dish-washing station. We determined a competitive standard for each of the job tasks our trainees learn. We do this by observing and measuring the productivity of nondisabled employees in the restaurants where our graduates will likely be working and by measuring the productivity of our trainers here at Touchstone. For example, we know a busperson in a full-service restaurant takes an average of 5 minutes to clear and reset a four-top table. So we don't feel one of our trainees has mastered table bussing until he consistently can do a four-top within a range of 4 to 6 minutes.

"But first, we focus on doing the job correctly," Grossi continues. "It doesn't do any good to try to go fast if you're making mistakes or finishing only half the job. Initially, a trainer is right alongside each trainee, modeling the job and providing prompts, assistance, and feedback as needed. These teaching trials are interspersed with probe trials to find out how the trainee is doing. During a probe trial, the trainer stands back and records the trainee's perfor-

the wages paid to workers but also the equipment needs, training costs, production rate, overhead, and so on.

Prime manufacturing involves the designing, producing, marketing, and shipping of a complete product. The advantage of prime manufacturing over contracting, assuming a successful product is being manufactured, is that the workshops do not have problems with downtime when they are between contracts. They can plan their training and labor requirements more directly. Most sheltered workshops, however,

A Touchstone trainee takes an order while his trainer looks on.

mance on each step of the task analysis for the given job—no help is given. If a customer gets the wrong soup . . . well, natural consequences are usually a pretty good teacher.

"When a trainee demonstrates he can perform the job accurately for five consecutive shifts, we begin working on productivity. For example, Chuck was taking almost 12 minutes to bus a four-person table. I showed him a graph of his times compared to what he'd be expected to do if hired by another restaurant. Chuck was given a stopwatch and taught how to time and graph his own performance and then to self-evaluate by comparing his time to the competitive standard. It didn't take him long to work consistently at a productivity level equal to what's expected in the workplace."

Follow-up and Natural Supports

An individual's relationship with Touchstone isn't over once he or she is employed by a local restaurant. Touchstone provides several follow-along services for their graduates and the restaurants who hire them. One is the Dessert Club, a twice-a-month pie and coffee session in which Touchstone graduates get together to talk of successes, discuss problem-solving strate-gies, and share the wisdom they've gained from competitive employment with current trainees. Another is a training package designed to assist supervisors and nondisabled co-work-ers who provide support to the employee with disabilities.

Risk Taking and Self-Esteem

Susan Berg, Touchstone's president, realizes that the program must survive as a viable restaurant if its early success is to continue. "It's always a balancing act between running a restaurant and a training program at the same time. We're a real restaurant, and we have to remember the needs of our customers. While some of our first-time customers come because they're interested, curi-ous, or want to support what we're doing, many who walk through the door don't know anything about our special mission. They come to Touch-stone for the same reasons they'd patronize any other restaurant—good food, good value, good service.

"It's our customers who make it real. We don't have to contrive any-thing in order to 'simulate' commu-nity-based instruction. This is it. Nerves get on edge when things get rushed, people are waiting for a table, food gets cold, customers change their minds too many times . . . it's great. Our trainees take risks. What we ask them to do is not easy. But the rewards are tremendous. The biggest reward for me is watching the almost daily growth in self-esteem and confidence in trainees." ✳

are neither staffed nor equipped to handle the more sophisticated business venture of prime manufacturing.

In a salvage or *reclamation* operation, a workshop purchases or collects sal-vageable material, performs the salvage or reclamation operation, and then sells the reclaimed product. Salvage and reclamation operations have proven successful for many sheltered workshops because they require a lot of labor, are low in overhead, and can usually continue indefinitely.

Another kind of sheltered work environment is called the **work activity center.** A work activity center offers programs of activities for individuals whose disabilities are viewed by local decision makers as too severe for productive work. Rehabilitation and training revolve around concentration and persistence at a task. Intervals of work may be short, perhaps only an hour long, interspersed with other activities—such as training in social skills, self-help skills, household skills, community skills, and recreation. It is estimated that approximately 100,000 adults with disabilities attend work activity centers, with about 40,000 being excluded from an opportunity to earn wages (Will, 1986). The remaining 60,000 earn an average of $1.00 per day, or $288 per year.

The Problems with Sheltered Workshops

Sheltered workshops and work activity centers have come under intense criticism. The theoretical purpose of sheltered workshops is to train individuals in specific job-related skills that will enable them to obtain competitive employment; however, few employees of sheltered workshops are ever placed in jobs in the community. Only about 10% of sheltered workshop employees were placed in community jobs from 1977 to 1987 (U.S. Congress, 1987; U.S. Department of Labor, 1979), and many who are placed do not keep their jobs for long (Brickey, Campbell, & Browning, 1985). By contrast, approximately 50% of all supported employees are still earning wages and paying taxes 1 year after placement while working alongside nondisabled co-workers (Rusch, 1990).

Some professionals believe that the poor competitive employment record of sheltered workshop graduates may be more indicative of limitations inherent in sheltered workshops than of the actual employment potential of persons with disabilities (McLoughlin, Gorner, & Callahan, 1987). Whitehead (1979) contends that the only individuals who attained competitive employment in the community were those who did not need skills training. Rusch and Schutz (1981) concluded that "training" in sheltered workshops often consisted of no more than "supervision with vague instructions and occasional prompts to stay on task" (p. 287). After conducting 9,000 hours of observation in a workshop for adults with mental retardation, Turner (1983) found that "the average individual in workshop society spends less than 50% of his or her time on the lines actually working" (p. 153). Turner found that on-task behavior varied tremendously as a function of the availability of subcontracts and that workers decreased their productivity rates to accommodate times when little subcontracted work was available.

Nisbet and Vincent (1986) compared the behavior of employees with moderate and severe mental retardation in sheltered and community work environments. They found that inappropriate behavior (e.g., hostility, aggression, inactivity, self-stimulation) was exhibited 8.8 times more frequently in sheltered environments than in the community work environments.

> In sheltered environments, inactivity accounted for 61% of the inappropriate behavior and in nonsheltered environments, it accounted for 3%. The lack of meaningful work or absence of work altogether due to contract procurement difficulties may, in part, account for the inactivity rather than the inability of the worker with a disability to perform at an acceptable rate over a measurable duration of time. (Nisbet & Vincent, 1986, p. 26)

Brown et al. (1984) are particularly critical of the lack of real work in sheltered workshops and work activity centers.

The average wage of all persons with mental retardation who worked in sheltered employment settings in 1987 was $1.02 per hour (Lakin et al., 1989). Sheltered workshop employees interviewed in 1988 as part of an Iowa follow-up study reported an average hourly wage of $1.59 (Frank & Sitlington, 1993).

Because sheltered workshop employment is conducted in segregated settings, affords limited opportunities for job placement in the community, and provides extremely low pay, it has been called a "dead-end street" for individuals with mental retardation (Frank & Sitlington, 1993; Frank, Sitlington, & Carson, 1992).

> Thousands of workers . . . are confined to activity centers and sheltered workshops where they are required to perform "simulated work," "prework," "could be work some day," and "looks like work" year after year. In the process, they are systematically and categorically denied access to the real world of work. (p. 266)

Although the concept of supported work is still relatively new, the positive results produced by a variety of supported work models implemented in both urban and rural communities under various economic conditions cause us to wonder, along with Wehman, Hill, et al. (1985), about the appropriateness of long-term sheltered employment.

> What this report indicates is that many more persons with mental retardation could be working competitively than currently are employed. . . . Furthermore, our data raise some serious questions about the appropriateness of long-term sheltered workshop employment and work activity center placements for individuals that are labeled mentally retarded who could be benefiting from the economic and social benefits of competitive employment. Specifically, one might reasonably ask: why should so many persons be placed in adult activity centers and sheltered workshops if they, in fact, can work competitively under appropriate support conditions? (p. 279)

> Murphy and Rogan (1995) describe a process by which agencies can convert sheltered workshops into integrated work settings.

✳ *Residential Alternatives*

Where one lives determines a great deal about how one lives. Where a person lives influences where she can work, what community services and resources will be available, who her friends will be, what the opportunities for recreation and leisure will be, and to a great extent, what feelings of self and place in the community will develop. Not long ago, the only place someone with mental retardation could live, if she did not live with family, was a large state-operated institution. Although she had done no wrong to society, an institution was considered the "best place" for the person. There were no other options—no such thing as residential alternatives.

Today, most communities provide a variety of residential options for adults with disabilities. Increased community-based residential services have meant a greater opportunity for adults with severe disabilities to live in a more normalized setting. Three residential alternatives for adults with mental retardation and related developmental disabilities—group homes, foster homes, and apartment living—help complete a continuum of possible living arrangements between the highly structured and typically segregated public institution and fully independent living. First, however, we consider the number of persons with mental retardation in large public institutions.

> About 330,000 persons (including children) with mental retardation/developmental disabilities live in institutions, group homes, foster homes, psychiatric facilities, and nursing homes (Amado, Lakin, & Menke, 1990). This number represents less than 0.15% of the U.S. population. Using a conservative estimate of 1% of the population with MR/DD, we can estimate that 85% of persons with MR/DD live with their families or on their own without support from the public residential care system.

Institutions

A survey of all 50 states and the District of Columbia found that 91,582 persons were living in 296 large state-operated institutions for individuals with mental retardation (White, Lakin, & Bruininks, 1989). This number represents the fewest people living in mental retardation institutions since 1934. A large residential facility is defined as one serving 16 or more residents; however, the average size of most institutions today is more than 300 residents. Other key findings from this survey were

- The number of persons with mental retardation living in state institutions has decreased steadily from a high of 228,500 in 1967.

- The annual cost of providing services to a person with mental retardation in a large institution in 1988 was $57,200, compared with an annual expenditure of $750 per person in 1950. Controlling for inflation, the increased cost is 15 times the 1950 level.
- Eighty percent of the residents of public institutions are classified with severe or profound mental retardation. Many have additional disabilities; for example, 39% have epilepsy, 12% have cerebral palsy, and 10% have visual and/or hearing impairments.
- Current residents in large state-operated institutions for individuals with mental retardation represent a wide range of abilities and disabilities: An estimated 24% can bathe or shower independently; 54% can use the toilet independently; 66% can feed themselves; 10% can use the telephone; 6% can manage money; 7% can shop for some personal items; and 7% can get around the community without assistance.
- Only about 25% of residents in large public facilities work for pay (5% off grounds), whereas an estimated 49% of residents of small residential facilities have paying jobs (47% away from where they live).

Most of our nation's public institutions were founded in the 19th or early 20th century, when it was generally believed that people with mental retardation could not be educated or trained. Large custodial institutions have kept people with mental retardation segregated from the rest of society; the institutions were never designed to train people to live in the community. Institutions have come under severe criticism for their general inability to provide individualized services in a comfortable, humane, and normalized environment (Blatt, 1976; Blatt & Kaplan, 1966; Kugel & Wolfensberger, 1969; Wolfensberger, 1969).

The complaints are not leveled against the concept of residential programs; there will probably always be persons whose disabilities are so severe that they require the kind of 24-hour support that residential facilities can offer. The problem lies with the inherent inability of large institutions to provide needed supports in a manner that allows a normalized lifestyle.

During the past 25 years, tremendous improvements have been made in the abysmal living conditions in institutions that Blatt and Kaplan exposed in their book *Christmas in Purgatory* (1966). During the 1970s, the U.S. Department of Health, Education and Welfare and the Joint Commission on the Accreditation of Hospitals developed extensive standards for residential facilities for individuals with mental retardation. A residential facility must meet these standards—which cover topics as diverse as building construction, staffing, and habilitative and educational programming—to qualify for federal and state Medicaid funding. Residential units that meet the standards are referred to as ICF-MR Medicaid facilities. Although the ICF-MR Medicaid system of rules and regulations has eliminated the inhumane, filthy conditions that were a defining feature of institutional life in the 1950s and 1960s, the system has become the target for increasing criticism:

> If Burton Blatt could spend a day in an ICF-MR today, he would likely see a smaller, more livable residence. It would be clean, well-appointed, even homelike. The people who live there would be appropriately dressed, and a few might be interacting with direct-care staff members. Professional staff members would probably be found absorbed in paperwork or in a meeting. Voluminous records would detail individualized programmatic goals and procedures, but there would be questions as to which

programs are actually being implemented and working. Further observation might reveal that the staff, as a whole, is not as organized or adept in teaching as the paperwork and expertise might suggest. However, the staff members might be quite sensitive and oriented to their own ICF-MR accountability requirements, giving the impression that regulation compliance is the predominant focus in the home, whereas habilitation and enhancing the quality of life are secondary. (Holburn, 1990, p. 65)

Many families of institutionalized persons with mental retardation, however, do not feel as negatively about institutions as do those in the professional community. A survey of the parent or nearest relative of 284 residents living in 40 institutions found that 88% believed the institution provided the kind of services and care their family members with mental retardation needed (Spreat, Telles, Conroy, Feinstein, & Colombatto, 1985). Eighty-seven percent of those who returned the questionnaire considered the staff at the facility to be "very good." When asked whether they would like their family members transferred out of the institution and into a community-based group home, 60% of the respondents indicated they were opposed to such a move; only 23% favored such a transfer. When asked under what conditions they would approve the move of their family members to a group home, 58% said they would never approve such a move.

These results should be interpreted in the context of the respondents' assessment of the ability of the persons with mental retardation to live and work in the community and the respondents' knowledge of community-based residential alternatives. Only half believed their relatives were able to learn more about getting along with others; only 21% believed their relatives could learn to work for pay; 61% considered group homes appropriate only for persons with mild mental retardation; and only 13% strongly agreed with the statement "I know a lot about group homes and other alternatives to large facilities." Interestingly, several studies have found that parents' views change dramatically after a family member has been transferred from a large institution to a smaller community-based residence (Braddock & Heller, 1985; Conroy & Bradley, 1985).

Deinstitutionalization—the movement of people with mental retardation out of large institutions and into smaller community-based living environments, such as foster or group homes—furthers the degree of normalization of persons who have previously resided in institutions. Deinstitutionalization is more than a philosophy or goal of concerned individuals; it has been an active reality during the past 30 years. Evidence of this is the dramatic decline in the number of persons with mental retardation living in large public institutions. Whereas 85% of all people with mental retardation in the residential services system lived in large state-run institutions in 1967, only 34% were still in institutions by 1988.

In summarizing the findings of their 1982 national census of the nation's MR/DD residential system, Hill, Lakin, and Bruininks (1984) predicted that

public facilities [institutions], which continue to depopulate at a fairly constant rate of 6,000 residents per year, are being replaced by smaller community-based programs that serve individuals with severely/profoundly handicapping conditions. . . . Efforts of this nature [federal and state regulations proposing acceleration of deinstitutionalization], as well as research and testimony, will undoubtedly continue to develop the perception that appropriate care is community-based care and that such a perception is no less true for people who are severely/profoundly retarded than for those who are mildly retarded or nonretarded. While a formal policy of noninstitu-

---

Results of an observational study by Repp and Barton (1980) support this concern. They compared the interactions (e.g., verbal instruction, custodial guidance, no interaction) between residents and staff and the behaviors of residents (e.g., on task, no programming, self-stimulatory) that took place in two licensed and six unlicensed cottages at a large state institution. The most striking finding was the overwhelming number of observations in which no interactions between residents and staff and no programming occurred. Whether licensed or not, few instances of praise or encouragement directed by staff toward the residents occurred. On the average, every resident, whether in a licensed or unlicensed cottage, spent more time engaging in self-stimulatory behaviors than in programming.

A person who has just left an institution needs support in the community. In the early days of the deinstitutionalization movement, too many former residents of state institutions experienced "relocation syndrome" (Cochran, Sran, & Varano, 1977) or "transition shock" (Coffman & Harris, 1980) as a result of being dumped into the community without the necessary skills to cope successfully in their new environment and without easy access to support and follow-up services to see that the transition was successful.

tionalization may not be imminent, there is considerable longitudinal evidence that through continuing program development efforts of the past few years, that end will be essentially realized by the turn of the century. (p. 249)

But what about the experiences of those who transfer from large institutions to smaller community residences? Does the quality of their lives improve? Given the complexity and variety of community residential programs and the many variables that play a part in determining quality of life and developmental progress, answering these important questions in a definitive, scientific manner is nearly impossible. Several studies, however, indicate generally positive outcomes for residents transferred from institutions to group homes. One of the most comprehensive studies was reported by Conroy and Bradley (1985), who monitored over a 5-year period the adjustment of 176 persons with mental retardation who were deinstitutionalized from the Pennhurst State School and Hospital in Pennsylvania and placed in community residences. Measures of the adaptive behavior growth of the individuals placed in the community showed gains 10 times greater than those of a matched comparison group remaining in the institution.

Conroy and Bradley also conducted interviews with family members and verbal residents before and after deinstitutionalization. While still in the institution, the residents described themselves as happy and satisfied with their life in the institution. When the same individuals were interviewed again after they had been placed in community-based living arrangements, however, they said they were happier in the community and did not want to return to the institution. Figure 15.5 shows the tremendous turnaround in attitude toward community placement on the part of the individuals' parents and families.

On the average, the people deinstitutionalized under the Pennhurst court order are better off in every way measured. This is an uncommon, but welcome, situation in social science. More often, evaluative results are mixed, and one must balance gains

FIGURE 15.5
Attitudes of parents and families regarding transfer of a family member with mental retardation from a state institution to a community-based residential setting—before and after deinstitutionalization.

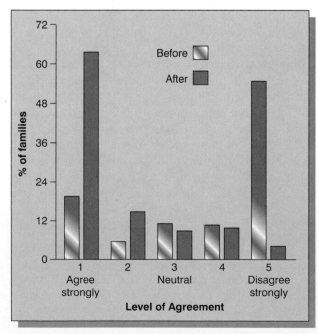

From J. W. Conroy and V. J. Bradley, "The Pennhurst Longitudinal Study: A Report on Five Years of Research and Analysis" 1985, p. 179. Philadelphia: Temple University Developmental Disabilities Center. Reprinted by permission.

in one area against losses in another. For the people who have moved from Pennhurst to small community residences, results are not mixed. They are conclusive. (Conroy & Bradley, 1985, p. 322)

Larson and Lakin (1989) reviewed 18 studies involving 1,358 persons who moved from large state institutions to small (15 or fewer people) community-based living arrangements. They found that, in all 8 of the experimental group versus contrast group studies and in 5 of the 10 longitudinal studies, moving from the institution to the community was associated with statistically significant improvements in either overall adaptive behavior or in the basic self-help/domestic domain. All 18 studies resulted in at least some improvement for groups moving to the community.

Group Homes

Small community-based group homes of six or fewer residents are the most rapidly growing residential model for adults with mental retardation in the United States. A survey in 1982 reported 15,700 persons living in 3,557 group homes (Hill & Lakin, 1986); by 1988, 80,800 persons with mental retardation and developmental disabilities were living in group homes (Amado et al., 1990). Most people who leave state-operated institutions move into group homes.

Group homes provide family-style living for a small group of individuals, usually three to six persons. Most group homes serve adults with mental retardation, although some have residents with other disabilities. Group homes vary as to purpose. Some are principally residential and represent a permanent home for their residents. Staff persons in a home of this type help the people who live there develop self-care and daily living skills, form interpersonal relationships, and learn recreational and leisure-time skills. During the day, most individuals are outside the group home, employed in the community or in a sheltered workshop.

Other group homes operate more as halfway houses. Their primary function is to prepare individuals with disabilities for a more independent living situation, such as a supervised apartment. These transitional group homes typically serve residents who have recently left institutions, bridging the gap between institutional and community living.

Two key aspects of group homes make them a much more normalized place to live than an institution: their size and their location (Wolfensberger, 1972). Most people grow up in a typical family-sized group, where there is opportunity for personal attention, care, and privacy. The massed-living arrangement common to many institutions cannot be said to be normalized, regardless of the efforts of hardworking, caring staff. By keeping the number of people in a group home small, there is a greater chance for a familylike atmosphere. Size is also directly related to the neighborhood's ability to assimilate the members of the group home into normal, routine activities within the community, which is a key element of normalization. Indeed, some evidence suggests that quality of life is better for persons residing in smaller rather than larger group homes (Rotegard, Hill, & Bruininks, 1983).

Although research on the effects of the size of group homes has been inconclusive, operators of community residential programs consistently state that residential settings of three or four individuals are much more likely to have their residents integrated into the community (Cooke, 1981). Bronston (1980) offers four arguments favoring small residential settings: (a) the group and the home do not attract undue attention by being larger than a large family; (b) the smaller the number of different individuals in a group home, the more likely the neighborhood will absorb them; (c)

Zirpoli and Wieck (1989) ask, "If the benefits of deinstitutionalization and integration are so overwhelming, why do states continue to spend enormous sums of money maintaining public institutions?" (p. 201). Their analysis of Minnesota's public institutions led them to conclude that the economic and political impact of institutional closure (e.g., loss of jobs, community support for institutions) may be slowing the rate of deinstitutionalization.

Low pay and little or no fringe benefits for direct care workers in privately operated residential programs are major problems in attracting and keeping good quality care providers. A national study found the average wage of direct care workers in public institutions was 46% higher than the wage earned by similar workers in privately operated community facilities ($8.72 vs. $5.97) and that half of privately operated community facilities reported starting wages for full-time workers that were below the poverty level for a family of three (Braddock & Mitchell, 1992). The same study found the annual turnover rate of staff at privately operated programs to be nearly three times the turnover of direct care workers in public institutions (70.7% vs. 24.8%).

large groups tend to become self-sufficient, orienting inward and thereby resisting movement outward into the community; and (d) in groups larger than six or eight, care providers can no longer relate properly to individuals.

The location and physical characteristics of the group home itself are also vital determinants of its ability to provide a normalized lifestyle. A group home must be located within the community, in a residential area, not in a commercially zoned district. It must be in an area where the people who live there can conveniently access shopping, schools, churches, public transportation, and recreational facilities. In other words, a group home must be located in a normal residential area where any one of us might live. And it must look like a home, not conspicuously different from the other family dwellings on the same street.

A significant problem for any residential option is securing, training, and keeping competent staff. Direct care staff in residential settings must fill a demanding role, often serving as family member, friend, counselor, and teacher to one individual, all in a day's time. The training that residential staff members receive varies considerably from one program to another. The more successful residential service programs place tremendous emphasis on staff training, making it mandatory and ongoing. Most training objectives are practical, as opposed to theoretical; they stress first aid, fire safety, nutrition, neighborhood relations, behavior management, instruction in daily living skills, and so on (Cooke, 1981).

Wetzel and Hoschouer (1984) offer an excellent model of program development and staff training that they call residential teaching communities. A central concept of their model is that naturally occurring, everyday activities are the most appropriate and effective opportunities for teaching the daily living and interpersonal skills that residents of community-based programs need to learn. For example, Gardner and Heward (1991) used the interactions that occurred naturally in a group home between a man with severe and multiple disabilities and other residents and staff as opportunities to teach appropriate personal interaction/conversational skills (e.g., hands to self, proper distance, ask a question just one time). As they take advantage of such naturally occurring teaching and learning opportunities, however, group home staff and other residential service providers must remember that the residence is, first and foremost, a home, not a school or training center.

Janicki and Zigman (1984) studied the location and design characteristics of 386 small group homes in New York State. They found that the homes exhibited a wide variety of styles and configurations, were located in all types of residential neighborhoods, and were in close proximity to commercial and recreational resources (e.g., two thirds of the residences were within one fourth of a mile of both a corner store and a bus or subway station). Janicki and Zigman concluded that the homes in their study were "normative, homelike dwellings in terms of their structural aspects, and as such they contribute to the physical integration of the residence program within its neighborhood. If this is true, then it is reasonable to assume that these aspects add to the social integration of their occupants as well" (p. 300).

New group homes are opening almost every day all across the country; however, they continue to encounter obstacles. Many communities have been slow to accept group homes into their neighborhoods. Most agencies, service groups, and individuals who have started (or attempted to start) group homes for persons with disabilities have encountered harsh resistance (Gelman, Epp, Downing, Twark, & Eyerly, 1989). Convinced that people with mental retardation are dangerous or crazy, that they will have a bad influence on neighborhood children, or that property values will go down if a group home comes into the area, neighborhood associations have too often been effective in keeping group homes from starting.

In 1985, the United States Supreme Court unanimously ruled that communities cannot use a discriminatory zoning ordinance to prevent the establishment of group homes for persons with mental retardation in an area already zoned for apartment and other congregate living facilities (*City of Cleburne v. Cleburne Living Center,* 1985). Lawyers for the city of Cleburne, Texas, argued that the nearby presence of a junior high school and the fact that the group home site was located on a 500-year flood plain permitted the city to exclude the group home from that site. City administrators were also concerned "about the legal responsibility for actions which the mentally retarded might take" and about fire safety, congestion, and the serenity of the neighborhood. In their analysis of the Cleburne decision, the attorneys who prepared a brief on behalf of the group home for the AAMD, CEC, TASH, and four other national disability groups said:

> In each instance, the Supreme Court concluded that the city's purported concerns were a smokescreen for prejudice and unconstitutional discrimination.
>
> Perhaps most significantly, the fears and objections of neighbors were held to be insufficient to support the ordinance because "mere negative attitudes, or fear, unsubstantiated by factors which are properly recognizable in a zoning proceeding, are not permissible bases for treating a home for people with mental retardation differently from" other uses that the law allows. As the Court observed, "Private biases may be outside the reach of the law, but the law cannot, directly or indirectly, give them effect."
>
> [This case] is a useful precedent for arguments that zoning laws cannot be used as a device to discriminate against the housing needs of people who are mentally retarded, and in particular that the fears and irrational prejudices of neighbors who may be opposed to such a group home will not justify its exclusion from the community. (Ellis & Luckasson, 1985, p. 250)

Foster Homes

When a family opens its home to an unrelated person for an extended period, the term *foster home* applies. Although foster homes have been used for years in providing temporary residential services and family care for children (usually wards of the court), more and more families are now beginning to share their homes with adults with disabilities. In return for providing room and board for their new family member, foster families receive a modest financial reimbursement.

For an adult with disabilities, life in a foster family home can have numerous advantages. Instead of interacting with paid group home staff, who may or may not actually live at the same address, the person with disabilities lives in a residence that is owned or rented by individuals or families as their primary domicile. The person can participate and share in the day-to-day activities of a normal family, receive individual attention from people vitally interested in his or her continued growth and development, and develop close interpersonal relationships. As part of a family unit, the adult with disabilities also has more opportunities to interact with and be accepted by the community at large. In their survey of small group homes and foster homes, Hill et al. (1989) found that 80% of foster home caregivers perceived residents with disabilities primarily as family members. In contrast, group home staff were more likely to view persons with disabilities as trainees or friends.

Apartment Living

A rented apartment is one of the most common places for people without disabilities to live in our society. In recent years, an increasing number of adults with disabilities

Two studies analyzing real estate transaction data have found that neighborhood property values were not adversely affected by group homes. One study examined the sale prices of 525 homes sold around 13 group homes in and around Omaha, Nebraska (Ryan & Coyne, 1985); a second study analyzed the sale of 388 properties near 19 group homes in the Pittsburgh, Pennsylvania, area (Gelman et al., 1989).

To learn more about foster family care for persons with mental retardation, see Borthwick-Duffy, Widaman, Little, and Eyman (1992).

are enjoying the freedom and independence that apartment living offers. Apartment living offers individuals with disabilities an even greater opportunity for integration into the community than do group homes. Whereas the resident of a group home interacts primarily with other persons with disabilities, in an apartment-living arrangement (assuming the apartment is in a regular apartment complex), the likelihood of interacting with persons without disabilities is greater. Burchard, Hasazi, Gordon, and Yoe (1991) found that people who lived in supervised apartments had about twice as many social and leisure activities in the community than did individuals who lived in small group homes or with their natural parents. They also found that persons living in supervised apartments were more likely to be accompanied in the community by peers who are not disabled than those living in group homes. Another study followed up on seven young adults with mental retardation who had moved from a campus-type residential setting to community-based apartments (Rose, White, Conroy, & Smith, 1993). Assessments of the young adults' social/communication skills, community-living skills, and general independence conducted at 6 and 12 months after the move found significant and continued gains over pre-move measures.

Some professionals believe that full integration into the community will be achieved only when all persons with disabilities are in private homes or apartments—that even small group homes are too institutional. Bronston (1980) has even suggested that apartment dwellings could handle the residential needs for all adults with disabilities. Three types of apartment living for adults with disabilities are most common: the apartment cluster, the coresidence apartment, and the maximum-independence apartment.

An *apartment cluster* consists of a small number of apartments housing persons with disabilities and another nearby apartment for a supervisory person or staff. An apartment cluster is an extremely workable arrangement because it allows for a great deal of flexibility in the amount and degree of supervision needed by residents in the various apartments. Whereas some people might require direct help with such things as shopping, cooking, or even getting dressed, others need only limited assistance or suggestions and prompts. To facilitate social integration, some apartments in an apartment cluster are also occupied by persons without disabilities.

A *coresidence apartment* is shared by an individual with disabilities and a roommate without disabilities. Although this arrangement is sometimes permanent, most coresidence apartments are used as a step toward independent living. The live-in roommates are often unpaid volunteers.

Many adults with developmental disabilities live at home with their parents. The monetary costs to society to support families in caring for their adult offspring with disabilities is small, compared with the cost of providing public out-of-home residential services (Fujiura, Roccoforst, & Braddock, 1994). These individuals, however, do not experience the same kinds of independence and change that characterize typical adulthood.

Judy and Kathy, who spent most of their lives in a state institution for people with mental retardation, have shared a maximum-independence apartment for the past five years.

Two to four adults with disabilities usually cohabit *maximum-independence apartments*. These adults have all of the self-care and daily living skills required to take care of themselves and their apartment on a day-to-day basis. A supervisory visit is made once or twice a week to help them deal with any special problems they may be having.

A follow-up study of 69 adults with mental retardation 5 years after they had been placed in independent living arrangements found 80% of the group still in their original independent housing placements (Schalock, Harper, & Carver, 1981). These adults reported that they were proud of their apartments and that they felt good about "doing their own thing". The results of another study, however, suggest that some adults with mental retardation need to learn to "do their own thing" more independently. Salend and Giek (1988) interviewed 25 landlords about their experiences renting to persons with mental retardation. A significant number of the landlords reported problems related to poor independent living skills, failure to maintain the apartment properly, and extreme dependence on the landlord for minor problems. The authors suggest guidelines for promoting the success of apartment living arrangements for adults with mental retardation. Several curricula and training programs for teaching persons with mental retardation and other disabilities housekeeping, domestic, and independent living skills are available (Wilcox & Bellamy, 1987; Dever, 1988; Falvey, 1989; Ford et al., 1989; Vogelsberg et al., 1980).

> For excellent information on how to help individuals with disabilities learn domestic and daily living skills, see Browder and Snell (1993) and Spooner and Test (1994).

Issues in Residential Services

During the early years of the group home movement, many thought that small community-based residences were appropriate only for more highly skilled persons experiencing mild or moderate levels of disability. But in their nationally representative survey of group homes, Hill et al. (1989) found that 41% of the residents were classified with severe or profound mental retardation. The national residential census conducted by Hauber et al. (1984) found a small percentage of persons with severe or profound mental retardation living in semi-independent apartments. Several studies have found that persons living in community-based residences are more likely than persons who reside in state institutions to have friends and engage in social relationships and leisure activities with individuals who are not staff or coresidents (Hill & Bruininks, 1981; Horner, Stoner, & Ferguson, 1988). Research has also shown that the smaller the residence, the more likely that individuals will participate in social and leisure activities (Burchard et al., 1991). Another study found that adults with disabilities living in small community homes of two to five residents had about the same number of close relationships as people without disabilities in a comparison group and more friends than those living in a large residential facility of 90 persons (Barber & Hupp, 1993).

As encouraging as results such as these are, simply placing a person with disabilities into a small community-based residence such as a group home does not automatically produce a normalized, adaptive lifestyle (Hayden, Lakin, Hill, Bruininks, & Copher, 1992). People with disabilities are often segregated by their activities and schedules, not only in the physical place where they live (Mount & Zwernick, 1988). For many persons with disabilities, the majority of opportunities they have for community-based recreation and leisure activities are with professional staff. It is not uncommon for adults with disabilities to develop close relationships with residential staff, but such relationships are typically not a true friendship. Friendships are reciprocal, with both parties giving and receiving support. If a friendship is not reciprocal, the relationship is closer to that of service provider and client (Lutfiyya, Shoultz, & O'Conner, 1989). One person in a small group home said, "Staff really

The *Home Observation for Measurement of the Environment* (HOME) is a 100-item scale that measures various aspects of a home environment and daily care practices of care providers (Bradley & Caldwell, 1979). The *Home Quality Rating Scale* (HRQS) is an attempt to measure the sense of love and attachment shown by care providers to the person with disabilities in a foster care setting and family participation in providing care (Meyers, Mink, & Nihira, 1981).

aren't my friends. Friends you do things with because you have fun and want to. I like my staff but we only work together." (Barber & Hupp, 1993, p. 20).

Evaluating the Normalization Quality of Residential Programs

The most well known and widely used method for evaluating the degree to which service programs such as community residential programs meet various criteria of normalization is the *Program Analysis of Service Systems* (PASS) (Wolfensberger & Thomas, 1983). Researchers and program developers have used different combinations and variations of the original 50 items included in PASS to evaluate a wide array of aspects of residential programs such as setting, program, administrative and staffing policies, and the facility's proximity and access to the community (Flynn, 1980). Pieper and Cappuccilli (1980) suggest the following set of questions, based on PASS, as a means of determining how appropriate a given residential setting may be. A community residential program would be considered normalized if all or most of these questions can be answered yes.

- Did the residents choose to live in the home?
- Is this type of setting usually inhabited by people in the residents' age-group?
- Do the residents live with others of their own age?
- Is the home located within a residential neighborhood?
- Does the residence look like the other dwellings around it?
- Can the number of people living in the residence be reasonably expected to be assimilated into the community?
- Are community resources and facilities readily accessible from the residence?
- Do the residents have a chance to buy the house?
- Do the managers of the place act in an appropriate manner toward the residents?
- Are the residents encouraged to do all they can for themselves?
- Are the residents encouraged to have personal belongings that are appropriate to their age?
- Are residents encouraged to use community resources as much as possible?
- Are all of the residents' rights acknowledged?
- Are the residents being given enough training and assistance to help them grow and develop as individuals?
- Would I want to live in the home? Here is the final test. If the residence appears good enough for you to want to live in it, it will probably be an appropriate living arrangement for persons with special needs. We should demand residential arrangements for persons with special needs that are comparable to those inhabited by most nondisabled citizens.

Supported Living

Most professionals agree that no one type of residential setting is best for all adults with disabilities; we need a continuum of options. But the continuum-of-services approach, with residential options ranging from most restrictive to least restrictive, is not without its problems and critics. The typical continuum of residential options does not guarantee there will be no gaps between one option and the next, nor does it recognize the possibility that other, perhaps more innovative, alternatives are appropriate for some individuals (Cooke, 1981). Also, continuum-of-service models usually assume that someone moves into the residential service system at the more restrictive end and must earn the right to the least restrictive living arrangement.

The underlying philosophy of this model is not at all consistent with civil rights decisions in other areas. The Supreme Court ruled in the 1960s that black people had a right to ride in the front of the bus and to go to their neighborhood schools, rights based simply on their citizenship—not rights they had to earn. But with "developmentally disabled" people we have said you must earn the right to live in an integrated setting. You must behave yourself before we'll ever give you this right. This is clearly a basic form of discrimination. (Hitzing, 1980, p. 84)

Several innovative models for residential services for adults with disabilities—based on the belief that residential placements must be adapted to the needs of the person with disabilities, not vice versa—have been developed (Apolloni & Cooke, 1981; Klein, 1994; Provencal, 1980). **Supported living** is the term used to describe a growing movement of helping people with disabilities live in the community in as independently and normalized a fashion as they possibly can. Similar to the way that supported employment provides continued supports to help individuals with disabilities perform meaningful work in real community-based employment settings, supported living involves a network of various kinds and levels of natural supports. Supported living is neither a place nor a single set of procedures to be provided for a person with disabilities.

Klein (1994) explains what supported living is by describing what it is not. Supported living does not revolve around a professional program. People should not live in a place referred to by an agency name or provider name (e.g., UCP Group Home, New Life Center). There are no criteria for participation (e.g., persons in this program must be able to cook for themselves, have a physical disability, need more or less than 3 hours per day of attendant care, have visual impairments). Supported living is not based on readiness and movement through a continuum. Participation in traditional residential services is based on a professional's assessment of the person's readiness or ability to live in a particular program, and a person must perform well (learn new skills on his or her Individual Habilitation Plan) in order to move ("earn" the right) to the next, less restrictive rung on the continuum. Persons who do not do well may be moved to a more restrictive setting.

Supported living, according to Klein (1994), is guided by these nine principles:

1. *Individualization.* Supported living must be something that is for one person without exception. This does not mean that everyone has to live alone. It does

Supported living provides flexible supports when and as they are needed. Twice per month, Judy and Kathy pay their bills and review their budget with the help of a support person.

mean that if people want to live with someone else, they choose with whom they live. The magic number becomes one.

2. *Everybody is ready.* There are no criteria to receive support because what occurs is individually designed. We must give up trying to make people ready by simulating how it is to live in a home and begin supporting people to have that home. If people cannot do a task, then we can find someone to do it for them, rather than require them to learn to do it before they will be ready.

3. *Future planning.* People who are assisting others must get to know the individuals they are supporting. What are their desires and preferences? Who are people in their lives who care about them? What would an ideal living situation look like for each person? After answers to these questions are determined, the people who care about the person get together regularly to develop a plan for getting as close as possible to that ideal living situation.

4. *Use of connections.* Traditional residential services rely on system solutions to problems, referring to the procedures and policy manual to "find out" what rules and regulations suggest. Supported living relies on the assistance of all who want to and can help. This means that professional "care providers" and "staff" are replaced by friends, family members, and neighbors whenever possible. "Who do we know who can help?" becomes a key question for planning and arranging needed supports.

5. *Flexible supports.* Supports are based and provided on the individual's schedule and needs, not on a program's schedule. Persons receive support where, when, how, and with whom it is needed. Supports must be flexible enough to be adjusted on the basis of the individual's changing needs, preference, and desires.

6. *Combining natural supports, learning, and technology.* As much as possible, supports used are natural to the time, place, and person. Individuals are given opportunities to learn to provide their own support and to use technology to gain control over their environment as much as possible.

7. *Focusing on what people can do.* Traditional residential programs often focus on what people cannot do and design treatment programs to try to remediate those skill deficiencies. Supportive living focuses on what people can do, provides support for things they cannot do, and provides opportunities for them to learn how to do the things they want to do.

8. *Using language that is natural to the setting.* The language of supported living is natural and promotes inclusion in the community. The places where people live are described as Joe's home or Mary's home. People clean their homes and do their laundry, rather than learn programs; people live with roommates, not with staff or care providers; friends, not volunteers, come over to visit; and people with disabilities are referred to as neighbors, friends, and citizens, rather than as clients, consumers, and residents.

9. *Ownership and control.* Last and most important, the home is the person's, and that person controls the support that is received. Home ownership does not mean that most individuals with disabilities who do not have many financial resources will hold the mortgage to a home. It does mean, however, that they sign the lease, that things in the home belong to them, and that the place is their home. Roommates sublet from the person, support people are hired by the person, and support people respond to the need for assistance when, where, and how it is needed as determined by the person. (adapted from Klein, 1994, pp. 17-18. Used by permission.)

Rather than a single approach or model, supported living is a philosophy about the kind of living experiences appropriate for citizens with disabilities and about commitment to figuring out how to best appropriate the ideal for each individual.

Supported living, supported employment, and full inclusion of school-age students in regular classrooms share several fundamental philosophical positions and procedural features: (a) Individuals with disabilities have the right to live, work, and learn in the same settings as everyone else; (b) benefits accrue to individuals with disabilities, to persons without disabilities, and to society at large when this occurs; (c) individuals with disabilities must be given opportunities to choose and self-determine the kinds of settings in which they wish to live, work, and learn and the kinds of lifestyle, job, and learning activities they wish to pursue; and (d) the kinds and levels of supports necessary to accomplish fully integrated and meaningful living, working, and learning must be determined and provided on an individual basis.

> Supported living is not a model, the answer, or some new magic. It is, however, a way of viewing people and assisting them in ways that enable these individuals to receive the support they need and to live in a home they want. When asked about what model they were using in North Dakota for 598 people who were receiving funding under a category called supported living, Russ Pitsley said, "We have 598 models." (Klein, 1994, p. 18)

✷ *Recreation and Leisure*

Many persons with disabilities need support in finding a self-satisfying lifestyle, and recreation and the enjoyable use of leisure time are primary means to that end. Most of us take for granted our ability to pursue leisure and recreational activities. We benefit from a lifetime of learning how to play and how to enjoy personal hobbies or crafts. But appropriate recreational and leisure-time activities do not come easily for many adults with disabilities; such activities may not even be available in some communities.

To use community recreational resources, one must have transportation, the physical ability or skills to play the game, and, usually, other willing and able friends to play with. These three variables, alone or in combination, often work together to limit the recreational and leisure-time activities available to the disabled adult. Transportation is not available; the person's disability does not allow her to swim, bowl, or play tennis; and she has no friends with similar skills and interests and no convenient way to make new friends. Because of these problems, the majority of recreational and leisure activities for adults with disabilities are segregated, "disabled only" outings.

Providing age-appropriate and otherwise normalized recreational and leisure-time activities is an important facet of extending services to adults with disabilities. Special educators must realize the importance of including training for recreation and leisure in curricula for school-age children with disabilities (Bigge, 1991; Peterson & Gunn, 1984). Professionals must also realize the importance that leisure activities hold for adults with disabilities, especially those who are unemployed (Fain, 1986). Too often, their so-called leisure activities consist of watching great amounts of television, listening to music in the solitude of their rooms, and spending discretionary time socially isolated (Shannon, 1985). As Bigge (1991) says,

> Choice is the most crucial element. Without choice, activities become simply tasks rather than providing elements of control that lead to leisure satisfaction. If television is the only choice, choice is neglected. Thus, awareness of options through leisure education must precede development of specific recreation-related skills. (p. 429)

Bigge describes how numerous games, hobbies, crafts, and projects can be adapted to become enjoyable, worthwhile leisure-time pursuits for persons with disabilities. Areas she suggests include raising guinea pigs, music appreciation and

Mahon and Bullock (1992) successfully taught adolescents with mild mental retardation to make choices and decisions during leisure.

See "Listen to the Birds" in Chapter 9.

Tom loves to fish. Choice is crucial to the enjoyment of leisure activities.

Special Olympics, the worldwide sports and physical development program for individuals with mental retardation, has been the target of criticism by some special educators for offering a segregated program only for athletes with mental retardation, which invites "sympathy" and limits opportunities for interaction with nondisabled peers, and for holding competitive events that are nonfunctional (Orelove, Wehman, & Wood, 1982; Polloway & Smith, 1978). These early criticisms were mostly on target because the Special Olympics program of the 1960s and 1970s was out of step with the changing philosophies in special education of integration and functional curriculum. In recent years, however, the Special Olympics has developed several innovative approaches toward *(continues on next page)*

study, photography, card games, and nature study. Suggestions are also available for adapting leisure activities for young adults who are deaf-blind, such as using permanent tactile prompts (e.g., attaching fabric to the flipper buttons of a pinball machine), adequately stabilizing materials, enhancing the visual or auditory input provided by the materials (e.g., using large-print, low-vision playing cards), and simplifying the requirements of the task (e.g., raising the front legs on a pinball machine, thereby reducing the speed with which the ball approaches the flippers) (Hamre-Nietupski, Nietupski, Sandvig, Sandvig, & Ayres, 1984).

Learning appropriate leisure skills is particularly important for adults with severe disabilities. Most persons with severe disabilities have ample free time but do not use it constructively, often engaging in inappropriate behaviors such as body rocking, hand flapping, or bizarre vocalizations (Wehman & Schleien, 1981). A number of promising studies have been reported in which age-appropriate leisure skills have been taught to adults with moderate and severe mental retardation (Johnson & Bailey, 1977; Nietupski & Svoboda, 1982; Schleien, Kiernan, & Wehman, 1981). Schleien, Wehman, and Kiernan (1981) successfully taught three adults with severe and multiple disabilities to throw darts; Hill, Wehman, and Horst (1982) taught a group of young adults with severe disabilities to play pinball machines. Vandercock (1991) taught five high school students with severe mental retardation and physical disabilities to play pinball and bowl with nondisabled peer partners. In another study, four teenagers and young adults with severe and profound mental retardation learned to perform a basic dance step (Lagomarcino, Reid, Ivancic, & Faw, 1984).

Horseback riding has become very popular with many individuals with physical and mental disabilities. Often called therapeutic horsemanship or equine therapy, horseback riding has given many people with disabilities the excitement and thrill of the sport while at the same time improving their gross motor functioning, social skills, and feelings of pride and self-esteem. The National Riding for the Disabled Association, founded in England in 1967 and now associated with groups in many countries, has developed a training program, exercises, and a variety of adaptive equipment to enable persons with just about any kind of disability to ride a horse.

Therapeutic Recreation

Therapeutic recreation uses recreation services for intervention in some physical, emotional, and/or social behavior to modify that behavior and to promote individual growth and development.

Many communities have therapeutic recreation programs. For example, the Division of Therapeutic Recreation of the Cincinnati Recreation Commission offers a full schedule of recreational activities throughout the year for children and adults with disabilities. Dancing, bicycling, swimming, softball, tennis, soccer, golf, fishing, camping, and hiking are just some of the activities that are offered for citizens with mental retardation, physical disabilities, autism, learning disabilities, and behavioral and emotional problems. One of the goals of the Cincinnati program is to help persons with disabilities move into the recreational mainstream—that is, to participate in integrated activities as much as possible. To help staff evaluate and monitor each participant's progress toward that goal, the Division of Therapeutic Recreation has developed a continuum of five levels.

Level I consists of activities for persons who require a 1:1 or 1:2 staff-to-participant ratio. Mat activities (e.g., tumbling), music, crafts, and camping are used to help participants increase their sensorimotor and self-help skills.

Level II is a program for people who have basic skills (e.g., running, throwing, striking) and are able to function in a group situation. Team sports such as volleyball and softball are used, but the emphasis is on group interaction, rather than on specific rules or skills.

promoting the inclusion of persons with disabilities in mainstream community recreation and sports activities. Two examples are the Unified Sports Program, in which teams made up of athletes with mental retardation and nondisabled teammates of similar age and skill levels compete in the local community, and Sports Partnerships, in which athletes with mental retardation become members of their local high school or club team and practice and receive training alongside nondisabled teammates. Block and Moon (1992) recommend that present-day critics of the Special Olympics "quit talking about what 'they' should do and start doing it themselves. . . . at this point in time, the organization so many of us have criticized may be doing as much as any of us to provide integrated recreation options" (p. 385).

Learning to ride a horse can provide physical, social, and emotional benefits.

At Level III, teamwork is assumed; the emphasis shifts to learning how to play the game or perform the activity well (e.g., learning to convert spares and to keep score in bowling). Skill improvement is the primary objective in Level III programs.

At Level IV, activities are held in regular community center facilities and are conducted by the regular staff of those facilities, instead of by therapeutic recreation specialists. However, the clients with disabilities still participate as a segregated group.

Finally, at Level V, individuals with disabilities participate in the recreational programs and activities offered by the Cincinnati Recreation Commission for everyone in the community. Staff from the Division of Therapeutic Recreation monitor and follow up on these mainstreaming efforts, working with regular recreation staff somewhat the same way resource room teachers work with regular classroom teachers to help ease the integration of students with disabilities into the regular classroom.

✳ *The Ultimate Goal: A Better Quality of Life*

A continuing problem for many adults with disabilities is lack of acceptance as full members of our society, with all the rights, privileges, and services granted to any citizen. Progress has been made in this regard—witness the litigation and legislation on behalf of persons with disabilities that have been discussed throughout this book—but we still have a long way to go. Courts can decree and laws can require, but neither can alter the way individuals feel toward and treat people with disabilities. Individuals with disabilities often "seem to be in the community but not of it" (Birenbaum, 1986 p. 145). As O'Conner (1983) states, "There is precious little evidence that . . . public support of normalization has gone so far that mentally retarded persons would be welcome or even tolerated in most 'nondeviate' social circles" (p. 192).

Handicapism

To read about the personal experiences of living and working in the community as described by people with disabilities, see Taylor, Bogdan, and Lutfiyya (1995).

Most adults with disabilities believe the biggest barriers to full integration into society are not inaccessible buildings or the actual restrictions imposed by their disabilities, but the differential treatment afforded them by nondisabled people. Just as the terms *racism* and *sexism* indicate prejudiced, discriminatory treatment of racial groups and women, the term **handicapism** has been coined to describe biased reactions toward a person with a disability. Those reactions are not based on an individual's qualities or performance, but on a presumption of what the disabled person must feel or must be like because of the disability.

Handicapism occurs on personal, professional, and societal levels. Biklen and Bogdan (1976) describe the following examples of handicapism in personal relations.

> First, there is a tendency to presume sadness on the part of the person with a disability. For example, one woman who has a physical disability, and who, incidentally, smiles a lot, told us of an encounter with a man who said, "It's so good that you can still smile. Lord knows, you don't have much to be happy for."
>
> Second, there is the penchant to pity. You might have heard, "It is a tragedy that it had to happen to her; she had so much going for her." Or people sometimes tell us, "It is so good of you to give up your lives to help the poor souls." Or "My, you must be so patient to work with them. I could never do it."

Third, people without disabilities sometimes focus so intensely on the disability as to make it impossible to recognize that the person with the disability is also simply another person with many of the same emotions, needs, and interests as other people. This attitude is reflected in the perennial questions, "What is it like to be deaf?" "It must be hard to get around in a wheelchair," and "You must really wish you could see sometimes."

Fourth, people with disabilities are often treated as children. Notice, for example, that feature films about people with mental retardation and physical handicaps are so frequently titled with first names: "Joey," "Charley," "Larry," and "Walter." We communicate this same message by calling disabled adults by first names when full names and titles would be more appropriate and by talking in a tone reserved for children.

Fifth is avoidance. Having a disability often means being avoided, given the cold shoulder, and stared at from a distance. The phrases "Sorry, I have to go now," "Let's get together sometime [but not now and not any specific time]," and, "I'd like to talk but I have to run" are repeated too consistently for mere coincidence.

Sixth, we all grow up amidst a rampage of handicapist humor. It must take a psychological toll. "Did you hear the one about the moron who threw the clock out the window?" "There was a dwarf with a sawed-off cane. . . . " "Two deaf brothers went into business with each other . . . and a blind man entered the store."

Seventh, people with disabilities frequently find themselves spoken for, as if they were not present or were unable to speak for themselves. In a similar vein, people without disabilities sometimes speak about people with disabilities in front of them, again as if they were objects and not people.

In terms of personal relations, then, if you are labeled "handicapped," handicapism is your biggest burden. It is a no-win situation. You are not simply an ordinary person.

Only when a man or woman with a disability is allowed to be simply an ordinary person—given the opportunity to strive and perhaps succeed, but also to be allowed the freedom and dignity to strive and sometimes fail—can normalization become a reality. Only then can people with disabilities enjoy a quality of life that citizens without disabilities take for granted.

Quality of Life

Without question, significant strides have been made in the lives of many people with disabilities. Tens of thousands of people who previously were relegated to life in an institution now live in real homes in regular neighborhoods. Thousands who never had an opportunity to learn meaningful job skills go to work each day and bring home a paycheck each week. But living in a community-based residence and having a real job in an integrated setting do not translate automatically into a better life (Landesman, 1986).

What is the quality of life for a young man who lives in a small group home in a residential neighborhood but who seldom or never gets to choose what will be served for dinner or when he will go to bed and whose only "friends" are the paid staff responsible for supervising him on his weekly trip to the shopping mall? One measure of the quality of a person's life is the extent to which she can make choices (Meyer, 1986). The choices we make play a significant role in defining our individual identities—from everyday matters, such as what to eat or wear, to the choices we make on larger matters, such as where to live or what kind of work to do (O'Brien,

There are numerous conceptions and definitions of quality of life, debates over how or whether it can be measured, and recommendations of what should or must be done to improve it (e.g., Dennis, Williams, Giangreco, & Cloninger, 1993; Halpern, 1993; Sands & Kozleski, 1994; Shalock & Bogale, 1990; Wehmeyer, 1994).

Maria Serrao won't let para-plegia get in the way of her quality of life. In her video, Everyone Can Exercise!, *Maria shows individuals with disabilities how to achieve fitness and enjoy a more active lifestyle.*

One study comparing the everyday choices and choice-making opportunities of 24 adults with mental retardation living in group homes with 42 adults without disabilities found the group home residents had significantly fewer choices about fundamental matters of daily living (e.g., what television show to watch, whether to make a phone call) (Kishi, Teelucksingh, Zollers, Park-Lee, & Meyer, 1988). Belfiore and Toro-Zambrana (1994) offer step-by-step instructions to help care providers recognize and provide choice-making opportunities for persons with disabilities in community settings.

1987). Opportunities to make choices for persons living in residential programs, however, "are generally absent from the daily routines" (Bercovici, 1983, p. 42).

How highly would we rate the quality of life for a woman who always sits alone during lunch and breaks at work because she has not developed a social relationship with her co-workers? Recent research on social interaction patterns in integrated work settings suggests that this is an all-too-common scenario. Several studies have found that the majority of contact between employees with disabilities and their nondisabled co-workers involves task performance; disabled workers are less involved in good-natured teasing and joking; and few workers with disabilities are befriended by their co-workers (e.g., Lignugaris/Kraft, Rule, Salzberg, & Stowitscheck, 1988; Rusch, Johnson, & Hughes, 1990; Shafer, Rice, Metzler, & Haring, 1989).

Most advocates and professionals now realize that the physical presence of individuals with disabilities in integrated residential and work settings is an important first step but that the only truly meaningful outcome of human service programs must be improved quality of life. Schalock, Keith, Hoffman, and Karan (1989) believe that "quality of life has recently become an important issue in human services and may replace deinstitutionalization, normalization, and community adjustment as the issue of the 1990s" (p. 25).

These authors propose an objective measure of quality of life. Table 15.4 shows the 28 criterion-referenced questions that comprise the Quality of Life Index. The questions are organized under three aspects: control of one's environment, involvement in the community, and social relationships. This approach to assessing the

TABLE 15.4

The Quality of Life Questionnaire. Each of the 28 questions is answered or scored on a 1- to 3-point scale. A person's Quality of Life Index can range from 28 (low) to 84 (high).

FACTOR 1: ENVIRONMENTAL CONTROL	FACTOR 2: COMMUNITY INVOLVEMENT	FACTOR 3: SOCIAL RELATIONS
1. How many people sleep in your bedroom?	14. Does your job make you feel good?	3. How about your neighbors? How do they treat you?
2. How much control do you have when you go to bed and when you get up?	15. Do you think that your work is important to your employer?	4. How do you like this town?
7. Who plans your meals?	17. How often do you use public transportation? (handibus, taxi, city bus, etc.)	5. How often do you talk with the neighbors, either in the yard or in their home?
8. Who shops for groceries?	18. Do you earn enough money to pay for all the things you need?	6. If there are staff or family where you live, or if you live with another client or spouse, do they eat meals with you?
9. Who chose the decorations in your bedroom?	19. Do you have friends over to visit your home?	10. Do you have any pets?
11. If you have a regular doctor, who chose your doctor?	27. How frequently do you spend time in recreational activities in town?	21. Are there people living with you who have dangerous or annoying behavior problems?
12. If you take medicines, who gives you the medicine?		25. What type of educational program are you involved in at the present time?
13. Who makes your doctor and dentist appointments?		
16. How do you usually get to work?		
20. Do you have a guardian or conservator?		
22. Do you have a key to your house?		
23. How many rooms or areas in your house are locked so that you cannot get in them?		
24. Can you do what you want to do?		
26. Who decides how you spend your money?		
28. When can friends visit your home?		

Source: From "Quality of Life: Its Measurement and Use" by R. L. Schalock, K. D. Keith, K. Hoffman, and O. C. Karan, 1989, *Mental Retardation, 27,* p. 27. Reprinted by permission.

quality of life differs from facility, or program-level, evaluations such as the Program Analysis of Service Systems (PASS; Wolfensberger & Thomas, 1983). The authors' goal is to "develop an instrument that can be used easily by (re)habilitation personnel to assess, monitor, and improve a person's quality of life" (p. 27). They note the Quality of Life Index is more appropriate for living rather than work environments and that generalizations across all types of living environments are not possible.

Self-Advocacy

Estimates of the number of adults with developmental disabilities over the age of 65 range from a low of 150,000 to more than 1 million (Gibson, Rabkin, & Munson, 1992). For research and recommendations on the supports needed to improve the quality of life of older citizens with disabilities, see Seltzer, Krauss, and Janicki (1994) and Sutton, Factor, Hawkins, Heller, and Seltzer (1993).

Advocacy on behalf of children and adults with disabilities has had tremendous impact, especially during the past 25 years. Indeed, most of the pervasive changes in education, employment opportunities, and residential services have occurred because of the efforts of advocates. Advocacy for persons with disabilities has traditionally been undertaken by family members, friends, professionals, and attorneys. Bigge (1991), however, is among a growing number of professionals and individuals with disabilities who believe that

> the age of "doing for" a person with a disability is rapidly diminishing. Increasingly, our society is viewing individuals with disabilities as integral and contributing members of the community in which they are a part. Federal and state legislation have provided and supported equal access of individuals with disabilities into all walks of life. . . . Along with the acquisition of these equal rights has come the responsibility for the utilization and protection of these rights. It is now necessary for those with disabilities, as individuals and as groups, to assert themselves as self-advocates. (p. 493)

Persons with disabilities have begun to assert their legal rights, challenging the view that persons with disabilities are incapable of speaking for themselves. Perhaps most conspicuous has been the self-advocacy of individuals with physical disabilities, who have been highly effective in their lobbying as part of the independent living movement. Individuals with sensory impairments have also engaged in self-advocacy. A striking and successful example is the refusal by students at Gallaudet University to accept the appointment of a hearing president who did not know American Sign Language. Persons with mental retardation, however, have engaged in little self-advocacy, perhaps because many have not learned to recognize when their rights are being violated and because they lack the verbal skills to advocate on their behalf in the natural environment.

Despite the importance of self-advocacy and the efforts of persons with disabilities to assert their rights, little research has been conducted on how to teach self-advocacy skills. A study by Sievert, Cuvo, and Davis (1988) is a notable exception. They taught eight adults with a variety of mild disabilities (mental retardation, learn-

Self-advocacy: responsibility for the utilization and protection of one's rights.

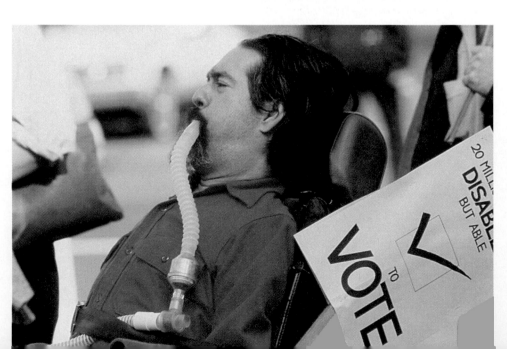

ing disability, cerebral palsy, speech impairment) to discriminate whether or not possible violations of legal rights occurred in up to 200 hypothetical scenarios involving 30 specific rights (e.g., right to help when voting) across four general areas: personal, community, human services, and consumer. Through role playing, the participants learned a 3-step procedure for redressing a violation that involved (a) asserting their rights directly to the person who violated them, (b) if this person did not resolve the problem, complaining to that person's supervisor, and (c) if the problem remained unsolved, seeking the assistance of a community advocacy agency. Participants were given a handbook describing each of the legal rights and the procedure for redressing violations. With one exception, the participants demonstrated generalization and maintenance of their newly learned self-advocacy skills by responding accurately to simulations and depictions of legal rights violations in natural settings.

Self-advocacy requires self-determination:

> Self-determined people know how to choose. They know what they want and use their self-advocacy skills to get it. From an awareness of personal needs, self-determined individuals choose goals and doggedly pursue those goals. This involves asserting their presence, making their needs known, evaluating progress toward meeting their goals, adjusting their performance, and creating unique approaches to solve problems. (Martin et al., 1993, p. 55)

This is a tall order for anyone, with or without disabilities. But along with these skills comes freedom.

> Freedom to choose, what kind of job to have, where to live, to have relationships, to make all of the everyday decisions (big and small), and the freedom to make mistakes. Dignity of failure.

Tony Coehlo, Chairperson of the President's Committee on Employment of People with Disabilities, opened the 1994 National Self-Advocacy Conference: Voices for Choices with these remarks:

> We want everything we are entitled to as citizens, nothing more, but nothing less. We want the privileges of full citizenship, but we also welcome its responsibilities. We want the respect we deserve, and we demand the rights we have been denied. We now recognize that empowerment is not a gift to be given, but a right to be demanded. (in Cone, 1994, p. 445)

Still a Long Way to Go

In general, the quality of life for most adults with disabilities today is better than it has ever been. Not only do more adults with disabilities live, work, and play in community-based, integrated environments, but more adults with disabilities have acquired or are acquiring the personal, social, work, and leisure skills that enable them to enjoy the benefits of those settings. But more persons with disabilities does not mean all persons with disabilities. And individuals don't live life "in general"; they experience specific instances of joy and sadness, success and failure. There is still a long way to go.

True, the quality of life for someone who now has his own bedroom in a group home and works for wages in a segregated sheltered workshop may be appreciably better than it was before he left the institution where he ate and slept communal style and his "work" consisted of an endless series of arts-and-crafts projects. Does favorable comparison with the unacceptable standards of the past mean a relatively better quality of life today is therefore good? Would it be good enough for mc or you?

Sebine: Twelve Years Later

"I Need a Vacation"

When we took her picture for the cover of the second edition of this textbook, Sebine Johnson was 10 years old and in the third grade. Now, she's 22 years old and experiencing the joys and responsibilities and facing the changes that lie ahead for any young adult. She works two jobs, juggles her checkbook, takes dance lessons, and hangs out with friends. Sebine is still living with her parents but will soon be moving into her own home as part of a supported living program. Before reading what Sebine had to say about her busy life, here's a brief biography of her educational experiences that helped prepare her for where she is today:

Early Childhood

Sebine was born in Minneapolis in 1972 and diagnosed with Down syndrome. The doctor strongly encouraged her parents to place her in an institution. When she was 1½ months old, her parents began taking her to a once per week "infant stimulation" program where they also received training on how to work with Sebine at home. At about 18 months of age, Sebine began attending the Reuben Lindh Learning Center, a full-time (5 hours per day, 5 days per week), center-based early intervention program. Even though this was 1974 and before PL 94-142, the Lindh Center (named after the founder of The Arc in Minneapolis) had IEPs for every child and offered multidisciplinary, family-ori-

ented services, including a speech therapist and social worker.

At age 5, Sebine's family moved to Columbus, Ohio, and she was enrolled in a half-day preschool. When Sebine was age 6, her parents met with the principal, school psychologist, and teaching staff of her neighborhood school to write her first IEP. There was some initial reluctance to having Sebine in the school because the school had never before had a child with Down syndrome and a county program operated separate schools for children with such disabilities. Nevertheless, school personnel agreed to create a full-day kindergarten program for Sebine. She spent mornings in the regular kindergarten classroom and afternoons going back and forth between the regular class, a resource room, music, art, the library, and gym. Sebine "sold herself" with her outgoing personality and was soon a regular part of the school. During that kindergarten year, the resource room teacher taught Sebine how to read with a phonics-based approach.

Elementary School

During her elementary years, Sebine spent about half of each school day with her regular classroom peers, being mainstreamed for music and art and some academic activities. In first grade, Sebine and her classmates participated in a research study evaluating a classwide peer tutoring system. Sebine did so well that she was featured in a journal article describing how peer tutoring could be used as a means to include children with disabilities in both the academic and social life of a regular classroom (Cooke, Heron, Heward, & Test, 1982). Several of Sebine's elementary teachers took the initiative to plan and adapt academic activities to include Sebine, particularly in social studies, creative writing, plays, and community activities. In fifth

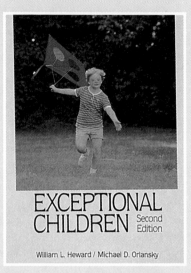

EXCEPTIONAL CHILDREN Second Edition

William L. Heward / Michael D. Orlansky

Sabine on the cover of the second edition.

grade, Sebine started playing drums in the school band.

Sebine's elementary school had only one resource room, and it served children in grades 1 to 6. Because of the large differences in the students' ages, skills, and special education needs, it was difficult to keep track of all of their schedules. The resource room teacher developed laminated, color-coded cards. Sebine learned to follow her own schedule, independently getting herself from the resource room, to the regular classroom, to the gym, to the music room, back to the resource room, and so on. Her parents believe this opportunity to be independent laid the foundation for the high level of self-determination and responsibility that Sebine displays as a young adult.

Junior High

To facilitate the transition to junior high school, Sebine's mother and her elementary special education teacher met with each of the teachers and staff that Sebine would come into contact with: the gym teacher, art teacher, librarian, cooks, school secretary, custodian, etc. They told of Sebine's experiences and success in elementary school, answered questions about her strengths and weaknesses, and suggested ways that people might support her inclusion in the school.

Sebine spent about one third to one half of her time in regular classes, went to school dances and sports events, and was generally a part of the school. She was treated well by her peers. Teachers reported that if a new student laughed or stared at Sebine, he would be "talked to" and corrected by those who knew Sebine.

Sebine began attending her IEP meetings during junior high. The meetings were sometimes difficult for her—as it would be for anyone to have to listen to a group of people who are important in your life talk about you and rehash every flaw and thing you cannot do, as well as some that you can.

High School

In high school, Sebine attended regular classes for health, art, music, gym, and home economics. Her extracurricular activities included taking part in several clubs, participating on the gymnastics team, and participating in the band for 2 years. She attended football and basketball games and went to the prom.

In her sophomore and junior years, Sebine's IEP included community-based job experiences, and she spent half of each school day working at different job experiences—dishwasher, laundry, supply room, etc.—at a local hospital. Sebine's transition program during her senior year included training at a Bob Evans Restaurant, which eventually led to competitive employment.

Here are some of the things Sebine has to say about her life today:

Work

Before I left school, I had an interview down at the Bob Evans on Olentangy River Road. They hired me for busing tables. I have worked there for over 3 years. Dave, the manager, has also trained me how to do tank [dish washing].

A cab takes me to work. I tell the driver my schedule. Sometimes they are late or forget to come, so I call the dispatcher. When I finish work, they give me a ride home.

When Sebine first started at the restaurant, she only worked during the afternoon, when it wasn't very busy. Her supervisor was concerned that she might not be able to keep up the pace required for the busy lunch or dinner hours. A job coach was brought in to help increase her productivity. But after 2 years, Sebine was only working 19 hours per week, so she decided to get a second job. Her parents helped her prepare a résumé.

I wrote the address on the envelope and mailed it to other restaurants. The owner called me, and I had an interview.

The second job was at Nickleby's Bookstore & Cafe, where Sebine worked as a "tanker." For several months, Sebine worked 7 days per week: Monday through Friday afternoons at Bob Evans and Saturday and Sunday afternoons at Nickleby's. Then trouble happened at Nickleby's. The concern was about Sebine's work rate and that she wasn't following her supervisor's directions to put dishes and other items in the right places.

I got fired. I was arguing. I put things not in the right place. I just put it where I feel like.

A week later, Sebine went back to apologize, on her own volition and by herself even though she had already found another job.

I rode my bike to the Spaghetti Shop. It was a store where I mailed my résumé before. The manager still had my résumé. He just gave me an application form and I signed it. Then he asked me what's my sched-

With two jobs and a busy social life, Sebine is on the go.

ule at Bob's. I started there a couple months ago. First they had me bus, but I'm really good at it, and so now they send me in the back to help wash dishes too. Now, Mondays and Tuesdays I work from 11-2, no, no, Mondays and Tuesday I work from 11 to 1, and Wednesday, Thursday and Friday I work 11 to 2.

In the meantime, Sebine's supervisor at Bob Evans gave her the additional hours she'd been asking for, increasing her work week there to 32 hours.

And I work late at Bob's now. Friday they have me work 5 to 9, Saturday 2 to 9, Sunday 2 to 9, Monday 2 to 9, Tuesday 2 to 9. Sometimes they change my schedule, have me come in on Wednesdays or holidays or to make up for someone who's missing.

Friends

Sebine's entire family, including her grandparents, recently had dinner at Bob Evans when she was on duty. Sebine proudly introduced them to all of her co-workers.

Yeah, I got friends there. I've got lots of friends from work, from church and dance too. We usually go out to eat, see a movie. If it's someone's birthday, I usually take them out. Sometimes we have a party.

Some of Sebine's friends have disabilities, and some do not.

I got lots of friends now. Well, I have some with handicaps, but some are not. I got some friends who are in

college, Jenny at Wittenberg. We mostly have dinner or a movie, or whatever. Susan lives in Cincinnati, and Kristin is in South America. I talk to her mom on the phone. Sometimes I write letters to my friends. My friend Barb is going to have her first baby. I talked to her last night. She said she's going to the hospital because her baby's coming soon.

Sebine chooses to participate in some of the recreation and leisure activities and outings offered by the community parks and recreation program.

Mostly I hang out with a few people who have handicaps. The adult group does activities. This fall we went to an Amish farm. We go to movies, have parties and dinners, baseball games. After they give me a flier, I usually look at them and pick the ones I want to go, and then take off from work. On the 12th, I have to find someone to work for me. We have a new guy at work, his name is Francis, and he's going to work for me on Monday and I can work for him on Tuesday.

I like to dance. Now this year I take only ballet, jazz, and tap. So I'm just taking three this year instead of

"I like to dance."

Summary

How Do Former Special Education Students Fare as Adults?

- Studies of graduates of secondary special education programs report high unemployment rates; most of the young adults who had found competitive employment were working in part-time, low-paying jobs.

- Only 58% of teenagers and young adults with disabilities who exited from the public schools during the 1991-92 school year graduated with a diploma or received a certificate of completion, and it is estimated that 30% of students with disabilities who enroll in high school drop out before they finish.

four. Ballet is only two people, but jazz is lots of people. Mostly I dance ballet and jazz with kids, but mostly I am taking tap with adults.

A Busy Life

Sebine goes to the grocery store, deposits her own paychecks at the bank, visits the hair salon, checks books out of the library, goes to the dance studio, and eats at fast-food restaurants by herself or with friends. All in all, she's a very busy young lady. She even spent 3 years working as a volunteer at a local nursing home, which recently recognized her for accumulating more than 500 service hours.

> I'm a volunteer there. I go there early in the morning, and I stay there until 11:00. I got friends over there. Mostly the residents and mostly people who work there. I don't know exactly how many. Mostly old people, but not that old I don't think. I come in the mornings and there are activities going on, like music. I push the wheelchairs and take my friends to their activities. Yeah. I did go there, but since I got my job at the Spaghetti Shop, there's no time anymore.

Saving for the Future

> Well, Spaghetti Shop don't pay me that much because I get short hours there, but I get more at Bob's. I put most of it in the bank. I pay Irene for my dance lessons. I go shopping. I save for a baby gift. I save for a flight ticket to Minnesota to see my rela-

tives and to go to Disney World. One time my checkbook got messed up and I got in big trouble with my mom. I'm paying for my rent when I move. I'll be moving into my own house pretty soon. Not too far away. It's kind of like crummy right now. They didn't fix it up yet. I'll have two roommates, Cristal and Lisa.

> There's two things I'm wondering about now. One big and other one just little. The big one is I will miss my mom, mostly. The little one is, I met this kid, this boy, he's from Worthington. I haven't seen him that much, but I'm thinking about him.

> I need a vacation.

Agreed. Sebine's busy life is pretty normal for these days: a hectic schedule, bills to pay, things to do, people to see, plans to make, and things to worry and wonder about. Sebine's full life represents the ultimate outcome for special education. She has learned the necessary skills, is sufficiently self-determined, and has access to the natural supports needed. Sebine has achieved significant autonomy, is an active member of her community, and can prepare for and cope with the changes she will experience as an adult. Sebine was fortunate to have parents who spent time with her, were interested and actively involved with her schooling, and who encouraged her from an early age to be as independent as she could be. But Sebine's success as a young adult must also be due, at least in part, to a special education that included the following:

- Intensive intervention that began while she was an infant and continued until she entered school and that included integrated preschool classes
- Regular home-school communication and cooperation between teachers and parents
- Being included in mainstream academic and social activities of her home school throughout her elementary, junior high, and high school years
- Systematic instruction in functional academic and daily living skills throughout her school years
- Early and frequent opportunities to make choices and to participate in the decision making that would affect her life
- Early career education and a systematic plan for the transition from school to adult life that included experience and training in real community-based jobs while she was still in school

An earlier edition of this textbook began with a picture of 10-year-old Sebine on the cover. During the 12 years since, both Sebine and special education have come a long way. Sebine is one of special education's success stories, but her story is not unique; there are many success stories like hers. But Sebine's story is as good a story as any with which to end this book. ✳

- Although the percentage of college students who indicate they have a disability has increased in recent years, compared to their peers without disabilities, fewer former special education students pursue post-secondary education.
- The NLTS reported that four out of every five former special education students had still not achieved the status of independent adulthood after being out of high school for up to 5 years.

Transition from School to Adult Life

- Transition from school to life in the community has become perhaps the most challenging issue in special education today. Models for school-to-adult-life transition stress the importance of a functional secondary school curriculum that provides work experience in integrated community job sites, systematic coordination between the school and adult service agencies, parental involvement and support, and a written individualized transition plan (ITP) to guide the entire process.

- Development of career awareness and vocational skills should begin in the elementary grades for children with severe disabilities.

- Middle school students should begin to spend time on actual community job sites.

- Secondary students should spend more time on actual community job sites, with in-school instruction focusing on the functional skills needed in the adult work, domestic, community, and recreational/leisure environments.

Employment

- Secondary school programs can enhance the competitive employment prospects for young adults with disabilities by (a) stressing functional, vocational skills, (b) conducting school-based instruction in integrated settings as much as possible, and (c) beginning community-based instruction as early as about age 12 for students with severe disabilities and for progressively extended periods as the student nears graduation.

- Supported employment is a relatively new concept that recognizes that many adults with severe disabilities require ongoing support to obtain and hold a job. Supported employment is characterized by performance of real paid work in regular, integrated work sites; it requires ongoing support from a supported work specialist.

- The role of the employment specialist/job coach is evolving from one of primary supporter for the employee with disabilities to one who works with the employer and co-workers to create innovative and natural support networks.

- Self-monitoring—observing, counting, recording one's performance—learning how to respond independently to the cues that occur naturally in the workplace are two ways that employees with disabilites can increase their job productivity and independence in the workplace.

- Many adults with disabilities work in sheltered workshops that provide one or a combination of three kinds of programs: training for competitive employment in the community, extended or long-term employment, and work activities.

Residential Alternatives

- More community-based residential services mean greater opportunities for adults with severe disabilities to live in more normalized settings.

- Despite deinstitutionalization—movement of persons with mental retardation out of large public institutions and into smaller community-based residences such as group homes—approximately 100,000 persons, mostly adults with severe or profound mental retardation, still live in large institutions.

- Foster home placement allows the adult with disabilities to participate in day-to-day activities of family life, to receive attention from people interested in his or her development, and to experience close personal relationships.

- Apartment living offers the greatest opportunities for integration into the community and interaction with people without disabilities. Three common forms of apartment living for adults with disabilities are the apartment cluster, the coresidence apartment, and the maximum-independence apartment.

- Supported living is an approach toward helping people with disabilities live in the community in as independently and normalized a fashion as they possibly can by providing a network of various kinds and levels of natural supports.

Recreation and Leisure

- Learning the skills needed to participate in age-appropriate recreational and leisure activities is necessary for a self-satisfying, normalized lifestyle.

- Too few community resources and recreation training programs are available for adults with severe disabilities. Communities are, however, beginning to develop therapeutic recreation programs for children and adults with disabilities.

The Ultimate Goal: A Better Quality of Life

- Adults with disabilities continue to face lack of acceptance as full members of society.

- Handicapism—discriminatory treatment and biased reactions toward someone with a disability—occurs on personal, professional, and societal levels. It must be eliminated before normalization can become a reality for every man and woman with a disability.

- Persons with disabilities have begun to assert their legal rights, challenging the view that persons with disabilities are incapable of speaking for themsleves.

For More Information

Journals

Behavioral Residential Treatment. Published quarterly by John Wiley & Sons, Inc., 605 Third Avenue, New York, NY 10158. Reports of research and descriptions of behavioral treatment programs in residential settings.

Career Development for Exceptional Individuals. Published two times per year by the Division on Career Development and Transition (DCDT), Council for Exceptional Children, 1920 Association Drive, Reston, VA 22091. Focuses on education and other programs for complete life experiences—including vocational, residential, and leisure activities—for children and adults with disabilities.

International Journal of Rehabilitation Research Quarterly. Published by the International Society for Rehabilitation of the Disabled, 432 Park Avenue South, New York, NY 10016.

Journal of Vocational Rehabilitation. Quarterly journal of research and ideas for practitioners published by Andover Medical Publishers, Inc., 80 Montvale Avenue, Stoneham, MA 02180.

Mainstream: Magazine of the Able-Disabled. Published by Exploding Myths, Inc., P.O. Box 370598, San Diego, CA 92137-0598. A monthly magazine of articles about and advertising directed toward persons with disabilities.

Mouth: The Voice of Disability Rights. A satirical and hard-hitting newsletter published by disability rights activists and aimed at human services professionals and the rehabilitation industry. Six issues per year. For subscriptions write: Mouth, 61 Brighton Street, Rochester, NY 14607.

Books

Bellamy, G. T., Rhodes, L. E., Mank, D. M., & Albin, J. M. (1988). *Supported employment: A community implementation guide.* Baltimore: Paul H. Brookes.

Brinkerhoff, L. C., Shaw, S. F., & McGuire, J. M. (1993). *Promoting postsecondary education for students with learning disabilities.* Austin, TX: PRO-ED.

Brolin, D. E. (1993). *Life-centered career education* (4th ed.). Reston, VA: Council for Exceptional Children.

Brolin, D. E. (1995). *Career education: A functional life skills approach* (3rd ed.). New York: Merrill/Macmillan.

Clark, G. M., & Kolstoe, O. P. (1995). *Career development and transition education for adolescents with disabilities* (2nd ed.). Needham Heights, MA: Allyn & Bacon.

Edgerton, R. B., & Gaston, M. A. (1990). *"I've seen it all!" Lives of older persons with mental retardation in the community.* Baltimore: Paul H. Brookes.

Gajar, A., Goodman, L., & McAfee, J. (1993). *Secondary schools and beyond: Transition of individuals with mild disabilities.* New York: Macmillan.

Halpern, A. S., Close, D. W., & Nelson, D. J. (1986). *On my own: The impact of semi-independent living programs for adults with mental retardation.* Baltimore: Paul H. Brookes.

Lovitt, T. C. (1991). *Preventing school dropouts.* Austin, TX: PRO-ED.

Ludlow, B. L., Turnbull, A. P., & Luckasson, R. (Eds.). (1988). *Transitions to adult life for people with mental retardation: Principles and practices.* Baltimore: Paul H. Brookes.

Moon, M. S., Inge, K. J., Wehman, P., Brooke, V., & Barcus, M. (1990). *Helping persons with severe mental retardation get and keep employment.* Baltimore: Paul H. Brookes.

Rusch, F. R. (1986). *Competitive employment: Issues and strategies.* Baltimore: Paul H. Brookes.

Rusch, F. R. (1990). *Supported employment: Models, methods, and issues.* Pacific Grove, CA: Brooks/Cole.

Rusch, F. R., DeStefano, L., Chadsey-Rusch, J., Phelps, A., & Szymanski, E. (1992). *Transition from school to adult life: Models, linkages, and policy.* Pacific Grove, CA: Brooks/Cole.

Seltzer, M. M., Krauss, M. W., & Janicki, M. P. (1994). *Life course perspectives on adulthood and old age.* Washington, DC: American Association on Mental Retardation.

Siegel, S., Robert, M., Greener, K., Meyer, G., Halloran, W., & Gaylord Ross, R. (1993). *Career ladders for challenged youths in transition from school to adult life.* Austin, TX: PRO-ED.

Smith, J. D. (1995). *Pieces of purgatory: Mental retardation in and out of institutions.* Pacific Grove, CA: Brooks/Cole.

Smith, M. D., Belcher, R. G., & Juhrs, P. D. (1994). *A guide to successful employment for individuals with autism.* Baltimore: Paul H. Brookes.

Thomas, C. H., & Thomas, J. L. (1986). *Directory of college facilities and services for the disabled* (2nd ed.). Phoenix, AZ: Oryx Press.

Wehman, P. (Ed.). (1992). *Life beyond the classroom: Transition for youth with disabilities.* Baltimore: Paul H. Brookes.

Wehman, P., Moon, M. S., Everson, J. M., Wood, W., & Barcus, J. M. (Eds.). (1988). *Transition from school to work: New challenges for youth with severe disabilities.* Baltimore: Paul H. Brookes.

West, L. L., Corbey, S., Boyer-Stephens, A., Jones, B., Miller, R. J., & Sarkees-Wircenski, M. (1992). *Integrating transition planning into the IEP process.* Reston, VA: Council for Exceptional Children.

Organizations

American Coalition of Citizens with Disabilities (ACCD), 346 Connecticut Avenue, NW, Washington, DC 20201.

Association on Handicapped Student Service Programs in Post-Secondary Education, P.O. Box 21192, Columbus, OH 43221. A young association devoted to providing accessibility and equal opportunities for college and university students with disabilities. Includes special interest groups on deafness, learning disabilities, community colleges, and rural institutions.

Clearinghouse on Disability Information, Office of Special Education and Rehabilitation Services, U.S. Department of Education, Room 3132, Switzer Building, Washington, DC 20202-1904.

Disability Rights Education and Defense Funds, Inc., 2212 Sixth Street, Berkeley, CA 94710.

Division on Career Development and Transition (DCDT), Council for Exceptional Children, 1920 Association Drive, Reston, VA 22091. A relatively new division of CEC that focuses on career and lifestyle education for persons with disabilities.

Postscript

All introductory textbooks contain a great deal of information. In that respect, this book is no different from others. I hope, however, that you have gained more than just some basic facts and information about learners with exceptional educational needs and special education, the discipline dedicated to meeting those needs. I hope you have examined your own attitudes toward and relationships with children and adults with disabilities. At the beginning of the book, I shared eight fundamental beliefs that underlie my personal, but by no means unique, view of special education. I would like to repeat those beliefs here.

A Personal View of Special Education

- People with disabilities have a fundamental right to live and participate fully in settings and programs—in school, at home, in the workplace, and in the community—that are as normalized as possible. A defining feature of normalized settings and programs is the integration of persons with and without disabilities.
- Individuals with disabilities have the right to as much independence as we can help them achieve. Special educators have no more important teaching task than helping children and adults with disabilities learn how to increase the level of decision making and control over their own lives.
- Special education must continue to expand and improve its efforts to respond appropriately to all learners with special needs and attributes—the gifted and talented child, the preschooler with a disability, the infant or toddler who is at risk for a future learning problem, the exceptional child from a different cultural, ethnic, or linguistic background, and the adult with disabilities.
- Professionals have too long ignored the needs of parents and families of exceptional children, treating them as patients, clients, or even adversaries instead of partners with the same goals. We have long neglected to recognize parents as their children's first—and in many ways best—teachers. Learning to work effectively with parents is one of the most important skills a special educator can acquire.
- Special educators' efforts are most effective when they incorporate the input and services of all of the disciplines in the helping professions.

- All students have the right to an effective education. As educators, our primary responsibility is to design and implement effective instruction for personal, social, vocational, and academic skills. Instruction is ultimately effective when it helps the individuals we serve acquire and maintain positive lifestyle changes. Or, to put it another way: the proof of the process is in the product. Therefore . . .

- Teachers must demand effectiveness from their instructional approaches. The belief that special educators require unending patience is a disservice to students with special needs and to the educators—both special and general education teachers—whose job it is to teach them. Teachers should not wait patiently for exceptional children to learn, but should modify the instructional program to improve its effectiveness.

- Finally, the future for individuals with disabilities holds great promise. We have only begun to discover the ways to improve teaching, to increase learning, to prevent some of the conditions that lead to disabilities, to encourage acceptance, and to use technology to compensate for disabilities. We have not come as far as we can in learning how to help exceptional individuals build and enjoy fuller, more independent lives in the school, community, and workplace.

✳ As a Member of the Profession

If you consider yourself a prospective special educator, view special education as a profession and yourself as a professional. View yourself as someone with special skills and knowledge; you are different from people without your special training. This has nothing to do with arrogance, but everything to do with the recognition that each of us must develop and responsibly use as much professional competence as we can muster.

It is commendable that you have a commitment and a desire to help children with exceptional educational needs. You will probably hear often that you are "wonderful" or "patient" because of this. Good intentions are fine, but desire and commitment are only a beginning. What learners with disabilities need more than anything are teachers who are *impatient*—impatient with lack of progress, impatient with methods, materials, and policies that do not help their students acquire and subsequently use the knowledge and skills required for successful functioning in the home, school, community, and workplace. So, don't be patient, be effective.

Teaching students with disabilities requires systematic instruction. It is demanding work. Prepare yourself for that work the best way you can. Demand relevant, up-to-date information and hands-on practical experiences from your teacher-education program. Continue your education and training throughout your career. Stay on top of the continual developments in special education by reading professional journals, participating in inservice training opportunities, and attending conferences. Even better, experiment with instructional methods and share the results of your research with colleagues through presentations and publications.

Special education is not a grim, thankless business. Quite the opposite— special education is an exciting, dynamic field that offers personal satisfaction and feelings of accomplishment unequaled in most areas of endeavor. Welcome aboard!

✳ *As a Member of the Community*

The degree of success that a person with disabilities enjoys in the normal routine of daily life does not depend solely on his or her skills and abilities. In large measure, the integration of people with disabilities into contemporary society depends on the attitudes and actions of citizens with little knowledge of or experience with exceptional learners. How can people come to accept and support a group they do not know?

Society controls who enters and who is kept out, much as a gatekeeper lets some visitors pass but refuses others. For a particular individual, society's gatekeeper may have been a doctor who urged parents to institutionalize their child or a teacher who resisted having any difficult-to-teach kids in class. It may have been a school psychologist who imposed a label of "trainable mentally retarded" or an employer who refused to hire workers with disabilities. It may have been a social worker, a school board member, a voter. Saddest of all, it may have been a parent whose low expectations kept the gate closed.

How society views people with disabilities influences how individual members of the community respond. Society's views are changing gradually for the better—they are being changed by people who believe that our past practices of exclusion and denial of opportunities were primitive and unfair. But to have maximum impact, the movement toward integration and opportunities described in this book must ultimately translate into personal terms for those of you who will not choose careers in special education. People with disabilities and people without disabilities do experience certain aspects of life differently, but they are more like one another than they are different. And the conclusion I hope you have reached is this: Every child and adult with disabilities must be treated as an individual, not as a member of a category or a labeled group.

✳ *In Sum*

Viewing every individual with disabilities first as a person and second as a person with disabilities may be the most important step in integrating the individual into the mainstream of community life. But a change in attitude will not diminish the disability. What it will do is give us a new outlook—more objective and more positive—and allow us to see a disability as a set of special needs. Viewing exceptional people as individuals with special needs tells us much about how to respond to them—and how we respond is the essence of special education.

$\mathcal{G}$lossary

Absence seizure — A type of epileptic seizure in which the individual loses consciousness, usually for less than half a minute; can occur very frequently in some children.

Acceleration — An educational approach that provides a child with learning experiences usually given to older children; most often used with gifted and talented children.

Accommodation — The adjustment of the eye for seeing at different distances; accomplished by muscles that change the shape of the lens to bring an image into clear focus on the retina.

Acquired immune deficiency syndrome (AIDS) — A fatal illness in which the body's immune system breaks down. At present there is no known cure for AIDS or a vaccine for the virus that causes it (see human immunodeficiency virus).

Acquisition stage of learning — The initial phase of learning when the student is learning how to perform a new skill or use new knowledge; feedback should focus on accuracy and topography of the student's response.

Active student response (ASR) — A frequency-based measure of a student's active participation during instruction; measured by counting the number of observable responses made to an ongoing lesson or to curriculum materials.

Adaptive device — Any piece of equipment designed to improve the function of a body part. Examples include standing tables and special spoons that can be used by people with weak hands or poor muscle control.

Adventitious — A disability that develops at any time after birth, from disease, trauma, or any other cause; most frequently used with sensory or physical impairments (contrasts with congenital).

Advocate — Someone who pleads the cause of a person with disabilities or group of people with disabilities, especially in legal or administrative proceedings or public forums.

Albinism — A congenital condition marked by deficiency in, or total lack of, pigmentation. People with albinism have pale skin; white hair, eyebrows, and eyelashes; and eyes with pink or pale blue irises.

Amblyopia — Dimness of sight without apparent change in the eye's structures; can lead to blindness in the affected eye if not corrected.

American Sign Language (ASL) — A visual-gestural language with its own rules of syntax, semantics, and pragmatics; does not correspond to written or spoken English. ASL is the language of the Deaf culture in the United States and Canada.

Amniocentesis — The insertion of a hollow needle through the abdomen into the uterus of a pregnant woman. Used to obtain amniotic fluid in order to determine the presence of genetic and chromosomal abnormalities. The sex of the fetus can also be determined.

Anoxia — A lack of oxygen severe enough to cause tissue damage; can cause permanent brain damage and mental retardation.

Aphasia — Loss of speech functions; often, but not always, refers to inability to speak because of brain lesions.

Applied behavior analysis — "The science in which procedures derived from the principles of behavior are systematically applied to improve socially significant behavior to a meaningful degree and to demonstrate experimentally that the procedures employed were responsible for the improvement in behavior" (Cooper, Heron, & Heward, 1987, p. 14).

Aqueous humor — Fluid that occupies the space between the lens and the cornea of the eye.

Articulation — The production of distinct language sounds by the vocal organs.

Asthma — A chronic respiratory condition characterized by repeated episodes of wheezing, coughing, and difficulty breathing.

Astigmatism — A defect of vision usually caused by irregularities in the cornea; results in blurred vision and difficulties in focusing. Can usually be corrected by lenses.

At risk — A term used to refer to children who are not currently identified as handicapped or disabled but who are considered to have a greater-than-usual chance of developing a disability. Physicians use the terms at risk or high risk to refer to pregnancies with a greater-than-normal probability of producing a baby with disabilities.

Ataxia — Poor sense of balance and body position and lack of coordination of the voluntary muscles; characteristic of one type of cerebral palsy.

Athetosis — A type of cerebral palsy characterized by large, irregular, uncontrollable twisting motions. The muscles may be tense and rigid or loose and flaccid. Often accompanied by difficulty with oral language.

Attention deficit disorder (ADD) — See attention deficit-hyperactivity disorder (ADHD).

Attention deficit-hyperactivity disorder (ADHD) — Diagnostic category of the American Psychiatric Association for a condition in which a child exhibits developmentally inappropriate inattention, impulsivity, and hyperactivity.

Audiogram — A graph of the faintest level of sound a person can hear in each ear at least 50% of the time at each of several frequencies, including the entire frequency range of normal speech.

Audiologist — A professional who specializes in the evaluation of hearing ability and the treatment of impaired hearing.

Audiology — The science of hearing.

Audiometer — A device that generates sounds at specific frequencies and intensities; used to examine hearing.

Audiometric zero — the smallest sound a person with normal hearing can perceive; also called the zero hearing-threshold level (HTL).

Audition — the act or sense of hearing.

Auditory canal (external acoustic meatus) — Slightly amplifies and transports sound waves from the external ear to the middle ear.

Auditory training — A program that works on listening skills by teaching individuals with hearing impairments to make as much use as possible of their residual hearing.

Augmentative and alternative communication (ACC) — a diverse set of nonspeech communication strategies and methods to assist individuals who are unable to meet their communication needs through speech; includes sign language, symbol systems, communication boards, and synthetic speech devices.

Auricle — External part of the ear; collects sound waves into the auditory canal.

Autism — A pervasive developmental disorder marked by severe impairment of intellectual, social, and emotional functioning. The essential features of the condition typically appear prior to 30 months of age, and consist of disturbances of (a) developmental rates and/or sequences; (b) responses to sensory stimuli; (c) speech, language, and cognitive capacities; and (d) capacities to relate to people, events, and objects (Autism Society of America, Ritvo & Freeman, 1978)

Baseline — A measure of the level or amount of a specific target behavior prior to implementation of an intervention designed to change the behavior. Baseline data are used as an objective measure against which to compare and evaluate the results obtained during intervention.

Behavior observation audiometry — A method of hearing assessment in which an infant's reactions to sounds are observed; a sound is presented at an increasing level of intensity until a response, such as head turning, eye blinking, or cessation of play, is reliably observed.

Behavioral contract — A written agreement between two parties in which one agrees to complete a specified task (e.g., a child agrees to complete a homework assignment by the next morning) and in return the other party agrees to provide a specific reward (e.g., the teacher allows the child to have 10 minutes of free time) upon completion of the task.

Behavioral disorder — A disability characterized by behavior that differs markedly and chronically from current social or cultural norms and adversely affects educational performance.

Bilingual special education — Using the child's home language and home culture along with English in an individually designed program of special education.

Binocular vision — Vision using both eyes working together to perceive a single image.

Blind — Having either no vision or only light perception; learning occurs through other senses.

Blindness, legal — See legally blind.

Braille — A system of writing letters, numbers, and other language symbols with a combination of six raised dots. A person who is blind reads the dots with his or her fingertips.

Cataract — A reduction or loss of vision that occurs when the crystalline lens of the eye becomes cloudy or opaque.

Catheter — A tube inserted into the body to permit injections or withdrawal of fluids or to keep a passageway open; often refers to a tube inserted into the bladder to remove urine from a person who does not have effective bladder control.

Cerebral palsy — Motor impairment caused by brain damage, which is usually acquired during the prenatal period or during the birth process. Can involve a wide variety of symptoms (see ataxia, athetosis, rigidity, spasticity, and tremor) and range from mild to severe. Neither curable nor progressive.

Choral responding — Each student in the class or group responding orally in unison to a question, problem, or item presented by the teacher.

Chorion villus sampling (CVS) — A procedure for prenatal diagnosis of chromosomal abnormalities that can be conducted during the first 8 to 10 weeks of pregnancy; fetal cells are removed from the chorionic tissue, which surrounds the fetus, and directly analyzed.

Cleft palate — A congenital split in the palate that results in an excessive nasal quality of the voice. Can often be repaired by surgery or a dental appliance.

Cochlea — Main receptor organ for hearing located in the inner ear; tiny hairs within the cochlea transform mechanical energy into neural impulses that then travel through the auditory nerve to the brain.

Communication — An interactive process requiring at least two parties in which messages are encoded, transmitted, and decoded by any means, including sounds, symbols, and gestures.

Complex partial seizure — A type of seizure in which an individual goes through a brief period of inappropriate or purposeless activity (also called psychomotor seizure). Usually lasts from 2 to 5 minutes, after which the person has amnesia about the entire episode.

Conduct disorder — A group of behavior disorders including disobedience, disruptiveness, fighting, and tantrums, as identified by Quay (1975).

Conductive hearing loss — Hearing loss caused by obstructions in the outer or middle ear or malformations that interfere with the conduction of sound waves to the inner ear. Can often be corrected surgically or medically.

Congenital — Any condition that is present at birth (contrasts with adventitious).

Constant time delay — A procedure for transferring stimulus control from teacher provided response prompts to the instructional item itself. The teacher begins by simultaneously presenting the stimulus being taught and a controlling response prompt (e.g., as the teacher holds up a flashcard with the word *ball* printed on it she says "ball"). After a number of 0-second delay trials the teacher waits for a fixed amount of time (e.g., 4 seconds) between presentation of the instructional stimulus and the response prompt. Practice trials are repeated with the constant delay until the student begins to respond correctly prior the teacher's prompt.

Continuum of services — The range of different placement and instructional options that a school district can use to serve children with disabilities. Typically depicted as a pyramid, ranging from the least restrictive placement (regular classroom) at the bottom to the most restrictive placement (residential school or hospital) at the top.

Convulsive disorder — See epilepsy.

Cornea — The transparent part of the eyeball that admits light to the interior.

Cri-du-chat syndrome — A chromosomal abnormality resulting from deletion of material from the fifth pair of chromosomes. It usually results in severe retardation. Its name is French for "cat cry," named for the high-pitched crying of the child due to a related larynx dysfunction.

Cued speech — A method of supplementing oral communication by adding cues in the form of eight different hand signals in four different locations near the chin.

Cultural pluralism — The value and practice of respecting, fostering, and encouraging the cultural and ethnic differences that make up society.

Cultural-familial mental retardation — See psychosocial disadvantage.

Culture — The established knowledge, ideas, values, and skills shared by a society; its program of survival and adaptation to its environment.

Curriculum-based assessment — Evaluation of a student's progress in terms of his or her performance on the skills that comprise the curriculum of the local school.

Cystic fibrosis — An inherited disorder that causes a dysfunction of the pancreas, mucus, salivary, and sweat glands. Cystic fibrosis causes severe, long-term respiratory difficulties. No cure is currently available.

Deaf — The result of a hearing loss severe enough so that speech cannot be understood through the ears alone, even with a hearing aid; some sounds may still be perceived.

Decibel (dB) — The unit of measure for the relative intensity of sound on a scale beginning at zero. Zero dB refers to the faintest sound a person with normal hearing can detect.

Deinstitutionalization — The social movement to transfer individuals with disabilities, especially persons with mental retardation, from large institutions to smaller, community-based residences and work settings.

Diabetes — See juvenile diabetes mellitus.

Diabetic retinopathy — Visual impairment caused by hemorrhages on the retina and other disorders of blood circulation in people with diabetes.

Dialect — A variety within a specific language; can involve variation in pronunciation, word choice, word order, and inflected forms.

Differential reinforcement of other behavior (DRO) — A procedure in which any behavior except the targeted inappropriate response is reinforced; results in a reduction of the inappropriate behavior.

Diplegia — Paralysis that affects the legs more often than the arms.

Disability — Condition characterized by functional limitations that impede typical development as the result of a physical or sensory impairment or difficulty in learning or social adjustment.

Double hemiplegia — Paralysis of the arms, with less severe involvement of the legs.

Down syndrome — A chromosomal anomaly that often causes moderate to severe mental retardation, along with certain physical characteristics such as a large tongue, heart problems, poor muscle tone, and a broad, flat bridge of the nose.

Duchenne muscular dystrophy — The most common form of muscular dystrophy, a group of long-term diseases that progressively weaken and waste away the body's muscles.

Due process — Set of legal steps and proceedings carried out according to established rules and principles; designed to protect an individual's constitutional and legal rights.

Duration (of behavior) — Measure of how long a person engages in a given activity.

Dyslexia — A disturbance in the ability to read or learn to read.

Echolalia — The repetition of what other people say as if echoing them; characteristic of some children with delayed development, autism, and communication disorders.

Electroencephalograph (EEG) — Device that detects and records brain wave patterns.

Encephalitis — Inflammation of the brain; can cause permanent damage to the central nervous system and mental retardation.

Endogenous — Refers to an inherited cause of a disability or impairment.

Enrichment — Educational approach that provides a child with extra learning experiences that the standard curriculum would not normally include. Most often used with gifted and talented children.

Epilepsy — A condition marked by chronic and repeated seizures, disturbances of movement, sensation, behavior, and/or consciousness caused by abnormal electrical activity in the brain (see generalized tonic-clonic seizure, complex partial seizure, simple complex seizure, and absence seizure). Can usually be controlled with medication, although the drugs may have undesirable side effects; may be temporary or lifelong.

Equal protection — Legal concept included in the 14th Amendment to the Constitution of the United States, stipulating that no state may deny any person equality or liberty because of that person's classification according to race, nationality, or religion. Several major court cases leading to the passage of PL 94-142 (IDEA) found that children with disabilities were not provided equal protection if they were denied access to an appropriate education solely because of their disabilities.

Ethnocentrism — The view that the practices of one's own culture are the natural and correct, while perceiving the practices of other cultures as odd, amusing, inferior, and/or immoral.

Etiology — The cause(s) of a disability, impairment, or disease. Includes genetic, physiological, and environmental or psychological factors.

Evoked-response audiometry — A method of testing hearing by measuring the electrical activity generated by the auditory nerve in response to auditory stimulation. Often used to measure the hearing of infants and children considered difficult to test.

Exceptional children — Children whose performance deviates from the norm, either below or above, to the extent that special educational programming is needed.

Exogenous — Refers to a cause of a disability or impairment that stems from factors outside the body such as disease, toxicity, or injury.

Extinction — A procedure in which reinforcement for a previously reinforced behavior is withheld. If the actual reinforcers that are maintaining the behavior are identified and withheld, the behavior will gradually decrease in frequency until it no longer, or seldom, occurs.

Facilitated communication (FC) — A type of augmentative communication in which a "facilitator" provides assistance to someone in typing or pointing to vocabulary symbols; typically involves an alphanumeric keyboard on which the user types out his message one letter at a time. To date, research designed to validate FC has repeatedly demonstrated either facilitator influence—correct or meaningful language is produced only when the facilitator "knows" what should be communicated—or no unexpected language competence compared to the participants' measured IQ or a standard language assessment.

Fetal alcohol effects (FAE) — Term used to identify the suspected etiology of developmental problems experienced by infants and toddlers who have some but not all of the diagnostic criteria for fetal alcohol syndrome (FAS) and have a history of prenatal alcohol exposure.

Fetal alcohol syndrome (FAS) — A condition sometimes found in the infants of alcoholic mothers; can involve low birth weight, developmental delay, and cardiac, limb, and other physical defects. Caused by excessive alcohol use during pregnancy, often produces serious physical defects and developmental delays; diagnosed when the child has two or more craniofacial malformations and growth is below the 10th percentile for height and weight. FAS is one of the leading known causes of mental retardation. In addition to physical problems, many children with FAS have neurological damage which contributes to cognitive and language delays.

Field of vision — The expanse of space visible with both eyes looking straight ahead, measured in degrees; 180 degrees is considered normal.

Fluency — A performance measure that includes both the accuracy and the rate with which a skill is performed; a fluent performer is both accurate and fast. In communication, the rate and smoothness of speech; stuttering is the most common fluency disorder in speech.

Foster home — A living arrangement in which a family shares its home with a person who is not a relative. Long used with children who for some reason cannot live with their parents temporarily, foster homes are now being used with adults with disabilities as well.

Fragile X syndrome — A chromosomal abnormality associated with mild to severe mental retardation. Thought to be the most common known cause of inherited mental retardation. Affects males more often and more severely than females; behavioral characteristics are sometimes similar to individuals with autism. Diagnosis can be confirmed by studies of the X chromosome.

Functional analysis — Refers to a variety of behavior assessment methodologies for determining the environmental variables that are setting the occasion for and maintaining challenging behaviors such as self-injury (see Iwata et al., 1994).

Generalization — Using previously learned knowledge or skill under conditions other than those under which it was originally learned. Stimulus generality occurs when a student performs a behavior in the presence of relevant stimuli (people, settings, instructional materials) other than those that were present originally. For instance, stimulus generality occurs when a child who has learned to label baseballs and beach balls as "ball" identifies a basketball as "ball." Response generality occurs when a person performs relevant behaviors that were never directly trained but are similar to the original trained behavior. For example, a child may be taught to say, "Hello, how are you?" and "Hi, nice to see you," as greetings. If the child combines the two to say, "Hi, how are you?" response generality has taken place.

Generalized tonic-clonic seizure — The most severe type of seizure, in which the individual has violent convulsions, loses consciousness, and becomes rigid. Formerly called grand mal seizure.

Genetic counseling — A discussion between a specially trained medical counselor and persons who are considering having a baby about the chances of having a baby with a disability, based on the prospective parents' genetic backgrounds.

Glaucoma — An eye disease characterized by abnormally high pressure inside the eyeball. If left untreated, it can cause total blindness, but if detected early most cases can be arrested.

Grand mal seizure — See generalized tonic-clonic seizure.

Group home — A community-based residential alternative for adults with disabilities, most often persons with mental retardation, in which a small group of people live together in a house with one or more support staff.

Group-oriented contingency — A type of behavior management and motivation procedure in which consequences (rewards and/or penalties) are applied to the entire group or class of students and are contingent upon the behavior of selected students or the entire group.

Guided notes — A handout which "guides" students through a lecture, presentation, or demonstration by providing a format that includes basic information and cues students to note key points.

Handicap — Refers to the problems a person with a disability or impairment encounters in interacting with the environment. A disability may pose a handicap in one environment but not in another.

Handicapism — Prejudice or discrimination based solely on a person's disability, without regard for individual characteristics.

Hard of hearing — Level of hearing loss that makes it difficult, although not impossible, to comprehend speech through the sense of hearing alone.

Hearing impaired — Describes anyone who has a hearing loss significant enough to require special education, training, and/or adaptations; includes both deaf and hard-of-hearing conditions.

Hemiplegia — Paralysis of both the arm and the leg on the same side of the body.

Hemophilia — An inherited deficiency in blood-clotting ability, which can cause serious internal bleeding.

Hertz (Hz) — A unit of sound frequency equal to one cycle per second; used to measure pitch.

Human immunodeficiency virus (HIV) — The virus that causes acquired immune deficiency syndrome (AIDS).

Hydrocephalus — An enlarged head caused by cerebral spinal fluid accumulating in the cranial cavity; often causes brain damage and severe retardation; a condition present at birth or developing soon afterward. Can sometimes be treated successfully with a shunt.

Hyperactive — Excessive motor activity or restlessness.

Hyperopia — Farsightedness; condition in which the image comes to a focus behind the retina instead of on it, causing difficulty in seeing near objects.

Hypertonia — Muscle tone that is too high; tense, contracted muscles.

Hypotonia — Muscle tone that is too low; weak, floppy muscles.

Immaturity — Group of behavior disorders, including short attention span, extreme passivity, daydreaming, preference for younger playmates, and clumsiness, as identified by Quay (1975).

Impedance audiometry — Procedure for testing middle ear function by inserting a small probe and pump to detect sound reflected by the eardrum.

Incidence — The percentage of people who, at some time in their lives, will be identified as having a specific condition. Often reported as the number of cases of a given condition per 1,000 people.

Individualized education program (IEP) — Written document required by the Individuals with Disabilities Education Act (PL 94-142) for every child with a disability; includes statements of present performance, annual goals, short-term instructional objectives, specific educational services needed, relevant dates, regular education program participation, and evaluation procedures; must be signed by parents as well as educational personnel.

Individualized family services plan (IFSP) — A requirement of PL 99-457, Education of the Handicapped Act Amendments of 1986, for the coordination of early intervention services for infants and toddlers with disabilities from birth to age 3. Similar to the IEP that is required for all school-age children with disabilities.

Inflection — Change in pitch or loudness of the voice to indicate mood or emphasis.

Inservice training — Any educational program designed to provide practicing professionals (such as teachers, administrators, physical therapists) with additional knowledge and skills.

Inter-observer agreement — The degree to which two or more independent observers record the same results when observing and measuring the same target behavior(s); typically reported as a percentage of agreement.

Inter-rater agreement — See inter-observer agreement.

Interdisciplinary team — Group of professionals from different disciplines (e.g., education, psychology, speech and language, medicine) who work together to plan and implement an individualized education program (IEP) for a child with disabilities.

Interindividual differences — Differences between two or more people in one skill or set of skills.

Intervention — Any effort made on behalf of children and adults with disabilities; may be preventive, remedial, or compensatory.

Intraindividual differences — Differences within one individual on two or more measures of performance.

Iris — The opaque, colored portion of the eye that contracts and expands to change the size of the pupil.

Juvenile diabetes mellitus — A children's disease characterized by inadequate secretion or use of insulin and the resulting excessive sugar in the blood and urine. Managed with diet and/or medication but can be difficult to control. Can cause coma and, eventually, death if left untreated or treated improperly. Can also lead to visual impairments and limb amputation. Not curable at the present time.

Kinesics — The study of bodily movement, particularly as it relates to and affects communication.

Klinefelter syndrome — A chromosomal anomaly in which males receive an extra X chromosome; associated with frequent social retardation, sterility, underdevelopment of male sex organs, and development of secondary female sex characteristics, and borderline or mild levels of mental retardation.

Language — A system used by a group of people for giving meaning to sounds, words, gestures, and other symbols to enable communication with one another. Languages can use vocal (speech sounds) or nonvocal symbols, such as

American Sign Language, use movements and physical symbols instead of sounds.

Learning trial — Consists of three major elements: (a) antecedent (i.e., curricular) stimuli, (b) the student's response to those stimuli, and (c) consequent stimuli (i.e., instructional feedback) following the response; serves as a basic unit of analysis for examining teaching and learning from both the teacher's perspective, as an opportunity to teach, and the student's perspective, as an opportunity to learn (Heward, 1994). Sometimes called a practice trial or learn unit.

Least restrictive environment (LRE) — The educational setting that most closely resembles a regular school program and also meets the child's special educational needs. For many students with disabilities, the regular classroom is the LRE; however, the LRE is a relative concept and must be determined for each individual student with disabilities.

Legally blind — Visual acuity of 20/200 or less in the better eye after the best possible correction with glasses or contact lenses, or vision restricted to a field of 20 degrees or less. Acuity of 20/200 means the eye can see clearly at 20 feet what the normal eye can see at 200 feet.

Lens — The clear part of the eye that focuses rays of light on the retina.

Longitudinal study — A research study that follows one subject or group of subjects over an extended period of time, usually several years.

Low vision — Visual impairment severe enough so that special educational services are required. A child with low vision is able to learn through the visual channel and generally learns to read print.

Low-incidence disability — A disability that occurs relatively infrequently in the general population; often used in reference to sensory impairments, severe and profound mental retardation, autism, and multiple disabilities.

Macular degeneration — A deterioration of the central part of the retina, which causes difficulty in seeing details clearly.

Magnitude (of behavior) — The force with which a response is emitted.

Mainstreaming — The process of integrating children with disabilities into regular schools and classes.

Meningitis — An inflammation of the membranes covering the brain and spinal cord; can cause problems with sight and hearing and/or mental retardation.

Meningocele — Type of spina bifida in which the covering of the spinal cord protrudes through an opening in the vertebrae, but the cord itself and the nerve roots are enclosed.

Mental retardation — Substantial limitations in present functioning; characterized by significantly subaverage intellectual functioning, existing concurrently with related limitations in two or more of the following applicable adaptive skill areas: communication, self-care, home living, social skills, community use, self-direction, health and safety, functional academics, leisure, and work. Mental retardation manifests before age 18. (AAMR, 1992).

Microcephalus — A condition characterized by an abnormally small skull with resulting brain damage and mental retardation.

Milieu teaching strategies — A variety of strategies used to teach speech and language that naturally occur during real or simulated activities in the home, school, or community environments in which a child normally functions; characterized by dispersed learning trials, following the child's attentional lead within the context of normal conversational interchanges, and teaching the form and content of language in the context of normal use.

Minimal brain dysfunction — A once-popular term used to describe the learning disabilities of children with no clinical (organic) evidence of brain damage.

Mobility — The ability to move safely and efficiently from one point to another.

Model program — A program that implements and evaluates new procedures or techniques in order to serve as a basis for development of other similar programs.

Monoplegia — Paralysis affecting one limb.

Morpheme — The smallest element of a language that carries meaning.

Multicultural education — An educational approach in which a school's curriculum and instructional methods are designed and implemented such that all children acquire an awareness, acceptance, and appreciation of cultural diversity and recognize the contributions of many cultures.

Multifactored assessment — Assessment and evaluation of a child with a variety of test instruments and observation procedures. Required by the IDEA when assessment is for educational placement of a child who is to receive special education services. Prevents the misdiagnosis and misplacement of a student as the result of considering only one test score.

Multiple-gating screening — A multi-step process for screening children who may have disabilities. The initial step casts the broadest net (e.g., a multiple-gated screening for children who may have emotional and behavior problems might begin with teacher nominations); children identified in the first step are assessed more closely in a second step (e.g., a behavior checklist); children who have passed through the first two "gates" are screened further (e.g., direct observations in the classroom).

Muscular dystrophy — A group of diseases that gradually weakens muscle tissue; usually becomes evident by the age of 4 or 5.

Myelomeningocele — A protrusion on the back of a child with spina bifida, consisting of a sac of nerve tissue bulging through a cleft in the spine.

Myopia — Nearsightedness; results when light is focused on a point in front of the retina, resulting in a blurred image for distant objects.

Neurologic impairment — Any physical disability caused by damage to the central nervous system (brain, spinal cord, ganglia, and nerves).

Normal curve — A mathematically derived curve depicting the theoretical probability or distribution of a given variable (such as a physical trait or test score) in the general population. Indicates that approximately 68.26% of the population will fall within one standard deviation above and below the mean; approximately 27.18% will fall between one and two standard deviations either above or below the mean; and less than 3% will achieve more extreme scores of more than two standard deviations in either direction.

Normalization — As a philosophy and principle: the belief that individuals with disabilities should, to the maximum extent possible, be physically and socially integrated into the mainstream of society regardless of the degree or type of disability. As an approach to intervention: the use of progressively more normal settings and procedures "to establish and/or maintain personal behaviors which are as culturally normal as possible" (Wolfensberger, 1972, p. 28).

Nystagmus — A rapid, involuntary, rhythmic movement of the eyes that may cause difficulty in reading or fixating on an object.

Occupational therapist — A professional who programs and/or delivers instructional activities and materials to help children and adults with disabilities learn to participate in useful activities.

Ocular motility — The eye's ability to move.

Operant conditioning audiometry — Method of measuring hearing by teaching the individual to make an observable response to sound. For example, a child may be taught to drop a block into a box each time a light and a loud tone are presented. Once this response is learned, the light is no longer presented and the volume and pitch of the tone are gradually decreased. When the child no longer drops the block into the box, the audiologist knows the child cannot hear the tone. Sometimes used to test the hearing of nonverbal children and adults.

Ophthalmologist — A physician who specializes in the diagnosis and treatment of diseases of the eye.

Optic nerve — The nerve that carries impulses from the eye to the brain.

Optometrist — A vision professional who specializes in the evaluation and optical correction of refractive errors.

Oral approach — A philosophy and approach to educating deaf children that stresses learning to speak as the essential element for integration into the hearing world.

Orientation — The ability to establish one's position in relation to the environment.

Orthopedic impairment — Any disability caused by disorders to the musculoskeletal system.

Ossicles — Three small bones (hammer, anvil, and stirrup) that transmit sound energy from the middle ear to the inner ear.

Osteogenesis imperfecta — A hereditary condition in which the bones do not grow normally and break easily; sometimes called brittle bones.

Otitis media — An infection or inflammation of the middle ear that can cause a conductive hearing loss.

Otologist — A physician who specializes in the diagnosis and treatment of diseases of the ear.

Overcorrection — A procedure in which the learner must make restitution for, or repair, the effects of his or her undesirable behavior and then put the environment in even better shape than it was prior to the misbehavior. Used to decrease the rate of undesirable behaviors.

Paraplegia — Paralysis of the lower part of the body, including both legs; usually results from injury to or disease of the spinal cord.

Paraprofessionals (in education) — Trained classroom aides who assist teachers; may include parents.

Partial participation — Teaching approach that acknowledges that even though an individual with severe disabilities may not able to independently perform all the steps of a given task or activity, he or she can often be taught to do selected components or an adapted version of the task.

Perceptual handicap — A term formerly used to describe some conditions now included under the term learning disabilities; usually referred to problems with no known physical cause.

Perinatal — Occurring at or immediately after birth.

Peripheral vision — Vision at the outer limits of the field of vision.

Personality disorder — A group of behavior disorders, including social withdrawal, anxiety, depression, feelings of inferiority, guilt, shyness, and unhappiness, as identified by Quay (1975).

Petit mal seizure — See absence seizure.

Phenylketonuria (PKU) — An inherited metabolic disease that can cause severe retardation; can now be detected at birth and the detrimental effects prevented with a special diet.

Phoneme — The smallest unit of sound that can be identified in a spoken language. There are 45 phonemes, or sound families, in the English language.

Photophobia — Extreme sensitivity of the eyes to light; occurs most notably in albino children.

Physical therapist (PT) — A professional trained to help people with disabilities develop and maintain muscular and orthopedic capability and make correct and useful movement.

Play audiometry — A method for assessing a child's hearing ability by teaching the child to perform simple but distinct activities, such as picking up a toy or putting a ball in a cup whenever she hears the signal, either pure tones or speech.

Positive reinforcement — Presentation of a stimulus or event immediately after a behavior has been emitted, which has the effect of increasing the occurrence of that behavior in the future.

Postlingual — Occurring after the development of language; usually used to classify hearing losses that begin after a person has learned to speak.

Postnatal — Occurring after birth.

Practice stage of learning — After the student has learned how to perform a new skill, he or she should work to develop fluency with the target skill. Feedback during the practice stage of learning should emphasize the rate or speed with which the student correctly performs the skill.

Prader-Willi syndrome — A condition linked to chromosomal abnormality that is characterized by delays in motor development, mild to moderate mental retardation, hypogenital development, an insatiable appetite that often results in obesity, small features and stature.

Pragmatics — Study of the rules that govern how language is used in a communication context.

Precision teaching — An instructional approach that involves (a) pinpointing the skills to be learned; (b) measuring the initial fluency with which the student can perform those behaviors; (c) setting an aim, or goal, for the child's improvement; (d) using direct, daily measurement to monitor progress made under an instructional program; (e) charting the results of those measurements; and (f) changing the program if progress is not adequate.

Prelingual — Describes a hearing impairment acquired before the development of speech and language.

Prenatal — Occurring before birth.

Prenatal asphyxia — A lack of oxygen during the birth process usually caused by interruption of respiration; can cause unconsciousness and/or brain damage.

Prevalence — The number of people who have a certain condition at any given time.

Projective tests — Psychological tests that require a person to respond to a standardized task or set of stimuli (e.g., draw a picture or interpret an ink blot); responses are thought to be a projection of the test-taker's personality and are scored according to the given test's scoring manual to produce a personality profile.

Prosthesis — Any device used to replace a missing or impaired body part.

Psychomotor seizure — See complex partial seizure.

Psychosocial disadvantage — Category of causation for mental retardation that requires evidence of subaverage intellectual functioning in at least one parent and one or more siblings (when there are siblings). Typically associated with impoverished environments involving poor housing, inadequate diets, and inadequate medical care. Often used synonymously with cultural-familial retardation; suggests that mental retardation can be caused by a poor social and cultural environment.

Pupil — The circular hole in the center of the iris of the eye, which contracts and expands to let light pass through.

Quadriplegia — Paralysis of all four limbs.

Rate (or frequency of behavior) — A measure of how often a particular action is performed; usually reported as the number of responses per minute.

Refraction — The bending or deflection of light rays from a straight path as they pass from one medium (e.g., air) into another (e.g., the eye). Used by eye specialists in assessing and correcting vision.

Regular education initiative (REI) — A position advocated by some special educators that students with disabilities can and should be educated in regular classrooms under the primary responsibility of the general education program.

Rehabilitation — A social service program designed to teach a newly disabled person basic skills needed for independence.

Reinforcement — See positive reinforcement.

Related services — Developmental, corrective, and other supportive services required for a child with disabilities to benefit from special education. Includes special transportation services, speech and language pathology, audiology, psychological services, physical and occupational therapy, school health services, counseling and medical services for diagnostic and evaluation purposes, rehabilitation counseling, social work services, and parent counseling and training.

Remediation — An educational program designed to teach a person to overcome a disability through training and education.

Residual hearing — The remaining hearing, however slight, of a person who is deaf.

Resource room — Classroom in which special education students spend part of the school day and receive individualized special education services.

Response cards — Cards, signs, or items which are simultaneously held up by all students to display their response to a question or problem presented by the teacher; response cards enable every student in the class to respond to each question or item.

Retina — A sheet of nerve tissue at the back of the eye on which an image is focused.

Retinitis pigmentosa (RP) — An eye disease in which the retina gradually degenerates and atrophies, causing the field of vision to become progressively more narrow.

Retinopathy of prematurity (ROP) — A condition characterized by an abnormally dense growth of blood vessels and scar tissue in the eye, often causing visual field loss and retinal detachment. Usually caused by high levels of oxygen administered to premature infants in incubators. Also called retrolental fibroplasia (RLF).

Retrolental fibroplasia (RLF) — See retinopathy of prematurity.

Reye's syndrome — A relatively rare disease that appears to be related to a variety of viral infections; most common in children over the age of 6. About 30% of children who contract it die; survivors sometimes show signs of neurological damage and mental retardation. The cause is unknown, although some studies have found an increased risk after the use of aspirin during a viral illness.

Rigidity — A type of cerebral palsy characterized by increased muscle tone, minimal muscle elasticity, and little or no stretch reflex.

Rubella — German measles; when contracted by a woman during the first trimester of pregnancy, may cause visual impairments, hearing impairments, mental retardation, and/or other congenital impairments in the child.

Schizophrenic — Describes a severe behavior disorder characterized by loss of contact with one's surroundings and inappropriate affect and actions.

Screening — A procedure in which groups of children are examined and/or tested in an effort to identify children who are most likely to have a disability; identified children are then referred for more intensive examination and assessment.

Selective mutism — Speaking normally in some settings or situations and not speaking in others.

Self-contained class — A special classroom, usually located within a regular public school building, that includes only exceptional children.

Self-monitoring — A behavior change procedure in which an individual observes and records the frequency and/or quality of his or her own behavior.

Semantics — The study of meaning in language.

Sensorineural hearing loss — A hearing loss caused by damage to the auditory nerve or the inner ear.

Severe disabilities — Term used to refer to challenges faced by individuals with severe and profound mental retardation, autism, and/or physical/sensory impairments combined with marked developmental delay. Persons with severe disabilities exhibit extreme deficits in intellectual functioning and need systematic instruction for basic skills such as self-care and communicating with others.

Sheltered workshop — A structured work environment where persons with disabilities receive employment training and perform work for pay. May provide transitional services for some individuals (e.g., short-term training for competitive employment in the community) and permanent work settings for others.

Shunt — Tube that diverts fluid from one part of the body to another; often implanted in people with hydrocephalus to remove extra cerebrospinal fluid from the head and send it directly into the heart or intestines.

Simple partial seizure — A type of seizure characterized by sudden jerking motions with no loss of consciousness. Partial seizures may occur weekly, monthly, or only once or twice a year.

Social validity — A desirable characteristic of the objectives, procedures, and results of intervention, indicating their appropriateness for the learner. For example, the goal of riding a bus independently would have social validity for students residing in most cities, but not for those in small towns or rural areas.

Socialized aggression — A group of behavior disorders, including truancy, gang membership, theft, and delinquency, as identified by Quay (1975).

Spasticity — A type of cerebral palsy characterized by tense, contracted muscles.

Special education — Individually planned, systematically implemented, and carefully evaluated instruction to help learners with special needs achieve the greatest possible personal self-sufficiency and success in present and future environments.

Speech — A system of using breath and muscles to create specific sounds for communicating.

Speech audiometry — Tests a person's detection and understanding of speech by presenting a list of two-syllable words at different decibel (sound volume) levels.

Speech reception threshold (SRT) — The decibel (sound volume) level at which an individual can understand half of the words during a speech audiometry test; the SRT is measured and recorded for each ear.

Speechreading — Process of understanding a spoken message by observing the speaker's lips in combination with information gained from facial expressions, gestures, and the context or situation.

Spina bifida — A congenital malformation of the spine in which the vertebrae that normally protect the spine do not develop fully; may involve loss of sensation and severe muscle weakness in the lower part of the body.

Spina bifida occulta — A type of spina bifida that usually does not cause serious disability. Although the vertebrae do not close, there is no protrusion of the spinal cord and membranes.

Standard deviation — A descriptive statistic that shows the average amount of variability among a set of scores. A small standard deviation indicates the scores in the sample are distributed close to the mean; a larger standard deviation indicates more scores in the sample fall farther from the mean.

Stereotype — An overgeneralized or inaccurate attitude held toward all members of a particular group, on the basis of a common characteristic such as age, sex, race, or disability.

Stereotypic behavior (stereotypy) — Repetitive nonfunctional movements (e.g., hand flapping, rocking).

Stimulus control — Occurs when a behavior is emitted more often in the presence of a particular stimulus than it is in the absence of that stimulus.

Strabismus — A condition in which one eye cannot attain binocular vision with the other eye because of imbalanced muscles.

Stuttering — A complex fluency disorder of speech, affecting the smooth flow of words; may involve repetition of sounds or words, prolonged sounds, facial grimaces, muscle tension, and other physical behaviors.

Supported employment — Providing ongoing, individualized supports to persons with disabilities to help them find, learn, and maintain paid employment at regular work sites in the community.

Syntax — The system of rules governing the meaningful arrangement of words in a language.

Systematic replication — A strategy for extending and determining the generality of research findings by changing one or more variables from a previous study to see if similar results can be obtained. For example, testing a particular instructional method with elementary students that a previous study found effective with secondary students.

Task analysis — Breaking a complex skill or chain of behaviors into smaller, teachable units.

Tay-Sachs disease — A progressive nervous system disorder causing profound mental retardation, deafness, blindness, paralysis, and seizures. Usually fatal by age 5. Caused by a recessive gene; blood test can identify carrier; analysis of enzymes in fetal cells provides prenatal diagnosis.

Time trials — A fluency-building procedure in which a student performs a new skill as many times as he or she can during a short period of time; 1-minute time trials are effective for most academic skills.

Time-out — A behavior management technique that involves removing the opportunity for reinforcement for a specific period of time following an inappropriate behavior; results in a reduction of the inappropriate behavior.

Token economy (token reinforcement system) — An instructional and behavior management system in which students earn tokens (e.g., stars, points, poker chips) for performing specified behaviors. Students accumulate their tokens and turn then at prearranged times for their choice of activities or items from a "menu" of backup rewards (e.g., stickers, hall monitor for a day).

Topography (of behavior) — The physical shape or form of a response.

Total communication — An approach to educating deaf students that combines oral speech, sign language, and fingerspelling.

Tremor — A type of cerebral palsy characterized by regular, strong, uncontrolled movements. May cause less overall difficulty in movement than other types of cerebral palsy.

Triplegia — Paralysis of any three limbs; relatively rare.

Turner's syndrome — A sex chromosomal disorder in females, resulting from an absence of one of the X chromosomes; lack of secondary sex characteristics, sterility, and short stature are common. Although not usually a cause of mental retardation, it is often associated with learning problems.

Tymphonic membrane (eardrum) — Located in the middle ear, the eardrum moves in and out to variations in sound pressure, changing acoustical energy to sound energy.

Usher's syndrome — An inherited combination of visual and hearing impairments. Usually, the person is born with a profound hearing loss and loses vision gradually in adulthood because of retinitis pigmentosa, which affects the visual field.

Visual acuity — The ability to clearly distinguish forms or discriminate details at a specified distance.

Visual efficiency — A term used to describe how effectively a person uses his or her vision. Includes such factors as control of eye movements, near and distant visual acuity, and speed and quality of visual processing.

Vitreous humor — The jellylike fluid that fills most of the interior of the eyeball.

Vocational rehabilitation — A program designed to help adults with disabilities obtain and hold employment.

Work activity center — A sheltered work and activity program for adults with severe disabilities; teaches concentration and persistence, along with basic life skills, for little or no pay.

References

Aaronson, D. W., & Rosenberg, M. (1985). Asthma: General concepts. In R. Paterson (Ed.), *Allergic diseases: Diagnosis and management.* Philadelphia: J. B. Lippincott.

Abrams, B. J. (1992). Values clarification for students with emotional disabilities. *Teaching Exceptional Children, 24*(3), 28-33.

Achenbach, T. M. (1991). *The Child Behavior Checklist: Manual for the teacher's report form.* Burlington, VT: University of Vermont, Department of Psychiatry.

Ackerman, A. M., & Shapiro, E. S. (1984). Self-monitoring and work productivity with mentally retarded adults. *Journal of Applied Behavior Analysis, 17*, 403-407.

Ada, A. F. (1986). Creative education for bilingual teachers. *Harvard Educational Review, 56*, 386-394.

Adelman, S. H. (1992). LD: The next 25 years. *Journal of Learning Disabilities, 25, 17 ΩΩ.*

Affleck, J. Q., Madge, S., Adams, A., & Lowenbraun, S. (1988). Integrated classroom vs. resource model: Academic viability and effectiveness. *Exceptional Children, 54*, 339-348.

Agosta, J., Brown, L., & Melda, K. (1993). *Job coaching and community integrated employment: Present conditions and emerging directions.* Salem, OR: Human Services Research Institute.

Agran, M., & Moore, S. C. (1994). *How to teach self-instruction of job skills.* Washington, D.C.: American Association on Mental Retardation.

Agran, M., Fodor-Davis, J., Moore, S., & Deer, M. (1989). The application of a self-management program on instruction-following skills. *Journal of the Association of Persons with Severe Handicaps, 14*, 147-154.

Agran, M., Marchand-Martella, N. E., & Martella, R. C. (Eds.). (1994). *Promoting health and safety: Skills for independent living.* Pacific Grove, CA: Brooks/Cole.

Aiello, B. (1976, April 25). *Up from the basement: A teacher's story.* New York Times, p. 14.

Alabama Institute for the Deaf and Blind. (1989). *Helping kids soar.* Talladega, AL: Author.

Alber, M. B. (1974). *Listening: A curriculum guide for teachers of visually impaired students.* Springfield, IL: Illinois Office of Education.

Alberto, P. A., & Troutman, A. C. (1995). *Applied behavior analysis for teachers* (4th ed.). Englewood Cliffs, NJ: Merrill/Prentice Hall

Alberto, P., Jobes, N., Sizemore, A., & Doran, D. (1980). A comparison of individual and group instruction across response tasks. *Journal of Association for the Severely Handicapped, 5*, 285-293.

Alberto, P., Sharpton, W., Briggs, A., & Stright, M. (1986). Facilitating task acquisition through the use of a self-operated auditory prompting system. *The Journal of the Association of Persons with Severe Handicaps, 11*, 85-91.

Algozzine, B. (1980). The disturbing child: A matter of opinion. *Behavioral Disorders, 5*, 112-115.

Algozzine, B. (1993). Splitting hairs and loose ends: Answering special education's wake-up call. *The Journal of Special Education, 26*, 462-468.

Algozzine, B., & Korinek, L. (1985). Where is special education for students with high prevalence handicaps going? *Exceptional Children, 51*, 388-394.

Algozzine, B., & Ysseldyke, J. (1981). Special education services for normal children: Better safe than sorry? *Exceptional Children, 48*, 238-243.

Algozzine, B., & Ysseldyke, J. E. (1983). Learning disabilities as a subset of school failure: The over sophistication of a concept. *Exceptional Children, 50*, 242-246.

Allen, C. P., White, J., & Test, D. W. (1992). Using a picture/symbol form for self-monitoring within a community based training program. *Teaching Exceptional Children, 24*(2), 54-56.

Allen, D. A., & Affleck, G. (1985). Are we stereotyping parents? A postscript to Blacher. *Mental Retardation, 23*, 200-202.

Allen, J. I. (1980). Jogging can modify disruptive behaviors. *Teaching Exceptional Children, 12*(2), 66-70.

Allen, K. E. (1980a). The language impaired child in the preschool: The role of the teacher. *The Directive Teacher, 2*(3), 6-10.

Allen, K. E. (1980b). *Mainstreaming in early childhood education.* Albany, NY: Delmar Pubs.

Allen, T. (1986). Patterns of academic achievement among hearing impaired students: 1974 and 1983. In A. Schildroth & M. Karchmer (Eds.), *Deaf children in America* (pp. 161-206). San Diego: Little, Brown.

Alley, G., & Deshler, D. (1979). *Teaching the learning disabled adolescent: Strategies and methods.* Denver: Love.

Allsop, J. (1980). Mainstreaming physically handicapped students. *Journal of Research and Development in Education, 13*(4), 37-44.

Alpern, G., Boll, T., & Shearer, M. (1986). *The Developmental Profile-II.* Los Angeles, CA: Western Psychological Association.

Alpert, C. L., & Kaiser, A. P. (1992). Training parents as milieu language teachers. *Journal of Early Intervention, 16*, 31-52.

Alzate, G. (1978). Analysis of testing problems in Spanish speaking children. In A. H. Fink (Ed.), *International perspectives on future special education* (pp. 77-79). Reston, VA: Council for Exceptional Children.

Amado, A. N., Lakin, K. C., & Menke, J. M. (1990). *1990 chartbook of services for people with developmental disabilities.* Minneapolis: University of Minnesota, Center for Residential and Community Services.

Ambrose, S. A., Hazzard, A., & Haworth, J. (1980). Cognitive-behavioral parenting groups for abusive families. *Child Abuse and Neglect, 4*, 119-125.

American Academy of Ophthalmology. (1985). Health alert. Journal of Visual Impairment and Blindness, 79, 234.

American Association on Mental Deficiency. (1973). *Rights of mentally retarded persons: An official policy statement of the American Association on Mental Deficiency.* Washington, DC: Author.

American Council on Science and Health. (1979, May). *Diet and hyperactivity: Is there a relationship?* New York: Author.

American Psychological Association. (1994). *Violence and youth: Psychology's response.* Washington, DC. Author.

American Psychological Association. (1994, August). *Resolution on facilitated communication by the American Psychological Association.* Washington, DC: Author.

American Speech-Language-Hearing Association. (1982). *Definitions: Communicative disorders and variations.* Rockville, MD: Author.

American Speech-Language-Hearing Association. (1983). Position paper on social dialects. *ASHA, 25*(9), 23-24.

Ames, L. B. (1977). Learning disabilities: Time to check our road maps? *Journal of Learning Disabilities, 10*, 328-330.

Ammer, J. J., & Littleton, B. R. (1983, April). *Parent advocacy: Now more than ever, active involvement in education decisions.* Paper presented at the 61st Annual International Convention of the Council for Exceptional Children, Detroit, MI.

Anderegg, M. L., Vergason, G. A., & Smith, M. C. (1992). A visual representation of the grief cycle for use by teachers with families of children with disabilities. *Remedial and Special Education, 13*(2), 17-23.

Anderson-Inman, L. (1986). Bridging the gap: Student-centered strategies for promoting the transfer of learning. *Exceptional Children, 52*, 562-572.

Anderson-Inman, L., Walker, H. M., & Purcell, J. (1984). Promoting the transfer of skills across settings: Transenvironmental programming for handicapped students in the mainstream. In W. L. Heward, T. E. Heron, D. S. Hill, & J. Trap-Porter (Eds.), *Focus on Behavior Analysis in Education* (pp. 17-37). Englewood Cliffs, NJ: Merrill/Prentice Hall.

Andrews, J. F., & Gonzalez, K. (1992). Free writing of deaf children in kindergarten. *Sign Language Studies, 74*, 63-78.

Anthony, D. (1971). *Seeing Essential English.* Anaheim, CA: Anaheim School District.

Antonak, R. F., Fiedler, C. R., & Mulick, J. A. (1989). Misconceptions relating to mental retardation. *Mental Retardation, 27*, 91-97.

Antonak, R. F., Fiedler, C. R., & Mulick, J. A. (1993). A scale of attitudes toward the application of eugenics to the treatment of people with mental retardation. *Journal of Intellectual Disability Research. 37*, 75-83.

Apolloni, T., & Cooke, T. P. (Eds.). (1981). *California housing resources for persons with special developmental needs.* Unpublished manuscript, California Institute on Human Services at Sonoma State University.

Archambault Jr., F. X., Westberg, K. L., Brown, S. W., Hallmark, B. W., Zhang, W., & Emmons, C. L. (1993). Classroom practices used with gifted third and fourth grade students. *Journal for the Education of the Gifted, 16*, 103-119.

Armstrong v. Kline, 476 F. Supplement 583 (E.D. PA 1979).

Arnold, K. M., & Hornett, D. (1990). Teaching idioms to children who are deaf. *Teaching Exceptional Children, 22*(4), 14-17.

Arnold, L. E., Christopher, J., Huestis, R. D., & Smeltzer, D. J. (1978). Megavitamins

for minimal brain dysfunction: A placebo controlled study. *Journal of the American Medical Association, 240*, 2642-2643.

Arreaga-Mayer, C., Carta, J. J., & Tapia, Y. (1994). Ecobehavioral assessment of bilingual special education settings: The opportunity to respond. In R. Gardner III, D. M. Sainato, J. O. Cooper, T. E. Heron, W. L. Heward, J. Eshleman, & T. A. Grossi (Eds.), *Behavior analysis in education: Focus on measurably superior instruction* (pp. 225-239). Pacific Grove, CA: Brooks/Cole.

Artiles, A. J., & Trent, S. C. (1994). Overrepresentation of minority students in special education: A continuing debate. *The Journal of Special Education, 27*, 410-437.

Ashley, J. R., & Cates, D. L. (1992). Albinism: Educational techniques for parents and teachers. *RE:view, 24*, 127-131.

Atkins, B. J. (1992). Transition for individuals who are culturally divers. In F. R. Rusch, L. DeStefano, J. Chadsey-Rusch, L. Allen Phelps, & E. Szymanski (Eds.), *Transition from school to adult life* (pp. 443-457). Pacific Grove, CA: Brooks/Cole.

Atkins, C. P., & Cartwright, L. R. (1982). National survey: Preferred language elicitation procedures used in five age categories. *Journal of the American Speech and Hearing Association, 24*, 321-323.

Ault, M. J., Gast, D. L., Wolery, M., & Doyle, P. M. (1992). Data collection and graphing method. *Teaching Exceptional Children, 24*(2), 28-33.

Ault, M. M., Graff, J. C., & Rues, J. P. (1993). Physical management and handling procedures. In M. E. Snell, *Instruction of students with severe disabilities* (2nd ed.) (pp. 215-247). Englewood Cliffs, NJ: Merrill/Prentice Hall.

Ayres, A. J. (1972). *Sensory integration and learning disorders.* Los Angeles: Western Psychological Services.

Baca, L. M., & Cervantes, H. T. (1989). *The bilingual special education interface* (2nd ed.). Englewood Cliffs, NJ: Merrill/Prentice Hall.

Baer, D. M. (1981a). *How to plan for generalization.* Lawrence, KS: H & H Enterprises.

Baer, D. M. (1981b). A hung jury and a Scottish verdict: "Not proven." *Analysis and Intervention in Developmental Disabilities, 1*, 91-97.

Baer, D. M. (1984). We already have multiple jeopardy; why try for unending jeopardy? In W. L. Heward, T. E. Heron, D. S. Hill, & J. Trap-Porter (Eds.). *Focus on behavior analysis in education* (pp. 296-299). Englewood Cliffs, NJ: Merrill/Prentice Hall.

Baer, D. M., & Fowler, S. A. (1984). How should we measure the potential of self-control procedures for generalized educational outcomes? In W. L. Heward, T. E. Heron, D. S. Hill, & J. Trap-Porter (Eds.), *Focus on behavior analysis in education* (pp. 145-161). Englewood Cliffs, NJ: Merrill/Prentice Hall.

Baer, D. M., & Wolf, M. M. (1970). The entry into natural communities of reinforcement. In R. Ulrich, T. Stachnik, & J. Mabry (Eds.), *Control of human behavior* (Vol. 2, pp. 319-324). Glenview, IL: Scott Foresman.

Bagnato, S. J., Neisworth, J. T., & Capone, A. (1986). Curriculum-based assessment of the young exceptional child: Rationale and review. *Topics in Early Childhood Special Education, 6*, 97-110.

Bailey, D. B. (1989). Case management in early intervention. *Journal of Early Intervention, 13*, 120-134.

Bailey, D. B. (1994). Working with families of children with special needs. In M. Wolery & J. S. Wilbers (Eds.), *Including young children with special needs in early childhood programs*. Washington, DC: National Association for the Education of Young Children.

Bailey, D. B., & Bricker, D. D. (1985). Evaluation of a three-year early intervention demonstration project. *Topics in Early Childhood Special Education, 5*(2), 52-65.

Bailey, D. B., & Simeonsson, R. J. (1988a). *Family assessment in early intervention*. Englewood Cliffs, NJ: Merrill/Prentice Hall.

Bailey, D. B., & Simeonsson, R. J. (1988b). Home-based early intervention. In S. L. Odom & M. B. Karnes (Eds.), *Early intervention for infants & children with handicaps* (pp. 199-215). Baltimore, MD: Paul H. Brooks Publishing Company.

Bailey, D. B., & Wolery, M. (1984). *Teaching infants and preschoolers with handicaps*. Englewood Cliffs, NJ: Merrill/Prentice Hall.

Bailey, D. B., & Wolery, M. (1989). *Assessing infants and preschoolers with handicaps*. Englewood Cliffs, NJ: Merrill/Prentice Hall.

Bailey, D. B., & Wolery, M. (1992). *Teaching infants and preschoolers with disabilities* (2nd ed.). Englewood Cliffs, NJ: Merrill/Prentice Hall.

Bailey, D. B., Winton, P. J., Rouse, L., & Turnbull, A. P. (1990). Family goals in infant

intervention: Analysis and issues. *Journal of Early Intervention, 14*, 15-26.

Bailey, Jr., D. B., Buysse, V., Edmondson, R., & Smith, T. M. (1992). Creating family-centered services in early intervention: Perceptions of professionals in four states. *Exceptional Children, 58*, 298-309.

Bailey, Jr., D. B., Palsha, S. A., & Simeonsson, R. J. (1991). Professional skills, concerns, and perceived importance of work with families in early intervention. *Exceptional Children, 58*, 156-165.

Bailey, J. S. (1992). Gentle teaching: Trying to win friends and influence people with euphemism, metaphor, smoke, and mirrors. *Journal of Applied Behavior Analysis, 25*, 879-883.

Baker, B. L. (1989). *Parent training and developmental disabilities*. Washington, DC: American Association on Mental Retardation.

Baker, B. L., & Brightman, A. J. (1989). *Steps to independence: A skills training guide for parents and teachers of children with special needs*. Baltimore, MD: Paul H. Brooks Publishing Company.

Baker, L., & Lombardi, B. R. (1985). Students' lecture notes and their relation to test performance. *Teaching of Psychology, 12*, 28-32.

Baldwin, V. (1991). Understanding the deaf-blind census. *TRACES Newsletter, 1*(2), 1-4.

Ball, E. & Harry, B. (1993). Multicultural education and special education: Parallels, divergences, and intersections. *Educational Forum, 57*, 430-436.

Balow, I. H., Farr, R., Hogan, T. P., & Prescott, G. A. (1978). *Metropolitan Achievement Tests: 1978 edition*. New York: Psychological Corp.

Bambara, L. M., & Ager, C. (1992). Using self-scheduling to promote self-directed leisure activity in home and community settings. *Journal of the Association for Persons with Severe Handicaps, 17*, 67-76.

Banbury, M. M., & Herbert, C. R. (1992). Do you see what I mean? *Teaching Exceptional Children, 24*(2), 34-38.

Banks, J. A. (1989). Multicultural education: Characteristics and goals. In J. A. Banks & C. A. Banks (Eds.), *Multicultural education: Issues and perspectives* (pp. 2-26). Boston, MA: Allyn & Bacon.

Banks, J. A. (1993). Multicultural education: Characteristics and goals. In J. A. Banks & C. A. M. Banks (Eds.), *Multicultural education: Issues and perspectives* (2nd. ed.) (pp. 3-28). Boston: Allyn & Bacon.

Banks, J.A. (1994a). *An introduction to multicultural education*. Boston: Allyn and Bacon.

Banks, J.A. (1994b). *Multiethnic education: Theory and practice* (3rd ed.). Boston: Allyn and Bacon.

Banks, J. A., & Banks, C. A. (Eds.). (1993). *Multicultural education: Issues and perspectives* (2nd ed.). Boston, MA: Allyn & Bacon.

Bankson, N. W. (1982). The speech and language impaired. In E. L. Meyen (Ed.), *Exceptional children and youth* (2nd ed.). Denver: Love.

Bannerman, D. J., Sheldon, J. B., Sherman, J. A., & Harchik, A. E. (1990). Balancing the right to habilitation with the right to personal liberties: The rights of people with developmental disabilities to eat too many doughnuts and take a nap. *Journal of Applied Behavior Analysis, 23*, 79-89.

Barber, D., & Hupp, S. C. (1993). A comparison of friendship patterns of individuals with developmental disabilities. *Education and Training in Mental Retardation, 28*, 13-22.

Barbetta, P. M. (1990a). GOALS: A group-oriented adapted levels system for children with behavior disorders. *Academic Therapy, 25*, 645-656.

Barbetta, P. M. (1990b). Red light-green light: A classwide management system for students with behavior disorders in the primary grades. *Preventing School Failure, 34*(4), 14-19.

Barbetta, P. M. (1991, February). Personal communication.

Barbetta, P. M., & Heron, T. E. (1991). Project SHINE: Summer home instruction and evaluation. *Intervention in School and Clinic, 26*, 276-281.

Barbetta, P. M., & Heward, W. L. (1993). Effects of active student response during error correction on the acquisition and maintenance of geography facts by elementary students with learning disabilities. *Journal of Behavioral Education, 3*, 217-233.

Barbetta, P. M., Heron, T. E., & Heward, W. L. (1993). Effects of active student response during error correction on the acquisition, maintenance, and generalization of sight words by students with developmental disabilities. *Journal of Applied Behavior Analysis, 26*, 111-119.

Barbetta, P. M., Heward, W. L., & Bradley, D. M. C. (1993). Relative effects of whole-word and phonetic error correction on the acquisition and maintenance of sight words by students with developmental disabilities. *Journal of Applied Behavior Analysis, 26*, 99-110.

Barbetta, P. M., Heward, W. L., Bradley, D. M. C., & Miller, A. D. (1994). Effects of immediate and delayed error correction on the acquisition and maintenance of sight words by students with developmental disabilities. *Journal of Applied Behavior Analysis, 27*, 177-178.

Barnes, D. M. (1986). Brain function decline in children with AIDS. *Science, 232*, 1196.

Barnett, H. (1989). What teachers should know about their classroom learners. *Foreign Language Annals, 22*, 199-201.

Barnett, W. S. (1986). Definition and classification of mental retardation: A reply to Zigler, Balla, and Hodapp. *American Journal of Mental Deficiency, 91*, 111-116.

Barney, L. G., & Landis, C. L. (1987). Development differences in communication. In J. T. Neisworth & S. J. Bagnato, (Eds.), *The young exceptional child: Early development and education* (pp. 262-296). Englewood Cliffs, NJ: Merrill/Prentice Hall.

Barr, M. W. (1913). *Mental defectives: Their history, treatment, and training.* Philadelphia: Blakiston.

Barraga, N. C. (1964). *Increased visual behavior in low vision children.* New York: American Foundation for the Blind.

Barraga, N. C. (1970). *Teacher's guide for development of visual learning abilities and utilization of low vision.* Louisville, KY: American Printing House for the Blind.

Barraga, N. C. (1980). *Source book on low vision.* Louisville, KY: American Printing House for the Blind.

Barraga, N. C. (1983). *Visual handicaps and learning* (rev. ed.). Austin, TX: Exceptional Resources.

Barrera, I. (1993). Effective and appropriate instruction for all children: The challenge of cultural/linguistic diversity and young children with special needs. *Topics in Early Childhood Special Education, 13*, 461-487.

Barton, L. E., & LaGrow, S. J. (1985). Reduction of stereotypic responding in three visually impaired children. *Education of the Visually Handicapped, 6*, 145-181.

Batshaw, M. L., & Perret, Y. M. (1992). *Children with disabilities: A medical primer* (3rd ed.). Baltimore, MD: Paul H. Brooks Publishing Company.

Bauer, M. S., & Balius Jr., F. A. (1995). Storytelling. *Teaching Exceptional Children, 27*(2), 24-28.

Baumgart, D., & Askvig, B. (1992). Job-related social skills interventions: Suggestions from managers and employees. *Education and Training in Mental Retardation, 27*, 345-353.

Baumgart, D., Brown, L., Pumpian, I., Nisbet, J., Ford, A., Sweet, M., Messina, R., & Schroeder, J. (1982). Principle of partial participation and individualized adaptations in educational programs for severely handicapped students. *Journal of the Association for the Severely Handicapped, 7*, 17-27.

Baumgart, D., Johnson, J., & Helmstetter, E. (1990). *Augmentative and alternative communication systems for persons with moderate and severe disabilities.* Baltimore, MD: Paul H. Brooks Publishing Company.

Bayley, N. (1969). *Bayley Scales of Infant Development.* New York: Psychological Corporation.

Beare, P. L. (1991). Philosophy, instructional methodology, training, and goals of teachers of teachers of the behaviorally disordered. *Behavioral Disorders, 16*, 211-218.

Beatty, L., Madden, R., & Gardner, E. (1966). *Stanford Diagnostic Arithmetic Test.* New York: Harcourt Brace Jovanovich.

Beck, J., Broers, J., Hogue, E., Shipstead, J., & Knowlton, E. (1994). Strategies for functional community-based instruction and inclusion for children with mental retardation. *Teaching Exceptional Children, 26*(2), 44-48.

Becker, W. C. (1964). Consequences of different kinds of parental discipline. In M. L. Hoffman & L. W. Hoffman (Eds.), *Review of child development research* (Vol. 1) (pp. 169-208). New York: Russell Sage Foundation.

Becker, W. C. (1971). *Parents are teachers.* Champaign, IL: Research Press.

Becker, W. C. (1992). Direct Instruction: A twenty-year review. In R. P. West & L. A. Hamerlunck (Eds.), *Designs for excellence in education* (pp. 71-112). Longmont, CA: Sopris West.

Becker, W. C., Engelmann, S., & Thomas, D. R. (1971). *Teaching: A course in applied psychology.* Chicago: Science Research Associates.

Beirne-Smith, M., Patton, J. R., & Ittenbach, R. (1994). *Mental retardation* (4th ed.). Englewood Cliffs, NJ: Merrill/Prentice Hall.

Belcastro, F. P. (1989). Use of Belcastro Rods to teach mathematical concepts to blind students. *RE:view, 21*, 71-79.

Belfiore, P. J., & Toro-Zambrana, W. (1994). *Recognizing significant choices in com-munity settings by people with significant disabilities.* Washington, D.C.: American Association on Mental Retardation.

Bellamy, G. T., & Horner, R. H. (1987). Beyond high school: Residential and employment options after graduation. In M. Snell (Ed.), *Systematic instruction of persons with severe handicaps* (3rd ed.) (pp. 491-510). Englewood Cliffs, NJ: Merrill/Prentice Hall.

Bellamy, G. T., & Wilcox, B. (1982). Secondary education for severely handicapped students: Guidelines for quality services. In K. P. Lynch, W. E. Kiernan, & J. A. Stark (Eds.), *Prevocational and vocational education for special needs youth: A blueprint for the 1980s.* Baltimore, MD: Paul H. Brooks Publishing Company.

Bellamy, G. T., Horner, R. H., & Inman, D. (1979). *Vocational training of severely retarded adults.* Baltimore, MD: Paul H. Brooks Publishing Company.

Bellamy, G. T., Rhodes, L. E., Mank, D. M., & Albin, J. M. (1988). *Supported employment: A community implementation guide.* Baltimore, MD: Paul H. Brookes.

Bellamy, G. T., Rhodes, L. E., Wilcox, B., Albin, J. M., Mank, D. M., Boles, S. M., Horner, R. H., Collins, M., & Turner, J. (1984). Quality and equality in employment services for adults with severe disabilities. *The Journal of The Association for Persons with Severe Handicaps, 9*, 270-277.

Benjamin, L. T. (1990). Leta Stetter Hollingsworth: Psychologist, educator, feminist. *Roeper Review, 12*(3), 145-150.

Benjamin, S. (1989). An ideascape for education: What futurists recommend. *Educational Leadership, 47*, 8-14.

Bennett, C. I., (1990). *Comprehensive multicultural education; Theory and practice.* Needham Heights, MA: Allyn & Bacon.

Bennett, L. M., & Hensen, F. O. (1977). *Keeping in touch with parents: The teacher's best friend.* Hingham, MA: Teaching Resources.

Bennett, R. E., & Ragosta, M. (1984). *A research context for studying admission tests and handicapped populations.* Princeton, NJ: Educational Testing Service.

Bennett, W. J. (1986). *First lessons: A report on elementary education in America.* Washington, DC: U.S. Department of Education.

Bensberg, G. J., & Sigelman, C. K. (1976). Definitions and prevalence. In L. L. Lloyd (Ed.), *Communication assess-*

ment and intervention strategies. Baltimore, MD: University Park Press.

Bensky, J., Shaw, S., Gouse, A., Bates, H., Dixon, B., & Beane, W. (1980). Public Law 94-142 and stress: A problem for educators. *Exceptional Children, 47*, 24-29.

Bercovici, S. M. (1983). *Barriers to normalization: The restrictive management of retarded persons.* Austin, TX: PRO-ED.

Berg, F. S. (1986). Characteristics of the target population. In F. S. Berg, J. C. Blair, S. H. Viehweg, & A. Wilson-Vlotman, *Educational audiology for the hard of hearing child* (pp. 1-24). Orlando, FL: Grune & Stratton.

Bergstrom, T., Pattavina, S., Martella, R. C., & Marchand-Martella, N. E. (in press). A number- and color-coded microwave oven and recipe cards for successful meal preparation. *Teaching Exceptional Children.*

Berman, J. L., & Ford, R. (1970). Intelligence quotients and intelligence loss in patients with phenylketonuria and some variant states. *Journal of Pediatrics, 77*, 764-770.

Bernabe, E. A., & Block, M. E. (1994). Modifying rules of a regular girls softball league to facilitate the inclusion of a child with severe disabilities. *Journal of the Association for Persons with Severe Handicaps, 19*, 24-31.

Bernthal, J. E., & Bankson, N. W. (1986). Phonologic disorders: An overview. In J. M. Costello & A. L. Holland (Eds.), *Handbook of speech and language disorders* (pp. 3-24). San Diego: College-Hill.

Betts, G. (1985). *The autonomous learner model.* Greeley, CO: Autonomous Learning Publications Specialists.

Betts, G. T. (1986). The autonomous learner model for the gifted and talented. In J. S. Renzulli (Ed.), *Systems and models for developing programs for the gifted and talented* (pp. 27-56). Mansfield Center, CT: Creative Learning Press.

Beukelman, D. (1988, November). Personal communication with S. Blackstone, Editor of Augmentative Communication News.

Bigge, J. L. (1991). *Teaching individuals with physical and multiple disabilities* (3rd ed.). Englewood Cliffs, NJ: Merrill/Prentice Hall.

Bigler, E. D. (Ed.). (1990). *Traumatic brain injury: Mechanisms of damage, assessment, intervention and outcome.* Austin, TX: PRO-ED.

Bijou, S. W. (1966). A functional analysis of retarded development. In N. R. Ellis

(Ed.), *International review of research in mental retardation* (Vol. 1). New York: Academic Press.

Bijou, S. W., & Dunitz-Johnson, E. (1981). Interbehavior analysis of developmental disabilities. *Psychological Record, 31*, 305-329.

Biklen, D. (1985). *Achieving the complete school: Strategies for effective mainstreaming.* New York: Teachers College Press.

Biklen, D. (1988). The myth of clinical judgment. *Journal of Social Issues, 44*, 127-140.

Biklen, D. (1990). Communication unbound: Autism and praxis. *Harvard Educational Review, 60*, 291-314.

Biklen, D. (1992). Typing to talk: Facilitated communication. *American Journal of Speech Language Pathology, 1*(2), 15-17.

Biklen, D. (1993). *Communication unbound: How facilitated communication is challenging traditional views of autism and ability-disability.* New York: Teachers College Press.

Biklen, D., & Bogdan, R. (1976). *Handicapism in America.* Syracuse, NY: WIN.

Bilken, D., & Zollers, N. (1986). The focus of advocacy in the LD field. *Journal of Learning Disabilities, 19*, 579-586.

Billingsley, F. F., & Kelley, B. (1994). An examination of the acceptability of instructional practices for students with severe disabilities in general education settings. *Journal of the Association for Persons with Severe Handicaps, 19*, 75-83.

Billingsley, F. F., Liberty, K. A., & White, O. R. (1994). The technology of instruction. In E. C. Cipani & F. Spooner (Eds.), *Curricular and instructional approaches for persons with severe disabilities* (pp. 81-116). Boston: Allyn & Bacon.

Bireley, M. (1995). The special characteristics and needs of gifted students with disabilities. In Genshaft, J. L., Bireley, M., & Hollinger, C. L. (Eds.). *Serving gifted and talented students: A resource for school personnel* (pp. 201-215). Austin, TX: PRO-ED.

Birenbaum, A. (1986). Symposium overview: Community programs for people with mental retardation. *Mental Retardation, 24*, 145-146.

Bishop, V. E. (1986). Identifying the components of successful mainstreaming. *Journal of Visual Impairment and Blindness, 80*, 939-946.

Blacher, J. (1984). A dynamic perspective on the impact of a severely handicapped child on the family. In J. Blacher (Ed.), *Severely handicapped children and*

their families (p. 3-50). Orlando, FL: Academic Press.

Blackburn, A. C., & Erickson, D. D. (1986). Predictable crises of the gifted student. *Journal of Counseling and Development, 64*, 552-555.

Blackburn, J. A. (1987). Cerebral palsy. In M. L. Wolraich (Ed.), *The practical assessment and management of children with disorders of development and learning.* Chicago: Yearbook Publishers.

Blackorby, J., Edgar, E., & Kortering, L. J. (1991). A third of our youth? A look at the problem of high school dropout among students with mild handicaps. *The Journal of Special Education, 25*, 102-113.

Blackstone, M. (1981). How parents can affect communitization, or, what do you mean I'm a troublemaker? In C. H. Hansen (Ed.), *Severely handicapped persons in the community* (pp. 29-52). Seattle: University of Washington, PDAS.

Blackstone, S. W. (Eds.). (1989). *Augmentative communication: Implementation strategies.* Rockville, MD: American Speech-Language-Hearing Association.

Blackstone, S. W., Cassatt-James, E. L., & Bruskin, D. M. (1988). *Augmentative communication implementation strategies.* Rockville, MD: American Speech-Language-Hearing Association.

Blair, J., Peterson, M., & Viehweg, S. (1985). The effects of mild hearing loss on academic performance of young school-age children. *Volta Review, 87*, 87-93.

Blalock, G. (1991). Paraprofessionals: Critical team members in our special education programs. *Intervention in School and Clinic, 26*(4), 200-214.

Blank, M. (1988). Classroom text: The next state of intervention. In R. L. Schiefelbusch & L. L. Lloyd (Eds.), *Language perspectives: Acquisition, retardation and intervention* (pp. 367-392). Austin, TX: PRO-ED.

Blatt, B. (1976). *Revolt of the idiots: A story.* Glen Ridge, NJ: Exceptional Press.

Blatt, B. (1987). *The conquest of mental retardation.* Austin, TX: PRO-ED.

Blatt, B., & Kaplan, F. (1966). *Christmas in purgatory: A photographic essay on mental retardation.* Boston: Allyn & Bacon.

Bleck, E. E. (1979). Integrating the physically handicapped child. *Journal of School Health, 49*, 141-146.

Bleck, E. E. (1987). *Orthopedic management of cerebral palsy—Clinics in developmental medicine No. 99/100.* Philadelphia: J. B. Lippincott.

Bledsoe, C. W. (1993). Dr. Samuel Gridley Howe and the family tree of residential schools. *Journal of Visual Impairment & Blindness, 87,* 174-176.

Bley, N. S., & Thornton, C. A. (1994). *Teaching mathematics to students with learning disabilities* (3rd ed.). Austin, TX: PRO-ED.

Blick, D. W., & Test, D. W. (1987). Effects of self-recording on high school students' on-task behavior. *Learning Disability Quarterly, 10,* 203-213.

Block, M. E., & Moon, M. S. (1992). Orelove, Wehman, and Wood revisited: An evaluative review of Special Olympics ten years later. *Education and Training in Mental Retardation, 27,* 379-386.

Bloom, L., & Lahey, M. (1978). *Language development and language disorders.* New York: John Wiley & Sons.

Board of Education of the Hendrick Hudson Central School District v. Rowley, 102 S. Ct. 3034 (1982).

Bogdan, R. (1986). Exhibiting mentally retarded people for amusement and profit, 1850-1940. *American Journal of Mental Deficiency, 91,* 120-126.

Book, D., Paul, T. L., Gwalla-Ogisi, N., & Test, D. W. (1990). No more bologna sandwiches. *Teaching Exceptional Children, 22*(2), 62-64.

Boone, D. R. (1977). Our profession: Where are we? *Journal of the American Speech and Hearing Association, 19,* 3-6.

Boone, R. S. (1992). Involving culturally diverse parents in transition planning. *Career Development for Exceptional Individuals, 15,* 205-221.

Bormaster, J. S., & Treat, C. L. (1994). *Building interpersonal relationships through talking, listening, communicating* (2nd ed.). Austin, TX: PRO-ED.

Borthwick, C., Morton, M., Crossley, R., & Biklen, D. (1992). Facilitated communication and disclosures of abuse. *Facilitated Communication Digest, 1*(1), 5-6.

Borthwick-Duffy, S. (1994). Review of mental retardation: Definition, causes, and systems of supports. *American Journal on Mental Retardation, 98,* 541-544.

Borthwick-Duffy, S. A., Widaman, K. F., Little, T. D., & Eyman, R. K. (1992). *Foster family care for persons with mental retardation.* Washington, DC: American Association On Mental Retardation.

Boshes, B., & Myklebust, H. R. (1964). A neurological and behavioral study of children with learning disorders. *Neurology, 14,* 7-12.

Bostow, D. E., & Bailey, J. (1969). Modification of severe disruptive and aggressive behavior using brief time-out and rein-forcement procedures. *Journal of Applied Behavior Analysis, 2,* 31-37.

Bower, E. M. (1960). *Early identification of emotionally handicapped children in the schools.* Springfield, IL: Charles C. Thomas.

Bower, E. M. (1981). *Early identification of emotionally handicapped children in school* (3rd ed.). Springfield, IL: Charles C. Thomas.

Bower, E. M. (1982). Defining emotional disturbance: Public policy and research. *Psychology in the Schools, 19,* 55-60.

Bower, E. M., & Lambert, N. M. (1962). *A process for in-school screening of children with emotional handicaps.* Princeton, NJ: Education Testing Service.

Braaten, S., Kauffman, J. M., Braaten, B., Polsgrove, L., & Nelson, C. M. (1988). The Regular Education Initiative (REI): Patent medicine for behavioral disorders. *Exceptional Children, 55,* 21-27.

Braddock, D., & Heller, T. (1985). The closure of mental retardation institutions II: Implications. *Mental Retardation, 23,* 222-229.

Braddock, D., & Mitchell, D.. (1992). *Residential services and developmental disabilities in the United States.* Washington, DC: American Association On Mental Retardation.

Braden, J. P., Maller, S. J., & Paquin, M. M. (1993). The effects of residential versus day placement on the performance IQs of children with hearing impairment. *The Journal of Special Education, 26,* 423-433.

Bradley, R. H., & Caldwell, B. M. (1979). Home observation for measurement of the environment: A revision of the preschool scale. *American Journal of mental Deficiency, 84,* 235-244.

Bradley, V. J. Knoll, J., & J. M. Agosta, J. M. (Eds.) (1992). *Emerging Issues in Family Support.* Washington, DC: American Association on Mental Retardation.

Bradley-Johnson, S., & Harris, S. (1990). Best practices in working with students with a visual loss. In A. Thomas & J. Grimes (Eds.), *Best practices in school psychology-II* (pp. 871-885). Washington, DC: National Association of School Psychologists.

Brady, M. P., Linehan, S. A., Neilson, W. L., & Campbell, P. C. (1992). Too high, too low, too young: An ethnography of teachers' curriculum and instruction decisions for students with severe disabilities. *Education and Training in Mental Retardation, 27,* 354-366.

Brandt, J. (1992). *Idea Bunny: Teaching special needs preschool children inde-pendent work skills with an audio prompt recording device.* Unpublished Masters Thesis, The Ohio State University, Columbus, Ohio.

Brandwein, H. (1973). The battered child: A definite and significant factor in mental retardation. *Mental Retardation, 11,* 50-51.

Brantliner, E. A., & Guskin, S. L. (1985). Implications of social and cultural differences for special education with specific recommendations. *Focus on Exceptional Children, 18,* 1-12.

Brazelton, T. B. (1973). *Neonatal Assessment Scale.* Philadelphia: J. B. Lippincott.

Bredekamp, S. (1993). The relationship between early childhood education and early childhood special education: Healthy marriage or family feud? *Topics in Early Childhood Special Education, 13,* 258-273.

Bredekamp, S., & Rosegrant, T. (Eds.). (1992). *Reaching potentials: Appropriate curriculum and assessment for young children* (Vol. 1). Washington, DC: National Association for the Education of Young Children.

Bricker, D. D. (1986). An analysis of early intervention programs: Attendant issues and future directions. In R. J. Morris & B. Blatt (Eds.), *Special education: Research and trends* (pp. 28-65). New York: Pergamon Press.

Bricker, D. D., Bailey, E. J., & Slentz, K. (1990). Reliability, validity, and utility of the Evaluation and Programming System: For Infants and Young Children (EPS-I). *Journal of Early Intervention, 14,* 147-158.

Bricker, D. D., Gentry, D., & Bailey, E. J. (1985). *The Evaluation and Programming System: For Infants and Young Children. Assessment level I: Developmentally 1 month to 3 years.* Eugene, OR: University of Oregon.

Brickey, M. P., Campbell, K. M., & Browning, L. J. (1985). A five-year follow-up of sheltered workshop employees placed in competitive jobs. *Mental Retardation, 23,* 67-73.

Brigance, A. (1982). *K & 1 screen for kindergarten and first grade.* N. Billerica, MA: Curriculum Associates.

Brigance, A. (1983). *BRIGANCE Diagnostic Inventory of Basic Skills.* N. Billerica, MA: Curriculum Associates.

Briggs, A., Alberto, P., Sharpton, W., Berlin, K., McKinley, C.,& Ritts, C. (1990). Generalized use of a self-operated audio prompt system. *Education and Training in Mental Retardation, 25,* 381-389.

Briggs, S. J. (1991). The multilingual/multicultural classroom. *Kappa Delta Pi Record*, *28*, 11-14.

Brinker, R. P. (1985). Interactions between severely mentally retarded students and other students in integrated and segregated public school settings. *American Journal of Mental Deficiency*, *89*, 587-594.

Brinkerhoff, L. C., Shaw, S. F., & McGuire, J. M. (1993). *Promoting postsecondary education for students with learning disabilities*. Austin, TX: PRO-ED.

Bristor, V. J. (1987). "But I'm not a teacher." *Academic Therapy*, *23*, 23-27.

Brolin, D. E. (1993). *Life-centered career education* (4th ed.). Reston, VA: Council for Exceptional Children.

Brolin, D. E. (1995). *Career education: A functional life skills approach* (3rd ed.). Englewood Cliffs, NJ: Merrill/Prentice Hall.

Bronicki, G. J., & Turnbull, A. P. (1987). Family-professional interactions. In M. E. Snell (Ed.), *Systematic instruction of persons with severe handicaps* (3rd ed.) (pp. 9-35). Englewood Cliffs, NJ: Merrill/Prentice Hall.

Bronston, W. (1980). Matters of design. In T. Apolloni, J. Cappuccilli, & T. P. Cooke (Eds.), *Achievements in residential services for persons with disabilities: Toward excellence*. Baltimore, MD: University Park Press.

Brophy, J. (1986). Teacher influences on student achievement. *American Psychologist*, *41*, 1069-1077.

Brophy, J., & Good, T. (1986). Teacher behavior and student achievement. In M. C. Wittrock (Ed.), *Handbook on research on teaching (3rd ed.)* (pp. 328-375). Englewood Cliffs, NJ: Merrill/Prentice Hall.

Browder, D. M. (1991). *Assessment of individuals with severe disabilities: An applied behavior approach to life skills assessment* (2nd. ed.). Baltimore, MD: Paul H. Brooks Publishing Company.

Browder, D. M., & Snell, M. E. (1993). Daily living and community skills. In M. E. Snell, *Instruction of students with severe disabilities* (4th ed.) (pp. 588-607). Englewood Cliffs, NJ: Merrill/Prentice Hall.

Browder, D. M., & Snell, M. E. (1993). Functional academics. In M. E. Snell, *Instruction of persons with severe disabilities* (4th ed.) (pp. 442-479). Englewood Cliffs, NJ: Merrill/Prentice Hall.

Browder, D. M., Lim, L., Lin, C. H., & Belfiore, P. J. (1993). Applying therbligs to task analytic instruction: A technology

to pursue? *Education and Training in Mental Retardation*, *28*, 242-251.

Browder, D., Lentz, F. E., Knoster, T., & Wilansky, C. (1988). Determining extended school year eligibility: From esoteric to explicit criteria. *The Journal of The Association for Persons with Severe Handicaps*, *13*, 235-243.

Brower, I. C. (1983). Counseling Vietnamese. IN D. R. Atkinson, G. Morten, & D. W. Sue (Eds.), *Counseling American minorities* (2nd ed.) (pp. 107-121). Dubuque, IA: Wm. C. Brown.

Brown v. Board of Education of Topeka. (1954). 347 U.S. 483.

Brown, D., & Moore, L. (1992). The Bama Bookworm Program. *Teaching Exceptional Children*, *24*(4), 17-20.

Brown, F. (1987). Meaningful assessment of people with severe and profound handicaps. In M. E. Snell (Ed.), *Systematic instruction of persons with severe handicaps* (3rd ed.) (pp. 39-63). Englewood Cliffs, NJ: Merrill/Prentice Hall.

Brown, F., & Lehr, D. H. (1993). Making activities meaningful for students with severe multiple disabilities. *Teaching Exceptional Children*, *25*(4), 12-16.

Brown, F., Holvoet, J., Guess, G., & Milligan, M. (1980). The individualized curriculum sequencing model (III): Small group instruction. *Journal of Association for the Severely Handicapped*, *5*, 352-367.

Brown, J. R. (1982). Assessment of the culturally different and disadvantaged child. In G. Ulrey & S. J. Rogers (Eds.), *Psychological assessment of handicapped infants and young children* (pp. 163-171). New York: Thieme-Stratton.

Brown, L. (1990). Who are they and what do they want? An essay on TASH. *TASH Newsletter*, *16*(9), 1.

Brown, L., Branston-McClean, M. B., Baumgart, D., Vincent, L., Falvey, M., & Shroeder, J. (1979). Using the characteristics of current and subsequent least restrictive environments in the development of curricular content for severely handicapped students. *AAESPH Review*, *4*, 407-424.

Brown, L., Ford, A., Nisbet, J., Sweet, M., Donnellan, A., & Gruenewald, L. (1983). Opportunities available when severely handicapped students attend chronological age appropriate regular schools. *Journal of The Association for Persons With Severe Handicaps*, *8*, 16-24.

Brown, L., Long, E., Udvari-Solner, A., Davis, L., VanDeventer, P., Ahlgren, C., Johnson, F., Gruenewald, L., & Jorgensen, J. (1989a). The home school: Why stu-

dents with severe disabilities must attend the schools of their brothers, sisters, friends, and neighbors. *The Journal of The Association for Persons with Severe Handicaps*, *14*, 1-7.

Brown, L., Long, E., Udvari-Solner, A., Davis, L., VanDeventer, P., Ahlgren, C., Johnson, F., Gruenewald, L., & Jorgensen, J. (1989b). Should students with severe intellectual disabilities be based in regular or in special education classrooms in home schools? *The Journal of The Association for Persons with Severe Handicaps*, *14*, 8-12.

Brown, L., Schwartz, P., Udvari-Solner, A., Kampschroer, E. F., Johnson, F., Jorgensen, J., & Gruenewald, L. (1991). How much time should students with severe intellectual disabilities spend in regular education classrooms and elsewhere? *Journal of the Association for Persons with Severe Handicaps*, *16*, 39-47.

Brown, L., Shiraga, B., York, J., Kessler, K., Strohm, B., Rogan, P., Sweet, M., Zanella, K., VanDeventer, P., & Loomis, R. (1984). Integrated work opportunities for adults with severe handicaps: The extended training option. *The Journal of The Association for Persons with Severe Handicaps*, *9*, 262-269.

Brown, S. C. (1986). Etiological trends, characteristics, and distributions. In A. N. Schildroth & M. A. Karchmer (Eds.), *Deaf children in America* (pp. 33-54). San Diego: College-Hill.

Brown, W., Thurman, S. K., & Pearl, L. W. (1993). *Family-centered intervention with infants and toddlers: Innovative cross-disciplinary approaches*. Baltimore, MD: Paul H. Brookes Publishing Company.

Bryan, T. H., & Bryan, J. H. (1978). Social interactions of learning disabled children. *Learning Disability Quarterly*, *1*, 107-115.

Bryan, W. H., & Jeffrey, D. L. (1982). Education of visually handicapped students in the regular classroom. *Texas Tech Journal of Education*, *9*, 125-131.

Buchanan, L., & Kochar, C. (1989). *The right to a free & appropriate public education (for some?): The case of Timothy vs. Rochester School District* (Policy Briefs in Special Education, Paper No. 1). Washington, DC: The George Washington University, School of Education and Human Development.

Bull, G. L., & Rushakoff, G. E. (1987). Computers and speech and language disordered individuals. In J. D. Lindsey (Ed.), *Computers and exceptional individuals* (pp. 83-104). Englewood Cliffs, NJ: Merrill/Prentice Hall.

Bullis, M., & Bull, B. (1986). *Review of research on adolescents and adults with deaf-blindness.* Washington, DC: Catholic University of America, DATA Institute.

Bullis, M., & Gaylord-Ross, R. (1991). *Moving on: Transitions for youth with behavioral disorders.* Reston, VA: Council for Exceptional Children.

Bullis, M., & Otos, M. (1988). Characteristics of programs for children with deaf-blindness: Results of a national survey. *The Journal of The Association for Persons with Severe Handicaps, 13,* 110-115.

Bullivant B. M. (1993). Culture: Its nature and meaning for educators. In J. A. Banks & C. A. M. Banks (Eds.), *Multicultural education: Issues and perspectives* (2nd. ed.) (pp. 29-47). Boston: Allyn & Bacon.

Burchard, S. N., Hasazi, J. S., Gordon, L. R., & Yoe, J. (1991). An examination of lifestyle and adjustment in three community residential alternatives. *Research in Developmental Disabilities, 12,* 127-142.

Burd, L., & Martsolf, J. T. (1989). Fetal alcohol syndrome: Diagnosis and syndrome variability. *Physiology & Behavior, 46,* 39-43.

Burgess, D. M., & Steissguth, A. P. (1992). Fetal alcohol syndrome and fetal alcohol effects: Principles for educators. *Phi Delta Kappan, 74,* 24-29.

Burkhardt, L. J. (1981). *Homemade battery powered toys and educational devices for severely disabled children.* Millville, PA: Burkhardt.

Burstein, N. D. (1986). The effects of classroom organization on mainstreamed preschool children. *Exceptional Children, 52,* 525-534.

Bushell, Jr., D. Baer, D. M. (1994). Measurably superior instruction means close, continual contact with the relevant outcome data. Revolutionary! In R. Gardner III, D. M. Sainato, J. O. Cooper, T. E. Heron, W. L. Heward, J. Eshleman, & T. A. Grossi (Eds.), *Behavior analysis in education: Focus on measurably superior instruction* (pp. 3-10). Pacific Grove, CA: Brooks/Cole.

Butler, C. (1988). High tech tots: Technology for mobility, manipulation, communication, and learning in early childhood. *Infants and Young Children, 1,* 66-73.

Buysse, V., & Bailey, Jr., D. B. (1993). Behavioral and developmental outcomes in young children with disabilities in integrated and segregated settings: A review of comparative studies. *The Journal of Special Education, 26,* 434-461.

Byers, J. (1989). AIDS in children: Effects on neurological development and implications for the future. *The Journal of Special Education, 23,* 5-16.

Calculator, S. N., & Jorgensen, C. M. (1991). Integrating augmentative and alternative communication instruction into regular education settings: Expounding on best practices. *Augmentative and Alternative Communication, 7,* 204-214.

Calhoun, M. L., & Calhoun, L. G. (1993). Age-appropriate activities: Effects on the social perception of adults with mental retardation. *Education and Training in Mental Retardation, 28,* 143-148.

Calkins, L. M. (1994). *The art of teaching writing* (2nd ed.) Portsmouth, NH: Heinemann.

Callahan, C. M., & Caldwell, M. S. (1993). Establishment of a national data bank on identification and evaluation instruments. *Journal for the Education of the Gifted, 16,* 201-219.

Callister, J. P., Mitchell, L., & Talley, G. (1986). Profiling family preservation efforts in Utah. *Children Today, 15,* 23-25, 36-37.

Calvert, D. R. (1986). Speech in perspective. In D. M. Luterman (Ed.), *Deafness in perspective* (pp. 167-191). San Diego: College-Hill.

Campbell, C., Campbell, S., Collicott, J., Perner, D., & Stone, J. (1988). Individualized instruction. *Education New Brunswick—Journal Education, 3,* 17-20.

Campbell, P. H. (1993). Physical management and handling procedures. In M. E. Snell, *Instruction of students with severe disabilities* (4th ed.) (pp. 248-263). Englewood Cliffs, NJ: Merrill/Prentice Hall.

Campbell, V., Smith, R., & Wool, R. (1982). Adaptive Behavior Scale differences in scores of mentally retarded individuals referred for institutionalization and those never referred. *American Journal of Mental Deficiency, 86,* 425-428.

Caputo, R. A. (1993). Using puppets with students with emotional and behavioral disorders. *Intervention in School and Clinic, 29,* 26-30.

Carlberg, C., & Kavale, K. (1980). the efficacy of special versus regular class placement for exceptional children: A meta-analysis. *The Journal of Special Education, 14,* 295-305.

Carmichael Olson, H. (1994). The effects of prenatal alcohol exposure on child development. *Infants and Young Children, 6(3),* 10-25.

Carnine, D. (1976). Effects of two teacher presentation rates on off-task behavior, answering correctly, and participation. *Journal of Applied Behavior Analysis, 9,* 199-206.

Carnine, D. W. (1980). Phonics versus whole-word correction procedures following phonic instruction. *Education and Treatment of Children, 3* (4), 323-330.

Carnine, D., & Kameenui, E. J. (1992). *Higher order thinking: Designing curriculum for mainstreamed students.* Austin, TX: PRO-ED.

Carr, E. G., & Durand, V. M. (1985). Reducing behavior problems through functional communication training. *Journal of Applied Behavior Analysis, 18,* 111-126.

Carr, E. G., Levin, L., McConnachie, G., Carlson, J. I., Kemp, D. C., & Smith, C. E. (1994). *Communication-based intervention for problem behavior: A user's guide for producing positive change.* Baltimore, MD: Paul H. Brookes Publishing Company.

Carr, M. N. (1993). A mother's thoughts on inclusion. *Journal of Learning Disabilities, 26,* 590-592.

Carrier, C. A. (1983). Notetaking research: Implications for the classroom. *Journal of Instructional Development, 6(3),* 19-25.

Carroll, M. E., Burnworth, C., Chambers, J., Cousino, D., Mahaney, P., & Trent, D. (1991). Classroom companies: The buck starts here. *Intervention in School and Clinic, 27(2),* 97-100.

Carta, J. J., Atwater, J. B., Schwartz, I. S., & McConnell, S. R. (1993). Developmentally appropriate practices and early childhood special education: A reaction to Johnson and McChesney Johnson. *Topics in Early Childhood Special Education, 13,* 243-254.

Carta, J. J., Atwater, J. B., Schwartz, I. S., & Miller, P. A. (1990). Applications of ecobehavioral analysis to the study of transitions across early education settings. *Education and Treatment of Children, 13,* 298-315.

Carter, J. F. (1993). Self-management. Education's ultimate goal. *Teaching Exceptional Children, 25(3),* 28-32.

Carter, J., & Sugai, G. (1989). Survey on prereferral practices: Responses from state departments of education. *Exceptional Children, 55,* 298-302.

Cartledge, G., & Cochran, L. L. (1993). Developing cooperative learning behavior in students with behavior disorders. *Preventing School Failure, 37,* 5-10.

Cartledge, G., & Milburn, J. F. (1995). *Teaching social skills to children and youth: Innovative approaches* (3rd ed.). Boston: Allyn and Bacon.

Case, L. P., Harris, K. R., & Graham, S. (1992). Improving the mathematical problem-solving skills of students with learning disabilities: Self-regulated strategy development. *The Journal of Special Education, 26,* 1-19.

Casto, G. (1988). Research and program evaluation in early childhood special education. In S. L. Odom & M. B. Karnes (Eds.), *Early intervention for infants & children with handicaps* (pp. 51-62). Baltimore, MD: Paul H. Brooks Publishing Company.

Casto, G., & Mastropieri, M. A. (1986). The efficacy of early intervention programs: A meta-analysis. *Exceptional Children, 52,* 417-424.

Cavan, R. S., & Ferdinand, T. N. (1975). *Juvenile delinquency* (3rd ed.). New York: J. B. Lippincott.

Cavanaugh, R. A. (1990). "I don't have any homework, and even if I did I don't remember what it was." *American Secondary Education, 19* (1) 2–8.

Cavanaugh, R. A., Heward, W. L., & Donelson, F. (1995). *Comparative effects of teacher-presented verbal review and active student response during lesson closure on the academic performance of high school students in an earth science course.* Manuscript submitted for publication review.

Center on Human Policy. (1986, December). Positive interventions for challenging behavior. *The Association for Persons with Severe Handicaps Newsletter 12(12), 4*

Center, D. B. (1990). Social maladjustment: An interpretation. *Behavioral Disorders, 15,* 141-148.

Chadsey-Rusch, J., Drasgow, E., Reinoehl, B., Halle, J., & Collet-Klingenberg, L. (1993). Using general-case instruction to teach spontaneous and generalized requests for assistance to learners with severe disabilities. *Journal of the Association for Persons with Severe Handicaps, 18,* 177-187.

Chaikind, S., Danielson, L. C., & Brauen, M. L. (1993). What do we know about the costs of special education? A selected review. *The Journal of Special Education, 26,* 344-370.

Chalfant, J. C., & Pysh, M. V. D. (1989). Teacher assistance teams: Five descriptive studies on 96 teams. *Remedial and Special Education, 10*(6), 49-58.

Chalifoux, L. M. (1991). Macular degeneration: an overview. *Journal of Visual Impairment & Blindness, 85,* 249-250.

Chandler, L. K. (1993). Steps in preparing for transition: Preschool to kindergarten. *Teaching Exceptional Children, 25*(4), 52-55.

Chaney, C., & Frodyma, D. A. (1982). A noncategorical program for preschool language development. *Teaching Exceptional Children, 14,* 152-155.

Charney, E. B. (1992). Neural tube defects: Spina bifida and myelomeningocele. In M. L. Batshaw & Y. M. Perret, *Children with disabilities: A medical primer* (3rd ed.) (pp. 471-488). Baltimore, MD: Paul H. Brooks Publishing Company.

Chase, J. B. (1986a). Application of assessment techniques to the totally blind. In P. J. Lazarus & S. S. Strichart (Eds.), *Psychoeducational evaluation of children and adolescents with low-incidence handicaps* (pp. 75-102). Orlando, FL: Grune & Stratton.

Chase, J. B. (1986b). Psychoeducational assessment of visually-impaired learners. In P. J. Lazarus & S. S. Strichart (Eds.), *Psychoeducational evaluation of children and adolescents with low-incidence handicaps* (pp. 41-74). Orlando, FL: Grune & Stratton.

Chesapeake Institute. (1994, September). *National Agenda for Achieving better Results for Children and Youth with Serious Emotional Disturbance.* Washington, DC: U.S. Department of Education.

Chinn, P. C., & Hughes, S. (1987). Representation of minority students in special education classes. *Remedial and Special Education, 8,* 41-46.

Chinn, P. C., & Kamp, S. H. (1982). Cultural diversity and exceptionality. In N. G. Haring (Ed.), *Exceptional children and youth* (3rd ed.) (pp. 371-390). Englewood Cliffs, NJ: Merrill/Prentice Hall.

Chinn, P. C., & McCormick, L. (1986). Cultural diversity and exceptionality. In N. G. Haring & L. McCormick (Eds.), *Exceptional children and youth* (4th ed.) (pp. 95-117). Englewood Cliffs, NJ: Merrill/Prentice Hall.

Christensen, C. M. (1992). Multicultural competencies in early intervention: Training professionals for a pluralistic society. *Infants and Young Children, 4,* 49-83.

Christenson, S. L., Ysseldyke, J. E., & Thurlow, M. L. (1989). Critical instructional factors for students with mild handicaps:

An integrative interview. *Remedial and Special Education, 10,* (5), 21-23.

Cipani, E. C., & Spooner, F. (Eds.). (1994). *Curricular and instructional approaches for persons with severe disabilities.* Boston: Allyn & Bacon.

Clarizio, H. F. (1990). Assessing severity in behavior disorders: Empirically based criteria. *Psychology in the Schools, 27*(1), 5-15.

Clark, B. (1986). The integrative education model. In J. S. Renzulli (Ed.), *Systems and models for developing programs for the gifted and talented* (pp. 57-91). Mansfield Center, CT: Creative Learning Press.

Clark, B. (1992). *Growing up gifted: Developing the potential of children at home and at school* (4th ed.). Englewood Cliffs, NJ: Merrill/Prentice Hall.

Clark, G. M. (1994). Is a functional curriculum approach compatible with an inclusive education model? *Teaching Exceptional Children, 26*(2), 36-39.

Clark, G. M., & Kolstoe, O. P. (1995). *Career development and transition education for adolescents with disabilities* (2nd ed.). Needham Heights, MA: Allyn & Bacon.

Clark, G. M., Carlson, B. C., Fisher, S., Cook, I. D., & D'Alonzo, B. J. (1991). Career development for students with disabilities in elementary schools: A position statement of the division on career development. *Career Development for Exceptional Individuals, 14,* 109-120.

Clark, L. A., & McKenzie, H. S. (1989). Effects of self-evaluation training of seriously emotionally disturbed children on the generalization of their classroom rule following and work behaviors across settings and teachers. *Behavioral Disorders, 14,* 89-98.

Clark, L., DeWolf, S., & Clark, C. (1992). Teaching teachers to avoid having culturally assaultive classrooms. *Young Children, 47,* (5), 4-9.

Clarke, B., & Leslie, P. (1980). Environmental alternatives for the hearing handicapped. In J. W. Schifani, R. M. Anderson, & S. J. Odle (Eds.), *Implementing learning in the least restrictive environment: Handicapped children in the mainstream* (pp. 199-240). Baltimore, MD: University Park Press.

Clarke, K. L. (1988). Barriers or enablers? Mobility devices for visually impaired and multihandicapped infants and preschoolers. *Education of the Visually Handicapped, 20,* 115-132.

Clarke, K. L., Sainato, D. M., & Ward, M. E. (1994). Travel performance of preschoolers: The effects of mobility training with a long cane versus a pre-cane. *Journal of Visual Impairment & Blindness, 88,* 19-30.

Clausen, J. A. (1967). Mental deficiency: Development of a concept. *American Journal of Mental Deficiency, 71,* 727-745.

Clausen, J. A. (1972). The continuing problem of defining mental deficiency. *The Journal of Special Education, 6,* 97-106.

Clearinghouse for Offender Literacy Programs. (1975). *Literacy: Problems and solutions: A handbook for correctional educators.* Washington, DC: American Bar Association.

Cleeland, L. K. (1984). The function of the auditory system in speech and language development. In R. K. Hull & K. I. Dilka (Eds.), *The hearing-impaired child in school* (pp. 7-17). Orlando, FL: Grune & Stratton.

Clements, S. D. (1966). Minimal brain dysfunction in children *(NINDS Monograph No. 3, Public Health Service Bulletin No. 1415).* Washington, DC: U.S. Department of Health, Education and Welfare.

Cline, D. H. (1990). Interpretations of emotional disturbance and social maladjustment as policy problems: A legal analysis of initiatives to exclude handicapped/disruptive students from special education. *Behavioral Disorders, 15,* 159-173.

Cochran, L., Feng, H., Cartledge, G., & Hamilton, S. (1993). The effects of cross-age tutoring on the academic achievement, social behaviors, and self-perceptions of low-achieving African-American males with behavioral disorders. *Behavioral Disorders, 18,* 292-302.

Cochran, W. E., Sran, P. K., & Varano, G. A. (1977). The relocation syndrome in mentally retarded individuals. *Mental Retardation, 15,* 10-12.

Coffman, T. L., & Harris, M. C. (1980). Transition shock and adjustments of mentally retarded persons. *Mental Retardation, 18,* 28-32.

Cohen, L. H. (1994). *Train go sorry: Inside a deaf world.* Boston: Houghton Mifflin.

Cohen, S. B., & deBettencourt, L. V. (1991). Dropout: Intervening with the reluctant learner. *Intervention in School and Clinic, 26*(5), 263-271.

Cohen, S., Agosta, J., Cohen, J., & Warren, R. (1989). Supporting families of children with severe disabilities. *The Journal of The Association for Persons with Severe Handicaps, 14,* 155-162.

Cole, D. A., & Meyer, L. H. (1991). Social integration and severe disabilities: A lon-gitudinal analysis of child outcomes. *The Journal of Special Education, 25,* 340-351.

Cole, E. B., & Paterson, M. M. (1986). Assessment and treatment of phonologic disorders. In J. M. Costello & A. L. Holland (Eds.), *Handbook of speech and language disorders* (pp. 93-127). San Diego: College-Hill.

Coleman, J. M., & Dover, G. M. (1989). *Rating inventory for screening kindergartners.* Austin, TX: PRO-ED.

Coleman, J. M., & Dover, G. M. (1993). The RISK screening test: Using kindergarten teachers' ratings to predict future placement in resource classrooms. *Exceptional Children, 59,* 468-477.

Coleman, J. M., & Minnett, A. M. (1993). Learning disabilities and social competence: A social ecological perspective. *Exceptional Children, 59,* 234-246.

Coleman, M., & Webber, J. (1988). Behavior problems? Try groups! *Academic Therapy, 23,* 265-274.

Collicott, J. (1991). Implementing multi-level instruction: Strategies for classroom teachers. In G. Porter & D. Richler (Eds.). *Changing Canadian schools: Perspectives on disability and inclusion* (pp. 191-218). Ottawa, Ontario, Canada: The Roeher Institute.

Colson, S. E., & Carlson, J. K. (1993). HIV/AIDS education for students with special needs. *Intervention in School and Clinic, 28,* 262-274.

Colvin, G., Sugai, G., & Patching, B. (1993). Precorrection: An instructional approach for managing predictable problem behaviors. *Intervention in School and Clinic, 28,* 143-150.

Commission on Education of the Deaf. (1988). *Toward equality: Education of the deaf, a report to the President and the Congress of the United States, February.* Washington, DC: U.S. Government Printing Office.

Commission on Education of the Deaf. (1988). *Toward equality: Education of the deaf.* Washington, D.C.: U.S. Government Printing Office.

Compton, M. V., & Niemeyer, J. A. (1994). Expressions of affection in young children with sensory impairments: A research agenda. *Education and Treatment of Children, 17,* 68-85.

Condon, M. E., York, R., Heal, L. W., & Fortschneider, J. (1986). Acceptance of severely handicapped students by non-handicapped peers. *The Journal of The Association for Persons with Severe Handicaps, 11,* 216-219.

Cone, A. A. (1994). Reflections on "Self-advocacy: Voices for choices." *Mental Retardation, 32,* 444-445.

Cone, J. D., Delawyer, D. D., & Wolfe, V. V. (1985). Assessing parent participation: The Parent/Family Involvement Index. *Exceptional Children, 51,* 417-424.

Cone, T. E., Wilson, L. R., Bradley, C. M., & Reese, J. H. (1985). Characteristics of LD students in Iowa: An empirical investigation. *Learning Disability Quarterly, 8,* 211-220.

Conners, F. A. (1992). Reading instruction for students with moderate mental retardation: Review and analysis of research. *American Journal on Mental Retardation, 96,* 577-597.

Connolly, A., Natchman, W., & Pritchett, E. (1973). *KeyMath Diagnostic Arithmetic Test.* Circle Pines, MN: American Guidance Service.

Connor, L. E. (1986). Oralism in perspective. In D. M. Luterman (Ed.), *Deafness in perspective* (pp. 116-129). San Diego: College-Hill.

Connors, C. K., Goyette, C., Southwick, D., Lees, J., & Andrulonis, P. (1976). Food additives and hyperkinesis: A controlled double blind study. *Pediatrics, 58,* 154-166.

Conroy, J. W., & Bradley, V. J. (1985). *The Pennhurst longitudinal study: A report on five years of research and analysis.* Philadelphia: Temple University Developmental Disabilities Center.

Conte, R., & Andrews, J. (1993). Social skills in the context of learning disability definitions: A reply to Gresham and Elliott and directions for the future. *Journal of Learning Disabilities, 26,* 146-153.

Cook, P. S., & Woodhill, J. M. (1976). The Feingold dietary treatment of the hyperkinetic syndrome. *Medical Journal of Australia, 2,* 85-90.

Cook, R. E., Tessier, A., & Klein, M. D. (1992). *Adapting early childhood curricula for children with special needs* (3rd ed.). Englewood Cliffs, NJ: Merrill/Prentice Hall.

Cooke, N. L., Heron, T. E., & Heward, W. L. (1983). *Peer tutoring: Implementing classwide programs in the primary grades.* Columbus, OH: Special Press.

Cooke, N. L., Heron, T. E., Heward, W. L., & Test, D. W. (1982). Integrating a Down syndrome student into a classwide peer tutoring system. *Mental Retardation, 20,* 22-25.

Cooke, N. L., Heward, W. L., Test, D. W., Spooner, F., & Courson, F. H. (1991). Student performance data in the special education classroom: Measurement and evaluation of student progress. *Teacher Education and Special Education, 13,* 155-161.

Cooke, T. P. (1981). Your place or mine? Residential options for people with developmental disabilities. In C. L. Hansen (Ed.), *Severely handicapped persons in the community* (pp. 103-145). Seattle: University of Washington PDAS.

Cooper, J. O., Heron, T. E., & Heward, W. L. (1987). *Applied behavior analysis.* Englewood Cliffs, NJ: Merrill/Prentice Hall.

Cooper, L. J., Peck, S., Wacker, D. P., & Millard, T. (1993). Functional assessment for a student with a mild mental disability and persistent behavior problems. *Teaching Exceptional Children, 25*(3), 56-57.

Corn, A. L. (1986). Low vision and visual efficiency. In G. T. Scholl (Ed.), *Foundations of education for blind and visually handicapped children and youth: Theory and practice* (pp. 99-117). New York: American Foundation for the Blind.

Corn, A. L. (1989). Instruction in the use of vision for children and adults with low vision: A proposed program model. *RE:view, 21,* 26-38.

Corn, A., & Ryser, G. (1989). Access to print for students with low vision. *Journal of Visual Impairment and Blindness, 83,* 340-349.

Cornett, R. O. (1974). What is cued speech? *Gallaudet Today, 5*(2), 3-5.

Correa, V. I. (1989). Involving culturally diverse families in the education of their limited English proficient handicapped and at risk children. In S. Fradd & M. J. Weismantel (Eds.), *Meeting the needs of culturally and linguistically different students: A handbook for educators* (pp. 130-144). San Diego: College-Hill Press.

Correa, V. I. (1989). Involving culturally diverse families in the education of their limited English proficient handicapped and at-risk children. In S. Fradd & M. J. Weismantel (Eds.), *Bilingual special education: An administrator's handbook* (pp. 130-144). San Diego, CA: College-Hill Press.

Correa, V. I. (1992). Cultural accessibility of services for culturally diverse clients with disabilities and their families. *Rural Special Education Quarterly, 7,* 6-12.

Correa, V. I., Blanes-Reyes, M., & Rapport, M. J. (1995). Minority issues. In (Eds.) H. R. Turnbull & A. P. Turnbull, *A compendium report to Congress.* Council for Disabilities, Lawrence, KS: Beach Center.

Correa, V. I., Gollery, T., & Fradd, S.. (1988). The handicapped undocumented alien student dilemma: Do we advocate or abdicate? *Journal of Educational Issues of Language Minority Students, 3,* 41-47.

Cott, A. (1972). Megavitamins: The orthomolecular approach to behavioral disorders and learning disabilities. *Academic Therapy, 7,* 245-258.

Coulter, D. L. (1994). Biomedical conditions: Types, causes, and results. In L. Sternberg (Ed.). *Individuals with profound disabilities: Instructional and assistive strategies* (3rd ed.) (pp. 41-58). Austin, TX: PRO-ED.

Council for Children with Behavior Disorders. (1987). Position paper on definition and identification of students with behavioral disorders. *Behavioral Disorders, 12,* 9-19.

Council for Children with Behavior Disorders. (1989). Best assessment practices for students with behavioral disorders: Accommodation to cultural diversity and individual differences. *Behavioral Disorders, 14,* 263-278.

Council for Learning Disabilities. (1986). Use of discrepancy formulas in the identification of learning disabled individuals. *Learning Disabilities Quarterly, 9,* 245.

Council for Learning Disabilities (1993). Concerns about the full inclusion of students with learning disabilities in regular education classrooms. *Journal of Learning Disabilities, 26,* 595.

Courson, F. H. (1989). *Comparative effects of short- and long-form guided notes on social studies performance by seventh grade learning disabled and at-risk students.* Unpublished doctoral dissertation. Columbus, OH: The Ohio State University.

Courson, F. H., & Heward, W. L. (1988). Increasing active student response through the effective use of paraprofessionals. *The Pointer, 33*(1), 27-31.

Couture, B. J. (1994, April). *The card connection.* Paper presented at the Annual Convention of the Council for Exceptional Children, Denver, CO.

Cox, B. G., & Ramirez, M., III. (1981). Cognitive styles: Implications for multiethnic education. In J. A. Banks (Ed.), *Education in the 80's: Multiethnic education* (pp. 61-71). Washington, DC: National Education Association.

Crank, J. N., & Bulgren, J. A. (1993). Visual depictions as information organizers for enhancing achievement of students with learning disabilities. *Learning Disabilities Research & Practice, 8,* 140-147.

Creaghead, N. A., Newman, P. W., & Secord, W. (1989). *Assessment and remediation of articulatory and phonological disorders* (2nd. ed.). Englewood Cliffs, NJ: Merrill/Prentice Hall.

Cremins, J. J. (1983). *Legal and political issues in special education.* Springfield, IL: Charles C. Thomas.

Cronin, M. E., Slade, D. L., Bechtel, C., & Anderson, P. (1992). Home-school partnerships: A cooperative approach to intervention. *Intervention in School and Clinic, 27,* 286-292.

Crossley, R. (1988). *Unexpected communication attainments by persons diagnosed as autistic and intellectually impaired.* Caulfield, Victoria: Deal Communication Centre.

Crossley, R., & Remington-Guerney, J. (1992). Getting the words out: Facilitated communication training. *Topics in Language Disorders, 12*(4), 29-45.

Cruickshank, W. M. (1986). *Disputable decisions in special education.* Ann Arbor, MI: University of Michigan Press.

Cullinan, D., Epstein, M. H., & Kauffman, J. M. (1984). Teachers' ratings of students behaviors: What constitutes behavior disorders in schools? *Behavioral Disorders, 10,* 9-19.

Cullinan, D., Epstein, M. H., & Lloyd, J. W. (1991). Evaluation of conceptual models of behavior disorders. *Behavioral Disorders, 16,* 148-157.

Cullinan, D., Epstein, M. H., & Sabornie, E. J. (1992). Selected characteristics of a national sample of seriously emotionally disturbed adolescents. *Behavioral Disorders, 17,* 273-280.

Culton, G. L. (1986). Speech disorders among college freshmen: A 13-year survey. *Journal of Speech and Hearing Disorders, 51,* 3-7.

Cummins, J. (1989). A theoretical framework for bilingual special education. *Exceptional Children, 56,* 111-119.

Curl, R. M. (1990). A demonstration project for teaching entry-level job skills: The Co-worker Transition Model for Youths with Disabilities. *Exceptional News, 13*(3), 3-7.

Curl, R. M., Lignugaris/Kraft, B., Pawley, J. M., & Salzberg, C. L. (1988). *"What's next?" A quantitative and qualitative analysis of the transition for trainee to valued worker.* Manuscript submitted for publication.

Curran, B. E. (1983). *Effects of one-to-one and small-group instruction on incidental learning by moderately/severely handicapped adults.* Unpublished master's thesis. Ohio State University, Columbus, OH.

Curran, J. J., & Algozzine, B. (1980). Ecological disturbance: A test of the matching hypothesis. *Behavioral Disorders, 5,* 159-174.

Currie, W. (1981). Teacher preparation for a pluralistic society. In J. A. Banks (Ed.), *Education in the 80's: Multiethnic education* (pp. 162-174). Washington, DC: National Education Association.

Curry, S., & Hatlen, P. (1988). Meeting the unique educational needs of visually impaired pupils through appropriate placement. *Journal of Visual Impairment and Blindness, 82,* 417-424.

Cusher, K., McClelland, A., & Safford, P. (1992). *Human diversity in education.* New York: McGraw-Hill.

Cusick, B. (1991). Therapeutic management of sensorimotor and physical disabilities. In J. L. Bigge, *Teaching individuals with multiple and physical disabilities* (3rd ed.) (pp. 16-49). Englewood Cliffs, NJ: Merrill/Prentice Hall.

Cutler, B. C. (1993). *You, your child, and "special" education: A guide to making the system work.* Baltimore, MD: Paul H. Brookes Publishing Company.

D'Amico, R. (1991). The working world awaits. In M. Wagner, L. Newman, R. D'Amico, E. D. Jay, P. Butler-Nalin, C. Marder, & R. Cox (Eds.). *Youth with disabilities: How are they doing? A comprehensive report from wave 1 of the National Longitudinal Transition Study of special education students.* Menlo Park, CA: SRI International.

D'Angelo, K. (1981). Wordless picture books and the young language-disabled child. *Teaching Exceptional Children, 14,* 34-37.

Dale, D. M. C. (1984). *Individualized integration: Studies of deaf and partially-hearing children and students in ordinary schools and colleges.* London: Hodder & Stoughton.

Dalrymple, A. J., & Feldman, M. A. (1992). Effects of reinforced directed rehearsal on expressive sign language learning by persons with mental retardation. *Journal of Behavioral Education, 2,* 1-16.

Dangle, R. F., & Polster, R. A. (Eds.). (1984). *Parent training: Foundations of research and practice.* New York: Guilford Press.

Dardig, J. C. (1981). Helping teachers integrate handicapped students into the regular classroom. *Educational Horizons, 59,* 124-130.

Dardig, J. C., & Heward, W. L. (1981). A systematic procedure for prioritizing IEP goals. *The Directive Teacher, 3,* 6-8.

Darrow, M. A., & Clark, G. M. (1992). Cross-state comparisons of former special education students: Evaluation of a follow-along model. *Career Development for Exceptional Individuals, 15,* 83-99.

Datillo, J., & Mirenda, P. (1987). An application of a leisure preference assessment protocol for persons with severe handicaps. *The Journal of The Association for Persons with Severe Handicaps, 12,* 306-311.

Davila, R. R., Williams, M. L., & MacDonald, J. T. (1991, September 16). *Clarification of policy to address the needs of children with attention deficit disorders within general and/or special education.* Washington, DC: Office of Special Education and Rehabilitation Services, U.S. Department of Education.

Davis, C. A., Brady, M. P., Williams, R. E., & Burta, M. (1992). The effects of self-operated auditory prompting tapes on the performance fluency of persons with severe mental retardation. *Education and Training in Mental Retardation, 27,* 39-50.

Davis, G. & Rimm, S. (1989). *Education of the gifted and talented* (2nd ed.). Englewood Cliffs, NJ: Merrill/Prentice-Hall.

Davis, H., & Silverman, S. R. (Eds.). (1970). *Hearing and deafness* (3rd ed.). New York: Holt, Rinehart & Winston.

Davis, H., & Silverman, S. R. (1978). *Hearing and deafness* (4th ed.). New York: Holt, Rinehart & Winston.

Davis, J. M. (1986). Academic placement in perspective. In D. M. Luterman (Ed.), *Deafness in perspective* (pp. 205-224). San Diego: College-Hill.

De La Rosa, D., & Maw, C. (1990). *Hispanic education: A statistical portrait 1990.* Washington, DC: National Council of La Raza. (ERIC Document Reproduction Services No. 325 562)

DeAvila, E. (1976). Mainstreaming ethnically and linguistically different children: An exercise in paradox or a new approach? In R. I. Jones (Ed.), *Mainstreaming and the minority child* (pp. 93-108). Reston, VA: Council for Exceptional Children.

deBettencourt, L., Zigmond, N., & Thornton, H. (1989). Follow-up of postsecondary-age rural learning disabled graduates and dropouts. *Exceptional Children, 56,* 40-49.

DeLeon, J. (1989). Cognitive style differences and the underrepresentation of Mexican-Americans in programs for the gifted. *Journal for the Education of the Gifted, 19*(3), 52-53.

Delisle, J. (1992). *Social and emotional needs of the gifted.* Boston: Longman.

Delquadri, J., Greenwood, C. R., Whorton, D., Carta, J. J., & Hall, R. V. (1986). Class-wide peer tutoring. *Exceptional Children, 52,* 535-542.

Demchak, M. A. (1994). Helping individuals with severe disabilities find leisure activities. *Teaching Exceptional Children, 27,* 48-52.

Dennis, R. E., Williams, W., Giangreco, M. F., & Cloninger, C. J. (1993). Quality of life as context for planning and evaluation of services for people with disabilities. *Exceptional Children, 53,* 499-512.

Dent, N. E. (1976). Assessing black children for mainstream placement. In R. L. Jones (Ed.), *Mainstreaming and the minority child* (pp. 77-91). Reston, VA: Council for Exceptional Children.

Denton, D. M. (1972, August 18). *A philosophical foundation for total communication.* Paper presented at the Indiana School for the Deaf, Preschool Parent Conference, Indianapolis.

Deshler, D. D., Schumaker, J. B., & Lenz, B. K. (1984). Academic and cognitive interventions for LD adolescents: Part I. *Journal of Learning Disabilities, 17,* 108-117.

DeStefano, L., & Wermuth, T. R. (1992). IDEA (PL 101-476): Defining a second generation of transition services. In F. R. Rusch, L. DeStefano, J. Chadsey-Rusch, L. Allen Phelps, & E. Szymanski (Eds.), *Transition from school to adult life* (pp. 537-549). Pacific Grove, CA: Brooks/Cole.

Dever, R. B. (1989). A taxonomy of community living skills. *Exceptional Children, 55,* 395-404.

Dever, R. B. (1990). Defining mental retardation from an instructional perspective. *Mental Retardation, 28,* 147-153.

Diamond, K. E., & Squires, J. (1993). The role of parental report in the screening and assessment of young children. *Journal of Early Intervention, 17,* 107-115.

Diem, R., & Katims, D. S. (1991). Handicaps and at risk: Preparing teachers for a growing populace. *Intervention in School and Clinic, 26*(5), 272-275.

DiFrancesca, S. (1972). *Academic achievement test results of a national testing program for hearing-impaired students* (Series D, No. 9). Washington, DC: Gallaudet University, Center for Assessment and Demographic Studies.

DiGiandomenico, J., & Carey, M. L. (1988). Special approaches for special needs. *Foreign Language News Notes, 4,* 1-2.

Division for Early Childhood. (1993). *DEC Recommended Practices.* Reston, VA: Council for Exceptional Children, Division for Early Childhood.

Division for Learning Disabilities of the Council for Exceptional Children.

(1993). *Inclusion: What does it mean for students with learning disabilities?* Reston, VA: Author.

Divoky, D. (1978). Can diet cure the LD child? *Learning, 3,* 56-57.

Dixon, M. E., & Rossi, J. C. (1995). A reading strategy for students with learning disabilities. *Teaching Exceptional Children, 27*(2), 11-14.

Dobelle, W. H. (1977). Current status of research on providing sight to the blind by electrical stimulation of the brain. *Journal of Visual Impairment and Blindness, 71,* 290-297.

Dodge, K. (1993). The future of research on conduct disorder. *Development and Psychopathology, 5*(1/2), 311-320.

Doernberg, N. L. (1978). Some negative effects on family integration of health and educational services for young handicapped children. *Rehabilitation Literature, 39,* 107-110.

Doll, E. A. (1941). The essentials of an inclusive concept of mental deficiency. *American Journal of Mental Deficiency, 46,* 214-219.

Doll, E. A. (1965). *Vineland Social Maturity Scale.* Circle Pines, MN: American Guidance Service.

Donnellan, A. (1984). The criterion of the least dangerous assumption. *Behavioral Disorders, 9,* 141-150.

Donnellan, A. M., & Mirenda, P. L. (1984). Issues related to professional involvement with families of individuals with autism and other severe handicaps. *The Journal of The Association for Persons with Severe Handicaps, 9,* 6-24.

Downing, J., & Bailey, B. (1990). Developing vision use within functional daily activities for students with visual and multiple disabilities. *RE:view, 21,* 209-221.

Downing, J., & Eichinger, J. (1990). Instructional strategies for learners with dual sensory impairments in integrated settings. *The Journal of The Association for Persons with Severe Handicaps, 15,* 98-105.

Doyle, P. M., Gast, D. L., Wolery, M., Ault, M. J., & Farmer, J. A. (1990). Use of constant time delay in small group instruction: A study of observational and incidental learning. *Journal of Special Education, 23,* 369-385.

Doyle, P. M., Wolery, M., Ault, M. J., & Gast, D. L. (1988). System of least prompts: A literature review of procedural parameters. *The Journal of The Association for Persons with Severe Handicaps, 13,* 28-40.

Drabman, R. S., Spitalnik, R., & O'Leary, K. D. (1973). Teaching self-control to disruptive children. *Journal of Abnormal Psychology, 82,* 10-16.

Dratner, Minor, Addicott, & Sunderland, 1971 p. 417.

Drevno, G. E., Kimball, J. W., Possi, M. K., Heward, W. L., Gardner III, R., & Barbetta, P. M. (1994). Effects of active student response during error correction on the acquisition, maintenance, and generalization of science vocabulary by elementary students: A systematic replication. *Journal of Applied Behavior Analysis, 27,* 179-180.

Dryfoos, J. G. (1994). *Full-service schools.* San Francisco: Jossey-Bass Inc., Publications.

DuBose, R. F. (1981). Assessment of severely impaired young children: Problems and recommendations. *Topics in Early Childhood Special Education, 1,* 9-12.

Dudley-Marling, C. C., & Edmiaston, R. (1985). Social status of learning disabled children and adolescents: A review. *Learning Disability Quarterly, 8,* 189-204.

Duffy, F. H., & McAnulty, G. B. (1985). Brain electrical activity mapping (BEAM): The search for a physiological signature of dyslexia. In F. H. Duffy & N. Geschwind (Eds.), *Dyslexia: A neuroscientific approach to clinical evaluation* (pp. 105-122). Boston: Little, Brown.

Dunlap, G., Kern-Dunlap, L., Clarke, S., & Robbins, F. K. (1991). Functional assessment, curricular revision, and severe behavior problems. *Journal of Applied Behavior Analysis, 24,* 387-397.

Dunn, L. (1968). Special education for the mildly retarded: Is much of it justifiable? *Exceptional Children, 35,* 5-22.

Dunn, L. M., & Markwardt, F. C. (1970). *The Peabody Individual Achievement Test.* Circle Pines, MN: American Guidance Service.

Dunst, C. J. (1986). Overview of the efficacy of early intervention programs: Methodological and conceptual considerations. In L. Bickman & D. Weatherford (Eds.), *Evaluating early intervention programs for severely handicapped children and their families.* Austin, TX: PRO-ED.

Dunst, C. J., & Snyder, S. W. (1986). A critique of the Utah State University early intervention meta-analysis research. *Exceptional Children, 53,* 269-276.

Dunst, C. J., Snyder, S. W., & Mankinen, M. (1986). Efficacy of early intervention. In M. Wang, H. Walberg, & M. Reynolds (Eds.), *Handbook of special education: Research and practice* (Vols. 1-3). Oxford, England: Pergamon Press.

Dunst, C. J., Trivette, C. M., & Deal, A. (1994). *Supporting and strengthening families: Volume 1: Methods, strategies and practices.* Cambridge, MA: Brookline Books.

Dunst, C. J., Trivette, C. M., & Deal, A. G. (1988). *Enabling and empowering families: Principles and guidelines for practice.* Cambridge, MA: Brookline Books.

DuPaul, G. J., & Stoner, G. (1994). *ADHD in the schools: Assessment and intervention strategies.* New York: Guilford Press.

DuPaul, G. J., Stoner, G., Tilly, W. D., & Putnam, D. (1991). Interventions for attention problems. In G. Stoner, M. Shinn, & H. M. Walker (Eds.), *Interventions for achievement and behavior problems.* (pp. 685-713). Silver Spring, MD: National Association for School Psychologists.

Durand, V. M. (1986). Review of strategies for educating students with severe handicaps. *The Journal of The Association for Persons with Severe Handicaps, 11,* 140-142.

Durrant, J. E. (1994). A decade of research on learning disabilities: A report card on the state of literature. *Journal of Learning Disabilities, 27,* 25-33.

Durrell, D. D. (1955). *Durrell Analysis of Reading Difficulty.* New York: Harcourt Brace Jovanovich.

Dykes, J. (1992). Opinions of orientation and mobility instructors about using the long cane with preschool-age children. *RE:view, 24,* 85-92.

Dyson, L., Edgar, E., & Crnic, K. (1989). Psychological predictors of adjustment by siblings of developmentally disabled children. *American Journal of Mental Retardation, 94,* 292-302.

Eakin, W. M., & McFarland, T. L. (1960). *Type, printing, and the partially seeing child.* Pittsburgh, PA: Stanwix.

Eastman, M. (1978). The Eden express doesn't stop here anymore. *American Pharmacy, 40,* 12-17.

Eden-Piercy, G. V. S., Blacher, J. B., & Eyman, R. K. (1986). Exploring parents' reactions to their young child with severe handicaps. *Mental Retardation, 24,* 285-291.

Edgar, E. (1987). Secondary programs in special education: Are many of them justifiable? *Exceptional Children, 53,* 555-561.

Edmonds, C. (1985). Hearing loss with frequent diving: Deaf divers. *Undersea Biomedical Research, 12,* 315-319.

Edwards, P. L. (1986). *Heterogeneous grouping effects on educational service deliv-*

ery for students with moderate, severe, and profound retardation. Unpublished manuscript, Kent State University, Kent, OH.

Egan, I., Fredericks, H. D., & Hendrickson, K. (1985). Teaching associated work skills to adolescents with severe handicaps. *Education & Treatment of Children*, *8*, 239-250.

Eichinger, J. (1990). Effects of goal structure on social interaction between elementary level nondisabled students and students with severe disabilities. *Exceptional Children*, *56*, 408-417.

Eikeseth, S., & Lovaas, O. I. (1992). The autistic label and its potentially detrimental effect on the child's treatment. *Journal of Behavioral Therapy and Experimental Psychiatry*, *23*(3), 151-157.

Elks, M. A., (1993). The "Lethal Chamber": Further evidence for the euthanasia option. *Mental Retardation*, *32*, 201-207.

Elksnin, L. K., & Elksnin, N. (1991). Helping parents solve problems at home and school through parent training. *Intervention in School and Clinic*, *26*(4), 230-233.

Ellett, L. (1993). Instructional practices in mainstreamed secondary classrooms. *Journal of Learning Disabilities*, *26*, 57-64.

Elliott, B. (1979). Look but don't touch: The problems blind children have learning about sexuality. *Disabled USA*, *3*(2), 14-17.

Ellis, E. S. (1993). Integrative strategy instruction: A potential model for teaching content area subjects to adolescents with learning disabilities. *Journal of Learning Disabilities*, *26*, 358-383, 398.

Ellis, E. S., Deshler, D. D., & Schumaker, J. B. (1989). Teaching adolescents with learning disabilities to generate and use task-specific strategies. *Journal of Learning Disabilities*, *22*, 108-119.

Ellis, J. W., & Luckasson, R. A. (1985). Discrimination against people with mental retardation: A comment on the Cleburne decision. *Mental Retardation*, *23*, 249-252.

Elmer, E. (1977). A follow-up study of traumatized children. *Pediatrics*, *59*, 273-279.

Emerick, L. L., & Haynes, W. O. (1986). *Diagnosis and evaluation in speech pathology* (3rd ed.). Englewood Cliffs, NJ: Merrill/Prentice-Hall.

Engelmann, S. (1977). Sequencing cognitive and academic tasks. In R. D. Kneedler & S. G. Tarver (Eds.), *Changing perspec-*

tives in special education* (pp. 46-61). Englewood Cliffs, NJ: Merrill/Prentice Hall.

Engelmann, S., & Bruner, E. C. (1988). *Reading mastery: Fast cycle (DISTAR)*. Chicago, IL: Science Research Associates.

Engelmann, S., & Carnine, D. W. (1982). *Theory of instruction: Principles and applications*. New York: Irvington.

Engelmann, S., & Carnine, D. W. (1990). *DISTAR Arithmetic*. Chicago, IL: Science Research Associates.

Engelmann, S., & Silbert, J. (1993). *Reasoning and writing D*. Chicago, IL: Science Research Associates.

Engelmann, S., Haddox, P., & Bruner, E. (1983). *Teach your child to read in 100 easy lessons*. New York: Simon & Shuster.

Epanchin, B. C., Townsend, B., & Stoddard, K. (1994). *Constructive classroom management: Strategies for creating positive learning environments*. Pacific Grove, CA: Brooks/Cole.

Epstein, L. G., Sharer, L. R., & Goudsmit, J. (1988). Neurological and neuropathological features of human immunodeficiency virus infection in children. *Annals of Neurology*, *23*, 19-23.

Epstein, M. H., Bursuck, W., & Cullinan, D. (1985). Patterns of behavior problems among the learning disabled: II. Boys aged 12-18, girls aged 6-11. *Learning Disability Quarterly*, *8*, 123-131.

Epstein, M. H., Cullinan, D., & Lloyd, J. W. (1986). Behavior-problem patterns among the learning disabled: III. Replication across age and sex. *Learning Disability Quarterly*, *9*, 43-54.

Epstein, M. H., Cullinan, D., & Rosemier, R. (1983). Patterns of behavior problems among the learning disabled: Boys aged 6-11. *Learning Disability Quarterly*, *6*, 305-312.

Epstein, M. H., Foley, R. M., & Cullinan, D. (1992). National survey of educational programs for adolescents with serious emotional disturbance. *Behavioral Disorders*, *17*, 202-210.

Ericsson, K. A., & Charness, N. (1994). Expert performance. Its structure and acquisition. *American Psychologist*, *49*(8), 725-747.

Erin, J. N., Dignan, K., & Brown, P. A. (1991). Are social skills teachable? A review of the literature. *Journal of Visual Impairment & Blindness*, *85*, 58-61.

Eshleman, J. W. (1985). Improvement pictures with low celeration: An early foray into the use of SAFMEDS. *Journal of Precision Teaching*, *6*(3), 54-63.

Espe-Sherwindt, M., & Crable, S. (1993). Parents with mental retardation: Moving beyond the myths. *Topics in Early Childhood Special Education*, *13*, 154-174.

Espin, C. A., & Deno, S. L. (1989). The effects of modeling and prompting feedback strategies on sight word reading of students labeled learning disabled. *Education and Treatment of Children*, *12*, 219-231.

Esposito, B. G., & Reed, T. M. (1986). The effects of contact with handicapped persons on young children's attitudes. *Exceptional Children*, *54*, 224-229.

Esposito, L., & Campbell, P. H. (1987). Computers and severely and physically handicapped individuals. In J. D. Lindsey (Ed.), *Computers and exceptional individuals* (pp. 105-124). Englewood Cliffs, NJ: Merrill/Prentice Hall.

Evans, I. M., Salisbury, C. L., Palombaro, M. M., Berryman, J., & Hollowood, T. M. (1992). Peer interactions and social acceptance of elementary-age children with severe disabilities in an inclusive school. *Journal of the Association for Persons with Severe Handicaps*, *17*, 205-212.

Fabian, E. S., Luecking, R. G., & Tilson, Jr., G. P. (1994). *A working relationship: The job development specialist's guide to successful partnerships with business*. Baltimore: Paul H. Brookes.

Fain, G. S. (1986). Leisure: A moral imperative. *Mental Retardation*, *24*, 261-263.

Fairweather, J. S., & Shaver, D. M. (1991). Making the transition to postsecondary education and training. *Exceptional Children*, *57*, 264-270.

Falvey, M. A. (1989). *Community-based curriculum: Instructional strategies for students with severe handicaps*. Baltimore: Paul H. Brooks Publishing Company.

Falvey, M. F. (1995). *Inclusive and heterogeneous schooling*. Baltimore, MD: Paul H. Brooks Publishing Company.

Farber, B. (1975). Family adaptations to severely mentally retarded children. In M. Begab & S. A. Richardson (Eds.), *The mentally retarded and society: A social science perspective* (pp. 247-266). Baltimore, MD: University Park Press.

Farlow, L. J., & Snell, M. E. (1994). *Making the most of student performance data*. Washington, DC: American Association on Mental Retardation.

Favell, J. E., Favell, J. E., & McGimsey, J. F. (1978). Relative effectiveness and efficiency of group vs. individual training of severely retarded persons. *American*

Journal of Mental Deficiency, 83, 104-109.

Featherstone, H. (1980). *A difference in the family: Living with a disabled child.* New York: Basic Books.

Federal Register. (1977, August 23). Washington, DC: U.S. Government Printing Office.

Federal Register. (1981, January 19). Washington, DC: U.S. Government Printing Office.

Federal Register. (1988). *Code of federal regulations. 34: Education: Parts 300-399, revised as of July 1, 1988.* Washington, DC: U.S. Government Printing Office.

Fehrenbach, C. R. (1993). Underachieving gifted students: Intervention programs that work. *Roeper Review, 16*, 88-90.

Feil, E. G., & Becker, W. C. (1993). Investigation of a multiple-gated screening system for preschool behavior problems. *Behavioral Disorders, 19*, 44-53.

Fein, D. J. (1983). The prevalence of speech and language impairments. *ASHA, 25*, 37.

Feingold, B. F. (1975a). Hyperkinesis and learning disabilities linked to artificial food flavors and colors. *American Journal of Nursing, 75*, 797-803.

Feingold, B. F. (1975b). *Why your child is hyperactive.* New York: Random House.

Feingold, B. F. (1976). Hyperkinesis and learning disabilities linked to ingestion of artificial food colors and flavorings. *Journal of Learning Disabilities, 9*, 551-559.

Feldhusen, J. F. (1992a). *Talent identification and development in education (TIDE).* Sarasota, FL: Center for Creative Learning.

Feldhusen, J. F. (1992b). Early admission and grade advancement. *Gifted Child Today, 15*, 45-49.

Feldhusen, J. F. (1992c). On acceleration. *Gifted Child Today, 15*, (2).

Feldhusen, J. & Kolloff, P. (1985). The Purdue three-stage enrichment model for gifted education at the elementary level. In J. Renzulli (Ed.), *Systems and models for developing programs for the gifted and talented*. Mansfield Center, CT: Creative Learning Press.

Feldhusen, J. F., & Moon, S. (1995). The educational continuum and delivery of services. In Genshaft, J. L., Bireley, M., & Hollinger, C. L. (Eds.). *Serving gifted and talented students: A resource for school personnel* (pp. 103-121). Austin, TX: PRO-ED.

Feldhusen, J., & Sokol, L. (1982). Extra school programming to meet the needs of gifted youth: Super-Saturday. *Gifted Child Quarterly, 26*, 51-56.

Feldhusen, J., Proctor, T. B., & Black, K. N. (1986). Guidelines for grade advancement of precocious children. *Roeper Review, 9*, 25-27.

Feldman, D. H. (1991). Has there been a paradigm shift in gifted education? In N. Colangelo, S. G. Assouline, & D. L. Ambroson (Eds.), *Talent development: Proceedings from the 1991 Henry B. and Jocelyn Wallace National Research Symposium on Talent Development* (pp. 89-94). Boston: Trillium Press.

Feldman, D., Kinnison, L., Jay, R., & Harth, R. (1983). The effects of differential labeling on professional concepts and attitudes toward the emotionally disturbed/behavior disordered. *Behavioral Disorders, 8*, 191-198.

Fellows, R. R., Leguire, L. E., Rogers, G. L., & Bremer, D. L. (1986). A theoretical approach to vision stimulation. *Journal of Visual Impairment and Blindness, 80*, 907-909.

Ferguson, D. L. (1994). Is communication really the point? Some thoughts on interventions and membership. *Mental Retardation, 1*, 7-18.

Ferguson, D. L., & Baumgart, D. (1991). Partial participation revisited. *Journal of the Association for Persons with Severe Handicaps, 16*, 218-227.

Ferguson, D. L., Meyer, G., Jeanchild, L., Juniper, L., & Zingo, J. (1992). Figuring out what to do with the grownups: How teachers make inclusion "work" for students with disabilities. *Journal of the Association for Persons with Severe Handicaps, 17*, 218-226.

Fernald, G. M. (1943). *Remedial techniques in basic school subjects.* New York: McGraw-Hill.

Ferrell, K. A. (1984). A second look at sensory aids in early childhood. *Education of the Visually Handicapped, 16*, 83-101.

Ferrell, K. A. (1985). *Reach out and teach.* New York: American Foundation for the Blind.

Ferrell, K. A. (1986). Infancy and early childhood. In G. T. Scholl (Ed.), *Foundations of education for blind and visually handicapped children and youth: Theory and practice* (pp. 119-135). New York: American Foundation for the Blind.

Fewell, R. R. (1991). Trends in the assessment of infants and toddlers with disabilities. *Exceptional Children, 58*, 166-173.

Fiedler, J. F., & Knight, R. R. (1986). Congruence between assessed needs and IEP goals of identified behaviorally disabled students. *Behavioral Disorders, 12*, 22-27.

Figueroa, R. A. (1989). Psychological testing of linguistic-minority students: Knowledge gaps and regulations. *Exceptional Children, 56*, 145-152.

Figueroa, R. A. (1991). Bilingualism and psychometrics. *Diagnostique, 17*, 70-85.

Figueroa, R. A., Fradd, S. H., & Correa, V. I. (1989). Bilingual special education and this special issue. *Exceptional Children, 56*, 174-178.

Finch, T. E. (1985). Introduction. In D. Assael (Ed.), *Directory, 1984-85 edition: Handicapped Children's Early Education Program* (pp. ix-xiii). Chapel Hill, NC: University of North Carolina, Technical Assistance Development System.

Finders, M. & Lewis, C. (1994). Why some parents don't come to school. *Educational Leadership, 51*, 50-57.

Finlan, T. G. (1992). Do state methods of quantifying a severe discrepancy result in fewer students with learning disabilities? *Learning Disability Quarterly, 15*, 129-134.

Fish, M. C. (1990). Family-school conflict: Implications for the family. *Journal of Reading, Writing, and Learning Disabilities International, 6*, 71-97.

Fisher, A. T. (1989). Independent living. In D. L. Harnish & A. T. Fisher (Eds.), *Transition literature review: Educational, employment, and independent living outcomes.* Champaign, IL: University of Illinois at Urbana-Champaign.

Fisher, C. S., Berliner, C. D., Filby, N. N., Marliave, R., Cahen, L. S., & Dishaw, M. M. (1980). Teaching behaviors, academic learning time, and student achievement. An Overview. In C. Denham & A. Lieberman (Eds.), *Time to learn* (pp. 7-22). Washington, DC: National Institute of Education.

Fisher, C. W., & Berliner, D. C. (Eds.). (1985). *Perspectives on instructional time.* New York: Longman.

Fitzgerald, E. (1929). *Straight language for the deaf.* Washington, DC: Alexander Graham Bell Association for the Deaf.

Flener, B. S. (1993). The consultative-collaborative teachers for students with visual handicaps. *RE:view, 25*, 173-182.

Florence, I. J., & LaGrow, S. J. (1989). The use of a recorded message for gaining assistance with street crossings for deaf-blind travelers. *Journal of Visual Impairment and Blindness, 83*, 471-472.

Florian, V. (1987). Cultural and ethnic aspects of family support services for parents of a child with a disability. In D. K. Libsky (Ed.), *Family supports for families with a disabled member* (pp. 37-52). New York: World Rehabilitation Fund.

Flynn, L. L., & McCollum, J. (1989). Support systems: Strategies and implications for hospitalized newborns and families. *Journal of Early Intervention, 13*, 173-182.

Flynn, R. J. (1980). Normalization, PASS, and service quality assessment. In R. J. Flynn & K. E. Nitsch (Eds.), *Normalization, social integration, and community services* (pp. 323-359). Baltimore: University Park Press.

Fontana, V. J. (1971). *The maltreated child.* Springfield, IL: Charles C. Thomas.

Ford, A., Schnorr, R., Meyer, L., Davern, L., Black, J., & Dempsey, P. (Eds.). (1989). *The Syracuse community-referenced curriculum guide for students with moderate and severe disabilities.* Baltimore: Paul H. Brooks Publishing Company.

Ford, B. A., & Jones, C. (1990). An ethnic feelings book: Created by students with developmental handicaps. *Teaching Exceptional Children, 22*(4), 36-39.

Forest, M., & Lusthaus, E. (1990). Everyone belongs with the MAPS Action Planning System. *Teaching Exceptional Children, 22*(2), 32-35.

Forness, S., & Knitzer, J. (1992). A new proposed definition and terminology to replace "serious emotional disturbance" in Individuals with Disabilities Education Act. *School Psychology Review, 21*, 12-20.

Foster-Johnson, L., & Dunlap, G. (1993). Using functional assessment to develop effective, individualized interventions for challenging behaviors. *Teaching Exceptional Children, 25*(3), 4450.

Fourqurean, J. M., & LaCourt, T. (1991). A follow-up of former special education students: A model for program evaluation. *Remedial and Special Education, 12*(1), 16-23.

Fowler, S. A., Dougherty, S. B., Kirby, K. C., & Kohler, F. W. (1986). Role reversals: An analysis of therapeutic effects achieved with disruptive boys during their appointments as peer monitors. *Journal of Applied Behavior Analysis, 19*, 437-444.

Fowler, S. A., Schwartz, I., & Atwater, J. (1991). Perspectives on the transition from preschool to kindergarten for children with disabilities and their families. *Exceptional Children, 58*, 136-145.

Fox, L., & Westling, D. (1991). A preliminary evaluation of training parents to use

facilitated strategies with their children with profound disabilities. *The Journal of the Association for Persons with Severe Handicaps, 16*, 168-176.

Fox, L., Brody, L., & Tobin, D. (Eds.) (1980). *Women and the mathematical mystique.* Baltimore, MD: Johns Hopkins University Press.

Foy, C. J., Von Scheden, M., & Waiculonis, J. (1992). The Connecticut Pre-cane: Case study and curriculum. *Journal of Visual Impairment & Blindness, 86*, 178-181.

Fradd, S. H., & Correa, V. I. (1989). Hispanic students at risk: Do we abdicate or advocate? *Exceptional Children, 56*, 105-110.

Fradd, S. H., & McGee, P. L. (1994). *Instructional assessment: An integrative approach to evaluating student performance.* Reading, MA: Addison-Wesley Publishing Company.

Frank, A. R., & Sitlington, P. L. (1993). Graduates with mental disabilities: The story three years later. *Education and Training in Mental Retardation, 28*, 30-37.

Frank, A., Sitlington, P., & Carson, R. (1992). Adult adjustment of persons with severe/profound mental disabilities: A longitudinal study. *Journal of Developmental and Physical Disabilities, 4*, 37-50.

Frank, D. A., Zuckerman, B. S., Amaro, H., Aboagye, K., Baucher, H., Cabral, H., Fried, L., Hingson, R., Kayne, H., Levenson, S. M., Parker, S., Reece, H., & Vinvi, R. (1988). Cocaine use during pregnancy: Prevalence and correlates. *Pediatrics, 82*, 888-895.

Frankenberger, W., & Fronzaglio, K. (1991). States' definitions and procedures for identifying children with mental retardation: Comparison over nine years. *Mental Retardation, 29*, 315-321.

Frankenburg, W. K., Dodds, J., & Fandal, A. (1975). *Denver Developmental Screening Test.* Denver: LADOCA Project and Publishing Foundation.

Frankenburg, W. K., Dodds, J., Archer, P., Shapiro, H., & Bresnick, B. (1990). *The Denver II—revision and restandardization of the DDST.* Denver: University of Colorado School of Medicine.

Franklin, M. E. (1992). Culturally sensitive instructional practices for African-American learners with disabilities. *Exceptional Children, 59,* 115-122.

Frasier, M. (1987). The identification of gifted black students: Developing new perspectives. *Journal for the Education of the Gifted, 10*(3), 155-180.

Freagon, S. (1982). Present and projected services to meet the needs of severely handicapped children [Keynote address]. In *Proceedings of the National*

Parent Conference on Children Requiring Extensive Special Education Programming. Washington, DC: U.S. Department of Education, Special Education Programs.

Freagon, S., Smith, B., Costello, C., Bay, J., Ahlgren, C., & Costello, D. (1986). *Procedures and strategies for program development leading to employment of students with moderate and severe handicaps.* DeKalb, IL: Northern Illinois University.

Fredericks, H. D., & Baldwin, V. (1987). Individuals with sensory impairments: Who are they? How are they educated? In L. Goetz, D. Guess, & K. Stremel-Campbell, (Eds.), *Innovative program design for individuals with dual sensory impairments* (pp. 3-14). Baltimore, MD: Paul H. Brooks Publishing Company.

Fredericks, H. D., Hanks, S., Makohon, L., Fruin, C., Moore, W., Piazza-Templeman, T., Blair, L., Dalke, B., Hawkins, P., Coen, M., Renfroe-Burton, S., Bunse, C., Farnes, T., Moses, C., Toews, J., McGuckin, A. M., Moore, B., Riggs, C., Baldwin, V., Anderson, V., Ashbacher, V., Carter, V., Gage, M. A., Rogers, G., & Samples, B. (1980a). *The teaching research curriculum for moderately and severely handicapped: Gross and fine motor.* Springfield, IL: Charles C. Thomas.

Fredericks, H. D., Makohon, L., Fruin, C., Moore, W., Piazza-Templeman, T., Blair, L., Dalke, B., Hawkins, P., Coen, M., Renfroe-Burton, S., Bunse, C., Farnes, T., Moses, C., Toews, J., McGuckin, A. M., Moore, B., Riggs, C., Baldwin, V., Anderson, V., Ashbacher, V., Carter, V., Gage, M. A., Rogers, G., & Samples, B. (1980b). *The teaching research curriculum for moderately and severely handicapped: Self-help and cognitive.* Springfield, IL: Charles C. Thomas.

Freeman, D. E., & Freeman, Y. S. (1993). Strategies for promoting the primary language of all students. *The Reading Teacher, 46*, 552-558.

Frey, K. S., Greenberg, M. T., & Fewell, R. R. (1989). Stress and coping among parents of handicapped children: A multidimensional approach. *American Journal on Mental Retardation, 94*, 240-249.

Frostig, M., & Horne, D. (1973). *The Frostig program for the development of visual perception* (rev. ed.). Chicago: Follett.

Frostig, M., Lefever, D. W., & Whittlesey, J. R. B. (1964). *The Marianne Frostig Development Test of Visual Perception.* Palo Alto, CA: Consulting Psychologists Press.

Fuchs, D., & Fuchs, L. S. (1988a). Evaluation of the Adaptive Learning Environments

Model. *Exceptional Children, 55,* 115-127.

Fuchs, D., & Fuchs, L. S. (1988b). Response to Wang and Walberg. *Exceptional Children, 55,* 138-146.

Fuchs, D., & Fuchs, L. S. (1994). Inclusive schools movement and the radicalization of special education reform. *Exceptional Children, 60,* 294-309.

Fuchs, D., Fuchs, L. S., & Bahr, M. W. (1990). Mainstream assistance teams: A scientific basis for the art of consultation. *Exceptional Children, 57,* 128-139.

Fuchs, D., Fuchs, L. S., Bahr, M. W., Fernstrom, P., & Stecker, P. (1990). Prereferral intervention: A prescriptive approach. *Exceptional Children, 56,* 493-513.

Fuchs, D., Fuchs, L. S., Fernstrom, P., & Hohn, M. (1991). Toward a responsible reintegration of behaviorally disordered students. *Behavioral Disorders, 16,* 133-147.

Fuchs, L. S., & Fuchs, D. (1986). Effects of systematic formative evaluation: A meta-analysis. *Exceptional Children, 53,* 199-209.

Fuchs, L. S., & Fuchs, D., & Bishop, N. (1992). Teacher planning for students with learning disabilities: Differences between general and special education. *Learning Disabilities Research and Practice, 7,* 120-128.

Furth, H. G. (1973). *Deafness and learning: A psychosocial approach.* Belmont, CA: Wadsworth Publishing.

Gadow, K. D. (1986). *Children on medication: Volume I. Hyperactivity, learning disabilities, and mental retardation.* San Diego: College-Hill.

Gajar, A., Goodman, L, & McAfee, J. (1993). *Secondary schools and beyond: Transition of individuals with mild disabilities.* Englewood Cliffs, NJ: Merrill/Prentice Hall.

Gajria, M., Salend, S. J., & Hemrick, M. A. (1994). Teacher acceptability of testing modifications for mainstreamed students. *Learning Disabilities: Research and Practice, 9,* 236-243.

Gajria, M., Salend, S. J., Hemrick, M. A. (1994). Teacher acceptability of testing modification for mainstreamed students. *Learning Disabilities Research & Practice, 9*(4), 236-243.

Gallagher, J. (1975). *Teaching the gifted child.* Boston: Allyn & Bacon.

Gallagher, J. J. (1981). Differential curriculum for the gifted. In A. H. Kramer, D. Bitan, N. Butler-Por, A. Eryatar, & E. Landau (Eds.), *Gifted children: Challenging their potential* (pp. 136-154). New York: World Council for Gifted and Talented Children.

Gallagher, J. J. (1984). The evolution of special education concepts. In B. Blatt & R. J. Morris (Eds.), *Perspectives in special education: Personal orientations* (pp. 210-232). Glenview, IL: Scott, Foresman.

Gallagher, J. J. (1990). Editorial: The public and professional perception of the emotional status of gifted children. [Special Issue], *Journal for the Education of the Gifted, 13,* 202-211.

Gallagher, J. J. (1994). The pull of societal forces on special education. *The Journal of Special Education, 27,* 521-530.

Gallagher, J. J., & Gallagher, S. (1994). *Teaching the gifted child* (4th ed.). Boston: Allyn & Bacon.

Gallaudet Research Institute. (1985). *Gallaudet Research Institute Newsletter.* Washington, DC: Gallaudet University Press.

Gallimore, R., Boggs, J., & Jordan, C. (1974). *Culture, behavior, and education.* Beverly Hills, CA: SAGE Publications.

Gallimore, R., Weisner, T. S., Bernheimer, L. P., Guthrie, D., & Nihira, K. (1993). Family responses to young children with developmental delays: Accommodation activity in ecological and cultural context. *American Journal on Mental Retardation, 98,* 185-206.

Gallivan-Fenlon, A. (1994). Integrated transdisciplinary teams. *Teaching Exceptional Children, 26*(3), 16-20.

Galton, F. (1869/1936). Genius as inherited. In A. Rothenberg & C. R. Hausman (Eds.), *The creativity question* (pp. 42-48). Durham, NC: Duke University. (Reprinted from *Hereditary genius: An inquiry into its laws and consequences,* 1869. Englewood Cliffs, NJ: Merrill/Prentice Hall.)

Gandell, T. S., & Laufer, D. (1993). Developing a telecommunications curriculum for students with physical disabilities. *Teaching Exceptional Children, 25*(2), 26-28.

Gannon, J. (1981). *Deaf heritage: A narrative history of deaf America.* Silver Spring, MD: National Association of the Deaf.

Ganschow, L., & Sparks, R. (1987). The foreign language requirement. *Learning Disabilities Focus, 2,* 116-123.

Garber, H. L. (1988). *The Milwaukee Project: Preventing mental retardation in children at risk.* Washington, DC: American Association on Mental Retardation.

Garber, H., & Heber, R. (1973). *The Milwaukee Project: Early intervention as a technique to prevent mental retardation* [Technical paper]. Storrs, CT: University of Connecticut.

Gardner, H. (1983). *Frames of mind.* New York: Basic Books.

Gardner, J. F. (1993). The era of optimism, 1850-1870: A preliminary reappraisal. *Mental Retardation, 31,* 89-95.

Gardner, R., III, (1990a). Life-space interviewing: It can be effective, but don't . . . *Behavioral Disorders, 15,* 111-118.

Gardner, R., III, (1990b). Sincere, but sincerely wrong: A reply to Nicholas Long. *Behavioral Disorders, 15,* 125-126.

Gardner, R., III, & Heward, W.L. (1991). Case study: Improving the social interaction of a group home resident with severe and multiple disabilities. *Behavioral Residential Treatment, 6,* 39-50.

Gardner R., III, Heward, W. L., & Grossi, T. A. (1994). Effects of response cards on student participation and academic achievement: A systematic replication with inner-city students during whole-class science instruction. *Journal of Applied Behavior Analysis, 27,* 63-71.

Gardner, R., III, Sainato, D. M., Cooper, J. O., Heron, T. E., Heward, W. L., Eshleman, J., & Grossi, T. A. (Eds.). (1994). *Behavior analysis in education: Focus on measurably superior instruction.* Monterey, CA: Brooks/Cole.

Gartner, A., & Lipsky, D. K. (1987). Beyond special education: Toward a quality system for all students. *Harvard Educational Review, 57,* 367-395.

Gast, D. L., & Wolery, M. (1987). Severe maladaptive behaviors. In M. E. Snell (Ed.), *Systematic instruction of persons with severe handicaps* (3rd ed.) (pp. 300-332). Englewood Cliffs, NJ: Merrill/Prentice Hall.

Gast, D. L., Collins, B. C., Wolery, M., & Jones, R. (1993). Teaching preschool children with disabilities to respond to the lures of strangers. *Exceptional Children, 59,* 301-311.

Gast, D. L., Doyle, P. M., Wolery, M., Ault, M. J., & Baklarz, J. L. (1991). Acquisition of incidental information during small group instruction. *Education and Treatment of Children, 14,* 1-18.

Gates, A. T., & McKillop, A. S. (1962). *Gates-McKillop Reading Diagnostic Test.* New York: Columbia University, Teachers College, Bureau of Publication.

Gay, G. (1995). African-American culture and contributions in American life. In C. A. Grant (Ed.), *Educating for diversity: An anthology of multicultural voices* (pp. 35-52). Boston: Allyn & Bacon.

Gaylord-Ross, R., & Chadsey-Rusch, J. (1991). Measurement of work-related outcomes for students with severe disabilities. *The Journal of Special Education*, *25*, 291-304.

Gaylord-Ross, R., Lee, M., Johnson, S., Lynch, K., Rosenberg, B., & Goetz, L. (1991). Supported employment for youth who are deaf-blind and in transition. *Career Development for Exceptional Individuals*, *14*, 77-89.

Gearheart, B. R., & Litton, F. W. (1975). *The trainable retarded: A foundations approach.* St. Louis, MO: C. V. Mosby.

Geers, A. E. (1985). Assessment of hearing impaired children: Determining typical and optimal levels of performance. In F. Powell, T. Finitzo-Hieber, S. Friel-Patti, & D. Henderson (Eds.), *Education of the hearing impaired child* (pp. 57-83). San Diego: College-Hill.

Geers, A., & Moog, J. (1989). Factors predictive of the development of literacy in profoundly hearing-impaired adolescents. *The Volta Review*, *91*, 69-86.

Gellhaus, M. M., & Olson, M. R. (1993). Using color and contrast to improve the education environment of students with visual impairments with multiple disabilities. *Journal of Visual Impairment & Blindness*, *87*, 19-20.

Gelman, S. R., Epp, D. J., Downing, R. H., Twark, R. D., & Eyerly, R. W. (1989). Impact of group homes on the values of adjacent residential properties. *Mental Retardation*, *27*, 127-134.

Gelof, M. (1963). Comparisons of systems of classification relating to degrees of retardation to measured intelligence. *American Journal of Mental Deficiency*, *68*, 297-317.

Gense, M. H., & Gense, D. J. (1994). Identifying autism in children with blindness and visual impairments. *RE:view*, *26*, 55-62.

Genshaft, J. L., Bireley, M., & Hollinger, C. L. (Eds.). (1995). *Serving gifted and talented students: A resource for school personnel.* Austin, TX: PRO-ED.

Genshaft, J. L., Greenbaum, S., & Borovosky, S. (1994). Stress and the gifted. In Genshaft, J. L., Bireley, M., & Hollinger, C. L. (Eds.). *Serving gifted and talented students: A resource for school personnel* (pp. 257-268). Austin, TX: PRO-ED.

Gentile, A., & DiFrancesca, S. (1969). *Academic achievement test performance of hearing-impaired students.* United States, Spring, 1969. (Series D, No. 1). Washington, DC: Gallaudet University, Center for Assessment and Demographic Studies.

George, J. D. (1988). Therapeutic intervention for grandparents and extended family of children with developmental delays. *Mental Retardation*, *26*, 369-375.

Gerring, J. P., & Carney, J. M. (1992). *Head trauma: Strategies for educational reintegration.* San Diego, CA: Singular.

Gersten, R. & Woodward, J. (1994). The language-minority student in special education: Issues, trends, and paradoxes. *Exceptional Children, 60*, 310-322.

Gersten, R., Carnine, D., & White, W. A. T. (1984). The pursuit of clarity: Direct instruction and applied behavior analysis. In W. L. Heward, T. E. Heron, D. S. Hill, & J. Trap-Porter (Eds.), *Focus on behavior analysis in education* (pp. 38-57). Englewood Cliffs, NJ: Merrill/Prentice Hall.

Geschwind, N., & Galaburda, A. M. (1987). *Cerebral lateralization: Biological mechanisms, associations, and pathology.* Cambridge, MA: MIT Press.

Gesell, A., & Associates. (1940). *Gesell Developmental Schedules. 1940 Series.* New York: Psychological Corp.

Giangreco, M. F. (1991). Curriculum in inclusion-oriented schools: Trends, issues, challenges, and potential solutions. In S. Stainback & W. Stainback (Eds.). *Teaching in the inclusive classroom: Curriculum design, adaptation and delivery.* Baltimore, MD: Paul H. Brooks Publishing Company.

Giangreco, M. F. (1992). Curriculum in inclusion-oriented schools: Trends, issues, challenges, and potential solutions. In S. Stainback & W. Stainback (Eds.), *Curriculum considerations in inclusive classrooms: Facilitating learning for all students* (pp. 239-263). Baltimore: Paul H. Brookes Publishing Co.

Giangreco, M. F., & Meyer, L. H. (1988). Expanding service delivery options in regular schools and classrooms for students with severe disabilities. In J. L. Graden, J. E. Zins, & M. J. Curtis (Eds.), *Alternative educational delivery systems: Enhancing instructional options for all students* (pp. 241-267). Washington, DC: National Association of School Psychologists.

Giangreco, M. F., & Putnam, J. W. (1991). Supporting the education of students with severe disabilities in regular education environments. In L. H. Meyer, C. A. Peck, & L. Brown (Eds.), *Critical issues in the lives of people with severe disabilities* (pp. 245-270). Baltimore: Paul H. Brookes Publishing Co.

Giangreco, M. F., Cloninger, C. J., & Iverson, V. S. (1993). *Choosing options and accommodations for children.* Baltimore: MD: Paul H. Brooks Publishing Company.

Giangreco, M. F., Cloninger, C. J., Dennis, R. E., & Edelman, S. W. (1994). Problem-solving methods to facilitate inclusive education. In J. S. Thousand, R. A. Villa, & A. I. Nevin (Eds.), *Creativity and collaborative learning* (pp. 321-346). Baltimore, MD: Paul H. Brookes Publishing Company.

Giangreco, M. F., Cloninger, C. J., Mueller, P. H., Yuan, S., & Ashworth, S. (1990, April). *A quest to be heard: Perspectives of parents whose children are dual sensory impaired.* Paper presented at the annual meeting of the Council for Exceptional Children, Toronto, Canada.

Giangreco, M. F., Dennis, R., Cloninger, C., Edelman, S., & Schattman, R. (1993). "I've counted Jon": Transformational experiences of teachers educating students with disabilities. *Exceptional Children*, *59*, 359-372.

Giangreco, M. F., Edelman, S., & Dennis, R. (1991). Common professional practices that interfere with the integrated delivery of related services. *Remedial and Special Education*, *12*(2), 16-24.

Giangreco, M. F., York, J., & Rainforth, B. (1989). Providing related services to learners with severe handicaps in educational settings: Pursuing the least restrictive option. *Pediatric Physical Therapy*, *1*(2), 55-63.

Gibson, J. W., Rabkin, J., & Munson, R. (1992). Critical issues in serving the developmentally disabled elderly. *Journal of Gerontological Social Work*, *19*(1), 35-48.

Giek, K. A. (1992). Monitoring student progress through efficient record keeping. *Teaching Exceptional Children*, *24*(3), 22-26.

Gies-Zaborowski, J., & Silverman, F. H. (1986). Documenting the impact of a mild dysarthria on peer perception. *Language, Speech, and Hearing Services in the Schools*, *17*, 143.

Gilgoff, I. S. (1983). Spinal cord injury. In J. Umbreit (Ed.), *Physical disabilities and health impairments: An introduction* (pp. 132-146). Englewood Cliffs, NJ: Merrill/Prentice Hall.

Gilhool, T. K. (1976). Changing public policies: Roots and forces. *Minnesota Education, 2*(2), 8.

Gillespie, E. B. (1981). *Student participation in the development of IEP's. Perspective of parents and students.* Unpublished doctoral dissertation, University of North Carolina at Chapel Hill.

Gillham, B. (Ed.). (1986). *Handicapping conditions in children.* London: Croom Helm.

Glascoe, F. P., & Byrne, K. E. (1993). The accuracy of three developmental screening tests. *Journal of Early Intervention*, *17*, 368-379.

Glenn, C. L. (1989). Just schools for minority children. *Phi Delta Kappan*, *10*, 777-779.

Goddard, H. H. (1928). *School training for gifted children*. New York: World Book.

Gold, M. W. (1976). Task analysis of a complex assembly task by the retarded blind. *Exceptional Children*, *43*, 73-85.

Gold, M. W. (1980). An alternative definition of mental retardation. In M. W. Gold (Ed.), *"Did I say that?" Articles and commentary on the Try Another Way System*. Champaign, IL: Research Press.

Golden, G. (1980). Nonstandard therapies in the developmental disabilities. *American Journal of Diseases of Children*, *134*, 487-491.

Goldman, R., & Fristoe, M. (1986). *Goldman-Fristoe test of articulation*. Austin, TX: PRO-ED.

Goldman, R., Fristoe, M., & Woodcock, R. W. (1990). *Goldman-Fristoe-Woodcock test of auditory discrimination*. Austin, TX: PRO-ED.

Goldstein, H. (1990). The future of language science: A plea for language intervention research. *ASHA Reports*, *20*, 41-50.

Goldstein, H. (1993). Use of peers as communication intervention agents. *Teaching Exceptional Children*, *25*(2), 37-40.

Goldstein, H., Kaczmarek, L., & Hepting, N. (1994). Communication interventions: The challenges of across-the-day implementation. In R. Gardner III, D. M. Sainato, J. O. Cooper, T. E. Heron, W. L. Heward, J. Eshleman, & T. A. Grossi (Eds.), *Behavior analysis in education: Focus on measurably superior instruction* (pp. 101-113). Pacific Grove, CA: Brooks/Cole.

Goldstein, H., Kaczmarek, L., Pennington, R., & Shafer, K. (1992). Peer-mediated intervention: Attending to, commenting on, and acknowledging the behavior of preschoolers with autism. *Journal of Applied Behavior Analysis*, *25*, 289-305.

Goldstein, S., Strickland, B., Turnbull, A. P., & Curry, L. (1980). An observational analysis of the IEP conference. *Exceptional Children*, *46*(4), 278-286.

Gollnick, D. M. & Chinn, P. C. (1994). *Multicultural education in a pluralistic society* (4th ed.). Englewood Cliffs, NJ: Merrill/Prentice Hall.

Gonzales, R. (1980). Mainstreaming your hearing impaired child in 1980: Still an oversimplification. *Journal of Research and Development in Education*, *13*(4), 14-21.

Goodman, G., & Poillion, M. J. (1992). ADD: Acronym for any dysfunction or difficulty. *The Journal of Special Education*, *26*, 37-56.

Goodman, J. F., & Bond, L. (1993). The individualized education program: A retrospective critique. *The Journal of Special Education*, *26*, 408-422.

Goodman, L. V. (1976). A bill of rights for the handicapped. *American Education*, *12*(6), 6-8.

Gordon, J., & Vaughn, S., & Schumm, S. J. (1993). Spelling interventions: A review of literature and implications for instruction for students with learning disabilities. *Learning Disabilities Research & Practice*, *8*, 175-181.

Gothelf, C. R., Crimmins, D. B., Mercer, C. A., & Finocchiaro, P. A. (1994). Teaching choice-making skills to students who are deaf-blind. *Teaching Exceptional Children*, *26*(4), 13-15.

Gottlieb, J., & Leyser, Y. (1981). Facilitating the social mainstreaming of retarded children. *Exceptional Education Quarterly*, *1*, 57-69.

Gottlieb, J., Alter, M., Gottlieg, B. W., & Wishner, J. (1994). Special education in urban America: It's not justifiable for many. *The Journal of Special Education*, *27*, 453-465.

Gradel, K., Thompson, M. S., & Sheehan, R. (1981). Parental and professional agreement in early childhood assessment. *Topics in Early Childhood Special Education*, *1*, 31-39.

Graden, J. L. (1989). Redefining "prereferral" intervention as intervention assistance: Collaboration between general and special education. *Exceptional Children*, *56*, 227-231.

Graden, J. L., Casey, A., & Christenson, S. L. (1985). Implementing a prereferral intervention system: Part I. The model. *Exceptional Children*, *51*, 377-384.

Grant, C. A., & Sleeter, C. E. (1989). Race, class, gender, exceptionality, and educational reform. In J. A. Banks & C. A. M. Banks (Eds.), *Multicultural education: Issues and perspectives* (pp. 46-65). Boston: Allyn & Bacon.

Grant, G., & McGrath, M. (1990). Need for respite-care services for caregivers of persons with mental retardation. *American Journal on Mental Retardation*, *94*, 638-648.

Graves, D. H. (1983). *Writing: Teachers and children at work*. Exeter, NH: Heinemann Books.

Gray, W. S. (1963). *Gray Oral Reading Tests*. Indianapolis: Bobbs-Merrill.

Green, G., & Shane, H. C. (1994). Science, reason, and facilitated communication. *Journal of the Association for Persons with Severe Handicaps*, *19*, 151-172.

Green, S. K., & Shinn, M. R. (1995). Parent attitudes about special education and reintegration: What is the role of student outcomes? *Exceptional Children*, *61*, 269-281.

Greenspan, S. (1994). Review of mental retardation: Definition, classification, and systems of supports. *American Journal on Mental Retardation*, *98*, 544-549.

Greenwood, C. R. (1991). Longitudinal analysis of time, engagement, and achievement in at-risk versus non-risk students. *Exceptional Children*, *57*, 521-535.

Greenwood, C. R., Carta, J. J., Hart, B., Kamps, D., Terry, D., Delquadri, J. C., Walker, D., & Risley, T. (1992). Out of the laboratory and into the community: Twenty-six years of applied behavior analysis at the Juniper Gardens Children's Center. *American Psychologist*, *47*, 1464-1474

Greenwood, C. R., Carta, J. J., Hart, B., Thurston, L. P., & Hall. R. V. (1989). A behavioral approach to research on psychosocial retardation. *Education & Treatment of Children*, *12*, 330-346.

Greenwood, C. R., Delquadri, J., & Hall, R. V. (1984). Opportunity to respond and student academic achievement. In W. L. Heward, T. E. Heron, D. S. Hill, & J. Trap-Porter (Eds.), *Focus on behavior analysis in education* (pp. 58-88). Englewood Cliffs, NJ: Merrill/Prentice Hall.

Greenwood, C. R., Hart, B., Walker, D., & Risley, T. (1994). The opportunity to respond and academic performance revisited: A behavioral theory of developmental retardation and its prevention. In R. Gardner III, D. M. Sainato, J. O. Cooper, T. E. Heron, W. L. Heward, J. Eshleman, & T. A. Grossi (Eds.), *Behavior analysis in education: Focus on measurably superior instruction* (pp. 213-223). Pacific Grove, CA: Brooks/Cole.

Greenwood, C. R., Maheady, L., & Carta, J. J. (1991). Peer tutoring programs in the regular classroom. In G. Stoner, M. R. Shinn, & H. M. Walker (Eds.), *Interventions for achievement and behavior problems* (pp. 179-200). Silver Spring, MD: The National Association of School Psychologists.

Greisbach, L. S., & Polloway, E. A. (1990). *Fetal alcohol syndrome: Research review and implications.* (Report No. EC232650). Lynchburg College. (ERIC Document Reproduction Service No. ED 326035).

Gresham, F. M. (1982). Misguided mainstreaming: The case for social skills training with handicapped children. *Exceptional Children, 48*, 422-433.

Gresham, F. M. (1993). Social skills and learning disabilities and a type III error: Rejoinder to Conte and Andrews. *Journal of Learning Disabilities, 26*, 154-158.

Gresham, F. M., & Elliot, S. N. (1989). Social skills deficits as a primary learning disability. *Journal of Learning Disabilities, 22*, 120-124.

Gresham, F. M., & Reschly, D. J. (1986). Social skill deficits and low peer acceptance of mainstreamed learning disabled children. *Learning Disability Quarterly, 9*, 23-32.

Griffing, B. L. (1986). Planning for the future: Programs and services for the blind and visually impaired children. In *Yearbook of the Association for Education and Rehabilitation of the Blind and Visually Impaired* (Vol. 3) (pp. 2-11). Alexandria, VA: Association for Education and Rehabilitation of the Blind and Visually Impaired.

Griffith, D. R. (1992). Prenatal exposure to cocaine and other drugs: Developmental and educational prognoses. *Phi Delta Kappan, 74*(1), 30-34.

Groht, M. A. (1958). *Natural language for deaf children.* Washington, DC: Alexander Graham Bell Association for the Deaf.

Grossi, T. A. (1991). *Effects of a self-evaluation treatment package on the work productivity of adults with disabilities in a restaurant training program.* Unpublished doctoral dissertation. Columbus, OH: the Ohio State University.

Grossi, T. A. (1995). [Effects of listening to tape-recorded music with interspersed verbal prompts to "keep working" on the work performance of a young woman with severe and multiple disabilities in a community job site.] Unpublished raw data.

Grossi, T. A., Kimball, J. W., & Heward, W. L. (1994). What did you say? Using review of tape-recorded interactions to increase social acknowledgments by trainees in a community-based vocational program. *Research in Developmental Disabilities, 15*, 457-472.

Grossi, T. A., Test, D. W., & Keul, P. (1991). Strategies for hiring, training, and managing job coaches. *Journal of Rehabilitation, 57*(3), 37-42.

Grossman, H. (1995). *Teaching in a diverse society.* Boston, MA: Allyn & Bacon.

Grossman, H. J. (Ed.) (1983). *Classification in mental retardation.* Washington, DC: American Association on Mental Deficiency.

Grove, N. M. (1982). Conditions resulting in physical disabilities. In J. L. Bigge (Ed.), *Teaching individuals with physical and multiple disabilities* (2nd ed.) (pp. 1-11). Englewood Cliffs, NJ: Merrill/Prentice Hall.

Guess, D., & Mulligan, M. (1982). The severely and profoundly handicapped. In E. L. Meyen (Ed.), *Exceptional children and youth: An introduction* (2nd ed.). Denver: Love.

Guess, D., Benson, H. A., & Siegel-Causey, E. (1985). Concepts and issues related to choice-making and autonomy among persons with severe disabilities. *The Journal of The Association for Persons with Severe Handicaps, 10*, 79-86.

Guilford, J. P. (1956). The structure of intellect. *Psychological Bulletin, 53*(4), 276-293.

Guilford, J. P. (1956). The structure of the intellect. *American Psychology, 14*, 469-479.

Guilford, J. P. (1959). Traits of creativity. In H. H. Anderson (Ed.), *Creativity and its cultivation* (pp. 142-161). New York: Harper & Brothers.

Guilford, J. P. (1959). Three faces of intellect. *American Psychology, 14*, 267-293.

Guilford, J. P. (1967). *The nature of human intelligence.* New York: McGraw-Hill.

Guilford, J. P. (1987). Creativity research: Past, present and future. In S. Isaksen (Ed.), *Frontiers of creativity research* (pp. 33-66). Buffalo, NY: Bearly Ltd.

Gunter, P. L., Denny, R. K., Jack, S. L., Shores, R. E., & Nelson, C. M. (1993). Aversive stimuli in academic interactions between students with serious emotional disturbance and their teachers. *Behavioral Disorders, 18*, 265-274.

Guralnick, M. J. (1988). Efficacy research in early childhood intervention programs. In S. L. Odom & M. B. Karnes (Eds.), *Early intervention for infants and children with handicaps: An empirical base* (pp. 75-88). Baltimore, MD: Paul H. Brooks Publishing Company.

Guralnick, M. J. (1990). Social competence and early intervention. *Journal of Early Intervention, 14*, 3-14.

Guralnick, M. J. (1991). The next decade of research on the effectiveness of early intervention. *Exceptional Children, 58*, 174-183.

Guskey, T. R., Passaro, P. D., & Wheeler, W. (1995). Mastery learning. *Teaching Exceptional Children, 27*(2), 15-18.

Gustason, G. (1985). Interpreters entering public school employment. *American Annals of the Deaf, 130*, 265-266.

Hagner, D., & Daning, R. (1993). Opening lines: How job developers talk to employers. *Career Development for Exceptional Individuals, 16*, 123-134.

Halgren, D. W., & Clarizio, H. F. (1993). Categorical and programming changes in special education services. *Exceptional Children, 59*, 547-555.

Hall, A., Scholl, G. T., & Swallow, R. M. (1986). Psychoeducational assessment. In G. T. Scholl (Ed.), *Foundations of education for blind and visually handicapped children and youth: Theory and practice* (pp. 187-214). New York: American Foundation for the Blind.

Hall, E. T. (1976). How cultures collide. *Psychology Today, 10*(2), 66-74, 97.

Hallahan, D. P. (1992). Some thoughts on why the prevalence of learning disabilities has increased. *Journal of Learning Disabilities, 25*, 523-528.

Hallahan, D. P., Keller, C. E., McKinney, J. D., Lloyd, J. W., & Bryan, T. (1988). Examining the research base of the regular education initiative: Efficacy studies and the adaptive learning environment model. *Journal of Learning Disabilities, 21*(1), 29-35, 55.

Halle, J. W., Gabler-Halle, D., & Bemben, D. A. (1989). Effects of a peer-mediated aerobic conditioning program on fitness measures with children who have moderate and severe disabilities. *The Journal of The Association for Persons with Severe Handicaps, 14*, 33-47.

Halpern, A. S. (1985). Transition: A look at the foundations. *Exceptional Children, 51*, 479-486.

Halpern, A. S. (1992). Transition: Old wine in new bottles. *Exceptional Children, 58*, 202-211.

Halpern, A. S. (1993). Quality of life as a conceptual framework for evaluating transition outcomes. *Exceptional Children, 59*, 486-498.

Ham, R.. (1986). *Techniques of stuttering therapy.* Englewood Cliffs, NJ: Prentice-Hall.

Hamayan, E. V., & Damico, J. S. (1991). *Limiting bias in the assessment of bilingual students.* Austin, TX: PRO-ED.

Hammill, D. D. (1976). Defining learning disabilities for programmatic purposes. *Academic Therapy, 12*, 29-37.

Hammill, D. D. (1990). On defining learning disabilities: An emerging consensus. *Journal of Learning Disabilities, 23,* 74-84.

Hammill, D. D., & Larsen, S. (1974). The effectiveness of psycholinguistic training. *Exceptional Children, 41,* 5-15.

Hammill, D. D., & Larsen, S. (1978). The effectiveness of psycholinguistic training: A reaffirmation of position. *Exceptional Children, 44,* 402-417.

Hammill, D. D., Goodman, L., & Wiederholt, J. L. (1974). Visual-motor processes: Can we train them? *Reading Teacher, 27,* 469-478.

Hammill, D. D., Leigh, J. E., McNutt, G., & Larsen, S. C. (1981). A new definition of learning disabilities. *Learning Disability Quarterly, 4,* 336-342.

Hamre-Nietupski, S., Nietupski, J., Sandvig, R., Sandvig, M. B., & Ayres, B. (1984). Leisure skills instruction in a community residential setting with young adults who are deaf/blind severely handicapped. *The Journal of The Association for Persons with Severe Handicaps, 9,* 49-54.

Hanline, M. F. (1993). Facilitating integrated preschool service delivery transitions for children, families, and professionals. In C. A. Peck, S. L. Odom, & D. D. Bricker (Eds.), *Integrating young children with disabilities into community programs* (pp. 133-146). Baltimore, MD: Paul H. Brooks Publishing Company.

Hanline, M. F. (1993). Inclusion of preschoolers with profound disabilities: An analysis of children's interactions. *Journal of the Association for Persons with Severe Handicaps, 18,* 28-35.

Hansen, J. B., & Linden, K. W. (1990). Selecting instruments for identifying gifted and talented students. *Roeper Review, 13*(1), 10-15.

Harchik, A. E. (1994). Self-medication skills. In M. Agran, N. E. Marchand-Martella, and R. C. Martella (Eds.), *Promoting health and safety: Skills for independent living* (pp. 55-69). Pacific Grove, CA: Brooks/Cole.

Harchik, A. E., Putzier, V. S. (1990). The use of high-probability requests to increase compliance with instructions to take medication. *Journal of the Association for Persons with Severe Handicaps, 15,* 40-43.

Haring, K. A., Lovett, D. L., Haney, K. F., Algozzine, B., Smith, D. D., & Clarke, J. (1992). Labeling preschoolers as learning disabled: A cautionary position. *Topics in Early Childhood Special Education, 12,* 151-173.

Haring, N. G. (Ed.). (1988). *Generalization for students with severe handicaps: Strategies and solutions.* Seattle, WA: University of Washington Press.

Harrell, R., Capp, R., Davis, D., Peerless, J., & Ravitz, L. (1981). Can nutritional supplements help mentally retarded children? An exploratory study. *Proceedings of the National Academy of Science, 100,* 29-45.

Harris, C. R. (1991). Identifying and serving the gifted new immigrant. *Teaching Exceptional Children, 23*(4), 26-30.

Harris, S. L., & Handleman, J. S. (Eds.). (1994). *Preschool programs for children with autism.* Austin, TX: PRO-ED.

Harris, W. J., & Schutz, P. N. B. (1986). *The special education resource program: Rationale and implementation.* Englewood Cliffs, NJ: Merrill/Prentice Hall.

Harrison, R., & Edwards, J. (1983). *Child abuse.* Portland, OR: Ednick.

Harry, B. (1992). Making sense of disability: Low-income, Puerto Rican parents' theories of the problem. *Exceptional Children, 59,* 27-40.

Harry, B. (1992a). *Cultural diversity, families, and the special education system: Communication and empowerment.* New York: Teachers College Press.

Harry, B. (1992b). Restructuring the participation of African-American parents in special education. *Exceptional Children, 59,* 123-131.

Hart, B., & Risley, T. R. (1975). Incidental teaching of language in the preschool. *Journal of Applied Behavior Analysis, 8,* 411-420.

Hart, B., & Risley, T. (1992). Variations in American parenting that predict child outcomes at three. *Developmental Psychology, 28,* 1096-1105.

Harvey Smith, M A. (1994). Nutrition and diet. In M. Agran, N. E. Marchand-Martella, and R. C. Martella (Eds.), *Promoting health and safety: Skills for independent living* (pp. 33-53). Pacific Grove, CA: Brooks/Cole.

Hasazi, S. B., Gordon, L. R., & Roe, C. A. (1985). Factors associated with the employment status of handicapped youth exiting high school from 1979 to 1983. *Exceptional Children, 51,* 455-469.

Hasazi, S. B., Johnson, R. E., Hasazi, J. E., Gordon, L. R., & Hull, M. (1989). Employment of youth with and without handicaps following high school: Outcomes and correlates. *The Journal of Special Education, 23,* 243-255.

Hasazi, S. B., Johnston, A. P., Liggett, A. M., & Schattman, R. A. (1994). A qualitative policy study of the least restrictive environment provision of the individuals with disabilities education act. *Exceptional Children, 60,* 491-507.

Haskew, P., & Donnellan, A. M. (1992). *Emotional maturity and well-being: Psychological lessons of facilitated communication.* Danbury, CT: DRI Press.

Hassett, M. E., Engler, C., Cooke, N. L., Test, D. W., Weiss, A. B., Heward, W. L., & Heron, T. E. (1984). A telephone-managed, home-based summer writing program for LD adolescents. In W. L. Heward, T. E. Heron, D. S. Hill, & J. Trap-Porter (Eds.), *Focus on behavior analysis in education* (pp. 89-103). Englewood Cliffs, NJ: Merrill/Prentice Hall.

Hatlen, P. H. (1976, Winter). Priorities in education programs for visually handicapped children and youth. *Division for the Visually Handicapped Newsletter,* 8-11.

Hatlen, P. H. (1978, Fall). The role of the teacher of the visually impaired: A self-definition. *Division for the Visually Handicapped Newsletter,* 5.

Hatten, J. T., & Hatten, P. W. (1975). *Natural language.* Tucson, AZ: Communication Skill Builders.

Hauber, F. A., Bruininks, R. H., Hill, B. K., Lakin, K. C., & White, C. C. (1984). *National census of residential facilities: Fiscal year 1982.* Minneapolis: University of Minnesota, Center for Residential and Community Services.

Hawkins, R. P. (1984). What is "meaningful" behavior change in a severely/profoundly retarded learner? The view of a behavior analytic parent. In W. L. Heward, T. E. Heron, D. S. Hill, & J. Trap-Porter (Eds.), *Focus on behavior analysis in education* (pp. 282-286). Englewood Cliffs, NJ: Merrill/Prentice Hall.

Hawkins, R. P., & Hawkins, K. K. (1981). Parental observations on the education of severely retarded children: Can it be done in the classroom? *Analysis and Intervention in Development Disabilities, 1,* 13-22.

Haycock, G. S. (1933). *The teaching of speech.* Stoke-on-Trent, England: Hill & Ainsworth.

Hayden, A. H., & Pious, C. G. (1979). The case for early intervention. In R. York & E. Edgar (Eds.), *Teaching the severely handicapped* (Vol. 4) (pp. 267-287). Seattle: American Association for the Education of the Severely/Profoundly Handicapped.

Hayden, M. F., Lakin, K. C., Hill, B. K., Bruininks, R. H., & Copher, J. I. (1992). Social and leisure integration of people with mental retardation in foster homes and small group homes. *Education and*

Training in Mental Retardation, *27*, 187-199.

Hebbeler, K. M., Smith, B. J., & Black, T. L. (1991). Federal early childhood special education policy: A model for the improvement of services for children with disabilities. *Exceptional Children*, *58*, 104-112.

Heber, R. F. (1961). A manual on terminology and classification in mental retardation (rev. ed.). Monograph Supplement, *American Journal of Mental Deficiency*, 64.

Heber, R. F., & Garber, H. (1971). An experiment in prevention of cultural-familial mental retardation. In D. A. Primrose (Ed.), *Proceedings of the Second Congress of the International Association for the Scientific Study of Mental Deficiency*. Warsaw: Polish Medical Publishers.

Hedlund, R. (1989). Fostering positive social interactions between parents and infants. *Teaching Exceptional Children*, *21*(4), 45-48.

Hegde, M. N. (1986). Treatment of fluency disorders: State of the art. In J. M. Costello & A. L. Holland (Eds.), *Handbook of speech and language disorders* (pp. 505-538). San Diego: College-Hill.

Hegde, M. N. (1993). *Treatment procedures in communicative disorders*. Austin, TX: PRO-ED.

Heiden, S. M. (1989). A ten year follow-up study of former students at the Wisconsin School for the Visually Handicapped. *RE:view*, *21*, 21.

Heinze, T. (1986). Communication skills. In G. T. Scholl (Ed.), *Foundations of education for blind and visually handicapped children and youth: Theory and practice* (pp. 301-314). New York: American Foundation for the Blind.

Heller, K. W., Ware, S., Allgood, M. H ., Castelle, M. (1994). Use of dual communication boards with students who are deaf-blind. *Journal of Visual impairment & Blindness*, July-August, 368-376.

Heller, T., Bond, M. S., & Braddock, D. (1988). Family reactions to institutional closure. *American Journal on Mental Retardation*, *92*, 336-343.

Hemming, H., Lavender, T., & Pill, R. (1981). Quality of life of mentally retarded adults transferred from large institutions to new small units. *American Journal of Mental Deficiency*, *86*, 157-169.

Henderson, C. (1992). *College freshmen with disabilities: A statistical profile*. Washington, DC: American Council on Education, HEATH Resource Center. (ERIC No. ED354792).

Henderson, J. (1986). *Making regular schools special*. New York: Schocken.

Henderson, L. W., & Meisels, S. J. (1994). Parental involvement in the developmental screening of their young children: A multiple-source perspective. *Journal of Early Intervention*, *18*, 141-154.

Hendrickson, J. M., Strain, P. S., Tremlay, A., & Shores R. E. (1982). Interactions of behaviorally handicapped children. In P. S. Strain, M. J. Gurlanick, & H. M. Walker (Eds.) *Children's social behavior: Development, assessment, and modification* (pp. 323-337) Orlando, Fl: Academic Press.

Heron, T. E., & Harris, K. C. (1993). *The educational consultant: Helping professionals, parents and mainstreamed students* (3rd ed.). Austin, TX: PRO-ED.

Heron, T. E., & Heward, W. L. (1988). Ecological assessment: Implications for teachers of learning disabled students. *Learning Disability Quarterly*, *11*, 117-125.

Heron, T. E., & Skinner, M. E. (1981). Criteria for defining the regular classroom as the least restrictive environment for LD students. *Learning Disability Quarterly*, *4*, 115-121.

Heron, T. E., Heward, W. L., Cooke, N. L., & Hill, D. S. (1983). Evaluation of a classwide peer tutoring system: First graders teach each other sight words. *Education & Treatment of Children*, *6*, 137-152.

Heward, W. L. (1987). Self-management. In J. O. Cooper, T. E. Heron, & W. L. Heward, *Applied behavior analysis* (pp. 515-549). Englewood Cliffs, NJ: Merrill/Prentice Hall.

Heward, W. L. (1994). Three "low-tech" strategies for increasing the frequency of active student response during group instruction. In R. Gardner III, D. M. Sainato, J. O. Cooper, T. E. Heron, W. L. Heward, J. Eshleman, & T. A. Grossi (Eds.), *Behavior analysis in education: Focus on measurably superior instruction* (pp. 283-320). Pacific Grove, CA: Brooks/Cole.

Heward, W. L., & Cavanaugh, R. A. (in press). Educational equality for students with disabilities. In J. A. Banks & C. A. M. Banks (Eds.), *Multicultural education: Issues and perspectives* (3rd ed.). Boston: Allyn & Bacon.

Heward, W. L., & Chapman, J. E. (1981). Improving parent-teacher communication through recorded telephone messages: Systematic replication in a special education classroom. *Journal of Special Education Technology*, *4*, 11-19.

Heward, W. L., Courson, F. H., & Narayan, J. S. (1989). Using choral responding to increase active student response during group instruction. *Teaching Exceptional Children*, *21*(3), 72-75.

Heward, W. L., & Dardig, J. C. (1978). Improving the parent-teacher relationship through contingency contracting. In D. Edge, B. J. Strenecky, & S. I. Mour (Eds.), *Parenting learning-problem children: The professional educator's perspective* (pp. 71-78). Columbus, OH: Ohio State University, National Center for Educational Materials and Media for the Handicapped.

Heward, W. L., Dardig, J. C., & Rossett, A. (1979). *Working with parents of handicapped children*. Englewood Cliffs, NJ: Merrill/Prentice Hall.

Heward, W. L., Heron, T. E., & Cooke, N. L. (1982). Tutor huddle: Key element in a classwide peer tutoring system. *Elementary School Journal*, *83*, 115-123.

Heward, W. L., Heron, T. E., Gardner III, R., & Prayzer, R. (1991). Two strategies for improving students' writing skills. In G. Stoner, M. R. Shinn, & H. M. Walker (Eds.), *A school psychologist's interventions for regular education* (pp. 379-398). Washington, DC: National Association of School Psychologists.

Hewett, F. M., & Forness, S. R. (1977). *Education of exceptional learners* (2nd ed.). Boston: Allyn & Bacon.

Hewett, F. M., & Taylor, F. D. (1980). *The emotionally disturbed child in the classroom: The orchestration of success* (2nd. ed.). Boston: Allyn & Bacon.

Hieronymus, A. N., & Lindquist, E. F. (1978). *Iowa Tests of Basic Skills*. Boston: Houghton Mifflin.

Higbee Mandlebaum, L. (1992). Frequently recommended books for students in preschool through high school. *Intervention in School and Clinic*, *27*, 170-184.

Hill, B. K., & Bruininks, R. H. (1981). *Family, leisure, and social activities of mentally retarded people in residential facilities*. Minneapolis: University of Minnesota, Department of Education Psychology.

Hill, B. K., & Lakin, K. C. (1986). Classification of residential facilities for mentally retarded people. *Mental Retardation*, *24*, 107-115.

Hill, B. K., Lakin, K. C., & Bruininks, R. H. (1984). Trends in residential services for people who are mentally retarded: 1977-1982. *The Journal of The Association for Persons with Severe Handicaps*, *9*, 243-250.

Hill, B. K., Lakin, K. C., Bruininks, R. H., Amado, A. N., Anderson, D. J., & Copher, J. I. (1989). *Living in the community: A comparative study of foster homes and small group homes for people with mental retardation.* Minneapolis, MN: Center for Residential and Community Services (Report #28), University of Minnesota.

Hill, E. W., & Jacobson, W. H. (1985). Controversial issues in orientation and mobility: Then and now. *Education of the Visually Handicapped, 17,* 59-70.

Hill, J. W., Wehman, P., & Horst, G. (1982). Toward generalization of appropriate leisure and social behavior in severely handicapped youth: Pinball machine use. *The Journal of The Association for the Severely Handicapped, 6*(4), 38-44.

Hill, R., Carjuzaa, J., Aramburo, D., & Baca, L. (1993). Culturally and linguistically diverse teachers in special education: Repairing or redesigning the leaky pipeline. *Teacher Education and Special Education, 16,* 258-269.

Hilliard, A. G. (1975). The strengths and weaknesses of cognitive tests for young children. In J. D. Andrews (Ed.), *One child indivisible* (pp. 17-33). Washington, DC: National Association for the Education of Young Children.

Hilliard, A. G. (1980). Cultural diversity and special education. *Exceptional Children, 46,* 584-588.

Hilliard, A. G. (1992). Behavioral style, culture, and teaching and learning. *Journal of Negro Education, 16,* 370-375.

Hinshelwood, J. (1895). Word-blindness and visual memory. *Lancet, 2,* 1564-1570.

Hitzing, W. (1980). ENCOR and beyond. In T. Apolloni, J. Cappuccilli, & T. P. Cooke (Eds.), *Achievements in residential services for persons with disabilities: Total excellence.* Baltimore, MD: University Park Press.

Ho, Y. (1991). The easy listener FM system: A new strategy for students with LD. *Intervention in School and Clinic, 27*(1), 56-59.

Hobbs, N. (1966). Helping the disturbed child: Psychological and ecological strategies. *American Psychologist, 21,* 1105-1115.

Hobbs, N. (1975). *The futures of children.* San Francisco: Jossey-Bass.

Hobbs, N. (Ed.). (1976a). *Issues in the classification of children* (Vol. 1). San Francisco: Jossey-Bass.

Hobbs, N. (Ed.). (1976b). *Issues in the classification of children* (Vol. 2). San Francisco: Jossey-Bass.

Hodapp, J. B., & Hodapp, A. F. (1991). ABC's of homework: Tips for parents. *Intervention in School and Clinic, 26*(5), 282-283.

Hodapp, R. M., & Dykens, E. M. (1994). Mental retardation's two cultures of behavioral research. *American Journal on Mental Retardation, 98,* 675-687.

Hoemann, H. W., & Briga, J. I. (1981). Hearing impairments. In J. M. Kauffman & D. P. Hallahan (Eds.), *Handbook of special education.* Englewood Cliffs, NJ: Prentice-Hall.

Hoisch, S. A., Karen, R. L., & Franzini, L. R. (1992). Two-year follow-up of the competitive employment status of graduates with developmental disabilities. *Career Development for Exceptional Individuals, 15,* 149-155.

Holbrook, M. C., & Koenig, A. J. (1992). Teaching braille reading to students with low vision. *Journal of Visual Impairment & Blindness, 86,* 44-48.

Holburn, C. S. (1990). Symposium overview: Our residential rules—have we gone too far? *Mental Retardation, 28,* 65-66.

Holland, A. L., & Reinmuth, O. M. (1982). Aphasia in adults. In G. H. Shames & E. H. Wiig (Eds.), *Human communication disorders: An introduction* (pp. 561-593). Englewood Cliffs, NJ: Merrill/Prentice Hall.

Hollander, R. (1989). Euthanasia and mental retardation: Suggesting the unthinkable. *Mental Retardation, 27,* 53-61.

Hollinger, C. L. (1995). Counseling gifted young women about educational and career choices. In Genshaft, J. L., Bireley, M., & Hollinger, C. L. (Eds.). *Serving gifted and talented students: A resource for school personnel* (pp. 269-283). Austin, TX: PRO-ED.

Hollingworth, L. (1942/1975). *Children above 180 IQ.* Yonkers-on-Hudson, NY: World Books.

Homeward Bound, Inc. v. Hissom Memorial Center, U.S. Court of Appeals for the Tenth Circuit, No. 88-1119, 88-1241 (October 3, 1988).

Hoover, J. J. (1993). Helping parents develop a home-based study skills program. *Intervention in School and Clinic, 28,* 238-245.

Horn, E. M. (1991). Basic motor skills instruction for children with neuromotor delays: A critical review. *The Journal of Special Education, 25,* 168-197.

Horner, J. (1986). Moderate aphasia. In J. M. Costello & A. L. Holland (Eds.), *Handbook of speech and language disorders* (pp. 891-915). San Diego: College-Hill.

Horner, R. H. (1994). Facilitated communication: Keeping it practical. *Journal of the Association for Persons with Severe Handicaps, 19,* 185-186.

Horner, R. H., & McDonald, R. S. (1982). Comparison of single instance and general case instruction in teaching of a generalized vocational skill. *Journal of the Association for Persons with Severe Handicaps, 7*(3), 7-20.

Horner, R. H., Day, H. M., Sprague, J. R., O'Brien, M., & Heathfield, L. T. (1991). Interspersed requests: A non-aversive procedure for reducing aggression and self-injury during instruction. *Journal of Applied Behavior Analysis, 24,* 265-278.

Horner, R. H., Dunlap, G., & Koegel, R. L. (1988). *Generalization and maintenance: Life-style changes in applied settings.* Baltimore, MD: Paul H. Brooks Publishing Company.

Horner, R. H., McDonnell, J. J., & Bellamy, G. T. (1986). Teaching generalized skills: General case instruction in simulation and community settings. In R. H. Horner, L. H. Meyer, & H. D. B. Fredericks (Eds.), *Education of learners with severe handicaps: Exemplary service strategies* (pp. 289-314). Baltimore, MD: Paul H. Publishing Company.

Horner, R. H., Stoner, S., & Ferguson, D. (1988). *an activity based analysis of deinstitutionalization: The effects of community reintegration on the lives of residents leaving Oregon's Fairview Training Center.* Salem, OR: Oregon Developmental Disabilities Office.

Horner, R. H., Williams, J. A., & Steveley, J. D. (1987). Acquisition of generalized telephone use by students with moderate and severe mental retardation. *Research in Developmental Disabilities, 8,* 229-247.

Horner, R. H., Eberhard, J. M., & Sheehan, M. R. (1986). Teaching generalized table bussing. *Behavior Modification, 10*(4), 457-471.

Horner, R. H., Sprague, J., & Wilcox, B. (1982). Constructing general case programs for community activities. In B. Wilcox, & G. T. Bellamy (Eds.), *Design of high school programs for severely handicapped students* (pp. 61-98). Baltimore: Paul H. Brooks Publishing Company, Inc.

Horst, G., Wehman, P., Hill, J. W., & Bailey, C. (1981). Developing age-appropriate leisure skills in severely handicapped adolescents. *Teaching Exceptional Children, 14,* 11-16.

Horton, S. V., & Lovitt, T. C. (1989). Construction and implementation of graphic organizers for academically handicapped and regular secondary students. *Academic Therapy*, *24*, 625-640.

Horton, S. V., Lovitt, T. C., & Bergerud, D. (1990). The effectiveness of graphic organizers for three classifications of secondary students in content area classes. *Journal of Learning Disabilities*, *23*, 12-22.

Houlihan, M., & Van Houten, R. (1989). Behavioral treatment of hyperactivity: A review and overview. *Education & Treatment of Children*, *12*, 265-275.

Howard, V. F., Williams, B. F., & McLaughlin, T. F. (1994). Children prenatally exposed to alcohol and cocaine: Behavioral solutions. In R. Gardner III, D. M. Sainato, J. O. Cooper, T. E. Heron, W. L. Heward, J. Eshleman, & T. A. Grossi (Eds.), *Behavior analysis in education: Focus on measurably superior instruction* (pp. 131-146). Pacific Grove, CA: Brooks/Cole.

Howard-Rose, D., & Rose, C. (1994). Students' adaptations to task environments in resource and regular class settings. *The Journal of Special Education*, *28*, 3-26.

Howe, K. R., & Miramontes, O. B. (1991). A framework for ethical deliberation in special education. *The Journal of Special Education*, *25*, 7-25.

Howell, K. W., & Lorson-Howell, K. A. (1990). What's the hurry? Fluency in the classroom. *Teaching Exceptional Children*, *22*(3), 20-23.

Howell, K. W., Fox, S. L., & Morehead, M. K. (1993). *Curriculum-based evaluation: Teaching and decision making* (2nd ed.). Pacific Grove, CA: Brooks/Cole.

Howell, R. D. (1995). Technological innovations in the education of gifted and talented students. In Genshaft, J. L., Bireley, M., & Hollinger, C. L. (Eds.). *Serving gifted and talented students: A resource for school personnel* (pp. 155-171). Austin, TX: PRO-ED.

Hubbell, R. (1985). Language and linguistics. In P. Skinner & R. Shelton (Eds.), *Speech, language, and hearing: Normal processes and disorders* (2nd ed.). New York: John Wiley & Sons.

Hudson, P., Lignugaris-Kraft, B., & Miller, T. (1993). Using content enhancements to improve the performance of adolescents with learning disabilities in content classes. *Learning Disabilities Research & Practice*, *8*, 106-126.

Huebner, K. M. (1986). Social skills. In G. T. Scholl (Ed.), *Foundations for education for blind and visually handicapped children and youth: Theory and practice* (pp. 341-362). New York: American Foundation for the Blind.

Hughes, C. (1994). Teaching generalized skills to persons with disabilities. In R. Gardner III, D. M. Sainato, J. O. Cooper, T. E. Heron, W. L. Heward, J. Eshleman, & T. A. Grossi (Eds.), *Behavior analysis in education: Focus on measurably superior instruction* (pp. 335-348). Pacific Grove, CA: Brooks/Cole.

Hughes, C., & Rusch, F. R. (1989). Teaching supported employees with severe mental retardation to solve problems. *Journal of Applied Behavior Analysis*, *22*, 365-372.

Hughes, C., Rusch, F. R., & Curl, R. M. (1990). Extending individual competence, developing natural support, and promoting social acceptance. In F. Rusch (Ed.), *Supported employment: Models, methods, and issues* (pp. 181-197). Sycamore, IL: Sycamore Publishing.

Hulit, L. M., & Howard, M. R. (1993). *Born to talk: An introduction to speech and language development*. Englewood Cliffs, NJ: Merrill/Prentice Hall.

Hull, F. M., Mielke, P. W., Willeford, J. A., & Timmons, R. J. (1976). *National speech and hearing survey* (Final report; Project No. 50978; Grant No. OE-32-15-0050-5010 [607]). Washington, DC: U.S. Department of Health, Education, and Welfare.

Hunsucker, P. F., Nelson, R. O., & Clark, R. P. (1986). Standardization and evaluation of the Classroom Adaptive Behavior Checklist for school use. *Exceptional Children*, *53*, 69-71.

Hunt, P., Alwell, M., & Goetz, L. (1991). Establishing conversational exchanges with family and friends: Moving from training to meaningful communication. *The Journal of Special Education*, *25*, 305-319.

Hunt, P., Farron-Davis, F., Beckstead, S., Curtis, D., & Goetz, L. (1994). Evaluating the effects of placement of students with severe disabilities in general education versus special education classes. *Journal of the Association for Persons with Severe Handicaps*, *19*, 200-214.

Hunt, P., Goetz, L., & Anderson, J. (1986). The quality of IEP objectives associated with placement on integrated versus segregated school sites. *The Journal of The Association for Persons with Severe Handicaps*, *11*, 125-130.

Huntze, S. L. (1985). A position paper of the Council for Children with Behavioral Disorders. *Behavioral Disorders*, *10*, 167-174.

Hurlbut, B. I., Iwata, B. A., & Green, J. D. (1982). Nonvocal language acquisition in adolescents with severe physical disabilities: Blissymbol versus iconic stimulus formats. *Journal of Applied Behavior Analysis*, *15*, 241-258.

Hurvitz, J. A., Pickert, S. M., & Rilla, D. C. (1987). Promoting children's language interaction. *Teaching Exceptional Children*, *19*(3), 12-15.

Hutchins, M. P., & Renzaglia, A. M. (1990). Developing a longitudinal vocational training program. In F. Rusch (Ed.), *Supported employment: Models, methods, and issues* (pp. 365-380). Sycamore, IL: Sycamore Publishing.

Hutinger, P. L., Marshall, S., & McCarten, K. (1983). *Core curriculum: Macomb 0-3 regional project* (3rd ed.). Macomb, IL: Western Illinois University.

Idol, L. (1989). The resource/consulting teacher: An integrated model of service delivery. *Remedial and Special Education*, *10*(6), 38-48.

Ireland, J. C., Wray, D., & Flexer, C. (1988). Hearing for success in the classroom. *Teaching Exceptional Children*, *20*(2), 15-17.

Irving Independent School District v. Tatro, 104 S. Ct. 3371, 82 L.Ed. 2d 664 (1984).

Iscoe, I., & Payne, S. (1972). Development of a revised scale for the functional classification of exceptional children. In E. P. Trapp & P. Himelstein (Eds.), *Readings on the exceptional child* (pp. 7-29). New York: Appleton-Century-Crofts.

Itard, J. M. G. (1962). *The wild boy of Aveyron*. (G. Humphrey & M. Humphrey, Eds. and Trans.). New York: Appleton-Century-Crofts. (Original work published 1894)

Iwata, B. A. (1988). The development and adoption of controversial default technologies. *The Behavior Analyst*, *11*, 149-157.

Iwata, B. A., Pace, G. M., Dorsey, M. F., Zarcone, J. R., Vollmer, T. R., Smith, R. G., Rodgers, T. A., Lerman, D. C., Shore, B. A., Mazaleski, J. L., Goh, H. L., Cowdery, G. E., Kalsher, M. J., McCosh, K. C., & Willis, K. D. (1994). The functions of self-injurious behavior: An experimental-epidemiological analysis. *Journal of Applied Behavior Analysis*, *27*, 215-240.

Jacobsen, J. W. (1994). Review of mental retardation: Definition, classification, and systems of supports. *American Journal on Mental Retardation*, *98*, 539-541.

Jacobsen, J. W., & Mulick, J. A. (1992). A new definition of mentally retarded or a new definition of practice. *Psychology in Mental Retardation and Developmental Disabilities*, *18*(2), 9-14.

Jacobson, W. H. (1993). *The art and science of teaching orientation and mobility to persons with visual impairments*. New York: American Federation for the Blind.

Jaklin, C. N. (1989). Female and male: Issues of gender. *American Psychologist, 44*, 127-133.

Janicki, M. P., & Zigman, W. B. (1984). Physical and environmental design characteristics of community residences. *Mental Retardation, 22*, 294-301.

Janzen, R. (1994). Melting pot or mosaic? *Educational Leadership, 51*, 9-11.

Jastak, J. F., & Jastak, S. R. (1965). *The Wide Range Achievement Test* (rev. ed.). Wilmington, DE: Guidance Associates.

Jastak, J. F., & Wilkinson, G. S. (1984). *The Wide Range Achievement Test—Revised.* Wilmington, DE: Jastak Associates.

Jenkins, J. R., & Pious, C. G. (1991). Full inclusion and the REI: A reply to Thousand and Villa. *Exceptional Children, 57*, 562-564

Jenkins, J. R., Speltz, M. L., & Odom, S. L. (1985). Integrating normal and handicapped preschoolers: Effects on child development and social interaction. *Exceptional Children, 52*, 7-17.

Jensen, B. F., & Potter, M. L. (1990). Best practices in communicating with parents. In A. Thomas & J. Grimes (Eds.), *Best practices in school psychology—II* (pp. 183-193). Washington, DC: National Association of School Psychologists.

Jitendra, A. K., & Kameenui, E. J. (1993). Dynamic assessment as a compensatory assessment approach: A description and analysis. *Remedial and Special Education, 14*(5), 6-18.

Johnson, B., & Cuvo, A. (1981). Teaching mentally retarded adults to cook. *Behavior Modification, 12*, 69-73.

Johnson, C. (1994, September). *The nightmare of facilitated communication: A survivor fights back.* Paper presented at the annual meeting of the Florida Association for Behavior Analysis, Orlando, FL.

Johnson, J. R., & Rusch, F. R. (1990). Analysis of hours of direct training provided by employment specialists to supported employees. *American Journal on Mental Retardation, 94*, 674-682.

Johnson, J. R., & Rusch, F. R. (1993). Secondary special education and transition services: Identification and recommendations for future research and demonstration. *Career Development for Exceptional Individuals, 16*, 1-18.

Johnson, K. M., & Johnson, J. E. (1993). Rejoinder to Carta, Atwater, Schwartz, and McConnell. *Topics in Early Childhood Special Education, 13*, 255-257.

Johnson, L. J., Gallagher, R. J., LaMontagne, M. J., Jordan, J. B., Gallagher, J. J.,

Hutinger, P. L., & Karnes, M. B. (Eds.). (1994). *Meeting early intervention challenges: Issues from birth to three.* Reston, VA: Council for Exceptional Children.

Johnson, M. J. (1992). What's basic in a student-centered reading, writing, and thinking approach: One teacher's perspective. *The Volta Review, 94*, 389-394.

Johnson, M., & Bailey, J. (1977). The modification of leisure behavior in a halfway house for retarded women. *Journal of Applied Behavior Analysis, 10*, 273-282.

Johnson, R. (1985). *The picture communication symbols—Book II.* Solana Beach, CA: Mayer-Johnson.

Johnson, T. P. (1986). *The principal's guide to the educational rights of handicapped students.* Reston, VA: National Association of Secondary School Principals.

Johnston, K. R., & Layng, T. V. J. (1994). The Morningside model of generative instruction. In R. Gardner III, D. M. Sainato, J. O. Cooper, T. E. Heron, W. L. Heward, J. Eshleman, & T. A. Grossi (Eds.), *Behavior analysis in education: Focus on measurably superior instruction* (pp. 173-197). Pacific Grove, CA: Brooks/Cole.

Jolly, A. C., Test, D. W., & Spooner, F. (1993). Using badges to increase initiations of children with severe disabilities in a play setting. *Journal of the Association for Persons with Severe Handicaps, 18*, 46-51.

Jonas, G. (1976). *Stuttering: The disorder of many theories.* New York: Farrar, Straus & Giroux.

Jones, K. H., & Bender, W. N. (1993). Utilization of paraprofessionals in special education: A review of the literature. *Remedial and Special Education, 14*(1), 7-14.

Jones, M. H. (1977). Physical facilities and environments. In J. B. Jordan, A. H. Hayden, M. B. Karnes, & M. M. Woods (Eds.), *Early childhood education for exceptional children: A handbook of exemplary practices.* Reston, VA: Council for Exceptional Children.

Jones, R. S. P., & McCaughey, R. E. (1992). Gentle teaching and applied behavior analysis: A critical review. *Journal of Applied Behavior Analysis, 25*, 853-867.

Jose, R. (1983). *Understanding low vision.* New York: American Foundation for the Blind.

Justen, J. E. (1976). Who are the severely handicapped? A problem in definition. *AAESPH Review, 1*(2), 1-12.

Justen, III, J. E., & Howerton, D. L. (1993). Clarifying behavior management termi-

nology. *Intervention in School and Clinic, 29*(1), 36-40.

Kaiser, A. P. (1993). Functional language. In Snell, M. E. (Ed.), *Instruction of students with severe disabilities* (4th ed.) (pp. 347-379). Englewood Cliffs, NJ: Merrill/Prentice Hall.

Kaiser, A. P., & Goetz, L. (1993). Enhancing communication with persons labeled severely disabled. *Journal of the Association for Persons with Severe Handicaps, 18*, 137-142.

Kaiser-Kupfer, M. I., & Morris, J. (1985). Advances in human genetics: The long range impact on blindness and the visually impaired. *Yearbook of the Association for Education and Rehabilitation of the Blind and Visually Impaired* (Vol. 2) (pp. 46-49). Alexandria, VA: Association for Education and Rehabilitation of the Blind and Visually Impaired.

Kameenui, E. J., & Darch, C. B. (1995). *Instructional classroom management: A proactive approach to behavior management.* White Plains, NY: Longman.

Kameenui, E. J., & Simmons, D. C. (1990). *Designing instructional strategies: The prevention of academic learning problems.* Englewood Cliffs, NJ: Merrill/Prentice Hall.

Kamps, D. M., Dugan, E. P., Leonard, B. R., & Daoust, P. M. (1994). Enhanced small group instruction using choral responding and student interaction for children with autism and developmental disabilities. *American Journal on Mental Retardation, 99*, 60-73.

Kaplan, S. (1988). Maintaining a gifted program. *Roeper Review, 11*(1), 35-37.

Karmody, C. S. (1986). Otology in perspective. In D. M. Luterman (Ed.), *Deafness in perspective* (pp. 1-13). San Diego: College-Hill.

Karnes, K. B, Beauchamp, K. D. F., & Pfaus, D. B. (1993). PEECH: A nationally validated early childhood special education model. *Topics in Early Childhood Special Education, 13*, 120-135.

Karnes, M. B., & Stayton, V. D. (1988). Model programs for infants and toddlers with handicaps. In J. B. Jordon, J. J. Gallagher, P. L. Hutinger, & M. B. Karnes (Eds.), *Early childhood special education: Birth to three* (pp. 67-108). Reston, VA: Council for Exceptional Children.

Katsiyannis, A. (1991). Extended school year policies. *Remedial and Special Education, 12*(1), 24-28.

Katsiyannis, A. (1992). Policy issues in school attendance of children with AIDS: A national survey. *The Journal of Special Education, 26*, 219-226.

Kauffman, J. M. (1977). *Characteristics of children's behavior disorders.* Englewood Cliffs, NJ: Merrill/Prentice Hall.

Kauffman, J. M. (1982). Social policy issues in special education and related services for emotionally disturbed children and youth. In M. M. Noel & N. G. Haring (Eds.), *Progress of change: Issues in educating the emotionally disturbed. Vol. 1: Identification and program planning* (pp. 1-10). Seattle: University of Washington.

Kauffman, J. M. (1985). An interview with James M. Kauffman. *The Directive Teacher,* 7(1), 12-14.

Kauffman, J. M. (1986). Educating children with behavior disorders. In R. J. Morris & B. Blatt (Eds.), *Special education: Research and trends* (pp. 249-271). New York: Pergamon Press.

Kauffman, J. M. (1993a). How we might achieve the radical reform of special education. *Exceptional Children,* 60, 6-16.

Kauffman, J. M. (1993b). *Characteristics of emotional and behavioral disorders of children and youth* (5th ed.). Englewood Cliffs, NJ: Merrill/Prentice Hall.

Kauffman, J. M. (Ed.). (1981). Special issue: Are all children educable? *Analysis and Intervention in Developmental Disabilities,* 1(1).

Kauffman, J. M., & Hallahan, D. K. (1994). *The illusion of full inclusion: A comprehensive critique of a current special education bandwagon.* Austin, TX: PRO-ED.

Kauffman, J. M., & Krouse, J. (1981). The cult of educability: Searching for the substance of things hoped for; the evidence of things not seen. *Analysis and Intervention in Developmental Disabilities,* 1(1), 53-61.

Kauffman, J. M., & Pullen, P. L. (1989). An historical perspective: A personal perspective on our history of service to mildly handicapped and at-risk students. *Remedial and Special Education,* 10(6), 12-14.

Kauffman, J. M., Cullinan, D., & Epstein, M. H. (1987). Characteristics of students placed in special programs for the seriously emotionally disturbed. *Journal of Special Education,* 13, 283-295.

Kauffman, J. M., Gerber, M. M., & Semmel, M. I. (1988). Arguable assumptions underlying the regular education initiative. *Journal of Learning Disabilities,* 21(1), 6-11.

Kauffman, J. M., Wong, K. L. H., Lloyd, J. W., Hung, L., Pullen, P. L. (1991). What puts pupils at risk? An analysis of classroom teachers' judgments of pupils' behavior. *Remedial and Special Education,* 12(5), 7-16.

Kaufman, A., & Kaufman, N. (1983). *Kaufman Assessment Battery for Children, interpretive manual.* Circle Pines, MN: American Guidance Service.

Kavale, K. A., & Reese, J. H. (1992). The character of learning disabilities: An Iowa profile. *Learning Disability Quarterly,* 15, 74-94.

Kavale, K. A., Forness, S. R., & Lorsbach, T. C. (1991). Definition for definitions of learning disabilities. *Learning Disability Quarterly,* 14, 257-266.

Kavale, K. A., Fuchs, D., & Scruggs, T. E. (1994). Setting the record straight on learning disability and low achievement: Implications for policy making. *Learning Disabilities Research & Practice,* 9, 70-77.

Kavale, K., & Mattson, P. D. (1983). One jumped off the balance beam: Meta-analysis of perceptual-motor training. *Journal of Learning Disabilities,* 16, 165-173.

Kazdin, A. (1993). Treatment of conduct disorder: Progress and directions in psychotherapy research. *Development and Psychopathology,* 5(1/2), 277-310.

Keel, M. C., & Gast, D. L. (1992). Small-group instruction for students with learning disabilities: Observational and incidental learning. *Exceptional Children,* 58, 357-368.

Kelker, K., Hecimovic, A., & LeRoy, C. H. (1994). Designing a classroom and school environment for students with AIDS: A checklist for teachers. *Teaching Exceptional Children,* 26(4), 52-55.

Keller, H. (1903). *The story of my life.* New York: Dell.

Keller, W. D., & Bundy, R. S. (1980). Effects of unilateral hearing loss upon educational achievement. *Child Care, Health & Development,* 6, 93-100.

Kelly, D. J., & Rice, M. L. (1986). A strategy for language assessment of young children: A combination of two approaches. *Language, Speech, and Hearing Services in the Schools,* 17, 83-94.

Kelly, M. L. (1990). *School-home notes.* New York: Guilford.

Kelly, R. R. (1987). Computers and sensory impaired individuals. In J. D. Lindsey (Ed.), *Computers and exceptional individuals* (pp. 125-146). Englewood Cliffs, NJ: Merrill/Prentice Hall.

Kennedy, C. H., & Itkonen, T. (1994). Some effects of regular class participation on the social contacts and social network of high school students with disabilities. *Journal of the Association for Persons with Severe Handicaps,* 19, 1-10.

Kennedy, C. H., Horner, R. H., & Newton, J. S. (1989). Social contacts of adults with severe disabilities living in the community: A descriptive analysis of relationship patterns. *The Journal of The Association for Persons with Severe Handicaps,* 14, 190-196.

Kenney, K. W., & Prather, E. M. (1986). Articulation development in preschool children: Consistency of productions. *Journal of Speech and Hearing Research,* 29, 29-36.

Kent, R. D. (1994). *Reference manual for communicative sciences and disorders.* Austin, TX: PRO-ED.

Keogh, B. K. (1990). Narrowing the gap between policy and practice. *Exceptional Children,* 57, 186-190.

Kephart, N. C. (1971). *The slow learner in the classroom* (2nd ed.). Englewood Cliffs, NJ: Merrill/Prentice Hall.

Kerr, B. (1985). Smart girls, gifted women: Special guidance concerns. *Roeper Review,* 8(1), 30-33.

Kerr, M. M., & Nelson, C. M. (1989). *Strategies for managing behavior problems in the classroom* (2nd ed.). Englewood Cliffs, NJ: Merrill/Prentice Hall.

Kershner, J., Hawks, W., & Grekin, R. (1977). *Megavitamins and learning disorders: A controlled double-blind experiment.* Unpublished manuscript, Ontario Institute for Studies in Education.

Kidd, J. W. (1979). An open letter to the Committee on Technology and Classification of AAMD from the Committee on Definition and Terminology of CEC-MR. *Education and Training of the Mentally Retarded,* 14, 74-76.

Kim, K. C., & Harh, W. M. (1983). Asian Americans and the "success" image: A critique. *Amerasia Journal,* 10, 3-21.

King-Stoops, J. (1980). *Migrant education: Teaching the wandering ones.* Bloomington, IN: Phi Delta Kappa Educational Foundation.

Kirk, S. A. (1958). *Early education of the mentally retarded: An experimental study.* Urbana, IL: University of Illinois.

Kirk, S. A. (1963). Behavioral diagnosis and remediation of learning disabilities. *In Proceedings of the Conference on Exploration into the Problems of the Perceptually Handicapped Child* (Vol. 1). Chicago: Perceptually Handicapped Children.

Kirk, S. A. (1978). Foreword. In D. F. Moores, *Educating the deaf: Psychology, principles, and practices.* Boston: Houghton Mifflin.

Kirk, S. A., & Elkins, J. (1975). Characteristics of children enrolled in the child service demonstration centers. *Journal of Learning Disabilities, 8,* 630-637.

Kirk, S. A., McCarthy, J. J., & Kirk, W. D. (1968). *Illinois Test of Psycholinguistic Abilities* (rev. ed.). Urbana, IL: University of Illinois Press.

Kirsten, I. (1981). *The Oakland picture dictionary.* Wauconda, IL: Don Johnston.

Kishi, G., Teelucksingh, B., Zollers, N., Park-Lee, S., & Meyer, L. (1988). Daily decision-making in community residences: A social comparison of adults with and without mental retardation. *American Journal on Mental Retardation, 92,* 430-435.

Kitano, M. K. (1991). A multicultural educational perspective on serving the culturally diverse gifted. *Journal for the Education of the Gifted, 15,* 14-19.

Klein, J. (1994). Supported living: Not just another "rung" on the continuum. *TASH Newsletter, 20*(7), 16-18.

Kleinberg, S. B. (1982). *Educating the chronically ill child.* Rockville, MD: Aspen.

Kleinberg, S. (1984). Facilitating the child's entry to school and coordinating school activities during hospitalization. In *Home care for children with serious handicapping conditions* (pp. 67-77). Washington, DC: Association for the Care of Children's Health.

Kleinman, D., Heckaman, K. A., Kimball, J. W., Possi, M. K., Grossi, T. A., & Heward, W. L. (May, 1994). *A comparative analysis of two forms of delayed feedback on the acquisition, generalization, and maintenance of science vocabulary by elementary students with learning disabilities.* Poster presented at the 20th Annual Convention, Association for Behavior Analysis, Atlanta, GA.

Klima, E., & Bellugi, U. (1979). *The signs of language.* Cambridge, MA: Harvard University Press.

Kline, C. S. (1986). *Effects of guided notes on academic achievement of learning disabled high school students.* Unpublished masters thesis. Columbus, OH: The Ohio State University.

Klinghammer, H. D. (1964). Social perception of the deaf and of the blind by their voices and their speech. In *Report of the proceedings of the International Congress on the Education of the Deaf and of the 41st meeting of the Convention of American Instructors of the Deaf.* Washington, DC: U.S. Government Printing Office.

Kluwin, T. N. (1985). Profiling the deaf student who is a problem in the classroom. *Adolescence, 20,* 863-875.

Kluwin, T. N. (1993). Cumulative effects of mainstreaming on the achievement of deaf adolescents. *Exceptional Children, 60,* 73-81.

Kluwin, T. N., & Kelly, A. B. (1992). Implementing a successful writing program in the public schools for students who are deaf. *Exceptional Children, 59,* 41-53.

Kluwin, T. N., & Moores, D. F. (1989). Mathematics achievement of hearing impaired adolescents in different placements. *Exceptional Children, 55,* 327-335.

Knapczyk, D. R. (1992). Effects of developing alternative responses on the aggressive behavior of adolescents. *Behavioral Disorders, 17,* 247-263.

Knitzer, J. (1982). *Unclaimed children: The failure of public responsibility to children and adolescents in need of mental health services.* Washington, DC: Children's Defense Fund.

Knitzer, J., Steinberg, Z., & Fleisch, B. (1990). *At the school house door: An examination of programs and policies for children with behavioral and emotional problems.* New York: Bank Street College of Education.

Knobloch, H., & Pasamanick, B. (1974). *Gesell's and Amatruda's developmental diagnosis: The evaluation and management of normal and abnormal neuropsychotic development in infancy and early childhood.* Hagerstown, MD: Harper & Row.

Knobloch, H., Pasamanick, B., & Sherard, E. S., Jr. (1966). *Developmental Screening Inventory.* New York: Psychological Corp.

Kobrick, J. W. (1972, April 19). The compelling case for bilingual education. *Saturday Review,* pp. 54, 58.

Kochanek, T. T., Kabacoff, R. I., & Lipsitt, L. P. (1990). Early identification of developmentally disabled and at-risk preschool children. *Exceptional Children, 56,* 528-538.

Koegel, R. L., & Frea, W. D. (1993). The treatment of social behavior in autism through the modification of pivotal social skills. *Journal of Applied Behavior Analysis, 26,* 369-377.

Koegel, R. L., & Kern Koegel, L. (1995). *Teaching children with autism.* Baltimore, MD: Paul H. Brooks Publishing Company.

Koestler, F. (1976). *The unseen minority: A social history of blindness in the United States.* New York: David McKay Co.

Kohler, F. W., & Greenwood, C. R. (1986). Toward a technology of generalization: The identification of natural contingencies of reinforcement. *The Behavior Analyst, 9,* 19-26.

Kohler, F. W., & Strain, P. S. (1993). The early childhood social skills program. *Teaching Exceptional Children, 25*(2), 41-42.

Kohler, P. D. (1994). On-the-job training: A curricular approach to employment. *Career Development for Exceptional Individuals, 17,* 29-40.

Kohn, A. (1989, November). Suffer the restless children. *The Atlantic,* pp. 90-98.

Koppelman, J. (Ed.). (1986). Reagan signs bill expanding services to handicapped preschoolers. *Report to Preschool Programs, 18*(21), 3-4.

Kovach, J. (1992). Tools for transition: Preparing students with LD for postsecondary education. *Intervention in School and Clinic, 28,* 54-60.

Kraemer, M. J., & Bierman, C. W. (1983). Asthma. In J. Umbreit (Ed.), *Physical disabilities and health impairments* (pp. 159-166). Englewood Cliffs, NJ: Merrill/Prentice Hall.

Krajicek, M., & Thompkins, R. (1993). *The medically fragile infant.* Austin, TX: PRO-ED.

Kratzer, D. A., Spooner, F., Test, D. W., & Koorland, M. A. (1993). Extending the application of constant time delay: Teaching a requesting skill to students with severe multiple disabilities. *Education and Treatment of Children, 16,* 235-253.

Kraus, J. E., Fife, D., & Conroy, D. (1987). Pediatric brain injuries: The nature, clinical course, and early outcomes in a defined United States population. *Pediatrics, 79,* 501-507.

Krauss, M. W. (1990). New precedent in family policy: Individualized Family Service Plan. *Exceptional Children, 56,* 388-395.

Krebs, P., & Coultier, G. (1992). Unified Sports: Run across the light. *Palaestra 8*(2), 42-45.

Kregel, J., Hill, M., & Banks, P. D. (1988). Analysis of employment specialist intervention time in supported competitive employment. *American Journal on Mental Retardation, 93,* 200-208.

Kregel, J., Wehman, P., & Banks, P. D. (1989). The effects of consumer characteristics and type of employment model on individual outcomes in supported employment. *Journal of Applied Behavior Analysis, 22,* 407-415.

Kress, J. S., & Elias, M. J. (1993). Substance abuse prevention in special education populations: Review and recommendations. *The Journal of Special Education, 27,* 35-51.

Krim, M. (1969). Scientific research and mental retardation. *President's Committee on Mental Retardation message* (No. 16). Washington, DC: U.S. Government Printing Office.

Kroth, R. L. (1981). Involvement with parents of behaviorally disordered adolescents. In G. Brown, R. L. McDowell, & J. Smith (Eds.), *Educating adolescents with behavior disorders* (pp. 123-139). Englewood Cliffs, NJ: Merrill/Prentice Hall.

Kugel, R. B., & Wolfensberger, W. (Eds.). (1969). *Changing patterns in residential services for the mentally retarded.* Washington, DC: Superintendent of Documents.

Kuhlman, F. (1924). Mental deficiency, feeble-mindedness, and defective delinquency. *American Association for the Study of the Feeble-Minded, 29,* 58-70.

Kuhn, T. S. (1970). *The structure of scientific revolutions* (2nd ed.). Chicago: The University of Chicago Press.

Kulick, J.A., & Kulick, C. L. (1984). Effects of accelerated instruction on students. *Review of Educational Research, 54*(3), 409-425.

Kurtz, G., & Kurtz, P. D. (1987). Child abuse and neglect. In J. T. Neisworth & S. J. Bagnato, *The young exceptional child: Early development and education* (pp. 206-229). Englewood Cliffs, NJ: Merrill/Prentice Hall.

Kusserow, R. P. (1990). *Crack babies. A report of the Office of Inspector General , Department of Health and Human Services, February,* Washington, D. C..

LaBlance, G. R., Steckol, K. F., & Smith, V. L. (1994). Stuttering: The role of the classroom teacher. *Teaching Exceptional Children, 26*(2), 10-12.

Labov, W. (1975). The logic of nonstandard English. In P. Stoller (Ed.), *Black American English: Its background and its usage in the schools and in literature.* New York: Dell.

LaCelle-Peterson, M., & Rivera, C. (1994). Is it really real for all kids? A framework for equitable assessment policies for English language learners. *Harvard Education Review, 64,* 55-75.

Ladson-Billings, G. (1994). What we can learn from multicultural education research. *Educational Leadership, 51,* 22-27.

Lagerström, M., Bremme, K., Eneroth, P., & Magnusson, D. (1991). Sex-related differences in school and IQ performance for children with low birth weight at ages 10 and 13. *The Journal of Special Education, 25,* 261-270.

Lagomarcino, A., Reid, D. H., Ivancic, M. T., & Faw, G. D. (1984). Leisure-dance instruction for severely and profoundly retarded persons: Teaching an intermediate community-living skill. *Journal of Applied Behavior Analysis, 17,* 71-84.

Lagomarcino, T. R., Hughes, C., & Rusch, F. R. (1989). Utilizing self-management to teach independence on the job. *Education and Training of the Mentally Retarded, 24,* 139-148.

LaGrow, S. J., & Mulder, L. (1989). Structured solicitation: A standardized method for gaining travel information. *Journal of Visual Impairment and Blindness, 83,* 469-471.

Lahey, M. (1988). *Language disorders and language development.* Englewood Cliffs, NJ: Merrill/Prentice Hall.

Lakin, K. C., Hill, B. K., Chen, T., & Stephens, S. A. (1989). *Persons with mental retardation and related conditions in mental retardation facilities: Selected findings for the 1987 National Medical Expenditure Survey.* Minneapolis: University of Minnesota, Center for Residential and Community Services.

Lamb, J., & Daniels, R. (1993). Gifted girls in a rural community: Math attitudes and career options. *Exceptional Children, 59,* 513-517.

Lamb, P., Kennedy, D., Chezem, J., Hopf, S., & Vaughn, V. (1993). Research skills for gifted elementary school pupils. *GCT, July/August,* 2-7.

Lambert, N., K. Nihira, K., & Leland, H. (1993). *Adaptive Behavior Scale-School* (2nd. ed.) by Austin, TX: PRO-ED.

Lancaster, J. (1806). *Improvement in education.* London: Collins & Perkins.

Landesman, S. (1986). Quality of life and personal life satisfaction: Definition and measurement issues. *Mental Retardation, 24,* 141-143.

Landesman, S., & Ramey, C. T. (1989). Developmental psychology and mental retardation: Integrating scientific principles with treatment practices. *American Psychologist, 44,* 409-415.

Lane, H. L. (1988). Is there a "psychology of the deaf"? *Exceptional Children, 55,* 7-19.

Lane, J. (1992). The use of the least restrictive environment principle in placement decisions affecting school-age students with disabilities. *University of Detroit Mercy Law Review, 69,* 291-322.

Langham, T. (1993). Tools of the trade. *RE:view, 25,* 137-141.

Larson, S. A., & Lakin, K. C. (1989). Deinstitutionalization of persons with mental retardation. *The Journal of The Associa-*

tion for Persons with Severe Handicaps, 14, 324-332.

LaVigna, G. W., & Donnellan, A. M. (1987). *Alternatives to punishment: Solving behavior problems with non-aversive strategies.* Los Angeles: Institute for Applied Behavior Analysis.

Lazar, I., & Darlington, R. (1982). Lasting effects of early education: A report from the consortium for longitudinal studies. *Monographs of the Society for Research in Child Development, 47*(2 & 3, Serial No. 195).

Lazarus, B. D. (1991). Guided notes, review, and achievement of secondary students with learning disabilities in mainstream content courses. *Education and Treatment of Children, 14,* 112-127.

Lazarus, B. D. (1993). Guided notes: Effects with secondary and post secondary students with mild disabilities. *Education and Treatment of Children, 16,* 272-289.

Lazzari, A. M., & Wood, J. W. (1993). Reentry to the regular classroom from pull-out programs: Reorientation strategies. *Teaching Exceptional Children, 25*(3), 62-65.

Learning Disabilities Association of America. (1993). Position Paper on Full Inclusion of All Students with Learning Disabilities in the Regular Classroom. *LDA Newsbrief, 28*(2), 1.

Lehr, D. H., & S. Macurdy, S. (1994). Meeting special health care needs of students. In M. Agran, N. E. Marchand-Martella, and R. C. Martella (Eds.), *Promoting health and safety: Skills for independent living* (pp. 71-84). Pacific Grove, CA: Brooks/Cole.

Lenz, B. K., Bulgren, J., & Hudson, P. J. (1990). Content enhancement: A model for promoting the acquisition of content by individuals with learning disabilities. In T. Scruggs & B. Y. L. Wong (Eds.), *Intervention research in learning disabilities* (pp. 122-165). New York: Springer-Verlag.

Leonard, L. B. (1986). Conversational replies of children with specific language impairments. *Journal of Speech and Hearing Research, 29,* 114-119.

Leone, P. E. (1994). Education services for youth with disabilities in a state-operated juvenile correctional system: Case study and analysis. *The Journal of Special Education, 28,* 43-58.

Leone, P., Lovitt, T. C., & Hansen, C. (1981). A descriptive follow-up study of learning disabled boys. *Learning Disability Quarterly, 4,* 152-162.

Leone, P. E., Rutherford, R. B., & Nelson, C. M. (1991). *Special education and juve-*

nile corrections. Reston, VA: Council for Exceptional Children.

Lerner, J. (1976). *Children with learning disabilities* (2nd ed.). Boston: Houghton Mifflin.

Lerner, J. W. (1993). *Learning disabilities: Theories, diagnosis, and teaching strategies* (6th ed.). Boston, Houghton Mifflin.

Lerner, J. W., Lowenthal, B., & Lerner, S. R. (1995). *Attention deficit disorders: Assessment and teaching.* Pacific Grove, CA: Brooks/Cole.

LeRoy, C. H., Powell, T. H., & Kelker, P. H. (1994). Meeting our responsibilities in special education. *Teaching Exceptional Children, 26*(4), 37-44.

Lerro, M. (1994). Teaching adolescents about AIDS. *Teaching Exceptional Children, 26*(4), 49-51.

Leung, E. K. (1988). Cultural and acultural commonalties and diversities among Asian Americans: Identification and programming considerations. In A. A. Ortiz & B. A. Ramirez (Eds.), *Schools and the culturally diverse exceptional student: Promising practices and future directions* (pp. 86-95). Reston, VA: Council for Exceptional Children.

Levin, J., & Scherfenberg, L. (1987). *Selection and use of simple technology in home, school, work, and community settings.* Minneapolis, MN: ABLENET.

Levine, P., & Edgar, E. (1994). An analysis by gender of long-term postschool outcomes for youth with and without disabilities. *Exceptional Children, 61,* 282-300.

Levitt, E. E. (1957). The results of psychotherapy with children: An evaluation. *Journal of Consulting Psychology, 21,* 189-196.

Levitt, E. E. (1963). Psychotherapy with children: A further evaluation. *Behavior Research and Therapy, 1,* 45-51.

Levitt, H. (1985). Technology and the education of the hearing impaired. In F. Powell, T. Finitzo-Hieber, S. Friel-Patti, & D. Henderson (Eds.), *Education of the hearing impaired child* (pp. 119-129). San Diego: College-Hill.

Lewis, R. B. (1993). *Special education technology: Classroom applications.* Pacific Grove, CA: Brooks/Cole.

Lewis, R. B., & Doorlag, D. H. (1991). *Teaching special students in the mainstream* (3rd ed.). Englewood Cliffs, NJ: Merrill/Prentice Hall.

Lewis, R. B., & Doorlag, D. H. (1995). *Teaching special students in the mainstream* (4th ed.). Englewood Cliffs, NJ: Merrill/Prentice-Hall.

Lewis, R. B., & Doorlag, D. H. (1995). *Teaching special students in the mainstream* (4th ed.). Englewood Cliffs, NJ: Merrill/Prentice-Hall.

Li, A. K. F., & Adamson, G. (1992). Gifted secondary students' preferred learning style: Cooperative, competitive, or individualistic? *Journal for the Education of the Gifted, 16,* 46-54.

Lichtenstein, S. (1993). Transition from school to adulthood: Case studies of adults with learning disabilities who dropped out of school. *Exceptional Children, 59,* 336-347.

Lichtenstein, S., & Michaelides, N. (1993). Transition from school to young adulthood: Four case studies of young adults labeled mentally retarded. *Career Development for Exceptional Individuals, 16,* 183-195.

Liebergott, J., Favors, A., von Hippel, C. S., & Needleman, H. L. (1978). *Mainstreaming preschoolers: Children with speech and language impairments.* (Stock No. 017-092-00033-2). Washington, DC: U.S. Government Printing Office.

Lieberman, L. M. (1982). The nightmare of scheduling. *Journal of Learning Disabilities, 15,* 57-58.

Lieberman, L. M. (1985). Special education and regular education: A merger made in heaven? *Exceptional Children, 51,* 513-516.

Light, L., Dumlao, C. M., & Stecker, P. M. (1993). Video Résumé: An application of technology for persons with severe disabilities. *Teaching Exceptional Children, 25*(3), 58-61.

Lignugaris/Kraft, B., Rule, S., Salzberg, C. L., & Stowitschek, J. J. (1988). Social-vocational skills of handicapped and nonhandicapped adults at work. *Journal of Employment Counseling, 23,* 20-31.

Likins, M., Salzberg, C. L., Stowitschek, J. J., Lignugaris/Kraft, R., & Curl, R. (1989). Co-worker implemented job training: The use of coincidental training and quality-control checking on the food preparation skills of trainees with mental retardation. *Journal of Applied Behavior Analysis, 22,* 381-393.

Lilly, M. S. (1986). The relationship between general and specific education: A new face on an old issue. *Counterpoint, 6*(1), 10.

Lim, L. H. F., & Browder, D. M. (1994). Multicultural life skills assessment of individuals with severe disabilities. *Journal of the Association for Persons with Severe Handicaps, 19,* 130-138.

Lindfors, J. W. (1987). *Children's language and learning* (2nd ed.). Englewood Cliffs, NJ: Prentice-Hall.

Lindley, L. (1990, August). Defining TASH: A mission statement. *TASH Newsletter, 16*(8), 1.

Lindman, F. T., & McIntyre, J. M. (1961). *The mentally disabled and the law.* Chicago: University of Chicago Press.

Lindsey, M. (1980). *Training teachers of the gifted and talented.* New York: Teachers College Press.

Lindsley, O. R. (1972). From Skinner to precision teaching: The child knows best. In J. B. Jordan & L. S. Robbins (Eds.), *Let's try doing something else kind of thing* (pp. 1-12). Arlington, VA: Council for Exceptional Children.

Linebaugh, C. W. (1986). Mild aphasia. In J. M. Costello & A. L. Holland (Eds.), *Handbook of speech and language disorders* (pp. 871-889). San Diego: College-Hill.

Ling, D. (1976). *Speech and the hearing-impaired child: Theory and practice.* Washington, DC: The Alexander Graham Bell Association for the Deaf.

Ling, D. (1986). Devices and procedures for auditory learning. *The Volta Review, 88*(5), 19-28.

Ling, D. (Ed.). (1984). *Early intervention for hearing-impaired children: Total communication options.* San Diego: College-Hill.

Lingwell, J. (1982, July 15). Remarks quoted in M. Kelly, *Parent's Almanac: Early Stutterers.* Washington Post, p. D5.

Little Soldier, L. (1990). The education of Native American students: Where makes a difference. *Equity & Excellence, 24*(4), 66-69.

Livingston-White, D., Utter, C., & Woodard, Q. E. (1985). Follow-up study of visually impaired students of the Michigan School for the Blind. *Journal of Visual Impairment and Blindness, 79,* 150-153.

Lloyd, J. W., Kauffman, J. M., & Concpeder, B. (1987). Differential teacher response to descriptions of aberrant behavior. In R. B. Rutherford, C. M. Nelson, & S. R. Forness (Eds.), *Severe behavior disorders of children and youth* (pp. 41-52). Boston: College Hill Press.

Lloyd, L. L., & Kangas, K. A. (1994). Augmentative and alternative communication. In G. H. Shames & E. H. Wiig, (Eds.), *Human communication disorders* (4th ed.) (pp. 606-657). Englewood Cliffs, NJ: Merrill/Prentice Hall.

Lloyd, L. L., Quist, R. W., & Windsor, J. (1990). A proposed augmentative and alternative communication model. *Augmentative and Alternative Communication, 6,* 172-183.

Lloyd, L., Spradlin, J., & Reid, M. (1968). An operant audiometric procedure for difficult-to-test patients. *Journal of Speech and Hearing Disorders, 33,* 236-245.

Logan, K. R., Alberto, P. A., Kana, & T. G., & Waylor-Bowen, T. (1994). Curriculum development and instructional design for students with profound disabilities. In L. Sternberg (Ed.). *Individuals with profound disabilities: Instructional and assistive strategies* (3rd ed.) (pp. 333-383). Austin, TX: PRO-ED.

Long, N. (1990). Comment on Ralph Gardner's article on life-space interviewing. *Behavioral Disorders, 15,* 119-125.

Lotter, V. (1966). Epidemiology of autistic conditions in young children—Part 1: Prevalence. *Social Psychiatry, 1*(3), 124-137.

Lotter, V. (1978). Follow-up studies. In M. Rutter & E. Schopler (Eds.), *Autism: A reappraisal of concepts and treatment.* London: Plenum Press.

Lovaas, O. I. (1981). *Teaching developmentally disabled children: The ME book.* Austin, TX: PRO-ED.

Lovaas, O. I. (1987). Behavioral treatment and normal educational and intellectual functioning in young autistic children. *Journal of Consulting and Clinical Psychology, 55,* 3-9.

Lovaas, O. I. (1994, October). Comments made during Ohio State University teleconference on applied behavior analysis, The Ohio State University, Columbus.

Lovaas, O. I., & Newsom, C. D. (1976). Behavior modification with psychotic children. In H. Leitenberg (Ed.), *Handbook of behavior modification and behavior therapy* (pp. 303-360). Englewood Cliffs, NJ: Prentice-Hall.

Lovitt, T. C. (1977). *In spite of my resistance . . . I've learned from children.* Englewood Cliffs, NJ: Merrill/Prentice Hall.

Lovitt, T. C. (1978). The learning disabled. In N. G. Haring (Ed.), *Behavior of exceptional children* (2nd ed.) (pp. 155-191). Englewood Cliffs, NJ: Merrill/Prentice Hall.

Lovitt, T. C. (1979). What should we call them? *Exceptional Teacher, 1*(1), 5-7.

Lovitt, T. C. (1982). *Because of my persistence . . . I've learned from children.* Englewood Cliffs, NJ: Merrill/Prentice Hall.

Lovitt, T. C. (1986). Oh! That this too too solid flesh would melt . . . the erosion of standardized tests. *The Pointer, 30*(2), 55-57.

Lovitt, T. C. (1989). *Introduction to learning disabilities.* Boston: Allyn & Bacon.

Lovitt, T. C. (1991). *Preventing school dropouts.* Austin, TX: PRO-ED.

Lovitt, T. C. (1995). *Tactics for teaching* (2nd. ed.). Englewood Cliffs, NJ: Prentice-Hall.

Lovitt, T. C. (in press). Curricular options and services for youth with disabilities. *Journal of Behavioral Education.*

Lovitt, T. Rudsit, J., Jenkins, J., Pious, C., & Benedetti, D. (1986). Adapting science materials for regular and learning disabled seventh graders. *Remedial and Special Education, 7*(1), 31-39.

Lowell, E. L., & Pollack, D. B. (1974). Remedial practices with the hearing impaired. In S. Dickson (Ed.), *Communication disorders: Remedial principles and practices.* Glenview, IL: Scott, Foresman.

Lowenfeld, B. (Ed.). (1973). *The visually handicapped child in school.* New York: John Day.

Lowitzer, A. C., Utley, C. A., & Baumeister, A. A. (1987). AAMD's 1983 classification in mental retardation as utilized by state mental retardation/developmental disabilities agencies. *Mental Retardation, 25,* 287-291.

Lucey, J., & Dangman, B. (1984). A reexamination of the role of oxygen in retrolental fibroplasia. *Pediatrics, 73,* 82-96.

Luckasson, R., Coulter, D. L., Polloway, E. A., Reiss, S., Schalock, R. L., Snell, M. E., Spitalnik D. M., & Stark, J. A. (1992). *Mental retardation: Definition, classification, and systems of supports* (9th ed.). Washington, DC: American Association on Mental Retardation.

Luckner, J. (1994). Developing independent and responsible behaviors in students who are deaf or hard of hearing. *Teaching Exceptional Children, 26*(2), 13-17.

Luckner, J. L., & Isaacson, S. C. (1990). Teaching expressive writing to hearing-impaired students. *Journal of Childhood Communication Disorders, 13,* 135-152.

Ludlow, B. L., & Sobsey, R. (1984). *The school's role in educating severely handicapped students.* Bloomington, IN: Phi Delta Kappa Educational Foundation.

Luetke-Stahlman, B., & Luckner, J. (1991). *Effectively educating students with hearing impairments.* New York: Longman.

Lund, K. A., & Bos, C. S. (1981). Orchestrating the preschool classroom: The daily schedule. *Teaching Exceptional Children, 14,* 120-125.

Lund, K. A., Foster, G. E., & McCall-Perez, F. C. (1978). The effectiveness of psycholinguistic training: A reevaluation. *Exceptional Children, 44,* 310-319.

Lusthaus, C. S., Lusthaus, E. W., & Gibbs, H. (1981). Parents' role in the decision process. *Exceptional Children, 48,* 256-257.

Lusthaus, E. (1985). "Euthanasia" of person with severe handicaps: Refuting the rationalizations. *Journal of the Association for Persons with Severe Handicaps, 10,* 87-94.

Luterman, D. M. (1991). *Counseling the communicatively disordered and their families.* Austin, TX: PRO-ED.

Luterman, D. M. (Ed.). (1986). *Deafness in perspective.* San Diego: College-Hill.

Lutfiyya, Z., Shoultz, B., & O'Connor S. (1989). Relationships and community: A resource review. *The Association for Persons with Severe Handicaps Newsletter, 15.*

Lutzker, J. R., & Campbell, R. (1994). *Ecobehavioral family interventions in developmental disabilities.* Pacific Grove, CA: Brooks/Cole.

Lynas, W. (1986). *Integrating the handicapped into ordinary schools: A study of hearing-impaired pupils.* London: Croom Helm.

Lynch, E. W., & Hanson, M. J. (1992). *Developing cross-cultural competence: A guide for working with young children and their families.* Baltimore: Paul H. Brooks Publishing Company.

Lynch, E. W., & Stein, R. (1982). Perspectives on parent participation in special education. *Exceptional Education Quarterly, 3*(2), 56-63.

Lynch, E. W., Lewis, R. B., & Murphy, D. S. (1993). Educational services for children with chronic illnesses: Perspectives of educators and families. *Exceptional Children, 59,* 210-220.

MacCarthy, A., & Connell, J. (1984). Audiological screening and assessment. In G. Lindsay (Ed.), *Screening for children with special needs* (pp. 63-85). London: Croom Helm.

MacDonald, L., & Barton, L. E. (1986). Measuring severity of behavior: A revision of Part II of the Adaptive Behavior Scale. *American Journal of Mental Deficiency, 90,* 418-424.

MacFadyen, J. T. (1986). Educated monkeys help the disabled to help themselves. *Smithsonian, 17*(7), 125-133.

Mack, J. H. (1980). *An analysis of state definitions of severely emotionally disturbed.* Reston, VA: Council for Exceptional Children. (ERIC Document Reproduction Service No. ED 201 135)

Macmann, G. M., & Barnett, D. W. (1992). Redefining the WISC-R: Implications for professional practice and public policy. *The Journal of Special Education, 26,* 139-161.

Macmann, G. M., Barnett, D. W., Lonbard, T. J., Belton-Kocher, E., & Sharpe, M. N. (1989). On the actuarial classification of children: Fundamental studies of classification agreement. *The Journal of Special Education, 23*, 127-149.

MacMillan, D. L. (1982). *Mental retardation in school and society* (2nd ed.). Boston: Little, Brown.

MacMillan, D. L. (1989). Mild mental retardation: Emerging issues. In G. A. Robinson, J. R. Patton, E. A. Polloway, & L. R. Sargent (Eds.), *Best practices in mild mental disabilities* (pp. 3-20). Reston, VA: Council for Exceptional Children.

MacMillan, D. L., Gresham, F. M., & Siperstein, G. N. (1993). Conceptual and psychometric concerns about the 1992 AAMR definition of mental retardation. *American Journal on Mental Retardation, 98*, 325-335.

MacMillan, D. L., Jones, R., & Aloia, G. (1974). The mentally retarded label: A theoretical analysis and review of the literature. *American Journal on Mental Retardation, 79*, 241-261.

MacMillan, D. L., Widaman, K. F., Balow, I. H., Borthwick-Duffy, S., Hendrick, I. G., & Hemsley, R. E. (1992). Special education students exiting the educational system. *The Journal of Special Education, 26*, 20-36.

Madden, N. A., & Slavin, R. E. (1983). Mainstreaming students with mild handicaps: Academic and social outcomes. *Review of Educational Research, 53*, 519-569.

Maddux, C. D., & Cummings, R. E. (1983). Parental home tutoring: Aids and cautions. *The Exceptional Parent, 13*(4), 30-33.

Maestas y Moores, J., & Moores, D. F. (1980). Language training with the young deaf child. In D. Bricker (Ed.), *Early language intervention with handicapped children.* San Francisco: Jossey-Bass.

Maheady, L., Mallete, B., Harper, G. F., & Saca, K. (1991). Heads together: A peer-mediated option for improving the academic achievement of heterogeneous learning groups. *Remedial and Special Education, 12*(2), 25-33.

Maheady, L., Sacca, M. K., & Harper, G. F. (1987). Classwide student tutoring teams: The effects of peer-mediated instruction on the academic performance of secondary mainstreamed students. *The Journal of Special Education, 21*, 107-121.

Maheady, L., Sacca, M. K., & Harper, G. F. (1988). Classwide peer tutoring with mildly handicapped high school students. *Exceptional Children, 55*, 52-59.

Mahon, M. J., & Bullock, C. C. (1992). Teaching adolescents with mild mental retardation to make decisions in leisure through the use of self-control techniques. *Therapeutic Recreation Journal, 26*, 9-26.

Maker, C. J. (1977). *Providing programs for the gifted handicapped*. Reston, VA: Council for Exceptional Children.

Maker, C. J. (1982). *Curriculum development for the gifted*. Austin, TX: PRO-ED.

Maker, C. J. (1982). Teaching models in education of the gifted. Rockville, MD: Aspen.

Maker, C. J. (1989). *Critical issues in gifted education: Defensible programs for cultural and ethnic minorities*. Austin, TX: PRO-ED.

Maker, C. J. (1989). Programs for gifted minority students: A synthesis of perspectives. In C. J. Maker & S. W. Schiever (Eds.), *Critical issues in gifted education: Defensible programs for cultural and ethnic minorities, Vol. II.* (pp.). Austin, TX: PRO-ED.

Maker, C. J. (1992). Intelligence and creativity in multiple intelligences: Identification and development. *Educating Able Learners, 17*(4), 12-19.

Maker, C. J. (1993). Creativity, intelligence, and problem solving: A definition and design for cross-cultural research and measurement related to giftedness. *Gifted Education International, 9*(2), 68-77.

Maker, C. J., & Schiever, S. W. (Eds.). (1989). *Critical issues in gifted education: Defensible programs for cultural and ethnic minorities, Vol. II*,. Austin, TX: PRO-ED.

Maker, C. J., Nielson, A. B., & Rogers, J. A. (1994). Giftedness, diversity, and problem-solving. *Teaching Exceptional Children, 27*(1), 4-10.

Malone, C. (Ed.). (1978). Disadvantaged and gifted handicapped. *Gifted Child Quarterly, 22*(3).

Mangrum, C. T., & Strichart, S. S. (1988). *College and the learning disabled student* (2nd ed.). Philadelphia: Grune & Stratton.

Mank, D., Buckley, J., Whaley, P., Cioffi, A., Albin, J., Slovic, R. (1993). *National forum on natural supports*. Eugene, OR: The Employment Network, University of Oregon.

Mansour, S. L. (1985). 1985 ASHA demographic update. *ASHA, 27*(7), 55.

Marbach, W. D. (1982, July 12). Building the bionic man. *Newsweek*, pp. 78-79.

Marchand-Martella, N. E., Martella, R. C., & Marchand, A. G. (1991). Teaching elementary students first-aid skills via interactive storytelling. *Teaching Exceptional Children, 24*(1), 30-33.

Margolis, H., & Brannigan, G. (1990). Calming the storm. *Learning, 18*, 40-42.

Margolis, L. H., & Meisels, S. J. (1987). Barriers to the effectiveness of EPSDT for children with moderate and severe developmental disabilities. *American Journal of Orthopsychiatry, 57*, 424-430.

Marland , S., Jr. (1972). *Education of the gifted and talented*. Report to the Congress of the United States by the U.S. Commissioner of Education. Washington, DC: U.S. Government Printing Office.

Marland, S. P. (1972). *Education of the gifted and talented.* Washington, DC: U.S. Office of Education.

Martin, E. W. (1993). Learning disabilities and public policies: Myths and outcomes. In G. R. Lyon, D. B. Gray, J. F. Kavanaugh, & N. A. Krasnegor (Eds.), *Better understanding learning disabilities: New views from research and their implications for education and public policies* (pp. 325-342). Baltimore, MD: Paul H. Brooks Publishing Company.

Martin, J. E., Marshall, L. H., & Maxson, L. L. (1993). Transition policy: Infusing self-determination and self-advocacy into transition programs. *Career Development for Exceptional Individuals, 16*, 53-61.

Martin, J., Marshall, L. H., Maxson, L., & Jerman, P. (1993). *Self-directed IEP*. Colorado Springs, CO: University of Colorado.

Martin, R. R., & Lindamood, L. P. (1986). Stuttering and spontaneous recovery: Implications for the speech-language pathologist. *Language, Speech, and Hearing Services in the Schools, 17*, 207-218.

Martin, S. L., Ramey, C. T., & Ramey, S. L. (1990). The prevention of intellectual impairment in children of impoverished families: Findings of a randomized trial of educational daycare. *American Journal of Public Health, 80*, 844-847.

Mason, M. A., & Gambrill, E. (1994). *Debating children's lives*. Hollywood, CA: Sage Publications.

Mastropieri, M. A., & Scruggs, T. E. 1992. Science for students with disabilities. *Review of Educational Research, 62,4*, 377-411.

Mastropieri, M. A., Jenne, T., & Scruggs, T. E. (1988). A level system for managing problem behaviors in a high school resource program. *Behavioral Disorders, 13*, 202-208.

Mather, N., & Roberts, R. (1994). Learning disabilities: A field in danger of extinction? *Learning Disabilities Research & Practice, 9*, 49-58.

Mathes, P. G., Fuchs, D., Fuchs, L. S., Henley, A. M., & Sanders, A. (1994). Increasing strategic reading practice with Peabody classwide peer tutoring. *Learning Disabilities Research & Practice, 9*, 44-48.

Matson, J. L. (Ed.). (1994). *Autism in children and adults: Etiology, assessment, and intervention.* Pacific Grove, CA: Brooks/Cole.

Mattes, L. J., & Omark, D. R. (1984). Speech and language assessment for the bilingual handicapped. San Diego: College-Hill.

Mayer-Johnson, R. (1986). *The Picture Communications Symbols* (Book 1). Solana Beach, CA: Mayer-Johnson Co.

Mayo, L. W. (1962). A proposed program for national action to combat mental retardation. *Report of the President's Committee on Mental Retardation.* Washington, DC: U.S. Government Printing Office.

McAdam, D. B., O'Cleirigh, C. M., & Cuvo, A. J. (1993). Self-monitoring and verbal feedback to reduce stereotypic body rocking in a congenitally blind adult. *RE:view, 24*, 163-172.

McAnally, P. L., Rose, S., & Quigley, S. P. (1994). *Language learning practices with deaf children* (2nd ed.). Austin, TX: PRO-ED.

McCollum, J. A., & Hughes, M. (1988). Staffing patterns and team models in infancy programs. In J. B. Jordon, J. J. Gallagher, P. L. Hutinger, & M. B. Karnes (Eds.), *Early childhood special education: Birth to three* (pp. 129-146). Reston, VA: Council for Exceptional Children.

McCollum, J. A., McLean, M., McCartan, K., & Kaiser, C. (1989). DEC White Paper: Recommendations for certification of early childhood special educators. *Journal of Early Intervention, 13*, 195-211.

McConnell, S. R. (1994). Social context, social validity, and program outcome in early intervention. In R. Gardner III, D. M. Sainato, J. O. Cooper, T. E. Heron, W. L. Heward, J. Eshleman, & T. A. Grossi (Eds.), *Behavior analysis in education: Focus on measurably superior instruction* (pp. 75-85). Pacific Grove, CA: Brooks/Cole.

McConnell, S. R., McEvoy, M. A., & Odom, S. L. (1992). Implementation of social competence interventions in early childhood special education classes. In S. L. Odom, S. R. McConnell, & M. A. McEvoy (Eds.),

Social competence of young children with disabilities: Nature, development and intervention (pp. 277-306). Baltimore, MD: Paul H. Brooks Publishing Company.

McCormick, L., & Schiefelbusch, R. L. (1990). *Early language intervention: An introduction* (2nd ed.). Englewood Cliffs, NJ: Merrill/Prentice Hall.

McCormick, M. E., & Wolf, J. S. (1993). Intervention programs for gifted girls. *Roeper Review, 16*, 85-88.

McCracken, K. (1987, October 5). 85 at TSD suspended in sign language dispute. Knoxville Journal, pp. 1, 10.

McCuin, D., & Cooper, J. O. (1994). Teaching keyboarding and computer skills to persons with developmental disabilities. *Behaviorology, 2*(1), 63-78.

McDermott, S. (1994). Explanatory model to describe school district prevalence rates for mental retardation and learning disabilities. *American Journal on Mental Retardation, 99*, 175-185.

McDonald, E. T. (1980). *Using and teaching Blissymbolics.* Toronto: Blissymbolics Communication Institute.

McDonnell, A., & Hardman, M. (1988). A synthesis of "best practice" guidelines for early childhood services. *Journal of Early Intervention, 12*, 328-341.

McDonnell, J. J., Hardman, M. L., & Hightower, J. (1989). Employment preparation for high school students with severe handicaps. *Mental Retardation, 27*, 396-405.

McDonnell, J. J., Wilcox, B., Boles, S. M., & Bellamy, G. T. (1985). Transition issues facing youth with severe disabilities: Parent's perspective. *The Journal of The Association for Persons with Severe Handicaps, 10*, 61-65.

McEachin, J. J., Smith, T., & Lovaas, I. O. (1993). Long-term outcome for children with autism who received early intensive behavioral treatment. *American Journal on Mental Retardation, 97*, 359-372.

McEvoy, M. A., & Yoder, P. (1993). Interventions to promote social skills and emotional development. In *DEC Recommended Practices* (pp. 77-81). Reston, VA: Council for Exceptional Children, Division for Early Childhood.

McGee, J. J. (1992). Gentle teaching's assumptions and paradigm. *Journal of Applied Behavior Analysis, 25*, 869-872.

McGee, J. J., & Gonzalez, L. (1990). Gentle teaching and the practice of human interdependence: A preliminary group study of 15 persons with severe behavioral disorders and their caregivers. In A. C. Repp & N. N. Singh (Eds.), *Current*

perspectives on the use of nonaversive and aversive interventions for persons with developmental disabilities (pp. 237-254). Sycamore, IL: Sycamore.

McGee, J. J., & Menolascino, F. J. (1991). *Beyond gentle teaching: A nonaversive approach to helping those in need.* New York: Plenum.

McGreevy, P. (1983). *Teaching and learning plain English* (2nd. ed.). Sarasota, FL: Precision Teaching Materials and Associates.

McGrew, K. S., Bruininks, R. H., & Thurlow, M. L. (1992). Relationship between measures of adaptive functioning and community adjustment for adults with mental retardation. *Exceptional Children, 58*, 517-529.

McIntire, J. C. (1985). The future role of residential schools for visually impaired students. *Journal of Visual Impairment and Blindness, 79*, 161-164.

McIntosh, R., Vaughn, S., Schumm, J. S., Haager, D., & Lee, O. (1994). Observations of students with learning disabilities in general education classrooms. *Exceptional Children, 60*, 249-261.

McIntyre, T. (1992). The culturally sensitive disciplinarian. In R. B. Rutherford, Jr. & S. R. Mathur (Eds.), *Severe Behavior Disorders of Children and Youth* (Vol. 15, pp. 112-120). Reston, VA: Council for Children with Behavior Disorders.

McIntyre, T. (1993a).Behaviorally disordered youth in correctional settings: Prevalence, programming, and teacher training. *Behavioral Disorders, 18*, 167-176.

McIntyre, T. (1993b). Reflections on the new definition for emotional or behavioral disorders: Who still falls through the cracks and why. *Behavioral Disorders, 18*, 148-160.

McKee, M., da Cunha, K., Echols, L., Starr, C., Naskrent, D., & Urbanovsky, J. (1983). *Occupational and physical therapy services in school-based programs: Organizational manual.* Houston, TX: Psychological Services Division, Harris County Department of Education.

McKelvey, J. L., Sisson, L. A., Van Hasselt, V. B., & Herson, M. (1992). An approach to teaching self-dressing to a child with dual-sensory impairment. *Teaching Exceptional Children, 25*(1), 12-15.

McKenzie, R. G., & Houk, C. S. (1993). Across the great divide. *Teaching Exceptional Children, 25*(2), 16-20.

McKeon, D. (1994). When meeting "common" standards is uncommonly difficult. *Educational Leadership, 51*, 45-49.

McLaren, J., & Bryson, S. E. (1987). Review of recent epidemiological studies of mental retardation: Prevalence, related disorders and etiology. *American Journal on Mental Retardation, 92*, 243-254.

McLean, M., Smith, B. J., McCormick, K., Schakel, J., & McEvoy, M. (1991). *Developmental delay: Establishing parameters for a preschool category of exceptionality*. Reston, VA: Council for Exceptional Children.

McLeskey, J. (1992). Students with learning disabilities at primary, intermediate, and secondary grade levels: Identification and characteristics. *Learning Disability Quarterly, 15*, 13-19.

McLeskey, J., & Grizzle, K. L. (1992). Grade retention rates among students with learning disabilities. *Exceptional Children, 58*, 548-554.

McLeskey, J., & Pacchiano, D. (1994). Mainstreaming students with learning disabilities: Are we making progress? *Exceptional Children, 60*, 508-517.

McLoughlin, J. A., & Kelly, D. (1982). Issues facing the resource teacher. *Learning Disability Quarterly, 5*, 58-64.

McLoughlin, J. A., & Lewis, R. B. (1994). *Assessing special students* (4th ed.). Englewood Cliffs, NJ: Merrill/Prentice Hall.

Mcloughlin, C. S., Garner, J. B., & Callahan, M. (1987). *Getting employed, staying employed: Job development and training for persons with severe handicaps*. Baltimore: Paul H. Brookes.

McNair, J., & Rusch, F. R. (1992). The coworker involvement instrument: A measure of indigenous workplace support. *Career Development for Exceptional Individuals, 15*, 23-36.

McNeish, T. J., & Naglieri, J. A. (1993). Identification of individuals with serious emotional disturbance using the Draw A Person: Screening procedure for emotional disturbance. *The Journal of Special Education, 27*, 115-121.

McReynolds, L. V. (1990). Articulation and phonological disorders. In G. H. Shames & E. H. Wiig, (Eds.), *Human communication disorders* (3rd ed.) (pp. 30-73). Englewood Cliffs, NJ: Merrill/Prentice Hall.

Meadow, K. P. (1980). *Deafness and child development*. Berkeley, CA: University of California Press.

Meadow-Orlans, K. P. (1985). Social and psychological effects of hearing loss in adulthood: A literature review. In H. Orlans (Ed.), *Adjustment to adult hearing loss* (pp. 35-57). San Diego: College-Hill.

Meadows, N. B., Neel, R. S., Scott, C. M., & Parker, G. (1994). Academic perfor-

mance, social competence, and mainstream accommodations: A look at mainstreamed and nonmainstreamed students with serious behavioral disorders. *Behavioral Disorders, 19*, 170-180.

Meddin, B. J., & Rosen, A. L. (1986). Child abuse and neglect: Prevention and reporting. *Young Children, 41*(4), 26-30.

Meisels, S. J., & Provence, S. (1989). *Screening and assessment: Guidelines for identifying young disabled and developmentally vulnerable children and their families*. Washington, DC: National Center for Clinical Infant Programs.

Meisels, S. J., & Shonkoff, J. P. (1990). *Handbook of early childhood intervention*. New York: Cambridge University Press.

Mercer, C. D. (1992). *Students with learning disabilities* (4th ed.). Englewood Cliffs, NJ: Merrill/Prentice Hall.

Mercer, C. D., & Mercer, A. R. (1993). *Teaching students with learning problems* (4th ed.). Englewood Cliffs, NJ: Merrill/Prentice Hall.

Mercer, C. D., King-Sears, P., & Mercer, A. R. (1990). Learning disabilities definitions and criteria used by state education departments. *Learning Disability Quarterly, 13*, 141-152.

Mercer, J. R. (1973a). *Labelling the mentally retarded*. Berkeley, CA: University of California Press.

Mercer, J. R. (1973b). The myth of 3% prevalence. In R. K. Eymon, C. E. Meyers, & G. Tarjon (Eds.), *Sociobehavioral studies in mental retardation*, (pp. 1-18). American Association on Mental Deficiency, No. 1.

Mercer, J. R. (1981). Testing and assessment practices in multiethnic education. In J. A. Banks (Ed.), *Education in the 80's: Multiethnic education* (pp. 93-104). Washington, DC: National Education Association.

Mesinger, J. F. (1985). Commentary on "A rationale for the merger of special and regular education" or, is it now time for the lamb to lie down with the lion? *Exceptional Children, 51*, 510-512.

Meyen, E. L. (Ed.). (1978). *Exceptional children and youth: An introduction*. Denver: Love.

Meyer, L. H. (1986, June). Creating options and making choices. *TASH Newsletter*, p. 1.

Meyer, L. H. (1991). Guest editorial-Why meaningful outcomes? *The Journal of Special Education, 25*, 287-290.

Meyer, L. H., & Evans, I. M. (1989). *Nonaversive intervention for behavior problems: A manual for home and community*. Baltimore, MD: Paul H. Brooks Publishing Company.

Meyer, L. H., Cole, D. A., McQuarter, R., & Reichle, J. (1990). Validation of the Assessment of Social Competence (ASC) for children and young adults with developmental disabilities. *The Journal of The Association for Persons with Severe Handicaps, 15*, 57-68.

Meyers, C. E., Mink, I. T., & Nihira, K. (1981). *Home Quality Rating Scale: User's manual*. Los Angeles: University of California, Neuropsychiatric Institute.

Michael, M. G., & Paul, P. V. (1991). Early intervention for infants with deaf-blindness. *Exceptional Children, 57*, 200-210.

Michael, R. J. (1992). Seizures: Teachers observations and record keeping. *Intervention in School and Clinic, 27*, 211-214.

Michaud, L. J., & Duhaime, A. (1992). Traumatic brain injury. In M. L. Batshaw & Y. M. Perret, *Children with disabilities: A medical primer* (3rd ed.) (pp. 525-546). Baltimore, MD: Paul H. Brooks Publishing Company.

Miller, A. D., Barbetta, P. M., & Heron, T. E. (1994). START tutoring: Designing, training, implementing, adapting, and evaluating tutoring programs for school and home settings. In R. Gardner III, D. M. Sainato, J. O. Cooper, T. E. Heron, W. L. Heward, J. Eshleman, & T. A. Grossi (Eds.), *Behavior analysis in education: Focus on measurably superior instruction* (pp. 75-85). Pacific Grove, CA: Brooks/Cole.

Miller, A. D., Hall, S. W., & Heward, W. L. (in press). Effects of sequential 1-minute time trials with and without intertrial feedback on general and special education students' fluency with math facts. *Journal of Behavioral Education*.

Miller, A. D., & Heward, W. L. (1992). Do your students really know their math facts? Using daily time trials to build fluency. *Intervention in School and Clinic, 28*, 98-104.

Miller, D. (1979). *Ophthalmology: The essentials*. Boston: Houghton Mifflin.

Miller, J. (1993). Augmentative and alternative communication. In Snell, M. E. (Ed.), *Instruction of students with severe disabilities* (4th ed.) (pp. 319-346). Englewood Cliffs, NJ: Merrill/Prentice Hall.

Miller, J., & Pfingst, B. (1984). Cochlear implants. In C. Berlin (Ed.), *Hearing science* (pp. 309-339). San Diego: College-Hill.

Miller, L. J., Strain, P. S., Boyd, K., McKinley, J., Hunsicker, S., & Wu, A. (1992). *Preschool mainstreaming: Outcomes for children with disabilities and typi-

cal children. Pittsburgh, PA: Allegheny-Singer Research Institute.

Miller, S. P., & Hudson, P. (1994). Using structured parent groups to provide parental support. *Intervention in School and Clinic, 29*, 151-155.

Miller, W. (1989, July). *Obstetrical issues.* Paper presented at Conference on Drugs, Alcohol, Pregnancy and Parenting: An Intervention Model, Spokane, WA.

Miller, W. H. (1985). The role of residential schools for the blind in educating visually impaired students. *Journal of Visual Impairment and Blindness, 79*, 160.

Milner, J. S., & Wimberley, R. C. (1980). Prediction and explanation of child abuse. *Journal of Clinical Psychology, 36*, 875-884.

Minke, K. M., & Scott, M. M. (1993). The development of individualized family service plans: Roles for parents and staff. *The Journal of Special Education, 27*, 82-106.

Minskoff, E. (1975). Research on psycholinguistic training: Critique and guidelines. *Exceptional Children, 42*, 136-144.

Mitchell, B. (1982). An update on the state of gifted/talented education in the U.S. *Phi Delta Kappan, 64*, 357-358.

Mitchell, D. C. (1983). Spina bifida. In J. Umbreit (Ed.), *Physical disabilities and health impairments: An introduction* (pp. 117-131). Englewood Cliffs, NJ: Merrill/Prentice Hall.

Mitchell, J. V. (Ed.). (1985). *The ninth mental measurements yearbook.* Lincoln, NE: University of Nebraska Press.

Mitchell, P. B. (Ed.). (1981). *A policymaker's guide to issues in gifted and talented education.* Washington, DC: National Association of State Boards of Education.

Mithaug, D. E., Horiuchi, C. N., & Fanning, P. N. (1985). A report on the Colorado statewide follow-up survey of special education students. *Exceptional Children, 51*, 397-404.

Mithaug, D. W., Martin, J. E., & Agran, M. (1987). Adaptability instruction: The goal of transitional programming. *Exceptional Children, 53*, 500-505.

Mithaug, D. W., Martin, J. E., Agran, M., & Rusch, F. R. (1988). *Why special education graduates fail: How to teach them to succeed.* Colorado Springs, CO: Ascent.

Moll, L. C. (1992). Bilingual classroom studies and community analysis: Some recent trends. *Educational Researcher, 21*(2), 20-24.

Moon, M. S. (1994). *Making school and community recreation fun for every-*

one: Places and ways to integrate. Baltimore, MD: Paul H. Brooks Publishing Company.

Moon, M. S., & Bunker, L. (1987). Recreation and motor skills programming. In M. E. Snell (Ed.), *Systematic instruction of persons with severe handicaps* (3rd ed.) (pp. 214-244). Englewood Cliffs, NJ: Merrill/Prentice Hall.

Moon, M. S., & Inge, K. (1993). Vocational preparation and transition. In M. E. Snell, *Instruction of students with severe disabilities* (4th ed.) (pp. 556-587). Englewood Cliffs, NJ: Merrill/Prentice Hall.

Moon, S. M., Feldhusen, J. F., Powley, S., Nidiffer, L., & Whitman, M. W. (1993). Secondary applications of the Purdue three stage model. *GCT, May/June*, 2-9.

Moore, P., & Hicks, D. M. (1994). Voice disorders. In G. H. Shames & E. H. Wiig, (Eds.), *Human communication disorders* (4th ed.) (pp. 292-335). Englewood Cliffs, NJ: Merrill/Prentice Hall.

Moores, D. F. (1985). Educational programs and services for hearing impaired children: Issues and options. In F. Powell, T. Finitzo-Hieber, S. Friel-Patti, & D. Henderson (Eds.), *Education of the hearing impaired child* (pp. 3-20). San Diego: College-Hill.

Moores, D. F. (1987). *Educating the deaf: Psychology, principles, and practices* (3rd ed.). Boston: Houghton Mifflin.

Moores, D. F., & Kluwin, T. N. (1986). Issues in school placement. In A. N. Schildroth & M. A. Karchmer (Eds.), *Deaf children in America* (pp. 105-123). San Diego: College-Hill.

Moores, D. F., & Maestas y Moores, J. (1981). Special adaptations necessitated by hearing impairments. In J. M. Kauffman & D. P. Hallahan (Eds.), *Handbook of special education.* Englewood Cliffs, NJ: Prentice-Hall.

Morgan, C. D., & Murray, H. A. (1935). A method for investigating fantasies: The Thematic Appreception Test. *Archives of Neurology and Psychiatry 34*, 289-306.

Morgan, S. R. (1987). *Abuse and neglect of handicapped children.* San Diego: College-Hill.

Morocco, C. C., Dalton, B., & Tivnan, R. A. (1990). *Interim report: Problem solving in science project.* Newton, MA: Education Development Center.

Morse, W. C. (1976). Worksheet on life-space interviewing for teachers. In N. Long, W. Morse, & R. Newman (Eds.), *Conflict in the classroom* (pp. 337-341). Belmont, CA: Wadsworth Publishing.

Morse, W. C. (1985). *The education and treatment of socioemotionally impaired children and youth.* Syracuse, NY: Syracuse University Press.

Morsink, C. V., Thomas, C. C., & Smith-Davis, J. (1987). Noncategorical special education programs: Process and outcomes. In M. C. Wang, M. C. Reynolds, & H. J. Walberg (Eds.), *The handbook of special education: Research and practice* (pp. 287-311). Oxford, England: Pergamon Press.

Mount, B., & Zwernick, K. (1988). *It's never too early, it's never too late.* St. Paul, MN: Metropolitan Council. Publication No. 421-88-109, 1-45.

Mow, S. (1973). How do you dance without music? In D. Watson (Ed.), Readings on deafness (pp. 20-30). New York: New York University School of Education, Deafness Research and Training Center.

Moyer, J. R., & Dardig, J. C. (1978). Practical task analysis for special educators. *Teaching Exceptional Children, 11*(1), 1-16.

Mudford, O. C. (1995). Review of the gentle teaching data. *American Journal on Mental Retardation, 99*, 345-355.

Mulick, J. A. (1990). The ideology and science of punishment in mental retardation. *American Journal on Mental Retardation, 95*, 142-156.

Mulick, J. A., & Antonak, R. (Eds.). (1994). *Life styles: Transitions in mental retardation* (Vol. 5). Norwood, NJ: Ablex Publishing Corporation.

Munk, D. D., & Repp, A. C. (1994). The relationship between instructional variables and problem behavior: A review. *Exceptional Children, 60*, 390-401.

Murphy, S. T., & Rogan, P. M. (1995). *Closing the shop: Conversion from sheltered to integrated work.* Baltimore: Paul H. Brookes.

Murray, J. (1990). Best practices in working with parents of handicapped children. In A. Thomas & J. Grimes (Eds.), *Best practices in school psychology—II* (pp. 823-836). Washington, DC: National Association of School Psychologists.

Myers, P. I., & Hammill, D. D. (1982). *Methods for learning disorders* (2nd ed.). New York: John Wiley.

Myers, P. I., & Hammill, D. D. (1990). *Learning disabilities: Basic concepts, assessment practices, and instructional strategies* (3rd ed.). Austin, TX: PRO-ED.

Myles, B. S., Moran, M. R., Ormsbee, C. K., & Downing, J. A. (1992). Guidelines for establishing and maintaining token economies. *Intervention in School and Clinic, 27*(3), 164-169.

Nagel, D., Schumaker, J. B., & Deshler, D. D. (1986). *The learning strategies curriculum: The FIRST-letter mnemonic strategy.* Lawrence, KS: Excel Enterprises.

Naglieri, J. A., & Das, J. P. (1987). Construct and criterion-related validity of planning, simultaneous, and successive cognitive processing tasks. *Journal of Psychoeducational Assessment, 4,* 353-363.

Naglieri, J. A., & Pfeiffer, S. I. (1992). Performance of disruptive behavior by behavior disordered and normal samples on the Draw A Person: Screening Procedure for Emotional Disturbance. *JCCP: Psychological Assessment, 4,* 156-159.

Naglieri, J. A., McNeish, T. J., & Bardos, A. N. (1991). *Draw A Person: Screening Procedure for Emotional Disturbance.* Austin, TX: PRO-ED.

Naisbitt, J., & Aburdene, P. (1990). *Megatrends 2000: Ten new directions for the 1990's.* New York: William Morrow.

Napier, L. A. (1992, November). *The Denver, Colorado Public School's American Indian focus schools pilot project.* Paper presented at the convention of the University Council for Educational Administration, Minneapolis, MN.

Napierkowski, H. (1981). The role of language in the intellectual development of the deaf child. *Teaching Exceptional Children, 14,* 106-109.

Narayan, J. S., Heward, W. L., Gardner, III, R. Courson, F. H., & Omness, C. (1990). Using response cards to increase student participation in an elementary classroom. *Journal of Applied Behavior Analysis, 23,* 483-490.

National Association of State Boards of Education. (1992, October). *Winners all: A call for inclusive schools.* Washington, DC: Author.

National Commission on Excellence in Education. (1984). *A nation at risk: The imperative for educational reform.* Washington, DC: U.S. Government Printing Office.

National Committee for Citizens in Education. (1979). Unpublished manuscript serving as basis for congressional testimony.

National Hotel and Restaurant Association. (1983). Personal communication with Dr. Philip Nelen, Washington, DC.

National Joint Committee on Learning Disabilities (1989, September 18). Letter from NJCLD to member organizations. Topic: Modifications to the NJCLD definition of learning disabilities.

National Joint Committee on Learning Disabilities. (1994). A reaction to full inclusion: A reaffirmation of the right of students with learning disabilities to a continuum of services. In *Collective perspectives on issues affecting learning disabilities* (pp. 95-96). Austin, TX: PRO-ED.

National Joint Committee on Learning Disabilities. (1994). *Collective perspectives on issues affecting learning disabilities: Position papers and statements.* Austin, TX: PRO-ED.

Needleman, H. L. (1992). childhood exposure to lead: A common cause of school failure. *Phi Delta Kappan, 74*(1), 35-37.

Neef, N. A., Parrish, J. M., Hannigan, K. F., Page, T. J., & Iwata, B. A. (1989). Teaching self-catheterization skills to children with neurogenic bladder complications. *Journal of Applied Behavior Analysis, 22,* 237-243.

Neel, R. S., & Billingsley, F. F. (1989). *IMPACT: A functional curriculum for students with moderate to severe disabilities.* Baltimore: Paul H. Brooks Publishing Company.

Neisworth, J. T., & Bagnato, S. J. (1992). The case against intelligence testing in early intervention. *Topics in Early Childhood Special Education, 12,* 1-20.

Neisworth, J. T., & Smith, R. M. (Eds.). (1978). *Retardation: Issues, assessment, and intervention.* New York: McGraw-Hill.

Nelson, C. M., Rutherford, R. B., Jr., & Wolford, B. I. (1987). *Special education in the criminal justice system.* Englewood Cliffs, NJ: Merrill/Prentice Hall.

Nelson, J. R., Smith, D. J., Young, R. K., & Dodd, J. M. (1991). A review of self-management outcome research conducted with students who exhibit behavioral disorders. *Behavioral Disorders, 16,* 169-179.

Nelson, K. B., & Ellenberg, J. H. (1986). Antecedents of cerebral palsy: Multivariate analysis of risk. *New England Journal of Medicine, 315,* 81-86.

Nevin, A., McCann, S., & Semmel, M. I. (1983). An empirical analysis of the regular classroom teacher's role in implementing IEP's. *Teacher Education and Special Education, 6,* 235-246.

Newborg, J., Stock, J., Wnek, J., Guidubaldi, J., & Suinicki, J. (1984). *Battelle Developmental Inventory Screening Test.* Allen, TX: DLM Teaching Resources.

Newcomber, P. L., & Hammill, D. D. (1988). *Tests of language development* (2nd ed.). Austin, TX: PRO-ED.

Newton, J. S., Horner, R. H., & Lund, L. (1991). Honoring activity preferences in individualized plan development. *Journal of the Association for Persons with Severe Handicaps, 16,* 207-212.

Newton, J. S., Horner, R. H., Ard, Jr., W. R., LeBaron, N., & Sappington, G. (1994). A conceptual model for improving the social life of individuals with mental retardation. *American Journal of Mental Retardation, 32,* 393-402.

Nietupski, J., & Svoboda, R. (1982). Teaching a cooperative leisure skill to severely handicapped adults. *Education and Training of the Mentally Retarded, 17,* 38-43.

Nietupski, J., & Verstegen, D., Hamre-Nietupski, S. (1992). Incorporating sales and business practices into job development in supported employment. *Education and Training in Mental Retardation, 27,* 207-218.

Nisbet, J., & Hagner, D. (1988). Natural supports in the workplace: A reexamination of supported employment. *The Journal of The Association for Persons with Severe Handicaps, 13,* 260-267.

Nisbet, J., & Vincent, L. (1986). The differences in inappropriate behavior and instructional interactions in sheltered and nonsheltered work environments. *The Journal of The Association for Persons with Severe Handicaps, 11,* 19-27.

Noonan, M. J., Brown, F., Mulligan, M., & Rettig, M. A. (1982). Educability of severely handicapped persons: Both sides of the issue. *The Journal of The Association for the Severely Handicapped, 7*(1), 3-12.

Norman, C. A., & Zigmond, N. (1980). Characteristics of children labeled and served as learning disabled in school systems affiliated with Child Service Demonstration centers. *Journal of Learning Disabilities, 13,* 542-547.

Norris, C. (Ed.). (1975). *Letters from deaf students.* Eureka, CA: Alinda Press.

Northcott, W. H., & Erickson, L. C. (1977). *The UNISTAPS Project.* St. Paul: Minnesota Department of Education.

Northern, J. L., & Lemme, M. (1982). Hearing and auditory disorders. In G. H. Shames & E. H. Wiig (Eds.), *Human communication disorders: An introduction.* Englewood Cliffs, NJ: Merrill/Prentice Hall.

Norton, L. S., & Hartley, J. (1986). What factors contribute to good examination marks? The role of notetaking in subsequent examination performance. *Higher Education, 15,* 355-371.

Notari, A. R., & Bricker, D. D. (1990). The utility of a curriculum-based assessment instrument in the development of Individualized Education Plans for infants and young children. *Journal of Early Intervention, 14*, 117-132.

Notari-Syverson, A. R., & Shuster, S. L. (1995). Putting real-life skills into IEP/IFSPs for infants and young children. *Teaching Exceptional Children, 27*(2), 29-32.

Nurss, J. R., & McGauvran, M. E. (1986). *Metropolitan Readiness Test.* Cleveland, OH: Psychological Corp.

O'Brien, J. (1971). How we detect mental retardation before birth. *Medical Times, 99*, 103.

O'Brien, J. (1987). A guide to life-style planning: Using the activity catalog to integrate services and natural life support systems. In B. Wilcox & G. T. Bellamy (Eds.), *A comprehensive guide to the activities catalog: An alternative curriculum for youth and adults with severe disabilities* (pp. 175-189). Baltimore, MD: Paul H. Brooks Publishing Company.

O'Brien, J., Forest, M., Snow, J., & Hasbury, D. (1989). *Action for inclusion.* Toronto: Frontier College Press.

O'Connell, J. C. (1986). Managing small group instruction in an integrated preschool setting. *Teaching Exceptional Children, 18*, 166-171.

O'Conner, G. (1983). Presidential address 1983: Social support of mentally retarded persons. *Mental Retardation, 21*, 187-196.

O'Connor, R. E., Jenkins, J. R., Cole, K. N., & Mills, P. E. (1993). Two approaches to reading instruction with children with disabilities: Does program design make a difference? *Exceptional Children, 59*, 312-323.

O'Leary, K. D. (1980). Pills or skills for hyperactive children. *Journal of Applied Behavior Analysis, 13*, 191-204.

O'Reilly, M. F., & Chadsey-Rusch, J. (1992). Teaching a social skills problem-solving approach to workers with mental retardation: An analysis of generalization. *Education and Training in Mental Retardation, 27*, 324-334.

O'Shea, D. J. (1994). Modifying daily practices to bridge transitions. *Teaching Exceptional Children, 26*(4), 29-34.

O'Shea, L. J., Sindelar, P. T., & O'Shea, D. J. (1985). The effects of repeated readings and attentional cues on reading fluency and comprehension. *Journal of Reading Behavior, 17*, 129-142.

Obiakor, F. E., Algozzine, B., & Ford, B. A. (1993). Urban education, the General Education Initiative, and service delivery

to African-American students. *Urban Education, 28*, 313-327.

Odom, S. L., & Karnes, M. B. (Eds.). (1988). *Early intervention for infants and children with handicaps: An empirical base.* Baltimore, MD: Paul H. Brooks Publishing Company.

Odom, S. L., McConnell, S. R. & McEvoy, M. M. (1992). *Social competence of young children with disabilities: Nature, development, and intervention.* Baltimore, MD: Paul H. Brookes Publishing Company.

Office of Technology Assessment. (1987). *Technology-dependent children: Hospital v. home care—A technical memorandum.* OTA-TM-H-38. Washington, DC: Author.

Ohio Department of Education. (1982). *Rules for the education of handicapped children.* Columbus, OH: Author.

Olson, J., Algozzine, B., & Schmid, R. E. (1980). Mild, moderate, and severe EH: An empty distinction? *Behavioral Disorders, 5*, 96-101.

Opp, G. (1994). Historical roots of the field of learning disabilities: Some nineteenth-century German contributions. *Journal of Learning Disabilities, 27*, 10-19.

Orelove, F. P. (1982). Acquisition of incidental learning in moderately and severely handicapped adults. *Education and Training of the Mentally Retarded, 17*, 131-136.

Orelove, F. P. (1984). The educability debate: A review and a look ahead. In W. L. Heward, T. E. Heron, D. S. Hill, & J. Trap-Porter (Eds.), *Focus on behavior analysis in education* (pp. 271-281). Englewood Cliffs, NJ: Merrill/Prentice Hall.

Orelove, F. P., Wehman, P., & Wood, J. (1982). An evaluative review of Special Olympics: Implications for community integration. *Education and Training in Mental Retardation, 17*, 325-329.

Orlansky, J. Z. (1979). *Mainstreaming the hearing impaired child: An educational alternative.* Ann Arbor, MI: University Microfilms International. (Catalog No. AU00322)

Orlansky, M. D. (1981). The deaf/blind and the severely/profoundly handicapped: An emerging relationship. In S. R. Walsh & R. Holzberg (Eds.), *Understanding and educating the deaf-blind/severely profoundly handicapped* (pp. 5-24). Springfield, IL: Charles C. Thomas.

Orlansky, M. D. (1986). Multiply handicapped. In J. V. Van Cleve (Ed.), *Gallaudet encyclopedia of deaf people and*

deafness (Vol. 2) (pp. 335-357). New York: McGraw-Hill.

Orlansky, M. D., & Bonvillian, J. D. (1985). Sign language acquisition: Language development in children of deaf parents and implications for other populations. *Merrill-Palmer Quarterly, 31*, 127-143.

Orlansky, M. D., & Heward, W. L. (1981). *Voices: Interviews with handicapped people.* Englewood Cliffs, NJ: Merrill/Prentice Hall.

Orlion, L. (1988). Enhancing the involvement of Black parents of adolescents with handicaps. In A. A. Ortiz & B. A. Ramirez (Eds.), *Schools and the culturally diverse exceptional student: Promising practices and future directions* (pp. 96-103). Reston, VA: Council for Exceptional Children.

Ortiz, A. A. (1986). Characteristics of limited English proficient Hispanic students served in programs of the learning disabled: Implications for policy and practice. *Bilingual Special Education Newsletter, 4*, 3-5. Austin, TX: University of Texas.

Ortiz, A. A. (1991a). *AIM for the BESt: Assessment and intervention model for the Bilingual exceptional student. A technical report for the Innovative Approaches Research Project.* Austin, TX: University of Texas (ERIC Document No. 341 194).

Ortiz, A. A. (1991b). *AIM for the BESt: Assessment and intervention model for the bilingual exceptional student. A Handbook for teachers and planners from the Innovative Approaches Research Project.* Austin, TX: University of Texas (ERIC Document No. 341 195).

Ortiz, A. A., & Garcia, S. B. (1986). Characteristics of limited-English-proficient Hispanic students served in programs for the learning disabled: Implications for policy and practice. *Counterpoint, 7*(1), 10-11.

Ortiz, A. A., & Garcia, S. (1988). A prereferral process for preventing inappropriate referrals of Hispanic students to special education. In A. Ortiz & B. A. Ramirez (Eds.), *Schools and the culturally diverse exceptional student: Promising practices and future directions* (pp. 6-18). Reston, VA: Council for Exceptional Children.

Ortiz, A. A., & Ramirez, B. A. (Eds.). (1988). *Schools and the culturally diverse exceptional student: Promising practices and future directions.* Reston, VA: Council for Exceptional Children.

Ortiz, A. A., & Yates, J. R. (1988). Characteristics of learning disabled, mentally retarded, and speech-language handicapped Hispanic students at initial evaluation and reevaluation. In A. A. Ortiz & B. A. Ramirez (Eds.), *Schools and the culturally diverse exceptional student: Promising practices and future directions* (pp. 50-62). Reston, VA: Council for Exceptional Children.

Ortiz, A. A., & Wilkerson, C. Y. (1991). Assessment and intervention model for the bilingual exceptional student (AIM for the BESt). *Teacher Education and Special Education, 14,* 35-42.

Ortiz, V., & Gonzales, A. (1991). Gifted Hispanic adolescents. In M. Bireley & J. Genshaft (Eds.), *Understanding the gifted adolescent* (pp. 240-247). New York: Teachers College Press.

Orton, S. T. (1925). Word-blindness in school children. *Archives of Neurology and Psychiatry, 14,* 581-615.

Osguthorpe, R. T., & Scruggs, T. E. (1986). Special education students as tutors: A review and analysis. *Remedial and Special Education, 7*(4), 15-26.

Oswald, D. P. (1994). Facilitator influence in facilitated communication. *Journal of Behavioral Education, 4,* 191-200.

Owens, R. E. (1994). Development of communication, language, and speech. In G. H. Shames & E. H. Wiig, (Eds.), *Human communication disorders* (4th ed.) (pp. 36-81). Englewood Cliffs, NJ: Merrill/Prentice Hall.

Pados, G. (1989). *A comparison of the effects of students' own notes and guided notes on the daily quiz performance of fifth-grade students.* Unpublished masters thesis. Columbus, OH: The Ohio State University.

Page, E. B. (1972). Miracle in Milwaukee: Raising the IQ. *Educational Researcher, 1,* 8-16.

Pallas, A. M., Natriello, G., & McDill, E. L. (1989). The changing nature of the disadvantaged population: Current dimensions and future trends. *Educational Researcher, 18,* 16-22.

Pancsofar, E., & Blackwell, R. (1986). *A user's guide to community entry for the severely handicapped.* Albany, NY: State University of New York Press.

Parette, H. P., Hofmann, A., & VanBiervliet, A. (1994). The professional's role in obtaining funding for assistive technology for infants and toddlers with disabilities. *Teaching Exceptional Children, 26*(3), 22-28.

Parette, Jr., H. P., & Hourcade, J. J. (1986). Management strategies for orthopedically handicapped students. *Teaching Exceptional Children, 18*(4), 282-286.

Parette, Jr., H. P., Hourcade, J. J., & Van-Biervliet, A. (1993). Selection of appropriate technology for children with disabilities. *Teaching Exceptional Children, 25*(3), 18-22.

Parham, J. L. (1983). *A meta-analysis of the use of manipulative materials and student achievement in elementary school mathematics.* (Doctoral dissertation, Auburn University, 1983.) Dissertation Abstracts International, 96, 44A.

Parsons, M. B., McCarn, J. E., & Reid, D. H. (1993). Evaluating and increasing meal-related choices throughout a service setting for people with severe disabilities. *Journal of the Association for Persons with Severe Handicaps, 18,* 253-260.

Passow, A. H., & Rudnitski, R. A. (1994). Transforming policy to enhance educational services for the gifted. *Roeper Review, 16*(4), 271-275.

Pattavina, S., Bergstrom, T., Marchand-Martella, N. E, & Martella, R. C. (1992). "Moving on" Learning to cross streets independently. *Teaching Exceptional Children, 25*(1), 32-35.

Patterson, G. R. (1979). *Living with children: New methods for parents and teachers* (rev. ed.). Champaign, IL: Research Press

Patterson, G. R. (1980). Mothers: The unacknowledged victims. *Monographs of the Society for Research in Child Development, 45* (5, Serial No. 186).

Patterson, G. R. (1982). *Coercive family process.* Eugene, OR: Castalia Press.

Patterson, G. R. (1986). Performance models for antisocial boys. *American Psychologist, 41,* 432-444.

Patterson, G. R., Cipaldi, D., & Bank, L. (1991). An early starter model for predicting delinquency. In D. J. Pepler & K. H. Rubin (Eds.), *the development and treatment of childhood aggression* (pp. 139-168). Hillsdale, NJ: Lawrence Erlbaum.

Patterson, G. R., Reid, J. B., & Dishion, T. J. (1992). *Antisocial boys: Vol. 4, A social interactional approach.* Eugene, OR: Castalia.

Patton, J. M. (1992). Assessment and identification of African-American learners with gifts and talents. *Exceptional Children, 59,* 150-159.

Patton, J. R., & Polloway, E. A. (1993). Learning disabilities: The challenges of adulthood. *Journal of Learning Disabilities, 25,* 410-415, 447.

Paul, P. V., & Jackson, D. W. (1993). *Toward a psychology of deafness: Theoretical and empirical perspectives.* Boston: Allyn and Bacon.

Paul, P. V., & Quigley, S. P. (1987). Some effects of early hearing impairment on English language development. In F. Martin (Ed.), *Hearing disorders in children: Pediatric audiology* (pp. 49-80). Austin, TX: PRO-ED.

Paul, P. V., & Quigley, S. P. (1990). *Education and deafness.* New York: Longman.

Paul, P. V., & Quigley, S. P. (1994). *Language and deafness* (2nd ed.). San Diego: Singular Publishing Group.

Pava, W. S. (1994). Visually impaired persons' vulnerability to sexual and physical assault. *Journal of Visual Impairment & Blindness, 88,* 103-112.

Pava, W. S., Bateman, P., Appleton, M. K., & Glascock, J. (1991). Self-defense training for visually impaired women. *Journal of Visual Impairment & Blindness, 85,* 397-401.

Pawlas, G. E. (1994). Homeless students at the school door. *Educational Leadership, 51,* 79-82.

Peacock Hill Working Group, The (1991). Problems and promises in special education and related services for children and youth with emotional or behavioral disorders. *Behavioral Disorders, 16,* 299-313.

Peck, C. A., Odom, S. L., & Bricker, D. D. (1993). *Integrating young children with disabilities into community programs.* Baltimore, MD: Brookes.

Peckham, V. C. (1993). Children with cancer in the classroom. *Teaching Exceptional Children, 26*(1), 27-32.

Peña, E., Quinn, R., & Iglesias, T. (1992). The application of dynamic methods to language assessment: A nonbiased procedure. *The Journal of Special Education, 26,* 269-280.

Pendergast, K., Dickey, S., Selmar, J., & Soder, A. (1984). *Photo articulation test.* Austin, TX: PRO-ED.

Pennhurst State School & Hospital v. Halderman, 446 F. Supp. 1295 (E. D. Pa. 1981).

Pennsylvania Association for Retarded Children v. Commonwealth of Pennsylvania. (1972). 343 F. Supp. 279.

Perkins School for the Blind. (1978). *Sign language curricula.* Watertown, MA: Author.

Perkins, W. H. (1977). *Speech pathology.* St. Louis, MO: C. V. Mosby.

Perlmutter, B. F., & Parus, M. V. (1983). Identifying children with learning disabilities: A comparison of diagnostic procedures across school districts. *Learning Disability Quarterly, 6,* 321-328.

Perry, M., & Garber, M. (1993). Technology helps parents teach their children with developmental delays. *Teaching Exceptional Children*, *25*(2), 8-11.

Pester, E. (1993). Braille instruction for individuals who are blind adventitiously: Scheduling, expectation, and reading interests. *RE:view*, *25*, 83-87.

Peters, C. C. (1994). Leta Stetter Hollingworth: Women and giftedness. *Gifted Education International*, *9*(3), 136-137.

Peters, M. T. (1990). Someone's missing: The student as an overlooked participant in the IEP process. *Preventing School Failure*, *34*(4), 32-36.

Peters, M. T., & Heron, T. E. (1993). When the best is not good enough: An examination of best practice. *Journal of Special Education*, *26*, 371–385.

Peterson, C. A., & Gunn, S. L. (1984). *Therapeutic recreation* (2nd ed.). Englewood Cliffs, NJ: Prentice-Hall.

Peterson, R., Benson, D., Edwards, L., Rosell, J., & White, M. (1986). Inclusion of socially maladjusted children and youth in the legal definition of the behaviorally disordered population: A debate. *Behavioral Disorders*, *11*, 213-222.

Pfeiffer, S. I. (1982). The superiority of team decision making. *Exceptional Children*, *49*, 68-69.

Phelps, D. L. (1981). Retinopathy of prematurity: An estimate of vision loss in the United States—1979. *Pediatrics*, *67*, 924-926.

Phillips, A. L., & Cole, E. B. (Eds.). (1993). Beginning with babies: A sharing of professional experience. *The Volta Review*, *95*.

Phillips, N. B., Hamlett, C. L., Fuchs, L. S., & Fuchs, D. (1993). Combining classwide curriculum-based measurement and peer tutoring to help general educators provide adaptive education. *Learning Disabilities Research & Practice*, *8*, 148-156.

Pieper, B., & Cappuccilli, J. (1980). Beyond the family and the institution: The sanctity of liberty. In T. Apolloni, J. Cappucilli, & T. P. Cooke (Eds.), *Achievements in residential services for persons with disabilities: Toward excellence*. Baltimore, MD: University Park Press.

Pieper, E. (1983). *The teacher and the child with spina bifida* (2nd ed.). Rockville, MD: Spina Bifida Association of America.

Piirto, J. (1992). *Understanding those who create*. Dayton, OH: Ohio Psychology Press.

Piirto, J. (1994). *Talented children and adults: Their development and education*. Englewood Cliffs, NJ: Merrill/Prentice Hall.

Plann, S. (1992). Roberto Francisco Pradez: Spain's first deaf teacher of the deaf. *American Annals of the Deaf*, *137*, 48-55.

Plummer, D. (1995). Serving the needs of gifted children from a multicultural perspective. In Genshaft, J. L., Bireley, M., & Hollinger, C. L. (Eds.). *Serving gifted and talented students: A resource for school personnel* (pp. 285-300). Austin, TX: PRO-ED.

Pogrund, R. L., & Rosen, S. J. (1989). The preschool child can be a cane user. *Journal of Visual Impairment and Blindness*, *83*, 431-439.

Pogrund, R. L., Fazzi, D. L., & Schreier, E. M. (1993). Development of a preschool "kiddy cane." *Journal of Visual Impairment & Blindness*, *87*, 52-54.

Polifka, J. C. (1981). Compliance with Public Law 94-142 and consumer satisfaction. *Exceptional Children*, *48*, 250-253.

Polloway, E. A. (1984). The integration of mildly retarded students in the schools: A historical review. *Remedial and Special Education*, *5*(4), 18-28.

Polloway, E. A., & J. R. Patton. (1993). *Strategies for teaching learners with special needs* (5th ed.). Englewood Cliffs, NJ: Merrill/Prentice Hall.

Polloway, E. A., & Smith, J. D. (1978). Special Olympics: A second look. *Education and Training in Mental Retardation*, *13*, 432-433.

Polloway, E. A., Cronin, M. E., & Patton, J. R. (1986). The efficacy of group versus one-to-one instruction: A review. *Remedial and Special Education*, *7*(1), 22-30.

Possi, M. K. (1994). *Effects of money counting fluency training on the acquisition and generalization of money counting and purchasing skills by high school students with mental retardation*. Unpublished doctoral dissertation, The Ohio State University, Columbus.

Potter, M. L., & Wamre, H. M. (1990). Curriculum-based measurement and developmental reading models: Opportunities for cross-validation. *Exceptional Children*, *57*, 16-25.

Potts, L., Eshleman, J. W., & Cooper, J. O. (1993). Ogden R. Lindsley and the historical development of precision teaching. *The Behavior Analyst*, *16*, 177-189.

Powell, T. H., & Ogle, P. A. (1985). *Brothers and sisters: A special part of exceptional families*. Baltimore, MD: Paul H. Brooks Publishing Company.

Prasse, D. P. (1986). Litigation and special education: An introduction. *Exceptional Children*, *52*, 311-312.

Prendergast, D. E. (1995). Preparing for children who are medically fragile in educational programs. *Teaching Exceptional Children*, *27*(2), 37-41.

Pressey, S. L. (1955). Concerning the nature and nurture of genius. *Scientific Monthly*, *80*, 123-129.

Pressey, S. L. (1962). Educational acceleration: Occasional procedure or major issue? *Personnel and Guidance Journal*, 12-17.

Prinz, P. M., & Nelson, K. E. (1985). "Alligator eats cookie": Acquisition of writing and reading skills by deaf children using the microcomputer. *Applied Psycholinguistics*, *6*, 283-306.

Prinz, P. M., & Prinz, E. A. (1979). Simultaneous acquisition of ASL and spoken English in a hearing child of a deaf mother and hearing father. *Sign Language Studies*, *25*, 283-296.

Provencal, G. (1980). The Macomb-Oakland regional center. In T. Apolloni, J. Cappucilli, & T. P. Cooke (Eds.), *Achievements in residential services for persons with disabilities: Toward excellence* (pp. 19-43). Baltimore, MD: University Park Press.

Pruess, J. B., Fewell, R. R., & Bennett, F. C. (1989). Vitamin therapy and children with Down syndrome: A review of research. *Exceptional Children*, *55*, 336-341.

Public Law 95-561. Gifted and Talented Children's Education Act. *Congressional Record* (1978, October 10). H-12179.

Pueschel, S. M. (1991). Ethical considerations relating to prenatal diagnosis of fetuses with Down syndrome. *Mental Retardation*, *29*, 185-190.

Pugach, M. C., & Johnson, L. J. (1989). Prereferral interventions: Progress, problems, and challenges. *Exceptional Children*, *56*, 217-226.

Pugach, M. C., & Warger, C. L. (1993). Curriculum considerations. In J. I. Goodlad & T. C. Lovitt (Eds.), *Integrating general and special education* (pp. 125-148). Englewood Cliffs, NJ: Merrill/Prentice Hall.

Pullis, M. (1991). Practical considerations of excluding conduct disordered students: An empirical analysis. *Behavioral Disorders*, *17*, 9-22.

Putnam, J. W. (1993). *Cooperative learning and strategies for inclusion: Celebrating Diversity in the classroom*. Baltimore: Paul H. Brookes.

Quay, H. C. (1968). The faces of educational exceptionality: Conceptual framework for assessment, grouping, and instruction. *Exceptional Children*, *35*, 25-31.

Quay, H. C. (1975). Classification in the treatment of delinquency and antisocial behavior. In N. Hobbs (Ed.), *Issues in the classification of children* (Vol. 1) (pp. 377-392). San Francisco: Jossey-Bass.

Quay, H. C. (1986). Classification. In H. C. Quay, & J. S. Werry, (Eds.). (1986). *Psychopathological disorders of childhood* (3rd ed.). New York: John Wiley & Sons.

Quay, H. C., & Peterson, D. R. (1987). *Manual for the Revised Behavior Problem Checklist*. (Available from H. C. Quay, P. O. Box 248185, University of Miami, Coral Gables, FL 33124-2070).

Quigley, S. P., & Paul, P. V. (1986). A perspective on academic achievement. In D. M. Luterman (Ed.), *Deafness in perspective* (pp. 55-86). San Diego: College-Hill.

Ramey, C. T., & Ramey, S. L. (1992). Effective early intervention *Mental Retardation, 30,* 337-345.

Ramey, C. T., Bryant, D. M., Wasik, B. H., & Sparling, J. J., Fendt, K. H., & LaVange, L. M. (1992). The Infant Health and Development Program for low birthweight, premature infants: Program elements, family participation, and child intelligence. *Pediatrics, 89,* 454-465.

Ramirez, B. A. (1988). Culturally and linguistically diverse children. *Teaching Exceptional Children, 20*(4), 45.

Ramirez, B. A., & Johnson, J. J. (1988). American Indian exceptional children: Improved practices and policy. In A. A. Ortiz & B. A. Ramirez (Eds.), *Schools and the culturally diverse exceptional student: Promising practices and future directions* (pp. 128-140). Reston, VA: Council for Exceptional Children.

Rapport, M. J. K., & Thomas, S. B. (1993). Extended school year: Legal issues and implications. *Journal of the Association for Persons with Severe Handicaps, 19,* 16-27.

Raskin, D. (1990). Fast brakes. *American Health, 9*(6), 24.

Raver, S. (1984). Modification of head droop during conversation in a 3-year-old visually impaired child: A case study. *Journal of Visual Impairment and Blindness, 78,* 307-310.

Rawlings, B. W., & King, S. J. (1986). Postsecondary educational opportunities for deaf students. In A. N. Schildroth & M. A. Karchmer (Eds.), *Deaf children in America* (pp. 231-257). San Diego: College-Hill.

Reagan, T. (1985). The deaf as a linguistic minority: Educational considerations. *Harvard Educational Review, 55,* 265-277.

Redmond, N. B., Bennett, C., Wiggert, J., & McLean, B. (1993). Using functional assessment to support a student with severe disabilities in the community. *Teaching Exceptional Children, 25*(3), 51-52.

Reed, V. A. (1986). *An introduction to children with language disorders.* Englewood Cliffs, NJ: Merrill/Prentice Hall.

Reed, V. A. (1994). *An introduction to children with language disorders* (2nd ed.). Englewood Cliffs, NJ: Merrill/Prentice Hall.

Reichle, J., & Keogh, W. J. (1986). Communication instruction for learners with severe handicaps: Some unresolved issues. In R. H. Horner, L. H. Meyer, & H. D. B. Fredericks (Eds.), *Education of learners with severe handicaps: Exemplary service strategies* (pp. 189-219). Baltimore, MD: Paul H. Brooks Publishing Company.

Reid, D. H., & Favell, J. (1984). Group instruction with persons who have severe disabilities: A critical review. *The Journal of The Association for Persons with Severe Handicaps, 9,* 167-177.

Reid, D. H., Parsons, M. B., McCarn, J. E., Green, C. W., Phillips, J. F., & Schepis, M. M. (1985). Providing a more appropriate education for severely handicapped persons: Increasing and validating functional classroom tasks. *Journal of Applied Behavior Analysis, 18,* 289-301.

Reid, R., Maag, J. W., & Vasa, S. F. (1994). Attention deficit hyperactivity disorder as a disability category: A critique. *Exceptional Children, 60,* 198-214.

Reiff, H. B., Gerber, P. J, & Ginsberg, R. (1993). Definitions of learning disabilities from adults with learning disabilities: The insiders' perspectives. *Learning Disability Quarterly, 16,* 114-125.

Reis, S. (1987). We can't change what we don't recognize: Understanding the needs of gifted females. *Gifted Child Quarterly, 31*(2), 83-89.

Reis, S. (1995). What gifted education can offer the reform movement: Talent development. In Genshaft, J. L., Bireley, M., & Hollinger, C. L. (Eds.). *Serving gifted and talented students: A resource for school personnel* (pp. 371-387). Austin, TX: PRO-ED.

Reis, S. M., & Cellerino, M. (1983). Guiding gifted students through independent study. *Teaching Exceptional Children, 15,* 136-139.

Reis, S. M., & Purcell, J. H. (1993). An analysis of content elimination and strategies used by elementary classroom teachers in the curriculum compacting process.

Journal for the Education of the Gifted, 16, 147-170.

Reisberg, L., Brodigan, D., & Williams, G. J. (1991). Classroom management: Implementing a system for students with BD. *Intervention in School and Clinic, 27*(1), 31-38.

Reiss, S. (1994). Issues in defining mental retardation. *American Journal on Mental Retardation, 99,* 1-7.

Renzulli, J. S. (1977). *The enrichment triad model: A guide for developing defensible programs for the gifted and talented.* Weathersfield, CT: Creative Learning Press.

Renzulli, J. S. (1978). What makes giftedness?: Reexamining a definition. *Phi Delta Kappan, 61,* 180-184.

Renzulli, J. S. (1982). What makes a problem real: Stalking the illusive meaning of qualitative differences in gifted education. *Gifted Child Quarterly, 26,* 147-156.

Renzulli, J. S. (1986). *Systems and models for developing programs for the gifted and talented.* Mansfield Center, CT: Creative Learning Press.

Renzulli, J., & Reis, S. (1986). The enrichment triad/revolving door model: A schoolwide plan for the development of creative productivity. In J. Renzulli (Ed.), *Systems and models for developing programs for the gifted and talented.* Mansfield Center, CT: Creative Learning Press.

Renzulli, J., Reis, S., & Smith, L. (1981). *The revolving door identification model.* Mansfield Center, CT: Creative Learning Press.

Repp, A. C., & Barton, L. E. (1980). Naturalistic observations of institutionalized retarded persons: A comparison of licensure decisions and behavioral observations. *Journal of Applied Behavior Analysis, 13,* 333-341.

Repp, A. C., & Singh, N. N. (Eds.). (1990). *Perspectives on the use of nonaversive and aversive interventions for persons with developmental disabilities.* Sycamore, IL: Sycamore Publishing.

Revell, W. G., Wehman, P., Kregel, J. West, M., & Rayfield, R. (1994). Supported employment for persons with severe disabilities: Positive trends in wages, models, and funding. *Education and Training in Mental Retardation, 29,* 256-264.

Reynolds, A. J. (1992). Comparing measures of parental involvement and their effects on academic achievement. *Research Quarterly, 7,* 441-462.

Reynolds, C. R. (1992). Two key concepts in the diagnosis of learning disabilities and the habilitation of learning. *Learning Disability Quarterly, 15,* 2-12.

Reynolds, M. C. (1989). An historical perspective: The delivery of special education to mildly disabled and at-risk students. *Remedial and Special Education, 10*(6), 7-11.

Reynolds, M. C., Wang, M. C., & Walberg, H. J. (1987). The necessary restructuring of special and regular education. *Exceptional Children, 53,* 391-398.

Reynolds, M. C., Zetlin, A. G., & Wang, M. C. (1993). ²⁰⁄₂₀ analysis: Taking a close look at the margins. *Exceptional Children, 59,* 294-300.

Rhoads, G. G., Jackson, L. G., Schlesselman, S. E., de la Cruz, F. F., Desnick, R. J., Golbus, M. S., Ledbetter, D. H., Lubs, H. A., Mahoney, M. J., Pergament, E., Simpson, J. L., Carpenter, R. J., Elias, S., Ginsberg, N. A., Goldberg, J. D., Hobbins, J. C., Lynch, L., Shiono, P. H. K., Wapner, R. J., & Zachary, J. M. (1989). The safety and efficacy of chorionic villus sampling for early prenatal diagnosis of cytogenetic abnormalities. *The New England Journal of Medicine, 320,* 609-617.

Rhode, G. (1981). *Generalization and maintenance of treatment gains on behaviorally/emotionally handicapped students from resource rooms to regular classrooms using self-evaluation procedures.* Unpublished doctoral dissertation, Utah State University.

Rhode, G., Jensen, W. R., & Reavis, H. K. (1993). *The Tough Kid Book: Practical Classroom Management Strategies.* Longmont, CO: Sopris West.

Rhode, G., Morgan , D. P., & Young, K. R. (1983). Generalization and maintenance of treatment gains of behaviorally handicapped students from resource rooms to regular classrooms using self-evaluation procedures. *Journal of Applied Behavior Analysis, 16,* 171-188.

Rhodes, L. E., & Valenta, L. (1985). Industry-based supported employment: An enclave approach. *The Journal of The Association for Persons with Severe Handicaps, 10,* 12-20.

Rhodes, W. C., & Head, S. (Eds.). (1974). *A study of child variance: Vol 3. Service delivery systems.* Ann Arbor: University of Michigan.

Rhodes, W. C., & Tracy, M. L. (Eds.). (1972a). *A study of child variance: Vol 1. Theories.* Ann Arbor: University of Michigan.

Rhodes, W. C., & Tracy, M. L. (Eds.). (1972b). *A study of child variance: Vol 2. Interventions.* Ann Arbor: University of Michigan.

Rhyne, J. M. (1982). Comprehension of synthetic speech by blind children. *Journal of Visual Impairment and Blindness, 76,* 313-316.

Rich, H. L., Beck, M. A., & Coleman, T. W., Jr. (1982). Behavior management: The psychoeducational model. In R. L. McDowell, G. W. Adamson, & F. H. Wood (Eds.), *Teaching emotionally disturbed children* (pp. 131-166). Boston: Little, Brown.

Richards, J. C., & Gipe, J. P. (1993). Spelling lessons for gifted language arts students. *Teaching Exceptional Children, 25*(2), 12-15.

Richardson, E. H. (1981). Cultural and historical perspectives in counseling American Indians. In D. W. Sue, *Counseling the culturally different: Theory and practice.* New York: John Wiley & Sons.

Richardson, J. (1993). Three classes of change to improve the daily living skills of persons with visual impairments. *Journal of Visual Impairment and Blindness, 87,* 402-404.

Richert, E. S., Alvino, J., & McDonnel, R. (1981). *The national report on identification: Assessment and recommendations for comprehensive identification of gifted and talented youth.* Sewell, NJ: Educational Information and Resource Center, for U.S. Department of Education.

Rieke, J. A., Lynch, L. L., & Soltman, S. F. (1977). *Teaching strategies for language development.* New York: Grune & Stratton.

Ries, P. (1986). Characteristics of hearing impaired youth in the general population and of students in special educational programs for the hearing impaired. In A. N. Schildroth & M. A. Karchmer (Eds.), *Deaf children in America* (pp. 1-31). San Diego: College-Hill.

Rieth, H., & Evertson, C. (1988). Variables related to the effective instruction of difficult-to-teach children. *Focus on Exceptional Children, 20* (5), 1-8.

Rieth, H. J., & Polsgrove, L. (1994). Curriculum and instructional issues in teaching secondary students with learning disabilities. *Learning Disabilities Research & Practice, 9,* 118-126.

Rikhye, C. H., Gothelf, C. R., & Appell, M. W. (1989). A classroom environment checklist for students with dual sensory impairments. *Teaching Exceptional Children, 22*(1), 44-46.

Rimland, B. (1993a). Beware the advozealots: Mindless good intentions

injure the handicapped. *Autism Research Review International, 7*(4), 1.

Rimland, B. (1993b). Inclusive education: Right for some. *Autism Research Review International, 7*(1), 3.

Rimmerman, A. (1989). Provision of respite care for children with developmental disabilities: Changes in maternal coping and stress over time. *Mental Retardation, 27,* 99-103.

Ring, B., & Shaughnessy, M. F. (1993). The gifted label, gifted children, and the aftermath. *Gifted Education International, 9*(1), 33-35.

Ritvo, E. R., & Freeman, B. J. (1978). National Society of Autistic Children definition of the syndrome of Autism. *Journal of Autism and Developmental Disorders, 8,* 162-170.

Roberds-Baxter, S. (1984). The parent connection: Enhancing the affective component of parent conferences. *Teaching Exceptional Children, 17*(1), 55-58.

Roberts, F. K. (1986). Education for the visually handicapped: A social and educational history. In G. T. Scholl (Ed.), *Foundations of education for blind and visually handicapped children and youth: Theory and practice* (pp. 1-18). New York: American Foundation for the Blind.

Roberts, J. E., Burchinal, M. R., & Bailey, D. B. (1994). Communication among preschoolers with and without disabilities in same-age and mixed-age classes. *American Journal on Mental Retardation, 99,* 231-249.

Robins, L. (1966). *Deviant children grown up.* Baltimore, MD: Williams & Wilkins.

Robins, L. N. (1979). Follow-up studies. In H. C. Quay & J. S. Werry (Eds.), *Psychopathological disorders of childhood* (2nd ed.). New York: John Wiley & Sons.

Robinson, D. (1982). The IEP: Meaningful individualized education in Utah. *Phi Delta Kappan, 64,* 205-206.

Robinson, D., Griffith, J., McComish, L., & Swasbrook, K. (1984). Bus training for developmentally disabled adults. *American Journal of Mental Deficiency, 89,* 37-43.

Robinson, N. M., & Noble, K. D. (1991). Social-emotional development and adjustment of gifted children. In M. C. Wang, M. C. Reynolds, & H. J. Walberg (Eds.), *Handbook of special education: Research and practice. Volume 4: Emerging programs* (pp. 57-76). New York: Pergamon Press.

Robinson, N. M., & Robinson, H. B. (1976). *The mentally retarded child: A psycho-

logical approach (2nd ed.). New York: McGraw-Hill.

Roeser, R., & Yellin, W. (1987). Pure-tone tests with preschool children. In F. Martin (Ed.), *Hearing disorders in children: Pediatric audiology* (pp. 217-264). Austin, TX: PRO-ED.

Rogers-Warren, A., & Warren, S. (1977). *Ecological perspectives in behavior analysis.* Baltimore, MD: University Park Press.

Rogers-Warren, A., & Warren, S. (1980). Mands for verbalization: Facilitating the generalization of newly trained language in children. *Behavior Modification, 4,* 320-245.

Romer, L. T., & Haring, N. G. (1994). The social participation of students with deaf-blindness in educational settings. *Education and Training in Mental Retardation and Developmental Disabilities, 29,* 134-144.

Rooney, K. J. (1991). Controversial therapies: A review and critique. *Intervention in School and Clinic, 26,* 134-142.

Rooney, T. E. (1982). Signing vs. speech: What's a parent to do? *SEE What's Happening, 1*(1), 6-8.

Roos, P. (1980). The handling and mishandling of parents of mentally retarded persons. In F. Menolascino (Ed.), *Bridging the gap.* New York: John Wiley & Sons.

Roos, P. (1985). Parents of mentally retarded children—misunderstood and mistreated. In A. P. Turnbull & H. R. Turnbull (Eds.), *Parents speak out: Views from the other side of the two-way mirror* (2nd. ed.) (pp. 245-257). Englewood Cliffs, NJ: Merrill/Prentice Hall.

Rorschach, H. (1942). *Rorschach psychodiagnostic plates.* New York: Psychological Corp.

Rose, K. C., White, J. A., Conroy, J., & Smith, D. M. (1993). Following the course of change: A study of adaptive and maladaptive behaviors in young adults living in the community. *Education and Training in Mental Retardation, 28,* 149-154.

Rose, T. L. (1978). The functional relationship between artificial food colors and hyperactivity. *Journal of Applied Behavior Analysis, 11,* 439-446.

Rose, T. L., & Calhoun, M. L. (1990). The Charlotte Circle Project: A program for infants and toddlers with severe/profound disabilities. *Journal of Early Intervention, 14,* 175-185.

Rose, T. L., Calhoun, M. L., & Ladage, L. (1989). Helping young children respond

to caregivers. *Teaching Exceptional Children, 21*(4), 48-51.

Rosenberg, G. (1994, March 17). *Hearing on inclusion reauthorization of The Individuals with Disabilities Education Act.* Testimony before the U.S. House of Representatives Select Education and Civil Rights Committee on Education and Labor.

Ross A. O. (1974). *Psychological disorders of children.* New York: McGraw-Hill.

Ross, M. (1981). Review, overview, and other educational considerations. In M. Ross & L. W. Nober (Eds.), *Educating hard of hearing children* (pp. 102-116). Reston, VA: Council for Exceptional Children.

Ross, M. (1986). A perspective on amplification: Then and now. In D. M. Luterman (Ed.), *Deafness in perspective* (pp. 35-53). San Diego: College-Hill.

Rotegard, L. L., Hill, B. K., & Bruininks, R. H. (1983). Environmental characteristics of residential facilities for mentally retarded persons in the United States. *American Journal of Mental Deficiency, 88,* 49-56.

Roth, M., McCaul, E., & Barnes, K. (1993). Who becomes an "At-risk" student? The predictive value of a kindergarten screening battery. *Exceptional Children, 59,* 348-358.

Rothman, E. P. (1977). *Troubled teachers.* New York: David McKay Co.

Rowitz, L. (1981). A sociological perspective on labeling and mental retardation. *Mental Retardation, 19,* 47-51.

Rowland, C. (1990). Communication in the classroom for children with dual sensory impairments: Studies of teacher and child behavior. *Augmentative and Alternative Communication, 7,* 262-274.

Rowland, C., & Schweigert, P. (1993). Analyzing the communication environment to increase functional communication. *Journal of the Association for Persons with Severe Handicaps, 18,* 161-176.

Rubin, R. A., & Balow, B. (1971). Learning and behavior disorders: A longitudinal study. *Exceptional Children, 38,* 293-299.

Rugow, S. (1984). The uses of social routines to facilitate communication in visually impaired and multihandicapped children. *Topics in Early Childhood Special Education, 3*(4), 67-70.

Ruhl, K. L., & Berlinghoff, D. H. (1992). Research on improving behaviorally disordered students' academic performance: A review of the literature. *Behavioral Disorders, 17,* 178-190.

Rumberger, R. W., Ghatak, R., Polous, G., Ritter, P. L., & Dornbush, S. M. (1990).

Family influences on dropout behavior in one California high school. *Sociology of Education, 63,* 283-299.

Rusch, F. (1990). *Supported employment: Models, methods, and issues.* Sycamore, IL: Sycamore Publishing.

Rusch, F. R., Chadsey-Rusch, J., & Lagomarcino, T. (1987). Preparing students for employment. In M. E. Snell (Ed.), *Systematic instruction of persons with severe handicaps* (3rd ed.) (pp. 471-490). Englewood Cliffs, NJ: Merrill/Prentice Hall.

Rusch, F. R., DeStefano, L., Chadsey-Rusch, J., Phelps, A., & Szymanski, E. (1992). *Transition from school to adult life: Models, linkages, and policy.* Pacific Grove, CA: Brookes/Cole.

Rusch, F. R., Hughes, C., McNair, J., & Wilson, P. G. (1990). *Co-worker involvement scoring manual and instrument.* Champaign, IL: University of Illinois, The Board of Trustees of the University of Illinois.

Rusch, F. R., Johnson, J. R., & Hughes, C. (1990). Analysis of co-worker involvement in relations to level of disability versus placement approach among supported employees. *The Journal of The Association for Persons with Severe Handicaps, 15,* 32-39.

Rusch, F. R., & Minch, K. E. (1988). Identification of co-worker involvement in supported employment: A review and analysis. *Research in Developmental Disabilities, 9,* 247-254.

Rusch, F. R., Rose, T. L., & Greenwood, C. R. (1988). *Introduction to behavior analysis in special education.* Englewood Cliffs, NJ: Prentice-Hall.

Rusch, F. R., & Shutz, R. P. (1981). Vocational and social work behavior: An evaluative review. In J. L. Matson & J. R. McCartney (Eds.), *Handbook of behavior modification with the mentally retarded* (pp. 247-280). New York: Plenum Press.

Rutherford, R., Chipman, J., DiGangi, S., & Anderson, K. (1992). *Teaching social skills: A Practical instructional approach.* Reston, VA: Council for Exceptional Children.

Rutter, M. (1970). Autistic children: Infancy to adulthood. *Seminars in Psychiatry, 2,* 435-450.

Rutter, M. (1976). *Helping troubled children.* New York: Plenum Press.

Rutter, M., & Schopler, E. (1987). Autism and pervasive developmental disorders: Concepts and diagnostic issues. *Journal of Autism and Developmental Disorders, 17,* 159-186.

Ryan, C. S., & Coyne, A. (1985). Effects of group homes on neighborhood property values. *Mental Retardation, 23,* 241-245.

Sabornie, E. J., & Kauffman, J. M. (1986). Social acceptance of learning disabled adolescents. *Learning Disability Quarterly, 9,* 55-60.

Sacks, O. (1986, March 27). Mysteries of the deaf. *New York Review of Books, 33*(5).

Safer, D. J., & Krager, J. M. (1988). A survey of medication treatment for hyperactive/inattentive students. *Journal of the American Medical Association, 260,* 2256-2258.

Sailor, W., & Guess, D. (1983). *Severely handicapped students: An instructional design.* Boston: Houghton Mifflin.

Sailor, W., & Haring, N. G. (1977). Some current directions in education of the severely/multiply handicapped. *AAESPH Review, 2,* 67-87.

Sailor, W., Anderson, J. L., Halvorsen, A. T., Doering, K., Filler, J., & Goetz, L. (1989). *The comprehensive local school: Regular education for all students with disabilities.* Baltimore, MD: Paul H. Brooks Publishing Company.

Sailor, W., Gee, K., Goetz, L., & Graham, N. (1988). Progress in educating students with the most severe disabilities: Is there any? *The Journal of The Association for Persons with Severe Handicaps, 13,* 87-89.

Sainato, D. M., & Lyon, S L. (1989). Promoting successful mainstreaming transitions for handicapped preschool children. *Journal of Early Intervention, 13*(4), 305-314.

Sainato, D. M., Goldstein, H., & Strain, P. S. (1992). Effects of self-evaluation on preschool children's use of social interaction strategies with their autistic peers. *Journal of Applied Behavior Analysis, 25,* 127-141.

Sainato, D. M., & Strain, P. S. (1993). Increasing integration success for preschoolers with disabilities. *Teaching Exceptional Children, 25*(2), 36.

Sainato, D. M., Strain, P. S., & Lyon, S. L. (1987). Increasing academic responding of handicapped preschool children during group instruction. *Journal of the Division of Early Childhood Special Education, 12,* 23-30.

Salend, S. J. (1990). A migrant education guide for special educators. *Teaching Exceptional Children, 22*(2), 18-21.

Salend, S. J. (1994). *Effective mainstreaming: Creating inclusive classrooms* (2nd ed.). Englewood Cliffs, NJ: Merrill/Prentice Hall.

Salend, S. J., & Giek, K. A. (1988). Independent living arrangements for individuals with mental retardation: The landlords' perspective. *Mental Retardation, 26,* 89-92.

Salend, S. J., & Longo, M. (1994). The roles of the education interpreter in mainstreaming. *Teaching Exceptional Children, 26*(4), 22-28.

Salend, S. J., Ellis, L. L., & Reynolds, C. J. (1989). Using self-instruction to teach vocational skills to individuals who are severely retarded. *Education and Training of the Mentally Retarded, 24,* 248-254.

Salend, S. J., Jantzen, N. R., & Giek, K. (1992). Using a peer confrontation system in a group setting. *Behavioral Disorders, 17,* 211-218.

Salend, S. J., Whittaker, C. R., & Reeder, E. (1993). Group evaluation: A collaborative peer-mediated behavior management system. *Exceptional Children, 59,* 203-209.

Salisbury, C. L. (1991). Mainstreaming during the early childhood years. *Exceptional Children, 58,* 146-155.

Salisbury, C. L., & Intaglia, J. (1986). *Respite care support for persons with developmental disabilities and their families.* Baltimore, MD: Paul H. Brooks Publishing Company.

Salisbury, C., & Chambers, A. (1994). Instructional costs of inclusive schooling. *Journal of the Association for Persons with Severe Handicaps, 19,* 215-222.

Salvia, J., & Hughes, C. (1990). *Curriculum-based assessment: Testing what is taught.* Englewood Cliffs, NJ: Merrill/Prentice Hall.

Salvia, J., & Ysseldyke, J. E. (1991). *Assessment in special and remedial education* (5th ed.). Boston: Houghton Mifflin.

Sameroff, A. J., & Chandler, M. J. (1975). Reproductive risk and the continuum of caretaking casualty. In F. D. Horowitz (Ed.), *Review of child development research* (Vol. 4) (pp. 187-244). Chicago: University of Chicago Press.

Samuels, S. J. & Miller, N. L. (1985). Failure to find attention differences between learning disabled and normal children on classroom and laboratory tasks. *Exceptional Children, 51,* 358-375.

Sandler, A. G., Arnold, L. B., Gable, R. A., & Strain, P. S. (1987). Effects of peer pressure on disruptive behavior of behaviorally disordered students. *Behavioral Disorders, 16,* 9-22.

Sandler, A., & Coren, A. (1981). Integrated instruction at home and school: Parents'

perspective. *Education and Training of the Mentally Retarded, 16*(3), 183-187.

Sands, D. J., & Kozleski, E. B. (1994). Quality of life differences between adults with and without disabilities. *Education and Training in Mental Retardation, 29,* 90-101.

Sansone, J., & Zigmond, N. (1986). Evaluating mainstreaming through an analysis of students' schedules. *Exceptional Children, 52,* 452-458.

Santos, K. E. (1992). Fragile X syndrome: An educator's role in identification, prevention, and intervention. *Remedial and Special Education, 13,* 32-39.

Saski, J., Swicegood, P., & Carter, J. (1983). Notetaking formats for learning disabled adolescents. *Learning Disability Quarterly, 6,* 265-270.

Sasser, E., & Zorena, N. (1991). Storytelling as an adjunct to writing: Experiences with gifted students. *Teaching Exceptional Children, 23*(2), 44-45.

Savage, R. C., & Wolcott, G. F. (Eds.). (1994). *Educational dimensions of acquired brain injury.* Austin, TX: PRO-ED.

Scanlon, C. A., Arick, J., & Phelps, N. (1981). Participation in the development of the IEP: Parents' perspective. *Exceptional Children, 47,* 373-374.

Scarcella, R. (1990). *Teaching language minority students in the multicultural classroom.* Englewood Cliffs, NJ: Merrill/Prentice-Hall.

Schalock, R. L., Harper, R. S., & Carver, G. (1981). Independent living placement: Five years later. *American Journal of Mental Deficiency, 86,* 170-177.

Schalock, R. L., Keith, K. D., Hoffman, K., & Karan, O. C. (1989). Quality of life: Its measurement and use. *Mental Retardation, 27,* 25-31.

Schalock, R. L., Stark, J. A., Snell, M. E., Coulter, D. L., Polloway, E. A., Luckasson, R., Reiss, S., & Spitalnik, D. M. (1994). The changing conception of mental retardation: Implications for the field. *Mental Retardation, 32,* 181-193.

Scheerenberger, R. C. (1984). *A history of mental retardation.* Baltimore, MD: Paul H. Brooks Publishing Company.

Schell, G. C. (1981). The young handicapped child: A family perspective. *Topics in Early Childhood Special Education, 1,* 21-27.

Schenck, S. (1980). The diagnostic/instructional links in individualized education programs. *The Journal of Special Education, 14,* 337-345.

Schiff-Myers, N. B., Djukic, J., McGovern-Lawler, J., & Perez, D. (1994). Assessment considerations in the evaluation of second-language learners: A case study. *Exceptional Children, 60,* 237-248.

Schildroth, A. N. (1986). Residential schools for deaf students: A decade in review. In A. N. Schildroth & M. A. Karchmer (Eds.), *Deaf children in America* (pp. 83-104). San Diego: College-Hill.

Schirmer, B. R. (1994). *Language and literacy development in children who are deaf.* Boston: Allyn & Bacon.

Schleien, S. J., & Ray, M. T. (1988). *Community recreation and persons with disabilities: Strategies for integration.* Baltimore, MD: Paul H. Brooks Publishing Company.

Schleien, S. J., Green, F. P., & Heyne, L. A. (1993). Integrated community recreation. In M. E. Snell, *Instruction of students with severe disabilities* (4th ed.) (pp. 526-555). Englewood Cliffs, NJ: Merrill/Prentice Hall.

Schleien, S. J., Kiernan, J., & Wehman, P. (1981). Evaluation of an age-appropriate leisure skills program for moderately retarded adults. *Education and Training of the Mentally Retarded, 16,* 13-19.

Schleien, S. J., Meyer, L. H., Heyne, L. A., & Brandt, B. B. (1995). *Lifelong leisure skills and lifestyles for persons with developmental disabilities.* Baltimore, MD: Paul H. Brooks Publishing Company.

Schleien, S. J., Wehman, P., & Kiernan, J. (1981). Teaching leisure skills to severely handicapped adults: An age-appropriate darts game. *Journal of Applied Behavior Analysis, 14,* 513-519.

Schlesinger, H. S. (1985). Deafness, mental health, and language. In F. Powell, T. Finitzo-Hieber, S. Friel-Patti, & D. Henderson (Eds.), *Education of the hearing impaired child* (pp. 103-116). San Diego: College-Hill.

Schlesinger, H. S., & Meadow, K. P. (1976). Emotional support for parents. In D. L. Lillie & P. L. Trohanis (Eds.), *Teaching parents to teach* (pp. 35-48). New York: Walker.

Schloss, P. J., Alexander, N., Hornig, E., Parker, K., & Wright, B. (1993). Teaching meal preparation vocabulary and procedures to individuals with mental retardation. *Teaching Exceptional Children, 25*(3), 7-12.

Schloss, P. J., Alper, S., & Jayne, D. (1994). Self-determination for persons with disabilities: Choice, risk, and dignity. *Exceptional Children, 60,* 215-225.

Schneider, B. H., & Leroux, J. (1994). Educational environments for the pupil with behavioral disorders: A "Best evidence"

synthesis. *Behavioral Disorders, 19,* 192-204.

Schneiderman, C. (1984). *Basic anatomy and physiology in speech and hearing.* San Diego: College-Hill.

Schnorr, R. (1990). "Peter? He comes and he goes . . . ": First-graders' perspectives of a part-time mainstream student. *Journal of The Association for Persons With Severe Handicaps, 15,* 231-240.

Scholl, G. T. (1986). Multicultural considerations. In G. T. Scholl (Ed.), *Foundations of education for blind and visually handicapped children and youth* (pp. 165-182). New York: American Foundation for the Blind.

Schonert-Reichl, K. A. (1993). Empathy and social relationships in adolescents with behavioral disorders. *Behavioral Disorders, 18,* 189-204.

Schopler, E., Reichler, R. J., & Renner, B. R. (1988). *The childhood autism rating scale.* Los Angeles: Western Psychological Services.

Schreier, E. M., Leventhal, J. D., & Uslan, M. M. (1991). Access technology for blind and visually impaired persons. *Technology and Disability, 1*(1), 19-23.

Schroeder, F. (1989). Literacy: the key to opportunity. *Journal of Visual Impairment & Blindness, 83,* 290-293.

Schroeder, S. (Ed.). (1987). *Toxic substances and mental retardation: Neurobiological toxicology and teratology.* Washington, DC: American Association on Mental Retardation.

Schulz, J. B. (1985). The parent-professional conflict. In H. R. Turnbull and A. P. Turnbull (Eds.), *Parents speak out: Then and now* (pp. 3-11). Englewood Cliffs, NJ: Merrill/Prentice Hall.

Schumaker, J. B., & Deshler, D. D. (1988). Implementing the regular education initiative in secondary schools: A different ball game. *Journal of Learning Disabilities, 21,* 43-52.

Schumaker, J. B., Hovell, M. F., & Sherman, J. A. (1977). An analysis of daily report cards and parent-managed privileges in the improvement of adolescents' classroom performance. *Journal of Applied Behavior Analysis, 10,* 449-464.

Schumaker, J. B., Pederson, C. S., Hazel, J. S., & Meyen, E. L. (1983). Social skills curricula for mildly handicapped adolescents: A review. *Focus on Exceptional Children, 4,* 1-16.

Schutter, L. S., & Brinker, R. P. (1992). Conjuring a new category of disability from prenatal cocaine exposure: Are the infants unique biological or caretaking

casualties? *Topics in Early Childhood Special Education, 11,* 84-111.

Scott, M. L., Ebbert, A., & Price, D. (1986). Assessing and teaching employability skills with prevocational work samples. *The Directive Teacher, 8*(1), 3-5.

Scruggs, T. E., & Mastropieri, M. A. (1992). Classroom applications of mnemonic instruction: Acquisition, maintenance, and generalization. *Exceptional Children, 58,* 219-229.

Scruggs, T. E., Mastropieri, M. A., Bakken, J. P., Brigham, F. J. 1993. Reading versus doing: The relative effects of text-book-based and inquiry-oriented approaches to science learning in special education classrooms. *The Journal of Special Education, 27,* 1, 1-16.

Scuccimarra, D. J., & Speece, D. L. (1990). Employment outcomes and social integration of students with mild handicaps: The quality of life two years after high school. *Journal of Learning Disabilities, 23,* 213-219.

Sears, P. S. (1979). The Terman genetic studies of genius, 1922-1972. In A. H. Passow (Ed.), *The gifted and the talented: Their education and development* (pp. 75-96). Chicago: University of Chicago Press.

Sears, R. R. (1977). Sources of life satisfaction of the Terman gifted men. *American Psychologist, 32*(2), 119-128.

Secord, W. (1981). *Test of Minimal Articulation Competence.* Englewood Cliffs, NJ: Merrill/Prentice Hall.

Seltzer, M. M., Krauss, M. W., & Janicki, M. P. (1994). *Life course perspectives on adulthood and old age.* Washington, DC: American Association On Mental Retardation.

Semel, E. M., & Wiig, E. H. (1980). *Clinical evaluation of language functions.* Englewood Cliffs, NJ: Merrill/Prentice Hall

Serna, L. (1993). Social skills instruction. In E. A. Polloway & J. R. Patton, *Strategies for teaching learners with special needs* (5th ed.) (pp. 437-458). Englewood Cliffs, NJ: Merrill/Prentice Hall.

Sexson, S. B., & Madan-Swain, A. (1993). School reentry for the child with chronic illness. *Journal of Learning Disabilities, 26,* 115-125.

Shafer, M. S., Rice, M. L., Metzler, H. M. D., & Haring, M. (1989). A survey of nondisabled employees' attitudes toward supported employees with mental retardation. *The Journal of The Association for Persons with Severe Handicaps, 14,* 137-146.

Shalock, R., & Bogale, M. J. (Eds.) (1990). *Quality of life: Perspectives and issues.*

Washington, DC: American Association on Mental Retardation.

Shannon, G. (1985). *Characteristics influencing current recreational patterns of persons with mental retardation.* Unpublished doctoral dissertation, Brandeis University.

Shapiro, E. S., & Cole, C. L. (1994). *Behavior change in the classroom: Self-management interventions.* New York: Guilford Press.

Shapiro, E. S., & Lentz, Jr., F. E. (1991). Vocational-technical programs: Follow-up of students with learning disabilities. *Exceptional Children, 58,* 47-59.

Shapiro, J. P., Loeb, P., & Bowermaster, D., & Toch, T. (1993, December 13). Separate and unequal: How special education programs are cheating our children and costing taxpayers billions of dollars. *US News and World Report, 115*(23), 46-60.

Shapiro, J., & Simonsen, D. (1994). Educational/support group for Latino families of children with Down syndrome. *Mental Retardation, 32,* 403-415.

Shaughnessy, M. F., & Fickling, K. L. (1993). Testing for giftedness: The pros, cons and concerns. *Gifted Education International, 9*(2), 82-84.

Shearer, D. E., & Snider, R. S. (1981). On providing a practical approach to the early education of children. *Child Behavior Therapy, 3,* 78-80.

Shearer, M. S., & Shearer, D. E. (1972). The Portage Project: A model for early childhood education. *Exceptional Children, 39,* 210-217.

Shepard, L. A. (1987). The new push for excellence: Widening the schism between regular and special education. *Exceptional Children, 53,* 327-329.

Shepard, L., & Smith, M. L. (1981, February). *Evaluation of the identification of perceptual-communicative disorders in Colorado: Final report.* Boulder, CO: Laboratory of Educational Research.

Shepard, L., & Smith, M. L. (1983). An evaluation of the identification of learning disabled students in Colorado. *Learning Disability Quarterly, 6,* 115-127.

Shevin, M., & Klein, N. K. (1984). The importance of choice-making skills for students with severe disabilities. *The Journal of The Association for Persons with Severe Handicaps, 9,* 159-166.

Shewan, C. M. (1986). Characteristics of clinical services provided by ASHA members. *ASHA, 28*(1), 29.

Shields, J., & Heron, T. E. (1989). Teaching organizational skills to students with learning disabilities. *Teaching Exceptional Children, 21*(2), 8-13.

Shivers, J. S., & Fait, H. F. (1985). *Special recreational services: Therapeutic and adapted.* Philadelphia: Lea & Febiger.

Shonkoff, J. P., & Meisels, S. J. (1990). Early childhood intervention: The evaluation of a concept. In S. J. Meisels & J. P. Shonkoff (Eds.), *Handbook of early childhood intervention* (pp. 3-32). New York: Cambridge University Press.

Shonkoff, J. P., & Meisels, S. J. (1991). Defining eligibility for services under PL 99-457. *Journal of Early Intervention, 15,* 21-25.

Shores, R. E., Gunter, P. L., & Jack, S. L. (1993). Classroom management strategies: Are they setting events for coercion? *Behavioral Disorders, 18,* 92-102.

Shymansky, J.A., Kyle, W. C., & Alport, J. M. 1983. The effects of the new science curricula on student performance. *Journal of Research in Science Teaching, 20,* 387-404.

Siccone, F. (1995). *Celebrating diversity: Building self-esteem in today's multicultural classrooms.* Boston, MA: Allyn & Bacon.

Sicley, D. (1993). Effective methods of communication: Practical interventions for classroom teachers. *Intervention in School and Clinic, 29,* 105-108.

Sidman, M. (1989). *Coercion and its fallout.* Boston: Authors Group.

Siegel, L. J., & Senna, J. J. (1991). *Juvenile delinquency: Theory, practice, and law.* St. Paul, MN: West.

Siegel, S., Robert, M., Greener, K., Meyer, G., Halloran, W., & Gaylord-Ross, R. (1993). *Career ladders for challenged youths in transition from school to adult life.* Austin, TX: PRO-ED.

Siegel, S., Robert, M., Waxman, M., & Gaylord-Ross, R. (1992). A follow-along study of participants in a longitudinal transition program for youths with mild disabilities. *Exceptional Children, 58,* 346-356.

Sievert, A. L., Cuvo, A. J., & Davis, P. K. (1988). Training self-advocacy skills to adults with mild handicaps. *Journal of Applied Behavior Analysis, 21,* 299-309.

Silver, L. B. (1993). On the occasion of the thirtieth anniversary of LDA: Learn from the past, look to the future. *LDA Newsbrief, 28*(2), 12-13.

Silverman, L. K. (1986). Parenting young gifted children. *Journal of Children in Contemporary Society, 18,* 73-87.

Silverman, L. K. (1989). The highly gifted. In J. F. Feldhusen, J. VanTassel-Baska, & K. Seeley (Eds.), *Excellence in educating the gifted* (pp. 71-83). Denver, CO: Love.

Silverman, L. K. (1995). Highly gifted children. In Genshaft, J. L., Bireley, M., & Hollinger, C. L. (Eds.). *Serving gifted and talented students: A resource for school personnel.* Austin, TX: PRO-ED.

Silverman, L. K. (Ed.). (1993). *Counseling the gifted and talented.* Denver, CO: Love.

Simeonsson, R. J., Olley, J. G., & Rosenthal, S. L. (1987). Early intervention for children with autism. In M. J. Guralnick & F. C. Bennett (Eds.), *The effectiveness of early intervention for at-risk and handicapped children* (pp. 275-296). Orlando, Fl: Academic Press.

Simmons, D. C., Fuchs, D., & Fuchs, L. S., Hodge, J. P., & Mathes, P. G. (1994). Inclusive schools movement and the radicalization of special education reform. *Learning Disabilities: Research and Practice, 9,* 203-212

Simon, R. (1987). *After the tears: Parents talk about raising a child with a disability.* San Diego: Harcourt Brace Jovanovich.

Simpson, R. G. (1991). Agreement among teachers of secondary students in using the revised behavior problem checklist to identify deviant behavior. *Behavioral Disorders, 17,* 66-71.

Simpson, R. G., & Halpin, G. (1986). Agreement between parents and teachers in using the revised behavior problem checklist to identify deviant behavior in children. *Behavioral Disorders, 12,* 54-59.

Simpson, R. L. (1990). *Conferencing parents of exceptional children* (2nd ed.). Austin, TX: PRO-ED.

Sinclair, E. (1993). Early identification of preschoolers with special needs in head start. *Topics in Early Childhood Special Education, 13,* 184-201.

Sinclair, E., Del'Homme, M., & Gonzalez, M. (1993). Systematic screening for preschool behavioral disorders. *Behavioral Disorders, 18,* 177-188.

Sindelar, P. T., & Deno, S. L. (1979). The effectiveness of resource programming. *The Journal of Special Education, 12,* 17-28.

Singer, G. H. S., & Powers, L. E. (1993). *Families, disability, and empowerment: Active coping skills and strategies for family interventions.* Baltimore, MD: Paul H. Brookes Publishing Company.

Singer, J. D., & Butler, J. A. (1987). The Education of All Handicapped Children Act: Schools as agents of social reform. *Harvard Educational Review, 57,* 125-152.

Singh, N. N., & Ellis, C. R. (1993). *Effects of school, child and family variables on drug responsiveness of children with ADHD.* A Proposal Funded by the Office of Special Education and Rehabilitative Services. CFDA No. 84.023C, Washington, DC.

Sirvis, B. P., & Heintz Caldwell, T. (1995). Physical disabilities and chronic health impairments. In E. L. Meyen & T. M. Skirtic (Eds.), *Special education and student disability: An introduction* (4th ed..). Denver: Love.

Sisk, D. (1984, October). *A national survey of gifted programs.* Presentation to the National Business Consortium for Gifted and Talented, Washington, DC.

Sisk, D. (1987). *Creative teaching of the gifted.* New York: McGraw-Hill.

Sitlington, P. L., Frank, A. R., & Carson, R. (1993). Adult adjustment among high school graduates with mild disabilities. *Exceptional Children, 59,* 221-233.

Sitlington, P., & Frank, A. (1990). Are adolescents with learning disabilities successfully crossing the bridge into adult life? *Learning Disability Quarterly, 13,* 97-111.

Skeels, H. M. (1966). Adult status of children with contrasting early life experiences. *Monographs of the Society for Research in Child Development, 31* (No. 3).

Skeels, H. M., & Dye, H. B. (1939). A study of the effects of differential stimulation on mentally retarded children. *Convention Proceedings, American Association on Mental Deficiency, 44,* 114-136.

Skellenger, A., Hill, E., & Hill, M. (1992). The social functioning of children with visual impairments. In S. L. Odom, S. R. McConnell, & M. A. McEvoy (Eds.), *Social competence of young children with disabilities: Issues and strategies for intervention* (pp. 165-188). Baltimore: Paul H. Brooks Publishing Company.

Skinner, B. F. (1974). *About behaviorism.* New York: Alfred A. Knopf.

Slade, J. C., & Conoley, C. W. (1989). Multicultural experiences for special educators. *Teaching Exceptional Children, 22*(1), 60-64.

Sleeter, C. E., & Grant, C. A. (1986). Success for all students. *Phi Delta Kappan, 68*(4), 297-299.

Slingerland, B. H. (1971). *A multi-sensory approach to language arts for specific language disability children: A guide for primary teachers.* Cambridge, MA: Educators Publishing Service.

Smith, B. J., & Strain, P. S. (1984). *The argument for early intervention.* Reston, VA: ERIC Information Service Digest, ERIC

Clearinghouse on Handicapped and Gifted Children.

Smith, D. D., & Luckasson, R. (1995). *Introduction to special education: Teaching in an age of challenge* (2nd ed.). Boston, MA: Allyn & Bacon.

Smith, D. D., & Rivera, D. M. (1993). *Effective discipline* (2nd ed.). Austin, TX: PRO-ED.

Smith, D. D., & Robinson, S. (1986). Educating the learning disabled. In R. J. Morris & B. Blatt (Eds.), *Special education: Research and trends* (pp. 222-248). New York: Pergamon Press.

Smith, E. J. (1981). Cultural and historical perspectives in counseling blacks. In D. W. Sue, *Counseling the culturally different: Theory and practice.* New York: John Wiley & Sons.

Smith, J. D. (1985). *Minds made feeble: The myth and legacy of the Kallikaks.* Rockville, MD: Aspen.

Smith, J. D. (1994). The revised AAMR definition of mental retardation: The MRDD position. *Education and Training in Mental Retardation, 29,* 179-183.

Smith, J. D. (1995). *Pieces of purgatory: Mental retardation in and out of institutions.* Pacific Grove, CA: Brooks/Cole.

Smith, J. D., & Polloway, E. A. (1993). Institutionalization, involuntary sterilization, and mental retardation: Profiles from the history of the practice. *Mental Retardation, 31,* 208-214.

Smith, J. O. (1992). Falling through the cracks: Rehabilitation services for adults with learning disabilities. *Exceptional Children, 58,* 451-460.

Smith, L., & Fowler, S. A. (1984). Positive peer pressure: The effects of peer monitoring on children's disruptive behavior. *Journal of Applied Behavior Analysis, 17,* 213-227.

Smith, M. D., Belcher, R. G., & Juhrs, P. D. (1994). *A guide to successful employment for individuals with autism.* Baltimore: Paul H. Brookes.

Smith, O. S. (1984). *Severely and profoundly physically handicapped students.* In P. J. Valletutti & B. M. Sims-Tucker (Eds.), Severely and profoundly handicapped students: Their nature and needs (pp. 85-152). Baltimore, MD: Paul H. Brooks Publishing Company.

Smith, R. M., Neisworth, J. T., & Hunt, F. M. (1983). *The exceptional child: A functional approach* (2nd ed.). New York: McGraw-Hill.

Smith, S. W. (1990a). Comparison of Individualized Education Programs (IEPs) of students with behavioral disorders and

learning disabilities. *The Journal of Special Education, 24*(1), 85-100.

Smith, S. W. (1990b). Individualized Education Programs (IEPs) in special education—From intent to acquiescence. *Exceptional Children, 57,* 6-14.

Smith, S. W., & Farrell, D. T. (1993). Level system use in special education: Classroom intervention with prima facie appeal. *Behavioral Disorders, 18,* 251-264.

Smith, S. W., & Simpson, R. L. (1989). An analysis of individualized education programs (IEPs) for students with behavioral disorders. *Behavioral Disorders, 14,* 107-116.

Smith, T. (1993). Autism. In T. R. Giles (Ed.) *Handbook of effective psychotherapy* (pp. 107-133). New York: Plenum.

Smith, T. E. C., & Hilton, A. (1994). Program design for students with mental retardation. *Education and Training in Mental Retardation, 29,* 3-8.

Smithdas, R. (1981). Psychological aspects of deaf-blindness. In S. R. Walsh & R. Holzberg (Eds.), *Understanding and educating the deaf- blind/severely and profoundly handicapped: An international perspective.* Springfield, IL: Charles C. Thomas.

Snarr, R. W., & Wolford, B. I. (1985). *Introduction to corrections.* Dubuque, IA: William C. Brown.

Snell, M. E. (Ed.). (1987). *Systematic instruction of persons with severe handicaps* (3rd ed.). Englewood Cliffs, NJ: Merrill/Prentice Hall.

Snell, M. E. (Ed.). (1993). *Instruction of students with severe disabilities* (4th ed.). Englewood Cliffs, NJ: Merrill/Prentice Hall.

Snell, M. E., & Beckman-Brindley, S. (1984). Family involvement in intervention with children having severe handicaps. *The Journal of The Association for Persons with Severe Handicaps, 9,* 213-230.

Snell, M. E., & Brown, F. (1993). Instructional planning and implementation. In M. E. Snell (Ed.), *Instruction of students with severe disabilities* (4th ed.) (pp. 99-151). Englewood Cliffs, NJ: Merrill/Prentice Hall.

Snell, M. E., Lewis, A. P., & Houghton, A. (1989). Acquisition and maintenance of toothbrushing skills by students with cerebral palsy and mental retardation. *The Journal of The Association for Persons with Severe Handicaps, 14,* 216-226.

Sonnenschein, P. (1981). Parents and professionals: An uneasy relationship. *Teaching Exceptional Children, 14,* 62-65.

Sontag, E., Sailor, W., & Smith, J. (1977). The severely/profoundly handicapped: Who are they? Where are we? *The Journal of Special Education, 11*(1), 5-11.

Sontag, J. C., & Schacht, R. (1994). An ethnic comparison of parent participation and information needs in early intervention. *Exceptional Children, 60*, 422-433.

Soodak, L. C., & Podell, D. M. (1994). A response to Reynolds, Zetlin, and Wang's "20/20 analysis: Taking a closer look at the margins." *Exceptional Children, 60*, 276-277.

Southern, W. T. & Jones, E. (1991). *The academic acceleration of gifted children.* New York: Teacher's College Press.

Sowell, V., Packer, R., Poplin, M., & Larsen, S. (1979). The effects of psycholinguistic training on improving psycholinguistic skills. *Learning Disability Quarterly, 2*, 69-77.

Sowers, J., Jenkins, C., & Powers, L. (1988). *Vocational education of persons with physical handicaps.* In R. Gaylord-Ross (Ed.), Vocational education for persons with handicaps (pp. 387-416). Mountain View, CA: Mayfield Publishing.

Sowers, J., Verdi, M., Bourbeau, P., & Sheehan, M. (1985). Teaching job independence to mentally retarded students through the use of a self-control package. *Journal of Applied Behavior Analysis, 18*, 81-85.

Spache, G. D. (1963). *Diagnostic Reading Scales.* Monterey, CA: California Test Bureau.

Sparrow, S. S., Balla, D. A., & Cicchetti, D. V. (1984). *Vineland Adaptive Behavior Scales.* Circle Pines, MN: American Guidance Service.

Spenciner, L. J. (1972). Differences between blind and partially sighted children in rejection by sighted peers in integrated classrooms, grades 2-8. Cited in B. W. Tuckman (Ed.), *Conducting educational research.* New York: Harcourt Brace Jovanovich.

Spivak, M. P. (1986). Advocacy and legislative action for head-injured children and their families. *Journal of Head Trauma Rehabilitation, 1*, 41-47.

Spooner, F. H., & Test, D. W. (1994). Domestic and community living skills. In E. Cipani & F. H. Spooner (Eds.), *Curricular and instructional approaches for persons with severe disabilities* (pp. 149-183). Boston: Allyn and Bacon.

Spooner, F., Enright, B. E., Haney, K., & Heller, H. W. (1993). A examination of classic articles in the education of persons with severe disabilities. *Education and Training in Mental Retardation, 28*, 23-29.

Spradlin, J. E., & Spradlin, R. R. (1976). Developing necessary skills for entry into classroom teaching arrangements. In N. G. Haring & R. L. Schiefelbusch (Eds.), *Teaching special children* (pp. 232-267). New York: McGraw-Hill.

Sprague, J. R., & Horner, R. H. (1984). The effects of single instance, multiple instance, and general case training on generalized vending machine used by moderately and severely handicapped students. *Journal of Applied Behavior Analysis, 17*, 273-278.

Sprague, J. R., & Horner, R. H. (1990). Preventing challenging behaviors. *Teaching Exceptional Children, 23*(1), 1-5.

Spreat, S., Telles, J. T., Conroy, J. W., Feinstein, C., & Colombatto, J. J. (1985). *Attitudes toward deinstitutionalization: A national survey of families of institutionalized mentally retarded persons, Occasional paper of the NASPRFMR.* Philadelphia: Temple University.

Spring, C., & Sandoval, J. (1976). Food additives and hyperkinesis: A critical evaluation of the evidence. *Journal of Learning Disabilities, 9*, 560-569.

Stafford, R. (1978). Education for the handicapped: A senator's perspective. *Vermont Law Review, 3*, 71-76.

Stainback, S., & Stainback, W. (1987). Integration versus cooperation: A commentary on "Educating children with learning problems: A shared responsibility." *Exceptional Children, 54*, 66-68.

Stainback, S., & Stainback, W. (1992). *Curriculum considerations in inclusive classrooms: Facilitating learning for all students.* Baltimore, MD: Paul H. Brooks Publishing Company.

Stainback, S., & Stainback, W. (Eds.). (1991). *Teaching in the inclusive classroom: Curriculum design, adaptation and delivery.* Baltimore, MD: Paul H. Brooks Publishing Company.

Stainback, S., Stainback, W., East, K., & Sapon-Shevin, M. (1994). A commentary on inclusion and the development of a positive self-identity by people with disabilities. *Exceptional Children, 60*, 486-490.

Stainback, W., & Stainback, S. (1984). A rationale for the merger of special and regular education. *Exceptional Children, 51*, 102-111.

Stainback, W., Stainback, S., Raschke, D., & Anderson, R. J. (1981). Three methods of encouraging interactions between severely retarded and nonhandicapped students. *Education and Training of the Mentally Retarded, 16*, 188-192.

Stanley, J. C. (1991). An academic model for educating the mathematically talented. Gifted Child Quarterly, 35, 36-42.

Stanley, N. V. (1993). The gifted and the "Zone of proximal development." *Gifted Education International, 9*(2), 78-81.

Stanovich, K. E. (1991). Conceptual and empirical problems with discrepancy definitions of reading disability. *Learning Disability Quarterly, 14*, 269-280.

Stark, L. J., Knapp, L. G., Bowen, A. M., Powers, S. W., Jelalian, E., Evans, S., Passero, M. A., Mulvihill, M. M., & Hovell, M. (1993). Increasing calorie consumption in children with cystic fibrosis: Replication with 2-year follow-up. *Journal of Applied Behavior Analysis, 26*, 435-450.

Staub, D., & Hunt, P. (1993). The effects of social interaction training on high school peer tutors of schoolmates with severe disabilities. *Exceptional Children, 60*, 41-57.

Stedt, J. D. (1992). Interpreter's wrist: Repetitive stress injury and Carpel Tunnel Syndrome in sign language interpreters. *American Annals of the Deaf, 137*, 40-43.

Steensma, M. (1992). Getting the student with head injuries back in school: Strategies for the classroom. *Intervention in School and Clinic, 27*, 207-210.

Stein, L. (1988). Hearing impairment. In V. B. Van Hasselt, P. S. Strain, & M. Hersen (Eds.), *Handbook of developmental and physical disabilities* (pp. 271-294). New York: Pergamon Press.

Stemley, J. (1993). *Idea Puppy: Teaching preschool age children with disabilities to build independent work skills with the use of a self-operated audio prompt recording device.* Unpublished Master's thesis, The Ohio State University, Columbus, Ohio.

Stephens, T. M. (1992). *Social skills in the classroom.* Odessa, FL: Psychological Assessment Resources.

Stephens, T. M., & Wolf, J. S. (1978). The gifted child. In N. G. Haring (Ed.), *Behavior of exceptional children: An introduction to special education* (2nd ed.) (pp. 387-405). Englewood Cliffs, NJ: Merrill/Prentice Hall.

Stephens, T. M., & Wolf, J. S. (1980). *Effective skills in parent/teacher conferencing.* Columbus, OH: Ohio State University, National Center for Educational Materials and Media for the Handicapped.

Stephens, T. M., Blackhurst, A. E., & Magliocca, L. A. (1982). *Teaching mainstreamed students*. New York: John Wiley & Sons.

Stern, L. M. (1990, July 10). The healthychild guide: Check-ups, immunizations, diet, safety. *Woman's Day*, p. 549.

Sternberg, L. (Ed.). (1994). *Individuals with profound disabilities: Instructional and assistive strategies*. Austin, TX: PRO-ED.

Sternberg, R. (1985). *Beyond IQ: A triarchic theory of human intelligence*. New York: Cambridge University Press.

Sternberg, R. (1988). *The triarchic mind: A new theory of human intelligence*. New York: Viking.

Sternberg, R. (1995). Changing conceptions of intelligence and their impact upon the concept of giftedness: The triarchic theory of intelligence. In Genshaft, J. L., Bireley, M., & Hollinger, C. L. (Eds.). *Serving gifted and talented students: A resource for school personnel*. Austin, TX: PRO-ED.

Stewart, D. A. (1992). Initiating reform in total communication programs. *The Journal of Special Education*, *26*, 68-84.

Stewart, J. L. (1977). Unique problems of handicapped Native Americans. In *The White House Conference on Handicapped Individuals* (Vol. 1) (pp. 438-444). Washington, DC: U.S. Government Printing Office.

Stile, S. W., Kitano, M., Kelley, P., & Lecrone, J. (1993). Early intervention with gifted children: A national survey. *Journal of Early Intervention*, *17*, 30-35.

Stocker, C. S. (1973). *Listening for the visually impaired: A teaching manual*. Springfield, IL: Charles C. Thomas.

Stokes, K. S. (1976). Educational considerations for the child with low vision. In E. Faye (Ed.), *Clinical low vision* (pp. 343-353). Boston: Little, Brown.

Stokes, T. F., & Baer, D. M. (1977). An implicit technology of generalization. *Journal of Applied Behavior Analysis, 10*, 349-367.

Stokes, T. F., & Osnes, P. G. (1989). An operant pursuit of generalization. *Behavior Therapy*, *20*, 337-355.

Stone, W. L., & La Greca, A. M. (1990). The social status of children with learning disabilities: A reexamination. *Journal of Learning Disabilities*, *23*, 32-37.

Stoner, G., Carey, S. P., Ikeda, M. J., & Shinn, M. R. (1994). The utility of curriculum-based measurement for evaluating the effects of methylphenidate on academic performance. *Journal of Applied Behavior Analysis*, *27, 101-113*.

Stoner, G., Hunt, M., Cornelius, P., Leventhal, P. Miller, P., & Murrary, T. (1994). Parents on the team. *TASH Newsletter*, *20*(5), 9-11.

Storey, K. (1993). A proposal for assessing integration. *Education and Training in Mental Retardation*, *28*, 279-287.

Storey, K., & Horner, R. H. (1991). An evaluating review of social validation research involving persons with handicaps. *The Journal of Special Education*, *25*, 352-401.

Story, C. (1985). Facilitator of learning: A microethnographic study of the teacher of the gifted. *Gifted Child Quarterly*, *29*(4), 155-159.

Stowell, L. J., & Terry, C. (1977). *Mainstreaming: Present shock*. Illinois Libraries, *59*, 475-477.

Strain, P. S. (1981). Peer-mediated treatment of exceptional children's social withdrawal. *Exceptional Education Quarterly*, *1*, 83-95.

Strain, P. S., & Odom, S. L. (1986). Peer social initiations: Effective intervention for social skills development of exceptional children. *Exceptional Children*, *52*, 543-551.

Strain, P. S., & Smith, B. J. (1986). A counter-interpretation of early intervention effects: A response to Casto and Mastropieri. *Exceptional Children*, *53*, 260-265.

Strain, P. S., Guralnick, M. J., & Walker, H. M. (Eds.). (1986). *Children's social behavior: Development, assessment, and modification*. Orlando, FL: Academic Press.

Straus, M. A., Gelles, R. J., & Steinmetz, S. K. (1980). *Behind closed doors: Violence in the American family*. New York: Anchor Press.

Streissguth, A. P., Aase, J. M., Clarren, S. K., Randels, S. P., LaDue, R. A., & Smith, D. F. (1991). Fetal alcohol syndrome in adolescents and young adults. *Journal of American Medical Association*, *265*, 1961-1967.

Stremel, K., Molden, V., Leister, C., Matthews, J., Wilson, R., Goodall, D. V., & Hoston, J. (1990). *Communication systems and routines: A decision making process*. Washington, DC: U. S. Office of Special Education.

Strickland, B. B., & Turnbull, A. P. (1993). *Developing and implementing Individualized Education Programs* (3rd ed.). Englewood Cliffs, NJ: Merrill/Prentice Hall.

Strickland, S. P. (1971). Can slum children learn? *American Education*, *7*(6), 3-7.

Stump, C. S., Lovitt, T. C., Fister, S., Kemp, K., Moore, R., & Schroeder, B. (1992). Vocabulary intervention for secondary-level youth. *Learning Disability Quarterly*, *15*, 207-222.

Sturdivant, C. (1992). Ownership, risk-taking, and collaboration in an elementary language arts classroom. *The Volta Review*, *94*, 371-375.

Sturmey, P., & Crisp, A. G. (1986). Portage guide to early education: A review of research. *Educational Psychology*, *6*(2), 139-157.

Suarez, T. M., Hurth, J. L., & Prestridge, S. (1988). Innovation in services for young children with handicaps and their families: An analysis of the Handicapped Children's Early Education Program projects from 1982 to 1986. *Journal of Early Intervention*, *12*, 224-237.

Subotnik, R. F. (1993). Talent developed: Conversations with masters of the arts and sciences. *Journal for the Education of the Gifted*, *16*, 311-322.

Sugai, G., & Maheady, L. (1988). Cultural diversity and individual assessment for behavior disorders. *Teaching Exceptional Children*, *21*, 28-31.

Sulzbacher, S., Haines, R., Peterson, S. L., & Swatman, F. M. (1987). Encourage appropriate coffee break behavior. *Teaching Exceptional Children*, *19*(2), 8-12.

Sulzer-Azaroff, B., & Mayer, G. R. (1991). *Behavior analysis for Lasting change*. New York: Holt, Rinehart & Winston.

Summers, M., Bridge, J., & Summers, C. R. (1991). Sibling support groups. *Teaching Exceptional Children*, *23*(4), 20-25.

Suritsky, S. K., & Hughes, C. A. (1991). Benefits of notetaking: Implications for secondary and post secondary students with learning disabilities. *Learning Disability Quarterly, 14*, 7-18.

Sutton, E., Factor, A. R., Hawkins, B. A., Heller, T. & Seltzer, G. B. (1993) *Older adults with developmental disabilities: Optimizing choice and change*. Baltimore, MD: Paul H. Brooks Publishing Company.

Swallow, R. M. (1978, May). *Cognitive development*. Paper presented at the North American Conference on Visually Handicapped Infants and Preschool Children, Minneapolis, MN.

Swallow, R. M., & Conner, A. (1982). Aural reading. In S. S. Mangold (Ed.), *A teacher's guide to the special educational needs of blind and visually handicapped children* (pp. 119-135). New York: American Foundation for the Blind.

Swan, W. W., & Sirvis, B. (1992). The CEC common core of knowledge and skills essential for all beginning special education teachers. *Teaching Exceptional Children, 25*(1), 16-20.

Swanson, H. L. (1991). Operational definitions and learning disabilities: An overview. *Learning Disability Quarterly, 14,* 242-254.

Swanson, J. M., McBurnett, K, Wigal, T., Pfiffner, L. J., Lerner, M. A., Williams, L., Christian, D. L., Tamm, L., Willcutt, E., Crowley, K., Clevenger, W., Khouzam, N., Woo, C., Crinella, F. M., & Fisher, T. D. (1993). Effect of stimulant medication on children with attention deficit disorder: A "Review of Reviews". *Exceptional Children, 60,* 154-161.

Swassing, R. (1994). (Guest Ed.). Affective dimensions of being gifted. *Roeper Review, 17*(2).

Swiatek, M. A. (1993). A decade of longitudinal research on academic acceleration through the study of mathematically precocious youth. *Roeper Review, 15*(3), 120-123.

Swiatek, M. A., & Benbow, C. P. (1991, November). *Acceleration: Does it cause academic or psychological harm?* Paper presented at the meeting of the National Association for Gifted Children, Little Rock, AR.

Swiatek, M. A., & Benbow, C. P. (1993). A ten-year longitudinal follow-up of participants in a fast-paced mathematics course. *Journal for Research in Mathematics Education, 22,* 138-150.

Szymanski, E. M. (1994). Transition: Life-span and life-space considerations for empowerment. *Exceptional Children, 60,* 402-410.

Tannenbaum, A. (1983). *Gifted Children: Psychological and educational perspectives.* Englewood Cliff, NJ: Merrill/Prentice Hall.

Tarnowski, K. J., & Drabman, R. S. (1987). Teaching intermittent self-catheterization to mentally retarded children. *Research in Developmental Disabilities, 8,* 521-529.

Tawney, J. W. (1984). The pragmatics of the educability issue: Some questions which logically precede the assumption of ineducability. In W. L. Heward, T. E. Heron, D. S. Hill, & J. Trap-Porter (Eds.), *Focus on behavior analysis in education* (pp. 287-295). Englewood Cliffs, NJ: Merrill/Prentice Hall.

Taylor, O. L., & Payne, K. T. (1994). Language and communication differences. In G. H. Shames & E. H. Wiig, (Eds.), *Human communication disorders* (4th ed.)

(pp. 136-173). Englewood Cliffs, NJ: Merrill/Prentice Hall.

Taylor, S. J. (1988). Caught in the continuum: A critical analysis of the principle of the least restrictive environment. *The Journal of The Association for Persons with Severe Handicaps, 13,* 41-53.

Taylor, S. J., Biklen, D., & Searl, S. J. (1986). *Preparing for life: A manual for parents on least restrictive environment.* Boston: Federation for Children with Special Needs.

Taylor, S. J., Bogdan, R., & Lutfiyya, Z. M. (1995). *The variety of community experience: Qualitative studies of family and community life.* Baltimore: Paul H. Brookes.

Teacher Education Division. (1986). *The national inquiry into the future of education for students with special needs.* Reston, VA: Council for Exceptional Children.

Tedder, N. E., Warden, K., & Sikka, A. (1993). Prelanguage communication of students who are deaf-blind and have other severe impairments. *Journal of Visual Impairment and Blindness, 87,* 302-307.

Terkel, S. (1974). *Working: People talk about what they do all day and how they feel about what they do.* New York: Pantheon Books.

Terman, L. (1925). Mental and physical traits of a thousand gifted children. In L. Terman (Ed.), *Genetic studies of genius* (Vol. I). Stanford, CA: Stanford University Press.

Terman, L. M. (1916). *The measurement of intelligence.* Boston: Houghton Mifflin.

Terman, L. M., & Merrill, M. A. (1973). *Stanford-Binet intelligence scale* (4th ed.). Boston: Houghton Mifflin.

Test, D. W., Keul, P. K., Williams, B., Slaughter, M., &, Allen, C. (1992). Evaluating performance in a workstation. *Education and Training in Mental Retardation, 27,* 335-344.

Test, D. W., Cooke, N. L., Weiss, A. B., Heward, W. L., & Heron, T. E. (1986). A home-school communication system for special education. *The Pointer, 30,* 4-7.

Test, D. W., Grossi, T., & Keul, P. (1988). A functional analysis of the acquisition and maintenance of janitorial skills in a competitive work setting. *The Journal of The Association for Persons with Severe Handicaps, 13,* 1-7.

Test, D. W., Hinson, K. B., Solow, J., & Keul, P. (1993). Job satisfaction of persons in supported employment. *Education and Training in Mental Retardation, 28,* 38-46.

Test, D. W., & Spooner, F. (in press). *Task analysis.* Washington, DC: American Association on Mental Retardation.

Test, D. W., Spooner, F. H., Keul, P. K., & Grossi, T. A. (1990). Teaching adolescents with severe disabilities to use the public telephone. *Behavior Modification, 14,* 157-171.

The Association for Persons with Severe Handicaps. (1990). Draft mission statement, June 27, 1990. *TASH Newsletter,* 16(8), 1.

The Association for Persons with Severe Handicaps. (1994/1995). Resolution on facilitated communication. *TASH Newsletter, 20/21,* p. 7.

The DLD Times (Fall, 1994). DLD takes a learning role in the reauthorization of IDEA. *Newsletter, 12*(1), 1-2.

Thomas, A., & Chess, S. (1984). Genesis and evolution of behavioral disorders: From infancy to early adult life. *American Journal of Psychiatry, 141,* 1-9.

Thomas, A., Chess, S., & Birch, H. G. (1968). *Temperament and behavior disorders in children.* New York: New York University Press.

Thomas, C. C., Correa, V. I., & Morsink, C. V. (1995). *Interactive teaming: Consultation and collaboration in special programs* (2nd ed.). Englewood Cliffs, NJ: Merrill/Prentice Hall.

Thomas, D. R., Becker, W. C., & Armstrong, M. (1968). Production and elimination of disruptive classroom behavior by systematically varying teachers' behavior. *Journal of Applied Behavior Analysis, 1,* 35-45.

Thomas, G., & Jackson, G. (1986). The whole-school approach to integration. *British Journal of Special Education, 13*(1), 27-29.

Thomas, S. B. (1985). *Legal issues in special education.* Topeka, KS: National Organization on Legal Problems in Education.

Thompson, K. (1984). The speech therapist and language disorders. In G. Lindsay (Ed.), *Screening for children with special needs: Multidisciplinary approaches* (pp. 86-97). London: Croom Helm.

Thorndike, R. L., Hagen, E. P., & Sattler, J. M. (1986). *Technical manual, The Stanford-Binet Intelligence Scale: Fourth edition.* Chicago: Riverside Publishing.

Thornton, C., & Krajewski, J. (1993). Death education for teachers: A refocused concern relative to medically fragile children. *Intervention in School and Clinic, 29,* 31-35.

Thousand, J. S., & Villa, R. A. (1990). Sharing expertise and responsibilities through teaching teams. In S. Stainback & W. Stainback (Eds.), *Support networks for inclusive schooling: Interdependent integrated education* (pp. 151-166). Baltimore, MD: Paul H. Brooks Publishing Company.

Thousand, J. S., & Villa, R. A. (1991). A futuristic view of the REI: A response to Jenkins, Pious, and Jewell. *Exceptional Children, 57*, 556-562.

Thousand, J. S., Villa, R. A., & Nevin, A. I. (1994). *Creativity and collaborative learning: A practical guide to empowering students and teachers.* Baltimore, MD: Paul H. Brooks Publishing Company.

Thurman, D. (1978). Mainstreaming and the visually impaired: A report from Atlantic Canada. *Education of the Visually Handicapped, 10*, 35-37.

Thurman, S. K., Brobeil, R. A., Ducette, J. P., & Hurt, H. (1994). Prenatally exposed to cocaine: Does the label matter? *Journal of Early Intervention, 18*, 119-130.

Thurston, L. P. (1989). Helping parents tutor their children: A success story. *Academic Therapy, 24*, 579-587.

Thurston, L. P., & Dasta, K. (1990). An analysis of in-home parent tutoring in children's academic behavior at home and in school and on parents' tutoring behaviors. *Remedial and Special Education, 11*(4), 41-52.

Todd, J. H. (1986). Resources, media, and technology. In G. T. Scholl (Ed.), *Foundations of education for blind and visually handicapped children and youth: Theory and practice* (pp. 285-296). New York: American Foundation for the Blind.

Todis, B., Severson, H. H., & Walker, H. M. (1990). The critical events scale: Behavioral profiles of students with externalizing and internalizing behavior disorders. *Behavioral Disorders, 15*, 75-86.

Tolan, P. H. (1987). Implications of age of onset for delinquency risk. *Journal of Abnormal Child Psychology, 15*, 47-65.

Tonemah, S. A. (1987). Assessing American Indian gifted and talented student's abilities. *Journal for the Education of the Gifted, 10*, 181-194.

Torrance, E. P. (1969). Creative positives of disadvantaged children and youth. *Gifted Child Quarterly, 13*(2), 71-81.

Torrance, E. P. (1977). Creatively gifted and disadvantaged children. In A. Baldwin, G. Gear, & L. Lucito (Eds.). *The gifted and the creative: A fifty-year perspective.* Baltimore, MD: Johns Hopkins University Press.

Torrance, E. P. (1977). *Discovery and nurturance of giftedness in the culturally different.* Reston, VA: Council for Exceptional Children.

Torrance, E. P. (1993). The beyonders in a thirty year longitudinal study of creative achievement. *Roeper Review, 15*(3), 131-135.

Trammel, D. L., Schloss, P. J., & Alper, S. (1994). Using self-recording, evaluation, and graphing to increase completion of homework assignments. *Journal of Learning Disabilities, 27*, 75-81.

Trask-Tyler, S. A., Grossi, T. A., & Heward, W. L. (1994). Teaching young adults with developmental disabilities and visual impairments to use tape-recorded recipes: Acquisition, generalization, and maintenance of cooking skills. *Journal of Behavioral Education, 4*, 283-311.

Tredgold, A. F. (1937). *A textbook on mental deficiency.* Baltimore, MD: Wood.

Tredgold, A. F. (1947). *A textbook of mental deficiency (amentia)* (7th ed.). New York: William Wood.

Trief, E., Duckman, R., Morse, A. R., & Silberman, R. K. (1989). Retinopathy of prematurity. *Journal of Visual Impairment and Blindness, 83*, 500-504.

Trybus, R., & Karchmer, M. (1977). School achievement scores of hearing impaired children: National data on achievement status and growth patterns. *American Annals of the Deaf, 122*, 62-69.

Tucker, B. (1993). Deafness: 1993 - 2013—The dilemma. *The Volta Review, 95*, 105-108.

Tucker, B. F., & Colson, S. E. (1992). Traumatic brain injury: An overview of school re-entry. *Intervention in School and Clinic, 27*, 198-206.

Tucker, J. A. (1985). Curriculum-based assessment: An introduction. *Exceptional Children, 52*, 199-204.

Turnbull, A., & Bronicki, G. J. (1986). Changing second graders' attitudes toward people with mental retardation: Using kid power. *Mental Retardation, 24*, 44-45.

Turnbull, A. P. (1983). Parent-professional interactions. In M. E. Snell (Ed.), *Systematic instruction of the moderately and severely handicapped* (2nd ed.) (pp. 18-43). Englewood Cliffs, NJ: Merrill/Prentice Hall.

Turnbull, A. P., & Morningstar, M. E. (1993). Family and professional interaction. In M. E. Snell, *Instruction of students with severe disabilities* (2nd ed.) (pp. 31-60). Englewood Cliffs, NJ: Merrill/Prentice Hall.

Turnbull, A. P., & Turnbull, H. R. (1982). Parent involvement in the education of

handicapped children: A critique. *Mental Retardation, 20*, 115-122.

Turnbull, A. P., & Turnbull, H. R. (1990). *Families, professionals, and exceptionality: A special partnership* (2nd ed.). Englewood Cliffs, NJ: Merrill/Prentice Hall.

Turnbull, A. P., Turnbull, H. R., Shank, M., & Leal, D. (1995). *Exceptional lives: Special education in today's schools.* Englewood Cliffs, NJ: Prentice-Hall.

Turnbull, H. R. (1986). Appropriate education and Rowley. *Exceptional Children, 52*, 347-352.

Turnbull, H. R., III. (1993). *Free appropriate public education: The law and children with disabilities* (4th ed.). Denver: Love.

Turnbull, H. R., III, & Turnbull, A. P. (1985). *Parents speak out: Then & now* (2nd ed.). Englewood Cliffs, NJ: Merrill/Prentice Hall.

Turnbull, K., & Bronicki, G. J. (1989). Children can teach other children. *Teaching Exceptional Children, 21*(3), 64-65.

Turner, J. (1983). Workshop society: Ethnographic observations in a work setting for retarded adults. In K. Kernan, M. Begab, & R. Edgerton (Eds.), *Environments and behavior: The adaptation of mentally retarded persons* (pp. 147-171). Austin, TX: PRO-ED.

Tuttle, D. W. (1984). *Self-esteem and adjusting with blindness: The process of responding to life's demands.* Springfield, IL: Charles C. Thomas.

Tyler, J. S., & Mira, M. P. (1993). Educational modifications for students with head injuries. *Teaching Exceptional Children, 25*(3), 24-27.

U. S. Bureau of the Census. (1990). *U.S. population estimates, by age, sex, race, and Hispanic origin: 1989.* (Current Population Reports, Series P-25, No. 1045). Washington, DC: U.S. Government Printing Office.

U.S. Commission on Civil Rights (1983, September). *Accommodating the spectrum of individual abilities* [Clearinghouse Publication 81]. Washington, DC: U.S. Government Printing Office.

U.S. Comptroller General. (1981, September 30). Disparities still exist in who gets special education. *Report to the chairman, Subcommittee on Select Education, Committee on Education and Labor, House of Representatives of the United States.*

U.S. Congress. (1987). *Promotion opportunities for blind and handicapped workers in sheltered workshops under the Javitz-Wagner-O'Day act.* Washington, DC: U.S. Government Printing Office.

U.S. Department of Commerce. (1990a). Persons arrested by crime, sex, and age: 1988. In *Statistical abstracts of the U.S.* p. 177. Washington, DC: Author.

U.S. Department of Commerce. (1990b). *Statistical abstracts of the United States* (110th ed.). Washington, DC: Author.

U.S. Department of Education. (1986). *Eighth annual report to Congress on the implementation of the Education of the Handicapped Act.* Washington, DC: Author.

U. S. Department of Education. (1989). *Eleventh annual report to Congress on the implementation of the Education of the Handicapped Act.* Washington, DC: Author.

U.S. Department of Education. (1990). *Twelfth annual report to Congress on the implementation of the Education of the Handicapped Act.* Washington, DC: Author.

U. S. Department of Education. (1990). *Survey of schools*. In Shapiro, J. P., Loeb, P., & Bowermaster, D. (1993, December 13). Separate and unequal: How special education programs are cheating our children and costing taxpayers billions of dollars. *U.S. News and World Report*, 46-60.

U. S. Department of Education. (1991). *America 2000, an Education Strategy Sourcebook.* Washington, DC.

U. S. Department of Education. (1991). Office of Educational Research and Improvement. *National Education Longitudinal Study (NELS: 88) on Gifted and Talented Education*, unpublished study, Washington, DC.

U. S. Department of Education, (1992). *To assure the free appropriate public education of all children with disabilities: Fourteenth annual report to Congress on the implementation of the Individuals with Disabilities Education Act.* Washington, DC: U.S. Government Printing Office.

U. S. Department of Education. (1993). *To assure the free appropriate public education of all children with disabilities: Fifteenth annual report to Congress on the implementation of the Individuals with Disabilities Education Act.* Washington, D.C.: Government Document Service.

U.S. Department of Education. (1993). Office of Educational Research and Improvement. *National Excellence: A Case for Developing America's Talent.*

U.S. Department of Education. (1994). *Sixteenth annual report to Congress on the implementation of the Individuals with Disabilities Education Act.* Washington, DC: Author.

U.S. Department of Labor. (1979). *Study of handicapped clients in sheltered workshops* (Vol. 2). Washington, DC: Author.

U.S. General Accounting Office. (1981). *Disparities still exist in who gets special education.* Washington, DC: Author.

U.S. Office of Education. (1977a). Implementation of Part B of the Education of the Handicapped Act. *Federal Register, 42,* 42474-42518.

U.S. Office of Education. (1977b). Procedures for evaluating specific learning disabilities. Federal Register, 42, 65082-65085.

Udvari-Solner, A., Jorgenson, J., & Courchane G. (1992). Longitudinal vocational curriculum: The foundations for effective transition. In F. R. Rusch, L. DeStefano, J. Chadsey-Rusch, L. Allen Phelps, & E. Szymanski (Eds.), *Transition from school to adult life* (pp. 285-320). Pacific Grove, CA: Brooks/Cole.

Ulicny, G. R., Thompson, S. K., Favell, J. E., & Thompson, M. S. (1985). The active assessment of educability: A case study. *The Journal of The Association for Persons with Severe Handicaps, 10,* 111-114.

Ulrey, G. (1982). Assessment considerations with language impaired children. In G. Ulrey & S. J. Rogers (Eds.), *Psychological assessment of handicapped infants and young children* (pp. 123-134). New York: Thieme-Stratton.

Uslan, M. M. (1992). Barriers to acquiring assistive technology: Cost and lack of information. *Journal of Visual Impairment & Blindness, 86,* 402-407.

Utley, C. (1995). Culturally and linguistically diverse students with mild disabilities. In C. A. Grant (Ed.), *Educating for diversity: An anthology of multicultural voices* (pp. 301-324). Boston: Allyn & Bacon.

Utley, C. A., Lowitzer, A. C., & Baumeister, A. A. (1987). A comparison of the AAMD's definition, eligibility criteria, and classification schemes with state department of education guidelines. *Education & Training in Mental Retardation, 22,* 35-43.

Vacc, N. A., Vallecorsa, A. L., Parker, A., Bonner, S., Lester, C., Richardson, S., & Yates, C. (1985). Parents' and educators' participation in IEP conferences. *Education & Treatment of Children, 8,* 153-162.

Valcante, G. (1986). Educational implications of current research on the syndrome of autism. *Behavioral Disorders, 11,* 131-139.

Valdes, K. A., Williamson, C. L., & Wagner, M. (1990). *The National Longitudinal Transition Study of special education students Vol. 3: Youth categorized as emotionally disturbed.* Palo Alto, CA: SRI International.

Van Dijk, J. (1983). *Rubella handicapped children: The effects of bilateral cataract and/or hearing impairment on behaviour and learning.* Lisse, Netherlands: Swets & Zeitlinger.

Van Dijk, J. (1985). An educational curriculum for deaf-blind multihandicapped persons. In D. Ellis (Ed.), *Sensory impairments in mentally handicapped people* (pp. 374-382). San Diego: College-Hill.

Van Houten, R. (1980). *Learning through feedback: A systematic approach for improving academic performance.* New York: Human Sciences Press.

Van Houten, R. (1984). Setting up performance feedback systems in the classroom. In W. L. Heward, T. E. Heron, D. S. Hill, & J. Trap-Porter (Eds.), *Focus on behavior analysis in education* (pp. 114-125). Englewood Cliffs, NJ: Merrill/Prentice Hall.

Van Reusen, A. K., & Bos, C. (1994). Facilitating student participation in individualized education programs through motivation strategy instruction. *Exceptional Children, 60,* 466-475.

Van Reusen, A. K., Bos, C. S. (1990). IPLAN: Helping students communicate in planning conferences. *Teaching Exceptional Children, 22*(4), 30-32.

Van Riper, C. (1972). *Speech correction: Principles and methods* (5th ed.). Englewood Cliffs, NJ: Prentice-Hall.

Van Riper, C., & Emerick L. L. (1984). *Speech correction: An introduction to speech pathology.* Englewood Cliffs, NJ: Prentice-Hall.

Van Tassel-Baska, J. (1983). The teacher as counselor for the gifted. *Teaching Exceptional Children, 15,* 144-150.

Van Tassel-Baska, J. (1986). Acceleration. In C. J. Maker (Ed.), *Critical issues in gifted education: Defensible programs for the gifted.* Rockville, MD: Aspen.

Van Tassel-Baska, J. (Ed.). (1990). *A practical guide to counseling the gifted in a school setting* (2nd ed.). Reston, VA: Council for Exceptional Children.

Van Tassel-Baska, J., Patton, J. M., & Prillaman, D. (1991). *Gifted youth at risk: A report of a national study.* Reston, VA: Council for Exceptional Children.

van den Pol, R. A., & Iwata, B. A., Ivancic, M. T., Page, T. J., Neef, N. A., & Whitley, F. P. (1981). Teaching the handicapped to eat in public places: Acquisition, generalization and maintenance of restaurant skills. *Journal of Applied Behavior Analysis, 14,* 61-69.

Vandercook, T. (1991). Leisure instruction outcomes: Criterion performance, positive interactions, and acceptance by typical high school peers. *The Journal of Special Education, 25,* 320-339.

Vandercook, T., York, J., & Forest, M. (1989). The McGill Action Planning System (MAPS): A strategy for building the vision. *The Journal of The Association for Persons with Severe Handicaps, 14,* 205-215.

Vanderheiden, G. C., & Lloyd, L. L. (1986). Non-speech modes and systems. In S. W. Blackstone (Ed.), *Augmentative communication* (pp. 49-161). Rockville, MD: American Speech-Language-Hearing Association.

Vaughn, S., & Hogan, A. (1994). The social competence of students with learning disabilities over time: A within-individual examination. *Journal of Learning Disabilities, 27,* 292-303.

Vaughn, S., Bos, C. S., Harrell, J. E., & Lasky, B. A. (1988). Parent participation in the initial placement/IEP conference ten years after mandated involvement. *Journal of Learning Disabilities, 21,* 82-89.

Vaughn, S., McIntosh, R., Schumm, J. S., Haager, D., & Callwood, D. (1993). Social status, peer acceptance, and reciprocal friendships revisited. *Learning Disabilities Research & Practice, 8,* 82-88.

Venn, J. (1994). *Assessment of students with special needs.* Englewood Cliffs, NJ: Merrill/Prentice Hall.

Venn, J., Morganstern, L., & Dykes, M. K. (1979). Checklists for evaluating the fit and function of orthoses, prostheses, and wheelchairs in the classroom. *Teaching Exceptional Children, 11,* 51-56.

Verhaaren, P. R., & Connor, F. P. (1981). Physical disabilities. In J. M. Kauffman & D. P. Hallahan (Eds.), *Handbook of special education.* Englewood Cliffs, NJ: Prentice-Hall.

Vernon, M. (1987). The primary causes of deafness. In E. Mindel & M. Vernon (Eds.), *They grow in silence: Understanding deaf children and adults* (2nd ed.) (pp. 31-38). San Diego: College-Hill.

Vernon, M., & Koh, S. D. (1970). Effects of manual communication of deaf children's educational achievement, linguistic competence, oral skills, and psychological adjustment. *American Annals of the Deaf, 115,* 527-536.

Villa, R. A., & Thousand, J. S. (1992). Student collaboration: An essential for curriculum delivery in the 21st century. In S. Stainback & W. Stainback (Eds.), *Curriculum considerations in inclusive classrooms: Facilitating learning for all students* (pp. 117-142). Baltimore, MD: Paul H. Brooks Publishing Company.

Villaronga, P. (1995). The so called. In C. A. Grant, *Educating for diversity: An anthology of multicultural voices* (pp. 255-260). Boston: Allyn & Bacon.

Villegas, A. M. (1988). School failure and cultural mismatch: Another view. *Urban Review, 20*(4), 253-265.

Vincent, L., Davis, J., Brown, P., Broome, K., Miller, J., & Grunewald, L. (1983). *Parent inventory of child development in non-school environments.* Madison, WI: Metropolitan School District Early Childhood Program, Active Decision Making by Parents Grant.

Vitello, S. J. (1986). The Tatro case: Who gets what and why. *Exceptional Children, 52,* 353-356.

Vogelsberg, R. T., Anderson, J., Berger, P., Haselden, T., Mitwll, S., Schmidt, C., Skowron, A. Ulett, P., & Wilcox, B. (1980). Selecting, setting up, and surveying in an independent living situation: An inventory and instructional approach for handicapped individuals. *AAESPH Review, 5,* 38-54.

Voltz, D. L., & Damiano-Lantz, M. (1993). Developing ownership in learning. *Teaching Exceptional Children, 25,* 18-28.

Vorrath, H. H., & Brendtro, L. K. (1985). *Positive peer culture* (2nd ed.). Hawthorne, NY: Aldine Publishing.

Wacker, D. P., Wiggins, B., Fowler, M., & Berg, W. K. (1988). Training students with profound or multiple handicaps to make requests via microswitches. *Journal of Applied Behavior Analysis, 21,* 331-343.

Wadsworth, D. E., Knight, D., & Balser, V. (1993). Children who are medically fragile or technology dependent: Guidelines. *Intervention in School and Clinic, 29,* 102-104.

Wagner, M. (1991). *Dropouts: What do we know? What can we do?* Menlo Park, CA: SRI International.

Wagner, M., Blackorby, J., Cameto, R., & Newman, L. (1994). *What makes a difference? Influences on postschool outcomes of youth with disabilities.* Menlo Park, CA: SRI International.

Wagner, M., D'Amico, R., Marder, C., Newman, L., & Blackorby, J. (1993). *What happens next? Trends in postschool outcomes of youth with disabilities. The second comprehensive report from the national Longitudinal Transition Study of Special Education Students.* Menlo Park, CA: SRI International.

Wagner, M., Newman, L., D'Amico, R., Jay, E. D., Butler-Nalin, P., Marder, C., & Cox, R. (1991). *Youth with disabilities: How are they doing? The first comprehensive report from the national Longitudinal Transition Study of Special Education Students.* Menlo Park, CA: SRI International.

Wagner-Lampl, A., & Oliver, G. W. (1994). Folklore of blindness. *Journal of Visual Impairment & Blindness, 88,* 267-276.

Wahler, R. G., & Dumas, J. E. (1986). "A chip off the old block": Some interpersonal characteristics of coercive children across generations. In P. S. Strain, M. J. Guralnick, & H. M. Walker (Eds.), *Children's social behavior: Development, assessment, and modification* (pp. 49-91). Orlando, FL: Academic Press.

Wainapel, S. F. (1989). Attitudes of visually impaired persons toward cane use. *Journal of Visual Impairment and Blindness, 83,* 446-448.

Walker, H. M. (1979). *The acting-out child: Coping with classroom disruption.* Boston: Allyn & Bacon.

Walker, H. M., & Buckley, N. K. (1973). Teacher attention to appropriate and inappropriate classroom behavior: An individual case study. *Focus on Exceptional Children, 5,* 5-11.

Walker, H. M., & Rankin, R. (1983). Assessing the behavioral expectations and demands of less restrictive settings. *School Psychology Review, 12*(3), 274-284.

Walker, H. M., & Severson, H. H. 1990. Systematic Screening for Behavior Disorders. Longmont, CO: Sopris West, Inc.

Walker, H. M., Colvin, G., & Ramsey, E. (1995). *Antisocial behavior in schools: Strategies and best practices.* Pacific Grove, CA: Brooks/Cole.

Walker, H. M., Severson, H. H., & Feil, E. G. (1994). *The Early Screening Project: A proven child-find process.* Longmont, CO: Sopris West.

Walker, H. M., Severson, H., Stiller, B., Williams, G., Haring, N., Shinn, M., & Todis, B. (1988). Systematic screening of pupils in the elementary age range at risk for behavior disorders: Development and trial testing of a multiple gating model. *Remedial and Special Education, 9*(3), 8-20.

Walker, H. M., Stieber, S., Ramsey, E., & O'Neill, R. E. (1991). Longitudinal prediction of the school achievement, adjustment, and delinquency of antisocial versus at-risk boys. *Remedial and Special Education, 12*(4), 41-51.

Walker, J. E., & Shea, T. M. (1995). *Behavior management: A practical approach for educators* (6th ed.). Englewood Cliffs, NJ: Merrill/Prentice Hall.

Walker, L. A. (1986). *A loss for words: The story of deafness in a family.* New York: Harper & Row.

Wallace, G., & McLoughlin, J. A. (1979). *Learning disabilities: Concepts and characteristics* (2nd ed.). Englewood Cliffs, NJ: Merrill/Prentice Hall.

Wang, M. C. (1980). Adaptive instruction: Building on diversity. *Theory Into Practice, 19*, 122-128.

Wang, M. C., & Walberg, H. J. (1988). Four fallacies of segregationism. *Exceptional Children, 55*, 128-137.

Wang, M. C., Reynolds, M. C., & Walberg, H. J. (1985, December). *Rethinking special education.* Paper presented at the Wingspread Conference on the Education of Students with Special Needs: Research Findings and Implications for Policy and Practice. Racine, WI.

Ward, M. C. (1994). *Effects of a self-operated auditory prompt system on the acquisition, maintenance and generalization of independent work skills of preschoolers with developmental disabilities.* Unpublished doctoral dissertation. The Ohio State University, Columbus, Ohio.

Ward, M. E. (1979). Children with visual impairments. In M. S. Lilly (Ed.), *Children with exceptional needs: A survey of special education* (pp. 320-361). New York: Holt, Rinehart & Winston.

Ward, M. E. (1986). The visual system. In G. T. Scholl (Ed.), *Foundations of education for blind and visually handicapped children and youth: Theory and practice* (pp. 35-64). New York: American Foundation for the Blind.

Warger, C. L., Aldinger, L. E., & Okun, K. A. (1983). *Mainstreaming in the secondary school: The role of the regular teacher.* Bloomington, IN: Phi Delta Kappa Educational Foundation.

Warren, S. F. (1992). Facilitating basic vocabulary acquisition with milieu teaching procedures. *Journal of Early Intervention, 16*, 235-251.

Warren, S. F., & Gazdag, G. (1990). Facilitating early language development with milieu intervention procedures. *Journal of Early Intervention, 14*, 62-86.

Warren, S. F., McQuarter, R. J., & Rogers-Warren, A. K. (1984). The effects of teacher mands on the speech of unre-

sponsive language-delayed children. *Journal of Speech and Hearing Research, 49*, 43-52.

Wasik, B. H., Ramey, C. T., Bryant, D. M., & Sparling, J. J. (1990). A longitudinal study of two early intervention strategies: Project CARE. *Child Development, 61*, 1682-1692.

Watkins, C. L. (1988). Project Follow Through: A story of the identification and neglect of effective instruction. *Youth Policy, 10*(7), 7-11.

Wayman, K., Lynch, E., & Hanson, M. (1990). Home based early childhood services: Cultural sensitivity in a family systems approach. *Topics in Early Childhood Special Education, 10*, 56-75.

Webber, J., Scheuermann, B., McCall, C., & Coleman, M. (1993). Research on self-monitoring as a behavior management technique in special education classrooms: A descriptive review. *Remedial and Special Education, 14*(2), 38-56.

Webster, A., & Ellwood, J. (1985). *The hearing-impaired child in the ordinary school.* London: Croom Helm.

Wechsler, D. (1974). *Manual for the Wechsler Intelligence Scale for Children—Revised.* New York: Psychological Corp.

Wedel, J. W., & Fowler, S. A. (1984). "Read me a story, Mom": A home-tutoring program to teach prereading skills to language-delayed children. *Behavior Modification, 8*, 245-266.

Weeks, M., & Gaylord-Ross, R. (1981). Task difficulty and aberrant behavior in severely handicapped students. *Journal of Applied Behavior Analysis, 14*, 449-463.

Wehby, J. H., Dodge, K. A., Valente Jr., E., & The Conduct Disorders Prevention Research Group. (1993). School behavior of first grade children identified as at-risk for development of conduct problems. *Behavioral Disorders, 19*, 67-78.

Wehman, P. (1983). Toward the employability of severely handicapped children and youth. *Teaching Exceptional Children, 15*, 220-225.

Wehman, P. (1992). Transition for young people with disabilities: Challenges for the 1990's. *Education and Training in Mental Retardation, 27*, 112-118.

Wehman, P., & Hill, J. W. (Eds.). (1985). *Competitive employment for persons with mental retardation.* Richmond, VA: Virginia Commonwealth University, Rehabilitation Research and Training Center.

Wehman, P., & Kregel, J. (1985). A supported work approach to competitive employment of individuals with moder-

ate and severe handicaps. *The Journal of The Association for Persons with Severe Handicaps, 10*, 3-11.

Wehman, P., & Schleien, S. J. (1981). *Leisure programs for handicapped persons: Adaptations, techniques, and curriculum.* Baltimore, MD: University Park Press.

Wehman, P., Hill, M., Goodall, P., Cleveland, P., Brooke, V., & Pentecost, J. H. (1982). Job placement and follow-up of moderately and severely handicapped individuals after three years. *The Journal of The Association for the Severely Handicapped, 7*(2), 5-16.

Wehman, P., Hill, M., Hill, J. W., Brooke, V., Pendleton, P., & Britt, C. (1985). Competitive employment for persons with mental retardation: A follow-up six years later. *Mental Retardation, 23*, 274-281.

Wehman, P., Kregel, J., & Barcus, J. M. (1985). From school to work: A vocational transition model for handicapped students. *Exceptional Children, 52*, 25-37.

Wehman, P., Kregel, J., & Seyfarth, J. (1985a). Employment outlook for young adults with mental retardation. *Rehabilitation Counseling Bulletin, 5*, 343-354.

Wehman, P., Kregel, J., & Seyfarth, J. (1985b). Transition from school to work for individuals with severe handicaps: A follow-up study. *The Journal of The Association for Persons with Severe Handicaps, 10*, 132-136.

Wehman, P., Kregel, J., Shafer, M., & West, M. (1989). *Emerging trends in supported employment: A preliminary analysis of 27 states.* Richmond, VA: Rehabilitation Research and Training Center, Virginia Commonwealth University.

Wehman, P., Renzaglia, A. M., & Bates, P. (1985). *Functional living skills for moderately and severely handicapped individuals.* Austin, TX: PRO-ED.

Wehmeyer, M. L. (1992). Self-determination and the education of students with mental retardation. *Education and Training in Mental Retardation, 27*, 302-314.

Wehmeyer, M. L. (1994). Perceptions of self-determination and psychological empowerment of adolescents with mental retardation. *Education and Training in Mental Retardation, 29*, 9-21.

Weinberg, R. (1989) Intelligence and IQ: Landmark issues and great debates. *American Psychologist, 44*(2), 98-104.

Weinstein, G., & Cooke, N. L. (1992). The effects of two repeated reading interventions on generalization of fluency. *Learning Disability Quarterly, 15*, 21-28.

Weintraub, F. J., & Abeson, A. (1974). New education policies for the handicapped: The quiet revolution. *Phi Delta Kappan*, 55, 526-529, 569.

Weisberg, P. (1994). Helping preschoolers from low-income backgrounds make substantial progress in reading through Direct Instruction. In R. Gardner III, D. M. Sainato, J. O. Cooper, T. E. Heron, W. L. Heward, J. Eshleman, & T. A. Grossi (Eds.), *Behavior analysis in education: Focus on measurably superior instruction* (pp. 115-129). Pacific Grove, CA: Brooks/Cole.

Weisman, M. L. (1994, July). When parents are not in the interest of the child. *The Atlantic*, 274(1), 43-44, 46-47, 50-54, 56-60, 62-63.

Weisz, J. R. (1981). Effects of the "mentally retarded" label on adult judgments about child failure. *Journal of Abnormal Psychology*, 4, 371-374.

Weisz, J. R., Bromfield, R., Vines, D. L., & Weiss, B. (1985). Cognitive development, helpless behavior, and labeling effects in the lives of the mentally retarded. *Applied Developmental Psychology*, 2, 129-167.

Wender, P. H. (1987). *The hyperactive child, adolescent, and adult*. New York: Oxford University Press.

Wepman, J. M. (1973). *Auditory discrimination test*. Chicago: Language Research Associates.

Wesson, C. L., King, R. P., & Deno, S. L. (1984). Direct and frequent measurement of student performance: If it's good for us, why don't we do it? *Learning Disability Quarterly*, 7, 45-48.

West, J. F., & Idol, L. (1990). Collaborative consultation in the education of mildly handicapped and at-risk students. *Remedial and Special Education*, 11(1), 22-31.

West, L. L., Corbey, S., Boyer-Stephens, A. Jones, B., Miller, R. J., & Sarkees-Wircenski, M. (1992). *Integrating transition planning into the IEP process*. Reston, VA: Council for Exceptional Children.

West, M. D., Rayfield, R. G., Clements, C., Unger, D., & Thornton, T. (1994). An illustration of positive behavioral support in the workplace for individuals with severe mental retardation. *Journal of Vocational Rehabilitation*, 4(4), 265-271.

West, R. P., Young, K. R., Callahan, K., Fister, S., Kemp, K., Freston, J., & Lovitt, T. C. (1995). The musical clocklight. *Teaching Exceptional Children*, 27(2), 46-51.

Westberg, K. L., Archambault Jr., F. X., Dobyns, S. M., & Salvin, T. J. (1993). The classroom practices observation study. *Journal for the Education of the Gifted*, 16, 120-146.

Westling, D. L., & Fox, L. (1995). *Teaching persons with severe disabilities*. Englewood Cliffs, NJ: Prentice-Hall/Merrill.

Westling, D. L., Ferrell, K., & Swenson, K. (1982). Intraclassroom comparison of two arrangements for teaching profoundly mentally retarded children. *American Journal of Mental Deficiency*, 86, 601-608.

Wetzel, R. J., & Hoschouer, R. L. (1984). *Residential teaching communities: Program development and staff training for developmentally disabled persons*. Glenview, IL: Scott, Foresman.

Weyhing, M. C. (1983). Parental reactions to handicapped children and familial adjustments to routines of care. In J. A. Mulick & S. M. Pueschell (Eds.), *Parent-professional partnerships in developmental disabilities* (pp. 125-138). Cambridge, MA: Ware Press.

Wheeler, D. L., Jacobson, J. W., Paglieri, R. A., & Schwartz, A. A. (1993). An experimental assessment of facilitated communication. *Mental Retardation*, 31, 49-60

Wheeler, J. J., Bates, P., Marshall, K. J., & Miller, S. R. (1988). Teaching appropriate social behaviors to a young man with moderate mental retardation in a supported competitive employment setting. *Education & Training in Mental Retardation*, 23, 105-116.

Whelan, R. J. (1981). Prologue. In G. Brown, R. L. McDowell, & J. Smith (Eds.), *Educating adolescents with behavior disorders* (pp. 1-9). Englewood Cliffs, NJ: Merrill/Prentice Hall.

White, B. L. (1975). *The first three years of life*. Englewood Cliffs, NJ: Prentice-Hall.

White, C. C., Lakin, K. C., & Bruininks, R. H. (1989). *Persons with mental retardation and related conditions in state-operated residential facilities: Year ending June 30, 1988 with longitudinal trends from 1950 to 1988*. (Report No. 30). Minneapolis: University of Minnesota, Center for Residential and Community Services.

White, D. M. (1991). *Use of guided notes to promote generalized note taking behavior of high school students with learning disabilities*. Unpublished masters thesis, The Ohio State University, Columbus.

White, K. R., Bush, D., & Casto, G. (1986). Let the past be prologue: Learning from previous reviews of early intervention efficacy research. *The Journal of Special Education*, 19(4), 417-428.

White, O. R. (1986). Precision teaching—precision learning. *Exceptional Children*, 52, 522-534.

White, O. R., & Haring, N. G. (1980). *Exceptional teaching* (2nd ed.). Englewood Cliffs, NJ: Merrill/Prentice Hall.

Whitehead, C. W. (1979). Sheltered workshops in the decade ahead: Work and wages, or welfare. In G. T. Bellamy, C. O'Connor, & O. C. Karan (Eds.), *Vocational rehabilitation of severely handicapped persons* (pp. 71-84). Baltimore, MD: University Park Press.

Whitmore, J. R. (1980). *Giftedness, conflict, and underachievement*. Boston: Allyn & Bacon.

Whitmore, J. R., & Maker, C. J. (1985). *Intellectual giftedness in disabled persons*. Rockville, MD: Aspen.

Widerstrom, A. H., Mowder, B. A., & Willis, W. G. (1989). The school psychologist's role in the early childhood special education program. *Journal of Early Intervention*, 13, 239-248.

Wiederholt, J. L., & Chamberlain, S. P. (1989). A critical analysis of resource programs. *Remedial and Special Education*, 10(6), 15-37.

Wiederholt, J. L., Hammill, D. D., & Brown, V. (1983). *The resource teacher: A guide to effective practice*. (2nd ed.). Boston: Allyn & Bacon.

Wiener, W. R., Deaver, K., DiCorpo, D., Hayes, J., Hill, E., Manzer, D., Newcomver, J., Pogrund, R., Rosen, S., & Uslan, M. (1990). The orientation and mobility assistant. *RE:view*, 22, 69-77.

Wiig, E. H., & Semmel, E. (1984). *Language assessment intervention for the learning disabled* (2nd ed.). Englewood Cliffs, NJ: Merrill/Prentice Hall.

Wikler, L. D. (1986). Periodic stresses of families of older mentally retarded children: An exploratory study. *American Journal of Mental Deficiency*, 90, 703-706.

Wilcox, B., & Bellamy, G. T. (1987). *A comprehensive guide to The Activities Catalog: An alternative curriculum for youth and adults with severe disabilities*. Baltimore: Paul H. Brooks Publishing Company.

Will, M. C. (1986). Educating children with learning problems: A shared responsibility. *Exceptional Children*, 52, 411-415.

Williams, B. F. (1992). Changing demographics: Challenges for educators. *Intervention in School and Clinic*, 27(3), 157-163.

Williams, B. F., & Howard, V. F. (1990, May). *Cocaine exposed infants: Current findings and implications*. Paper presented at the 16th Annual Convention of the Association for Behavior Analysis, Nashville, TN.

Williams, B. F., & Howard, V. F. (1993). Children exposed to cocaine: Characteristics and implications for research and intervention. *Journal of Early Intervention, 17,* 61-72.

Williams, G. E., & Cuvo, A. J. (1986). Training apartment upkeep skills to rehabilitation clients: A comparison of task analytic strategies. *Journal of Applied Behavior Analysis, 19,* 39-51.

Williams, J. (1977). The impact and implication of litigation. In G. Markel (Ed.), *Proceedings of the University of Michigan Institute on the Impact and Implications of State and Federal Legislation Affecting Handicapped Individuals.* Ann Arbor: University of Michigan, School of Education.

Williamson, G. G. (1978). The individualized education program: An interdisciplinary endeavor. In B. Sirvis, J. W. Baken, & G. G. Williamson (Eds.), *Unique aspects of the IEP for the physically handicapped, homebound, and hospitalized.* Reston, VA: Council for Exceptional Children.

Willoughby, D. M. (1980). *A resource guide for parents and educators of blind children.* Baltimore, MD: National Federation of the Blind.

Willoughby, D. M., & Duffy, S. (1989). *Handbook for itinerant and resource teachers of blind and visually impaired students.* Baltimore, MD: National Federation of the Blind.

Wilson, J., Blacher, J., & Baker, B. L. (1989). Siblings of children with severe handicaps. *Mental Retardation, 27,* 167-173.

Wilson, P. G., Schepis, M. M., & Mason-Main, M. (1987). In vivo use of picture prompt training to increase independent work at a restaurant. *The Journal of The Association for Persons with Severe Handicaps, 12,* 145-150.

Wilson, W. M. (1992). The Stanford-Binet: Fourth edition and form L-M in assessment of young children with mental retardation. *Mental Retardation, 30,* 81-84.

Winer, M. (1978). A course on resources for the newly blind. *Journal of Visual Impairment and Blindness, 72,* 311-315.

Winter, R. J. (1983). Childhood diabetes mellitus. In J. Umbreit (Ed.), *Physical disabilities and health impairments: An introduction* (pp. 117-131). Englewood Cliffs, NJ: Merrill/Prentice Hall.

Winton, P. J. (1986). Effective strategies for involving families in intervention efforts.

Focus on Exceptional Children, 19(2), 1-12.

Winton, P. J., & Bailey, D. B. (1988). The family-focused interview: A collaborative mechanism for family assessment and goal-setting. *Journal of Early Intervention, 12,* 195-207.

Winton, P. J., & Turnbull, A. P. (1981). Parent involvement as viewed by parents of preschool handicapped children. *Topics in Early Childhood Special Education, 1,* 11-19.

Wittenstein, S. H. (1993). Braille training and teacher attitudes: Implications for personnel preparation. *RE:view, 25,* 103-111.

Witty, P. A. (1930). A study of one hundred gifted children. *University of Kansas Bulletin of Education, 2*(7).

Witty, P. (1940). Some considerations in the education of gifted children. *Educational Administration and Supervision, 26,* 512-521.

Witty, P. A. (Ed.) (1951). *The gifted child.* Boston: D.C. Heath & Company.

Witty, P. A. (1958). Who are the gifted? In W. B. Henry (Ed.), *Education of the gifted, fifty-seventh yearbook of the National Society for the Study of Education, part II.* Chicago: University of Chicago Press.

Wolery, M. (1991). Instruction in early childhood special education: "Seeing through a glass darkly . . . knowing in part." *Exceptional Children, 58,* 127-135.

Wolery, M. , Werts, M. G., Snyder, E. D., & Caldwell, N. K. (1994). Efficacy of constant time delay implemented by peer tutors in general education classrooms. *Journal of Behavioral Education, 4,* 415-436.

Wolery, M., & Dyk, L. (1984). Arena assessment: Description and preliminary social validity data. *The Journal of The Association for Persons with Severe Handicaps, 9,* 231-235.

Wolery, M., & Haring, T. G. (1994). Moderate, severe, and profound disabilities. In N. G. Haring, L. McCormick, & T. G. Haring (Eds.), *Exceptional children and youth* (6th ed.) (pp. 258-299). Englewood Cliffs, NJ: Merrill/Prentice Hall.

Wolery, M., & Sainato, D. M. (1993). General curriculum and intervention strategies. In *DEC Recommended Practices* (pp. 50-57). Reston, VA: Council for Exceptional Children, Division for Early Childhood.

Wolery, M., & Sainato, D. M. (in press). General curriculum and intervention strategies. In S. L. Odom & M. McClean (Eds.), *Recommended practices in early intervention.* Austin, TX: PRO-ED.

Wolery, M., & Wilbers, J. S. (1994). *Including young children with special needs in early childhood programs.* Washington, DC: National Association for the Education of Young Children.

Wolery, M., Ault, M. J., & Doyle, P. M. (1992). *Teaching students with moderate to severe disabilities.* New York: Longman.

Wolery, M., Bailey, D. B., & Sugai, G. M. (1988). *Effective teaching: Principles and procedures of applied behavior analysis.* Boston: Allyn and Bacon.

Wolery, M., Strain, P. S., & Bailey, Jr., D. B. (1992). Reaching potentials of children with special needs. In S. Bredekamp & T. Rosegrant (Eds.), *Reaching potentials: Appropriate curriculum and assessment for young children* (Vol. 1) (pp. 92-111). Washington, DC: National Association for the Education of Young Children.

Wolf, E. G., Delk, M. T., & Schein, J. D. (1982). *Needs assessment of services to deaf-blind individuals.* (Contract No. 300-81-0426). Silver Spring, MD: REDEX, Inc.)

Wolfensberger, W. (1969). The origin and nature of our institutional models. In R. B. Kugel & W. Wolfensberger (Eds.), *Changing patterns in residential services for the mentally retarded* (pp. 59-71). Washington, DC: President's Committee on Mental Retardation.

Wolfensberger, W. (1972). *Normalization: The principle of normalization in human services.* Toronto, Canada: National Institute on Mental Retardation.

Wolfensberger, W. (1976). The origin and nature of our institutional models. In R. B. Kugel & A. Shearer (Eds.), *Changing patterns in residential services for the mentally retarded* (pp. 35-82). Washington, DC: President's Committee on Mental Retardation.

Wolfensberger, W. (1983). Social role valorization: A proposed new term for the principle of normalization. *Mental Retardation, 21,* 234-239.

Wolfensberger, W., & Thomas, S. (1983). *Program Analysis of Service Systems implementation of normalization goals: Normalization criteria and ratings manual. Vol. 2.* Toronto: National Institute on Mental Retardation.

Woliver, R., & Woliver, G. M. (1991). Gifted adolescents in the emerging minorities: Asians and Pacific Islanders. In M. Bireley and J. Genshaft (Eds.), *Understanding the gifted adolescent* (pp. 248-258). New York: Teachers College Press.

Wolk, S., & Schildroth, A. N. (1986). Deaf children and speech intelligibility: A national study. In A. N. Schildroth & M. A. Karchmer (Eds.), *Deaf children in America* (pp. 139-159). San Diego: College-Hill.

Wolman, C., Thurlow, M. L., & Bruininks, R. H. (1989). Stability of categorical designation for special education students: A longitudinal study. *The Journal of Special Education, 23*, 213-222.

Wolraich, M. L., Lindgren, S., Stromquist, A., Milich, R., Davis, C., & Watson, D. (1990). Stimulant medications use by primary care physicians in the treatment of attention deficit hyperactivity disorder. *Pediatrics, 86*, 95-101.

Wong, K. L. H., Kauffman, J. M., & Lloyd, J. W., (1991). Choices for integration: Selecting teachers for mainstreamed students with emotional or behavioral disorders. *Intervention in School and Clinic, 27*(2), 108-115.

Wood, D. A., Rosenberg, M. S., & Carran, D. T. (1993). The effects of tape-recorded self-instruction cues on the mathematics performance of students with learning disabilities. *Journal of Learning Disabilities, 26*, 250-258.

Wood, F. H. (1985). Issues in the identification and placement of behaviorally disordered students. *Behavioral Disorders, 10*, 219-228.

Wood, J. W. (1992). *Adapting instruction for mainstreamed students* (2nd ed.). Englewood Cliffs, NJ: Merrill/Prentice Hall.

Wood, J. W. (1993). *Mainstreaming: A practical approach for teachers* (2nd ed.). Englewood Cliffs, NJ: Merrill/Prentice Hall.

Wood, M. E. (1981). Costs of intervention programs. In G. Garland, N. W. Stone, J. Swanson, & G. Woodruff (Eds.), *Early intervention for children with special needs and their families: Findings and recommendations* (pp. 15-32). *Westar Series Paper No. 11.* Seattle WA: University of Washington. (ERIC Document Reproduction Service No. 207278)

Wood, M. M., & Long, N. J. (1991). *Life space intervention: Talking with children and youth in crisis.* Austin, TX: PRO-ED.

Woodcock, R. (1974). *Woodcock Reading Mastery Tests.* Circle Pines, MN: American Guidance Service.

Woodcock, R. W. (1978). *Woodcock-Johnson Psychoeducational Battery.* Allen, TX: DLM Teaching Resources.

Woodruff, G. (1994). Serving the needs of children with AIDS and their families: A

case for comprehensive community-based and family-centered programs. *Teaching Exceptional Children, 26*(4), 45-48.

Woodruff, G., & McGonigel, M. J. (1988). Early intervention team approaches: The transdisciplinary model. In J. B. Jordon, J. J. Gallagher, P. L. Hutinger, & M. B. Karnes (Eds.), *Early childhood special education: Birth to three* (pp. 163-181). Reston, VA: Council for Exceptional Children.

Woodward, J., & Gersten, R. (1992). Innovative technology for secondary students with learning disabilities. *Exceptional Children, 58*, 407-421.

Wright, C., & Bigge, J. L. (1991). Avenues to physical participation. In J. L. Bigge, *Teaching individuals with multiple and physical disabilities* (3rd ed.) (pp. 132-174). Englewood Cliffs, NJ: Merrill/Prentice Hall.

Wright, C., & Momari, M. (1985). *From toys to computers: Access for the physically disabled child.* San Jose, CA: Wright.

Wright, J. E., Cavanaugh, R. A., Sainato, D. M., & Heward, W. L. (in press). Somos todos ayudantes y estudiantes: Evaluation of a classwide peer tutoring program in a modified Spanish class for secondary students identified as learning disabled or academically at-risk. *Education & Treatment of Children.*

Wu, L. Y. (1993). Suggestions for refining the Chinese braille system. *Journal of Visual Impairment & Blindness, 87*, 289-294.

Wyatt v. Stickney, 344 F. Supp. 387, 344 F. Supp. 373 (M.D. Ala. 1972), 334 F. Supp. 1341, 325 F. Supp. 781 (M.D. Ala. 1971), aff'd sub nom. Wyatt v. Aderholt, 503 F. 2d 1305 (5th Cir. 1974).

Yang, F. M. (1988). *Effects of guided lecture notes on sixth graders' scores on daily science quizzes.* Unpublished master's thesis. Columbus, OH: The Ohio State University.

Yaremko, R. L. (1993). Cochlear implants and children under the age of three. *The Volta Review, 95*, 51-61.

Yates, J. R., & Ortiz, A. A. (1991). Professional development needs of teachers who serve exceptional language minorities in today's schools. *Teacher Education and Special Education, 14*, 11-18.

Yee, L. Y. (1988). Asian children. *Teaching Exceptional Children, 20*(4), 49-50.

Yell, M. L. (1991). Reclarifying *Honig v. Doe* . *Exceptional Children, 57*, 364-368.

Yell, M. L. (1995). Least restrictive environment, inclusion, and students with disabilities: A legal analysis. *Journal of Special Education, 28*, 389-404.

Ylvisaker, M. (1986). Language and communication disorders following pediatric head injury. *Journal of Head Trauma Rehabilitation, 1*, 48-56.

York, J., Vandercook, T., MacDonald, C., Heise-Neff, C., & Caughey, E. (1992). Feedback about integrating middle-school students with severe disabilities in general education classes. *Exceptional Children, 58*, 244-258.

Ysseldyke, J. E., Algozzine, B., & Epps, S. (1983). A logical and empirical analysis of current practice in classifying students as handicapped. *Exceptional Children, 50*, 160-166.

Ysseldyke, J., Algozzine, B., Richey, L., & Graden, J. (1982). Declaring students eligible for learning disability services: Why bother with the data? *Learning Disability Quarterly, 5*, 37-44.

Ysseldyke, J. E. & Algozzine, B., Thurlow, M. L., (1992). *Critical issues in special education* (2nd ed.). Boston: Houghton Mifflin.

Ysseldyke, J. E., & Salvia, J. (1974). Diagnostic-prescriptive teaching: Two models. *Exceptional Children, 41*, 181-186.

Ysseldyke, J. E., Thurlow, M., Graden, J., Wesson, C., Algozzine, B., & Deno, S. (1983). Generalizations from five years of research on assessment and decision making: The University of Minnesota Institute. *Exceptional Education Quarterly, 4*(1), 75-93.

Yurt, R. W., & Pruitt, B. A. (1983). Burns. In J. Umbreit (Ed.), *Physical disabilities and health impairments: An introduction* (pp. 175-184). Englewood Cliffs, NJ: Merrill/Prentice Hall.

Zambone, A. M., & Huebner, K. M. (1992). Service for children and youths who are deaf-blind: An overview. *Journal of Visual Impairment & Blindness, 86*, 287-290.

Zangwill, I. (1909). *The melting pot.* Englewood Cliffs, NJ: Merrill/Prentice Hall.

Zaragoza, N., Vaughn, S., & McIntosh, R. (1991). Social skills intervention and children with behavior problems: A review. *Behavioral Disorders, 16*, 260-275.

Zawolkow, E., & DeFiore, S. (1986). Educational interpreting for elementary- and secondary-level hearing-impaired students. *American Annals of the Deaf, 131*, 26-28.

Zelski, R. F. K., & Zelski, T. (1985). What are assistive devices? *Hearing Instruments, 36*, 12.

Zetlin, A., & Murtaugh, M. (1990). What ever happened to those with borderline IQs? *American Journal on Mental Retardation, 94*, 463-469.

Zigler, E., Balla, D., & Hodapp, R. (1984). On the definition and classification of mental retardation. *American Journal of Mental Deficiency, 89,* 215-230.

Zigler, E., Hodapp, R. M., & Edison, M. R. (1990). From theory to practice in the care and education of mentally retarded individuals. *American Journal of Mental Retardation, 95,* 1-12.

Zigmond, N., & Baker, J. (1987). *Project MELD grant application to OSERS.* Pittsburgh, PA: University of Pittsburgh.

Zigmond, N., & Baker, J. (1990). Mainstream experiences for learning disabled students (Project MELD): Preliminary report. *Exceptional Children, 57,* 176-185.

Zigmond, N., & Baker, J. M. (1994). Is the mainstream a more appropriate educational setting for Randy? A case study of one student with learning disabilities. *Learning Disabilities Research & Practice, 9,* 108-117.

Zigmond, N., & Miller, S. E. (1986). Assessment for instructional planning. *Exceptional Children, 52,* 501-509.

Zigmond, N., & Thornton, H. (1985). Follow-up of postsecondary age learning disabled graduates and drop-outs. *Learning Disabilities Research, 1,* 50-55.

Zirpoli, T. J. (1987). Child abuse and children with handicaps. *Remedial and Special Education, 7*(2), 39-48.

Zirpoli, T. J. (1990). Physical abuse: Are children with disabilities at greater risk? *Intervention in School and Clinic, 26-*(1), 6-11.

Zirpoli, T. J. (1995). *Understanding and affecting the behavior of young children.* Englewood Cliffs, NJ: Merrill/Prentice Hall.

Zirpoli, T. J., & Wieck, C. (1989). Economic and political factors affecting deinstitutionalization: One state's analysis. *The Journal of Special Education, 23,* 201-211.

Name Index

672

Subject Index